Contents

KU-051-930

PART II

THE GENDER SYSTEM: Its Effects on Our Private Lives and Public Institutions 247

CHAPTER SIX

The Effects of Sexism on Women's Private Lives 249

CHAPTER SEVEN

The Effects of Sexism on Public Institutions 344

CHAPTER EIGHT

How Sexist Ideology Affects Our Understanding of the World–and How Feminists Respond 445

PART III
WOMEN ON THE MOVE 503

CHAPTER NINE

Our Feminist Foremothers: Events and Arguments 505

Preface

When I was preparing the first edition of *Issues in Feminism* early in the 1970s, I wrote:

Women's studies was born out of the women's movement, which was born out of the concrete experiences, realities, and possibilities of women's lives. No matter how much a part of the traditional, "respectable" university the research, faculty, or students of women's studies become, we never lose sight of our beginnings or continuing rootedness in women's liberation, because it is the rootedness in its issues that gives impetus and meaning to our work.

Those of us engaged in what is currently called women's studies (research and learning in a feminist context) have come along different routes, yet almost without exception each of us is here because at some time in our personal history we have specifically experienced events or ideas that have propelled us into a reappraisal of our lives as women. Generally it was the power of those experiences and the shock of the appraisal that created in us the desire and the commitment to know more about women, womanhood, and the consequences of gender definition.

In the years since this book's beginnings, although many things have changed, others have not. Women's studies has changed: it has grown and developed and influenced the intellectual and academic landscape to a degree we could barely have imagined in the early 1970s. Society too has changed. In the Western world, the women's movement has profoundly altered the lives of women and men, mostly for the better, but not sufficiently. Elsewhere, in different ways and to various degrees, not only feminism is vital and growing, but women's studies as well.

I too have changed; I am now past 60, an "older generation" second-wave feminist, considered by some to be a "mother" of women's studies. Over the years, my colleagues and students have deepened my understanding of the complexity of navigating the range of issues embedded in women's experience, and this, of course, has altered for the better the terms of my analyses. What has not changed is my passionate belief in women's movement(s) and feminist analysis, in the need for feminist activism and radical social change, in the positive possibilities of the future. I am still rooted, by choice, in the spirit of (dare I still use the phrase?) women's liberation. It is still my conviction that women's studies must be firmly grounded in the women's movement. Feminist analysis that is not anchored in women's concrete experiences may serve academia, but it will not serve women or the world.

An unregenerate feminist, I have not at all altered my original conviction that there is something radically wrong with the direction civilization has taken; that it is grounded in the condition of women around the world and intimately related to the definition of masculinity that has become prevalent; that urgent effort is needed, in Sojourner Truth's words, to turn the world right side up again; and that feminism—its insights *together with* its action, has the tools to do it.

I still believe that women, *as women*, share a commonality of problems—in varying degrees and expressions, to be sure, but we share them nonetheless, and we must solve them together. Different though we may be, all women are burdened by violence, subordination, misogyny, discrimination, and so on, as our daughters will be, as the planet will be, if we do not act together. For many reasons, women, as women, are in a unique position to see into the heart of what has gone wrong and to change it. We have moved in that direction, but the women's movement has not come nearly close enough to accomplishing sufficiently deep changes in our world. This requires that we continue to gain ever deeper understanding, and that is a primary goal of women's studies.

Developments in methodology and analysis have brought us sharp tools, new issues, and increasing sophistication. Theorizing grows ever more complex, schools of thought ever more numerous. Few would not delight in our growth; however, we must take care lest our sophistication degenerate into the vacuity we deplore in other fields. Women's studies must not be allowed to devolve into just another academic board game—full of cryptic lore and rules but having little to do with life. That would destroy its appeal as well as its primary reason for being.

> The education promoted by women's studies engages its public because it promises to enhance—or rather, to restore—the role of the university in giving meaning to people's lives and moral direction to society. The arguments for sex equity are ethical as well as legal and economic. . . . Women's studies gives new meaning to the lives of its students, faculty, and community associates, and it brings to higher education new possibilities for questions, answers, and interpretations of personal and social relationships.

—Marilyn Jacoby Boxer[1]

> The grass roots/community women's movement has given women's studies its life. How do we relate to it? How do we bring our gifts and our educational privilege back to it? Do we realize also how very much there is to learn in doing this essential work? Ask yourself what the women's movement is working on in your town or city. Are you a part of it? Ask yourself which women are living in the worst conditions in your town and how your work positively affects and directly touches their lives. If it doesn't, why not?

—Barbara Smith[2]

Women within and outside the academy find ourselves in an environment that is in many ways improved but in others is far more hostile. There has been marked economic improvement for certain groups of women; yet, contrary to the images portrayed in the media, women's overall progress has been slow and inadequate, and for some there has been desperate deterioration of means. In other countries around the world, women find themselves in like circumstances: improvement for some women in some places, deterioration for others. American women have inched forward, but our gains haven't accomplished anything close to what is needed. There are more women in government and the professions, but they still represent a very small percentage of the whole. Racism has received permission from various quarters to become more overt, as has homophobia, and poor women have been demonized and placed at risk in terms of health, freedom, and economic opportunity.

Socially, antifeminist, antiwoman forces on the right have whittled away at our demands for human parity, for reproductive autonomy, and for racial justice, and they promise continued assault. Violence of all kinds against women, including homophobic and other hate crimes, is increasing, and yet a corporately controlled network of media regales us ceaselessly with statistics touting that "crime is down." Women are ever more targeted for media and industry assaults on our appearance and well-being; eating disorders are nearly epidemic among girls. Viagra is everywhere; RU-486 is . . . where? The infamous backlash of the last two decades has been very effective.

It is against this backdrop that we must consider the fact that the majority of young people, including university students, continue to be for the most part apolitical, and that many young women accept the proposition, advanced by the media and forces on the right, that feminism has become either irrelevant, all important battles having been settled, or that it is contrary to the best interests of women and the country. Indeed, it has become unfashionable for women to use the *f* word at all, even among young, progressive women who clearly are feminist in orientation—the "I'm not a feminist, but . . ." phenomenon.

Women's studies is faced with a vast responsibility: to counter the misinformation and to restore in our students the awareness, the commitment, and the ability to participate in the struggle for social justice. It is a tall order, but it is what women's studies was designed to do. As you will see, these beliefs underlie this edition of *Issues in Feminism* as they have every previous edition.

The focus of this text, both in the introductory essays and in the readings, is on *issues*, exactly as its title states: *Issues in Feminism* is an introduction to some of the most important themes of the feminist movement. Newspaper articles, scholarly papers, manifestos, political papers, personal narratives, and all the rest are here to serve the purpose of unfolding the important questions and engaging their critiques. To simply know the facts of women's various lives is an important beginning, but it is not sufficient. For students to grow in self-awareness and social responsibility, they must understand those facts; they must have a context and create an analysis.

The underlying themes of the book, both in the text and in the readings, are twofold. First, to make sense of the consequences of gender in our lives and in our world, we must know our history. We must have access to all the influential beliefs and ideas, past and present, regarding women, both negative and positive, from the academic to the popular, from the scientific to the pseudoscientific, from the complex to the simplistic, and from the thoughtful to the downright silly. Second, to counter the misogyny that is embedded in many of those ideas, we must comprehend their impact on our lives in a profound and personal way, and that requires critical analysis of even the homeliest events of our day-to-day lives.

This book is designed for beginners in feminism and women's studies, for those who have not yet had the "click" of recognition and reappraisal, or who have had it only in the most inchoate way. Its intention is not only to impart information but also to precipitate the student into an awareness of the self in the context of social constructions of gender. This is a primer in the most exact sense: It is directed at the prime, the spring, the level of consciousness out of which come the need and the decision to understand. It aims to engage students by revealing the gender issues embedded in the most familiar facets of life: family relationships, work, education, media, religion, popular culture, and more.

Selections here are purposely diverse in character. They range across several fields of study— literature, anthropology, biology, theology, and others. They represent various viewpoints, from the "radically" feminist to the antifeminist and in between. They include scientific papers, learned analyses, political arguments, and personal narratives. Some are funny, others despicable. Some will take little effort to understand; others are fairly demanding. It is hoped that every student, at whatever level of ability or accomplishment, may find a challenge here.

These are not necessarily the most recent pieces, the most erudite, or even the most reputable. They are statements from the past and the present that are representative of the prevailing notions that have had a terrific impact on our lives as women (and the lives of men as well). These readings, diverse as they are, go together. They have been selected for their collective power to provide a picture of the pattern of ideas about women, to reveal issues in their interrelatedness. They are meant to educate in the broadest sense—to bring students face-to-face with their own experiences of gender, and to provide them with a context within which to understand them.

Although the material represents a range of academic fields, from psychology to economics, from politics to anthropology, its treatment is primarily out of the humanities. The driving questions presented here are: What do we see? What does this mean? How does this affect the quality of our lives? What would be better? Why does it matter?

The methodology is essentially Socratic—we pose questions, articulate various responses, assess them, set the stage for further questions, and so on. The goal is understanding. Its consequence is growth in wisdom and spirit. Nonetheless, what we will be doing here is women's studies, a nondisciplinary, multidisciplinary, counterdisciplinary feminist exploration of the conditions of our lives, where we ourselves set the boundaries of what may be asked and what we may ultimately do with the answers we devise.

In broadest strokes, the outline of the text is this: Part I first introduces women's studies itself, then essential theoretical concepts, terminology, and issues; Part II follows with examples of how these theoretical concepts are played out concretely in our lives, both personally and institutionally; and Part III closes with some of the important documents and events of women's history.

Specifically, Chapter 1 introduces women's studies, its relationship to feminism and to the women's movement, something of its history and reason for being, its goals, and its internal issues. Part I (Chapters 2 through 5) provides an explication of the major *themes* of sex-role arrangements: the male and female ideals, the roles and expectations of gender as they have been expressed in various aspects of our culture and as they crisscross with class, race, ethnicity, sexual identity, and other social categories. The book begins with these images, as coarsely defined as they are—the Mars and Venus ideals—because, in one variation or another, they are at the root of social beliefs and attitudes toward the sexes. They have great explanatory value—both for the traditionalist, as a justification for sexist structures, and for the feminist, as a schema to be explored. Chapter 2 explores the nature of patriarchy, masculinity, and the evolving notion of "masculinities." Chapter 3 begins the unpacking of patriarchal conceptions of women—stereotyping, misogyny, subordination, oppression. Chapter 4 provides examples of some of the responses women have made to patriarchal ideas and some of the ways women resist their impact. Chapter 5 describes the kinds of explanations various thinkers have devised regarding the origin of female subordination and furnishes some examples.

In Part II, the gender system is traced through its reflection in such concrete aspects of life as family structures, sexual mores, education, work, politics, health, and so on. Chapter 6 introduces issues usually taken to be "personal"—personal identity, love relationships, motherhood, and so on. Although feminist theory years ago exploded the myth that there was a line between the personal and the political, young women need very much to explore that relationship. Chapter 7 examines the appearance of sexism in major social institutions, and Chapter 8 explores the way sexist ideology supports it and feminist activism resists it. Finally, Chapter 9 is a compilation of important feminist documents.

Of course, in reality, it is impossible to separate the elements of these chapters into discrete little packets; they overlap and weave into one another, and there are many ways in which they could be presented. For this reason, one chapter does not assume knowledge of the selections contained in any other. Also, there are more issues and selections here than can usually be managed in one semester.

The intention is to provide the instructor latitude in choosing the material best suited for the students and assigning it in whatever order best satisfies the goals and makeup of the class.

Issues in Feminism began as a collection of reading handouts for an experimental course I was "permitted" provisionally to offer in 1973, when academic feminism was in its infancy and I was as yet an untenured assistant professor in philosophy. Over the years, having been instructed by the work, by my students and my colleagues (I dare still to use the word *sisters*), both the book and I have changed. I have lost many, although not all, of my blind spots. I am becoming, for example, increasingly aware of my own particularity—an older White, middlish-class, professional, Midwesterner, crusted around a working-class, Jewish, loner, Bronx kid. I understand better what that enables me to say and what I should leave for others to say: I tend to be more careful in my speech—measuring, qualifying. I know how much I don't know, and how much I must learn from others. I hope that this is reflected in this edition of *Issues in Feminism*.

Many reviewers of this text have asked for a greater range of voices in the selections. That I have gladly provided. Others, remarking that the book was "too feminist" for their students or courses, asked for a change in "tone." That will not be forthcoming. A too feminist women's studies course is, I believe, an oxymoron.

To complete a project like *Issues in Feminism* requires many kinds of help and support. I am grateful to many colleagues who have reviewed the manuscript for the previous editions and offered guidance and suggestions including Joseph J. Arpad, California State University at Fresno; Susan Arpad, California State University at Fresno; Anne M. Butler, Utah State University; Carol Coburn, University of Kansas; Joan Hagman, Concordia College; Barbara S. Havira, Western Michigan University; Annis H. Hopkins, Arizona State University; Lynn Kamenitsa, Northern Illinois University; Betty C. Safford, California State University at Fullerton; Pamela S. Thoma, Colby College; Tim Weinfeld, Western Maryland College; and Barbara A. White, University of New Hampshire. I would also like to thank the reviewers of this fifth edition including Cathryn Bailey, Minnesota State University, Mankato; Susan Gail Baker, Oakland University, Rochester, MI; Shereen G. Bingham, University of Nebraska, Omaha; Jodi Brodsky, The New School for Social Research & The College of New Jersey; Suzanne Cataldi, Southern Illinois University, Edwardsville; Amy C. Lind, Arizona State University; Sheila Nyhus, University of Wyoming; and Karin Suesser, University of Wisconsin, Green Bay. At Southern Illinois University in Edwardsville, I am indebted to my colleagues in the Department of Philosophical Studies for their support and friendship over more than 30 years.

To my girls, Amity and Kendra, goes appreciation for the joy of seeing women of a new generation—feminist women—making their own way, continuing the process, and flourishing in the legacy my generation wanted so much for them. To

Michael Allaband goes my deepest gratitude for the certainty that love and partnership between the sexes is a possible and worthy ideal.

Notes

1. Marilyn Jacoby Boxer, *When Women Ask the Questions: Creating Women's Studies in America* (Baltimore: Johns Hopkins University Press, 1998), p. 251.

2. Barbara Smith, "Racism and Women's Studies," in *All the Women Are White, All the Blacks Are Men, But Some of Us Are Brave,* ed. Gloria T. Hull, Patricia Bell Scott, and Barbara Smith (Old Westbury, NY: The Feminist Press, 1982); quoted in *Making Face, Making Soul, Haciendo Caras: Creative and Critical Perspectives by Women of Color,* ed. Gloria Anzaldua (San Francisco: Aunt Lute Foundation Books, 1990), p. 27.

CHAPTER ONE

Women's Studies, Feminism, and the Women's Movement

WHAT IS WOMEN'S STUDIES?

In the mid- to late 1960s, a scattering of courses focusing on feminist issues began to appear on college campuses. In 1970, the terms *women's studies* and *feminist studies* were first used to refer to them. Against strong resistance, two or three courses developed into thousands of courses, into programs, into a whole new educational and intellectual enterprise.

According to an early study by Florence Howe, by 1980 university faculty were teaching more than twenty thousand such courses in institutions all over the country,[1] and the number is still increasing. Today there are programs at all levels of study—from the undergraduate minor to the doctorate. According to the National Women's Studies Association (NWSA), the number of undergraduate programs listed between 1988 and 1990 increased by 23 percent (creating a total of more than 500 programs!), and by 1990 there were 102 programs offering work at the graduate level.[2] In the United States today, women's studies is offered at over two-thirds of universities, half of four-year colleges, and more than 40 percent of institutions of higher education,[3] and its extent is even greater if we consider the thousands of noncredit courses offered through extension and continuing education programs. Nor is women's studies confined to the United States. As you will read in the selection by Florence Howe at the end of this chapter, women's studies is a major intellectual force in universities all over the world, in countries on every continent. What is more, in the thirty or so years since its inception, women's studies has transformed not only the curriculum, the topics, and the material we teach but also our thinking about knowledge itself. Marilyn Boxer tells us:

> *Whether alluding to the Renaissance or the Enlightenment, to Copernicus or Darwin, several scholars have compared the impact of women's studies to the major intellectual transformations that mark human history. In the sense that such great moments in human experience give rise to an immense flowering of art, literature, and science, and to the challenging of previously accepted authorities of text or tradition, these comparisons are apt. The term* feminist enlightenment, *first suggested by the late sociologist Jessie*

Bernard, is appropriate to those meanings, although not insofar as it may evoke a search for universal laws or rules to define the world. Feminist enlightenment stands instead for the mental "click," the spiritual conversion, the realization of a new capacity for vision that illuminates the dark and enlarges the landscape. By posing new questions and seeking answers that place women in the center, it allows altogether new ways of viewing women and the world to emerge.[4]

From the beginning, the growth of women's studies as a discipline was extraordinary. In 1977, barely a decade after its birth, the number of people involved in feminist research had grown so large and their interests were so diverse that it became necessary to establish some formal means of communication and support. In January of that year, delegates from institutions all over the country participated in the founding of the NWSA, which now has thousands of members, individual and institutional.[5] NWSA's constitution, formulated in 1982, clearly identifies the close association between *the women's movement*, a social process, and *women's studies*, an intellectual or academic enterprise:

Because

> —*Feminist education is a process deeply rooted in the women's movement and remains accountable to that community;*
> —*Feminist aims include the elimination of oppression and discrimination on the basis of sex, race, age, class, religion, ethnicity, and sexual orientation, as well as other barriers to human liberation inherent in the structure of our society;*
> —*Feminist education is not only the pursuit of knowledge about women, but also the development of knowledge for women, a force which furthers the realization of feminist aims;*

Therefore

> —*The National Women's Studies Association actively supports and promotes feminist education and supports the persons involved in that effort, at any educational level and in any educational setting.*[6]

For contemporary university education, and for some high schools, women's studies is a fact of life.

But what is the nature of this new enterprise? What precisely does it do?

Because women's studies is still very young—slightly more than thirty years old—it is difficult to give it an absolute definition. One reason is that scholars are still only beginning to articulate the challenging new insights and methods that are developing within the field. Also, women's studies is a field that has few models. It consciously rejects many traditional forms of inquiry, concepts, and explanatory systems; at the same time, it is developing new and sometimes unique traditions and authorities of its own.

In this chapter, you will learn how feminist researchers are discovering that most accepted theories in all traditional fields—even methods of pursuing knowledge—are rife with prejudice and misunderstandings about women in particular and humanity in general. Because the task of uncovering this bias and restoring balance in knowledge is so complex, feminist thinkers are extremely hesitant to impose artificial limits on those who pursue this work. We are committed to being tolerant toward new methodologies and analyses to avoid creating additional rigid principles that would discourage research. Therefore, we place a high value on freedom and self-determination. Ideologically, and often temperamentally, we are suspicious of hierarchies and control in either social relations or intellectual pursuits. Self-disciplined freedom and cooperative efforts, we believe, are more apt to produce constructive results in most endeavors. Thus, most of us try to encourage and be open to ideas, even when they are very different from our own. You will see that openness and freedom from rigid preconception is not easy to attain, and the work is far from complete.

For many reasons then—the rich diversity of perspectives and people engaged in women's studies; the newness of feminist research; the hesitancy to embrace constricting standards; and the unusually strong desire for tolerance, experimentation, and growth—the ideas, methods, curricula, and theories of women's studies exhibit great variety and resist easy definition. Those of us now working in women's studies have called it variously a process, a field of inquiry, a critical perspective, a center for social action, and the academic arm of the women's movement. It is all of these and more.

THE "STUDY OF WOMEN"

For centuries, women have been "studied." Aristotle theorized that we were "misbegotten males," conceived instead of men when the winds were not propitious. Aquinas agreed that women were flawed humans, but he decided that since women were at least necessary for procreation, God had not after all made some terrible mistake in creating us. Freud discovered the vengeful, castrating, penis-envying character of us all, and the philosopher Karl Stern speculated about our "nonreflective," cosmically tied life of nature.[7]

Such concepts in past studies of women reflect their origin: They were conceived almost exclusively by men working together in institutions and disciplines absolutely closed to women. An examination of the many traditional works on women reveals certain characteristics:

- Women are generally looked *at;* rarely have we done our own looking, and still more rarely are we asked for our opinions concerning our own experience. Ideas that women have offered tend to be ignored or debunked unless they reinforce existing beliefs.

- Women are generally "studied" in a separate section or subsection of a work, as though we are some kind of extra appendage or anomaly, not readily understood within the general context of the inquiry. In Aristotle's *Politics,* for example, following a discussion of *human* excellence, is a separate section asking whether women as well as men might have "excellence," and if so, in what this excellence might consist.[8] (Aristotle decided that unlike men, who should be intelligent, rational, dutiful, honest, generous, etc., women are valued for two characteristics alone: obedience and silence.) An *Introduction to Islam*[9] contains fifteen chapters describing the fundamental beliefs and practices of the Muslim *people.* One chapter is entitled "The Muslim Woman"; there is no chapter on "The Muslim Man."

- Professional and academic studies of women reflect the prejudices and attitudes that exist in the wider culture. Without women's own perspectives to balance the historical fund of ignorance and superstition surrounding our lives, conventional (misogynist) "wisdom" has been carried into research by so-called authorities on the subject, has hardened into accepted theory, and has ultimately become "science." As science, these myths about women have been used to justify all sorts of oppression, from witch-hunts to clitoridectomy.

Until recently, the accepted studies of women from primitive times to the present have examined women as if we were senseless, semihuman creatures unable to speak for ourselves. We have been prodded, dissected, categorized and filed, researched and resolved. No wonder the traditional products of the "study of women" are distorted.

Such an approach to understanding women's lives necessarily produces poor information. Try reversing the gender, and treat the male as the adjunct of humanity instead of the female. Can you imagine a history of westward expansion containing a chapter on the pioneer husband or the pioneer male? Or how would you evaluate an anlysis of masculine attitudes on impotence that was researched and written entirely by women and was based on their observations alone, with no input from men?

WOMEN'S STUDIES AND THE ISSUE OF DIVERSITY AMONG WOMEN

Gaining freedom from rigid preconceptions is not easy. This is true for any thinker. As has the wider society, feminist scholars have been subject to bias and misconception, to prejudice, and to narrowness of vision, and our work has reflected this. Women's studies and the women's movement are now engaged in the arduous process of correcting serious errors. Among the isms with which we have been struggling are racism, ethnocentrism, heterosexism, ableism, classism, and ageism.

Early enthusiasm for "sisterhood," for cohesion among women *as* women, blinded many to the importance of understanding the *differences* among women as well as the similarities, and it led to serious theoretical and practical mistakes. In 1988, Elizabeth Spelman delineated the problem very sharply when she said that there is *a tendency in dominant Western feminist thought to posit an essential "womanness" that all women have and share in common despite the racial, class, religious, ethnic, and cultural differences among us. I try to show that the notion of a generic "woman" functions in feminist thought much the way the notion of generic "man" has functioned in Western philosophy: it obscures the heterogeneity of women and cuts off examination of the significance of such heterogeneity for feminist theory and political activity.*[10]

Spelman summed the issue up quite succinctly in citing Audre Lorde (whose selection you will see in Chapter 4): "There is a pretense to a homogeneity of experience covered by the word *sisterhood* that does not in fact exist."[11]

Sociologist Jessie Bernard, author of several books about women's experiences, had earlier addressed the issue this way:

. . . Ruth Useem, a sociologist, once commented on the inadequacy of the single mark she had to make on all documents asking for "sex." All she could do was check the F box. But she knew that this "mark of Eve" told the reader very little about her. There were so many kinds of F: $F_1, F_2, \ldots F_n$. . . . Whatever the difference may be between M and F, and whatever the origin of these differences may be, they are matched and in some cases exceeded by differences among women themselves. A woman may in many ways be more like the average man than she is like another woman. . . . In many situations F_1 may have more in common with M_1 than with any of the Fs. Rank, for example, is more important than sex in many situations. A princess has more in common with a prince than with a domestic; a professional woman often has more in common with a colleague than with a cleaning woman; an heiress with an heir than with a woman receiving welfare payments. Sometimes F_1 and F_2 have not only different but opposing points of view, each seeing the other as a threat either to a vested interest or to opportunity for achievement. The wife of a workingman may not agree with the woman worker on the principle of equal pay for equal work; she believes her husband should get more because he has to support his family. . . .

It would, then, be more in line with the facts of life if, instead of compressing all women into the F

category, the diversity among them could be recognized by allowing for $F_1, F_2, \ldots F_n$.[12]

For feminist research, understanding the diverse circumstances among women is critical. Obviously, we cannot allow ourselves to make the same mistakes we so abhor in other fields of study and in the wider society. Comprehending differences in perspective and circumstances among women is not only required to maintain the kind of relationships we desire among ourselves, it is a prerequisite for making credible sense of reality. Masculine bias among men not only impairs women's lives, it deforms men's own lives as well because it distorts their discernment of reality. The pernicious isms among and in women have the same effect: They injure the women who are marginalized, and they diminish the lives of all women, including those of the dominant group.

The reason racism is a feminist issue is easily explained by the inherent definition of feminism. Feminism is the political theory and practice that struggles to free all women: women of color, working-class women, poor women, disabled women, lesbians, old women—as well as white, economically privileged, heterosexual women. Anything less than this vision of total freedom is not feminism, but merely female self-aggrandizement.

. . . White women don't work on racism to do a favor for someone else, solely to benefit Third World women. You have to comprehend how racism distorts and lessens your own lives as white women— that racism affects your chances for survival, too, and that it is very definitely your issue. Until you understand this, no fundamental change will come about.

—BARBARA SMITH, *Racism and Women's Studies*[13]

Our particular perspective affects the way we experience our lives in a patriarchal society, how we see ourselves, how we understand ourselves in relation to different groups of women and men, and how we seek solutions to our problems as women. When we explore women's studies, then, we all must come to terms with "particularity." In *Women's Realities, Women's Choices*, the Hunter College Women's Studies Collective explains the issue this way:

Individuals come to women's studies and feminism from a variety of cultural and social backgrounds. As members of different races, ethnic groups, economic classes, and age groups, we bring with us different interests and preoccupations which sometimes make it difficult to arrive at a consensus.

Those of us who were brought up as members of oppressed racial and ethnic groups and social classes may find it particularly difficult to see what we have in common with those whom we have learned to classify as members of privileged, dominant groups. . . .

Our identity as black, Jew, Chicana, Puerto Rican, Native American, Asian American, or member of a less privileged economic class depends on our consciousness of the history of our oppression by others. Freedom from racist, ethnic, or class oppression may rank highest among our priorities, and to focus attention on a division within our groups, between women and men, may seem to us a betrayal of our common cause. How can we concern ourselves with the problems of the women among our oppressors or even with our own experiences of sexism in our particular group when the men in our group daily suffer oppression from more privileged groups and classes?[14]

Yet we are becoming more sophisticated in our analyses, and as we grow, we encompass and integrate more diverse perspectives, enlarge our understanding, and create the possibilities of connection. Says Robin Morgan, feminist theorist, activist, and past editor of *Ms. Magazine*:

After all, on the one hand, as feminists we celebrate our diversity. On the other hand, we've all experienced how difficult attempts at dialogue among different women can be. So what do we mean when we say we "speak feminism"?

It's nothing so sentimental (or arrogant) as presuming our differences don't exist. But it's nothing so cowardly (or lazy) as overemphasizing them to the point of justifying not engaging each other across them.

It's a complex, delicate kind of "feminist diplomacy" that we're still in the process of developing. It involves respect, courtesy, risk, curiosity, and patience. It means doing one's homework in advance, being willing to be vulnerable, and attentively listening to one another. (A sense of humor never

hurts, either.) Skill improves with practice, and practicing feminist diplomacy is challenging, exhilarating, rewarding—and at times exhausting.

Feminism itself dares to assume that, beneath all our (chosen or forced) diversity, we are in fact much the same—yet the ways in which we are similar are not for any one woman or group of women to specify, but for all of us, collectively, to explore and define—a multiplicity of feminisms. In other words, our experience as female human beings in patriarchy may be the same, but our experiences of the experience differ.[15]

WOMEN'S STUDIES AND FEMINISM

What transforms the "study of women" into women's studies is reflected in the terms themselves. In the *"study of women,"* women are objects; in *women's studies,* we are subjects.

Women's studies has a feminist base. Feminists do not agree among themselves on one all-inclusive and universally acceptable definition of *feminism.* Depending on a number of factors, the term *feminism* can mean different things and have a variety of functions. We shall see later that several different theories of feminism exist, and considerable discussion centers on what it means to be a feminist, what goals feminism should have, and how feminists should behave. Feminism may be a perspective, a worldview, a political theory, a spiritual focus, or a kind of activism. Actually, one learns best what feminism means by listening to women who consider themselves to be feminists and by understanding how they respond to events and conditions.

Just how much range in meaning there can be for the term is reflected in this partial list of the definitions of *feminism,* as reported in Cheris Kramarae and Paula A. Treichler's *Feminist Dictionary:*[16]

May be defined as a movement seeking the reorganization of the world upon a basis of sex-equality in all human relations; a movement which would reject every differentiation between individuals upon the ground of sex, would abolish all sex privileges and sex burdens, and would strive to set up the recognition of the common humanity of woman and man as the foundation of law and custom.

—THERESA BILLINGTON-GREIG, "Feminism and Politics," *The Contemporary Review,* Nov. 1911

. . . has as yet no defined creed . . . [Is] the articulate consciousness of mind in women . . . in its different forms of expression.

—"THE FREEWOMAN" 1911, *Votes for Women*

Feminism at heart is a massive complaint. Lesbianism is the solution. . . . Until all women are lesbians there will be no true political revolution. No feminist per se has advanced a solution outside of accommodation to the man.

—JILL JOHNSTON, *Lesbian Nation*, 1973

Begins but cannot end with the discovery by an individual of her self-consciousness as a woman. It is not, finally, even the recognition of her reasons for anger, or the decision to change her life, to go back to school, to leave a marriage. . . . Feminism means finally that we renounce our obedience to the fathers and recognize that the world they have described is not the whole world. . . . Feminism implies that we recognize fully the inadequacy for us, the distortion, of male-created ideologies, and that we proceed to think, and act, out of that recognition.

—ADRIENNE RICH, *Of Woman Born*, 1976

A method of analysis as well as a discovery of new material. It asks new questions as well as coming up with new answers. Its central concern is with the social distinction between men and women, with the fact of this distinction, with its meanings, and with its causes and consequences.

—JULIET MITCHELL and ANNE OAKLEY, *The Rights and Wrongs of Women*, 1976

Is a mode of analysis, a method of approaching life and politics, a way of asking questions and searching for answers, rather than a set of political conclusions about the oppression of women.

—NANCY HARTSOCK, "Feminist Theory and the Development of Revolutionary Strategy," in Zillah Eisenstein, *Capitalist Patriarchy and the Case for Socialist Feminism*, 1979

Feminism is the political theory and practice to free all women; women of color, working-class women, poor women, physically challenged women, lesbians, old women, as well as white economically privileged heterosexual women. Anything less than this is not feminism, but merely female self-aggrandizement.

—BARBARA SMITH in Cherríe Moraga and Gloria Anzaldúa, *This Bridge Called My Back*, 1981

Is a commitment to eradicating the ideology of domination that permeates Western culture on various levels—sex, race, and class, to name a few—and a commitment to reorganizing U.S. society, so that the self-development of people can take precedence over imperialism, economic expansion, and material desires.

—BELL HOOKS, *Ain't I a Woman*, 1981

Is an entire world view or gestalt, *not just a laundry list of "women's issues." Feminist theory provides a basis for understanding every area of our lives, and a feminist perspective can affect the world politically, culturally, economically, and spiritually.*

—CHARLOTTE BUNCH, *Learning Our Way*, 1983

Third World feminism is about feeding people in all their hungers.

—CHERRÍE MORAGA, *Loving in the War Years*, 1983

From Alice Walker we have this strong, jubilant definition of a *womanist*, a term that has become associated with the feminism of some women of color, as you will see in the selection by Patricia Hill Collins at the end of this chapter:

Womanist 1. From womanish. *(Opp. of "girlish," i.e., frivolous, irresponsible, not serious.) A black feminist or feminist of color. From the black folk expression of mothers to female children, "You acting womanish," i.e., like a woman. Usually referring to outrageous, audacious, courageous or* willful *behavior. Wanting to know more and in greater depth than is considered "good" for one. Interested in grown-up doings. Acting grown up. Being grown up. Interchangeable with another black folk expression: "You trying to be grown." Responsible. In charge. Serious.*
2. Also: A woman who loves other women, sexually and/or nonsexually. Appreciates and prefers women's culture, women's emotional flexibility (values tears as natural counterbalance of laughter), and women's strength. Sometimes loves individual men, sexually and/or nonsexually. Committed to survival and wholeness of entire people, male and female. Not a separatist, except periodically, for health. Traditionally universalist, as in: "Mama, why are we brown, pink, and yellow, and our cousins are white, beige, and black?" Ans.: "Well, you know the colored race is just like a flower garden,

with every color flower represented." Traditionally capable, as in: "Mama, I'm walking to Canada and I'm taking you and a bunch of other slaves with me." Reply: "It wouldn't be the first time."
3. Loves music. Loves dance. Loves the moon. Loves the Spirit. Loves love and food and roundness. Loves struggle. Loves the Folk. Loves herself. Regardless.
4. Womanist is to feminist as purple to lavender.[17]

"Feminism," says Phyllis Chesler, psychologist, activist, theorist, "is a way of *understanding* reality, not just a series of things to do. Feminism challenges our predilection for one right answer, one right God, one size fits all."[18]

Notwithstanding our diversity, certain beliefs, values, and attitudes are common to all feminists. To set a context for comprehending the rich variety of feminist/womanist thought, these common points might be articulated as follows:

- *Feminism* means literally *"woman-ism."* Feminists value women, not in the hypocritical fashion of centuries of male-dominated cultures in which women were valued for the work they could produce, the price they could bring, or the services they could render; nor do feminists value women provided they behave according to some externally imposed set of requirements. Rather we value women in and of themselves, as ends in themselves, and for themselves.

- As feminists we value the fact of being women as highly as we value the fact of being human. We do not accept the cultural images of women as incompetent, petty, irresponsible, or weak. In contrast, we affirm our capacities to be strong, capable, intelligent, successful, ethical human beings. Many of us believe that our history and special forms of experience have set the conditions for making us particularly "excellent" human beings.

- As feminists we value autonomy for ourselves as individuals and for women as a group. We mean to develop the conditions in ourselves and in our societies that will enable us to control our own political, social, economic, and personal destinies.

- As feminists we reject attitudes that regard the traditionally ascribed masculine characteristics of aggression, power, and competition as good and desirable and the ascribed feminine characteristics of compassion, tenderness, and compromise as weak and ridiculous. We tend to reject both the practice of separating human qualities into two categories—one of them for men and one for women—and the valuing of one of those categories above the other. Instead we recognize that all such characteristics may appear in either sex, and we evaluate each of them on its own merit.

- As feminists we understand that the majority of beliefs and attitudes regarding women both in our own culture and in most other cultures are false or wrongheaded, based on myth, ignorance, hate, and fear. It is necessary to replace myth with reality and ignorance with knowledge about women created by women, first for women and finally for all people.

- As feminists we point out that for centuries women have been denied our rights as citizens and as human beings. The right to vote, the right to earn a substantive living commensurate with effort, the freedom to determine whether to bear children—the denial of these and other freedoms constitutes concrete instances of oppression. We recognize that women possess persistent strength and spirit in the face of such oppression and are optimistic about the possibilities of change. Many of the qualities developed by women in the face of denial are precious and unique.

It is this feminist base—on the one hand, a realization that women's reality has been distorted, on the other, a positive and affirming stance toward women and womanhood—that transforms the "study of women" into women's studies. Women's studies might have been called feminist studies, and in some institutions it is. Although some feminist educators consider the term to be strategically imprudent (since it evokes resistance from entrenched and powerful antifemale forces within institutions), others believe that it reflects the connection that should always be maintained between women's studies and the women's movement. Indeed, a considerable number of feminist authors and activists have been concerned that while feminist scholarship continues to grow in complexity and influence, it may be in danger of detaching itself from the concrete goals of the feminist movement.

> *The question is: what is dying in Women's Studies—or killing it? I know this begs another question and appears absurd when Women's Studies is growing all the time, developing in universities, research institutions, even schools, publishing (of a certain type), beginning to get funding from "established" sources, credence, credibility. But if the profile has never been higher, what is that profile, who's constructing and projecting it and who's it aimed at? What is the price we pay for growth? It would be naive indeed to think there is no price. . . . What is the politics of Women's Studies? Why do I feel, experience, such disconnection between Women's Studies and political action? Is there a wilful disengagement from activism? What is the meaning of feminism (in all its global plurality) within Women's Studies?*

> —Ailbhe Smyth[19]

What *is* the meaning of feminism within women's studies? It will be in the hands of emerging women's studies scholars and the new generation of feminist activists, sometimes called the "third wave," to answer this most pressing of questions.

RESISTANCE TO WOMEN'S STUDIES

Women's programs, academic and nonacademic—even after three decades of excellence—are still often met with derision or intolerance. The same forces that limit the freedom, status, and power of women in the wider society tend to limit women within academe. For reasons we shall explore in this book, a pro-woman stance is threatening to traditional attitudes and institutional structures. The very word *feminism* carries fearful connotations for many people and evokes a defensive response.

Remarks that the student of women's studies may encounter express that defensive posture:

- "Are you taking that stuff?! What are you, a *man-hater*?"

- "Women's studies? What good is that going to do you?"

- "Since you've been reading that stuff you've been hard to get along with. I don't want to hear any more about it."

Faculty hear the same kinds of comments, cast a little differently:

- "Feminism is biased. How do you expect to teach a course like that fairly? You can't be objective."

- "You were hired to teach political science, not to waste your time getting sidetracked on trivia. *Women in Politics* is just too esoteric a course for this department to spend resources on."

- "Women's studies! Are you serious? When are we going to get a men's studies program?"

- "We've got to get back to basics. Women's studies is just a faddish trend that is destroying the very fabric of education and the works and ideas that the Western World is built upon."

It is interesting, and a little depressing, to note that after more than thirty-five years of a women's movement and thirty years of women's studies, the issue of harassment of women, not just in universities but *in the women's studies classroom in particular*, is looming large enough to warrant increased attention. Citing an expanding body of literature that examines various forms of harassment that are generally directed at female students and faculty by male students, professors of women's studies Marcia Bedard and Beth Hartung raise the question of how to deal with the growing harassment of women faculty and students in women's studies classrooms.[20] They characterize the women's studies classroom as often a "specific site of harassment" on campus, sometimes a *"Blackboard Jungle* revisited." Feminist teachers and scholars report adversarial relationships, taunting of instructors and female students, passive resistance, and disruption of classes (among others) as examples of the hostile behavior they encounter. Pointing out that many of these behaviors need to be understood "in the larger context of campus violence against women," Bedard and Hartung describe some of the forms classroom harassment can take:

- Claiming male victim status or challenging facts with particularistic anecdotes to undermine the credibility of feminist reading materials and instructors.

- Dominating class discussions (talking too much and too long so that no one else has a chance to express their views or speaking so loudly and aggressively that other students are silenced and the instructor is irritated).

- Aggressively pointing out minor flaws in statements of other students or the instructor, stating the exception to every generalization, and finding something wrong with everything from quizzes to books.

- Changing the topic abruptly in the middle of a class discussion, often to claim male victim status or shift discussion to a less threatening topic.

- Formulating a challenge after the first few sentences of an instructor's lecture, not listening to anything from that point on, and leaping in to argue at the first pause.

- Taking intransigent and dogmatic stands on even minor positions and insisting that the instructor recognize the validity of the rigid positions.[21]

Although women constitute more than half the human population, serious examination of women's world and its implications for all humanity is simply not considered meaningful and important from an *androcentric* (male-centered, from *andros,* the Greek name for man) or sexist perspective. Feminist contentions that both women and the wider society are being deprived of female power are not seen as valid; the argument is dismissed, just as women are often dismissed. Too seldom do the fruits of feminist research find their way from women's studies into the wider curriculum or the classrooms of other instructors—a situation that becomes a point of frustration for women's studies students and teachers alike.

BIAS IN ACADEME

Bias—which means prejudice, the absence of objectivity—derives from a term that means oblique, slanted, not standard or true, off-center. Bias implies some kind of distortion, usually unconscious. It is ironic that the enterprise of women's studies should be charged with bias.

When it is argued that feminist thinkers (or women's studies practitioners, as they are sometimes called) and women's studies are biased, at least two things are being said: (1) that feminists hold a set of beliefs that is somehow off-center, askew from "the truth"; and (2) that either we are unaware of having a distorted perspective, or we deliberately intend to impose slanted views on unsuspecting and vulnerable minds.

Feminism is perceived as a skewing of reality. Feminists would argue, however, that it is the traditional, androcentric image of reality that is skewed.

Centuries ago, discerning thinkers in science, theology, and philosophy recognized the fallacy of mistaking the part for the whole. In philosophy and theology, it was recognized that to mistake human values and perspectives for universal ones was to be misled in our analyses of God and reality. This mistake was called *anthropocentrism,* and cautious thinkers learned to avoid it. More recently, social scientists have become aware of the dangers of *ethnocentrism,* the practice of imposing the standards of one's own culture on another. *Egocentrism,* whether conceptual (as when an individual assumes that others see reality as he or she does) or ethical, also distorts understanding. The error here lies in assuming that one's own special view of the world is the true and only one, applicable everywhere to everyone and everything. Universally acknowledged to be fallacious, all such isms are guarded against—all, that is, except the most pervasive and distorting ism of all: *masculinism.*

Masculinism has many facets. We shall explore them in Chapter 2. Here we need only say that it is in part the mistaking of male perspectives, beliefs, attitudes, standards, values, and perceptions for all human perceptions. Masculinism is pervasive, except for the feminist challenge, and it is frequently unconscious.

In almost every culture, the tools and conditions necessary for learning, the means of communication, and the forms of legitimization of knowledge have been jealously and effectively kept from women. In some societies, the artifacts of history, the symbols of religious significance, and the activities of power are all secreted in a special hut, the men's hut, taboo to women. In other cultures, men speak a private language that the women of the tribe are forbidden to utter; in that language, the policies of the tribe are decided. In our own culture, until relatively recently—the nineteenth century—serious reading and study were deemed dangerous for women, contributing to discontent and rebellion against our "natural" roles as wives and helpmates. Too much learning, it was said, would drain away the physical energies we needed to produce children. Mathematics and science were particularly dangerous. They might rob women of a meek and gentle loveliness. Women were not supposed to have the stomach or the wit for politics. Such views have functioned as justifications for denying women the education, tools, and power to sustain ourselves and to direct society.

Women have been systematically barred from contributing all that we could to the intellectual landscape. Historically that has been reserved for men, and particular men with particular views at that, as we shall see in the next chapter. Even today, when many people claim that the battle is over and there is no longer a need for a women's movement, few feminist women or men are in a position to control institutional policy. Traditionalists are, for the most part, still in control of the academic disciplines, the universities, the learned societies, the large publishing houses, and the research foundations. With feminist views still severely restricted in the political and intellectual power centers of the world, the (androcentric) minority opinion is fallaciously taken to be standard. The masculinist establishment has, in essence, appropriated reality for itself.

All over the world, men as a group have dominated their societies. Their needs and goals have become official social goals. Until the advent of feminist analysis, in learning, male thought had become official thought, and the male stance was the official human stance. Until feminist criticism penetrated the accepted ways of understanding, the errors of masculinism were omnipresent and, for the most part, undetected. Consider, for example, the following analysis of the concept of respect written in 1973 by Joel Feinberg, a contemporary philosopher (emphasis added):[22]

In olden days, when power and authority went hand in hand . . . the scale of respect was one with the scales of power and status. This was the background against which the earliest moralists could begin demanding that respect be shown to various classes of the deserving weak, too. Hence our rude and unimpressed ancestors were urged to "show respect" for women, for the aged, for the clergy. . . . Christianity gave dignity even to the meek and humble. Respect could then be extended to the aged, to women, to the clergy. . . .

To see a woman as having dignity now is to see her as in a moral position to make claims against our conduct, even though she may lack physical or political power over us. Certain minimal forms of consideration are her due, something she has coming, and can rightfully claim, even when she is in no position to make demands in the gunman sense. Insofar as we think of her that way we have respect for her . . . and insofar as she shares this image of herself she has self respect.[23]

Today an argument so insensitive to gender blindness would probably not be written except by one determined to ignore feminist insights, and then it might be more amusing than shocking. Not so before women's studies! When I first read this piece in 1973, I was shocked, and it was my developing feminist consciousness that provided me with the tools to see and to clarify for others the androcentric skewing. As I read this argument, not only as a philosopher but also from my woman's (feminist) perspective, I thought: Indeed! And would any *man* in such a position—weak, meek, humble, and powerless—perceive himself with self-respect? Who is this author to speak for me? And who are the *we* (*us, our*) of whom Feinberg speaks? He is a philosopher addressing philosophers. But he could not mean that only philosophers grant respect in this fashion. (Besides, I am a philosopher.) No, Feinberg is analyzing the concept of respect as it is used, given, and granted in society, among people. Which people? Society surely must include women. Do women grant respect that way? Am I part of that *we, us*? I certainly do not think of women and our worthiness that way. Generic *we*? Rather not.

Feinberg's essay and his use of *we* (*us, our*) in juxtaposition to the term *women* is only one example among many of a worldview that constitutes humanity as male and relegates women to the status of out-group. This essay, confident that "we boys" are "we everyone," exhibits the masculinist usurpation of universality, conveniently masked by the linguistic device of generic *man,* so generally accepted that it is invisible to the naked (that is, nonfeminist) eye. Prior to the incursion of feminism into the intellectual world, such examples were commonplace. A film entitled *Why Man Creates* (1968), produced for the Kaiser Corporation and ostensibly an inquiry into the nature and motivation of *human* creativity, was composed of sequences in which scientists, artists, inventors, and symbols were all male; women appeared only as wives, foils, or the subject of art. *The Uncommitted: Alienated Youth in Modern American Society* (1960), a sociopsychological study by Kenneth Keniston based on profiles of alienated young people, contained not one female profile yet purported to be a study of alienated *youth.* The jacket of the book stated that "Mr. Keniston starts from an intensive study of alienated *youth,* asking why a group of talented and privileged young *men* should reject . . ." (italics added). An advertisement described a work entitled *The States of Human Life: A Biography of Entire Man* (1974) as follows: "In this study of the career of the *individual,* the age-grades are considered as escarpments. . . . The perspective of *the individual* . . . shifts radically as *he* grows from infancy to young *manhood* and from maturity to old age" (italics added). In another example, a logic textbook (used in my department) asked the supposedly general reader, "She won't give you a date?" Finally, the Constitution of the United States had declared, "We the people," although at the time women were totally disfranchised. The examples are endless, and they continue in the present, as you will see as you read further. A major task today of women's studies research is to uncover such errors and correct their consequences.

The conceptual confusing of *human* and *male,* historically and in the present, in all disciplines and inquiries, has been so pervasive as to be the rule rather than the exception. Only since the advent of feminist criticism have traditional disciplines and scholars—with considerable resistance—become somewhat sensitive to their own inaccuracies. Feminist criticism reveals male bias; it does not create a female one, as charged. Women's studies seeks to

be the prophylactic of bias, not the cause. Noted historian Gerda Lerner explains how replacing the missing perspective of women's insight transforms knowledge:

> [W]hen we see with one eye, our vision is limited in range and devoid of depth. When we add to it the single vision of the other eye, our range of vision becomes wider, but we still lack depth. It is only when both eyes see together that we accomplish full range of vision and accurate depth perception. . . .
>
> Seeing as we have seen, in patriarchal terms, is two-dimensional. "Adding women" to the patriarchal framework makes it three-dimensional. But only when the third dimension is fully integrated and moves with the whole, only when women's vision is equal with men's vision, do we perceive the true relations of the whole and the inner connectedness of the parts. . . .
>
> . . . We now know that man is not the measure of that which is human, but men and women are. Men are not the center of the world, but men and women are. This insight will transform consciousness as decisively as did Copernicus's discovery that the earth is not the center of the universe.[24]

Some researchers contend there are areas of investigation directly relevant to women's lives that may be pursued without a political perspective or a sex-theoretical stance: the female endocrine system, for example, or human reproduction. Such subjects, it is argued, are simply factual. It does not matter whether they are pursued by feminists or nonfeminists. Their content, being neutral in this respect, might be considered women's studies, but not feminist studies.

Feminist theoreticians in every field, however, are convinced that no purely factual studies exist. The way knowledge has been ordered, the methods of asking and answering questions, and the constructs used to understand data have all developed within a framework of male bias. Even an apparently true statement like the following becomes problematic from a feminist perspective: "The Renaissance took place during the fourteenth, fifteenth, and sixteenth centuries." A feminist historian illustrated the effect of a woman-oriented perspective on this traditionally accepted, so-called historical truth:

A young specialist in the Renaissance spoke to the obvious but unasked question, "Did women have a renaissance?" Her response was a jolt, for she suggested that the bourgeoisification of Italian society deprived women of power, created a patriarchal culture, and, in general, set women back in their quest for human liberty and autonomy. So what "renaissance" can be considered? What is progress, after all, if the transformation to a modern social order is achieved at the expense of half a population?

Such questions would never have been asked within the context of traditional political and economic history, nor would they emerge in ordinary considerations of intellectual "revolutions." The Renaissance becomes problematic only as a question of social history, and it is precisely that field with which the women's movement has merged to create a wholly new way to regard the human past.[55]

An interesting development of the past decade or so has been the growth of two new fields, offshoots of women's studies: men's studies, involving the analysis and critique of various conceptions of masculinity, and gender studies, said to be an umbrella enterprise, encompassing both women's studies and men's studies.

Prompted by the insights and new perspectives of feminist scholarship, some male scholars have begun to rethink the nature of masculinity, much as women have been analyzing the meanings of femininity and womanhood. Harry Brod, a theorist in men's studies, explains:

An acceptance of the obvious fact that most scholarship, in the conventional sense, has been about men, and the contention that such scholarship, in perhaps a more significant sense, has not really been about men at all. In my attempt to make "The Case for Men's Studies," I offer the following formulation:

While seemingly about men, traditional scholarship's treatment of generic man as the human norm in fact systematically excludes from consideration what is unique to men qua *men. The over generalization from male to generic human experience not only distorts our understanding of what, if anything, is truly generic to humanity but also precludes the study of masculinity as a* specific male *experience, rather than a universal paradigm for human experience. The*

most general definition of men's studies is that it is the study of masculinities and male experiences as specific and varying social-historical-cultural formations. Such studies situate masculinities as objects of study on a par with femininities, instead of elevating them to universal norms.

Men's studies questions assumptions that have passed beyond the horizons of usual scholarly inquiry to bring them back under critical purview. These assumptions about masculinity are so widely shared that they cease to appear as assumptions.[26]

Most feminist theoreticians agree that it is desirable that "masculinity" or masculinities (different versions of masculine ideals) and men's behavior be investigated in the same critical way as femininity has been, and by men as well as by women. That would benefit men as individuals, and it would accelerate the development of more humane societies. Furthermore, it is not surprising that feminist insight should spur men to look into their own lives. Men's studies can have real value and can complement and deepen feminist critique.

But some women's studies scholars are justifiably concerned about the development of gender studies programs. They argue that although women's studies is gender scholarship, not all gender scholarship can be or should be thought of as women's studies. Women's studies is and must be feminist, they point out. Gender studies may not be. If women's studies allows itself to be absorbed into gender studies, they ask, will it lose its feminist-activist foundations? Will its perspectives and goals be diluted or co-opted by men's interests under the guise of "universal" concerns, as they are in the wider curriculum and society? Might its women scholars and teachers, its methodologies, and its theories likewise be co-opted or displaced? Is gender studies one more example of women's interests being pushed to the peripheries of society, supplanted by the needs and desires of men?

I am both interested in and wary of the emerging field of Gender Studies, which is in some places replacing efforts to develop Women's Studies. Just as many people early on encouraged us to stop focusing on women, to move quickly to the goal of studying humankind, others today are urging an immediate move to a study of gender. We need to notice that the pressure is to ensure that what we study includes men (as subject matter, as teachers, as students). Some give that advice in good faith, trying to get to what seems a deeper level of analysis, to look at what makes us women and men in a way that recognizes their profound mutual implication. For others, I fear, the motivation is akin to that of people who get nervous when we talk "too much" about women. There are threads here from the old tangle: study that does not involve men cannot really be significant, cannot become general enough, cannot raise "the basic and most important" questions or introduce works that are "good" enough to merit all that attention. Studying women feels like studying a kind *of human, and a highly particular one at that . . . so let's hurry on to the "real stuff," which means that men* must *be more than present and in all roles.*

But if we do not study women, we will not become able to think about humans well, nor will our work on gender be equally informed by knowledge of and about women. It has taken millennia for the knowledge we have from and about men to develop; we can hardly critique it adequately in twenty or even a hundred years, nor can we discover or create knowledge of and about the equally diverse creatures who inhabit the category of women. I know very well how uncomfortable it makes men and some women to remain in the company of women for long, but that discomfort is precisely why we need to do so. Gender Studies requires Women's Studies, just as Women's Studies requires the study of gender. One does not substitute for the other; they are mutually enriching.

—Elizabeth Minnich, *Transforming Knowledge*[27]

Another issue raised in regard to men's studies is the matter of separatism, a strategy designed to maintain the independence of women's theorizing, and adopted during the early part of twentieth-century feminism. Sandra Bartky, a feminist philosopher, argues in favor of profeminist men, "gender traitors," having "a place at our table: They have listened and learned from us; there is much that we can learn from them."

While I no longer accept the overgeneralized claim that "all men oppress all women," I still believe that patriarchy, like racism, is a lethal, and,

unless we act with some dispatch, quite possibly a terminal illness of the social body. I still believe that a movement for the liberation of women should be led by women and answerable to them. . . .

Nevertheless, I feel that the profoundly separatist moment that animated radical feminist organizing twenty-five years ago is a moment that is passing. The reasons for this are manifold. First of all, we have discovered in the course of over two decades of feminist agitation that many men have been stalwart, committed, and politically effective allies, while many women, even some self-styled feminists (the proverbial wolves in sheep's clothing), have made crude and uninformed criticisms of feminism, trivialized our ideas, distorted what we say almost beyond recognition, and called for the defunding of women's studies programs. Second, younger feminists appear not to have the same need for separation of the genders that feminists of my generation needed so badly. I do not think that this is a result of "false consciousness" on the part of younger women. We are at a different historical moment now: many of the insights that my feminist generation wrested with such difficulty out of the confusion of our lives, insights that needed a protective space in which to come to consciousness and then to word, are now accepted by younger feminists as obvious, even self-evident.[28]

The problem is summed up well by Imelda Whelehan:

The central question must be—if feminism is to remain a politics as well as a polemic . . . what are the political consequences of "male feminism"? This question is an ethical one ranging from the issue of whether the woman's voice will again be suppressed in favour of the male authoritative one, to whether in the academic institution (the last bastion of feminism's growth) women's tenure—even in the "ghetto" of women's studies—will face renewed threat.[29]

In 1994, Ronni Sandroff, then editor of a feminist quarterly called *On the Issues*, wrote in her editorial:

BEWARE OF PHALLIC DRIFT. A compass needle always drifts to the North, no matter how you turn the instrument. Phallic Drift is the similar, powerful tendency for public discussion of gender issues to drift, inexorably, back to the male point of view.

Phallic Drift is when television coverage of incest concentrates on the injustices done to a few falsely accused male victims, while the masses of genuine (female) victims fade to invisibility.

Phallic Drift is when the "radical feminists" invited to talk shows are the women who take the "enough already" male-friendly point of view that the gender wars are won and feminism is already victorious. . . .[30]

More recently we could add, Phallic Drift is when wife battering is renamed "domestic violence" and discussion—in the media, in research, and in the courts—slides increasingly into concern for men who (according to certain widely publicized "pioneering" studies) are just as likely as women to be victimized by abusive female partners as vice versa.[31] Phallic Drift is when deliberation on how to protect young women from date rape turns into worry about young men's confusion in expressing their sexuality during these times of women's freedom. Phallic Drift is a clever name for the tendency of patriarchal society, ever resilient, to erase women's perspective and, when that is not possible, to metamorphose things to men's advantage. It is real and problematic for women's growing awareness, and it is at least a considerable portion of what women's studies scholars think about when they hesitate to embrace the advantages of gender studies or men in women's studies.

THE GOALS OF WOMEN'S STUDIES

Of course, in women's studies, as in any other field of study, the primary goal is discovery and enlightenment, the creation of new knowledge, and the correction of error in what is already believed. Specifically, feminist research aims to uncover masculinist bias in the history of knowledge; to employ a feminist perspective in gaining new information and new insight into the relations of women, men, and society; and to allow people to form new values about ourselves and our societies through research into the construction and consequences of gender, particularly women's experience of gender.

For women, women's studies seeks:

- To change our sense of ourselves—our self-image, our sense of worth and rights, our presence in the world.

- To change women's aspirations based on an increased sense of self-confidence and self-love, to allow women to create for ourselves new options in our own personal goals as well as in our commitments and/or contributions to society.

- To alter the relations between women and men, to create true friendship and respect between the sexes in place of "the war between the sexes."

- To give all people, women and men, a renewed sense of human worth, to restore to the center of human endeavors a love for beauty, kindness, justice, and quality in living.

- To erase from the world all the representations of unwholesome, illegitimate power of one group over another: sexism, racism, heterosexism, classism, and so on.

- Through values that are not contaminated with an aggressive, patriarchal worldview, to end the race toward the destruction of the planet and to reaffirm in society the quest for harmony, peace, and humane compassion.

Such goals may appear presumptuous or at least not obviously related to the study of women's lives. But feminists have found that the movement that began in the concrete events of women's daily lives has implications that reach to the very foundations and quality of all life.

THE ENFRANCHISEMENT OF WOMEN IN THE UNIVERSITY

Earlier, in the discussion of bias, reference was made to the exclusion of women from all the powerful policy-making institutions of our society and culture. That women all over the world should not have won suffrage until the turn of the century (New Zealand being first in 1893) is an indication of our exclusion from power in public life.

Until the end of the nineteenth century—except for the lowest paid, lowest status jobs—most women anywhere in the world had little access to economic independence. Within the family, they had small power over their possessions, their work, or their reproductive capacities. Legally they were at the mercy of male judges, lawyers, jurors, and legislators. Women of any race or class found higher education barred to them. Oberlin was the first American college to admit women, in 1833, but its earliest programs for women were largely composed of home economics, religion, and other "female" subjects.

Today in this country, because it is illegal to bar women from admission to any public educational institution on the basis of sex, we are entering universities and professional schools in increasing numbers, although the numbers are still disproportionate in terms of race and ethnicity; and the fruits of feminist research are increasingly penetrating the academy. One would think, therefore, that on campus the priorities of women would become significantly more important than they have been and that the character of the institutions too would reflect the results of our particular input. But strong forces impel many thinkers to be absorbed into the old worldview rather than to create a new one. The masculinist perspective in education, the continuing preponderance of male faculty and administrators, masculinist textbooks and curricular materials, the pressures of husband care and child care for female faculty and administrators, the conflicts between women's family roles and educational needs, the general contempt for women's views—all conspire to prevent women (particularly feminist women) from enjoying truly full participation in policy making or a sufficiently powerful intellectual/spiritual influence.

Certainly it is a major goal of women's studies to reverse discriminatory conditions in the educational system, and campus feminists engage in a number of activities to accomplish this end. Besides increasing the university community's awareness of the conceptual issues, we are often involved in activities directed toward changing policies in administration that have direct bearing on women's abilities to attend school: policies regarding admissions, affirmative action, financial assistance, health facilities, sexual harassment, child-care programs, part-time attendance, scheduling, and more. Feminist faculty, in or outside women's studies, move for fairer decisions on salaries, promotion, and hiring, and we work toward increasing women's participation in decision making by seeking important administrative or committee appointments. The intent is to create balance and to eradicate the historical accumulation of masculinist control.

Women have the right to full educational and professional opportunity, and this is the primary reason for ending university discrimination. But there is another reason as well, also profound and far-reaching: a desperately needed transformation of the university itself.

THE RESTORATION OF HUMANE COMMITMENTS

It has already been pointed out that historically, all over the world, education and research have been the private preserve of men; that today, knowledge and the formation of knowledge are still largely in the hands of men; and that masculinism distorts conceptualization. But as we shall see in Chapter 2, masculinism goes well beyond conceptual bias, beyond the universalization of male perspectives in thought, to a universalization of male perspectives and attitudes in values and behavior.

Masculinism is not only the cause of misinterpretations of women's nature, it is also the reflection of a disdain for women themselves and for a whole set of characteristics historically ascribed to women, especially in Western culture; to name a few, sensitivity, compassion, compromise, and aesthetic sensibility. These qualities, although officially regarded with respect, are actually only minimally valued except in women. In men, except in special circumstances and in measured amounts, they are often regarded with contempt. The complementary qualities have been prescribed for and encouraged in men, the warrior virtues—strength, competitiveness, power, emotional reserve—and these are the qualities expected in the public sphere. In any environment dominated by men, the warrior virtues are likely to prevail. The university is no exception.

For decades, educators have been decrying a growing dehumanization in universities, a waning of aesthetic and ethical commitment. Of course something *is* wrong, and we can look to many factors involved. But as we shall see, the androcentric university is a microcosm of the wider society, and its character defects reflect those of society.

Universities are products of the cultures that provide the individuals who people them and the ideas that govern them. In turn, by contributing the leaders of government, industry, art, and communication, and by bequeathing scientific and social theories or inventions and discoveries to society, the universities help to mold and direct cultural consciousness. An exchange of authority takes place between society and the halls of knowledge.

It can be easy to lose sight of the tremendous impact of much that is said and done in academe. What researchers and professors have learned and created in their institutions is passed on to their students, who in turn pass it to others through their work—in business, in government, in every phase of social life. The theories developed in lunchrooms and offices become tomorrow's "science," the "truths" that ultimately govern legal policy, psychotherapeutic techniques, media expression, and, finally, social behavior. If the truths of academe, developed in a masculinist environment, seem to reflect and reinforce the warrior qualities, it is small wonder.

Consider the tone of university experience. It is not difficult to see that human compassion and caring, personal sensitivity, authenticity, love, and openness are not highly prized in formal education. Even talk of such things tends to embarrass people, to make them uneasy. Academic language is distant, cold, rife with jargon. Instructional faculty combat with administrators. Professors bore and bombard their students with disconnected facts not clearly relevant to life experience. Students distrust and deceive faculty. They are wary of participation in class or intimacy with one another. Courses and programs die and are born and die again, fitting students (however poorly) to meet the requirements of industry or government but rarely giving them the tools to live well. Although it purports to be, academia is not typically a loving, caring environment.

It is, however, competitive, sometimes ruthless. Students learn to be "successful." Faculty spar at intellectual gatherings, guard their positions, and compete for salary, status, and power. We are all reluctant to reveal our feelings and admit vulnerability. The warrior virtues prevail in contemporary education, blotting out the humane—a condition becoming increasingly obvious.

HUMAN REDEFINITION AND SOCIAL VALUES

Many feminists believe that women's reclamation of ourselves and our power may bring about a whole new way of being, a redefinition of human values. I agree but have to point out that such an idea must be based on a belief that is much debated within women's studies—the idea that women are somehow in a special position with regard to values and better able to make ethical or humane judgments than most or many men.

For centuries, culminating in the Victorian period, a certain kind of woman—one who was removed from or had risen above her "carnal" nature—was thought to be especially sacred, especially like the Virgin Mary, a mother of the generations, a keeper of morality. In the nineteenth century, enshrined within the family, middle-class women were charged with the responsibility for maintaining human morality by keeping their own lives "pure," by investing the young with a love for virtue, and by creating a home where it could flourish. Women were to furnish society with a place and experience apart from the harsh realities of work and government.

The image of woman as keeper of morality was, however, double-edged. As we shall see in Chapter 3, it was based on all kinds of myths and misconceptions; and it placed impossible burdens on women, denying them their own freedom and requiring them to maintain public morality when they had no power to do so. Feminists quite rightly reject this image.

That women might be especially predisposed to human virtue may carry yet another assumption that is problematic: that women and men really are different by nature, at least in this respect. The idea that women and men have essential, unchanging (or unchangeable) natures, based in biology, is termed *essentialism*; it is generally rejected among feminist theorists, who for the most part believe that gender is socially constructed.[32] After all, the contention that women and men are *constitutionally* different has been used as the main justification for rigid role distinctions and female subordination for centuries, and feminists have taken great pains to gather evidence against it.

Yet the belief that the classes of women and men are different in values and social outlook, that many women may be in a special position with regard to certain kinds of judgments, is not necessarily based on biological essentialism. Rather it may be based on one or more of the following arguments: (1) In many cultures, women are trained and encouraged to develop caring or nurturing values and aesthetic sensibilities; (2) women's position outside the realms of power has kept us from being fully absorbed into the psychodynamics of power and warrior values; (3) women's history of oppression makes us especially sensitive to the abuses of power and domination; (4) the concrete realities of women's lives—the creation of life, the intimate connection with rites of passage, the maintenance of the necessities of living—give us different perspectives on what is valuable and important in existence.

From infancy onward, women's lives are suffused with the affective (feeling, experiential, noncognitive) aspects of living. Considerations of beauty, tenderness, warmth, compassion, and love have been prescribed as the special province of women. No doubt a masculinist society's motivation is not to make women especially humane, but to make us excellent servants. Nonetheless, our intimate relationship with the nonwarrior (or antiwarrior) virtues, our inculcated avoidance of domination together with our intact intellectual capacities may indeed render women especially insightful in matters of human value.

Women, particularly feminist women, hold a key to new perspectives on society. If new goals, values, and visions are to be infused into society, we must win for women access to all the centers of power and policy, from science and industry to art and communication. This a major goal of women's studies.

CHANGES IN LIFESTYLES AND SELF-CONCEPTS

Nothing goes deeper in one's personal awareness or has more far-reaching implications for the whole of one's existence than her or his sexual identity. This accounts in part for the great resistance to feminism;

it also accounts for the impact feminist learning and consciousness-raising have on students. Propelled into self-examination by the intensity of the search and the research, women and men alike report changes in attitudes and lifestyles that represent tremendous emotional, intellectual, spiritual, and professional growth.

Consciousness-raising means what it says: It raises the level of consciousness, of awareness one has about the feelings, behaviors, and experiences surrounding sex roles. The woman who learns how much of her personal being emanates from her social and political status as a woman must ask herself how much of that being she wants to keep, how much she wants to change, and how she plans to do it. Bewilderment, surprise, pain, joy, anger, and love accompany this growth.

Feminist instructors and students alike have been chided about consciousness-raising in women's studies courses. It has been argued that consciousness-raising (1) makes the courses "soft," (2) belongs in the women's movement, not in school, (3) is not a legitimate part of formal university education, (4) is brainwashing, and (5) sometimes causes great anguish with which some students are unable to cope.

You will discover as you read this book that women's studies is anything but soft. You will find that consciousness-raising occurs as a result of new insights and innovative ideas. Rather than brain-*washing*, raised consciousness comes as a result of brain-*opening*. Susan Bordo explains:

> [F]eminist cultural criticism is not a blueprint for the conduct of personal life (or political action, for that matter) and does not empower (or require) individuals to "rise above" their culture or to become martyrs to feminist ideals. It does not tell us what to do. . . . Its goal is edification and understanding, enhanced consciousness of the power, complexity, and systemic nature of culture, the interconnected webs of its functioning. It is up to the reader to decide how, when, and where (or whether) to put that understanding to further use, in the particular, complicated, and ever-changing context that is his or her life and no one else's.
>
> The goal of consciousness-raising may seem, perhaps, to belong to another era. I believe, however,

*that in our present culture of mystification—a cul-
ture which continually pulls us away from systemic
understanding and inclines us toward constructions
that emphasize individual freedom, choice, power,
ability—simply becoming more conscious is a tremendous achievement.*[33]

Consciousness-raising can be painful. Yet pain
is not in itself something to avoid at all times, for
there are two kinds of pain: destructive and constructive. Destructive pain is suffered in a no-win
situation. Embedded in the status quo, it leads to no
benefits, no improvements. It just hurts. Such pain
is best avoided. Constructive pain differs dramatically. It is like the physical distress we feel when we
decide to get our bodies in shape after some disuse.
Our muscles ache; we strain and groan, but we
grow stronger. Much the same thing happens when
we grow emotionally or intellectually. Our insight,
memories, and feelings—not accustomed to such
use—may cause us pain. Our new sense of autonomy and freedom, and the attendant responsibility,
may make us anxious. We hurt, but we grow
stronger. Emotional and spiritual strength are necessary to well-being.

Consider some of the comments taken from the
journals of students in an introductory course in
women's studies:

- "I feel like a ton of bricks has been lifted off
  my shoulders. I finally found me. For the first
  time in my life, I really looked at myself and
  said, 'I like you!' I decided that there is only
  one companion that you can count on all
  through your life—yourself. If I don't like
  me, who will? I took a full survey of myself
  and decided what I liked and what I would
  like to change, not because I wanted to look
  good in someone else's eyes, but because I
  wanted to look good in *my* own eyes. I feel
  so free, happy; like I could lick the world.
  This is the way I want to stay—this is the
  way I always want to feel. And I will because
  I like me."

- "I have more pride; I am more confident in
  myself as a woman. I used to wonder if my
  womanhood would be a slight handicap. I
  now realize it is my strongest asset!"

- "While we were talking about fear and pain
  being all a part of growing, I found a great
  deal of consolation because I had felt both. . . .
  It took a while, but I now realize that all the
  things I learned and have become aware of
  will not allow me to keep silent. Also, those
  feelings of understanding and support will
  never really be left behind because I'll carry
  those feelings inside of me forever."

THE TERMS AND TECHNIQUES OF WOMEN'S STUDIES

Women's studies must be pursued on its own terms
if it is to maintain its integrity. Although the integration of feminist perspectives and insights into the
regular curriculum is an ultimate goal of most feminist educators, the absorption of women's studies
into the masculinist domain is not something we
seek. That might involve a loss of the unique configuration of methods and approaches we have developed. The feminist classroom typically differs from
others, and feminist research bears the mark of its
status outside the mainstream.

Feminist Pedagogy

Feminist faculty, like any other, gather information
and ideas and impart them to students. Often they
do this in traditional ways: They lecture, lead group
discussions, show films, assign term papers, and
give exams. Just as often, however, they opt for
other, sometimes unorthodox, procedures.

Feminist faculty frequently diverge from their
colleagues in attitudes, experiences, or methods.
Many of us have come to academia from the learning laboratories of social action outside the university—from civil rights organizations, from feminist
groups, from political parties and social change associations. From these experiences we have come to
understand the strength of the entrenched power
structures. Others of us, having lived within the established system and having tried its regular channels and found them resistant, have learned the same
lesson in another way. Experiencing life, as philosopher Mary Daly puts it, "on the boundaries of patriarchal space,"[34] we have developed ways that are
often in opposition to traditional academic etiquette.

Although women's studies is beginning to generate some kinds of formal credentials, for the most part we enter this field as thinkers entered any field centuries ago—through experience and self-directed research. We have few models on which to style our activities. The criterion for our methods is productivity.

The result of these factors and others is a highly innovative, spontaneous, and authentic modus operandi. In a feminist classroom, one is apt to find group projects, small-group discussions, self-directed or student-directed study, credit for social change activities or for life experience, contracts or self-grading, diaries and journals, even meditation or ritual. Noticeable in a feminist classroom are two factors not typical in college classrooms: an acceptance of, and even emphasis on, the personal-affective element in learning; and a warm, human relationship among persons in the class, students and teacher. Feminist teachers are no longer at pains to maintain the manly aura of distance—from their work or from one another. Recognizing, too, that hierarchical structures can belie what is common to female experience, feminist faculty often seek alternatives to the traditional student-teacher dichotomy. These different strategies and perspectives often bring criticism on us, but we believe that they are sufficiently advantageous to maintain them.

The Interdisciplinary Nature of Women's Studies

Almost all women's studies programs, curricula, and analyses are interdisciplinary. For the most part, the programs have avoided separating into discrete departments. Although this has raised some serious practical problems—of funding, staffing, and scheduling, for example—it serves important purposes. Some of these are pragmatic, having to do with survival in the institution, professional flexibility for instructors, and the like; but the most important reasons for the interdisciplinary structure of women's studies are philosophical.

Feminist theorists have found that insights into the elements of women's lives and their effects on the progress of humanity do not sensibly divide into the traditional academic disciplines. Understanding, for example, how the concept *human na-*

ture is distorted by the omission of women from the subject requires sophisticated knowledge of history, sociology, psychology, linguistics, philosophy, and other fields. Feminist analysis requires global knowledge.

Sensitized by our own investigations, many feminists have gone on to challenge the entire departmental or disciplinary structure as it exists today. Some of us suggest that the division of knowledge into neat areas with boundaries that ought not to be crossed is analogous to (and possibly derived from) the warrior behavior of separating land into territories that then must be justified and guarded. Intellectual boundaries, we may argue, are not only artificial, they are destructive.

Feminist theoreticians then, recognizing the importance of global knowledge and not typically given to territorial competition, are at least interdisciplinary; I tend to think of us as counterdisciplinary. Elizabeth Janeway, feminist author and educator, comments:

> Women have both history and reality on their side. Our knowledge of the world as it is is really quite formidable, broadly based, aware of detail, and not afraid to make connections between areas which the traditionally minded see as separate. Our experience makes us interdisciplinary. Well, this is a most useful and needed ability in a fragmented society, and particularly in an educational system where the trend for years has been to know more and more about less and less. Research is valuable—if it is used; and to be used, it must be allowed to connect with other research and, even more, with everyday life.[35]

The Scope of Women's Studies

Given what has been said about the global nature of feminist research, you can see how broad a scope women's studies must have. It ranges across history, psychology, art, economics, literature, philosophy, sociology, political science, biology, mathematics, law, and on through every area called an academic discipline. Of course, no one can be conversant with the details of all fields, but the study of women's experience requires some sophistication in each. Thus, women's studies scholars must be multifaceted in perspectives.

At the same time, however, there is specialization. A feminist psychologist is a psychologist with a woman-defined orientation. She pursues her work with a feminist perspective and challenges the sexist bias and beliefs in her field, often—though not always—focusing on issues most pertinent to women. As a feminist philosopher, I have the traditional interests in metaphysics, ethics, and epistemology, but I add to their study my special feminist awareness. I might, for example, challenge the validity of Hobbes's argument that life is "a war of all against all," wondering whether this may be so for men (warriors?) but perhaps not so for women. I question the traditionally accepted basic assumptions of philosophy—its definition of *objectivity,* for example—and its relationship to prescribed male emotional reserve. But beyond a feminist analysis of traditional questions, I am involved in raising other questions crucial for women. What does the feminist idea of *matriarchy* imply for utopian visions? How does a notion of God as female change theology (thealogy?). What does my woman's understanding of the dehumanizing effect of rape tell me about the ethical implications of physical integrity?

Women's Studies and Feminist Theory[36]

Women's studies is the *academic* arm of the women's movement. As such, it is engaged in, among other things, discovery—learning about the world. Discovery is not only the uncovering of facts, although it includes that. More importantly, it is coming to understand those facts. Understanding, at any level beyond the very simple, involves theory.

Theory and *theorizing* can be very complex concepts, and there are several ways to use or define them. For our purposes, let us say that a theory is a system of concepts and principles designed to enhance the understanding of a collection of events, facts, and phenomena.[37] We observe certain facts (the constitution of the United States was not originally formulated so that women had the right to vote), or events (during the 1920s, feminist movements became increasingly active in many countries of the Western world), or phenomena (women are the victims of male violence everywhere around the world), and we want to "make sense" of them; we want to "understand." There may be a variety of

reasons to understand, to change things perhaps, or to put an idea in context. There may be a variety of *ways* to understand: to determine what gives rise to something, or to place some event in the context of other events we already know. For this reason, there are different kinds of theories. Some, called descriptive theories, *describe*; they tell us what is going on. Others, called normative theories, *prescribe*; they guide our actions by telling us what should be going on. Yet other theories are combinations of both. Most feminist theories fall into this third category.

A theory can help us to understand by providing a system of explanation, a framework, a way of looking at things so that we may know not only *that* something is a certain way but also *why* it is that way, either in the sense of giving reasons for it (for example, Susan is praised for her "sweetness" to induce her to comply with the expectations placed on her) or in the sense of revealing its causes, that is, what gives rise to it (for example, sexual abuse gives rise to latent anger). This is crucial, for should we decide to influence events (change them or eliminate them, for example), we do this by manipulating the conditions that precede and give rise to them. In other words, through explanations, theories give us ways to predict events and to control them.

As an example, suppose feminists note that poor, single women are being used as scapegoats in an election campaign (we *observe* it), and we want to stop it from happening again (*change* or influence events). We must comprehend why women are being used as scapegoats in this way (come to *identify what factors* in the makeup of society *give rise* to individuals taking this tack) and find ways to alter their behavior, perhaps by making scapegoating unsuccessful, or by changing voters' reactions, or what have you (that is, by *manipulating the elements* that give rise to the behavior we are concerned about). The more consistently we are able to *influence outcomes* as we wish, the more confident we may be that we have correctly understood (*explained*) what has been taking place. When we are able to accumulate a group of related *explanations* of this kind, we can weave them into increasingly complex explanations, which we call a theory. The goal is to create patterns of explanations broad enough to answer more and more questions, even ones we had not thought of before.

Now descriptive theories do not tell us that we *should* do a certain thing, like eliminate scapegoating—that lies in another realm, the realm of normative theory, which is in the province of ethics—but ethical values may affect the development of a theory by influencing the researcher in a variety of ways, such as the "facts" she chooses to explain, the information she finds relevant, the kind of evidence she will accept, and so on. Value may be "presupposed," assumed in implicit ways in the terminology or interpretation of "facts" (observations). The word *scapegoating,* for example, is not value neutral.

A theory contains a number of elements and strategies that lead to its success in reaching its goal (dependable information): It sets forth a series of assumptions or presuppositions, ideas that are taken to be true from the outset, without proof, such as, "What has happened consistently in the past is likely to happen in the future" or "Women's experience is more dependable in this study than men's." A theory provides a kind of rulebook to help us proceed, what we call method; it tell us what kind of information we may use and how we are to use it. For example, it might say that one may use only data that can be measured, or instead, one may use material that cannot be measured or even verified in the traditional way, such as first-person accounts, stories that people tell about their own experiences. A theory provides principles to determine which facts may be considered relevant and important and which will be deemed less so. Or it may tell us how to determine if a discovery is reliable or not; for example, it may set forth a rule that an idea is taken to be true if it is consistent with experience, or an idea is taken to be true if one can use it to predict the future. A theory describes, analyzes, interprets, and tests. Ultimately, it provides a framework within which to comprehend what we observe. Experientially (how it "feels" inside, how it strikes us), it clarifies, it elucidates, it makes events meaningful. When a theory becomes highly developed, it may be able to predict events, and then it is capable of showing us how to control events, how to change outcomes as described above.

Notice that a theory is not simply an unproven fact, as it is sometimes taken to be in everyday language. A theory is a conceptual tool for making sense of things and for giving us some purchase in participating in the direction that events may take.

Whether a theory is considered "successful" or not depends on its capabilities, on what it can do, and, of course, on what one wants it to do. That, obviously, will be determined by the theorist. For example, if I were looking at theories of violence, hoping to find a way to secure women's safety on the streets and at home, then a theory of violence that did not speak specifically to gender issues, particularly men's violence against women, would not be a "good" theory, so far as I was concerned. If possible, I might try to improve it—change or augment it. If not, I might discard it entirely as not being a proper (dependable? true? adequate?) theory of violence.

Gender theories, like any others, contain assumptions, guide observation, choose what is relevant, provide tests, and so on. Considering this, one can see how much a theory can be a reflection of its creator(s), especially in the social sciences, where observations and evidence depend on one's perspective, and testing is difficult. One can see why it would distort analyses of femaleness and women's relations to men to prohibit women from participating in the making of gender theories. The frame of reference of the researchers (men) would be skewed because it would be partial. Important observations would be missing, and matters of relevance (what counts) would be determined by those not in a position to make such judgments. Male researchers might make certain procedural choices that women would not make because of different attitudes or interests. The first selection in this chapter, "The Myth of the Male Orgasm," humorously demonstrates just these issues.

For a very long time, the prevailing theories about gender were thoroughly masculinist. Purporting to describe or explain women's lives, they contained almost nothing of women's observations or insight. Indeed, the men who created and controlled "explanatory theories" about women and men, about society, about life in general strenuously resisted women's incursion into "their" domain. Many still do, and there are many ways that they can keep women's views out of the process: by denying women education, by barring us from entry into the professions, by refusing to publish our work, and so on. Mary Daly argues that the masculinist systems of explanation that have predominated for so long have "amounted to a kind of gang rape of [women's] minds."[38] In *Beyond God the Father*, she explains:

> One of the false gods of theologians, philosophers, and other academics is called Method. It commonly happens that the choice of a problem is determined by method, instead of method being determined by the problem. This means that thought is subjected to an invisible tyranny. . . .
>
> The tyranny of methodolatry hinders new discoveries. It prevents us from raising questions never asked before and from being illumined by ideas that do not fit into pre-established boxes and forms. The worshippers of Method have an effective way of handling data that does not fit into the Respectable Categories of Questions and Answers. They simply classify it as nondata, thereby rendering it invisible.
>
> It should be noted that the god Method is in fact a subordinate deity, serving Higher Powers. These are social and cultural institutions whose survival depends upon the classification of disruptive and disturbing information as nondata. Under patriarchy, Method has wiped out women's questions so totally that even women have not been able to hear and formulate our own questions to meet our own experiences. Women have been unable even to experience our own experience.[39]

Masculinist science and philosophy not only barred women from participating in the creation of knowledge about the world, it barred us from participating in the creation of knowledge about ourselves, even knowledge that would be used for ourselves. It told us that we didn't see what we saw or feel what we felt, and it damned or ridiculed us when we disagreed with it. Women were silenced, and our experience was rendered nondata; our issues, questions, and insights did not fit into the "respectable" (that is, masculinist) categories, so they were rejected or erased, which served patriarchy very well. Feminism, in one of its aspects, is the rejection of that erasure. Enter feminist theory: We would ask our own questions, form our own categories, develop our own methods and theories, test hypotheses to our satisfaction, and create our own (more accurate) knowledge.

During the early years of women's studies, controversy arose between activists and academics over whether theory was necessary for women's liberation, or even desirable. Some activists, then oc-

casionally called "street activists" (the women who created and served in women's shelters, health clinics, rape crisis centers, food collectives, and so on), argued that theorizing was a waste of time, that it was masculinist, merely an obsession with empty abstraction, and that it could sidetrack feminists from engaging in the really important work of changing society and improving women's lives. Feminist theorists responded that without theory there could indeed be action but no understanding of causes, and without an understanding of causes, action might be misdirected, and there could be no consistently effective work for social change.

From the theory/activism debate, which still goes on in some form, it emerged that the distinction between academic and activist was not a good one: The women who work "in the streets" do theory in some form, and academics can be activists in different venues. Further, activism becomes more effective when guided by reliable theory, and theorizing ought not to proceed unless informed by substantive observation of the concrete realities of women's lives. In fact, theory and action participate in a dynamic: Theory grows within action, and action proceeds as guided by theory.

Charlotte Bunch, an important feminist theorist and activist since the early days of the second wave,* describes her entry into feminist theorizing:

> When I left the university to do full-time work in "the movement" in the 1960s, it didn't occur to me that I would return one day to teach or write feminist theory. Like many others who chose to become movement activists then, I felt that I was leaving behind not only the academic world, but also what I saw as irrelevant theorizing. However, as I experienced the problems of movement organizing when an overall analysis was lacking, felt the frustration of conflicts where issues were not clear, and observed people dropping out of political activity, I became aware of the critical role of theory in the movement. I began to see feminist theory not as academic, but as a process based on understanding and advancing the activist movement.

---

*The women's movement of the twentieth century beginning in the early 1960s is referred to as the second wave of feminism. The first wave refers to the period of activism beginning in the early part of the nineteenth century and continuing into the suffrage movement.

While my growing sense of the importance of theory applied to all my feminist work, the urgency that I felt about it became clearest during my involvement with lesbian-feminism. When the lesbian issue became a major controversy in the women's movement in the 1970s, I realized that in order for lesbians to function openly, we would have to understand why *there was so much resistance to this issue. It was not enough to document discrimination against homosexuals or to appeal to fairness. We had to figure out why lesbianism was taboo, why it was a threat to feminists, and then devise strategies accordingly. I saw that my life as a lesbian in the movement depended on, among other things, the development of a theory that would explain our immediate conflicts in the context of a long-term view of feminism. This theoretical perspective developed along with our activism. . . .*[40]

Bunch's story reveals important elements in theory: She and others could observe the fact of resistance to lesbian-feminism, but they didn't know *why* there was resistance; that is, they did not know what gave rise to it, what caused it, and without understanding causes, they could not respond effectively to it, couldn't "devise strategies" to either change it or deal with it.

Most theory is not monolithic. Because theories are tools, there can be more than one theory (effectively) explaining the same thing in different ways at the same time, just as there can be more than one tool for the same job. They may start from different points of view or contexts; they may operate on varying levels of complexity; they may frame the issues differently, or they may use different terminologies. For example, it is possible to "explain" a slap on the face from the point of view of psychology, or biology, or chemistry, or physics. They may all be correct, each in its own way, but their uses vary. These are large explanatory systems, different but not competing. Within these large systems, there can be subordinate systems—various theories within the larger system. For example, in psychology—a major system focusing on the individual behavior of living beings—we might explain in several different ways (from within several different explanatory systems) how a person might come to deliver a slap on the face: We might speak as a behaviorist or a Freudian or a mechanist. Actually, a multiplicity of theories is a benefit to the researcher, for in the clash of contending theories, new insights occur and progress can be made.

As it is with traditional explanatory systems, so it is with feminist theory. Feminism is a major system, crisscrossing through many fields of study—political science, sociology, psychology, and so on. It is an encompassing framework or perspective, with presuppositions, assumptions, starting points, and accepted beliefs. As a large worldview, it is a way of seeing the world. But within the worldview that is feminism, there are various theoretical stances or approaches to understanding gender, different ways of patterning explanations. There are theories and theories within the theories, some of them competing, some of them not.

As women's studies has matured, several theoretical stances have emerged, diverse ways of framing the issues to explain what women experience and to account for women's oppression. To help us understand those different approaches in relation to one another, and to give us a context in which to view the approaches themselves, some researchers have devised names or categories for them. It is difficult to categorize such a vast field of study as feminist theory, and most of the writers who attempt it admit several problems: Any categorization will omit important lines of thought, some theorists will fit nowhere, and others will straddle groupings. Additionally, feminist theory is in constant change, so categories must be created and recreated again and again. Finally, often we have little choice but to use patriarchal labels and criteria. They are problematic because they may be misleading, hinting at ideas that feminists do not intend, and because they may suggest that one or another theory evolved out of a patriarchal framework when it did not.

Mary Maynard, a contemporary feminist theorist, tells us that until recently it was customary to place feminist theories of gender relations into three main groups: *liberal feminism, radical feminism,* and *Marxist/socialist feminism.*[41] Most schemas of feminist theory include these three categories (and variations on their themes). Although some students of feminist theory tend to associate these three types of feminism with the early years of the second wave, they all have their roots in periods before the twentieth century.

Liberal feminism could be thought of as the classic feminism of human rights and egalitarianism, values that were at the heart of eighteenth-century Enlightenment ethics. Mary Wollstonecraft, author of *A Vindication of the Rights of Woman,* comes to us out of this tradition, as does John Stuart Mill and Harriet Taylor, nineteenth-century authors of the famous *The Subjection of Women.* Liberal feminism takes women and men to be equals in worth, dignity, and ability and therefore deserving of equal opportunity in society, education, work, and political authority. Social arrangements grounded in history—legal, political, and economic—are the problem, it claims, and if women and men would work together to remove the social barriers to women's full participation in all aspects of human endeavor, the world would be better for all people. Emphasis for action, then, is placed on acquiring equality for women by gradually extending to women the same opportunities and rights that men already enjoy. This is the philosophy expressed in the "Statement of Purpose" of the National Organization for Women (see the extract later in this section); it is also the reason why early members of NOW chose to call themselves the National Organization *for* Women and not the National Organization *of* Women—men were seen to be potential allies, friends.

Radical feminism takes a different tack, reaching deeper into the psychology of the relations of women and men for its explanations. It posits a virulent sexism, rife with misogyny (hatred of women) and masculinist obsession with power, as the primary ground of all oppression, not only of women but of less dominant men as well. It argues that *patriarchy,* a society built on those masculinist values, as our society is, must be hopelessly flawed, aggressive, hierarchical, and violent. Contempt for women, an element essential to patriarchy, results in the exploitation and abuse of women in both the private and the public sphere—in the appropriation of women's time and bodies in traditional heterosexual relationships, including marriage, in sexual violence, in the manipulation and misuse of our reproductive capacities, in economic exploitation, political subordination, and so on. Closely related to the contempt for women is disdain for the so-called "feminine" virtues—cooperation, receptivity, tenderness, and so on—particularly in men themselves. The fear of being perceived or treated as woman-like, *un*manly, both causes and reflects violent, competitive behavior among men. Pervading our social institutions, masculine competitiveness is a major source of war, abuse of the environment, and indifference to the sufferings of the weak. Worse, the ideology of sexism, the entire belief system that maintains a patriarchal worldview, is embedded in the psyches of women as well as men. The solution, then, must be sought not in equality (for who would want to be equal, even if possible, with such destructiveness?), but in *radical* transformation, change at the *root* of society as a whole and of both women and men individually. To accomplish this, women must somehow disentangle their minds from the social landscape (through consciousness-raising), perhaps separating themselves from interaction with men, some or all, temporarily or permanently. *Sexual Politics,* by Kate Millett, was one of the first works of the second wave to set out systematically an argument of this kind.

One segment of radical feminism has been termed *cultural feminism,* which celebrates femaleness and character traits that have been associated with women and "the feminine principle." It tends to hold that women *are* different from men, in some sense better people than men, because we are not attracted to violence and competitiveness as men are socialized to be, and because our lives are grounded in what Mary Daly calls the "biophilic"—the life-serving aspects of existence, such as regeneration, instead of what is life destroying, such as war and environmental abuse. Cultural feminists have been criticized for "essentialism," for assuming that there is an essential (perhaps inborn) female nature. However, cultural feminists often argue, as suggested earlier, that one does not have to be a biological essentialist to claim that women as a group often do have different values and exhibit different behaviors from men as a group. The differences have been developed precisely because women's social roles, opportunities, and circumstances have been structured differently from men's by patriarchal society.

Some, but not all, radical feminists are *separatists* (nor are all separatists radical feminists). Separatism, a view that tended to appear more typically in the early years of the second wave but still has adherents, can be argued on various grounds, among them: Women need space and distance from men and male perspectives to develop a worldview uniquely female; the misogynistic and aggressive socialization men undergo makes it difficult (or impossible) for them not to drive thought and action in their own direction, and women spend more time engaged in teaching and defense than is productive; it is pleasant and meaningful to spend time with women alone; and women who spend their energy among and for other women become more woman-identified, more biophilic, more inclined toward activism.

Lesbian feminists, for whom lesbianism and feminism are logically and materially related, may or may not be radical feminists and may or may not be separatist. Women who do identify as radical lesbians and radical lesbian separatists have developed a very rich, very productive body of analysis and theory. Lesbian feminists point out that thoroughly woman-identified, unflinching, and incisive analysis has been developed within lesbian feminism because its perspectives are grounded in a life that is centered in women's existence, lived outside male-identified values and social expectation and outside the mainstream (what many second-wave feminists from a variety of perspectives refer to as life "on the margins").

The third theoretical stance of what Maynard calls the "big three," *Marxist/socialist feminism,* employs the terms and concepts of classic socialism, but they are adapted to work within a feminist framework to explain women's oppression, which the socialists, including Engels and Marx, understood only partially. Generally, socialist feminists accept the thesis that capitalism distorts social relations, that society is divided into groups, or classes: One class is wealthy and powerful, possessing and directing the means to use and create wealth; the other class is oppressed and exploited, possessing only their labor, which is used by the powerful to amass greater and greater wealth for themselves. Socialist feminists tend to agree, too, that the increasing concentration of power and wealth in the hands of a few leads to a dehumanization of all people, rich and poor, which renders them cruel and exploitative of any who are subordinate to them. Unlike radical feminists, however, socialist feminists believe that such a system is not grounded in masculinist attitudes and beliefs alone but in the material conditions of society itself, such as technol-

ogy, natural resources, geographic location, and so on. What feminism adds to the socialist analysis is that there is another division of society into classes that is at least as basic as owner and worker. Grounded in and maintained by the institutions of marriage and the nuclear family there is a division of men and women into separate and opposing classes that is analogous to that of owners and workers. In patriarchy, women are used as a material "resource" to be managed and harvested. Our work, time, energy, and any other "wealth" we may produce or possess, including our capacity to bear children, are regulated and appropriated by the dominant class (men). Because they are designated as "private" or personal services, women's labors in the *domestic* sphere are not considered "work," in the commercial sense, and, therefore, they earn no salary. Confined to the domestic sphere, and without the financial resources that paid labor might otherwise procure, women are made dependent, and, thus, can be controlled. This is the source of women's oppression. Changes in our circumstances, therefore, cannot be accomplished only by changing belief systems (which are products of the social system), but by changing the material conditions and institutions of society.

The foregoing descriptions, of course, can offer only very brief sketches of systems that can be quite complex. Even granting that, there are systems that do not fit into these categories. Maynard recognizes that these categories now require augmentation and adds that especially in the last two decades several contemporary philosophies have changed the way many feminists do theory. First, she argues, the schema of the "big three" captures essentially a "White, Western" endeavor, and does not give sufficient place to the work of Black feminists, women of color, non-Western, and colonialized feminists. Second, it fails to give attention to the work of the postmodernists that has made such an impact on feminist theory since the 1980s and 1990s.

In her book *Feminist Thought,* philosopher Rosemary Tong gives us that augmentation. Admitting that it is difficult to categorize feminist thought but nonetheless useful to help us understand its historical evolution and its strategies, Tong proposes eight major categories (and then categories within those). To the "big three"—liberal, radical, and Marxist/socialist feminism—Tong adds *psychoanalytic feminism,* which uses Freudian concepts as a base but alters them to reflect feminist insight; *existentialist feminism,* building on the works of Beauvoir and other existentialists; *postmodern feminism,* which focuses on the complexity of thought and language and its implications for the construction of meaning; *multicultural/global feminism,* a huge and important category that presents feminist issues from the perspectives of women from different parts of the world, women of various races, religions, and ethnic groups, especially those identified as "subordinate," and women in other "marginalized" categories; and finally, *ecofeminism,* an approach to feminist social theory that focuses not only on the oppression of women but also on its correlation with the oppression of the ecosphere and all living things, and that often includes elements of environmentalism, antimilitarism, feminist spirituality, or anti-imperialism (or all of these).

Of Tong's five added categories, the most influential have been multicultural feminism, sometimes called identity feminism, and postmodern feminism.

There can be little question in feminist theory regarding the salutary consequences of *multicultural* or *identity* feminism, which has provided a corrective to a kind of blindness that plagued both the women's movement and feminist theory for at least the first fifteen years of the second wave. An extremely valuable contribution rests in its methodological focus—study of the intersection of the consequences of race, class, and gender for women's lives. Multicultural feminism points out that women differ tremendously from one another, in our experiences, our circumstances, our needs, our goals, our relations to men and to the rest of society, even our views of what feminism is, where it should go, or how it should position itself toward other—perhaps competing—activisms. No one group of women may speak for all women because we are "diverse." Our differences arise not only from our individuality and the uniqueness of our personal experience, but from our membership in certain groups. To posit *woman* as some ultimate, uniform category and then to derive from that category descriptions of all women's circumstances and interests is to commit an error of *essentialism,* the idea that there is one essential female nature and condition, biological or otherwise, constant in every

woman in any "location." One must not assume that what is advantageous to one group of women will be advantageous to all. Thus, one must not assume that there is one understanding of "feminism" or one women's movement with a single direction or agenda. Many categories "intersect" with sex or gender—race, class, sexual identity, ethnicity, age, nationality, and so on. Like a giant kaleidoscope, each multiple intersection creates new categories and new issues. Not only each woman, but each group must characterize its identity, carry out its own social analysis, and decide its interests and direction.

In contrast to theories that ground themselves in personal or collective experience, postmodernism expressly challenges the reliability of experience as an indicator of reality and rejects the idea of a unified identity drawn from it.

Postmodernism is a composite philosophy deriving from the work of Jacques Derrida, Jacques Lacan, Michel Foucault, and others, many of whom are related in thought to the French existentialist movement, particularly the insights of Simone de Beauvoir and her discussion of "otherness." Postmodern feminists do not deny the diversity of women. They agree that there are indeed differences among us that are grounded in our diverse experiences, but they argue much of our experience, perhaps all of it, is permeated by the *discourses* of the cultures we inhabit. (Discourses are the various expressions of belief systems, worldviews, canons, and so on.) Women are subject to a plurality of discourses, both dominant (for example, masculinist, White) and oppositional, those outside and in opposition to the dominant culture (for example, feminist, Hispanic). Both our experiences and the identities that grow out of them are constructed (formed) through and by these discourses. Analysis, then, should focus on examining and critiquing them. Those who are "others," outsiders in society, have an advantage, argue the postmodernists: They are in an excellent position to view the most deeply held convictions and behaviors of the dominant culture with a profoundly critical eye, and thence to "deconstruct" them, to pull them apart, show their error, and by so doing, to disempower them. This is accomplished through a variety of techniques but especially through linguistic analysis. Liberation lies in the direction of analysis and response to the dominant groups' discourses and the various systems of expression it uses to "construct" our realities. Emily Martin's selection, *The Egg and the Sperm,* is an example of such analysis, showing how the dominant ideology of masculinism embeds itself in the discourse of Western science, masquerading as fact or truth, promoting a particular perception of, and ultimately a particular "experience" of, gender.

There is a great deal of debate regarding the consequences of postmodernist theory for feminism. On the one hand, theorists point to the sharpness of its analysis, the utility of certain of its concepts for other theories, and the lessons it has taught us regarding the exquisite care we must take to guard against confusing particular social constructions with "truth." Postmodernist methodology provides us with a highly refined analytic tool. On the other hand, critics argue that by shifting the focus of discussion away from the concrete realities of women's lives to the analysis of language and symbols, it has pushed women's studies, as the academic arm of the women's movement, off track—away from attention to improving women's lives and toward producing only meticulous, and perhaps needlessly arcane, argumentation.

Surely this preceding schema cannot encompass all feminist thought, which you will see, is marvelously diverse, often highly original, and rich with insight. It is no easy task to wrap one's mind around all the ideas and systems of thought feminist thinkers are responsible for and we cannot attempt it here in one part of one chapter. You are at the beginning of a huge enterprise. Comprehending these approaches comes as you encounter the concepts that will be brought before you. Interact with them on the basis of your own experience and assess them within that context. As you look at each of the selections that follow in this collection, you might see if you can identify any of the elements of the various theoretical approaches.

"Radicalism" in the Women's Movement

A final note needs to be added to the discussion of theory regarding the use of the term *radical* in the women's movement, especially when it is applied not to a particular theoretical orientation, as described above, but rather to what one might characterize as an entire stance toward the women's movement in general. It is a term that bears scrutiny for several reasons: It is frequently misunderstood, it is used by antifeminists to create negative attitudes toward the women's movement, and it represents an approach to women's activism that has been at the heart of some controversy even within feminism. Feminists are often assailed by our detractors for being radical, meaning fanatical, extreme, destructive. The term is meant to create fear and hatred. Many feminists, on the other hand, cherish the term, take pride in thinking of themselves as radical in orientation. What accounts for the difference?

The word *radical* comes out of the Latin word *radix,* meaning root. The term, then, means going to the root or having to do with the root of something. Radical action would mean action directed at the root or base of an issue at hand; radical change in society would be change that is basic, fundamental, not on the surface of things, but rather far below the surface, where social elements originate. *Radical* does not mean the same thing as *extreme,* in the sense of immoderate or drastic, although radical change (or action, or what have you) can be of a very great degree. Obviously, we can see that *radical* is a relative term. Where anyone or anything is placed on the spectrum of radical to conservative has at least as much to do with the person doing the placing—with what she desires or finds tolerable—as it does with the person or action described.

Within the women's movement, then, there are two uses of the term: One identifies a particular theoretical approach, radical feminism. The other refers to a degree of intensity regarding any number of elements, material as well as theoretical: the extent of social change needed to redress women's grievances (for example, total social redefinition versus removal of legal barriers to women's equality with men), the kinds of strategy feminists ought to employ (for example, militant demonstrations and strikes versus painstaking political or legal action), the desirable procedural rules (for example, complete separatism versus male participation in organizations), or even language used (for example, reform versus revolution).

Even beyond theory, some have associated moderation or conservatism with the women's rights organizations aimed at securing equality for women and men through institutional reform. They have reserved the term *radical* for those groups who wish to go beyond institutional reform, beyond equality, to bring about profound changes in the culture as well as a complete redefinition of gender itself. It has been said that moderate feminists want to secure for women a piece of the pie; radical feminists want to change the pie. We must, however, use even this characterization with care, for clearly there is overlap. Radical feminists usually support institutional reform that improves women's condition, and moderate or conservative activists realize that even small changes in society beget profound alterations in our lives.

The differences between radicals and moderates are based not only on their theories, but also on their general philosophical orientation, ethical priorities, cultural vision, and even temperament. Compare, for example, the sharp differences in the tone, attitudes, explanatory constructs, strategies, and goals of the following documents: Ann Koedt's statement, which was adopted as the manifesto of the New York Radical Feminists in 1969, and the "manifesto" of the National Organization for Women, generally thought of as a classic example of liberal (moderate) feminism:

> *Radical feminism recognizes the oppression of women as a fundamental political oppression wherein women are categorized as an inferior class based upon their sex. It is the aim of radical feminism to organize politically to destroy this sex class system. . . .*
>
> *A political power institution is set up for a purpose. We believe that the purpose of male chauvinism is primarily to obtain psychological ego satisfaction, and that only secondarily does this manifest itself in economic relationships. For this reason we do not believe that capitalism, or any other economic system, is the cause of female oppression, nor do we believe that female oppression will disappear as a result of a purely economic revolution. The political oppression of women has its own class dynamic; and that dynamic must be understood in terms previously called "non-political"— namely the politics of the ego.*[42]

—ANN KOEDT, "Politics of the Ego"[43]

> *We, men and women who hereby constitute ourselves as the National Organization for Women, believe that the time has come for a new movement toward true equality for all women in America, and toward a fully equal partnership of the sexes, as part of the worldwide revolution of human rights now taking place within and beyond our national borders.*
>
> *The purpose of NOW is to take action to bring women into full participation in the mainstream of American society now, exercising all the privileges and responsibilities thereof in truly equal partnership with men. . . .*
>
> *We realize that women's problems are linked to many broader questions of social justice; their solution will require concerted action by many groups. Therefore, convinced that human rights for all are indivisible, we expect to give active support to the common cause of equal rights for all those who suffer discrimination and deprivation, and we call upon other organizations committed to such goals to support our efforts toward equality for women.*

—FROM THE NATIONAL ORGANIZATION FOR WOMEN'S "Statement of Purpose," 1966[44]

SOME BASIC CONCEPTS FOR THE WORK THAT FOLLOWS

This book is primarily about women—our experience, history, present situation, and future. It is about men, too, insofar as men's lives affect women. When we say that we are going to talk about women and men, when we use the words *woman, man, female, male, feminine, masculine,* what do we mean? What is a woman or a man? What possible different meanings do the terms *feminine* and *masculine* involve?

Perhaps the questions seem odd, their answers obvious. Yet it will become increasingly clear that such words as *woman, man, female,* and *male* are used in a variety of ways; they connote all sorts of meanings and, therefore, have wide-ranging implications—psychological, political, social, and so on. Unless this is understood, one is apt to encounter a great deal of confusion in the analyses of sex roles.

To inquire into what it is to be a woman or a man, one must understand that various contexts exist in which to formulate definitions and make analyses, and though these may impinge on one another, their viewpoints are not the same. For example, the fact that females bear offspring (a biological aspect of womanhood) may be partly responsible for the kind of work a woman engages in (a cultural aspect), and that may have tremendous bearing on her status (political and social aspects). Furthermore, to understand that arrangements of these variables may vary within cultures by several factors— class, age, race, and ethnicity, for example—and change from culture to culture (an anthropological aspect), it is necessary to know which economic and historical factors affect the others and how.

Before we continue, certain terms should be clearly understood because they are essential tools of our analysis. These are: *sex, gender, role, stereotype,* and *ideal.*

Sex is a term used by social scientists and biologists to refer to certain biological categories: female and male. Identification of sex is based on a variety of factors, including chromosomal patterns, hormonal makeup, and genital structure. The determination of sex is considerably more complex than is generally understood, but it is the least ambiguous of the five concepts we are considering.

Gender, on the other hand, is a social, not a physiological, concept. *Femininity* and *masculinity,* the terms that denote one's gender, refer to a complex set of characteristics and behaviors prescribed for a particular sex by society and learned through the socialization experience. For example, femininity (female gender) for certain groups of women in our culture requires passivity, fragility, and proclivities for nurturance. A little girl—given dolls to play with, prohibited from engaging in wild play, dressed in frilly or constricting clothing, and rebuked for so-called unladylike behavior—is reinforced in those behavior patterns here called feminine, and she learns to be passive, fragile, and nurturing.

The exact relation between sex and gender is controversial. Some argue that sexual characteristics are fixed in nature and account for gender and role arrangements; others disagree sharply. (This is part of what is called the "nature/nurture controversy.") Lionel Tiger, for example, argues that leadership or dominance is a characteristically male trait in animals as well as in human communities.[45] He contends that the trait is inheritable, therefore biological, and thus accounts for the dominance of men over women in human society. In other words, dominance or submission are biological (sexual) characteristics that account for the gender prescrip-

tion of passivity in women and aggressiveness in men. Tiger is challenged by those who point to the tremendous variation of behavior both in the animal kingdom and in different societies. These commentators argue that the observed malleability and diversity of behavior imply a loose association between sex and gender.[46]

Gender is composed of a set of socially defined character traits. *Role* is composed of a pattern of behaviors prescribed for individuals playing a certain part in the drama of life. The sociologist Theodore R. Sarbin defined role as "The organized actions of a person in a given position."[47] For example, the role of teacher in our society requires such actions as imparting knowledge to students, attending classes, counseling, and grading papers; it might also include certain attitudes, values, and even appearance.

In almost every society, females and males—on the basis of their sex—are assigned separate and specific roles: the sex roles. Differing from culture to culture, and within a culture by a variety of factors (class, religion, race, age, and so on), the sex roles are made up of a set of expected behaviors, with accompanying gender traits. The role of a middle-class white female in our society includes playing with dolls, helping mother, getting married, having children, cooking and cleaning, being sexy, and so on. Many of these behaviors in their turn form other role configurations. Marrying, for example, requires that one be a wife, which entails another whole set of behaviors. The role of a woman, then, includes a series of subroles such as daughter, wife, mother, office worker, and so on. In this book, we shall be largely concerned with analyses of sex roles: their nature, composition, effects, and implications.

Stereotype is a concept related to role yet distinct. Defined by one author as a "picture in our heads,"[48] a stereotype is a composite image of traits and expectations pertaining to some group (such as teachers, police officers, Jews, or women)—an image that is persistent in the social mind though it is somehow off-center or inaccurate. Typically, the stereotype is an overgeneralization of characteristics that may or may not have been observed in fact. Often containing a kernel of truth that is partial and thus misleading, the stereotype need not be self-consistent, and it has a remarkable resistance to change by new information; to wit, Walter Lipp-mann's remark:

> *If the experience contradicts the stereotype, one of two things happens. If the man is no longer plastic, or if some powerful interest makes it highly inconvenient to rearrange his stereotypes, he pooh-poohs the contradiction as an exception that proves the rule, discredits the witness, finds a flaw somewhere, and manages to forget it. But if he is still curious and open-minded, the novelty is taken into the picture, and allowed to modify it. Sometimes, if the incident is striking enough, and if he has felt a general discomfort with his established scheme, he may be shaken to such an extent as to distrust all accepted ways of looking at life, and to expect that normally a thing will not be what it is generally supposed to be.*[49]

Not all stereotypes are pejorative, but many are. For example, one stereotypical image of a feminist is a woman incapable of fulfilling the traditional role requirements for femininity, unable to "catch a man," homely, dirty, aggressive, strident, shrill, sexually promiscuous (or frigid or a lesbian or all three), unkempt, ill-clothed, middle or upper middle class, childish, making speeches, carrying banners, and burning underwear. It is this image that is meant when clearly feminist women demur, "Now, I'm no feminist, but. . . ." Many feminists are not middle class or white or college educated. Feminists wear a variety of costumes and have differing sexual codes and identities.

Stereotypes can have wide-ranging effects on both the stereotyped group and those with whom the members of the group interact. Stereotypes can and do direct behavior.

An *ideal* is much like a stereotype. It, too, is a "picture in our heads"; it is resistant to change, frequently inconsistent, generally fits a very few, and is frequently based on false information. But the ideal contains only traits the society deems desirable. It functions as a standard and a goal, such as a "lady" or "the American girl."

All of these concepts are involved in the analyses of women's experience. Feminist investigators ask: What are the biological, physiological, and anatomical characteristics that distinguish women from men, and what are their implications? Are the sexes inherently different in makeup and behavior? What are

the major psychological factors in women's lives; which, if any, are based on femaleness per se, and which come as a consequence of women's role in this and other societies? Since women's lives are apt to be markedly different across economic, educational, or racial lines, what traits or qualities, if any, can be said to characterize the category of women in general? How and why do they operate? How are the perceived female ideals different from the perceived stereotypes? What is their origin? How do they affect the daily lives of women in particular and people in general? In the following chapters, we shall be using the concepts of sex, gender, role, stereotype, and ideal to explore these and other questions.

Notes

1. Florence Howe, "The Power of Education," in *Women's Studies in the Curriculum* (Winston-Salem, NC: Salem College, 1983), p. 24; quoted in Catharine R. Stimpson with Nina Kressner Cobb, *Women's Studies in the United States* (New York: Ford Foundation, 1986), p. 4.

2. According to the National Women's Studies Association *Directory of Women's Studies Programs, Women's Centers, and Women's Research Centers;* cited in "Revolution and Reaction," *Women's Review of Books,* IX, no. 5 (February 1992), p. 13.

3. Marilyn Jacoby Boxer, *When Women Ask the Questions: Creating Women's Studies in America* (Baltimore, MD: The Johns Hopkins University Press, 1998), p. 5.

4. Boxer, *When Women Ask the Questions,* p. 225.

5. Mariam Chamberlain, "Enriching the Curriculum: Women's Studies," *Thought and Action: The NEA Higher Education Journal* IV, no. 2 (Fall 1988), p. 24; and *National Women's Studies Association Membership Directory: 1998–1999* (National Women's Studies Association, 7100 Baltimore Avenue, #500, University of Maryland, College Park, MD 20740).

6. From the Statement of Purpose, National Women's Studies Association, presented and passed at the February 1982 meeting of the Coordinating Council, passed at the Delegate Assembly in June 1982, and ratified by the membership in September 1982. Reprinted with permission of the National Women's Studies Association.

7. Karl Stern, *The Flight from Woman* (New York: Farrar, Straus & Giroux, 1965), pp. 21–22.

8. Aristotle, *Politics,* Book 1, Chap. 13, 1259b–60a.

9. Muhammad Hamidullah, *Introduction to Islam,* 2nd ed. (Paris: Centre Culturel Islamique, 1968; c/o The Mosque, Place Puits de l'Ermite, Paris, France).

10. Elizabeth V. Spelman, *Inessential Woman: Problems of Exclusion in Feminist Thought* (Boston: Beacon Press, 1988), p. ix.

11. Spelman, *Inessential Woman,* p. 1.

12. Jessie Bernard, *Women and the Public Interest* (New York: Aldine Publishing Company, 1971), pp. 7–13, passim.

13. *All the Women Are White, All the Blacks Are Men, But Some of Us Are Brave,* ed. Gloria T. Hull, Patricia Bell Scott, and Barbara Smith (Old Westbury, New York: The Feminist Press, 1982; quoted in *Making Face, Making Soul, Haciendo Caras: Creative and Critical Perspectives by Women of Color,* ed. Gloria Anzaldúa (San Francisco: Aunt Lute Foundation Books, 1990), p. 27.

14. Hunter College Women's Studies Collective, *Women's Realities, Women's Choices* (New York: Oxford University Press, 1983), p. 11.

15. "Feminist Diplomacy," *Ms. Magazine* I, no. 6 (May/ June, 1991), p. 1.

16. Cheris Kramarae and Paula A. Treichler, with the assistance of Ann Russo, *A Feminist Dictionary* (New York: Pandora Press, 1985), pp. 158–160, passim. Copyright © Cheris Kramarae and Paula A. Treichler, 1985. Reprinted with permission of Unwin Hyman Ltd. (A newer version of this book was published in 1992: *Amazons, Bluestockings, and Crones: A Feminist Dictionary,* by Cheris Kramarae and Paula A. Treichler, with the assistance of Ann Russo [London: Pandora].)

17. "Definition of a Womanist" from *In Search of Our Mothers' Gardens: Womanist Prose.* Copyright © 1983 by Alice Walker. Reprinted by permission of Harcourt Brace & Company.

18. Phyllis Chesler, *Letters to a Young Feminist* (New York: Four Walls Eight Windows, 1997), p. 14.

19. "A (Political) Postcard from a Peripheral Pre-Postmodern State (of Mind) or How Alliteration and Parentheses Can Knock You Down Dead in Women's Studies," in *Radically Speaking: Feminism Reclaimed,* ed. Diane Bell and Renate Klein (Australia: Spinifex, 1996), p. 172; originally published in *Women's Studies International Forum* (May/ June 1992).

20. Marcia Bedard and Beth Hartung, "Blackboard Jungle Revisited," *Thought and Action: The NEA Higher Education Journal* VII, no. 1 (Spring 1991), pp. 7–20.

21. Bedard and Hartung, "Blackboard Jungle Revisited," p. 11.

22. Some of the following discussion is included in my paper, "Methodocracy, Misogyny, and Bad Faith: Sexism in the Philosophic Establishment," *Metaphilosophy* 10, no. 1 (January 1979), pp. 48–61.

23. Joel Feinberg, "Some Conjectures About the Concept of Respect," *Journal of Social Philosophy* 3, no. 2 (April 1973), pp. 1–3.

24. *The Creation of Patriarchy,* Vol. I of *Women and History* (New York: Oxford University Press, 1986), pp. 11–14, passim.

25. Bari Watkins, "Women and History," in *Women on Campus: The Unfinished Liberation,* ed. *Change Magazine* editors (New York: *Change Magazine,* 1975).

26. Harry Brod, "Introduction," *The Making of Masculinities: The New Men's Studies* (Boston: Allen & Unwin, 1987), p. 2.

27. Elizabeth Kamarck Minnich, *Transforming Knowledge* (Philadelphia: Temple University Press, 1990), p. 139.

28. Sandra Bartky, "Foreword," *Men Doing Feminism,* ed. Tom Digby (New York: Routledge, 1998), pp. xi–xii.

29. Imelda Whelehan, *Modern Feminism Thought: From the Second Wave to "Post-Feminism"* (New York: New York University Press, 1995), p. 186.

30. Ronni Sandroff, "Beware of Phallic Drift," *On the Issues: The Progressive Woman's Quarterly* III, no. 2 (Spring 1994), p. 2.

31. See Jennifer L. Pozner, "Not All Domestic Violence Studies Are Created Equal," *Extra* 12, no. 6 (November/ December 1999), pp. 14–16, for her analysis of the trend as well as for references to several articles and examples.

32. For a good description and discussion of essentialism versus constructionism, see Imelda Whelehan, *Modern Feminist Thought,* pp. 205 ff. Also, for criticisms of the concepts of essentialism and post-modernism, see sections two and three of *Radically Speaking, Feminism Reclaimed,* ed. Diane Bell and Renate Klein (North Melbourne, Victoria: Spinifex, 1996).

33. Susan Bordo, *Unbearable Weight: Feminism, Western Culture, and the Body* (Berkeley and Los Angeles: University of California Press, 1993), p. 30.

34. Mary Daly, *Beyond God the Father* (Boston: Beacon Press, 1973).

35. Elizabeth Janeway, "Women on Campus: The Unfinished Liberation," in *Women on Campus,* ed. *Change Magazine* editors (New York: *Change Magazine,* 1975), p. 27.

36. For their kindness and invaluable assistance in reading and commenting on this discussion, I am grateful to Professor Carole McCann, Director of Women's Studies at the University of Maryland, Baltimore County, and Professors John Barker and Suzanne Cataldi of the Department of Philosophical Studies at Southern Illinois University Edwardsville.

37. I am particularly indebted to Professor Barker for this formulation of the concept of *theory.*

38. Mary Daly, *Beyond God the Father,* p. 9.

39. Mary Daly, *Beyond God the Father,* pp. 11–12.

40. Charlotte Bunch, "Not By Degrees," in *Learning Our Way: Essays in Feminist Education,* ed. Charlotte Bunch and Sandra Pollack (Trumansburg, NY: Crossing Press, 1983); quoted in *Feminist Theory: A Reader,* ed. Windy Kolmar and Frances Bartkowski (Mountain View, CA: Mayfield Publishing Company, 2000), p. 12.

41. Mary Maynard, "Women's Studies," in *Contemporary Feminist Theories,* ed. Stevi Jackson and Jackie Jones (New York: New York University Press, 1998), pp. 253–54.

42. *ego:* We are using the classical definition rather than the Freudian—that is, the sense of individual self as distinct from others. [Footnote in original source.]

43. "Politics of the Ego" was adopted as the manifesto of the New York Radical Feminists at its founding meeting in December 1969.

44. Reprinted in *Up from the Pedestal,* ed. Aileen S. Kraditor (Chicago: Quadrangle, 1968), pp. 363ff.

45. Lionel Tiger, *Men in Groups* (New York: Random House, 1969).

46. See, for example, Margaret Mead, *Sex and Temperament in Three Primitive Societies* (New York: Morrow, 1935).

47. Theodore R. Sarbin, "Role Theory," in *Handbook of Social Psychology* I, ed. Gardner Lindzey (Reading, MA: Addison-Wesley, 1954), p. 225.

48. Walter Lippmann, *Public Opinion* (New York: Harcourt, Brace, 1922).

49. Walter Lippmann, *Public Opinion,* p. 100.

The Myth of the Male Orgasm

Bette-Jane Raphael

Bette-Jane Raphael, author of Can This Be Love? And Other Quandaries of Love in the Eighties *(1985), has been senior editor for* Viva *magazine and for* Working Woman.

Here Raphael presents with wonderful humor the absurdity of research and theories based on myth, false assumptions, and misplaced objectivity. Parodying Freud and other "experts" who presume to explain and describe the female sexual experience from their armchairs, so to speak, she shows what nonsense might have been produced if the tables had been turned and all that we knew about male sexuality (or, for that matter, male anything) had been created by women looking at men.

IS THERE SUCH A THING as male orgasm? For decades, scientists have argued about it, written tracts about it, philosophized about it, and, in more recent years, conducted countless studies. But as Dr. Mary Jane Grunge, president of SMOS (the Society for Male Orgasmic Studies), said in her opening statement of the society's ninth annual cookout: "We still don't know."

But do we? Recent findings by Dr. Fern Herpes and her colleague, Dr. Lavinia Shoot, indicate that the mystery is at last on the brink of being unmasked. Working under a grant from NASA, which was disturbed by the cleaning bills for its last Apollo mission, Dr. Herpes and Dr. Shoot conducted a study of 300 middle-class men between the ages of 14 and 23. Their findings seem to indicate that not only is there a male orgasm, there may actually be two distinct kinds!

While 43 percent of the men in the Herpes/Shoot study were found to have trouble attaining orgasm consistently, or did not attain orgasm at all, and while another 4½ percent had no opinion, a whopping 50½ percent (four men fell asleep during their interviews, which accounts for the other two percent) admitted they had two distinctly different kinds of orgasms. After careful questioning, psychological testing, and physical examinations, Dr. Herpes came to the following conclusion (Dr. Shoot came to a different conclusion and left in a huff): there are two types of male orgasm. For purposes of clarification, Dr. Herpes called these penile orgasm and the spherical orgasm.

Of the two orgasms, Dr. Herpes hypothesizes that the spherical orgasm is the more mature. "Men who are enamored of their penises, who see their penises as the seat of all sexual pleasure, are just a bunch of babies. I hate them. Only the spherically oriented male can be thought of as mature because he can identify with the female to a much greater extent than the penile-oriented male. Thus the former's identification with his balls, which are the closest thing he has to female breasts."

Dr. Shoot, who consented to speak in rebuttal to Dr. Herpes, had this to say: "That woman is crazy. Men don't have two types of orgasm. They just think they do. My own findings reveal that they don't even have one kind of orgasm. Actually, there is no such thing as the male orgasm. What passes for orgasm in the male is really a mild form of St. Vitus dance. This afflicts more than 55 percent of the male population in this country, and if Herpes wasn't so hipped on orgasm she'd admit she's wrong. But as far as she's concerned, *everything* is orgasm!"

It should be noted that Dr. Amelia Leviathan is in close agreement with Dr. Shoot. She too believes that what passes for male orgasm is actually a disease. But contrary to Dr. Shoot, she believes the affliction is actually a form of epilepsy localized in the groin. She feels she proved this in her much publicized recent study of 100 male rats, 50 of whom had epilepsy. The epileptic rats, Dr. Leviathan found, could mate with the female rats, even if the female rats didn't want to. The nonepileptic rats just sat around exposing themselves.

Confusing the question of male orgasm even further is Dr. Jennifer Anis, who conducted a study of nearly 700 married males in their late 20s and 30s. According to the results of her study, the issue of male orgasmic or nonorgasmic capacity is clouded by the fact that many men simulate orgasm in order to please their partners. Nearly 25 percent of the men in the Anis group admitted they had at some time in their marriage faked orgasm either because they were tired, or because they knew their partners would be hurt if they didn't climax, or because they had headaches.

Nearly half the men in the Anis study had mild to severe orgasmic difficulties. (It was this group, incidentally, whose psychological profiles appeared in Dr. Anis's widely acclaimed paper, "The Prostate, the Penis, and You-oo," wherein it was revealed that all the orgasmically troubled men shared a common fear of their mothers' cuticles, a hatred of Speed-writing ads in subways, and a horror of certain kinds of peaked golf hats.) What has not been revealed until now, however, is that a great many of these men lead perfectly satisfactory sex lives *without* orgasm, a finding which would seem to put to rest the theory that men must achieve orgasm in order to enjoy sex.

Well, if men can enjoy sex without orgasm, can they also become fathers without achieving climax?

Here again the answer is by no means clear. Dr. Herpes and Dr. Shoot, of course, disagree. Dr. Shoot says yes, they can, if they think they can. Dr. Herpes says no, not unless they have either a penile or a spherical orgasm. Dr. Anis believes they can fake it.

Lastly there is the question of the multiple orgasm. Do men have them? Unfortunately, here we are still very much in the dark. The only person ever to do research in this area was Dr. Helen Hager-Bamf, in 1971. From January through April of that year, Dr. Hager-Bamf personally tested more than 3,000 randomly selected men for duration and number of orgasms. Tragically dead at the age of 28, she never recorded her findings.

So where do we stand? Is there such a thing as male orgasm? Can men enjoy sex without it? Is a low orgasmic capacity psychologically or physiologically induced? To quote Dr. Grunge at her recent press conference, "Who knows?"

Perhaps the answers are not as important as the fact that the questions are finally being taken seriously. So that, someday, the boy who sells shoes, the young fellow in upholstery, and the man who sews alligators on shirts will no longer have to walk around in perplexity, confused and unnerved by the myth of the male orgasm.

When that day arrives, perhaps male sexuality will come out of the bathroom and into the bedroom where it belongs.

Womanism and Black Feminism

Patricia Hill Collins

Patricia Hill Collins is the Charles Phelps Taft Professor of Sociology in the Department of African-American Studies at the University of Cincinnati. Her works include Black Feminist Thought: Knowledge, Consciousness, and the Politics of Empowerment *(1990) and* Race, Class and Gender: An Anthology *(1992), which she edited with Margaret L. Andersen.*

Black feminism and womanism are two terms used to denote African-American women's feminist theorizing. How are they different, and why is it important?

Professor Collins tells us that a rich tradition of Black women intellectuals of the past thirty years has created a "voice" for Black women as "agents of knowledge" regarding core themes for women, including family, work, motherhood, and sexual politics. The work is in the wide tradition of feminist analysis, but it is unique to the African-American community. The name given to a "Black women's standpoint" and "intellectual production" regarding gender, womanism *or* Black feminism, *is important, she tells us, because it will reflect different perspectives and priorities, different agendas, and different relationships to the rest of the African-American community and to the global women's movement.*

WOMANISM

Alice Walker's multiple definitions of the term *womanist* shed light on the issue of why many African-American women prefer the term *womanism* to *Black feminism*. Walker offers two seemingly contradictory meanings of *womanist*. On the one hand, Walker clearly sees womanism as rooted in Black women's particular history of racial and gender op-

pression in the United States. Taking the term from "You acting womanish," the southern Black folk expression of mothers to female children, Walker suggests that Black women's concrete history fosters a womanist worldview accessible primarily and perhaps exclusively to African-American women. Womanish girls acted in outrageous, courageous, and willful ways, using attributes that freed them from the conventions long limiting White women. Womanish girls wanted to know more and in greater depth than what was considered good for them. They were responsible, in charge, and serious (1983, xi).

On the other hand, Walker aspires to a universal meaning of *womanist* that transcends particular histories, including that of African-American women. Walker sees womanists as being "traditionally universalist," a philosophy invoked by her metaphor of the garden, where room exists for all flowers to bloom equally and differently. Despite this disclaimer, Walker implies that African-American women are somehow superior to White women because of their Black folk tradition. Defining *womanish* as the opposite of the "frivolous, irresponsible, not serious" *girlish* (1983, xi), Walker constructs Black women's experiences in opposition to those of White women. This meaning presents womanism as different from and superior to feminism, a difference allegedly stemming from Black and White women's different histories within American racism. Walker's much cited phrase, "Womanist is to feminist as purple to lavender" (xii) clearly seems designed to set up this type of comparison—Black women are womanist, whereas White women remain merely feminist.

This usage sits squarely in Black nationalist traditions premised on the belief that Blacks and Whites cannot function as equals while inhabiting the same territory or participating in the same social institutions (Van Deburg 1992). Since Black nationalist philosophies posit that Whites as a group have a vested interest in continuing a system of institutionalized racism, they typically see little use for African-American integration or assimilation into a system predicated on Black subjugation. Black nationalist approaches also support a Black moral superiority over Whites because of Black suffering (Pinkney 1976; Moses 1978).

Walker's use of the term *womanist* promises to African-American women who operate within these Black nationalist assumptions yet see the need to address women's issues within African-American communities a partial reconciliation of two seemingly incompatible philosophies. Although womanism raises the issue of gender, it simultaneously offers a distance from the "enemy," in this case, Whites generally and White women in particular. Because of its seeming endorsement of racial separatism, this interpretation of womanism offers a vocabulary for addressing gender issues within African-American communities without violating norms of racial solidarity of Black civil society. Geneva Smitherman's understanding of womanism taps this meaning. For Smitherman, a womanist refers to an "African-American woman who is rooted in the Black community and committed to the development of herself and the entire community" (1996, 104). This usage provides Smitherman and others continuity with earlier generations of "race women" who worked on behalf of Black civil society.

This use of womanism sidesteps an issue central to many White feminists, namely, finding ways to foster interracial cooperation among women. African-American women who embrace Black nationalist philosophies typically express little interest in working with White women—in fact, White women are defined as part of the problem (see, e.g., Welsing 1991). Moreover, womanism appears to provide an avenue for fostering stronger relationships between Black women and Black men in the United States, another very important issue for African-American women regardless of their political perspective. Again, Walker's definition provides guidance when she notes that womanists are "committed to survival and wholeness of entire people, male *and* female" (1983, xi). Many Black women in the United States view feminism as a movement that, at best, is exclusively for women and, at worst, is dedicated to attacking or eliminating men. Shirley Williams

takes this view when she notes that in contrast to feminism, "womanist inquiry . . . assumes that it can talk both effectively and productively about men" (1990, 70). Womanism seemingly supplies a way for Black women to address gender oppression without attacking Black men.

Walker also presents a visionary meaning for womanism that dovetails with Black civil society's norms concerning the centrality of moral, ethical principles to Black political struggle. As part of her second definition of *womanist*, Walker has a Black girl pose the question "Mama, why are we brown, pink, and yellow, and our cousins are white, beige, and black?" (1983, xi). The response, "The colored race is just like a flower garden, with every color flower represented" (xi), both criticizes colorism within African-American communities and broadens the notion of humanity to make all people "people of color." Reading this passage as a metaphor, womanism thus furnishes a vision wherein women and men of different colors coexist like flowers in a garden yet retain their cultural distinctiveness and integrity.

This meaning of womanism also invokes another major political tradition within African-American politics, namely, a pluralist version of Black empowerment (Van Deburg 1992). Pluralism views society as being composed of various ethnic and interest groups, all of whom compete for goods and services. Equity lies in providing equal opportunities, rights, and respect to all groups. By retaining Black cultural distinctiveness and integrity, pluralism offers a modified version of racial integration premised not on individual assimilation but on group integration. Clearly rejecting what they perceive as the limited vision of feminism projected by North American White women, many Black women theorists have been attracted to the joining of pluralism and racial integration in this interpretation of Walker's womanism. Black women theologians, in particular, illustrate this use (Cannon 1988; Townes 1993; Sanders 1995). As an ethical system, womanism is always in the making—it is not a closed, fixed system of ideas but one that continually evolves through its rejection of all forms of oppression and its commitment to social justice.

Walker's definition thus manages to invoke three important yet seemingly contradictory philosophies that frame Black social and political thought in the United States. By claiming a moral and epistemological superiority for Black women because of their suffering under racial and gender oppression, Walker invokes Black nationalism. Through the metaphor of the garden, she embraces pluralism, and her claims that Black women are "traditionally universalist" call up integration and assimilation (Van Deburg 1992). Just as Black nationalism and racial integration coexist in uneasy partnership, with pluralism occupying the contested terrain between the two, Walker's definition of womanism demonstrates comparable tensions. By both grounding womanism in the concrete experiences of African-American women and generalizing about the potential for realizing a humanist vision of community via the experiences of African-American women, Walker depicts the potential for oppressed people to possess a moral vision and a standpoint on society that grows from their situation of oppression. This standpoint also emerges as an incipient foundation for a more humanistic, just society. Overall, these uses of Walker's term *womanist* create conceptual space to explore philosophical differences that exist among African-American women.

One particularly significant feature of African-American women's use of *womanist* concerns the part of Walker's definition that remains neglected. A troublesome line for many Black women who self-define as womanists precedes the often cited passage "committed to survival and wholeness of entire people, male *and* female." Just before Walker offers this admonition that womanists, by definition, are committed to wholeness, she states that a womanist is also "a woman who loves other women, sexually and/or nonsexually" (1983, xi). The relative silence of womanists on this dimension of womanism speaks to many African-American women's continued ambivalence in dealing with the links between race, gender, and sexuality, in this case, the "taboo" sexuality of lesbianism. In her essay "The Truth That Never Hurts: Black Lesbians in Fiction in the 1980s" (1990), Black feminist critic Barbara Smith points out that African-American women have yet to come to terms with homophobia in African-American communities. Smith applauds the growth of Black women's fiction in the 1980s but also observes that within Black feminist intellectual production, Black lesbians continue to be ignored. Despite the fact that some of the most prominent

and powerful Black women thinkers claimed by both womanists and Black feminists were and are lesbians, this precept often remains unacknowledged in the work of African-American writers. In the same way that many people read the Bible, carefully selecting the parts that agree with their worldview and rejecting the rest, many people engage in selective readings of Walker's womanism.

Another significant feature of African-American women's multiple uses of womanism concerns the potential for a slippage between the real and the ideal. To me, there is a distinction between describing Black women's responses to racial and gender oppression in the United States as womanist, and using *womanism* as a visionary term delineating an ethical or ideal vision of humanity for all people. Identifying the liberatory *potential* within Black women's communities that emerges from concrete, historical experiences differs from claiming that these same communities have already *arrived* at this ideal, "womanist" end point. Refusing to distinguish carefully between these two meanings of womanism thus collapses the historically real and the future ideal into one privileged position for African-American women in the present. Taking this position is reminiscent of the response of some Black women to the admittedly narrow feminist agenda forwarded by White women in the early 1970s. Those Black women proclaimed that they were already "liberated," although this was far from the truth.

BLACK FEMINISM

African-American women who use the term *Black feminism* also attach varying interpretations to this term. According to Black feminist theorist and activist Pearl Cleage, feminism is "the belief that women are full human beings capable of participation and leadership in the full range of human activities—intellectual, political, social, sexual, spiritual and economic" (1993, 28). In its broadest sense, feminism constitutes both an ideology and a global political movement that confronts sexism, a social relationship in which men as a collectivity have authority over women as a collectivity.

Globally, a feminist agenda encompasses several major areas. First and foremost, the economic status of women and issues associated with women's poverty, such as educational opportunities for girls, industrial development, employment policies, prostitution, and inheritance laws concerning property, constitute important women's issues globally. Political rights for women, such as the right to vote, to assemble, to travel in public, and to hold office, as well as the rights of political prisoners, and basic human rights violations against women, such as rape and torture, constitute a second area of concern. A third area of global attention consists of marital and family issues, such as marriage and divorce laws, child custody policies, and domestic labor. Women's health and survival issues, such as reproductive rights, pregnancy, sexuality, and AIDS constitute another area of global feminist concern. This broad global feminist agenda finds varying expressions in different regions of the world and among diverse populations.

Using the term *Black feminism* positions African-American women to examine how the particular constellation of issues affecting Black women in the United States are part of issues of women's emancipation struggles globally (Davis 1989; James and Busia 1994). In the context of feminism as a global political movement for women's rights and emancipation, the feminism that African-American women encounter in the United States represents a narrow segment refracted through the binary thinking of American racial politics. Because the media in the United States portray feminism as a for-Whites-only movement and because many White women have accepted racially segregated institutions of all types, including feminist organizations, feminism is often viewed by American Blacks and Whites as the cultural property of White women (Caraway 1991). Despite considerable ideological heterogeneity that operates within the term *feminism,* unfortunately racial segregation in the United States and the hegemonic ideologies that accompany it typically obscure this plurality.

Despite their erasure in the media, many African-American women have long struggled against this exclusionary American feminism and have participated in what appear to be for-Whites-only feminist activities. In some cases, Black women have directly challenged the assumptions guiding feminist organizations controlled by White women in order to generate more inclusive feminist agendas (see, e.g.,

Matthews 1989 and Poster 1995). At other times, even though Black women's past and present participation in feminist organizations remains largely invisible—for example, Pauli Murray made many contributions as a founding member of the National Organization for Women—African-American women have participated in women's organizations. In still other cases, Black women have combined allegedly divergent political agendas. For example, Pearl Cleage observes that Black feminist politics and Black nationalist politics need not be contradictory: "I don't think you can be a true Black Nationalist, dedicated to the freedom of Black people *without* being a feminist, Black *people* being made up of both men and *women,* after all, and feminism being nothing more or less than a belief in the political, social and legal equality of women" (1993, 180).

In the United States, the term *Black feminism* also disrupts the racism inherent in presenting feminism as a for-Whites-only ideology and political movement. Inserting the adjective *Black* challenges the assumed Whiteness of feminism and disrupts the false universal of this term for both White and Black American women. Since many White women think that Black women lack feminist consciousness, the term *Black feminist* both highlights the contradictions underlying the assumed Whiteness of feminism and reminds White women that they are neither the only nor the normative "feminists." Because it challenges Black women to confront their own views on sexism and women's oppression, the term *Black feminism* also makes many African-American women uncomfortable. Even though they may support global feminist ideas, large numbers of African-American women reject the term *feminism* because of its perceived association with Whiteness. They are not alone in this rejection, since women of color globally have questioned the association of the term *feminism* with Western domination. Within this context, many Black women in the United States see feminism as operating exclusively within the term *White American* and perceive its opposite as being *Black American.* When given these two narrow and false choices, Black women routinely choose "race" and let the lesser question of "gender" go. In this situation, those Black women who identify with feminism must be recoded as either non-Black or less authentically Black.[8]

The term *Black feminist* also disrupts a long-standing and largely unquestioned reliance on racial solidarity in Black civil society (Dyson 1993). Using family rhetoric that views Black family, community, race, and nation as a series of nested boxes, each gaining meaning from the other, certain rules apply to all levels of this "family" organization (Gilroy 1992). Just as families have internal, naturalized hierarchies that give, for example, older siblings authority over younger ones or males over females, groups defining themselves as racial families invoke similar rules (Collins forthcoming 1998b). Within African-American communities, one such rule is that Black women will support Black men no matter what, an unwritten family rule that was manipulated quite successfully during the Clarence Thomas confirmation hearings. Even if Anita Hill was harassed by Clarence Thomas, many proclaimed in barbershops and beauty parlors, she should have kept her mouth shut and not "aired dirty laundry." Even though Thomas recast the life of his own sister through the framework of an unworthy welfare queen, Black women should have kept their collective mouths shut in deference to rules of racial solidarity (McKay 1992). By counseling Black women not to remain silent in the face of abuse no matter who does it, Black feminism comes into conflict with codes of silence such as these.

Several difficulties accompany the use of the term *Black feminism.* One involves balancing the genuine concerns of African-American women against continual pressures to absorb and recast such interests within White feminist frameworks. For example, gaining quality educations, jobs, and health care remains a strong focal point in the feminism of African-American women. Yet within some academic feminist circles, the emphasis on individualism, individual subjectivity, and personal advocacy implied in the politics of postmodernism saps Black feminism of its critical edge as a group-based, critical social theory. Contemporary Black women thinkers' efforts to explicate a long-standing African-American women's intellectual tradition bearing the label "Black feminism" can attract the attention of White women advancing different feminist agendas. Issues raised by Black women that are not seen as explicitly "feminist" ones (i.e., issues that do not affect only women) receive much less sanction. Even well-meaning White feminists can inadver-

tently consume the limited resources of African-American women who claim Black feminism. The constant drumbeat of supporting White women in their efforts to foster an antiracist feminism diverts Black women's energy away from addressing social issues facing African-American communities. Because Black feminism appears to be so well received by White women, in the context of the segregated racial politics of the United States, some African-American women quite rightly suspect its motives.

Another difficulty with Black feminism concerns the direct conflict between Black feminism and selected elements of Black religious traditions in the United States. Given the significance of Christianity for African-American women (see, e.g., Gilkes 1985 and Higginbotham 1993), any social movement that criticizes such a fundamental element of Black civil society will remain suspect. Moreover, the visibility of White lesbians within North American feminism overall directly conflicts with many Black women's article of faith that homosexuality is a sin. Although individual African-American women may be accepting of gays, lesbians, and bisexuals as individuals, especially if such individuals are African-American, Black women as a collectivity have distanced themselves from social movements perceived as requiring acceptance of homosexuality. Feminism in the United States appears to be one such movement. As one African-American female student queried, "Why do I have to accept lesbianism in order to support Black feminism?" The association of feminism with lesbianism remains a problematic one for many Black women. Reducing Black lesbians to their sexuality, one that chooses women over men, reconfigures Black lesbians as enemies of Black men. This reduction not only constitutes a serious misreading of Black lesbianism—African-American lesbians have fathers, brothers, and sons of their own and are often embedded in a series of relationships as complex as those of their Black heterosexual counterparts—it simultaneously diverts attention away from more important issues (Lorde 1984). One might ask, who ultimately benefits when the presence of Black lesbians in any Black social movement leads to its rejection by African-Americans?

The theme of lesbianism and its association with feminism in the minds of many African-Americans also overlaps with another concern of many African-

American women, namely, their commitment to African-American men. Sensitive to the specific issues confronting Black men generally (see, e.g., Madhubuti 1990a and Dyson 1993) and, as mothers, Black sons in particular (see, e.g., Golden 1995), Black women in the United States routinely reject philosophies and social movements that portray Black men as adversaries or enemies. Thus, another difficulty confronting Black feminism concerns its perceived separatism—many African-Americans define Black feminism as being exclusively for Black women and as rejecting Black men. In explaining her preference for *womanism*, Shirley Williams notes, "One of the most disturbing aspects of current black feminist criticism [is] its separatism—its tendency to see not only a *distinct* black female culture but to see that culture as a separate cultural form having more in common with white female experience than with the facticity of Afro-American life" (1990, 70). Geneva Smitherman offers a similar criticism. In response to a press conference of Black women intellectuals who denounced the alleged sexism of the 1995 Million Man March in Washington, D.C., Smitherman notes, "Black women must be wary of the seductive feminist trap. White males hold the power in this society, not Black ones. . . . To launch an attack against the first mass-based, sorely needed, long overdue, positive effort by Black men on the grounds of sexism is to engage in a misguided, retrogressive brand of feminism" (1996, 105). Smitherman's criticism cannot be dismissed as the ideas of a woman who lacks feminist consciousness. Involved for years as a community activist and scholar in Detroit, Smitherman knows firsthand what is happening to Black youth in inner cities. Until White and Black feminists show some concern for those issues, they are likely to have little support from Smitherman and other self-defined womanists.

Williams and Smitherman offer a valid criticism of Black feminism in the United States, one that, in my mind, must be addressed if Black feminism is to avoid the danger of becoming increasingly separated from African-American women's experiences and interests. It also speaks to the larger issue of the continuing difficulty of positioning Black feminism between Black nationalism and North American White feminism. In effect, Black feminism must come to terms with a White feminist agenda incapable of seeing its own racism, as well as a Black nationalist one resistant to grappling with its own sexism (White 1990). Finding a place that accommodates these seemingly contradictory agendas remains elusive (Christian 1989b).

Notes

8. Black feminism has a different meaning in Britain and elsewhere. For an analysis of alternative meanings of *Black* not attached to essentialist identities, see Nain (1991) and Anthias and Yuval-Davis (1992).

Works Cited

Anthias, Floya, and Nira Yuval-Davis. 1992. *Racialized Boundaries: Race, Nation, Gender, Colour, and Class in the Anti-racist Struggle.* New York: Routledge.

Cannon, Katie G. 1988. *Black Womanist Ethics.* Atlanta: Scholars Press.

Caraway, Nancie. 1991. *Segregated Sisterhood: Racism and the Politics of American Feminism.* Knoxville: University of Tennessee Press.

Christian, Barbara. 1989b. "But Who Do You Really Belong To—Black Studies or Women's Studies?" *Women's Studies* 17 (1–2): 17–23.

Cleage, Pearl. 1993. *Deals with the Devil and Other Reasons to Riot.* New York: Ballantine.

Collins, Patricia Hill. Forthcoming, 1998b. "It's All in the Family: Intersections of Gender, Race, Class, and Nation." *Hypatia.*

Davis, Angela Y. 1989. *Women, Culture, and Politics.* New York: Random House.

Dyson, Michael Eric. 1993. *Reflecting Black: African-American Cultural Criticism.* Minneapolis: University of Minnesota Press.

Gilkes, Cheryl Townsend. 1985. "'Together and in Harness': Women's Traditions in the Sanctified Church." *Signs* 10 (4): 678–99.

Gilroy, Paul. 1992. "It's a Family Affair." In *Black Popular Culture,* edited by Michele Wallace and Gina Dent, 303–16. Seattle: Bay Press.

Golden, Marita. 1995. *Saving Our Sons: Raising Black Children in a Turbulent World.* New York: Anchor.

Higginbotham, Evelyn Brooks. 1993. *Righteous Discontent: The Women's Movement in the Black Baptist Church, 1880–1920.* Cambridge: Harvard University Press.

James, Stanlie, and Abena Busia, eds. 1994. *Theorizing Black Feminisms.* New York: Routledge.

Lorde, Audre. 1984. *Sister Outsider.* Trumansburg, N.Y.: Crossing Press.

Madhubuti, Haki R. 1990a. *Black Men: Obsolete, Single, Dangerous?* Chicago: Third World Press.

Matthews, Nancy A. 1989. "Surmounting a Legacy: The Expansion of Racial Diversity in an Anti-rape Movement." *Gender and Society* 3 (4): 518–32.

McKay, Nellie. 1992. "Remembering Anita Hill and Clarence Thomas: What Really Happened When One Black Woman Spoke Out." In *Race-ing Justice, En-gendering Power,* edited by Toni Morrison, 269–89. New York: Pantheon.

Moses, Wilson Jeremiah. 1978. *The Golden Age of Black Nationalism, 1850–1925.* New York: Oxford University Press.

Nain, Gemma Tang. 1991. "Black Women, Sexism, and Racism: Black or Antiracist Feminism?" *Feminist Review* 37 (spring): 1–22.

Pinkney, Alphonso. 1976. *Red, Black, and Green: Black Nationalism in the United States.* London: Cambridge University Press.

Poster, Winifred R. 1995. "The Challenges and Promises of Class and Racial Diversity in the Women's Movement: A Study of Two Women's Organizations." *Gender and Society* 9 (6): 659–79.

Sanders, Cheryl J. 1995. *Empowerment Ethics for a Liberated People: A Path to African American Social Transformation.* Minneapolis: Fortress.

Smith, Barbara. 1990. "The Truth That Never Hurts: Black Lesbians in Fiction in the 1980s." In *Wild Women in the Whirlwind,* edited by Joanne Braxton and Andree Nicola McLaughlin, 213–45. New Brunswick, N.J.: Rutgers University Press.

Smitherman, Geneva. 1996. "A Womanist Looks at the Million Man March." In *Million Man March/Day of Absence,* edited by Haki R. Madhubuti and Maulana Karenga, 104–7. Chicago: Third World Press.

Townes, Emilie M., ed. 1993. *A Troubling in My Soul: Womanist Perspectives on Evil and Suffering.* Maryknoll, N.Y.: Orbis.

Van Deburg, William L. 1992. *New Day in Babylon: The Black Power Movement and American Culture, 1965–1975.* Chicago: University of Chicago Press.

Walker, Alice. 1983. *In Search of Our Mothers' Gardens,* New York: Harcourt Brace Jovanovich.

Welsing, Frances Cress. 1991. *The Isis Papers: The Keys to the Colors.* Chicago: Third World Press.

White, E. Frances. 1990. "Africa on My Mind: Gender, Counter Discourse, and African-American Nationalism." *Journal of Women's History* 2 (1), spring: 73–97.

Williams, Shirley. 1990. "Some Implications of Womanist Theory." In *Reading Black, Reading Feminist: A Critical Anthology,* edited by Henry Louis Gates Jr., 68–75. New York: Meridian.

Beyond Bean Counting

JeeYeun Lee

Born in Japan and raised in Chicago, Korean-American JeeYeun Lee specialized in cultural studies in the Ethnic Studies Program at the University of California at Berkeley.

During her first undergraduate women's studies course, JeeYeun Lee tells us, she experienced a profound tension between the exhilaration of developing feminist awareness and the uncomfortable experience of "marginalization," the "nearly complete exclusion of Asian/ Pacific American women" from the focus of her course. That encounter shaped her feminism. Today, she argues, although (and because) most feminists are sensitized to the importance of the differences among women, the tension that prevails in women's movements and women's studies is between the goal of inclusivity and the risks of tokenism.

I CAME OUT AS A woman, an Asian American and a bisexual within a relatively short span of time, and ever since then I have been guilty of the crime of bean counting, as Bill Clinton oh-so-eloquently phrased it. Every time I am in a room of people gathered for any reason, I automatically count those whom I can identify as women, men, people of color, Asian Americans, mixed-race people, whites, gays and lesbians, bisexuals, heterosexuals, people with disabilities. So when I received the call for submissions for this anthology, I imagined opening up the finished book to the table of contents and counting beans; I then sent the call for submissions to as many queer Asian/Pacific American women writers as I knew.

Such is the nature of feminism in the 1990s: an uneasy balancing act between the imperatives of outreach and inclusion on the one hand, and the risk of tokenism and further marginalization on the other. This dynamic has indelibly shaped my personal experiences with feminism, starting from my very first encounter with organized feminism. This encounter happened to be, literally, Feminist Studies 101 at the university I attended. The content of the class was divided into topics such as family, work, sexuality and so forth, and for each topic we studied what various feminist paradigms said about it: "liberal feminism," "socialist feminism," "radical feminism" and "feminism and women of color."

Taking this class was an exhilarating, empowering and very uneasy experience. For the first time I found people who articulated those murky half-formed feelings that I could previously only express incoherently as "But that's not fair!" People who agreed, sympathized, related their own experiences, theorized, helped me form what I had always known. In seventh grade, a teacher made us do a mock debate, and I ended up arguing with Neil Coleman about whether women or men were better cooks. He said more men were professional chefs, therefore men were better. I responded that more women cooked in daily life, therefore women were better. He said it was quality that mattered, not quantity, and left me standing there with nothing to say. I knew there was something wrong with his argument, something wrong with the whole issue as it was framed, and felt extremely betrayed at being made to consent to the inferiority of my gender, losing in front of the whole class. I could never defend myself when arguments like this came up, invariably with boys who were good at debates and used to winning. They left me seething with resentment at their manipulations and frustrated at my speechlessness. So to come to a class that addressed these issues directly and gave me the words for all those pent-up feelings and frustrations was a tremendously affirming and empowering experience.

At the same time, it was an intensely uncomfortable experience. I knew "women of color" was supposed to include Asian American women, but I could not find any in the class readings. Were there no Asian American feminists? Were there none who could write in English? Did there even exist older Asian American women who were second or third generation? Were we Asian American students in the class the first to think about feminism? A class about women, I thought, was a class about me, so I looked for myself everywhere and found nothing. Nothing about Asian American families, immigrant women's work patterns, issues of sexuality and body image for Asian women, violence against Asian American women, Asian American women in the seventies feminist movement, nothing anywhere. I wasn't fully conscious then that I was searching for this, but this absence came out in certain feelings. First of all, I felt jealous of African American and Chicana feminists. Their work was present at least to some degree in the readings: They had research and theories, they were eloquent and they *existed.* Black and Chicana women in the class could claim them as role models, voices, communities—I had no one to claim as my own. My emerging identification as a woman of color was displaced through the writings of black and Chicana women, and I had to read myself, create my politics, through theirs; even now, to a certain extent, I feel more familiar with their issues than those of Asian American women. Second, I felt guilty. Although it was never expressed outright, I felt that there was some pressure on me to represent Asian American issues, and I could not. I felt estranged from the Asian American groups on campus and Asian American politics and activism in general, and guilty about this ignorance and alienation.

Now mind you, I'm still grateful for this class. Feminism was my avenue to politics: It politicized me; it raised my consciousness about issues of oppression, power and resistance in general. I learned a language with which I could start to explain my experiences and link them to larger societal structures of oppression and complicity. It also gave me ways that I could resist and actively fight back. I became interested in Asian American politics, people of color politics, gay/lesbian/bisexual politics and other struggles because of this exposure to feminism. But there is no excuse for this nearly complete exclusion of Asian/Pacific American women from the class. Marginalization is not simply a polit-

ically correct buzzword, it is a material reality that affects people's lives—in this case, my own. I would have been turned off from feminism altogether had it not been for later classes that dealt specifically with women of color. And I would like to name names here: I went to Stanford University, a bastion of privilege that pretends to be on the cutting edge of "multiculturalism." Just under twenty-five percent of the undergraduate population is Asian/Pacific American, but there was no mention of Asian/Pacific American women in Feminist Studies 101. All the classes I took on women of color were taught by graduate students and visiting professors. There was, at that time, only one woman of color on the feminist studies faculty. I regret that I realized the political import of these facts only after I left Stanford.

I understand that feminists in academia are caught between a rock and a hard place—not too many of us hold positions of decision-making power in universities. And I must acknowledge my gratitude for their struggles in helping to establish feminist studies programs and produce theories and research about women, all of which create vital opportunities and affirmation. But other women's organizations that are not constrained by such explicit forces are also lily-white. This obviously differs from group to group, and I think many of them are very conscientious about outreach to historically marginalized women. But, for instance, in 1992 and 1993, at the meetings I attended of the Women's Action Coalition (WAC) in New York City, out of approximately two hundred women usually fewer than twenty women of color were present.

But this is not a diatribe against feminism in general. I want to emphasize that the feminism that I and other young women come to today is one that is at least sensitive to issues of exclusion. If perhaps twenty years ago charges of racism, classism and homophobia were not taken seriously, today they are the cause of extreme anguish and soul-searching. I am profoundly grateful to older feminists of color and their white allies who struggled to bring U.S. feminist movements to this point. At the same time, I think that this current sensitivity often breeds tokenism, guilt, suspicion and self-righteousness that have very material repercussions on women's groups. I have found these uneasy dynamics in all the women's groups I've come across, addressed to varying degrees. At one extreme, I have seen groups that deny the marginalizing affects of their practices, believing that issues of inclusion really have nothing to do with their specific agendas. At the other extreme, I have seen groups ripped apart by accusations of political correctness, immobilized by guilt, knowing they should address a certain issue but not knowing how to begin, and still wondering why "women of color just don't come to our meetings." And tokenism is alive and well in the nineties. Those of us who have been aware of our tokenization often become suspicious and tired of educating others, wondering if we are invested enough to continue to do so, wondering if the overall goal is worth it.

In this age when "political correctness" has been appropriated by conservative forces as a derogatory term, it is extremely difficult to honestly discuss and confront any ideas and practices that perpetuate dominant norms—and none of us is innocent of such collusion. Many times, our response is to become defensive, shutting down to constructive critiques and actions, or to individualize our collusion as solely a personal fault, as if working on our individual racist or classist attitudes would somehow make things better. It appears that we all have a lot of work to do still.

And I mean *all.* Issues of exclusion are not the sole province of white feminists. I learned this very vividly at a 1993 retreat organized by the Asian Pacifica Lesbian Network. It has become somewhat common lately to speak of "Asian and Pacific Islanders" or "Asian/Pacific Americans" or, as in this case, "Asian Pacifica." This is meant to be inclusive, to recognize some issues held in common by people from Asia and people from the Pacific Islands. Two women of Native Hawaiian descent and some Asian American allies confronted the group at this retreat to ask for more than lip service in the organization's name: If the group was seriously committed to being an inclusive coalition, we needed to educate ourselves about and actively advocate Pacific Islander issues. And because I don't want to relegate them to a footnote, I will mention here a few of these issues: the demand for sovereignty for Native Hawaiians, whose government was illegally overthrown by the U.S. in 1893; fighting stereotypes of women and men that are different from those of

Asian people; decrying U.S. imperialist possession and occupation of the islands of Guam, the Virgin Islands, American Samoa, the Marshall Islands, Micronesia, the Northern Mariana Islands and several others.

This was a retreat where one would suppose everyone had so much in common—after all, we were all queer API women, right? Any such myth was effectively destroyed by the realities of our experiences and issues: We were women of different ethnic backgrounds, with very different issues among East Asians, South Asians, Southeast Asians and Pacific Islanders; women of mixed race and heritage; women who identified as lesbians and those who identified as bisexuals; women who were immigrants, refugees, illegal aliens or second generation or more; older women, physically challenged women, women adopted by white families, women from the Midwest. Such tangible differences brought home the fact that no simplistic identity politics is *ever* possible, that we had to conceive of ourselves as a coalition first and foremost; as one woman on a panel said, our identity as queer API women must be a *coalitional* identity. Initially, I thought that I had finally found a home where I could relax and let down my guard. This was true to a certain degree, but I discovered that this was the home where I would have to work the hardest because I cared the most. I would have to be committed to push myself and push others to deal with all of our differences, so that we *could* be safe for each other. And in this difficult work of coalition, one positive action was taken at the retreat: We changed the name of the organization to include "bisexual," thus becoming the Asian Pacifica Lesbian and Bisexual Network, a name that people started using immediately.

All this is to say that I and other young women have found most feminist movements today to be at this point, where there is at least a stated emphasis on inclusion and outreach with the accompanying risk of tokenism. I firmly believe that it is always the margins that push us further in our politics. Women of color do not struggle in feminist movements simply to add cultural diversity, to add the viewpoints of different kinds of women. Women of color feminist theories challenge the fundamental premises of feminism, such as the very definition of "women," and call for recognition of the constructed racial nature of *all* experiences of gender. In the same way, heterosexist norms do not oppress solely lesbians, bisexuals and gay men, but affect all of our choices and non-choices; issues posed by differently abled women question our basic assumptions about body image, health care, sexuality and work; ecofeminists challenge our fundamental ideas about living on and with the earth, about our interactions with animals, plants, food, agriculture and industry. Many feminists seem to find the issues of class the most difficult to address; we are always faced with the fundamental inequalities inherent to late-twentieth-century multinational capitalism and our unavoidable implication in its structures. Such an overwhelming array of problems can numb and immobilize us, or make us concentrate our energies too narrowly. I don't think that we have to address everything fully at the same time, but we *must* be fully aware of the limitations of our specific agendas. Progressive activists cannot afford to do the masters' work for them by continuing to carry out oppressive assumptions and exclusions.

These days, whenever someone says the word "women" to me, my mind goes blank. What "women"? What is this "women" thing you're talking about? Does that mean me? Does that mean my mother, my roommates, the white woman next door, the checkout clerk at the supermarket, my aunts in Korea, half of the world's population? I ask people to specify and specify, until I can figure out exactly what they're talking about, and I try to remember to apply the same standards to myself, to deny myself the slightest possibility of romanticization. Sisterhood may be global, but who is in that sisterhood? None of us can afford to assume anything about anybody else. This thing called "feminism" takes a great deal of hard work, and I think this is one of the primary hallmarks of young feminists' activism today: We realize that coming together and working together are by no means natural or easy.

"Promises to Keep": Trends in Women's Studies Worldwide

Florence Howe

Florence Howe, activist, teacher, and scholar, is one of the leading foremothers of women's studies. After actively participating in the antiwar and civil rights movements of the 1960s, she became closely involved with the women's movement, and in the 1970s and 1980s she became an important voice in the founding of women's studies. Now professor of English and women's studies at the Graduate Center/City University of New York, she is director and publisher of The Feminist Press at CUNY. Among other works, she is the author of Myths of Coeducation *and recently the editor of* The Politics of Women's Studies: Testimony from Thirty Founding Mothers, *the first volume in* The Women's Studies History Series *(New York: The Feminist Press at CUNY, 2000).*

Women's studies and the women's movement has always been multicultural, Howe argues, for although important differences exist among women, so do characteristics that unite us, and that has created a worldwide women's movement. The future of women's studies is international, and we must think, teach, and publish cross-culturally. Although patriarchy is amazingly powerful and resilient, women's studies is emerging as a counterforce in countries all over the world, establishing centers in teaching, research, and activism. In Howe's words, there are now many peaceful, liberated women and men with "promises to keep."

IN 1994 I WAS INVITED by *Vina Mazumdar, emerita director of the Centre for Women's Development Studies in New Delhi, India, to give the annual J. P. Naik Memorial Lecture. J. P. Naik was the father of women's studies in India. He urged that educated women and men had*

"promises to keep," responsibilities to assure the education of others. He believed in the significance of research as a strategy for change, even when political power would seemingly silence all change. He dared Vina Mazumdar to open the center in the mid-1970s by saying, "Good work that needs to be done never gets held up for lack of resources, only for lack of determination." He was also fond of telling Vina Mazumdar that "men will never be liberated until women are liberated."

The essay that follows, revised for publication here in February 1997, is based on the lecture delivered in December 1994. The Centre for Women's Development Studies has published the original text of the lecture as a monograph.

I come to this topic from thirty years in women's studies in the United States, from fifty-two national reports on women's studies from individual countries, from my own travels to Japan, Korea, Argentina, Australia, India, and various countries in Europe, as well as from participation in a score of international conferences over the past fifteen years.[1] By now, women's studies in its various forms may be found in scores of countries on every continent, among thousands of scholar/activists, and millions of students. I believe that the development of women's studies as an arm of the worldwide women's movement is as important for the future of world peace as disarmament, and as important for the health of the planet's air, water, trees, and other resources as the ecology movement itself.

Education is a human right, and women as well as men need an education free of gender bias and containing an understanding of women's history and culture. We know that women who have had such education not only understand the world's fragility—that ethnic wars and the misuse of the planet's resources will destroy the world for generations to come—but also understand the power of women to change not only their own personal lives but the social order.

Florence Howe, " 'Promises to Keep': Trends in Women's Studies Worldwide" is reprinted by permission of the author and The Feminist Press at the City University of New York, from *Women's Studies Quarterly* 25, nos. 1 & 2 (spring/summer 1997): 404–421, special issue, *Looking Back, Moving Forward: Twenty-five Years of Women's Studies,* edited by Elaine Hedges and Dorothy O. Helly. Copyright © 1997 by Florence Howe.

The connections between the women's movement and worldwide movements for peace have been evident not only in the last three decades but in the early years of this century, when peace and suffrage were twin goals that women's movement leaders discussed and worked to establish. In our time, I see as additional goals a woman's right to control her body, including the right to bear children as well as the right not to, and the right to equal opportunities in employment for equal pay, with provisions for childcare. Central to these goals and movements has been the rise of women's studies. It is not possible to ignore the body of knowledge now available even to those who would want to turn the clock back, to urge women to leave the workforce, for example, and care for a single child or possibly two, and ignore the world's turmoil. Indeed, what I see happening worldwide now is different: the march of feminist women into public office via politics.[2] And again, I see this connected to the worldwide study of history, and the energy released by knowledge about women that ends their invisibility—individually and collectively. As the American historian Mary Beard said fifty years ago, but as some of us understand today palpably, women have been a "force" in history.

I read the worldwide backlash against individual women, and against feminism in general, as evidence of the strength of this actual and potential force. Even the Republican right wing in the United States—ready to promote prayers in the schools and orphanages for indigent children of mothers under the age of eighteen or twenty—will not take a formal stand on the issue of abortion, since it affects women of all social classes. It remains to be seen whether women inside and outside the women's movement can rally to support indigent women and children as the Republican right moves to end what they are calling "the welfare state."

Trends in women's studies worldwide connect us despite regional and national differences, even despite significant differences in the forms of our educational institutions. These trends connect us even over time and space, as I was recently reminded by reading *Changing Lives,* a group of essays by Asian pioneers in women's studies.[3]

If one begins with the obvious question, Where did women's studies come from? there are striking commonalities. Again and again, I hear them embedded in the echoes of worldwide experiences. Characteristically, two types of "passages"—moments of awareness or a deepening in consciousness inspired by experience—move faculty into women's studies; both are visions from the rocks of inequality. The first I shall call personal, the second, intellectual or work related.

The personal passage into women's studies typically narrates a critical experience that makes visible the inequality between professional husband and professional wife. In an essay in *Changing Lives,* Li Xiaojiang, director of the Center for Women's Studies at Zhengzhou University and professor of Chinese literature and language, describes her life as a young girl, outachieving all the boys in her class, working hard at studies and sports and citizenry, and succeeding. But then, after gaining a significant academic position, she marries, has a child, and finds herself, unlike her husband, expected to do all the housework and child care, as well as her academic work, while he does only his academic work. How is she to deal with this? She writes most poignantly of her conflict—her love and her burden:

> As long as I was unwilling to part with my husband and family, I had to assume all the consequences. . . . I was forced to . . . carry a load which would be twice as much as that usually carried by a man.
>
> All modern women are doomed to fall into such a trap. Most are wallowing in it silently and in a docile manner. . . . But the question baffles me: why are women alone made to suffer in this manner?[4]

Li Xiaojiang eventually asks her husband to share some chores, but she goes on to the main point of consciousness for women's studies pioneers:

> In an age that boasts equality between the sexes, why do women lead a painfully laborious and depressing life? . . . Despite the fact that women's inherent status and value have been completely obliterated by the writers of history and society, I harbor the hope that my academic studies may contribute to the rediscovery of that status and value.[5]

It is a painfully familiar story, with many variations. I have my own: back at the end of the 1960s, in Baltimore, Maryland, my former husband and I drove off in two directions each morning to our two different teaching jobs and drove back in the evening. One evening I forgot to pick up the laundry, and my husband charged me fiercely the next morning with negligence. I apologized and said I'd remember that evening. But all day long something troubled me about the morning's scene, even about my humble apology, for the laundry lay in *his* direction, not mine. Nevertheless, I picked up the laundry that evening, and presented it to him, with the following statement: "This is the last time I will pick up the laundry. It occurred to me today that the shop lies in your direction, not mine. You could pick up the laundry far more easily. Further, the laundry is yours, not mine—I wash mine by hand—and we both use the bed and bath linen. It's now your turn to deal with the laundry." Change hardly transpired overnight. For most of that year I bought new sheets and towels, for my husband wouldn't at first take the laundry in, and I kept my word.

The second passage to women's studies is an intellectual or work-related passage. My own came from several sources, one of which I will describe to you. In a 1968 study of sex-role stereotypes, male and female clinical psychologists were asked to check off on a bipolar scale of 132 items those that described the "healthy American male," the "healthy American female," and the "healthy American person." Years later, the findings are still shocking: the items checked for "male" and "person" were identical in every respect; those checked for "female" were entirely different. Thus, women were "religious"; men and persons were "not religious." Thus, men and persons were "rational" and "not emotional"; women were "irrational" and "emotional."[6]

I'll return again to *Changing Lives,* in which there are several examples of the ways intellectual effort has inspired consciousness. Sometimes these moments are painful. In one of them, at the end of her research project, when Malavikar Karlekar tells the sweepers who had been her subjects that "they had been of considerable help" to her, one of them responds: "You will write your book, but what will happen to us?"[7] In Korea, when Cho Hyoung presents a research proposal on poor urban women, a senior male sociologist remarks, "Why should a promising young sociologist like you spend so much time and energy on such trivial matters as

women and poverty?" "Gradually," Cho Hyoung writes, she "became grateful to this man who had unintentionally prepared me to face the anti-feminist world."[8] It is, of course, not only an antifeminist world but often antireformist and antidemocratic, especially with regard to poor women or women of different races or ethnicities. These passages make wonderful stories—of blinders removed from vision, of what we have been calling re-visioning, and, of course, of idealism. These are features of women's studies worldwide.

So, in fact, I have begun with my conclusion. That though we in the West may have begun with the idea that women's studies, as an arm of the women's movement, was a strategy for changing education, it has, throughout the world, become far more than that. We've known that women's studies changes individual lives, but, and I am speaking for myself here, I have not before now understood how women's studies may turn academics and researchers into activists—that women's studies itself may galvanize a movement. At first this idea seemed strange to me, since I came to women's studies already an activist, with a decade of experience in the civil rights and antiwar movements. I had always thought of women's studies as growing out of movements. But, as I have seen, women's studies in some countries in Asia and Africa as well as in Eastern Europe has been a strategic force to energize and develop a nascent women's movement. In other words, a raised consciousness may be the cause as well as the consequence of activism.

The good news is that it is hard to find a country without some women's studies center or program just beginning, or of an age between one and twenty-five. When the planners of women's studies sessions came from the United States, Canada, and India to Copenhagen in 1980 for the United Nations' NGO (nongovernmental organization) Forum with a modest program of panels and roundtables, we hoped to be joined by perhaps fifty others; none of us expected the hundreds that flocked to major sessions and came as well to roundtables and announced their own programs. Fourteen hundred people from fifty-five countries registered in what, thanks to Vina Mazumdar's vision, became Women's Studies International: A Network and Educational Project of The Feminist Press. Joined by twenty-five women's studies programs from as many countries, Women's Studies International went on to organize panels and roundtables for Nairobi's NGO Forum in 1985 and for Beijing in 1995.

There we met with women's studies pioneers from China and Korea, from Latvia and Hungary, from Uganda, Ghana, and South Africa, from Peru and Argentina, from Turkey, Norway, Germany, France, and Russia.[9] It is difficult to think of a country without a women's studies center or an academic women's studies program of some sort. The spread of women's studies since 1985 and Nairobi has been especially rapid: we can count some ten African countries with women's studies projects or programs. Since the end of the Cold War, we can count programs in most of the countries of Eastern Europe. And, since the mid- to late 1980s, we can count mainland China, as well as Taiwan, Hong Kong, and Vietnam—all with some women's studies programs or centers. So the first trend is proliferation, the spread of women's studies worldwide, which, I have no doubt, will continue for many years to come.

These programs or centers, regardless of their geography and even their institutionalization, have three characteristics in common: they are research centered, formally or informally; they are teaching institutions, formally or informally; and they are centers of activism, again formally or informally. A fourth characteristic is not as universal as the other three, but it is growing in importance: publishing of journals or even books—again formally and independently, or informally, or through other channels. Often, one activity is more important than the others; often one activity leads the way to the others.

Significantly, I see the presence of research worldwide as more ubiquitous than teaching, which is, of course, where women's studies began in the United States. In India, Professor Naik urged the Indian Social Science Research Council (ISSRC) to study the status of women in India at a moment that coincided with the beginnings of the worldwide women's movement, following the UN meetings in Mexico City in 1975. Just as women's studies began in India with research on women, so in Russia did women's studies pioneers spend their first two years in research that challenged the newly established government's attempt to change laws regard-

ing women's rights to education, employment, and even abortion.[10] Scandinavian women's studies centers report that they work on problems posed by politicians, bureaucrats, and other researchers, and are supported by government grants rather than the university.[11] And in the United States, Mariam K. Chamberlain at the Ford Foundation as early as the mid-1970s envisioned "centers for research on women" as adjuncts to the women's studies teaching programs on campus. There are now seventy-seven of these in the United States alone; some of them are on campuses, and one-third of them are separate nonprofit institutions like The Feminist Press in New York or the Center for Women Policy Studies in Washington, D.C., or the Centre for Women's Development Studies in New Delhi, or the Center for Women's Studies in Buenos Aires, Argentina.

In Argentina, in the late 1970s, when fascism ruled the universities as well as the nation, women's studies began in an independent NGO, composed chiefly of psychologists and other social scientists, with a program of action-oriented research.[12] In Africa the pattern for women's studies—in Botswana, Tanzania, and Nigeria, for example—begins with university faculty setting up a research group with an agenda that includes major social issues, seminars both for researchers and for dissemination, and a publishing program.[13] In Japan, where women's studies teaching is quite well established, research is now turning to a study of Japanese women, including minority women and the past two decades of feminism.[14]

Certain themes may be found in research programs worldwide. These include the need for better nationally and internationally gathered statistics and the need for more statistics-driven studies to galvanize the women's studies movement. Ubiquitous also is an emphasis on what is often called "participatory research"; the effort to design research that serves women, especially the least privileged, rather than uses them to benefit the researcher. With regard to this type of research, there are increased efforts to use research not only to effect education locally but to change public policies—to educate communities to politics and political activism. Increasingly researchers are turning to history, both the history of women in communities and nations and the history of the women's movement over the past century. Finally, there is worldwide concern about the human rights of women, and researchers are increasingly focused on violence against women in all its forms—in peace and during war. I see this renewed emphasis on human rights as one aspect of women's increasing participation in ecological struggles to preserve the trees of Africa or to provide clean water to the children of India.

As I turn to teaching, which is where my own work and the work of many women's studies pioneers in the United States began, I want to add at once that, even where there were no formal teaching programs—as in many of the independent centers that were founded off campus and outside the mainstream of university life—there were always seminars, public lectures, and the dissemination of research findings. Of course, these also teach. But worldwide, women's studies has built on research to create teaching programs, especially for college and university students, and even to create teaching programs for faculty, very often male faculty, who would not, on their own, find their way into the new research on women or into women's studies courses. And in some countries—the United States, Britain, New Zealand, and Argentina come quickly to mind—such teaching programs extend themselves into primary and secondary education and into the preparation of teachers.[15]

While undergraduate teaching programs have been women's studies' most visible form in the United States, such programs have not been exportable as such, simply because the U.S. organization of undergraduate education does not translate itself into other systems. There are now approximately 620 of these teaching programs in the United States, one-third of them offering some graduate degrees as well as undergraduate degrees. I should add that there is hardly a college in the United States that does not at least offer some courses in women's studies. (Courses are small units in the U.S. system; whereas programs or majors are what in most parts of the world would be called "courses."[16]) Almost all of the 1,800 four-year colleges and universities in the United States offer some women's studies courses; one-third of these institutions offer programs, comparable to what one might think of as departments, but with some differences. Most of the

larger programs are located in the 160 universities that offer graduate degrees as well as undergraduate degrees. The U.S. system of higher education incorporates additions to the curriculum in processes usually described as "difficult" or "complex" by those attempting to work through them. On the other hand, there is a process, and, in more than 2,000 two- and four-year colleges and universities, countless thousands of individual faculty members have been able to add countless women's studies courses to the curriculum. I remember a conversation with Vina Mazumdar many years ago, in which she said that such easy additions to the curriculum might just as easily be eliminated. Quite so, for when specialists capable of teaching such courses move from one campus to another, often the courses disappear with them, especially if there is not an organized program standing guard.

But what do women's studies programs teach? In the United States some single units—what we call courses—are arranged as interdisciplinary introductions to women's studies as an area of study. But the curriculum that follows may be disciplinary and may consist of courses in any one of fifteen or sixteen broad fields, disciplines, or interdisciplinary areas. They may range from a course called "U.S. Women Writers in the 19th Century" (cross-listed in English and women's studies) to "Women in Politics" (cross-listed in political science and women's studies) to "Women and the Family" (cross-listed, depending on emphasis, with history or sociology and women's studies), to "Women and Violence" to "Women in Developing Countries." And I am merely skimming the surface of the curriculum here. The important point is that, because of the U.S. educational structure, women's studies faculty have not thus far had to choose between "autonomy" or "integration," or between "separation" or "ghettoization" and "inclusion."

In India, as well as in most countries of the world, there are two or three strategies with which to create teaching programs, all of them difficult to achieve. Years ago Vina Mazumdar was hopeful about the institutional route through which questions on women could be appended to the degree examination in history, political science, and sociology, among other fields, thus forcing the inclusion of lectures on women through those fields. But few women's studies pioneers have been sanguine about introducing whole new degrees in women's studies into the university structure. There are at least two obstacles: the theorizing of women about such institutional strategies and, of course, an even more difficult obstacle, the patriarchal university.

I can name a few success stories, despite such obstacles and reservations. In India, for example, there are "courses" and "papers" on women, chiefly at postgraduate levels in selected departments—sociology in Bombay, political science and history in Delhi. While there are thirty-seven research units in India and twenty independent research centers, there are relatively few degree-granting teaching programs. My experience in Hyderabad, and even in Delhi, in 1994, convinced me that women's studies faculty were not especially interested in teaching programs, even at the graduate level, and were not thinking about the fact that, without teaching programs, there will not be subsequent generations of researchers in women's studies. And there seems to be no easy route—given the undergraduate system of education—to allow the adding of a new area of inquiry called women's studies.

On the other hand, in Argentina, for example, after a long hiatus outside university structures, Gloria Bonder and her colleagues in the independent Center for Women's Studies in Buenos Aires, were invited into the faculty of psychology at the University of Buenos Aires, and asked to establish an M.A. course in women's studies for practicing psychologists or others who wanted that degree. The faculty has now been invited to establish a second degree-granting program in women's studies, this one for health professionals.

One of the important elements in women's studies in the United States has been an emphasis on changing pedagogical practices in the classroom to encourage independent thinking and long-lasting integration of the content of the curriculum. In other words, feminist educators were especially aware that the passivity of women students in the classroom merely reflected and reinforced social conditioning. Much has been done to change this. When I was asked, however, to consult with Argentine educators devising a new graduate curriculum, and wanting some new pedagogical ideas, I was dismayed to learn that all of what we have been taking

for granted in the United States since the mid-1970s seemed very "radical" to them.

Had I been preparing this paper a decade ago, I would have begun with activism. I would have said that the very first trend was a significant relationship between women's studies and women's movements. I would have said that women's studies has emerged and has continued to emerge from women's movements all over the world. In the United States, for example, one can date the women's movement from Betty Friedan's 1963 book, *The Feminine Mystique,* or from the founding of the National Organization for Women in 1966. While I began teaching courses in 1964 that eventually I came to see as women's studies courses, that phrase—"women's studies"—did not come into use until 1969 at the earliest, and it was somewhat later that women's studies named itself "the academic arm of the women's movement." I would say that all the programs founded before the mid-1980s—in India and Japan, in Argentina and elsewhere in Latin America, all over Western Europe, in Canada, Australia, and New Zealand, as well as in the United States—came out of women's movements.

On the other hand, programs founded since then, especially in Eastern Europe, Africa, and parts of Asia, *are—or are becoming*—women's movements. In some ways, this is interesting, baffling, exciting, and worrisome. It is interesting and exciting because, of course, those of us who have been in women's studies for twenty to thirty years know that one of the problems in India, in Canada, in parts of Europe, and in the United States is the widening separation between the women's movements and women's studies. Older women's studies programs share a trend that is potentially very dangerous: the split between the women's movement and women's studies, brought on in part by the development of highly specialized fields of scholarly inquiry and in part by what I can only call a "generation gap," differences between the activist pioneers who began women's studies and the young graduate students becoming instructors in the field. The new generation of scholar/teachers in the university often is as little aware of the history of the women's studies movement as their students. The research findings they teach, the theorizing they are often totally absorbed by, may be as remote from women's lives as the traditional male agenda has been for centuries. So, as a real trend, this is a significant worry for all of us in women's studies.

On the other hand, from reports of developing women's studies perspectives in Asian and African countries, one gets the impression of women's studies *as the women's movement,* or perhaps assuming leadership in, or teaching future leaders of, a nascent women's movement. Perhaps you understand at once why this worries me, especially in countries where all academics, researchers or teachers, would be a tiny minority of a specially privileged class: can these women's studies pioneers *be* or *become* a women's movement? In other places, for example, some countries of Latin America, women's studies practitioners have been viewed by members of some parts of the women's movement as out of touch with reality, like other academics.

Perhaps one way to begin to understand these trends is to consider what has happened in the world over the past decade. While some walls came down in Europe and in the Middle East, fiery nationalisms have begun to burn in their place and radical fundamentalisms to grow more boldly visible. Carnage and the religious right affect women even more adversely than they affect men. It is as though, since women have been traditionally the vessels of culture and the vehicles through which it is carried into the next generation, they must be the bloodiest and most brutalized victims of culture wars.

In certain environments, therefore, it is understandable that there is too much political turbulence or just plain danger for a women's movement to develop in ways that it did in the West, for example, or in India. Rather, scholars, some of them teachers as well, touched by the international movements now opened to them—as in Eastern Europe, China, parts of Africa, and the Middle East—have seized on women's studies as a relatively nonthreatening, even seemingly nonactivist form of women's movement. After all, seminars and publications are different from street demonstrations.

In some of these countries, these activists have decided to substitute the term "gender studies" for "women's studies" or "feminist studies," especially in Eastern Europe where the communists allegedly

settled "the woman question" decades ago, and where the term is linked to the old order and hence anathema to the new. As Anastasia Posadskaya, formerly an economist at the Moscow Academy of Science and one of the pioneers of women's studies in Russia, tells the story, when she first mentioned "gender studies," which is what she and her colleagues determined to call their new program several years ago, she was inevitably asked, "What is this 'gender'?" There is no Russian word for "gender," and so she and her colleagues could describe their perspective—one we would call feminist or women's studies—under this new label "gender studies," which is how women's studies is known in Russia.[17]

Though my own experience in the United States could have told me that a publishing arm moved women's studies forward rapidly and coherently, and though I have long urged the establishment of feminist presses in many countries throughout the world, only this past year have I come to the conclusion that publishing needs to be named as the fourth essential arm of women's studies. In some ways, we've all known this: take the publications program of the women's studies unit of the Shrimati Nathibai Damodar Thackersey Women's University or *Samyit Shakti,* the original journal of the Centre for Women's Development Studies in Delhi, now known as *The Indian Journal of Women's Studies.* But there are a couple of new indicators I'd like to mention. First, with respect to Latin America, I have continued to wonder why the profile of women's studies in Latin America is not more visible, even to Latin Americans. One reason may be that there is no press, no journal that circulates through the region. On the other hand, there are new efforts, in Peru, Chile, Argentina, Mexico, to found feminist presses and even scholarly journals. In China, where women's studies began in the mid-1980s, the first major activity of Li Xiaojiang, director of the first center, was to edit and publish the *Women's Studies Series,* more than twenty volumes by and about women to be used in teaching.[18]

I want to turn now to the unfinished agenda: what are the trends that need more than naming, and not simply for their ubiquitous presence, but for other reasons?

When women's studies first began more than two decades ago in the United States, pioneers envisioned significant change in consciousness and knowledge. Women—and men—were to be reeducated in women's history. They were to rediscover the lost literature once important to various cultures. They were to rework almost a century of male-focused social science, to allow into experimental design and data the female half of the population. At the same time, since the United States is a multicultural nation, from the first, women's studies claimed that race and class, and later sexual orientation, age, and disability, also needed to be considered along with patriarchal omissions and distortions. The explosion of women's studies—both in research and teaching—was an explosion not only in consciousness and knowledge. It was as though we were following Simone de Beauvoir's message at the conclusion of *The Second Sex:* one could not change the status of women by fiat, as the Chinese or the Russians had attempted early in their separate revolutions; one had to change consciousness either first or at least at the same time.

Certainly, we seemed to have heard her message: it explained for us why, regardless of revolutionary goals, in post-revolutionary societies, women remained "the second sex." We were going to begin from the other end: changing consciousness, and more than that, producing a revolution in epistemology that some have compared to the Copernican. Feminist philosopher Elizabeth Minnich has said that one could not simply "add" the idea that the world is round to the previous idea that the world was flat; the new idea changed, indeed eradicated, the old idea—which is why it was revolutionary.[19] Similarly, the idea that women are not inferior creatures either in brain or body cannot be "added" on to the idea of women as "the second sex." Feminism displaces patriarchy—at least where it is allowed to live.

But then we come to the hard question: Where is it allowed to live? If women's studies pioneers can be faulted—and I count myself among these pioneers—it is for a failure of long-range *institutional* imagination, *strategic institutional imagination.* In the United States, we knew what *not* to do. That is, to take myself as an early strategist, I was strongly opposed to separatism, what has been called "autonomy." I knew that home economics had been a dismal failure, not only because of the limitations in its intellectual vision but also because its institutional strategy had called for separate departments, even "schools." I knew also, from a study in the 1960s of efforts to reform higher education in the United States, that separate islands of excellence called "experimental colleges," spawned by large universities themselves, had had no significant impact on the host institutions. Large, sprawling institutions were not about to "imitate" the intellectual successes of academic Edens, even when they had established these Edens in their own backyards. Further, I could see the isolation and budgetary penury suffered by Black studies departments formed as separate enclaves in response to the demands of Black students in the second half of the 1960s. And so, when I could, I recommended a very different kind of institutional model for women's studies in United States' higher education.[20]

I said, let women's studies be a strategy for change. Let women's studies form programs, not departments. Let women's studies form programs with a strong administrative center, a director, an office, a staff, a budget that will pay for faculty to teach in the program, even a budget that will pay half the salaries of faculty located half in women's studies, half in traditional departments of sociology, history, English, etc. Let women's studies expect that each year its outreach into traditional departments and into professional schools of the university will broaden and deepen until every part of the college or university has been reached and changed. Let women's studies expect also that those brave faculty within departments with a strong allegiance to women's studies will begin to transform their own discipline-based courses, and perhaps also begin to interest their colleagues in change.

Further, even as early as the middle of the 1970s, intrepid faculty members were thinking about how to change their colleagues, mostly male, mostly unacquainted with what was happening in the world of feminist scholarship. This movement, originally called "mainstreaming," gathered force in the 1980s, and has had some modest affect upon the traditional curriculum in perhaps a hundred institutions of higher education. This kind of work, slow at best, was generally paid for in the late 1970s and through the 1980s by the federal government and by private foundations, chief among them the Ford Foundation. Some of this work continues into the 1990s. But it is clear that none of it speaks to questions of long-range significant institutional change. As Cora Kaplan, formerly at Rutgers University, said at a City University of New York conference in 1994, the university has not changed at all in the twenty years we in women's studies have changed our minds and hearts. But the university in the United States has, I would add, made room for us in women's studies, and sometimes in privileged positions.[21]

Throughout the discussion of institutionalizing women's studies over the past twenty years has run the refrain of "autonomy" versus "integration." I have been one of those who claimed that neither position was tenable, that one had to have a hybrid, which I described as an interdisciplinary program inside a university, with certain ingredients—a director, an office, a budget, an approved course of study, and students earning degrees—but without the right to tenure faculty, though one might hire them either temporarily or through the cooperation of many departments in the university.[22]

What is the next step for women's studies in higher education? Or are we in the United States and elsewhere to remain as fixed in our semiautonomous/semi-integrated pattern as home economics remained as a separate department/division? And are others in the rest of the world to continue to try to change degree examinations? This question takes for granted, of course, that the male-privileged university moves forward as it always has, making room for women's studies, and that we continue to educate another generation of scholar/activists to do our work. It is certainly true that the U.S. system of higher education is uniquely suited to absorbing change from without *without* changing itself. Despite the presence of over 600 women's studies programs, the campus moves on as before, having "absorbed" or "added" women's studies along with such new areas as African studies, African-American studies, Asian studies, Asian-American studies. And in the rest of the world, where universities are organized to resist easy change from within or without, where they are structured to withstand side attacks, boring from within, or establishing enclaves inside and yet outside power structures—in such institutions, change is more difficult still.

This is a discussion not confined to the United States. European women's studies faculty raised these questions at a United Nations meeting in Vienna in October 1994. In Europe, women's studies teaching and research programs are twenty years old, or older. In some countries, especially the Nordic and the Netherlands, women's studies can be found in a variety of formations, often on the margins of universities, sometimes in well-funded, well-staffed centers, producing significant research. Yet I heard little satisfaction expressed. Rather, I heard ugly stories, painful accounts of rejections of women's studies scholars by the university "fraternity." I was somewhat surprised by these complaints, and for two reasons. First, in the United States such complaints were commonplace a decade ago. But feminist scholarship in some fields has become vanguard enough to attract male scholars, and feminist female scholars have gained positions at the most elite universities in the country. Moreover, U.S. feminists have created their own networks and institutions outside the patriarchal ones, and many of them are now able to function in both worlds.

Second, I heard nothing from the Europeans that spoke to action, to how to move their agendas forward. Indeed, the only account that I have found that prescribes institutional change is one from Australia. In a lecture on the occasion of the twentieth anniversary of the first women's studies "topic," or "paper" for a course of study, in an Australian university, Lyndall Ryan of Flinders University describes the "fragility" of women's studies in Australia, though thirty of the forty-three higher education institutions in the country offer women's studies "topics" and programs at the undergraduate or graduate level, and though there are also seven research centers. The "fragility" she describes is institutional: she describes the units as "additive," dependent on "voluntary" labor of feminist faculty she depicts in the "category of unpaid housework." She sees women's studies through university administrators' eyes as "an academic hobby with no clear long-term purpose." She depicts women's studies as "dwelling on the margins of the academy where it has ceased to be a threat to the mainstream because it uses few resources."

And not unexpectedly, her demand is for resources: the establishment of permanent, well-funded professorships and permanent, well-funded departments. The senior positions would reflect the importance of women's studies as a research area, and the "administrative coherence" would allow for the appropriate education of "the next generation of feminists."[23]

The education of the next generation of feminists is my concluding topic and my all-encompassing concern, as it is, I am sure, your own. What shall we make of the idea of "difference," wiping out "essentialism," and in some quarters of the women's studies world forbidding the very connections that made for the movement in the first place? I worry these days about "amnesia," forgetting—or never knowing about—the first twenty-five years of women's studies and, in the process, losing all that has been recovered during that period. And so I will conclude with some prescriptives for women's studies education.

First, remember and honor your foremothers, in literature and history, and in the recent period of pioneering women's studies. Whatever your specialty, teach and learn history, including the history of the past thirty years. Unless we know this history, unless we carry it with us, we will lose what we have gained, and generations long after we have gone will need to begin again.

Second, remember that women's studies has been multicultural from the start, despite its "essentialism," and that without "essentialism" we would not have had a movement. While significant differences separate women, significant characteristics connect them, not only across race and class, for example, but across nations.

Third, remember that the future of women's studies is international, which means that, beyond the women's history and culture of one's own country, one must begin to teach, to do research, and publish cross-culturally.

Fourth, remember that still largely untapped body of students, professors, and researchers who are the other half of the human race, the men some of us live with, mother, and love. How are we, in the next century, to teach them? Or will they teach themselves?

Fifth, and finally, remember and never underestimate the strength of patriarchy, that it is far more complexly entrenched ideologically and institution-

ally than we had imagined some thirty years ago. In the late 1960s, when some women of my generation first began to see that patriarchy controlled every aspect of women's and men's lives, we naively believed that visibility was the answer. If we could make everyone see it, we could, through vision alone, destroy it. Very simple, very wrong. It will take countless visions, innumerable sightings and namings in our lives and our books to help us see the strategies for changing the patriarchal world into one fit for humans.

But of course we have what we did not have twenty-five or thirty years ago: we have countless adherents, pioneers, and the daughters and granddaughters of pioneers on every continent, prepared for educational battle. We stand with J. P. Naik, a peaceful army of liberated women and men, with many "promises to keep."

Notes

1. These national reports on women's studies have been published in three issues of *Women's Studies Quarterly*: *Women's Studies in Europe*, edited by Tobe Levin and Angelica Koster-Lossack; *Women's Studies: A World View*, edited by Florence Howe and Mariam K. Chamberlain; and *Beijing and Beyond: Toward the Twenty-first Century for Women*, edited by Florence Howe with the assistance of Mariam K. Chamberlain, Tobe Levin, and Gloria Bonder; see, respectively, *Women's Studies Quarterly* 20, nos. 3 & 4 (Fall/Winter 1992), *Women's Studies Quarterly* 22, nos. 3 & 4 (Fall/Winter 1994), and *Women's Studies Quarterly* 24, nos. 1 & 2 (Spring/Summer 1996). Also, for further information on the status of women's studies in developing countries in Asia, see Mariam K. Chamberlain and Florence Howe, "Women's Studies and Developing Countries: Focus on Asia," in *The Women and International Development Annual*, vol. 4, edited by Rita Gallin, Ann Ferguson, and Janice Harper (Boulder, Colorado: Westview Press, 1995).

2. See Alida Brill, ed., *A Rising Public Voice: Women in Politics Worldwide* (New York: The Feminist Press at The City University of New York, 1995).

3. See Committee on Women's Studies in Asia, ed., *Changing Lives: Life Stories of Asian Pioneers in Women's Studies* (New York: The Feminist Press at The City University of New York, 1995). Kali for Women published this book in 1994 in India under the title *Women's Studies, Women's Lives*.

4. Li Xiaojiang, "My Path to Womanhood," in *Changing Lives*, 114.

5. Ibid., 115.

6. See Inge K. Broverman, Donald M. Broverman, Frank E. Clarkson, Paul S. Rosenkrantz, and Susan R. Vogel, "Sex-Role Stereotypes and Clinical Judgements of Mental Health," *Journal of Consulting and Clinical Psychology* 34 (1970): 1–7.

7. Malavika Karlekar, "A Fieldworker in Women's Studies," in *Changing Lives,* 141.

8. Cho Kyoung, "To Grow with Women's Studies," in *Changing Lives,* 55.

9. See *Women's Studies Quarterly* 24, nos. 1 & 2 (Spring/Summer 1996).

10. See Anastasia Posadskaya, "Women's Studies in Russia: Prospects for a Feminist Agenda," *Women's Studies Quarterly* 22, nos. 3 & 4 (Fall/Winter 1994): 157–170.

11. See Tove Beate Pedersen, *Women's Studies Quarterly* 24, nos. 1 & 2 (Spring/Summer 1996): 343–350.

12. See Gloria Bonder, "Women's Studies in Argentina: Keeping the Feminist Spirit Alive," *Women's Studies Quarterly* 22, nos. 3 & 4 (Fall/Winter 1994): 89–102.

13. See Marjorie Mbilinyi, Ruth Meena, Athaliah Molokomme, Bolanle Awe, Nina Mba, E. Maxine Ankrah, and Peninah D. Bizimana, "Reports from Four Women's Groups in Africa," *Signs: Journal of Women in Culture and Society* 16, no. 4 (1991): 846–869.

14. See Kazuko Watanabe, "Japanese Women's Studies," *Women's Studies Quarterly* 22, nos. 3 & 4 (Fall/Winter 1994): 73–88.

15. See *Women's Studies Quarterly* 22, nos. 3 & 4 (Fall/Winter 1994).

16. The term "course" in the United States has nothing in common with the word "course" as it is used to describe an entire program of study in certain countries. A U.S. course is a small unit, one of thirty-two to forty that undergraduates need to complete their bachelor's degrees. Undergraduates take four or five such courses each semester, generally for eight semesters. Some of these might be in a "major" area of study, usually a discipline like economics or history or English or biology. Since the mid-1960s, it has also been possible at some colleges and universities in the United States to major in an interdisciplinary area of study: Black studies, for example, or Asian studies, or women's studies, just to name a few.

17. See Posadskaya, "Women's Studies in Russia."

18. See Li Xiaojiang, "My Path to Womanhood."

19. See Elizabeth Minnich, *Transforming Knowledge* (Philadelphia: Temple University Press, 1990).

20. See Florence Howe, *Myths of Coeducation: Selected Essays, 1964–1983* (Bloomington, Indiana: Indiana University Press, 1984).

21. I will add that where there once had been a handful of women college presidents, most of them at women's colleges, there are now more than 600, some of them at major universities like Duke and the University of Pennsylvania.

22. See Howe, *Myths of Coeducation.*

23. See Lyndall Ryan, "Women's Studies in the University Seminar," *Newsletter, Australian Women's Studies Association* 8, no. 2 (November 1993).

Get Out of the Kitchen

Marcia Ann Gillespie

Long-time activist in the women's movement and author of many articles on gender, Marcia Ann Gillespie is currently the editor of Ms. Magazine. *Here she reminds us that feminists cannot afford to divert our energies from the business of battling sexists and sexism. They are busy; we must be vigilant and active.*

SEVERAL MONTHS AGO I RECEIVED a letter from a disgruntled reader chastising me for not concentrating on women's issues in the pages of this magazine. The idea that everything under the sun is a women's issue obviously held little appeal. As far as she was concerned, discussions about the economy, immigration, race, poverty, welfare reform, lesbian and gay rights, or factory workers here or in Mexico or in Malaysia had no place in *Ms.* because, concerned only with economic issues as they affect the middle class, she didn't feel they had anything to do with her life. Angry as that letter made me—and I was seeing red—it served to remind me that some women's feminism ends not much further than their front door. Some women have to feel the heat in their own kitchens. It's not until a divorce, a lost job, or a catastrophic illness catapults them onto the welfare line that these concerns resonate. Meanwhile, others simply feel overwhelmed by all the many issues and injustices and problems that women struggle with and against in this world.

Who doesn't wish that it could all be simpler? That we could take on issues one by one by one, and solve each sequentially and be done. You know, like those Year of . . . or Decade of . . . campaigns that the U.N. always seems to be launching. However, unlike those efforts, at the end of the time period the problems would truly be addressed and redressed. No child would go to bed hungry; be abused; or be

denied education, medical attention, decent housing, and a safe environment.

Yes, it's true that this movement of ours often feels way too splintered, what with all the many passionately held beliefs and causes that swirl under the banner of feminism: domestic violence, sexual assault, incest, war and nuclear armaments, women's health, electoral politics, the death penalty, censorship, pornography, poverty, ageism, racism, classism. Wiccans and vegans and womanists. Lesbian and gay rights, disability rights, animal rights, welfare rights, reproductive rights, girls' rights, children's rights . . . the list goes on and on and on. Sometimes it's hard to figure out what unites us, what issue or issues will bring us to our feet, out into the streets en masse, and into sustained activism.

By and large, the one issue that seems to ignite us is the right to safe, legal abortion. Hundreds of thousands of us have marched the streets of Washington to declare our commitment to keep this hard-fought right. We have used choice as the litmus test for candidates, dug deep into our pockets to support organizations that focus on this issue when it seemed the Supreme Court was going to reverse *Roe v. Wade.* And yet, even with this critical issue, our fervor ebbs and flows depending on major catastrophic events. Meanwhile, anti-choice fanatics kill doctors and clinic workers, harass patients and providers, and steadily chip away at our rights. Abortion is legal, but it is not available anywhere and everywhere to every woman as a standard medical procedure. Abortion is legal, but fewer and fewer doctors are willing to perform it. Abortion is legal, but the Republican party's soon-to-be-crowned presidential candidate is anti-choice and has made it clear that he would not stand in the way of legislation that would further limit access to this service.

Four years ago, the memory of Anita Hill and the Senate Judiciary Committee fresh in our minds, we were galvanized into political activism on a grand scale, determined to bring more women into the political process, exercise our electoral muscles by putting our candidates into office, and sensitize male politicians to our issues with our voting clout. We turned out at the polls in record numbers, but too many women wanted to believe that we needed to do that only once, and the problems would be solved. So two years later they stayed home, and we ended up with a Congress hell-bent on serving us with a reactionary Contract with America.

For two decades, the conservatives and religious fundamentalists have been busy torching the neighborhood—targeting women's reproductive rights, curtailing abortion services, demonizing poor women, pinning scarlet letters on sexually ac-tive teen girls while blaming feminists for the problem of teen pregnancy, playing the race card to kill affirmative action, keeping the lid on the minimum wage, busting unions, undermining public education, targeting immigrants, seeking to deprive lesbians and gay men of their civil rights, trashing the environment, and eliminating social welfare programs—all in the name of God, Country, and Family Values. This is no time to be picking and choosing our feminisms, waiting for the issue to get up close and personal before we become politically engaged. We can't afford to stay in our kitchens stirring our individual pots, arguing about what is and is not a women's issue, because when they come for me in the morning, don't be fooled, sooner or later they will be coming for you.

PART 1

THE GENDER SYSTEM: CONCEPTUAL AND THEORETICAL ISSUES

Men know a lot about dying, but they don't know enough about living.

—Margaret Mead, speech before the Fourth Plenary Session, First National Women's Conference, International Women's Year, Houston, 20 November 1977

We begin with an examination of the abstract elements that underlie our gender identities—the expectations, images, stereotypes, and ideals that tell us how our genderedness should be expressed.

We examine first in Chapter 2 the dynamics of patriarchy, the masculinist society in which we live. It is both the setting in which traditional images of womanhood were created and the foil against which new, feminist ideals are being forged. In Chapters 3 and 4 we explore patriarchal images, stereotypes and ideals of womanhood, as well as feminist women's responses to them. Chapter 5 closes this part with some of the theories that attempt to explain the origins of the asymmetrical relations of the sexes.

CHAPTER TWO

Patriarchy, Sexism, and Masculinity

CONCEPTIONS OF PATRIARCHY

The terms *patriarchy* and *matriarchy* can have a multiplicity of meanings. Since the suffix *-archy* literally means "the rule of," patriarchy means literally "the rule of the fathers" and matriarchy "the rule of the mothers." In the social sciences, particularly in anthropology, the terms have meanings very close to this literal sense: A patriarchy is a society in which formal power over public decision and policy making is held by adult men; a matriarchy is a society in which policy is made by adult women.

Many contemporary anthropologists contend that although there have been, and still are, societies that are matrilineal (societies in which descent is traced through the females) and matrilocal (in which domicile after marriage is with the wife's family), there is little if any evidence to show that actual matriarchies—societies ruled by women—ever existed, yet *matriarchy* (with its alter, *patriarchy*) is a term commonly used in feminist theories.

This seeming contradiction could be confusing unless one realizes that feminists use the terms *patriarchy* and *matriarchy* in various ways. Depending on the context, the terms may be scientific (as in anthropology, above), political, philosophic, or even poetic. In feminist thought, matriarchy can mean not only an actual society ruled by women, but also the rule of what historically has been taken to be the traits of the female principle—in other words, the rule of feminist ideals. Patriarchy, then, would refer not simply to a society where men hold power, but rather to a society ruled by a certain kind of men wielding a certain kind of power—a society reflecting the values underlying a particular male ideal, the warrior, which will be appraised more fully below. Thus, feminists frequently use the term *patriarchy* to denote a culture that embodies masculinist ideals and practices. Contemporary radical theorists Robyn Rowland and Renate Klein explain:

> *Patriarchy is a system of structures and institutions created by men in order to sustain and recreate male power and female subordination. Such structures include: institutions*

*such as the law, religion, and the family; ideologies
which perpetuate the "naturally" inferior position of
women; socialisation processes to ensure that
women and men develop behavior and belief systems
appropriate to the powerful or less powerful group
to which they belong.*[1]

The social *structures* they speak of, for example the
legal profession (and within that, the courts), or
marriage (and within that, reproduction) are maintained by patriarchal *ideology.*

*The family is maintained through the concept of ro-
manic love between men and women, when in fact
marriage contracts have traditionally had an economic base. Women's labour within the family,
which has been unpaid and unacknowledged, and
which includes the emotional servicing of members
of the family as well as their physical servicing, continues to be defined as a "labour of love." Men have
managed to create an ideology which defines men as
the "natural" owners of intellect, rationality, and
the power to rule. Women "by nature" are submissive, passive, and willing to be led. Processes such
as the socialisation of children encourage this situation to continue. So, for example, in playground
games, boys soon learn that they are to act and girls
to create an "audience" for male performance.*[2]

Note that above, patriarchy is described as a society embodying the values of "a certain kind of
men wielding a certain kind of power." In the past
several years, research into masculinity has revealed several versions, or forms, of masculinity,
across time periods and within and across societies,
just as there are with femininity. And these forms of
masculinity are often influenced by the same set of
factors described in Chapter 1 regarding the diversity of women: race, class, sexual identity, age, nationality, and so on. For this reason, many male
theorists in gender studies prefer to speak of "masculinities" rather than masculinity. There is not one
male ideal, they point out, but many. For example,
Chinese-American ideals of manhood at the beginning of the twenty-first century might require
different traits than Jewish-American ideals, and
the image of manly perfection in thirteenth-century
France might have been quite different from the
frontier ideals of nineteenth-century America. Yet
there is agreement that a particular form of mascu-

linity has been dominant for centuries, especially
in the West, and, as you will see in the selection by
R. W. Connell, it has tended to "globalize." In other
words, by a number of means, it has tended to push
aside or "destabilize" other forms of masculinity all
over the world and replace it. That dominant masculinity will be described more fully below. For the
present, we can say that it is hierarchical, competitive, driven by power, often violent, suspicious of
feelings, egocentric, and it subordinates women's
interests to men's. It is this masculinity that informs
masculinism and this set of characteristics that feminists intend when they speak of patriarchy and the
masculinist male ideal.

Feminists argue that contemporary Western culture is a patriarchy, both in the anthropological and
in the political, feminist sense. Patriarchal values
have informed the character of our society, including the place and image of women within it and the
relation between the sexes. Thus, to comprehend
our lives, we must understand the dynamics of
patriarchy—what it is and how it works. To do this,
we must ask the following questions:

- Since patriarchy is an embodiment of the
  masculinist ideal, what is that ideal? How is
  it derived from the traditionally dominant
  picture of ideal masculinity?

- What are the underlying themes of the masculinist ideal? How and why do they actually
  function in the real world?

- What is the effect of the masculinist ideal—
  on men, on women, and on society in
  general?

Let us begin then with an examination of the
masculinist ideal, what it looks like, what it believes, and what it demands. We can then burrow
more deeply, examining its underlying dynamic, to
reveal its consequences for the way we live.

THE MASCULINIST IDEAL

We must begin with a caution: In studying the male
ideals, we are examining *masculinity,* not human excellence. Because masculinist society has historically considered men to be the only fully human
creatures, and because—as we saw in Chapter 1—
the concepts *human* and *male* have frequently been

confused, the concept of the human ideal has been similarly confused with that of the masculine. This blurring of concepts has led to a good deal of misunderstanding and mischief.

The "Human" and the "Male": A Preliminary Distinction

When I have asked students (women and men alike) to name people whom they believed represented human ideals, they have named Mahatma Gandhi, Abraham Lincoln, Martin Luther King, Jr., Jesus, and others they believe to be great-hearted individuals. When I have asked them to name "ideal men," they have again listed Gandhi, Lincoln, King, and Jesus, but the same lists have also included such names as John Wayne, Brad Pitt, and Indiana Jones. Even the students were perplexed by the disparity of their choices. What, they asked, accounts for this confusion?

According to sociologists Michael S. Kimmel and Michael A. Messner, until the modern women's movement, most men had not been accustomed to thinking of themselves as "gendered." Although men as well as women come to know themselves "through the prism of gender," for men that prism is generally invisible because they are the dominant group. That is, maleness does not "marginalize" men, press them to the edges of society, and does not cause them pain and dislocation as femaleness does women, thus it goes essentially unnoticed. In their book *Men's Lives*, Kimmel and Messner recount the story of Kimmel's shock of awareness during a seminar he attended on feminist theory several years ago:

> A discussion between a white woman and a black woman revolved around the question of whether their similarities as women were greater than their racial differences as black and white. The white woman asserted that the fact that they were both women bonded them, in spite of their racial differences. The black woman disagreed.
>
> "When you wake up in the morning and look in the mirror, what do you see?" she asked.
>
> "I see a woman," replied the white woman.
>
> "That's precisely the issue," replied the black woman. "I see a black woman. For me, race is visible every day, because it is how I am not privileged in this culture. Race is invisible to you, which is

> why our alliance will always seem somewhat false to me."
>
> Witnessing this exchange, Michael Kimmel was startled. When he looked in the mirror in the morning, he saw, as he put it, "a human being: universally generalizable. The generic person." What had been concealed—that he possessed both race and gender—had become strikingly visible. As a white man, he was able not to think about the ways in which gender and race had affected his experiences.[3]

Because of the long history of men's not thinking of themselves as gendered, there is a great deal of ambiguity surrounding the term *man*, which has come to mean in our language either *human* or *male*. Such usage, feminists point out, derives from the ancient masculinist presumption that humanity and masculinity are one and the same. If that were true, then excellence in humanity would be the same as excellence in masculinity, and if a man enhanced his masculine qualities, he would also be enhancing his "human" qualities. As he developed excellence in human character, so would he also become more "manly." Recognizing this ambiguity, we can understand why the terms *male ideal* and *ideal man* might not be distinguished and thus how Tarzan and Mahatma Gandhi might appear on the same list.

Until feminists crystallized the problem, researchers had given almost no consideration to the masculine element distinct from the human. But once the simple fact is realized that *human* and *masculine* are not the same, it is evident that ideal masculinity and ideal humanity are different, too, and that no sense can be made of either one until they are separated and compared.

The intellectual community has spent considerable energy identifying the qualities of human excellence. Philosophers of classical antiquity included intelligence, independence, temperance, honesty, courage, responsibility, altruism, justice, and rationality in their vision. Modern thinkers have added more characteristics, particularly the affective traits, such as humor, compassion, and sensibility. Now, to fully comprehend "the male ideal," we must ask how these qualities of human excellence are related to the requirements of the dominant masculinity. Which of them are retained and which discarded? How are they adapted to the image, and how are they changed? In a conflict between masculine and human ideals, which takes precedence for most men? Under what conditions? These are questions that must be explored if we are to understand more than superficially what contemporary images of masculinity mean to men and ultimately to women.

The Masculine Ideal

Consider the men, real or fanciful, who have come to be known as masculine heroes in our culture—figures like Babe Ruth, Tarzan, the Lone Ranger, Hulk Hogan, Sam Malone, Mel Gibson, Rambo, 007, Elliot Ness, Axel Foley, and Batman.

An examination of these images begins to reveal the qualities of the masculinist ideal male. Typically, our hero exhibits some version of the classical traits of human excellence, adapted though they may be to contemporary circumstances: He is intelligent (or canny), competent, courageous, essentially forthright (at least with the "right" people and under the "right" circumstances), healthy, and strong. Responsible and persevering, he pursues right as he sees it and lets no one deter him from his course. He has spirit or backbone. Thus, from the shores of Iwo Jima to the hills of Montana, soldier or cowboy or rugged ex-fighter-come-home, John Wayne gets the job done. Not an intellectual, though natively intelligent, he always knows just how to make things come out right. Fearless in the face of danger, he speaks truth to his adversaries—captors, crooks, townspeople—and always triumphs.

It becomes apparent that our image is not fully drawn using only the classical qualities of intelligence, honesty, courage, and so on. Added dimensions are required to transform it from the merely human to the masculine: This hero needs to be (1) "sexy" and (2) "tough,"—that is, violent in a socially approved way. (As we shall see later, for masculinists, these two factors—sex and violence—coalesce.)

For the most part, the masculine heroes in our culture can be grouped into just a few categories: soldiers (warriors); cops, detectives, and international spies (warriors against crime); cowboys (pioneer warriors against bad guys, Indians, and the untamed environment); tough doctors (warriors against disease, ignorance, or the hospital administration); rough but basically good crooks (warriors

against . . . [fill in the blank]); and now a new, high-tech version, the half-man, half-machine warrior like Robo-Cop and others. Our hero may be handsome or rugged, young or graying or bald, a good guy or a good bad guy, a learned professional or a street-educated bum, but one thing is certain—he is tough in a special and desirable way: He is in charge. He isn't afraid of pain; he doesn't shun a "necessary" fight; he can't be pushed; he perseveres in his will; he wins. Taciturn or talkative, he doesn't mince (words or movement); and whether in a lab coat, a uniform, a loin cloth, or a three-piece suit, like the Incredible Hulk, he communicates the untamed animal within, under control but nonetheless ready to surface should a challenge present itself.

The Warrior Imperative

Masculinity, manhood, is symbolized by the astrological symbol ♂, which represents Mars, the ancient god of war. That is no accident, for the essence of this masculine ideal is the warrior image. The "real man," the "man's man," the virile, exciting hero is a winning warrior, the guy on top, regardless of what he battles. Without the aura of the fighter, a man may be important or influential, or even humanly excellent, but he will not be masculine in the traditional sense. Indiana Jones is a scholar, a professor, successful in his profession, intelligent, capable. He is quiet, one might even say reserved and conservative. He is transformed into a symbol of potent masculinity, however, by the alter character within: the fearless, never defeated, unorthodox, knock-'em-down, take charge, shoot-'em-up, get-the-girl wise guy. Harrison Ford played the same character in *Witness* in a different venue: a competent, successful cop who succeeds because he is tough, relentless in a fight, breaks rules when he chooses, gives them what for, and gets the girl.

From *Lethal Weapon* to "NYPD Blue," from *The Last of the Mohicans* to "Law and Order," male heroes are fighters. They won't be pushed around; they don't take orders, they give them. Aggressive—often downright truculent and even violent—they epitomize the ideal of the primal warrior, the prototype of pure masculinity. In the words of Marc Feigen Fasteau, a lawyer and feminist, "men are brought up with the idea that there *ought* to be some part of them, under control until released by neces- sity, that thrives on [violence]. This capacity, even affinity, for violence, lurking beneath the surface of every real man, is supposed to represent the primal, untamed base of masculinity."[4]

But a proclivity for violence, though a necessary part, is not all there is to the warrior-hero. Within the ideal lies a further, nearly hidden prescription. It is the reverse side of the coin: The "real man" must never exhibit the complementary characteris- tics of the masculinist ideal, those qualities that would render him unfit for battle—delicacy, sensi- tivity, fastidiousness, pity, emotionality, fearfulness, need, tenderness toward other men, and certain other humane traits. These are exactly the qualities reserved for women, expected and required of women, and symbolized by ♀, the sign of Venus, goddess of life. The masculine ideal is *all* "man," *all* Mars, *none* of Venus. Ultimately, it comes to this: The warrior virtues together with the negation of their complements (the affective qualities) compose the patriarchal ideal of masculinity.

Patriarchal Ideal of Masculinity

Warrior Virtues	*Not-Male (Complement)*
aggressiveness	passivity
courage	timidity
physical strength and health	fragility and delicacy
self-control and emotional reserve	expressiveness
perseverance and endurance	frailty
competence and rationality	emotionality
independence	needfulness
self-reliance and autonomy	dependence
individuality	humility
sexual potency	chastity, innocence, or receptivity

The ideal patriarchal male must be not only brave but never timid; not only independent but never needful; not only strong but never weak. Committed to victory in battle, which is his first pri- ority, he is a man of constraint and restraint, for vi- olent emotions of any kind might deter him from his rationally designed course or strategy. For this man, control over himself and his needs or feelings is perceived to be the key to control over events, which is crucial to his sense of self.

This current patriarchal superhero is super- sexed; yet with all the emphasis on potency (as a sign of strength and power), the version of sex pre- sented by this masculinist imperative is devoid of sensuality. According to the precepts of Mars, the warrior must not involve himself with commit- ments other than success; nor can he allow himself the luxury of compliance, of shared control or surrender—to himself or to his partner. If feeling must be denied—if sensitivity, delicacy, and need- fulness are prohibited—then surely an experience as profoundly emotional and affective as full sen- suality must also be denied. Instead of yielding to the affective self, as implied by sensuality, the warrior-hero must fight another battle, treating sex as war (between the sexes), making conquests and gaining victories. Even the contemporary image of the sexual expert is more a matter of a "mission accomplished" than of shared delight. "Cheers" hero Sam Malone (Ted Danson) drove women mad with his rugged good looks and his adolescent charm, yet we could see that his own involvement was less than complete; even when "in love," he was distant, ambivalent, frequently exploitative.

Malone is an interesting character because he represents a bridge between the formal image of ideal masculinity (perfectly represented by John Wayne) and another of its aspects—culturally sub- liminal, slightly illicit, and only grudgingly ack- nowledged—the good guy who is so bad or the guy who is good because he's so bad, sharply character- ized by such images as Silvester Stallone in *Rambo*, Bruce Willis in *Die Hard*, James Bond, or to some extent Andy Sipowicz of "NYPD Blue."

The official portrait of the perfect patriarchal man, à la Wayne, depicts a man accomplished and successful, a warrior, a fighter in socially approved arenas, strong, powerful, and dominating, fully controlled, emotionally detached, logical, orderly, duty-bound, and committed to the "right" side. He is law-abiding (for the most part) and motivated by the altruistic values of his society. He is, in the strict- est sense, a hero.

Sam Malone, and a score of others quite like him—Crocodile Dundee, Rocky, and the Beverly Hills Cop, for example—represent a uniquely contemporary variation on the theme, halfway between the classic strong man and the contemporary "new man." On the outside, this man is tough, cool, slick, proud; he is hot stuff. He charms women, takes what he wants, does what he likes, fights the system. As far as women are concerned, as one undergraduate woman put it, "he's a dick, but it's okay, because he's actually only half a dick (which is sexy) and half not a dick." That is, under the traditional masculinist exterior roams a character more appealing (at least to this young woman), the boy inside the man—playful, sensitive, confused, needy, messing up by the numbers ("a tear not quite on the cheek"). He is Star Man, an advanced being, yet a baby; Rocky, oh so tough but oh so dependent on his lady; Dundee, king of the outback, wielder of the big knife, who cannot fathom a bidet; Malone, jock and lady killer, brought down by his attraction to the wrong (bright, independent, educated, but safely goofy) woman; Sipowicz, tough cop, nasty fighter, willing to do the necessary not quite legal dirty work of his squad (in a good cause), embarrassed by sex and intimacy, managed—for his own good—by a strong, bright woman that, finally, he is lost without.

Actually, although very up-to-date, this is not a new image. In the 1930s and '40s, Jimmy Stewart, Cary Grant, and Clark Gable played this type very well. The 1990s element is the degree of tension between the two poles and also perhaps the sheer immaturity of the personalities depicted.

On the far end resides the darker aspect of maleness, the character who is most defined by the martial ideals—the tough, hard, uncompromising, totally controlled warrior-man. On the "good" side of this role is James Bond, sex symbol of the 1970s. He strayed a bit: He beat women (but only those of the other side), he killed (with a license), he was "b-a-a-a-d." In the 1980s he was replaced by Charles Bronson (*Death Wish*, et cetera) or by Rambo and Rocky, in the 1990s by Steven Seagal (*Under Siege*) or Arnold Schwarzenegger—more savage, less controlled, less suave, reflecting perhaps the frustrations of their decade. These men are released from the rules of civilization by the unconscionable crimes of the enemy. That is, with "justification" they kill without quarter, pleasure themselves with the fruits of their fury, and bring order out of chaos with brute force, as proper warriors should.

But what happens when the justification dissolves or the control goes awry? Then we have the monster-sergeant of *Platoon*, who is just a shade away from his acceptable counterpart.

The dark side of the masculinist imperative is an alliance between violence, sexuality, a certain baseness, and mischief, pointedly manifest in events like the one during the Vietnam war described here:

> Some of the GIs who conducted the My Lai massacre raped women before they shot them. The day after that "mission," an entire platoon raped a woman caught fleeing a burning hut. And a couple of days later a helicopter door gunner spotted the body of a woman in a field. She was spread-eagled, with an Eleventh Brigade patch between her legs. Like a "badge of honor," reported the gunner. "It was obviously there so people would know the Eleventh Brigade had been there."[5]

Machismo: Bad Is Good

Under the gloss of the classic heroic ideal is a hidden agenda, a group of themes spawned by the warrior ideal and containing the underlying realities of patriarchal manliness. They take precedence over, or transform, the classical values, and they constitute the concrete fleshing out of the abstract formal ideal. A term American feminists have borrowed from Latin America and adapted for use in referring to this aspect of masculinity is *machismo*. Violeta Sara-Lafosse explains the origin of the term:

> This [is a] form of masculine behavior, which comprises the man's desire to take sexual advantage of women, the failure to assume responsibility for the consequences of such actions, and the self-praise for sexual exploits within the subculture of the peer group. . . .
>
> Machismo and patriarchy are both forms of sexist behavior, for both treat the woman as a sexual object and thus as a person subject to domination. The fundamental difference lies in the fact that the patriarch becomes responsible for the children he begets from that woman, while the macho man is not interested in them and does not recognize them as his offspring. He considers the children the concern of the woman.
>
> This irresponsibility toward the children is a basic feature of machismo, a term that arose in Latin

America and has no equivalents in other languages. Therefore, those who use it elsewhere tend to use it, erroneously, as a synonym for sexism.[6]

As the term is used by feminists of the second wave, *machismo* denotes a configuration of attitudes, values, and behaviors related to its original intent, but wider. It is clearly articulated by a Michael Jackson video of the 1990s: "I'm bad," he sings joyfully, skipping around with his buddies, menacing and leering at women, and bumping his hips and groin. All the associations are made: masculinity, genitalia, bad, . . . desirable.

The machismo element of masculinity is that of the bad boy, of mischief that can and sometimes does slip into downright evil. This configuration is not an aberration, peripheral to martial masculinity. It is essential to it. Encouraged by parents ("Trouble, trouble, trouble, isn't he *all* boy?"), tolerated in school, and enhanced by sports, military traditions, and many rites of passage—for example, the bachelor dinner, Friday night with the boys, or "sowing wild oats"—machismo is real and present. Although its expression may vary with class, race, or location, it forms an important part of the masculinist worldview, for its alternate is the sissy or goody-two-shoes, an object of ridicule and rejection.

Though the expression and the intensity of mischief may vary, the components are relatively stable:

- *General naughtiness; breaking the rules.* El Macho does what he chooses, often the opposite of what is required. Christian society requires certain attitudes of temperance; el Macho drinks too much, spends too much, gambles, and engages in excessive and/or illicit sex. In the extreme, he may steal or kill; in polite society, he swears and fools around. The point of the behavior is in the fact of breaking the rules; too much concern for submission is clearly effeminate.
- *Sexual potency.* Machismo is a cultural image, a human type, but it is a sexual identity as well. Potency—defined as the ability to have sex often and as rapidly as possible, to impregnate with ease—is tightly integrated into the other components described. Violence and sexuality are *not* juxtaposed in this con-

text. Instead, they are different facets of the same thing. El Macho uses his sex like a weapon. In street language, you "deck 'em and dick 'em," you "tear off a piece," or you "bang 'em" or "hit 'er"—all intensely violent metaphors. In the extreme, one rapes or gangbangs; ordinarily, one simply exploits or insults.

- *Contempt for women.* Since masculinity requires a commitment to Mars and an aversion to Venus, it is hardly surprising that el Macho should be contemptuous of Venus's earthly manifestations, women. The official macho attitude requires that women—in their delicacy, dependence, timidity, gullibility, and softness—be used and enjoyed, like a peach plucked from a tree and just as easily discarded. A young man told me that his father advised him to practice the four *f*'s: "Find 'em, feel 'em, fuck 'em, and forget 'em." Contempt blossoms into hatred: Women are stupid, dangerous, wheedling. The only exceptions are those who cannot be contemplated as sexual partners—mothers and sisters, for example, or nuns.

The women's movement reserves the word *macho* for behavior and attitudes expressive of these values wherever they appear. He who even jokingly brags of his macho orientation (and there are those who do) either misunderstands what he is saying or else he deserves the contempt he receives, for it is this aspect of the masculine imperative that transforms an inadequate lifestyle (the martial hero) into a destructive one.

THE MALE ROLE IN THE TWENTIETH CENTURY

In a book that includes a variety of writings on the male role, Deborah S. David and Robert Brannon have translated the concepts given in the previous section into the concrete dictates of patriarchal masculinity for the contemporary Western man.[7] They contend that four major themes underlie prescribed behavior for men and boys. These themes appear early in life, function powerfully in the socialization process, and pervade boys' conceptual environment.

1. "No sissy stuff"—the rejection of any of the characteristics reserved for femininity, either in the male's own behavior or in other men. This includes the fear of being labeled a sissy and discomfort in female environments, the rejection of vulnerability, and the flight from close male friendships.
2. "The Big Wheel"—the quest for wealth, fame, success, and signs of importance.
3. "The Sturdy Oak"—the aura of confidence, reliability, unshakable strength and toughness: "I can handle it."
4. "Give 'em hell"—the enjoyment and expression of aggression, violence, and daring.[8]

The Effects of Patriarchy

Thus, a two-part image of masculinity pervades Western culture: on the one hand, the warrior-hero, a compilation of classical ideals and warrior qualities; on the other hand, the machismo syndrome, the undercurrent of mischief, composed of a predilection for violence, intemperate and exploitative sex, and recklessness.

THE COMMANDMENTS OF MARS ARE:

Dominate and control—people, events, objects.

Succeed at any cost. Never admit defeat or error.

Control your emotions. Avoid strong feelings.

Strive for distance—from others and from self.

Banish needfulness (called weakness).

Be contemptuous of needfulness in others.

Guard against the female within and without.

Protect your image (or ego).

ADD THE MACHISMO ORIENTATION:

Exhibit a kind of reckless unconcern for rules.

Embrace violence.

Place sexuality in a power context.

Such are the imperatives of the masculinist ideal in Western patriarchy.

As we explore the imperatives of this masculine mystique, it is essential to remember that we are dealing with an image, an ideal, or a stereotype. The image functions as a standard; it does not represent any individual or even a group of individuals. Although a man may strive to meet the requirements of the image, he cannot become the image in reality any more than a real woman can actually become all that is implied by the title "Playmate of the Year."

The gender ideals function as powerful social mores in the culture. These are, as the sociologist William G. Sumner showed, values and attitudes that begin dimly somewhere in the past, become so habitualized that they take on an aura of cosmic validity, and ultimately become so embedded in the social fabric that they cannot allow for deviation or rejection.[9] They are usually perceived not as social rules but as enduring truths and realities. Learned through the process of socialization, mores—including sex-role prescriptions—are internalized by individuals and become extremely powerful determinants of behavior. As David and Brannon's discussion points out, the young boy learns truculence as a value for men the same way he learns that Americans eat beef but not horse meat. The picture of ideal manhood is presented to him as a required model, not as a choice.

Yet a variety of factors affect a male's response to the model: how insistently it is presented to him, the successes (or failures) he has within it, the values that are juxtaposed to it, the alternative lifestyles he may learn about and try, and many more. One way or another, by adoption, rejection, or adaptation, each male must reckon with these idealized images of masculinity. Insofar as he internalizes the masculinist ideal, he will exhibit its characteristics, will try to control others with them, and will be controlled by them.

The sex-role prescriptions function in this way: Although they are created by men, they are in large part independent of individual men; and although men may benefit or suffer from them and have a stake in maintaining or ending them, men as social beings are nevertheless subject to them, as are women.

Men Under Patriarchy

Men are not the greatest victims of patriarchy (as I have heard it said), but they are certainly victimized. If the sex roles, both female and male, are destructive, as feminists believe they are, then men as well as women are afflicted.

One might hypothesize that any externally imposed role model would create difficulties. After all, any prescriptive set of values will inevitably contain elements contrary to existing patterns and "natural" inclinations in individuals. What makes these sex roles particularly difficult to deal with, however, is their tremendous scope, the intensity of feelings surrounding them, their inflexibility, and the aspect of one's identity that they affect.

A role model for a pop musician, let us say, requires certain standards of competence with music and with instruments. It also prescribes other values related to the work, such as a tolerance of mobility and a willingness to hustle for engagements. Going a little deeper, one expects as well a particular personal style. To be really popular, a musician needs to look a certain way, talk a certain way, and so on, depending on the era. If the musician fails to meet these expectations, the penalty for deviation may adversely affect his or her musical career, but it is unlikely to be extreme beyond that point. That is, it is unlikely to ruin the player's very sense of being and human worth.

But deviation from the sex roles can have just that effect. In our culture, and possibly for all people, the sense of one's sexual identity and of one's sexual desirability are powerful components of the sense of self and worth. Accordingly, deviation from sexual norms incurs severe penalties, not only from others but often from oneself as well. In other words, the inability or even the refusal to meet particular sex-role prescriptions, for whatever reason, creates serious conflicts for the individual. Whether in terms of adapting to the culture or in terms of resolving inner confusion, the person who deviates from gender expectations experiences real difficulty.

In a genuine way, then—and in several respects—men in patriarchy encounter a painful situation.[10] Certainly, should a man fail to adopt the dominant masculine role expectations, either by default (because he cannot meet them) or by choice (because he rejects them on principle), he must confront and resolve both the social traumas and the conflicts within himself. Through rejection, ostracism, ridicule, or more formidable signs of hostility, people will punish him for his deviation. Because he is not a "man's man" or a "real man," he is apt to find himself ill received both in traditional male environments and among many traditional women. Male students who do not submit to the masculine mold have described their surprise at being rejected not only by men (as they expected) but also by women, who consider them unmanly or unattractive as sexual partners.

If the pain of rejection from without is hard to bear, so is the pain of rejection from within. From childhood on, from our membership in the culture, we carry with us beliefs and attitudes that are extremely difficult to change. Even after we have deliberately altered our opinions in the light of a better-considered set of ideals, the old, internalized value judgments continue in force, thwarting our resolve through doubt and self-contention and raising both anxieties and emotional turmoil. Breaking habits is hard; breaking these ancient and heavily prescribed habits of thought, feeling, and action is particularly hard. While part of the person opts for a new style, the other part rejects it. The result is inner war.

The problems entailed in rejecting traditional gender ideals are obvious; they are much the same problems involved in trying to reject any highly valued cultural norm. The problems that follow *accepting* the patriarchal image are far less obvious because they are so fully integrated into the culture, yet they are considerably more severe in their effects. The supermale image of macho masculinity is not a human image; machismo is not humane. The masculine mystique is directly at odds with a good portion of the classical and apostolic Christian ideals of human excellence; it is at odds with many of the known components of mental health; and it is certainly at odds with many elements that both philosophers and social scientists believe are essential to human happiness.

The classical ideal, although inadequate because it fails to treat the affective qualities of human life, still includes a certain tranquillity of spirit born of temperance, a strong commitment to the rights and needs of other individuals through social order, and thoughtful ethical awareness and responsibility. It is an ideal of intelligent, rational behavior, and although it contains a goodly element of physical strength, courage, and spirit, it is not given to violence or pugnacity as an end in itself.

The ideal of apostolic Christianity, too, is one of temperance and tranquillity. With greater emphasis on peace and gentleness than the classical ideal, it is yet disciplined and highly concerned with law.

The masculine mystique, however—particularly the machismo component—values violence, recklessness, intemperance, exploitativeness, and aggressive pursuit of success at all costs. Surely the man raised under the imperatives of both the classical and the martial visions suffers considerable conflict. Because our society officially teaches him the classical virtues and at the same time requires the martial, he is asked to exhibit incompatible qualities and behaviors: to love his neighbor or brother but to carry a bayonet; to be charitable and loving but also to succeed in business; to be a responsible father and husband but to prove his potency through untrammeled sex. To be pulled between contradictory values is not unusual in our changeable, diverse society. In fact, some social commentators suggest that the most important capacity for people in the coming era will be the capacity to adapt. But the martial imperative is such that it denies men the means to adapt in a substantive, meaningful, integrative way.

Adaptation and growth at the spiritual and emotional level requires a great deal of reflection, introspection, self-awareness, self-criticism, and emotional integrity. To flourish under conditions of stress and change, one must be capable of understanding one's feelings, of seeking assistance, and of nurturing an enduring internal sense of self. But these very capacities are denied by the masculinist male ideal. The proper warrior has neither the time nor the patience for reflection and introspection. His imperative is direct action. He considers thinking as effete and equates it with indecisiveness.

And feelings? We all "know" that big boys don't cry. They also don't get scared and don't need anyone to help them. Although the martial virtue of emotional reserve refers primarily to feelings not convenient for a warrior—such as fear, anguish, grief, and hurt—the truly "manly" man is expected to be reserved in all his feelings. Anger and lust might be acceptable, but even these ought never to operate spontaneously, independent of plan, for they must not interfere with success. Even the so-called positive emotions of humor, love, and joy must be controlled lest they interfere with duty. (Have we not been regaled with tales of foolish men who forsook their commitments for love and were

dashed into dishonor? Think of *Anthony and Cleopatra* or *Of Human Bondage.*) Young boys are trained early not to feel but to "take it like a man" and to "keep a stiff upper lip."

The key word in this image is *distance*—from the self, from one's feelings and needs, from other men, and from women. The perfect warrior trusts no one and has one loyalty: the battle and its success. He succeeds or he is worthless. In business, in science or debate, in relationships, or in sex, a man under patriarchy must win or set himself to winning. That is why weakness is contemptible: The "weak" (the needful, the feeling, or the tender) do not win (that is, dominate, control, overwhelm). A man must push, strive, never let up, and loathe himself if he fails.

Where Mars triumphs, men are shorn of their affective elements, impelled toward distance and truculence, and robbed of many precious experiences of life and self. They find themselves consigned to an arena of striving, pressure, anxiety, and threat. They must content themselves with the prescribed fruits of patriarchal success: status, power, and public praise. In such a context, even pleasure is transitory and shallow—not a happy prospect. But happiness, in terms that Aristotle or Plato or Buddha might understand—an ongoing, profound experience—is not the issue for the warrior. He has no time for that kind of experience. He is too busy winning.

This is not a wholesome picture, to be sure. Men who pursue the macho ideal indeed lose a good deal in life, yet we must not be blind to a harsh reality: They hold a tremendous advantage in power, privilege, and position. And because masculinist men have the presiding power in society, their perspectives and values, including the martial ideal, permeate our culture. These have become, in fact, the guiding ethos of much social behavior. That is why, feminists argue, we inhabit a patriarchy.

MEN'S CRITIQUE OF MASCULINITY

Because of the women's movement, definitions of masculinity are changing. Thirty years of feminist critique of gender could not have occurred without men finally coming to recognize and analyze their own genderedness. Their appraisals have taken various directions, from the scholarly investigations of men's studies to an assortment of reactionary men's "liberation" movements. "Men's studies," similar to women's studies, deconstructs the cultural definitions of manhood, considers their effects on men (and women), and ultimately seeks change and improvement in men's lives, relationships, and actions. Its investigations have focused on such diverse topics as race, class, and ethnic prescriptions for manliness, the impact on boys of sports and athletics, the meaning of heterosexism, the abuses of "toughness," the influence of the military, coming-of-age rituals, economic power, and many others.

A different tack is taken by "mythopoetic" theorists like Sam Keen or Robert Bly, author of *Iron John*[11], a symbolic analysis of the quest for adult manhood and self-affirmation. In many ways, Bly's title reveals his approach. His story contains many of the classic elements of patriarchal masculinity: differentiation and separation from the female, male-to-male bonding, assertions of strength and power, the celebration of "wild" maleness. In groups for men only, Bly often prompts participants to reconnect with their fathers and other male elders, dance and pound drums to release the primal man within, and reaffirm their inner warrior and essential manliness. While most feminists tend to welcome men's studies—its scholarship is often in harmony with our own—regarding movements like Bly's, there are differences of opinion. Some reason that they reflect the primitive beginning of men's reevaluation of their participation in traditional masculinity. Others, like myself, believe that they constitute a negative reaction to feminism, born of resentment toward women's growing awareness and strength, and a movement to reestablish the traditional "me Tarzan, you Jane" relationship between men and women. Declares Robert Bly in *Iron John*:

> The male of the past twenty years has become more thoughtful, more gentle. But by this process he has not become more free. He's a nice boy who pleases not only his mother but also the young woman he is living with.[12]

Men's apologists and groups hostile to the goals and achievements of the women's movement have popped up like Hydra's heads in the last several years, some of them small, crazy, and ineffectual, others gaining considerable influence (we have all been treated to the rantings of "angry white males"), but none have grown so fast or have so much potential for power as the religious right's Promise Keepers.

The Un-"sissified" Men of the Religious Right (The More Things Change, the More They Remain the Same)

The men of the Promise Keepers are not friends to feminism. According to their rhetoric, they mean to restore men to their lost masculinity, make them more responsible to their families and communities, return them to God. Further, they mean to save women from "wimpy" men, from too much or the wrong kind of responsibility, from too much or the wrong kind of work; they mean to draw husbands closer to their wives and children. A closer examination of their writings, however, reveals a different program: Their intention is to reassert the traditional relations between the sexes, to rebuild the patriarchal system under the rubric of "family values," and to restore the power of men over women, of husbands over wives.

According to Randy Phillips, president of the group, Promise Keepers was founded in 1990 by football coach Bill McCartney of Colorado University in Boulder with just 70 men. Two years later, 50,000 men attended an assembly in Boulder, and now such conferences take place all over the country. In *Seven Promises of a Promise Keeper*, Phillips explains that the group's express purpose, at its beginning and still today, is to bring "hundreds of thousands" of men together to "enter into the struggle for righteousness and, shoulder to shoulder, seize the divine opportunity to further the kingdom of God."[13] As this is a movement designed for men, for males, a great deal of energy goes into defining the manly male: He is a "godly" man, he "loves Jesus," he is devoted to "God's word," to other men, to the Church, to "purity," to strong marriages, close relationships with his children, and a commitment to evangelize the world.

This "manly man" of the Promise Keepers may sound good at first blush, but he may be too good to be true. We must read on. Careful attention to what is said about women and wives must give us pause. Wives have become altogether too powerful in the American family. Through no fault of their own, mind you, women have taken over responsibility for their children and their homes. This is because men have failed to be "men," have abrogated both their obligations and their rights, leaving an absence of "leadership" (read, "power"?). Cries Dr. Howard G. Hendricks, "We need leaders in our homes, too. The American family is unraveling like a cheap sweater."[14] Dr. Tony Evans also decries the demise of the American family. He explains:

> *I am convinced that the primary cause of this national crisis is the feminization of the American male. When I say* feminization, *I am not talking about sexual preference. I'm trying to describe a misunderstanding of manhood that has produced a nation of "sissified" men who abdicate their role as spiritually pure leaders, thus forcing women to fill the vacuum. . . .*
>
> *. . . much has been said about liberating women, when what we really need are* men *who are liberated from the distorted images conjured up by our corrupt culture.*[15]

Finally, men have to climb out of the backseat to which corrupt (feminist? liberal?) culture has relegated them.

RECLAIMING YOUR MANHOOD

> *I can hear you saying, "I want to be a spiritually pure man. Where do I start?"*
>
> *The first thing you do is sit down with your wife and say something like this: "Honey, I've made a terrible mistake. I've given you my role. I gave up leading this family, and I forced you to take my place. Now I must reclaim that role."*
>
> *Don't misunderstand what I'm saying here. I'm not suggesting that you* ask *for your role back, I'm urging you to* take *it back.*
>
> *. . . there can be no compromise here. If you're going to lead, you must lead. Be sensitive. Listen. Treat the lady gently and lovingly. But* lead!*[16]*

We should know that this is not a new image of masculinity, born of the current fundamentalist revival. This sort of man appeared in the religious revivals of the nineteenth and earlier twentieth centuries, called by various commentators "muscular Christianity," a brand of Christianity that abhorred

and attempted to expunge an alleged "feminization" of the church.

Note the inversion in the reasoning: To be a "real man," a godly man, is to relieve women of the *burden* of "leadership" that we have been *forced* to take because of men's terrible error—allowing women a portion of power in our own homes. Presumably, women cannot or must not be leaders, and once women have only the task of following (obeying) and no longer have to make decisions regarding our own lives and that of our children's, we will all be much happier, the world will have been turned right side up once more, God will be pleased, and men will have rid themselves of the sin of sissification. A spiritually pure man is one who maintains control over his wife.

Here, in different apparel, is the same principle you will see articulated in Chapter 3 by the medieval philosopher St. Thomas Aquinas. What is striking is its resurgence in the same form in the late twentieth century in many places around the world, a fact that attests to the incredible resiliency of patriarchal ideology: Women were made by God as "helpers" to man, not in the business of culture, but in the (biological) work of the human race. Our job is to care for our husbands' and children's *bodies*, their shelter, their food, while our husbands "care for" our souls and that of the wider world.

Despite the rhetoric, despite the glossing over, the reality is clear: As far as women are concerned, Promise Keepers represents the old order, struggling hard to reestablish itself.

SOCIAL PRIORITIES IN PATRIARCHY

To reiterate: We have seen that the essential element of the patriarchal masculine ideal is warrior aggressiveness. The rationale is as follows: "Because this is a violent world, the man of the world must be violent." It is rarely considered that the world is violent because the ideal man of the world is violent. Feminists, however—both female and male—have suggested just that.

Shulamith Firestone, Andrea Dworkin, Gloria Steinem, Brian Easlea, and countless others have commented on the principle of violence in patriarchal culture. Some argue that this element of masculinism is the root of all the other destructive forces that plague us: war, racism, rape, and environmental abuse. Mary Daly argues that all of these problems are manifestations of patriarchy's "phallocentric" commitment to domination (of people, events, and things). She calls the configuration of power-through-violence "phallic morality," and sees it expressed through "The Most Unholy Trinity: Rape, Genocide, and War."[17] If Daly's language seems extreme or exceptional, her thesis is not.

SEXISM, MASCULINISM, AND PATRIARCHY

Before going on, let us pause to review some important concepts. Sexism, masculinism, and patriarchy are related, as we have seen, but the terms may not always be used interchangeably.

Sexism is a way of seeing the world in which actual or alleged differences between males and females are perceived as profoundly relevant to important political, economic, and social arrangements. One way to more easily understand the meaning of the term *sexism,* is to think of some human trait that is not typically treated as relevant to such things and substitute it for sex differences— hair color, for example. To continue the analogy, *hairism* becomes a way of seeing the world in which differences in hair color are thought to be profoundly relevant to important political, economic, and social structures. In that case, ego identities, social roles, work assignments, rights and obligations, and human relationships would all be determined in large measure by the color of one's hair.

It seems absurd, doesn't it? After all, the color of one's hair has nothing to do with one's functioning in society. Hair color as a sociopolitically relevant trait is recognized as absurd because in our culture there are no claims that it is related in any way to other traits that *are* important to social function, such as intelligence, character, competence, maturity, and responsibility.

But this is exactly what happens in sexism. Sexists claim that important traits such as character, competence, and so on are related to, and in fact determined by, one's biological sexual identity: Males are intelligent, responsible, courageous; females are emotional, dependent, and flighty—hence, males rather than females are suited to authority.

Of course, the maintenance of such claims does not constitute the full meaning of sexism. If it did, sexism would simply be a strategy for ordering social functions that were essentially neutral in value. Men and women would be different and have different things to do, but they would still have equal worth. The argument would be much like this: Bananas and apples are different and, respectively, go better with certain foods, but neither fruit is superior to the other. In fact, many sexists claim that this is precisely what they do believe about sexual arrangements. However, their claim is false.

The essence of sexism (as of racism, nativism, heterosexism, and similar bigotries) is its inherent evaluative element. The term *sexism* may appear to be neutral, and some maintain that women, too, may be sexist (that is, female chauvinistic), but that is not the way sexism functions in our society. "Separate but equal" is a lie between the races; "complementary but equal" is a lie between the sexes. Sexists believe and require that men are superior to women in every way that matters. Both a dichotomy of sexual characteristics and a negative judgment about women (misogyny) are essential features of our culture's particular brand of sexism, *masculinism.*

Masculinism (or *androcentrism*) is the elevation of the masculine, conceptually and physically, to the level of the universal and the ideal. It is the valuing of men above women. It is, as well, an honoring of a male principle (conceived of as Mars, a warring configuration of qualities) above the female (conceived of as Venus, a serving and nurturing configuration). Some feminists have referred to this honoring of the male and the male principle as phallic worship, or *phallocentrism*, because male identity in a martial context is so intricately bound up with and expressed through their sexuality, more specifically, genital sexuality.

WOMEN UNDER PATRIARCHY

Masculinism in a political context is *patriarchy.* A consideration of the condition of women under patriarchy will fill the remainder of this book, but some general remarks are appropriate here because the misogynist, patriarchal treatment of women and womanhood is the quintessence of masculinism, its culmination and fullest expression.

If masculinism is at heart the worship of Mars and the embracing of phallic morality to the exclusion of its complement, then the rejection of Venus and the rejection of the traits symbolized by her—love, beauty, tenderness—as well as the rejection of woman, her earthly manifestation, becomes predictable. No "real man" may tolerate (within himself, at least) the tender qualities. He must deny himself any tendency toward them, any personal experience of them. Instead, these traits must be projected outward. The complement of his masculine character is settled on his sexual complement, woman: "I am man; she is woman. I am strong; she is weak. I am tough; she is tender. I am self-sufficient; she is needful."

Woman serves this important function in patriarchy. As the negative image of man, his complement, she is the receptacle of all the traits he cannot accept in himself yet cannot, as a *human* being, live without. The image Woman contains that element of humanity ripped from Man—an element she keeps for him, still in the world, available when and where needed, but sufficiently distant to avoid interfering with business. Yet even as negation, woman's place is not safe. As a man must flee from the Venus principle within himself, as he must hold that configuration in contempt, so he must hold woman in contempt as well, for *in patriarchy* she is the incarnation of Venus and nothing else. The outcome of this arrangement for man is ambivalence. He is both drawn to and repelled by patriarchal woman. Although she represents love, tenderness, compassion, nurturance, passion, beauty, and pleasure, she is also, fashioned by him, the composite of all the reasons why these traits were banned for men: She is weak, emotional, dependent, imprudent, incompetent, timid, and undependable.

Woman's place, then, as we shall see in detail in Chapter 3, is precarious. She is the object of love and hate, fascination and horror. As Venus, she carries traits that are for men both beautiful and terrible, seductive and dangerous; hence, she may be desired and tolerated by men but only so long as she serves and is controlled, like feelings within. Adored and reviled, worshiped and enslaved, the image of woman as well as her "place" in patriarchy is the natural outcome of masculinist values and needs. More than a convenience (which it is), the subordination of women is a necessity in patriarchy. Economically, politically, biologically, and psychologically, it is the foundation on which the entire structure rests.

Notes

1. Robyn Rowland and Renate Klein, "Radical Feminism: History, Politics, Action," *Radically Speaking: Feminism Reclaimed* (Australia: Spinifex Press, 1996), p. 14.

2. Rowland and Klein, "Radical Feminism," p. 14.

3. Michael S. Kimmel and Michael A. Messner, eds., *Men's Lives,* 2nd ed. (New York: Macmillan, 1992), pp. 2–3.

4. Marc Feigen Fasteau, *The Male Machine* (New York: McGraw-Hill, 1974), p. 144.

5. Lucy Komisar, "Violence and the Masculine Mystique," *Washington Monthly* 2, no. 5 (July 1970), p. 45.

6. Violeta Sara-Lafosse, "Machismo in Latin America and the Caribbean," *Women in the Third World: An Encyclopedia of Contemporary Issues* (New York: Garland Publishing, 1998), p. 107.

7. Deborah S. David and Robert Brannon, eds., *The Forty-Nine Percent Majority: The Male Sex Role* (Reading, MA: Addison-Wesley, 1976).

8. David and Brannon, *The Forty-Nine Percent Majority,* pp. 13–35.

9. William G. Sumner, *Folkways* (Boston: Ginn and Co., 1907).

10. In Chapter 3, you will see that women face many of the same problems, although cast differently, that men face in dealing with their sex roles.

11. Robert Bly, *Iron John: A Book About Men* (Reading, MA: Addison-Wesley, 1990).

12. Quoted in Michael Kimmel, *Manhood in America: A Cultural History* (New York: The Free Press, 1996), p. 291.

13. Randy Phillips, "Seize the Moment," in *Seven Promises of a Promise Keeper,* ed. Al Janssen (Colorado Springs, CO: Focus on the Family Publishing, 1994), p. 6.

14. "A Mandate for Mentoring," in *Seven Promises,* p. 49.

15. "Spiritual Purity," in *Seven Promises,* p. 73.

16. "Spiritual Purity," pp. 79–80.

17. Mary Daly, *Beyond God the Father* (Boston: Beacon Press, 1973), ch. 4.

What Are Little Boys Made Of?

Michael Kimmel

Professor of sociology at the State University of New York at Stony Brook, Michael Kimmel is one of the most perceptive scholars in the study of gender. He has authored several articles and books on masculinity and gender in society, among them Manhood in America: A Cultural History *(Free Press, 1995);* The Gendered Society *(Oxford University Press, 2000); and, with Thomas E. Mosmiller,* Against the Tide: Pro-Feminist Men in the United States 1776–1990 *(Beacon Press, 1993). He has edited several other works, including* Changing Men: New Directions in Research on Men and Masculinity *(Sage, 1987);* Men Confront Pornography *(New American Library, 1991); and* The Politics of Manhood: Profeminist Men Respond to the Mythopoetic Men's Movement *(Temple University Press, 1995).*

Yes, says Professor Kimmel, there is indeed a boy's crisis in the United States. But, contrary to certain opinion, it is not the feminist movement that has created the problems but the way masculinity has been constructed—with destructive pressures from within and without. The "ideology of manhood" must be challenged; it can be changed, and it should.

TO HEAR SOME TELL IT, there's a virtual war against boys in America. Best-sellers' subtitles counsel us to "protect" boys, to "rescue" them. Inside, we hear how boys are failing at school, where their behavior is increasingly seen as a problem. Therapists advise anguished parents about boys' fragility, their hidden despair and despondence. Boys, we read, are depressed, suicidal, emotionally shut down.

And why? It depends on whom you ask. The backlash chorus—the cultural right as well as the authors of some of these books—chant "feminism." Because of feminism, they say, America has been so focused on girls that we've forgotten about the boys. Other writers blame patterns of male development, while still others find in feminism not the problem but its solution.

There's no question that there's a boy crisis. Virtually all the books cite the same statistics: boys are four to five times more likely to kill themselves than girls, four times more likely to be diagnosed as emotionally disturbed, three times more likely to be diagnosed with attention deficit disorder, and 15 times more likely to be victims of violent crime. The debate concerns the nature of the crisis, its causes, and, of course, its remedies. The startling number of advice manuals that have appeared in the past couple of years—almost all by male therapists—alternate between psychological diagnoses and practical advice about how to raise boys.

One group, epitomized by therapist Michael Gurian (*A Fine Young Man, The Wonder of Boys*), suggests that boys are both doing worse than ever and doing worse than girls—thanks to feminists' efforts. Gurian argues that as feminists have changed the rules, they've made boys the problem. By minimizing the importance of basic biological differences, and establishing girls' standards as the ones all children must follow, feminists have wrecked boyhood. Along with Australian men's movement guru Steve Biddulph (*Raising Boys*), Gurian argues that our educational system forces naturally rambunctious boys to conform to a regime of obedience. With testosterone surging through their little limbs, boys are commanded to sit still, raise their hands, and take naps.

To hear these critics tell it, we're no longer allowing boys to be boys. We've misunderstood boy biology, and cultural meddling—especially by misinformed women—won't change a thing. It's nature, not nurture, that propels boys toward obnoxious behavior, violence, and sadistic experiments on insects. What makes boys boys is, in a word, testosterone, that magical, catch-all hormone that drives them toward aggression and risk-taking, and challenging this fact gives them the message, Gurian says, that "boyhood is defective."

This facile biological determinism mars otherwise insightful observations. Gurian adroitly points out the nearly unbearable pressure on young boys to conform, to resort to violence to solve problems, to disrupt classroom decorum. But he thinks it's entirely due to biology—not peer culture, media violence, or parental influence. And Biddulph agrees: "Testosterone equals vitality," he writes. All we have to do is "honor it and steer it into healthy directions." This over-reliance on biology leads both writers to overstate the differences between the sexes and ignore the differences among boys and among girls. To argue that boys have a harder time in school ignores all reliable evidence from sources such as Myra and David Sadker's *Failing at Fairness: How America's Schools Cheat Girls.*

These misdiagnoses lead to some rather bizarre excuses for boys' behavior, and to the celebration of all things masculine as the simple product of that pubertal chemical elixir. In *The Wonder of Boys*, Gurian cites bewilderingly incongruous rites of passage, such as "military boot camp, fraternity hazings, graduation day, and bar mitzvah," as essential parts of every boy's life. Hazing and bar mitzvahs? Have you read any reports of boys dying at the hands of other boys at bar mitzvahs? Biddulph explains boys' refusal to listen to adult authority by reference to the "fact" that their ear canals develop in irregular spurts, "leading to a period of hearing loss." And did you know that baritone singers in Welsh choruses have more testosterone than tenors—and have more sex! Where do they get this stuff?

More chilling, though, are their strategies for intervention. Gurian suggests reviving corporal punishment both at home and at school—but only when administered privately with cool indifference and never in the heat of adult anger. (He calls it "spanking responsibly.") Biddulph, somewhat more moderately, proposes that boys start school a year later than girls, so they'll be on a par intellectually.

The problem is, there's plenty of evidence that boys are not "just boys" everywhere and in the same ways. If it's all biological, why is the slightest deviation from expected manly behavior so cruelly punished? Why aren't Norwegian or French or Swiss boys as violent, homophobic, and misogynist

as many are in the U.S.? Boys are not doomed to be victims of what Alan Alda once facetiously called "testosterone poisoning." On the contrary, they can become men who express their emotions and treat their partners respectfully, who listen as well as act, and who love and nurture their children.

But how do we get there? Another group of therapists, including Dan Kindlon and Michael Thompson, and William Pollack, eschew testosterone-tinged testimonials and treat masculinity as an ideology to be challenged. For them, we need to understand the patterns of boys' development to more effectively intervene and set boys on the path to a manhood of integrity.

To do that, Kindlon and Thompson write in *Raising Cain,* we must contend with the "culture of cruelty" that forces a boy to deny emotional neediness, "routinely disguise his feelings," and end up emotionally isolated. In *Real Boys*, Pollack calls it the "Boy Code" and the "mask of masculinity"—a kind of swaggering attitude that boys embrace to hide their fears, suppress dependency and vulnerability, and present a stoic front.

These two books are the biggest sellers and their authors the most visible experts on boyhood. Pollack's book is far better. The most influenced by feminism, his observations provide an important parallel to psychologist Carol Gilligan's work on how assertive, confident, and proud girls "lose their voices" when they hit adolescence. At the same moment, Pollack says, boys find the inauthentic voice of bravado, of constant posturing, of foolish risk-taking and gratuitous violence. The Boy Code teaches them that they are supposed to be in power and thus to act like it. They "ruffle in a manly pose," as Yeats once put it, "for all their timid heart."

Unfortunately, these therapists' explanations don't always track. For one thing, they all use examples drawn from their clinical practices but then generalize casually from their clients to all boys. And, alas, "all" is limited almost entirely to middle-class, suburban white boys. Cute blond boys stare at us from the books' covers, while inside the authors ignore large numbers of boys whose pain and low self-esteem may have to do with insecurities and anxieties that are more economically and politically rooted. Gurian's books disingenuously show one boy of color on each cover, but there's nary a mention of them inside. Kindlon and Thompson generalize from their work at an elite prep school.

If all the boys are white and middle class, at least they're not all straight. Most therapists treat homosexuality casually, dropping in a brief reference, "explaining" it as biological, and urging compassion and understanding before returning to the more "important" stuff. Only Pollack devotes a sensitive and carefully thought-out chapter to homosexuality, and he actually uses the term "homophobia."

The cause of all this posturing and posing is not testosterone, of course, but privilege. In adolescence, both boys and girls get their first real dose of gender inequality, and that is what explains their different paths. The interventions recommended by Kindlon and Thompson—allowing boys to have their emotions; accepting a high level of activity; speaking their language; treating them with respect; using discipline to guide and build; modeling manhood as emotionally attached (all of which are good suggestions and applicable to girls, also)—don't address male entitlement. Indeed, of the male therapists, only Pollack and James Gilligan (*Violence*) even seem to notice it. For the others, boys' troubles are all about fears suppressed, pain swallowed. Kindlon and Thompson write that the "culture of cruelty imposes a code of silence on boys, requiring them to suffer without speaking of it and to be silent witnesses to acts of cruelty to others."

The books that are written with an understanding of male privilege—and the need to challenge it—are the ones that offer the most useful tools to improve boys' lives. Books by Myriam Miedzian and by Olga Silverstein and Beth Rashbaum, published several years ago, offer critiques of traditional boyhood and well-conceived plans for support and change. Eschewing biological determinism, these books see in feminism a blueprint for transforming both boyhood and manhood. Feminism encourages men—and their sons—to be more emotionally open and expressive, to develop empathic skills, and to channel emotional outbursts away from violence. And feminism demands the kinds of societal changes that make this growth possible.

That's all the more necessary, because there really is a boy crisis in America—not the crisis of inverted proportions that claims boys are the new victims of a feminist-inspired agenda run amok. The real boy crisis usually goes by another name. We call it "teen violence," "youth violence," "gang violence," "violence in the schools." Let's face facts: men and boys are responsible for 85 percent of all violent crimes in this country, and their victims are overwhelmingly male as well. From an early age, boys learn that violence is not only an acceptable form of conflict resolution, but one that is admired. Four times more teenage boys than teenage girls think fighting is appropriate when someone cuts into the front of a line. Half of all teenage boys get into a physical fight each year.

"Rescuing" or "protecting" isn't the answer, say British high school teachers Jonathan Salisbury and David Jackson. As their title, *Challenging Macho Values*, shouts, they want to take issue with traditional masculinity, to disrupt the facile "boys will be boys" model, and to erode boys' sense of entitlement. And for Paul Kivel (*Boys Will Be Men*), raising boys to manhood means confronting racism, sexism, and homophobia—both in our communities and in ourselves. These books are loaded with hands-on practical advice to help adolescents raise issues, confront fears, and overcome anxieties, and to help teachers dispel myths, encourage cooperation, and discourage violent solutions to perceived problems. Salisbury and Jackson's book will be most valuable to teachers seeking to transform disruptive behavior; Kivel's is geared more to parents, to initiate and continue those sensitive and difficult conversations. The most valuable material helps parents and teachers deconstruct sexuality myths and challenge sexual harassment and violence. "We believe that masculine violence is intentional, deliberate, and purposeful," write Salisbury and Jackson. "It comes from an attempt by men and boys to create and sustain a system of masculine power and control that benefits them every minute of the day." Forget testosterone; it's sexism! Even if these two books are less gracefully written and more relentlessly critical of traditional boyhood, they are the only ones to recognize that not all boys are the same, and that one key to enabling boys to express a wider range of emotions is to challenge the power and privilege that is part of their cultural heritage.

Gilligan and Miedzian, along with James Garbarino (*Lost Boys*), understand that the real boy crisis is a crisis of violence—specifically the cultural prescriptions that equate masculinity with the capacity for violence. Garbarino's fortuitously timed study of youthful offenders locates the origins of men's violence in the way boys swallow anger and hurt. Among the boys he studied, "deadly petulance usually hides some deep emotional wounds, a way of compensating through an exaggerated sense of grandeur for an inner sense of violation, victimization, and injustice." In other words, as one prison inmate put it, "I'd rather be wanted for murder than not wanted at all."

Gilligan is even more specific. In his insightful study of violence, he places its origins in "the fear of shame and ridicule, and the overbearing need to prevent others from laughing at oneself by making them weep instead." The belief that violence is manly is not carried on any chromosome, not soldered into the wiring of the right or left hemisphere, not juiced by testosterone. (Half of all boys don't fight, most don't carry weapons, and almost all don't kill: are they not boys?) Boys learn it. Violence, Gilligan writes, "has far more to do with the cultural construction of manhood than it does with the hormonal substrates of biology."

That's where feminism comes in. Who, after all, has offered the most trenchant critique of that cultural construction but feminists? That's why the books written by women and men that use a feminist perspective (Gilligan, Kivel, Miedzian, Pollack, Salisbury and Jackson, and Silverstein and Rashbaum) are far more convincing than those that either repudiate it (Gurian, Biddulph) or ignore it (Kindlon and Thompson).

Frankly, I think the antifeminists such as Gurian and Biddulph (and the right wing in general) are the real male bashers. When they say boys will be boys, they mean boys will be uncivilized animals. In their view, males are biologically propelled to be savage, predatory, sexually omnivorous creatures, hard-wired for violence. As a man, I find this view insulting.

Feminists imagine, and demand, that men (and boys) can do better. Feminism offers the possibility of a new boyhood and a new masculinity based on a passion for justice, a love of equality, and the expression of a full range of feelings.

Patriarchy, Scientists, and Nuclear Warriors

Brian Easlea

Brian Easlea received a doctorate in mathematical physics from London University in 1961 and, during the 1960s, taught nuclear physics in various countries. He later studied the history, philosophy, and social studies of science, which he taught at Sussex University until 1987. He has published on issues relating to both capitalism and science, and gender and science. Since 1987, he has devoted his time to birdwatching and to the writing of his new book, Divinity and Nature: A View Through Five Centuries of Western Science, c. 1500– c. 2000.

Lest anyone believe that masculism, martial values, or patriarchy is either not real or not important, this frightening piece should bring them up short. Easlea shows that the present "masculinity of science" may very well kill us. What is more, he offers an alternative perspective.

IN A LECTURE AT THE University of California in 1980, the Oxford historian Michael Howard accused the world's scientific community, and particularly the Western scientific community, of an inventiveness in the creation and design of weapons that has made, he believes, the pursuit of a "stable nuclear balance" between the superpowers virtually impossible. At the very least, he found it curious that a scientific community that had expressed great anguish over its moral responsibility for the development of the first crude fission weapons "should have ceased to trouble itself over its continuous involvement with weapons-systems whose lethality and effectiveness make the weapons that destroyed Hiroshima and Nagasaki look like clumsy toys."[1] On the other hand, in the compelling pamphlet *It'll Make a Man of You: A Feminist View of the Arms Race,* Penny Strange expresses no surprise at the militarization of science that has occurred since the Second

World War. While acknowledging that individual scientists have been people of integrity with a genuine desire for peace, she tersely states that "weapons research is consistent with the attitudes underlying the whole scientific worldview" and that she looks forward to "an escape from the patriarchal science in which the conquest of nature is a projection of sexual dominance."[2] My aim in this article is to explore the psychological attributes of patriarchal science, particularly physics, that contribute so greatly to the apparent readiness of scientists to maintain the inventive momentum of the nuclear arms race.

My own experiences as a physicist were symptomatic of the problems of modern science. So I begin with a brief account of these experiences followed by a look at various aspects of the masculinity of science, particularly physics, paying special attention to the ideology surrounding the concept of a scientific method and to the kinds of sexual rhetoric used by physicists to describe both their "pure" research and their contributions to weapons design. I conclude with some thoughts on the potential human integrity of a life in science—once patriarchy and its various subsystems have become relics of history.

A PERSONAL EXPERIENCE OF PHYSICS

Growing up in the heart of rural England, I wanted in my early teens to become a professional birdwatcher. However, at the local grammar school I was persuaded that boys who are good at mathematics become scientists: people just don't become birdwatchers. I did in fact have a deep, if romantic, interest in physics, believing that somehow those "great men" like Einstein and Bohr truly understood a world whose secrets I longed to share. So I went to University College London in 1954 to study physics and found it excruciatingly boring. But I studied hard and convinced myself that at the post-

From Michael Kaufman, *Beyond Patriarchy.* Toronto: Oxford University Press, 1987. Reprinted by permission of the author.

graduate level it would be different if only I could "do research"—whatever that mysterious activity really was. It didn't seem remarkable to me at the time that our class consisted of some forty men and only three or four women. At that time, I was both politically conservative and politically naive, a situation not helped by the complete absence of any lectures in the physics curriculum on "science and society" issues.

In my final year it was necessary to think of future employment. Not wanting to make nuclear weapons and preferring to leave such "dirty" work to other people, I considered a career in the "clean and beautiful" simplicity of the electronics industry. I came very close to entering the industry but in the end, to my great happiness, was accepted back at University College to "do research" in mathematical physics. It was while doing this research that I was to begin my drift away from a career in physics.

One event in my graduate years stands out. As an undergraduate I had only twice ever asked about the nature of reality as presented by modern physics, and both times the presiding lecturer had ridiculed my question. However, one day a notice appeared announcing that a famous physicist, David Bohm, together with a philosopher of science were inviting physics students to spend a weekend in a large country house to discuss fundamental questions of physics. That weekend was an enlightening experience that gave me the confidence to believe that physics was not solely a means for manipulating nature or a path to professional mundane achievement through the publication of numerous, uninteresting papers, but ideally was an essential part of human wisdom.

In the early 1960s, while I was on a two-year NATO Fellowship at the Institute of Theoretical Physics in Copenhagen, the first cracks and dents began to appear in my worldview. I met scientists from around the world, including the Soviet Union, who engaged me in animated political discussions. With a group of physicists I went on a ten-day tour of Leningrad and Moscow and, equipped with a smattering of Russian, I left the group to wander about on my own and kept meeting people who, at this high point of the Cold War, implored me to believe that Russia wanted peace. I couldn't square this image of Russia and the Russian people with what I had become accustomed to in Britain and

would soon be exposed to while teaching at the University of Pittsburgh.

It seemed to be a world gone mad: my new university in Pittsburgh awarded honorary degrees to Werner von Braun, the former Nazi missile expert, and to Edward Teller, the father of the H-bomb. The Cuban blockade followed; Kennedy, Khrushchev, and physics were going to bring about the end of the world. I kept asking myself how the seemingly beautiful, breathtaking physics of Rutherford, Einstein, Heisenberg, and Niels Bohr had come to this.

New experiences followed which deepened my frustration with physics and increased my social and philosophic interests. University appointments in Brazil gave me a first-hand experience with the type of military regime that the United States so liked to support to save the world from communism. In the end I returned to the University of Sussex, where I taught "about science" courses to non-science students and "science and society" courses to science majors.

The more I learned, the more I became convinced that the reason physics was so misused and the reason the nuclear arms race existed was the existence of capitalist societies, principally the United States, that are based on profit making, permanent war economies, and the subjugation of the Third World. My pat conclusion was that if capitalism could be replaced by socialism, human behavior would change dramatically. But I felt uneasy with this belief since oppression and violence had not first appeared in the world in the sixteenth century. As the years went by and the feminist movement developed, I came to explore the profound psychological connections between the discipline of physics and the world of the warriors—connections that are ultimately rooted in the social institutions of patriarchy. That is the focus of this paper.

THE MASCULINITY OF PHYSICS

Indisputably, British and American physics is male-dominated. In Britain in the early 1980s, women made up only 4 percent of the membership of the Institute of Physics, and in the United States women made up only 2 percent of the faculty of the 171 doctorate-awarding physics departments.[3] This male domination of physics has obviously not come about by chance; not until recently have physicists made serious attempts to encourage women to study the discipline and enter the profession. Indeed, in the first decades of the twentieth century strenuous attempts by physicists to keep women out of their male preserve were not unknown. Symbolic of such attempts in the 1930s was that of no less a man than the Nobel laureate Robert Millikan, who in 1936 wrote to the President of Duke University questioning the wisdom of the University's appointment of a woman to a full physics professorship.[4] As the statistics amply demonstrate, the male domination of physics continues despite publicized attempts by physicists to eliminate whatever prejudice still exists against the entry of women into the profession.

A second aspect of the masculinity of physics is that the men who inhabit this scientific world—particularly those who are successful in it—behave in culturally masculine ways. Indeed, as in other hierarchical male-dominated activities, getting to the top invariably entails aggressive, competitive behavior. Scientists themselves recognize that such masculine behavior, though it is considered unseemly to dwell upon it, is a prominent feature of science. The biologist Richard Lewontin even goes so far as to affirm that "science is a form of competitive and aggressive activity, a contest of man against man that provides knowledge as a sideproduct."[5] Although I wouldn't agree with Lewontin that knowledge is a mere "sideproduct" of such competition, I would, for example, agree with the anthropologist Sharon Traweek, who writes that those most prestigious of physicists—the members of the high-energy physics "community"—display the highly masculine behavioral traits of "aggressive individualism, haughty self-confidence, and a sharp competitive edge."[6] Moreover, Traweek's verdict is supported by the remarks of the high-energy physicist Heinz Pagels, who justifies such masculine behavior by explaining that a predominant feature in the conduct of scientific research has to be intellectual aggression, since, as he puts it, "no great science was discovered in the spirit of humility."[7] Scientists, then, physicists included, behave socially in a masculine manner.

A third aspect of the masculinity of physics is the pervasiveness of the ideology and practice of the conquest of nature rather than a human goal of re-

spectful interaction and use. Although, of course, many attitudes (including the most gentle) have informed and continue to inform the practice of science, nevertheless a frequently stated masculine objective of science is the conquest of nature. This was expressed prominently by two of the principal promoters and would-be practitioners of the "new science" in the seventeenth century, Francis Bacon and René Descartes, the former even claiming that successful institutionalization of his method would inaugurate the "truly masculine birth of time." Although modern scientists usually attempt to draw a distinction between "pure" and "applied" science, claiming that pure science is the attempt to discover the fundamental (and beautiful) laws of nature without regard to possible application, it is nevertheless widely recognized that it is causal knowledge of nature that is sought, that is, knowledge that in principle gives its possessors power to intervene successfully in natural processes. In any case, most "pure" scientists know very well that their work, if successful, will generally find application in the "conquest of nature." We may recall how the first investigators of nuclear energy wrote enthusiastically in the early years of the twentieth century that their work, if successful, would provide mankind with an almost limitless source of energy. Both the "pure" and the technological challenges posed by the nucleus proved irresistible: the nucleus was there to be conquered and conquest was always incredibly exciting. Even in today's beleaguered domain of nuclear power for "peaceful" purposes, the ideology and practice of the conquest of nature has not disappeared. Thus, rallying the troops in 1979 at the twenty-fifth anniversary of the formation of the UK Atomic Energy Authority, the physicist chairman of the Authority, Sir John Hill, said that we will be judged "upon our achievements and not upon the plaintive cries of the faint-hearted who have lost the courage and ambitions of our forefathers, which made mankind the master of the earth."[8]

The masculine goal of conquest undoubtedly makes its presence felt in our images of nature and beliefs about the nature of reality; this constitutes a fourth aspect of the masculinity of physics and of science in general. That which is to be conquered does not usually emerge in the conqueror's view as possessing intrinsically admirable properties that need to be respected and preserved. Much, of course, could be written on specific images of nature, particularly with respect to "pure" and "applied" research objectives, and the subject does not lend itself to obvious generalizations. Nevertheless, it is clear that from the seventeenth century onwards, natural philosophers, men of science, and scientists tended to see the "matter" of nature as having no initiating, creative powers of its own (a point of view maintained only with some difficulty after the development of evolutionary theory in the nineteenth century). The historian of science, R. S. Westfall, is certainly not wrong when he writes that "whatever the crudities of the seventeenth century's conception of nature, the rigid exclusion of the psychic from physical nature has remained as its permanent legacy."[9] No matter what the cognitive arguments in favor of science's generally reductionist conception of "matter" and nature, it is clear that a nature that is seen as "the mere scurrying of matter to and fro" is a nature not only amenable to conquest but also one that requires no moral self-examination on the part of its would-be conqueror. "Man's place in the physical universe," declared the Nobel laureate physical chemist (and impeccable Cold-War warrior) Willard Libby, "is to be its master . . . to be its king through the power he alone possesses—the Principle of Intelligence."[10]

A fifth aspect of the masculinity of physics lies in the militarization the discipline has undergone in the twentieth century. Optimistically, Francis Bacon had expressed the hope in the seventeenth century that men would cease making war on each other in order to make collective warfare on nature. That hope has not been realized, nor is it likely to be. We may, after all, recall C. S. Lewis's opinion that "what we call Man's power over nature turns out to be a power exercised by some men over other men [and women] with nature as its instrument."[11] In the overall militarization of science that has occurred largely in this century and that was institutionalized during and after the Second World War, physics and its associated disciplines have indeed been in the forefront. For example, in a courageous paper to the *American Journal of Physics,* the physicist E. L. Woollett reported that at the end of the 1970s some 55 percent of physicists and astronomers carrying out research and development in the United States worked on projects of direct military value and he complained bitterly that physics had become a largely silent partner in the nuclear arms race.[12] It is estimated that throughout the world some half million physical scientists work on weapons design and improvement. As the physicist Freeman Dyson has reported, not only is the world of the scientific warriors overwhelmingly male-dominated but he sees the competition between physicists in weapons creation, allied to the (surely masculine) thrill of creating almost limitless destructive power, as being in large part responsible for the continuing qualitative escalation of the nuclear arms race.[13] Moreover, competition between weapons physicists is still a powerful motivating force in the nuclear arms race. Commenting on the rivalry at the Livermore Weapons Laboratory between two physical scientists, Peter Hagelstein and George Chapline, as to who would be the first to achieve a breakthrough in the design of a nuclear-bomb-powered X-ray laser, the head of the Livermore "Star Wars" Group, Lowell Wood, alleged: "It was raw, unabashed competitiveness. It was amazing—even though I had seen it happen before . . . two relatively young men . . . slugging it out for dominance in this particular technical arena."[14] And he then went on to agree with Richard Lewontin's unflattering description of motivation throughout the world of science:

> I would be very surprised if very many major scientific endeavors, maybe even minor ones, happen because a disinterested scientist coolly and dispassionately grinds away in his lab, devoid of thoughts about what this means in terms of competition, peer esteem, his wife and finally, prizes and recognition. I'm afraid I'm sufficiently cynical to think that in excess of 90 percent of all science is done with these considerations in mind. Pushing back the frontiers of knowledge and advancing truth are distinctly secondary considerations.[15]

One might, no doubt naively, like to believe that male scientists do not compete among themselves for the privilege of being the first to create a devastating new weapon. That belief would certainly be quite wrong.

Given such a sobering description of the masculine world of physics in Britain and North America, it isn't altogether surprising if girls, whose gender socialization is quite different from that of boys, are reluctant to study physics at school.

What's more, it is in no way irrational, as British science teacher Hazel Grice points out, for girls to reject a subject that appears to offer "as the apex of its achievement a weapon of mass annihilation."[16]

SCIENTIFIC METHOD FOR SCIENTISTS AND WARRIORS

One common description of physics is that it is a "hard," intellectually difficult discipline, as opposed to "soft" ones, such as English or history. The hard-soft spectrum spanning the academic disciplines is, of course, well-known, and within the sciences themselves there is also a notorious hard-soft spectrum, with physics situated at the hard end, chemistry somewhere toward the middle, biology toward the soft end, and psychology beyond. Insofar as mind, reason, and intellect are (in a patriarchy) culturally seen as masculine attributes, the hard-soft spectrum serves to define a spectrum of diminishing masculinity from hard to soft.

But what is held to constitute intellectual difficulty? It seems that the more mathematical a scientific discipline, the more intellectually difficult it is believed to be and hence the "harder" it is. Mathematics not only makes a discipline difficult, it seems: it also makes it rigorous; and the discipline is thus seen to be "hard" in the two connecting senses of difficult and rigorous. The fact that physics, and especially theoretical physics, makes prodigious use of sophisticated mathematics no doubt contributes to their enviable position at the masculine end of the hard-soft spectrum. It is perhaps of more relevance, however, that mathematics and logical rigor are usually seen as essential components of the "scientific method" and it is the extent to which a discipline is able to practice the "scientific method" that determines its ultimate "hardness" in the sense of intellectual difficulty, the rigor of its reasoning, and the reliability and profundity of its findings. Physics, it is widely believed, is not only able to but does make excellent use of the "scientific method," which thus accounts for its spectacular successes both in the understanding of physical processes and in their mastery. While, of course, all the scientific disciplines aspire to practice the "scientific method," it is physics and related disciplines that are held to have succeeded best.

But does such a procedure as the "scientific method" really exist? If it does, it is deemed to enjoy masculine rather than feminine status insofar as it rigorously and inexorably arrives at truth about the natural world and not mere opinion or wishful thinking. Such a method must therefore, it seems, be ideally characterized by logically rigorous thinking aided by mathematics and determined by experimental, that is, "hard" evidence with no contamination by feminine emotion, intuition, and subjective desires. "The scientific attitude of mind," explained Bertrand Russell in 1913, "involves a sweeping away of all other desires in the interests of the desire to know—it involves the suppression of hopes and fears, loves and hates, and the whole subjective emotional life, until we become subdued to the material, able to see it frankly, without preconceptions, without biases, without any wish except to see it as it is."[17] Such a view of the scientific method remains incredibly influential. In 1974 the sociologist Robert Bierstedt could confirm that "the scientist, *as such,* has no ethical, religious, political, literary, philosophical, moral, or marital preferences. . . . As a scientist he is interested not in what is right or wrong, or good and evil, but only in what is true or false."[18] Numerous examples could be given. Emotion, wishful thinking, intuition, and other such apparent pollutants of cognition are held to betray and subvert the objectivity of the scientific method, which is the hard, ruthless application of logic and experimental evidence to the quest to understand and master the world. Thus while the philosopher of science Hans Reichenbach could tell the world in 1951 that "the scientific philosopher does not want to belittle the value of emotions, nor would he like to live without them" and that the philosopher's own life could be as passionate and sentimental as that of any literary man, nevertheless the truly scientific philosopher "refuses to muddle emotion and cognition, and likes to breathe the pure air of logical insight and penetration."[19] Perhaps that is why the Nobel laureate physicist, Isidor Rabi, then eighty-four years of age, could confide in the early 1980s to Vivian Gornick that women were temperamentally unsuited to science, that the female nervous system was "simply different." "It makes it impossible for them to stay with the thing," he explained. "I'm afraid there's no use quarrelling with it, that's the way it is."[20]

Now the view of successful "scientific method" as masculine logic, rigor, and experimentation necessarily untainted and uncontaminated with feminine emotion, intuition, and wishful thinking is completely and hopelessly wrong. Such a scientific method is as elusive as "pure" masculinity. If nothing else, the invention of theories demands considerable intuition and creative imagination, as every innovative scientist knows and often has proclaimed. Does this therefore mean that the masculine "objectivity" of scientific method is intrinsically compromised? The philosopher of science, Carl Hempel, explains that it doesn't, since "scientific objectivity is safeguarded by the principle that while hypotheses and theories may be freely invented and *proposed* in science [the so-called context of discovery], they can be *accepted* into the body of scientific knowledge only if they pass critical scrutiny [the context of justification], which includes in particular the checking of suitable test implications by careful observation and experiment."[21] Alas for this typical defense of scientific objectivity, for ever since the work of Thomas Kuhn in his 1962 essay *The Structure of Scientific Revolutions,* it is generally accepted that no hard and fast distinction can be readily drawn between such a feminine context of discovery and a masculine context of justification.[22]

For this is what seems to be at issue. Not only does the notion of scientific objectivity appear to entail a clear-cut distinction between the masculine investigator and the world of "feminine" or "female" matter, within the psyche of the masculine investigator there also appears to be a pressing need to establish an inviolable distinction between a masculine mode of "hard," rigorous reasoning determined by logic and experimental evidence and, should it operate at all, a feminine mode characterized by creative imagination, intuition, and emotion-linked preferences. However, such clear-cut distinctions neither exist nor are possible in scientific practice, no matter how much the masculine mode appears paramount in normal research. What certainly does exist (although not uniformly so) is a very impassioned commitment to deny an evaluative subjective component to scientific practice; we may see such a masculine commitment as stemming from an emotional rejection and repudiation of the feminine within masculine inquiry. In other words, the impassioned claim that there exists an unemotional, value-free scientific method (or context of justification) may be interpreted as an emotional rejection and repudiation of the feminine and, if this is so, it would mean that scientific practice carried out (supposedly) in an "objective," value-free, unemotional way is in fact deeply and emotionally repressive of the feminine. This is a hornets' nest with all kinds of implications, but it may help to explain why much of modern science has, I shall argue, been embraced so uncritically by a society that is misogynistic and, in the case of the war industries, misanthropic as well. It is partly because patriarchal science is fundamentally antifeminine that its practitioners are psychologically vulnerable to the attractions of the "defense" industry.

We learn from Freeman Dyson that the world of the warriors, which comprises military strategists, scientists, and Pentagon officials, is ostentatiously defined by a "deliberately cool," quantitative style that explicitly excludes "overt emotion and rhetoric"—it is a style modelled on "scientific method" and directly opposed to, for example, the "emotional, anecdotal" style of the anti-nuclear campaigner Helen Caldicott, whose arguments, according to Dyson, the warriors find unacceptable even when they manage to take them seriously.[23] For her part, Helen Caldicott believes that great rage and hatred lie suppressed behind the seemingly imperturbable, "rational" mask of scientific military analysis.[24] The military historian Sue Mansfield has posed the problem at its starkest: the stress placed in the scientific world on "objectivity" and a quantitative approach as a guarantee of truth, together with the relegation of emotions to a peripheral and unconscious existence, has, she maintains, carried "from its beginnings in the seventeenth century the burden of an essential hostility to the body, the feminine, and the natural environment."[25]

SEXUAL RHETORIC BY SCIENTISTS AND WARRIORS

The stereotype of the sober male scientist dispassionately investigating the properties of matter with, obviously, not a single sexual thought in mind is singularly undermined by the extent to which scientists portray nature as female in their informal prose, lectures, and talks. Indeed, according to the historian of science, Carolyn Merchant, the most powerful image in Western science is "the identification of nature with the female, especially a female harbouring secrets."[26] Physicists often refer to their "pure" research as a kind of sexual exploration of the secrets of nature—a female nature that not only possesses great subtlety and beauty to be revealed only to her most skilful and determined admirers and lovers, but that is truly fearsome in her awesome powers.

"Nature," wrote the high-energy physicist Frank Close in the *Guardian*, "hides her secrets in subtle ways." By "probing" the deep, mysterious, unexpectedly beautiful submicroscopic world, "we have our eyes opened to her greater glory."[27] The impression is given of a non-violent, male exploration of the sexual secrets of a mysterious, profoundly wonderful female nature. From the end of the nineteenth century to the middle 1980s, such sentiments have frequently been expressed by famous physicists. Thus, addressing the annual meeting of the British Association in 1898, the physicist Sir William Crookes announced to his audience, "Steadily, unflinchingly, we strive to pierce the inmost heart of nature, from what she is to reconstruct what she has been, and to prophesy what she yet shall be. Veil after veil we have lifted, and her face grows more beautiful, august, and wonderful, with every barrier that is withdrawn."[28]

But no matter how many veils are lifted, ultimately the fearsome and untameable "femaleness" of the universe will remain.[29] Even if female nature is ultimately untameable, scientific research and application can reveal and make usable many of nature's comparatively lesser secrets. It is striking how successful scientific research is frequently described in the language of sexual intercourse, birth, and claims to paternity in which science or the mind of man is ascribed the phallic role of penetrating or probing into the secrets of nature—with the supposed hardness of successful scientific method now acquiring an obvious phallic connotation. Accounts of the origins of quantum mechanics and nuclear physics in the first decades of the twentieth century illustrate this well. In 1966 the physicist, historian, and philosopher of science, Max Jammer, admiringly announced that those early achievements of physicists in quantum mechanics clearly showed "how far man's intellect can penetrate into the se-

crets of nature on the basis of comparatively inconspicuous evidence"; indeed, Victor Weisskopf, Nobel laureate, remembers how the physicists at Niels Bohr's institute were held together "by a common urge to penetrate into the secrets of nature."[30] While Frederick Soddy was already proudly convinced by 1908 that "in the discovery of radioactivity . . . we had penetrated one of nature's innermost secrets,"[31] it was Soddy's collaborator in those early years, Sir Ernest Rutherford, who has been adjudged by later physicists and historians to have been the truly masculine man behind nuclear physics' spectacular advances in this period. Referring to Rutherford's triumphant hypothesis in 1911 that the atom consisted of an extremely concentrated nucleus of positively charged matter surrounded by a planetary system of orbiting electrons, one of Rutherford's assistants at the time, C. G. Darwin, later wrote that it was one of the "great occurrences" of his life that he was "actually present half-an-hour after the nucleus was born."[32] Successful and deep penetration, birth, and ensuing paternity: these are the hallmarks of great scientific advance.

At first sight it might seem that there is little untoward in such use of sexual, birth, and paternity metaphors, their use merely demonstrating that nuclear research, like scientific research in general, can be unproblematically described by its practitioners as a kind of surrogate sexual activity carried out by male physicists on female nature. However, not only did all the early nuclear pioneers (Rutherford included) realize that enormous quantities of energy lay waiting, as it were, to be exploited by physicists—"it would be rash to predict," wrote Rutherford's collaborator, W. C. D. Whetham, "that our impotence will last for ever"[33]—but, ominously, some of the sexual metaphors were extremely aggressive, reminding one forcibly of the ideology of (masculine) conquest of (female) nature. Indeed, since Rutherford's favorite word appears to have been "attack" it does not seem startling when one of the most distinguished physicists in the United States, George Ellery Hale, who was convinced that "nature has hidden her secrets in an almost impregnable stronghold," wrote admiringly to Rutherford in astonishingly military-sexual language. "The rush of your advance is overpowering," he congratulated him, "and I do not wonder that nature has retreated from trench to trench, and from height to height, until she is now capitulating in her inmost citadel."[34]

The implications of all this were not lost on everyone. Well before the discovery of uranium fission in 1939, the poet and Cambridge historian Thomas Thornely expressed his great apprehension at the consequences of a successful scientific assault on nature's remaining nuclear secrets:

> *Well may she start and desperate strain,*
> *To thrust the bold besiegers back;*
> *   If they that citadel should gain,*
> *What grisly shapes of death and pain*
> *May rise and follow in their track!*[35]

Not surprisingly, just as military scientists and strategists have adopted the formal "scientific style" of unemotional, quantitative argument, so they also frequently make informal use of sexual, birth, and paternity metaphors in their research and testing. Now, however, these metaphors become frighteningly aggressive, indeed obscene: military sexual penetration into nature's nuclear secrets will, the metaphors suggest, not only shake nature to her very foundations but at the same time demonstrate indisputable masculine status and military paternity. We learn that the first fission bomb developed at the Los Alamos laboratory was often referred to as a "baby"—a baby boy if a successful explosion, a baby girl if a failure. Secretary of War Henry Stimson received a message at Potsdam after the successful Trinity test of an implosion fission weapon which (after decoding) read:

> *Doctor has just returned most enthusiastic and confident that the little boy [the uranium bomb] is as husky as his big brother [the tested plutonium bomb]. The light in his eyes discernible from here to Highhold and I could have heard his screams from here to my farm.*[36]

Examples are abundant: the two bombs (one uranium and one plutonium) exploded over Japanese cities were given the code names "Little Boy" and "Fat Man"; a third bomb being made ready was given the name "Big Boy." Oppenheimer became known as the Father of the A-Bomb and indeed the National Baby Institution of America made Oppenheimer its Father of the Year. Edward Teller, publicly seen as the principal physicist behind the successful design of the first fusion weapon or H-bomb, seem-

ingly takes pains in his memoirs to draw readers' attention to the fact that it was a "phallic" triumph on his part.[37] After the enormous blast of the first H-bomb obliterated a Pacific island and all its life, Teller sent a triumphant telegram to his Los Alamos colleagues, "It's a boy."[38] Unfortunately for Teller, his paternity status of "Father of the H-Bomb" has been challenged by some physicists who claim that the mathematician Stanislaw Ulam produced the original idea and that all Teller did was to gestate the bomb after Ulam had inseminated him with his idea, thus, they say, making him the mere Mother.

Following the creation of this superbomb, a dispute over two competing plans for a nuclear attack against the Soviet Union occurred between strategists in the RAND think tank and the leading generals of the Strategic Air Command (SAC) of the U.S. Air Force. In a circulated memorandum the famous strategist Bernard Brodie likened his own RAND plan of a limited nuclear strike against military targets while keeping the major part of the nuclear arsenal in reserve to the act of sexual penetration but with withdrawal before ejaculation; he likened the alternative SAC plan to leave the Soviet Union a "smoking radiating ruin at the end of two hours" to sexual intercourse that "goes all the way."[39] His colleague Herman Kahn coined the term "wargasm" to describe the all-out "orgastic spasm of destruction" that the SAC generals supposedly favored.[40] Kahn's book *On Escalation* attempts, like an elaborate scientific sex manual, a precise identification of forty-four (!) stages of increasing tension culminating in the final stage of "spasm war."[41] Such sexual metaphors for nuclear explosions and warfare appear to be still in common use. In 1980 General William Odom, then a military adviser to Zbigniew Brzesinski on the National Security Council, told a Harvard seminar of a strategic plan to release 70 to 80 percent of America's nuclear megatonnage "in one orgasmic whump,"[42] while at a London meeting in 1984, General Daniel Graham, a former head of the Defense Intelligence Agency and a prominent person behind President Reagan's Strategic Defense Initiative, brought some appreciative chuckles from his nearly all-male audience in referring to all-out nuclear "exchange" as the "wargasm."[43]

What is one to make of such metaphors and in particular of an analogy that likens ejaculation of semen during sexual intercourse (an act, one hopes, of mutual pleasure and possibly the first stage in the creation of new life) with a nuclear bombardment intended to render a huge country virtually lifeless, perhaps for millennia to come? And what conception of pleasure was foremost in Kahn's mind when he coined the term "wargasm"—surely the most obscene word in the English language—to describe what he sees as the union between Eros and Thanatos that is nuclear holocaust? I find such comparisons and terminology almost beyond rational comment. Simone de Beauvoir's accurate observation that "the erotic vocabulary of males" has always been drawn from military terminology becomes totally inadequate.[44] Brodie's and Kahn's inventiveness has surely eclipsed Suzanne Lowry's observation in the *Guardian* that "'fuck' is the prime hate word" in the English language.[45] Indeed, given the sexual metaphors used by some of the nuclear warriors, one can understand Susan Griffin's anguished agreement with Norman Mailer's (surprising) description of Western culture as "drawing a rifle sight on an open vagina"—a culture, Griffin continues, "that even within its worship of the female sex goddess hates female sexuality."[46] We may indeed wonder why a picture of Rita Hayworth, "the ubiquitous pinup girl of World War II," was stenciled on the first atomic bomb exploded in the Bikini tests of 1946.[47]

UNCONSCIOUS OBJECTIVES OF PATRIARCHY AND PATRIARCHAL PHYSICS

There has been much analysis of the Catholic Church's dichotomization of women into two stereotypes: the unattainable, asexual, morally pure virgin to which the Christian woman could aspire but never reach and the carnal whore-witch representing uncontrollable sexuality, depravity, wickedness, and the threat of universal chaos and disorder. During the sixteenth and seventeenth centuries such a fear and loathing of women's apparent wickedness came to a head in the European witch craze that was responsible for the inquisition and execution of scores of thousands of victims, over 80 percent of them female. A major historian of the witch craze, H. C. E. Midelfort, has noted that "one cannot begin to understand the European witch craze without

recognizing that it displayed a burst of misogyny without parallel in Western history."[48]

Whatever the causes of the European witch craze, what may be particularly significant is that it coincided with the first phase of the scientific revolution, the peak of the witch craze occurring during the decades in which Francis Bacon, René Descartes, Johannes Kepler, and Galileo Galilei made their revolutionary contributions. In *one* of its aspects, I believe that the scientific revolution may be seen as a secularized version of the witch craze in which sophisticated men either, like Francis Bacon, projected powerful and dangerous "femaleness" onto nature or, like René Descartes, declared nature to be feminine and thus totally amenable to manipulation and control by (the mind of) man. We recall how Simone de Beauvoir declared that woman is seemingly "represented, at one time, as pure passivity, available, open, a utensil"—which is surely Descartes's view of "feminine" matter—while "at another time she is regarded as if possessed by alien forces: there is a devil raging in her womb, a serpent lurks in her vagina, eager to devour the male's sperm"—which has more affinity to Francis Bacon's view of "female" matter.[49] Indeed, Bacon likened the experimental investigation of the secrets of "female" nature to the inquisition of witches on the rack and looked forward to the time when masculine science would shake "female" nature to her very foundations. It is, I believe, the purified natural magical tradition advocated by Bacon (with considerable use of very aggressive sexual imagery) that contributed in a major way to the rise of modern science. Believing firmly in the existence of the secrets of nature that could be penetrated by the mind of man, Bacon predicted that eventually the new science would be able to perform near miracles. And indeed the momentous significance of the scientific revolution surely lies in the fact that, unlike the rituals of preliterate societies which in general failed to give their practitioners power over nature (if this is what they sought), the male practitioners of modern science have been rewarded with truly breathtaking powers to intervene successfully in natural phenomena (we have become blasé about the spectacular triumphs of modern science, but what a near miracle is, for example, a television picture). Bacon's prediction that the new science he so passionately advocated would inaugurate the "truly masculine birth of time" and eventually shake nature to her very foundations has been triumphantly borne out by the achievements of modern physics and the sad possibility of devastating nature with environmental destruction, nuclear holocaust, and nuclear winter.

Clearly modern science possesses what might be called a rational component. In this article I am taking for granted the fact that modern science produces knowledge of nature that "works" relative to masculine (and other) expectations and objectives and that the intrinsic interest and fascination of scientific inquiry would render a non-patriarchal science a worthy and central feature of a truly human society. What I am here concerned with is the "truly masculine" nature of scientific inquiry involving the discipline's would-be rigid separation between masculine science and "female" nature and the possibility of an underlying, if for the most part unconscious, hostility to "dangerous femaleness" in the minds of some, or many, of its practitioners—a hostility presumably endemic to patriarchal society. A case can be made—and has been both by Carolyn Merchant and myself—that a powerful motivating force, but not the only one, behind the rise of modern science was a kind of displaced misogyny.[50] In addition a case can be made that a powerful motivating force behind some (or much) modern science and particularly weapons science is a continuation of the displaced misogyny that helped generate the scientific revolution.

Certainly a counterclaim is possible that modern science might have had some misogynistic origins, but that this has no relevance today. In disagreement with such a counterclaim, however, it can be plausibly argued that the industrialized countries have remained virulently misogynistic, as seen in the prevalence of violence practiced and depicted by men against women. If there is indeed a link between misogyny, insecure masculinity, and our conceptions of science, particularly weapons science, then we are given a way to understand why nuclear violence can be associated in warriors' minds with sexual intercourse and ejaculation. Moreover, not only does Sue Mansfield suggest that at a deep level the scientific mentality has carried from its inception in the seventeenth century "the burden of an essential hostility to the body, the feminine, and the natural environment," but she also

points out that, if human life survives at all after a nuclear holocaust, then it will mean the total restoration of the power of arm-bearing men over women. This leads her to make a significant comment that "though the reenslavement of women and the destruction of nature are not conscious goals of our nuclear stance, the language of our bodies, our postures, and our acts is a critical clue to our unexamined motives and desires."[51]

Of course, at the conscious level the scientific warrior today can, and does, offer a "rational" explanation for his behavior: his creation of fission and fusion weapons, he maintains, has made the deliberate starting of world war unthinkable and certainly has preserved peace in Europe for the last forty years. Whatever financial gain comes his way is not unappreciated but is secondary to the necessity of maintaining his country's security; likewise whatever scientific interest he experiences in the technological challenge of his work is again secondary to the all-important objective of preserving the balance of terror until world statesmen achieve multilateral disarmament. While well-known arguments can be made against the coherence of such a typical rationalization, what I am suggesting is that at a partly conscious, partly unconscious, level the scientific warrior experiences not only an almost irresistible need to separate his (insecure) masculinity from what he conceives as femininity but also a compulsive desire to create the weapons that unmistakably affirm his masculinity and by means of which what is "female" can, if necessary and as a last resort, be annihilated. (And it must be noted that scientific warriors can be supported by women or even joined by female warriors in their largely unconscious quest to affirm masculine triumph over the feminine and female.)

CONCLUSION

Looking over the history of humanity—the "slaughter-bench of history" as Hegel called it—I feel compelled to identify a factor—beyond economic and territorial rationales—that could help explain this sorry escalation of weaponry oppression, and bloodshed. It seems to me of paramount importance to try to understand why men are generally the direct oppressors, oppressing other men and women, why in general men allow neither themselves nor women the opportunity to realize full humanity.

While the political scientist Jean Bethke Elshtain may well be correct when she writes skeptically that no great movement will ever be fought under the banner of "androgyny," I suggest that it could well be fought under the banner of "a truly human future for everyone."[52] And that would entail the abolition of the *institutionalized* sexual division of labor. Men and women must be allowed the right to become complete human beings and not mutilated into their separate masculine and feminine gender roles. At the same time, I agree with Cynthia Cockburn when she writes in her book *Machinery of Dominance* that "men need more urgently to learn women's skills than women need to learn men's" and that "the revolutionary step will be to bring men down to earth, to domesticate technology and reforge the link between making and nurturing."[53]

In such a world "education" could not remain as it is now in Britain and the United States (and elsewhere). Certainly there would be no "physics" degree as it exists today, although there would be studies that would eventually take "students" to the frontiers of research in "physics." Needless to say, such an educational system would not be male-dominated (or female-dominated), it would not institutionalize and reward socially competitive aggressive behavior, and there would be no objective in "physics" education of the "conquest of nature," although it would certainly recognize the need to find respectful, ecologically sound ways of making use of nature. Moreover, images of nature would, I suspect, undergo some profound changes (with probably major changes to some theories as well), and clearly in a truly human world there would be no militarization of physics. As for the "scientific method," this would be recognized to be a somewhat mysterious activity, perhaps never completely specifiable, certainly an activity making use of the full range of *human* capacities from creative intuition to the most rigorous logical reasoning.

As for sexual imagery, that would surely thrive in the new truly human activity of scientific research, given that sexual relations—deprived of the hatred that now so greatly distorts sexuality—would continue to provide not only much of the motivation but also the metaphors for describing

scientific activity (and much else). Consider, for example, the language of a woman who was awarded just about every honor the discipline of astrophysics could bestow (but only after she spent years challenging blatant sexism and discrimination). The images invoked by Cecilia Payne-Gaposchkin are more directly erotic than the "equivalent" sexual imagery used by male scientists and physicists (not to mention their frequent aggressive imagery); her language was of her friendship, her love, her delight, her ecstasy with the world of "male" stars and galaxies. Writing of nature as female, Payne-Gaposchkin advises her fellow researchers: "Nature has always had a trick of surprising us, and she will continue to surprise us. But she has never let us down yet. We can go forward with confidence,

Knowing that nature never did betray
The heart that loved her."[54]

But it was an embrace of relatedness that Payne-Gaposchkin had sought and which had given her great satisfaction throughout her life, the satisfaction arising, in the words of Peggy Kidwell, from a sustained impassioned, loving endeavor "to unravel the mysteries of the stars."[55] In a truly human world, the principal purpose and result of science, as Erwin Schrödinger once said, will surely be to enhance "the general joy of living."[56]

Notes

I am most grateful to Michael Kaufman for his extremely skillful pruning of a very long manuscript.

1. Michael Howard, "On Fighting a Nuclear War," in Michael Howard, *The Causes of War and Other Essays* (London: Temple Smith, 1983), 136.

2. Penny Strange, *It'll Make a Man of You* (Nottingham, England: Mushroom Books with Peace News, 1983), 24–5.

3. These statistics are taken from *Girls and Physics: A Report by the Joint Physics Education Committee of the Royal Society and the Institute of Physics* (London, 1982), 8, and Lilli S. Hornig, "Women in Science and Engineering: Why So Few?" *Technology Review* 87 (November/December, 1984), 41.

4. See Margaret W. Rossiter, *Women Scientists in America: Struggles and Strategies to 1940* (Baltimore: Johns Hopkins University Press, 1982), 190–1.

5. Richard Lewontin, "'Honest Jim' Watson's Big Thriller, about DNA," Chicago *Sun Times*, 25 Feb. 1968, 1–2,

reprinted in James D. Watson, *The Double Helix . . . A New Critical Edition,* edited by Gunther S. Stent (London: Weidenfeld, 1981), 186.

6. Sharon Traweek, "High-Energy Physics: A Male Preserve," *Technology Review* (November/December, 1984), 42–3; see also her *Beamtimes and Lifetimes: The World of High-Energy Physicists* (Boston: Harvard University Press, 1988).

7. Heinz Pagels, *The Cosmic Code: Quantum Physics as the Language of Nature* (London: Michael Joseph, 1982), 338.

8. Sir John Hill, "The Quest for Public Acceptance of Nuclear Power," *Atom,* no. 273 (1979): 166–72.

9. Richard S. Westfall, *The Construction of Modern Science* (1971; Cambridge: Cambridge University Press, 1977), 41. It should be noted, however, that quantum mechanics is essentially an antireductionist theory; see, for example, the (controversial) book by Fritjof Capra, *The Tao of Physics* (London: Fontana, 1976).

10. Willard Libby, "Man's Place in the Physical Universe," in John R. Platt, ed., *New Views of the Nature of Man* (Chicago: University of Chicago Press, 1965), 14–15.

11. C. S. Lewis, *The Abolition of Man* (1943; London: Geoffrey Bles, 1946), 40.

12. E. L. Woollett, "Physics and Modern Warfare: The Awkward Silence," *American Journal of Physics* 48 (1980): 104–11.

13. Freeman Dyson, *Weapons and Hope* (New York: Harper and Row, 1984), 41–2.

14. William J. Broad, *Star Warriors: A Penetrating Look into the Lives of the Young Scientists Behind Our Space Age Weaponry* (New York: Simon and Schuster, 1985), 204.

15. *Ibid.*

16. Hazel Grice, letter to the *Guardian,* 9 Oct. 1984, 20.

17. Bertrand Russell, "Science in a Liberal Education," the *New Statesman* (1913) reprinted in *Mysticism and Logic and Other Essays* (Harmondsworth: Penguin, 1953), 47–8.

18. Robert Bierstedt, *The Social Order* (1957; New York: McGraw-Hill, 1974), 26.

19. Hans Reichenbach, *The Rise of Scientific Philosophy* (1951; Berkeley and Los Angles: California University Press, 1966), 312.

20. Vivian Gornick, *Women in Science: Portraits from a World in Transition* (New York: Simon and Schuster, 1984), 36.

21. Carl Hempel, *Philosophy of Natural Science* (Englewood Cliffs, N.J.: Prentice-Hall, 1966), 16.

22. See, for example, Imre Lakatos and Alan Musgrave, eds., *Criticism and the Growth of Knowledge* (Cambridge: Cambridge University Press, 1970): Sandra Harding, "Is Gender a Variable in Conceptions of Rationality? A Survey of Issues," *Dialectica: International Journal of Philosophy of Knowledge* 36 (1982): 225–42: and Harry M. Collins, ed., special issue of *Social Studies of Science* 11 (1981): 3–158, "Knowledge and Controversy: Studies of Modern Natural Science."

23. Freeman Dyson, *Weapons and Hope,* 4–6.

24. Helen Caldicott, "Etiology: Missile Envy and Other Psychopathology," in her *Missile Envy: The Arms Race and Nuclear War* (New York: William Morrow, 1984).

25. Sue Mansfield, *The Gestalts of War: An Inquiry into Its Origins and Meaning as a Social Institution* (New York: Dial Press, 1982), 224.

26. Carolyn Merchant, "Isis' Consciousness Raised," *Isis* 73 (1982): 398–409.

27. Frank Close, "And now at last, the quark to top them all," the *Guardian,* 19 July 1984, 13, and "A shining example of what ought to be impossible," the *Guardian,* 8 Aug. 1985, 13.

28. Sir William Crookes, quoted in E. E. Fournier d'Albe, *The Life of Sir William Crookes* (London: Fisher Unwin, 1923), 365.

29. See, for example, the physicist Paul Davies's account of "black holes," "naked singularities," and "cosmic anarchy" in his *The Edge of Infinity: Naked Singularities and the Destruction of Space-time* (London: Dent, 1981), especially 92–3, 114, 145.

30. Max Jammer, *The Conceptual Development of Quantum Mechanics* (New York: McGraw-Hill, 1966), 61, and Victor Weisskopf, "Niels Bohr and International Scientific Collaboration," in S. Rozenthal, ed., *Niels Bohr: His Life and Work as Seen by His Friends and Colleagues* (Amsterdam: North Holland, 1967), 262.

31. Frederick Soddy, *The Interpretation of Radium* (London, 1909), 234.

32. C. G. Darwin quoted in A. S. Eve, *Rutherford* (Cambridge: Cambridge University Press, 1939), 199, 434.

33. W. C. D. Whetham, *The Recent Development of Physical Science* (London: Murray, 1904), 242.

34. G. E. Hale quoted in Helen Wright, *Explorer of the Universe: A Biography of George Ellery Hale* (New York: Dutton, 1966), 283, and in A. S. Eve, *Rutherford,* 231.

35. "The Atom" from *The Collected Verse of Thomas Thornely* (Cambridge: W. Heffer, 1939), 70–1, reprinted in John

Heath-Stubbes and Phillips Salmon, eds., *Poems of Science* (Harmondsworth: Penguin, 1984), 245.

36. Richard G. Hewlett and Oscar E. Anderson, *A History of the United States Atomic Energy Commission* (Pennsylvania State University Press, 1962), vol. 1, *The New World, 1939–1946,* 386.

37. Edward Teller with Allen Brown, *The Legacy of Hiroshima* (London: Macmillan, 1962), 51–3.

38. Edward Teller, *Energy from Heaven and Earth* (San Francisco: W. H. Freeman, 1979), 151. See also Norman Moss, *Men Who Play God* (Harmondsworth: Penguin, 1970), 78. For general detail see my *Fathering the Unthinkable: Masculinity, Scientists and the Nuclear Arms Race* (London: Pluto Press, 1983), ch. 3.

39. Bernard Brodie's memorandum is referred to by Fred Kaplan in *The Wizards of Armageddon* (New York: Simon and Schuster, 1983), 222. I have not seen the text of Brodie's memorandum. The chilling phrase "smoking, radiating ruin at the end of two hours" comes from a declassified Navy memorandum on a SAC briefing held in March 1954; see David Alan Rosenberg, "A Smoking Radiating Ruin at the End of Two Hours: Documents on American Plans for Nuclear War with the Soviet Union 1954–55," *International Security* 6 (1981/82), 3–38.

40. Herman Kahn, *On Escalation: Metaphors and Scenarios* (London: Pall Mall, 1965), 194.

41. Note that Gregg Herken in *Counsels of War* (New York: Knopf, 1985), 206, writes that Bernard Brodie objected to Herman Kahn's "levity" in coining the term "wargasm."

42. Quoted in Thomas Powers, "How Nuclear War Could Start," *New York Review of Books,* 17 Jan. 1985, 34.

43. Roger Hutton, (personal communication), who attended the meeting when researching the Star Wars project.

44. Simone de Beauvoir, *The Second Sex* (1949; Harmondsworth: Penguin, 1972), 396.

45. Suzanne Lowry, "O Tempora, O Mores," the *Guardian,* 24 May 1984, 17.

46. Susan Griffin, *Pornography and Silence: Culture's Revenge Against Nature* (London: Women's Press, 1981), 217.

47. Paul Boyer, *By the Bomb's Early Light: American Thought and Culture at the Dawn of the Atomic Age* (New York: Pantheon, 1985), 83.

48. H. C. E. Midelfort, "Heartland of the Witchcraze: Central and Northern Europe," *History Today* 31 (February 1981): 28.

49. Simone de Beauvoir, *The Second Sex,* 699.

50. See, for example, Carolyn Merchant, *The Death of Nature: Women, Ecology and the Scientific Revolution* (San Francisco: Harper and Row, 1980), and my *Science and Sexual Oppression: Patriarchy's Confrontation with Women and Nature* (London: Weidenfeld, 1981), ch. 3 and *Fathering the Unthinkable,* ch. 1.

51. Sue Mansfield, *The Gestalts of War,* 223.

52. Jean Bethke Elshtain, "Against Androgyny," Telos 47 (1981), 5–22.

53. Cynthia Cockburn, *Machinery of Dominance* (London: Pluto Press, 1985), 256–7.

54. Katherine Haramundanis, ed., *Cecilia Payne-Gaposchkin: An Autobiography and Other Recollections* (Cambridge: Cambridge University Press, 1984), 237.

55. *Ibid.,* 28.

56. "Science, Art and Play," reprinted in E. C. Schrödinger, *Science, Theory and Man* (New York: Dover, 1957), 29; see, for example, Euan Squires, *To Acknowledge the Wonder: The Story of Fundamental Physics* (Bristol: Adam Hilger, 1985).

Child Violence: It's a Male Thing

Karla Mantilla

Karla Mantilla has been a collective member of off our backs, *the longest continuously publishing women's paper in the United States, since 1994. She holds a master's degree in sociology from George Mason University and is the mother of two, a son and a daughter. She tells us that as one who felt that feminism saved her life, she is proud to be a radical lesbian feminist at a time when radical feminism is dismissed by many as no longer relevant.*

Children shoot their schoolmates; workers murder their colleagues; buddies shoot buddies; family members shoot, stab, and bludgeon spouses, parents, and offspring. Massacres have taken place in schools, homes, workplaces, restaurants, railroad cars, streets. Mantilla asks us to note that the eruption of violence we have witnessed in the United States in recent years has had a common characteristic that few, if any, have commented on: It has been perpetrated nearly exclusively by boys and men. Only if we look at the way boys are turned into men can we make sense of the slaughter and stop it.

IN THE PAST SIX MONTHS, young boys have gunned down two students and wounded seven at a high school in Pearl, Mississippi; killed three students in West Paducah, Kentucky; killed four students and a teacher in Jonesboro, Arkansas; and killed a teacher and wounded a student in Edinboro, Pennsylvania. What is going on?

All the murders, but in particular the Jonesboro murders have been much debated in the popular press. The mainstream press has tended to attribute the cause to the proliferation of guns, Southern culture (?), violent television, violent movies and video games, or even to the abolition of prayer in schools. But no one in the mainstream media has mentioned the most glaring feature of these massacres: it's a male thing.

What strikes me as remarkable in nearly every case of violence is that the mainstream media somehow neatly refuse to notice that acts of violence are nearly always committed by men (or boys). There have been articles in newspapers and discussions on TV earnestly searching for the reasons why *children* kill and wondering what the real cause could be of the increase in such crimes by *children.*

Some people, some feminists included, want so badly for the genders to be equal that they will deny in the face of overwhelming evidence any actual differences between the behavior of boys and girls. (To say that actual differences exist is not to say that such differences are biologically based.)

I have read such breathtaking denials of the predominantly male phenomenon of violence as a recent *Time* magazine article asking the question "Why do kids kill?" The article is rife with references to "kids," "youngsters," and "juveniles" who are violent, rather than to *boys.* When there *was* a reference (late in the article) to the fact that it is boys and not girls who are gunning down their fellow students, the writer explained, "Girls are more likely to decline into such inward-directed aggressions as depression or eating disorders." Rather than simply admit that violence is a male thing, girls are seen to be just as "violent" except they turn their "aggressions" inward. Never mind that such behavior no longer qualifies as aggression since, by definition, aggression is violent behavior turned upon *others.* While it may be bad, destructive, and harmful to be depressed or have an eating disorder, it is ludicrous and a strange twist of meanings for these behaviors to be construed as aggression. These are the lengths the mainstream media will go to to deny that men are more violent than women.

Even many feminists seem to have missed this point. There has been an outcry that we must notice

Karla Mantilla, "Child Violence: It's a Male Thing," *off our backs* XXVIII, no. 5 (May 1998), p. 5. Reprinted with the permission of the author.

that this was an attack on *girls* and not just a random attack. This is certainly important to note, and violence directed at women and girls is certainly a feminist issue. Some feminists have also pointed out that one of the boys became violent in response to a *girl's* rejection of him. It is also a feminist issue that boys and men do often kill a girl or woman upon her leaving him; certainly the Jonesboro boy had many examples of such behavior in the larger culture to emulate.

But although it is important to notice that it is girls who were murdered in the Jonesboro massacre, I think it is more important to notice that *it is boys who did the killing*. I don't think as feminists we can say that a crime is more terrible because girls or women were murdered than boys or men. Certainly acts of violence against women are abhorrent to the maximum degree, but are acts of violence against men less abhorrent? I believe that violence against any person, woman or man, girl or boy, assaults the human dignity of us all.

The important fact to note, then, is not the gender of the victims, but the gender of the perpetrators. As people theorize the causes of these events and wonder what we should do about "children killing children," there is very little hope of discovering the answer if we ignore the most salient aspect of these young killers—their gender.

Once we can admit that it is boys who perpetrate such aggression (and not inwardly upon themselves), we then can start to look at the ways boys (as opposed to girls) are raised, socialized, and exposed to influences which could lead them to such abhorrent acts. We can then look at the ways we turn boys into men through toughening them up, through hunting rituals with older men, through encouraging them to fight, through tolerating "boys will be boys" attitudes, and many other things. But if we ignore the fact that it is, after all, boys who are the problem, we eliminate all hope of finding out what it is we can do differently *with boys* that can lead to the solution.

The Gender Knot: What Drives Patriarchy?

Allan G. Johnson

Sociologist Allan G. Johnson received his Ph.D. in 1972 from the University of Michigan. He teaches at Hartford College for Women and conducts training courses and seminars on gender for business and educational institutions. Besides The Gender Knot, *he has authored several books, including* Human Arrangements: An Introduction to Sociology, *in its fourth edition (1996), and* The Forest and the Trees: Sociology as Life, Practice, and Promise *(1997).*

Patriarchy is oppressive and counterproductive, Johnson acknowledges. Given that men and women depend on each other for life and existence, it is also puzzling: Why does it exist at all? Johnson argues that although it affects both women and men, patriarchy originates with men, driven by what is inside them. The task, then, is to understand the factors in men that impel them to the values and behaviors we recognize as patriarchal.

PATRIARCHY IS FULL OF PARADOX, not least of which is the mere fact that it exists at all. Consider this. Female and male are two halves of the human species. In union they bring new life into the world; they live and work together to make families and communities; they trace their deepest time-space sense of who they are and where they came from through ties of blood and marriage that join them as children, parents, siblings, or life partners who bring with them some of the profoundest needs for intimacy, belonging, and caring that humans can have. And yet here we are, stuck in patriarchy, surrounded by gender prejudice and oppression, fundamentally at odds. Obviously, something powerful is going on here and has been for a long time. What kind of social engine could create and sustain

such an oppressive system in the face of all the good reasons against it? Why patriarchy?

The answer that first occurs to many people is that patriarchy is rooted in the natural order of things. As such, it reflects "essential" differences between women and men based on biology or genetics (which is why such arguments are often called "essentialist").[1] Men tend to be physically stronger than women, for example, which might explain their dominance. Or men must protect pregnant or lactating women from wild beasts and other men, and female dependency somehow requires men to be in charge. Or men are naturally predisposed to dominance, and patriarchy simply *is* men and what they do to one another and to women. In other words, patriarchy comes down to guys just being guys.

If we take such arguments seriously, it's hard not to conclude that gender oppression is simply part of who we are as a species. This will appeal to anyone who wants to perpetuate patriarchy or who wants to blame men for it in a way that leaves men no room to maneuver. For people like me, who sometimes feel overwhelmed by men's violence, it is also hard to resist the idea that there's something fundamentally wrong with maleness itself. Unfortunately, though, essentialism offers us little hope short of changing human nature, getting rid of men, or finding a way for women and men to live completely apart (which won't do anything about the awful things many men do to one another).[2] Given this, it makes little sense to embrace essentialism unless there's solid evidence to support it. But there isn't. Essentialism requires us to ignore much of what we know about psychology, biology, genetics, history, and how social life actually works. We have to be willing to reduce incredibly complex patterns of social life not just to biology and genetics, but to the even thinner slice of human life that defines sex, a position that gets little support even from biologists, including sociobiologists like E. O. Wilson.[3]

And if we believe in evolution, essentialism backs us into the corner of arguing that oppression is actually a *positive* adaptation, that societies organized around gender oppression will thrive more than those that aren't.

Essentialism also implies that patriarchy is the only system that's ever been, since what makes something "essential" is its universal and inescapable nature. Some things, of course, are essentially human, such as small children's unavoidable period of dependence on adults to feed, protect, and care for them. When it comes to patriarchy, however, all kinds of evidence from anthropology, archaeology, and history point to anything but a universal natural order. There is, for example, a lot of archaeological evidence from prepatriarchal times that dates back to about seven thousand years ago, when goddess imagery held a central place throughout modernday Europe, Africa, and the Middle East.[4] We also know that the status of women varies a great deal among pre-industrial tribal societies. In many cases, for example, kinship is traced through women, not men; women are neither subordinated nor oppressed; misogyny and sexual violence are unheard of; and women control property and have political authority.[5] Since essentialism assumes that all humans share the same human "essence," it falls apart in the face of such striking and widespread variations.

The best reason to pass up essentialism may be that it doesn't fit with what we know about how patriarchy and gender actually work. Essentialism, for example, can't account for the enormous variability we find *among* women and *among* men, or for the similarities between men and women in similar situations.[6] On various measures of mental ability, men differ as much from other men as they do from women; and men and women placed in the same situation, such as having sole responsibility for child care, tend to respond in ways that are far more similar than different.[7] Essentialism also can't explain why so much coercion and violence are needed to keep patriarchy going. If gender oppression is rooted in some male essence, for example, then why do many men experience such pain, confusion, ambivalence, and resistance during their training for patriarchal manhood and their lives as adult men?[8] And if women's essence is to be subordinate, how do we explain their long history of re-

sisting oppression and learning to undermine and counteract male dominance?[9]

In spite of its appeal, essentialism doesn't hold up as a way to understand patriarchy. The alternative takes us into the deep root structures of society and social forces powerful enough to drive patriarchy in spite of all the good reasons against it. And it takes us deep into ourselves, where the terms of life under patriarchy often seem to permeate to the core of who we are.

MISSING LINKS: CONTROL, FEAR, AND MEN

More than anything else, patriarchy is based on control as a core principle around which entire societies are organized. What drives patriarchy as a system—what fuels competition, aggression, and oppression—is a dynamic relationship between control and fear.[10] Patriarchy encourages men to seek security, status, and other rewards through control; to fear other men's ability to control and harm them; and to identify being in control as both their best defense against loss and humiliation and the surest route to what they need and desire. In this sense, although we usually think of patriarchy in terms of women and men, it is more about what goes on *among men*. The oppression of women is certainly an important part of patriarchy, but, paradoxically, it may not be the *point* of patriarchy.

It would be misleading to suggest that control is inherently bad or inevitably leads to oppression. Control is, after all, one of the hallmarks of our species. It is our only hope to bring some order out of chaos or to protect ourselves from what threatens our survival. We imagine, focus, and act—from baking bread to composing music to designing a national health plan—and all of this involves control. Even small children delight in a sense of human agency, in being able to make things happen. Under patriarchy, however, control is more than an expression of human essence or a way to get things done; it's valued and pursued to a degree that gives social life an oppressive form by taking a natural human capacity to obsessive extremes.

Under patriarchy, control shapes not only the broad outlines of social life but also men's inner lives. It does this through its central place in the definition of masculinity: a real man is in control or at least gives the impression of being in control. The more men see control as central to their sense of self, well-being, worth, and safety, the more driven they feel to go after it and to organize their inner and outer lives around it. This takes men away from connection to others and themselves and toward disconnection. This is because control involves a relationship between controller and controlled, and disconnection is an integral part of that relationship. In order to control something, we have to see it as a separate "other." Even if we're controlling ourselves, we have to mentally split ourselves into a "me" that's being controlled and an "I" that's doing the controlling. And if we're controlling other people, we have to justify the control and protect ourselves from an awareness of how our control affects them.

As a result, controllers come to see themselves as subjects who intend and decide what will happen, and to see others as objects to act upon. The controlled are seen without the fullness and complexity that define them as human beings; they have no history, no dimensions to give them depth; there's nothing there to command the controllers' *attention* or *understanding* except what might interfere with control. When parents control small children, for example, they often act as though children aren't full human beings, and justify physical punishment by saying that children can't reason and don't understand anything else. As the ability to see children as "other" breaks down, control becomes more difficult, especially in that memorable moment when a parent looks at a maturing child and sees a person looking back. Suddenly, control that once seemed justified may feel awkward, inappropriate, or even foolish.

Since patriarchy isn't organized simply around the idea of control, but of *male* control, the more men participate in the system, the more they come to see themselves as separate, autonomous, and disconnected from others. They can become versions of the western hero who rides into town from nowhere, with no past, and leaves going nowhere, with no apparent future. Women's lives, of course, also involve control, especially in relation to children. But the idea and practice of control as a core principle of social life is part of what defines patriarchal *man*hood, not womanhood, and so women are less driven to pursue it and are criticized if they

do. A woman perceived as controlling a man is typically labeled a "castrating bitch" or a "ball buster," and the man she supposedly controls is looked down upon as "henpecked," "pussy whipped," and barely a man at all. But there are no insulting terms for a man who controls a woman—by having the last word, not letting her work outside the home, deciding when she'll have sex, or limiting her time with other women—or the woman he controls. There is no need for such words because men controlling women is what patriarchal manhood is all about.

Why does control have such cosmic importance under patriarchy? One possibility is that control may be inherently so terrific that men just can't resist organizing their lives around it. In other words, men control because they *can*. But this puts us back in the arms of dead-end essentialism and up against the fact that the more people try to control other people and themselves, the more miserable they seem to be. And the idea that what men might get through control, such as wealth or prestige, is inherently so appealing that they would participate routinely in the oppression of their mothers, sisters, daughters, and wives isn't much better. For that to be true, we would first have to explain how control and its rewards could possibly outweigh the horrendous consequences of social oppression, especially involving groups as intimately involved as women and men are. A common explanation is "That's the way people (men) are: they'll always compete for wealth, power, and prestige." But that's the kind of circular reasoning that essentialism so often gets us into: Men are that way because that's the way men are.

An essentialist approach also ignores the prominent role that fear plays in most men's lives. Unlike control, fear may be one of the most powerful and primal of all human motivations, more deeply rooted than greed, desire, lust, or even love. Nothing matches fear's potential to twist us out of shape, to drive us to abandon everything we otherwise hold dear, to oppress and do violence to one another—fear of death, of loss, of pain, of what we don't know or don't understand. And the most powerfully oppressive systems are those organized to promote fear. What patriarchy accomplishes is to make men fear what other men might do to them, how control might be turned on them to do them harm and deprive them of what matters most to them. This encourages men to feel afraid that other men will ridicule us and deprive us of recognition as real men.[11] We're afraid they'll use economic power to take away jobs or hold us back or make our work lives miserable. We're afraid they'll beat us up or kill us if we're unlucky enough to provoke the wrong one. We're afraid they'll wage war against us, destroy our communities and homes, beat, torture, rape, and kill those we love. In short, we're afraid of all the things that men can do to exert control and thereby protect and enhance their standing as real men in relation to other men.

Women, of course, have many reasons to fear men, but this isn't what shapes and defines patriarchy as a way of life. Men's fear of other men is crucial because *patriarchy is driven by how men both cause and respond to it.* Since patriarchy is organized around male-identified control, men's path of least resistance is to protect themselves by increasing their own sense of control, and patriarchy provides many ways to do it. Men learn to hold their own in aggressive male banter, for example, whatever their particular group's version of "doing the dozens"[12] happens to be. They learn to keep their feelings to themselves rather than be vulnerable at the wrong moment to someone looking for an advantage. They learn to win an argument, always have an answer, and never admit they're wrong. They learn early on not to play with girls unless it's in the back seats of cars, and go out of their way to avoid the appearance that women can control them. They pump iron, talk and follow sports, study boxing and martial arts, learn to use guns, play football or hockey or rugby. In all these ways they cope with their own fear and inspire it in others, while still maintaining an underlying commitment to men, what men do, and the system that binds them together.

Men's participation in patriarchy tends to lock them in an endless pursuit of and defense against control, for *under patriarchy control is both the source of and the only solution they can see to their fear.* The more invested a man is in the control-fear spiral, the worse he feels when he doesn't feel in control. And so on some level he's always on the lookout for opportunities to renew his sense of control while protecting himself from providing that same kind of opportunity for others, especially men. As each man pursues control as a way to defend and ad-

vance himself, he fuels the very same response in *other* men. This dynamic has provided patriarchy with an escalating and seemingly unending driving force for thousands of years.[13]

Men pay an enormous price for participating in patriarchy. The more in control men try to be, for example, the less secure they feel. They may not know it because they're so busy trying to be in control, but the more they organize their lives around being in control, the more tied they are to the fear of *not* being in control. As Marilyn French put it, "A religion of power is a religion of fear, and . . . those who worship power are the most terrified creatures on the earth."[14] Dig beneath the surface appearance of "great men," and you'll often find deep insecurity, fear, and a chronic need to prove themselves to other men. As president of the United States, for example, one of the most powerful positions on Earth, George Bush was obsessed that people might think he was a "wimp." And rather than making men feel safe, great power makes them need still greater control to protect themselves from still more powerful men locked into the same cycle. To make matters worse, control itself is a fleeting, momentary experience, not a natural, stable state, and so is always on the edge of slipping away or falling apart:

> [P]ower is not what we think it is. Power is not substantial; not even when it takes substantive form. The money you hold in your hand can be devalued overnight. . . . A title can be removed at the next board meeting. . . . A huge military establishment can disintegrate in a few days . . . a huge economic structure can collapse in a few weeks.[15]
>
> All power is unstable. . . . There is never power, but only a race for power. . . . Power is, by definition, only a means . . . but power seeking, owing to its essential incapacity to seize ahold of its object, rules out all consideration of an end, and finally comes . . . to take the place of all ends.[16]

The religion of fear and control also blocks men's need for human connection by redefining intimacy. Men are encouraged to see everything and everyone as other, and to look on every situation in terms of how it might enhance or threaten their sense of control. Every opportunity for control, however, can also be an occasion for a failure of control, a fact that can inject issues of control and power into the most unlikely situations. Intimacy is lost as a chance to be open and vulnerable on the way to a deeper connection. Sexual intimacy in particular can go from pleasure in a safe place to a male performance laced with worry about whether the penis—that notorious and willful "other" that so often balks at men's efforts at control—will "perform" as it's supposed to. Dictionaries typically define impotence as a man's *inability to achieve or sustain an erection,* as if an erection were something a man *did* and not something he experienced, like sweating or having his heart beat rapidly or feeling happy. The more preoccupied with control men are, the more lovers recede as full people with feelings, thoughts, will, and soul, and become vehicles for bolstering manhood and relieving anxiety. And even though a woman's opinion of a man's sexual "performance" may seem to be what matters, her words of reassurance are rarely enough, for it's always a patriarchal male gaze that's looking at him over her shoulder.

Patriarchy is grounded in a Great Lie that the answer to life's needs is disconnection and control rather than connection, sharing, and cooperation. The Great Lie separates men from what they need most by encouraging them to be autonomous and disconnected when in fact human existence is fundamentally relational. What is a "me" without a "you," a "mother" without a "child," a "teacher" without a "student"? Who are we if not our ties to other people—"I *am* . . . a father, a husband, a worker, a friend, a son, a brother"?[17] But patriarchal magic turns the truth inside out, and "self-made man" goes from oxymoron to cultural ideal. And somewhere between the need for human connection and the imperative to control, the two merge, and a sense of control becomes the closest many men ever come to feeling connected with anything, including themselves.

PATRIARCHY AS A MEN'S PROBLEM

Patriarchy is usually portrayed as something that's primarily between women and men. At first blush this makes a lot of sense, given that "male" and "female" define each other and that women occupy an oppressed position in relation to men. Paradoxically, however, the cycle of control and fear that drives patriarchy has more to do with relations among men than with women, for it's men who control men's standing *as men.* With few exceptions, men look to other men to affirm their manhood, whether as coaches, friends, teammates, coworkers, sports figures, fathers, or mentors.

This contradicts the conventional wisdom that women hold the key to heterosexual men's sense of manhood. It's true that men often use women to show they measure up—especially by controlling women sexually—but the standards that are used are men's, not women's. Men also may try to impress women as "real men" in order to start and keep relationships with them, to control them, or to get sexual access and personal care. This doesn't prove they're real men, however. For affirmation they have to go to a larger male-identified world—from the local bar to sports to work—which is also where they're most vulnerable to other men. Whether in school locker rooms or in the heat of political campaigns, when a man is accused of being a "wimp" or of otherwise failing to measure up, it almost always comes from another man. And when a man suspects *himself* of being less than a real man, he judges himself through a patriarchal male gaze, not from a woman's perspective.

Although men often use women as scapegoats for their bad feelings about themselves, women's role in this is indirect at most. If other men reject a man's claim to "real man" standing, how his wife or mother sees him usually makes little difference, and if women's opinions *do* matter to him, his manhood becomes all the more suspect to other men.[18] Women's marginal importance in the manhood question is plain to see in the risks men take to prove themselves in spite of objections from wives, mothers, and other women who find them just fine the way they are. The record books are full of men who seize upon *anything*—from throwing frisbees to flagpole sitting to being the first to get somewhere or discover something—as a way to create competitive arenas in which they can jockey for position and prove themselves among men.[19] If a man must choose between men's and women's views of what makes a real man, he'll choose men's views most of the time. "A man's gotta do what a man's gotta do" is typically spoken by a man to a woman (often as he goes off to do something with other men); and just what it is that he's got to do is determined by men and patriarchy, not by women. It isn't up to women to decide what a real man is. Her role is to reassure men that they meet the standards of a patriarchal culture she doesn't control.

When a woman does question or attack a man's masculinity, the terms of the attack and the power behind it are based on men's standards of patriarchal manhood. She's not going to attack his manhood, for example, by telling him he isn't caring enough. When she uses what are culturally defined as *women's* terms—"You're not sensitive, nurturing, open, or vulnerable and you're *too* controlling"— the attack has much less weight and produces far less effect. But when women don't play along— when they criticize or question or merely lose enthusiasm for affirming patriarchal manhood—they risk the wrath of men, who may feel undermined, abandoned, and even betrayed. Men may not like being criticized for failing to measure up to "women's" ideas of what men should be, but it's nothing compared to how angry and violent men can be toward women who dare to use "men's" weapons against them.

In the patriarchal cycle of control and fear, no man is safe from challenges to his real-man standing, which is why even the rich and powerful can be quick to defend themselves. In his analysis of John F. Kennedy's presidency, for example, David Halberstam argues that Kennedy initiated U.S. involvement in the Vietnamese civil war in part because he failed to appear sufficiently tough and manly at his 1961 Vienna summit meeting with Soviet Premier Nikita Khrushchev. Khrushchev challenged Kennedy from the start, and Kennedy, surprised, responded in kind only toward the end. Upon returning home, he felt the need for an opportunity to right the impression he'd made and remove any doubts about his manhood. "If he [Khrushchev] thinks I'm inexperienced and have no guts," Kennedy told *New York Times* reporter James Reston, ". . . we won't get anywhere with him. So we have to act . . . and Vietnam looks like the place."[20] And so the horror and tragedy of America's involvement in Vietnam turned on a political system organized in part around men's ability to impress one another with their standing as real men. And this no doubt played a prominent role in the tortured progress of that war and the stubborn refusal of all sides to compromise or admit defeat.

In addition to what Kennedy's dilemma says about patriarchal politics, it also challenges the stereotype that macho displays of manhood are largely confined to lower- and working-class subcultures. The roots of men proving their manhood run deep in the upper classes, from the enthusiastic stampede of Britain's elite to the killing fields of World War I to Kennedy's sexually compulsive private behavior to the San Francisco Bohemian Grove retreats where captains of business and government gather to make deals, mock women in cross-dressing skits, and otherwise relax in the comfort of male privilege.[21] Men, of course, aren't born to this; they must be trained and given ongoing incentives.

In the early 1960s, for example, I was a middle-class freshman at an all-male Ivy League college, a training ground for the sons of the elite. Among my classmates' fathers were prominent figures in business, government, and the professions, who fully expected their sons to follow in their footsteps. In late fall, dorm residents who'd been accepted to fraternities prepared for "sink night," a time to celebrate their newfound "brotherhood" by getting very drunk. Before they went off, they warned freshmen not to lock our doors when we went to bed because they intended to pay us a visit later on and didn't expect to be stopped by a locked door. We didn't know what was coming, but there was no mistaking the dense familiar weight of men's potential for violence.

When they returned that night, screaming drunk, they went from door to door, rousting us from our beds and herding us into the hall. They lined us up and ordered us to drop our pants. Then one held a metal ruler and another a *Playboy* magazine opened to the centerfold picture, and the two went down the line, thrusting the picture in our faces, screaming "Get it up!" and resting our penises on the ruler. The others paced up and down the hall behind them, yelling, screaming, and laughing, thickening the air with a mixture of alcohol and the potential for violence. None of us protested, and of course none of us "measured up." We weren't supposed to (any man who'd managed an erection would have become a legend on the spot). That, after all, was the point: to submit to the humiliation, to mirror (like women) men's power to control and terrorize in what we later learned was a rite of passage called "the peter meter."

For them, perhaps, it was a passage to a fraternal bond forged in their shared power over the "others"; for us, it was a grant of immunity from having to submit again, at least in this place, to these men, in this way. But our lack of outrage and the general absence of talk about it afterward suggest we got something else as well. As outrageous as the peter meter was, it touched a core of patriarchal truth about men, power, and violence that, as men, we found repellant yet ultimately acceptable. The truth is, we, too, got a piece of real-man standing that night, for by deadening and controlling ourselves in the face of an assault, we showed that we had the right stuff. Had anyone protested, he wouldn't have been seen as the more manly for his courage; more likely he'd have been called a sissy, a pussy, a little mama's boy who couldn't take it. And so we both lost and gained during our late-night dip in the patriarchal paradox of men competing and bonding at the same time.[22]

WHAT ABOUT WOMEN?

In one sense, women, like all else in patriarchy, are something for men to control. The consequences of this are enormous because of the damage it does to women's lives, but controlling women is neither the point of patriarchy nor the engine that drives it. This means that women's place is more complicated than it might seem, especially in relation to competition among men.[23]

This works in several ways. First, heterosexual men are encouraged to use women as badges of success to protect and enhance their standing in the eyes of other men. People routinely compliment a man married to a beautiful woman, for example, not because he had a hand in making her beautiful but because he has proprietary rights of access to her. In contrast, people are much less likely to compliment a man whose wife is financially successful—especially if she earns more than he does—because this threatens rather than enhances his status as a real man.

Men's use of women as badges of success is a prime example of how men can compete and ally with one another at the same time.[24] On the one hand, they may compete over who has the highest standing and is therefore least vulnerable to other men's control, as when they vie for a specific woman or use women in general as a way to keep score on their manhood. A man who lacks enthusiasm for pursuing women may have his masculinity questioned, if not attacked, especially by being "accused" of being gay. In this sense, "getting laid" is more than a badge of success; it's also a safe-conduct pass through perpetually hostile territory.

At the same time that men may compete with one another, they're also encouraged to bond around a common view of women as objects to be competed for, possessed, and used. When men tell sexist jokes, for example, or banter about women's bodies, they usually can count on other men to go along (if only in silence), for a man who objects risks becoming an outcast. Even if the joke is directed at his wife or lover, he's likely to choose his tie to men over loyalty to her by letting it pass with a shrug and perhaps a good-natured smile that leaves intact his standing as one of the guys. In this sense, the competitive dynamic of patriarchal heterosexuality brings men together and promotes feelings of solidarity by acting out the values of control and domination. This is partly why there is so much male violence against gay men: since gays don't use women in this way, their sexual orientation challenges not so much heterosexuality per se but *male solidarity* around the key role of control and domination in *patriarchal* heterosexuality.[25] John Stoltenberg argues that violence against gays also protects male solidarity by protecting men from sexual aggression at the hands of other men:

> *Imagine this country without homophobia: There would be a woman raped every three minutes and a man raped every three minutes. Homophobia keeps that statistic at a manageable level. The system is not fool-proof. It breaks down, for instance, in prison and in childhood—when men and boys are often subject to the same sexual terrorism that women live with almost all the time. But for the most part homophobia serves male supremacy by keeping males who act like real men safe from sexual assault.[26]*

A second part that women play in men's struggle for control is to support the idea that men and women are fundamentally different, because this gives men a clear and unambiguous turf—masculinity—on which to pursue control in competition with one another.[27] Women do this primarily by supporting (or at least not challenging) femininity as a valid view of women and how they're supposed to be. The idea that male sexuality is inherently aggressive, predatory, and heterosexual, for example, defines a common ground for men in relation to both women and other men. To protect this, it's important that women *not* be sexually aggressive or predatory because this would challenge the idea of a unique male sexuality as a basis for male solidarity and competition.

When women challenge stereotypically feminine ways of acting, it makes it harder for men to see themselves clearly as men. This muddles men's relationships with women and their standing as real men under patriarchy. In the film *Fatal Attraction*, for example, the villain embodies a predatory, violent female sexuality that sent shock waves through audiences across the country. The history of film includes legions of obsessive, murderous men, but with the appearance of the first such woman there was a rush to analyze and explain how such a thing could happen. Perhaps her greatest transgression was to trespass on male turf by violating the strictures of cultural femininity. How fitting, then, that everything should be "set right" when her lover's wife—who embodies all the feminine virtues of good mother, faithful wife, and constrained sexuality—kills the madwoman who's invaded the sanctity of this normal patriarchal household.

In a third sense, a woman's place is to support the key patriarchal illusion that men are independent and autonomous. An unemployed wife who sees herself as dependent, for example, props up images of male independence that mask men's considerable dependence on women for emotional support, physical comfort, and a broad range of practical services. On the average, for example, married men are both mentally and physically healthier than single men and live longer, whereas for women just the opposite is true.[28] Men also tend to have a much harder time adjusting to the loss of a spouse than women do, especially at older ages. And the standard model for a career still assumes a wife at home to perform support work, and any man (or woman) who doesn't have one is at a disadvantage.

The illusion of male independence and female dependence is amplified by men's complaints about the burdens of the breadwinner role. In fact, however, most husbands would have it no other way, because for all its demands, the provider role brings with it power and status and exempts men from domestic work such as cleaning and child care. As a result, many men feel threatened when their wives earn as much or more than they do. They cling to the idea that breadwinning is a man's responsibility that anchors male gender identity, and that women are little more than helpers in that role[29] if not "little women" waiting for a man to bring home the bacon. This arrangement, however, was created largely by working- and middle-class white men who fought for the "family wage" in the early 1900s. This enabled them to support their families by themselves and justified keeping wives at home, where they would be financially dependent and available to provide personal services.[30]

You might think that such arrangements are a thing of the past, that with so many married women working outside the home, the breadwinner role is no longer male-identified. But the superficial appearance of gender equity and balance masks a continuing imbalance that's revealed when we consider how men and women would be affected by leaving paid employment. If the woman in a two-earner household were to give up breadwinning, it might create hardships and negative feelings, but these probably wouldn't include making her feel less than a real woman. But for a man to give up the breadwinning role, he'd have to contend with far more serious threats to his sense of himself as a real man, and both women and men know it. This is why, when someone in a marriage has to leave paid employment—to take care of children or ailing relatives, for example—it is generally understood that it will be the woman, regardless of who earns more.[31]

A fourth aspect of women's place is to help contain men's resentment over being controlled *by other men* so that it doesn't overpower the male solidarity that's so essential to patriarchy. Most men are dominated by other men, especially at work, and yet judge their manhood by how much control they have in their own lives. It's a standard against which they're bound to fall short. If they rebel against other men—as in worker strikes—the risks are often huge and the gains short-lived. A safer alternative is to accept as compensation social support to control and feel superior to women. This provides both individual men and patriarchy with a safety valve for the frustration and rage that might otherwise be directed toward other men and at far greater risk to both individuals and the system as a whole.[32] No matter what other men do to a man or how deeply they control his life, he can always feel culturally superior to women and take out his anger and frustration on them.[33]

In this way, men are allowed to dominate women as a kind of compensation for their being subordinated to other men because of social class, race, or other forms of inequality. Ironically, however, their dominance of women supports the same principles of control that enable other men to subordinate them, a contradiction that is typical of oppressive systems. Men may buy into this so long as they can, in turn, enjoy the dominance that comes with applying those principles to women. The use of such compensation to stabilize systems also works with race and class inequality where one oppression is used to compensate for another. Working-class people, for example, can always look down on people receiving welfare, just as lower-class whites can feel superior to people of color. The playing off of one oppression against another helps explain why overt prejudice is most common among the most disadvantaged groups, because these are the people most in need of some kind of compensation.[34]

Related to men's use of women as compensation is the expectation that women will take care of men who have been damaged by other men. When he comes home from work, he wants a woman there to greet and take care of him, whether or not she's been at work all day herself. On a deeper level, he wants her to make him feel whole again, to restore what he loses through his disconnected pursuit of control, to calm his fears—all, of course, without requiring him to face the very things about himself and patriarchy that produce the damage in the first place. When women fail to "make it better"—and they are bound to fail eventually—they are also there to accept the blame and receive men's disappointment, pain, and rage. Men who feel unloved, incomplete, disconnected, battered, humiliated, frightened, and anxious routinely blame women for not supporting or loving them enough. It's a responsibility women are encouraged to accept,

which is one reason so many victims of domestic violence stay with the men who abuse them.

MISOGYNY

These days even the slightest criticism of men or male dominance can prompt accusations of "man hating" or "male bashing"; but only feminists seem to care about the cultural woman hating that's been around for millennia as part of everyday life under patriarchy.[35] Men's hypersensitivity is typical of dominant groups such as whites who often react strongly when blacks refer to whites as "honkies" or merely express anger over continuing white resistance to dealing with the everyday reality of racism. But whites barely notice the racial hostility that pervades the lives of minorities, for part of white privilege is the subtle arrogance of not having to pay attention to how that privilege affects others. What men don't get about gender, white people don't get about race: whites don't have to go out of their way to *act* hatefully in order to participate in a society that produces hateful consequences for people of color. Simply flowing with the mainstream and going about business as usual is enough.

The cultural expression of misogyny—the hatred (*mis-*) of femaleness (*gyny*)—takes many forms.[36] It's found in ancient and modern beliefs that women are inherently evil and a primary cause of human misery—products of what the Greek philosopher and mathematician Pythagoras called the "evil principle which created chaos, darkness, and woman."[37] There is misogyny in the violent pornography that portrays women as willing victims of exploitation and abuse, in jokes about everything from mothers-in-law to the slapping around or "good fuck" that some women "need." Misogyny shaped the historical transformation of ancient wise-women healers into modern-day images of witches who roast and eat children; in the torture and murder of millions of women from the witch hunts of the Middle Ages to recent Serb terrorism in Bosnia; in the everyday reality of sexual coercion, abuse, violence, and harassment; in the mass media display of women's bodies as objects existing primarily to please men and satisfy the male gaze; in cultural ideals of slenderness that turn women against their own bodies and inspire self-hatred and denial; in the steady stream of sensationalized and sexualized mass media "entertainment" in which men terrorize, torture, rape, and murder women.[38]

Not to be overlooked is the routine of insulting males with names that link them to females—sissy (sister), girl, pussy, son of a bitch, mama's boy. Notice, however, that the worst way to insult a woman isn't to call her a man or a "daddy's girl"; it's to call her a woman by another name by highlighting or maligning femaleness itself—bitch, whore, cunt.[39] The use of such words as insults is made even worse by the fact that prior to patriarchy many had neutral or positive meanings for women. A "whore" was a lover of either sex; "bitch" was associated with the pre-Christian goddess of the hunt, Artemis-Diana; and "cunt" derives from several sources, including the goddesses Cunti and Kunda, the universal sources of life.[40]

It's difficult to accept the idea that in the midst of wanting, needing, and loving women—if only as sons in relation to mothers—men are involved in a system that makes misogynist feelings, thoughts, and behavior paths of least resistance. Most men would probably deny this affects them in any way; often the most sexist men are among the first to say how much they love women. But there's no escaping misogyny, because it isn't a personality flaw; it's part of patriarchal culture. We're like fish swimming in a sea laced with it, and we can't breathe without passing it through our gills.[41] Misogyny infuses into our cells and becomes part of who we are because by the time we know enough to reject it, it's too late. As with everything else in a culture, some people are exposed to more of it than others; but to suppose that anyone escapes untouched is both wishful and disempowering. It's wishful because it goes against what we know about socialization and the power of culture to shape reality; it's disempowering because if we believe that misogyny doesn't involve us, we won't feel compelled to do anything about it.

Misogyny plays a complex role in patriarchy. It fuels men's sense of superiority, justifies male aggression against women, and works to keep women on the defensive and in their place. Misogyny is especially powerful in encouraging women to hate their own femaleness, an example of internalized oppression. The more women internalize misogynist images and attitudes, the harder it is to challenge male privilege or patriarchy as a system. In

fact, women won't tend to see patriarchy as even problematic since the essence of self-hatred is to focus on the self as the sole cause of misery, including the self-hatred.

In another sense, patriarchy promotes the hatred of women as a reaction to men's fear of women. Why should men fear women? Every oppressive system depends to some degree on subordinate groups being willing to go along with their own subordination. The other side of this, however, is the potential to undermine and rebel. This makes oppression inherently unstable and makes dominant groups vulnerable. Throughout the slave-holding South, for example, white people's fear of slave revolts was woven into the fabric of everyday life and caused many a restless night. And I suspect that much of the discomfort that whites feel around blacks today, especially black men, also reflects a fear that the potential for challenge and rebellion is never far from the surface.[42] For men, the fear is that women will stop playing the complex role that allows patriarchy to continue, or may even go so far as to challenge male privilege directly. Women's potential to disrupt patriarchy and make men vulnerable is why it's so easy for women to make men feel foolish or emasculated through the mildest humor that focuses on maleness and hints at women's power to stop going along with the status quo. Making fun of men, however, is just the tip of the iceberg of what women can do to disturb the patriarchal order, and on some level most men know this and have reason to feel threatened by it.

In more subtle ways, misogyny arises out of a system that offers women to men as a form of compensation. Because patriarchy limits men's emotional and spiritual lives, and because men rarely risk being vulnerable with other men, they often look to women as a way to ease their sense of emptiness, meaninglessness, and disconnection. However, the patriarchal expectation that "real men" are autonomous and independent sets men up to both want and resent women at the same time. This is made all the worse by the fact that women can't possibly give men what they want. Caught in this bind, men could face the truth of the system that put them in it in the first place. They could look at patriarchy and how their position in it creates this dilemma. The path of least resistance, however, is to resent and blame women for what men lack, by accusing women of not being loving or sexual enough, of being manipulative, withholding, selfish bitches who deserve to be punished.[43]

In a related sense, misogyny can reflect male envy of the human qualities patriarchy encourages men to devalue and deny in themselves as they avoid association with anything remotely female. Under patriarchy, women are viewed as trustees of all that makes a rich emotional life possible—of empathy and sympathy, vulnerability and openness to connection, caring and nurturing, sensitivity and compassion, emotional attention and expressiveness—all of which are driven out by the cycle of control and fear. On some level, men know the value of what they don't have and see women as privileged for being able to hold on to it. As a result, women live a double bind: the patriarchal ideology that supports women's oppression devalues the human qualities associated with being female, yet it also sets men up to envy and resent women for being able to weave those same qualities into their lives.[44]

Finally, misogyny can be seen as a cultural result of men's potential to feel guilty about women's oppression. Rather than encourage men to feel guilty, patriarchal culture projects negative judgments about men onto women. When men do feel guilty, they can blame women for making them feel this way: "If you weren't there reminding me of how oppressed women are, then I wouldn't have to feel bad about myself as a member of the group that benefits from it." Anger and resentment play this kind of role in many oppressive systems. When middle-class people encounter the homeless on the street, for example, it's not uncommon for them to feel angry simply for being reminded of their privilege and their potential to feel guilty about it. It's easier to hate the messenger than it is to take some responsibility for doing something about the reality behind the message.

As a mainstay of patriarchal culture, misogyny embodies some of the most contradictory and disturbing aspects of gender oppression. When love and need are bound up with fear and envy, hate and resentment, the result is an explosive mixture that can twist our sense of ourselves and one another beyond recognition. If misogyny were merely a problem of bad personal attitudes, it would be relatively easy to deal with. But its close connection to the cycle of control and fear that makes patriarchy work will make it part of human life as long as patriarchy exists.

Notes

1. See, for example, Steven Goldberg, *The Inevitability of Patriarchy,* new ed. (New York: William Morrow, 1993); and Lionel Tiger, *Men in Groups* (London: Nelson, 1969). For a view of feminist essentialism, see Rosemarie Tong, *Feminist Thought: A Comprehensive Introduction* (Boulder, Colo.: Westview Press, 1989).

2. Which, of course, some feminists, lesbian separatists in particular, have suggested.

3. E. O. Wilson, "Biology and the Social Sciences," *Daedalus* 106 (fall 1977): 127–140. See also Ruth Bleier, *Science and Gender: A Critique of Biology and Its Theories on Women* (New York: Pergamon Press, 1984); Anne Fausto-Sterling, *Myths of Gender: Biological Theories about Men and Women* (New York: Basic Books, 1985); Katharine B. Hoyenga and Kermit T. Hoyenga, *Gender-Related Differences: Origins and Outcomes* (Needham Heights, Mass.: Allyn and Bacon, 1993); and Eleanor E. Maccoby and Carol N. Jacklin, *The Psychology of Sex Differences* (Stanford: Stanford University Press, 1974).

4. See Riane Eisler, *The Chalice and the Blade* (New York: Harper and Row, 1987); Elizabeth Fisher, *Woman's Creation: Sexual Evolution and the Shaping of Society* (New York: McGraw-Hill, 1979); Marilyn French, *Beyond Power: On Men, Women, and Morals* (New York: Summit Books, 1985); Marija Gimbutas, *The Civilization of the Goddess: The World of Old Europe* (San Francisco: Harper and Row, 1991); idem, *The Language of the Goddess* (New York: HarperCollins, 1989); Richard Lee and Richard Daly, "Man's Domination and Woman's Oppression: The Question of Origins," in *Beyond Patriarchy: Essays by Men on Pleasure, Power, and Change,* ed. Michael Kaufman (New York: Oxford University Press, 1987), 30–44; Gerda Lerner, *The Creation of Patriarchy* (New York: Oxford University Press, 1986); and Merlin Stone, *When God Was a Woman* (New York: Harcourt Brace Jovanovich, 1976).

5. See, for example, Maria Lepowsky, "Women, Men, and Aggression in an Egalitarian Society," *Sex Roles* 30, nos. 3/4 (1994): 199–211; Margaret Mead, *Sex and Temperament in Three Primitive Societies* (New York: William Morrow, 1963); Henrietta L. Moore, *Feminism and Anthropology* (Minneapolis: University of Minnesota Press, 1988); Peggy Sanday, *Female Power and Male Dominance: On the Origins of Sexual Inequality* (Cambridge: Cambridge University Press, 1981); and Peggy Sanday, "The Socio-Cultural Context of Rape: A Cross-Cultural Study," *Journal of Social Issues* 34, no. 7 (1981): 5–27.

6. See Fausto-Sterling, *Myths of Gender.*

7. See, for example, W. T. Bielby and D. D. Bielby, "Family Ties: Balancing Commitments to Work and Family in Dual Earner Households," *American Sociological Review* 54, no. 5 (1989): 776–789; Maccoby and Jacklin, *The Psychology of Sex Differences;* B. J. Risman, "Intimate Relationships from a Microstructuralist Perspective: Men Who Mother," *Gender and Society* 1, no. 1 (1987): 6–32; and Naomi Weisstein, "Psychology Constructs the Female," in *Woman in Sexist Society,* ed. Vivian Gornick and Barbara K. Moran (New York: Basic Books, 1971).

8. See, for example, Deborah S. David and Robert Brannon, eds., *The Forty-Nine Percent Majority: The Male Sex Role* (Reading, Mass.: Addison-Wesley, 1976); Clyde W. Franklin, *Men and Society* (Chicago: Nelson-Hall, 1988); Michael Kaufman, ed., *Beyond Patriarchy: Essays by Men on Pleasure, Power, and Change* (New York: Oxford University Press, 1987); Sam Keen, *Fire in the Belly: On Being a Man* (New York: Bantam, 1991); Michael S. Kimmel and Michael A. Messner, eds., *Men's Lives,* 2nd ed. (New York: Macmillan, 1992); Joseph H. Pleck and Jack Sawyer, *Men and Masculinity* (Englewood Cliffs, N.J.: Prentice-Hall, 1974); and Andrew Tolson, *The Limits of Masculinity* (New York: Harper and Row, 1977).

9. For a history of European women's early awareness of and resistance to patriarchal oppression, see Gerda Lerner, *The Creation of Feminist Consciousness: From the Middle Ages to Eighteen Seventy* (New York: Oxford University Press, 1993).

10. The following discussion draws on many sources, especially Eisler, *The Chalice and the Blade;* Fisher, *Woman's Creation;* French, *Beyond Power;* David D. Gilmore, *Manhood in the Making: Cultural Concepts of Masculinity* (New Haven: Yale University Press, 1990); Lerner, *The Creation of Patriarchy;* Lee and Daly, "Man's Domination"; Miriam M. Johnson, *Strong Mothers, Weak Wives: The Search for Gender Equality* (Berkeley: University of California Press, 1988); and Robert Connell, *Gender and Power: Society, the Person, and Sexual Politics* (Stanford: Stanford University Press, 1987).

11. For more on this see, for example, Michael Kaufman, "The Construction of Masculinity and the Triad of Men's Violence," in Kaufman, ed., *Beyond Patriarchy,* 1–29.

12. A form of ritual aggression most often associated with African American males in which the contest is to trade progressively harsher insults until one or the other contestant either gives up or cannot better the previous insult.

13. It is, of course, possible for women to identify with patriarchal values and pursue power just as men do, but this is the exception that proves the rule and does not therefore do much to help us understand how patriarchy works as a system. Like Elizabeth I and Margaret Thatcher, under patriarchy such women can never be more than guests in an essentially male terrain.

14. French, *Beyond Power,* 337.

15. Ibid., 508.

16. Simone Weil, "Analysis of Oppression," in *Oppression and Liberty,* trans. Arthur Wills and John Petrie (Amherst: University of Massachusetts Press, 1973), quoted in French, *Beyond Power,* 508.

17. This was the subject of a now classic experiment in social psychology. See Manford Kuhn and Thomas McPartland, "An Empirical Investigation of Self Attitudes," *American Sociological Review* 19 (1954): 68–76.

18. Anyone who doubts this need look no further than the nearest school playground and the persecution endured by boys who show any interest in playing with girls. Among adults, woe betide the man who openly prefers the company of women. See Barrie Thorne, *Gender Play: Girls and Boys in School* (New Brunswick, N.J.: Rutgers University Press, 1993).

19. I haven't done the research, but I'd guess that men comprise the overwhelming majority of entries in the *Guiness Book of Records.*

20. David Halberstam, *The Best and the Brightest* (New York: Random House, 1972), 76.

21. See William G. Domhoff, *The Bohemian Grove and Other Retreats* (New York: Harper and Row, 1974).

22. Women in this position, of course, would only lose.

23. See Joseph H. Pleck, "Men's Power with Women, Other Men, and Society: A Men's Movement Analysis," in *Men's Lives,* ed. Michael S. Kimmel and Michael A. Messner, 2nd ed. (New York: Macmillan, 1992), 25.

24. See Johnson, *Strong Mothers, Weak Wives,* 117–118, and Pleck, "Men's Power with Women," 22–25.

25. See, for example, Tim Carrigan, Robert Connell, and John Lee, "Hard and Heavy: Toward a New Sociology of Masculinity," in Kaufman, ed., *Beyond Patriarchy,* 139–192; Frank Browning, *The Culture of Desire: Paradox and Perversity in Gay Lives Today* (New York: Crown Publishers, 1993); and Suzanne Pharr, *Homophobia: A Weapon of Sexism* (Inverness, Calif.: Chardon Press, 1988).

26. John Stoltenberg, "Pornography and Freedom," in *Men's Lives,* ed. Michael S. Kimmel and Michael A. Messner (New York: Macmillan, 1989), 482–488.

27. This is a confused area of thinking about gender that I try to clear up in Chapter 3.

28. See J. M. Golding, "Division of Household Labor, Strain, and Depressive Symptoms among Mexican American and Non-Hispanic Whites," *Psychology of Women Quarterly* 14, no. 1 (1990): 103–117; E. Litwak and P. Messeri, "Organizational Theory, Social Supports, and Mortality Rates," *American Sociological Review* 54, no. 1 (1989): 49–66; and J. Mirowsky and C. E. Ross, *Social Causes of Psychological Distress* (New York: Aldine de Gruyter, 1989).

29. See, for example, Jessie Bernard, "The Good Provider Role," *American Psychologist* 36, no. 1 (1981): R. C. Kessler and J. A. McRae, Jr., "The Effects of Wives' Employment on the Mental Health of Married Men and Women," *American Sociological Review* 47 (April 1982): 216–227; W. Michelson, *From Sun to Sun: Daily Obligations and Community Structure in the Lives of Employed Women and Their Families* (Totowa, N.J.: Rowman and Allanheld, 1985); and J. R. Wilkie, "Changes in U.S. Men's Attitudes Towards the Family Provider Role, 1972–1989," *Gender and Society* 7, no. 2 (1993): 261–279.

30. See Heidi I. Hartmann, "The Unhappy Marriage of Marxism and Feminism: Towards a More Progressive Union," in *Women and Revolution,* ed. Lydia Sargent (Boston: South End Press, 1981), 1–41.

31. For some revealing case studies of how this works, see Arlie Hochschild, *The Second Shift: Working Parents and the Revolution at Home* (New York: Viking/Penguin, 1989).

32. Men do, of course, direct a great deal of anger at each other. For example, men are far more likely to murder other men than they are to murder women.

33. This phenomenon is part of most oppressive systems, including racist ones. See Gerda Lerner, "Reconceptualizing Differences Among Women," in *Feminist Frameworks,* ed. Alison M. Jaggar and Paul S. Rothenberg, 3rd ed. (New York: McGraw-Hill, 1993), 237–248.

34. See David R. Roediger, *The Wages of Whiteness: Race and the Making of the American Working Class* (New York: Verso, 1991).

35. See Andrea Dworkin, *Woman Hating* (New York: E. P. Dutton, 1974); Susan Faludi, *Backlash: The Undeclared War Against Women* (New York: Crown Publishers, 1991); Marilyn French, *The War Against Women* (New York: Summit Books, 1992); and Catharine A. MacKinnon, *Only Words* (Cambridge: Harvard University Press, 1993).

36. It is notable that although a word for the hatred of maleness exists—misandry—it wasn't included in most dictionaries until very recently. The closest the English language comes to the hatred of males is "misanthropy," which actually refers to the hatred of people in general. Once again, patriarchal culture identifies males as the standard of humanity while women are marginalized as a hate-worthy "outgroup."

37. See B. Dijkstra, *Idols of Perversity: Fantasies of Feminine Evil* (New York: Oxford University Press, 1987); and S. Pomeroy, *Goddesses, Whores, Wives, and Slaves* (New York: Schocken, 1975).

38. See N. Ben-Yehuda, "The European Witch Craze of the 14th and 17th Centuries: A Sociologist's Perspective," *American Journal of Sociology* 86, no. 1 (1980): 1–31; Kim Chernin, *The Obsession: Reflections on the Tyranny of Slenderness* (New York: Harper and Row, 1981); C. P. Christ, "Heretics and Outsiders: The Struggle over Female Power in Western Religion," in *Feminist Frontiers,* ed. L. Richardson and V. Taylor (Reading, Mass.: Addison-Wesley, 1983), 87–94; Dworkin, *Woman Hating;* Barbara Ehrenreich and Deidre English, *For Her Own Good: 150 Years of Experts' Advice to Women* (New York: Anchor Books/Doubleday, 1978); Faludi, *Backlash;* French, *War Against Women;* MacKinnon, *Only Words.*

39. It's true that "prick" is a form of insult, but it doesn't have nearly the weight of likening men to women.

40. Barbara G. Walker, *The Woman's Encyclopedia of Myths and Secrets* (San Francisco: Harper and Row, 1983).

41. A metaphor I first heard from Nora L. Jamieson.

42. For some accounts of how this works, see Studs Terkel, *Race* (New York: New Press, 1992).

43. It should come as no surprise that abusive men tend to be very emotionally dependent on the women they abuse. See Thomas J. Scheff and Suzanne M. Retzinger, *Emotions and Violence: Shame and Rage in Destructive Conflicts* (Lexington, Mass.: Lexington, 1991). See also Claire M. Renzetti, *Violent Betrayal: Partner Abuse in Lesbian Relationships* (Newbury Park, Calif.: Sage, 1992).

44. I suspect a similar phenomenon occurs in other forms of oppression. Whites, for example, often look upon stereotypical characteristics of people of color with a mixture of contempt and envy. I've heard some whites say they would like to have the feeling of deep strength and wisdom that many African Americans have developed in order to survive in a racist society.

A New Response to "Angry Black (Anti) Feminists": Reclaiming Feminist Forefathers, Becoming Womanist Sons

Gary Lemons

Gary Lemons teaches African-American literature and feminist studies at Eugene Lang College at the New School University. He has authored many articles on gender, race, and feminism, including "Teaching the (Bi)Racial Space that Has No Name: Reflections of a Black Male Feminist Teacher" (in Maureen T. Reddy, ed., Everyday Acts Against Racism*); "Young Man, Tell Our Stories of How We Made It Over: Beyond the Politics of Identity" (in Katherine J. Mayberry, ed.,* Identity Politics in Higher Education*); "To Be Black, Male, and Feminist: Making Womanist Space for Black Men,"* International Journal of Sociology and Social Policy.*

In opposition to a view that feminism is inherently racist and Black feminist women have sold out the racial struggle, Lemons responds that Black profeminism has a long tradition in the struggle for racial justice. Racial domination and sexist oppression are related, Lemons argues, and as Blacks call for Whites to give up racial supremacy, Black men must give up male supremacy.

REVISITING "THE BLACK SEXISM DEBATE"

Since 1979, when *The Black Scholar* published "The Black Sexism Debate," controversy continues to rage around the idea of *black* feminism. Black antifeminist men have charged black women feminists with creating a racial/gender rift between black men and women, arising from the feminist positionality they have claimed. Thus, black feminist women have been accused of such Machiavellian plots as conspiring with white feminists against black men, with promoting lesbianism, and selling out black struggle against racism (a move tantamount to black cultural genocide). Stated another

way, the single most virulent critique of black women in feminist movement has come with the perception by some black men that "feminism" is itself a racist ideology solely fixed in a manhating ideology ultimately leading to the castration and "feminization" of all black men.

It was Robert Staples' "The Myth of Black Macho: A Response to Angry Black Feminists," appearing in the March/April 1979 issue of *The Black Scholar*, which declared a black male antifeminist stance that framed the parameters for a "debate on black sexism" (published in the following issue of the same journal). The Staples article, nothing short of a diatribe against Michele Wallace and Ntozake Shange, couched itself as a "response to angry black feminists"—stating that:

> Since white feminists could not marshal an all-out attack on black males, and well-known black female activists such as Joyce Ladner and Angela Davis would not, how could they be put in their place. Enter Ntozake Shange and Michele Wallace. (24)

This statement, in tandem with those that defined Staples' anti-feminist position, prompted (upon the essay's publication) an outpouring of response to Staples from black women and men. In reaction, *The Black Scholar* reconstructed these responses in the form of a "Reader Forum" under the aforementioned title. Bringing together commentaries of twenty-three respondents[1] (and a rejoinder by Staples) on the essay's polemics, the editors stated:

> We are now entering a phase in which the oppression of women by men, and all aspects of that sexism, is the subject of considerable criticism and analysis by the women's movement. Black feminists have raised just criticisms of black male sexism, and this has strengthened the understanding of conscientious black men and women who seek to improve not only the collective black human condition, but

the quality of their lives in terms of their individual personal relationships. We believe that the effort to clarify the nature of black male/female relationships is an important step in the process of re-uniting our people and revitalizing the struggle against oppression. (Quoted from the editorial statement, "The Black Sexism Debate.")

Considering the continued sexual abuse, exploitation, racist, and sexist oppression of black women in the U.S.—"conscientious" black women in feminist movement have confronted sexism and sexist practice in and outside black communities. Those black men in the 1979 "debate" who wrote in solidarity with black women against black antifeminist ideology must today be joined by those of us black men who declare ourselves in feminist alliance with black women—writing, speaking, and acting in comradeship against women's oppression. We must critique sexism perpetrated by black men (as well as other men)—calling out sexism and misogynist behavior wherever we encounter it.

While my objective here is not to give a full reading to the commentary of the Reader Forum respondents, I believe it necessary to reclaim the courageous words of one black male respondent—Kalamu ya Salaam who wrote:

> *The facts of life are that African-American women are more economically exploited than our men, white women/or white men. Additionally, our women face a sexist discrimination, exploitation and harassment which our men do not. To deny these facts only aids in perpetuating sexism as we can not eradicate it or its effects and influences until we face and fight sexism head on.*

Acknowledging the often complicitous relation between black sexism and white supremacy in the oppression of black women, Salaam resists the idea that black men cannot be sexist because we have no power to institutionalize sexism.

> *It is equally inappropriate and down-right reactionary to resist the criticism that we African-American men have generally adopted a sexist outlook and behavior vis-à-vis our women. Our lack of the power to institutionalize sexism means little because* sexism is already embedded into nearly every institution in America. Regardless of our lack of power, the fact is that we routinely act our sex-

ist behavior *(my emphasis) and the controllers of society at large condone, seldom punish and even sometimes reward such sexist behavior. . . . (21)*

I respond to Salaam's words as a contemporary call for black men to recognize and resist sexism as a misogynist weapon employed to dehumanize all women. I hear his words as an echo of W.E.B. DuBois' exhortation to black men of his time to take up the cause of woman suffrage and women's rights. For those of us black men already committed to feminist movement, we must begin a more vocal and demonstrative declaration of a "pro-womanist" stand (a term I will use interchangeably with the phrase "black [male] feminist positionality" throughout this study to name a relationship of women's rights advocacy articulated by black men in the first, second, and present stage of U.S. feminist movement). I do, however, view the term "womanism" in nuanced relationship to "feminism." Evoking Alice Walker's name for the self-autonomized position occupied by black women and other women of color (see *In Search of Our Mothers' Gardens*), I apply it to the pro-woman writings of W.E.B. DuBois. As a race-specific representation of feminism, I believe "womanism" more closely approximates the Africanist vision of womanhood he defended.

Whether we name ourselves in solidarity with "feminism" or "womanism," collectively, black men must—as did black men in the woman suffrage movement—actively combat antifeminist thinking that privileges anti-racist work over women's struggle to end sexual oppression. As we know, sexism in the black power movement of the 1960s represented itself as a political move to "regain black manhood" to the exclusion of black *women's* struggle in the cause of black liberation. The movement reduced the place of black women in the struggle to the identical position they occupy in white supremacist capitalist patriarchy. Toward a new gender/race politic in black communities, we must work to eradicate the notion that black women (and men) active in feminism is synonymous with the emasculation of black men. Only when we begin to acknowledge the dehumanizing effects of sexism and misogyny on women, children, and ourselves can we participate in a life-affirming dialogue with black women to strategize an end to female oppression. Coming to recognize, as Kalamu Ya Salaam maintained, that—even as we struggle against our racial oppression—we possess power as *men* in a culture driven by patriarchal hegemony.

Contrary to popular black antifeminist belief, feminism conceived by black women has never been rooted in anti-male rhetoric, theory, or practice— nor has it ever been antithetical to the struggle against racism. Black men acknowledging this enables transformed thinking, where the narrow identity politics of male-centered black nationalism is displaced and disavowed. When we begin strategizing ways to end sexism, we bring about a form of self-healing that promotes a liberatory gender healing that affects all (black) women and men.

I employ the stated objectives of "The Black Sexism Debate" as the central premise upon which this study rests—that "[b]lack feminists have raised just criticisms of black male sexism . . . to improve . . . the collective black human condition . . . to clarify the nature of black male/female relationships . . . in the process of re-uniting our people and revitalizing the struggle against oppression." Today, nearly twenty years after "The Debate," the need still exists (perhaps more than before)—not just to discuss black sexism, but to create a dialogue of intervention. We need to return to the debate—critically dialoguing on the necessity of feminist agency in black communities and the primacy of feminist movement in the liberation of all black people.

Thinking about the editorial commentary *The Black Scholar* set in place to frame "The Black Sexism Debate," during the second wave of U.S. feminist movement, I am compelled to ponder its contemporary implications. Anti-racist activism conceived by many black men in the nineteenth century fostered the idea that the eradication of racism could not be fought solely in terms of racial stratagems. Along with Frederick Douglass, many other black men (including Martin Delany, Charles Lenox Redmond, James Forten, Jr. and Sr., Robert Purvis, William Whipper, Alonzo Ranzier, William Henry Johnson, and Alexander Crummell) perceived black women's issues in the black liberation movement to be a priority, believing that they too had to rally around them, understanding the fact that black women had to battle both racism and sexism. In 1910, as editor of *The Crisis*, W.E.B. DuBois ran a forum on woman suffrage. "[I]t was," he declared, "to be regarded as one of the strongest cumulative attacks on sex and race discrimination in politics ever written" (vol. 10, 177). Representing black men of distinction in religion, law, government, politics, and literature, pro-woman suffragists included Bishop John Hurst, Reverend Francis J. Grimké (who officiated in the wedding of Frederick Douglass and Helen Pitts), Benjamin Brawley (then Dean of Morehouse College), J. W. Johnson (the foreign U.S. Consul to Nicaragua), Robert H. Terrell (prominent judge in Washington, D.C., and husband of Mary Church Terrell), and noted novelist and short story writer Charles Chesnutt.

DOCUMENTING THE HISTORY OF BLACK MEN IN THE WOMAN SUFFRAGE MOVEMENT

Black men in the woman suffrage movement during the nineteenth and early twentieth centuries proved to be significant allies in women's struggle for voting rights. Black men advocating woman suffrage, almost from the movement's inception, believed strategically that a battle against racism linked to the campaign for female voting rights would create a stronger political power base. The African- and Anglo-American women and men who worked for a gender/race coalition believed abolitionism and feminism combined the principles that would lead to race and gender liberation. The woman suffrage movement formed in the North during the 1850s framed its emerging agenda around an anti-sexist, anti-racist platform.

From the alliance formed between abolitionists and feminists came one of the nineteenth century's most outspoken, black male advocates of woman suffrage—Frederick Douglass. Moreover, in the early twentieth century W.E.B. DuBois would become a leading spokesperson, not only for woman suffrage but for black women's rights. As woman suffrage activists, however, both Douglass and Du Bois discoursed extensively on the necessity of women's voting rights and issues of race/gender equality. What marks the distinctiveness of their "pro-woman texts" is what I choose to identify as a *black (male) feminist positionality*.

Chiefly, this study embarks upon an interrogation of Douglass, and DuBois' pro-woman writings, along with activist expressions by other black male advocates of woman suffrage, to ascertain the discursive features and particularities of an historic black male standpoint located in a theoretical and pragmatic alliance with feminism. I employ an analytical perspective that draws upon contemporary black feminist thought asserting the notion that gender, in and of itself, cannot be an exclusive analytical category in the critique of women's oppression—that sex oppression interrelates with racism and classism to form a system of triadic domination.

I aim to figure ways black male resistance against racism in the nineteenth and early twentieth centuries coalesced with, diverged from, and made further complex the already complex race/gender relationship between white and black women—whose struggle for voting rights never solely cohered around gender. Mapping the contours and production of black men's profeminist discourse during the woman suffrage movement brings forth an analysis that seeks to delineate the gender politics that men like Frederick Douglass and W.E.B. DuBois hoped to achieve, in light of the position each held as a "race" man. I argue precisely that from the early writings and actions of black men advocating race and gender rights that a black men's profeminist position came into being.

In pronouncing an historic relation between African-American men and feminism, I displace (as earlier stated) the myth, originating with the rise of the black power movement that black men are inherently anti-feminist. Counter to prevailing black nationalist rhetoric, all black men do not view our resistance to racism as a more urgent priority than feminist struggle to end patriarchal sexist domination, oppression, and exploitation of women. The aim of this study is to (en)gender a "race talk" among black men that seriously acknowledges the pervasiveness of sexism in black communities, as much as it is to establish Frederick Douglass and W.E.B. DuBois as proto-feminist black men. In reconstructing the history of each man in the woman suffrage movement, I replicate the move by contemporary black feminist scholars to reclaim their pivotal place in U.S. women's movement. I read the various discursive forms (speeches, autobiographies, formal essays, newspaper articles, and fiction) black men engaged to represent their personal and political commitment to women's rights.

Rather than writing a vindication of black men in which profeminist men like Douglass and Du Bois obtain the status of idealized icons of radically progressive gender politics, I examine them in the context of complex public and private lives where their theory and praxis sometimes failed to convey the idea(l)s they at other times maintained about the equality of women. In reality, neither Douglass nor Du Bois ever completely freed themselves from the trappings of patriarchal thinking about women, gender, masculinity, and manhood. Encoded in their feminist discourse is a race/gender "twoness." On the one hand, it represented itself as liberatory in tone and sentiment. On the other, it reinforced a paternalistic and traditionally male-centered ethos that privileged their power as men (despite the racial inequality they experienced). I argue that in pro-woman writings by Douglass and Du Bois there surfaces at times a race/gender anxiety having to [do] with their own ambivalence toward a sustained coalition struggle in which racism and sexism figure coterminately. The desire to legitimate black manhood, in a culture where manhood and masculinity were racially inscribed in "whiteness," drives a competing (race/gender) agenda in both men's writings—to such an extent that the lines between "blackness" and patriarchy blurs.

A black (male) feminist impulse generated in pro-woman writings by Douglass and DuBois registered in a race/gender expression that was always already given to masculine bias. Yet it signaled each man's attempt to assert his identity as an exemplary figure of black manhood—as a master rhetorician, a "spokes(man) for the race," and a man of progressive gender politics. Even while struggling to represent themselves as "manly" men against white supremacist denial of their right to manhood, both Douglass and DuBois resisted patriarchal ideas that labeled women the weaker sex. And in spite of the patriarchal position each occupied in his lifetime, he articulated an impassioned and liberatory vision of equality between the sexes. In so doing, he transformed the meanings of (black) manhood, one linked to the empowerment of women. Considering the status of race and sex in the U.S. during the time in which each lived, his progressive race/gender ideas certainly generated controversy (See Davis and Giddings). What did it mean for a black man to support women's rights when black women and men had not been enfranchised as American citizens, who during slavery had been commodified as chattel to be bought and sold? What did it mean for a black man to assert himself as a "man" who embraced feminist ideas in a culture of white supremacist patriarchy where he was perceived as a threat to white womanhood? What did it mean for a black man to ally himself in the cause of black women's rights in particular when black women were excluded from the category "woman"—sexually, physically, and psychologically brutalized in a system of enslavement that reduced them to exoticized objects of white male capitalist consumption, their bodies forced into labor as breeding machines?

In the dehumanized space that names the racialized/gendered history of African-American women and men, ap(praising) the history of black men in feminist movement, I work to revalue the political imperatives that inform the nature of black (male) profeminism. Frederick Douglass and W.E.B. DuBois, among other black men, claimed it as a standpoint for black liberation understanding that the status of all women in the U.S. (determined differently according to their relation to white ruling class patriarchy). Douglass and DuBois "moved" incisively to empower themselves as *black men* in feminist terms. Demystifying black men's relation to feminism and reclaiming the history of black male support of woman suffrage, can be a powerful means to engage contemporary black men in dialogue about the viability of feminist movement focused on the liberation of all black people. Black men reading and talking about our legacy in the woman suffrage movement carries with it transformative possibilities related to gender, race, and sexual oppression. A concept of black manhood and masculinity linked personally and politically to progressive antiracist-feminist thinking calls for a radical reordering of black male and female relationship. Remembering our feminist past enables the potential for liberatory thinking that supports coalition struggle across race and gender, advocates resistance to black male sexist and misogynist behavior, and embraces notions of sexual difference where heterosexism and homophobia are actively contested.

"RE–MEMBER(ING)" NOT TO FORGET AND THE IDEA OF A USABLE PAST: FEMINISM AND A TRANSFORMED VISION OF BLACK LIBERATION: LESSON #1

Our histories may be irretrievable, but they invite imaginative reconstruction.

—HENRY LOUIS GATES (231)

Restating my opening assertion that black men (and women)—across economic, sexual, class, and religious borders—hold on to a distorted belief that feminism is about middle class white women and manhating/castrating black women, in contest to this representation, I assert that black people must begin a critical reassessment of liberation struggle. Many black men (particularly those with nationalist and/or religious notions of black liberation) continue to situate anti-racist work in opposition to anti-sexist activism. Similarly, many black women have rejected feminism privileging racial solidarity over the need to combat gender inequality. We must envision black liberation as a radical space of transformation where domination is opposed—whether rooted in gender oppression, (hetero)sexist discrimination, class bias, and/or any other form of treatment that denies the basic humanity of the individual.

We can create a progressive agenda for emancipatory struggle based on a space of negotiation in which issues of race, gender, sexuality, and class are not filtered through a patriarchal hierarchy. Moving freely within a liberatory framework where black women and men operate in a partnership of mutual respect and recognition—we give rise to a visionary consciousness that is genuinely revolutionary. Progressive black men working toward a liberated consciousness no longer invest in ideas of manhood and masculinity in patriarchy and the subjugation of women. We must fully realize the meaning of our battle as black men resisting the dehumanization of racism when we begin divesting ourselves of *male* supremacist power. Reciting black men's pro-active stance in the woman suffrage movement, I rely upon the concept of a usable feminist past in service to a contemporary vision of unity among difference(s) in black communities as sites of individual and collective empowerment.

Black men supporting women's rights in the past serves as a model for their place in contemporary black liberation struggle. Black male profeminist activism in political solidarity with black women obtains as a powerful legacy for a new vision of unity in black communities. Contemporary black women and men struggling together against racism and sexism challenges the dogma of male-centered nationalism. When gender oppression is again placed on the agenda of black liberation as a crucial location for resistance, we invoke the past as an empowering force for change. Calling black men and women into critical remembrance of liberatory moments in history, such as the woman suffrage movement and its relation to abolitionism, serves as a complex but necessary lesson in the effectiveness of coalition strategizing. bell hooks calls us to a transformative "re-member(ing)" each other. Such a process may be employed as a political strategy to oppose sexism, as well as sexist and misogynist behavior in black communities. It means, in hooks' words, coming to

> the point of connection between black women and men [that is the] space of recognition and understanding, where we know one another so well, our histories, that we can take the bits and pieces, the fragments of who we are, and put them back together, re-member them (my emphasis). (19)

Recollecting the history of black women and men working together for women's voting rights evokes a powerful image of political solidarity. Remembering the past, serving as an active agent in the creation of spaces where "we can take the bits and pieces, the fragments of who we are" enables progressive dialogues to happen around issues of race and gender. Black feminist women and men need to create spaces in our communities where we can talk openly about sexism and its particular manifestations in the lives of black people. More importantly, we need to establish locations where antisexist activism can take place, illustrating the integral role political work opposing gender oppression plays in the liberation of black people.

The goal of any movement to end oppression should have as a priority the welfare of all those oppressed within its ranks—whether by race, gender, class, sexuality, or any other form of domina-

tion that seeks to devalue life. Black people in the U.S. possess a history of shared struggle across borders. Yet today many black men and women find ourselves battling each other, having internalized racist and sexist myths that perpetuate a gulf between us. In black communities, sexism continues to be a battle ground where black women must defend themselves, opposing black men who deny that sexism is less a problem than racism and that feminism has no place in work opposing racial oppression. Progressive black men disrupt antifeminist sentiment when we claim a profeminist relationship. Reclaiming the history of black men as advocates of women's rights, black male feminists establish a politic of remembrance in which the past intervenes powerfully on the present toward a new vision of black liberation.

My desire to situate a history of black male support of women's rights in relation to the present is generated by the lack of a sustained, vocal presence in the contemporary period of black men speaking in opposition to sexist and misogynist behavior—especially that perpetuated by many of us. As a feminist black man, I am particularly concerned about how we begin to educate black men about the hurtful effects of male supremacy. As rap has become a pervasive signifier of popular black youth culture, we have witnessed a young, black male-dominated mode of expression whose ladder of success, for the most part, has been placed on the backs of black women. Black female sexual denigration and misogynist objectification played out in gangsta rap is a prime example. In its anti-woman lyrics, black females occupy the status of "bitch" and "ho"—served up in a sexist minstrel show of black male supremacist, masturbatory fantasy. Supported by a white male-dominated sexist and racist music industry, colonized black men exploit black women and female sexuality for self-advancement in a system based on the capitalist exploitation of the black body. "Feminist critiques of the sexism and misogyny in gangsta rap, and in all aspects of popular culture," hooks asserts, "must continue to be bold and fierce" (123). Contemporary black men need to know that the early history of black liberation movement represented itself in coalition strategy where men like Frederick Douglass and W.E.B. DuBois envisioned the struggle for racial equality successfully won when women gained political freedom.

IN THE CAUSE OF WOMEN'S RIGHTS: FREDERICK DOUGLASS AND W.E.B. DUBOIS AS WOMAN SUFFRAGISTS: LESSON #2

Politicizing pro-woman speeches, essays, autobiographical narratives, and journalistic media by black men in the woman suffrage movement, contemporary profeminist black men become important allies to women fighting to end sexism. As "pro-woman" black men, our speaking and acting in feminist alliance not only challenge antifeminism in black communities but contests the myth of black macho that all black men endorse patriarchy and sexism.

Paula Giddings acknowledges Frederick Douglass and W.E.B. DuBois as the leading black male feminists of their times. As advocates of woman suffrage, each man crafted his own version of pro-woman discourse. On the one hand, Douglass viewed the subjugated status of (white) women as comparable to the condition of the (male and female) slave. Along with woman suffrage leaders Elizabeth Cady Stanton and Susan B. Anthony, among others, he strategized the idea of a joint movement based on the interrelation of race and sex oppression. The same strategy informed the feminist ideas of DuBois. However, he conceived women's liberation in a specifically racialized manner. Comparing the pro-womanist texts of these men reveals a particular race/gender problematic located in the very idea of "male" feminism. What does it mean for a man to occupy a feminist position—to speak and write from a feminist standpoint? What is at stake for the feminist man? What if anything must he give up? What are the benefits being a (male) feminist? These questions take on more resonance when asked in relation to black men.

Understanding the rhetorical tactics Douglass and DuBois crafted as black male woman suffragists means examining the political relationship between gender and race in their pro-woman writings. To show the discursive strategy each man employed to put forth a radical discourse of women's

rights and racial liberation, I engage Houston Baker's discussion of the subversive nature of the black discursive tradition. Baker theorizes a history of black textuality formulated in two modes of literary discourse known as the "mastery of form" and the "deformation of mastery." In *Modernism and the Harlem Renaissance* (1987) he suggests, for example, that the writing styles of Booker T. Washington and W.E.B. DuBois displayed a conscious play of rhetorical subversion where the writing act established black (author)ity. Illustrating the skillful manner in which Washington conveyed the merits of his political program for black progress to white benefactors, Baker argues that his deceptively humble style bore the signs of a sophisticated command of Western literary convention. DuBois, on the other hand, by infusing certain "Africanisms" into his writings on race, purposely undermined the cultural hegemony of the West. Baker maintains that the insurgent stylistics of Washington and DuBois operate as models for the beginning of "black modernism."

Thinking about the established tradition of black men's writing on racial progress, I argue for the importance of establishing a history of black men writing pro-woman texts. The emergence of black modernism and the rise of black male profeminism bare a striking relation when viewed through the model Baker proposes. As mentioned earlier, I apply it to the problematics of DuBois and Douglass writing feminist texts to clarify the complex relationship between race and gender in them, as it informed the men's conception of women's rights.

Frederick Douglass' assertion of manhood (through his woman suffrage writings) is accomplished in a "mastery of form," or a *mastery* of the "master's forms" (to play on Baker's subversive intent, as I will go on to illustrate). DuBois, on the other hand, collapses traditional discursive categories to create a *black* feminist discourse to address the specific historical condition of black women. Troping on DuBois' radical departure from conventional form, Baker refers to his mode of writing as a "deformation of mastery"—a conscious subversion of Eurocentricity. It is achieved by the "(mask)ing" of form. Baker's mask trope, connotatively connected to his definition of form, acts as the illustrating device to convey his theory of the source for the modern black writer's "literary" agency. It is the *minstrel mask*, "a governing object in a ritual of *non-sense*" (21) that Baker establishes as the initial site of modern African-American literary form-"ing" (form in the active, moving sense). The minstrel mask

> *is a space of habitation not only for repressed spirits of sexuality, ludic play, id satisfaction, castration anxiety, and a mirror stage of development, but also for that deep-seated denial of the indisputable humanity of inhabitants of and descendants from the continent of Africa.* And it is first and foremost, the master of the minstrel mask by blacks that constitutes a primary move in Afro-American discursive modernism [my emphasis]. (17)

The minstrel mask, the historical embodiment of the black's nonhuman, objectified figuration in the minstrel show was, Baker states, "designed to remind white consciousness that black men and women are *mis-speakers* bereft of humanity—carefree devils strumming and humming all day—unless, in a gaslight misidentification, they are violent devils fit for lynching, a final exorcism that will leave whites alone" (21). As black men, Douglass and DuBois "played" within the minstrel mask for different reasons—the former manipulating its interior to advance his claim to manhood as a "self-made" man, the latter "Africanizing" it to empower black women (and men). Further defining the minstrel mask as prime device for black discursive legitimation, Baker insists that:

> *Obviously, an Afro-American spokesperson who wished to engage in a* masterful *(my emphasis) and empowering play within the minstrel spirit house needed the uncanny ability to manipulate bizarre phonic legacies. For he or she had the task of transforming the mask and its sounds into negotiable discursive currency. In effect, the task was the production of a manual of black speaking, a book of speaking "back and black."* (24)

I draw on the minstrel mask's "formative" premise to suggest that both Douglass and DuBois wrote pro-woman texts that represented themselves as "manual(s) of black speaking" to talk "back and black" to white supremacy and sexism, but where the two men diverged in motive had to do with the audience they looked to for support. Douglass wrote mainly for a white middle class, female edu-

cated constituency; DuBois composed primarily for its emerging black counterpart. And the writing strategies each employed to advocate woman suffrage reflected his particular relationship to the race of the women to whom they appealed.

As I have already argued, Douglass' woman suffrage discourse affirmed his participation and status in a predominately white woman suffrage movement. Long-time personal friends of Douglass, Elizabeth Cady Stanton, and Susan B. Anthony (as well as many other Northern white women feminists of the day), heralded him for his support. DuBois' womanist stance enabled a race/gender movement counter to the dominant culture—affecting his personal/political vision of black liberation through the revaluation and celebration of black womanhood. His pro-woman texts subverted the power and privilege of a Eurocentric view of "woman" to reveal the beauty of black women. On the other hand, the women's rights discourse of Douglass worked implicitly to erase a personal and political association with black women, though he on occasion assisted in black women's political organizing.

It may be seen that discursively Douglass and DuBois stood at opposite poles. Rhetorically, the politics of their writing strategies mirror the difference in the ideological positions each occupied in feminism. Located in Afrocentric nationalism, DuBois' womanist stance constructs a "literary" black female subjectivity figured in African mythology (focused on an eternal black feminine). He resituates it within the existing (author)ized tradition of the white Western imagination. In this way, he performs a "deforming" mastery. Rather than a manipulation of the position of the writer's voice inside the "minstrel mask"—as Douglass had done—DuBois radically re(forms) it, to speak beyond its racialized boundaries. Frankly speaking, DuBoisian black feminist nationalism opposes the assimilationist woman suffrage politics Douglass avowed.

(Re)writing *gender*, as a political category into the discourse of race (from a nationalist feminist standpoint), DuBois, I argue, works out a mastery of subversion. It functions not only to subvert the power of white supremacy but to disrupt the domination of patriarchy in the lives of (black) women. He seizes the minstrel mask and transforms it into a more authentically gendered, African one. The most performative text representing this oppositional gesture is exemplified in *The Quest of the Silver Fleece* (1911), his first novel.

The novel's protagonist, Zora Creswell is purposely imaged as *dark-skinned* black woman. Figuring her in "blackness," DuBois goes against the grain of African-American literary tradition, in which there exists a long history of "light-skinned" female representation. Zora, however, is the first black female hero in black literature. Troping on black female dark skin color, the author embodies her as the literal and "figurative" representative of an African goddess, mythic supernatural power. The "deformation of the mask" Baker claims DuBois affects in *The Souls of Black Folk* is ultimately realized in the image of Zora. Fittingly wearing the ancestral mask, she "distinguishes rather than conceals" (51) the particular attributes of a dark-skinned black female subjectivity. Defining them through Zora, DuBois achieves a discursive mastery that was (he believed) indigenous to Africa and the *African*-American. Baker observes:

> *The deformation of mastery refuses a master's* nonsense. *It returns—often transmuting "standard" syllables—to the common sense of the tribe. Its relationship to masks is radically different from the mastery of form. The spirit house occupying the deformer is not minstrelsy, but the sound and space of an African ancestral past. For the Afro-American spokesperson, the most engaging repository for deformation's sounding work is the fluid and multiform mask of African ancestry.* (56–57)

As Douglass constructs himself as a "master of form"; DuBois (as Baker suggests) stood at the beginning of the twentieth century as its "most articulate adherent of African sound" (57). I agree with Baker that *The Souls of Black Folk* is the prototypic textual illustration of the "mask of African ancestry," but there can be no doubt that it exists in a precursorial relation to *The Quest*—DuBois' most sophisticated realization and most provocative display of deformative ancestralism.

LOOKING FOR FEMINIST FATHERS, BECOMING WOMANIST SONS: LESSON #3

In 1920, DuBois published "The Damnation of Women"—his most pronounced statement of women's rights support. Ten years before its publication, he had emphatically stated in "Votes for Women: A Symposium By Leading Thinkers of Colored America" that *"votes for women, means votes for black women"* (my emphasis). In his womanist prose, there obtains an unequivocal advocacy of woman suffrage even as he promoted himself as personal arbiter of black culture. And while his ideas of black manhood were rooted in patriarchal tradition, he constructed a self-image in which his nationalist agenda for black progress remained integrally linked to the liberation of black women as represented in "The Damnation of Women." Written over seventy years ago, as it spoke to the urgent need for black men to support the woman suffrage movement, its message of radical gender alliance speaks to black men today as a wo(man)ist manifesto. It calls for a new generation of black men to take up the cause of women's rights as comrades in feminist struggle.

Black men conscious of the relation between sexist domination and racial oppression in the lives of black women come to understand the necessity of joint resistance. We can no longer strategize a movement for black empowerment solely in terms of race. Insisting that white people divest themselves of the power of white supremacy, we should demand that black men rid ourselves of the hegemony of male supremacy. As profeminist black men wrote in support of feminist black women in 1979 who opposed Robert Staples' invective against Michele Wallace and Ntozake Shange, today we must write more and speak louder with (black) women who refuse to be sexually exploited, objectified, and devalued for misogynist pleasure. The moment has come for us to "remember." When black men begin to reclaim our feminist inheritance, carrying on the legacy of Frederick Douglass and W.E.B. DuBois, we share in a brotherhood founded not on a flawed quest for lost manhood (driven by a fear of masculine inferiority) but one anchored in the confidence that who we are as men does not depend upon our ability to subjugate, control, exploit, batter, dominate, and/or sexually violate women.

Contemporary feminist black men, like our pro-woman predecessors, can offer a transformed vision of black manhood—one in which we disclaim the need for patriarchy to affirm our masculinity. At this particular historical moment when the rhetoric of the Million Man March compels black men to atone for not having lived up to the patriarchal, capitalist ideas voiced by Louis Farrakhan—a progressive counter movement is needed that defies narrow (hetero)sexist notions of blackness and offers gender and sexual freedom for all black people. The need for black men's feminist alliance has not changed since the days of Douglass and DuBois. As profeminist black men, we must continue to wage war against sexual oppression as vigorously as we fight against racism. Only then will we sense the full meaning of a unified movement for black empowerment. Only then will we be able to assume fully our inheritance as "womanist sons" of Frederick Douglass and W.E.B. DuBois, our "feminist forefathers."

Note

1. The respondents in the Readers Forum included the following persons: Robert Allen, S. E. Anderson, Bonnie M. Daniels, Harry Edwards, Sarah Fabio, Chidi Ikonne, Terry Jones, June Jordan, M. Ron Karenga, Audre Lorde, Julianne Malveaux, Mark D. Matthews, Rosemary Mealy, E. Ethelbert Miller, George Mosby, Jr., Alvin F. Poussant, Kalamu Ya Salaam, Andrew Salkey, Ntozake Shange, Sabrina Sojourner, Robert Staples, Pauline T. Stone, Askia Toure, and Sherley Williams.

Bibliography

Baker, Houston. 1987. *Modernism and the Harlem Renaissance*. Chicago: University of Chicago Press.

DuBois, W. E. B. 1910. "Votes for Women: A Symposium by Leading Thinkers of Colored America." *The Crisis* 10, p. 177.

Gates, Henry L. 1993. "The Black Man's Burden" in *Fear of a Queer Planet: Queer Politics and Social Theory.* ed. Michael Warner. Minneapolis: University of Minnesota Press.

hooks, bell. 1994. *Outlaw Culture.* New York: Routledge.

Staples, Robert. 1979. "The Myth of Black Macho: A Response to Angry Black Feminists." *The Black Scholar: Journal of Black Studies and Research* 10, Nos. 6, 7 (March/April).

"The Black Sexism Debate." Editorial. *The Black Scholar: Journal of Black Studies and Research* 10, Nos. 8–9 (May/June 1979).

Ya Salaam, Kalamu. 1979. "Revolutionary Struggle/Revolutionary Love." *The Black Scholar: Journal of Black Studies and Research* 10, Nos. 8–9 (May/June).

Masculinities and Globalization

R. W. Connell

R. W. Connell is professor of education at the University of Sydney. He is past president of the Sociological Association of Australia and New Zealand and has written widely on subjects in education, sociology, and gender studies. His books include Gender and Power *(1987) and* Masculinities *(1995).*

Connell explains that current research, moving away from the broad generalizations of the 1970s and '80s, tends to focus on understanding masculinity in a specific "locality," a particular time, place, or circumstance—among members of a sports team, for example, or children of a clergyman. There is not one "masculinity" to explore but many, because different cultures and times define masculinity differently. To understand any of these "local masculinities," however, one must think globally, because "what happens in localities is affected by the history of whole countries, and what happens in countries is affected by the history of the world." Individuals are influenced by the events and conditions around the entire world, by wars, labor migrations, or global markets, for example, and "this fundamental fact [must] be built into our analysis of men and masculinities."

THE ETHNOGRAPHIC MOMENT IN STUDIES OF MASCULINITY

To understand local masculinities, we must think in global terms. But how? That is the problem pursued in this article. I will offer a framework for thinking about masculinities as a feature of world society and for thinking about men's gender practices in

Excerpted from R. W. Connell, "Masculinities and Globalization," Men and Masculinities I, no. 1 (July 1998), pp. 3–23. Copyright © 1998 Sage Publications, Inc. Reprinted by permission of Sage Publications, Inc.

Author's Note: *This article is revised from an address "Men in the World: Masculinities and Globalization" given at the Colloquium on "Masculinities in Southern Africa." University of Natal-Durban, July 1997.*

terms of the global structure and dynamics of gender. This is by no means to reject the ethnographic moment in masculinity research. It is, rather, to think how we can use its findings more adequately.

THE WORLD GENDER ORDER

Masculinities do not first exist and then come into contact with femininities; they are produced together, in the process that constitutes a gender order. Accordingly, to understand the masculinities on a world scale, we must first have a concept of the globalization of gender.

This is one of the most difficult points in current gender analysis because the very conception is counterintuitive. We are so accustomed to thinking of gender as the attribute of an individual, even as an unusually intimate attribute, that it requires a considerable wrench to think of gender on the vast scale of global society. Most relevant discussions, such as the literature on women and development, fudge the issue. They treat the entities that extend internationally (markets, corporations, intergovernmental programs, etc.) as ungendered in principle—but affecting unequally gendered recipients of aid in practice, because of bad policies. Such conceptions reproduce the familiar liberal-feminist view of the state as in principle gender-neutral, though empirically dominated by men.

But if we recognize that very large scale institutions such as the state are themselves gendered, in quite precise and specifiable ways (Connell 1990b), and if we recognize that international relations, international trade, and global markets are inherently an arena of gender formation and gender politics (Enloe 1990), then we can recognize the existence of a world gender order. The term can be defined as the structure of relationships that interconnect the gender regimes of institutions, and the gender orders of local society, on a world scale. That is, however, only a definition. The substantive questions remain: what is the shape of that structure, how tightly are its elements linked, how has it arisen historically, what is its trajectory into the future?

Current business and media talk about globalization pictures a homogenizing process sweeping across the world, driven by new technologies, producing vast unfettered global markets in which all participate on equal terms. This is a misleading image. As Hirst and Thompson (1996) show, the global economy is highly unequal and the current degree of homogenization is often overestimated. Multinational corporations based in the three major economic powers (the United States, European Union, and Japan) are the major economic actors worldwide.

The structure bears the marks of its history. Modern global society was historically produced, as Wallerstein (1974) argued, by the economic and political expansion of European states from the fifteenth century on and by the creation of colonial empires. It is in this process that we find the roots of the modern world gender order. Imperialism was, from the start, a gendered process. Its first phase, colonial conquest and settlement, was carried out by gender-segregated forces, and it resulted in massive disruption of indigenous gender orders. In its second phase, the stabilization of colonial societies, new gender divisions of labor were produced in plantation economies and colonial cities, while gender ideologies were linked with racial hierarchies and the cultural defense of empire. The third phase, marked by political decolonization, economic neocolonialism, and the current growth of world markets and structures of financial control, has seen gender divisions of labor remade on a massive scale in the "global factory" (Fuentes and Ehrenreich 1983), as well as the spread of gendered violence alongside Western military technology.

The result of this history is a partially integrated, highly unequal and turbulent world society, in which gender relations are partly but unevenly linked on a global scale. The unevenness becomes clear when different substructures of gender (Connell 1987; Walby 1990) are examined separately.

The division of labor. A characteristic feature of colonial and neocolonial economies was the restructuring of local production systems to produce a male wage worker–female domestic worker couple (Mies 1986). This need not produce a "housewife"

in the Western suburban sense, for instance, where the wage work involved migration to plantations or mines (Moodie 1994). But it has generally produced the identification of masculinity with the public realm and the money economy and of femininity with domesticity, which is a core feature of the modern European gender system (Holter 1997).

Power relations. The colonial and postcolonial world has tended to break down purdah systems of patriarchy in the name of modernization, if not of women's emancipation (Kandiyoti 1994). At the same time, the creation of a westernized public realm has seen the growth of large-scale organizations in the form of the state and corporations, which in the great majority of cases are culturally masculinized and controlled by men. In *comprador* capitalism, however, the power of local elites depends on their relations with the metropolitan powers, so the hegemonic masculinities of neocolonial societies are uneasily poised between local and global cultures.

Emotional relations. Both religious and cultural missionary activity has corroded indigenous homosexual and cross-gender practice, such as the native American *berdache* and the Chinese "passion of the cut sleeve" (Hinsch 1990). Recently developed Western models of romantic heterosexual love as the basis for marriage and of gay identity as the main alternative have now circulated globally—though as Altman (1996) observes, they do not simply displace indigenous models, but interact with them in extremely complex ways.

Symbolization. Mass media, especially electronic media, in most parts of the world follow North American and European models and relay a great deal of metropolitan content; gender imagery is an important part of what is circulated. A striking example is the reproduction of a North American imagery of femininity by Xuxa, the blonde television superstar in Brazil (Simpson 1993). In counterpoint, exotic gender imagery has been used in the marketing strategies of newly industrializing countries (e.g., airline advertising from Southeast Asia)—a tactic based on the long-standing combination of the exotic and the erotic in the colonial imagination (Jolly 1997).

Clearly, the world gender order is not simply an extension of a traditional European-American gender order. That gender order was changed by colonialism, and elements from other cultures now circulate globally. Yet in no sense do they mix on equal terms, to produce a United Colours of Benetton gender order. The culture and institutions of the North Atlantic countries are hegemonic within the emergent world system. This is crucial for understanding the kinds of masculinities produced within it.

THE REPOSITIONING OF MEN AND THE RECONSTITUTION OF MASCULINITIES

The positioning of men and the constitution of masculinities may be analyzed at any of the levels at which gender practice is configured: in relation to the body, in personal life, and in collective social practice. At each level, we need to consider how the processes of globalization influence configurations of gender.

Men's bodies are positioned in the gender order, and enter the gender process, through body-reflexive practices in which bodies are both objects and agents (Connell 1995)—including sexuality, violence, and labor. The conditions of such practice include where one is and who is available for interaction. So it is a fact of considerable importance for gender relations that the global social order distributes and redistributes bodies, through migration, and through political controls over movement and interaction.

The creation of empire was the original "elite migration," though in certain cases mass migration followed. Through settler colonialism, something close to the gender order of Western Europe was reassembled in North America and in Australasia. Labor migration within the colonial systems was a means by which gender practices were spread, but also a means by which they were reconstructed, since labor migration was itself a gendered process—as we have seen in relation to the gender division of labor. Migration from the colonized world to the metropole became (except for Japan) a mass process in the decades after World War II. There is also migration within the periphery, such as the creation of a very large immigrant labor force, mostly from other Muslim countries, in the oil-producing Gulf states.

These relocations of bodies create the possibility of hybridization in gender imagery, sexuality, and other forms of practice. The movement is not always toward synthesis, however, as the race/ethnic hierarchies of colonialism have been recreated in new contexts, including the politics of the metropole. Ethnic and racial conflict has been growing in importance in recent years, and as Klein (1997) and Tillner (1997) argue, this is a fruitful context for the production of masculinities oriented toward domination and violence. Even without the context of violence, there can be an intimate interweaving of the formation of masculinity with the formation of ethnic identity, as seen in the study of Poynting, Noble, and Tabar (1997) of Lebanese youths in the Anglo-dominant culture of Australia.

At the level of personal life as well as in relation to bodies, the making of masculinities is shaped by global forces. In some cases, the link is indirect, such as the working-class Australian men caught in a situation of structural unemployment (Connell 1995), which arises from Australia's changing position in the global economy. In other cases, the link is obvious, such as the executives of multinational corporations and the financial sector servicing international trade. The requirements of a career in international business set up strong pressures on domestic life: almost all multinational executives are men, and the assumption in business magazines and advertising directed toward them is that they will have dependent wives running their homes and bringing up their children.

At the level of collective practice, masculinities are reconstituted by the remaking of gender meanings and the reshaping of the institutional contexts of practice. Let us consider each in turn.

The growth of global mass media, especially electronic media, is an obvious "vector" for the globalization of gender. Popular entertainment circulates stereotyped gender images, deliberately made attractive for marketing purposes. The example of Xuxa in Brazil has already been mentioned. International news media are also controlled or strongly influenced from the metropole and circulate Western definitions of authoritative masculinity, criminality, desirable femininity, and so on. But there are limits to the power of global mass communications. Some local centers of mass entertainment differ from the Hollywood model, such as the

Indian popular film industry centered in Bombay. Further, media research emphasizes that audiences are highly selective in their reception of media messages, and we must allow for popular recognition of the fantasy in mass entertainment. Just as economic globalization can be exaggerated, the creation of a global culture is a more turbulent and uneven process than is often assumed (Featherstone 1995).

More important, I would argue, is a process that began long before electronic media existed, the export of institutions. Gendered institutions not only circulate definitions of masculinity (and femininity), as sex role theory notes. The functioning of gendered institutions, creating specific conditions for social practice, calls into existence specific patterns of practice. Thus, certain patterns of collective violence are embedded in the organization and culture of a Western-style army, which are different from the patterns of precolonial violence. Certain patterns of calculative egocentrism are embedded in the working of a stock market; certain patterns of rule following and domination are embedded in a bureaucracy.

Now, the colonial and postcolonial world saw the installation in the periphery, on a very large scale, of a range of institutions on the North Atlantic model: armies, states, bureaucracies, corporations, capital markets, labor markets, schools, law courts, transport systems. These are gendered institutions and their functioning has directly reconstituted masculinities in the periphery. This has not necessarily meant photocopies of European masculinities. Rather, pressures for change are set up that are inherent in the institutional form.

To the extent that particular institutions become dominant in world society, the patterns of masculinity embedded in them may become global standards. Masculine dress is an interesting indicator: almost every political leader in the world now wears the uniform of the Western business executive. The more common pattern, however, is not the complete displacement of local patterns but the articulation of the local gender order with the gender regime of global-model institutions. Case studies such as Hollway's (1994) account of bureaucracy in Tanzania illustrate the point; there, domestic patriarchy articulated with masculine authority in the state in ways that subverted the government's formal commitment to equal opportunity for women.

We should not expect the overall structure of gender relations on a world scale simply to mirror patterns known on the smaller scale. In the most vital of respects, there is continuity. The world gender order is unquestionably patriarchal, in the sense that it privileges men over women. There is a patriarchal dividend for men arising from unequal wages, unequal labor force participation, and a highly unequal structure of ownership, as well as cultural and sexual privileging. This has been extensively documented by feminist work on women's situation globally (e.g., Taylor 1985), though its implications for masculinity have mostly been ignored. The conditions thus exist for the production of a hegemonic masculinity on a world scale, that is to say, a dominant form of masculinity that embodies, organizes, and legitimates men's domination in the gender order as a whole.

The conditions of globalization, which involve the interaction of many local gender orders, certainly multiply the forms of masculinity in the global gender order. At the same time, the specific shape of globalization, concentrating economic and cultural power on an unprecedented scale, provides new resources for dominance by particular groups of men. This dominance may become institutionalized in a pattern of masculinity that becomes, to some degree, standardized across localities. I will call such patterns *globalizing masculinities,* and it is among them, rather than narrowly within the metropole, that we are likely to find candidates for hegemony in the world gender order.

MASCULINITY POLITICS ON A WORLD SCALE

Recognizing global society as an arena of masculinity formation allows us to pose new questions about masculinity politics. What social dynamics in the global arena give rise to masculinity politics, and what shape does global masculinity politics take?

The gradual creation of a world gender order has meant many local instabilities of gender. Gender instability is a familiar theme of poststructuralist theory, but this school of thought takes as a universal condition a situation that is historically specific. Instabilities range from the disruption of men's local cultural dominance as women move into the public realm and higher education, through the disruption of sexual identities that produced "queer" politics in the metropole, to the shifts in the urban intelligentsia that produced "the new sensitive man" and other images of gender change.

One response to such instabilities, on the part of groups whose power is challenged but still dominant, is to reaffirm *local* gender orthodoxies and hierarchies. A masculine fundamentalism is, accordingly, a common response in gender politics at present. A soft version, searching for an essential masculinity among myths and symbols, is offered by the mythopoetic men's movement in the United States and by the religious revivalists of the Promise Keepers (Messner 1997). A much harder version is found, in that country, in the right-wing militia movement brought to world attention by the Oklahoma City bombing (Gibson 1994), and in contemporary Afghanistan, if we can trust Western media reports, in the militant misogyny of the Taliban. It is no coincidence that in the two latter cases, hardline masculine fundamentalism goes together with a marked anti-internationalism. The world system—rightly enough—is seen as the source of pollution and disruption.

Not that the emerging global order is a hotbed of gender progressivism. Indeed, the neoliberal agenda for the reform of national and international economies involves closing down historic possibilities for gender reform. I have noted how it subverts the gender compromise represented by the metropolitan welfare state. It has also undermined the progressive-liberal agendas of sex role reform represented by affirmative action programs, anti-discrimination provisions, child care services, and the like. Right-wing parties and governments have been persistently cutting such programs, in the name of either individual liberties or global competitiveness. Through these means, the patriarchal dividend to men is defended or restored, without an *explicit* masculinity politics in the form of a mobilization of men.

Within the arenas of international relations, the international state, multinational corporations, and global markets, there is nevertheless a deployment of masculinities and a reasonably clear hegemony. The transnational business masculinity described above has had only one major competitor for hegemony in recent decades, the rigid, control-oriented masculinity of the military, and the military-style

bureaucratic dictatorships of Stalinism. With the collapse of Stalinism and the end of the cold war, Big Brother (Orwell's famous parody of this form of masculinity) is a fading threat, and the more flexible, calculative, egocentric masculinity of the fast capitalist entrepreneur holds the world stage.

We must, however, recall two important conclusions of the ethnographic moment in masculinity research: that different forms of masculinity exist together and that hegemony is constantly subject to challenge. These are possibilities in the global arena too. Transnational business masculinity is not completely homogeneous; variations of it are embedded in different parts of the world system, which may not be completely compatible. We may distinguish a Confucian variant, based in East Asia, with a stronger commitment to hierarchy and social consensus, from a secularized Christian variant, based in North America, with more hedonism and individualism and greater tolerance for social conflict. In certain arenas, there is already conflict between the business and political leaderships embodying these forms of masculinity: initially over human rights versus Asian values, and more recently over the extent of trade and investment liberalization.

If these are contenders for hegemony, there is also the possibility of opposition to hegemony. The global circulation of "gay" identity (Altman 1996) is an important indication that nonhegemonic masculinities may operate in global arenas, and may even find a certain political articulation, in this case around human rights and AIDS prevention.

Critiques of dominant forms of masculinity have been circulating for some time among heterosexual men, or among groups that are predominantly heterosexual. English-language readers will be most familiar with three Anglophone examples: the antisexist or profeminist men's groups in the United States, with their umbrella group NOMAS (National Organization for Men Against Sexism), which has been running since the early 1980s (Cohen 1991); the British new left men's groups, which produced the remarkable magazine *Achilles Heel* (Seidler 1991); and the Canadian White Ribbon campaign, the most successful mass mobilization of men opposing men's violence against women (Kaufman 1997).

There are parallel developments in other language communities. In Germany, for instance, feminists launched a discussion of the gender of men in the 1980s (Metz-Goeckel and Mueller 1986; Hagemann-White and Rerrich 1988), which has been followed by an educational (Kindler 1993), a popular-psychology (Hollstein 1992), and a critical (*Widersprueche* 1995; BauSteineMaenner 1996) debate among men about masculinities and how to change them. In Scandinavia, gender reform and debates about men (Oftung 1994) have led to the "father's quota" of parental leave in Norway (Gender Equality Ombudsman 1997) and to a particularly active network of masculinity researchers. In Japan, a media debate about men's liberation and some pioneering books about changing masculinities (Ito 1993; Nakamura 1994) have been followed by the foundation of a men's center and diversifying debates on change.

These developments at national or regional levels have very recently begun to link internationally. An International Association for Studies of Men has begun to link men involved in critical studies of masculinity. Certain international agencies, including the United Nations Educational, Scientific and Cultural Organization (UNESCO) (1997), have sponsored conferences to discuss the policy implications of new perspectives on masculinity.

Compared with the concentration of institutional power in multinational businesses, these initiatives remain small scale and dispersed. They are, nevertheless, important in potential. I have argued that the global gender order contains, necessarily, greater plurality of gender forms than any local gender order. This must reinforce the consciousness that masculinity is not one fixed form. The plurality of masculinities at least symbolically prefigures the unconstrained creativity of a democratic gender order.

CONCLUDING NOTE ON RESEARCH

If the perspective set out in this article holds well, it suggests a significant refocusing of the research agenda on masculinities. There is already a move beyond strictly local studies in the direction of comparative studies from different parts of the world (Cornwall and Lindisfarne 1994; UNESCO 1997). My argument suggests moving beyond this again, to study of the global arena itself, both as a venue for the social construction of masculinities and as a powerful force in local gender dynamics. Such a

move will require a reconsideration of research methods, since the life-history and ethnographic methods that have been central to recent work on masculinities give limited grasp on the very large scale institutions, markets, and mass communications that are in play on the world scale. Finally, the typical researcher of recent years—the individual scholar with a personal research project—will need to be supplemented by international teams, able to work together for significant periods, to investigate issues of the scale and complexity we must now address.

References

Altman, Dennis. 1996. Rupture or continuity? The internationalisation of gay identities. *Social Text* 48 (3): 77–94.

BauSteineMaenner, ed. 1996. *Kritische Maennerforschung* [Critical research on men]. Berlin: Argument.

Cohen, Jon. 1991. NOMAS: Challenging male supremacy. *Changing Men* (Winter/Spring): 45–46.

Connell, R. W. 1987. *Gender and power.* Cambridge, MA: Polity.

———. 1990b. The state, gender and sexual politics: Theory and appraisal. *Theory and Society* 19:507–44.

———. 1995. *Masculinities.* Cambridge, MA: Polity.

Cornwall, Andrea, and Nancy Lindisfarne, eds. 1994. *Dislocating masculinity: Comparative ethnographies.* London: Routledge.

Enloe, Cynthia. 1990. *Bananas, beaches and bases: Making feminist sense of international politics.* Berkeley: University of California Press.

Featherstone, Mike. 1995. *Undoing culture: Globalization, postmodernism and identity.* London: Sage.

Fuentes, Annette, and Barbara Ehrenreich. 1983. *Women in the global factory.* Boston: South End.

Gender Equality Ombudsman. 1997. *The father's quota.* Information sheet on parental leave entitlements, Oslo.

Gibson, J. William. 1994. *Warrior dreams: Paramilitary culture in post-Vietnam America.* New York: Hill and Wang.

Hagemann-White, Carol, and Maria S. Rerrich, eds. 1988. *FrauenMaennerBilder* (Women, Imaging, Men). Bielefeld: AJZ-Verlag.

Hinsch, Bret. 1990. *Passions of the cut sleeve: The male homosexual tradition in China.* Berkeley: University of California Press.

Hirst, Paul, and Grahame Thompson. 1996. *Globalization in question: The international economy and the possibilities of governance.* Cambridge, MA: Polity.

Hollstein, Walter. 1992. *Machen Sie Platz, mein Herr! Teilen statt Herrschen* [Sharing instead of dominating]. Hamburg: Rowohlt.

Hollway, Wendy. 1994. Separation, integration and difference: Contradictions in a gender regime. In *Power/gender: Social relations in theory and practice,* edited by H. Lorraine Radtke and Henderikus Stam, 247–69. London: Sage.

Holter, Oystein Gullvag. 1997. Gender, patriarchy and capitalism: A social forms analysis. Ph.D. diss., University of Oslo, Faculty of Social Science.

Ito Kimio. 1993. *Otokorashisa-no-yukue* [Directions for masculinities]. Tokyo: Shinyo-sha.

Jolly, Margaret. 1997. From point Venus to Bali Ha'i: Eroticism and exoticism in representations of the Pacific. In *Sites of desire, economies of pleasure: Sexualities in Asia and the Pacific,* edited by Lenore Manderson and Margaret Jolly, 99–122. Chicago: University of Chicago Press.

Kandiyoti, Deniz. 1994. The paradoxes of masculinity: Some thoughts on segregated societies. In *Dislocating masculinity: Comparative ethnographies,* edited by Andrea Cornwall and Nancy Lindisfarne, 197–213. London: Routledge.

Kaufman, Michael. 1997. Working with men and boys to challenge sexism and end men's violence. Paper presented at UNESCO expert group meeting on Male Roles and Masculinities in the Perspective of a Culture of Peace, September, Oslo.

Kindler, Heinz. 1993. *Maske(r)ade: Jungen- und Maennerarbeit fuer die Praxis* [Work with youth and men]. Neuling: Schwaebisch Gmuend und Tuebingen.

Klein, Uta. 1997. Our best boys: The making of masculinity in Israeli society. Paper presented at UNESCO expert group meeting on Male Roles and Masculinities in the Perspectives of a Culture of Peace, September, Oslo.

Messner, Michael A. 1997. *The politics of masculinities: Men in movements.* Thousand Oaks, CA: Sage.

Metz-Goeckel, Sigrid, and Ursula Mueller. 1986. *Der Mann: Die Brigitte-Studie* [The male]. Beltz: Weinheim & Basel.

Mies, Maria. 1986. *Patriarchy and accumulation on a world scale: Women in the international division of labour.* London: Zed.

Moodie, T. Dunbar. 1994. *Going for gold: Men, mines, and migration.* Johannesburg: Witwatersrand University Press.

Nakamura Akira. 1994. *Watashi-no Danseigaku* [My men's studies]. Tokyo: Kindaibugei-sha.

Oftung, Knut, ed. 1994. *Menns bilder og bilder av menn* [Images of men]. Oslo: Likestillingsradet.

Poynting, S., G. Noble, and P. Tabar. 1997. "Intersections" of masculinity and ethnicity: A study of male Lebanese immigrant youth in Western Sydney. Paper presented at the conference Masculinities: Renegotiating Genders, June, University of Wollongong, Australia.

Seidler, Victor J. 1991. *Achilles heel reader: Men, sexual politics and socialism.* London: Routledge.

Simpson, Amelia. 1993. *Xuxa: The mega-marketing of gender, race and modernity.* Philadelphia: Temple University Press.

Taylor, Debbie. 1985. Women: An analysis. In *Women: A world report,* 1–98. London: Methuen.

Tillner, Georg. 1997. Masculinity and xenophobia. Paper presented at UNESCO meeting on Male Roles and Masculinities in the Perspective of a Culture of Peace, September, Oslo.

United Nations Educational, Scientific and Cultural Organization (UNESCO). 1997. *Male roles and masculinities in the perspective of a culture of peace: Report of expert group meeting, Oslo, 24–28 September 1997.* Paris: Women and a Culture of Peace Programme, Culture of Peace Unit, UNESCO.

Walby, Sylvia. 1990. *Theorizing patriarchy.* Oxford, U.K.: Blackwell.

Wallerstein, Immanuel. 1974: *The modern world-system: Capitalist agriculture and the origins of the European world-economy in the sixteenth century.* New York: Academic Press.

Widersprueche, 1995. Special issue: Maennlichkeiten. Vol. 56/57.

Bob Connell is professor of education at the University of Sydney and was formerly professor of sociology at the University of California, Santa Cruz, and professor of sociology at Macquarie University. He received his B.A. Hons from the University of Melbourne and his Ph.D. from the University of Sydney. He is author or coauthor of fifteen books, including Class Structure in Australian History, Making the Difference, Gender and Power, *and* Schools and Social Justice. *He is past president of the Sociological Association of Australia and New Zealand, and a contributor to research journals in sociology, education, political science, and gender studies. His most recent book,* Masculinities, *was published on three continents and is being translated into Italian, German, Japanese, and Swedish.*

CHAPTER THREE

The Portrayal of Women in Patriarchy: Ideals, Stereotypes, and Roles

THE "NAMING" OF WOMEN

It is necessary to grasp the fundamental fact that women have had the power of naming stolen from us. We have not been free to use our own power to name ourselves, the world, or God. The old naming was not the product of dialogue—a fact inadvertently admitted in the Genesis story of Adam's naming the animals and the women. Women are now realizing that the universal imposing of names by men has been false because partial. That is, inadequate words have been taken as adequate.

To exist humanly is to name the self, the world, and God.

—MARY DALY[1]

In a society where men have controlled the conceptual arena and have determined social values as well as the structure of institutions, it is not surprising that women should have lost the power of *naming,* of explaining and defining for ourselves the realities of our own experience, including ourselves. In this context, to say that men, not women, are responsible for the naming of women is to say that masculine interests, values, perspectives, and activities have created what postmodern theorists would call the *social construction* of woman. In a patriarchal culture, men define (construct, explain, analyze, describe) what "the female" is, just as they define nearly everything else. The problem is not only that men perceive women from this masculine point of view but also, given the nature of socialization, that all members of society—including women—may perceive the female from the prevailing masculine perspective.

The Male Identification of Women

Feminists point out that women—sometimes directly, often indirectly—have had considerable impact on the development of civilization.[2] In primitive times, women were very likely the inventors of pottery, food preservation, and other "domestic" technology; hence, they probably also originated early forms of social organization.

As those who care for the young, women have always done much to form the individual attitudes and values within the community, and our personal influence on one another and on men has long been recognized (although often maligned).

But informal networks and personal power are not political power, and the influence that women do wield in patriarchy is frequently deflected and counterbalanced—often distorted—by the subordinate and peripheral place we are assigned in society. The attitudes and values we teach, the influences we mean to effect are often alien to us, originating not in our own perspectives but in worldviews we inherit and internalize. We learn our roles and their attendant behaviors from mothers who themselves were bent to the yoke as we are meant to be. Although it varies in intensity and range, men's authority to control women's values, beliefs, and behaviors is a constant in almost every society. In the West, we read books, manuals, and bibles written mainly by men for male interests. We are exhorted and chastised by male priests. We learn about and care for our bodies through male physicians, institutions, and medical societies. We attend male-dominated schools and universities. We model ourselves after images presented in media controlled almost entirely by men, who publish newspapers and magazines, manage advertising agencies, produce and direct films, and determine fashion trends in the great couture houses of Europe. Finally, through societally cultivated dependence, we place ourselves in the position of bartering our right to self-definition for "protection" or "love."

The naming of women has been effected by men primarily through control of the social institutions that determine behavior and attitudes. As social beings subject to those institutions, we commonly (although not without exception) tend to adopt the images wrought by that naming, often unaware that those ideals are not of our own creation or to our benefit. Whether we may live them concretely or not—whether they are economically or socially within our reach or not, whether they are mandated for our class or race or sexual identity or what have you, or instead are prohibited—the pictures of perfect femininity, the dominant female ideal, drawn in the public consciousness by a variety of media dance in our heads and lead us toward conformity. In America, from our first breath—from our entry into a world enamored of pink and white ruffles; of dolls and docility; of behaving like a lady; of loving strokes for submission, quiet, and gentility; of cut-out dolls in wedding gowns and Barbie dolls that develop oversized breasts; of cheering on the sidelines; of applause for being picked; of frowns for "tomboy" behavior, assertiveness, intelligence, and independence—from that earliest time before we can even question, we absorb an environment that teaches us a vision of femininity so pervasive and complete that it appears real; it appears to be our own.

> *Being good at what was expected of me was one of my earliest projects. . . . Girls were different from boys, and the expression of that difference seemed mine to make clear. Did my loving, anxious mother, who dressed me in white organdy pinafores and Mary Janes and who cried hot tears when I got them dirty, give me my first instruction? Of course. Did my doting aunts and uncles with their gifts of pretty dolls and miniature tea sets add to my education? Of course. But even without the appropriate toys and clothes, lessons in the art of being feminine lay all around me, and I absorbed them all: the fairy tales that were read to me at night, the brightly colored advertisements I pored over in magazines before I learned to decipher the words, the movies I saw, the comic books I hoarded, the radio soap operas I happily followed whenever I had to stay in bed with a cold. I loved being a little girl, or rather I loved being a fairy princess, for that was who I thought I was.*

—SUSAN BROWNMILLER[3]

Here is a vision designed for girls of a privileged class, girls whose families can afford "dress-up" clothes, white organdy pinafores and Mary Janes, who are given pretty dolls and tea sets, who are destined to grow up and go to real teas and wear the adult equivalent of Mary Janes. Nonetheless, the fantasy pervades even the lives of those less privileged by birth or caste, who are not and never will be fairy princesses, and the lessons train and control no less by the dream being out of reach.

By the time we are old enough, wise enough, and angry enough to discard the visions, the seed planted in infancy and constantly tended has so taken root, become so integral a part of us, that to reject it has almost the force of rejecting ourselves.

Such is the meaning of a saying coined in the 1970s that it is easier to fight an external enemy than one who has "outposts in your head."[4] High-heeled shoes and tight brassieres hurt our bodies and limit our movement, but most women wear them. The fashion for skinniness has become so extreme that it endangers women's health and haunts our daily lives with guilt and frustration, but few women question or resist it. If women acted only for themselves or other women, would they conform to such expectations? Whether we are expected to cover our faces with veils or makeup, whether the rule is enforced by a whip or a media image that embeds itself inside our minds, it is not created by or for women's interests.

The alien definition of women, even more extreme than it first appears, goes beyond merely the producing and imposing of foreign images, beyond women's accepting these images as our own; it proceeds all the way to our accepting the status of not only less-than-standard humanity but of less-than-standard *being,* of "otherness." Otherness, in existentialist terms, is a social-moral as well as a personal-psychological assignment of women to the role of a less than primary, less than completely worthy human being. Otherness defines women as the "other half" of humanity, the "distaff," the half that "helps," that *assists* in the work of society, whether by staying out of the way, or by relieving the primary beings (men) of chores that would impede their work, or even by carrying *their* offspring in our bodies for them so they don't have to (as St. Thomas argued in his selection at the end of this chapter). Otherness defines woman as satellite, adjunct, alter to man, but not as an end in herself. It accounts for women being willing to accept a servant consciousness, such as the one presented below by Darlene Wilkinson (described as "the wife of Bruce H. Wilkinson, founder and president of Walk Thru the Bible Ministries" in a *1996* sort of companion book to *Seven Promises of a Promise Keeper* described in Chapter 2). Pointing out that in the Genesis story of the Old Testament, God creates woman as a "helper for man," not as an equal, she concludes that the divine intention is for man to be a "leader" and woman a "helper," her life lived "in service" to her husband. Here are some "affirmations" worthy of a perfect helper, that is, a perfect wife: "I am the perfect helper for my husband, for I

share his hopes and dreams and bear his hurts and frustrations along with him. . . . I encourage him in strategic moments. . . . I put his sexual and emotional needs ahead of my own. . . . I love him unconditionally."[5] Finally, she provides an acrostic to help us remember:

H   *Have dinner ready when he gets home.*
E   *Encourage him to talk about his life's goals.*
L   *Listen to him with my undivided attention.*
P   *Pray for him every day.*
E   *Embrace his ideas enthusiastically.*
R   *Respect him by how I talk to him and about him before others.*[6]

What makes these injunctions so destructive is that there are no similar directives for the perfect husband. He is not enjoined to adopt her ideas enthusiastically or put her needs ahead of his. He is not expected to be a servant to her, a "helper," perfect or otherwise. After all, he is the "leader." This is not meant to be a two-way street. It is one way, and that way is the man's. Rather convenient for the husband, one might think. We must wonder on what grounds we are to believe that we were ordained to be servants.

Although there are many versions—giving, sacrificing wife, mother, nurse, teacher, lover, and others—the patriarchal role for women is to *care for* before being *cared for,* and we are not only to submit to this role but submit graciously; we are to revel in it, as Wilkinson describes. Our role is to keep to the background rather than foreground, to yield to man's will, which is valued in itself directly *for* the world, whereas woman is only *in* the world. It accounts for women in some cultures being bought and sold as wives or concubines, like so much cattle. It accounts for women being kept in seclusion in certain societies so that they cannot be seen by any men other than their "protectors." It accounts for families—here and elsewhere, mothers included—hoping for sons and deeming daughters less valuable, killing them in some cases. In America it accounts for women being told not to take jobs away from men, as if the jobs were somehow the cosmically ordained property of men.

The term *otherness* was coined by French existentialist Simone de Beauvoir (1908–1986), one of the foremothers of the second wave. In 1949, in *The Second Sex* (*Le Deuxieme Sexe*), Beauvoir wrote:

It amounts to this: just as for the ancients there was an absolute vertical with reference to which the oblique was defined, so there is an absolute human type, the masculine. . . . "The female is a female by virtue of a certain lack *of qualities," said Aristotle; "we should regard the female nature as afflicted with a natural defectiveness." And St. Thomas for his part pronounced woman to be an "imperfect man," an "incidental" being. . . .*

Thus humanity is male and man defines woman not in herself but as relative to him; she is not regarded as an autonomous being. . . . And she is simply what man decrees; thus she is called "the sex," by which is meant that she appears essentially to the male as a sexual being. For him she is sex—absolute sex, no less. She is defined and differentiated with reference to man and not he with reference to her; she is the incidental, the inessential as opposed to the essential. He is the Subject, he is the Absolute—she is the Other.[7]

Woman Identification Versus Male Identification: The Alternatives

The woman created in and by the male perspective, subject to masculine interests, is called by the women's movement the *male-identified woman.* Her behavior and interests are identified (defined) by patriarchy, and she defines herself according to patriarchal values. The alternative, the woman-identified woman, is surely a feminist vision. She is a person who indeed understands herself to be subject (self), not object (other); she respects both her womanhood and her humanity; she takes her direction and definition from values that are her own, born of her own self-perceived qualities and goals as well as those of other women; she contributes to society that which she takes to be meaningful and does so in her own way. She defines herself and is defined by a community of women.

Such a woman is only now evolving. In a patriarchal environment, hostile as it is to assertive, self-defined women, the processes of woman identification and of growth toward that new identity are perplexing and arduous. The new images that feminists are laboring to draw are necessarily influenced by the struggle in which we are engaged.

What we shall see, then, in this chapter and the next, is a contest of visions: on the one hand, the male-identified ideals and masculinist stereotypes; on the other, feminist responses and affirmations. The pictures of womanhood that are created by women defining women are intricately interwoven by circumstance, race, class, nationality, religion, sexuality, age, and a host of other factors, yet they are so different from masculinist ideals as to entail two separate realities; patriarchal perspective and feminist consciousness.

IDEALS AND IMAGES: THE MASCULINIST DEFINITION

It is an extraordinary fact of women's lives that for centuries, across space and time and from culture to culture, women have been consistently treated with ambivalence, misogyny, and subordination.[8] These constant themes in the naming of women by patriarchal societies may find different expressions and may vary in intensity and effect, but they recur almost universally.

Although there are many hypotheses, ranging from the scientific to the religious and from the ridiculous to the not quite adequate, the origins and causes of women's subordination have never been explained. Certain things are clear, however. The masculinist images of women and the roles that these images support are socially constructed to create circumstances that privilege men in many ways. The patriarchal definitions of femininity provide the masculinist with excellent rationales for using women as they do as well as for granting themselves potent advantages. The female role of helpmeet is said to follow "naturally" from women's nature; it provides men with tremendous entitlement, power, and pleasure. Women are expected to be delighted to serve men: physically, taking care of their homes, property, children, clothing, or persons; economically, doing countless jobs for which women are ill paid or not paid at all; sexually, as wives, mistresses, or prostitutes; and reproductively, assuring men of paternity through female chastity. Because in patriarchal society women are socialized to volunteer for "women's work" (work that men do not wish to do), privileged men are freed to spend their time on socially valued activities for which they receive all kinds of material and psychological rewards. From this use of women, men accrue extra time, energy, and power.

The image of woman as man's complement offers an extremely effective support mechanism for the masculinist self-image: The softer, weaker, and more dependent the woman is, the stronger and more powerful the man appears; the more a servant the woman, the more a master the man. And the more the woman withdraws into home and gentility, the more the arenas of government and industry are left to the iron grasp of warriors and warrior values.

The misogynist picture of women as inferior—not quite human, incompetent, petty, evil, and lacking in responsibility and moral aptitude—stands as clear justification to the masculinist for our subordination and suffering. After all, because we cause all the trouble in the world and instigate misfortune and disaster (Eve taking the apple, Pandora opening the box), it is natural and fitting that we should be punished for our deeds and controlled, lest we do further harm.

> *in sorrow thou shalt bring forth children; and thy desire shall be to thy husband, and he shall rule over thee.*
>
> —Genesis 3:16

Patriarchal society has been well served indeed by these masculinist ideas; it behooves us to understand them. However, because they are "mystified" (covered over, their true nature hidden by a veil of misleading language and images), this is no easy task. The origins of these images cannot be traced definitively, but feminists have proposed cogent speculations that help to clarify them.

Ambivalence: An Undercurrent

The images of women in our culture are fraught with contradiction: Woman is the sublime, the perfect, the beautiful; she is the awful, the stupid, the contemptible. She is the mother of God as well as the traitor of the garden. She is the tender young creature man marries and protects as well as the treacherous, manipulative sneak who tricks him into a union he never sought. Keeper of virtue, she is yet a base and petty creature, incapable of rational moral judgment, cosmically wise, concretely stupid. Explicitly or implicitly, women are represented as having dual natures, of being all that is desirable, fascinating, and wonderful yet also being extremely destructive and dangerous. Ambivalence toward a whole range of real and alleged female powers (birth, menstruation, seduction, intuition) expresses itself in a subliminal patriarchal belief that women have a great deal of "big magic," very much worth having but destined to go awry if not controlled and subdued.

No doubt, there are many sources for such attitudes, but, feminists argue, we must understand them all within this important context: In patriarchy, images of women—like other conceptualizations—have been male-created. The stereotypes of women, contradictory and conflicting, are male projections. As such, we must understand them as outward expressions of masculine attitudes. The dichotomy in the representation of women, therefore, is a strong indication of extreme ambivalence on the part of men.

In literature, psychology, philosophy, or religion, one comes face-to-face, again and again, with the ambivalence men feel toward women. They seek her, the eternal feminine. They want and desire her, but oh so much the worse for them! Men are exhorted by the stronger and more stoic among them to beware the lures and entrapments of females. In the first century C.E., Paul proclaimed the dangers of sin, sex, and uncontrolled women (all related). Centuries later, in language altered for "science" yet reminiscent of primitive mythology—toothed vaginas and grasping spiders—Freud advised the same caution.

Students of many disciplines try to account for the origin of these attitudes. Certain sociologists, for example, have pointed out that ambivalence is typical of feelings experienced by any dominant group toward those it colonizes or exploits—a mixture of need and contempt, guilt, anger, and fear.

Many anthropologists, tracing a long history of male fear of women, place great emphasis on attitudes toward female regenerative powers and organs, so magical, so powerfully important and stirring, yet so utterly female, and both mysterious and alien to men. Anthropologists such as H. R. Hays, Wolfgang Lederer, and Joseph Campbell point to the frequency of myths crediting the *first* human birth to a man (like Adam). They point to menstrual taboos and blood magic, and they postulate that men feel strong envy for a power they themselves can never have.

Psychologists, from classical times to the present, have pointed to male fears surrounding the sex act: fear of impotence, detumescence, vaginal containment, and other, more abstract matters, such as absorption by the partner, possession, or even castration. That the act of intercourse[9] is simultaneously perceived as a most desirable and also a fearsome or dangerous experience may account for male ambivalence, in the view of many psychologists.[10]

That all these factors contribute to ambivalence is likely the case, yet like many other feminists, I am more apt to seek the major source of masculinist attitudes toward women or womanhood in the intricate, primal dimensions of men's own gender identity, in the dynamics of the martial ideal.

Masculinity as defined in patriarchy, you remember, requires men to repudiate in themselves most of the affective components of human experience: It is imprudent to feel. It is very difficult, however, not to acknowledge feeling, and as a result at least two major facets of life are thrown into severe conflict for men: sex and an entire configuration of experience we may call *the tender.* These conflicts have direct bearing on male attitudes toward women.

Although it is surely true that the sex act is surrounded with certain fears and danger, I contend that it is not intercourse itself that provides the greatest conflict but rather what sex represents. It is not the mechanical act of sex that has usually been presented as the great source of "sin" but rather the *enjoyment* of the act, the surrender to sex; it is sensuality and its attendant implications—fun, caprice, relaxation, nonstriving. Whether the language be religious (Paul warning against sin and damnation) or psychological (Freud fretting about the id and sublimation), sensuality and pleasure have been consistently presented as the foe of duty, the primary value of the martial ideal. The message is always the same: A man has a choice between duty (manhood) and indulgence (sensuality, pleasure, and self). If he chooses the former, he gains pride, identity, praise, and worthiness; if he chooses the latter, all he may expect is dissipation and disgrace.

For the masculinist, *woman* and *sex* are nearly synonymous terms. The rejection of sensuality necessitates, then, a rejection of the object and instigator of sensuality: woman. If sex evokes mixed feelings—of approach and avoidance—most certainly woman must evoke the same feelings.

But the problem does not end here. The ambivalence goes further. Besides sensuality and pleasure, the warrior must also expunge from his character the parts of himself that either express vulnerability or render him vulnerable: fear, sensitivity, need, desire, grief, hurt, trust, and all the other traits, qualities, and feelings that are part of the tender. Because the tender is not allowable in men but is impossible to live without, patriarchy splits this element off from men and instead invests it in women, where men may enjoy it in greater safety. Yet even in this externalized form, the tender remains a danger that each man must guard against because he knows—though he would probably deny it—how easily he might yield to it, how much he wishes to yield.

In this light, we can understand masculinist contempt for women's "emotionalism" as a rejection of emotions within; ridicule of female timidity as flight from timidity within; hatred of the woman without as of the woman within. The ambivalence, then, that men may feel toward women is something we can understand, at least in part, as a displaced expression of an inner conflict so frustrating and frightening that it cannot be contained but must instead be projected outward, onto women.

That we should be the recipients of all these negative feelings is not surprising; it is common for minorities or out-groups to serve as scapegoats for the masters. But that we should function as the object of this particular displaced ambivalence is even more to be expected: Patriarchy decrees that we are, after all, the repository of the entire configuration the male is required to excise.

Martial man has ordained woman as the carrier of all he dare not entertain in himself—and he hates her for it. It is as if he has said to woman: "Woman—be tenderness, be nurture, be vulnerability, be laughter, play, and fun for me, because I cannot be these things myself"; but then "You are all the things the great Mars has deemed evil and dangerous; and therefore you are evil and dangerous."

Misogyny: The Expression

Attitude is easily converted into judgment: *Woman is desirable* is quickly transformed into *woman is good; woman is frightening* readily becomes *woman is bad.*

Misogyny—the hatred or distrust of women—is an integral part of masculinism and patriarchy. Veiled by chivalry or a mythic masking of female roles (called *mystification* in the women's movement), it is nonetheless a potent force in the relations of men and women—and readily apparent should the veil or mask be rent even slightly. It is misogyny that underlies not only "honor" killings, beatings, rape, invective, and abuse but also beauty contests, work segregation, menstrual taboos, mother-in-law jokes, "old bag" themes, "Hooters" restaurants, patronizing etiquette, and current sexual mores.

Misogyny includes the beliefs that women are stupid, petty, manipulative, dishonest, silly, gossipy, irrational, incompetent, undependable, narcissistic, castrating, dirty, overemotional, unable to make altruistic or moral judgments, oversexed, undersexed, and a host of other ugly things. Such beliefs culminate in attitudes that demean our bodies, our abilities, our characters, and our efforts, and so imply that we must be controlled, dominated, subdued, abused, and used, not only for male benefit but for our own. St. Jerome, Freud, the Rolling Stones, and numerous others have all agreed that when it comes to punishment, women need it and love it.

The image of woman as victim is nowhere more acutely portrayed than in *Story of O,*[11] originally published in France and described by reviewers variously as "pornographic," "political,"[12] or "mystical."[13] The plot is simple: O is a young woman subjected by her lover and his comrades to continual sadosexual torture and humiliation unto death, all of which (vividly portrayed in "erotic" images) both O and her lover willingly, consciously, even joyfully, accept as proof of O's love as well as punishment for her "wantonness" (any little bits of self-assertion). During the course of the book, O is transformed from an individual to a totally degraded, totally pliant, totally selfless (in the worst sense) creature—a sexual garbage pail, for "love."

Many feminists have pointed out that what is important about the book is not the plot but the theme, as it is interpreted and responded to by its commentators. Jean Paulhan, in a prefacing essay significantly titled "Happiness in Slavery," describes the "mystical" theme in these familiar terms:

At last a woman who admits it![14] *Who admits what? Something that women have always refused till now to admit (and today more than ever before). Something that men have always reproached them with: That they never cease obeying their nature, the call of their blood, that everything in them, even their minds, is sex. That they have constantly to be nourished, constantly washed and made up, constantly beaten. That all they need is a good master, one who is not too lax or kind: for the moment we make any show of tenderness they draw upon it, turning all the zest, joy, and character at their command to make others love them. In short, that we must, when we go to see them, take a whip along.*[15]

Paulhan praises woman's uniqueness, her greater "understanding" born of childlikeness, her more primitive decency, requiring "nothing less than hands tied behind the back . . . the knees spread apart and bodies spread-eagled, than sweat and tears."[16] The other "official" commentator, Mandiargues, proposes that the theme is "the tragic flowering of a woman."[17]

It is important that we look at such talk. It is not simply an aberration but rather the expression of a vital and common principle of masculinism: that woman is most adored, most exquisite, most revered when she is sufficiently selfless to be martyred. In O, self-effacement that would be repulsive in men, inimical to all the classical values of human excellence, is deemed mystically beautiful, fulfilling, and sacrificial. *The Sacred Principle of Victimization,* Andrea Dworkin's term,[18] means that women are more conveniently exploitable and indeed more sexually exciting when they are stripped not only of clothing but also of power, strength, assertiveness, and sense of self. Should one doubt the relevance of such an attitude for us today, consider how titillating many men find the newspaper stories of rape, the torture-murders of slasher movies, the bent-over beauties in girlie magazines and porno films, the tough sex of current movies and television series, and increasingly the abusive images in rock lyrics and videos. Because women are bad, they must be controlled. They must be punished. Misogyny earns women torture of one kind or another.[19]

STEREOTYPES: GOOD WOMEN AND BAD

The ultimate ambivalence finally expresses itself in the ultimate bifurcation into good women and bad.

The judgments of good and bad, like the images themselves, are masculinist projections, resting not only on the extent to which any woman meets the specifications of her role requirements or adheres to the standards set for her but also on a particular man's needs and his attitudes toward that role configuration at some moment in time. That is, an image may be judged good at one time and bad at another, depending on its serviceability to those making the judgment. As the image is judged, so is the woman expressing that image. Meeting the complex imperatives of femininity is a tenuous affair at best.

All male-identified ideals of women rest on one basic presupposition: that women are and ought to be completely defined and understood within our biological capacities, sexual or reproductive. These capacities determine our "place" in the world, and we are only "good," one way or another, when we are (willingly or unwillingly) in that place. Should we instead stray—particularly through our own assertiveness but even by accident—then we are bad women and can be redeemed only if we are returned to our proper sphere.

In patriarchy, for women, "anatomy is destiny," and our physical capacities determine for us two separate and often conflicting roles: that of procreator-mother and that of sexual partner.[20] The "good" woman, then, is she who serves, each in a different sense: either in the capacity of excellent mother or of excellent mistress or both.

Mother: The Primary Ideal

Named for Mary, mother of Jesus, the Marian image, Mother, nurture incarnate, is patriarchy's most positive image for women. Although the term *Marian* (*marianismo* in Hispanic cultures) is decidedly Western, the ideal it refers to is ubiquitous, ancient, appearing in non-Western cultures as well. This lady is the complement of male power—she is tenderness, fragility, love, charity, loyalty, submission, and sacrifice. Carrier of man's seed, she is the essence of purity, totally absorbed in the activities and qualities of caring. Serene and satisfied within her role, placing the needs of her charges above her own, she busies herself with feeding them, watching over them, making them happy. Intuitive, cosmically linked with lunar cycles, she

has special powers and therefore little need for rationality.

Just as in sexual physiology the female principle is one of receiving, keeping and nourishing—woman's specific form of creativeness, that of motherhood, is tied up with the life of nature, with a non-reflective bios. . . . Indeed, the four-week cycle of ovulation, the rhythmically alternating tides of fertility . . . the nine months of gestation . . . ties woman deeply to the life of nature, to the pulse beat of the cosmos.[21]

I think, perhaps, that insofar as insight—the seeing into, the throwing of light into darkness, the intellectual illumination—aims at greater self-awareness and a more conscious functioning, it belongs into the mode or sphere of male development. The eternal feminine, static, perfect in itself, does not and need not develop. What any given woman does not know about it, insight therapy cannot ever teach her. Insight therapy, even in women, can only address itself to the masculine aspect. A given woman, through insight, can become more aware and more conscious, but not more feminine—although the balance of male and female within her may at times be shifted through insight which enables her to place less stress on male modes of functioning; in that case a covered-up femininity may emerge: but only as much of it as was there in the first place. One is a woman, one learns to be a man. Therapeutic theories stressing insight deal primarily with men because only men—and the masculine aspects of women—can be approached by and can utilize insight.[22]

Womanhood, it would seem then, is closer to nature (or the divine) than manhood, more compelling as well as more disastrous if denied. One might wonder (and feminists do) how anything so "natural" and "instinctive" *could* be denied. Yet according to theory, it sometimes is, and then not only do women themselves suffer, but the whole world goes topsy-turvy; it is askew, even in danger. Men lose their manhood, children become psychotic, society dissolves, and the natural order is disturbed!

In the language of the women's movement, the Marian role is *mystified*, covered over with a whole set of myths, fantasies, and images that hide many realities of the role and the persons who live it.

Playmate: The Illicit Ideal

Mother is the *official* good woman of the Western world. But another kind of "good" woman exists, good in a different sense, good in an elbow-in-the-ribs or slightly déclassé kind of way—a sexy, naughty, fun-loving lady: the Playmate.

The Marian image, the classic model of femininity in the West, born out of the fear and loathing of sex and sensuality rampant in the early Christian church, is pointedly asexual: pure, chaste, and virginal, despite marriage, wifehood, and childbirth. The good woman in this image, the Mother, is an asexual or even antisexual ideal, too pure for carnality. Sex is beneath her. She is patient, enduring, dutiful, submissive, and nurturing, *and she doesn't play around*. She's not supposed to, and she doesn't want to, not even with her husband. Hence her converse, the Playmate.

For the Playmate, playing around is a raison d'être. She is built "to take it" and to give it. You can tell by the seductive, compliant look in her eyes, the parted lips, the knowing smile, the receptive, open posture of her opulent young body. But the Playmate is no ordinary whore. She is interesting (bright enough to be companionable but not so bright as to be uncooperative or threatening). She is independent (able to take care of herself but needful enough to succumb to male power). She is choosy (nobody wants something that anyone can have). She is even a little aggressive, a little dangerous—enough to make her a worthy trophy.

"There are two kinds of girls," a saying goes, "the kind you bring home to Mother and the kind you bring home to Father." To each of these types is attached a distinct set of male expectations and responses. The Playmate is for playing, for fun, not for seriousness and heavy obligation. She has waived her claims to adulation from afar. She isn't chaste, so one need not hide "baser" motivations and appetites. Because she's not timid or naive, one needn't be solicitous or protective. She's worldly wise—no need for protocol, courtship, and protestations of love. Having opted out of "purity" and the category of the primary ideal, she has abandoned the status and prerogatives of the "official" good woman. Mother and Playmate, lady and tramp, Mary and Eve, the dichotomy—familiar in novels, movies, and sermons—creates tension that puts women in a bind.

The Wife

It should be obvious by now that the two female ideals, perfect mother and perfect mistress, are incompatible. No one can be chaste, submissive, timid, needful, innocent, loyal, tender, and serene and *at the same time* sexually wise, perky, naughty, independent, and so on. Yet that is exactly the position into which American patriarchy places women, for to be both Mary/Mother and Playmate is the prescribed role and image of the dominant ideal—girlfriend, roommate, date, or wife. Like the "hell of a woman" in a popular song lyric, she is supposed to be all things to her hell of a man: not just *act* all things, but *be* them: "woman, baby, witch, lady." It's a difficult game, for even if she wins, she loses—her identity, her self-concept, her sense of autonomy, cohesion, and direction. It is a schizophrenic setup.

THE DICHOTOMY DICHOTOMIZES: THE MISOGYNIST FLIP

All that effort, and as often as not, it doesn't even work. Any of us may choose between a life modeled on Mary or a life modeled on Playmate, settling for the rewards of either role. We may even manage to negotiate the tricks and turns of playing both, but that still cannot guarantee us undying love.

Circumstances arise over which none have control and in which Mary, the Playmate, or even Helluvawoman may become a pain in the neck, an object of contempt, a creature to be avoided. Reflected visions, after all, ultimately depend on the minds of those who reflect. And the extent to which any of these roles is prized (and consequently the woman playing it praised) depends on how well it serves the function for which it was created and how long that function endures. Mary is desirable to one seeking nurture, understanding, and mothering (for himself or his children). But she rapidly becomes a nuisance when that same man sets out to find exuberant or illicit sex. The Playmate is fun when playing is what he wants, but she is an unsuitable companion at the company dinner.

BASIC FEMALE STEREOTYPES

	Nonsexual	*Sexual*
	The Virgin Mary/Mother-Wife	*The Playmate/Lover*
Serviceable	chaste, pure, innocent, good	sensuous, sexually wise, experienced
	proper-looking, conservative, matronly	sexy, "built," stylish
	nurturing, selfless, loving, gentle, "mother of his children"	satisfying, eager, earthy, mysterious, slightly dangerous
	submissive, pliable, receptive	sexually receptive, agreeable, "game"
	compromising, tactful, loyal	challenging, exciting
	fragile, needful, dependent	independent, carefree, "laid back"
	feeling, nonrational, aesthetic, spiritual	bright, fun-loving, playful, carnal
	understanding, supportive	responsive, ego-building
	The Old Ball and Chain/Wif'nkids	*Eve/The Witch-Bitch Temptress*
Nonserviceable	frigid, sexually uninteresting	promiscuous, bad
	frumpy or slatternly	coarse, vulgar, trampy
	cloying, suffocating, obligating	tempting, leads one into sin and evil
	incapable of decision, changeable, scatterbrained	undiscriminating
	dumb, passive	she's "anybody's"
	nagging, shrewish, harping	bitchy, demanding, selfish; she "asks for it"
	helpless, burdensome	immoral, makes trouble
	overemotional, irrational, unreasonable	thoughtless, sinful, evil
	shrewd, manipulative, sneaky	immodest, unladylike

Each ideal is subject to a "serviceability" factor: The status of the role itself, its value and meaning, and even the language used to refer to it can shift radically as its utility shifts or its context changes. She who is "the little woman" in church becomes "the old lady" at the bar; she who was seen as "a good old girl" in graduate school may be seen as "a slut" when he joins the club.

Within a single moment, depending on changing attitudes or interests, the image may shift—good becomes bad, bad becomes good. The nurturing Mary becomes the old ball and chain, and very easily her innocence becomes stupidity; her chastity, frigidity; her nurture, suffocation; her loyalty, imprisonment; her beauty, vanity; her earthiness, carnality; her children, obligation. The Playmate becomes Eve, the Traitor of the Garden, she who is trouble—and contempt mushrooms into hatred.

> *And I have found a woman more bitter than death, who is the hunter's snare, and her heart is a net, and her hands are bonds. . . .*

> *More bitter than death, again, because that is natural and destroys only the body; but the sin which arose from woman destroys the soul . . . bodily death is an open and terrible enemy, but woman is a wheedling and secret enemy.*[23]

This serviceability factor in women's role in patriarchy manifests more clearly than all the rest—including the images that allege to portray her—that under patriarchy women's lives are meant to be lived not for ourselves, but for men's needs, and our cultural images are defined by that fact. The major factor in the flip from good to bad (that is, serviceable to not serviceable) is the matter of intrusiveness into male affairs; it has to do with women's self-assertion, self-direction, and will. It is important to have Mary; it is fun to have Playmates—just so long as neither gets in the way. When a woman moves toward her own needs, gets "pushy," or stands in the way of *his* wishes, Mary becomes the ball and chain (alias the Wif'nkids), and the Playmate becomes the Bitch.

As you look at the chart on page 133, remember that any or all of these images may be expected from any one woman, sometimes at the same time.

Variations on the Theme: Ethnic Overlay

Because the men who make up and direct the patriarchy in which we live are mostly white, Christian, and middle class, it is not surprising that the primary models of womanhood in our society are markedly WASP. Across racial, ethnic, and class lines, one composite image prevails. The fragile, pale-skinned Madonna and the saucily tanned Playmate with flowing blond hair are clearly white, Christian images not even marginally attainable for the very large segment of the female population comprising members of racial or ethnic subgroups. Yet, viable or not, these images continue to function as models, held up to us either as ideals we must strain to copy in whatever meager way possible or as evidence of our inferiority.

The WASP quality of the cultural ideal puts minority women—African-American, Asian, Chicana, Jew, or other—in an even more constricted double bind. Not only are we subject to all the usual contradictions of the bifurcated female image—sexual/nonsexual, good/bad—but we must also deal with a second set of problems compounded and enlarged by our particular ethnic status and circumstances. Oppressed as women, oppressed again as minorities, and oppressed in the nexus between the two, we are expected to choose between loyalties, between liberations. Caught between minority men's anger at WASP behavior and their unconscious acceptance of WASP ideals, minority women "cannot win for losing": If we strain to meet prevailing stan-

dards, we are selling out; if we do not, we are unattractive.

Whichever way we choose to go, however we resolve the cultural loyalties, the issue of our own self-image also arises. The traditional minority woman, as any other, seeks desirability as a mate, seeks the whole range of rewards that comes with being thought "beautiful." Should those standards be even further removed from her real self than they are from other women, she must either work harder to meet them, risking proportionately deeper self-alienation, or she must accept defeat and wrestle with an intense sense of inferiority.

I vividly remember, as an adolescent Jewish girl of the 1950s—hooked on Marilyn Monroe and Ava Gardner, Debbie Reynolds and Liz Taylor—how I fretted at my unfashionable curly hair, trying tirelessly to straighten its resilient black locks. I remember, too, staring enviously at my *shiksa* girlfirends' straight noses. Anything, I thought, even being old, would be better than having this awful bumpy nose. At nineteen, I had it "fixed."

For the Jewish women who fix their noses, for the Black women who straighten their hair, for the millions of us who attempt or contemplate "corrections" to body and character that must ever remain inadequate, there must always be a severe sense of either deceit or defeat. The experience is more than self-diminishing; it is crushing.

Although ideals and models rarely vary from one group to another, the pejorative stereotypes, born of particular history and circumstance, admit of a good deal of variation and adjustment. For example, the Jewish woman, as a woman, may still function as the old ball and chain or the bitch temptress; but she may, as well, be placed within some other disparaging categories, exotic variations on the traditional themes. The young Jewish woman who is ethnically identified and hence esteemed by the Jewish community (and therefore *less* desirable to her male compatriots for the reasons pointed out above) is known as the Nice Jewish Girl—the NJG. Her more chic, less ethnically identified counterpart, the Jewish-American Princess (the JAP) is disparaged precisely because she avoids the social pitfalls of ethnic identification and strives so diligently to meet the WASP model.

In either case, the racist, masculinist mythology will ultimately turn both women into the Jewish Mother: aggressive, brassy, domineering, suffocating, unwholesomely self-inclined. If she cares too little, she's a shrew; if she cares too much, she's sick. Finally, any Jewish woman may be typed the Pushy Jewish Broad, projecting onto her female self all the worst traits of the Jewish stereotype—a classic example of how an image, created by an external dominant group and internalized within the minority group, is applied to women by any men, in and out of the group, and even by women themselves.

Just as entangled in the dilemma of ethnic identification is the African-American woman, bound on one hand by White images of Black women and on the other by Black images of White women. For men, Black or White, who adopt the traditional WASP models, the Black woman functions both as a symbol of racial difference and as the usual receptacle of misogyny. Pejorative images of her only intensify the traditional dichotomies.

In the African-American context, the mother-nurturer gone wrong is not only the frigid nuisance, the nag of White society; she is also the destroyer of the race—the matriarch of the Moynihan Report, who controls the family, castrates the African-American man by displacing him as head of the household, and thereby contributes to the destruction of his manhood, the family unit, and African-American pride.[24] Rather than being prized and lauded, the strength, resiliency, and independence developed in the African-American woman through centuries of hardship are in true masculinist style deflected and turned against her.

These same traits—strength and assertiveness—are the very ones that mark the African-American version of Eve. In this context, Eve is still the Playmate gone awry, only worse. Here we have the Hot Black Bitch, an image obviously constructed by the White overlord, yet at least partially reflected in the African-American community as well. Whereas the White Playmate is naughty, her stereotypic Black counterpart is depicted as without morals, without limits, sexually voracious, undiscriminating, and hard as nails, her behavior and character placing her completely outside the bounds of chivalry and masculine protection.

Each woman can and should analyze the particular version of the stereotype applicable to her background. This is certain: Whatever the ethnic, racial, and class variations, however the images are adapted and reflected, they all are born of masculinist experience to serve masculinist needs. They have little to do with who women are.

EFFECTS OF THE STEREOTYPE

The patriarchal images of women—whether sexual or nonsexual, working class or middle class, black or white—have a common denominator. They all say that women as human beings are substandard: less intelligent; less moral; less competent; less able physically, psychologically, and spiritually; small of body, mind, and character; often bad or destructive. The images argue that we have done little in society (besides reproduce) to earn our keep; that we have made only small contributions to culture, high or low, yet always push for more than we deserve. Sometimes cute or adorable, sometimes consoling, but only in a controlled context, we are pleasant baubles to have around. In any other guise, we are a nuisance at best, a disaster at worst.

These and other stereotypical images of women work to destroy us. In their positive aspects, they are impossible to meet; in the negative, they are deprecatory and ugly, flourishing in the minds of women who are forced to live them. Functioning in large part as social norms, they have great power to direct attitudes and behavior among the group stereotyped, as well as in the larger community. The tragedy of the female stereotype is that it impels women not only to appear substandard but also to become substandard; it moves to form us into the loathed monster. If the work of the stereotype be done, we are reduced to the weak, hapless creatures required by social lore, living in the mold, even experiencing ourselves according to the myth.

Limited experience, opportunity, and education, deemed appropriate for beings who must not become "too smart for our own good"; restrictive clothing and play, tailored for our more "alluring" and refined bodies; disapproval for behavior (for example, sports, competition, and assertiveness) that might strengthen body or character; suitors who require subservience and fragility; adolescent girl-friends straining to become "desirable" women; parents prompting us to marriage or marriageability; media and advertisers seducing us into buying their products; these and countless other influences combine to make us believe the myth and copy the model.

The model requires that we be pretty, gentle, and kind; we can become pretty, gentle, and kind. If, however, the model also requires that we be silly, weak, and incompetent, are we not required to become silly, weak, and incompetent? Haven't some of us tried? If we work to fit the mold and exhibit the expected traits, we reinforce the stereotype and so perpetuate the cycle and give "truth" to the lie. And if the lie be true, then everything follows. Because women are incompetent and weak, we must be protected, set apart, and given a safe "place," guarded by "our" men. Since we are petty and evil, unable to get along even with each other, we must be controlled for the good of ourselves and society. We deserve the contempt in which we are held.

Clearly, to live in the shadow of such attitudes is intolerable, even when they are hidden by chivalry or mystification, even when they are temporarily suspended for our good behavior. Life and personhood defined within such constraints is necessarily distorted, out of phase with even the barest elements of emotional and physical health, spiritual transcendence, and joy. But the misery brought on by these ideals extends beyond the psychological and spiritual elements of life. Because we are speaking here only about images, we have not yet raised the issue of more concrete oppression: poverty and physical abuse. That appears in Chapter 6.

In the next chapter, we examine feminist responses to these images, feminist insights into the nature and effects of patriarchal stereotypes, the struggles women experience in freeing ourselves, and the alternative, woman-identified images we are forging in the struggle.

Notes

1. Mary Daly, *Beyond God the Father* (Boston: Beacon Press, 1973), p. 8.

2. See, for example, Mary R. Beard, *Woman as Force in History* (New York: Macmillan, 1946). Some contemporary feminists make this argument from a cross-cultural perspective, pointing out that "power" is a highly complex notion that varies within and across social groups.

3. Susan Brownmiller, *Femininity* (New York: Fawcett Columbine, 1984), pp. 13–14.

4. Sally Kempton's terminology in "Cutting Loose," *Esquire*, July 1970, p. 57.

5. Darlene Wilkinson, "A Wife's Role," *Promises Promises: Understanding and Encouraging Your Husband,* edited by Liz Heaney (Gresham, OR: Vision House Publishing, 1996), pp. 28–29.

6. Wilkinson, "A Wife's Role," p. 30.

7. Simone de Beauvoir, *The Second Sex,* translated and edited by H. M. Parshley (New York: Alfred A. Knopf, 1953), pp. xvii–xviii.

8. There is a school of feminists who question the thesis of the universal subordination of women within patriarchal culture. They contend that women's power in some societies is different but real; hence, *subordination* is a term not universally applicable. I am not of this opinion.

9. For an interesting analysis of the meaning of the relation of carnality and femaleness for men, see Beauvoir, *Second Sex,* chap. 9.

10. Whether there are oedipal components to male fear of sex I hesitate to conjecture, although others have. Certainly it ought to be considered but in another, wider study of this problem.

11. Pauline Réage, *Story of O,* trans. Sabine d'Estrée (New York: Grove Press, 1965).

12. Andrea Dworkin, *Woman Hating* (New York: E. P. Dutton, 1974), pp. 55–63.

13. André Pieyre de Mandiargues, "A Note on *Story of O,*" in Réage, *Story of O,* p. xvi.

14. It is a sport among the readers and commentators of *Story of O* to guess at the sex of its author (who uses a pen name). Actually, it matters little whether it was written by a man or a woman; the book is the expression of one fully steeped in the perspectives and values of masculism, and, as I have pointed out, these are not gender-specific.

15. Jean Paulhan, "Happiness in Slavery," in Réage, *Story of O,* p. xxv.

16. Paulhan, "Happiness in Slavery,", p. xxviii.

17. Mandiargues, "A Note," in Réage, *Story of O,* p. vii.

18. The idea that victimization per se is an essential principle of female excellence in patriarchy appeared in Andrea Dworkin's *Woman Hating.*

19. Some of this discussion appeared in Sheila Ruth, "Sexism, Patriarchy, and Feminism: Toward an Understanding of Terms" (paper delivered at Pioneers for Century III Conference, Cincinnati, Ohio, March 1976).

20. "Anatomy is destiny," argued Sigmund Freud. For the female, he contended, the body, its makeup and potential, determines personality and character in a far more definitive way than is true for men.

21. Karl Stern, *The Flight from Woman* (New York: Farrar, Straus & Giroux, 1964), pp. 21–22.

22. Wolfgang Lederer, *The Fear of Women* (New York: Grune & Stratton, 1968), pp. 269-70. Note that Beauvoir argued just the opposite in *The Second Sex*, that one is "not born, but becomes a woman."

23. K. Kramer and J. Sprenger, *Malleus Maleficarum*, trans. M. Summers (London: Arrow Books, 1971), p. 112.

24. Daniel Patrick Moynihan, *The Negro Family: The Case for National Action* (U.S. Department of Labor, Office of Policy Planning and Research, 1965). Moynihan wrote this analysis of African-American needs and problems for the president of the United States, thereby launching many of the economic programs of the sixties. Moynihan argued that "In essence, the Negro community has been forced into a matriarchal structure, which . . . imposes a crushing burden on the Negro male, and in consequence on a great many Negro women as well" (p. 29).

Myth America Grows Up

Rita Freedman

Psychologist Rita Freedman studied at Cornell University and the State University of New York at Albany, where she took her doctorate. After some years teaching psychology and women's studies, she opened a practice in clinical psychology. In addition to Beauty Bound *(1986), she authored* Bodylove: Learning to Like Our Looks—and Ourselves *(1988) and has long been concerned with the place of appearance in the formation of women's self-concept.*

Feminists have long held that we are not born "women" but rather are made into the beings our societies intend, learning early to embrace the appearance, behaviors, and roles for which we are destined. In this selection, Freedman details how many girls in American society learn to please with their looks and mannerisms, and by extension, how we are all taught to manage the trappings of "femininity."

I COMBED THE BEACHES LAST summer counting topless toddlers. Few could be found. On the Riviera, women freely bare their breasts to the Mediterranean sun. Here at home, the uncomplicated chests of little girls are discreetly covered. In this way young bodies are draped in gender, poured into the female mold, to be shaped, reshaped, and misshapen by it. Three-year-olds veiled behind bikini tops learn a small lesson in body awareness, one that often leads to heightened self-consciousness and sometimes to tormenting obsessions.

In every society, certain behaviors are considered more appropriate for one sex than for the other. Gender divergence includes occupational, recreational, and legal distinctions, as well as decorative and ornamental ones. How do children acquire this complex set of gender rules? A five-year-old confidently tells me that "girls play at being pretty, but boys play cars. . . ." How did she learn these components of masculinity and femininity so soon?

The socialization of gender begins in infancy, continues through adolescence, and involves almost every aspect of experience, including toys, clothes, media images, and, of course, parental expectations and behavior. Although studies of infants reveal few sex-based differences in emotional and cognitive functions, parents believe that their sons and daughters are quite different right from birth. Girls and boys do grow up in different "climates of expectation."

During pregnancy, parents prepare not just for a new baby but for a strong masculine son or a beautiful feminine daughter. Consequently, these are the qualities that they project onto their newborns. As noted . . . earlier . . . when parents rated firstborn infants, they saw their daughters as beautiful, soft, pretty, cute, and delicate, whereas they viewed their sons as strong, better coordinated, and hardier, even though the male and female infants had been carefully matched for equivalent physical characteristics.[1] People who played with a three-month-old dressed in yellow more often judged it a boy because of "the strength of his grasp and his lack of hair." Those who thought the baby was a girl remarked on her "roundness, softness, and fragility."[2] The cuter the baby, the more likely it is to be judged a girl.

Long before birth, babies are imagined through fantasies that devalue girls even while idealizing their appearance. In a song from the show *Carousel*, Bill ponders his unborn child. First a son "with head held high, feet planted firm"; a boy who, in his father's daydream, "grows tall and tough as a tree." Then, in the softer tones of an afterthought, Bill considers a daughter, "pink, and white as peaches and cream"; a girl with "ribbons in her hair, brighter than girls are meant to be," yet still needing to be "sheltered and dressed in the best that money can buy."

Old autograph books sometimes "wish you hope, wish you joy, wish you first a baby boy." A widespread preference for male offspring persists. In a recent American sample, over 90 percent of the couples wanted a firstborn son. Nearly all the men and three-fourths of the women said they would want a boy if they were to have only one child.[3] A frequent reason given by those few women who did prefer a girl was that "it would be fun to dress her and fuss with her hair."[4] When asked what kind of a person they want their child to become, parents mentioned "being attractive" far more often for daughters than for sons.

Imagine a growing girl who represents the collective experiences of many youngsters whose lives were studied for this chapter. The composite experiences of Linda typify the socialization process which teaches girls their role as members of the fair sex. Linda is initiated into the beautified female world through the subtle lessons of daily life. Her few strands of baby hair are swept into a curl in the hospital nursery. Her ears are pierced before her first birthday, her nails polished for her second. She is securely wrapped in a strawberry-shortcake universe: roses on her walls, ribbons in her hair, ruffles on her shirts. "Early in life, the pink world starts to process the girls to value it."[5]

Intuitively, children sense when and how they are touched or avoided, admired or ignored, complimented or criticized. Girls are initially sturdier than boys and developmentally ahead of them, but are perceived as more fragile. Handled more delicately, they receive less physical stimulation and less encouragement for energetic or exploratory behavior. Parents show greater anxiety about a girl's safety even while she is still in diapers. Fathers begin by engaging in more rough-and-tumble play with sons and by spending nearly twice as much time with sons as with daughters.[6] As Bill concludes in his song, "You can have fun with a son, but you gotta be a father to a girl."

Interestingly, fathers seem to sex-type youngsters even more consciously than mothers do, for example by giving children toys that are more gender-stereotyped. Men show greater anxiety over effeminate behavior in sons, while actively encouraging it in daughters. Fathers seem to want their little girls to fit their own personal image of an attractive female, within the bounds of what is appropriate for a child. Wives report that husbands urge them to keep their daughters' hair long and to "doll them up" even when the mothers themselves don't feel that these things are very important. Linda's father echoes the voices of many dads who describe their preschool daughters as "a bit of a flirt": "she cuddles and flatters in subtle ways"; "she's coy and sexy."[7]

Whether such descriptions of "daddy's little girl" are accurate, fathers enjoy and encourage seductive appearance in their daughters, which in turn enhances these Oedipal flirtations. In this way, Linda is more or less explicitly directed toward a kind of "predatory coquetry." Her enactment of the beauty role is therefore shaped by the way her father reinforces Linda's appearance, independently of how her mother may model feminine beauty.

According to Piaget's theory of intellectual growth, children strive to adapt to life by trying to understand their experiences. We are biologically programmed, says Piaget, to mentally reconstruct the world by forming concepts about ourselves and our surroundings. Mental file cards are written and rewritten to conform ever more closely to social "reality." Concepts of masculinity and femininity are learned as part of this general process of intellectual growth.

In acquiring her sense of gender, Linda first develops a rudimentary idea that people come in two separate forms. Her mental file cards are scribbled with vague notions of mommy/daddy, boy/girl, man/woman, along with perceptions about clothing, hair styles, and other gender markers. By her third birthday, she is well aware that girls and boys look and act differently, apart from any underlying genital structure. An anecdote describes two toddlers looking at a statue of Adam and Eve. "Which is which?" asks one. "I could tell if only they had their clothes on," replies the other.

Though she does not yet understand gender constancy (once a girl, always a girl), Linda knows her own gender membership. Confidently she asserts, "I'm a girl," because she has written "me" on the file card that is filled with "feminine" concepts. Once gender has been established internally, Linda begins to strive for consistency between what she knows about herself and what she knows about girls in general. The dialogue in her head runs something like this: "Since I'm a girl, and since girls look and act in certain ways, then I, too, should look and act the way they do." And so she begins to enact her feminine role. The need to establish consistency between oneself and one's gender role is the same for the toddler as for the adult. The problem for Linda (as for all women) is how to bring together her self-perception as a female with an understanding of gender role.

Femininity soon becomes associated with beauty, and to the internal dialogue a subtheme is added. "Since I'm a girl," Linda thinks intuitively, "and since girls are pretty, then I, too, should be (will be, must be) pretty, just like Mommy." In this way, beauty becomes part of her self-perception as a female. When she confirms the belief that she is a girl by enacting some part of the beauty role (such as putting ribbons in her hair), she achieves a sense of cognitive consistency that in turn feels satisfying. Hence, the inner dialogue concludes with the sentiment "I enjoy being a girl!" By maintaining harmony between two concepts (self-image and feminine image), Linda keeps her mental file cards in order, and in this way makes the world more comfortable and predictable.

Piaget explains that knowledge of one's gender role is partly imposed from within, that is, self-motivated through the basic drive to create intellectual order out of chaotic experiences. But gender role is also externally imposed. It is culturally conditioned through the direct experience of hearing Cinderella tales, dressing Barbie dolls, watching Miss America, Miss Teen, Miss Hémisphere. It is also overtly reinforced. Throughout the elementary school years, girls receive more compliments than boys on their appearance. They are given a bigger wardrobe to choose from and are admired especially when they wear dresses.[8] Linda repeatedly hears others say "You look so pretty," and eventually greets her own reflection with "I'm so pretty" or "Am I pretty? . . . as pretty as other girls? . . . as pretty as others expect me to be?" Finally she begins to wonder, "How can I be prettier?" *Pretty* becomes a framework within which she paints her feminine self-image.

Although parents are beginning to treat sons and daughters more similarly, they still give their children sex-typed clothing, toys, and books. These act as powerful conditioning agents that socialize the importance of female beauty. Emphasis on feminine attractiveness is obvious in fairy tales and in picture books for preschoolers, in which female animals are depicted with long curly eyelashes and ribbons on their tails. A study of school texts found that these books traditionally portrayed women as mothers who wear aprons and who "seem to want and do nothing personally for themselves." The notable exception was cited of a mother who "treated herself to some earrings on a shopping trip."[9]

Before 1970, textbooks rarely showed females engaged in independent activities. When the occupational world of women was presented, it consisted of either service jobs (nurse, teacher) or "glamour" jobs (model, dancer, actress), in which body display is an important component. A popular children's book of the 1970s shows a small boy and girl fantasizing about their future: when the boy becomes a jungle explorer and captures a lion, the girl "curls the lion's mane in her beauty shop for animals"; when he dreams of being a deep-sea diver, she becomes "a mermaid who serves him tea and ice cream."[10]

Books are somewhat less stereotyped today, although children's toys remain highly gender-typed. While boys are given action dolls equipped to capture the enemies of outer space, girls are given fashion dolls equipped with exotic outfits for capturing attention. Over 250 million Barbies have been sold in the past twenty-five years, a doll population that equals the number of living Americans. Over 20 million outfits a year are bought for Barbie and her friends, as the seeds of clothing addiction are sown. One collector concludes that Barbie remains the most popular fashion doll simply because she is the prettiest. (Barbie is both thinner and "sexier looking" than when first created in 1959.) Fashions for Barbie in 1984 featured her in elegant gowns because "glamour is back." Toy stores also sell makeup for dolls. With "Fashion Face," Linda can "put on Barbie's face, wash it off, change her look again and again." A single tube costs several dollars, and remember, this is makeup for a doll!

On Christmas morning, Linda eagerly unwraps her very own superdeluxe makeup set, "just like Mommy's." Here, packaged innocently with fun titles like "Fresh and Fancy" and "Pretty Party" are the sugar and spice that feed the beauty myth. These high-priced glamour rehearsal kits contain the essential tools of the trade. For Linda's hair there are rollers, styling combs, curling irons, "falls," wash-in color, and sparkles. For her face there are paints, gloss, frosting, liners, blush, shadow, and mascara. For her hands there are lotions, polish, nail crayons, and decals. Also included is gold foil for "beauty accents" and glitter for "today's metallic look." The tubes smell like candy and taste like soda pop. They come complete with magnifying mirror in a convenient carrying case so that she can take it anywhere and check her looks perpetually. Here is the making of a mirror junkie. The box covers of cosmetic kits carry reassuring messages to parents. "These toys are suitable for children as young as three"; they will help your child "personalize her own pretty face"; help her "create dozens of fashion looks and become a beauty consultant for her friends"; teach her the "fun way to learn beauty secrets."

What else do they teach Linda about herself and her role in society? That feminine beauty requires many faces and she can cultivate them all; that the easy way to impersonate a real grown-up lady is to put on the same disguise that Mommy wears; that playtime means narcissistic preening; that fantasy fun means enacting Cinderella; that spending time and money on beautifying oneself is approved by parents; that others like her to look fresh, fancy, and seductive; that her own face, though pretty, is somehow inadequate and needs to be made even lovelier—a double message that fosters negative body image and self-doubt.

For some girls, "glamouring up" is not just child's play. There has been a phenomenal growth in children's beauty contests since those protestors picketed the Miss America Pageant in 1968. Paradoxically, during the very years when the women's movement became a pervasive social force, beauty pageants for children . . . also gained in popularity. The Miss Hemisphere Pageant, with numerous divisions for girls ages three to twenty-seven, has mushroomed in size from a few hundred contestants in 1963 to hundreds of thousands of participants today. It is billed as the largest single beauty pageant in the world. Toddlers barely out of diapers (sometimes wearing false eyelashes and tasseled bikinis) are paraded before judges who scrutinize their "beauty, charm, poise and personality." The separate "masters" division for boys up to age nine attracts far fewer contestants.

Why do parents pay sizable entrance fees, invest in elaborate outfits, and drive hundreds of miles to these contests? Besides seeking prizes and modeling opportunities, many sincerely believe that they are helping girls to develop into "ambitious but feminine women, like Bess Myerson." Some experience a strong element of vicarious achievement. They describe the thrill of seeing their daughters on display. One father remarked, "Taking my girls around to pageants is my activity, like a hobby. The contests are flashier than Little League and the children don't get hurt."[11]

But perhaps they do get hurt, in ways less obvious yet more odious than a sprained ankle in a ballgame. Pediatrician Lee Salk warns that children's beauty contests do more harm than good. He describes them as perfect setups for failure, as girls experience tremendous pressure to accept and identify with exaggerated physical stereotypes. Realizing that they lack the winning look, many suffer deep feelings of inadequacy.

"GIRLS LIKE RAINBOWS, BOYS DON'T"

Although children start with only rudimentary concepts of masculinity and femininity, they soon fill in the details. Awareness of gender dualism expands and crystallizes with age, as cognitive file cards are refined. Each day, children learn from their books and toys, from parental reaction to their behavior, and from models that constantly surround them, that beauty is a critical part of femininity. When asked how boys and girls are different from each other, children's compositions show a clear understanding that beauty belongs to females. Although genital and reproductive differences are rarely mentioned, youngsters universally say that girls wear makeup, have pretty hair, "don't get as dirty and aren't as tough" as boys. It is tempting to think that times have changed, that the next generation is already liberated from gender stereotypes and is no longer bound by beauty myths. But consider this response written in 1982 by a fifth-grader:

Because I am a girl I am different in many ways. Girls put on eye shoudo and boys ware nothing like eye shoudo. And girls ware gowns and shoes and take a pocket book around. Boys don't do that. Alls they have to do is put on a tie and shine shoes. Girls

*put lipstick on their lips and girls put on earings,
then they put on stockings and put thier hair in a
bun or fix up the hair. Girls do housework and take
care of a baby if they have one. Boys just sit around
and watch football games and other sports.*

The following comments from seven- and eight-year-olds are cited because they particularly reflect an awareness that beauty is central to the female role.[12]

"HOW ARE BOYS AND GIRLS DIFFERENT?"

- Girls play at being pretty but boys play cars. Boys' voices are louder. Girls wear more jewelry.

- Girls like pink, boys like blue. Boys take their shirts off when it's hot but girls don't.

- Girls are prettier and boys are bossy. Boys stay outside as long as they want, but girls can't.

- Boys don't clean house and girls don't get dirty. Most girls do not get hit by their mothers because girls are more beautiful.

- Girls are cute and harmless, don't get as muddy as boys. Girls like rainbows, but boys don't.

- Boys don't dance, or play hopscotch. Girls don't play rough or get sweaty (but they have the same rights as us).

More articulate ten- and eleven-year-olds made the following observations:

- Girls are very sensitive and delicate. They like perfume and like looking good and sweet. Boys are rough, tough, and insensitive.

- Girls can wear anything they like, but boys can only wear pants. Girls have more clothes. They are more into pink rooms and looking pretty.

- Girls put on makeup and boys don't because they don't want to look pretty. Girls like to stay clean and neat. Some boys say they don't want to take a bath and they want to stay smelly and dirty.

- Girls don't have a mustache, boys don't have a baby. Boys have short hair and drive better than girls. Girls can cook better but boys are stronger.

- Girls are soft like cotton but boys are rough like a truck. But we are nice to each other—that's what counts.

Clearly, these children believe that the male body is to be strengthened and developed, while the female body is to be protected and beautified. In fact, young children evaluate physical attractiveness in much the same way as adults do.[13] In nursery school, they can reliably judge the attractiveness of classmates and prefer to play with those who are better-looking.[14] Preschoolers also connect sex-related personality traits to appearance. They rate unattractive boys as more "scary and aggressive" but rate unattractive girls as more "fearful of things." (Good looks may inhibit assertive behavior in pretty girls who feel out of character when behaving more actively or aggressively than others expect.)

Children sex-typed a pretty face as feminine and a strong muscular physique as masculine. These stereotypes in turn influence the self-concepts of boys and girls in different directions. In a survey of eight- to fifteen-year-olds, girls at each age level worried more about their appearance than boys. Over half the fifth-grade girls in another sample ranked themselves as the least attractive person in their class. Follow-up interviews showed they were not simply motivated by modesty but were truly troubled by their "poor appearance."[15] The older the girl, the greater the influence of attractiveness on her popularity, as if children's understanding of the disproportionate social value of beauty to females gradually increases.

Linda grows up dressing and undressing Barbie, playing with her "Pretty Party" glamour kit, watching the selection of Miss Universe each year. She believes that beauty is something that happens at adolescence. Patiently she awaits it. While marking time, Linda may try on the role of the tomboy. Why do so many tomboys appear only to disappear? What can they teach us about the growing of little Myth America?

Tomboyism is a temporary detour on the road to female development, a last adventure before the final commitment to womanhood. Tomboys are familiar figures. Bred in every neighborhood, they roam like tomcats over the noisy, competitive, outdoor masculine turf. High on energy, they use their bodies freely to explore the world of people and things. The term *tomboy* traces back to the 1600s, when it was first directed at boys to censure them for "rude, boisterous or forward behavior." Soon the label was transferred to "girls who behave like unruly boys," and girls have worn it ever since.[16]

Tomboys not only act the part, they look it as well. We recognize them by their smudged faces and ragged clothes. The frills of Miss Muffet are not for them. Patched, scruffy, and unkempt, they need shoes they can run in, pants they can climb in. A tomboy's appearance enables the very behavior it proclaims. For packaging can create both the image *and* the limits of a person. A female is what she looks like as much as what she does.

One of the most striking aspects of tomboyism is its current popularity. A majority of female college students describe themselves as former tomboys. With bright eyes and a tinge of nostalgia, they recount their tomboy adventures without shame or embarrassment. Tomboyism is the rule rather than the exception. More than half the adult women surveyed recall having been tomboys. Among growing girls, nearly three out of four currently place themselves in the tomboy category.[17]

Although tomboyism is almost universal in Western cultures, it has no counterpart among males. Parents, especially fathers, react strongly against effeminate appearance in sons. A young boy in mommy's high heels, pearls, and nail polish, makes parents fidgety, to say the least. Such adornments remain a gender distinction reserved for the other sex. The term *sissy* is sometimes suggested as a parallel to *tomboy,* although the two are not really equivalent. Any child, whether boy or girl, who is noncombative, fearful, prim, and proper can be dubbed a sissy and ridiculed for possessing such "effeminate" qualities. Whereas *sissy* is clearly perjorative for both sexes, the term *tomboy* confers little stigma before puberty; it is never directed at boys and is often considered a tacit compliment for girls. Differences between the two terms clearly reflect the bias that male attributes are normative.

Why does our culture produce so many tomboys? Why do we first dichotomize gender roles and then permit and even encourage girls to "cross over" temporarily? Why do we set them apart with a distinct label?

Answers to these questions lead back to the belief in female deviance. Recall that one strategy women use to normalize their social position is to become one of the boys. Tomboyism has survived for centuries because it serves a purpose: to defer the full impact of being just another girl. As a tomboy, Linda straddles two gender roles and thereby expands the territory of the self into the valued male domain.

Both boys and girls internalize the cultural devaluation of females. Even preschoolers are aware that masculine traits are accorded higher value and yield greater rewards. In tests where children can express a preference for being one sex or the other, only one boy in ten chooses to be female, whereas one girl in three chooses to be male.[18] Similar results are found in age groups ranging from toddlers to adults. Fewer boys than girls believe it would be better to have been born the opposite sex. As one boy remarked, "If I'd been born a girl, I would have to be pretty and no one would be interested in my brains." Nearly a quarter of adult women surveyed recall a conscious desire to be a boy during childhood, but fewer than 5 percent of adult men remember ever wanting to be female.[19] At twelve Linda writes:

> I am a female. I play football and baseball with a lot of boys. They sometimes beg me to play with them. I don't think it is fair that boys can do everything and girls can't. Boys have a baseball league but girls can't. . . . Nobody knows if girls could do more than boys or if boys could do than girls. . . . Girls have to wash the dishes and suffer by doing everything while the boys have all the fun. One day, I want it to be fair.

Tomboys gain temporary access to the valued masculine world. As "one of the boys," they shake off the girlish stigma and enjoy membership in a privileged club. In fact, rejection of personal adornment and adoption of a boyish look accomplishes for the prepubertal girl very much what beauty rituals accomplish for the adult woman. Both facilitate access to male company; both influence body image and self-esteem; and both defend against an underlying feeling of inferiority. Adopting tomboyism, like cultivating beauty, brings similar tangible rewards: visibility, attention, adventure.

Some young girls (like their mothers) maintain a dual repertoire of tomboy togs along with more coquettish drag, using one or the other as events require. In fact, such role diversity and flexibility may epitomize the best of an androgynous gender model. However, a time comes during adolescence when tomboyism evokes more anxiety than satisfaction, and its rewards no longer balance its costs. Though tolerated before puberty, tomboyism becomes increasingly threatening and is usually abandoned as gender file cards are updated. By the late teens, few girls continue to wear the title. When asked why they gave it up, college students replied:

> *I just outgrew it. It was more or less a natural process that happened over a long period of time. . . . I started wearing more dresses because I like them and because Mom decided I should look nice. . . . When dating, it was difficult to be myself, so I had to change my image in dressing and mannerisms.*

Their responses convey an underlying feeling of loss. Some young women are searching for new labels that can link them to their former selves. At age nineteen Linda says, "If a tomboy is a woman who is very assertive or aggressive, I guess I'm still a tomboy. . . . I don't use the term *tomboy* because that connotes being very young, but I'm still very active, though less athletic, and still consider myself androgynous." The effects of tomboyism reach into adulthood. A survey showed that women who had been overtly tomboyish as children preferred a more tailored style of dress, wore more muted colors, and decorated their homes with a nonfrilly, functional design. Women who had never been tomboys preferred more ruffly clothes, were more marriage-oriented and less career-minded.

ATTRACTING AN IDENTITY

"A boy expands into a man; a girl contracts into a woman." So goes an old saying. With each contraction Linda sheds a piece of her comfortable old skin to emerge naked and pink into the pastel shades of womanhood. Transforming into the fair sex, she delivers a new self. Yet labor is painful. Adolescence marks a major crisis in gender acquisition. Puberty

rings out, sounding the death knell for a tomboy. Gentle curves on breast and hip expose her. In poetry, Anne Sexton assures her daughter: "There is nothing in your body that lies / All that is new is telling the truth."[20] Revealed as woman, Linda can no longer masquerade as an impostor in a tomboy's costume. Contracting, she abandons the ballfield for the prince's ball, trades in her old uniform, learns to play new games and to compete in new arenas. Contracting, she must outfit herself with the eleven traits that professionals in the Broverman study judged as feminine and must gradually abandon the long list of thirty-eight attributes they rated as masculine.

Puberty arrives uninvited—sometimes prematurely, other times long overdue. Many girls experience it as a turning point in their self-image. At age eleven, Linda was asked to describe herself by making a series of statements starting with "I am a . . ." She began: "I am a human being, I am a girl, I am a truthful person, I am not pretty. . . ." One of the striking sex differences to emerge at adolescence is a greater self-consciousness in females. Girls find it harder than boys do to measure up against the idealized norms for their own sex. In a study of fourth- through tenth-graders, the oldest girls had the poorest self-image of any group in the sample.[21] Nearly half the girls in a survey of twenty thousand teenagers reported they frequently felt ugly.[22] To the extent that adolescent girls dislike their bodies, they also dislike themselves.

Twice as many high school girls as boys want to change their looks. Girls are dissatisfied with a greater number of body parts than boys. They generally see themselves as less attractive than other girls, whereas boys tend to rate themselves as better-looking than their peers.[23] A correlation exists between intelligence and body satisfaction in boys, that is, the brighter the boy, the more satisfied he is with his appearance. No such relationship is found in girls, possibly because bright girls are all too aware that they can never attain the beauty ideal.[24]

By college age, 75 percent of males report they feel good about their overall looks and facial features, as compared with only 45 percent of females.[25] Adolescent girls are tormented by poor body image, partly because they have learned during childhood to overvalue, display, and mistrust their appearance. They enter puberty with a strong need to feel attractive, and therefore suffer greater insecurity than boys do when their developing bodies feel awkward and out of control. Moreover, girls are socialized to search for self-identity through male attention. To transform from tomboy to Tom's girl, Linda must depend in large part on being pretty.

Since good looks are stereotypically associated with desirable personality traits, an "unattractive" changing body threatens self-esteem. The connection between appearance and worthiness for females can become so deeply ingrained during puberty that it remains throughout a woman's life, making her continuously insecure about her appearance and, consequently, about herself. Looking back, women describe their teens as a time filled with awkwardness, embarrassment, feelings of inadequacy, fear of sexuality and of separation. Some become frozen into the negative body images that develop during this transitional stage and are never able to accept themselves as attractive women.

Even those girls who are naturally well endowed with beauty (or who manage to achieve it) report that good looks can be a mixed blessing. Pretty is nice but not always better. Nubile beauties become vulnerable to sexual exploitation, sometimes at a very young age. They may be shown off by parents or "used" by peers who seek social prestige through contacts with them. Many begin to resent attention that is based solely on looks and that disregards who they are as people. Good-looking boys rarely suffer from these special hazards. . . .

In their quest for a separate identity, adolescent girls become especially vulnerable to beauty problems that threaten their health and well-being. For example, sophisticated medical techniques now lure girls into cosmetic surgery even before they are fully grown. Nose jobs, chin implants, and breast reductions are being performed on minors as modern medicine perpetuates the myth of female beauty. The vast majority of teenage aesthetic surgery patients are girls, not boys. Before they can adjust to their own changing profiles, growing girls are considered suitable candidates for cosmetic overhaul. Parents are paying for it; professionals are providing it.

Girls as young as age fourteen are now undergoing breast alterations. This is a good example of how beauty stereotypes interact with the matura-

tional process, producing adjustment problems that in turn prompt cosmetic surgery. Because breasts are so symbolic of feminine beauty (in Western cultures), many physically normal girls experience an almost paralyzing self-consciousness during breast development. Advertisements for bust "improvement" products abound in teen magazines. Breast development begins early in puberty, often by age ten. Girls start to mature before boys, and can be several years ahead of boys in the same grade. Full-breasted girls must carry the burden of their early maturation "up front." They suffer embarrassment, ostracism, and overt ridicule. (In fact, large-breasted females of any age are stereotyped as unintelligent, incompetent, immoral, and immodest.)[26] To these young girls, surgical correction of their breast problem seems to be a wonderful solution. In rare cases such a solution may be justifiable; usually it is pre-mature. . . .

The use of cosmetics is another beauty transformation that poses a special health hazard for adolescents. Makeup serves as a critical initiation rite into womanhood. It is an essential fashion prop that helps to exaggerate gender differences. An estimated one-third of the girls who regularly use cosmetics will develop a condition dermatologists are now calling acne cosmetica. Genetic in origin, acne is triggered by increasing hormone production during puberty. The potent ingredients used in cosmetics can induce serious skin problems even in girls who are not genetically prone. Since it takes several months for cosmetic acne to develop, the cause may go unsuspected. Once the acne has developed, a vicious cycle ensues: as it becomes worse, more makeup is used to cover it, which only further escalates the condition.[27] . . .

Pursuit of mythical beauty turns the adolescent girl into an active consumer. Giant industries create, define, and cater to her special beauty "needs" and siphon her babysitting money into the purchase of bust developers and Ultralash. A *New York Times* editorial asked, "Why does a fourteen-year-old Brooklyn girl need to spend $40 on a manicure and $700 on pants, sweaters, headbands and makeup to complete her back-to-school wardrobe?"[28] The very next day this newspaper carried a full back-page ad directed at potential advertisers for *Seventeen* magazine: "*Seventeen* readers don't love you and leave you. As adults 34% still rinse with the same mouthwash and

33% use the same nail polish. Talk to them in their teens and they'll be customers for life."

After analyzing magazine ads aimed at female adolescents, a researcher concludes that girls are bombarded with one essential message about their purpose in life: "learning the art of body adornment through clothing, cosmetics, jewelry, hair products, perfumes."[29] In these ads cosmetic transformations are made to seem a natural accentuation of what already exists. "I look myself, only better," says the young model, confiding the secret formula that brought out the highlights of her hair. Narcissism is fostered by ads that focus again and again on appearance as the primary source of female identity. Cosmetic advertisements have been shown to affect the "conception of social reality" of teenage girls. A single fifteen-minute exposure to a series of beauty commercials increased the degree to which they perceived beauty as being "important to their own personality and important to being popular with boys."[30]

Ads attempt to convince Linda that she must make up and make over in order to make it in life. She is directed to her mirror to discover herself. In effect, the question "Who am I?" is translated into "What should I look like?" Her natural adolescent drive to attain a personal identity is distorted into a need to package herself as a product. In the end, costly and painful beauty rituals do not produce a sense of individuality. Just the opposite occurs: girls wind up all looking the same and are thus more easily stereotyped. "They look alike, think alike, and even worse . . . believe they are not alike."[31]

Notes

1. Rubin, J. et al., 1974.
2. Seavy, C. et al., 1975.
3. Hoffman, L., 1977.
4. Coombs, C. et al., 1975.
5. Bernard, J., 1981, 479.
6. Lamb, M., 1976.
7. Maccoby, E., & Jacklin, C., 1974, 329.
8. Joffe, C., 1971.
9. Weitzman, L. et al., 1972.
10. Williams, J., 1977, 176.
11. Vespa, M., 1975 and 1976.
12. Author's unpublished data.
13. Unger, R., & Madar, T., as cited in Unger, R., 1985.
14. Dion, K., 1973.
15. Simmons, R., & Rosenberg, F., 1975.
16. Fried, B., 1979, 37.
17. Hyde, J. et al., 1977.
18. Williams, J., 1983, 161.
19. Ibid., 161.
20. Sexton, A., "Little Girl, My String Bean, My Lovely Woman," 1966.
21. Bohan, J., 1973.
22. Offer, D. et al., 1981.
23. Musa, K., & Roach, M., 1973.
24. Offer, D. et al., 1981.
25. Dacey, J., 1979.
26. Kleinke, C., & Staneski, R., 1980.
27. Fulton, J., & Black, E., 1983.
28. *New York Times,* Sept. 13, 1983, editorial page.
29. Umiker-Sebeok, J., 1981, 226.
30. Tan, A., 1977.
31. Firestone, S., 1970, 151.

Bibliography

Bernard, J. 1981. *The Female World.* New York: Free Press.

Bohan, J. 1973. Age and sex difference in self-concept. *Adolescence, 8,* 379–384.

Coombs, C., Coombs, L., & McClelland, G. 1975. Preference scales for number and sex of children. *Population Studies, 29,* 273–298.

Dacey, J. 1979. *Adolescents Today.* Santa Monica, Calif.: Goodyear.

Dion, K. 1973. Young children's stereotyping of facial attractiveness. *Developmental Psychology, 10,* 772–778.

Firestone, S. 1970. *The Dialectic of Sex.* New York: William Morrow.

Hoffman, L. 1977. Changes in family roles, socialization and sex differences. *American Psychologist, 32,* 644–657.

Hyde, J., Rosenberg, B., & Behrman, J. 1977. "Tomboyism." *Psychology of Women Quarterly, 2,* 73–75.

Joffe, C. 1971. Sex role socialization and the nursery school: As the twig is bent. *Journal of Marriage and the Family, 33,* 467–475.

Kleinke, C., & Staneski, R. 1980. First impressions of female bust size. *Journal of Social Psychology, 10,* 123–124.

Lamb, M. 1976. (Ed.), *The Role of the Father in Child Development.* New York: Wiley.

Maccoby, E., & Jacklin, C. 1974. *The Psychology of Sex Differences.* Stanford, Calif.: Stanford University Press.

Musa, K., & Roach, M. 1973. Adolescent appearance and self-concept. *Adolescence, 8,* 385–394.

Offer, D., Ostrov, E., & Howard, K. 1981. *The Adolescent: A Psychological Self-Portrait.* New York: Basic Books.

Rubin, J., Provenzano, F., & Luria, Z. 1974. The eye of the beholder: Parents' views on sex of newborns. *American Journal of Orthopsychiatry, 44,* 512–519.

Seavey, C., Katz, P., & Zalk, S. 1975. Baby X: The effect of gender labels on adult responses to infants. *Sex Roles, 1,* 103–110.

Sexton, A. 1966. *Live or Die.* Boston: Houghton Mifflin.

Simmons, R., & Rosenberg, F. 1975. Sex, sex-roles, and self-image. *Journal of Youth and Adolescence, 4,* 229–258.

Tan, A. 1977. TV beauty ads and role expectations of adolescent female viewers. *Journalism Quarterly, 56,* 283–288.

Umiker-Sebeok, J. 1981. The seven ages of women. In C. Mayo & N. Henley (Eds.), *Gender and Non-Verbal Behavior* (pp. 220–239). New York: Springer-Verlag.

Unger, R., Hilderbrand, M., & Madar, T. 1982. Physical attractiveness and assumptions about social deviance: Some sex-by-sex comparisons. *Personality and Social Psychology Bulletin, 8,* 293–301.

Vespa, M. 1975, Feb. 9. The littlest vamps. *New York Sunday News.*

Vespa, M. 1976, Sept. A two year old in false eyelashes. *Ms.,* pp. 61–63.

Weitzman, L., Eifler, D., Hokada, E., & Ross, C. 1972. Sex role socialization in picture books for preschool children. *American Journal of Sociology, 77,* 1125–1150.

Williams, J. 1977. *Psychology of Women* (First Edition). New York: W. W. Norton.

———. 1983. *Psychology of Women* (Second Edition). New York: W. W. Norton.

Whether Woman Should Have Been Made in the First Production of Things

St. Thomas Aquinas

St. Thomas Aquinas (1227–1274), medieval philosopher and theologian, was named the official philosophic authority of the Catholic church by Pope Leo XIII in 1879. His reasoning forms the basis of Catholic doctrine and pervades much of Protestant theology as well. As such, it has exerted tremendous influence on Western culture and hence on women's lives. Through the church, Aquinas's ideas continue in importance today, having their effect on arguments regarding contraception and abortion, women's place in the priesthood, women's role in the family, and in the economy, and so on.

In the following discussion, Aquinas asks whether one could say that because women are defective and sinful (more so than men), they ought not to have been created in the first innocent beginning of things by an all-perfect God. Certainly, women should have been created, he replies, for nature decrees that men must have "helpers," not in cultural works but in reproduction. That is, women are necessary as biological assistants.

Aquinas was known for his reconciliation of Christian doctrine with the philosophy of Aristotle, increasingly important in the thirteenth century. The philosopher he refers to in his opening remarks is Aristotle, who theorized that "females are weaker and colder in nature, and we must look upon the female character as being a sort of natural deficiency" (De Generatione Animalium, IV, 6, 775a 15). Aristotle's analysis of woman as "misbegotten male" is one of a whole genre of theories, popular through the centuries, treating womanhood as a partial or defective instance of manhood.

St. Thomas Aquinas, *Summa Theologicae.* Part I, Q. 92, Art. 1, in *Basic Writings of St. Thomas Aquinas,* ed. Anton C. Pegis (NY: Random House, 1945). Reprinted by permission of the estate of Anton C. Pegis.

QUESTION XCII
THE PRODUCTION OF WOMAN

First Article
Whether Woman Should Have Been Made in the First Production of Things?

WE PROCEED THUS TO THE FIRST ARTICLE:—

Objection 1. It would seem that woman should not have been made in the first production of things. For the Philosopher says that the *female is a misbegotten male.*[1] But nothing misbegotten or defective should have been in the first production of things. Therefore woman should not have been made at that first production.

Obj. 2. Further, subjection and limitation were a result of sin, for to the woman was it said after sin (*Gen.* iii. 16): *Thou shalt be under the man's power;* and Gregory says that, *Where there is no sin, there is no inequality.*[2] But woman is naturally of less strength and dignity than man, *for the agent is always more honorable than the patient,* as Augustine says.[3] Therefore woman should not have been made in the first production of things before sin.

Obj. 3. Further, occasions of sin should be cut off. But God foresaw that woman would be an occasion of sin to man. Therefore He should not have made woman.

On the contrary, It is written (*Gen.* ii. 18): *It is not good for man to be alone; let us make him a helper like to himself.*

I answer that, It was necessary for woman to be made, as the Scripture says, as a *helper* to man; not, indeed, as a helpmate in other works, as some say,[4] since man can be more efficiently helped by another man in other works; but as a helper in the work of generation. This can be made clear if we observe the mode of generation carried out in various living things. Some living things do not possess in themselves the power of generation, but are generated by an agent of another species; and such are those plants and animals which are generated, without seed, from suitable matter through the active power of the heavenly bodies. Others possess the active and passive generative power together, as we see in plants which are generated from seed. For the noblest vital function in plants is generation, and so we observe that in these the active power of generation invariably accompanies the passive power. Among perfect animals, the active power of generation belongs to the male sex, and the passive power to the female. And as among animals there is a vital operation nobler than generation, to which their life is principally directed, so it happens that the male sex is not found in continual union with the female in perfect animals, but only at the time of coition; so that we may consider that by coition the male and female are one, as in plants they are always united, even though in some cases one of them preponderates, and in some the other. But man is further ordered to a still nobler work of life, and that is intellectual operation. Therefore there was greater reason for the distinction of these two powers in man; so that the female should be produced separately from the male, and yet that they should be carnally united for generation. Therefore directly after the formation of woman, it was said: *And they shall be two in one flesh* (Gen. ii. 24).

Reply Obj. 1. As regards the individual nature, woman is defective and misbegotten, for the active power in the male seed tends to the production of a perfect likeness according to the masculine sex; while the production of woman comes from defect in the active power, or from some material indisposition, or even from some external influence, such as that of a south wind, which is moist, as the Philosopher observes.[5] On the other hand, as regards universal human nature, woman is not misbegotten, but is included in nature's intention as directed to the work of generation. Now the universal intention of nature depends on God, Who is the universal Author of nature. Therefore, in producing nature, God formed not only the male but also the female.

Reply Obj. 2. Subjection is twofold. One is servile, by virtue of which a superior makes use of a subject for his own benefit; and this kind of subjection began after sin. There is another kind of subjection, which is called economic or civil, whereby the superior makes use of his subjects for their own benefit and good; and this kind of subjection existed even before sin. For the good of order would have been wanting in the human family if some were not governed by others wiser than themselves. So by such a kind of subjection woman is naturally subject to man, because in man the discernment of reason predominates. Nor is inequality among men excluded by the state of innocence, as we shall prove.[6]

Reply Obj. 3. If God had deprived the world of all those things which proved an occasion of sin, the universe would have been imperfect. Nor was it fitting for the common good to be destroyed in order that individual evil might be avoided; especially as God is so powerful that He can direct any evil to a good end.

Notes

1. *De Gener. Anim.,* II, 3 (737a 27).

2. *Moral.,* XXI, 15 (PL 76, 203).

3. *De Genesi ad Litt.,* XII, 16 (PL 34, 467).

4. Anonymously reported by St. Augustine, *De Genesi ad Litt.,* IX, 3 (PL 34, 395).

5. Aristotle, *De Gener. Anim.,* IV, 2 (766b 33).

6. Q.96, a.3.

The Church and the Second Sex

Mary Daly

Radical feminist Mary Daly, who holds degrees in philosophy and theology, is one of the most brilliant and original thinkers of the second wave. Her second book, Beyond God the Father: Toward a Philosophy of Women's Liberation *(1973), introduced insights so piercing and language analysis so innovative it generated a unique form of inquiry in women's studies for more than two decades. Among the books that followed are* Gyn/Ecology: The Metaethics of Radical Feminism *(1978),* Pure Lust: Elemental Feminist Philosophy *(1984),* Outercourse: The Be-Dazzling Voyage *(1992), and* Quintessence . . . Realizing the Archaic Future: A Radical Elemental Feminist Manifesto *(1998).*

The Church and the Second Sex *was Daly's first book; it created a furor at Boston College, where she taught, because in it Daly made a "case against the Church," arguing that it supported destructive views of women. Here she chronicles the misogynist attitudes and beliefs of the Judeo-Christian tradition, from the Old Testament, to the New Testament, and through the early Fathers of Christianity.*

I. SCRIPTURE

THE BIBLE MANIFESTS THE UNFORTUNATE—often miserable—condition of women in ancient times. The authors of both the Old and the New Testaments were men of their times, and it would be naïve to think that they were free of the prejudices of their epochs. It is therefore a most dubious process to construct an idea of 'feminine nature' or of 'God's plan for women' from biblical texts. As one theologian expressed it: 'Let us be careful not to transcribe into terms of nature that which is written in terms of history.'[1]

An example will illustrate this point. The New Testament gave advice to women (and to slaves) which would help them to bear the subhuman (by today's standards) conditions imposed upon them. It would be foolish to erect, on this basis, a picture of 'immutable' feminine qualities and virtues. Thus, although obedience was required of women and slaves, there is nothing about obedience which makes it intrinsically more appropriate for women than for men. The idea of taking feminine 'types' from the Bible as models for modern women may be an exercise for the imagination, but it is difficult to justify as a method. Any rigid abstraction of types from history implies a basic fallacy.

Old Testament

The Bible contains much to jolt the modern woman, who is accustomed to think of herself as an autonomous person. In the writings of the Old Testament women emerge as subjugated and inferior beings. Although the wife of an Israelite was not on the level of a slave, and however much better off she was than wives in other near-eastern nations, it is indicative of her inferior condition that the wife addressed her husband as a slave addressed his master, or a subject his king.

According to Fr Roland de Vaux:

'The Decalogue includes a man's wife among his possessions, along with his house and land, his male and female slaves, his ox and his ass (Ex 20:17; Dt 5: 21). Her husband can repudiate her, but she cannot claim a divorce; all her life she remains a minor. The wife does not inherit from her husband, nor daughters from their father, except when there is no male heir. (Nb 27:8). A vow made by a girl or married woman needs, to be valid, the consent of father or husband and if this consent is withheld, the vow is null and void (Nb 30:4–17).'[2]

Whereas misconduct on the part of the wife was severely punished, infidelity on the part of the man was punished only if he violated the rights of another man by taking a married woman as his accomplice. In the rabbinical age, the school of Shammai permitted a husband to get a divorce only on the grounds of adultery and misconduct. However, some teachers of the more liberal school of Hillel would accept even the most trivial excuse. If the husband charged that his wife had cooked a dish badly, or if he simply preferred another woman, he could repudiate his wife. Even earlier than this it was written in Sirach 25:26: 'If thy wife does not obey thee at a signal and a glance, separate from her.'

Respect for the woman increased once she became a mother, especially if she produced males, since these were, of course, more highly valued. A man could, indeed, sell his daughter as well as his slaves. If a couple did not have children, it was assumed to be the fault of the wife. Briefly, although Hebrew women were honored as parents and often treated with kindness, their social and legal status was that of subordinate beings. It is understandable that Hebrew males prayed: 'I thank thee, Lord, that thou hast not created me a woman.' From the point of view of the modern woman, the situation of women in the ancient Semitic world—and, indeed, in the ancient world in general—has the dimensions of a nightmare.

Christian authors through the centuries have made much of the Genesis accounts of the creation of Eve and the geographical location of the rib. This, together with her role as temptress in the story of the Fall, supposedly established beyond doubt woman's immutable inferiority, which was not merely physical but also intellectual and moral. So pervasive was this interpretation that through the ages the antifeminist tradition has justified itself on the basis of the origin and activities of the 'first mother' of all mankind. . . .

New Testament

In the New Testament it is significant that the statements which reflect the antifeminism of the times are never those of Christ. There is no recorded speech of Jesus concerning women 'as such.' What is very striking is his behavior toward them. In the passages describing the relationship of Jesus with various women, one characteristic stands out starkly: they emerge as persons, for they are treated as persons, often in such contrast with prevailing custom as to astonish onlookers. The behavior of Jesus toward the Samaritan woman puzzled even his disciples, who were surprised that he would speak to her in public (John 4:27). Then there was his defense of the adulterous woman, who according to the law of Moses should have been stoned (John 8:1–11). There was the case of the prostitute whose many sins he forgave because she had loved much (Luke 7:36–50). In the Gospel narratives the close friendship of Jesus with certain women is manifested in the context of the crucifixion and resurrection. What stands out is the fact that these, his friends, he saw as persons, to whom he gave the supreme yet simple gift of his brotherhood.

The contemporary social inferiority of women was, indeed, reflected in the New Testament. Although the seeds of emancipation were present in the Christian message, their full implications were not evident to the first century authors. The most strikingly antifeminist passages are, of course, in the Pauline texts, which are all too familiar to Catholic women, who have heard them cited approvingly *ad nauseam*. We now know it is important to understand that Paul was greatly preoccupied with *order* in society and in Christian assemblies in particular. In modern parlance, it seemed necessary to sustain a good 'image' of the Church. Thus it appeared to him an important consideration that women should not have too predominant a place in Christian assemblies, that they should not 'speak' too much or unveil their heads. This would have caused scandal and ridicule of the new sect, which already had to face accusations of immorality and effeminacy. In ancient Corinth, as one scholar has pointed out, for a woman to go out unveiled would be to behave like a prostitute.[3] Paul was concerned with protecting the new Church against scandal. Thus he repeatedly insisted upon 'correct' sexual behavior, including the subjection of wives at meetings. Once this is understood, it becomes evident that it is a perversion to use Pauline texts, which should be interpreted within their own social context, to support the claim that even today, in a totally different society, women should be subject.

Paul looked for theological justification for the prevailing customs, such as the custom that women should wear veils. This partially accounts for his reference to Genesis 2 in I Corinthians II:7ff, which he interprets to mean that woman is for man and not the contrary. We have here the idea that man is the 'image and glory of God', whereas woman is 'the glory of man'. Then there is his biased statement which has been quoted with relish by preachers ever since: 'For man was not made from woman, but woman from man. Neither was man created for woman, but woman for man.' Modern scripture scholars do not, of course, agree with this interpretation of Genesis. Moreover, Paul himself evidently noticed that there was something wrong and corrected himself immediately afterward: 'Nevertheless, in the Lord woman is not independent of man nor man of woman; for as woman was made from man, so man is now born of woman. And all things are from God.' However, the damage was done. For two thousand years women have endured sermons on the 'glory of man' theme, and we still receive a yearly harvest of theological essays and books dealing with the 'theology of femininity', which rely heavily upon the 'symbolism of the veil' and 'God's plan for women' as made known through Paul.

A similar procedure of using the then current interpretation of Genesis to buttress convention is seen in another text, which is no longer generally thought to have been written by Paul, although it surely was written under the influence of the Pauline tradition:

> '[I desire] also that women should adorn themselves modestly and sensibly in seemly apparel, not with braided hair or gold or pearls or costly attire but by good deeds, as befits women who profess religion. Let a woman learn in silence with all submissiveness. I permit no woman to teach or to have authority over men; she is to keep silent. For Adam was formed first, then Eve; and Adam was not deceived, but the woman was deceived and became a transgressor. Yet woman will be saved through bearing children, if she continues in faith and love and holiness, with modesty' (I Timothy 2:9–15).

The author tries to support the androcentric attitudes and practices of his times by reference to Genesis. The fact is, of course, that there is no evidence that God made woman subordinate or that the social facts of the past should be prolonged and erected into an immutable destiny.

It is interesting to observe that those who have been fond of quoting such texts down through the ages to keep women 'in their place' have been obliged to adapt their interpretations. For example, that famous 'I permit no woman to teach' was used in the past against women who attempted to teach the catechism. It was later used by some to support prohibitions against their taking theological degrees. Today, women do take such degrees and do in fact teach theology. The same text, however, is still used by some writers to support their exclusion from the hierarchy, although it has been refuted. Moreover, it is evident that a certain selectivity is operative in the use of such texts on the subject of women. Few of those who cite this passage in justification of women's traditional silence would, for example, go so far as to argue that women should not braid their hair, nor wear gold or pearls or expensive clothing. To go to this extent would be considered absurd. On the other hand, many still cite Paul's words to support the custom of women covering their heads in Church. Such inconsistencies demonstrate the unreliability of the process of applying culturally conditioned texts within changed and changing social contexts.

One of the most frequently quoted texts is, of course, the following:

> 'Wives, be subject to your husbands, as to the Lord. For the husband is the head of the wife as Christ is the head of the Church, his body, and is himself its Saviour. As the Church is subject to Christ, so let wives also be subject in everything to their husbands' (Eph 5:22–24).

. . .

2. THE PATRISTIC PERIOD

An examination of the writings of the Church Fathers brings vividly into sight the fact that there is, indeed, a problem of women and the Church. The following statement of Jerome strikes the modern reader as weird:

> 'As long as woman is for birth and children, she is different from man as body is from soul. But when she wishes to serve Christ more than the world, then

she will cease to be a woman and will be called man (vir).'⁴

A similar idea is expressed by Ambrose, who remarks that

'she who does not believe is a woman and should be designated by the name of her sex, whereas she who believes progresses to perfect manhood, to the measure of the adulthood of Christ. She then dispenses with the name of her sex, the seductiveness of youth, the garrulousness of old age.'⁵

These strange utterances can be understood only if one realizes the lowness of women in the commonly held view. The characteristics which the Fathers considered to be typically feminine include fickleness and shallowness,⁶ as well as garrulousness and weakness,⁷ slowness of understanding,⁸ and instability of mind.⁹ For the most part, the attitude was one of puzzlement over the seemingly incongruous fact of woman's existence. Augustine summed up the general idea in saying that he did not see in what way it could be said that woman was made for a help for man, if the work of child-bearing be excluded.¹⁰ Clement of Alexandria was also evidently baffled. Although he was somewhat more liberal than Augustine and concluded that men and women have the same nature, he inconsistently upheld masculine superiority.¹¹

In Genesis the Fathers found an 'explanation' of woman's inferiority which served as a guarantee of divine approval for perpetuating the situation which made her inferior. John Chrysostom thought it followed from the later creation of Eve that God gave the more necessary and more honorable role to man, the more petty and the less honorable to woman.¹² Ambrosiaster remarks that woman is inferior to man, since she is only a portion of him.¹³ Thus there was an uncritical acceptance of the androcentric myth of Eve's creation. Linked to this was their refusal, in varying degrees of inflexibility, to grant that woman is the image of God, an attitude in large measure inspired by Paul's first epistle to the Corinthians. Ambrosiaster states baldly that man is made to the image of God, but not woman.¹⁴ Augustine wrote that only man is the image and glory of God. Since the believing woman, who is co-

heiress of grace, cannot lay aside her sex, she is restored to the image of God only where there is no sex, that is, in the spirit.¹⁵

Together with the biblical account, the Fathers were confronted with an image of woman produced by oppressive conditions which were universal. In contrast to their modern counterparts, women in the early centuries of the Christian era—and, in fact, throughout nearly all of the Christian era—had a girlhood of strict seclusion and of minimal education which prepared them for the life of mindless subordinates. This was followed by an early marriage which effectively cut them off for the rest of their lives from the possibility of autonomous action. Valued chiefly for their reproductive organs, which also inspired horror, and despised for their ignorance, they were denied full personhood. Their inferiority was a fact; it appeared to be 'natural'. Thus, experience apparently supported the rib story, just as the myth itself helped 'explain' the common experience of women as incomplete and lesser humans. The vicious circle persisted, for the very emancipation which would prove that women were not 'naturally' defective was denied them in the name of that defectiveness which was claimed to be natural and divinely ordained. Thus, Augustine taught that the order of things subjugates woman to man.¹⁶ Jerome wrote that it is contrary to the order of nature, or of law, that women should speak in the assembly of men.¹⁷ He maintained that the man should be commanded to love his wife, whereas the woman should fear her husband:

'For love befits the man; fear befits the woman. As for the slave, not only fear is befitting him, but also trembling.'¹⁸

Thus the 'ideal' marital situation proposed by Jerome—an 'ideal' suited to encourage such perversities as the sadomasochistic couple—appears highly abnormal to the modern person. It is significant that he was unable to find an adequate difference between the roles of wife and slave other than the fact that the fear of the latter should be so strong as to be accompanied by trembling.

The presumed defectiveness of woman extended also, and perhaps especially, into the moral sphere. The primary grievance against her was her supposed guilt in the Fall. The violence of some of the tirades on this subject has psychoanalytic implications. Tertullian, for example, wrote for the edification of his contemporaries:

'Do you not know that you are Eve? . . . You are the devil's gateway. . . . How easily you destroyed man, the image of God. Because of the death which you brought upon us, even the Son of God had to die.'[19]

Clement of Alexandria taught that it is shameful for woman to think of what nature she has.[20] Augustine cynically complained that man, who was of superior intelligence, couldn't have been seduced, and so the woman, who was small of intellect, was given to him.[21] The logical inconsistencies implied in this seem to have escaped him: this dull-witted creature could hardly have been too responsible. Moreover, she was clever enough to seduce man, which the ingenious devil could not do. Why did that paragon of intelligence and virtue succumb so easily? It is all too evident that logic is not operative in such invective, which neurotically projects all guilt upon the woman. For the Fathers, woman is a temptress of whom men should beware. That the problem might be reciprocal is not even considered.

There were attempts to balance the alleged guilt-laden condition of the female sex, but these, unfortunately, did not take the form of an admission of guilt shared by the sexes. Instead, Eve was balanced off by Mary. Thus, for example, Origen remarks that as sin came from the woman so does the beginning of salvation.[22] Augustine wrote that woman is honored in Mary.[23] He claimed that since man (*homo*) fell through the female sex, he was restored through the female sex. 'Through the woman, death; through the woman, life.'[24] This type of compensation produced an ambivalent image of woman. Mary was glorified, but she was unique. Women in the concrete did not shake off their bad reputation and continued to bear most of the burden of blame. The sort of polemic, therefore, which attempts to cover the antifeminism of the Fathers by pointing to their glorification of Mary ignores the important point that this did not improve their doctrine about concrete, living women. In fact there is every reason to suspect that this compensation unconsciously served as a means to relieve any possible guilt feelings about injustice to the other sex.

In the mentality of the Fathers, woman and sexuality were identified. Their horror of sex was also

a horror of woman. There is no evidence that they realized the projection mechanisms involved in this misogynistic attitude. In fact, male guilt feelings over sex and hyper-susceptibility to sexual stimulation and suggestion were transferred to 'the other', the 'guilty' sex. The idea of a special guilt attached to the female sex gave support to the double moral standard which prevailed. For example, in cases of adultery, the wife had to take back her unfaithful husband, but if the wife was unfaithful, she could be rejected.

Even in the face of such oppressive conditions a few women managed to attain stature. Jerome admitted that many women were better than their husbands.[25] But more significant is the fact that the existence of exceptions, no matter how numerous, did not change the generalizations about feminine 'nature'. Hence the strange ambivalence which we have noted.

On the whole, then, the Fathers display a strongly disparaging attitude toward women, at times even a fierce misogynism. There is the recurrent theme that by faith a woman transcends the limitations imposed by her sex. It would never occur to the Fathers to say the same of a man. When woman achieves this transcendence which is, of course, not due to her own efforts but is a 'supernatural' gift, she is given the compliment of being called 'man' (*vir*). Thus there is an assumption that all that is of dignity and value in human nature is proper to the male sex. There is an identification of 'male' and 'human'. Even the woman who was elevated by grace retained her abominable nature. No matter what praise the Fathers may have accorded to individuals, it is not possible to conclude that in their doctrine women are recognized as fully human. . . .

3. THE MIDDLE AGES

Theological opinion of women was hardly better in the Middle Ages, although some of the fierceness of tone was mitigated. The twelfth century theologian, Peter the Lombard, whose *Sentences* became a standard textbook to be commented upon by teachers of theology, went so far as to write that woman is sensuality itself, which is well signified by woman, since in woman this naturally prevails.[26] Bonaventure repeated many of the standard ideas. He thought that the image of God is realized more in man than in woman, not in its primary meaning, but in an accidental way.[27] He repeats the old idea that woman signifies the 'inferior part' of the soul; man, the 'superior part'.[28]

What was new in the picture in the Middle Ages was the assimilation into theology of Aristotelianism, which provided the conceptual tools for fixing woman's place in the universe and which, ironically, could have been used to free her. In the writings of Thomas Aquinas, which later came to have a place of unique pre-eminence in the Church, Aristotelian thought was wedded to the standard biblical interpretations, so that the seeming weight of 'science' was added to that of authority. Thus, following Aristotle, Aquinas held that the female is defective as regards her individual nature. He wrote that she is, in fact, a misbegotten male, for the active force in the male seed tends to the production of a perfect likeness in the masculine sex. Her existence is due to some defect in the active force (that of the father), or to some material indisposition, or even to some external influence, such as that of the south wind, which is moist. He adds that, as regards human nature in general, woman is not misbegotten, but is included in nature's intention as directed to the work of generation.[29] She has, then, a reason for being—that is, she is needed in the work of generation. It seems that this really is all she is good for, 'since a man can be more efficiently helped by another man in other works'.[30]

It would be a mistake, however, to conclude that Thomas thought woman has a major or even an equal role, even in her one specialty, i.e. reproduction. He wrote:

> 'Father and mother are loved as principles of our natural origin. Now the father is principle in a more excellent way than the mother, because he is the active principle, while the mother is a passive and material principle. Consequently, strictly speaking, the father is to be loved more.'[31]

Notes

1. Louis-Marie Orrieux, O.P., 'Vocation de la femme: recherche biblique', *La femme; nature et vocation. Recherches et débats* (Paris: Librairie Arthème Fayard), cahier n. 45, décembre, 1963, p. 147.

2. Roland de Vaux, *Ancient Israel, its Life and Institutions,* translated by John McHugh (New York: McGraw Hill Book Co., 1961), p. 39.

3. Pastor André Dumas, *op. cit.,* p. 28.

4. PL 26, 567. *Comm. in epist. ad Ephes.,* III, 5.

5. PL 15, 1844. *Expos. evang. sec. Lucam,* lib. X, n. 161.

6. John Chrysostom, PG, 61, 316. *In epist. I ad Cor.,* cap. 14, v. 35., *Homilia* XXXVII.

7. John Chrysostom, PG, 62, 544–5. *In epist. I ad Tim.,* cap. 2, v. II. *Homilia* IX.

8. Cyril of Alexandria, PL 74, 691. *In Joannis evang.,* lib. XII, xx, 15.

9. Gregory the Great, PL 76, 453. *Moral.,* lib. XXVIII, cap. 3.

10. PL 34, 395–6. *De Genesi ad litteram* IX, cap. 5.

11. PG 8, 1271–5. *Stromatum,* lib. IV, cap. 8.

12. PG 51, 231. *Quales ducendae sint uxores,* 4.

13. PL 17, 240. *Commentaria in epist. ad Corinth. primam.*

14. *Ibid.*

15. PL 42, 1003–5. *De Trinitate* XII, 7.

16. PL 34, 204. *De Genesi contra Manich.* II, II.

17. PL 30, 794. *Expos. in epist. I ad Cor.,* cap. 14.

18. PL 26, 570. *Comm. in epist. ad Ephes.* III, 5.

19. PL I, 1418b–19a. *De cultu feminarum, libri duo* I, I.

20. PG 8, 430. *Paedagogi* II, 2 (end).

21. PL 34, 452. *De Genesi ad litteram* XI, 42.

22. PG 13, 1819 C. *In Lucam homilia* VIII.

23. PL 40, 186. *De fide et symbolo,* 4.

24. PL 38, 1108. *Sermo* 232, 2.

25. PL 26, 536. *Comm. in epist. ad Ephes.,* III, 5.

26. PL 191, 1633. *Collectanea in epist. D. Pauli in epist. ad Cor.,* cap. XI, 8–10.

27. *Comm. in Sec. Librum Sententiarum Petri Lombardi* (Quaracchi edition), dist. XVI, art. 2, q. 2.

28. *Ibid.,* dist. XVIII, art. I, q. I.

29. *Summa Theologiae,* I, 92, I, ad I. Albert the Great also wrote that woman is misbegotten: in II P. *Sum. Theol.* (Borgnet), tract. 13, q. 80, membrum I.

30. Thomas Aquinas, *Summa Theologiae,* I, 92, I c.

31. *Ibid.,* II–II, 26, 10 c.

Femininity

Sigmund Freud

The Austrian psychologist Sigmund Freud (1856–1939) was one of the earliest theorists and probably the most influential in the areas of clinical psychology and psychoanalysis. Although extraordinarily creative and insightful as ground-breaker in a new dimension, his work has been severely criticized for its ethnocentricity, its lack of objective verification (or perhaps even verifiability), and, more recently, its thorough sexism. Freud's theories on the nature of women's psychology include the following themes: (1) that for women, anatomy is destiny—more so than for men, women's lives and personalities are prescribed by their biological and reproductive nature; (2) that women are not only fundamentally different from men in character but inferior to them physically (in sexual capacity and equipment), emotionally (in stability and control), and ethically (in the sense of honesty and justice).

The essay reprinted here (written about 1933) is Freud's most famous treatise on femininity. It was at one time (until quite recently—into the 1940s or '50s) the official word on female psychology. Although Freud and this analysis have been challenged roundly from all quarters, its themes are still highly influential and pervade much of both contemporary clinical and popular thought.

LADIES AND GENTLEMEN,[1]—ALL THE while I am preparing to talk to you I am struggling with an internal difficulty. I feel uncertain, so to speak, of the extent of my licence. It is true that in the course of fifteen years of work psycho-analysis has changed and grown richer; but, in spite of that, an introduction to psycho-analysis might have been left without alteration or supplement. It is constantly in my mind that these lectures are without a *raison d'être.*

From *New Introductory Lectures on Psycho-Analysis* by Sigmund Freud, translated by James Strachey. Translation copyright © 1965, 1964 by James Strachey. Reprinted by permission of W. W. Norton & Company, Inc.

For analysts I am saying too little and nothing at all that is new; but for you I am saying too much and saying things which you are not equipped to understand and which are not in your province. I have looked around for excuses and I have tried to justify each separate lecture on different grounds. The first one, on the theory of dreams, was supposed to put you back again at one blow into the analytic atmosphere and to show you how durable our views have turned out to be. I was led on to the second one, which followed the paths from dreams to what is called occultism, by the opportunity of speaking my mind without constraint on a department of work in which prejudiced expectations are fighting to-day against passionate resistances, and I could hope that your judgement, educated to tolerance on the example of psycho-analysis, would not refuse to accompany me on the excursion. The third lecture, on the dissection of the personality, certainly made the hardest demands upon you with its unfamiliar subject-matter; but it was impossible for me to keep this first beginning of an ego-psychology back from you, and if we had possessed it fifteen years ago I should have had to mention it to you then. My last lecture, finally, which you were probably able to follow only by great exertions, brought forward necessary corrections—fresh attempts at solving the most important conundrums; and my introduction would have been leading you astray if I had been silent about them. As you see, when one starts making excuses it turns out in the end that it was all inevitable, all the work of destiny. I submit to it, and I beg you to do the same.

To-day's lecture, too, should have no place in an introduction; but it may serve to give you an example of a detailed piece of analytic work, and I can say two things to recommend it. It brings forward nothing but observed facts, almost without any speculative additions, and it deals with a subject which has a claim on your interest second almost to no other. Throughout history people have knocked their heads against the riddle of the nature of femininity—

> *Häupter in Hieroglyphenmützen,*
> *Häupter in Turban und schwarzem Barett,*
> *Perückenhäupter und tausend andre*
> *Arme, schwitzende Menschenhäupter. . . .*[2]

Nor will *you* have escaped worrying over this problem—those of you who are men; to those of you who are women this will not apply—you are yourselves the problem. When you meet a human being, the first distinction you make is 'male or female?' and you are accustomed to make the distinction with unhesitating certainty. Anatomical science shares your certainty at one point and not much further. The male sexual product, the spermatozoon, and its vehicle are male; the ovum and the organism that harbours it are female. In both sexes organs have been formed which serve exclusively for the sexual functions; they were probably developed from the same [innate] disposition into two different forms. Besides this, in both sexes the other organs, the bodily shapes and tissues, show the influence of the individual's sex, but this is inconstant and its amount variable; these are what are known as the secondary sexual characters. Science next tells you something that runs counter to your expectations and is probably calculated to confuse your feelings. It draws your attention to the fact that portions of the male sexual apparatus also appear in women's bodies, though in an atrophied state, and vice versa in the alternative case. It regards their occurrence as indications of *bisexuality*,[3] as though an individual is not a man or a woman but always both—merely a certain amount more the one than the other. You will then be asked to make yourselves familiar with the idea that the proportion in which masculine and feminine are mixed in an individual is subject to quite considerable fluctuations. Since, however, apart from the very rarest cases, only one kind of sexual product—ova or semen—is nevertheless present in one person, you are bound to have doubts as to the decisive significance of those elements and must conclude that what constitutes masculinity or femininity is an unknown characteristic which anatomy cannot lay hold of.

Can psychology do so perhaps? We are accustomed to employ 'masculine' and 'feminine' as mental qualities as well, and have in the same way transferred the notion of bisexuality to mental life. Thus we speak of a person, whether male or female, as behaving in a masculine way in one connection and in a feminine way in another. But you will soon perceive that this is only giving way to anatomy or to convention. You cannot give the concepts of 'masculine' and 'feminine' *any* new connotation. The distinction is not a psychological one; when you say 'masculine', you usually mean 'active', and when you say 'feminine', you usually mean 'passive'. Now it is true that a relation of the kind exists. The male sex-cell is actively mobile and searches out the female one, and the latter, the ovum, is immobile and waits passively. This behaviour of the elementary sexual organisms is indeed a model for the conduct of sexual individuals during intercourse. The male pursues the female for the purpose of sexual union, seizes hold of her and penetrates into her. But by this you have precisely reduced the characteristic of masculinity to the factor of aggressiveness so far as psychology is concerned. You may well doubt whether you have gained any real advantage from this when you reflect that in some classes of animals the females are the stronger and more aggressive and the male is active only in the single act of sexual union. This is so, for instance, with the spiders. Even the functions of rearing and caring for the young, which strike us as feminine *par excellence*, are not invariably attached to the female sex in animals. In quite high species we find that the sexes share the task of caring for the young between them or even that the male alone devotes himself to it. Even in the sphere of human sexual life you soon see how inadequate it is to make masculine behaviour coincide with activity and feminine with passivity. A mother is active in every sense towards her child; the act of lactation itself may equally be described as the mother suckling the baby or as her being sucked by it. The further you go from the narrow sexual sphere the more obvious will the 'error of superimposition'[4] become. Women can display great activity in various directions, men are not able to live in company with their own kind unless they develop a large amount of passive adaptability. If you now tell me that these facts go to prove precisely that both men and women are bisexual in the psychological sense, I shall conclude that you have decided in your own minds to make 'active' coincide with 'masculine' and 'passive' with 'feminine'. But

I advise you against it. It seems to me to serve no useful purpose and adds nothing to our knowledge.[5]

One might consider characterizing femininity psychologically as giving preference to passive aims. This is not, of course, the same thing as passivity; to achieve a passive aim may call for a large amount of activity. It is perhaps the case that in a woman, on the basis of her share in the sexual function, a preference for passive behaviour and passive aims is carried over into her life to a greater or lesser extent, in proportion to the limits, restricted or far-reaching, within which her sexual life thus serves as a model. But we must beware in this of underestimating the influence of social customs, which similarly force women into passive situations. All this is still far from being cleared up. There is one particularly constant relation between femininity and instinctual life which we do not want to overlook. The suppression of women's aggressiveness which is prescribed for them constitutionally and imposed on them socially favours the development of powerful masochistic impulses, which succeed, as we know, in binding erotically the destructive trends which have been diverted inwards. Thus masochism, as people say, is truly feminine. But if, as happens so often, you meet with masochism in men, what is left to you but to say that these men exhibit very plain feminine traits?

And now you are already prepared to hear that psychology too is unable to solve the riddle of femininity. The explanation must no doubt come from elsewhere, and cannot come till we have learnt how in general the differentiation of living organisms into two sexes came about. We know nothing about it, yet the existence of two sexes is a most striking characteristic of organic life which distinguishes it sharply from inanimate nature. However, we find enough to study in those human individuals who, through the possession of female genitals, are characterized as manifestly or predominantly feminine. In conformity with its peculiar nature, psycho-analysis does not try to describe what a woman is— that would be a task it could scarcely perform—but sets about enquiring how she comes into being, how a woman develops out of a child with a bisexual disposition. In recent times we have begun to learn a little about this, thanks to the circumstance that several of our excellent women colleagues in anal-

ysis have begun to work at the question. The discussion of this has gained special attractiveness from the distinction between the sexes. For the ladies, whenever some comparison seemed to turn out unfavourable to their sex, were able to utter a suspicion that we, the male analysts, had been unable to overcome certain deeply-rooted prejudices against what was feminine, and that this was being paid for in the partiality of our researches. We, on the other hand, standing on the ground of bisexuality, had no difficulty in avoiding impoliteness. We had only to say: 'This doesn't apply to *you*. You're the exception; on this point you're more masculine than feminine.'

We approach the investigation of the sexual development of women with two expectations. The first is that here once more the constitution will not adapt itself to its function without a struggle. The second is that the decisive turning-points will already have been prepared for or completed before puberty. Both expectations are promptly confirmed. Furthermore, a comparison with what happens with boys tells us that the development of a little girl into a normal woman is more difficult and more complicated, since it includes two extra tasks, to which there is nothing corresponding in the development of a man. Let us follow the parallel lines from their beginning. Undoubtedly the material is different to start with in boys and girls: it did not need psycho-analysis to establish that. The difference in the structure of the genitals is accompanied by other bodily differences which are too well known to call for mention. Differences emerge too in the instinctual disposition which give a glimpse of the later nature of women. A little girl is as a rule less aggressive, defiant and self-sufficient; she seems to have a greater need for being shown affection and on that account to be more dependent and pliant. It is probably only as a result of this pliancy that she can be taught more easily and quicker to control her excretions: urine and faeces are the first gifts that children make to those who look after them, and controlling them is the first concession to which the instinctual life of children can be induced. One gets an impression, too, that little girls are more intelligent and livelier than boys of the same age; they go out more to meet the external world and at the same time form stronger object-cathexes. I cannot say whether this lead in development has been confirmed by exact observations, but in any case there is no question that girls cannot be described as intellectually backward. These sexual differences are not, however, of great consequence: they can be outweighed by individual variations. For our immediate purposes they can be disregarded.

Both sexes seem to pass through the early phases of libidinal development in the same manner. It might have been expected that in girls there would already have been some lag in aggressiveness in the sadistic-anal phase, but such is not the case. Analysis of children's play has shown our women analysts that the aggressive impulses of little girls leave nothing to be desired in the way of abundance and violence. With their entry into the phallic phase the differences between the sexes are completely eclipsed by their agreements. We are now obliged to recognize that the little girl is a little man. In boys, as we know, this phase is marked by the fact that they have learnt how to derive pleasurable sensations from their small penis and connect its excited state with their ideas of sexual intercourse. Little girls do the same thing with their still smaller clitoris. It seems that with them all their masturbatory acts are carried out on this penis-equivalent, and that the truly feminine vagina is still undiscovered by both sexes. It is true that there are a few isolated reports of early vaginal sensations as well, but it could not be easy to distinguish these from sensations in the anus or vestibulum; in any case they cannot play a great part. We are entitled to keep to our view that in the phallic phase of girls the clitoris is the leading erotogenic zone. But it is not, of course, going to remain so. With the change to femininity the clitoris should wholly or in part hand over its sensitivity, and at the same time its importance, to the vagina. This would be one of the two tasks which a woman has to perform in the course of her development, whereas the more fortunate man has only to continue at the time of his sexual maturity the activity that he has previously carried out at the period of the early efflorescence of his sexuality.

We shall return to the part played by the clitoris; let us now turn to the second task with which a girl's development is burdened. A boy's mother is the first object of his love, and she remains so too during the formation of his Oedipus complex and,

in essence, all through his life. For a girl too her first object must be her mother (and the figures of wet-nurses and foster-mothers that merge into her). The first object-cathexes occur in attachment to the satisfaction of the major and simple vital needs,[6] and the circumstances of the care of children are the same for both sexes. But in the Oedipus situation the girl's father has become her love-object, and we expect that in the normal course of development she will find her way from this paternal object to her final choice of an object. In the course of time, therefore, a girl has to change her erotogenic zone and her object—both of which a boy retains. The question then arises of how this happens: in particular, how does a girl pass from her mother to an attachment to her father? or, in other words, how does she pass from her masculine phase to the feminine one to which she is biologically destined?

It would be a solution of ideal simplicity if we could suppose that from a particular age onwards the elementary influence of the mutual attraction between the sexes makes itself felt and impels the small woman towards men, while the same law allows the boy to continue with his mother. We might suppose in addition that in this the children are following the pointer given them by the sexual preference of their parents. But we are not going to find things so easy; we scarcely know whether we are to believe seriously in the power of which poets talk so much and with such enthusiasm but which cannot be further dissected analytically. We have found an answer of quite another sort by means of laborious investigations, the material for which at least was easy to arrive at. For you must know that the number of women who remain till a late age tenderly dependent on a paternal object, or indeed on their real father, is very great. We have established some surprising facts about these women with an intense attachment of long duration to their father. We knew, of course, that there had been a preliminary stage of attachment to the mother, but we did not know that it could be so rich in content and so long-lasting, and could leave behind so many opportunities for fixations and dispositions. During this time the girl's father is only a troublesome rival; in some cases the attachment to her mother lasts beyond the fourth year of life. Almost everything that we find later in her relation to her father was already present in this earlier attachment and has been transferred subsequently on to her father. In short, we get an impression that we cannot understand women unless we appreciate this phase of their pre-Oedipus attachment to their mother.

We shall be glad, then, to know the nature of the girl's libidinal relations to her mother. The answer is that they are of very many different kinds. Since they persist through all three phases of infantile sexuality, they also take on the characteristics of the different phases and express themselves by oral, sadistic-anal and phallic wishes. These wishes represent active as well as passive impulses; if we relate them to the differentiation of the sexes which is to appear later—though we should avoid doing so as far as possible—we may call them masculine and feminine. Besides this, they are completely ambivalent, both affectionate and of a hostile and aggressive nature. The latter often only come to light after being changed into anxiety ideas. It is not always easy to point to a formulation of these early sexual wishes; what is most clearly expressed is a wish to get the mother with child and the corresponding wish to bear her a child—both belonging to the phallic period and sufficiently surprising, but established beyond doubt by analytic observation. The attractiveness of these investigations lies in the surprising detailed findings which they bring us. Thus, for instance, we discover the fear of being murdered or poisoned, which may later form the core of a paranoic illness, already present in this pre-Oedipus period, in relation to the mother. Or another case: you will recall an interesting episode in the history of analytic research which caused me many distressing hours. In the period in which the main interest was directed to discovering infantile sexual traumas, almost all my women patients told me that they had been seduced by their father. I was driven to recognize in the end that these reports were untrue and so came to understand that hysterical symptoms are derived from phantasies and not from real occurrences. It was only later that I was able to recognize in this phantasy of being seduced by the father the expression of the typical Oedipus complex in women. And now we find the phantasy of seduction once more in the pre-Oedipus prehistory of girls; but the seducer is regularly the mother. Here, however, the phantasy touches the ground of reality, for it was really the mother who by her activities over the child's bodily hygiene inevitably stimulated, and perhaps even roused for the first time, pleasurable sensations in her genitals.[7]

I have no doubt you are ready to suspect that this portrayal of the abundance and strength of a little girl's sexual relations with her mother is very much overdrawn. After all, one has opportunities of seeing little girls and notices nothing of the sort. But the objection is not to the point. Enough can be seen in the children if one knows how to look. And besides, you should consider how little of its sexual wishes a child can bring to preconscious expression or communicate at all. Accordingly we are only within our rights if we study the residues and consequences of this emotional world in retrospect, in people in whom these processes of development had attained a specially clear and even excessive degree of expansion. Pathology has always done us the service of making discernible by isolation and exaggeration conditions which would remain concealed in a normal state. And since our investigations have been carried out on people who were by no means seriously abnormal, I think we should regard their outcome as deserving belief.

We will now turn our interest on to the single question of what it is that brings this powerful attachment of the girl to her mother to an end. This, as we know, is its usual fate: it is destined to make room for an attachment to her father. Here we come upon a fact which is a pointer to our further advance. This step in development does not involve only a simple change of object. The turning away from the mother is accompanied by hostility; the attachment to the mother ends in hate. A hate of that kind may become very striking and last all through life; it may be carefully overcompensated later on; as a rule one part of it is overcome while another part persists. Events of later years naturally influence this greatly. We will restrict ourselves, however, to studying it at the time at which the girl turns to her father and to enquiring into the motives for it. We are then given a long list of accusations and grievances against the mother which are supposed to justify the child's hostile feelings; they are of varying validity which we shall not fail to examine. A number of them are obvious rationalizations and the true sources of enmity remain to be found.

I hope you will be interested if on this occasion I take you through all the details of a psycho-analytic investigation.

The reproach against the mother which goes back furthest is that she gave the child too little milk—which is construed against her as lack of love. Now there is some justification for this reproach in our families. Mothers often have insufficient nourishment to give their children and are content to suckle them for a few months, for half or three-quarters of a year. Among primitive peoples children are fed at their mother's breast for two or three years. The figure of the wet-nurse who suckles the child is as a rule merged into the mother; when this has not happened, the reproach is turned into another one—that the nurse, who fed the child so willingly, was sent away by the mother too early. But whatever the true state of affairs may have been, it is impossible that the child's reproach can be justified as often as it is met with. It seems, rather, that the child's avidity for its earliest nourishment is altogether insatiable, that it never gets over the pain of losing its mother's breast. I should not be surprised if the analysis of a primitive child, who could still suck at its mother's breast when it was already able to run about and talk, were to bring the same reproach to light. The fear of being poisoned is also probably connected with the withdrawal of the breast. Poison is nourishment that makes one ill. Perhaps children trace back their early illnesses too to this frustration. A fair amount of intellectual education is a prerequisite for believing in chance; primitive people and uneducated ones, and no doubt children as well, are able to assign a ground for everything that happens. Perhaps originally it was a reason on animistic lines. Even to-day in some strata of our population no one can die without having been killed by someone else—preferably by the doctor. And the regular reaction of a neurotic to the death of someone closely connected with him is to put the blame on himself for having caused the death.

The next accusation against the child's mother flares up when the next baby appears in the nursery. If possible the connection with oral frustration is preserved: the mother could not or would not give the child any more milk because she needed the nourishment for the new arrival. In cases in which the two children are so close in age that lactation is prejudiced by the second pregnancy, this reproach acquires a real basis, and it is a remarkable fact that a child, even with an age difference of only 11 months, is not too young to take notice of what is happening. But what the child grudges the unwanted intruder and rival is not only the suckling but all the other signs of maternal care. It feels that it has been dethroned, despoiled, prejudiced in its rights; it casts a jealous hatred upon the new baby and develops a grievance against the faithless mother which often finds expression in a disagreeable change in its behaviour. It becomes 'naughty', perhaps, irritable and disobedient and goes back on the advances it has made towards controlling its excretions. All of this has been very long familiar and is accepted as self-evident; but we rarely form a correct idea of the strength of these jealous impulses, of the tenacity with which they persist and of the magnitude of their influence on later development. Especially as this jealousy is constantly receiving fresh nourishment in the later years of childhood and the whole shock is repeated with the birth of each new brother or sister. Nor does it make much difference if the child happens to remain the mother's preferred favourite. A child's demands for love are immoderate, they make exclusive claims and tolerate no sharing.

An abundant source of a child's hostility to its mother is provided by its multifarious sexual wishes, which alter according to the phase of the libido and which cannot for the most part be satisfied. The strongest of these frustrations occur at the phallic period, if the mother forbids pleasurable activity with the genitals—often with severe threats and every sign of displeasure—activity to which, after all, she herself had introduced the child. One would think these were reasons enough to account for a girl's turning away from her mother. One would judge, if so, that the estrangement follows inevitably from the nature of children's sexuality, from the immoderate character of their demand for love and the impossibility of fulfilling their sexual wishes. It might be thought indeed that this first love-relation of the child's is doomed to dissolution for the very reason that it is the first, for these early object-cathexes are regularly ambivalent to a high degree. A powerful tendency to aggressiveness is always present beside a powerful love, and the more passionately a child loves its object the more sensitive does it become to disappointments and frustrations from that object; and in the end the love must succumb to the accumulated hostility. Or the idea that there is an original ambivalence such as this in erotic cathexes may be rejected, and it may be pointed out that it is the special nature of the mother-child relation that leads, with equal inevitability, to the destruction of the child's love; for even the mildest upbringing cannot avoid using compulsion and introducing restrictions, and any such intervention in the child's liberty must provoke as a reaction an inclination to rebelliousness and aggressiveness. A discussion of these possibilities might, I think, be most interesting; but an objection suddenly emerges which forces our interest in another direction. All these factors—the slights, the disappointments in love, the jealousy, the seduction followed by prohibition—are, after all, also in operation in the relation of a *boy* to his mother and are yet unable to alienate him from the maternal object. Unless we can find something that is specific for girls and is not present or not in the same way present in boys, we shall not have explained the termination of the attachment of girls to their mother.

I believe we have found this specific factor, and indeed where we expected to find it, even though in a surprising form. Where we expected to find it, I say, for it lies in the castration complex. After all, the anatomical distinction [between the sexes] must express itself in psychical consequences. It was, however, a surprise to learn from analyses that girls hold their mother responsible for their lack of a penis and do not forgive her for their being thus put at a disadvantage.

As you hear, then, we ascribe a castration complex to women as well. And for good reasons, though its content cannot be the same as with boys. In the latter the castration complex arises after they have learnt from the sight of the female genitals that the organ which they value so highly need not necessarily accompany the body. At this the boy recalls to mind the threats he brought on himself by his doings with that organ, he begins to give credence to them and falls under the influence of fear of castration, which will be the most powerful motive force in his subsequent development. The castration complex of girls is also started by the sight of the

genitals of the other sex. They at once notice the difference and, it must be admitted, its significance too. They feel seriously wronged, often declare that they want to 'have something like it too', and fall victim to 'envy for the penis', which will leave ineradicable traces on their development and the formation of their character and which will not be surmounted in even the most favourable cases without a severe expenditure of psychical energy. The girl's recognition of the fact of her being without a penis does not by any means imply that she submits to the fact easily. On the contrary, she continues to hold on for a long time to the wish to get something like it herself and she believes in that possibility for improbably long years; and analysis can show that, at a period when knowledge of reality has long since rejected the fulfilment of the wish as unattainable, it persists in the unconscious and retains a considerable cathexis of energy. The wish to get the longed-for penis eventually in spite of everything may contribute to the motives that drive a mature woman to analysis, and what she may reasonably expect from analysis—a capacity, for instance, to carry on an intellectual profession—may often be recognized as a sublimated modification of this repressed wish.

One cannot very well doubt the importance of envy for the penis. You may take it as an instance of male injustice if I assert that envy and jealousy play an even greater part in the mental life of women than of men. It is not that I think these characteristics are absent in men or that I think they have no other roots in women than envy for the penis; but I am inclined to attribute their greater amount in women to this latter influence. Some analysts, however, have shown an inclination to depreciate the importance of this first instalment of penis-envy in the phallic phase. They are of opinion that what we find of this attitude in women is in the main a secondary structure which has come about on the occasion of later conflicts by regression to this early infantile impulse. This, however, is a general problem of depth psychology. In many pathological—or even unusual—instinctual attitudes (for instance, in all sexual perversions) the question arises of how much of their strength is to be attributed to early infantile fixations and how much to the influence of later experiences and developments. In such cases it is almost always a matter of complemental series such as we put forward in our discussion of the aetiology of the neuroses.[8] Both factors play a part in varying amounts in the causation; a less on the one side is balanced by a more on the other. The infantile factor sets the pattern in all cases but does not always determine the issue, though it often does. Precisely in the case of penis-envy I should argue decidedly in favour of the preponderance of the infantile factor.

The discovery that she is castrated is a turning-point in a girl's growth. Three possible lines of development start from it: one leads to sexual inhibition or to neurosis, the second to change of character in the sense of a masculinity complex, the third, finally, to normal femininity. We have learnt a fair amount, though not everything, about all three.

The essential content of the first is as follows: the little girl has hitherto lived in a masculine way, has been able to get pleasure by the excitation of her clitoris and has brought this activity into relation with her sexual wishes directed towards her mother, which are often active ones; now, owing to the influence of her penis-envy, she loses her enjoyment in her phallic sexuality. Her self-love is mortified by the comparison with the boy's far superior equipment and in consequence she renounces her masturbatory satisfaction from her clitoris, repudiates her love for her mother and at the same time not infrequently represses a good part of her sexual trends in general. No doubt her turning away from her mother does not occur all at once, for to begin with the girl regards her castration as an individual misfortune, and only gradually extends it to other females and finally to her mother as well. Her love was directed to her *phallic* mother; with the discovery that her mother is castrated it becomes possible to drop her as an object, so that the motives for hostility, which have long been accumulating, gain the upper hand. This means, therefore, that as a result of the discovery of women's lack of a penis they are debased in value for girls just as they are for boys and later perhaps for men.

You all know the immense aetiological importance attributed by our neurotic patients to their masturbation. They make it responsible for all their troubles and we have the greatest difficulty in persuading them that they are mistaken. In fact, however, we ought to admit to them that they are right, for masturbation is the executive agent of infantile sexuality, from the faulty development of which they are indeed suffering. But what neurotics mostly blame is the masturbation of the period of puberty; they have mostly forgotten that of early infancy, which is what is really in question. I wish I might have an opportunity some time of explaining to you at length how important all the factual details of early masturbation become for the individual's subsequent neurosis or character: whether or not it was discovered, how the parents struggled against it or permitted it, or whether he succeeded in suppressing it himself. All of this leaves permanent traces on his development. But I am on the whole glad that I need not do this. It would be a hard and tedious task and at the end of it you would put me in an embarrassing situation by quite certainly asking me to give you some practical advice as to how a parent or educator should deal with the masturbation of small children.[9] From the development of girls, which is what my present lecture is concerned with, I can give you the example of a child herself trying to get free from masturbating. She does not always succeed in this. If envy for the penis has provoked a powerful impulse against clitoridal masturbation but this nevertheless refuses to give way, a violent struggle for liberation ensues in which the girl, as it were, herself takes over the role of her deposed mother and gives expression to her entire dissatisfaction with her inferior clitoris in her efforts against obtaining satisfaction from it. Many years later, when her masturbatory activity has long since been suppressed, an interest still persists which we must interpret as a defence against a temptation that is still dreaded. It manifests itself in the emergence of sympathy for those to whom similar difficulties are attributed, it plays a part as a motive in contracting a marriage and, indeed, it may determine the choice of a husband or lover. Disposing of early infantile masturbation is truly no easy or indifferent business.

Along with the abandonment of clitoridal masturbation a certain amount of activity is renounced. Passivity now has the upper hand, and the girl's turning to her father is accomplished principally with the help of passive instinctual impulses. You can see that a wave of development like this, which clears the phallic activity out of the way, smooths the ground for femininity. If too much is not lost in the course of it through repression, this femininity may turn out to be normal. The wish with which the girl turns to her father is no doubt originally the wish for the penis which her mother has refused her and which she now expects from her father. The feminine situation is only established, however, if the wish for a penis is replaced by one for a baby, if, that is, a baby takes the place of a penis in accordance with an ancient symbolic equivalence. It has not escaped us that the girl has wished for a baby earlier, in the undisturbed phallic phase: that, of course, was the meaning of her playing with dolls. But that play was not in fact an expression of her femininity; it served as an identification with her mother with the intention of substituting activity for passivity. *She* was playing the part of her mother and the doll was herself: now she could do with the baby everything that her mother used to do with her. Not until the emergence of the wish for a penis does the doll-baby become a baby from the girl's father, and thereafter the aim of the most powerful feminine wish. Her happiness is great if later on this wish for a baby finds fulfilment in reality, and quite especially so if the baby is a little boy who brings the longed-for penis with him.[10] Often enough in her combined picture of 'a baby from her father' the emphasis is laid on the baby and her father left unstressed. In this way the ancient masculine wish for the possession of a penis is still faintly visible through the femininity now achieved. But perhaps we ought rather to recognize this wish for a penis as being *par excellence* a feminine one.

With the transference of the wish for a penis-baby on to her father, the girl has entered the situation of the Oedipus complex. Her hostility to her mother, which did not need to be freshly created, is now greatly intensified, for she becomes the girl's rival, who receives from her father everything that she desires from him. For a long time the girl's Oedipus complex concealed her pre-Oedipus attachment to her mother from our view, though it is nevertheless so important and leaves such lasting fixations behind it. For girls the Oedipus situation is the outcome of a long and difficult development; it is a kind of preliminary solution, a position of rest which is not soon abandoned, especially as the beginning of the latency period is not far distant. And we are now struck by a difference between the two sexes, which is probably momentous, in regard to

the relation of the Oedipus complex to the castration complex. In a boy the Oedipus complex, in which he desires his mother and would like to get rid of his father as being a rival, develops naturally from the phase of his phallic sexuality. The threat of castration compels him, however, to give up that attitude. Under the impression of the danger of losing his penis, the Oedipus complex is abandoned, repressed and, in the most normal cases, entirely destroyed, and a severe super-ego is set up as its heir. What happens with a girl is almost the opposite. The castration complex prepares for the Oedipus complex instead of destroying it; the girl is driven out of her attachment to her mother through the influence of her envy for the penis and she enters the Oedipus situation as though into a haven of refuge. In the absence of fear of castration the chief motive is lacking which leads boys to surmount the Oedipus complex. Girls remain in it for an indeterminate length of time; they demolish it late and, even so, incompletely. In these circumstances the formation of the super-ego must suffer; it cannot attain the strength and independence which give it its cultural significance, and feminists are not pleased when we point out to them the effects of this factor upon the average feminine character.

To go back a little. We mentioned as the second possible reaction to the discovery of female castration the development of a powerful masculinity complex. By this we mean that the girl refuses, as it were, to recognize the unwelcome fact and, defiantly rebellious, even exaggerates her previous masculinity, clings to her clitoridal activity and takes refuge in an identification with her phallic mother or her father. What can it be that decides in favour of this outcome? We can only suppose that it is a constitutional factor, a greater amount of activity, such as is ordinarily characteristic of a male. However that may be, the essence of this process is that at this point in development the wave of passivity is avoided which opens the way to the turn towards femininity. The extreme achievement of such a masculinity complex would appear to be the influencing of the choice of an object in the sense of manifest homosexuality. Analytic experience teaches us, to be sure, that female homosexuality is seldom or never a direct continuation of infantile masculinity. Even for a girl of this kind it seems necessary that she should take her father as an object for some time and enter the Oedipus situation. But afterwards, as a result of her inevitable disappointments from her father, she is driven to regress into her early masculinity complex. The significance of these disappointments must not be exaggerated; a girl who is destined to become feminine is not spared them, though they do not have the same effect. The predominance of the constitutional factor seems indisputable; but the two phases in the development of female homosexuality are well mirrored in the practices of homosexuals, who play the parts of mother and baby with each other as often and as clearly as those of husband and wife.

What I have been telling you here may be described as the prehistory of women. It is a product of the very last few years and may have been of interest to you as an example of detailed analytic work. Since its subject is woman, I will venture on this occasion to mention by name a few of the women who have made valuable contributions to this investigation. Dr. Ruth Mack Brunswick [1928] was the first to describe a case of neurosis which went back to a fixation in the pre-Oedipus stage and had never reached the Oedipus situation at all. The case took the form of jealous paranoia and proved accessible to therapy. Dr. Jeanne Lampl-de Groot [1927] has established the incredible phallic activity of girls towards their mother by some assured observations, and Dr. Helene Deutsch [1932] has shown that the erotic actions of homosexual women reproduce the relations between mother and baby.

It is not my intention to pursue the further behaviour of femininity through puberty to the period of maturity. Our knowledge, moreover, would be insufficient for the purpose. But I will bring a few features together in what follows. Taking its prehistory as a starting-point, I will only emphasize here that the development of femininity remains exposed to disturbance by the residual phenomena of the early masculine period. Regressions to the fixations of the pre-Oedipus phases very frequently occur; in the course of some women's lives there is a repeated alternation between periods in which masculinity or femininity gains the upper hand. Some portion of what we men call 'the enigma of women' may perhaps be derived from this expression of bisexuality in women's lives. But another question

seems to have become ripe for judgement in the course of these researches. We have called the motive force of sexual life 'the libido'. Sexual life is dominated by the polarity of masculine-feminine; thus the notion suggests itself of considering the relation of the libido to this antithesis. It would not be surprising if it were to turn out that each sexuality had its own special libido appropriated to it, so that one sort of libido would pursue the aims of a masculine sexual life and another sort those of a feminine.one. But nothing of the kind is true. There is only one libido, which serves both the masculine and the feminine sexual functions. To it itself we cannot assign any sex; if, following the conventional equation of activity and masculinity, we are inclined to describe it as masculine, we must not forget that it also covers trends with a passive aim. Nevertheless the juxtaposition 'feminine libido' is without any justification. Furthermore, it is our impression that more constraint has been applied to the libido when it is pressed into the service of the feminine function, and that—to speak teleologically—Nature takes less careful account of its [that function's] demands than in the case of masculinity. And the reason for this may lie—thinking once again teleologically—in the fact that the accomplishment of the aim of biology has been entrusted to the aggressiveness of men and has been made to some extent independent of women's consent.

The sexual frigidity of women, the frequency of which appears to confirm this disregard, is a phenomenon that is still insufficiently understood. Sometimes it is psychogenic and in that case accessible to influence; but in other cases it suggests the hypothesis of its being constitutionally determined and even of there being a contributory anatomical factor.

I have promised to tell you of a few more psychical peculiarities of mature femininity, as we come across them in analytic observation. We do not lay claim to more than an average validity for these assertions; nor is it always easy to distinguish what should be ascribed to the influence of the sexual function and what to social breeding. Thus, we attribute a larger amount of narcissism to femininity, which also affects women's choice of object, so that to be loved is a stronger need for them than to love. The effect of penis-envy has a share, further, in the physical vanity of women, since they are bound to value their charms more highly as a late compensation for their original sexual inferiority.[11] Shame, which is considered to be a feminine characteristic *par excellence* but is far more a matter of convention than might be supposed, has as its purpose, we believe, concealment of genital deficiency. We are not forgetting that at a later time shame takes on other functions. It seems that women have made few contributions to the discoveries and inventions in the history of civilization; there is, however, one technique which they may have invented—that of plaiting and weaving. If that is so, we should be tempted to guess the unconscious motive for the achievement. Nature herself would seem to have given the model which this achievement imitates by causing the growth at maturity of the pubic hair that conceals the genitals. The step that remained to be taken lay in making the threads adhere to one another, while on the body they stick into the skin and are only matted together. If you reject this idea as fantastic and regard my belief in the influence of lack of a penis on the configuration of femininity as an *idée fixe,* I am of course defenceless.

The determinants of women's choice of an object are often made unrecognizable by social conditions. Where the choice is able to show itself freely, it is often made in accordance with the narcissistic ideal of the man whom the girl had wished to become. If the girl has remained in her attachment to her father—that is, in the Oedipus complex—her choice is made according to the paternal type. Since, when she turned from her mother to her father, the hostility of her ambivalent relation remained with her mother, a choice of this kind should guarantee a happy marriage. But very often the outcome is of a kind that presents a general threat to such a settlement of the conflict due to ambivalence. The hostility that has been left behind follows in the train of the positive attachment and spreads over on to the new object. The woman's husband, who to begin with inherited from her father, becomes after a time her mother's heir as well. So it may easily happen that the second half of a woman's life may be filled by the struggle against her husband, just as the shorter first half was filled by her rebellion against her mother. When this reaction has been lived through, a second marriage may easily turn out very much more satisfying.[12] Another alteration in

a woman's nature, for which lovers are unprepared, may occur in a marriage after the first child is born. Under the influence of a woman's becoming a mother herself, an identification with her own mother may be revived, against which she had striven up till the time of her marriage, and this may attract all the available libido to itself, so that the compulsion to repeat reproduces an unhappy marriage between her parents. The difference in a mother's reaction to the birth of a son or a daughter shows that the old factor of lack of a penis has even now not lost its strength. A mother is only brought unlimited satisfaction by her relation to a son; this is altogether the most perfect, the most free from ambivalence of all human relationships.[13] A mother can transfer to her son the ambition which she has been obliged to suppress in herself, and she can expect from him the satisfaction of all that has been left over in her of her masculinity complex. Even a marriage is not made secure until the wife has succeeded in making her husband her child as well and in acting as a mother to him.

A woman's identification with her mother allows us to distinguish two strata: the pre-Oedipus one which rests on her affectionate attachment to her mother and takes her as a model, and the later one from the Oedipus complex which seeks to get rid of her mother and take her place with her father. We are no doubt justified in saying that much of both of them is left over for the future and that neither of them is adequately surmounted in the course of development. But the phase of the affectionate pre-Oedipus attachment is the decisive one for a woman's future: during it preparations are made for the acquisition of the characteristics with which she will later fulfil her role in the sexual function and perform her invaluable social tasks. It is in this identification too that she acquires her attractiveness to a man, whose Oedipus attachment to his mother it kindles into passion. How often it happens, however, that it is only his son who obtains what he himself aspired to! One gets an impression that a man's love and a woman's are a phase apart psychologically.

The fact that women must be regarded as having little sense of justice is no doubt related to the predominance of envy in their mental life; for the demand for justice is a modification of envy and lays down the condition subject to which one can put envy aside. We also regard women as weaker in their social interests and as having less capacity for sublimating their instincts than men. The former is no doubt derived from the dissocial quality which unquestionably characterizes all sexual relations. Lovers find sufficiency in each other, and families too resist inclusion in more comprehensive associations.[14] The aptitude for sublimation is subject to the greatest individual variations. On the other hand I cannot help mentioning an impression that we are constantly receiving during analytic practice. A man of about thirty strikes us as a youthful, somewhat unformed individual, whom we expect to make powerful use of the possibilities for development opened up to him by analysis. A woman of the same age, however, often frightens us by her psychical rigidity and unchangeability. Her libido has taken up final positions and seems incapable of exchanging them for others. There are no paths open to further development; it is as though the whole process had already run its course and remains thenceforward insusceptible to influence—as though, indeed, the difficult development to femininity had exhausted the possibilities of the person concerned. As therapists we lament this state of things, even if we succeed in putting an end to our patient's ailment by doing away with her neurotic conflict.

That is all I had to say to you about femininity. It is certainly incomplete and fragmentary and does not always sound friendly. But do not forget that I have only been describing women in so far as their nature is determined by their sexual function. It is true that that influence extends very far; but we do not overlook the fact that an individual woman may be a human being in other respects as well. If you want to know more about femininity, enquire from your own experiences of life, or turn to the poets, or wait until science can give you deeper and more coherent information.

Notes

1. [This lecture is mainly based on two earlier papers: 'Some Psychical Consequences of the Anatomical Distinction between the Sexes' (1925*j*) and 'Female Sexuality' (1931*b*). The last section, however, dealing with women in adult life, contains new material. Freud returned to the subject once again in Chapter VII of the posthumous *Outline of Psycho-Analysis* (1940*a* [1938]).]

2. Heads in hieroglyphic bonnets,
    Heads in turbans and black birettas,
    Heads in wigs and thousand other
    Wretched, sweating heads of humans. . . .
        (Heine, *Nordsee* [Second Cycle, VII, 'Fragen'].)

3. [Bisexuality was discussed by Freud in the first edition of his *Three Essays on the Theory of Sexuality* (1905*d*). The passage includes a long footnote to which he made additions in later issues of the work.]

4. [I.e., mistaking two different things for a single one. The term was explained in *Introductory Lectures*, XX.]

5. [The difficulty of finding a psychological meaning for 'masculine' and 'feminine' was discussed in a long footnote added in 1915 to Section 4 of the third of his *Three Essays* (1905*d*), and again at the beginning of a still longer footnote at the end of Chapter IV of *Civilization and its Discontents* (1930*a*).]

6. [Cf. *Introductory Lectures,* XXI.]

7. [In his early discussions of the aetiology of hysteria Freud often mentioned seduction by adults as among its commonest causes (see, for instance, Section I of the second paper on the neuro-psychoses of defence (1896*c*), and Section II (*b*) of 'The Aetiology of Hysteria' (1896*c*). But nowhere in these early publications did he specifically inculpate the girl's father. Indeed, in some additional footnotes written in 1924 for the *Gesammelte Schriften* reprint of *Studies on Hysteria,* he admitted to having on two occasions suppressed the fact of the father's responsibility. He made this quite clear, however, in the letter to Fliess of September 21, 1897 (Freud, 1950*a*, Letter 69), in which he first expressed his scepticism about these stories told by his patients. His first published admission of his mistake was given several years later in a hint in the second of the *Three Essays* (1905*d*), but a much fuller account of the position followed in his contribution on the aetiology of the neuroses to a volume of Löwenfeld (1906*a*). Later on he gave two accounts of the effects that this discovery of his mistake had on his own mind—in his 'History of the Psycho-Analytic Movement' (1914*d*), and in his *Autobiographical Study* (1925*d*), (Norton, 1963). The further discovery which is described in the present paragraph of the text had already been indicated in the paper on 'Female Sexuality' (1931*b*).]

8. [See *Introductory Lectures,* XXII and XXIII.]

9. [Freud's fullest discussion of masturbation was in his contributions to a symposium on the subject in the Vienna Psycho-Analytical Society (1912*f*).]

10. [See below.]

11. [Cf. Section II of 'On Narcissism' (1914*c*).]

12. [This had already been remarked upon earlier, in 'The Taboo of Virginity' (1918a).]

13. [This point seems to have been made by Freud first in a footnote to Chapter VI of *Group Psychology* (1921c). He repeated it in the *Introductory Lectures,* XIII, and in Chapter V of *Civilization and its Discontents* (1930a). That exceptions may occur is shown by the example above.]

14. [Cf. some remarks on this in Chapter XII (D) of *Group Psychology* (1921c).]

Twenty–Seven Reasons Why a Beer Is Better Than a Woman!

Anonymous

Little comment can be made except that this is a classic piece of misogyny, not at all unusual.

So much for perfect wifeliness and the eternal feminine.

1. You can enjoy beer all month long.
2. Beer stains wash out.
3. You don't have to wine and dine a beer.
4. Your beer will always wait patiently for you in the car while you play a sport.
5. When a beer goes flat, you toss it.
6. Beer is never late.
7. Hangovers go away.
8. A beer doesn't get jealous when you grab another beer.
9. Beer never has a headache.
10. When you go to a bar, you know you can always pick up a beer.
11. After a beer, the bottle is still worth a nickel.
12. A beer won't get upset when you come home with beer on your breath.
13. If you pour a beer right, you know you'll always get good head.
14. You can have more than one beer a night and not feel guilty.
15. You can share a beer with your friend.
16. A beer always goes down easy.
17. You always know you're the first one to pop a beer.
18. A beer is always wet.
19. Beer doesn't demand equality.
20. You can have a beer in public.
21. A beer doesn't care when you come.
22. A frigid beer is a good beer.
23. You don't have to wash a beer before it tastes good.
24. It's good to get a case of beer.
25. It's acceptable to be in public with a dark beer.
26. Aging is good for beer.
27. Having a beer with nuts is all right.

This piece was provided by an undergraduate women's studies student, who said it was being passed around her boyfriend's fraternity house.

CHAPTER FOUR

Feminist Resistance to Sexist Ideology

THE CHALLENGERS

Subtract the effort to meet the stereotypic model; undo much of the indoctrination; add a streak of independence, self-affirmation, and self-respect; toss in a growing knowledge of women's history and circumstance, pride in womanhood, and concern for other women; wrap all in a strong awareness of the entire process and you have some picture of the feminist woman who today is challenging old images and building new ones. If patriarchy is hostile to women in general, even those who conform to its standards and regulations, one can imagine the attitudes it takes toward the feminist woman who rejects patriarchy's constraints, refuses to accept the "place" constructed for her, and aspires instead to a place of her own regardless of its acceptability to the patriarchs. To the masculinist, a feminist woman is their worst nightmare, the "feminazi" of Rush Limbaugh fame. According to this mythology, a woman unfettered by "respectable" convention—by the watchful eyes of fathers, brothers, and husbands—is dangerous. Now here are women not only unredeemed by their servitude but also questioning convention, rebelling, refusing their appointed labors, lusting after male jobs, intruding on male territory, demanding preposterous freedoms, and worst of all, making headway!

To verify this hostility, one need only turn to TV stories, letters to the editor in newspapers and magazines, commentaries in books and magazines, political campaign rhetoric and election results, church sermons, in-group jokes, and the other usual sources. Notice how the feminist and her demands are presented. Either ridiculed or despised, she is first of all *unfeminine*. This term implies not only a lack of "charm" and expertise in certain "womanly" behaviors, it suggests as well a particular appearance: either hard, "glitzy," and slick or else dirty, unkempt, badly dressed, and not pretty—she is clearly disadvantaged in whatever it takes to attract men. According to this presentation, the feminist woman has trouble with sex and problems relating to men, perhaps because of bad experiences in childhood (with her father) or later on (with husband, lover, or rapist). In short, she is maladjusted. From a representative cross section of such hostile comments, one gathers that feminists want

- To become like men, "sleep around," reject their maternal prerogatives and special "power," emasculate men, and destroy civilization (George Gilder)[1]
- To indulge themselves, abrogate familial responsibility, and avoid sex (Midge Decter)[2]
- To reject their true "femininity," castrate men, have a penis of their own, and disrupt society (Sigmund Freud)[3]
- To surrender their womanliness, become "phallic women," and distort the innate balance of complementarity in life and nature (Karl Stern)[4]
- To destroy the universities, academic freedom, scholarship, etc. (those against affirmative action)
- To give up all "the wonderful privileges" women in this country now enjoy (Phyllis Schlafly)
- To foster the "suppression of modesty" and the "naturally given" sexual differentiation that makes "men and women always men and women"[5] and the "dismantling" of men's souls.[6] (Allan Bloom)
- To take jobs away from those who are "really oppressed"
- To turn their children over to others to care for
- To enable women to have babies they can't afford and live like queens on the largesse of the state
- To fight battles (the women's movement) that are already won
- To kill babies

Feminists, it is said, tend to get "shrill" or "strident," which means literally high-pitched, grating on the ear. These are terms one would expect masculinists to use; they are—and are meant to be—deprecating. They not only refer to the higher pitch of the female voice, but they also conjure up images of whining old crones and nagging shrews. They are a means of ridiculing and discounting feminist arguments: "Not only do I not accept the things you

are saying, but I don't even take them seriously; I reduce them simply to the ugly noises of thwarted, aggressive women."

Yet I believe that, in a sense different from the intended one, the terms *shrill* and *strident* are accurate, for they reveal a deeper, perhaps unconscious, truth. Feminists' arguments *are* extremely grating—to the masculinist mind-set. Feminists are striking at values and feelings that run deep and have powerful impact. If even the smallest changes in gender images (such as altering hair length) provoke marked reactions, which they have, then greater shifts will certainly beget proportionately greater response. Feminists can and do expect to incur a great deal of anger and abuse, whether that is expressed as ridicule or as outright attack.

Although we have made gains in the last thirty years, women—feminist or nonfeminist—still live in a hostile environment, within a struggle. Feminists work within this struggle: We philosophize, analyze, act, and grow there. Our development—the way we grow, the things we learn, and the visions we create—all bear that mark.

To one degree or another, most feminists see themselves as revolutionaries. In Shulamith Firestone's words, "If there were another word more all-embracing than *revolution* we would use it."[7] Yet we are revolutionaries on peculiar terrain, for we do not typically seek battle, and we do not wish to exchange one hierarchy for another. We rarely hate our "enemies." In fact, we usually hesitate to call anyone "enemy," not quite certain who or what that enemy might be. It is said that many women live intimately in the homes of their oppressors, loving and caring for them. We have not decided on a firm, far-reaching revolutionary program, for we have not agreed on one set of strategies or goals. Yet notwithstanding all of this, we *are* revolutionaries, for in altering the relationships between women and men, in challenging masculinist values, we mean to change the very nature of life for all people.

The women's movement has a saying: The personal is the political. This means several things. First, no gulf truly exists between the personal and social/political elements of our lives. It also means that much of what is generally taken to be private matters—problems of communication with mates, for example, or difficulties in sexual relationships—are actually not purely personal but also social and political, a consequence of gender constructions. "The personal is the political" means also that the insights we gain into our private circumstances can ultimately have widespread political and social consequences.

Kate Millett defines politics as "power-structured relationships, arrangements whereby one group of persons is controlled by another."[8] If that is the case, then such questions as, "Why do I get up earlier than he does and prepare breakfast for the family before we both go off to our jobs?" are political questions because they refer to men's use of women's time and effort. It is a political issue that most women, even those who have jobs in the marketplace, are still expected to wash, cook, clean, and serve and yet not be paid for their labors or even be recognized as working two jobs. It is a political issue that society places the class of women in such a position and not so the class of men. This is no small matter, for it represents one symptom of the exploitation and domination of 51 percent of the world population by the remaining 49 percent. If the exploitation of women by men is both model and manifestation of other forms of exploitation and oppression, as many feminists believe, then understanding male-female roles is profoundly important, and the challengers' analyses of sexism, rather than being petty and inconsequential as charged, are highly significant, not only for the 51 percent but for all humanity.

THE PROCESS: COMING TO UNDERSTAND

The process of learning and unlearning, of coming to recognize the consequences that the images of women have and of reorienting oneself toward them, is difficult, painstaking, and time-consuming. Considering how long each of us has lived with these images and the extent of their power in our culture, it is not surprising that this should be so.

Consciousness-Raising

Each of us has come to the task of becoming aware from her own set of circumstances and in her own way. Most women report a first moment, an event, when they experienced "the explosion" or the "click," the first rush of awareness or insight into

sexism and its intimate connection with them. Perhaps triggered by a personal crisis—an unwanted pregnancy and the social cruelties that often follow, a divorce that led to impoverishment, abandonment by a family that would not tolerate a female lover, or perhaps job discrimination, or social humiliation, or even a feminist speech that freed the woman from some damaging beliefs—the explosion or insight, once begun, is almost always followed by a growing awareness. Often the growth is conscious and cultivated. Sometimes it happens despite resistance, for the awareness, though freeing and exciting, may be painful as well.

This process of coming to understand sexism fully, at the highest level of awareness, is called "consciousness-raising." It both intensifies awareness of the implications of sexism and stimulates the search for alternatives. Consciousness-raising takes a variety of forms: It follows from various techniques (for example, self-examination, role reversal, shared discussion, reading), and it takes different paths.

The Insight: It's a Lie

How does consciousness-raising proceed? Suppose you spent your youth learning the trade of "femininity." Suppose Mom and Dad taught you to make yourself just right so you could attract just the right man so he would care for you and make you happy because that is what women and men do, and it is right and proper and wonderful that it should be that way. Suppose you do just what is expected: You become sweet and sexy, and you find that man (or, rather, he finds you), and you marry and have three lovely children, and he has a lovely job and you have a lovely house and . . . then suppose it suddenly ends. Now suppose you find yourself in your thirty-third year with three lovely children, no husband, meager or no support, no income, no skills, no joy. Suppose you see him with freedom, mobility, job skills, income, future. What do you say? Usually, you first say, "What did I do wrong?" But perhaps in time you gain some insight and recognize that what went wrong wasn't you—it was the whole thing: beliefs, assumptions, and expectations. Seeing this, you say, "Oh, it was a lie."

Suppose it doesn't end. Suppose you have the lovely children, the lovely home, the lovely husband, but you aren't happy. You're depressed or restless or grouchy. You're always busy, but you're also bored. What do you say? You say, "What's wrong with me? Why am I unsatisfied?" Or perhaps you look around and say, "It was a lie."

Suppose you did all the things you were advised to do in *Cosmopolitan* or *Woman's Day:* You were kind, thoughtful, playful, sexy, and supportive—but instead of undying love, you got misunderstanding, neglect, hostility. Or suppose you got slapped, punched, kicked. What do you say?

Suppose it all went a different way. Suppose your youth was poor and hard. You learned to scratch and scrape. Now jobs are hard to find, and when they do come along they pay even less than a man's, and your men come and go, and you have some babies to support, but when you go to court and ask for support, the (male) judge decides that, after all, Mr. X has a new family to support and cannot be left penniless! Or Mr. X is ordered to pay support for his children, but no one can find him, and few care. What do you say?

Suppose none of the things you were being taught about yourself or your future seemed to fit. You knew from the beginning that you were "different," that it wasn't men you were drawn to but women. Suppose you confide in your parents and they cry and tell you that they hope you get over it; maybe "treatment" will help. Suppose you find that it's unsafe to walk the street with the woman you love, or rent an apartment, or care for the children you had before. . . . What do you say?

Suppose you spent your youth learning and preparing and studying, and the future is bright because America is a land of opportunity. You know things are harder for a woman and you have to be twice as good, but you *are* twice as good. But suppose you can't find the kind of job you want. They just ask how many words per minute you can type. Or suppose they do give you that job (EEOC and Title IX, you know), but you find you're the only associate answering the telephone or preparing customer forms. What do you say?

Or suppose you do find the job you want. You're very good at what you do; you're bright, energetic, highly committed, and that professional position you've dreamed of does come your way. You give it everything you've got, and you're pretty successful. And you find yourself in your mid- to late thirties,

and you want a family, too (and you listen to your biological clock going tick, tick, tick). But because women make the babies—and feed them, and clean them, and teach them, and need to be there for them—you fear you can't have it all, and you need to choose. Or perhaps you decide that you can have both and will have both, a job you love and a family you love, but it costs so much, and you can't do it all and still be a "trophy wife," or you can, but you're so stretched and tired, and you wonder why he doesn't have such choices to make or prices to pay. . . . What do you say?

When at last, for whatever reason and in whatever way, you recognize one lie, you get suspicious, and you begin to look at it all. Soon you see just how many lies there are. Then you think: If women are stupid, incompetent, and petty, as they say, but I am female and I am *not* those things, either I am not a woman or it's a lie. And if it's a lie about me, it's a lie about other women; and if that's a lie, then perhaps the rest is a lie. Perhaps it's a lie that women aren't smart enough or strong enough to be trusted to do this job or that—or women are strong enough, but then they destroy their men. Perhaps it's a lie that for women, love is more important than anything; that pushy women are destroying the family structure; that women are best satisfied in the home of a he-male; that women don't need jobs or incomes; that poor women are just plain lazy; that motherhood is so delightful it's enough to satisfy any woman; that men should make the decisions; that women have to choose between loyalty to our man (or men) and loyalty to ourselves; that women should *never* be "easy" or "pushy" or "ambitious" or "shrill"; that God said that we should "graciously submit."

Once begun, the questioning has no limits. We discover lie upon lie, myth upon myth. The response? If it is not true that women are bad or incompetent, then all our subordination is just plain wrong. If the role won't work, we'll have to find something else.

Where is it written that it must be the way it is?

WHAT WE LEARN: THE IMAGES TELL US

The heading of this section is presumptuous. What we learn when we begin to ask these kinds of questions is so vast that it could not be told in a thousand volumes. Different women learn different things and make different choices. Discoveries vary, reactions vary, feelings vary. What I would like to describe here, though, are some of the insights feminists have had into themselves as women, into the effects of the myths and stereotypes, and into the possibilities open to women without them.

The Splitting of the Androgyne: Complements

The term *androgyne* is composed of the two ancient Greek words *andros* and *gyne, man* and *woman.* In certain feminist theories, it refers to a person of either sex characterized by a combination of qualities that traditionally have been taken to be only male or only female.[9] The androgyne, or the androgynous person, may be strong *and* tender, rational *and* feeling, independent *and* receptive, and so on. Or they may be none of these but exhibit other traits true to their individuality, not simply the ones prescribed for them. Although considerable controversy surrounds the notion of an "androgenous" ideal, no feminists prescribe a division of character traits along gender lines.

As we saw earlier, what patriarchy decrees ideally for women and men is the exact opposite of androgyny, *complementarity.* Women and men are expected to exhibit opposite and exclusive traits and behavior (see list of patriarchal ideals on p. 175).

The following quotations are from a book entitled, *Safe Counsel or Practical Eugenics*[10], which offers us "Practical advice about sex, sin and sane living—Our grandfathers' (notice it does not say grandmothers') priceless legacy to our wayward world." Its preface tells us that it was written originally in 1893, had no fewer than thirty-nine editions, and sold over a million copies during an era when that would have been extraordinary. The authors tell us that this is a book for "right-thinking" modern people who can handle a bit of frank language and candid talk. Here are methods to improve the race and help a young man or woman to make choices that will lead to a happy life: he to go from a boyhood of study and cleanliness, to purity and economy at 25, honorable success at 36, and a venerable old age at 60; she to grow from a girlhood of study and obedience at 13, virtue and devotion at

20, to a loving mother at 26, and an honored grandmother at 60.[11] The pictures painted here of perfect men and women may seem hilarious to us, but they are not so old or out of date as one might think, and remember, they were taken very seriously in their time. These are the "musts" my mother taught me, that I resisted and feminism struggled against. They make very clear the gender rules out of which today's norms were born. Although they are adapted to today's culture, these images are still found in the present scene.

Men and women are radically different, we are told:

> *Man is the creature of interest and ambition. His nature leads him forth into the struggle and bustle of the world. Love is but the embellishment of his early life. . . . He seeks for fame, for fortune, for space in the world's thoughts, and dominion over his fellowmen. But a woman's whole life is a history of the affections. The heart is her world; it is there her ambition strives for empire; . . . she embarks her whole soul in the traffic of affection; and if shipwrecked her case is hopeless, for it is bankruptcy of the heart.*[12]

And what do men and women seek in each other (that is, what *is* the ideal)?

> *Women naturally love courage, force and firmness in men. The ideal man in a woman's eye must be heroic and brave. Woman naturally despises a coward, and she has little or no respect for a bashful man. . . . Man is naturally the protector of woman; as the male wild animal of the forest protects the female. . . . Women naturally love men of strength, size and fine physique, a tall, large and strong man . . . a generous man. . . . Women love strong, vigorous men. . . . Weak and delicate fathers have puny and sickly children. . . .*
>
> *Men love beautiful women. . . . A beautiful form, a graceful figure, graceful movements and a kind heart. . . . Good looks and good and pure conduct. . . . No weakly, poor-bodied woman can draw a man's love like a strong, well developed body. A round, plump figure with an overflow of animal life. . . . A woman with a large pelvis has a superior and significant appearance, while a narrow pelvis always indicates weak sexuality. . . . Small feet and small ankles are very attractive . . . and indicate modesty and reserve, while large feet and ankles*

indicate coarseness, physical power, authority, pre-
dominance. . . . a well shaped arm, small hands and
small wrists, with full muscular development, is a
charm. . . . If a woman desires to be loved, she must
cultivate her intellectual gifts, be interesting and
entertaining in society, and practical and helpful in
the home. . . .[13]

Patriarchal Ideals

Ideal Man	*Ideal Woman*
powerful, creative	nurturant, supportive
intelligent, rational	intuitive, emotional, cunning
independent, self-reliant	needful, dependent
strong	tender
courageous, daring	timid, fragile
responsible, resolute	capricious, childlike
temperate, cautious, sober	ebullient, exuberant
honest, forthright	tactful, evasive, artful
active, forceful	passive, receptive
honorable, principled, just	obedient, loyal, kind, merciful
self-affirming	self-abnegating
authoriative, decisive	compliant, submissive
successful, task-oriented	contented, serene, being-oriented
does	cares
lives in the mind	lives in the heart
confronts the world	withdraws from the world

Commonly, sexist ideologies, like the preceding one or that of Darlene Wilkinson quoted in Chapter 3, say that men and women are complements to one another; that their complementarity is natural, desirable, and beautiful, even divinely ordained; that together these two, different but interlocking, provide for themselves, their families, and society all that is necessary and harmonious for human living. Actually, the theory of complementarity is based on a division of labor: Men and women are different, each having their own special character and abilities. (In some versions of this argument, the traits are given by nature, in others they are divinely ordained.) Because they are not the same, their jobs and responsibilities are likewise not the same, dif-

ferent (though equally important) and appropriate to their "natures."

Feminists argue that this argument is a mystification, intentionally camouflaging ugly truths with euphemistic social myths. They counter with concrete criticisms of this complementary arrangement:

- It may be appealing to envision two interlocking creatures walking hand in hand down life's highway, but in reality, half a person plus half a person equals two half-persons, not one whole one.

- As Plato pointed out in the third century B.C.E., human beings require balance and excellence in all of their qualities to function well. The ideal man of patriarchy may be eminently successful so far as society is concerned, but if he lacks the ability to feel and to experience fully the affective elements of living, he gains only half of what life has to offer, and he is apt to be a rather unbalanced and unpleasant person. The ideal patriarchal woman may be very fetching and capable of deep feeling, but she is also unable to take care of herself in the material aspects of life, and hence she is at the mercy of other people and events.

- It is unrealistic to believe that two people, entirely different in capacity and outlook, could successfully manage meaningful communication, mutual respect, and love. Rather than interlocking, these people are locked together in a destructive, though symbiotic, partnership. The traditional complementary arrangement is logical and functional only in terms of social and economic efficiency, not in terms of human needs. Complementarity, a division of labor, may be an effective way of accomplishing a variety of social tasks; and when marriage functioned as a social arrangement for satisfying certain community needs, complementarity might have been a productive perspective. But if marriage is to function as a satisfying *personal* arrangement, as a primary source of emotional support and profound human interchange, then complementarity is dysfunctional, and "interlocking" symbiosis is a psychological and spiritual disaster.

- Even if it were possible for two people to relate well in complementarity, women would
still be at a marked disadvantage in this
schema because it assigns authority to men
and subordination to women.

In the first place, the thesis that in our society
the two elements, male and female, are different but
equal in value and importance is a lie. The system—
patriarchal in origin and serving patriarchal ends—
is built on the principle that men rule and women
obey. Even in the most benevolent of all worlds, that
is not a highly promising arrangement for women.

In the second place, although it is true that in a
system of complementarity, men and women are
both in the position of using half and only half of
their human capacities (and so losing half as well),
the half that men keep is the half valued by society,
and the half that women keep is devalued (which
stands to reason, given the control of society by the
masculinists). Though women are praised, a patronizing undertone always accompanies that praise.
The praise is awarded for traits that (masculinist)
society as a whole deems less valuable.

Human Versus Female

In Chapter 2, we looked at the historical confusion
of the concepts *man* and *human.* In fact, the patriarchal schema of complementary ideals is both cause
and effect of that confusion. The configuration of
traits and qualities reserved for ideal men is the configuration expected of excellent human beings: intelligence, independence, courage, honor, strength.
Not so the configuration for a woman. Womanly
perfection and human excellence in this schema are
incompatible.

In effect, in this schema, women are being asked
to choose between their human selves and their sexual identities. Unlike men, who develop and improve their masculinity and humanity concurrently,
women in patriarchy only destroy their acceptability as females if they develop their human excellence or else destroy their human potential if they
become more "feminine."

An important early feminist study translated
this issue into the language of psychology:

*A study by Inge Broverman and her colleagues sug-
gests that many clinicians today view their female*

*patients the way Freud viewed his. They gave 79
therapists (46 male and 33 female psychiatrists,
psychologists and social workers) a sex-role-stereo-
type questionnaire. This test consists of 122 pairs of
traits such as "very subjective . . . very objective" or
"not at all aggressive . . . very aggressive."*

*The investigators asked the subjects to rate each
set of traits on a scale from one to seven, in terms of
where a healthy male should fall, a healthy female,
or a healthy adult (sex unspecified). They found:*

1. *There was a high agreement among these clinicians on the attributes that characterize men,
women and adults.*

2. *There were no major differences between the male
and the female clinicians.*

3. *Clinicians have different standards of mental
health for men and women. Their standards for
a "healthy adult man" looked like those for a
"healthy adult"; but healthy women differed
from both by being: submissive, emotional, easily
influenced, sensitive to being hurt, excitable,
conceited about their appearance, dependent, not
very adventurous, less competitive, unaggressive, unobjective—and besides, they dislike math
and science. This "healthy woman" is not very
likeable, all in all! (In fact, other studies have
shown that these traits, characteristic of normal
women, are the least socially desirable.) For a
woman to be "healthy," then, she must adjust to
the behavioral norms for her sex even though
these norms are not highly valued by her society,
her men—or her therapist.*[14]

Thus, behavior considered healthy for men was
not considered healthy for women, and vice versa.
Men and women were expected to display opposite characteristics. But the traits deemed *generally*
healthy, desirable for *people* without regard to sex,
were those expected of, or prescribed for, men.
Women displaying those traits would be deemed
"unfeminine." At the same time, women who were
"feminine," who would be deemed healthy or adjusted as women, would by this schema have to be
judged sick as people!

What an impossible dilemma. Women may
choose to be considered "feminine," or we may
choose to be mature, healthy human beings, but we
may not be both. Put a slightly different way: While

men may be thought of as human beings who happen to be male, women are cast as females who happen to be (in a lesser sense) human.

Feminists argue that complementarity is a disaster for both sexes, that the healthy person (of either sex) is the human being who excels in both configurations—or perhaps rejects *any* configuration—who has the wherewithal to cope with the necessities and challenges of life, as well as the sensibilities to do it in a way that is *for* life.

WHAT'S WRONG WITH "FEMININITY"?

In the preceding chapter, we noted that the dichotomy in the female ideal required women to exemplify at once two incompatible characterizations, Mary and the Playmate, and we could see how destructive such a contradiction is. However, more is wrong with patriarchal female images, or "femininity," than just the contradictions wrought by dichotomy. For one thing, feminists argue, the pejorative stereotype of "Woman the Inferior" is false. For another, neither of the supposedly nonpejorative images, Mary or Playmate, is a desirable model. In fact, both are demeaning and destructive.

The Myth of Female Inferiority

According to misogynist ideology, women are inferior in two ways: (1) women are morally inferior; we are evil, sinful, dangerous, and (believe it or not) dirty; (2) women are inferior in ability—physically, intellectually, and spiritually.

Women Are Evil   That women are morally inferior to the point of being positively evil is a well-worn theme that comes down to us today from antiquity:

Woman is a pitfall—a pitfall, a hole, a ditch. Woman is a sharp iron dagger that cuts a man's throat.

—MESOPOTAMIAN POEM[15]

Man who trusts womankind trusts deceivers.

—HESIOD[16]

The beauty of woman is the greatest snare.

—ST. JOHN CHRYSOSTOM[17]

You are the devil's gateway . . . the first deserter of the divine law; you are she who persuaded him

whom the devil was not valiant enough to attack. You destroyed so easily God's image, man. On account of your desert—that is, death—even the son of God had to die.

—TERTULLIAN[18]

I have not left any calamity more detrimental to mankind than woman.

—ISLAMIC SAYING[19]

Art thou not formed of foul slime? Art thou not full of uncleanness?

—RULE FOR ANCHORESSES[20]

God made Adam master over all creatures, to rule over all living things, but when Eve persuaded him that he was lord even over God she spoiled everything. . . . With tricks and cunning women deceive men.

—MARTIN LUTHER[21]

I cannot escape the notion . . . that for women the level of what is ethically normal is different from what it is in man.

—SIGMUND FREUD[22]

So much for woman on a pedestal. These historical statements have only scratched the surface. Further evidence of the belief in female malevolence abounds—no less virulent today than it has been for centuries. In the past were the stories of Delilah and Salome, Bible temptresses who destroyed good men; Medusa, the Gorgon, who turned men into stone; Maenads, who tore men apart and ate them during drunken orgies; Sirens, who lived in the sea and lured sailors to their death with covert promises. Which of us did not grow up on the wicked women of the fairy tales: vain and murderous queens, dark fairies, bad witches, malevolent stepsisters and their cruel, ambitious, self-centered mothers. What these women all had in common was that they were not "good" like Snow White and Sleeping Beauty and Cinderella. They were not young and fair and victimized; they were not "sweet" and pliant, vulnerable, dependent, and utterly passive. Indeed, they were women on their own: autonomous, self-directed, unowned, *and therefore uncontrolled.* And that is why, furthermore, they all came to no good.

How different are these characters and these tales from those of today? Are there not still good, sweet, wholesome, back-home kinds of girls who follow their hearts and their men and their prescribed roles and win (the prince) in the end? The poor, sweet, innocent, good-hearted creatures of *Pretty Woman* and *My Best Friend's Wedding* remain loyal and loving even in the face of rejection and shame—and they triumph; they get their man. Another fate befalls the tougher women in, say, *Fatal Attraction* or *Working Girl*, or even *My Best Friend's Wedding*, where the "bad" girl is the very appealing Julia Roberts. They must lose; after all, they rebelled, said no to their "place," refused to be "feminine." In each film, a powerful, willful, independent, beautiful woman seems *for a while* to be in control. But she is vanquished in the end, supplanted by the sweet and proper lady. In each case, the fates of the contenders are settled by the decision of the male, who moves easily between them and always acts for his own interests in his own way.

To allegations of evil, feminists retort: Nonsense! While patriarchal society prattles about women's destructiveness, feminists ask: Who creates weapons and marches off to war? Who hunts and kills living creatures for fun? Who fights for kicks? Who pillages the earth for profit? Who colonizes and exploits? What destruction could we have wrought that even nearly compares?

If Eve we will be called, then let us be Eve in our own sense, in the best sense, reconstructed according to our feminist perspectives.

> They say: she violated the taboo, surrendered to the snake, ate the apple, corrupted the man, brought about the expulsion from the Father's garden, was responsible for the Fall, called down the Father's curse. Upon earth, upon labor, upon childbirth, upon woman. So far as they were concerned they told a tale of sin and its punishment, of gluttony and its consequences, of disobedience and the revenge taken by the primal father against those who eat.

> I say: Eve dared to break the taboo against eating, embraced the temptation offered by the snake, ate the apple, and returned symbolically to the maternal breast to regain an identity with the Mother Goddess. If eating caused her to be expelled from her Father's house, that precisely is what allowed her to give birth to the Woman Who Is Not Yet.

> Eve's dilemma: a choice between obedience and knowledge. Between renunciation and appetite. Between subordination and desire. Between security and risk. Between loyalty and self-development. Between submission and power. Between hunger as temptation and hunger as vision.

> It is the dilemma of modern women.
> —Kim Chernin[23]

Women Are Incompetent   The charge that both requires and easily admits of refutation is that women are simply not as able as men, not as competent at any task except those traditionally designated "women's work." It is said that women are less capable than men of doing any kind of work requiring a high degree of rationality, abstraction, and intelligence because women are intellectually inferior and are characteristically not given to rationality and logic. It is said that, in even the best of circumstances, even unusually intelligent women are still not the equals of men in important and difficult work because they are temperamentally unsuited to seriousness of purpose, sustained effort, and strain. It is said that women are unable to withstand the pressure of competition, either with people or with ideas, and are therefore always destined to defeat. And finally, it is said that women who are not thus characteristically inferior are not "normal," are not attractive or natural or feminine, and are not even really women—another double bind.

As evidence of women's inferiority, it is asserted that the great scientists, inventors, legislators, entrepreneurs, artists, humorists, authors, athletes, and warriors have always been men. Where are the female geniuses—the Beethovens, Shakespeares, and Platos? We are told that in business and industry, in the professions and professional schools, it is men who outrank women, who achieve. Even today, argue the sexists, when women have the opportunities of men, they still do not make it as often or as big. Why? Because women do not have the intelligence, the instincts, the grit, the motivation, the stamina, or the strength of men. In every way that counts, women are inferior.

This is how the schema goes:

Part I—It is unnatural and undesirable for women to do what men do; women must expend their energies serving, supporting, and pleasing; they must not be allowed to do what men do.

Part II—Because women do not do the things men do, it is evident that they cannot do what men do and are therefore obviously inferior.

The argument is circular, superficial, and fallacious. It does, however, hold tremendous power in society—at least as a rationale for the status quo, and a majority, both female and male, believe it.

Feminists refute these arguments. We contend that the socialization process and the structure of society, not "natural" capacities, account for the different levels of achievement and motivation in women and men. Although the literature is mixed and the research inconclusive, there is no evidence that men and women differ in intellectual capacity or IQ, and a good deal of evidence to the contrary. Apparently males excel earlier in spatial ability and females in verbal ability, but even this difference may be accounted for by social conditions. It is certainly not sufficient to account for the wide divergence in interest, abilities, motivations, and achievements.

A great deal of evidence suggests that "feminine" ideals—the images and values described in Chapter 3, including the constraints and circumstances imposed on women from childhood—are far more responsible for women's alleged and actual lack of motivation, grit, and aggressiveness than any inherent childlikeness or timidity. Differences in training, expectations, and experience produce ineffectualness and defeatism in women, as they do in men. Yet there are and always have been women of incredible courage, stamina, and commitment, too many to mention, women known and not known, in the past and in the present, enough to fill an encyclopedia, yet often ignored or forgotten.

Not now nor ever has equality of opportunity existed for women, in business, the professions, education, the arts, or any other socially prized and male-controlled venture. Today, doors are still only grudgingly opening to women. The glass ceiling is not a fantasy. Even if this were not so, the separate but not equal conditioning of females and the hostility and ignorance of the men already in positions of power make any claims to equality of opportunity a farce.

Women's dual roles and incompatible cultural requirements render success in the community or in a profession painfully expensive if not impossible, physically, emotionally, spiritually.

> *I was a child when I first heard someone say, "Men work from sun to sun, but women's work is never done." For years I thought it proof that women, rather than being the "weaker" sex, were if anything superior to, stronger than men. I was a woman, very much grown, before I realized how heavy those words can weigh—the reality, the burden.*
>
> *Black women work! Yet the gruesome truth is that "women's work" is often dismissed, taken for granted or devalued. It's almost as if never-ending hard work and bearing burdens is what we were born to. Our plates are piled high with things we have to do or are expected to do or want to do or are pushed to.*
>
> *The pressures we women are under are intense. We are bombarded from all sides with all manner of things we gotta do: Gotta make ways for lasting meaningful social, economic and political change. Gotta stop analyzing and amening and get to practical solutions, then make 'em happen. Gotta do well on our jobs, gotta keep 'em or get better ones or make the ones we have pay off. Gotta keep our relationships thriving or get some going. Gotta look good and stay healthy. Told that we gotta be in control of our lives and our destinies. Gotta be past, present and future women all at the same time. Gotta keep our spirits and our sanity. Most important, or so it often seems, is that we Black women gotta be good women, gotta be strong.*
>
> —Marcia Ann Gillespie[24]

The married woman who works outside the home usually has two jobs, one paid (however humbly), one not paid. She is clerk (teacher, doctor, pilot, dental assistant . . .), and she is homemaker and mother. The price of such demands, both for her job and her personal health, are obvious. The unmarried working woman faces different costs: slurs on her womanhood, social disapprobation, at times loneliness. According to the image, ideal women are intuitive but not rational, lovely but not effectual. The successful professional, according to the myth, is the unsuccessful *femme.* To opt for a career, the story goes, is to relinquish one's happily-ever-after. Such visions, even unfounded, are disturbing. They do not do much for professional motivation. Men do not generally face these choices or endure these slurs, and again it is women who are disadvantaged.

To the questions "Why haven't women produced any geniuses? and Why are there no female Shakespeares or Beethovens?" feminists respond that these are two different questions. The first assumes that there are no female geniuses. In fact, greatness among women is rarely acknowledged, let alone celebrated. In a patriarchal world, only accomplishments that matter to the patriarchs and serve them are lauded. Furthermore, generally throughout history, only genius that appeared in men was encouraged and given the means to flourish, a fact that answers the second question: Where are the Shakespeares and Beethovens? How were great writers, painters, poets, leaders to develop among women when they weren't even taught to read and write, or allowed to travel and study, when they were not free to use their time as they wished? Great thinkers did emerge in the convents, where women were able to use their minds and energies without interference from parents, husbands, and children, and now and then it appeared among the aristocracy, but rarely could it exist in the ordinary lives of ordinary women. Virginia Woolf wrote that women have not been allowed a "room of our own." We have been accorded bread but not roses. We have not been allowed the spiritual atmosphere, the creative space men are given, the amenities (not to mention the financial circumstances) that raise life above the mundane and encourage one to creativity.

The issues treated here all point to an important feminist argument: A range of factors in the environment conspire to impede women's competence and accomplishments in many areas: the hostile or deprecating attitudes of men in power, lack of support and assistance from all quarters, dual and/or incompatible professional and nonprofessional functions, pervasiveness of the masculinist (alien, inhospitable) ambience, and socialization that erodes confidence and self-assertion. Rather than being inferior, women are hampered in developing competence in the most profound ways. To overcome the obstacles put in our way, we must indeed be twice

as good as men, but in more ways than we expected. It is not surprising that so many of us do not "succeed." What is extraordinary is that any of us do.

And what we do accomplish often disappears! In the history books, women of achievement are rarely given more than a few lines, and the experiences of ordinary women, unlike those of "the common man," are simply not considered. Our successes have often gone underground, to be attributed to men or thought to be anonymous because women were not permitted either to have or to advertise their success. Female authors or artists often used male pen names or "protectors" or "co-authors" who frequently co-authored them right out of their due. Ancient accomplishments are simply usurped by the patriarchy. Male historians and anthropologists "forget" to research the contributions of women to early civilization: the introduction of pottery, weaving, food preservation and preparation, perhaps even agriculture itself. Current anthologies of the arts do not bother to include women's works because these are "inferior," "narrow," or "lacking in grandeur" (in the eyes of their male reviewers). In the Blackstone Audiobooks catalogue for the year 2000, a *New York Times* reviewer of Ayn Rand is quoted: "A writer of great power. . . . This is the only novel of ideas written by an American woman that I can recall."[25] Really? The only one?! It takes the breath away—even if his comment was made in the 1950s, when Rand published her novels, before the explosion of writing precipitated by the women's movement. Apparently he had never heard of Harriet Beecher Stowe, Kate Chopin, Zora Neale Hurston, Edith Wharton, Tillie Olsen, and a host of others who wrote "novels of ideas" before 1950, and that, of course, is just the point. Why didn't he? Did he think that the ideas women wrote about did not count as ideas? Or did he simply not bother to read women's novels?

It is telling too how many "novels of ideas" have been written by women since 1950, since feminist activism opened up opportunities for higher education to greater numbers of women and established presses that would make women's writing available to a constantly growing audience of women, and finally of men. It is no accident that only now, when feminist researchers are recovering the history and highlighting its importance, are women of great accomplishment being recognized by the world, women like Simone de Beauvoir and Eleanor Roosevelt.

We must not forget that at times in our past and still in some places it has been dangerous for women to succeed, that women die for visibility or assertiveness. In the Middle Ages, midwives were burned as witches. Rebellious wives and daughters were, and in some places in the world still are, imprisoned or beaten or stabbed or burned alive. Feminists in Nazi Germany were sent to concentration camps. On the streets or in their homes almost anywhere in the world, uppity women—independent women, gay women, nonconformist women—may be raped, battered, or murdered. Or they may be executed by the state.

> *In December of 1970, Ms. Farrokhrou Parsa, the first woman to serve in the Iranian cabinet, was executed after a trial by hooded judges—a trial at which no defense attorney was permitted, no appeal possible, and the defendant had been officially declared guilty before the proceedings began. She was charged with "expansion of prostitution, corruption on earth, and warring against God." Aware of the hopelessness of her case, she delivered a reasoned, courageous defense of her career decisions, among them a directive to free female schoolchildren from having to be veiled and the establishment of a commission for revising textbooks to present a nonsexist image of women. A few hours after sentence was pronounced she was wrapped in a dark sack and machine-gunned. . . .*
>
> *. . . The years ahead will be difficult. To unite a torn and battered nation and rebuild what had been destroyed is a monumental task. But as I contemplate the future of Iran, a reassuring image gives me hope. I recall a young women I met in the southern village of Zovieh. She had finished her military service in the literacy corps to return to her home and establish a school in which she taught all subjects to all four grades. On the day I saw her, she was walking out of a village meeting in her faded uniform, flushed, and proud, followed by the old men who had just selected her* Kadkhoda, *or "elderman," of the village.*
>
> *Those who have struggled and those who have died sacrificed so that women like her may exist.*
>
> *She is the future.*
>
> —Mahnaz Afkhami[26]

The Dark Side of the "Good" Woman

Refuting the claim that women as a class are inferior does not constitute the entire feminist offensive against patriarchal female images. The so-called positive images of women in patriarchy are as much a target, for even the ideals, Perfect Woman, Mary, or the Playmate, are destructive. Despite the apparent veneration these ideals receive, at their heart they actually disparage women's humanness and cause us to disparage ourselves. In so doing, they diminish our lives.

Consider once again the major requirements of traditional femininity: beauty, self-effacement, fragility, and domesticity. History, poetry, literature, philosophy, and even science have eulogized the woman who embodies these qualities, but feminists have taken a closer look. Demystifying the image, we have seen the dark side of this image.

Beauty   Attractiveness in people is by and large culturally determined; that is, beauty is socially defined. In patriarchy, men construct the ideal in their own interests, and women, whose lives have no purpose outside of being chosen, or whose identities and fortunes have been made subject to their appeal to men, have little choice but to struggle with the requirements of "beauty," even if the ideal is impossible or destructive, like the current obsession with a starved-looking body profile. No human being can be "perfect" in hair, skin, teeth, shape, proportion, and scent and, furthermore, be so both "naturally" and endlessly. Constant comparison with the made-up and reconstructed figures of screen and magazine that more nearly realize the ideal always leaves us defeated, always at a disadvantage, always self-deprecating.

Women are called narcissistic. We are chided for our obsession with clothing and fashion. We are ridiculed for slathering cream on our skin and dye in our hair. And yet that is precisely what is demanded *if we accept* the traditional role that bids us to use our appearance to attract and keep a mate. Can we reject that option if any life other than "being chosen" is deemed undesirable or even unacceptable, if "attractive" and "sexy" are society's best terms for women?

Self-effacement   The concept of submissiveness for women has changed since the Middle Ages. Few today would expect a women to lower her head and whisper, "Yes, sir." Yet the ideal survives in somewhat changed form: No one, we hear, likes an aggressive (pushy) woman. We may quarrel, we may fight, but in the end, if we don't give in often enough, we will lose our man. Assertiveness, the kind that goes beyond a little pluckiness, is still not considered acceptable in women; it is always translated into aggression.

And self-effacement? The husband who taunts in public is teasing. The wife who does the same is destroying her man's ego. She is not expected to say, "Yes, dear," but she is expected to yield to him the major decisions of their lives (or pretend to), to follow his job, to entertain his friends. He drives the car when they are together—to show he is in charge. He works late when he needs to. He storms out of the house when angry. She screams or she cries, but she stays put.

Women, it is said, are prone to depression. We get "neurotic," clingy, and nagging. What man who could not make his own decisions, place his own needs high in priority, satisfy his desires and wishes, please himself, and follow his goals would not get depressed and "neurotic"? What man barred from following his own inclinations wouldn't nag others for entertainment? The logical outcome of self-effacement is depression.

Fragility   Very close to self-effacement is fragility. Women are to be submissive because we are weaker, needing protection and guidance. In gratitude and in our understanding of our best interests, we are to take direction from the stronger. Fragility—physical smallness, timidity, delicacy, needfulness—entails vulnerability. It is, to be sure, very appealing to the male. But vulnerability of the sort required of women also entails dependence. To be fearful of strange situations, to be hesitant when decisions are called for, to avoid risk, to learn *not* to defend oneself, to feign or even encourage physical weakness, to shrink from the world, to do these things are to place oneself at the mercy of circumstances, to make oneself dependent on others. Even if those on whom one depends are completely trustworthy, marvelously competent, and around forever, any-

one in such a situation must feel some lack of self-respect, a sense of ineffectualness. For such people, life is truncated; the pleasures and rewards of independence, accomplishment, and power are unknown. Further, in a culture that clearly values competence, independence, and self-reliance, the endlessly vulnerable and dependent person is a figure of ridicule and contempt.

Domesticity   *Kinder, Kirche, Küche*—"children, church, cooking"—was the slogan of ideal womanhood in Hitler's Germany, the Third Reich. In patriarchy, masculinists decree that the only acceptable work for women is care of children, including teaching, child care, and nursing (Kinder); housekeeping, and related work, including food preparation (Küche); and obedient worship, including maintenance of moral rules for one's self and one's household, and dutiful care of the physical symbols of worship—chalices, candlesticks, benches, vestments, and so on (Kirche). Theology, of course, or any other work that presumes to "name" reality, is prohibited. Women's work is to be task-oriented, not policy-oriented; that is, we are to execute our jobs according to prescribed procedure, not to define those jobs or to create their meaning. Ours is to carry out that part of any job that is repetitive, routine, uninteresting. Work that transcends the mundane belongs to men. Women may be cooks, not chefs; dressmakers, not designers; secretaries, not executives. We may busy ourselves with the "craft" of making curtains or vases, but we are not to presume to art. (In fact, in the United States, until the women's movement fought to widen women's occupational opportunities, these were the jobs most women had to settle for.)

Women, the sexists say, haven't the minds or spirit for highly creative activities, such as art (or engineering, or . . .). Besides, we haven't the time for it, or we should not, if we are doing our primary tasks properly. Women were designed to reproduce and care for our children (see the reading from Aquinas in the preceding chapter), which takes a great deal of time, and thus we are meant to stay at home, where we can do what we were designed to do and serve our men, who protect us and enable us to meet our divinely ordained responsibilities. (Unless, of course, we are poor and need assistance, in which case we ought to leave our children, take any job we can get, and remember not to have any more children.)

Philosophers tell us that the imminent (as the existentialists call it), the mundane, the here-and-now, the "what," is dull and petty unless it is lifted by the transcendent, the eternal, the why and the wherefore. Tasks and things do not have the scope or the breadth of ideas. Interest, scope, and depth belong to creativity. Interesting people are living, growing people; they are people who are themselves interested, excited, challenged and challenging, learning and experiencing. *Kinder, Kirche, Küche,* however taxing of time and energy, cannot be creative unless so treated. In closing women to freedom of experience and movement, in disallowing as "unfeminine" interest in the transcendent, in constricting our limits and our power, patriarchy confines us to the narrow and then condemns us for our "narrowness."

Patriarchal feminine ideals are monstrous. When successful, they destroy; and when we become the most perfect realizations of them, we are most damaged.

RESPONSES: FEMINIST REACTIONS AND IDEALS

When feminist women look over the history of the tyranny of these beliefs and visions, when we note the destruction they have wrought and the exploitation they have legitimized, we are appalled and filled with anger, pain, grief, shock, and finally, determination.

Some call feminists petty, prattling noisily about inconsequentials. But is the loss of potential, self-respect, and autonomy inconsequential? Are economic deprivation and financial dependency inconsequential, or the use and abuse of our bodies for the interests of others? What about infanticide, physical mutilation, footbinding, clitoridectomy, and other physical torture? Is ten thousand years of domination and exploitation of over half of humanity inconsequential? Is it inconsequential to claim that women are not quite as human as men and therefore ought not to have choices, or freedom, or autonomy, or dreams, or opportunity, or power like men?

We are advised to be ladylike, to go slowly, to ask nicely, and to develop a sense of humor. Are we to swallow our pride once again and plead prettily for our liberation from those who have withheld it for ten millennia until this day? Are we to chuckle good naturedly at centuries of exploitation, at restrictive clothing, chastity belts, and whalebone corsets, at enforced fatigue of body and mind, at slave labor and sexual servitude, at prostitution and rape and physical abuse? Are we to take these images in our stride, once more play the peacemakers, maintain the hated postures just a little longer while the masculinists slowly adjust to the idea of change?

No, say the feminists, we will not do it. If we are angry, it is because we have seen the assault. If we are noisy, it is because women are suffering. If we sound strident, it is because the affirmation of women grates on the ears of masculinists. "It is not that we are so radical," said Gloria Steinem, "but that there is something radically wrong with our world."

We have seen the visions of *woman the oppressed, woman the exploited, woman the outsider, woman the lost, woman the debased*—and we reject them all, opting instead for positive visions.

Feminists are building new visions, throwing away the demands of "femininity" so badly conceived, canceling "ladylikeness." We are redefining what is desirable for us, what is commendable, what is possible. Our new role models include *woman rediscovering herself in history* and for today; *woman redeeming herself* in her own eyes; *woman rightfully angry,* rightfully fighting for change; and *woman the leader,* the pillar, who in the words of Wilma Scott Heide may "create the kind of world where the power of love exceeds the love of power."[27] Indeed, our ideals include our own free selves, to whom we are saying, yes!

What we shall be, what we should and can be, remains an open question. Feminists are still very much involved in the matter of what we are not and should not be. We have been asked what we would wish to be, how life would be if we could have our way, and many have answered that it is hard to say. We have never known a time when we have not been subordinated and devalued; we have never known a time of freedom and self-determination. We are only beginning to learn our history and to conceive our future—with few known models and precious little experience. In very large part, the question of what we ought to be is the question philosophers have pursued for centuries: What is human excellence and virtue? Women are, after all, human beings, and our strivings and hopes are those of all humanity. How our ideals may differ from those of men or how our insights may alter the notion of human excellence is yet to be discovered.

Certain things we do know: We are being born, coming into life. We are struggling, and in this birth struggle is joy. Feminist writer Germaine Greer expresses it eloquently:

The surest guide to the correctness of the path that women take is joy in the struggle. Revolution is the festival of the oppressed. For a long time there may be no perceptible reward for women other than their new sense of purpose and integrity. Joy does not mean riotous glee, but it does mean the purposive employment of energy in a self-chosen enterprise. It does mean pride and confidence. It does mean communication and cooperation with others based on delight in their company and your own. To be emancipated from helplessness and need and walk freely upon the earth that is your birthright. To refuse hobbles and deformity and take possession of your body and glory in its power, accepting its own laws of loveliness. To have something to desire, something to make, something to achieve, and at last something genuine to give. To be freed from guilt and shame and the tireless self-discipline of women. To stop pretending and dissembling, cajoling and manipulating, and begin to control and sympathize. To claim the masculine virtues of magnanimity and generosity and courage. It goes much further than equal pay for equal work, for it ought to revolutionize the conditions of work completely. It does not understand the phrase "equality of opportunity," for it seems that the opportunities will have to be utterly changed and women's souls changed so that they desire opportunity instead of shrinking from it. The first significant discovery we shall make as we racket along our female road to freedom is that men are not free, and they will seek to make this an argument why nobody should be free. We can only reply that slaves enslave their masters, and by securing our own manumission we may show men the way that they could follow when they jumped off their own treadmill. Privileged women will pluck at your sleeve and seek to enlist you in the "fight" for reforms, but reforms are retrogressive. The old process must be broken, not made new. Bitter women will call you to rebellion, but you have too much to do. What will you do?[28]

What might I, as one feminist, include in an ideal? I would like to see

- Women bearing all the marvelous traits of excellence chronicled by the great philosophers: strength, intelligence, temperance, independence, courage, principle, honor, and the rest

- Women, beautiful and healthy in our bodies, comfortable with them, understanding them, proud of them, defining their "fitness" for ourselves

- Women free of the fetters of possession and exploitation, free to define our own female beings, to direct the rites, events, and progress of our own lives and experience

- Women caring for one another, proud of our womanhood, caring for any living thing in the way that is meaningful to us

- Women contributing to civilization wholeheartedly and equally with men in whatever way we enjoy and believe to be right

What would you like to see in an ideal woman?

Notes

1. George Gilder, *Sexual Suicide* (New York: Quadrangle, 1973), chap. 1.

2. Midge Decter, *The New Chastity and Other Arguments Against Women's Liberation* (New York: Coward, McCann & Geoghegan, 1972).

3. Especially in Sigmund Freud, "Femininity," Lecture XXXIII, in *The Standard Edition of the Complete Psychological Works of Sigmund Freud,* trans. and ed. James Strachey et al. (London: Hogarth Press, 1964), vol. 22.

4. Karl Stern, *The Flight from Woman* (New York: Farrar, Straus & Giroux, 1965).

5. Allan Bloom, *The Closing of the American Mind* (New York: Simon & Schuster, 1987), pp. 101–102.

6. Bloom, *Closing,* p. 129.

7. Shulamith Firestone, *The Dialectic of Sex* (New York: Bantam, 1971), p. 1.

8. Kate Millett, *Sexual Politics* (New York: Doubleday, 1970), p. 23.

9. The meaning and utility of the concept of androgyny is much debated. See Joyce Trebilcot, "Two Forms of Androgynism," in *Feminism and Philosophy,* ed. Mary Vetterling-Braggin, Frederick A. Elliston, and Jane English (Totowa, NJ: Littlefield, Adams, 1977), among others.

10. B. G. Jefferis, M.D., Ph.D. and J. L. Nichols, A.M., *Safe Counsel or Practical Eugenics* (New York: Intext Press, date unknown).

11. Jefferis and Nichols, *Safe Counsel,* back cover.

12. Jefferis and Nichols, *Safe Counsel,* pp. 39–40.

13. Jefferis and Nichols, *Safe Counsel,* pp. 47–51, *passim.*

14. Reported by Phyllis Chesler, "Men Drive Women Crazy," in *The Female Experience,* ed. Carol Tavris (Del Mar, CA: Communications Research Machines, 1973), p. 83.

15. Quoted in Vern L. Bullough, Brenda Shelton, and Sarah Slavin, *The Subordinated Sex* (Athens: University of Georgia Press, 1988), p. 24.

16. Quoted in Bullough, *Subordinated Sex,* p. 49.

17. Quoted in Bullough, *Subordinated Sex,* p. 84.

18. Quoted in Bullough, *Subordinated Sex,* p. 96–97.

19. Quoted in Bullough, *Subordinated Sex,* p. 122.

20. Quoted in Bullough, *Subordinated Sex,* p. 150.

21. Quoted in Bullough, *Subordinated Sex,* p. 169.

22. Quoted in Chesler, "Men Drive Women Crazy," p. 82.

23. Kim Chernin, *Reinventing Eve: Modern Woman in Search of Herself* (New York: Harper & Row, 1987), p. 182.

24. Marcia Ann Gillespie, "The Myth of the Strong Black Woman," *Essence Magazine* (August 1982), p. 58.

25. *Blackstone Audiobooks: Unabridged Recordings of Great Books,* Vol. XII, 2000, p. 16.

26. Mahnaz Afkhami, "Iran: A Future in the Past," from *Sisterhood Is Global: The International Women's Movement Anthology,* ed. Robin Morgan, supra, pp. 330, 337. By permission of Edite Kroll Literary Agency. Copyright © 1984 by Robin Morgan.

27. Wilma Scott Heide, in the "Introduction" to *Hospitals, Paternalism, and the Role of the Nurse,* by JoAnn Ashley (New York: Teachers College Press, 1976), p. viii.

28. Germaine Greer, *The Female Eunuch* (New York: McGraw-Hill, 1971), pp. 328–329. Reprinted by permission of Aitken & Stone, Ltd. Copyright © 1971 by Germaine Greer.

Woman–Which Includes Man, of Course

Theodora Wells

Theodora Wells, who took an MBA at the University of Southern California, taught management and communication at the University of California at Los Angeles and at the University of Southern California. President of Wells Associates, a management consulting firm, she is also coauthor of Breakthrough: Women into Management *(1972) and* Keeping Your Cool Under Fire: Communicating Non-Defensively *(1980).*

The following selection is an "experience in awareness." Read and feel it slowly and deeply.

THERE IS MUCH CONCERN TODAY about the future of man, which means, of course, both men and women—generic Man. For a woman to take exception to this use of the term "man" is often seen as defensive hair-splitting by an "emotional female."

The following experience is an invitation to awareness in which you are asked to feel into, and stay with, your feelings through each step, letting them absorb you. If you start intellectualizing, try to turn it down and let your feelings again surface to your awareness.

Consider reversing the generic term Man. Think of the future of Woman which, of course, includes both women and men. Feel into that, sense its meaning to you—as a woman—as a man.

Think of it always being that way, every day of your life. Feel the everpresence of woman and feel the nonpresence of man. Absorb what it tells you about the importance and value of being woman—of being man.

Recall that everything you have ever read all your life uses only female pronouns—she, her—meaning both girls and boys, both women and men. Recall that most of the voices on radio and most of the faces on TV are women's—when important events are covered—on commercials—and on the

late talk shows. Recall that you have no male senator representing you in Washington.

Feel into the fact that women are the leaders, the power-centers, the prime-movers. Man, whose natural role is husband and father, fulfills himself through nurturing children and making the home a refuge for woman. This is only natural to balance the biological role of woman who devotes her entire body to the race during pregnancy.

Then feel further into the obvious biological explanation for woman as the ideal—her genital construction. By design, female genitals are compact and internal, protected by her body. Male genitals are so exposed that he must be protected from outside attack to assure the perpetuation of the race. His vulnerability clearly requires sheltering.

Thus, by nature, males are more passive than females, and have a desire in sexual relations to be symbolically engulfed by the protective body of the woman. Males psychologically yearn for this protection, fully realizing their masculinity at this time—feeling exposed and vulnerable at other times. The male is not fully adult until he has overcome his infantile tendency to penis orgasm and has achieved the mature surrender of the testicle orgasm. He then feels himself a "whole man" when engulfed by the woman.

If the male denies these feelings, he is unconsciously rejecting his masculinity. Therapy is thus indicated to help him adjust to his own nature. Of course, therapy is administered by a woman, who has the education and wisdom to facilitate openness leading to the male's growth and self-actualization.

To help him feel into his defensive emotionality, he is invited to get in touch with the "child" in him. He remembers his sister's jeering at his primitive genitals that "flop around foolishly." She can run, climb and ride horseback unencumbered. Obviously, since she is free to move, she is encouraged to develop her body and mind in preparation for her active responsibilities of adult womanhood. The male vulnerability needs female protection, so he is taught the less active, caring, virtues of homemaking.

Because of his clitoris-envy, he learns to strap up his genitals, and learns to feel ashamed and unclean because of his nocturnal emissions. Instead, he is encouraged to keep his body lean and dream of getting married, waiting for the time of his fulfillment—

when "his woman" gives him a girl-child to carry on the family name. He knows that if it is a boy-child he has failed somehow—but they can try again.

In getting to your feelings on being a woman—on being a man—stay with the sensing you are now experiencing. As the words begin to surface, say what you feel from inside you.

The Transformation of Silence into Language and Action

Audre Lorde

Audre Lorde—poet, essayist, fiction writer, activist—was born in New York City of West Indian parents. Her writing is powerful, searingly honest—and always directed toward positive social change and personal action. In her essay "Eye to Eye," she says:

> *To search for power within myself means I must be willing to move through being afraid to whatever lies beyond. If I look at my most vulnerable places and acknowledge the pain I have felt, I can remove the source of that pain from my enemies' arsenals. My history cannot be used to feather my enemies' arrows then, and that lessens their power over me. Nothing I accept about myself can be used against me to diminish me. I am who I am, doing what I came to do, acting upon you like a drug or a chisel or remind you of your me-ness, as I discover you in myself.[1]*

Those are important words to hear after the preceding chapter's heavy load of misogyny and untruth.

In this essay, Lorde admonishes us to be warriors, to wage war with the forces of death, to bring hope and life by breaking destructive silences, by acting.

I HAVE COME TO BELIEVE over and over again that what is most important to me must be spoken, made verbal and shared, even at the risk of having it bruised or misunderstood. That the speaking profits me, beyond any other effect. I am standing here as a Black lesbian poet, and the meaning of all that waits upon the fact that I am still alive, and might not have been. Less than two months ago I was told by two doctors, one female and one male, that I would have to have breast surgery, and that there was a 60 to 80 percent chance that the tumor was malignant. Between that telling and the actual sur-

gery, there was a three-week period of the agony of an involuntary reorganization of my entire life. The surgery was completed, and the growth was benign.

But within those three weeks, I was forced to look upon myself and my living with a harsh and urgent clarity that has left me still shaken but much stronger. This is a situation faced by many women, by some of you here today. Some of what I experienced during that time has helped elucidate for me much of what I feel concerning the transformation of silence into language and action.

In becoming forcibly and essentially aware of my mortality, and of what I wished and wanted for my life, however short it might be, priorities and omissions became strongly etched in a merciless light, and what I most regretted were my silences. Of what had I *ever* been afraid? To question or to speak as I believed could have meant pain, or death. But we all hurt in so many different ways, all the time, and pain will either change or end. Death, on the other hand, is the final silence. And that might be coming quickly, now, without regard for whether I had ever spoken what needed to be said, or had only betrayed myself into small silences, while I planned someday to speak, or waited for someone else's words. And I began to recognize a source of power within myself that comes from the knowledge that while it is most desirable not to be afraid, learning to put fear into a perspective gave me strength.

I was going to die, if not sooner then later, whether or not I had ever spoken myself. My silences had not protected me. Your silence will not protect you. But for every real word spoken, for every attempt I had ever made to speak those truths for which I am still seeking, I had made contact with other women while we examined the words to fit a world in which we all believed, bridging our differences. And it was the concern and caring of all those women which gave me strength and enabled me to scrutinize the essentials of my living.

The women who sustained me through that period were Black and white, old and young, lesbian, bisexual, and heterosexual, and we all shared a war against the tyrannies of silence. They all gave me a strength and concern without which I could not have survived intact. Within those weeks of acute fear came the knowledge—within the war we are all waging with the forces of death, subtle and otherwise, conscious or not—I am not only a casualty, I am also a warrior.

What are the words you do not yet have? What do you need to say? What are the tyrannies you swallow day by day and attempt to make your own, until you will sicken and die of them, still in silence? Perhaps for some of you here today, I am the face of one of your fears. Because I am woman, because I am Black, because I am lesbian, because I am myself—a Black woman warrior poet doing my work—come to ask you, are you doing yours?

And of course I am afraid, because the transformation of silence into language and action is an act of self-revelation, and that always seems fraught with danger. But my daughter, when I told her of our topic and my difficulty with it, said, "Tell them about how you're never really a whole person if you remain silent, because there's always that one little piece inside you that wants to be spoken out, and if you keep ignoring it, it gets madder and madder and hotter and hotter, and if you don't speak it out one day it will just up and punch you in the mouth from the inside."

In the cause of silence, each of us draws the face of her own fear—fear of contempt, of censure, or some judgment, or recognition, of challenge, of annihilation. But most of all, I think, we fear the visibility without which we cannot truly live. Within this country where racial difference creates a constant, if unspoken, distortion of vision, Black women have on one hand always been highly visible, and so, on the other hand, have been rendered invisible through the depersonalization of racism. Even within the women's movement, we have had to fight, and still do, for that very visibility which also renders us most vulnerable, our Blackness. For to survive in the mouth of this dragon we call america, we have had to learn this first and most vital lesson—that we were never meant to survive. Not as human beings. And neither were most of you here today,

Black or not. And that visibility which makes us most vulnerable is that which also is the source of our greatest strength. Because the machine will try to grind you into dust anyway, whether or not we speak. We can sit in our corners mute forever while our sisters and our selves are wasted, while our children are distorted and destroyed, while our earth is poisoned; we can sit in our safe corners mute as bottles, and we will still be no less afraid.

In my house this year we are celebrating the feast of Kwanza, the African-american festival of harvest which begins the day after Christmas and lasts for seven days. There are seven principles of Kwanza, one for each day. The first principle is Umoja, which means unity, the decision to strive for and maintain unity in self and community. The principle for yesterday, the second day, was Kujichagulia—self-determination—the decision to define ourselves, name ourselves, and speak for ourselves, instead of being defined and spoken for by others. Today is the third day of Kwanza, and the principle for today is Ujima—collective work and responsibility—the decision to build and maintain ourselves and our communities together and to recognize and solve our problems together.

Each of us is here now because in one way or another we share a commitment to language and to the power of language, and to the reclaiming of that language which has been made to work against us. In the transformation of silence into language and action, it is vitally necessary for each one of us to establish or examine her function in that transformation and to recognize her role as vital within that transformation.

For those of us who write, it is necessary to scrutinize not only the truth of what we speak, but the truth of that language by which we speak it. For others, it is to share and spread also those words that are meaningful to us. But primarily for us all, it is necessary to teach by living and speaking those truths which we believe and know beyond understanding. Because in this way alone we can survive, by taking part in a process of life that is creative and continuing, that is growth.

And it is never without fear—of visibility, of the harsh light of scrutiny and perhaps judgment, of pain, of death. But we have lived through all of those already, in silence, except death. And I remind myself all the time now that if I were to have been born mute, or had maintained an oath of silence my whole life long for safety, I would still have suffered, and I would still die. It is very good for establishing perspective.

And where the words of women are crying to be heard, we must each of us recognize our responsibility to seek those words out, to read them and share them and examine them in their pertinence to our lives. That we not hide behind the mockeries of separations that have been imposed upon us and which so often we accept as our own. For instance, "I can't possibly teach Black women's writing—their experience is so different from mine." Yet how many years have you spent teaching Plato and Shakespeare and Proust? Or another, "She's a white woman and what could she possibly have to say to me?" Or, "She's a lesbian, what would my husband say, or my chairman?" Or again, "This woman writes of her sons and I have no children." And all the other endless ways in which we rob ourselves of ourselves and each other.

We can learn to work and speak when we are afraid in the same way we have learned to work and speak when we are tired. For we have been socialized to respect fear more than our own needs for language and definition, and while we wait in silence for that final luxury of fearlessness, the weight of that silence will choke us.

The fact that we are here and that I speak these words is an attempt to break silence and bridge some of those differences between us, for it is not difference which immobilizes us, but silence. And there are so many silences to be broken.

Notes

1. "Eye to Eye: Black Women, Hatred and Anger" in *Sister Outsider: Essays and Speeches by Audre Lorde* (New York: Crossing Press, 1984), p. 147.

2. Paper delivered at the Modern Language Association's "Lesbian and Literature Panel," Chicago, Illinois, December 28, 1977. First published in *Sinister Wisdom* 6 (1978) and *The Cancer Journals* (San Francisco: Spinsters Ink, 1980).

Myths to Divert Black Women from Freedom

Barbara Smith

*Barbara Smith is a Black feminist writer and activist
who has been politically active since the 1960s. She was
one of the founders of the Combahee River Collective, a
Black feminist and lesbian group that did political organizing in Boston from 1974 to 1980. Afterwards she
served on the board of the National Coalition of Black
Lesbians and Gays and cofounded Kitchen Table:
Women of Color Press, the only U.S. publisher for
women of color.*

*Smith's articles, essays, literary criticism, and short
stories have appeared in a variety of publications, in-
cluding* Gay Community News, The New York
Times Book Review, Ms., The Black Scholar, The
Guardian, The Village Voice, *and* The Nation. *She
has edited three major collections about Black women:*
Conditions: Five, The Black Women's Issue *(with
Lorraine Bethel) (1979),* All the Women Are White,
All the Blacks Are Men, but Some of Us Are Brave:
Black Women's Studies *(with Gloria T. Hull and
Patricia Bell Scott) (1982), and* Home Girls: A Black
Feminist Anthology *(1983). She is the coauthor with
Elly Bulkin and Minnie Bruce Pratt of* Yours in Strug-
gle: Three Feminist Perspectives on Anti-Semitism
and Racism *(1984). She is currently a general editor of*
The Reader's Companion to U.S. Women's History
*with Wilma Mankiller, Gwendolyn Mink, Maryea
Navarro, and Gloria Steinem.*

*A guest on "Donahue," "Charlie Rose," and "Tony
Brown's Journal," Smith has appeared in several films,
including* Pink Triangles *and Marlon Riggs's* Black Is,
Black Ain't. *She has lectured on college campuses
throughout the country.*

*"Black feminism is, on every level, organic to Black
experience," argues Smith. The history, culture, and experience of African-American women is innately femi-*
*nist, yet many Third World women have not been
attracted to the contemporary women's movement.
Smith addresses the reasons this may be so: among others, a set of myths designed to divert women of color
from organizing around specifically women's political
issues.*

SOURCES

THERE IS NOTHING MORE IMPORTANT to me than
home.

The first house we lived in was in the rear. Hidden between other houses, it had a dirt yard that
my twin sister Beverly and I loved to dig in, and a
handful of flowers my grandmother had planted.
We lived there with our mother and grandmother
and with one of our great-aunts named Phoebe,
whom we called Auntie. We seldom saw Auntie because she was a live-in cook for rich people. The
house, however, was considered to be hers, not because she owned it, but because Auntie was the one
who had originally rented it. She had been the first
of the family to come North in the late 1920s, followed by the rest of her sisters and their children all
during the 30s and 40s.

The house was old and small, but I didn't know
it then. It had two bedrooms. The big one was
Auntie's, though she only used it on her occasional
visits home. The small one was where my grandmother, Bev, and I slept, our cribs and her bed
crowding together. Our mother, who worked full
time, slept downstairs on a daybed which she
folded in half each morning, covered with a faded
maroon throw, and pushed back against the wall.
The kitchen, where we ate every meal except Sunday dinner, was the room Bev and I liked best. Our
grandmother did most of the cooking. Unlike her
sister Phoebe she was a "plain" cook, but she did
make a few dishes—little pancakes with Alaga
syrup and bacon, vanilla-ey boiled custards—

which appealed even to Bev and my notoriously fussy appetites.

The house was on 83rd Street between Central and Cedar Avenues in what was called the Central Area, one of Cleveland's numerous ghettos. The church the family had belonged to ever since they'd come North, Antioch Baptist, was a few blocks away at 89th and Cedar. Aunt LaRue, our mother's sister, also lived on 89th Street, on the second floor of a house half a block from the church.

When Bev and I were six we moved. Aunt LaRue and her husband had bought a two-family house (five rooms up, five rooms down) on 132nd Street off of Kinsman for us all to live in. They lived upstairs and the five of us lived downstairs, including Auntie, who became increasingly ill and was eventually bedridden. The "new" house was old too, but it was in a "better" neighborhood, had a front and a back yard, where my aunt and uncle planted grass, and there was more space.

One thing that was different about being at the new house was that for the first time we lived near white people. Before this we only saw them downtown, except for some of the teachers at school. The white people, mostly Italians and Jews, quickly exited from our immediate neighborhood but some remained in the schools. Most of our white classmates, however, were Polish, Czech, Yugoslavian, or Hungarian. Their families had emigrated from Eastern Europe following the World Wars. Despite the definite racial tensions between us, we had certain things in common. Cleveland was new to their people as it was to ours; the church figured heavily in their lives as both a spiritual and social force; they were involved in close-knit extended families; and they were working people many rungs below the rich white people who lived on the Heights.

Beverly and I lived in the house on 132nd Street until we were eighteen and went away to college. It is this house that I remember clearly when I think of home. It is this place that I miss and all the women there who raised me. It was undoubtedly at home that I learned the rudiments of Black feminism, although no such term even existed then. We were "Negroes" or "colored people." Except for our uncle, who lived upstairs briefly and soon departed because "LaRue was too wrapped up in her family," we were all women. When I was growing up I was surrounded by women who appeared able to do

everything, at least everything necessary to maintain a home. They cleaned, cooked, washed, ironed, sewed, made soap, canned, held jobs, took care of business downtown, sang, read, and taught us to do the same. In her essay, "Women In Prison: How We Are," Assata Shakur perfectly describes the kind of women who filled my childhood. She writes:

> *I think about North Carolina and my home town and [I] remember the women of my grandmother's generation: strong, fierce women who could stop you with a look out the corners of their eyes. Women who walked with majesty. . . .*
>
> *Women who delivered babies, searched for healing roots and brewed medicines. Women who darned sox and chopped wood and layed bricks. Women who could swim rivers and shoot the head off a snake. Women who took passionate responsibility for their children and for their neighbors' children too.*
>
> *The women in my grandmother's generation made giving an art form. "Here, gal, take this pot of collards to Sister Sue"; "Take this bag of pecans to school for the teacher"; "Stay here while I go tend Mister Johnson's leg." Every child in the neighborhood ate in their kitchens. They called each other sister because of feeling rather than as the result of a movement. They supported each other through the lean times, sharing the little they had.*
>
> *The women of my grandmother's generation in my home town trained their daughters for womanhood.*[1]

The women in my family, and their friends, worked harder than any people I have known before or since, and despite their objective circumstances, they believed. My grandmother believed in Jesus and in sin, not necessarily in that order; my mother believed in education and in books; my Aunt LaRue believed in beauty and in books as well; and, their arguments aside, they believed in each other. They also seemed to believe that Beverly and I could have a future beyond theirs, although there was little enough indication in the 40s and 50s that Negro girls would ever have a place to stand.

Needless to say, they believed in home. It was a word spoken often, particularly by my grandmother. To her and her sisters, home meant Georgia. One of the last to leave, my grandmother never considered Cleveland anything but a stopping place.

My older relatives' allegiance to a place we'd never seen was sometimes confusing, but their loyalty to their origins was also much to our benefit, since it provided us with an essentially Southern upbringing, rooting us solidly in the past and at the same time preparing us to face the unknowable future.

In the spring of 1982 I visited Georgia for the first time and finally saw the little town of Dublin where they had lived and farmed. Being in rural Georgia, I thoroughly understood their longing for it, a longing they had implanted sight unseen in me. It is one of the most beautiful, mysterious landscapes I have ever seen. I also understood why they had to leave. Though lynching and segregation are officially past, racial lines are unequivocally drawn. Dublin has become very modern and unmistakably prosperous, yet many streets in the Black section of town are, to this day, unpaved. I took a handful of red clay from the side of the road in Dublin and brought it home to remind me of where my family had walked and what they had suffered.

I learned about Black feminism from the women in my family—not just from their strengths, but from their failings, from witnessing daily how they were humiliated and crushed because they had made the "mistake" of being born Black and female in a white man's country. I inherited fear and shame from them as well as hope. These conflicting feelings about being a Black woman still do battle inside of me. It is this conflict, my constantly " . . . seeing and touching/Both sides of things" that makes my commitment real.[2]

In the fall of 1981, before most of this book was compiled, I was searching for a title. I'd come up with one that I knew was not quite right. At the time I was also working on the story which later became "Home" and thought that I'd like to get some of the feeling of that piece into the book. One day while doing something else entirely, and playing with words in my head, "home girls" came to me. Home Girls. The girls from the neighborhood and from the block, the girls we grew up with. I knew I was onto something, particularly when I considered that so many Black people who are threatened by feminism have argued that by being a Black feminist (particularly if you are also a Lesbian) you have left the race, are no longer a part of the Black community, in short no longer have a home.

I suspect that most of the contributors to *Home Girls* learned their varied politics and their shared commitment to Black women from the same source I did. Yet critics of feminism pretend that just because some of us speak out about sexual politics *at home*, within the Black community, we must have sprung miraculously from somewhere else. But we are not strangers and never have been. I am convinced that Black feminism is, on every level, organic to Black experience.

History verifies that Black women have rejected doormat status, whether racially or sexually imposed, for centuries. Not only is there the documented resistance of Black women during slavery followed by our organizing around specific Black women's issues and in support of women's rights during the nineteenth century, there is also the vast cultural record of our continuously critical stance toward our oppression. For example, in the late nineteenth and early twentieth centuries, poets Frances E. W. Harper (1825–1911), Angelina Weld Grimké (1880–1958), Alice Dunbar-Nelson (1875–1935), Anne Spencer (1882–1975), and Georgia Douglas Johnson (1886–1966) all addressed themes of sexual as well as racial identity in some of their work.

. . .

I have always felt that Black women's ability to function with dignity, independence, and imagination in the face of total adversity—that is, in the face of white America—points to an innate feminist potential. To me the phrase, "Act like you have some sense," probably spoken by at least one Black woman to every Black child who ever lived, is a cryptic warning that says volumes about keeping your feet on the ground and your ass covered. Alice Walker's definition of "womanist" certainly makes the connection between plain common sense and a readiness to fight for change. She writes:

> WOMANIST: (*According to Walker*) *From* womanish. (*Opp. of "girlish," i.e. frivolous, irresponsible, not serious.*) *A black feminist or feminist of color. From the colloquial expression of mothers to daughters, "You're acting womanish," i.e., like a woman. Usually referring to outrageous, audacious, courageous or* willful *behavior. Wanting to know more and in greater depth than is considered "good" for one. Interested in grown-up doings. Acting*

grown-up. Being grown-up. Interchangeable with other colloquial expression: "You're trying to be grown." Responsible. In charge. Serious. . . .

2. Also: Herstorically capable, as in "Mama, I'm walking to Canada and I'm taking you and a bunch of other slaves with me." Reply: "It wouldn't be the first time."[3]

Black women as a group have never been fools. We couldn't afford to be. Yet in the last two decades many of us have been deterred from identifying with a liberation struggle which might say significant things to women like ourselves, women who believe that we were put here for a purpose in our own right, women who are usually not afraid to struggle.

Although our involvement has increased considerably in recent years, there are countless reasons why Black and other Third World women have not identified with contemporary feminism in large numbers.[4] The racism of white women in the women's movement has certainly been a major factor. The powers-that-be are also aware that a movement of progressive Third World women in this country would alter life as we know it. As a result there has been a concerted effort to keep women of color from organizing autonomously and from organizing with other women around women's political issues. Third World men, desiring to maintain power over "their women" at all costs, have been among the most willing reinforcers of the fears and myths about the women's movement, attempting to scare us away from figuring things out for ourselves.

It is fascinating to look at various kinds of media from the late 1960s and early 1970s, when feminism was making its great initial impact, in order to see what Black men, Native American men, Asian American men, Latino men, and white men were saying about the irrelevance of "women's lib" to women of color. White men and Third World men, ranging from conservatives to radicals, pointed to the seeming lack of participation of women of color in the movement in order to discredit it and to undermine the efforts of the movement as a whole. All kinds of men were running scared because they knew that if the women in their midst were changing, they were going to have to change too. In 1976 I wrote:

Feminism is potentially the most threatening of movements to Black and other Third World people because it makes it absolutely essential that we examine the way we live, how we treat each other, and what we believe. It calls into question the most basic assumption about our existence and this is the idea that biological, i.e., sexual identity determines all, that it is the rationale for power relationships as well as for all other levels of human identity and action. An irony is that among Third World people biological determinism is rejected and fought against when it is applied to race, but generally unquestioned when it applies to sex.[5]

In reaction to the "threat" of such change, Black men, with the collaboration of some Black women, developed a set of myths to divert Black women from our own freedom.

MYTHS

Myth No. 1: The Black woman is already liberated.

This myth confuses liberation with the fact that Black women have had to take on responsibilities that our oppression gives us no choice but to handle. This is an insidious, but widespread myth that many Black women have believed themselves. Heading families, working outside the home, not building lives or expectations dependent on males, seldom being sheltered or pampered as women, Black women have known that their lives in some ways incorporated goals that white middle-class women were striving for, but race and class privilege, of course, reshaped the meaning of those goals profoundly. As W.E.B. DuBois said so long ago about Black women: ". . . our women in black had freedom contemptuously thrust upon them."[6] Of all the people here, women of color generally have the fewest choices about the circumstances of their lives. An ability to cope under the worst conditions is not liberation, although our spiritual capacities have often made it look like a life. Black men didn't say anything about how poverty, unequal pay, no childcare, violence of every kind including battering, rape, and sterilization abuse, translated into "liberation."

Underlying this myth is the assumption that Black women are towers of strength who neither feel nor need what other human beings do, either emotionally or materially. White male social scientists, particularly Daniel P. Moynihan with his "matriar-chy theory," further reinforce distortions concerning Black women's actual status.

. . .

Myth No. 2: Racism is the primary (or only) oppression Black women have to confront. (Once we get that taken care of, then Black women, men, and children will all flourish. Or as Ms. Luisah Teish writes, we can look forward to being "the property of powerful men.")[7]

This myth goes hand in hand with the one that the Black woman is already liberated. The notion that struggling against or eliminating racism will completely alleviate Black women's problems does not take into account the way that sexual oppres-sion cuts across all racial, nationality, age, reli-gious, ethnic, and class groupings. Afro-Americans are no exception.

It also does not take into account how oppres-sion operates. Every generation of Black people, up until now, has had to face the reality that no matter how hard we work we will probably not see the end of racism in our lifetimes. Yet many of us keep faith and try to do all we can to make change now. If we have to wait for racism to be obliterated *before* we can begin to address sexism, we will be waiting for a long time. Denying that sexual oppression exists or requiring that we wait to bring it up until racism, or in some cases capitalism, is toppled, is a bankrupt position. A Black feminist perspective has no use for ranking oppressions, but instead demonstrates the simultaneity of oppressions as they affect Third World women's lives.

Myth No. 3: Feminism is nothing but man-hating. (And men have never done anything that would legiti-mately inspire hatred.)

It is important to make a distinction between attacking institutionalized, systematic oppression (the goal of any serious progressive movement) and attacking men as individuals. Unfortunately, some of the most widely distributed writing about Black women's issues has not made this distinction suffi-ciently clear. Our issues have not been concisely defined in these writings, causing much adverse re-action and confusion about what Black feminism re-ally is.[8]

This myth is one of the silliest and at the same time one of the most dangerous. Anti-feminists are incapable of making a distinction between being critically opposed to sexual oppression and simply hating men. Women's desire for fairness and safety in our lives does not necessitate hating men. Trying to educate and inform men about how their feet are planted on our necks doesn't translate into hatred either. Centuries of anti-racist struggle by various people of color are not reduced, except by racists, to our merely hating white people. If anything it seems that the opposite is true. People of color know that white people have abused us unmercifully and it is only sane for us to try to change that treatment by every means possible.

Likewise the bodies of murdered women are strewn across the landscape of this country. Rape is a national pastime, a form of torture visited upon all girls and women, from babies to the aged. One out of three women in the U.S. will be raped during her lifetime. Battering and incest, those home-based crimes, are pandemic. Murder, of course, is men's ultimate violent "solution." And if you're thinking as you read this that I'm exaggerating, please go get today's newspaper and verify the facts. If anything is going down here it's woman-hatred, not man-hatred, a war against women. But wanting to end this war still doesn't equal man-hating. The feminist movement and the anti-racist movement have in common trying to insure decent human life. Oppo-sition to either movement aligns one with the most reactionary elements in American society.

Myth No. 4: Women's issues are narrow, apolitical concerns. People of color need to deal with the "larger struggle."

This myth once again characterizes women's oppression as not particularly serious, and by no means a matter of life and death. I have often wished I could spread the word that a movement committed to fighting sexual, racial, economic, and heterosexist oppression, not to mention one which opposes imperialism, anti-Semitism, the oppres-sions visited upon the physically disabled, the old and the young, at the same time that it challenges militarism and imminent nuclear destruction is the very opposite of narrow. All segments of the women's movement have not dealt with all of these issues, but neither have all segments of Black peo-ple. This myth is plausible when the women's movement is equated only with its most bourgeois and reformist elements. The most progressive sectors of the feminist movement, which includes some radical white women, have taken the above issues, and many more, quite seriously. Third World women have been the most consistent in defining our politics broadly. Why is it that feminism is considered "white-minded" and "narrow" while socialism or Marxism, from verifiably white origins, is legitimately embraced by Third World male politicos, without their having their identity credentials questioned for a minute?

Myth No. 5: Those feminists are nothing but Lesbians.

This may be the most pernicious myth of all and it is essential to understand that the distortion lies in the phrase "nothing but" and not in the identification Lesbian. "Nothing but" reduces Lesbians to a category of beings deserving of only the most violent attack, a category totally alien from "decent" Black folks, i.e., not your sisters, mothers, daughters, aunts, and cousins, but bizarre outsiders like no one you know or *ever* knew.

Many of the most committed and outspoken feminists of color have been and are Lesbians. Since many of us are also radicals, our politics, as indicated by the issues merely outlined above, encompass all people. We're also as Black as we ever were. (I always find it fascinating, for example, that many of the Black Lesbian-feminists I know still wear their hair natural, indicating that for us it was more than a "style.") Black feminism and Black Lesbianism are not interchangeable. Feminism is a political movement and many Lesbians are not feminists. Although it is also true that many Black feminists are not Lesbians, this myth has acted as an accusation and a deterrent to keep non-Lesbian Black feminists from manifesting themselves, for fear it will be hurled against them.

Fortunately this is changing. Personally, I have seen increasing evidence that many Black women of whatever sexual preference are more concerned with exploring and ending our oppression than they are committed to being either homophobic or sexually separatist. Direct historical precedent exists for such commitments. In 1957, Black playwright and activist Lorraine Hansberry wrote the following in a letter to *The Ladder*, an early Lesbian periodical:

I think it is about time that equipped women began to take on some of the ethical questions which a male-dominated culture has produced and dissect and analyze them quite to pieces in a serious fashion. It is time that "half the human race" had something to say about the nature of its existence. Otherwise—without revised basic thinking—the woman intellectual is likely to find herself trying to draw conclusions—moral conclusions—based on acceptance of a social moral superstructure which has never admitted to the equality of women and is therefore immoral itself. As per marriage, as per sexual practices, as per the rearing of children, etc. In this kind of work there may be women to emerge who will be able to formulate a new and possible concept that homosexual persecution and condemnation has at its roots not only social ignorance, but a philosophically active anti-feminist dogma.[9]

I would like a lot more people to be aware that Lorraine Hansberry, one of our most respected artists and thinkers, was asking in a Lesbian context some of the same questions we are asking today, and for which we have been so maligned.

Black heterosexuals' panic about the existence of both Black Lesbians and Black gay men is a problem that they have to deal with themselves. A first step would be for them to better understand their own heterosexuality, which need not be defined by attacking everybody who is not heterosexual.

HOME TRUTHS

Above are some of the myths that have plagued Black feminism. The truth is that there is a vital movement of women of color in this country. Despite continual resistance to women of color defining our specific issues and organizing around them, it is safe to say in 1982 that we have a movement of our own. I have been involved in building that movement since 1973. It has been a struggle every step of the way and I feel we are still in just the beginning stages of developing a workable politics and practice. Yet the feminism of women of color, particularly of Afro-American women, has wrought many changes during these years, has had both obvious and unrecognized impact upon the development of other political groupings and upon the lives and hopes of countless women.

The very nature of radical thought and action is that it has exponentially far-reaching results. But because all forms of media ignore Black women, in particular Black feminists, and because we have no widely distributed communication mechanisms of our own, few know the details of what we have accomplished. The story of our work and contributions remains untold. One of the purposes of *Home Girls* is to get the word out about Black feminism to the people who need it most: Black people in the U.S., the Caribbean, Latin America, Africa—everywhere. It is not possible for a single introduction or a single book to encompass all of what Black feminism is, but there is basic information I want every reader to have about the meaning of Black feminism as I have lived and understood it.

In 1977, a Black feminist organization in Boston of which I was a member from its founding in 1974, the Combahee River Collective, drafted a political statement for our own use and for inclusion in Zillah Eisenstein's anthology, *Capitalist Patriarchy and the Case for Socialist Feminism.* In our opening paragraph we wrote:

> The most general statement of our politics at the present time would be that we are actively committed to struggling against racial, sexual, heterosexual, and class oppression and see as our particular task the development of integrated analysis and practice based upon the fact that the major systems of oppression are interlocking. The synthesis of these oppressions creates the conditions of our lives. As Black women we see Black feminism as the logical political movement to combat the manifold and simultaneous oppressions that all women of color face.

The concept of the simultaneity of oppression is still the crux of a Black feminist understanding of political reality and, I believe, one of the most significant ideological contributions of Black feminist thought.

We examined our own lives and found that everything out there was kicking our behinds—race, class, sex, and homophobia. We saw no reason to rank oppressions, or, as many forces in the Black community would have us do, to pretend that sexism, among all the "isms," was not happening to us. Black feminists' efforts to comprehend the complexity of our situation as it was actually occurring, almost immediately began to deflate some of the cherished myths about Black womanhood, for example, that we are "castrating matriarchs" or that

we are more economically privileged than Black men. Although we made use of the insights of other political ideologies, such as socialism, we added an element that has often been missing from the theory of others: what oppression is comprised of on a day-to-day basis, or as Black feminist musician Linda Tillery sings, ". . . what it's really like/To live this life of triple jeopardy."[10]

This multi-issued approach to politics has probably been most often used by other women of color who face very similar dynamics, at least as far as institutionalized oppression is concerned. It has also altered the women's movement as a whole. As a result of Third World feminist organizing, the women's movement now takes much more seriously the necessity for a multi-issued strategy for challenging women's oppression. The more progressive elements of the left have also begun to recognize that the promotion of sexism and homophobia within their ranks, besides being ethically unconscionable, ultimately undermines their ability to organize. Even a few Third World organizations have begun to include the challenging of women's and gay oppression on their public agendas.

Approaching politics with a comprehension of the simultaneity of oppressions has helped to create a political atmosphere particularly conducive to coalition building. Among all feminists, Third World women have undoubtedly felt most viscerally the need for linking struggles and have also been most capable of forging such coalitions. A commitment to principled coalitions, based not upon expediency, but upon our actual need for each other is a second major contribution of Black feminist struggle. Many contributors to *Home Girls* write out of a sense of our ultimate interdependence. Bernice Johnson Reagon's essay, "Coalition Politics: Turning the Century," should be particularly noted. She writes:

> You don't go into coalition because you just like it. The only reason you would consider trying to team up with somebody who could possibly kill you, is because that's the only way you can figure you can stay alive. . . . Most of the time you feel threatened to the core and if you don't you're not really doing no coalescing.

The necessity for coalitions has pushed many groups to rigorously examine the attitudes and ignorance within themselves which prevent coalitions from succeeding. Most notably, there has been the commitment of some white feminists to make racism a priority issue within the women's movement, to take responsibility for their racism as individuals, and to do anti-racist organizing in coalition with other groups. Because I have written and spoken about racism during my entire involvement as a feminist and have also presented workshops on racism for white women's organizations for several years during the 1970s, I have not only seen that there are white women who are fully committed to eradicating racism, but that new understandings of racial politics have evolved from feminism, which other progressive people would do well to comprehend.[11]

Having begun my political life in the Civil Rights movement and having seen the Black liberation movement virtually destroyed by the white power structure, I have been encouraged in recent years that women can be a significant force for bringing about racial change in a way that unites oppressions instead of isolating them. At the same time the percentage of white feminists who are concerned about racism is still a minority of the movement, and even within this minority those who are personally sensitive and completely serious about formulating an *activist* challenge to racism are fewer still. Because I have usually worked with politically radical feminists, I know that there are indeed white women worth building coalitions with, at the same time that there are apolitical, even reactionary, women who take the name of feminism in vain.

One of the greatest gifts of Black feminism to ourselves has been to make it a little easier simply to *be* Black and female. A Black feminist analysis has enabled us to understand that we are not hated and abused because there is something wrong with us, but because our status and treatment is absolutely prescribed by the racist, misogynistic system under which we live. There is not a Black woman in this country who has not, at some time, internalized and been deeply scarred by the hateful propaganda about us. There is not a Black woman in America who has not felt, at least once, like "the mule of the world," to use Zora Neale Hurston's still apt phrase.[12] Until Black feminism, very few people besides Black women actually cared about or took seriously the demoralization of being female *and* colored *and* poor *and* hated.

When I was growing up, despite my family's efforts to explain, or at least describe, attitudes prevalent in the outside world, I often thought that there was something fundamentally wrong with me because it was obvious that me and everybody like me was held in such contempt. The cold eyes of certain white teachers in school, the Black men who yelled from cars as Beverly and I stood waiting for the bus, convinced me that I must have done something horrible. How was I to know that racism and sexism had formed a blueprint for my mistreatment long before I had ever arrived here? As with most Black women, others' hatred of me became self-hatred, which has diminished over the years, but has by no means disappeared. Black feminism has, for me and for so many others, given us the tools to finally comprehend that it is not something we have done that has heaped this psychic violence and material abuse upon us, but the very fact that, because of who we are, we are multiply oppressed. Unlike any other movement, Black feminism provides the theory that clarifies the nature of Black women's experience, makes possible positive support from other Black women, and encourages political action that will change the very system that has put us down.

The accomplishments of Black feminism have been not only in developing theory, but in day-to-day organizing. Black feminists have worked on countless issues, some previously identified with the feminist movement and others that we, ourselves, have defined as priorities. Whatever issues we have committed ourselves to, we have approached them with a comprehensiveness and pragmatism which exemplify the concept "grassroots." If nothing else, Black feminism deals in home truths, both in analysis and in action. Far from being irrelevant or peripheral to Black people, the issues we have focused on touch the basic core of our community's survival.

Some of the issues we have worked on are reproductive rights, equal access to abortion, sterilization abuse, health care, child care, the rights of the disabled, violence against women, rape, battering, sexual harassment, welfare rights, Lesbian and gay rights, educational reform, housing, legal reform, women in prison, aging, police brutality, labor organizing, anti-imperialist struggles, anti-racist organizing, nuclear disarmament, and preserving the environment.

Notes

1. Shakur, Assata. "Women in Prison: How We Are," in *The Black Scholar,* Vol. 9, No. 7 (April, 1978), pp. 13 & 14.

2. Rushin, Donna Kate. "The Bridge Poem," in *This Bridge Called My Back: Writings by Radical Women of Color,* eds. Moraga and Anzaldúa. Watertown: Persephone Press, Inc., 1981, p. xxi.

3. Walker, Alice. *In Search of Our Mothers' Gardens* (Forthcoming, 1983). Cited from manuscript, n.p. [*Note:* Alice Walker's book was published by Harcourt Brace Jovanovich (New York, 1983).—S. Ruth]

4. The terms Third World women and women of color are used here to designate Native American, Asian American, Latina, and Afro-American women in the U.S. and the indigenous peoples of Third World countries wherever they may live. Both the terms Third World women and women of color apply to Black American women. At times in the introduction Black women are specifically designated as Black or Afro-American and at other times the terms women of color and Third World women are used to refer to women of color as a whole.

5. Smith, Barbara. "Notes for Yet Another Paper on Black Feminism, Or Will the Real Enemy Please Stand Up?" in *Conditions: Five, The Black Women's Issue,* eds. Bethel & Smith. Vol. 2, No. 2 (Autumn, 1979), p. 124.

6. DuBois, W.E.B. *Darkwater, Voices from Within the Veil,* New York: AMS Press, 1969, p. 185.

7. Teish, Luisah. "Women's Spirituality: A Household Act," in *Home Girls,* ed. Smith. Watertown: Persephone Press, Inc., 1983. All subsequent references to work in *Home Girls* will not be cited.

8. See Linda C. Powell's review of Michele Wallace's *Black Macho and the Myth of the Super Woman* ("Black Macho and Black Feminism") in this volume and my review of Bell Hooks' (Gloria Watkins) *Ain't I A Woman: Black Women and Feminism* in *The New Women's Times Feminist Review,* Vol. 9, no. 24 (November, 1982), pp. 10, 11, 18, 19 & 20 and in *The Black Scholar,* Vol. 14, No. 1 (January/February 1983), pp. 38–45.

9. Quoted from *Gay American History: Lesbians and Gay Men in the U.S.A.,* ed. Jonathan Katz. New York: T.Y. Crowell, 1976, p. 425. Also see Adrienne Rich's "The Problem with Lorraine Hansberry," in "Lorraine Hansberry: Art of Thunder, Vision of Light," *Freedomways,* Vol. 19, No. 4, 1979, pp. 247–255 for more material about her woman-identification.

10. Tillery, Linda. "Freedom Time," *Linda Tillery,* Oakland: Olivia Records, 1977, Tuizer Music.

11. Some useful articles on racism by white feminists are Elly Bulkin's "Racism and Writing: Some Implications for White Lesbian Critics." *Sinister Wisdom 13* (Spring, 1980), pp. 3–22; Minnie Bruce Pratt's "Rebellion." *Feminary,* Vol. 11, Nos. 1 & 2 (1980), pp. 6–20; and Adrienne Rich's "Disloyal to Civilization: Feminism, Racism, Gynephobia." *On Lies, Secrets and Silence: Selected Prose 1966–1978.* New York: W.W. Norton, 1979, pp. 275–310.

12. Hurston, Zora Neale. *Their Eyes Were Watching God.* Urbana: University of Illinois, 1937, 1978, p. 29.

Empathy Among Women on a Global Scale

Mahnaz Afkhami

Mahnaz Afkhami is executive director of the Foundation for Iranian Studies in Bethesda, Maryland, and a member of the Advisory Committee for the Women's Project of the Human Rights Watch. Founder of the Iranian University Women's Association, she was also the secretary-general of the Women's Organization of Iran and Minister of State for Women's Affairs of Iran from 1976 to 1979. She is the author of many articles about feminism and women in the Middle East. Among her books are Women in Exile *(1994) and* Faith and Freedom: Women's Human Rights in the Muslim World *(1995).*

Afkhami argues that because there is a "universality of the feminine condition," in which women are subordinated, reduced to creatures of procreation, our entire social life mediated by patriarchy, there is a potential for women everywhere to share experience and concern. If we are to communicate, there must be a "global feminist discourse" that must transcend religion, economics, and culture.

In the "Foreword" to In the Eye of the Storm, *Robin Morgan tells us:*

> *Women in the Islamic world—who they really are, and how and why they are being used on so many fronts—are central to any possibility of global political understanding. This is not only because the Middle East region and its environs are so geopolitically important and engaged in such upheaval, but also because Muslim women have borne the brunt of especially invidious stereotyping (by men of their own cultures, by westerners, and even, sadly, by western feminists). It is also because, contrary to those stereotypes, Muslim women are poised courageously on the cutting edge of change, both in their*

own societies and in the international Women's Movement.

THE HISTORY OF IRANIAN WOMEN is bound inextricably to the history of Shii Islam and to the myths that emotionally and intellectually sustain it. As a practical philosophy of life, contemporary Shii Islam is a product of a historical process and, like all historical processes, has gone through many changes. The ruling clerics, however, present it as timeless dogma. By presenting it ahistorically, they suggest that Islam is qualitatively different from other religions. Islam, they argue, defines all aspects of life and the Quran, as God's Word, prescribes for all time the proper pattern of relationships within and among all social institutions. Furthermore, what Islam has prescribed as the word of God, they say, corresponds to the order of nature.[1] This is particularly stressed in the case of women and their position relative to men in the household and in society. Major Islamic 'myths'—the *sunna* or the custom of the Prophet and the *hadith*, the compiled sayings of the Prophet and Imams[2]—were designed to uphold this particular interpretation of 'reality' and in the course of time the interpretation itself, as content and process, was established as the center of historical reality. Consequently, Shiism is now what the Shii clerics who dispose of political and moral power say it is.

The ulema defined early and, over the years, precisely the proper place of woman in Iranian society. The late Ayatollah Morteza Motahhari (d. 1979), one of the more enlightened Iranian Shii clerics and probably the foremost authority on contemporary Shii jurisprudence regarding women, provides a modern example of the Shii formulation of woman's proper place. He argues the *naturalness* of the differences between the sexes and the conformity of Islamic law with the purpose of divine (natural) creation.[3] From the idea of purpose and

Mahnaz Afkhami, "Women in Post-Revolutionary Iran: A Feminist Perspective" in *In the Eye of the Storm: Women in Post-Revolutionary Iran*, eds. Mahnaz Afkhami and Erika Friedl (Syracuse: Syracuse University Press, 1994), by permission of the publisher.

order in the process of divine creation he deduces, among others, formally structured criteria of justice and beauty and concludes what amounts to the proposition that God, in His encompassing wisdom and justice, formally wills woman's subordinate position in accordance with the requirements of nature.

This 'natural' position for women has been asserted by all patriarchal religions throughout history. Indeed, the process of the subjugation of women appears remarkably similar in all cultures. The originary myth usually treats man and woman more equitably, but once the historical process begins, woman is reduced to a vehicle of procreation—the axis around which woman's history as myth or religion is organized.[4]

The theology of procreation emphasizes the family. Within the family, woman achieves value primarily as mother, and secondarily as wife, daughter, or sister. The more society grows, differentiates, and becomes structured, the more the originary concepts yield to systems of mores and regulations that define woman's subordinate place in increasing detail. In time, her contact with the larger society is totally mediated by man.

In the originary Zoroastrian sources, for example, the *Gatha,* the *Yashts* and other early religious texts as well as in parts of the *Matikan-e Hazar Datastan (The Digest of a Thousand Points of Law),* a later text compiled during the Sasanian period, woman is treated with respect, if not quite as an equal of man.[5] Women in Iranian epics—Sindokht, Rudabeh, Tahmineh, Gordafarid, Manijeh, and a host of others whose names are perpetuated in the *Shahnameh*—are invariably brave, aggressive, and full of initiative.[6] By the middle of the Sasanian period, however, under a dominant Zoroastrian clergy, women had lost many of their rights and privileges.[7]

Abrahamic religions also accord woman an important position in originary sources. Genesis, in fact, seems to treat Eve as the more resourceful of the first pair, man and woman, created in God's image. If human history is said to have begun with the fall of Adam, then Eve, in the act of leading Adam to the forbidden fruit, may be said to have taken upon herself the burden of a civilizing mission. In the Talmudic tradition, however, the laws apply only to men because in the course of time the Isra-

elite woman was relegated to 'a dependent existence derived from that of her father or her husband.'[8] In the Gospels, the very 'idea' of Christ suggests a leveling of inequities that to be meaningful must have included women. After Paul, however, Christianity steadily moved toward the affirmation of patriarchy and by the second Christian century the patriarchal interpretation had become, for all practical purposes, established dogma.[9]

This pattern is repeated in Islam. . . .

The universality of the feminine condition at present suggests the possibility of empathy among women on a global scale—a humanizing process that to succeed must be empowered to travel over time and space, as all successful discourses have historically done. Zoroastrianism, Buddhism, Judaism, Christianity, and Islam moved over many countries across many centuries, nourishing and receiving nourishment from the cultures they encountered. Saint Augustine was a Manichaean at first; Thomas Aquinas received Aristotle's teachings through the intermediary of Muslim scholars. During the nineteenth and twentieth centuries, as we have seen, secular ideas derived from the European Enlightenment traveled east and south. Each transmission produced contradiction, agony, and despair as well as hope. New and unfamiliar ideas broke into established systems and clashed with tradition, merging with indigenous thought, energizing it to overcome intellectual inertia and to produce new form and content that challenged and often changed the established norms and values.

Waging their struggle in the colonial environment, Third World feminist thinkers have achieved a multicultural ethical and intellectual formation and a plethora of experience relevant to the development of an internationally valid and effective discourse addressing women's condition on a global scale. The question is whether this foundation can become a springboard for a global discourse. By definition, such a discourse must transcend the boundaries of Christian, Jewish, Muslim, Buddhist, socialist, capitalist, or any other particular culture. It will be feminist rather than patriarchal, humane rather than ideological, balanced rather than extremist, critical as well as exhortatory.[10] The global feminist discourse recognizes that the problem of women constitutes an issue in its own right, not as a subsidiary of other ideologies, no matter how structurally comprehensive or textually promising they might seem to be. It insists in relating concepts to the historical contexts in which they are embedded.[11] Since 'traditional' concepts are by definition founded in patriarchal discourse, global feminism must be skeptical of propositions that present them as liberating. This feminism is not anti-man; rather, it sees the world in humane terms, that is, it seeks a redefinition of social, economic, and political principles of societal organization on the basis of non-paternalistic models. Realizing that such a feat cannot be accomplished without or against men's participation, it does not hesitate to engage men politically in favor of the feminist cause. On the other hand, given the present effects of the historical process, feminism will be critically aware of and fight against patriarchal structures and institutions.[12]

The global feminist discourse rejects the notion that 'East' and 'West' constitute mutually exclusive paradigms; rather, it looks at life as evolving for all and believes that certain humane and morally defensible principles can and should be applied in the West and in the East equally. The point is not that Iranian women should forget the problems that are obviously 'Iranian' and intensely present. It is, rather, that unless Iranian feminists think globally, they will neither be able to mobilize world opinion for their cause, nor succeed in breaking out of the boundaries of patriarchal discourse on their own, and, therefore, they will likely fail to address their problems in a way that will lead to their solution.[13]

At present, of course, reality belies the potential. The disparity in physical and material power between the developed and less-developed countries forces Third World women to withdraw to reactive positions, formulating their discourse in response to the West and its challenge. Consequently, they fail to think globally, that is, to move beyond the indigenous culture they have objectively outgrown. Their discourse remains nationalistic, parochial, fearful, tradition-bound, and rooted in the soil of patriarchy. The world, however, is undergoing a qualitative change, an important aspect of which may be the tumbling of nation-states qua culture boundaries. In the process, women may gain a chance to promote on a world scale the kinds of ideas that are applicable to women everywhere. If they do, Third World women will be able to critique

women's condition in the West from a vantage point that transcends the cultures of Abraham, Buddha, and Confucius and thus will help the women of all 'worlds of development', including Iran.

I am not suggesting therefore that the West be taken as the standard for the evaluation of women's conditions in Iran. On the contrary, it seems to me that there are significant issues of commission and omission in the western discourse that can be addressed profitably only from the global feminist position. The virtue of the global position is that it partakes of the wisdom of all cultures and that it accommodates differences in the levels of economic and social development without succumbing to either the normlessness of cultural relativism or the self-righteous parochialism of any particular culture.

The heightened awareness of female human rights that exists today throughout the world makes possible a more unified and effective approach to the global feminist movement. Western feminists can help this process but only to an extent, because they are burdened by two severe handicaps. First, they carry the onus of historical western hegemony, even though they themselves are the victims of a taxing patriarchal order.[14] Second, their problems as women are often of a different order than the problems of women in Third World countries. Consequently, they appear alternately as self-righteous promoters of their own western culture, when they advocate principles and rights that differ with the tenets of Third World societies, or as self-deprecating defenders of atrociously anti-feminist conditions, when they explain away oppressive behavior in the developing world on the grounds of cultural relativism.

Non-western feminists can be instrumental in the development of a viable global feminism despite their historical handicap. As the world moves from a disjointed society of nation-states to an increasingly interconnected economic and technological system, and as the symmetry of the enclaves of poverty and backwardness in the developed and developing countries is increasingly apparent, it becomes easier for Third World feminists to develop a sense of empathy with their sisters in other parts of the globe. Indeed, unless such empathy is effected and expanded, patriarchal norms, for all practical purposes, will not be transcended and feminism, global or otherwise, will not fully succeed.

It is from this vantage point that the originary myth in the Shii lore may be successfully engaged. Here is a chance for Iranian women to transcend the parochial discourse. By showing at once the similarity in the historical treatment of women in all societies and the need for women to deny the legitimacy of the patriarchal order in all cultures, Iranian women can challenge the claim that there is something unique in Islam that separates it from other human experiences. The goal is to contest the right and legitimacy of Iran's patriarchal clerical order to be the sole interpreters of the values, norms, and aesthetic standards of Shii Islam—a religion that lies at the core of Iranian culture. The truth is that there is nothing sacred about a limited and highly protected discourse, developed over centuries by a society of zealous men in order to produce and maintain a regime of control, a major function of which is to keep women in bondage—for ever.

Notes

Author's note: I wish to thank Guity Nashat, Miriam Cooke, Shahla Haeri and Seyyed Vali Reza Nasr for reading an earlier version of this paper. Their comments have been of great help to me.

1. The correspondence between Divine Law (*Jus Divine*) and Natural Law (*Jus Naturale*) is a commonplace of most religions, including the Abrahamic. For a general discussion of the essentials of Shii Islam see Allameh Sayyid Muhammad Husain Tabataba'i, *Shiite Islam,* trans S. H. Nasr (Houston: Free Islamic Literature, 1979). For a discussion of women in Islam see Morteza Motahhari, *The Rights of Women in Islam* (Tehran: World Organization for Islamic Services, 1981) part vii; John L. Esposito, *Women in Muslim Family Law* (Syracuse: Syracuse University Press, 1982).

2. The theory of *hadith,* or tradition, did not take definite shape until late in the second century after Islam. Since its inception, its method and authority have been matters for disagreement among Muslim scholars as well as others in terms of the reliability of its raconteurs and continuity of chains of transmission. Furthermore, there has always been a conflict among the various Sunni and Shii schools. Thus, the time factor involved and the differences between the compilers on the authenticity of the sayings or the chains opens the validity of much of the *hadith* to serious doubt even among Muslim ulema. For Shiis, perhaps the most celebrated compiler of tradition is Mohammad Baqer Majlesi, a *mojtahed* of the Safavid era. For the meaning and a concise discussion of the theory and development of *hadith* see J. Robson's article in *The Encyclopaedia of Islam*

(Leiden: E. J. Brill, 1971), vol 3, pp 23–9. For a brief history of imamite jurisprudence, particularly a survey of important Shii jurists, see A. A. Sachedina, *The Just Ruler in Shiite Islam: The Comprehensive Authority of the Jurist in Imamite Jurisprudence* (Oxford: Oxford University Press, 1988), pp 9–25. For a Marxist discussion see I. P. Petrushevski, *Islam in Iran* (Albany: State University of New York Press, 1985), pp 101ff.

3. Motahhari: *Rights of Women in Islam.*

4. See Yvonne Yazbeck Haddad and Ellison Banks Findly (eds) *Women, Religion and Social Change* (Albany: State University of New York Press, 1985); also chapters by Denise L. Carmody, Rosemary R. Ruether and Jane I. Smith on Judaism, Christianity and Islam respectively in Arvind Sharma (ed), *Women in World Religions* (Albany: State University of New York Press, 1987).

5. See the *Laws of Ancient Persians As Found in the Matikan-i Hazar Datastan or the Digest of A Thousand Points of Law,* trans S. J. Bulasara (Tehran: Imperial Organization for Social Services, 1976), first published by Hoshang T. Anklesaria, Bombay, 1937.

6. For women in *Shahnameh* see Khojasteh Kia, *Sokhanan-e Sezavar-e Zanan dar Shahnameh-ye Pahlavani (Words Deserving of Women in the Epic Shahnameh)* (Tehran: Nashr-e Fakhteh, 1371). For a comparative rendition of Iranian and non-Iranian female character see Saidi Sirjani, *Sima-ye Do Zan (A Portrait of Two Women)* (Tehran: 1367), where an Iranian and non-Iranian woman as portrayed in Nezami's *Khamseh* are compared.

7. See A. Perikhanian, 'Iranian Society and Law,' in *The Cambridge History of Iran,* vol 3 (2), ed. Ehsan Yarshater (Cambridge: Cambridge University Press, 1983), particularly pp 646–55.

8. Judith Baskin, 'The Separation of Women in Rabbinic Judaism,' in Haddad and Findly: *Women, Religion and Social Change,* pp 3–18 and Denise L. Carmody in Sharma: *Women in World Religions,* p 192.

9. Rosemary R. Ruether in Sharma: *Women in World Religions,* p. 209.

10. I realize that these terms are problematic. The function of a global discourse is to define and clarify the concepts invoked by these terms in a way that is suitable to the requirements of an equitable system of gender relations in the twenty-first century, if not earlier in the so-called 'new world order.' For a critique of approaches to feminism, patriarchy, and Islam see Deniz Kandiyoti, 'Islam and Patriarchy: A Comparative Perspective,' in Nikkie R. Keddie and Beth Baron (eds), *Women in Middle Eastern History: Shifting Boundaries in Sex and Gender* (New Haven: Yale University Press, 1991), pp 23–42.

11. For a relevant critique see Christine Delphy, 'Proto-feminism and antifeminism,' in Moi: *French Feminist Thought,* pp 80–109. See also Linda Kauffman (ed), *Gender and Theory: Dialogues on Feminist Criticism* (New York: Basil Blackwell, 1989).

12. For some possibilities of what might constitute a discourse that has a chance of transcending fixed sexual polarities see Julia Kristeva, 'Woman's Time,' in Belsey and Moore: *The Feminist Reader,* pp 198–217.

13. What appear as obstacles to the development of a global approach to a feminist social and literary criticism, namely, the contemporary emphasis in universities on cultural relativism, on one hand, and on textual and deconstructionist analysis, on the other, may prove a positive force for the future involvement of Third World women in the construction of a global discourse. The transition from parochial/relativistic to a global approach is already taking place as more and more feminist positions are advanced mutually through intellectual representatives of western and non-western cultures.

14. Nupur Chaudhuri and Margaret Strobel (eds), *Western Women and Imperialism: Complicity and Resistance* (Bloomington: Indiana University Press, 1992).

Antifeminism

Andrea Dworkin

For more than two decades, radical feminist Andrea Dworkin has been a powerful speaker, activist, and the author of many influential books, including Mercy *(1990),* Letters from a War Zone *(1988),* Pornography: Men Possessing Women *(1981),* Ice and Fire *(1986),* Intercourse *(1987),* Right-Wing Women *(1983),* Our Blood: Prophecies and Discourses on Sexual Politics *(1976), and* Woman-Hating *(1974). With Catharine MacKinnon, she co-authored the first law recognizing pornography as a violation of women's civil rights.*

As a speaker or a writer, Dworkin never minces words. In the following piece, she argues that because feminism is the philosophy of liberation for women, antifeminism, in any guise, is an expression of misogyny, the hatred of women. Antifeminism supports the present abusive gender system as natural and desirable: it opposes women's freedom and it denigrates our selfhood.

FEMINISM IS A MUCH-HATED POLITICAL philosophy. This is true all along the male-defined, recognizable political spectrum from far Right to far Left. Feminism is hated because women are hated. Antifeminism is a direct expression of misogyny; it is the political defense of woman hating. This is because feminism is the liberation movement of women. Antifeminism, in any of its political colorations, holds that the social and sexual condition of women essentially (one way or another) embodies the nature of women, that the way women are treated in sex and in society is congruent with what women are, that the fundamental relationship between men and women—in sex, in reproduction, in social hierarchy—is both necessary and inevitable. Antifeminism defends the conviction that the male

abuse of women, especially in sex, has an implicit logic, one that no program of social justice can or should eliminate; that because the male use of women originates in the distinct and opposite natures of each which converge in what is called "sex," women are not abused when used as women—but merely used for what they are by men as men. It is admitted that there are excesses of male sadism—committed by deranged individuals, for instance—but in general the massive degradation of women is not seen to violate the nature of women as such. For instance, a man's nature would be violated if anyone forcibly penetrated his body. A women's nature is not violated by the same event, even though she may have been hurt. A man's nature would not provoke anyone to forcibly penetrate his body. A woman's nature does provoke such penetration—and even injury is no proof that she did not want the penetration or even the injury itself, since it is her nature as a woman to desire being forcibly penetrated and forcibly hurt. Conservatively estimated, in the United States a woman is raped every three minutes, and in each and every rape the woman's nature is at issue first and foremost, not the man's act. Certainly there is no social or legal recognition that rape is an act of political terrorism.

Antifeminism can accommodate reform: a recognition that some forms of discrimination against women are unfair to women or that some kinds of injustice to women are not warranted (or entirely warranted) by the nature of women. But underneath the apparent civility, there are facile, arrogant assumptions: that the remedies are easy, the problems frivolous; that the harm done to women is not substantial nor is it significant in any real way; and that the subordination of women to men is not in and of itself an egregious wrong. This assessment is maintained in the face of proved atrocities and the obvious intractability of the oppression.

Antifeminism is always an expression of hating women: it is way past time to say so, to make the equation, to insist on its truth. Antifeminism throws women to the wolves; it says "later" or "never" to those suffering cruel and systematic deprivations of liberty; it tells women that when their lives are at stake, there is no urgency toward either justice or decency; it scolds women for wanting freedom. It is right to see woman hating, sex hatred, passionate contempt, in every effort to subvert or stop an improvement in the status of women on any front, whether radical or reform. It is right to see contempt for women in any effort to subvert or stop any move on the part of women toward economic or sexual independence, toward civil or legal equality, toward self-determination. Antifeminism is the politics of contempt for women as a class. This is true when the antifeminism is expressed in opposition to the Equal Rights Amendment or to the right to abortion on demand or to procedures against sexual harassment or to shelters for battered women or to reforms in rape laws. This is true whether the opposition is from the Heritage Foundation, the Moral Majority, the Eagle Forum, the American Civil Liberties Union, the Communist Party, the Democrats, or the Republicans. The same antifeminist contempt for women is expressed in resistance to affirmative action or in defenses of pornography or in the acceptance of prostitution as an institution of female sex labor. If one sees that women are being systematically exploited and abused, then the defense of anything, the acceptance of anything, that promotes or continues that exploitation or abuse expresses a hatred of women, a contempt for their freedom and dignity; and an effort to impede legislative, social, or economic initiatives that would improve the status of women, however radical or reformist those measures are, is an expression of that same contempt. One simply cannot be both for and against the exploitation of women: for it when it brings pleasure, against it in the abstract; for it when it brings profit, against it in principle; for it when no one is looking, against it when someone who might notice is around. If one sees how exploited women are—the systematic nature of the exploitation, the sexual base of the exploitation—then there is no political or ethical justification for doing one whit less than everything—using every resource—to stop that exploitation. Antifeminism has been the cover for outright bigotry and it has been the vehicle of outright bigotry. Antifeminism

has been a credible cover and an effective vehicle because the hatred of women is not politically anathema on either the Right or the Left. Antifeminism is manifest wherever the subordination of women is actively perpetuated or enhanced or defended or passively accepted, because the devaluation of women is implicit in all these stances. Woman hating and antifeminism, however aggressive or restrained the expression, are empirical synonyms, inseparable, often indistinguishable, often interchangeable; and any acceptance of the exploitation of women in any area, for any reason, in any style, is both, means both, and promotes both.

. . .

To achieve a single standard of human freedom and one absolute standard of human dignity, the sex-class system has to be dismembered. The reason is pragmatic, not philosophical: nothing less will work. However much everyone wants to do less, less will not free women. Liberal men and women ask, Why can't we just be ourselves, all human beings, begin now and not dwell in past injustices, wouldn't that subvert the sex-class system, change it from the inside out? The answer is no. The sex-class system has a structure; it has deep roots in religion and culture; it is fundamental to the economy; sexuality is its creature; to be "just human beings" in it, women have to hide what happens to them as women because they are women—happenings like forced sex and forced reproduction, happenings that continue as long as the sex-class system operates. The liberation of women requires facing the real condition of women in order to change it. "We're all just people" is a stance that prohibits recognition of the systematic cruelties visited on women because of sex oppression.

Feminism as a liberation movement, then, demands a revolutionary single standard of what humans have a right to, and also demands that the current sexual bifurcation of rights never be let out of sight. Antifeminism does the opposite: it insists that there is a double standard of what humans have a right to—a male standard and a female standard; and it insists at the same time that we are all just human beings, right now, as things stand, within this sex-class system, so that no special attention should be paid to social phenomena on account of sex. With respect to rape, for instance, the feminist starts out with a single standard of freedom and dignity: everyone, women as well as men, should have a right to the integrity of their own body. Feminists then focus on and analyze the sex-class reality of rape: men rape, women are raped; even in those statistically rare cases where boys or men are raped, men are the rapists. Antifeminists start out with a double standard: men conquer, possess, dominate, men take women; women are conquered, possessed, dominated, and taken. Antifeminists then insist that rape is a crime like any other, like mugging or homicide or burglary: they deny its sex-specific, sex-class nature and the political meaning undeniably implicit in the sexual construction of the crime. Feminists are accused of denying the common humanity of men and women because feminists refuse to fudge on the sex issue of who does what to whom, how often, and why. Antifeminists refuse to acknowledge that the sex-class system repudiates the humanity of women by keeping women systematically subject to exploitation and violence as a condition of sex. In analyzing the sex-class system, feminists are accused of inventing or perpetuating it. Calling attention to it, we are told, insults women by suggesting that they are victims (stupid enough to allow themselves to be victimized). Feminists are accused of being the agents of degradation by postulating that such degradation exists. This is a little like considering abolitionists responsible for slavery, but all is fair when love is war. In ignoring the political significance of the sex-class system except to defend it when it is under attack, antifeminists suggest that "we're all in this together," all us human beings, different-but-together, a formulation that depends on lack of clarity for its persuasiveness. Indisputably, we're all in rape together, some of us to great disadvantage. Feminism especially requires a rigorous analysis of sex class, one that is ongoing, stubborn, persistent, unsentimental, disciplined, not placated by fatuous invocations of a common humanity that in fact the sex-class system itself suppresses. The sex-class system cannot be undone when those whom it exploits and humiliates are unable to face it for what it is, for what it takes from them, for what it does to them. Feminism requires precisely what misogyny destroys in women: unimpeachable bravery in confronting male power. Despite the impossibility of it, there is such bravery: there are such women, in some periods millions upon millions of them. If

male supremacy survives every effort of women to overthrow it, it will not be because of biology or God; nor will it be because of the force and power of men per se. It will be because the will to liberation was contaminated, undermined, rendered ineffectual and meaningless, by antifeminism: by specious concepts of equality based on an evasion of what the sex-class system really is. The refusal to recognize the intrinsic despotism of the sex-class system means that that despotism is inevitably incorporated into reform models of that same system: in this, antifeminism triumphs over the will to liberation. The refusal to recognize the unique abuses inherent in sex labor (treating sex labor as if it were sex-neutral, as if it were not intrinsically part of sex oppression and inseparable from it) is a function of antifeminism; the acceptance of sex labor as appropriate labor for women marks the triumph of antifeminism over the will to liberation. The sentimental acceptance of a double standard of human rights, responsibilities, and freedom is also the triumph of antifeminism over the will to liberation; no sexual dichotomy is compatible with real liberation. And, most important, the refusal to demand (with no compromise being possible) one absolute standard of human dignity is the greatest triumph of antifeminism over the will to liberation. Without that one absolute standard, liberation is mush; feminism is frivolous and utterly self-indulgent. Without that one absolute standard as the keystone of revolutionary justice, feminism has no claim to being a liberation movement; it has no revolutionary stance, goal, or potential; it has no basis for a radical reconstruction of society; it has no criteria for action or organization; it has no moral necessity; it has no inescapable claim on the conscience of "mankind"; it has no philosophical seriousness; it has no authentic stature as a human-rights movement; it has nothing to teach. Also, without that one absolute standard, feminism has no chance whatsoever of actually liberating women or destroying the sex-class system. Refusing to base itself on a principle of universal human dignity, or compromising, retreating from that principle, feminism becomes that which exists to stop it: antifeminism. No liberation movement can accept the degradation of those whom it seeks to liberate by accepting a different definition of dignity for them and stay a movement for their freedom at the same time. (Apologists for pornography:

take note.) A universal standard of human dignity is the only principle that completely repudiates sex-class exploitation and also propels all of us into a future where the fundamental political question is the quality of life for all human beings. Are women being subordinated to men? There is insufficient dignity in that. Are men being prostituted too? What is human dignity?

Two elements constitute the discipline of feminism: political, ideological, and strategic confrontation with the sex-class system—with sex hierarchy and sex segregation—and a single standard of human dignity. Abandon either element and the sex-class system is unbreachable, indestructible; feminism loses its rigor, the toughness of its visionary heart; women get swallowed up not only by misogyny but also by antifeminism—facile excuses for exploiting women, metaphysical justifications for abusing women, and shoddy apologies for ignoring the political imperatives of women.

One other discipline is essential both to the practice of feminism and to its theoretical integrity: the firm, unsentimental, continuous recognition that women are a class having a common condition. This is not some psychological process of identification with women because women are wonderful; nor is it the insupportable assertion that there are no substantive, treacherous differences among women. This is not a liberal mandate to ignore what is cruel, despicable, or stupid in women, nor is it a mandate to ignore dangerous political ideas or allegiances of women. This does not mean women first, women best, women only. It does mean that the fate of every individual woman—no matter what her politics, character, values, qualities—is tied to the fate of all women whether she likes it or not. On one level, it means that every woman's fate is tied to the fate of women she dislikes personally. On another level, it means that every woman's fate is tied to the fate of women whom she politically and morally abhors.

For instance, it means that rape jeopardizes communist and fascist women, liberal, conservative, Democratic, or Republican women, racist women and black women, Nazi women and Jewish women, homophobic women and homosexual women. The crimes committed against women because they are women articulate the condition of women. The eradication of these crimes, the transformation of the condition of women, is the purpose of feminism: which means that feminism requires a most rigorous definition of what those crimes are so as to determine what that condition is. This definition cannot be compromised by a selective representation of the sex class based on sentimentality or wishful thinking. This definition cannot exclude prudes or sluts or dykes or mothers or virgins because one does not want to be associated with them. To be a feminist means recognizing that one is associated with all women not as an act of choice but as a matter of fact. The sex-class system creates the fact. When that system is broken, there will be no such fact. Feminists do not create this common condition by making alliances: feminists recognize this common condition because it exists as an intrinsic part of sex oppression. The fundamental knowledge that women are a class having a common condition—that the fate of one woman is tied substantively to the fate of all women—toughens feminist theory and practice. That fundamental knowledge is an almost unbearable test of seriousness. There is no real feminism that does not have at its heart the tempering discipline of sex-class consciousness: knowing that women share a common condition as a class, like it or not.

What is that common condition? Subordinate to men, sexually colonized in a sexual system of dominance and submission, denied rights on the basis of sex, historically chattel, generally considered biologically inferior, confined to sex and reproduction: this is the general description of the social environment in which all women live.

CHAPTER FIVE

Patriarchy and Women's Subordination: Explanations from Feminist Theory, Science, and Myth

ASKING THE QUESTION

The more one studies women's circumstances around the world, the more one is likely to ask: How did this situation come to be, and why is it so resistant to change? Although great diversity exists among peoples of the world, with few exceptions, in society after society and across time and space, men dominate the upper levels of political, economic, and social power, and women are rarely or only partially included.[1] The work of men is generally more highly valued than that of women and usually more highly compensated. Men are typically valued more in themselves as persons, a fact often expressed in social customs, rites, and laws. Men tend to outrank women in social status, and often their comfort and privilege is built on the service of women; the reverse is rarely the case.

Men are dominant; women are subordinated by them. Why do men as a group dominate and disparage women, and why do women submit? Has it always been this way, or was there a time in the past when women were the equals of men or even, as some have suggested, the leaders of civilization? If the subordination of women did not always exist, what could account for its coming into existence? Was there a primordial revolution of magnificent proportions, as ancient myths sometimes depict, or did a gradual erosion of female power and autonomy occur, and, if so, what could have caused such an erosion? Is it true, as the patriarchs contend, that men simply were superior to women, or did they win their place by the choice of the gods?

Many have argued that men and women are "different" in a variety of ways and that these differences account for women's position. Are women different in ways that influenced the direction civilization has taken? Or did the way civilization evolve create the differences? Are behavioral differences grounded in biology or in culture? And what difference do the differences make, or *should* they make, for the way a society is presently structured—in apportioning political authority, economic benefits, and the enjoyment of life's amenities?

There are theories that attempt to answer these questions. Some are scientific or quasi-scientific; some pretend to be science but are actually pseudo-science (false science), theories inconsistent with accepted scientific beliefs and methods; others are mythic, in the most positive sense of that term—they are stories that are meant to capture a society's deeply felt and revered truths or psychological truths that otherwise could not be put into words. Some theories speak in purely pragmatic terms, arguing social efficiency or orderliness, whereas others may posit cosmic significance to gender, suggesting divine plans or great schemes of nature.

These questions have been asked before, but now the women's movement has focused on them afresh, and the analyses are becoming more balanced and more sophisticated. In religious communities, feminist theologians are challenging the traditional interpretations of language, dogma, and beliefs. In the sciences, feminists and nonfeminists alike are carrying on new and vigorous research into aspects of these issues barely touched before or else treated prejudicially. Controversy and debate are sharp. New, more reliable information and new research methods and techniques are generating fresh ways to deal with these ancient questions.

New Data

Researchers in almost every field of intellectual endeavor are collecting new information regarding women's contributions to culture, past and present. Anthropologists have thrown new light on women's discoveries and inventions in early civilization—pottery, food preservation, tanning, and so on. Feminist historians have unearthed data on women never before recognized, events whose importance had been overlooked, activities never before understood. Psychologists and biologists are carefully reexamining studies of female-male differences to deal in a more objective way with traditional assumptions and theories. Linguists are discovering new connections between speech patterns and social effectiveness and power.

New Perspectives

The addition of feminist critique to intellectual dialogue is bringing a new degree of sophistication to the inquiry. Having challenged the reliability of traditional knowledge collected solely by men or within male perspectives, feminists are now posing questions that considerably alter the research. How

viable and/or complete is much of the information we have on prehistory and primitive cultures, interpreted as it has been through masculinist bias? Can we depend on men to have asked the pertinent questions about women; would women have confided freely in male researchers? Would the male researcher have properly evaluated the female data he collected? If the masculinist psychologist has imposed his expectations on his research findings, won't they have been distorted, and won't most of the theories of sex differences be unreliable? Might not there then have to be entirely new ways of piecing together the information about the origins of patriarchy?[2]

Terminology, for example, has been sharply challenged. The term *domestic*, for example, means literally "pertaining to the home," and social scientists use it to describe tasks, artifacts, or behavior directly related to the home site, to the group's family or living arrangements. Anthropologists generally agree that women have almost universally carried on the "domestic" activities of society. However, evidence shows that almost any task assigned to women is likely to be deemed "domestic" by social scientists, whereas the same task assigned to men is likely to be categorized differently. For example, an ethnographer might categorize creating pottery for the tribe as a "domestic" activity when it is done by women but as an "artistic" activity if done by men. In other words, because the assumption is that women do the domestic work of the group, their tasks are automatically categorized as domestic; then, in a real round-robin, because women's work is termed "domestic," researchers feel safe in reporting that the domestic work of the tribe is always done by women!

One may realistically challenge such traditionally accepted claims as the one that women are oppressed because they have never united in their own self-interest. Recent discussions have highlighted many circumstances where women did fight in their own behalf, events that were either unknown before the surge of feminist history rediscovered them or else misunderstood and therefore neglected as irrelevant, Events such as the Roman women's opposition to the Oppian Laws, the movement of the Beguines in the Middle Ages, or the later fights for temperance, birth control, and abortion rights are examples of women uniting in their own interests. If this information is ignored, how reliable is the final thesis?

The current interest in finding explanations for gender systems gives us reason to be optimistic about making more sense of things, but not without careful attention to the many complicated problems before us. First, no one as yet knows "the answers" to many factual questions. Vast gaps in data and analyses exist. Second, there may not be one source of patriarchy but many. Third, the several theories presented here represent only examples of those that exist, and even the challenges put to them do not constitute the full array of possibilities. This book has room only for an introduction to the issue.

THE MATTER OF DEFINITION

No one as yet knows "the answer" to what? That is, what exactly is our question? Are we asking why women and men are "unequal"? Unequal in what? In political or personal power? What do we mean by power? What kind of power do women not have? Unequal in opportunity? Opportunity for what? We have opportunity to gain income—we can marry it. From a value-free standpoint, why is that mode of opportunity less acceptable than any other? Are we unequal in status? Or are we just "different," that is, separate but "equal"? To compare different levels of status, we have to measure it. How does one do that? How does one compare the power and status of one group of women in a culture (say, middle-class White American women) with another (perhaps, wealthy Black British women)?

If we ask why women are subordinate to men, what do we mean by *subordinate,* and how do we indicate and include differences in subordination from culture to culture? How is subordination different from oppression, exploitation, discrimination, domination? What does the term *subordination* mean in the context of power? If it is true, as some have suggested, that though men hold formal power, women frequently hold great informal power over men, then who is subordinate to whom, and in what way?

As you can see, there are many relevant concepts and terms, and each has its nuances and implications. One must be extraordinarily careful about how they are used.

Any good researcher will point out that effective problem solving requires an accurate statement of the problem itself as well as careful definitions of the terms employed. Consider the following two sentences, each of which has actually been used as a statement of the problem: How did it come about that men usurped the autonomy and labor of women? Why are men superior to women both in power and accomplishments? Neither of these formulations defines the problem adequately. Each contains assumptions and value judgments; each expresses a particular perspective; and each contains research expectations that have not been critically explored. In short, each is biased and circular, assuming an answer before beginning to search.

In tracking down reliable explanations, one must guard against hidden assumptions and values, charged language (*usurped, equality, superior*), and bias-prone terminology (*domestic, aggressive, technological*). This in itself is a monumental task. How does one ask a question that is free of prior assumptions and value-laden concepts yet is still meaningful? For example: "Under what conditions did the present cultural sexual arrangements come into existence?" Which arrangements? What culture? What kind of origin—in time? in causative factors? Whereas the two formulations in the previous paragraph are too narrow and prejudicial, this one is too broad and omits the essence of the problem, which *is* valuational. Clearly, a balance of attention must exist between constructing formulations that are relatively objective and free of assumption yet sufficiently concrete in perspective to be substantive.[3]

Sexual Asymmetry

Searching for an expression that captures all the issues we have been raising, that is broad enough and relatively objective, some feminists and social scientists have been using the term *sexual asymmetry,* which simply means a disproportion or dissimilarity based on sex. The term functions in a number of different contexts—scientific, political, religious, and so on—and also avoids many pitfalls. It is both meaningful and scientifically productive to ask, "What are the origins and causes of sexual asymmetry?" Yet, in its scientific purity, the term *sexual asymmetry* tends to be vague, and without the support of related concepts for fleshing it out (charged though they may be), discussion within its limits might tend to be thin.

For purposes of our discussion, let us say that sexual asymmetry refers to a whole range of situations where (1) policies regarding control over the wider community and the freedom to participate in activities affecting all members of the group are determined solely or primarily on the grounds of sex, and (2) judgments of worth are made solely or primarily on the basis of sex. For example, in a society where the legal right to vote for a leader of the entire group is limited to men *because they are men* (not bright men or strong men or educated men) and prohibited to women *because they are women* (not stupid women or poor women or malicious women), political sexual asymmetry exists. In a society where men are deemed intrinsically more valuable than women, more worthy humans, more desirable *solely on the ground of maleness,* valuational sexual asymmetry exists.

Asymmetry takes many forms. In most cultures, as we have said, the work of men is more highly prized than that of women; women are considered to be the inferiors of men (in a variety of ways); and people tend to disparage both the work and the personhood of women. Such societies are termed *misogynist,* woman-hating. In our society, signs of misogyny range from the subtle to the blatant. Women are reputed to be stupid, petty, incompetent, or deceptive; relative to men doing the same jobs, women are underpaid and excluded from many activities. Other societies have featured such signs of misogyny as infibulation or clitoridectomy (the broadest category of these practices is called *female genital mutilation*),[4] the chastity belt, purdah, female infanticide, and suttee.

Although in some societies women have considerable power within the family group or over other women, in every known society, men make the policy, for the most part, that affects the group as a whole. Men make policy for women (and for some other men), but women do not formally make policy for the majority of men. In such a case, women are *subordinate* to men; that is, women inhabit a lower order of rank, power, and privilege. For example, men in our society control the institutions that determine the rules of our lives: the legislature,

the judiciary, the police, the law, the economy. Women control the home, though *formally* only with the approval of the men they live with.

Oppression differs from subordination in that one person may be subordinate to another and yet not be oppressed, as when a child is subordinate to a benevolent parent or when a worker of lesser ability must yield to policy set by a more highly qualified person in a position of higher rank. To oppress means to bear down, to weigh on, to burden. One is oppressed when one experiences life as a burden, when one is emotionally or spiritually crushed or tyrannized. A culture that demeans a woman's self-image, destroys her pride, misuses her person for ends not her own, or appropriates the fruits of her labor without proper compensation (that is, exploits her labor) is an oppressive culture. Many cultures oppress and exploit their women, as our culture oppresses and exploits at least some of us, if not all (as many feminists argue). Through *discrimination* (different, disadvantageous treatment before the law), outright slavery, or social customs that serve to solidify male privilege, women are oppressed and exploited in most cultures.

When we ask here, "What are the origins and causes of sexual asymmetry?" we are seeking an answer to the entire range of asymmetry, from discrimination to misogyny.

PROBLEMS OF METHOD

How do we find reliable answers to the questions we have asked? We are, after all, pursuing a situation that in myth is without beginning and in social science traces back at least ten thousand years into prehistory, that traverses diverse cultures around the globe, and that may even have parallels in other species.

Scientifically, how do we deal with origins when the beginnings are lost? And where shall we count the beginnings? With recorded history? With early primitive peoples? With primates and hominoids? How helpful is information gleaned from current "primitive" groups when they diverge so much even among themselves?

Under what circumstances and to what degree is the practice of drawing analogies between humans and other animals to count? And if they count, which animals? Shall we select those that meet one set of expectations, like the aggressive, asymmetrical gibbon, or shall we focus on the ever-faithful, one-time-mating greylag goose, or perhaps the lion with its tough female hunter? Shall we confine ourselves to primates? And to what degree are any animal studies helpful when investigating a creature as uniquely malleable as the human being?

A great deal of important information is coming from new research into certain primate groups such as the chimpanzees, which are believed to be closely related to the kind of African ape that some four million years ago may have given rise to the hominids (the earliest members of the human family, such as *Australopithecus* and *Homo erectus*). Because fossil records (bones and teeth, for example, or organic tools) of this period are scarce, and because it is difficult to speculate reliably on behavior patterns of groups that are not observable, anthropologists use several kinds of evidence to generate hypotheses about the nature of early human social activities. For example, changes in the relative size of canine and molar teeth, within and across sexual categories, may tell us about diet (and therefore food-getting patterns) or about modes of defense or even about degrees of sociability. Such speculations, supported or enlarged by the observation of existent populations of highly developed primates, offer possibilities for piecing together a picture of the evolution of early human organization.

Some social scientists, however, approach the problem differently. They contend that because *Homo sapiens* is a far more advanced and complex creature in terms of intelligence than the earliest hominids, and because reflective thinking is unique to humans, *Homo sapiens* is qualitatively different from its ancestors. Its behavior patterns and social organization, therefore, require a different kind and level of explanation, perhaps psychological or even mythic.

Studying the art and artifacts of lost civilizations farther along the evolutionary scale, some claim that advanced cultures existed before our own that were matriarchal and matrilineal. Argued primarily from inferential information, such theories are very controversial.

What counts as evidence? It is commonly understood that personal testimony (called *emic* data) may be unreliable; issues of subjectivity, of perspec-

tive, of lack of insight, even of deceit arise. Yet even purely objective, researcher-based analysis (called *etic* data) may suffer from ethnocentrism or oversimplification; and even with physical evidence, the problem of interpretation remains. How then are such speculations or hypotheses to be verified?

A SERIES OF HYPOTHESES

So far, all we have for "answers" to our problem is conjecture. There are hypotheses, no firm theories. The hypotheses, except for certain themes that appear to be common to all, range across a variety of perspectives, levels of explanation, and conclusions, some of them quite contradictory.

Biological Approaches

When one argues that asymmetry occurs because women and men have different capacities and behaviors based on the *innate, inherited physical differences* (such as hormonal patterns, brain size, or bone structure), then one is arguing from the biological perspective or level. This approach has included arguments that females and males differ *constitutionally* in such varied factors as intelligence, temperament, IQ, capacity to lead, physical endurance, propensity to "bond" with members of the same sex, sexuality, aggressiveness, and even sense of justice. Some have contended that these biologically based differences account for *and justify* sexual asymmetry.

Such a point of view has the advantage of focusing on factors that are more easily observable, hence more amenable to study and to verification than some others. And, as some of the discussion in the preceding chapter pointed out, research does indicate that real physical, behavior-related differences may exist between females and males. What remains, however, is to determine what these differences mean, and more important, what they should mean. If it should be found, for example, that males are constitutionally more aggressive and hence more likely to compete than females (there is some evidence to this effect) and thus more inclined to dominate or lead, one ought reasonably to ask whether this means that men *should* lead;[5] or, since the world now suffers from an overabundance of aggressiveness, whether less aggressive persons (females?) should be socially encouraged to lead and males be discouraged from doing so.

To say that women are "naturally" this and men are "naturally" that (leaving aside the question of the truth of such propositions) is an argument that is frequently used to maintain the status quo. Yet one must remember that the terms *natural* and *desirable* are different. It is natural for animals to kill or maim (usually for food or protection but sometimes for other reasons), but that does not make this behavior desirable. It is natural for humans to die painfully of disease, but that does not make this desirable. The human species has never rested content with what is "natural." That is our splendor as well as our infamy. We have survived because of adaptations that were not "natural." Cultures evolve because humans are malleable. We must not confuse the muddy scientific concept *natural* with the equally muddy ethical notion *desirable.*

Sociological or Cultural Theories

The factor of malleability raises the familiar issue of the "nature/nurture" controversy. Which is more responsible for human behavior, nature (physiological, inborn components) or nurture (the effects of society—socialization, enculturation, learning)? Although nature, our physical selves and our genes, constitutes the raw material of our beings and thus imposes its own limits on our development, social scientists generally agree that nurture contributes the lion's share to our development.

In a famous cross-cultural study of three existing societies, Margaret Mead described extremely divergent gender-based behavior.[6] The Arapesh society approved behavior for both men and women that our culture would term *feminine*: unaggressive, maternal, and cooperative rather than competitive. In contrast, Mundugumor men and women were expected to be extremely aggressive, violent, and nonmaternal. The Tchambuli culture, a mirror image of our own, prized dominant, impersonal, and managing women and emotionally dependent, less effective men. Mead concluded that such data threw great doubt on the biological basis of gender difference and strongly supported the thesis that sex-linked behavioral characteristics are the result of social conditions.

The emphasis on enculturation as the main source of sex-role behavior continues today, yet both nonfeminists and feminists are moving toward reappraising biological and physiological factors. Sociological theories like Mead's generally argue that female-male behavioral differences are more a matter of social than of biological degree: The traits we take to be feminine or masculine are prescribed by the mores of our culture and are learned or internalized through formal education, religion, media, and all the other institutions that define experience. Unlike biological explanations, which account for the beginnings of asymmetry by saying simply, "It has always been that way, decreed by nature," sociological theories need additional elaboration to deal with origins. It is one thing to say that I as a woman have trait x because my society teaches it, and another to account for *why* my society teaches x. How and why did my society choose to teach x, and why does this society teach x while another teaches y?

There are those, feminist and otherwise, who say that it is not necessary to ask why or how gender norms originated. They argue that we need only evaluate them in the present context from the point of view of ethics (is it right, fair, or just to subordinate women?) or of social efficacy (does it benefit our society to maintain the present arrangement?). In common sense, this argument carries weight. One need not ask when or how the first war began in order to decide that war is undesirable and must be ended. A medical researcher need not ask who had the first cancer in order to search for its cause. But origins and causes are logically related. As we saw earlier in the discussion of theory, if we know how something comes to be, if we can determine *what factors precede and precipitate an event,* in effect we have found the cause, and only in understanding causes of events can we hope to control them.

The problem, however, becomes complicated. Just as some people confuse natural with desirable, others confuse origin with justification. For example, George Gilder, a well-known writer of antifeminist theories, argued that asymmetry originates in the males' exclusion from childbearing and in their drive to achieve parity through other modes of creativity.[7] This, he argued, explains why men feel the need to exclude women from their activities, why they become unpleasant if women refuse the place men have made for them, and *why women should not refuse that place.* Whatever one thinks of Gilder's first contention—that men dominate women to achieve reproductive parity—we can plainly see that the thesis cannot stand as a justification, an ethical argument, for asymmetry. To say that *people commit murder because they are hostile, antisocial, and pressured* may explain why they do it—how their murderous impulses originate—but it does not support the thesis that *they should do it*; that is, the explanation does not serve as a justification. Clearly, it is helpful to explore the origins of sexual asymmetry, but one must carefully distinguish what the exploration accomplishes and what it leaves undone. By and large, sociological-cultural theories of origin are either *evolutionary* or *psychomythic.* Evolutionary theories argue that individuals or entire cultures or both have developed certain traits or norms as adaptations, or survival mechanisms, in answer to the requirements of their environment.

Individual-Evolutionary Theories A famous example of the individual-evolutionary explanation is the "man-the-hunter" theory. Food, it begins, was the most important survival commodity in primitive society, and because scarce, meat was the most prized. As women in primitive circumstances were always with child or caring for their young, it was not practical for them to go on the hunt, which often took one miles and days away from the safety of the home site and required activities hard to perform with an attached small child. For this reason, women stayed at home, raising children, foraging for vegetables and small game, and tending the hearth while men went hunting. Finally, each sex developed (evolved) physical and behavioral traits appropriate to their tasks. This, some evolutionists say, explains not only work segregation based on sex but also why men are prized above women (*they* brought the meat). It also reveals the origin of the different capabilities, traits, and personalities of females and males: Men are aggressive and bonding so they can hunt, whereas women are compliant and gentle because "the overall mood arising from such organic orientation, from so much waiting and letting grow and gentling and encouraging but never forcing, is a mood of compliance."[8]

For a time, this theory was in great vogue with many people, feminists and nonfeminists alike. But now the entire perspective has come into question.

One may ask whether the male became aggressive because he had to hunt or hunted because he was aggressive. (After all, other sources of protein existed, usually provided by the woman, than what was sought in the hunt—even meat.) Which came first, man the hunter or man the warrior, and are the two related? Did women really evolve "compliance" because that temperament is necessary to raising children, and who says that it is necessary? Mead's Mundugumors certainly do not believe so. Their women are aggressive, their children survive, and female aggressiveness does not lead to male unagressiveness as some theories suggest. How does one account for male aggressiveness and rites of courage in cultures (for example, in Polynesia) where food (including protein) is plentiful and hunting unnecessary?

Evolutionary theories that focus on the development of individual (male-female) differences are certainly more sophisticated than biological theories, but they leave much to be desired. Still paying scant attention to the power of socialization, they fail to take into account the changes in individual behavior that would be wrought by changing environments. Men no longer go off to hunt (however widely one chooses to define the term), and brute strength, size, and aggressiveness are no longer adaptive traits for social survival, yet the value persists. Some other, wider factor may be needed to explain the cultural definitions of woman and man.

Cultural-Evolutionary Theories Variations of the preceding kind of explanation, cultural-evolutionary theories, take the society rather than the individual as the basic unit to be explored.[9] In this case, it is the entire culture, as well as the individual, that evolves adaptive mechanisms; sexual mores, role definitions, and gender expectations are part of them. For example, if a society were located in an environment where conditions were particularly hard, with a high death rate, such a society would probably require a high birth rate to maintain an adequate population, and it might well develop values that encouraged women to conceive and bear many children, to view themselves primarily in their childbearing capacity, and so on. The cultural-evolutionary approach, then, seeks to understand sexual mores, attitudes, and behaviors in terms of the environmental conditions that give rise to them.

Psychomythic Theories   None of the theories thus far developed fully accounts for the whole range of sexual asymmetry. Too many puzzling questions are left unanswered. The kinds of explanations we have considered do not adequately explain the reasons for sex segregation, political subordination, or the divisions of labor based on sex. They do not even begin to explain the other, more virulent aspect of asymmetry: misogyny.

It is one thing to categorize people on the basis of a certain trait—old people do this, young people do that; large people do this, small people do that—but what gives sexism its essential characteristic is the element of valuation. Not only are tasks separated by sex, but men's tasks are also judged more valuable, women's less valuable. Not only is the male's role to lead and the female's to follow, but leading is valued and following is disparaged. Not only are men and women to exhibit complementary character traits, but male traits are praised and female traits are held in contempt. Nor is it only that men tend to do or be better things and hence are more deserving of praise. Rather, it is the reverse: The things that are praised are simply the things that men do; they are praised *because men do them*. For the most part, a task socially assigned to women is debased. Cross-cultural studies bear this out.

We hear much of the fact, for example, that 75 percent of all physicians in the former USSR were women. However, it is rarely pointed out that in that society the practice of medicine, except for some highly specialized fields, was considered merely a technical job and was not highly paid; for the most part, the higher-paid specialists and surgeons were men. In the United States, secretarial work had high status and was highly paid until it became a female occupation; so was teaching. Nursing, historically female, has always suffered in power, prestige, and pay. The men who are now moving into the nursing field are being rewarded with preference in the highest paid, most select positions. Men are "encouraged" to enter nursing to "raise the level of the profession." Women are "permitted" to enter medicine or law because it is not just or legal to bar them; nothing is said about raising the level of the profession. More and more it becomes apparent that it is not simply that women do what feminists used to call the "shitwork" of so-

ciety, but it is equally the other way around: Tasks are deemed unworthy if women do them.

We can make the same analysis of human behaviors. For example, when men ask their wives more than once to do something, they are "reminding." Women who ask repeatedly are "nagging." When men are firm and resolute, they have backbone; women who act the same way are stubborn or bitchy. When a man raises his voice in argument he is angry but a woman is hysterical. Menstruation in most societies is surrounded with taboos, disgust, and even horror. In today's modern society, where people can utter any obscenity, freely discuss publicly any body function from nose blowing to orgasm, open admission of having one's period is still an occasion for shock and embarrassment. Would that be the case if menstruation were a male function? Erections are a source of pride to their owners. Much fuss is made over the length and breadth of a penis. What is analogous for women? The breast? But that is meant to be a joy to men, not to women ourselves. In patriarchy, it is as though the female carries with her an evil effusion and contaminates all that she touches.

Theories that explain only the *fact* of separation or categorization (men do this, women do that) and omit the *judgment* of devaluation (men and what they do are good; women and what they do are contemptible), or theories that disclaim the existence or importance of devaluation are missing the central point. The misogyny in sexual asymmetry is what renders it sexist and makes it oppressive. It is true that analyses of asymmetry are highly charged with value. One could argue that one's misogyny is another man's reality—it is not misogyny to say that women are inferior; it is true! Many of us, however, know better, and the fact of misogyny, almost universal though varying in degree, must be explained.

Psychomythic explanations function on a level where this issue can be treated. A myth is a story that serves to explain and/or to express some important reality of life or nature that is not easily explainable (or perhaps not explainable at all) in ordinary ways. The creation story in the Bible, for example, represented the ancient Hebrew explanation of the origin of the world, of life, and of human suffering. Sometimes the stories are avowedly fictitious; others are regarded as true.

Several theories try to explain myths: that they represent certain human verities, common to all people (such as the confrontation with one's own mortality); that they are modes of expressing experiences or feelings inexpressible in ordinary language; or that they symbolize beliefs and needs in a person that are too deep, too intense, or too socially bizarre to express directly. Their relation to psychological explanation, then, is clear.

A myth is generally taken to be an accurate representation of common, perhaps universal, human beliefs and attitudes. For this reason, myths are important for the analysis of sexual asymmetry. We study them to reveal their hidden message about attitudes toward women, and feminists often explain certain arrangements regarding women as the social acting out of basic psychomythic beliefs or psychological needs. The Adam and Eve story, for example, is a powerfully revealing myth that has parallels in many cultures. Many societies, primitive and otherwise, have stories that credit the first human life and the power of birth to a male and then relegate the life-giving function to women as a discredited and burdensome task. Does this story reveal a universal male envy of female procreative powers? Does it perhaps hark back to a primitive matriarchy, if not a historical one then a symbolic one (as in the paradigmatic Mother)? And does this tale not neatly justify the subordination and oppression of women? Have not numerous churchmen contended that women's suppression justly results from the primordial betrayal in the Garden of Eden? Does this story not express a statement of women's evil, untrustworthiness, guile, naivete, seduceability, and unworthiness before God? Does it not justify hatred and contempt?

Although the story expresses misogyny and presents a "justification" for the believer, we are still left with a question: Why is it necessary to create stories to justify the subordination and hatred of women? That is, why do men control and condemn women? The psychomythic theories attempt to approach this central issue through various themes, such as a yearning for maternal safety (Elizabeth Janeway), the model of family aggression—man upon woman (Shulamith Firestone), or even penis envy (Sigmund Freud). Each theory seeks some universal theme, some common human reality to explain this universal behavior: misogynous sexual asymmetry.

The major strength of psychomythic theories is that they seek wide-ranging explanations, sufficiently inclusive to cover all the variations of sexism. Also, they treat psychological events—attitudes and beliefs—on a psychological level. The problem with psychomythic theories, however, is that they are almost impossible to verify, and if used exclusively, they omit references to the very essential sociocultural elements.

CONCLUSION

If we have no definitive theories of explanation, what can we do? Search the following explanations carefully. Ponder the points they have in common, such as the centrality of childbearing or of hunting, and consider whether these themes are viable and/or sufficient. Notice the gaps in all the theories; use these as further points of departure.

Ultimately, we can probably develop reliable explanations from a combination of levels and perspectives. Such explanations will undoubtedly require a great deal more in the way of research and data than is now available.

Notes

1. In the social sciences today, particularly anthropology, energetic dialogue surrounds the issue of the universality or near universality of female subordination. Well known in this debate is the work of Alice Schlegel (see *Sexual Stratification: A Cross-Cultural View,* ed. Alice Schlegel [New York: Columbia University Press, 1977]) and of Michelle Rosaldo and Nancy Chodorow in the anthology *Women, Culture, and Society,* ed. Michelle Rosaldo and Louis Lamphere (Stanford, CA: Stanford University Press, 1974).

2. For an interesting discussion of the relation of politics to scientific inquiry, see Donna Haraway, "Animal Sociology and a Natural Economy of the Body Politic, Part I: A Political Physiology of Dominance," *Signs* 4, no. 1 (Autumn 1978), 21–36.

3. For two very different but good approaches to the matter of definitions, see Cheris Kramarae and Paula A. Treichler, *A Feminist Dictionary* (Boston: Pandora Press, 1985), and Gerda Lerner, "Definitions" in the "Appendix" of *Creation of Patriarchy* (New York: Oxford University Press, 1986), pp. 231–243.

4. *Infibulation:* the practice of excising the clitoris and labia of the vagina and sewing together the vulva to ensure chastity; *clitoridectomy:* the removal of the clitoris; *purdah:* the practice in Islam of totally sequestering women; *suttee:* the practice in Hindu India, surviving now only in rural areas, of widows immolating themselves on the burning funeral pyres of their husbands.

5. Steven Goldberg, in *The Inevitability of Patriarchy* (New York: Morrow, 1974), argued precisely that: Males are constitutionally more aggressive, more likely to compete energetically and hence to win. Thus, women are discouraged from competing with them to spare them the agony of defeat. Socialization patterns merely recognize and sup-

port this reality. Patriarchy, therefore, is the inevitable arrangement because it is the most orderly, stable, and reflective of nature.

6. Margaret Mead, *Sex and Temperament in Three Primitive Societies* (New York: Morrow, 1935).

7. George Gilder, *Sexual Suicide* (New York: Quadrangle, 1973).

8. Wolfgang Lederer, *The Fear of Women* (New York: Grune & Stratton, 1968), p. 87.

9. For an excellent review of these kinds of theories (and others), see Virginia Sapiro, *Women in American Society,* 3rd ed. (Mountain View, CA: Mayfield, 1994), chaps. 2 and 3.

Genesis

The myth that the origin of male authority rested in some great cataclysmic female sin is not peculiar to the Judeo-Christian tradition or to the Western world. Again and again, this idea appears in primitive and highly advanced societies: Woman is evil and dangerous, and to make things right, the gods decree that man should maintain order through control.

[26]AND GOD SAID, LET US make man in our image, after our likeness: and let them have dominion over the fish of the sea, and over the fowl of the air, and over the cattle, and over all the earth, and over every creeping thing that creepeth upon the earth. [27]So God created man in his *own* image, in the image of God created he him; male and female created he them.

[28]And God blessed them, and God said unto them, Be fruitful, and multiply, and replenish the earth, and subdue it: and have dominion over the fish of the sea, and over the fowl of the air, and over every living thing that moveth upon the earth.

[29]And God said, Behold, I have given you every herb bearing seed, which *is* upon the face of all the earth, and every tree, in which *is* the fruit of a tree yielding seed; to you it shall be for meat. [30]And to every beast of the earth, and to every fowl of the air, and to every thing that creepeth upon the earth, wherein *there is* life, *I have given* every green herb for meat: and it was so.

[31]And God saw every thing that he had made, and, behold, *it was* very good. And there was evening and there was morning, the sixth day.

2 Thus the heavens and the earth were finished, and all the host of them. [2]And on the seventh day God ended his work which he had made; and he rested on the seventh day from all his work which he had made. [3]And God blessed the seventh day, and sanctified it: because that in it he had rested from all his work which God created and made.

The Holy Scriptures, rev. by Alexander Harkavy (New York: Hebrew Publishing Company, 1951).

[4]These *are* the generations of the heavens and of the earth when they were created, in the day that the Lord God made the earth and the heavens.

[5]And no plant of the field was yet on the earth, and no herb of the field had yet grown: for the Lord God had not caused it to rain upon the earth, and *there was* not a man to till the ground. [6]But there went up a mist from the earth, and watered the whole face of the ground. [7]And the Lord God formed man *of* the dust of the ground, and breathed into his nostrils the breath of life; and man became a living soul.

[8]And the Lord God planted a garden eastward in Eden; and there he put the man whom he had formed. [9]And out of the ground made the Lord God to grow every tree that is pleasant to the sight, and good for food; the tree of life also in the midst of the garden, and the tree of knowledge of good and evil. [10]And a river went out of Eden to water the garden; and from thence it was parted, and became into four heads. [11]The name of the first *is* Pishon: that *is* it which compasseth the whole land of Havilah, where *there is* gold; [12]And the gold of that land *is* good: there *is* bdellium and the onyx stone. [13]And the name of the second river *is* Gihon: the same *is* it that compasseth the whole land of Ethiopia. [14]And the name of the third river *is* Hiddekel: that *is* it which goeth toward the east of Assyria. And the fourth river is Euphrates.

[15]And the Lord God took the man, and put him into the garden of Eden to till it and to keep it. [16]And the Lord God commanded the man saying, Of every tree of the garden thou mayest freely eat: [17]But of the tree of the knowledge of good and evil, thou shalt not eat of it; for in the day that thou eatest thereof thou shalt surely die.

[18]And the Lord God said, *it is* not good that the man should be alone; I will make a help meet for him. [19]And out of the ground the Lord formed every beast of the field, and every fowl of the air; and brought *them* unto Adam to see what he would call them: and whatsoever Adam called every living creature, that *was* the name thereof. [20]And Adam

gave names to all cattle, and to the fowl of the air, and to every beast of the field; but for Adam there was not found a help meet for him. ²¹And the Lord God caused a deep sleep to fall upon Adam, and he slept: and he took one of his ribs, and closed up the flesh instead thereof; ²²And the rib, which the Lord God had taken from man, made he a woman, and brought her unto the man. ²³And Adam said, This *is* now bone of my bones, and flesh of my flesh: she shall be called Woman, because she was taken out of Man. ²⁴Therefore shall a man leave his father and his mother, and shall cleave unto his wife: and they shall be one flesh.

²⁵And they were both naked, the man and his wife, and were not ashamed.

3 Now the serpent was more subtle than any beast of the field which the Lord God had made. And he said unto the woman, Yea, hath God said, Ye shall not eat of every tree of the garden? ²And the woman said unto the serpent, We may eat of the fruit of the trees of the garden: ³But of the fruit of the tree which *is* in the midst of the garden, God hath said, Ye shall not eat of it, neither shall ye touch it, lest ye die. ⁴And the serpent said unto the woman, Ye shall not surely die: ⁵For God doth know that in the day ye eat thereof, then your eyes shall be opened, and ye shall be as gods, knowing good and evil. ⁶And when the woman saw that the tree *was* good for food, and that it *was* pleasant to the eyes, and a tree to be desired to make *one* wise, she took of the fruit thereof, and did eat, and gave also unto her husband with her; and he did eat. ⁷And the eyes of them both were opened, and they knew that they *were* naked; and they sewed fig leaves together, and made themselves aprons. ⁸And they heard the voice of the Lord God walking in the garden in the cool of the day: and Adam and his wife hid themselves from the presence of the Lord God amongst the trees of the garden. ⁹And the Lord God called unto Adam, and said unto him, Where *art* thou? ¹⁰And he said, I heard thy voice in the garden, and I was afraid, because I *was* naked; and I hid myself. ¹¹And he said, Who told thee that thou *wast* naked?

Hast thou eaten of the tree, whereof I commanded thee that thou shouldest not eat? ¹²And the man said, The woman whom thou gavest *to be* with me, she gave me of the tree, and I did eat. ¹³And the Lord God said unto the woman, What *is* this *that* thou hast done? And the woman said, The serpent beguiled me, and I did eat. ¹⁴And the Lord God said unto the serpent, Because thou hast done this, thou *art* cursed above all cattle, and above every beast of the field; upon thy belly shalt thou go, and dust shalt thou eat all the days of thy life: ¹⁵And I will put enmity between thee and the woman, and between thy seed and her seed; he shall bruise thy head, and thou shalt bruise his heel. ¹⁶Unto the woman he said, I will greatly multiply thy sorrow and thy conception; in sorrow thou shalt bring forth children; and thy desire *shall be* to thy husband, and he shall rule over thee. ¹⁷And unto Adam he said, Because thou hast hearkened unto the voice of thy wife, and hast eaten of the tree, of which I commanded thee, saying, Thou shalt not eat of it; cursed *is* the ground for thy sake; in sorrow shalt thou eat *of* it all the days of thy life; ¹⁸Thorns also and thistles shall it bring forth to thee, and thou shalt eat the herb of the field; ¹⁹In the sweat of thy face shalt thou eat bread, till thou return unto the ground; for out of it wast thou taken; for dust thou *art*, and unto dust shalt thou return.

²⁰And Adam called his wife's name Eve; because she was the mother of all living.

²¹Unto Adam also and to his wife did the Lord God make coats of skins, and clothed them.

²²And the Lord God said, Behold, the man is become as one of us, to know good and evil: and now, lest he put forth his hand, and take also of the tree of life, and eat, and live for ever: ²³Therefore the Lord God sent him forth from the garden of Eden, to till the ground from whence he was taken. ²⁴So he drove out the man; and he placed at the east of the garden of Eden the Cherubim, and a flaming sword which turned every way, to keep the way of the tree of life.

Rape

Susan Brownmiller

*Born in Brooklyn, New York, in 1935, Susan Brown-
miller was educated at Cornell University, worked as a
freelance writer, a reporter for NBC-TV, and a news-
writer for ABC-TV. She authored* Shirley Chisholm
*(1970); the landmark book from which this excerpt is
taken,* Against Our Will: Men, Women, and Rape
(1975); Femininity *(1984);* Waverly Place *(1989); and
most recently,* In Our Time: Memoir of a Revolution
(1999).

*In this selection, Brownmiller's treatment of rape is
at once historical, political, psychological, and anthropological. She argues that forcible rape, in its violence and
cruelty, is a conscious act of intimidation by which "all
men keep all women in a state of fear." Men rape
because they can; women have always been vulnerable.
In primitive times, speculates Brownmiller, a woman's
one form of protection, perhaps the only one, might have
been to choose one among the predators to be her owner
and protector. Could this be the origin of women's subordination to men?*

MAN'S STRUCTURAL CAPACITY TO RAPE and woman's
corresponding structural vulnerability are as basic
to the physiology of both our sexes as the primal act
of sex itself. Had it not been for this accident of biology, an accommodation requiring the locking together of two separate parts, penis and vagina,
there would be neither copulation nor rape as we
know it. Anatomically one might want to improve
on the design of nature, but such speculation appears to my mind as unrealistic. The human sex act
accomplishes its historic purpose of generation of
the species and it also affords some intimacy and
pleasure. I have no basic quarrel with the procedure. But, nevertheless, we cannot work around the
fact that in terms of human anatomy the possibility

of forcible intercourse incontrovertibly exists. This
single factor may have been sufficient to have
caused the creation of a male ideology of rape.
When men discovered that they could rape, they
proceeded to do it. Later, much later, under certain
circumstances they even came to consider rape a
crime.

In the violent landscape inhabited by primitive
woman and man, some woman somewhere had a
prescient vision of her right to her own physical
integrity, and in my mind's eye I can picture her
fighting like hell to preserve it. After a thunderbolt
of recognition that this particular incarnation of
hairy, two-legged hominid was not the Homo
sapiens with whom she would like to freely join
parts, it might have been she, and not some man,
who picked up the first stone and hurled it. How
surprised he must have been, and what an unexpected battle must have taken place. Fleet of
foot and spirited, she would have kicked, bitten,
pushed and run, *but she could not retaliate in kind.*

The dim perception that had entered prehistoric
woman's consciousness must have had an equal but
opposite reaction in the mind of her male assailant.
For if the first rape was an unexpected battle
founded on the first woman's refusal, the second
rape was indubitably planned. Indeed, one of the
earliest forms of male bonding must have been the
gang rape of one woman by a band of marauding
men. This accomplished, rape became not only a
male prerogative, but man's basic weapon of force
against woman, the principal agent of his will and
her fear. His forcible entry into her body, despite her
physical protestations and struggle, became the vehicle of his victorious conquest over her being, the
ultimate test of his superior strength, the triumph of
his manhood.

Man's discovery that his genitalia could serve as
a weapon to generate fear must rank as one of the
most important discoveries of prehistoric times,
along with the use of fire and the first crude stone

axe. From prehistoric times to the present, I believe, rape has played a critical function. It is nothing more or less than a conscious process of intimidation by which *all men* keep *all women* in a state of fear.

IN THE BEGINNING WAS THE LAW

From the humblest beginnings of the social order based on a primitive system of retaliatory force—the *lex talionis:* an eye for an eye—woman was unequal before the law. By anatomical fiat—the inescapable construction of their genital organs—the human male was a natural predator and the human female served as his natural prey. Not only might the female be subjected at will to a thoroughly detestable physical conquest from which there could be no retaliation in kind—a rape for a rape—but the consequences of such a brutal struggle might be death or injury, not to mention impregnation and the birth of a dependent child.

One possibility, and one possibility alone, was available to woman. Those of her own sex whom she might call to her aid were more often than not smaller and weaker than her male attackers. More critical, they lacked the basic physical wherewithal for punitive vengeance; at best they could maintain only a limited defensive action. But among those creatures who were her predators, some might serve as her chosen protectors. Perhaps it was thus that the risky bargain was struck. Female fear of an open season of rape, and not a natural inclination toward monogamy, motherhood or love, was probably the single causative factor in the original subjugation of woman by man, the most important key to her historic dependence, her domestication by protective mating.

Once the male took title to a specific female body, and surely for him this was a great sexual convenience as well as a testament to his warring stature, he had to assume the burden of fighting off all other potential attackers, or scare them off by the retaliatory threat of raping *their* women. But the price of woman's protection *by some men* against an abuse *by others* was steep. Disappointed and disillusioned by the inherent female incapacity to protect, she became estranged in a very real sense from

other females, a problem that haunts the social organization of women to this very day. And those who did assume the historic burden of her protection—later formalized as husband, father, brother, clan—extracted more than a pound of flesh. They reduced her status to that of chattel. The historic price of woman's protection by man against man was the imposition of chastity and monogamy. A crime committed against her body became a crime against the male estate.

The earliest form of permanent, protective conjugal relationship, the accommodation called mating that we now know as marriage, appears to have been institutionalized by the male's forcible abduction and rape of the female. No quaint formality, bride capture, as it came to be known, was a very real struggle: a male took title to a female, staked a claim to her body, as it were, by an act of violence. Forcible seizure was a perfectly acceptable way—to men—of acquiring women, and it existed in England as late as the fifteenth century. Eleanor of Aquitaine, according to a biographer, lived her early life in terror of being "rapt" by a vassal who might through appropriation of her body gain title to her considerable property. Bride capture exists to this day in the rain forests of the Philippines, where the Tasadays were recently discovered to be plying their Stone Age civilization. Remnants of the philosophy of forcible abduction and marriage still influence the social mores of rural Sicily and parts of Africa. A proverb of the exogamous Bantu-speaking Gusiis of southwest Kenya goes "Those whom we marry are those whom we fight."

It seems eminently sensible to hypothesize that man's violent capture and rape of the female led first to the establishment of a rudimentary mate-protectorate and then sometime later to the full-blown male solidification of power, the patriarchy. As the first permanent acquisition of man, his first piece of real property, woman was, in fact, the original building block, the cornerstone, of the "house of the father." Man's forcible extension of his boundaries to his mate and later to their offspring was the beginning of his concept of ownership. Concepts of hierarchy, slavery and private property flowed from, and could only be predicated upon, the initial subjugation of woman.

The Mystery of How We Got Here

Allan G. Johnson

In Chapter 2 of this text, we looked at sociologist Allan G. Johnson's analysis of what drives patriarchy—fear and a need for control that proceed from a masculinist construction of masculinity. Here Johnson addresses the origin of patriarchy. He argues that just as the cycle of fear and control drive modern patriarchy, it is reasonable to surmise that it must have done so in the past. A combination of the same male psychology he described earlier and the social forces acting on them perhaps gave rise to the subordination of women.

THE MYSTERY OF HOW WE GOT HERE

WHENEVER I SPEAK ABOUT PATRIARCHY, someone always asks where the system came from in the first place. The question usually comes from a man, and I suspect he's saying that if he's going to give up the essentialist idea that patriarchy is universal and inevitable, he wants something to put in its place. If patriarchy isn't hard-wired into the species, then it had to *start* for some reason. The problem is that what we know as history doesn't reach back very far and can't tell us what we want to know without a lot of speculation mixed in. That won't stop us from wondering about where patriarchy came from, however, because this huge hole in our understanding nags for something to fill it up. And we need to feel hope that something better is possible, which we can't have if we settle for essentialist explanations. What, after all, is the point of trying to change something that's inevitable?

Another reason to look at the question of where patriarchy came from is that whatever model we use to explain what drives patriarchy now is more credible if it fits with a plausible argument about

where it came from in the first place. If we're right about patriarchy as it *is*, we should be able to extend our understanding back in time and see a connection between how it is now and how it most likely *was*. This won't *prove* anything, for the forces that bring a social system into being aren't necessarily the same as those that keep it going. But if one framework can make sense of patriarchy's past *and* its present, we can quiet some nagging questions that distract us from doing something about it.

What, then, do we know about nonpatriarchal societies, and how do we know it?[1] Some evidence comes from anthropological and historical studies of tribal societies, from the !Kung in Africa to Native American tribes to the New Guinea Arapesh.[2] From these we know of numerous societies in which women have not been devalued or subordinated but have, in fact, played prominent roles in social life. Matrilineal and matrilocal societies[3] have been quite common and have often included substantial female control over land and other property. Although every known society divides some tasks by gender, there is often a great deal of overlap, and in either case men's and women's work are valued equally. Sexual violence and the treatment of women as property are almost unknown in these societies, and historically have increased only with advances in male dominance.[4]

If we consider the rich store of archaeological evidence from prehistoric civilizations such as ancient Crete, it's difficult to deny that something other than patriarchy existed as recently as seven thousand or so years ago.[5] Artifacts dating to before that time, for example, suggest the existence of Middle Eastern societies in which women and men were equally well-regarded. Women's graves were as centrally located and richly appointed with statues and other artifacts as those of men. In addition, the accumulation of statuary from ancient sites shows far more female than male figures. These consist mostly of women with prominent breasts, belly, and

Excerpted and reprinted from "Why Patriarchy?" included in *The Gender Knot: Unraveling Our Patriarchal Legacy*, by Allan G. Johnson, by permission of Temple University Press. Copyright © 1997 by Temple University. All rights reserved.

vagina, suggesting a clear focus on women's role in renewing life. Only in later periods of emerging male dominance do artistic themes shift away from women and begin to portray phallic images. Evidence also suggests that organized warfare was rare if not unknown. Excavations in ancient Crete, for example, find no evidence of fortifications in the prepatriarchal period.

It's reasonable to argue from such evidence that for most of humanity's 250,000 years on Earth, social life has not been organized around control and domination. It is also reasonable to argue that male dominance and gender oppression are relatively recent. Not only has women's work been regarded as central to social life, but on a deeper level, the belief that women could create life seems to have placed female imagery at the core of religious traditions.[6] The abundant goddess imagery found in archaeological digs, for example, suggests that prepatriarchal societies were organized around a world view centered on the idea of the female as a symbolic link between humanity and the flow of nature from which all life comes. This doesn't mean that men were marginalized or subordinated, only that there was reverence for cultural *principles* associated with femaleness:

> *Matrifocality [a cultural focus on mothers] . . . does not refer to domestic maternal dominance so much as it does to the relative cultural prestige of the* image *of mother, a role that is culturally elaborated and valued. . . . It is not the absence of males (males may be quite present) but the centrality of women as mothers and sisters that makes a society matrifocal, and this matrifocal emphasis is accompanied by a minimum of differentiation between women and men.*[7]

Nonetheless, we're so used to the patriarchal obsession with control that it's hard to imagine that a society might exist without a dominant group. From our narrow perspective, the logical conclusion is that if the world was ever nonpatriarchal, it must have been matriarchal, especially if femaleness was valued and even revered.

Once we accept the idea that something came before patriarchy and that valuing women and gender equality was one of its core aspects, then we have to deal with the question of what happened to turn all of this into a system based on control and

gender oppression. What social engine could be powerful enough to break down bonds of equality between women and men? What could create new forms of family life in which women and children became men's property? How could kinship systems organized around mothers and their blood relatives become exclusively male-identified?[8] Why would systems of cooperation and peaceful coexistence give way to systems of competition and warfare?

Although we can never answer such questions once and for all, Riane Eisler, Elizabeth Fisher, Marilyn French, Gerda Lerner, and others have made a good case that certain social conditions played an important part.[9] The first was the discovery of how to grow crops, which took place some nine thousand years ago. As using plows to cultivate large fields replaced small-garden horticulture, societies could produce a surplus of goods. This, in turn, made it possible for some people to accumulate wealth at the expense of others. This didn't *cause* inequality, since sharing is as much a possibility as hoarding. Surpluses were, however, a precondition that made inequality *possible*.[10] Perhaps even more important, agriculture introduced the *idea* of control into many human cultures as people settled into more permanent communities and discovered they could affect their environment through such practices as clearing forests and cultivating the soil. Some degree of control had always been part of human life, but never before had the concept of control emerged so forcefully as part of culture, or been so conducive to seeing the rest of the natural world as a nonhuman "other" to be controlled.[11]

This changing relationship of humans to nature was related to the discovery, some nine thousand to eleven thousand years ago, of how reproduction worked in both plant and animal species, and the resulting domestication of goats, cattle, and other animals. Elizabeth Fisher believes this helped lay the groundwork for patriarchy in several ways. First, it transformed a relatively equal and balanced relation between humans and other animals into one of control and dominance. When hunters killed wild animals for food, they had reason to see them as creatures of equal standing in the nature of things whose deaths warranted appreciation, often in the form of ritual honoring. The lives of domesticated animals, however, are from the start dominated and controlled by people, their entire existence subordinated to human needs and ends.

Second, when animals were bred for slaughter or work, reproduction took on an economic value it didn't have before.[12] From this it was a short leap to the idea that human reproduction also has economic value, especially given how much labor was needed to cultivate large fields. This, in turn, created an incentive to control women's reproductive potential, for the more children a man had, the more workers there were to produce surplus goods, which men invariably came to control.

Third, domesticating animals created an emotional dilemma around nurturing and caring for animals with the intention of slaughtering them later.[13] Short of letting the animals live, the only way people could resolve the tension was to distance themselves from both the nurturing and the killing, to see nature as a separate and alien exploitable resource, an object of control and domination, or even an adversary—all of which more advanced patriarchies have done to greater and greater degrees.

Fisher believes the split between humanity and the rest of nature sowed the seeds for a more general and profound disconnection in social life. It did this by providing a model for control and domination based on the distinction between self and other, an "us" and a "them." Instead of seeing all life as an undifferentiated whole, the stage was now set for dividing the world into the controllers and the controlled. This was crucial to the development of patriarchy, especially given how an understanding of reproduction must have undermined the cultural reverence for women's reproductive powers. If reproduction wasn't a matter of female magic and could be controlled like anything else, then women's special connection to the universal life force was lost and men could put themselves at the center of things. Knowledge that men played a role in reproduction, for example, opened the door to the belief that men, not women, are the source of life, who plant their seed in the passive, fertile fields of women's wombs.

Fisher's arguments fit quite well with the observations that the first known patriarchies were nomadic herding societies (the first to depend on raising livestock) and that gender oppression reaches its height in advanced agrarian societies with their heavy dependence on both human labor and animal breeding.[14] As Riane Eisler reads the evidence, aggressive herding tribes from the northern reaches of Eurasia swept down on goddess civilizations such as that at Crete and converted them by force to the patriarchal model.[15] In this we can see various factors coming together to set the stage for the emergence of patriarchy: surplus production and the possibility of inequality; development of control as a human potential and cultural ideal; an economic value placed on reproduction and the ability to control it; and the potential for competition among tribes for grazing land, water, and other resources. But the puzzle still has missing pieces, for although these conditions made patriarchy *possible*, they aren't the social engine we're looking for.

The problem is that just because control and oppression became possible, it did not follow that they had to take over social life, just as people don't necessarily do something just because they can, whether it be hoarding wealth, killing disobedient children, or conquering neighbors. It might seem that conflict and aggression among nomadic tribes or expanding settlements were inevitable,[16] since these are ways to deal with conditions of scarcity. But cooperation, compromise, and sharing are even more effective solutions to the problem of scarcity, especially in the long run. Being able to produce a surplus makes it possible for some to hoard at the expense of others, but surpluses also can be used to create leisure and plenty for all. But isn't it human nature to hoard, compete, and aggress? Of course it is, but compromise, cooperation, and compassion are also part of human nature, although under patriarchy they are culturally associated with women and devalued as not fitting the male-identified standard of "human nature." If a society is organized around one set of human capabilities rather than another, human nature won't tell us why. The answer lies in the social forces that shaped it in this way.[17]

All of which brings us back to the nagging question of what could be powerful enough to move humanity toward gender oppression. This is where we need to connect what we know about the present with what is reasonable to suppose about the past. What both have in common is the patriarchal cycle of fear and control. Modern patriarchy is driven by the dynamic between control and fear, of men seeking status through control, fearing other men's control over them, and seeing still more control as the only solution. And if we look at our reasonable speculations about the past, it is more than credible to suppose that this same dynamic provided the key to the origins and evolution of patriarchy. Just as men are at the center of this powerful cycle now, so too were they at the center when that cycle emerged thousands of years ago.

But why would men be the ones at the center of the fear-control whirlwind? For men to be at the center, they had to be more likely than women to embrace the emerging cultural idea of control and to run with it. For this to happen, they had to be more likely to experience themselves and others in a disconnected way. There is no reason to believe that men did not feel a strong connection to the nature-centered goddess cultures of their societies. But there are good reasons to believe that men's connection was weaker than women's and that this left them more open to the cycle of control and fear and the religion of power that patriarchy embodied. Men's connection to the creation of new life is invisible—they must imagine how intercourse produces a child rather than feel it in their own bodies—and prepatriarchal cultures lacked even the abstract knowledge of how reproduction works. Nor do men bleed in monthly cycles in tune with the moon. As a result, men have fewer reminders of the body and its relation to natural rhythms of birth, renewal, and death. This makes it easier to live as though it were possible to stand apart from such rhythms, and this is the first step to rising above, transcending, and ultimately trying to control the self and everything else as "other." None of this means that men can't feel deeply connected to nature and the body, or that women can't feel disconnected and separate. But it does mean that men are more open to feeling this way and more vulnerable to being drawn into the cycle of control and fear that became patriarchy.

Since pursuing control goes hand in hand with disconnection from the object of control, it is reasonable to suppose that as the *idea* of control emerged as a natural part of cultural evolution, men were more likely than women to see it as something to develop and exploit. Women's lives, of course, also involved the idea of control—over children, for example, or gardens, or materials involved in producing goods and services that have always met a huge portion of human needs. But women have more to

overcome in order to develop a sense of disconnection, and for this reason they would be less likely to pursue control to its extremes. This would fall to men, and the result would be patriarchy.

At first, the idea of control was most likely applied to the simple mechanics of altering the environment by making things and growing food. It was only a matter of time, however, before the potential to control other people became apparent. Women and children may have been the first human objects of this new potential as husbands and fathers looked for ways to enhance their resources and standing in relation to other men. But why would men do this, given all the good reasons not to? How could the idea of control be powerful enough to re-order a world rooted in connection, unity, and equality? Why couldn't the powerful and complex bonds that joined people together in pre-patriarchal societies withstand the allure of control?

I believe the answer lies in the same dynamic that drives patriarchy today. It seems reasonable to suppose that as populations grew and nomadic societies moved about in search of food, they must have gotten in one another's way. If men were most open to the idea of control as a solution to such problems, then they must have learned to fear what other men might do to them as well as women and children in their societies. It wouldn't take much to realize how control could be used to do them harm, to deprive them of their liberty, to deny them their means of survival. It's here that men find themselves caught in a cycle, for the same reliance on control that created the fear in the first place is also what will occur to them as the most effective response to it. And so men respond to their fear of other men by increasing their own ability to control and dominate, gradually making this a central focus of social life. Once this dynamic is set in motion, it forms the basis for an upward spiral of control and fear. The result is an extended patriarchal history marked not only by the great accomplishments that control makes possible, but also by domination, warfare, and oppression, all of which are male-dominated, male-identified, male-centered pursuits that revolve around affirming, protecting, and enhancing men's standing in relation to other men.

Maybe it all happened this way and maybe it didn't. But our inability to prove where patriarchy came from won't stop us from reaching our own conclusions about it. The argument that patriarchy is rooted in a cycle of fear, control, and domination is no less plausible than alternative explanations, and far more plausible than many. It also has the advantage of enabling us to feel some continuity between what we can reasonably know and speculate about the past and how patriarchy works today. This gives us a more hopeful and more solid base to push off from as we work toward change. After all, if control and domination are inherently so appealing to men that they'd oppress half the human race in pursuit of them, then working for change is a hopeless war against men's "nature." But what if patriarchy is rooted in men's paradoxical fixation on control, fear, competition, and solidarity with other men? Then the way is open to changing not men per se, but the patriarchal system and its paths of least resistance, which we can see as only one of many possible forms that the natural human potential for control can take.

Notes

1. I base what follows on my understanding of a sizable literature that, for reasons of space, I won't try to summarize in a comprehensive way. Readers who want more should consult these fascinating and well-written sources and decide for themselves.

2. See, for example, Jack Goody, *Production and Reproduction* (New York: Cambridge University Press, 1976); Ruby Leavitt, "Women in Other Cultures," in *Woman in Sexist Society*, ed. Vivian Gornick and Barbara K. Moran (New York: Mentor, 1971), 393–427; Margaret Mead, *Sex and Temperament in Three Primitive Societies* (New York: William Morrow, 1963); Henrietta L. Moore, *Feminism and Anthropology* (Minneapolis: University of Minnesota Press, 1988); and M. Kay Martin and Barbara Voorhies, *Female of the Species* (New York: Columbia University Press, 1975).

3. In matrilineal societies, lineage is traced through the mother's blood relatives, not the father's; in matrilocal societies, a married couple must live near and be integrated with the wife's family.

4. See Peggy Reeves Sanday, "The Socio-Cultural Context of Rape: A Cross-Cultural Study," *Journal of Social Issues* 37 (1981): 5–27; idem, "Rape and the Silencing of the Feminine," in *Rape: An Historical and Social Enquiry*, ed. Sylvana Tomaselli and Roy Porter (Oxford: Basil Blackwell, 1986), 84–101.

5. See, for example, Eisler, *The Chalice and the Blade*; Fisher, *Woman's Creation*; French, *Beyond Power*; Gimbutas, *The Language of the Goddess* and *The Civilization of the Goddess*; Lee and Daly, "Man's Domination"; Lerner, *The Creation of Patriarchy*; and Stone, *When God Was a Woman*.

6. There are fairly recent historical records of societies in which the male reproductive role was unknown. It also would seem beyond dispute that knowledge of reproductive biology was something humans had to discover, perhaps through the domestication of animals. See Fisher, *Woman's Creation*.

7. Miriam M. Johnson, *Strong Mothers, Weak Wives: The Search for Gender Equality* (Berkeley: University of California Press, 1988), 266. See also French, *Beyond Power*, 46–47, 65.

8. The "locality" of family systems refers to marriage rules governing where married couples live—matrilocal (with the wife's mother) and patrilocal (with the husband's father). Together with the way in which lineage is figured, locality has profound effects on the degree to which social relationships are woman-identified or man-identified.

9. Much of the discussion that follows depends on my interpretation of several sources, the most important of which are Eisler, *The Chalice and the Blade*; Fisher, *Woman's Creation*; French, *Beyond Power*; Lee and Daly, "Man's Domination"; and Lerner, *The Creation of Patriarchy*. For an important sociological discussion of the origins of social inequality in general, see Gerhard Lenski, *Power and Privilege: A Theory of Social Stratification* (New York: McGraw-Hill, 1966).

10. This is based on Lenski, *Power and Privilege*. For a recent test of Lenski's theory, see A. Haas, "Social Inequality in Aboriginal North America: A Test of Lenski's Theory," *Social Forces* 72, no. 2 (1993): 295–313.

11. See French, *Beyond Power*, 47.

12. See Fisher, *Woman's Creation*.

13. Ibid.

14. This is also true of racism in some respects. Slavery, for example, is most common in agricultural societies. See Gerhard Lenski, Jean Lenski, and Patrick Nolan, *Human Societies*, 6th ed. (New York: McGraw-Hill, 1991).

15. Eisler, *The Chalice and the Blade*.

16. See, for example, Keen, *Fire in the Belly*, and Lee and Daly, "Man's Domination."

17. See Brittan, *Masculinity and Power*, 88–92.

The "Patriarchalization" of Native American Tribes— When Women Throw Down Bundles: Strong Women Make Strong Nations

Paula Gunn Allen

Paula Gunn Allen was born in 1939. The daughter of a Laguna Pueblo, Sioux, and Scottish mother and a Lebanese-American father, she was raised in a small New Mexican village boundedby the Laguna Pueblo reservation on one side and an Acoma reservation on another. Paula spent eleven years at a convent school from the age of six to seventeen, yet she was strongly influenced by her mother's stories about Native American goddesses and traditions.

As one of the country's most visible spokespersons for Native American culture, she is also an award-winning writer and a professor of English at UCLA. A major Native American poet, writer, lecturer, and scholar, she has written numerous works, including Off the Reservation: Reflections on Boundary-Busting, Border-Crossing Loose Canons *(1998);* Grandmothers of the Light: A Medicine Woman's Sourcebook *(1991);* Spider Woman's Granddaughters: Native American Women's Traditional and Short Stories *(1989); a book of poetry,* Skins and Bones *(1988);* The Sacred Hoop: Recovering the Feminine in American Indian Traditions *(1986); the novel* The Woman Who Owned the Shadows *(1983); and an anthology,* Studies in American Indian Literature *(1982).*

In this essay, Allen shows us that the subordination and deprecation of women was not universal but had its origins in particular cultures and particular philosophies. In detailing the enforced "patriarchalization" of one society, the overthrow of one gynocracy, she gives us a clue as to how the current subordination of women may have been accomplished, and she defeats the idea that patriarchy is natural or inevitable.

NOT UNTIL RECENTLY HAVE AMERICAN Indian women chosen to define themselves politically as Indian *women*—a category that retains American Indian women's basic racial and cultural identity but distinguishes women as a separate political force in a tribal, racial, and cultural context—but only recently has this political insistence been necessary. In other times, in other circumstances more congenial to womanhood and more cognizant of the proper place of Woman as creatrix and shaper of existence in the tribe and on the earth, everyone knew that women played a separate and significant role in tribal reality.

This self-redefinition among Indian women who intend that their former stature be restored has resulted from several political factors. The status of tribal women has seriously declined over the centuries of white dominance, as they have been all but voiceless in tribal decision-making bodies since reconstitution of the tribes through colonial fiat and U.S. law. But over the last thirty years women's sense of ourselves as a group with a stake in the distribution of power on the reservations, in jobs, and within the intertribal urban Indian communities has grown.

As writer Stan Steiner observes in *The New Indians*, the breakdown of women's status in tribal communities as a result of colonization led to their migration in large numbers into the cities, where they regained the self-sufficiency and positions of influence they had held in earlier centuries. He writes, "In the cities the power of women has been recognized by the extra-tribal communities. Election of tribal women to the leadership of these urban Indian centers has been a phenomenon in modern Indian life."[1]

Since the 1960s when Steiner wrote, the number of women in tribal leadership has grown immensely. Women function as council members and tribal chairs for at least one-fourth of the federally recognized tribes. In February 1981, the Albuquerque *Journal* reported that sixty-seven American Indian tribes had women heads of state. In large measure, the urbanization of large numbers of American Indians has resulted in their reclaiming their traditions (though it was meant to work the other way when in the 1950s the Eisenhower administration developed "Relocation" and "Termination" policies for Indians).

The coming of the white man created chaos in all the old systems, which were for the most part superbly healthy, simultaneously cooperative and autonomous, peace-centered, and ritual-oriented. The success of their systems depended on complementary institutions and organized relationships among all sectors of their world. The significance of each part was seen as necessary to the balanced and harmonious functioning of the whole, and both private and public aspects of life were viewed as valuable and necessary components of society. The private ("inside") was shared by all, though certain rites and knowledge were shared only by clan members or by initiates into ritual societies, some of which were gender-specific and some of which were open to members of both sexes. Most were male-dominated or female-dominated with helping roles assigned to members of the opposite gender. One category of inside societies was exclusive to "berdaches"—males only—and "berdaches"*—female only. All categories of ritual societies function in present-day American Indian communities, though the exclusively male societies are best recorded in ethnographic literature.

The "outside" was characterized by various social institutions, all of which had bearing on the external welfare of the group. Hunting, gathering, building, ditch cleaning, horticulture, seasonal and permanent moves, intertribal relationships, law and policy decisions affecting the whole, crafts, and childrearing are some of the areas governed by outside institutions. These were most directly affected by

white government policies; the inside institutions were most directly affected by Christianization. Destruction of the institutions rested on the overthrow or subversion of the gynocratic nature of the tribal system, as documents and offhand comments by white interveners attest.

Consider, for example, John Adair's remark about the Cherokee, as reported by Carolyn Foreman: "The Cherokee had been for a considerable while under petticoat government and they were just emerging, like all of the Iroquoian Indians from the matriarchal period."[2] Adair's idea of "petticoat government" included the power of the Women's Council of the Cherokee. The head of the Council was the Beloved Woman of the Nation, "whose voice was considered that of the Great Spirit, speaking through her."[3] The Iroquoian peoples, including the Cherokee, had another custom that bespoke the existence of their "petticoat government," their gynocracy. They set the penalty for killing a woman of the tribe at double that for killing a man. This regulation was in force at least among the Susquehanna, the Hurons, and the Iroquois; but given the high regard in which the tribes held women and given that in killing a woman one killed the children she might have borne, I imagine the practice of doubling the penalty was widespread.[4]

The Iroquois story is currently one of the best chronicles of the overthrow of the gynocracy. Material about the status of women in North American groups such as the Montagnais-Naskapi, Keres, Navajo, Crow, Hopi, Pomo, Turok, Kiowa, and Natchez and in South American groups such as the Bari and Mapuche, to name just a few, is lacking. Any original documentation that exists is buried under the flood of readily available, published material written from the colonizer's patriarchal perspective, almost all of which is based on the white man's belief in universal male dominance. Male dominance may have characterized a number of tribes, but it was by no means as universal (or even as preponderant) as colonialist propaganda has led us to believe.

The Seneca prophet Handsome Lake did not appreciate "petticoat government" any more than did John Adair. When his code became the standard for Iroquoian practice in the early nineteenth century, power shifted from the hands of the "meddling old women," as he characterized them, to men. Under

---

*The term *berdache* is applied (or rather misapplied) to both lesbians and gay males. It is originally an Arabic word meaning sex-slave boy, or a male child used sexually by adult males. As such it has no relevance to American Indian men or women.

the old laws, the Iroquois were a mother-centered, mother-right people whose political organization was based on the central authority of the Matrons, the Mothers of the Longhouses (clans). Handsome Lake advocated that young women cleave to their husbands rather than to their mothers and abandon the clan-mother–controlled longhouse in favor of a patriarchal, nuclear family arrangement. Until Handsome Lake's time, the sachems were chosen from certain families by the Matrons of their clans and were subject to impeachment by the Matrons should they prove inadequate or derelict in carrying out their duties as envisioned by the Matrons and set forth in the Law of the Great Peace of the Iroquois Confederacy. By provision in the Law, the women were to be considered the progenitors of the nation, owning the land and the soil.[5]

At the end of the Revolutionary War, the Americans declared the Iroquois living on the American side of the United States–Canadian border defeated. Pressed from all sides, their fields burned and salted, their daily life disrupted, and the traditional power of the Matrons under assault from the missionaries who flocked to Iroquois country to "civilize" them, the recently powerful Iroquois became a subject, captive people. Into this chaos stepped Handsome Lake who, with the help of devoted followers and exigencies of social disruption in the aftermath of the war, encouraged the shift from woman-centered society to patriarchal society. While that shift was never complete, it was sufficient. Under the Code of Handsome Lake, which was the tribal version of the white man's way, the Longhouse declined in importance, and eventually Iroquois women were firmly under the thumb of Christian patriarchy.

The Iroquois were not the only Nation to fall under patriarchalization. No tribe escaped that fate, though some western groups retained their gynecentric egalitarianism[6] until well into the latter half of the twentieth century. Among the hundreds of tribes forced into patriarchal modes, the experiences of the Montagnais-Naskapi, the Mid-Atlantic Coastal Algonkians, and the Bari of Colombia,[7] among others, round out the hemisphere-wide picture.

Among the Narragansett of the area now identified as Rhode Island was a woman chief, one of the six sachems of that tribe. Her name was Magnus, and when the Narragansetts were invaded by

Major Talcot and defeated in battle, the Sunksquaw Magnus was executed along with ninety others. Her fate was a result of her position; in contrast, the wife and child of the sachem known as King Philip among the English colonizers were simply sold into slavery in the West Indies.[8]

This sunksquaw, or queen (hereditary female head of state), was one of scores in the Mid-Atlantic region. One researcher, Robert Grumet, identifies a number of women chiefs who held office during the seventeenth and eighteenth centuries. Grumet begins his account by detailing the nonauthoritarian character of the Mid-Atlantic Coastal Algonkians and describes their political system, which included inheritance of rank by the eldest child through the maternal line. He concludes with the observation that important historians ignore documented information concerning the high-status position of women in the leadership structure of the Coastal Algonkians:

Both Heckewelder (1876) and Zeisberger (1910) failed to mention women in their lengthy descriptions of Delawaran leadership during the westward exile. Eight out of the eleven sources listed in Kinietz (1946) noted that women could not be chiefs. The remaining three citations made no mention of women leaders. These same sources stated that "women had no voice in council and were only admitted at certain times." Roger Williams translated the Narragansett term saunks *as "the Queen, or Sachims Wife," with the plural "Queenes" translating out as* sauncksquuaog *(1866). He nowhere indicated that these* sauncksquuaog *were anything more than wives.*

The ethnographic record has indicated otherwise. Even a cursory scanning of the widely available primary documentation clearly shows the considerable role played by Coastal Algonkian women throughout the historic contact period. Many sources state that women were able to inherit chiefly office. Others note that women sachems were often the sisters of wives of male leaders who succeeded them upon their decease. This does not mean that every "sunksquaw's" husband or brother was a leader. Many women sachems were married to men who made no pretension to leadership.[9]

The first sunksquaw Grumet mentions was noted in John Smith's journal as "Queene of Appamatuck." She was present during the council that decided on his death—a decision that Pocahontas, daughter of one of the sachems, overturned.[10] The Wampanoag Confederacy's loss of control over the Chesapeake Bay area did not cause an end to the rule of sunksquaws or of the empress: George Fox, founder of the Quaker religion, recorded that "the old Empress [of Accomack] . . . sat in council" when he was visiting in March 1673.[11] In 1705, Robert Beverley mentioned two towns governed by queens: Pungoteque and Nanduye. Pungoteque, he said, was a small Nation, even though governed by a Queen, and he listed Nanduye as "a seat of the Empress." He seemed impressed. For while Nanduye was a small settlement of "not above 20 families," the old Empress had "all the Nations of this shore under Tribute."[12]

From before 1620 until her death many years later, a squaw-sachem known as the "Massachusetts Queen" by the Virginia colonizers governed the Massachusetts Confederacy.[13] It was her fortune to preside over the Confederacy's destruction as the people were decimated by disease, war, and colonial manipulations. Magnus, the Narragansett sunksquaw whose name was recorded by whites, is mentioned above. Others include the Pocasset sunksquaw Weetamoo, who was King Philip's ally and "served as war chief commanding over 300 warriors" during his war with the British.[14] Queen Weetamoo was given the white woman Mary Rowlandson, who wrote descriptions of the sunksquaw in her captivity narrative.

Awashonks, another queen in the Mid-Atlantic region, was squaw-sachem of the Sakonnet, a tribe allied with the Wampanoag Confederacy. She reigned in the latter part of the seventeenth century. After fighting for a time against the British during King Philip's War, she was forced to surrender. Because she then convinced her warriors to fight with the British, she was able to save them from enslavement in the West Indies.[15]

The last sunksquaw Grumet mentions was named Mamanuchqua. An Esopus and one of the five sachems of the Esopus Confederacy, Mamanuchqua is said to be only one name that she used. The others include Mamareoktwe, Mamaroch, and Mamaprocht,[16] unless they were the names of other Esopus sunksquaws who used the same or a similar mark beside the written designation. Grumet wisely

comments on the presence of women chiefs and the lack of notice of them in secondary documents—that is, in books about the region during those centuries.

Ethnohistorians have traditionally assigned male gender to native figures in the documentary record unless otherwise identified. They have also tended to not identify native individuals as leaders unless so identified in the specific source. This policy, while properly cautious, has fostered the notion that all native persons mentioned in the documentation were both male and commoners unless otherwise identified. This practice has successfully masked the identities of a substantial number of Coastal Algonkian leaders of both sexes.[17]

And that's not all it successfully achieves. It falsifies the record of people who are not able to set it straight; it reinforces patriarchal socialization among all Americans, who are thus led to believe that there have never been any alternative structures; it gives Anglo-Europeans the idea that Indian societies were beneath the level of organization of western nations, justifying colonization by presumption of lower stature; it masks the genocide attendant on the falsification of evidence, as it masks the gynocidal motive behind the genocide. Political actions coupled with economic and physical disaster in the forms of land theft and infection of native populations caused the Mid-Atlantic Algonkians to be overwhelmed by white invaders.

Politics played an even greater role in the destruction of the Cherokee gynocracy, of a region that included parts of Georgia, Mississippi, and North Carolina. Cherokee women had the power to decide the fate of captives, decisions that were made by vote of the Women's Council and relayed to the district at large by the War Woman or Pretty Woman. The decisions had to be made by female clan heads because a captive who was to live would be adopted into one of the families whose affairs were directed by the clan-mothers. The clan-mothers also had the right to wage war, and as Henry Timberlake wrote, the stories about Amazon warriors were not so farfetched considering how many Indian women were famous warriors and powerful voices in the councils.[18]

The war women carried the title Beloved Women, and their power was so great "that they can, by the wave of a swan's wing, deliver a wretch condemned by the council, and already tied to the stake," Lieutenant Timberlake reports.[19] A mixed-blood Cherokee man who was born in the early nineteenth century reported knowing an old woman named Da'nawa-gasta, or Sharp War, which meant a fierce warrior.[20]

The Women's Council, as distinguished from the District, village, or Confederacy councils, was powerful in a number of political and socio-spiritual ways, and may have had the deciding voice on what males would serve on the Councils, as its northern sisters had. Certainly the Women's Council was influential in tribal decisions, and its spokeswomen served as War Women and as Peace Women, presumably holding those offices in the towns designated red towns and white towns, respectively. Their other powers included the right to speak in men's Council, the right to inclusion in public policy decisions, the right to choose whom and whether to marry, the right to bear arms, and the right to choose their extramarital occupations.

During the longtime colonization of the Cherokee along the Atlantic seaboard, the British worked hard to lessen the power of women in Cherokee affairs. They took Cherokee men to England and educated them in English ways. These men returned to Cherokee country and exerted great influence on behalf of the British in the region. By the time the Removal Act was under consideration by Congress in the early 1800s, many of these British-educated men and men with little Cherokee blood wielded considerable power over the Nation's policies.

In the ensuing struggle women endured rape and murder, but they had no voice in the future direction of the Cherokee Nation. The Cherokee were by this time highly stratified, though they had been much less so before this period, and many were Christianized. The male leadership bought and sold not only black men and women but also men and women of neighboring tribes, the women of the leadership class retreated to Bible classes, sewing circles, and petticoats that rivaled those worn by their white sisters. Many of these upper-strata Cherokee women married white ministers and other opportunists, as the men of their class married white women, often the daughters of white ministers. The traditional strata of Cherokee society became rigid and modeled on Christian white social organization of upper, middle, and impoverished classes usually composed of very traditional clans.

In an effort to stave off removal, the Cherokee in the early 1800s, under the leadership of men such as Elias Boudinot, Major Ridge, and John Ross (later Principal Chief of the Cherokee in Oklahoma Territory), and others, drafted a constitution that disenfranchised women and blacks. Modeled after the Constitution of the United States, whose favor they were attempting to curry, and in conjunction with Christian sympathizers to the Cherokee cause, the new Cherokee constitution relegated women to the position of chattel. No longer possessing a voice in the Nation's business, women became pawns in the struggle between white and Cherokee for possession of Cherokee lands.

The Cherokee, like their northern cousins, were entirely represented by men in the white courts, in the U.S. Congress, and in gatherings where lobbying of white officials was carried on. The great organ of Cherokee resistance, the *Cherokee Phoenix*, was staffed by men. The last Beloved Woman, Nancy Ward, resigned her office in 1817 sending her cane and her vote on important questions to the Cherokee Council, and "thus renounced her high office of Beloved Woman, in favor of written constitutional law."[21]

In spite of their frantic attempts to prevent their removal to Indian Territory by aping the white man in patriarchal particulars, the Cherokee were removed, as were the other tribes of the region and those living north and west of them, whom the Cherokee thought of as "uncivilized." Politics does make strange bedfellows, as the degynocratization of the Cherokee Nation shows. Boudinot and Ridge were condemned as traitors by the newly reconstituted Cherokee government in Indian Territory and were executed (assassinated, some say). The Cherokee got out from under the petticoats in time to be buried under the weight of class hierarchies, male dominance, war, and loss of their homeland.

While the cases cited above might be explained as a general conquest over male Indian systems that happened to have some powerful women functioning within them rather than as a deliberate attempt to wipe out female leadership, the case of the Montagnais women clarifies an otherwise obscure issue. The Montagnais-Naskapi of the St. Lawrence Valley was contacted early in the fifteenth century by fur traders and explorers and fell under the sway of Jesuit missionizing in the mid-sixteenth century. The Jesuits, under the leadership of Fr. Paul Le Jeune (whose name, appropriately, means The Little or The Young One), determined to convert the Montagnais to Christianity, resocialize them, and transform them into peasant-serfs as were the Indians' counterparts in France centuries earlier.

To accomplish this task, the good fathers had to loosen the hold of Montagnais women on tribal policies and to convince both men and women that a woman's proper place was under the authority of her husband and that a man's proper place was under the authority of the priests. The system of vassalage with which the Frenchmen were most familiar required this arrangement.

In pursuit of this end, the priests had to undermine the status of the women, who, according to one of Le Jeune's reports, had "great power . . . A man may promise you something and if he does not keep his promise, he thinks he is sufficiently excused when he tells you that his wife did not wish him to do it."[22] Further, the Jesuit noted the equable relations between husbands and wives among the Montagnais. He commented that "men leave the arrangement of the household to the women, without interfering with them; they cut and decide to give away as they please without making the husband angry. I have never seen my host ask a giddy young woman that he had with him what became of the provisions, although they were disappearing very fast."[23]

Undaunted, Paul Le Jeune composed a plan whereby this state of affairs could be put aright. His plan had four parts, which, he was certain, would turn the Montagnais into proper, civilized people. He figured that the first requirement was the establishment of permanent settlements and the placement of officially constituted authority in the hands of one person. "Alas!" he mourned. "If someone could stop the wanderings of the Savages, and give authority to one of them to rule the others, we would see them converted and civilized in a short time."[24] More ominously, he believed that the institution of punishment was essential in Montagnais social relations. How could they understand tyranny and respect it unless they wielded it upon each other and experienced it at each other's hands? He

was most distressed that the "Savages," as he termed them, thought physical abuse a terrible crime.

He commented on this "savage" aberration in a number of his reports, emphasizing his position that its cure rested only in the abduction or seduction of the children into attendance at Jesuit-run schools located a good distance from their homes. "The Savages prevent their [children's] instruction; they will not tolerate the chastisement of their children, whatever they may do, they permit only a simple reprimand," he complains.[25]

What he had in mind was more along the lines of torture, imprisonment, battering, neglect, and psychological torment—the educational methods to which Indian children in government and mission schools would be subjected for some time after Conquest was accomplished. Doubtless these methods were required, or few would have traded the Montagnais way for the European one. Thus his third goal was subsumed under the "education" of the young.

Last, Le Jeune wished to implement a new social system whereby the Montagnais would live within the European family structure with its twin patriarchal institutions of male authority and female fidelity. These would be enforced by the simple expediency of forbidding divorce. He informed the men that in France women do not rule their husbands, information that had been conveyed by various means, including Jesuit education, to other tribes such as the Iroquois and the Cherokee.

Le Jeune had his work cut out for him: working with people who did not punish children, encouraged women in independence and decision making, and had a horror of authority imposed from without—who, in Le Jeune's words could not "endure in the least those who seem desirous of assuming superiority over the others, and place all virtue in a certain gentleness or apathy,"[26] who

imagine that they ought by right of birth, to enjoy the liberty of wild ass colts, rendering no homage to anyone whomsoever, except when they like. They have reproached me a hundred times because we fear our Captains, while they laugh at and make sport of theirs. All the authority of their chief is in his tongue's end, for he is powerful insofar as he is eloquent; and even if he kills himself talking and haranguing, he will not be obeyed unless he pleases the Savages.[27]

The wily Le Jeune did not succeed entirely in transforming these gentle and humorous people into bastard Europeans, but he did succeed in some measure. While the ease of relationships between men and women remains and while the Montagnais retain their love of gentleness and nurturing, they are rather more male-centered than not.[28] Positions of formal power such as political leadership, shamanhood, and matrilocality, which placed the economic dependence of a woman with children in the hands of her mother's family, had shifted. Shamans were male, leaders were male, and matrilocality had become patrilocality. This is not so strange given the economics of the situation and the fact that over the years the Montagnais became entirely Catholicized.

With the rate of assimilation increasing and with the national political and economic situation of Indians in Canada, which is different in details but identical in intent and disastrous effect to that of Indians in the United States, the Montagnais will likely be fully patriarchal before the turn of the next century.

As this brief survey indicates, the shift from gynecentric-egalitarian and ritual-based systems to phallocentric, hierarchical systems is not accomplished in only one dimension. As Le Jeune understood, the assault on the system of woman power requires the replacing of a peaceful, nonpunitive, nonauthoritarian social system wherein women wield power by making social life easy and gentle with one based on child terrorization, male dominance, and submission of women to male authority.

Montagnais men who would not subscribe to the Jesuit program (and there were many) were not given authority backed up by the patriarchy's churchly or political institutions. Under patriarchy men are given power only if they use it in ways that are congruent with the authoritarian, punitive model. The records attest, in contrast, that gynecentric systems distribute power evenly among men, women, and berdaches as well as among all age groups. Economic distribution follows a similar pattern; reciprocal exchange of goods and services among individuals and between groups is ensured because women are in charge at all points along the distribution network.

Effecting the social transformation from egalitarian, gynecentric systems to hierarchical, patriarchal systems requires meeting four objectives. The first is accomplished when the primacy of female as creator is displaced and replaced by male-gendered creators (generally generic, as the Great Spirit concept overtakes the multiplicitous tribal designation of deity). This objective has largely been met across North America. The Hopi goddess Spider Woman has become the masculine Maseo or Tawa, referred to in the masculine, and the Zuñi goddess is on her way to malehood. Changing Woman of the Navajo has contenders for her position, while the Keres Thought Woman trembles on the brink of displacement by her sister-goddess-cum-god Utset. Among the Cherokee, the goddess of the river foam is easily replaced by Thunder in many tales, and the Iroquois divinity Sky Woman now gets her ideas and powers from her dead father or her monstrous grandson.

The second objective is achieved when tribal governing institutions and the philosophies that are their foundation are destroyed, as they were among the Iroquois and the Cherokee, to mention just two. The conqueror has demanded that the tribes that wish federal recognition and protection institute "democracy," in which powerful officials are elected by majority vote. Until recently, these powerful officials were inevitably male and were elected mainly by nontraditionals, the traditionals being until recently unwilling to participate in a form of governance imposed on them by right of conquest. Democracy by coercion is hardly democracy, in any language, and to some Indians recognizing that fact, the threat of extinction is preferable to the ignominy of enslavement in their own land.

The third objective is accomplished when the people are pushed off their lands, deprived of their economic livelihood, and forced to curtail or end altogether pursuits on which their ritual system, philosophy, and subsistence depend. Now dependent on white institutions for survival, tribal systems can ill afford gynocracy when patriarchy—that is, survival—requires male dominance. Not that submission to white laws and customs results in economic prosperity; the unemployment rates on most reservations is about 50 to 60 percent, and the situation for urban Indians who are undereducated (as many are) is almost as bad.

The fourth objective requires that the clan structure be replaced, in fact if not in theory, by the nuclear family. By this ploy, the women clan heads are replaced by elected male officials and the psychic net that is formed and maintained by the nature of nonauthoritarian gynecentricity grounded in respect for diversity of gods and people is thoroughly rent. Decimation of populations through starvation, disease, and disruption of all social, spiritual, and economic structures along with abduction and enforced brainwashing of the young serve well in meeting this goal.

Along the way, each of these parts of the overall program of degynocraticization is subject to image control and information control. Recasting archaic tribal versions of tribal history, customs, institutions, and the oral tradition increases the likelihood that the patriarchal revisionist versions of tribal life, skewed or simply made up by patriarchal non-Indians and patriarchalized Indians, will be incorporated into the spiritual and popular traditions of the tribes. This is reinforced by the loss of rituals, medicine societies, and entire clans through assimilation and a dying off of tribal members familiar with the elder rituals and practices. Consequently, Indian control of the image-making and information-disseminating process is crucial, and the contemporary prose and poetry of American Indian writers, particularly of woman-centered writers, is a major part of Indian resistance to cultural and spiritual genocide.

Notes

1. Stan Steiner, *The New Indians* (New York: Dell, Delta Books, 1968), p. 224. Steiner's chapter on Indian women, "Changing Women," is an important contribution to our understanding of the shift in women's positions under colonization. It should be read by those interested in learning about contemporary processes of patriarchalization and tribal resistance or acquiescence to it.

2. Carolyn Foreman, *Indian Women Chiefs* (Washington, D.C.: Zenger Publishing Co., 1976), p. 7.

3. John P. Brown, *Old Frontiers* (Kingsport, Tenn.: State of Wisconsin, State Historical Society, Draper Manuscripts, 1938), p. 20. Cited in Foreman, *Indian Women Chiefs*, p. 7.

4. Foreman, *Indian Women Chiefs*, p. 9.

5. See William Brandon, *The Last Americans: The Indian in American Culture* (New York: McGraw-Hill, 1974), p. 214, for more detail. Also see "Red Roots of White Feminism" in Part 3 of this volume.

6. The terms *gynecentric* and *egalitarianism* are not mutually exclusive; in fact, I doubt that egalitarianism is possible without gynecentrism at its base.

7. See Elisa-Buenaventura-Posso and Susan E. Brown, "Forced Transition from Egalitarianism to Male Dominance: The Bari of Colombia," in *Women and Colonization: Anthropological Perspectives,* eds. Mona Etienne and Eleanor Leacock (New York: Praeger, 1980), pp. 109–134, for an informative discussion of contemporary attempts to force the last remaining traditional group of Bari to shift their social structure to authoritarian male dominance.

8. Foreman, *Indian Women Chiefs*, p. 32. *Squaw* is not a derogatory word in its own language. Like the Anglo-Saxon "forbidden" word *cunt*, which is mostly used as an insult to women, *squaw* means "queen" or "lady," as will be seen in the following discussion. The fact that it has been taken to mean something less is only another example of patriarchal dominance, under which the proudest names come to be seen as the most degrading epithets, which the conquered and the conquerer alike are forbidden to use without the risk of sounding racist.

9. Robert Steven Grumet, "Sunksquaws, Shamans, and Tradeswomen: Middle Atlantic Coastal Algonkian Women During the 17th and 18th Centuries," in Etienne and Leacock, *Women and Colonization*, p. 49. In his note to this passage, Grumet comments that Regina Flannery ("An Analysis of Coastal Algonquian Culture," *Catholic University Anthropological Series,* no. 7 [1939], p. 145) "listed women's inheritance of chiefly rank among the Massachusett, Natick, Caconnet, Martha's Vineyard (Wampanoag), Narragansett, Western Niantic, Scaticook, Piscataway, and Powhatan groups" (p. 60n).

10. Grumet, "Sunksquaws," p. 60.

11. Grumet, "Sunksquaws," p. 50.

12. Grumet, "Sunksquaws," p. 50.

13. Grumet, "Sunksquaws," p. 50.

14. Grumet, "Sunksquaws," p. 51.

15. Grumet, "Sunksquaws," pp. 51–52.

16. Grumet, "Sunksquaws," pp. 51–52.

17. Grumet, "Sunksquaws," pp. 52–53.

18. Lieutenant Henry Timberlake, *Lieut. Henry Timberlake's Memoirs* (Marietta, Ga., 1948), p. 94 and n. 56. Cited in Foreman, *Indian Women Chiefs*, p. 76.

19. Timberlake, *Memoirs*, p. 94 and n. 56. Cited in Foreman, *Indian Women Chiefs*, p. 77.

20. Colonel James D. Wofford, whose name is frequently spelled Wafford, cited in Foreman, *Indian Women Chiefs*, p. 85.

21. Foreman, *Indian Women Chiefs*, p. 79.

22. Eleanor Leacock, "Montagnais Women and the Jesuit Program for Colonization," in Etienne and Leacock, *Women and Colonization*, p. 27. She is citing R. G. Thwaites, ed., *The Jesuit Relations and Allied Documents*, 71 vols. (Cleveland: Burrows Brothers Co., 1906), 2:77.

23. Leacock, "Montaignais Women," p. 27. Le Jeune's remarks from Thwaites, *Jesuit Relations*, 6:233.

24. Leacock, "Montaignais Women," p. 27. Thwaites, *Jesuit Relations*, 12:169.

25. Leacock, "Montaignais Women," p. 28. Thwaites, *Jesuit Relations*, 5:197.

26. Leacock, "Montaignais Women," p. 30. Thwaites, *Jesuit Relations*, 16:165.

27. Leacock, "Montaignais Women," p. 30. Thwaites, *Jesuit Relations*, 6:243.

28. Leacock, "Montaignais Women," pp. 40–41.

A Working Hypothesis

Gerda Lerner

Noted historian Gerda Lerner is the author of ten books on women's history, among them Black Women in White America *(1972),* The Female Experience *(1979), and* The Majority Finds Its Past *(1979). Her latest work is* The Feminist Thought of Sarah Grimké *(1998). She was a founding member of the National Organization for Women (NOW) and one of the creators of Women's History Month. She is past president of the Organization of American Historians and is Robinson-Edwards Professor of History, Emerita, at the University of Wisconsin-Madison. The following selection is drawn from* The Creation of Patriarchy *(1986), the first of a two-volume work,* Women and History. *(The second volume,* The Creation of Feminist Consciousness, *was published in 1993.)*

Professor Lerner tells us that we must investigate the "historicity" of patriarchy—how it came to be and why it took the form it did. To do so is to demystify it, to rob it of its apparent immutability. We must seek the origins of masculine dominance among a complex of social factors and events, and we must approach the task "as historians," as scientists, with careful scrutiny and subtlety of mind.

THE BASIC ASSUMPTION WITH WHICH we must start any theorizing about the past is that men and women built civilization jointly.[1] Starting as we do from the end result and reasoning back, we thus ask a different question than that of a single-cause "origin." We ask: how did men and women in their society-building and in the construction of what we call Western civilization arrive at the present state? Once we abandon the concept of women as historical victims, acted upon by violent men, inexplicable "forces," and societal institutions, we must explain

the central puzzle—woman's participation in the construction of the system that subordinates her. I suggest that abandoning the search for an empowering past—the search for matriarchy—is the first step in the right direction. The creation of compensatory myths of the distant past of women will not emancipate women in the present and the future.[2] The patriarchal mode of thought is so built into our mental processes that we cannot exclude it unless we first make ourselves consciously aware of it, which always means a special effort. Thus, in thinking about the prehistoric past of women, we are so much locked into the explanatory androcentric system that the only alternate model that readily comes to mind is that of reversal. If not patriarchy, then there must have been matriarchy. Undoubtedly there were many different modes in which men and women organized society and allocated power and resources. None of the archaeological evidence we have is conclusive and sufficient to allow us to construct a scientifically sound model of that important period of the transition from Neolithic hunting/gathering to sedentary agricultural societies. The way of the anthropologists, who offer us examples of contemporary hunting/gathering societies and draw from them inferences about societies in the fifth millennium B.C., is no less speculative than is that of the philosopher and the specialist in religious studies who reason from literature and myths. The point is that most of the speculative models have been androcentric and have assumed the naturalness of patriarchy, and the few feminist models have been ahistorical and therefore, to my mind, unsatisfactory.

A correct analysis of our situation and how it came to be what it is will help us to create an empowering theory. We must think about gender historically and specifically as it occurs in varied and changeable societies. The anthropologist Michelle Rosaldo arrived at similar conclusions, although starting from a different vantage point. She wrote:

*To look for origins is, in the end, to think that what
we are today is something other than the product of
our history and our present social world, and, more
particularly, that our gender systems are primordial,
transhistorical and essentially unchanging in their
roots.*[3]

Our search, then, becomes a search for the history of the patriarchal system. To give the system of male dominance historicity and to assert that its functions and manifestations change over time is to break sharply with the handed-down tradition. This tradition has mystified patriarchy by making it ahistoric, eternal, invisible, and unchanging. But it is precisely due to changes in the social and educational opportunities available to women that in the nineteenth and twentieth centuries large numbers of women finally became capable of critically evaluating the process by which we have helped to create the system and maintain it. We are only now able to conceptualize women's role in history and thereby to create a consciousness which can emancipate women. This consciousness can also liberate men from the unwanted and undesired consequences of the system of male dominance.

Approaching this quest as historians, we must abandon single-factor explanations. We must assume that if and when events occur simultaneously their relationship to each other is not necessarily causal. We must assume that changes as complex as a basic alteration in kinship structures most likely occurred as the result of a variety of interacting forces. We must test whatever hypothesis we have developed for one model comparatively and cross-culturally. Women's position in society must be viewed always also in comparison with that of the men of their social group and of their time.

We must prove our case not only by material evidence but by evidence from written sources. While we will look for the occurrence of "patterns" and similarities, we must be open to the possibility that similar outcomes, deriving from a variety of factors, might occur as the result of very different processes. Above all, we must view the position of women in society as subject to change over time, not only in its form but also in its meaning. For example, the social role of "concubine" cannot be evaluated by twentieth- or even nineteenth-century standards when we are studying it in the first millennium B.C. This is so obvious an example that to cite it may seem unnecessary, and yet just such errors occur frequently in the discussion of women's past. In particular, gender has, in most societies, such a strong symbolic as well as ideological and legal significance that we cannot truly understand it unless we pay attention to all aspects of its meaning.

The hypothetical construct I will offer is intended only as one of a number of possible models. Even on the limited geographic terrain of the Ancient Near East there must have been many different ways in which the transition to patriarchy took place. Since we will most likely never know just what happened, we are constrained to speculate on what might have been possible. Such utopian projections into the past serve an important function for those who wish to create theory—to know what might have been possible opens us up to new interpretations. It allows us to speculate about what might be possible in the future, free of the confines of a limited and entirely outdated conceptual framework.

Let us begin with the transitional period when hominids evolved from primates, some three million years ago, and let us consider the most basic dyad, mother and child. The first characteristic distinguishing humans from other primates is the prolonged and helpless infancy of the human child. This is the direct result of bipedalism, which led to the narrowing of the female pelvis and birth canal due to upright posture. One result of this was that human babies were born at a greater stage of immaturity than other primates, with relatively smaller heads in order to ease passage through the birth canal. Further, in contrast to the most highly developed apes, human babies are born naked and therefore must experience a greater need for warmth. They cannot grasp their mothers for steady support, lacking the apes' movable toe, so mothers must use their hands or, later, mechanical substitutes for hands to cradle their infants against them.[4] Bipedalism and upright posture led also to the finer development of the hand, the grasping thumb, and greater sensory–hand coordination. One consequence of this is that the human brain develops for many years during the child's period of infancy and complete dependency, and that it is therefore subject to modification through learning and intense cultural molding in a way that is decisively different from animal development. The neurophysiologist Ruth Bleier uses these facts in a telling argument against any theories claiming "innate" human characteristics.[5]

The step from foraging to gathering food for later consumption, possibly by more than one individual, was crucial in advancing human development. It must have fostered social interaction, the invention and development of containers, and the slow evolutionary increase in brain size. Nancy Tanner suggests that females caring for their helpless infants had the most incentive to develop these skills, while males may have, for a long period, continued to forage alone. She speculates that it was these activities which led to the first use of tools for opening and dividing plant food with children and for digging for roots. At any rate, the infant's survival depended on the quality of maternal care. "Similarly, a mother's gathering effectiveness improved her own nutrition and thereby increased her life expectancy and fertility."[6]

We postulate, as Tanner and Bleier do, that in the slow advance from upright hominids to the fully developed humans of the Neanderthal period (100,000 B.C.) the role of females was crucial. Sometime after that period large-scale hunting by groups of men developed in Africa, Europe, and Northern Asia; the earliest evidence for the existence of bows and arrows can be dated only to 15,000 years ago. Since most of the explanations for the existence of a sexual division of labor postulate the existence of hunting/gathering societies, we need to look more closely at such societies in the Paleolithic and early Neolithic periods.

It is from the Neolithic that we derive surviving evidence of cave paintings and sculptures suggesting the pervasive veneration of the Mother-Goddess. We can understand why men and women might have chosen this as their first form of religious expression by considering the psychological bond between mother and child. We owe our insights into the complexities and importance of that bond largely to modern psychoanalytic accounts.[7] As Freud has shown us, the child's first experience of the world is one in which the total environment and the self are barely separated. The environment, which consists mostly of the mother as the source of food, warmth, and pleasure, only gradually becomes differentiated from the self, as the infant

smiles or cries to secure gratification of its needs. When the infant's needs are not met and it experiences anxiety and pain associated with cold and hunger, it learns to acknowledge the overwhelming power of "the other out there," the mother. Modern psychological studies have given us detailed accounts of the complex interaction between mother and child and of the ways in which the mother's body response, her smile, her speech help to form the child's concept of world and self. It is in this humanizing interaction that the infant begins to derive pleasure in its ability to impose its will on the environment. The striving for autonomy and the recognition of selfhood are produced in the infant's struggle against the overwhelming presence of the mother.

The psychoanalytic accounts on which these generalizations are based derive from the study of motherhood in modern Western societies. Even so, they stress the crucial importance of the infant's experience of utter dependency and of the mother's overwhelming power for the character formation and identity of the individual. At a time when laws against infanticide as well as the availability of bottle feeding, heated rooms, and blankets provide infants with societal protection, regardless of the mother's inclinations, this "overwhelming power of the mother" seems more symbolic than real. For over two hundred years or more, other caretakers, male and female, could, if the need arose, provide maternal services to an infant without endangering that infant's chances of survival. Civilized society has interposed itself between mother and child and has altered motherhood. But under primitive conditions, before the institutions of civilized society were created, the actual power of the mother over the infant must have been awesome. Only the mother's arms and care sheltered the infant from cold; only her breast milk could provide the nourishment needed for survival. Her indifference or neglect meant certain death. The life-giving mother truly had power over life and death. No wonder that men and women, observing this dramatic and mysterious power of the female, turned to the veneration of Mother-Goddesses.[8]

My point here is to stress the *necessity*, which created the initial division of labor by which women do the mothering. For millennia group survival depended upon it, and no alternative was available.

Under the extreme and dangerous conditions under which primitive humans lived, the survival into adulthood of at least two children for each coupling pair necessitated many pregnancies for each woman. Accurate data on prehistoric life span are hard to come by, but estimates based on skeletal studies place the average Paleolithic and Neolithic life-span between thirty and forty years. In the detailed study of 222 adult skeletons from Čatal Hüyük earlier cited, Lawrence Angel arrives at an average adult male life length of 34.3 years, with a female life length of 29.8 years. (This excludes from consideration those who died in childhood.)[9]

Women would need to have had more pregnancies than live births, as continued to be the case also in historic times in agricultural societies. Infancy was much prolonged, since mothers nursed their infants for two to three years. Thus, we may assume that it was absolutely essential for group survival that most nubile women devote most of their adulthood to pregnancy, child-bearing, and nursing. One would expect that men and women would accept such necessity and construct beliefs, mores, and values within their cultures to sustain such necessary practices.

It would follow that women would choose or prefer those economic activities which could be combined easily with their mothering duties. Although it is reasonable to assume that some women in every tribe or band were physically able to hunt, it would follow that women would not want to hunt regularly for big game, because of their being physically encumbered by children carried in the womb, on the hip, or on the back. Further, while a baby slung on the back might not prevent a mother from participating in hunting, a crying baby might. Examples cited by anthropologists of hunting/gathering tribes in the contemporary world, in which alternate arrangements are made for child care and in which women occasionally do take part in hunting, do not contradict the above argument.[10] They merely show what it is possible for societies to arrange and to try; they do not show what was the likely historically predominant mode which enabled societies to survive. Obviously, given the precarious and short life spans I have cited above for the Neolithic period, tribes which put the lives of their nubile women at risk by hunting or by participating in warfare, thereby also increasing the like-

lihood of their injury in accidents, would not tend to survive as well as tribes in which these women were otherwise employed. Thus, the first sexual division of labor, by which men did the big-game hunting and children and women the small-game hunting and food gathering, seems to derive from biological sex differences.[11] These biological sex differences are not differences in the strength and endurance of men and women but solely reproductive differences, specifically women's ability to nurse babies. Having said this, I want to stress that my acceptance of a "biological explanation" holds only for the earliest stages of human development and does not mean that a later sexual division of labor based on women's mothering is "natural." On the contrary, I will show that male dominance is a *historic* phenomenon in that it arose out of a biologically determined given situation and became a culturally created and enforced structure over time.

My synthesis does not mean to imply that all primitive societies are so organized as to prevent mothers from economic activity. We know from the study of past and present primitive societies that groups find various ways of structuring the division of labor for childrearing so as to free mothers for a great variety of economic activities. Some mothers take their children with them over long distances; in other cases older children and old people act as child-tenders.[12] Clearly, the link between child-bearing and child-rearing for women is culturally determined and subject to societal manipulation. My point is to stress that the earliest sexual division of labor by which women *chose* occupations compatible with their mothering and child-raising activities were *functional*, hence acceptable to men and women alike.

Prolonged and helpless human infancy creates the strong mother-child bond. This socially necessary relationship is fortified by evolution during the earliest stages of humankind's development. Faced with new situations and changing environments, tribes and groups in which women did not mother well or which did not guard the health and survival of their nubile women, probably could not and did not survive. Or, seen another way, groups that accepted and institutionalized a functional sexual division of labor were more likely to survive.

We can only speculate on the personalities and self-perceptions of people living under such conditions as prevailed in the Neolithic. Necessity must have imposed restraints on men as well as on women. It took courage to leave the shelter of cave or hut to confront wild animals with primitive weapons, to roam far from home and risk encounters with potentially hostile neighboring tribes. Men and women must have developed the courage necessary for self-defense and the defense of the young. Because of their culture-bound tendency to focus on the activities of men, ethnographers have given us much information about the consequences for the development of self-confidence and competence in man the hunter. Basing herself on ethnographic evidence, Simone de Beauvoir has speculated that it was this early division of labor from which the inequality between the sexes springs and which has doomed woman to "immanence"—to the pursuit of daily, never-ending repetitious toil—as against the daring exploits of man, which lead him to "transcendence." Toolmaking, inventions, the development of weapons are all described as deriving from man's activities in pursuit of subsistence.[13] But the psychological growth of women has received far less attention and has usually been described in terms befitting a modern housewife more than a member of a Stone Age tribe. Elise Boulding, in her overview of women's past, has synthesized anthropological scholarship to present a considerably different interpretation. Boulding sees in the Neolithic societies an egalitarian sharing of work, in which each sex developed appropriate skills and knowledge essential for group survival. She tells us that food gathering demanded elaborate knowledge of the ecology, of plants and trees and roots, their properties as food and as medicine. She describes primitive woman as guardian of the domestic fire, as the inventor of clay and woven vessels, by means of which the tribe's surpluses could be saved for lean times. She describes woman as having elicited from plants and trees and fruits the secrets of transforming their products into healing substances, into dyes and hemp and yarn and clothing. Woman knew how to transform the raw materials and dead animals into nurturing products. Her skills must have been as manifold as those of man and certainly as essential. Her knowledge was perhaps greater or at least as great as his; it is easy to imagine that it would have seemed to her quite sufficient. In the development of ritual and rites, of music and dance

and poetry, she had as much of a part as he did. And yet she must have known herself responsible for life-giving and nurturance. Woman, in precivilized society, must have been man's equal and may well have felt herself to be his superior.[14]

Psychoanalytic literature and most recently Nancy Chodorow's feminist reinterpretation provide us with useful descriptions of the process by which gender is created out of the fact that women do the mothering of children. Let us see if these theories have validity for describing a process of historical development. Chodorow argues that "the relationship to the mother differs in systematic ways for boys and girls, beginning in the earliest periods."[15] Boys and girls learn to expect from women the infinite, accepting love of a mother, but they also associate with women their fears of powerlessness. In order to find their identity, boys develop themselves as other-than-the-mother; they identify with the father and turn away from emotional expression toward action in the world. Because it is women who do the mothering of children, Chodorow says:

> . . . *growing girls come to define and experience themselves as continuous with others; their experience of self contains more flexible or permeable ego boundaries. Boys come to define themselves as more separate and distinct, with a greater sense of rigid ego boundaries and differentiation. The basic feminine sense of self is connected to the world, the basic masculine sense of self is separate.*[16]

By the way in which their selfhood is defined against the nurturant mother, boys are prepared for participation in the public sphere. Girls, identifying with the mother and always keeping their close primary relationship with her, even as they transfer their love interest to men, are prepared for greater participation in "relational spheres." Gender-defined boys and girls are prepared "to assume the adult gender roles which situate women primarily within the sphere of reproduction in a sexually unequal society."[17]

Chodorow's sophisticated feminist reinterpretation of the Freudian explanation for the creation of gendered personalities is grounded in industrial Western society and its kinship and familial relations. It is doubtful that it is even applicable to people of color living within such societies, which should make us cautious about generalizing from it. Still, she makes a strong argument for the psychological undergirding upon which social relations and institutions rest. She and others argue convincingly that we must look to "motherhood" in patriarchal society, its structure and the relationships it engenders, if we wish to alter the relations of the sexes and end the subordination of women.[18]

I would speculate that the kind of personality formation Chodorow describes as the result of women mothering children in present-day industrialized societies did not occur in primitive societies of the Neolithic. Rather, women's mothering and nurturing activities, associated with their self-sufficiency in food gathering and their sense of competence in many, varied life-essential skills, must have been experienced by men and women as a source of strength and, probably, magic power. In some societies women jealously guarded their group "secrets," their magic, their knowledge of healing herbs. The anthropologist Lois Paul, reporting on a twentieth-century Guatemalan Indian village, says that the mystery and awe surrounding menstruation contributes in women "to a sense of participation in the mystic powers of the universe." Women manipulate men's fear that menstrual blood will threaten their virility by making of menstruation a symbolic weapon.[19]

In civilized society it is girls who have the greatest difficulty in ego formation. I would speculate that in primitive society that burden must have been on boys, whose fear and awe of the mother had to be transformed by collective action into identification with the male group. Whether mothers and their young children bonded with other such mother-child groups for their gathering and food-processing activities or whether men took the initiative in bringing young boys within their group must remain a matter of conjecture. The evidence from surviving primitive societies shows many different ways in which the sexual division of labor is structured into societal institutions, which bond young boys to males: sex-segregated preparation for initiation rites; membership in same-sex lodges and participation in same-sex rituals are just some of the examples. Inevitably, big-game hunting bands would have led to male bonding, which must have been greatly strengthened by warfare and the

preparation necessary to turn boys into warriors. Just as effective mothering skills of women were essential to ensuring tribal survival and must have therefore been greatly appreciated, so were the hunting and warfare skills of men. One can easily postulate that those tribes which did not develop men skilled in warfare and defense eventually succumbed to those tribes that fostered these skills in their men. These evolutionary arguments have frequently been made, but I am here arguing also in favor of a psychological argument based on changing historical conditions. The ego formation of the individual male, which must have taken place within a context of fear, awe, and possibly dread of the female, must have led men to create social institutions to bolster their egos, strengthen their self-confidence, and validate their sense of worth.

Theorists have offered a variety of hypotheses to explain the rise of man, the warrior, and the propensity of men to create militaristic structures. These have ranged from biological explanations (men's higher testosterone levels and greater strength make them more aggressive) to psychological ones (men compensate for their inability to bear children by sexual dominance over women and by aggression toward other men). Freud saw the origin of male aggressiveness in the Oedipal rivalry of father and son for the love of the mother and postulated that men built civilization to compensate for the frustration of their sexual instincts in early childhood. Feminists, beginning with Simone de Beauvoir, have been greatly influenced by such ideas, which made it possible to explain patriarchy as caused either by male biology or by male psychology. Thus, Susan Brownmiller sees man's *ability* to rape women leading to their *propensity* to rape women and shows how this has led to male dominance over women and to male supremacy. Elizabeth Fisher ingeniously argued that the domestication of animals taught men their role in procreation and that the practice of the forced mating of animals led men to the idea of raping women. She claimed that the brutalization and violence connected with animal domestication led to men's sexual dominance and institutionalized aggression. More recently, Mary O'Brien built an elaborate explanation of the origin of male dominance on men's psychological need to compensate for their inability to bear children through the construction of institutions of dominance and, like Fisher, dated this "discovery" in the period of the discovery of animal domestication.[20]

These hypotheses, while they lead us in interesting directions, all suffer from the tendency to seek single-cause explanations, and those basing their arguments on the discoveries connected with animal husbandry are factually wrong. Animal husbandry was introduced, at least in the Near East, around 8000 B.C., and we have evidence of relatively egalitarian societies, such as in Çatal Hüyük, which practiced animal husbandry 2000 to 4000 years later. There cannot therefore be a causal connection. It seems to me far more likely that the development of intertribal warfare during periods of economic scarcity fostered the rise to power of men of military achievement. As we will discuss later, their greater prestige and standing may have increased their propensity to exercise authority over women and later over men of their own tribe. But these factors alone could not have been sufficient to explain the vast societal changes which occurred with the advent of sedentarism and agriculture. To understand these in all their complexity our theoretical model must now take into consideration the practice of the exchange of women.[21]

The "exchange of women," a phenomenon observed in tribal societies in many different areas of the world, has been identified by the anthropologist Claude Lévi-Strauss as the leading cause of female subordination. It may take many different forms, such as the forceful removal of women from their home tribe (bride stealing); ritual defloration or rape; negotiated marriages. It is always preceded by taboos on endogamy and by the indoctrination of women, from earliest childhood on, to an acceptance of their obligation to their kin to consent to such enforced marriages. Lévi Strauss says:

> The total relationship of exchange which constitutes marriage is not established between a man and a woman . . . but between two groups of men, and the woman figures only as one of the objects in the exchange, not as one of the partners. . . . This remains true even when the girl's feelings are taken into consideration, as, moreover, is usually the case. In acquiescing to the proposed union, she precipitates or allows the exchange to take place; she cannot alter its nature.[22]

Lévi-Strauss reasons that in this process women are "reified"; they become dehumanized and are thought of more as things than as humans.

A number of feminist anthropologists have accepted this position and have elaborated on this theme. Matrilocality structures kinship in such a way that a man leaves his family of origin to reside with his wife or his wife's family. Patrilocality structures kinship in such a way that a woman must leave her family of birth and reside with her husband or her husband's family. This observed fact has led to the assumption that the kinship shift from matriliny to patriliny must be a significant turning point in the relation of the sexes, and must be coincident with the subordination of women. But how and why did such arrangements develop? We have already discussed the scenario by which men, possibly recently risen to power due to their warfare skills, coerced unwilling women. But why were women exchanged and not men? C. D. Darlington offers one explanation. He sees exogamy as a cultural innovation, which becomes accepted because it offers an evolutionary advantage. He postulates an instinctive desire in humans to control population to "optimum density" for a given environment. Tribes achieve this by sexual control, by rituals structuring males and females into appropriate sex roles, and by resorting to abortion, infanticide, and homosexuality when necessary. According to this essentially evolutionist reasoning, population control made control over female sexuality mandatory.[23]

There are other possible explanations: supposing grown men were exchanged among tribes, what would ensure their loyalty to the tribe to which they were traded? Men's bond to their offspring was not, then, strong enough to ensure their submission for the sake of their children. Men would be capable of violence against members of the strange tribe; with their experience in hunting and long distance travel they might easily escape and then return as warriors to seek vengeance. Women, on the other hand, would be more easily coerced, most likely by rape. Once married or mothers of children, they would give loyalty to their children and to their children's relatives and would thus make a potentially strong bond with the tribe of affiliation. This was, in fact, the way slavery developed historically, as we will see later. Once again, woman's biological function made her more readily adaptable for this new, culturally created role of pawn.

One might also postulate that not women but children of both sexes might have been used as pawns for the purpose of assuring intertribal peace, as they were frequently used in historical time among ruling elites. Possibly, the practice of the exchange of women got started that way. Children of both sexes were exchanged and on maturity married into the new tribe.

Boulding, always stressing women's "agency," assumes that it was women—in their function of keepers of the homeplace—who engaged in the necessary negotiations which led to intertribal coupling. Women develop cultural flexibility and sophistication by their intertribal linkage role. Women, removed from their own culture, straddle two cultures and learn the ways of both. The knowledge they derive from this may give them access to power and certainly to influence.[24]

I find Boulding's observations useful for reconstructing the gradual process by which women may have initiated or participated in establishing the exchange of women. In anthropological literature we have some examples of queens, in their role of head of state, acquiring many "wives" for whom they then arranged marriages which serve to increase the queen's wealth and influence.[25]

If boys and girls were exchanged as pawns and their offspring were incorporated into the tribe to which they had been given, clearly the tribe holding more girls than boys would increase in population more rapidly than the tribe accepting more boys. As long as children were a threat to the survival of the tribe or, at best, a liability, such distinctions would not be noticed or would not matter. But if, due to changes in the environment or in the tribal economy, children became an asset as potential labor power, one would expect the exchange of children of both sexes to give way to the exchange of women. The factors leading to this development are well explained, I believe, by Marxist structuralist anthropologists.

The process we are now discussing occurs at different times in different parts of the world; yet it shows regularity of causes and outcome. Approximately at the time when hunting/gathering or horticulture gives way to agriculture, kinship arrangements tend to shift from matriliny to patriliny,

and private property develops. There is, as we have seen, disagreement about the sequence of events. Engels and those who follow him think that private property developed first, *causing* "the world historic overthrow of the female sex." Lévi-Strauss and Claude Meillassoux believe that it is the exchange of women through which private property is eventually created. Meillassoux offers a detailed description of the transition stage.

In hunting/gathering societies men, women, and children engage in production and consume what they produce. The social relations among them are unstable, unstructured, voluntary. There is no need for kinship structures or for structured exchanges among tribes. This conceptual model (for which it is somewhat difficult to find actual examples) gives way to a transition model, an intermediate state—horticultural society. The harvest, based on roots and cuttings, is unstable and subject to climatic variations. Their inability to preserve crops over several years makes people dependent on hunting, fishing, and gathering as food supplements. In this period, when matrilineal, matrilocal systems abound, group survival demands the demographic equalization of men and women. Meillassoux argues that women's biological vulnerability in childbirth led tribes to procure more women from other groups, and that this tendency toward the theft of women led to constant intertribal warfare. In the process, a warrior culture emerged. Another consequence of this theft of women is that the conquered women were protected by the men who had conquered them or by the entire conquering tribe. In the process, women were thought of as possessions, as things—they became reified—while men became the reifiers because they conquered and protected. Women's reproductive capacity is first recognized as a tribal resource, then, as ruling elites develop, it is acquired as the property of a particular kin group.

This occurs with the development of agriculture. The material conditions of grain agriculture demand group cohesiveness and continuity over time, thus strengthening household structure. In order to produce a harvest, workers of one production cycle are indebted for food and seeds to workers of a previous production cycle. Since the amount of food depends on the availability of labor, production becomes the chief concern. This has two consequences: it strengthens the influence of older males and it increases the tribes' incentive for acquiring more women. In the fully developed society based on plow agriculture, women and children are indispensable to the production process, which is cyclical and labor intensive. Children have now become an economic asset. At this stage tribes seek to acquire the reproductive potential of women, rather than women themselves. Men do not produce babies directly; thus it is women, not men, who are exchanged. This practice becomes institutionalized in incest taboos and patrilocal marriage patterns. Elder males, who provide continuity in the knowledge pertaining to production, now mystify these "secrets" and wield power over the young men by controlling food, knowledge, and women. They control the exchange of women, enforce restrictions on their sexual behavior, and acquire private property in women. The young men must offer labor services to the old men for the privilege of gaining access to women. Under such circumstances women also become the spoil for the warriors, which encourages and reinforces the dominance of older men over the community. Finally, "women's world historic defeat" through the overthrow of matriliny and matrilocality is made possible, and it proves advantageous to the tribes who achieve it. . . .

Notes

1. My concepts here are grounded in the approach first formulated by Mary Beard in *Woman as Force in History* (New York, 1946). I have elaborated on this theme throughout my historical work. See especially Gerda Lerner, *The Majority Finds Its Past: Placing Women in History* (New York, 1979), chaps. 10–12.

2. See Paula Webster, "Matriarchy: A Vision of Power," in Rayna Reiter, *Toward an Anthropology of Women* (New York, 1975), pp. 141–56, for a thorough discussion of the psychological needs of contemporary women to have a vision of matriarchy in the distant past.

3. Michelle Rosaldo, "The Use and Abuse of Anthropology: Reflections on Feminism and Cross-Cultural Understanding," *SIGNS*, vol. 5, no. 3 (Spring 1980), 393.
    Rosaldo elaborates on these views in her unpublished paper, "Moral/Analytical Dilemmas Posed by the Intersection of Feminism and Social Science," prepared for the Conference on the Problem of Morality in the Social Sciences, Berkeley, March 1980. The following statement seems to me particularly apt: "By challenging the view

that we are either victims of cruel social rule or the unconscious products of a natural world that (most unfortunately) demeans us, feminists have highlighted our need for theories that attend to the ways that actors shape their worlds; to interactions in which significance is conferred, and to the cultural and symbolic forms in terms of which expectations are organized, desires articulated, prizes conferred, and outcomes given meaning" (p. 18).

4. See Nancy Makepeace Tanner, *On Becoming Human* (Cambridge, Eng., 1981), pp. 157–58. See also Nancy Tanner and Adrienne Zihlman, "Women in Evolution, Part I: Innovation and Selection in Human Origins," *SIGNS*, vol. 1, no. 3 (Spring 1976), 585–608.

5. Ruth Bleier, *Science and Gender: A Critique of Biology and Its Theories on Women* (New York, 1984), chap. 3, esp. pp. 55 and 64–68. The same point is made in Clifford Geertz, "The Impact of the Concept of Culture on the Concept of Man," in *The Interpretation of Cultures* (New York, 1973), pp. 33–54.

6. *Ibid.*, pp. 144–45; quote, p. 145.

7. Cf. Chapter One above, fn. 11. Also: Karen Horney, *Feminine Psychology* (New York, 1967); Clara Thompson, *On Women* (New York, 1964); Harry Stack Sullivan, *The Interpersonal Theory of Psychiatry* (New York, 1953), chaps. 4–12.

8. Conversely, one of the first powers men institutionalized under patriarchy was the power of the male head of the family to decide which infants should live and which infants should die. This power must have been perceived as a victory of law over nature, for it went directly against nature and previous human experience.

9. Information about prehistoric populations is unreliable and can be expressed only in rough quantitative terms. Cipolla thinks that "indirect evidence supports the view that Paleolithic populations had very high mortality. Since the species survived, we must admit that primitive man also had very high fertility. A study of 187 Neanderthal fossil remains reveals that one-third died before reaching the age of 20. An analysis of 22 fossil remains of the Asiatic Sinanthropus population revealed that 15 died when less than 14 years old, 3 before age 29 and 3 between the ages of 40 and 50." Carlo M. Cipolla, *The Economic History of World Population* (New York, 1962), pp. 85–86.
    Lawrence Angel, "Neolithic Skeletons from Čatal Hüyük," *Anatolian Studies*, vol. 21 (1971), 77–98; quote on p. 80.
    In contemporary hunting/gathering societies we find infant mortality rates as high as 60 percent in the first year. See F. Rose, "Australian Marriage, Land Owning Groups and Institutions," in R. B. Lee and Irven DeVore (eds.), *Man, the Hunter* (Chicago, 1968), p. 203.

10. Cf. Karen Sacks, *Sisters and Wives: The Past and Future of Sexual Equality* (Urbana, 1982), chap. 2.

There is, additionally, the possibility that menstruation presented an obstacle to women's hunting, not because it physically incapacitated women, but because of the effect of the scent of blood on the animal. This possibility came to my attention during a recent trip to Alaska. The National Park Service in its leaflets to campers and backpackers advises menstruating women to stay away from the wilderness areas, since grizzly bears are attracted by the scent of blood.

11. The anthropologist Marvin Harris argues to the contrary that "hunting is an intermittent activity and there is nothing to prevent lactating women from leaving their infants in someone else's care for a few hours once or twice a week." Harris argues that man's hunting specialty arose from his warfare training and that it is in men's warfare activities that we must seek the cause for male supremacy and sexism. Marvin Harris, "Why Men Dominate Women," *Columbia* (Summer 1978), 9–13, 39. It is unlikely and we have no evidence to show that organized warfare preceded big-game hunting, but I would argue that in any case both hunting and military activities would not be chosen by women for the reasons I have cited.

For a feminist interpretation of the same material, which makes no concessions to "biological determinism," see Bleier, *Science and Gender,* chaps. 5 and 6.

12. Cf. M. Kay Martin and Barbara Voorhies, *Female of the Species* (New York, 1975), pp. 77–83; Sacks, *Sisters and Wives,* pp. 67–84; Ernestine Friedl, *Women and Men: An Anthropologist's View* (New York, 1975), pp. 8, 60–61.

13. Simone de Beauvoir, *The Second Sex* (New York, 1953; 1974 reprint ed.).

14. While there is no hard proof for these claims to the originality of woman's contributions, neither is there proof for man's inventiveness. Both claims rest on speculation. For our purposes, it is important to allow ourselves the freedom to speculate on woman's contributions as equals. The only danger in this exercise is that we may claim for our speculations, because they sound convincing and logical, that they represent actual proof. This is what men have done; we should not repeat that mistake.

Elise Boulding, *The Underside of History: A View of Women Through Time* (Boulder, Colo., 1976), chaps. 3 and 4. See also V. Gordon Childe, *Man Makes Himself* (New York, 1951), pp. 76–80.

For a somewhat similar synthesis based on later anthropological work see Tanner and Zihlman, and Sacks, cited above in notes 4 and 10.

15. Nancy Chodorow, *The Reproduction of Mothering: Psychoanalysis and the Sociology of Gender* (Berkeley, 1978), p. 91.

16. *Ibid.,* p. 169. For a similar analysis based on different evidence see Carol Gilligan, *In a Different Voice: Psychological Theory and Women's Development* (Cambridge, Mass., 1982).

17. Chodorow, *The Reproduction of Mothering,* pp. 170, 173.

18. Adrienne Rich, in her analyses of "the institution of motherhood under patriarchy" and of "enforced heterosexuality," and Dorothy Dinnerstein, in her interpretation of Freudian thought, come to similar conclusions. See Adrienne Rich, *Of Woman Born: Motherhood As Experience and Institution* (New York, 1976); Adrienne Rich, "Compulsory Heterosexuality and Lesbian Existence," *SIGNS,* vol. 5, no. 4 (Summer 1980), 631–60; Dorothy Dinnerstein, *The Mermaid and the Minotaur: Sexual Arrangements and Human Malaise* (New York, 1977).

M. Rosaldo in "Dilemmas" (see note 3, above) criticizes these psychological theories because they slight or ignore the social context in which parenting takes place. Although I admire Chodorow's and Rich's work I agree with this criticism and add to it that in both cases generalizations applicable to middle-class people in industrialized nations are made to appear as universal.

19. Lois Paul, "The Mastery of Work and the Mystery of Sex in a Guatemalan Village," in M. Z. Rosaldo and Louise Lamphere, *Woman, Culture and Society* (Stanford, 1974), pp. 297–99.

20. Cf.: Sigmund Freud, *Civilization and Its Discontent* (New York, 1962); Susan Brownmiller, *Against Our Will: Men, Women and Rape* (New York, 1975); Elizabeth Fisher, *Woman's Creation, Sexual Evolution and the Shaping of Society* (Garden City, N.Y., 1979), pp. 190, 195.

21. My thinking on the subject of the rise and consequences of male warfare were influenced by Marvin Harris, "Why Men Dominate Women," and by a stimulating exchange of letters and dialogue with Virginia Brodine.

22. Claude Lévi-Strauss, *The Elementary Structures of Kinship* (Boston, 1969), p. 115.

For a contemporary illustration of the workings of this process and of the way the girl indeed "cannot alter its nature," see Nancy Lurie (ed.), *Mountain Wolf Woman, Sister of Crashing Thunder* (Ann Arbor, 1966), pp. 29–30.

23. C. D. Darlington, *The Evolution of Man and Society* (New York, 1969), p. 59.

24. Boulding, *Underside,* chap. 6.

25. See, for example, the case of the Lovedu in Sacks, *Sisters and Wives,* chap. 5.

PART 2

THE GENDER SYSTEM: ITS EFFECTS ON OUR PRIVATE LIVES AND PUBLIC INSTITUTIONS

We have been foreigners not only to the fortresses of political power but also to those citadels in which thought processes have been spun out. . . . Women are beginning to recognize that the value system that has been thrust upon us by the various cultural institutions of patriarchy has amounted to a kind of gang rape of minds as well as of bodies.

—MARY DALY, *Beyond God the Father*

SO FAR, WE HAVE BEEN examining the worldview (the "consciousness") of patriarchy, the abstract concepts, the myths, beliefs, and values that underlie the sexual caste system. We now turn to the material expression of that worldview, the effects it has on women's concrete lives. In a patriarchal society, sexism is built into almost everything that women do or that is done to us. It is lodged in the most personal facets of our lives as well as in the public. In the following chapters, we explore the outward expressions of sexist ideology, the social structures, both institutional and private, that give our female lives their particular color and shape.

Chapter 6 focuses on the part of women's lives ordinarily called the private sphere—personal appearance, relationships, marriage (or unmarriage, or nonmarriage), love, romance, and sex.

Chapter 7 directs attention to the institutional sphere—work and economics, health care, women's legal and political status, and women's participation in public policy making, all of which are intricately interrelated.

Finally, Chapter 8 treats some of the strategies through which patriarchy creates a sexist consciousness, not only in men but in women, not only in individuals but in the institutions of society.

CHAPTER SIX

The Effects of Sexism
on Women's Private Lives

THE LADY IN PATRIARCHAL SPACE

Earlier we looked at the images and the "place" patriarchy constructs for women, but we have not yet explored the impact these ideas have for the woman within that space. How do these forces shape our private lives, the way we think and the way we live on the most intimate level with ourselves and others?

Although sexists have difficulty wrapping their minds around the idea, we, of course, know that women are simply people, human beings, with the needs, dreams, and desires of any people. How we relate to others on a one-to-one basis; how we relate to ourselves, our bodies, and our feelings; and how we relate to the physical space around us are the concrete realities that make up our daily lives. But certain aspects of our lives as *women*, particularly women in a sexist world, profoundly influence those concrete human realities. It is in the tension between the two, our experience simply as people and our experience as women in a sexist world, that we live out our days. Let us turn, then, to examine women's personal lives in a patriarchal society.

A STORY

Once upon a time there lived a very beautiful little girl named Cinderella (Snow White, Sleeping Beauty, Rapunzel . . .). Her nature was as lovely as her face. Gentle, kind, accepting, modest, obedient, and sweet, she never complained or became peevish, though she suffered greatly at the hands of circumstance and of cruel people. Because she was good-natured and uncomplaining, because she asked for little and gave a great deal, her beauty shone, and a handsome prince came along, fell in love with her, and took her away to his castle, where the pair lived happily ever after. Here the story always ends.

This is a story that in its many tellings is dear to the hearts of most little girls, who hear it almost from the crib, read and repeat it endlessly, playact and live it vicariously, and dream of its realization in their own lives. It tells us a great deal about the way women are expected to be and the way we learn to see our existence.

The story teaches us that we are born to be chosen, admired, and sought after, and that to succeed in this goal of being chosen, certain attributes are required: physical "beauty" (according to the fashion of the day), "good nature" (willingness to take unwarranted abuse), modesty, self-effacement, piety, vulnerability, suffering, and good luck. We learn that even if we do not have these attributes, or for that matter, dislike them, we had better appear to have them—for the essence of the story is the fact of *being chosen* rather than choosing, of being noticed for our "feminine qualities," and of gaining success from endurance and patience rather than initiative, which belongs to men. The story goes beyond the facade of his asking and her assenting, straight to the unvarnished truth: It is the prince who picks what he wants; the woman's chief responsibility is to make herself "pickable," as worthy of his interest as she can. Our only allowable direct action lies in the orchestrating of an effect. The story teaches us, by extending the principles of passivity, that it is not by our own efforts that we are to be happy (or safe or comfortable), but rather through the intervention of a powerful protector who alone can bestow status and security on us. Only he has the power to make us happy, for clearly we are (or ought to be) unable to do that for ourselves.

In these tales, it is the willingness to relinquish initiative as well as the power to make ourselves happy or safe that is so potent a factor in molding the approved feminine character. We are to believe not only that we are too weak and small to take care of ourselves, that we are and must be dependent, that we should relish and cultivate this fragility, but also that it is wrong to be any other way. Self-assertive women like Cinderella's stepmother and sisters are portrayed as wicked and ugly, and because of this they come to bad ends. These and other stories fix in our minds the idea that women who take for themselves, by themselves, are selfish and wicked, whereas admirable females earn for themselves through renunciation what they do not take directly.

The attitude born of all this is a sense that only through intercession of another can we *be made* happy, that we are to receive the positive goods in life only from another in return for beauty of face,

passivity of nature, and for services rendered. Most of us do not learn until much later that in giving up the right of, as well as the responsibility for, framing our own fortunes, we place ourselves at the mercy of circumstance and of anyone who may wish to exercise the power we have abrogated. We do not hear until later, after the pain it brings, that we have bartered our souls for the illusion of protection.

But this is an old story, one might say, an archaic ideal, no longer applicable for women of the twenty-first century. And it was never applicable for many women who fell outside its range. First, we must never forget that the ideal of the subordinate woman is still very much alive in many places around the world, where "modern" Western ideals either do not apply or are thoroughly rejected. Second, within the Western world and within the United States, conservative ideologies, like those of the Promise Keepers described in Chapter 2, insist that precisely the ideal of the subordinated woman needs to be reasserted to save families, nations, morality, and the world. Third, even images in the media and elsewhere of "thoroughly modern women" do not stray very far from Cinderella and her cohorts: Movie and television female FBI agents may carry guns, do judo, and burn down buildings, but they usually get themselves into trouble and require saving by dashing *male* FBI agents, with whom they ultimately fall in love; very up-to-date female cartoon characters find themselves getting lost, tripping over themselves, or angering monsters and require rescuing by male characters; and female bad guys may build empires, kick butt, and rule men, but they too, like fairy-tale witches, come to no good. Fourth, although many women indeed may have fallen outside of the reaches of Cinderella expectations—because of class, or race, or appearance—none of us has ever fallen out of the category of *subordinate*. And none of us has escaped the influence of the model as a model, reachable or not.

THE MATTER OF MARRIAGE

Enter Mr. Right (alias the "prince" or the "one"). He will "come along," we will "fall in love," we will know instinctively that we belong together—forever. We will marry, have children, and live happily ever after. "The End."

That fantasy—the marriage myth, a mystical tale of love, romance, and forever—for women who marry, for women who do not, and for those who unmarry, exercises incredible power over how we live our lives. Even though the very smallest minority of families fits the fairy-tale version—Mama at home, Papa at work—and even though the very smallest minority of couples lives the happily-ever-after forever romance, the myth functions as it always has, right up to the present, right into and through the second wave of feminism, right into the era of professional women and egalitarian couples. It undergirds our expectations and colors our relationships. It may seep into the relationships of lesbian couples as well as heterosexual couples, and it influences the legislators who decide (and determine) who may or may not marry and/or have children, who may or may not deserve insurance coverage, and so on. The marriage myth operates on our consciousness even when it is completely absent from reality, even though the story may be utterly false.

The Myth

During the early 1960s, in a course I was teaching in introductory philosophy, I used to ask the students to begin the term's work with an essay entitled, "What I Want Out of Life." Those were the years before I had acquired what now is known as a feminist consciousness, and the results surprised me. With great regularity, the papers of the men in the class differed categorically from the women's. The men's papers generally followed a familiar theme: I want to finish school, get a good job, have a good income, a nice place to live, friends, fun things to do. Many said they wanted to be happy; a few remembered to hope for health. The women, too, said they wanted to be happy. They wanted to finish school, have an interesting career, fall in love, get married. Finis. Did the men, I asked, mean to get married? Oh sure, they said. That was understood: It came along the way. For the women, it *was* the way. Career, possessions, health, and all were only satisfying thoughts against the certainty of marriage. To play the successful "bachelorette" for a time was a kick—but then the Cinderella tale took over: the ultimate goal was "happily ever after."

In current classes, not so much has changed as one might imagine. Today's young women are more aware, more wary. Yet, in one way or another, for the majority, the dream still has powerful influence. Among heterosexual women, the majority hope, and often claim, that their marriages will be different from the average; that is, they will be happy, free, and loving, and they will survive, because their partners are "different" from other men—their partners want strong, bright women who will help them. Another large group of women, considering the statistics, accepts the probability that any marriage, theirs included (should there be one), has at best a fifty-fifty chance of survival. Marriage is risky. Even for them, however, singlehood is rarely a desirable option. By their own admission, very likely they will hope for the best, marry, and perhaps repeat the pattern, perhaps more than once. Even those women who most strenuously reject the Cinderella future rarely propose an alternative vision of equal power, desirability, and influence. Except occasionally among lesbian women, one rarely hears of "contract" relationships, female support systems, or women's communities, some of the alternatives proposed in the early days of the current women's movement.

Lest anyone think that the traditional myths are passé, we might turn to the popular media. *My Best Friend's Wedding*,[1] a movie of the late 1990s that was especially in favor among young women, featured two women: Jules, a strong, sleekly beautiful redhead, intelligent, ambitious, a successful professional, accustomed to self-reliance, and rarely sentimental; and Kimberly (Kimmy), a college student, considerably younger than Jules (who is 28), also beautiful and bright but ditzy, completely guileless, openly affectionate, rather childlike. In fact, the two characters embody the stereotypes, modern feminist woman (tough, worldly wise, and off-putting to men) and traditional girl ("sweet," "good," self-abnegating, very fetching). Both the women are in love with the same man, described in the film as an "insensitive doofus," a sort of good-natured, vaguely attractive, beer-drinking, egocentric jock who must choose between them. It is a war of the titans as each woman does her best to capture the hero's heart: Jules, unscrupulous, scheming ruthlessly, and Kimmy, always in character, subverting her own interests and inclinations to make her lover happy, meet his needs, and be *his* girl. No need to wonder who wins. In the final scene, here is Kimmy, chosen, radiant in white, glowing warmly with good-natured tolerance for her fallen rival. There is Jules, beaten, sad, but brave in defeat, gamely delivering the wedding toast to the happy couple, allowing now that Kimmy is indeed the "best woman." As the happy bride and doofus in a magnificent limousine drive away between two rows of dancing fountains (that look suspiciously like erupting orgasms), our modern heroine dances away with her ever-faithful friend and rescuer, her boss, an extraordinarily handsome and clever man who is, unfortunately for Jules, gay and therefore destined to provide for her only platonic affection. The film ends as he whispers to Jules, "Maybe there won't be marriage, maybe there won't be sex, but by God, there will be dancing." Moral of the tale, anyone? No, the traditional story is not dead. Good, sweet Cinderella will triumph over her wicked rivals, always.

It is most telling, I think, that the traditional fairy tales, just as this up-to-date film version, end with the wedding, and all else is subsumed under the heading of "ever after." It is as though these stories teach us that our whole existence is to be wrapped up in the quest for a mate; that once we acquire the mate, all else is decided; that the definition of what follows after the wedding is irrelevant because it is indistinguishable from any other "ever after"; that what follows really has little importance because we have already done the all-important; that no matter what else we do, life with the prince in his castle is the only "happily ever after" that is important for us, there being no viable alternatives; that all the other aspects of our lives, public as well as private, are determined in large measure by the overwhelming pervasiveness of the wifely estate. This is, after all, the prevailing myth.

As children listening to stories and as young women creating our own, how closely do we really look at ever-after land? The dream tells us that we will be loved and appreciated, sharing a husband's life, supporting him as he encourages and helps us, fulfilling ourselves in the haven of our world. But is this so?

Even today, when the terms of marriage, families, and relationships are shifting so dramatically, this vision of "happily ever after" persists. The demographics of families have become more than familiar; trends include

> *declining rates of marriage, later ages at first marriage, higher divorce rates, an increase in female-headed households, a higher proportion of births to unmarried mothers, larger percentages of children living in female-headed families, and a higher percentage of children living in poverty.*[2]

In 1972, 73 percent of children lived with their original parents, who were married to one another, and the most common household arrangement was married couples living with their children. By 1998, 51.7 percent of children lived with both parents and only 26 percent of households fit the earlier image.[3] Today more than half of all first marriages end in divorce.[4] Young women are painfully aware of that statistic, and it frightens them. Yet 90 percent of young people will marry,[5] and three out of four divorced women remarry,[6] half within four years.[7] What is more, divorced people are even more likely to marry (again) than those who have never married,[8] a fact cynically called the "triumph of hope over experience."[9] Notwithstanding all the frightening news, in surveys of high school students, 81 percent of females reported that they would choose to marry (compared to 74 percent of males).[10]

For even those few who do not or are not married, the dream often pervades their lives as a nightmare search: "Maybe tomorrow I'll find the right one." In the heterosexual community, and even to some extent in the gay community, the image of the perfect mate in the perfect eternal relationship provides the model against which most measure their personal lives.

Promise and Disillusionment

The traditional American mystique of marriage promises women a roster of assurances:

- You will have someone to *make you happy.*
- You will be loved and cherished.
- You will be cared for and protected from all the dangers of the world.
- You will have sexual intimacy and satisfaction.
- You will have someone to understand and support you.

- You will have companionship and safety from loneliness.
- You will have a father for your children.
- You will be socially secure as part of a couple.
- You will have a place in this world, a meaning, and you will love it.
- You will gain status and prestige as someone's chosen wife. You will not be an "old maid."
- You will be financially secure.
- You will be happy.

That's the promise.

Feminists cast a more objective glance at the promise. "Demystifying" marriage, we have drawn up a roster of our own: the data that tell the hard facts, the untruths and half-truths, the traps and games, the dissimulations and dangers of the traditional marriage mystique. It is not that feminism is in principle incompatible with marriage. (Although some feminists believe that it is, others do not, and many feminists marry.) Rather, it is that these presuppositions and traditional marriage arrangements can be destructive to women's lives in the most concrete ways, and feminists, discovering these realities, seek to both warn and redress.

The Case Against Traditional Marriage

Following the nineteenth-century sociologist Emile Durkheim, Jessie Bernard, a feminist sociologist, comments that "marriage is not the same for women as for men; it is not nearly as good."[11] Following extensive research, Bernard concluded that although men ridicule married life and pretend to have contempt for it, they benefit considerably from marriage, whereas women lose a great deal. Several studies, for example, found that married men have better emotional health than single men, suffer depression and anxiety less frequently than their single counterparts, advance faster professionally and socially, and have greater incomes than single men. Furthermore, the remarriage rate for divorced men and widowers is very high; they remarry more often and sooner than either women or never-married men.[12] Apparently, they know what is good for them.

Married women, on the other hand, experience greater depression, anxiety, and fear than single women, are more apt to experience severe neurotic symptoms, and have lower self-esteem than single women or married men. What is also interesting, as Carol Tavris and Carole Offir report, is that homemakers are even more apt to exhibit these problems than working wives, and single men in any category (never married, divorced, or widowed) are more likely to suffer from psychological difficulties than are single women.[13]

After all the ball-and-chain jokes, all the tavern mythology about carefree bachelors and manipulative women, and all the masculinist assertions that marriage is a terrific deal for women and a disaster for men, are not these findings a revelation? Yet, they should really come as no surprise. In so many ways—in terms of emotional exchange, economics, work, independence, freedom and mobility, autonomy and authenticity—traditional marriage offers to women and men a double standard, and women's part of that standard is truly the less advantaged.

Conjugal Obligation

In the patriarchal myth, a man and a woman marry, each taking on certain responsibilities. He agrees to love, honor, cherish, and provide her with the physical necessities of life. She agrees to love and obey (a term now mostly out of vogue in modern marriage ceremonies except among the religious right, although the power relationship in which it originated is not), and she takes on a whole composite of responsibilities that are diverse, unspecified, and generally lumped under the heading of being a wife or housewife. Though it might superficially appear to be an even exchange, it is actually rather an extraordinary exchange, and an enigmatic one, for at base it differs radically from what it appears to be. Overladen with social mythology, marriage is rarely seen for what it is, and the parties concerned often perceive it very differently.

In the patriarchal barroom myth, marriage is a trap for men. A man in the excellent condition of bachelorhood, free and unencumbered, encounters a lady, wily and manipulative, who tricks him into "falling in love." He becomes so besotted with her that he loses his good sense and marries her. The door slams shut; he will find out only later that he has been entrapped and is now the captive of a "ball and chain" who, for the rest of his life, will nag him, keep tabs on him, spend his money, and bring him no end of difficulties. The lady, on the other hand, has a "good deal," having snared a meal ticket and a respectable place in life. Actually, of course, both women and men know the myth to be false, yet both are unclear as to just how false because at some level of awareness, in some form, and to some degree, the myth is believed (or else Jessie Bernard's findings would not surprise us). Because of this, it exerts considerable pressure on the attitudes and behaviors of husbands and wives.

Let us take a more objective look at the patriarchal portrayal of traditional marriage—"demystified." In patriarchy, a man and a woman marry; they strike a bargain, make an exchange (not fully understood at the time of marriage), and each takes on certain responsibilities and privileges. The bare bones of the agreement require that the husband be the main provider of the physical necessities of life through his income—shelter, food, clothing, and so on—and that in return for these the wife provides care of the home and family and sometimes, if absolutely necessary, a secondary income. But what do these respective duties, obligations, and privileges actually entail for each?

The patriarchal husband's responsibilities are explicit: He must work or in some fashion secure financial maintenance of the home and family. Because he is "out in the world," and therefore worldly wise, he must act as "head of household," making policy decisions for the family and bearing responsibility for them. He is to protect his wife and children from danger, whatever that might be in their circumstances, and guide and mold their behavior and character. Although the law does not specify the quantity or quality of the provisions a man must secure for his family, the culture does, for according to the imperatives of Mars, a man proves his worthiness through success in the marketplace (the modern hunt). Society—and often his wife or children—may judge a man ill if he does not provide according to the standard of living decreed by the media. There is, then, an intense pressure on husbands to provide always bigger and better, and this pressure may be both burdensome and unremitting. What is more, such pressure may not be much reduced even when there are two incomes, since the marriage myth operates regardless of actual circumstances.

A different aspect to the prescription to "provide" is often overlooked, however, in discussions about masculine responsibility. "Provision" means work. It means one must have a job, of whatever nature, and must remain regularly at a job to obtain all one needs. Husbands frequently point out that they work very hard "to get you what you need" and therefore should be loved, respected, served, and accorded the right to make family decisions. What they do not say is that they would work in any event, married or unmarried, for one still needs to eat, dress, and have shelter. They do not say that they work for more than income, that even routine or laborious jobs provide a satisfaction in earning, and that life without work outside the house would drive them mad. They do not say that a tremendous satisfaction comes in looking about one's family home and noting that whatever is there, whatever its condition, has been provided by one's efforts and that because of those efforts, one is autonomous and worthy. We need not denigrate the value and importance of giving or the pressure of provision. We need only consider that such labor carries with it a highly positive and meaningful reward that we must not overlook in evaluating its claims to compensation. This satisfying experience of autonomy and self-worth that comes from providing is the reason many women give for returning to work outside the home or even for leaving "comfortable" marriages.

The husband's duty to protect is enigmatic in the twentieth century. Certainly, protection from physical danger is impossible in such a complex society. "Protection" is now largely passed to public institutions, and the remainder of the responsibility is equally shared by husband and wife. In terms of children's safety, the mother usually accomplishes the lion's share of that work, typically taking almost total charge of her offspring. Even when she is not with them, it is she who worries and protects through vigilance with regard to a ride to school, an adequate babysitter, a competent physician, dental appointments, birthday parties, and countless other matters. It is she, too, who "guides"; fathers could hardly be expected to provide much guidance in the average twelve minutes a day they spend with their children![14]

Head of household, then, becomes an interesting concept. If it does not mean protection, guidance, or modeling, what it means in essence is power, control over household and family in return for breadwinning, which is neither all sacrifice nor peculiar to marriage. The head of household also has certain real privileges that he enjoys both as husband and as male: considerably more freedom, autonomy, and service—the service, by and large, provided by his wife.

One of the most extraordinary features of being a traditional wife in patriarchy is the unification of certain aspects of the role: The married woman *is* a housewife; she doesn't *do* housewifing. She is not simply a mate, a coworker, and a partner in the business of life; she is a certain identity, one that carries with it a particular (mixed) status, a "place," and some identifiable and rather unchanging tasks. Upon marriage, the patriarchal wife yields her own individual identity (a fact attested to by her change of name), subsumes it under her husband's, and commits her life—her time, interests, and energies—to the needs of the family group, husband and offspring. Regardless of whatever else a wife may do—work in the marketplace or in community affairs, or pursue a professional career—patriarchy defines as her first priorities her duties as wife/housewife. Should she choose not to keep house, she is no less the housewife; she is simply a housewife not doing her job.

A husband barters some of his income and freedom for the kinds of services and satisfactions a wife provides. What does a wife barter? For the financial security (now not a clear return for the more than 60 percent of all married women who work outside the home[15]), for the status of being married, for love and companionship, women take on almost limitless labors of service to their home and family. Whereas a husband takes on a "job" involving specifiable hours, tasks, and rewards, a wife takes on a lifestyle. Her tasks are not wholly specified, but instead comprise the satisfaction of almost every kind of physical and emotional need her husband and children voice, as well as the many more services required for smooth maintenance of family life. Her labor is limited by neither time nor personal need. She is expected to perform at whatever hour needs arise—breakfast at whatever time the family must rise, dinner when they return home. Were this job to be advertised outside the home, it might carry the warning that the job makes tremendous demands on one's personal time, including split shifts and a great deal of overtime.

Unlike her husband, whose skills and education define the kind of work he will do, the wife is assigned work that is elemental and undifferentiated by ability. College-educated or illiterate, the common denominator is housework—sweeping floors, washing clothes, scouring ovens, cleaning toilets, washing dishes, dumping garbage—and she who performs such menial tasks earns for herself the status incumbent upon them: low. She is "a housewife." Even if she works outside the home, as most women today do, she is no less the housewife in her household; she is simply a housewife who works both at home and in the marketplace, or a "working wife." (Note that the husband is not referred to as a "working husband.")

The tasks of housekeeping are themselves no joy. However glorified in the media, housework in the real world is boring, ugly, tiresome, repetitive, unsatisfying, and lonely work. Factory or office work may be dull and tiresome, but there are people around; one can see and be seen, talk and interact, change scenes. One of the worst aspects of housewifing is the awful sense of being locked up with the sameness day after day or, if the woman has a job, evening after evening, weekend after weekend.

Labor to maintain the house itself is not the wife's only responsibility. Besides being responsible for the care of the home, she is also expected to manage the inhabitants of the home—and this really remarkable assignment makes the contemporary wife's role what it is. Most wives have nearly complete responsibility for the care of their children—not only to feed, clothe, and teach them but also to monitor the quality of their school experience; organize their religious, social, and health needs; provide for child care when parents are not at home; and so on. More to the point, the mother is held responsible for the emotional needs of her children, and it is left very unclear at which point needs become demands. Given current child-centered sensitivities deriving from the warnings of gurus Freud and Spock, not to mention a "kids"-obsessed media, no matter how tired or time-pressed they are, many mothers are extremely hesitant to deny their children any demands on their time, privacy, or strength without suffering considerable worry and guilt. In essence, the endless demands of parenting are shared but little, and most mothers—working out of the home or not—function for the most part as single parents. Thus, though both men and women have families, women are ultimately responsible for family life.

Care of the inhabitants does not end with children, however, for a wife is also expected to care for her husband in much the same way as she cares for their offspring. She is to feed him, cook his favorite dishes, buy and maintain his clothes, arrange his home to suit him, pack his suitcase when he goes on trips, arrange entertainment for him on Saturday nights, entertain his business friends, arrange doctor's appointments for him (even against his will), listen to him, and support and "understand" him.

In some circles, a wife is even responsible for the spiritual health of her husband. Priests in some parishes advise that it is sinful for a wife to deny her husband sex lest he be led into temptation outside the home, and Jews believe it to be a wife's duty to provide a living environment for her husband in which he may successfully seek blessings from God. Within the religious right, growing ever more numerous and powerful (for it is allied with the political right, now in control of the Republican party), a wife's role, ordained by God, is to be a "perfect helper," as we saw in Chapter 3.

Whereas a husband's contributions to family maintenance are "public" or communal, much of the wife's work is frequently personal or private, and it is this aspect of her labor, added to the rest, that renders it a form of service (in the sense of a servant). The husband may mow a lawn, repair a door, or dump garbage, tasks pertaining to the household collectively, but he would not be expected to mend his wife's slacks or to gauge and replenish her toiletries. In the traditional household, wives render to their husbands a plethora of personal services; the reverse is rarely true.

Wives do not receive salaries for their work, although husbands usually share their incomes with their wives, and sometimes generously. But a great deal of difference exists between receiving an established and agreed-on sum of money in return for one's labor and receiving money as a "gift"—that is, at the giver's choosing. Although wife labor is extensive, time-consuming, often taxing, and absolutely necessary for the household, and although most husbands could not advance professionally or be half so productive without it, wives laboring in the home are not perceived as earning; hence, they are not "salaried." Both institutions and individuals regard money wives "receive" from their husbands—for household goods or for personal use—as grants. Therefore, they must endure the disadvantages and indignities of pensioners. Dependent wives are cautioned as to how they are to spend their *husband's* money; they are to express gratitude for sums earmarked for their own personal use (such as clothing), and they must wait until their husbands decide it is time to replace the washer. To put aside savings of their own out of "granted" money is perceived as deceptive and is rarely done, and, as a result, wives working only in the home can find themselves trapped in intolerable marriages by finances—their lack thereof.

The cruelest jab in the wife's situation (and one not often recognized) is derogating this labor to the status of nonwork. Because our society (unlike some others) affords no economic recognition of housework (such as social security or compensation), because the work is accomplished at home in the service of the family rather than in the public marketplace, and because "women's work" is *always* devalued and demeaned, housework is perceived and treated as nonwork, as nonproductive—with all the stigmas and trials the term entails. "Does your wife work?" one might ask. "No, she stays home." "Do you work?" one woman asks another. "No, I'm just a housewife." "What do you do?" a woman might be asked. She might answer that she is a saleswoman or an engineer, but she will not add that she cooks for a family of five, vacuums carpets, irons shirts, shops for groceries, or plans dinners, because she is not paid for that labor. Even women, housewives themselves, must be reminded that, paid or not, recognized or not, *homemaking is a job.*

The effects of classifying homemaking as nonwork are far-reaching and powerful. The full-time housewife or the wife who works as a "supplement" is reduced to a state of financial dependence, which in turn diminishes her power in the family, her own self-image, and her standing in society. The problems, however, go much farther. By allowing herself to be dependent on her husband's income, by accruing little formally recognized history of labor (such as Social Security benefits or a pension) that could compensate her in later years, and by collecting no savings of her own, a wife makes her future financial security subject to the continuance of her marriage or her husband's goodwill. By reducing herself in the labor force and by not developing or enhancing marketable skills, she further erodes the possibility of financial independence in or out of marriage.

Consider a woman who, after twenty years as a traditional wife, finds herself in an intolerable marriage situation. With dependent children, no savings, a poorly paying job or none at all, and limited marketable skills, what can she do? She may remain trapped and unhappy, or she may leave. Divorced, she then suffers not only the loss of companionship and social status; she must also expect a terribly diminished standard of living, severe strains of economic survival with little experience to withstand them, and no career or professional interests to sustain her. Furthermore, alimony and child support are largely inadequate or nonexistent.[16]

The circumstances of a wife within a traditional marriage are difficult enough, but by 1990, fewer than 16 percent of families with minor children conformed to the traditional "Leave It to Beaver" model; by 1995, 76 percent of all mothers were employed.[17] Just as the traditional housewife often finds herself in a double bind, so the wife who opts for an alternative to dependence by working outside the home may also find herself severely hampered by the nonwork status of homemaking. As of 1994, more than 60 percent of all married women were doing paid work outside the home. Over 76 percent had children between six and seventeen years of age, and nearly 60 percent had children under three, with the number steadily rising.[18] Such women share the responsibilities of economic maintenance with their husbands. Do they commonly receive a proportional increase in status, power, privilege, and autonomy? Do they, in return, receive from their husbands equal participation in homemaking efforts? In this country, as in nearly every other in the world, most wives usually answer no.

Regardless of circumstances, husbands rarely take equal responsibility for maintaining the household. Research shows that working women spend two and a half to three times as many hours at housework as their husbands do, and men married

to women who work spend the same amount of time on housework as men married to full-time homemakers.[19] Furthermore, in the two-career family, fathers still spend less time with their children than their wives do and even *less* time intensely interacting with them at the end of the day than fathers in traditional families![20] Does the time men spend in housework come out of the time they would be spending with their children? Do women have that option?

In the case of the wife working only at home, the logic goes this way: If homemaking is nonwork, it is not a job with visible, recognized, and acknowledged demands. The homemaker has no right, therefore, to expect her husband to share in household tasks, for she is "not working," and he is! How can she legitimately expect him to add her responsibilities to his burden? The same logic holds even when the wife is publicly employed. Such a wife actually carries two jobs, a salaried and a nonsalaried one, but since homemaking is not recognized as "work," her two-job status is also not recognized. She merely has certain wifely "responsibilities" at home, and the husband's contributions are most usually treated as a gift or favor rather than a *bona fide* responsibility. (He "helps" with the laundry. He "babysits" the children.)

We are familiar with the media images of the (double) working wife: She must "organize her time" very carefully to meet all her responsibilities and not "neglect" her family. Smiling all the while, diligently dieting and exercising to maintain her sex appeal, she also hurries home from work each evening to get supper on and spends her nights and weekends cleaning, washing, and ferrying her children from one activity to another; somehow she also finds time to use sexy perfume and carry on all that follows. Husbands who "help" place already-prepared casseroles into the microwave. (Guess who prepared them.)

Two jobs, however, are more than taxing. Working for a salary as well as parenting, cleaning, cooking, shopping, putting oneself last, and rarely getting sufficient sleep take their toll: Physically, psychologically, and creatively, one runs down. It is a truism in the business and professional world that one cannot produce at peak performance if one is cut in too many ways. For this reason, most institutions have formal prohibitions against moonlighting.

Yet moonlighting is a way of life for most married working women or single mothers. Worse, it is never even clear which job is *the* job and which is moonlighting, because so many women never even realize that they are handling two full-time jobs simultaneously.

But many women are becoming sensitive to their circumstances. They have begun to recognize that a cultural construction, not a cosmic imperative, burdens them with homemaking. They have begun to expect their mates to share the work at home. Many husbands have come to recognize the unfairness, too, and some of them are moving (however grudgingly) toward carrying *some* of the load. Full sharing is painfully rare.

The Emotional Economy

If the fairy-tale image of marriage promises women anything, it promises abundant satisfaction of emotional needs. When the prince arrives, he is supposed to bring with him love everlasting, constant attention, affection, devotion, understanding, companionship, appreciation, and, most of all, the desire and wherewithal to make his princess happy. To be sure, a great deal of this fantasy is wrongheaded and ill-conceived. No one can make another person happy, however much he or she might want to, and no one can provide another with complete solace and total understanding. Neither can nor should anyone shower another with constant attention. Yet people still can and do care for one another. Sociologists tend to agree that marriage as an institution survives today primarily because it is seen as providing the major source of caring interactions.

Love, as we know, is an enigmatic idea. Love is different things to different people in varied circumstances, and it is often experienced and expressed in very individual ways. It is not as enduring, dependable, and consistent as it has been reputed to be, nor can it conquer all or justify every kind of action. Yet it would be wrong to lapse into cynicism. However difficult it is to understand or define, however changeable and distorted by myth, love as a concept persists in the human vocabulary. Ample evidence shows that human beings cannot thrive without the kind of succor provided by what is generally called love, and that life can be arid and unwholesome without some measure of love's joy.

Certainly, we can glean the intense personal contact that either is or begets love from many different kinds of relationships. However, our society rarely affords us an environment in which such relationships can grow, and we are discouraged rather than encouraged to participate in the kind of encounter crucial to love. Marriage (and living arrangements like marriage), though, does include an expectation that the partners will have at least this: a sharing of communication, concern, and mutual support and an exchange of sensitivity, compassion, and nurture. We can term such sharing and mutuality the emotional economy of the relationship.

For various reasons, all lodged in patriarchy, it is in this exchange that women often experience their greatest disappointment in the traditional relationship. The emotional economy, like the work economy, is out of balance, and once more the woman typically occupies the disadvantaged position. Although women usually express a greater interest in love and emotional exchange, and although women are thought to need and want more open expressions of affection, in the patriarchal marriage, women are apt to receive considerably less personal affection than their partners. Despite or because of the high priority women often place on the love relationship, women are more apt to love than be loved, support than be supported, nurture than be nurtured—even though they appear to seek the exchanges more than men do. The sexist role and character definitions of Venus and Mars decree that women should become more bound up with the behaviors and feelings of interpersonal contact. Ultimately, women become very good at loving, but for the patriarchal male, it is a clumsy business at best. In 1971, Shulamith Firestone, one of the founders of the women's liberation movement, wrote in *The Dialectic of Sex*:

> That women live for love and men for work is a truism. . . . There is also much truth in the clichés that "behind every man there is a woman," and that "women are the power behind [read: voltage in] the throne." (Male) culture was built on the love of women, and at their expense. Women provided the substance of those male masterpieces; and for millennia they have done the work, and suffered the costs, of one-way emotional relationships the benefit of which went to men and to the work of men. . . .

Simone de Beauvoir said it: "The word love has by no means the same sense for both sexes, and this is one cause of the serious misunderstandings which divide them."... [In] parlor discussions of the "double standard,"... it is generally agreed: That women are monogamous, better at loving, "clinging," more interested in (highly involved) "relationships" than in sex per se, and they confuse affection with sexual desire. That men are interested in nothing but a screw (Wham, bam, thank you M'am!), or else romanticize the woman ridiculously; that once sure of her, they become notorious philanderers, never satisfied; that they mistake sex for emotion. . . .

I draw three conclusions based on these differences:

1. *That men can't love. (Male hormones?? Women traditionally expect and accept an emotional invalidism in men that they would find intolerable in a woman.)*
2. *That women's "clinging" behavior is necessitated by their objective social situation.*
3. *That this situation has not changed significantly from what it ever was.*[21]

Men cannot love? Emotional invalidism? One-way emotional relationships built at women's expense?

Are women "better at loving"? There is a good deal of controversy in the women's movement over whether women do or do not have any special ability for love and feeling. Sexists have used that idea to exclude us from any activity *not* based on serving, *not* based on feeling. But such a division is more patriarchal than rational; the idea that one who is capable of emotion is incapable of discipline or reason is absurd. We need not be afraid to consider whether women's experiences in the world may have developed in us a particular ability to live more lovingly, more considerately. It bespeaks no *undesirable* softness (again, the martial belief that "softness" is contemptible), no lack of intellect or strength.

It appears that women are very much concerned with the human and the loving, and that most of us do exercise an immense ability to nurture and support, a fact of which we may be duly proud. A problem does arise, however, with our concern for caring, because in patriarchy, our ability to love can become distorted. Because love and service are prescribed as women's only allowable activities, they

are forced out of proportion. Loving can become disproportionate in at least two ways: the first, when loving and serving others is not balanced with loving and caring for oneself; and the second, when the interests of love are not balanced by other kinds of interests and indeed crowd out other sources of pleasure, satisfaction, and meaning. Such a situation is destructive, creating an overdependence on the exchanges of love (or some distorted facsimile) and an inability to draw on other resources.

Romance and love are important to men, but so are a lot of other things. Woman's prescribed role as subordinate and the prescription that she be passive, dependent, and emotional are at the heart of the saying that love is central for women but peripheral for men; that for women, love is abstract, emotional, and spiritual, whereas for men it is concrete, physical, and sexual. In relation to love, women and men move in two different realities, and there is the rub.

Let us look at how the traditional relationship turns the differences in male and female loving into the asymmetry of its emotional economy. Women and men both need love and nurture, although their expression of that need and the way they relate to it may differ. But given traditional female-male role definitions, men are far more likely than women to have that need well satisfied. Women, trained as we are for caring and service, often treat fulfilling another's needs not only as a responsibility or task but also as something we want to do. We are in a sense assertive about taking the initiative in caring: ferreting out, anticipating, or pursuing the emotional needs of those we love. We want to "help." Just as we might to a child, we often communicate to a lover (although not necessarily in these words), "Let me take care of you, let me 'mother' you."

But if that lover is a traditional man, who is mothering Mother? Trained to see tenderness as effeminate, uncomfortable with feelings in general and need in particular, the traditional male is not usually adept at that aspect of the emotional exchange termed *psychological nurturance*. For men in patriarchy, love is not to be expressed directly, emotionally, on a one-to-one basis, but rather indirectly through providing, modeling, and caring for the family's material well-being. Such indirect provision can be a form of expressing love, but in the traditional division of labor, it is a form of caring in which the woman makes equal, if not greater, contributions. Men work, but women work also, only their work is not acknowledged. Furthermore, in terms of the emotional economy, a woman's work is considerably more direct, personal, and expressive. She not only prepares food but prepares his favorite food; not only cleans clothes but maintains his personal items in an intimate and personal way; not only listens but hears.

It is often said that men express their most intimate feelings through their sexual lovemaking, and this may be true; one cannot presume to know how often or in what degree. Yet in journals, conferences, workshops, and consciousness-raising groups, women of all ages have revealed that they very often sense a lack of emotional connection with their mates even during sex. Although women and men are both capable of separating love and sex, women are apparently considerably less apt to do so, particularly with their mates.

Yet if there were no qualifications, if it were true that a man typically expresses his love equally, though differently, through providing and through sex, it would still not change the fact of his woman's not receiving adequate emotional support and nurturance. The need for intimate connection in the realm of feeling is profound and important; few can do well without it. The fact is that women report less of this kind of connection, less attention, less direct concern. Great imbalance characterizes the emotional economy of the patriarchal couple.

After-Marriage: Divorce and Widowhood

Few consider as they "walk down the aisle" that marriages often end, in either divorce or death. Because, in our culture, one is never free of a once-married state but instead is always perceived as a "formerly married person," when a marriage ends, a period of after-marriage follows. This is a time with its own particular character, a time that ends in either remarriage or death. More women than men experience this time because men are less frequently widowed than men, more men than women remarry after widowhood or divorce, and men remarry sooner. Women also experience this time very differently than men do, because social attitudes toward the unmarried person, customs (such as dating behavior), and economic circumstances are frequently determined by sex.

The character and quality of one's experience in after-marriage are largely determined by the life decisions the partners made earlier. Quite naturally, the seeds sown in marriage continue to be harvested after its end. As we might expect, the woman of a traditional marriage, who has built her life around the prescribed patriarchal model—truncated and distorted as it is—is apt to find her condition similarly truncated and distorted after marriage. Traditional expectations, even for the average working wife, fix a woman's whole identity within her marriage and make her dependent on it in a very profound way; the more traditional the arrangements of the relationship, the more profound the dependence. Passivity, economic or psychological dependence on one's mate, withdrawal from public life, and discouragement from developing resources outside the couple do not bode well for life; discouragement from developing resources outside the couple is not a good prognosis for life outside marriage—that is, after-marriage. To live life alone well and happily requires personal strength, preparation, and experience, none of which women in patriarchal marriage are encouraged to develop. Hence, the wife as ex-wife or widow is likely to suffer tremendously at her marriage's end and for some time thereafter, even if she grows considerably, for she has lost valuable time.

Although divorce and widowhood have some fundamental and important differences, in patriarchy these experiences have much in common. A widow and a divorcee are both "once-were wives," having had similar roles and identities in their former lives. They both may be treated as half-beings, anomalies in a universe of couples. They are generally unprepared both economically and psychologically for life alone; and they frequently have the same burdens: children to raise alone, hostility or tolerant contempt from outsiders, and increased responsibilities with decreased resources.

The Feminine Role in Traditional Marriage: A Setup

Generally in our culture, a woman marries young, typically in her twenties. Often before or without settling career questions, before becoming independent or self-sufficient, she moves out of her parents' home, or away from her roommates, into the home she shares with her husband. Directly she settles into the wife's role and lifestyle, forming her adult character, norms, and expectations and determining her future through decisions made within the economic and social structures of her marriage.

The Economic Setup Whether wives work only at home or work both at home and in the marketplace, as is most common, patriarchal marriage will likely cause her to be economically disadvantaged after marriage. If she works only at home, for a large portion of her life, parenting and housekeeping are her primary occupations. In such work at home, she accrues neither savings of her own nor salary nor Social Security benefits nor worker's compensation nor pension. She develops no special marketable skills, no experience, no work history, no seniority. In the job market, she's worth little or nothing, and the longer she has remained at home, the less she is worth outside.

A traditional wife may work outside the home, especially if her income is absolutely necessary for the family's subsistence, but her salary is generally treated as a supplement to her husband's. If neither mate perceives the wife's job as primary, very likely neither will pay much attention to the quality of the job situation, its potential for growth or advancement, its salary, benefits, or status in the work world. Even professionally trained women often make decisions that subordinate their careers to the needs of their husbands and families. In one study of dual-career families, for example, where both husbands and wives were working as managers in large corporations, W. B. O'Reilly found that wives accommodated their careers to those of their husbands *even when both "professed an 'egalitarian' ideology."*[22] O'Reilly found that although the couples philosophically valued both their careers equally, their actions furthered the men's careers over their wives' because of a "web of factors" that functioned in their private lives as well as at work.

> *The web begins with Steihm's*[23] *observations about "invidious intimacy." Even among highly educated men and women, marriage choices are made such that the man is older, often taller, and perceived to be "smarter." The edge in age, even if the men and women are in the same occupation with the same opportunities (which is frequently not the case), gives the husband more work experience and hence higher earnings than his wife has. If, in addition, the couple believes that the husband's opportunities for promotion are greater than the wife's, which is frequently a correct perception, the couple will seek to maximize their joint income by furthering the career of the husband.*

> *O'Reilly found two behavior patterns that favored husbands' careers over wives'. First, in determining whether or not to accept promotions that required geographical moves, couples made decisions that favored husbands' careers, even at the expense of their wives' careers.*[24] *Second, the pattern of labor division in the home favored the husband's career, especially in families where there were children. Even when husbands participated in housework and child care, wives typically fulfilled the time- and energy-consuming role of home manager and also did more of those home tasks that tended to conflict with work. . . . And of course, the more the wife's career progress was slowed, the more "sense" it made for the joining-maximizing couple to favor the husband's career.*[25]

Because patriarchy prescribes that the husband's job is more important than the wife's, wives must quit work to follow transferred husbands; because women are charged with the primary care of children, wives are more likely the ones who stay home from work to care for sick children (or, for that matter, for a sick spouse or parent); they accommodate their work around the needs of their families. It has become common for many women to quit working for periods of time, sometimes several years, to care for their children when they are young. Such actions do not make for professionalism or the rewards that follow it. In essence, during marriage, a husband builds a career, a future, marketable skills, experience, and seniority. But a wife who neglects her professional interests or one who invests her time, energy, and service in promoting her husband's financial future—mistakenly believing it to be her own—is impoverishing her own earning potential and independent economic security.

A majority of wives work as procurement officers for their households. They shop not only for groceries but also for furniture, household goods, and private and personal needs. For this reason, they often pay the bills, keep the checkbook and the records, and do the banking. Yet, despite claims to the contrary, wives do not "control" the money in the family or the nation, except as delegated. They execute policy; they do not form it. Patriarchal wives may make such decisions as which toilet paper to buy or where to purchase their vegetables (hence their manipulation by advertising media), but they must wait for their husbands to outline the larger budget: how *much* money to spend on food or clothes or mortgage and when to replace an appliance. The intricacies of insurance, long-range planning and budgeting, and investments are generally left to the male in the traditional household.

Furthermore, although the wife may sign the check or the credit card, she usually does so under her husband's name. Until recently (since the successes of the present women's movement), wives could not even have their own charge accounts, and the homemaker without salary still cannot. The result: The wife may accrue little credit of her own; it goes to Mr. and Mrs. X (or, more succinctly, to Mr. X). The bottom line in the economics of the traditional marriage is that when the marriage ends, the wife's "bottom line" is apt to be substantially lower than her husband's.

The Social Setup   One of the really delightful aspects of marriage, when it goes well, is the friendly companionship—the opportunity to talk and do things with one another, interact with others in a kind of community, share in work and play. And yet this very positive facet of the relationship is a two-edged sword; unbalanced by the functioning existence of two separate realms of being for each partner, "togetherness" can be a trap. In patriarchy, the wife usually lacks any separate realm of being.

A traditional wife's lifestyle, made up of the concrete details of her day, is built around her husband. She sleeps with him, rises with him, eats breakfast and dinner with him. She plans her day around him, work and play. Rarely does a traditional wife socialize in mixed company without her husband. Outside of occasional all-female events, socializing occurs in couples: One invites the Smiths and the Joneses for dinner or goes out for an evening with the Browns, two by two. It would be un-

usual for the typical wife to go to a party by herself, unescorted at least by another couple. She is not likely to travel any distance alone or to vacation or play or dine out or go to a theater by herself—or even with another woman except in rare instances. A traditional married friend of mine laughingly reported that she and her husband were "joined at the hip." In traditional marriage, coupledom reigns.

Such a "togetherness" marriage does not encourage women to develop companionship or buddy relationships with other women, or even with men, and it inhibits the growth of a life outside of marriage. In her workplace or at home during the day, with the children and/or her husband in the evening, with couples on the weekend, the traditional wife develops a social existence that is based almost entirely within marriage and the world of couples.

A patriarchal wife's social status and identity, too, are solidly grounded within her marriage. She is John's wife—John the mechanic, John whose last name (and therefore hers) is Smith, John whose social status (and therefore hers) is X. Her friends are friends of the marriage, attached to the couple collectively, rarely to either individually. These things are more true for a woman in marriage than for a man. It is generally she who takes on his name and the social standing of his work, who must live where his work is, who entertains his business friends or working buddies. It is she, moreover, with all her responsibilities at home, with reduced opportunity for people contact, with little interest in her own job or economic future, who builds her life around the world of her husband, whatever its character and potential.

Feminists often quip, "In marriage, two become one, and he's the one!" In the traditional household, this is very nearly so. Imagine the extent of the trauma to a person completely absorbed in a marriage if that union should end.

Dénouement: The Experience of After-Marriage

Typically, the patriarchal wife has put all her eggs into one basket. If she has built her life around her marriage, how will she fare at that marriage's end?

The Divorcée   The longer and more traditionally a woman has lived as a patriarchal wife, the more her whole being has adapted itself to one kind of existence, and the harder her transition into and the experience of a new life will be. A great proportion of divorces occur well into marriage, after ten, twenty, even thirty years.

The divorced patriarchal wife is apt to find herself financially strapped. She has probably been left with the house (after all, there are children who must be sheltered), but maintenance of that home is likely to pose problems. Mortgage payments are usually too high for her salary if she has one (between 60 and 80 percent of former wives do not receive child support or alimony), and she is usually unable to deal with repairs herself. Because she is inexperienced, she must hire maintenance people, usually at exorbitant rates. Perhaps she has been awarded the family car. But how long before it, too, begins to fail, and how able will she be to replace it and maintain payments?

If the former homemaker has not worked outside the home, a job is in order. But what is she trained for or ready for? Who wants her after ten or twenty years outside the job market? What salary is she likely to earn? If she worked during her marriage at an "auxiliary" job, how likely is her income to supply the entire needs of her family now, if it was only an auxiliary income earlier? If her children are young, she must bear the burden of full-time work and full-time single parenting in the intensely difficult emotional environment of after-marriage. If she is one of the minority of women who receive some financial contributions from their ex-husbands, she must bear the burden of continued dependence, fretful interactions with him, and all the problems that follow from that circumstance.

Responsibility lies heavily on her life. She must meet her children's psychological, financial, and material needs. She must work as sole earner—an alien experience—while maintaining the semblance of a stable home and at the same time dealing with her own sense of loss and anxiety. Altogether too little time, too little money, and too little peace are available to her.

Loneliness closes in. Inexperienced at cultivating friendships, at seeking out and encouraging camaraderie, and uncomfortable with the different modes of interaction in single life, she finds at the same time that her old friends are dropping away. They are couples; she, a single, is no longer part of

their world, the world she had with her husband. To the community of couples, the single woman is a pariah—more so the divorcée, because the image she carries is of wantonness and threat. Seeking new relationships, she often finds something different from what she wants. When a women leaves her marriage, she takes on a new image and a new status in male-female encounters. It is assumed that she is "on the prowl," and she often finds herself treated as a sexual mark. A new "meaningful relationship"? The later the divorce, the more limited her range of options are, particularly if she has children still at home.

Resentful, lonely, frightened, the divorced patriarchal wife has a good deal of building to do. She can do it, many have, but the prescriptions of patriarchy—"femininity," wifely subordination, and social discrimination—make this an intensely difficult challenge.

The Widow   Much that is true of the divorcée also fits the widow. Just as financially limited,[26] thrust into loneliness and new responsibilities, the widow discovers she has lost more than a husband. She has lost status and identity as well. No longer part of a couple, she too becomes a pariah in her singleness, intensified as it is by the stigma of death that she is perceived to carry. Friends who were so kind "at the end" drift away, embarrassed by her grief, uncomfortable with her new condition as not quite whole.

Living with Oneself

Women have two alternatives: married or . . . What? Unmarried? Unhusbanded? Single? In our society, each of these terms has the ring of "wrongness." *Unmarried* is clearly the negative of married, which is the norm—the "natural," acceptable, positive state in our society. *Single* implies that there must be a double. The wrongness of the terms is the wrongness assigned to the state, and I cannot find a term in our language for the unmarried state in women (*bachelor* is male) that is accurate and does not carry with it a social stigma.

It would be better, feminists believe, to think of the matter in a wholly different way. The crucial question (although our culture would disagree) is not whether we are married or unmarried or after-married, but whether we are whole or not whole, whether we are living fully and well or not. If we can be successful at living *with* ourselves, then the matter of whether or not we live *by* ourselves becomes secondary (though not unimportant). The ability to function well and happily with oneself and for oneself, encouraged to some extent in men, is discouraged in women in patriarchy. Self-sufficient, viable women do not make good servants. They make happier people, however, and, should they choose, better companions.

Living well, achieving peace and what happiness may be afforded, requires many hard-earned qualities: personal strength, courage, discipline, balance, perspective, endurance, humor, compassion, and intelligence. It requires a sense of self-worth and pride, a sense of the integrity and inviolability of one's own being, what one man I know refers to as personal "sovereignty." It requires self-awareness and understanding. It requires preparation, training, and experience, the wherewithal to use one's power for one's advantage in whatever circumstances one finds oneself. It requires a commitment made to the self to live well, to choose life for its own sake. When a person comes to see that there is good in the individual experiencing of life, that there is joy in doing what is personally meaningful, then that person is prepared to live with herself, alone or in company. When one keeps in mind that ultimately we walk quite by ourselves in this life, that for many reasons other people and other circumstances come and go, that we must always depend first on ourselves to meet our needs, emotional or material, then one does not relinquish one's power or safety into another's keeping.

A woman, as well as a man, must foster and maintain her own personal integrity and viability whatever her circumstances or relationships and however much she may love another or commit herself. In that case, she does not, as a female, take on herself any greater risks than are already presented to women quite naturally by life and society; rather, she diminishes them and greatly increases the likelihood of happiness. A woman so described—independent, capable, viable—may not be the darling of patriarchy. She may find herself out of step with many and even rejected by some. But she is far more a person, more fully able to relate to those who would accept her, more likely to contribute to her whole community. Besides, the alternative is self-destructive.

OUR BODIES: NEGOTIABLE CHATTEL

With few exceptions, the history of ideas has rarely given much consideration to the way one relates to one's own body in the formation of self-image. Possibly because of masculinist fear of sensuality and feelings, or because men as a class have so long had control over their own bodies as well as ours, "intellectuals" (until very recently) have given the subject short shrift. Nonetheless, our bodies are the material representations of our selves, both to others and to ourselves. On many levels, from the superficial (such as the way we dress) to the deeply profound (such as the way we encounter and treat our own aging), the attitudes directed toward our bodies often determine how we see other aspects of ourselves. The relationship between our physical selves and our psychosocial selves is very close.

If we look, we can see many examples that show the importance to self-image of control over one's body and its needs. One of the first and most compelling forms of control the military exercises over new recruits, one that molds them into obedience and dependence, is the control over their physical selves, through appearance (in dress and hair), through management of body functions (eating, sleeping, elimination), and through providing for bodily needs (from medical treatment to cigarettes). It has been reported that one of the major factors in breaking the resistance of victims in Nazi concentration camps was the removal of their clothing and their subjection to other physical humiliations. To a lesser extent, the same thing is true in prisons. Studies in the psychology of nursing and hospital care show that a patient's loss of control over the care of her or his own body, apart from the illness itself, often leads to a reduced sense of health and well-being; as a result, patients are encouraged as soon as possible to meet as many of their own physical needs as they can. Nowhere, of course, can we more clearly see the close relationship between body control and confident, independent maturity than in the development of children. With each new step toward meeting physical needs, with each step away from control through physical discipline, the child grows in independence.

But in patriarchy, in our world, it is the class of men as a whole, and not women, that wields power over the circumstances and exigencies of women's physical selves. Because of this, women can be reduced to the status of dependent children. Through the institutionalization of masculine authority—in medicine, education, politics, communication, and law enforcement—and through brute power, men have obtained for themselves the use, maintenance, even "protection" of women's bodies. Until conditions change, women are in the childlike position of seeking out the *pater* for the satisfaction of physical needs and for the disposition of our bodies.

Appearance

Let us begin with something that might seem superficial but is not: our appearance. We saw in Chapter 3 that women are taught very early that the way we come into this world is not the way we ought to remain. In our society, unlike men, who are expected to groom and reorder themselves only in small ways, we are pressed to conform significantly to whatever the current ideal is of feminine physical attractiveness. Who sets the standards of female beauty? Certainly not women; properly conditioned and prodded, we avidly acquiesce to the entire business of "beauty" to gain the patriarchs' approval.

It is men who determine not only how we must behave but also how we must present ourselves. Through fashion, through law, through "science" or religion, we are told how we ought to appear. The bound foot, the pierced ear and nose, the covered head or face, the enormous breast, the excised clitoris, the never-too-thin torso—are these ours? The near nakedness of jeans and bathing suits, the oppressive discomfort of spiked heels and garter belts; the obsession with youth, size, "sexiness"—are any of these ours? Do we do this to please ourselves? It is men who design fashions and control the media, the advertising, the magazines, the films, the cosmetic firms, the "fitness" industry, and the department stores, and who ultimately manipulate women into believing that it is we who set the trends.

It is difficult in a society so controlled by men for us to distinguish between what we think and feel genuinely, freely, and what we think and feel as accommodation to social expectation. We "love" the

little bikini that leaves us practically undressed, but do we love it because it is a joyous expression of self or do we love it because it draws approval from men? What is that bathing suit meant to accomplish? What do we have to do to our physical selves over the long term to look in that suit the way we are required to look—diet, starve, guard our movements?

We are told that today the average woman would like to lose 10 or 15 pounds, even when she is not objectively "overweight"; that fashion models weigh 23 percent less than the average woman (as opposed to 8 percent less a generation ago); that 20 to 25 percent of college women suffer from severe eating disorders; that according to the federal Centers for Disease Control, "nearly half of all teenage girls are on diets, even though the majority of them are not overweight"; that an astonishing number of young girls and women rely on diet pills, vomiting, and other destructive strategies to control their weight.[27]

What would happen if we chose *not* to wear that little bikini but instead selected a swimsuit for privacy and comfort? Would we have to choose between approval and autonomy? What is the significance of that? What does it tell us? Why do we choose as we do?

To adorn one's body out of a *self-defined* love of play and color may be self-expressive and healthy. To reject one's natural self and instead subject it to the requirements of an *alien* mold created by a separate reigning group for their interests, to surrender one's physical appearance for another's approval and protection—these are destructive because they are terribly close to surrendering one's entire sense of self. "I am, physically and nonphysically, who I am" is authentic. "I am and will become what the gaze of another wishes me to be, no matter what the cost" is fatally close to spiritual suicide. It may also be fatally close to physical suicide, captured nowhere more dramatically than in the growing willingness of women to submit to cosmetic surgery. Following the congressional hearings on the silicone implant industry and the consequences of breast reconstruction for women's health, Merle Hoffman, editor of *On the Issues*, wrote:

> It appears that having a potentially fatal disease
> like breast cancer and being small breasted or flat

chested have taken on the same life and death proportions to many women. While one can empathize with the ambivalence of the women on the panel who had to make choices about whether or not to allow one class of women to potentially risk their health and lives to have breast reconstruction, one also has to question the reality that women so eagerly make life-threatening decisions to fit someone else's definition of being sexually acceptable—an external definition that has been integrated into their own psychologies. . . . It was a purely democratic decision, one which said that all women should have the right to make the wrong choices for the wrong reasons. . . .

It was a decision that in one sweeping move reinforced and imprinted once again that women were defined, judged and found wanting or acceptable according to the size of their breasts. The women on the panel who so agonized over disqualifying the implants for purely cosmetic reasons seemed not to give a thought to the system, culture or society that spawned these ideas in the first place, that created the need and the market for women to desire reconstructed breasts even at the risk of their own lives. The fact that these decisions on implants are made more for internal rather than external approval only reinforces the insidious nature of the conditioning.[28]

Health

When children are troubled with physical ailments, they must seek out their guardians for help. So must women. Because relatively few women set or control health-care policy (a situation deftly arranged by patriarchy), when we are ill or face physical changes and "passages," *by law* and by custom we must turn to those formally charged with our care—for the most part, men. Consider how absurd and humiliating men would think it if they had to ask women for assistance whenever they had a urinary disorder, a dysfunction of the penis, or a sexual or reproductive problem! In any sane world, such exclusively female events as pregnancy and childbirth would be women's province alone. Yet in our world it is men, through such agencies as the American Medical Association (AMA) and the American Hospital Association (AHA), insurance companies, and legislatures, who determine almost entirely how these experiences are to proceed: where and how,

for example, we may give birth, what procedures will be followed, who may accompany us, who may assist. Women, at home or in clinics, may not legally contribute even informally to these affairs unless they are licensed by male-controlled agencies of various kinds.

Research into female medical needs, into surgical techniques and drug therapy for a variety of female experiences from menopause to depression, is carried on almost exclusively by males with the aid and support of the giant (male-dominated) research and grant agencies. Under policy written by men, male physicians develop, prescribe, and test contraceptives for women and may withhold them if they choose. They research and develop policy and procedures for treating conditions of the breast, uterus, and ovaries (no wonder so many of them wind up in jars!); they write theories about women's attitudes during menopause and debate the use of estrogen therapy and tranquilizers. They inform their patients that severe menstrual cramping is a problem of the mind. They tell women how to mother children. Now they manipulate women's reproductive systems to make babies in test tubes and create parents or transfer parenthood from one to another or "modify" results for more control over the process.

Through entrance into medical schools, licensing, lobbying, and legislation, patriarchy limits the participation and authority of women in health care—hence, over our own care. Historically, the AMA and AHA have fought any growth of power and prestige in the nursing associations. Now men are being encouraged to join the nursing profession to "raise the level of the profession," and, in passing, to capture the more highly skilled and highly paid positions in hospital nursing programs and in the American Nursing Association.

Control over our reproductive and medical needs is exacerbated by masculinist-masculine control over the law. Women have little power in the making of policy because, as you will see in the following chapter, we are systematically excluded from anything like full participation in government. Legal policy regarding reproduction, contraception, abortion, and illegitimacy is written, interpreted, and executed essentially by men on the advice and perspectives of "scientists" (men) and in response to their (most powerful and wealthy) constituencies (insurance companies, for example, or drug companies, legal associations, and political action committees, or PACs), which have the inclination and wherewithal to make substantial contributions to campaigns and administrations.

In matters of health and reproduction, almost more than anywhere else, women as "other" are objectified, reduced to "things," denied our own interests, and robbed of our personhood. In the current intense interest in women's reproductive lives, we are increasingly being treated as "delivery systems" of the young. The treatment of Jennifer Clarise Johnson, single mother and cocaine addict, is a perfect case in point.

> *Sanford, Fla.—A judge has opened a new avenue for the criminal prosecution of cocaine-using mothers by finding a woman guilty of delivering the drug to her newborn children through the umbilical cord.*
>
> *The decision Thursday marks the first time in the nation that a law normally used against drug dealers has been applied to a mother giving birth, a legal expert said. It applies only to the Florida judicial circuit where the woman lives, but could be applied by prosecutors in other jurisdictions, even outside Florida.*[29]

Johnson was sentenced to thirty years in prison under a law making it a felony to deliver drugs to a minor. The prosecutor, delighted with his "new tool" for solving this "great problem," centered the matter on the issue of whether newborns may be considered persons after birth and before the umbilical cord is cut. The judge decided that they may be and that drug "delivery" could mean passing cocaine to a fetus through the umbilical cord! A nice argument. Never mind that the woman has a serious and viciously difficult health problem. Never mind that the woman did not use drugs with the intention of passing drugs to her offspring, nor did she profit from it. Never mind that the law was not meant to cover such a case or that this interpretation of the law involves a most extraordinary use of the term *deliver.*

Johnson—poor, powerless, female, a "delivery system" gone wrong—is now incarcerated in a drug treatment center apart from her children, who are being raised by someone else, and denied her place and her desire to "mother." In a television interview, the prosecutor said that he saw this as a case of child abuse, pure and simple, *no different* from the intentional beating or burning of a child. How are men treated when they *do* abuse children? Are they typically given thirty-year prison sentences, whether they be drunk or sober? How are male athletes treated when they become addicted to drugs? What does the difference in treatment say about the way (the male) judge and prosecutor view women, as childbearers, as mothers (quite a different concept), and as selves—as individual, independent human persons?

Abortion

The matter of reducing women to "delivery systems," of ignoring the fact that women are people, with needs, feelings, goals, values, even when we are reproducing, is a crucial concept, for it is the heart of the antiabortion argument. It is the erasing of our personhood, together with a similar but opposite logical maneuver—the elevation of a fetus to the status of a "person"—that makes the antichoice campaign work. It is what makes the rhetoric so effective, even though it is often false and generally misleading. It is what drives the slogans and makes them appear convincing to the unpracticed eye: "Abortion is murder!" screams a highway sign. But murder is defined as the "illegal killing of one human being by another, especially with premeditated malice" (*Webster's II New Riverside University Dictionary*). If a fetus is *not* a human being—that is, a fully existent person (regardless of whether it is a potential person)—then *murder* is a misleading term. And if the intention of a woman choosing to abort a pregnancy is to care for her life, her happiness, her well-being (and in some cases the well-being of her present and future family and children), then it is not malevolence that is motivating her, and malice has nothing to do with her choice. In other words, there is very good reason to think that abortion is not at all murder, and the slogan is a lie.

"It is a baby, not a choice!" reads a popular bumper sticker. Leaving aside the grammatical games being played here, this slogan also lies. Were it not for people's perceptions being deceitfully manipulated, would anyone deny that there is a world of difference between the mass of tissue that is a fetus (especially an early fetus) and a living, breathing, experiencing *baby*. For centuries, philosophers and scientists have written about the differences between entities that are *potential* and entities that are *actual*. Do we really want to say, "It is a baby"? There are very thoughtful and moral people who believe that *it* is not a baby. Not a choice? Of course, there *is* a choice to be made—by the woman, by the person in the equation who has been erased. Put her back into the picture, and either choice is a legitimate consideration, or motherhood by coercion is the only logical end. The issue is whether women are going to be treated as intrinsically valuable, self-determining persons, "ends in themselves," as philosophers call fully functioning human beings, or, instead, once again we will be objectified and treated simply as resources for society, providers of reproduction and child care.

There are more complex issues in the question of abortion than the great majority of the antichoice contingent want anyone to think about; but think we must, for the reality is critical to women's lives.

> *As a nation, we are being asked to deny women the fundamental right to control their own bodies. We are being asked to reformulate a major policy that has broad social consequences. We are being asked to return to a time when women got abortions from motorcycle mechanics and dishwashers. . . .*
>
> *Dr. Kinsey found that in 1955, when abortion was almost entirely illegal, almost one in four American women had had an abortion by the time she was forty-five. By 1992, nineteen years after* Roe, *more than twenty-four million American women had had legal abortions in their own country and often in their own hometown. An even greater number of women have come of age, in a biological sense, since 1973. For the most part, they have no knowledge of what abortion was like when it was against the law.*
>
> *Many of today's legislators and policymakers were not old enough to hold office or perhaps even to vote in the years before Roe. When these newcomers formulate abortion policy, they often have no idea what abortion was like in the United States before 1973. How many of them know the barbaric and dangerous techniques of the abortion underground. How many know about the untold millions of*

> *women who terminated their pregnancies by whatever means available for reasons known only to them? How many know about the sheer numbers of women who died from illegal abortions? How many know anything at all about the public health consequences of recriminalizing abortion? Indeed, how many understand that the real public policy question is not whether we will have abortions but what kind of abortions we will have?*
>
> —Patricia G. Miller, *The Worst of Times*[30]

For the most part, the abortion debate is characterized by more noise than light. The most vocal antiabortion activists have tended to deflect reasonable discussion by focusing on issues that are either already apparent but moot, or for the most part irrelevant, but extremely inflammatory: Of course, life exists at conception; cells are alive. Of course, the fetus is *human* life; it certainly isn't canine or vegetable. But isn't it reasonable to ask whether it is *a* human life: that is, is it a person? Does it think, know, remember, make decisions, relate to others, and all the hundreds of things that persons do that constitute them as persons? What does one mean by *a life*, a person? A tumor is a lump of human life. Is it *a* life? Is it morally sinful to remove it from its host? A human ovum is a potential human being. Morally, must I help it to be fertilized lest it not come to fruition?

Does a potential human being become a person simply by fiat, by creating a fiction, labeling it a baby or a child (as opposed to determining if it is a baby or a child), and granting this fiction all the legal and moral rights of personhood, *all the rights denied the woman*? As women, we must ask, why is the woman less worthy of society's protection than an alleged or potential "baby"? Because it is "innocent," we are told. Here is an odd thought. How can a being that hasn't the capacity to do evil (because it has not yet lived and acted) be regarded as innocent? Doesn't innocence presuppose the ability to decide on virtue instead of vice?

Does a fetus quit being innocent upon birth? Why is that same potential baby, carried to term, born and alive and perhaps starving, less worthy of protection than it was in the womb? Why is there so much clamor directed at a woman's completing a pregnancy but not then sustained in regard to the feeding, sheltering, and aiding of that child and its mother? The great majority of America's poor, homeless, and desperate are women and their dependent children. To be substantively "prolife"— that is, *for life*—wouldn't one would need to actively care for such people? Where are their "rescuers"?

> *Here in St. Louis, where the anti-abortion movement is one of the strongest in the nation, the infant mortality rate ranks among the highest in the industrialized world—and for each white infant who dies two black infants die. Although many doctors sign the anti-abortion ads each year, I could not find an obstetrician to care for a homeless refugee woman with a complicated pregnancy who wanted her baby. There has been no demand by the heavily funded Missouri "pro-life" movement for improved prenatal care, no outrage at the decline in health-clinic services for the poor. . . .*
>
> *Here in Missouri, a mother with two children receives $282 maximum AFDC cash income, $228 maximum in food stamps. Even if she is lucky enough to have subsidized housing (and thus receive fewer benefits) she is poor, and she and her children are more likely to be ill, malnourished, and badly educated than their middle-class peers.*
>
> *Here in Missouri, one-fourth of the children who begin high school do not graduate, and one out of every five children lives at the poverty level. . . .*
>
> *Where are the thousands of marchers, led by bishops, when Emerson Electric and McDonnell Douglas and General Dynamics hold their annual meetings here to proclaim the money they have made from the arms industry? . . .*
>
> *My own fear, based on signs I have seen carried at demonstrations, is that many anti-abortion activists see birth as a punishment for sex, not as a gift.*

—MARY ANN MCGIVERN[31]

In a series on "The Changing American Family" in Missouri, the home state of the Webster case, the *St. Louis Post-Dispatch* told the story of Dawn Smith and her infant son, Benjamin. Abandoned by her boyfriend early in her pregnancy, with no place of her own to live, not yet out of business school, she was "at the point where if I couldn't talk to someone about my situation, I would explode." A Baptist crisis pregnancy center gave her a "sympathetic ear, a few baby care items," and a companion through delivery. When she went home after the delivery, however, "reality set in":

> *The phone had been disconnected because of a mix-up over her last payment. Instead of spending the next few weeks recuperating from childbirth and getting to know her son, Smith spent the time settling bills, finding a baby sitter, hauling laundry and checking out social programs that might provide them with help. . . .*
>
> *"By the time he was 3 weeks old, I was out of money. Completely out," Smith said. Although she had hoped to take a six-week maternity leave from her job, she was forced to return to work Feb. 13 (the leave had paid her only $50 a week). Benji was 33 days old.*
>
> *"I cried all the way to work, and I cried all day," Smith said. "When I left that day, I wanted to drive 90 miles per hour to get home."*
>
> *Smith now spends all of her free time with her baby. "There are 10 hours a day that I'm not with him, and I worry that some day when I go to pick him up he'll want to stay with the baby sitter instead of come with me," she said. "I want to spend all my time holding and loving him, but there are also times when I'm so tired that I just want him to go to sleep."*
>
> *The $672 Smith takes home each month barely covers her fixed bills—$295 for rent, $150 for a baby sitter, $90 for electricity, $25 for telephone service, and $13.20 for water. There's little left for food, gas and diapers, and nothing to make a dent in her outstanding bills—$200 for electricity, $250 for a 12-year-old car, $700 for past medical treatment and more than $7,000 for school loans.*
>
> *On the day she was interviewed, Smith had $35 to her name, $32 of which was needed to pay a bill. For the second week in a row, she had been unable to buy groceries. Her refrigerator contained a jar of jelly, a frozen pizza and some stale doughnuts bought for 25 cents a box. Besides baby formula, her pantry held a box of tea bags, a jar of peanut butter, a jar of honey, a box of crackers and two cans of green beans. Payday was 13 days away.[32]*

Somehow, after the delivery, when reality set in, the "helpers" were gone.

Rarely, for single mothers, poor mothers, working mothers, are there "helpers"; in fact, sometimes the "helpers" arrange things so you can't win for losing:

Church Closes Day Care, Wants Moms at Home

Little Rock, Ark. (AP)—A Baptist church board says it shut down its day care center to get mothers to stay at home because working mothers "neglect their children, damage their marriages and set a bad example.". . .

In a letter . . . [to parents], the church said that although it was sensitive to the plight of single parents, it could not continue the center because its existence encouraged mothers to work outside the home.

The letter added that families could get by on one salary if luxuries such as "big TVs, a microwave, new clothes, eating out and nice vacations" were forfeited.

"God intended for the home to be the center of a mother's world," the church said. "In Titus 2:5, women are instructed to be 'discreet, chaste, keepers at home, good and obedient to their own husbands'. . . ."[33]

The foregoing reveals an insidious intent. For the antichoice contingent, women must finish every pregnancy, whether they want children or not, whether they are prepared for them or not, whether their circumstances favor them or not. What is more, after the children arrive, they must expect no assistance, and if their lives become harder or less fulfilling, that's just the breaks. If the children suffer, that also is just too bad. One must wonder, is the ultimate commitment here to "life," or to ensuring that women remain "discreet, chaste, keepers at home, good and obedient to their own husbands"?

For several years and with growing intensity, the antifeminist, antichoice advocates have thrown up a smoke screen against their very real agenda: control over women's lives, our self-determination, our right to make decisions for ourselves, and our personal, economic, and social destinies. The issue for us as women is not only whether we wish to carry a pregnancy to term, but whether we wish to bear or raise a child. For whether we raise a child or give it up, whether it is healthy or disabled, whether we live with its father or not, few things can change one's life more dramatically or more permanently than having a child.

We are told that there is a "simple" alternative to aborting an unwanted pregnancy—we can give a child to someone else to raise, to a "loving and good couple who desperately want that baby." Women who have taken that route often describe it as far less than "simple."

The loss of a child to adoption is a unique and unnatural one. Unlike death, which is final, adoption creates a loss that is renewed daily, as each day is a new day of trying to live with the surrendered child whose life continues separately. It is a limbo loss, in which there are constant questions but no answer. Is my child well or ill? Happy or miserable? Alive or dead?[34]

Who is to decide, besides each of us ourselves, whether we should lend our life to those changes? On what moral grounds do we make that decision? Who besides the woman involved should have the right to do that?

Since 1973, when abortion was legalized through Roe v. Wade, the anti-abortion movement has worked to limit the ability of women to "choose" abortion. These efforts became part of a larger backlash which opposed gains made in the late 1960s and early 1970s by the women's liberation movement. Legalized abortion was fought for and won by that movement as part of a new and comprehensive vision of women's potential. In the 1970s and 1980s, abortion came to symbolize that vision as the New Right, driven by anti-feminism, made opposition to abortion the centerpiece of its own social and political program. The attack on abortion was part of an overall attack on women's freedom. This included a successful campaign to defeat the Equal Rights Amendment; efforts to constrain the rights of teenage girls through "Squeal Laws" which would force providers to notify parents if a minor sought contraception or a pregnancy test; the "Chastity Bill," which provided 30 million federal dollars to promote chastity among teens; gutting of affirmative action programs; and, most recently, efforts to control women's behavior during pregnancy by incarceration and other punitive measures.

In both the propaganda and policies of the Right, hostility to women's autonomy is the unifying link between opposition to abortion and opposi-

tion to other feminist goals. Abortion rights are central to and have come to symbolize women's control. The Right opposes that control in the broadest sense. That is why they oppose sex education, government-funded contraception and family planning clinics, gay rights, and government programs directed at the battering of women and children within their homes. But their fight against abortion is the most virulent, and they have made real gains.

—MARLENE GERBER FRIED, *From Abortion to Reproductive Freedom*[35]

Perhaps the most important gain that the antiabortion, antiwoman forces have made is to push the discussion about pregnancy decision making off-center. Women have begun to speak in whispers, where once we shouted for the right to determine our destinies. Even feminists, even prochoice activists, can be heard to say, "Well, of course, abortion is a terrible thing, but it's better than . . ." or "Sometimes it's necessary" or "It's the better of two terrible choices." Once we say yes, of course abortion is terrible, we have conceded the question, for expediency is probably not a sufficient moral counter to evil.

In fact, however, there are good reasons to think that abortion is not terrible, not merely expedient. There are many reasonable, ethical people who believe that although abortion may be emotionally trying, it can be a most positive, moral, life-loving choice.

From time immemorial women have risked their lives, have placed themselves in the most dreadful of situations when they felt it was necessary, and moral, to secure an abortion. I don't think we should ever believe that these women will allow themselves to be denied abortions by people who do something as simple as get arrested in front of clinics. Prochoice opponents need to be told that in no uncertain terms. Indeed their actions are remarkably trivial when they are weighed against the courage and decency and dedication and tenacity of women who need this service and persevere to get it.

As you reflect on this phenomenon, try to envision Operation Rescue's antecedents. The exponents of Operation Rescue compare themselves to U.S. civil rights demonstrators of the 1960s, but they don't summon a positive picture for me. Instead, I

see a group of school children trying to enter a school in the South, and I see two lines of people, adults, mothers and fathers, on either side of those children. There are people screaming, people hating, people with meanness and ruthlessness in their faces screaming at little children who want to enter a school and exercise the right to a quality, equal education. If we want to use the comparison of the civil rights movement, the comparison is very simple. Screaming people do not parallel the civil rights activists who were trying to exercise their rights; these screamers today parallel those zealots who were trying to prevent other citizens from exercising rights they legitimately held.

I think these are the images we need to keep before us: images of women willing to do whatever necessary to secure needed abortions; images of women acting unselfishly and with as much compassion as possible. They are courageous images that clearly contrast with pictures of individuals who are prepared to force or coerce others into following their ways and their visions of righteousness.

—FRANCES KISSLING, "Operation Rescue," *Conscience: A Newsjournal of Prochoice Catholic Opinion.*[36]

What is the proper response to those who would rob us of our right to choose? To those filled with hate and the need for power, the answer is obvious. For those whose arrogance is born of a belief in their own right to speak for God, the clearest rebuke would be to require them to look at their own hidden needs:

"Rescue" Activist Speaks

Twenty-five-year-old Mary Ann Baney is on the staff of Operation Rescue (OR) in Binghamton, New York. A Pittsburgh native, Baney has been active in the antiabortion movement since September, 1987. After hearing Randall Terry speak at a rally, she says, she was moved to activism. "I agreed with him that we have to act like abortion is murder. We have to do something."

Her first involvement took her to Cherry Hill, New Jersey, OR's first "rescue" site, a practice run for the week-long assault on New York City clinics that took place in May, 1988. "I saw men and women coming to kill their children," says Baney. "I cared about them and their children. Out of love for them, and obedience to God, I sat down. I know murder is against God's commandments."

Baney found her participation empowering. "It was the most valuable thing I ever did. It took courage to sit down. But I know one couple who changed their minds and had the baby; a boy was born a few months ago. He would not have been alive without that 'rescue'".

Raised Catholic, Baney is now part of the Roman Catholic Charismatic Renewal movement. "In a sense it's like being born again," says Baney. "I'm spirit filled."

After the Cherry Hill protest—at which 211 Operation Rescue members were arrested—Baney returned to Pittsburgh and helped form a local OR group there. Then in May she spent a week doing daily "rescues" in New York City. This was followed by participation in two "rescues" in Philadelphia. "The week before July 19, the start of the Democratic Convention in Atlanta, I was laid off by the lawn care company I worked for. Since I was free, I went to Atlanta and ended up spending 36 days in jail for protesting abortion. It was one of the highlights of my life. I grew so much spiritually because I was doing God's will. It was so valuable. I felt a great sense of doing something worthwhile."

Baney says she was particularly impressed by the sense of community forged during her month-long incarceration. "God moved in the jail. The pastors all worshipped together. As the group got smaller we were moved in with the other inmates and we shared the love of God with them. God's presence changed the jail to a place of peace and love." (OR members were released from prison when they gave the authorities their real names and addresses. Most identified themselves to police as Baby Jane or Baby John Doe when they were initially arrested. OR staffer Marti Hendrickson told me that this alias was used to allow participants to "take a stand on behalf of the unborn; to be their voice and show that we won't let any more babies be murdered.")

Baney started working with OR full-time upon her release from jail. There's nothing, she says, that she'd rather be doing. Single and childless, she sees herself as part of a generation that has come to its senses, the generation that came of age in the 1980s

and "found out the hard way about love and values. Many of my friends wish they'd remained pure, waited till marriage to have intercourse," she says. "They now know that they are to obey God, rather than men. They read the Bible and know that they are to render to God things that are God's. These children we "rescue" are the children of God. It's God's will."[37]

Apparently such absolute belief justifies arson and chemical attacks, physical and verbal harassment, stalking of pregnant women, medical workers, and their families, and even murder. A student in one of my ethics courses told the class that he'd like to "shake the hand of the guy that murdered that doctor in Florida." He was that prolife! And what's more, he didn't want to talk about it anymore. He was sick of the whole thing.

The matter of abortion is extremely complex, both ethically and legally, and the reasonable arguments both for and against (and there *are* reasonable arguments both for and against) are numerous and complicated. The following three points are crucial: First, in determining the matter of abortion laws and statutes, Supreme Court decisions, and constitutional amendments, we must take great care to distinguish legal rights and responsibilities from what we perceive to be moral obligations. Many acts one might wish performed or not performed, on moral or ethical grounds, cannot and should not be compelled or prohibited by law. Second, we must pay attention to the matter of consistency. People not actively or even ideologically opposed to killing real adult human beings in war or by capital punishment are clamoring for laws against killing a fetus. People little concerned with the quality of the ensuing life of either mother or child, pressing hard for welfare "reform," for example, are determined to maintain biological life at any cost. Although it is fallacious to attack an argument on the basis of who proposes it, in ethics the question of motivation is always pertinent. Third, it is valuable to place the issue of reproductive freedom into historical context. Strong analogies exist between the reproductive freedom movement of today and the movement in the 1930s to legalize the prescription, use, and sale of contraceptives. Those in favor argued then, as today, on the grounds of constitutionality, personal freedom, the quality of life for all, and the benefits of population control to society. Then, as now, their opponents accused them of immorality, murder (of future generations), opposition to God's will, and the destruction of the family and the social order.

Antirights activists have cast the issue in the context of good versus evil, godly versus ungodly, the forces of religion and morality opposing the forces of evil, as if all who opposed abortion were speaking for and with God and those who are pro-choice are immoral or atheistic or both. It goes without saying that not all antirights people are good or godly. It does, however, need to be emphasized that the decision to have an abortion or to support others' right to do so can be a highly positive and moral choice. The decision to end a pregnancy comes to many women (and men) through serious ethical reflection, and/or moral or religious meditation. Further, many highly moral people support women's personal and *legal* right to choose, even though they may oppose abortion for themselves or be unsure about where they might stand should the situation arise. Additionally, many religious organizations and institutions are on record supporting women's right to choose. One organization, The Religious Coalition for Reproductive Choice, provides statements supporting abortion rights by more than thirty organizations, among them: American Baptist Churches (USA), American Ethical Union, American Friends Service Committee, American Jewish Committee, American Jewish Congress, Disciples of Christ, Episcopal Church, Lutheran Women's Caucus, Presbyterian Church (USA), Reorganized Church of Jesus Christ of Latter Day Saints, United Church of Christ, and United Methodist Church. The Coalition states:

> For communities of faith, reproductive rights issues are difficult ones. People with equally committed religious convictions differ greatly in their opinions on these sensitive issues.
>
> Widespread denominational support exists for the right of women to choose safe and legal abortion, but the public has been falsely led to believe that all religions are opposed to abortion rights. The religious pro-choice community has a deep respect for the value of potential human life and an equally deep commitment to women as responsible, moral decision makers. . . .

> The Coalition believes that the right of reproductive freedom is intrinsically tied to religious liberty. . . .[38]

Sexuality

The matter of women's sexuality is a many-faceted topic, rarely treated either sanely or seriously outside women's studies. Yet in the analysis of our life space, our sexuality is an extremely important issue. It is ironic, as well as indicative of the role women play in a patriarchal society, that the aspect of our being by which we are most defined by the male hegemony—our sexuality—is also the aspect most alienated.

Everywhere around the world, women's bodies are made use of by men: Men buy and sell women's bodies in prostitution, in so-called gentlemen's bars, in marriage and concubinage, in pornography, in music videos, and in other ways, or they take it in rape, abuse, stalking, and harassment. Through laws governing reproductive rights, they control or attempt to control our reproductive systems and the children we produce. In many parts of the world, our children are not considered ours—they (and their mothers) are under the control of their fathers and community patriarchs.

Men may direct their own sexuality, and they may determine how women's sexuality is to be used. Women who have sex when and how they wish, for their own reasons and in their own interests, are at risk in various ways. Women's "lust" has been blamed for unwanted pregnancy. During a discussion in an ethics class about the moral issues in abortion, a *female* student, opposed to abortion rights, argued that "if women want to go out and have sex any time they feel like it, they should take the consequences." She had bought the patriarchal program. Against her own interests, she was proposing motherhood as punishment for unregulated sex. A male student concurred. The best way, he argued, to avoid unwanted pregnancy was to abstain from sex. I countered that his solution would mean that many women who wanted no more children or wanted none for a long time would have to give up sex indefinitely. His answer: "So?" "Would you give up sex?" I asked him. "I don't have to," he answered. "I don't get pregnant." Indeed.

In the United States, so-called conservative politicians have been advocating an aggressive "premarital abstinence movement"; through the Republican Party, they have managed to make federal grants to high schools conditional upon their willingness to make "abstinence education" a central part of their sex education programs. They are scoring victories, and it hardly requires effort to imagine on whom that program will fall hardest.

In Chapter 3, we saw that, except for our role as mother and caretaker (procreator or nurturer), our only function in patriarchy is to serve as sexual playmate. In the patriarchal environment, we are submerged in that guise. Our clothing is designed, our movements are trained, and our behavior is coached to be seductive. Though sex and appearing "sexy" is a prescribed part of the curriculum, women have been prohibited from enjoying sex or sensuality, from using sex to our own ends.

The women's movement has argued that in patriarchy, women are all reduced to the status of "sex objects." That does not mean simply that we are sometimes the object of sexual interest or desire (which most of us, on some occasion, have wished to be) but that we are formally perceived and treated as objects for sex: sex-things. Unlike a human being, a thing is not thought to have feelings, needs, and rights because a thing is not thought of as a subjectivity, as a self.

In patriarchy, women in our sexual roles ideally function not as self-affirming, self-fulfilling human beings but rather as beautiful dolls to be looked at, touched, felt, experienced for arousal, used for titillation (for sexual release or the sale of merchandise), to be enjoyed, consumed, and ultimately used up and traded in for a different model. We may respond to sexual contact or even enjoy it, but not for our own pleasure (only bad women are so "selfish"), only for the greater pleasure of the user. Our sexual role in patriarchy is to be acted on, not to act ourselves, except insofar as this serves the users' interests or needs. Nothing offers more proof of this than the practice euphemistically called female circumcision—actually a variety of forms of female genital mutilation involving excision of the clitoris, performed on millions of women to "make them more beautiful," to make them "clean," to "prepare them for marriage." The procedure can, and usually does, make sexual intercourse very painful, perhaps even dangerous, for the woman; and, of course, without a clitoris, the seat of sexuality in women, orgasm is impossible.

Full sexuality and sensuality are utterly conscious and healthily self-centered as well as other-centered. As long as we accept the patriarchal image of women as copulating machines, so long as we allow ourselves to be washed, perfumed, painted, and dressed, playing a part, totally selfless, we will experience alienation in sex and alienation from our bodies. In patriarchy, women are objectified, passive, and self-abnegating, but authentic sexuality is subjective, active, and self-affirming.

There is much to learn from lesbian views on love and sex. As women loving women because they are women, lesbians point out that they are in a special position with regard to liberating female sexuality. Free of the heterosexual politics of the usual gender-based roles and prescriptions, more positive and self-affirming as women, more acutely aware of the needs of their partners because, in a sense, they are their partners, lesbian women contend that they are more able to discover and express authentic female sexuality than heterosexual counterparts. Although lesbian couples share the conflicts of any two people in an intimate relationship, the experiences of many lesbian couples have valuable implications for creating nonexploitative relationships.

VIOLENCE

Canadian novelist Margaret Atwood once asked a male friend why men feel threatened by women. He replied: "They are afraid women will laugh at them." She then asked a group of women why they felt threatened by men. They answered: "We're afraid of being killed."

—JANE CAPUTI AND DIANA E. H. RUSSELL[39]

The right of men to control the female body is a cornerstone of patriarchy. . . . There is a different kind of terrorism, one that so pervades our culture that we have learned to live with it as though it were the natural order of things. Its targets are females—of all ages, races and classes. It is the common characteristic of rape, wife battery, incest, pornography, harassment, and all forms of sexual violence. I call it sexual terrorism because it is a system by which *males frighten and, by frightening, control and dominate females.*

—CAROL J. SHEFFIELD[40]

Rape is the logical outcome if men act according to the "masculine mystique" and women act according to the "feminine mystique."

—DIANNE HERMAN[41]

Man's discovery that his genitalia could serve as a weapon to generate fear must rank as one of the most important discoveries of prehistoric times . . . I believe rape has played a critical function. It is nothing more or less than a conscious process of intimidation by which all men *keep* all women *in a state of fear.*

—SUSAN BROWNMILLER[42]

Woman abuse is viewed here as an historical expression of male domination manifested within the family and currently reinforced by the institutions, economic "arrangements," and sexist division of labor within capitalist society.

—SUSAN SCHECHTER[43]

Violence against wives—indeed, violence against women in general—is as old as recorded history, and cuts across all societies and socioeconomic groups. There are few phenomena so pervasive and yet so ignored.

—LORI HEISE[44]

Male survivors charge that feminists see rape as a "man vs. woman" issue, emphasizing the central role male violence plays in stunting and destroying women's lives, and they're right. The distinction is that while many women, and some men, are victimized by rape, all women are oppressed by it, and any victimization of women occurs in a context of oppression most men simply do not understand. Rape for men is usually a bizarre, outrageous tear in the fabric of reality. For women, rape is often a confirmation of relative powerlessness, of men's contempt for women, and its trauma is reinforced every day in a thousand obvious and subtle ways.

—FRED PELKER[45]

There is no question within the women's movement that we live in a society permeated by male violence and that a great deal of that violence is directed against women.

FACTS
IN THE UNITED STATES:

One rape is reported every six minutes.[46]

Only one out of every ten rapes is reported.[47]

According to *Uniform Crime Reports,* published by the FBI, one in four women are raped. One in ten rape victims brings charges. Of the cases that are reported, only 20 percent make it to court. Half of these lead to a conviction (D.C. Rape Crisis Center). In the end, an estimated 97 to 98 percent of all rapists go free. Most rape again. Men who are caught have committed, on average, 14 rapes. Nor is a conviction any guarantee that they'll stop. Convicted rapists have one of the highest recidivism rates of any class of criminals.[48]

One in three females will be sexually assaulted by age 18, 70 percent by men they know.[49]

Reported in the higher education section of *What Counts: The Complete Harper's Index,* 35 percent of male college students say they might commit rape if there were no chance of being caught. Eighty-four percent say that some women look as though they're just asking to be raped.[50]

Nearly 20 percent of all American women were sexually abused as children. In cases of incest, nine times out of ten, the victim is a girl. The first sexual abuse generally occurs at age ten— although 37 percent report abuse at an even earlier age. Approximately 70 percent of young prostitutes and 80 percent of female drug users were victims of incest.[51]

Within the next decade, 25 million girls will be sexually abused, half of them under the age of eleven.[52]

Bureau of Justice figures show approximately 456,000 cases of domestic violence per year, more than half committed by a spouse or ex-spouse. It is estimated that only one case in ten is reported.[53]

A woman is abused every eighteen seconds.[54]

One in every five women involved in an intimate relationship with a man is beaten repeatedly by that man.[55]

Four women are killed by their boyfriends or husbands every day.[56]

Twenty-two to 35 percent of women who seek help in emergency rooms show signs of battering. Among 18- to 20-year-old women who appear at the emergency room door for trauma injuries, 42 percent have been battered. And battered women don't try to keep it a secret; 75 percent will reveal the cause of their injuries if asked. But doctors, unless educated about what to look for and what to do about it, are able to recognize abuse only 3 to 6 percent of the time.[57]

Three to four million women . . . become victims of domestic abuse every year, about 1,320 of them fatally. . . . Domestic violence is the leading cause of injury and violent death for American women, resulting in more injuries than rape, auto accidents and muggings combined, according to the National Woman Abuse Prevention Project.[58]

Forty percent of all women who are murdered are killed by their male partners.[59]

At least four women are murdered by their partners every day (National Coalition Against Domestic Violence, 1988). . . . American homicide statistics compiled by the Centers for Disease Control in Atlanta, Georgia, were analyzed by psychologist Angela Browne and sociologist Kirk Williams. They found an increase in the number of women being killed by abusive partners in 35 states; in 25 states, most of these women were killed after they separated from or divorced their male partners.[60]

Some studies have found that at least 40 percent of women who kill do so in self-defense (*WIN News*). A California state prison study found that 93 percent of the women who had killed their mates had been battered by them; 67 percent of these women indicated the homicide resulted from an attempt to protect themselves or their children (National Woman Abuse Prevention Project, 1989).[61]

In the 1980s, almost half of all homeless women were refugees of domestic violence (*Time*, Special Issue, Fall 1990). As of 1988, one-third of the one million battered women who sought emergency shelter each year could find none (Women and Housing Task Force, National Low-Income Housing Coalition). In the United States, there are three times as many animal shelters as there are shelters for victims of domestic abuse (Senate Judiciary Committee).[62]

More than one million women are stalked each year, according to a Justice Department study. One in twelve, or 8.2 million women, will be stalked at some point in their lives. Fifty-nine percent are stalked by current or former partners. Eighty percent of the women stalked by intimates had been physically assaulted by them. According to Attorney General Janet Reno, "Stalking is an act of terror that builds a prison of fear around its victims."[63]

AROUND THE GLOBE:

Every year in Pakistan, hundreds of women of all ages are reported killed in the name of honor. . . . Many more of these murders undoubtedly go unreported. Almost all go unpunished. So-called honor killings are, in fact, the most extreme example of how Pakistani women's lives are circumscribed by traditions enforcing seclusion and submission to men.[64]

Every day, 6,000 girls are genitally mutilated.[65] The procedure has been performed on 85–114 million girls and women worldwide.[66]

Every year in India, 5,000 brides are murdered or commit suicide because their marriage dowries are considered inadequate.[67]

In Russia, half of all murder victims are women killed by their male partners.[68]

Large-scale surveys in ten countries estimate that 17 to 33 percent of women have been physically assaulted by an intimate partner. In Papua, New Guinea, 18 percent of married women receive hospital treatment for injuries inflicted by their husbands.[69]

Domestic violence is one of the leading causes of female injuries in almost every country in the world, and it accounts in some countries for the largest percentage of hospital visits by women.[70]

Thousands of Burmese women and girls have been trafficked into what amounts to female sexual slavery in Thailand. As of January 1994, estimates of Burmese girls working in brothels in Thailand ranged from 20,000 to 30,000, with approximately 10,000 new recruits brought in each year.[71]

Women in the North and the South live with the risk of physical harm in ways that have no direct parallels for men. The experience and fear of violence are threads in women's lives that intertwine with their most basic human-security needs at all levels—personal, community, environmental, economic, and political. In virtually every nation, violence or the threat of it, particularly at home, shrinks the range of choices open to women and girls, limiting not only their mobility and their control over their own lives but, ultimately, their ability to imagine mobility and control over their lives.

Experts tell us this is exactly the aim of violence against women. It may not be the conscious intention of each batterer, or every rapist, but, as research on gender violence mounts, it points ever more forcefully to the conclusion that, as a social phenomenon, violence against women is not about sex; it is not even about conflict. It is about control. It is not an aberration; rather, it is an extension of the ideology that gives men the right to control women's behavior, their mobility, their access to material resources, and their labor, both productive and reproductive.

—Charlotte Bunch, Roxanna Carrillo, and Rima Shore[72]

Feminists agree: Male violence against women is an integral part of the gender system; it is largely sanctioned and reinforced by social institutions—the courts, the media, the economic system, religions, and others; it has an agenda, a goal—the control of women by men through fear. What is more, the social system has been manipulated so that women have been prohibited from defending ourselves. Not until the women's movement created women's self-help groups, coalitions against violence, rape crisis centers, and battered women's shelters did we have any recourse besides protection by men.

Protection

In the system of chivalry, men protect women against men. This is not unlike the protection relationship which the Mafia established with small businesses in the early part of this century. Indeed, *chivalry is an age-old protection racket which depends for its existence on rape.*

—Susan Griffin, *Rape: The Power of Consciousness*[73]

Ordinarily, nations and cultures grant their citizens the right of self-protection. Self-defense is deemed a natural and appropriate right. In patriarchy, however, so far as women are concerned, that is not true. No written law prohibits us from defending ourselves against attack; that would be unthinkable! Instead, we are kept from defending ourselves by two main devices. First, the kinds of attacks directed specifically against women (such as rape and many forms of prostitution) are simply defined away as not attacks or not crimes. The burden is shifted to the victim to prove not only that certain acts took place but that they are indeed criminal. Second, the entire set of rules and behaviors imposed on women through the requirements of "femininity" render us either passive or weak (or both) and thus unable to defend ourselves; nor are we allowed by law to compensate for our lesser strength and size with weapons or similar protective devices. In patriarchy, men as a class are charged with the protection of women. This is ironic because, for the most part, it is men as a class from whom we must be protected. It is men who rape, batter, exploit, and prostitute women for their own interests.

Nor is the issue easily explained away by the proposition that the part of the group that attacks is different from the part that defends. The same man who rapes may also be a husband or lover, though not necessarily of the raped woman. The same man who batters and beats a woman may be her own husband or lover. When one accepts friendship or companionship from a man—a date, a ride, a dinner—one cannot be sure what payment may be exacted, even forcibly, in return.

Those who, like slaves or prisoners, are not permitted or are not able to defend themselves against any kind of attack by any thing or person are deprived of a basic prerequisite to freedom, integrity, confidence, viability, and independence. It matters little whether the prohibition to self-defense is imposed by law or by lore. Total dependence on others for protection, particularly when those others are the very persons from whom one must be protected, does not work.

It may be said that women are not protected simply by men but by law, the courts, judges, and the police. Feminists point out that the percentage of women in legislatures, courts, and police forces is still far too small; the number who have any power in those areas is even smaller, and they are hampered by a legacy of masculinist decision making.

Women beaten and battered by their male partners are only recently beginning to receive even meager attention by society, much of it reversed by the Reagan-Bush years. Women raped or abused—by strangers, lovers, or relatives—have had little recourse in the courts and received little restitution. A patriarchal economy and society forces women to barter their bodies for goods and survival, and they are harassed and imprisoned. The use of brute force by men against women, in an environment in which we may not defend ourselves, is an act of political terror meant to keep us in the "place" devised for us.

CONCLUSION

This chapter has barely begun to lay open the many layers of women's private experiences in patriarchy. Much more remains to examine, much more to tell. Until now, much of the story has been painful, but as feminists point out, recognition of some of the harsh realities is the first spur to change.

There are some important thoughts to keep firmly in mind. Having been excluded from the inner power circle of patriarchy, women have also not been absorbed by it. Women have a unique position in society in that we have a more rounded, more balanced perception of it. Having lived and grown and studied in patriarchy, we know it intimately. Having lived on its periphery, often in contest with it, we also understand it more critically. With our "consciousnesses" raised, we are in a much stronger position to change patriarchy than those in the center who are more its captives. We have extraordinary social contributions to make.

We have, too, special options in our personal lives. Many have contended that a more satisfying life flows from challenge. I believe that, and so do many other feminists.

It is extremely difficult to break from the familiar, which is comfortable even in its inadequacy. It is hard indeed to alter behaviors, relationships, and

values that hold at least some attraction for us in order to move toward something that we can only dimly see at times, but something that we know must be better. May Sarton has said, "It is only when we can believe that we are creating the soul that life has any meaning, but when we can believe it—and I do and always have—then there is nothing we do that is without meaning and nothing that we suffer that does not hold the seed of creation in it."[74] Because the oppression of women has in large part been an oppression of our souls (our character, integrity, and spirit), feminist activism is as much as anything else an attempt to reclaim our souls, to rebuild them. This is the source of the buoyant excitement so many feminists carry, even side by side with the pain of recognition. It is the source of our pride in the achievements and successes we win. Rewards are only as great as the risks one has to take to gain them.

Notes

1. *My Best Friend's Wedding*, directed by P. J. Hogan, produced by Jerry Zucker and Ronald Bass, Tristar Pictures.

2. Quoted in Timothy H. Brubaker and Judy A. Kimberly, "Challenges to the American Family," in *Family Relations: Challenges for the Future,* ed. Timothy H. Brubaker (Newbury Park, CA: Sage, 1993), p. 4.

3. "Marriage losing key role in families," *USA Today,* (11/24/99), p. 1.

4. Sanford M. Dornbusch and Myra H. Strober, "Our Perspective," in *Feminism, Children and the New Families,* ed. Sanford M. Dornbusch and Myra H. Strober (New York: Guilford Press, 1988), pp. 3–24, passim.

5. Dornbusch and Strober, "Our Perspective."

6. Dornbusch and Strober, "Our Perspective."

7. Dornbusch and Strober, "Our Perspective."

8. Dornbusch and Strober, "Our Perspective."

9. Dornbusch and Strober, "Our Perspective," p. 17.

10. Kristine M. Baber and Katherine R. Allen, *Women and Families: Feminist Reconstructions* (New York: Guilford Press, 1992), p. 36.

11. Jessie Bernard, "The Paradox of the Happy Marriage," in *Women in Sexist Society,* ed. Vivian Gornick and Barbara Moran (New York: Basic Books, 1971), p. 147.

12. Jessie Bernard, "The Paradox," p. 147. See also Jessie Bernard, *The Future of Marriage* (New York: Bantam Books, 1972).

13. Carol Tavris and Carole Offir, *The Longest War* (New York: Harcourt Brace Jovanovich, 1977), p. 222.

14. Tavris and Offir, *Longest War,* p. 232.

15. U.S. Bureau of the Census (Washington, DC: Government Printing Office, 1994).

16. For statistics on alimony and child support, see the reading, "Women and the American Economy," by Elyce Rotella, in Chapter 7 of this book.

17. U.S. Bureau of the Census and Bureau of Labor Statistics (Washington, DC: Government Printing Office, 1999).

18. Rotella, "Women and the American Economy," in Chapter 7 of this book.

19. Dornbusch and Strober, "Our Perspective," p. 14.

20. Harriet Nerlove Mischel and Robert Fuhr, "Maternal Employment: Its Psychological Effects on Children and Their Families," in Dornbusch and Strober, *Feminism, Children and the New Families,* pp. 194–195.

21. Shulamith Firestone, *The Dialectic of Sex: The Case for Feminist Revolution* (New York: Bantam Books, 1971), pp. 127, 135.

22. W. B. O'Reilly, "Where Equal Opportunity Fails: Corporate Men and Women in Dual-Career Families" (Ph.D. dissertation, Stanford University, 1983), quoted in Myra H. Strober, "Two-Earner Families," in Dornbusch and Strober, *Feminism, Children, and the New Families,* p. 178.

23. [In Strober, "Two-Earner Families"] J. Steihm, "Invidious Intimacy," *Social Policy* 6, no. 5: 12–16.

24. [In Strober, "Two-Earner Families"] "The empirical evidence is unclear on whether two-earner couples are less likely to move than one-earner couples, even when their occupations and incomes are relatively similar." See W. T. Markham, "Sex, Relocation, and Occupational Advancement," *Women and Work: An Annual Review* 2, ed. A. H. Stromberg, L. Larwood, and B. A. Gutek (Beverly Hills, CA: Sage, 1987).

25. Strober, "Two-Earner Families."

26. Carol J. Barrett, "Women in Widowhood," *Signs* 2, no. 4 (Summer 1978), p. 856.

27. *St. Louis Post-Dispatch,* November 4, 1991, p. 2B.

28. Merle Hoffman, "Editorial," *On the Issues* 22 (Spring 1992), p. 38.

29. *St. Louis Post-Dispatch,* July 17, 1989, p. 5A. Copyright © 1989 Pulitzer Publishing Company. Reprinted with permission.

30. Patricia G. Miller, *The Worst of Times* (New York: HarperCollins, 1993), pp. 1–2.

31. Mary Ann McGivern, *St. Louis Post-Dispatch,* February 17, 1989.

32. *St. Louis Post-Dispatch,* March 26, 1989, pp. 5D, 9D. Copyright © 1989 Pulitzer Publishing Company. Reprinted with permission.

33. *St. Louis Post-Dispatch,* April 4, 1997, p. 4A.

34. Carole Anderson and Lee Campbell, with Mary Anne Cohen, "Adoption Abuse," *Womenwise* 5, no. 3 (Fall 1983).

35. Marlene Gerber Fried, *From Abortion to Reproductive Freedom* (Boston: South End Press, 1990), p. 3.

36. Frances Kissling, "Operation Rescue," in *Conscience: A Newsjournal of Prochoice Catholic Opinion* 10, no. 1 (January/February 1989), p. 8.

37. Reported by Eleanor J. Bader in *New Directions for Women* 18, no. 2 (March/April 1989), p. 14. Reprinted with permission of *New Directions for Women.*

38. "We Affirm," Religious Coalition for Abortion Rights, 100 Maryland Avenue, N.E., Washington, DC 20002.

39. Jane Caputi and Diana E. H. Russell, "Femicide: Sexual Terrorism Against Women," in *Femicide: The Politics of Woman Killing,* ed. Jill Radford and Diana E. H. Russell (New York: Twayne, 1992), p. 13.

40. Carol J. Sheffield, "Sexual Terrorism," in *Women: A Feminist Perspective,* 4th ed., ed. Jo Freeman (Mountain View, CA: Mayfield, 1984), p. 3.

41. Dianne Herman, "Rape Culture," in *Women: A Feminist Perspective,* p. 34.

42. Susan Brownmiller, *Against Our Will* (New York: Bantam Books, 1976), p. 5.

43. Susan Schechter, *Women and Male Violence* (Boston: South End Press, 1982), p. 209.

44. Lori Heise, "Crimes of Gender," *World-Watch* (March/April 1989), p. 12.

45. Fred Pelker, "Raped: A Male Survivor Breaks His Silence," *On the Issues* 22 (Spring 1992), p. 40.

46. Pelker, "Raped," 40.

47. Illinois Coalition Against Sexual Assault (ICASA).

48. Tiffany Devitt, "Media Circus at Palm Beach Rape Trial," *Extra! A Publication of FAIR,* Special Issue (1992), p. 9.

49. Devitt, "Media Circus," 9.

50. "The Hard Facts," statistics reprinted from the higher education section of *What Counts: The Complete Harper's Index,* published by Henry Holt. Reported in *Lingua Franca* 2, no. 1 (October 1991), p. 5.

51. Susan Dworkin, "Can We Save the Girls?" *New Directions for Women* 20, no. 5 (September/October 1991), p. 3.

52. NOW Legal Defense and Education Fund.

53. Louise Bausch and Mary Kimbrough, *Voices Set Free: Battered Women Speak from Prison* (St. Louis: Women's Self-Help Center, 1986), p. ix.

54. Bausch and Kimbrough, *Voices Set Free*, p. 3.

55. Illinois Coalition Against Sexual Assault and the Illinois Coalition Against Domestic Violence, "Male Violence Against Women," pamphlet.

56. Geri Redden, founder and director of the Education Center on Family Violence in St. Louis, reported in the *St. Louis Post-Dispatch*, May 6, 1992, p. 10A.

57. *Ms.* 2, no. 5 (March/April 1992), p. 39.

58. Martha Shirk, "Domestic Violence Is a Leading Hazard for Women," *St. Louis Post-Dispatch*, May 6, 1992, p. 10A.

59. Shirk, "Domestic Violence," p. 10A.

60. Constance A. Bean, *Women Murdered by the Men They Loved* (Binghamton, NY: Haworth Press, 1992), p. 6.

61. Merle Hoffman, "Editorial," *On the Issues: The Progressive Woman's Quarterly* 21 (Winter 1991), p. 3.

62. *Extra! A Publication of FAIR*, Special Issue (1992).

63. Gary Fields, "The Nation," *USA Today*, November 14, 1997, p. 3A.

64. *Amnesty International USA* 24, no. 1 (Winter 2000), p. 1.

65. SIGI (Sisterhood Is Global Institute), R.E.S.O.U.R.C.E.S., 8/24/99. Http://www.sigi.org/Resources/stats.htm

66. Rabia Terri Harris, "Women, Spirituality, and Nonviolence," *Fellowship* 61, no. 11–12 (November/December 1996), p. 3.

67. SIGI, R.E.S.O.U.R.C.E.S.

68. SIGI, R.E.S.O.U.R.C.E.S.

69. Harris, "Women, Spirituality, and Nonviolence," p. 3.

70. "Domestic Violence," *The Human Rights Watch Global Report on Women's Human Rights* (New York: Human Rights Watch, 1995), p. 341

71. "Trafficking of Women and Girls," *The Human Rights Watch Global Report on Women's Human Rights* (New York: Human Rights Watch, 1995), p. 205.

72. Charlotte Bunch, Roxanna Carrillo, and Rima Shore, "Violence Against Women," *Women in the Third World: An Encyclopedia of Contemporary Issues*, ed. Nelly P. Stromquist (New York: Garland, 1998), pp. 59–60.

73. Susan Griffin, *Rape: The Power of Consciousness* (San Francisco: Harper & Row, 1979), p. 10.

74. May Sarton, *Journal of a Solitude* (New York: Norton, 1973), p. 67.

Carnival Queen

Mavis Hara

The poems and stories of Mavis Hara have been published in Bamboo Ridge, A Hawaii Writers' Quarterly. *Her work has been anthologized in* Home to Stay *(Greenfield Review Press) and* Growing Up Asian American *(Morrow).*

The author tells us that "Carnival Queen" is a fictional piece set in the 1960s, and that the high schools in Hawaii that inspired the story no longer have beauty contests. They have replaced them with women's athletics programs.

"Carnival Queen" is nonetheless no less relevant today than it was in the 1960s. Don't most women still struggle to meet the standards of appearance and fashion decreed by media and culture? Are not minority women still subjected to the expectations and stereotypes of the dominant group? Are not women still pitted against one another? Don't most of us still struggle with self-deprecation if we do not or cannot conform—if we aren't skinny enough, or young enough, or . . . ? If Scotch tape is no longer an issue, what about plastic surgery, push-up bras, and wrinkle creams?

MY FRIEND TERRY AND I both have boy's nicknames. But that's the only thing about us that is the same. Terry is beautiful. She is about 5'4" tall, which is tall enough to be a stewardess. I am only 5 feet tall, which is too short, so I should know.

My mother keeps asking me why Terry is my friend. This makes me nervous, because I really don't know. Ever since we had the first senior class officers' meeting at my house and my mother found the empty tampax container in our waste basket she has been really asking a lot of questions about Terry. Terry and I are the only girls who were elected to office. She's treasurer and I'm secretary. The president, the vice-president, and the sergeant-at-arms

are all boys. I guess that's why Terry and I hang out together. Like when we have to go to class activities and meetings she picks me up. I never even knew her before we were elected. I don't know who she used to hang around with, but it sure wasn't with me and my friends. We're too Japanese girl, you know, plain. I mean, Terry has skin like a porcelain doll. She has cheekbones like Garbo, a body like Ann Margaret, she has legs like, well, like not any Japanese girl I've ever seen. Like I said, she's beautiful. She always dresses perfectly, too. She always wears an outfit; a dress with matching straw bag and colored leather shoes. Her hair is always set, combed, and sprayed; she even wears nylon stockings under her jeans, even on really hot days. Terry is the only girl I know who has her own Liberty House charge card. Not that she ever goes shopping by herself. Whenever she goes near a store, her mother goes with her.

Funny, Terry has this beautiful face, perfect body, and nobody hates her. We hate Valerie Rosecrest. Valerie is the only girl in our P.E. class who can come out of the girl's showers, wrap a towel around herself under her arms and have it stay up by itself. No hands. She always takes the longest time in the showers and walks back to her locker past the rest of us, who are already dry and fumbling with the one hook on the back of our bras. Valerie's bra has five hooks on the back of it and needs all of them to stay closed. I think she hangs that thing across the top of her locker door on purpose just so we can walk past it and be blinded by it shining in the afternoon sun. One time, my friend Tina got fed up and snatched Val's bra. She wore it on top of her head and ran around the locker room. I swear, she looked like an albino Mickey Mouse. Nobody did anything but laugh. Funny, it was Terry who took the bra away and put it back on Val's locker again.

I don't know why we're friends, but I wasn't surprised when we ended up together as contestants

Mavis Hara, "Carnival Queen," in *Sister Stew: Fiction and Poetry by Women,* edited by Juliet S. Kono and Cathy Song (Honolulu: Bamboo Ridge Press, 1991). Reprinted by permission of the author.

in the Carnival Queen contest. The Carnival Queen contest is a tradition at McKinley. They have pictures of every Carnival Queen ever chosen hanging in the Auditorium corridor right next to the pictures of the senators, governors, politicians, and millionaires who graduated from the school. This year there are already five portraits of queens up there. All the girls are wearing long ball gowns and the same rhinestone crown which is placed on their heads by Mr. Harano, the principal. They have elbow length white gloves and they're carrying baby's breath and roses. The thing is, all the girls are *hapa*.* Every one.

Every year, it is the same tradition. A big bunch of girls gets nominated to run, but everybody knows from intermediate school on which girl in the class is actually going to win. She has to be *hapa*.

"They had to nominate me," I try to tell Terry. "I'm a class officer, but you, you actually have a chance to be the only Japanese girl to win." Terry had just won the American Legion essay contest the week before. You would think that being fashionable and coordinated all the time would take all her energy and wear her out, but her mother wants her to be smart too. She looks at me with this sad face I don't understand.

"I doubt it," she says.

Our first orientation meeting for contestants is today in the library after school. I walk to the meeting actually glad to be there after class. The last after school meeting I went to was the one I was forced to attend. That one had no contestants. Just potential school dropouts. The first meeting, I didn't know anybody there. Nobody I know in the student government crowd is like me and has actually flunked chemistry. All the guys who were coming in the door were the ones who hang around the bathrooms that I'm too scared to use. Nobody ever threatened me though, and after a while, dropout class wasn't half bad, but I have to admit, I like this meeting better. I sit down and watch the other contestants come through the door. I know the first name of almost every girl who walks in. Terry, of course, who is wearing her blue suede jumper and silk blouse, navy stockings and navy patent leather shoes. My friend Trudye, who has a great figure for

an Oriental girl but who wears braces and coke bottle glasses. My friend Linda, who has a beautiful face but a basic *musubi*-shaped* body. The Yanagawa twins, who have beautiful *hapa* faces, but pretty tragic, they inherited their father's genes and have government-issue Japanese-girl legs. Songleaders, cheerleaders, ROTC sponsors, student government committee heads, I know them all. Krissie Clifford, who is small and blonde, comes running in late. Krissie looks like a young version of Beaver's mother on the TV show. She's always running like she just fell out of the screen, and if she moves fast enough, she can catch up with the TV world and jump back in. Then she walks in. Leilani Jones. As soon as she walks in the door, everybody in the room turns to look at her. Every body in the room knows that Leilani is the only girl who can possibly win.

Lani is *hapa*, Japanese-*haole*.† She inherited the best features from everybody. She is tall and slim, with light brown hair and butter frosting skin. I don't even know what she is wearing. Leilani is so beautiful it doesn't matter what she is wearing. She is smooth, and gracefully quiet. Her smile is soft and shiny. It's like looking at a pearl. Lani is not only beautiful, when you look at her all you hear is silence, like the air around her is stunned. We all know it. This is the only girl who can possibly win.

As soon as Leilani walks in, Mrs. Takahara, the teacher advisor says, "Well, now, take your seats everyone. We can begin."

We each take a wooden chair on either side of two rows of long library tables. There is a make-up kit and mirror at each of the places. Some of Mrs. Takahara's friends who are teachers are also sitting in.

"This is Mrs. Chung, beauty consultant of Kamedo cosmetics," Mrs. Takahara says, "she will show us the proper routines of skin cleansing and make-up. The Carnival Queen contest is a very special event. All the girls who are contestants must be worthy representatives of McKinley High School. This means the proper make-up and attitude. Mrs. Chung . . ."

---

hapa—literally, "half," that is, of mixed ancestry [editor's note].

---

musubi—rice ball [editor's note].
†*haole*—white person, thus Japanese-white [editor's note].

I have to admire the beauty consultant. Even though her makeup is obvious as scaffolding in front of a building, it is so well done, kind of like the men who dance the girls' parts in Kabuki shows, you look at it and actually believe that what you are seeing is her face.

"First, we start with proper cleansing," she says. We stare into our own separate mirrors.

"First, we pin our hair so that it no longer hangs in our faces." All of the girls dig in handbags and come up with bobby pins. Hairstyles disappear as we pin our hair straight back. The teachers look funny, kind of young without their teased hair. Mrs. Chung walks around to each station. She squeezes a glop of pink liquid on a cotton ball for each of us.

"Clean all the skin well," she says. "Get all the dirt and impurities out." We scrub hard with that cotton ball, we all know that our skin is loaded with lots of stuff that is impure. My friend Trudye gets kind of carried away. She was scrubbing so hard around her eyes that she scrubbed off her scotch tape.* She hurries over to Mrs. Takahara's chair, mumbles something and excuses herself. I figure she'll be gone pretty long, the only bathroom that is safe for us to use is all the way over in the other building.

"Now we moisturize," Mrs. Chung is going on. "We use this step to correct defects in the tones of our skins." I look over at Terry. I can't see any defects in any of the tones of her skin.

"This mauve moisturizer corrects sallow undertones," Mrs. Chung says.

"What's shallow?" I whisper to Terry.

"SALLOW," she whispers back disgusted. "Yellow."

"Oh," I say and gratefully receive the large glop of purple stuff Mrs. Chung is squeezing on my new cotton ball. Mrs. Chung squeezes a little on Terry's cotton ball too. When she passes Lani, she smiles and squeezes white stuff out from a different tube.

I happily sponge the purple stuff on. Terry is sponging too but I notice she is beginning to look like she has the flu. "Next, foundation," says Mrs. Chung. She is walking around, narrowing her eyes at each of us and handing us each a tube that she is

sure is the correct color to bring out the best in our skin. Mrs. Chung hands me a plastic tube of dark beige. She gives Terry a tube of lighter beige and gives Lani a different tube altogether.

"Just a little translucent creme," she smiles to Lani who smiles back rainbow bubbles and strands of pearls.

Trudye comes rushing back and Linda catches her up on all the steps she's missed. I got to admit, without her glasses and with all that running, she has really pretty cheekbones and nice colored skin. I notice she has new scotch tape on too, and is really concentrating on what Mrs. Chung is saying next.

"Now that we have the proper foundation, we concentrate on the eyes." She pulls out a rubber and chrome pincer machine. She stands in front of Linda with it. I become concerned.

"The eyelashes sometimes grow in the wrong direction," Mrs. Chung informs us. "They must be trained to bend correctly. We use the Eyelash Curler to do this." She hands the machine to Linda. I watch as Linda puts the metal pincer up to her eye and catches her straight, heavy black lashes between the rubber pincer blades.

"Must be sore if they do it wrong and squeeze the eyelid meat," I breathe to Terry. Terry says nothing. She looks upset, like she is trying not to bring up her lunch.

"Eyeshadow must be applied to give the illusion of depth," says Mrs. Chung. "Light on top of the lid, close to the lashes, luminescent color on the whole lid, a dot of white in the center of the iris, and brown below the browbone to accentuate the crease." Mrs. Chung is going pretty fast now. I wonder what the girls who have Oriental eyelids without a crease are going to do. I check out the room quickly, over the top of my make-up mirror. Sure enough, all the Oriental girls here have a nice crease in their lids. Those who don't are wearing scotch tape. Mrs. Chung is passing out "pearlescent" eyeshadow.

"It's made of fish scales," Terry says. I have eyelids that are all right, but eyeshadow, especially sparkling eyeshadow, makes me look like a gecko, you know, with protruding eye sockets that go in separate directions. Terry has beautiful deep-socketed eyes and browbones that don't need any help to look well defined. I put on the stuff in spite

---

*Author Mavis Hara tells us that Asian American women used Scotch tape in the 1960s to widen their eyes.

of my better judgment and spend the rest of the time trying not to move my eyeballs too much, just in case anybody notices. Lani is putting on all this makeup too. But in her case, it just increases the pearly glow that her skin is already producing.

"This ends the makeup session," Mrs. Chung is saying. "Now our eyes and skins have the proper preparation for our roles as contestants for Carnival Queen."

"Ma, I running in the Carnival Queen contest," I was saying last night. My mother got that exasperated look on her face.

"You think you get chance!"

"No, but the teachers put in the names of all the student council guys." My mother is beginning to look like she is suffering again.

"When you were small, everybody used to tell me you should run for Cherry Blossom contest. But that was before you got so dark like your father. I always tell you no go out in the sun or wear lotion like me when you go out but you never listen."

"Yeah, Ma, but we get modeling lessons, make-up, how to walk."

"Good, might make you stand up straight. I would get you a back brace, but when you were small, we paid so much money for your legs, to get special shoes connected to a bar. You only cried and never would wear them. That's why you still have crooked legs."

That was last night. Now I'm here and Mrs. Takahara is telling us about the walking and modeling lessons.

"Imagine a string coming out of the top of your skull and connected to the ceiling. Shorten the string and walk with your chin out and back erect. Float! Put one foot in front of the other, point your toes outward and glide forward on the balls of your feet. When you stop, place one foot slightly behind the other at a forty-five degree angle. Put your weight on the back foot . . ." I should have worn the stupid shoes when I was small. I'm bow-legged. Just like my father. Leilani is not bow-legged. She looks great putting one long straight tibia in front of the other. I look kind of like a crab. We walk in circles around and around the room. Terry is definitely not happy. She's walking pretty far away from me. Once, when I pass her, I could swear she is crying.

"Wow, long practice, yeah?" I say as we walk across the lawn heading toward the bus. Terry, Trudye, Linda, and I are still together. A black Buick pulls up to the curb. Terry's Mom has come to pick her up. Terry's Mom always picks her up. She must have just come back from the beauty shop. Her head is wrapped in a pink net wind bonnet. Kind of like the cake we always get at weddings that my mother keeps on top of the television and never lets anybody eat.

"I'll call you," Terry says.

"I'm so glad that you and Theresa do things together," Terry's mother says. "Theresa needs girlfriends like you, Sam." I'm looking at the pink net around her face. I wonder if Terry's father ever gets the urge to smash her hair down to feel the shape of her head. Terry looks really uncomfortable as they drive away.

I feel uncomfortable too. Trudye and Linda's make-up looks really weird in the afternoon sunlight. My eyeballs feel larger than tank turrets and they must be glittering brilliantly too. The Liliha-Puunui bus comes and we all get on. The long center aisle of the bus gives me an idea. I put one foot in front of the other and practice walking down. Good thing it is late and the guys we go to school with are not getting on.

"You think Leilani is going to win?" Trudye asks.

"What?" I say as I almost lose my teeth against the metal pole I'm holding on to. The driver has just started up, and standing with your feet at a forty-five degree angle doesn't work on public transportation.

"Lani is probably going to win, yeah?" Trudye says again. She can hide her eye make-up behind her glasses and looks pretty much OK. "I'm going to stay in for the experience. Plus, I'm going to the orthodontist and take my braces out, and I asked my mother if I could have contact lenses and she said OK." Trudye goes on, but I don't listen. I get a seat by the window and spend the whole trip looking out so nobody sees my fish scale eyes.

I am not surprised when I get home and the phone begins to ring.

"Sam, it's Terry. You stay in the contest. But I decided I'm not going to run."

"That's nuts, Terry," I am half screaming at her, "you are the only one of us besides Lani that has a chance to win. You could be the first Japanese Carnival Queen that McKinley ever has." I am going to argue this one.

"Do you know the real name of this contest?" Terry asks.

"I don't know, Carnival Queen. I've never thought about it I guess."

"It's the Carnival Queen Scholarship Contest."

"Oh, so?" I'm still interested in arguing that only someone with legs like Terry even has a chance.

"Why are you running? How did you get nominated?" Terry asks.

"I'm Senior Class secretary, they had to nominate me, but you . . ."

"And WHY are you secretary," she cuts me off before I get another running start about chances.

"I don't know, I guess because I used to write poems for English class and they always got in the paper or the yearbook. And probably because Miss Chuck made me write a column for the newspaper for one year to bring up my social studies grade."

"See . . . and why am I running?"

"OK, you're class officer, and sponsor, and you won the American Legion essay contest . . ."

"And Krissy?"

"She's editor of the yearbook, and a sponsor and the Yanagawa twins are songleaders and Trudye is prom committee chairman and Linda . . ." I am getting into it.

"And Lani," says Terry quietly.

"Well, she's a sponsor I think . . ." I've lost some momentum. I really don't know.

"I'm a sponsor, and I know she's not," Terry says.

"Student government? No . . . I don't think so . . . not cheering, her sister is the one in the honor society, not . . . hey, not, couldn't be . . ."

"That's right," Terry says, "the only reason she's running is because she's supposed to win." It couldn't be true. "That means the rest of us are all running for nothing. The best we can do is second place." My ears are getting sore with the sense of what she says. "We're running because of what we did. But we're going to lose because of what we look like. Look, it's still good experience and you can still run if you like."

"Nah . . ." I say still dazed by it. "But what about Mrs. Takahara, what about your mother?" Terry is quiet.

"I think I can handle Mrs. Takahara," Terry finally says.

"I'll say I'm not running, too. If it's two of us, it won't be so bad." I am actually kind of relieved that this is the last day I'll have to put gecko eye make-up all over my face.

"Thanks, Sam . . ." Terry says.

"Yeah . . . My mother will actually be relieved. Ever since I forgot the ending at my piano recital in fifth grade, she gets really nervous if I'm in front of any audience."

"You want me to pick you up for the carnival Saturday night?" Terry asks.

"I'll ask my Mom," I say. "See you then . . ."

"Yeah . . ."

I think, "We're going to lose because of what we look like." I need a shower, my eyes are itching anyway. I'm glad my mother isn't home yet. I think best in the shower and sometimes I'm in there an hour or more.

Soon, with the world a small square of warm steam and tile walls, it all starts going through my head. The teachers looked so young in the make-up demonstration with their hair pinned back—they looked kind of like us. But we are going to lose because of what we look like. I soap the layers of make-up off my face. I guess they're tired of looking like us; *musubi* bodies, *daikon** legs, *furoshiki*-shaped,[†] home-made dresses, *bento*[‡] tins to be packed in the early mornings, mud and sweat everywhere. The water is splashing down on my face and hair. But Krissy doesn't look like us, and she is going to lose too. Krissy looks like the Red Cross society lady from intermediate school. She looks like Beaver's mother on the television show. Too *haole*. She's going to lose because of the way she looks. Lani doesn't look anything like anything from the past. She looks like something that could only have been born underwater where all motions are slow and all sounds are soft. I turn off the water and towel off. Showers always make me feel clean and secure. I guess I can't blame even the teachers, everyone wants to feel safe and secure.

---

*daikon—white Japanese radish, shaped long and thick [editor's note].
[†] *furoshiki*—square cloth for carrying small objects [editor's note].
[‡] *bento*—packed lunch [editor's note].

My mother is sitting at the table peeling an orange. She does this almost every night and I already know what she's going to say.

"Eat this orange, good for you, lots of vitamin C."

"I don't want to eat orange now, Ma." I know it is useless, but I say it anyway. My mother is the kind of Japanese lady who will hunch down real small when she passes in front of you when you're watching TV. Makes you think she's quiet and easy going, but not on the subject of vitamin C.

"I peeled it already. Want it." Some people actually think that my mother is shy.

"I not running in the contest. Terry and I going quit."

"Why?" my mother asks, like she really doesn't need to know.

"Terry said that we running for nothing. Everybody already knows Lani going win." My mother looks like she just tasted some orange peel.

"That's not the real reason," she hands me the orange and starts washing the dishes.

There's lots of things I don't understand. Like why Terry hangs out with me. Why my mother is always so curious about her and now why she doesn't think this is the real reason that Terry is quitting the contest.

"What did the mother say about Terry quitting the contest?" my mother asks without turning around.

"I donno, nothing I guess."

"Hmmmmmmm . . . that's not the real reason. That girl is different. The way the mother treats her is different." Gee, having a baby and being a mother must be really hard and it must really change a person because all I know is that my mother is really different from me.

Terry picks me up Saturday night in her brother's white Mustang. It's been a really busy week. I haven't even seen her since we quit the contest. We had to build the Senior class Starch Throwing booth.

"Hi, Sam. We're working until ten o'clock on the first shift, OK?" Terry is wearing a triangle denim scarf in her hair, a workshirt and jeans. Her face is flushed from driving with the Mustang's top down and she looks really glamorous.

"Yeah, I thought we weren't going to finish the booth this afternoon. Lucky thing my Dad and Lenny's Dad helped us with the hammering and Valerie's committee got the cardboard painted in time. We kind of ran out of workers because most of the girls . . ." I don't have to finish. Most of the student council girls are getting dressed up for the contest.

"Mrs. Sato and the cafeteria ladies finished cooking the starch and Neal and his friends and some of the football guys are going to carry the big pots of starch over to the booth for us." Terry is in charge of the manpower because she knows everybody.

"Terry's mother is on the phone!" my mother is calling to us from the house. Terry runs in to answer the phone. Funny, her mother always calls my house when Terry is supposed to pick me up. My mother looks out at me from the door. The look on her face says, "Checking up." Terry runs past her and jumps back in the car.

"You're lucky, your mother is really nice," she says.

We go down Kuakini Street and turn onto Liliha. We pass School Street and head down the freeway on-ramp. Terry turns on K-POI and I settle down in my seat. Terry drives faster than my father. We weave in and out of cars as she guns the Mustang down H-1. I know this is not very safe, but I like the feeling in my stomach. It's like going down hills. My hair is flying wild and I feel so clean and good. Like the first day of algebra class before the symbols get mixed up. Like the first day of chemistry before we have to learn molar solutions. I feel like it's going to be the first day forever and I can make the clean feeling last and last. The ride is too short. We turn off by the Board of Water Supply station and we head down by the Art Academy and turn down Pensacola past Mr. Feiterra's green gardens and into the parking lot of the school.

"I wish you were still in the contest tonight," I tell Terry as we walk out toward the Carnival grounds. "I mean you are so perfect for the Carnival Queen. You were the only Japanese girl that was perfect enough to win."

"I thought you were my friend," Terry starts mumbling. "You sound like my mother. You only like me because of what you think I should be." She starts walking faster and is leaving me behind.

"Wait! What? How come you getting so mad?" I'm running to keep up with her.

"Perfect, perfect. What if I'm NOT perfect. What if I'm not what people think I am? What if I can't be what people think I am?" She's not making any sense to me and she's crying. "Why can't you just like me? I thought you were different. I thought you just liked me. I thought you were my friend because you just liked ME." I'm following her and I feel like it's exam time in chemistry. I'm flunking again and I don't understand.

We get to the Senior booth and Terry disappears behind the cardboard. Valerie Rosecrest is there and hands me a lot of paper cupcake cups and a cafeteria juice ladle.

"Quick, we need at least a hundred of these filled, we're going to be open in ten minutes."

"Try wait, I got to find Terry." I look behind the cardboard back of the booth. Terry is not there. I run all around the booth. Terry is nowhere in sight. The Senior booth is under a tent in the midway with all the games. There are lots of lightbulbs strung like kernels of corn on wires inside the tent. There's lots of game booths and rows and rows of stuffed animal prizes on clothes lines above each booth. I can't find Terry and I want to look around more, but all of a sudden the merry-go-round music starts and all the lights come on. The Senior booth with its handpainted signs, "Starch Throw—three script" looks alive all of a sudden in the warm Carnival light.

"Come on, Sam!" Valerie is calling me. "We're opening. I need you to help!" I go back to the booth. Pretty soon Terry comes back and I look at her kind of worried, but under the soft popcorn light, you cannot even tell she was crying.

"Terry, Mr. Miller said that you're supposed to watch the script can and take it to the cafeteria when it's full." Val's talking to her, blocking my view. Some teachers are arriving for first shift. They need to put on shower caps and stick their heads through holes in the cardboard so students can buy paper cupcake cups full of starch to throw to try to hit the teachers in the face. Terry goes in the back to help the teachers get ready. Lots of guys from my drop-out class are lining up in the front of the booth.

"Eh, Sam, come on take my money. Ogawa's back there. He gave me the F in math. Gimme the starch!" Business is getting better and better all night. Me, Val, and Terry are running around the booth, taking script, filling cupcake cups, and getting out of the way fast when the guys throw the starch. Pretty soon, the grass in the middle of the booth turns into a mess that looks like thrown-up starch, and we are trying not to slip as we run around trying to keep up with business.

"Ladies and gentlemen, McKinley High School is proud to present the 1966 Carnival Queen and her court." It comes over the loudspeaker. It must be the end of the contest, ten o'clock. All the guys stop buying starch and turn to look toward the tent. Pretty soon, everyone in the tent has cleared the center aisle. They clap as five girls in evening dresses walk our way.

"Oh, great," I think. "I have starch in my hair and I don't want to see them." The girls are all dressed in long gowns and are wearing white gloves. The first girl is Linda. She looks so pretty in a maroon velvet A-line gown. Cannot see her *musubi*-shaped body and her face is just glowing. The rhinestones in her tiara are sparkling under each of the hundreds of carnival lights. The ribbon on her chest says "Third Princess." It's neat! Just like my cousin Carolyn's wedding. My toes are tingling under their coating of starch. The next is Trudye. She's not wearing braces and she looks so pretty in her lavender gown. Some of the guys are going "Wow," under their breath as she walks by. The first Princesses pass next. The Yanagawa twins. They're wearing matching pink gowns and have pink baby roses in their hair, which is in ringlets. Their tiaras look like lace snowflakes on their heads as they pass by. And last. Even though I know who this is going to be I really want to see her. Sure enough, everybody in the crowd gets quiet as she passes by. Lani looks like her white dress is made of sugar crystals. As she passes, her crown sparkles tiny rainbows under the hundreds of lightbulbs from the tent and flashbulbs popping like little suns.

The court walks through the crowd and stops at the Senior booth. Mr. Harano, the principal, steps out.

"Your majesty," he's talking to Lani who is really glowing. "I will become a target in the Senior booth in your honor. Will you and your Princesses please take aim and do your best as royal representatives of our school?"

I look around at Terry. The principal is acting so stupid. I can't believe he really runs the whole school. Terry must be getting so sick. But I look at her and she's standing in front of Lani and smiling. This is weird. She's the one who said the contest was fixed. She's the one who said everyone knew who was supposed to win. She's smiling at Lani like my grandmother used to smile at me when I was five. Like I was a sweet *mochi** dumpling floating in red bean soup. I cannot stand it. I quit the contest so she wouldn't have to quit alone. And she yells at me and hasn't talked to me all night. All I wanted was for her to be standing there instead of Lani.

The Carnival Queen and four Princesses line up in front of the booth. Val, Terry, and I scramble around giving each of them three cupcake cups of starch. They get ready to throw. The guys from the newspaper and the yearbook get ready to take their picture. I lean as far back into the wall as I can. I know Trudye didn't have time to get contacts yet and she's not wearing any glasses. I wonder where Val is and if she can flatten out enough against the wall to get out of the way. Suddenly, a hand reaches out and grabs my ankle. I look down, and Terry, who is sitting under the counter of the booth with Val, grabs my hand and pulls me down on the grass with them. The ground here is nice and clean. The Carnival Queen and Princesses and the rows of

_____
mochi—rice cake [editor's note].

stuffed animals are behind and above us. The air is filled with pink cupcake cups and starch as they throw. Mr. Harano closes his eyes, the flashbulbs go off, but no one comes close to hitting his face. Up above us everyone is laughing and clapping. Down below, Terry, Val, and I are nice and clean.

"Lani looks so pretty, Sam," Terry is looking at me and smiling.

"Yeah, even though the contest was juice she looks really good. Like a storybook," I say, hoping it's not sounding too fake.

"Thanks for quitting with me." Terry's smile is like the water that comes out from between the rocks at Kunawai stream. I feel so clean in that smile.

"It would have been lonely if I had to quit by myself," Terry says, looking down at our starch-covered shoes. She looks up at me and smiles again. And even if I'm covered with starch, I suddenly know that to her, I am beautiful. Her smile tells me that we're friends because I went to drop-out class. It is a smile that can wash away all the F's that Mr. Low, my chemistry teacher, will ever give. I have been waiting all my life for my mother to give me that smile. I know it is a smile that Terry's mother has never smiled at her. I don't know where she learned it.

It's quiet now, the Carnival Queen and her Princesses have walked away. Terry stands up first as she and Val and I start to crawl out from our safe place under the counter of the booth. She gives me her hand to pull me up and I can see her out in the bright Carnival light. Maybe every girl looks like a queen at one time in her life.

The Body Politic

Abra Fortune Chernik

Abra Fortune Chernik is described in Listen Up *as having grown up in Manhattan and on the beaches of Fire Island. She has written a screenplay,* Portrait of an Invisible Girl, *and she is a frequent speaker on the topic of eating disorders.*

Here Fortune describes her own harrowing experience with anorexia. She contemplates the elements in a sexist society that propel so many women into eating disorders and most women into war with their own bodies: "As long as society resists female power, fashion will call healthy women physically flawed." She tells us that we each must claim our own body as it is, care for it, nourish it, and accept it unconditionally.

MY BODY POSSESSES SOLIDNESS AND curve, like the ocean. My weight mingles with Earth's pull, drawing me onto the sand. I have not always sent waves into the world. I flew off once, for five years, and swirled madly like a cracking brown leaf in the salty autumn wind. I wafted, dried out, apathetic.

I had no weight in the world during my years of anorexia. Curled up inside my thinness, a refugee in a cocoon of hunger, I lost the capacity to care about myself or others. I starved my body and twitched in place as those around me danced in the energy of shared existence and progressed in their lives. When I graduated from college crowned with academic honors, professors praised my potential. I wanted only to vanish.

It took three months of hospitalization and two years of outpatient psychotherapy for me to learn to nourish myself and to live in a body that expresses strength and honesty in its shape. I accepted my right and my obligation to take up room with my figure, voice, and spirit. I remembered how to

tumble forward and touch the world that holds me. I chose the ocean as my guide.

Who disputes the ocean's fullness?

Growing up in New York City, I did not care about the feminist movement. Although I attended an all-girls high school, we read mostly male authors and studied the history of men. Embracing mainstream culture without question, I learned about womanhood from fashion magazines, Madison Avenue and Hollywood. I dismissed feminist alternatives as foreign and offensive, swathed as they were in stereotypes that threatened my adolescent need for conformity.

Puberty hit late; I did not complain. I enjoyed living in the lanky body of a tall child and insisted on the title of "girl." If anyone referred to me as a "young woman," I would cry out, horrified, "Do not call me the *W* word!" But at sixteen years old, I could no longer deny my fate. My stomach and breasts rounded. Curly black hair sprouted in the most embarrassing places. Hips swelled from a once-flat plane. Interpreting maturation as an unacceptable lapse into fleshiness, I resolved to eradicate the physical symptoms of my impending womanhood.

Magazine articles, television commercials, lunchroom conversation, gymnastics coaches and write-ups on models had saturated me with diet savvy. Once I decided to lose weight, I quickly turned expert. I dropped hot chocolate from my regular breakfast order at the Skyline Diner. I replaced lunches of peanut butter and Marshmallow Fluff sandwiches with small platters of cottage cheese and cantaloupe. I eliminated dinner altogether and blunted my appetite with Tab, Camel Lights, and Carefree bubble gum. When furious craving overwhelmed my resolve and I swallowed an extra something, I would flee to the nearest bathroom to purge my mistake.

Within three months, I had returned my body to its preadolescent proportions and had manipulated my monthly period into drying up. Over the next five years, I devoted my life to losing my weight. I came to resent the body in which I lived, the body that threatened to develop, the body whose hunger I despised but could not extinguish. If I neglected a workout or added a pound or ate a bite too many, I would stare in the mirror and drown myself in a tidal wave of criticism. Hatred of my body generalized to hatred of myself as a person, and self-referential labels such as "pig," "failure" and "glutton" allowed me to believe that I deserved punishment. My self-hatred became fuel for the self-mutilating behaviors of the eating disorder.

As my body shrank, so did my world. I starved away my power and vision, my energy and inclinations. Obsessed with dieting, I allowed relationships, passions, and identity to wither. I pulled back from the world, off of the beach, out of the sand. The waves of my existence ceased to roll beyond the inside of my skin.

And society applauded my shrinking. Pound after pound the applause continued, like the pounding ocean outside the door of my beach house.

The word "anorexia" literally means "loss of appetite." But as an anorexic, I felt hunger thrashing inside my body. I denied my appetite, ignored it, but never lost it. Sometimes the pangs twisted so sharply, I feared they would consume the meat of my heart. On desperate nights I rose in a flannel nightgown and allowed myself to eat an unplanned something.

No matter how much I ate, I could not soothe the pangs. Standing in the kitchen at midnight, spotlighted by the blue-white light of the open refrigerator, I would frantically feed my neglected appetite: the Chinese food I had not touched at dinner; ice cream and whipped cream; microwaved bread; cereal and chocolate milk; doughnuts and bananas. Then, solid sadness inside my gut, swelling agitation, a too-big meal I would not digest. In the bathroom I would rip off my shirt, tie up my hair, and prepare to execute the desperate ritual, again. I would ram the back of my throat with a toothbrush handle, crying, impatient, until the food rushed up. I would vomit until the toilet filled and I emptied,

until I forgave myself, until I felt ready to try my life again. Standing up from my position over the toilet, wiping my mouth, I would believe that I was safe. Looking in the mirror through puffy eyes in a tumescent face, I would promise to take care of myself. Kept awake by the fast, confused beating of my heart and the ache in my chest, I would swear I did not miss the world outside. Lost within myself, I almost died.

By the time I entered the hospital, a mess of protruding bones defined my body, and the bones of my emaciated life rattled me crazy. I carried a pillow around because it hurt to sit down, and I shivered with cold in sultry July. Clumps of brittle hair clogged the drain when I showered, and blackened eyes appeared to sink into my head. My vision of reality wrinkled and my disposition turned mercurial as I slipped into starvation psychosis, a condition associated with severe malnutrition. People told me that I resembled a concentration camp prisoner, a chemotherapy patient, a famine victim or a fashion model.

In the hospital, I examined my eating disorder under the lenses of various therapies. I dissected my childhood, my family structure, my intimate relationships, my belief systems. I participated in experiential therapies of movement, art, and psychodrama. I learned to use words instead of eating patterns to communicate my feelings. And still I refused to gain more than a minimal amount of weight.

I felt powerful as an anorexic. Controlling my body yielded an illusion of control over my life; I received incessant praise for my figure despite my sickly mien, and my frailty manipulated family and friends into protecting me from conflict. I had reduced my world to a plate of steamed carrots, and over this tiny kingdom I proudly crowned myself queen.

I sat cross-legged on my hospital bed for nearly two months before I earned an afternoon pass to go to the mall with my mother. The privilege came just in time; I felt unbearably large and desperately wanted a new outfit under which to hide gained weight. At the mall, I searched for two hours before finally discovering, in the maternity section at Macy's, a shirt large enough to cover what I perceived as my enormous body.

With an hour left on my pass, I spotted a sign on a shop window: "Body Fat Testing, $3.00." I suggested to my mother that we split up for ten minutes; she headed to Barnes & Noble, and I snuck into the fitness store.

I sat down in front of a machine hooked up to a computer, and a burly young body builder fired questions at me:

"Age?"

"Twenty-one."

"Height?"

"Five nine."

"Weight?"

"Ninety-nine."

The young man punched my statistics into his keyboard and pinched my arm with clippers wired to the testing machine. In a moment, the computer spit out my results. "Only ten percent body fat! Unbelievably healthy. The average for a woman your age is twenty-five percent. Fantastic! You're this week's blue ribbon winner."

I stared at him in disbelief. *Winner? Healthy? Fantastic?* I glanced around at the other customers in the store, some of whom had congregated to watch my testing, and I felt embarrassed by his praise. And then I felt furious. Furious at this man and at the society that programmed him for their ignorant approbation of my illness and my suffering.

"I am dying of anorexia," I whispered. "Don't congratulate me."

I spent my remaining month in the hospital supplementing psychotherapy with an independent examination of eating disorders from a social and political point of view. I needed to understand why society would reward my starvation and encourage my vanishing. In the bathroom, a mirror on the open door behind me reflected my backside in a mirror over the sink. Vertebrae poked at my skin, ribs hung like wings over chiseled hip bones, the two sides of my buttocks did not touch. I had not seen this view of myself before.

In writing, I recorded instances in which my eating disorder had tangled the progress of my life and thwarted my relationships. I filled three and a half Mead marble notebooks. Five years' worth of: *I wouldn't sit with Daddy when he was alone in the hospital because I needed to go jogging; I told Derek not to* *visit me because I couldn't throw up when he was there; I almost failed my comprehensive exams because I was so hungry; I spent my year at Oxford with my head in the toilet bowl; I wouldn't eat the dinner my friends cooked me for my nineteenth birthday because I knew they had used oil in the recipe; I told my family not to come to my college graduation because I didn't want to miss a day at the gym or have to eat a restaurant meal.* And on and on for hundreds of pages.

This honest account of my life dissolved the illusion of anorexic power. I saw myself naked in the truth of my pain, my loneliness, my obsessions, my craziness, my selfishness, my defeat. I also recognized the social and political implications of consuming myself with the trivialities of calories and weight. At college, I had watched as classmates involved themselves in extracurricular clubs, volunteer work, politics and applications for jobs and graduate schools. Obsessed with exercising and exhausted by starvation, I did not even consider joining in such pursuits. Despite my love of writing and painting and literature, despite ranking at the top of my class, I wanted only to teach aerobics. Despite my adolescent days as a loud-mouthed, rambunctious class leader, I had grown into a silent, hungry young woman.

And society preferred me this way: hungry, fragile, crazy. *Winner! Healthy! Fantastic!* I began reading feminist literature to further understand the disempowerment of women in our culture. I digested the connection between a nation of starving, self-obsessed women and the continued success of the patriarchy. I also cultivated an awareness of alternative models of womanhood. In the stillness of the hospital library, new voices in my life rose from printed pages to echo my rage and provide the conception of my feminist consciousness.

I had been willing to accept self-sabotage, but now I refused to sacrifice myself to a society that profited from my pain. I finally understood that my eating disorder symbolized more than "personal psychodynamic trauma." Gazing in the mirror at my emaciated body, I observed a woman held up by her culture as the physical ideal because she was starving, self-obsessed and powerless, a woman called beautiful because she threatened no one except herself. Despite my intelligence, my education, and my supposed Manhattan sophistication, I had believed all of the lies; I had almost given my life in order to achieve the sickly impotence that this culture aggressively links with female happiness, love, and success. And everything I had to offer to the world, every tumbling wave, every thought and every passion, nearly died inside me.

As long as society resists female power, fashion will call healthy women physically flawed. As long as society accepts the physical, sexual and economic abuse of women, popular culture will prefer women who resemble little girls. Sitting in the hospital the summer after my college graduation, I grasped the absurdity of a nation of adult women dying to grow small.

Armed with this insight, I loosened the grip of the starvation disease on my body. I determined to recreate myself based on an image of a woman warrior. I remembered my ocean, and I took my first bite.

Gaining weight and getting my head out of the toilet bowl was the most political act I have ever committed.

I left the hospital and returned home to Fire Island. Living at the shore in those wintry days of my new life, I wrapped myself in feminism as I hunted sea shells and role models. I wanted to feel proud of my womanhood. I longed to accept and honor my body's fullness.

During the process of my healing, I had hoped that I would be able to skip the memory of anorexia like a cold pebble into the dark winter sea. I had dreamed that in relinquishing my obsessive chase after a smaller body, I would be able to come home to rejoin those whom I had left in order to starve, rejoin them to live together as healthy, powerful women. But as my body has grown full, I have sensed a hollowness in the lives of women all around me that I had not noticed when I myself stood hollow. I have made it home only to find myself alone.

Out in the world again, I hear the furious thumping dance of body hatred echoing every place I go. Friends who once appeared wonderfully carefree in ordering late-night french fries turn out not to eat breakfast or lunch. Smart, talented, creative women talk about dieting and overeating and hating the beach because they look terrible in bathing suits. Famous women give interviews insulting their bodies and bragging about bicycling twenty-four miles the day they gave birth.

I had looked forward to rejoining society after my years of anorexic exile. Ironically, in order to preserve my health, my recovery has included the development of a consciousness that actively challenges the images and ideas that define this culture. Walking down Madison Avenue and passing emaciated women, I say to myself, *those women are sick.* When smacked with a diet commercial, I remind myself, *I don't do that anymore.* I decline invitations to movies that feature anorexic actors, I will not participate in discussions about dieting, and I refuse to shop in stores that cater to women with eating-disordered figures.

Though I am critical of diet culture, I find it nearly impossible to escape. Eating disorders have woven their way into the fabric of my society. On television, in print, on food packaging, in casual conversation and in windows of clothing stores populated by ridiculously gaunt mannequins, messages to lose my weight and control my appetite challenge my recovered fullness. Finally at home in my body, I recognize myself as an island in a sea of eating disorder, a sea populated predominantly by young women.

A perversion of nature by society has resulted in a phenomenon whereby women feel safer when starving than when eating. Losing our weight boosts self-esteem, while nourishing our bodies evokes feelings of self-doubt and self-loathing.

When our bodies take up more space than a size eight (as most of our bodies do), we say, *too big.* When our appetites demand more than a Lean Cuisine, we say, *too much.* When we want a piece of a friend's birthday cake, we say, *too bad.* Don't eat too much, don't talk too loudly, don't take up too much space, don't take from the world. Be pleasant or crazy, but don't seem hungry. Remember, a new study shows that men prefer women who eat salad for dinner over women who eat burgers and fries.

So we keep on shrinking, starving away our wildness, our power, our truth.

Hiding our curves under long T-shirts at the beach, sitting silently and fidgeting while others eat dessert, sneaking back into the kitchen late at night to binge and hating ourselves the next day, skipping breakfast, existing on diet soda and cigarettes, adding up calories and subtracting everything else. We accept what is horribly wrong in our lives and fight what is beautiful and right.

Over the past three years, feminism has taught me to honor the fullness of my womanhood and the solidness of the body that hosts my life. In feminist circles I have found mentors, strong women who live with power, passion, and purpose. And yet, even in groups of feminists, my love and acceptance of my body remains unusual.

Eating disorders affect us all on both a personal and a political level. The majority of my peers—including my feminist peers—still measure their beauty against anorexic ideals. Even among feminists, body hatred and chronic dieting continue to consume lives. Friends of anorexics beg them to please start eating; then these friends go home and continue their own diets. Who can deny that the millions of young women caught in the net of disordered eating will frustrate the potential of the next wave of feminism?

Sometimes my empathy dissolves into frustration and rage at our situation. For the first time in history, young women have the opportunity to create a world in our image. But many of us concentrate instead on recreating the shape of our thighs.

As young feminists, we must place unconditional acceptance of our bodies at the top of our political agenda. We must claim our bodies as our own to love and honor in their infinite shapes and sizes. Fat, thin, soft, hard, puckered, smooth, our bodies are our homes. By nourishing our bodies, we care for and love ourselves on the most basic level. When we deny ourselves physical food, we go hungry emotionally, psychologically, spiritually and politically. We must challenge ourselves to eat and digest, and allow society to call us too big. We will understand their message to mean too powerful.

Time goes by quickly. One day we will blink and open our eyes as old women. If we spend all our energy keeping our bodies small, what will we have to show for our lives when we reach the end? I hope we have more than a group of fashionably skinny figures.

The Strength of My Rebellion

Gloria E. Anzaldúa

Gloria E. Anzaldúa is coeditor of This Bridge Called My Back: Writings by Radical Women of Color *(1983), editor of* Making Face, Making Soul—Haciendo Caras: Creative and Critical Perspectives by Feminists of Color *(1990), and author of* Borderlands/La Frontera: The New Mestiza *(1987), from which this excerpt is taken. She has taught creative writing, Chicano studies, and women's studies at several universities.*

In her essay "Towards a New Consciousness," also in Borderlands, *Anzaldúa describes the consciousness of a new* mestiza *as a "struggle of borders," a constant shifting from the points of view, experiences, and values of one culture to those of another, from Mexican, to Indian, to Anglo. To integrate, to cope with such dizzying possibilities of perception requires flexibility, tolerance of ambiguity, strength, courage, and creativity. Therefore, the future belongs to the* mestiza *because survival depends on the ability to heal splits, to move among diverse cultures—not only for the* mestiza, *not only for women, but for humankind itself.*

In this essay, Anzaldúa reveals another aspect of feminism for women of color: the intersection of different—sometimes opposing—perspectives, interests, and loyalties.

ESOS MOVIMIENTOS DE REBELDÍA QUE tenemos en la sangre nosotros los mexicanos surgen como ríos desbocanados en mis venas. Y como mi raza que cada en cuando deja caer esa esclavitud de obedecer, de callarse y aceptar, en mi está la rebeldía encimita de mi carne. Debajo de mi humillada mirada está una cara insolente lista para explotar. Me costó muy caro mi rebeldía—acalambrada con desvelos y dudas, sintiendome inútil, estúpida, e impotente.

"Movimientos de rebeldía y las culturas que traicionan," *Borderlands/La Frontera: The New Mestiza* (San Francisco: Spinsters/Aunt Lute Book Company, 1987). © 1987 by Gloria Anzaldúa. Reprinted with permission from Aunt Lute Books and the author.

Me entra una rabia cuando alguien—sea mi mamá, la Iglesia, la cultura de los anglos—me dice haz esto, haz eso sin considerar mis deseos.

Repele. Hable pa' 'tras. Fuí muy hocicona. Era indiferente a muchos valores de mi cultura. No me deje de los hombres. No fuí buena ni obediente.

Pero he crecido. Ya no soló paso toda mi vida botando las costumbres y los valores de mi cultura que me traicionan. También recojo las costumbres que por el tiempo se han provado y las costumbres de respeto a las mujeres. But despite my growing tolerance, for this Chicana *la guerra de independencia* is a constant.

THE STRENGTH OF MY REBELLION

I have a vivid memory of an old photograph: I am six years old. I stand between my father and mother, head cocked to the right, the toes of my flat feet gripping the ground. I hold my mother's hand.

To this day I'm not sure where I found the strength to leave the source, the mother, disengage from my family, *mi tierra, mi gente,* and all that picture stood for. I had to leave home so I could find myself, find my own intrinsic nature buried under the personality that had been imposed on me.

I was the first in six generations to leave the Valley, the only one in my family to ever leave home. But I didn't leave all the parts of me: I kept the ground of my own being. On it I walked away, taking with me the land, the Valley, Texas. *Gané mi camino y me largué. Muy andariega mi hija.* Because I left of my own accord *me dicen, "¿Cómo te gusta la mala vida?"*

At a very early age I had a strong sense of who I was and what I was about and what was fair. I had a stubborn will. It tried constantly to mobilize my soul under my own regime, to live life on my own terms no matter how unsuitable to others they were. *Terca.* Even as a child I would not obey. I was "lazy." Instead of ironing my younger brothers' shirts or cleaning the cupboards, I would pass many hours studying, reading, painting, writing. Every bit of self-faith I'd painstakingly gathered took a beating daily. Nothing in my culture approved of me. *Había agarrado malos pasos.* Something was "wrong" with me. *Estabá más allá de la tradición.*

There is a rebel in me—the Shadow-Beast. It is a part of me that refuses to take orders from outside authorities. It refuses to take orders from my conscious will, it threatens the sovereignty of my rulership. It is that part of me that hates constraints of any kind, even those self-imposed. At the least hint of limitations on my time or space by others, it kicks out with both feet. Bolts.

CULTURAL TYRANNY

Culture forms our beliefs. We perceive the version of reality that it communicates. Dominant paradigms, predefined concepts that exist as unquestionable, unchallengeable, are transmitted to us through the culture. Culture is made by those in power—men. Males make the rules and laws; women transmit them. How many times have I heard mothers and mothers-in-law tell their sons to beat their wives for not obeying them, for being *hociconas* (big mouths), for being *callajeras* (going to visit and gossip with neighbors), for expecting their husbands to help with the rearing of children and the housework, for wanting to be something other than housewives?

The culture expects women to show greater acceptance of, and commitment to, the value system than men. The culture and the Church insist that women are subservient to males. If a woman rebels she is a *mujer mala.* If a woman doesn't renounce herself in favor of the male, she is selfish. If a woman remains a *virgen* until she marries, she is a good woman. For a woman of my culture there used to be only three directions she could turn: to the Church as a nun, to the streets as a prostitute, or to the home as a mother. Today some of us have a fourth choice: entering the world by way of education and career and becoming self-autonomous persons. A very few of us. As a working class people our chief activity is to put food in our mouths, a roof over our heads and clothes on our backs. Educating our children is out of reach for most of us. Educated

or not, the onus is still on woman to be a wife/mother—only the nun can escape motherhood. Women are made to feel total failures if they don't marry and have children. *"¿Y cuándo te casas, Gloria? Se te va a pasar el tren."* Y yo les digo, *"Pos si me caso, no va ser con un hombre."* Se quedan calladitas. Sí, soy hija de la Chingada. I've always been her daughter. *No 'tés chingando.*

Humans fear the supernatural, both the undivine (the animal impulses such as sexuality, the unconscious, the unknown, the alien) and the divine (superhuman, the god in us). Culture and religion seek to protect us from these two forces. The female, by virtue of creating entities of flesh and blood in her stomach (she bleeds every month but does not die), by virtue of being in tune with nature's cycles, is feared. Because, according to Christianity and most other major religions, woman is carnal, animal, and closer to the undivine, she must be protected. Protected from herself. Woman is the stranger, the other. She is man's recognized nightmarish pieces, his Shadow-Beast. The sight of her sends him into a frenzy of anger and fear.

La gorra, el rebozo, la mantilla are symbols of my culture's "protection" of women. Culture (read males) professes to protect women. Actually it keeps women in rigidly defined roles. It keeps the girlchild from other men—don't poach on my preserves, only I can touch my child's body. Our mothers taught us well, *"Los hombres nomás quieren una cosa";* men aren't to be trusted, they are selfish and are like children. Mothers made sure we didn't walk into a room of brothers or fathers or uncles in nightgowns or shorts. We were never alone with men, not even those of our own family.

Through our mothers, the culture gave us mixed messages: *No voy a dejar que ningún pelado desgraciado maltrate a mis hijos.* And in the next breath it would say, *La mujer tiene que hacer lo que le diga el hombre.* Which was it to be—strong, or submissive, rebellious or conforming?

Tribal rights over those of the individual insured the survival of the tribe and were necessary then, and, as in the case of all indigenous peoples in the world who are still fighting off intentional, premeditated murder (genocide), they are still necessary.

Much of what the culture condemns focuses on kinship relationships. The welfare of the family, the community, and the tribe is more important than the welfare of the individual. The individual exists first as kin—as sister, as father, as *padrino*—and last as self.

In my culture, selfishness is condemned, especially in women; humility and selflessness, the absence of selfishness, is considered a virtue. In the past, acting humble with members outside the family ensured that you would make no one *envidioso* (envious); therefore he or she would not use witchcraft against you. If you get above yourself, you're an *envidiosa*. If you don't behave like everyone else, *la gente* will say that you think you're better than others, *que te crees grande*. With ambition (condemned in the Mexican culture and valued in the Anglo) comes envy. *Respeto* carries with it a set of rules so that social categories and hierarchies will be kept in order: respect is reserved for *la abuela, papá, el patrón,* those with power in the community. Women are at the bottom of the ladder one rung above the deviants. The Chicano, *mexicano,* and some Indian cultures have no tolerance for deviance. Deviance is whatever is condemned by the community. Most societies try to get rid of their deviants. Most cultures have burned and beaten their homosexuals and others who deviate from the sexual common.[1] The queer are the mirror reflecting the heterosexual tribe's fear: being different, being other and therefore lesser, therefore sub-human, inhuman, non-human.

HALF AND HALF

There was a *muchacha* who lived near my house. *La gente del pueblo* talked about her being *una de las otras*, "of the Others." They said that for six months she was a woman who had a vagina that bled once a month, and that for the other six months she was a man, had a penis and she peed standing up. They called her half and half, *mita' y mita'*, neither one nor the other but a strange doubling, a deviation of nature that horrified, a work of nature inverted. But there is a magic aspect in abnormality and so-called deformity. Maimed, mad, and sexually different people were believed to possess supernatural powers by primal cultures' magico-religious thinking. For them, abnormality was the price a person had to pay for her or his inborn extraordinary gift.

There is something compelling about being both male and female, about having an entry into both worlds. Contrary to some psychiatric tenets, half and halfs are not suffering from a confusion of sexual identity, or even from a confusion of gender. What we are suffering from is an absolute despot duality that says we are able to be only one or the other. It claims that human nature is limited and cannot evolve into something better. But I, like other queer people, am two in one body, both male and female. I am the embodiment of the *hieros gamos:* the coming together of opposite qualities within.

FEAR OF GOING HOME: HOMOPHOBIA

For the lesbian of color, the ultimate rebellion she can make against her native culture is through her sexual behavior. She goes against two moral prohibitions: sexuality and homosexuality. Being lesbian and raised Catholic, indoctrinated as straight, I *made the choice to be queer* (for some it is genetically inherent). It's an interesting path, one that continually slips in and out of the white, the Catholic, the Mexican, the indigenous, the instincts. In and out of my head. It makes for *loquería*, the crazies. It is a path of knowledge—one of knowing (and of learning) the history of oppression of our *raza.* It is a way of balancing, of mitigating duality.

In a New England college where I taught, the presence of a few lesbians threw the more conservative heterosexual students and faculty into a panic. The two lesbian students and we two lesbian instructors met with them to discuss their fears. One of the students said, "I thought homophobia meant fear of going home after a residency."

And I thought, how apt. Fear of going home. And of not being taken in. We're afraid of being abandoned by the mother, the culture, *la Raza*, for being unacceptable, faulty, damaged. Most of us unconsciously believe that if we reveal this unacceptable aspect of the self our mother/culture/race will totally reject us. To avoid rejection, some of us conform to the values of the culture, push the unacceptable parts into the shadows. Which leaves only one fear—that we will be found out and that the Shadow-Beast will break out of its cage. Some of us take another route. We try to make ourselves conscious of the Shadow-Beast, stare at the sexual lust and lust for power and destruction we see on its face, discern among its features the undershadow that the reigning order of heterosexual males project on our Beast. Yet still others of us take it another step: we try to waken the Shadow-Beast inside us. Not many jump at the chance to confront the Shadow-Beast in the mirror without flinching at her lidless serpent eyes, her cold clammy moist hand dragging us underground, fangs barred and hissing. How does one put feathers on this particular serpent? But a few of us have been lucky—on the face of the Shadow-Beast we have seen not lust but tenderness; on its face we have uncovered the lie.

INTIMATE TERRORISM: LIFE IN THE BORDERLANDS

The world is not a safe place to live in. We shiver in separate cells in enclosed cities, shoulders hunched, barely keeping the panic below the surface of the skin, daily drinking shock along with our morning coffee, fearing the torches being set to our buildings, the attacks in the streets. Shutting down. Woman does not feel safe when her own culture, and white culture, are critical of her; when the males of all races hunt her as prey.

Alienated from her mother culture, "alien" in the dominant culture, the woman of color does not feel safe within the inner life of her Self. Petrified, she can't respond, her face caught between *los intersticios*, the spaces between the different worlds she inhabits.

The ability to respond is what is meant by responsibility, yet our cultures take away our ability to act—shackle us in the name of protection. Blocked, immobilized, we can't move forward, can't move backwards. That writhing serpent movement, the very movement of life, swifter than lightning, frozen.

We do not engage fully. We do not make full use of our faculties. We abnegate. And there in front of us is the crossroads and choice: to feel a victim where someone else is in control and therefore responsible and to blame (being a victim and transferring the blame on culture, mother, father, ex-lover, friend, absolves me of responsibility), or to feel strong, and, for the most part, in control.

My Chicana identity is grounded in the Indian woman's history of resistance. The Aztec female rites of mourning were rites of defiance protesting the cultural changes which disrupted the equality and balance between female and male, and protesting their demotion to a lesser status, their denigration. Like *la Llorona*, the Indian woman's only means of protest was wailing.

So *mamá, Raza,* how wonderful, *no tener que rendir cuentas a nadie.* I feel perfectly free to rebel and to rail against my culture. I fear no betrayal on my part because, unlike Chicanas and other women of color who grew up white or who have only recently returned to their native cultural roots, I was totally immersed in mine. It wasn't until I went to high school that I "saw" whites. Until I worked on my master's degree I had not gotten within an arm's distance of them. I was totally immersed *en lo mexicano,* a rural, peasant, isolated, *mexicanismo.* To separate from my culture (as from my family) I had to feel competent enough on the outside and secure enough inside to live life on my own. Yet in leaving home I did not lose touch with my origins because *lo mexicano* is in my system. I am a turtle, wherever I go I carry "home" on my back.

Not me sold out my people but they me. So yes, though "home" permeates every sinew and cartilage in my body, I too am afraid of going home. Though I'll defend my race and culture when they are attacked by non-*mexicanos, conosco el malestar de mi cultura.* I abhor some of my culture's ways, how it cripples its women, *como burras,* our strengths used against us, lowly *burras* bearing humility with dignity. The ability to serve, claim the males, is our highest virtue. I abhor how my culture makes *macho* caricatures of its men. No, I do not buy all the myths of the tribe into which I was born. I can understand why the more tinged with Anglo blood, the more adamantly my colored and colorless sisters glorify their colored culture's values—to offset the extreme devaluation of it by the white culture. It's a legitimate reaction. But I will not glorify those aspects of my culture which have injured me and which have injured me in the name of protecting me.

So, don't give me your tenets and your laws. Don't give me your lukewarm gods. What I want is an accounting with all three cultures—white, Mexican, Indian. I want the freedom to carve and chisel my own face, to staunch the bleeding with ashes, to fashion my own gods out of my entrails. And if going home is denied me then I will have to stand and claim my space, making a new culture— *una cultura mestiza*—with my own lumber, my own bricks and mortar and my own feminist architecture.

THE WOUNDING OF THE *INDIA*–MESTIZA

Estas carnes indias que despreciamos nosotros los mexicanos asi como despreciamos y condenamos a nuestra madre, Malinali. Nos condenamos a nosotros mismos. Esta raza vencida, enemigo cuerpo.

Not me sold out my people but they me. *Malinali Tenepat*, or *Malintzin*, has become known as *la Chingada*—the fucked one. She has become the bad word that passes a dozen times a day from the lips of Chicanos. Whore, prostitute, the woman who sold out her people to the Spaniards are epithets Chicanos spit out with contempt.

The worst kind of betrayal lies in making us believe that the Indian woman in us is the betrayer. *We, indias y mestizas,* police the Indian in us, brutalize and condemn her. Male culture has done a good job on us. *Son los costumbres que traicionan. La india en mí es la sombra: La Chingada, Tlazolteotl, Coatlicue. Son ellas que oyemos lamentando a sus hijas perdidas.*

Not me sold out my people but they me. Because of the color of my skin they betrayed me. The dark-skinned woman has been silenced, gagged, caged, bound into servitude with marriage, bludgeoned for 300 years, sterilized and castrated in the twentieth century. For 300 years she has been a slave, a force of cheap labor, colonized by the Spaniard, the Anglo, by her own people (and in Mesoamerica her lot under the Indian patriarchs was not free of wounding). For 300 years she was invisible, she was not heard. Many times she wished to speak, to act, to protest, to challenge. The odds were heavily against her. She hid her feelings; she hid her truths; she concealed her fire; but she kept stoking the inner flame. She remained faceless and voiceless, but a light shone through her veil of silence. And though she was unable to spread her limbs and though for her right now the sun has sunk under the earth and there is no moon, she continues to tend the flame. The spirit of the fire spurs her to fight for her own skin and a piece of ground to stand on, a ground from which to view the world— a perspective, a homeground where she can plumb the rich ancestral roots into her own ample *mestiza* heart. She waits till the waters are not so turbulent and the mountains not so slippery with sleet. Battered and bruised she waits, her bruises throwing her back upon herself and the rhythmic pulse of the feminine. *Coatlalopeuh* waits with her.

> *Aquí en la soledad prospera su rebeldía.*
> *En la soledad Ella prospera.*

Note

1. Francisco Guerra, *The Pre-Columbian Mind: A Study into the Aberrant Nature of Sexual Drives, Drugs Affecting Behaviour, and the Attitude Towards Life and Death, with a Survey of Psychotherapy in Pre-Columbian America* (New York: Seminar Press, 1971).

The Lesbian Perspective

Julia Penelope

The works of well-known lesbian feminist poet and author Julia Penelope include Speaking Freely: Unlearning the Lies of the Fathers' Tongues *(1990);* For Lesbians Only: A Separatist Anthology, *coedited with Sarah Lucia-Hoagland (1992); and* Flying Wide the Eyed Universe, *with Susan J. Wolfe (1998). Her writing has appeared in several feminist magazines and journals.*

Penelope celebrates the joy of being lesbian and the potentials of life outside "heteropatriarchy." Following the primary task for Lesbians, self-definition, is the creation of community, and a healthier way and place to live. She tells us: "I want to emphasize the unique potential inherent in the Lesbian experience, a potential so dangerous to the heterosexual body politic that it's exhilarating."

I CALL THIS ESSAY "THE Lesbian Perspective," not because I imagine there is *one* Lesbian perspective, but to suggest the possibility of a Lesbian consensus reality—a Lesbian-centered view of the world—and to indicate that there are aspects of Lesbian experience on which we can ground a self-defined consensus reality. When Lesbians work and create together, we live a vision of Lesbian community. "That is the whole meaning of Lesbian works, magazines, videos, movies, research, all of which shape our collectivity into reality. A collectivity becomes flesh and bone each time one of us thinks of herself as partaking in an actual Lesbian community" (Grimard-Leduc, 494). Given the depth of the differences in the ways we understand ourselves, can there be such a being as "The Lesbian"? I think yes. Our perspective inheres in all our works. If we are not trying to articulate a Lesbian view of the world,

why do we create the artifacts of a self-realizing culture? Although I am unable to flesh out the anatomy of the Lesbian Body, I want to emphasize the unique potential inherent in the Lesbian experience, a potential so dangerous to the heterosexual body politic that it's exhilarating.

Easy generalizations about *all* Lesbians are impossible; each of us participates in heteropatriarchal culture to varying degrees. We make different social, economic, and political choices in the context of our backgrounds and experiences and our interpretations of them. But I cannot use that fact to avoid generalizing. If we think that any generalizing about Lesbians is wrong, then we should also stop identifying ourselves as *Lesbian* and *Dyke*, and adopt the point of view that there is nothing significant about being Lesbians. By placing the Lesbian experience clearly in relation to male culture, however, I will show how our political differences arise from specific contexts and our responses to those contexts. I want to outline the common ground on which I think we can create a Lesbian community that will support even those who may not want it or know that it exists.

What I call the "Lesbian Perspective" is a "turn of mind," a stance in the world, that asks unpopular questions, that can be comfortable only when it confronts the sources of its discomfort, a frame of mind that refuses to accept what most people believe to be "true." This turn of mind I identify as "Lesbian." It is what enabled us to reject heterosexual bribery. It is a mind that must have its own integrity on its own terms. Just as being a living, breathing Lesbian exposes the lie of heterosexuality as "normal" and "natural," the Lesbian Perspective challenges *every* lie on which male society is founded. And there are lots of those. We don't submit willingly to the dogmas of authority. Even when we try to hide our "bad attitude" from those who have power over us by retreating into silence, we stand out like dandelions in neatly manicured lawns. Lesbians are the weeds that blossom proudly, stubbornly, in heterosexual families; no matter what lethal methods they use to eradicate us, we keep springing back. We are resilient, and our roots go deep.

WHAT'S WRONG WITH THIS PICTURE?

Where do we begin to define our Selves? How are Lesbians unique? In spite of an occasional craving to be "like everybody else," we know that we *aren't*. If we were, we wouldn't be Lesbians. Some deep-seated consciousness knows that the world presented to us as "real" is false. There's something wrong with the picture. The Lesbian Perspective originates in our sense of "difference"—however vague the feeling may be, however much we resist that knowledge—and in our certainty that what others seem happy to accept as "real" is seriously flawed. In order to conceive and define ourselves as Lesbians, we have to defy the "wisdom of the ages." Nobody held up a picture of a wonderful Dyke for us and said, "*You* could grow up to be strong and defiant like her." From the day a girl child is born, everyone who exercises control and authority in her life assumes that she will grow up to "fall in love" with a male (the verb *fall* suggests that it is an "accidental" misstep), and that she will inevitably marry one. All the messages she hears about *who* she is and *who* she's expected to become assume that there's only one kind of love and one kind of sexuality, and that's *heterosexual*. One of those messages informs us that we possess a biologically determined "maternal instinct"; another croons at us, "Every woman needs a man." Imagine how many Lesbians there would be in the world if we got the kind of airtime and publicity that heterosexuality gets. In spite of liberal feminist proclamations to the contrary, we're a long, long way from Marlo Thomas's world of "Free to Be You and Me." What we're "free to be" is heterosexual. That, and that only.

If we must speak of choice, it is the Lesbian who *chooses* to accept the terms of the heterosexual imperative, not the heterosexual. Heterosexuals don't choose their sexuality; they believe it's "natural"—the only way there is to be. Only Lesbians can choose how to define ourselves. Being a Lesbian or a heterosexual isn't a matter of "choosing" a lifestyle or a "sexual preference" from the table spread before us by parents, teachers, and other authority figures. There's only one dish on the social menu—heterosexuality—and we're given to understand that we swallow it or go without. The only options we have are those we create for ourselves because we must do so. Who we decide we are isn't a matter of "taste," although some Lesbians do try to acquire a "taste" for heterosexuality.

There's a large difference between "being heterosexual" and "being a Lesbian." "Being" heterosexual means conforming, living safely, if uncomfortably, within the limits established by men. "Being" a Lesbian means living marginally, often in secrecy, often shamefully, but always as different, as "deviant." Some Lesbians have sex with men, may marry one, two, three, or four men, have numerous children, and live as heterosexuals for some portion of their lives. Lesbians are coming out at every age, and, regardless of how old we are when we decide to act on our self-knowledge, we say: "I've always been a Lesbian." Some Lesbians die without once acting on their deep feelings for other wimmin. Some Lesbians live someone else's life. Deciding to act on our emotional and sexual attractions to other wimmin is usually a long-drawn-out process of introspection and self-examination that can take years, because the social and emotional pressure surrounding us is powerful and inescapable. There's no visible, easily accessible support in our society for being Lesbians, which explains why we have so much trouble imagining what "being Lesbian" means. In many ways, we remain opaque even to our Selves because we haven't yet developed a language that describes our experiences.

Some of our political differences (I'm not referring here to differences arising from ethnic, racial, or class backgrounds, although they influence those I'm talking about) have to do with our level of tolerance for discomfort, how thoroughly we've learned to mistrust and deny our Lesbian selves. Lesbians can deny ourselves endlessly because we're told that we "should." Being heterosexual is the only identity offered, coerced, supported and validated by male society. Male society makes it easy to deny our inner selves, to disbelieve the integrity of our feelings, to discount the necessity of our love for each other, at the same time making it difficult for us to act on our own behalf. Ask a Lesbian who has lived as a heterosexual if she knew she was a Lesbian early in her life, and most will say "yes." Maybe some didn't know the word *Lesbian,* but they'll talk about their childhood love for teachers and girlfriends. Most will say, after they've named themselves Lesbians, "I've always been a Lesbian." Most will say, "I didn't believe there were others like me. I thought I was the only one." This is reinterpretation of experience from a new perspective, *not* revision.

Once a Lesbian identifies herself as *Lesbian,* she brings all of her earlier experiences with and feelings for other women into focus; she crosses the conceptual line that separates the known (the "safe") of the social validation awarded to heterosexuals and the tabooed unknown of deviance. Crossing into this territory, she begins to remember experiences she had "forgotten," recalling women and her feelings for them that she had analyzed or named differently; she examines memories of her past from a new perspective. Events and experiences that once "made no sense" to her are now full of meanings she had ignored, denied, or discarded. Reconceiving herself as Lesbian, she doesn't change or revise women, events, and experiences in her past; she reinterprets them, understanding them anew from her Lesbian Perspective in the present.

When we fail to be visible to each other, we invalidate the Lesbian Perspective and the meanings it attaches to our experiences. Each of us pays a price for Lesbian invisibility in our self-esteem, in years of our lives, in energy spent trying to deny our Selves. But it is a fact that millions of us name ourselves "Lesbian" even when we have no sense of a community, when we know no one else who is like us, when we believe we will live as outcasts and alone for the remainder of our lives. How do we become that which is nameless, or, once named, shameful, sinful, despised? The Lesbian stands against the world created by the male imagination. What *willfulness* we possess when we claim our lives!

The Lesbian Perspective develops directly out of our experiences in the world: how other people treat us as Lesbians, the negative and positive reactions we get in specific situations, what we're told (and believe) we "ought" to feel about ourselves as Lesbians, and the degree of honesty we come to feel

we can exercise in our various relationships. What appear to be important differences among Lesbians are survival skills that enable us to survive in hostile territory. Some of us, for example, have had mostly positive, or at least less damaging, reactions to our Lesbianism from others who "count" in our estimation. Some Lesbians have experienced varying degrees of acceptance, tolerance, and open-heartedness from their heterosexual families and friends. Some Lesbians say they've had "no problems" in their lives connected with their Lesbianism. Not every Lesbian has had portions of her mind destroyed by drugs and repeated shock treatments, or been disowned by her genetic family, or had to survive on her own in the streets, but lots of Lesbians have suffered greatly, have been abused, rejected, ridiculed, committed to psychiatric hospitals, jailed, and tortured. For some, the pain of living as a Lesbian made death a reasonable choice, and many Lesbians have killed themselves rather than endure an existence that seemed to have no hope. Suicide is a valid choice. Whatever our personal experience is, we are always at risk in this society.

CHOOSING OUR SELVES

Being a Lesbian isn't a "choice." We *choose* whether or not we'll live as *who we are.* Naming ourselves *Lesbian* is a decision to *act* on our truest feelings. The Lesbian who decides to live as a heterosexual does so at great cost to her self-esteem. Heterosexuals don't have to question the assumptions on which they construct their lives and then defend them to a hostile society. I can't estimate the damage done to our emotional lives by the dishonesty forced on us by male dogma, but I know how much of my own life has been lies, lies, and more lies.

We live in a society where dishonesty is prized above honesty, and Lesbians learn the necessity of lying early on. Parents may tell us to "be ourselves," but we find out quickly, after only one or two "experiments," that honesty is punished, that "being ourselves" really means "Be who we want you to be." I know how much of myself I've tried to cover up, deny, and lie about in order to escape the most violent, lethal methods of suppression. The people who represent "society" for us when we're growing up teach us all we need to know about what being an "adult" means. "Growing up" for females in male societies means *choosing men*, and then lying about how "happy" they are. Naming ourselves Lesbian is one of the most significant steps we take to affirm our integrity, to choose honesty over deception, and to become real to ourselves. This is why the consensus reality of heteropatriarchy describes Lesbianism as "a phase," as something we're supposed to "grow out of." Adopting the protective coloration of heterosexuality is thus equated with "maturity." "Growing up" is a code phrase signaling one's willingness to perform in specific ways: compromise principles, deny feelings, provide *and* accept descriptions one knows to be false, and read along from the heteropatriarchal script. Some people are more adept and credible at acting "mature," but adults lie, and they lie all the time—to their children, loved ones, friends, bosses—but mostly to themselves.

Even after we've begun to explore and expand the meanings of our Lesbian Perspective, we bring our painful experiences about the cost of being honest and the resulting dishonesty we've learned into our communities. Unlearning years of heterosexual training isn't something we can expect to accomplish quickly or easily. Staying honest about ourselves takes lots of practice. We bring our lessons about the necessity of disguising ourselves, of lying about our innermost feelings, and a sincere reluctance to self-disclose with us when we become members of Lesbian society. The results can be far more damaging to our attempts to communicate and create a community than they are in male society.

On the one hand, lying, not being honest about who we are or how we feel, is a *survival skill* we have developed. We have to lie to get by in most heterosexual contexts. I realize there are exceptions to this. But a majority of Lesbians—today—are still *afraid* to be honest about their Lesbian identity, and with good reason. As an out-front Lesbian, I want to validate their fear. It's real, it's based on actual or likely experiences, and no Lesbian should feel she's expected to apologize for protecting herself in the only way she knows.

On the other hand, we've learned the ethic of fear and secrecy so thoroughly that we discover we can't simply shed it when we're in Lesbian contexts. Again, though, previous experiences suggest that self-disclosure and honesty aren't entirely wise even among Lesbians. Too many Lesbians simply don't feel "safe" among other Lesbians on an emotional level, and so we're constantly on guard, prepared to protect ourselves. If we're committed to creating Lesbian communities in which we can work together, we have to deal up front with the fact that Lesbians hurt other Lesbians, not just sometimes, but frequently. We can only stop it when we recognize it, name it for what it is, resolve not to do it, and eliminate it as a behavior.

CHOOSING EACH OTHER

Those of us who call ourselves *Dyke* or *Lesbian* talk often about a Lesbian community, whether we're "in" or "out" of it, whether or not a community can be said to exist, whether we approve or disapprove of some events or behaviors. Some of our talk may be negative, bitter, wishful, even fanciful, but it is based in our experiences as well as our desire. However we feel about Lesbian community—negative, positive, or indifferent—we call it into existence because we *do* talk about it.

One Lesbian or another can be heard denying that there's any such thing as a Lesbian "community" because she hasn't gotten support for one thing or another. Denying the existence of something acknowledges its potential existence. It's easy to deny ourselves, to remove ourselves from a Lesbian context, to refuse to argue with each other. Those who say the Lesbian community doesn't exist are simultaneously asserting that it *should* exist, thereby calling it into being. I think we deny the existence of Lesbian community when someone or some group fails to meet our expectations of what we believe a Lesbian community *should* be. Rather than risk exposing our expectations of ourselves and other Lesbians, we elide the community we're working hard to create. Something that doesn't exist cannot be blamed for betraying or failing us.

However we conceive our Selves, when each of us decided to name ourselves Lesbians, we were simultaneously estranged from our first "community," the male society into which we were born and in which we were raised. Our decision to be Lesbians cut us off from the forms of validation available to non-Lesbians. Even if a Lesbian gladly embraces male values in every other aspect of her life, if her only act of rebellion is her decision to relate sexually and emotionally with other Lesbians, she will never be rewarded as heterosexuals are. Our Lesbianism isn't valued by male society; it's systematically devalued—discouraged, derided, punished—no matter how we choose, individually, to accommodate estrangement in our lives. We may find occasional support and validation here and there among heterosexuals, but it's not something we can rely on or count as permanent. Our greatest hope for steady, reliable support lies with each other, within the Lesbian community.

COMMUNITY AND COMMUNICATION

I'm going to suggest that a lot, not all, but a lot of our internal dis-eases, are essentially language problems. They originate in how we talk or don't talk to each other and how we listen or don't listen to each other. Talking, which implies the desire to share ideas, opinions, and feelings, is the essential feature of two pairs of words: *communicate* and *community*, and *relate* and *relationship*. The word *community*, after all, has the same Latin root as the verb to *communicate*, *communicare*, 'to share', and its adjective, *communis*, meaning 'common'. In addition to their more specialized meanings in English, these words also mean 'to share with' and 'to be connected'. If we break the words *community* and *communicate* down further, the prefix *com-*, as in *complete* and *commute*, means 'with', and *-mun-* is the root of the Latin verb *munire*, meaning 'to fortify'. If we think about all these meanings—being connected, sharing, having something in common, and being fortified—we can better understand why a word like *community* resonates in us. We communicate most comfortably with those with whom we have something in common, and we're most likely to find them within a community. By sharing with other Lesbians, we fortify ourselves and grow stronger.

Relationship, that tired, overused word, sounds empty these days, having been heterosexually reified as though it were an autonomous entity, or therapized into a banal abstraction. Whether we can save it or not, we need to remember what it once meant: the willing telling of our Selves to those we connect with. Our relationships aren't limited to

those that're sexual; sexual intimacy isn't the defining characteristic of a "relationship." Our friendships are "relationships," and our disagreements are relationships, too. Both our individual relationships as Lesbians and our community are premised on the same sharing: our willingness to *tell* our Selves, our stories, our fears, and our imaginings. The more we talk and listen to each other, the stronger each of us becomes. The stronger we are, the stronger our community. Too often, though, we talk *around* or *at* each other rather than *to* or *with*. Arguing is one kind of communication, but it's something we seem reluctant to do publicly, as if by suppressing our disagreements we can coerce unity from silence.

When we disagree, when we criticize other Lesbians, we're sharing ourselves and our own ideas and opinions. Disagreement isn't only a way of affirming ourselves; we also affirm the significance of the individuals we criticize. Arguing and disagreeing are ways of paying attention to the ideas and beliefs of others. When we argue, we're implying that the ideas we disagree with are important and merit attention. Silence often signals indifference. What we don't find worth responding to, we ignore. When we argue with other Lesbians, we also grow. Total agreement is total stagnation and boredom.

Consider this: In this society, we learn to think of argument as war (Lakoff and Johnson, 4–6). ARGUMENT IS WAR is a cultural metaphor that turns up in the ways we describe the process of arguing. We talk about feeling "defensive," "defending our position," "shooting holes in someone else's argument," "holding opposing views," "demolishing an argument," "winning" and "losing arguments," having "weak points" in an argument, making claims that're "indefensible," "going on the offensive," and "being right on target." If we argue with each other as though ARGUMENT IS WAR, it's no wonder that criticisms are felt as "attacks" and disagreements are felt as "hostility." But arguing doesn't have to be experienced as a war. It's only the male description that makes the equation seem to be "inevitable" and "accurate."

If we believe that criticism is an "attack," and arguing is inherently "hostile," we're also likely to confuse unquestioning support with nurturance. If someone questions our opinions, behaviors, or attitudes, we may dismiss them as "unsupportive."

Much is possible once we stop expecting to agree with each other on every single aspect of our lives. Like the members of any other society, we're not going to agree completely, ever. Yet, as a community, we don't handle our disagreements as well as we could.

I believe that inside each Lesbian is the headstrong, willful core of Self that enabled her to choose to act on her Lesbianism, and we need to reclaim that initial certainty, to fulfill the promises we made to our Selves. A first step toward a real Lesbian community must be relearning honesty, a difficult project when all we know is lies. If we are to talk to each other, we must be able to believe that what we're hearing is honesty, even if we don't like it. Let's drop the fine rhetoric and the pretense to perfect understanding. If we're going to make a commitment to a viable, strong, Lesbian community, we have to begin by talking honestly to each other and listening carefully, too. We must take responsibility for articulating and acting on Lesbian values, values that empower our Lesbian Selves.

THE BIG PICTURE

The 1980s were a scary decade for Lesbians, and many of us slipped into an uneasy silence or slammed shut the doors of the closets behind us for a second or third time. We need to keep reminding each other that, as far as we know, *nothing like us has ever happened before. As far as we know,* there has never been a Lesbian Move-ment, and we are *global* in our connectedness. Too many Lesbians have learned, again, to think of ourselves as insignificant. We've heard so much about "broader issues" and "the big picture" that some may think that the Lesbian Perspective is a "narrow" one, restricted to an "insignificant" minority.

Narrow, when applied to concrete, physical dimensions, is used positively, because it refers to slenderness in width, and being 'slender' in heteropatriarchal society is a virtue for those born female. But *narrow,* used abstractly to describe ideas, implies a primarily negative evaluation of whatever concepts it's attached to. We speak, for example, of "narrow opinions," "narrow perspectives," "narrow concerns," and we're much taken by points of view that advertise themselves as part of "the

broader picture," as affording us "a broader perspective," a "wider scope," or an opportunity to join the "larger revolution." The word *narrow* is used to trivialize, diminish, and discredit a point of view that some people, usually those with socially-validated power, find threatening, repugnant, and downright outrageous. It is my intention to be outrageous. The Lesbian Perspective is certainly no less "real" or compelling than the dominant perspective of the white, heterosexual majority, and it's by no means as "narrow" in the negative sense of that word. We rightly avoid the "straight and narrow path."

Our unacknowledged allegiance to male thought patterns can hypnotize us into passivity, and men frequently succeed in freezing us with the word *narrow* (and others). There is nothing "narrow" about being and thinking *Lesbian.* What I'm warming up to here is a discussion of "category width" in English and where we think we might "fit" into the categories of man-made frameworks. The language most Lesbians in the U.S. speak, by choice or coercion, is English (native American, black, Latina, Chicana, and Asian-American Lesbians know first-hand about the cultural imperialism of imposed language), and it's the semantic structure of English that binds our minds, squishing our ideas into tidy, binary codes: not-this/this, female/male, small/big, black/white, poor/rich, fat/thin, unseeing/seeing, insane/sane, powerless/powerful, narrow/broad, guilty/innocent. These are narrow concepts in the most negative sense of the word, but they are the semantic basis of the pale male perspective, and we need to understand the conceptual territory those semantic categories map before we can set about the task of creating a new map that charts the territory of the Lesbian Perspective.

Learning a first language socializes us, and we're dependent creatures when our minds are guided into the conceptual grooves created by the map of the territory men want us to follow. The language forces us to perceive the world as men present it to us. If we describe some behaviors as "feminine" and others as "masculine," we're perceiving ourselves in male terms. Or, we fail to perceive what is not described for us and fall back on male constructs, such as "butch" and "femme," as inherently explanatory labels for our self-conceptions.

Those of us raised speaking English weren't offered any choice in the matter. However, while we were passive in the indoctrination process for the first few years, there comes a time when we have to put aside the fact that we began as innocent victims, and undertake the active process of self-reclamation that starts with understanding what happened to us and questioning the conceptual premises on which male societies are based. Learning to think around categorial givens is hard, but it's something we have to do in order to think well of ourselves. If we refuse to do this, we abandon ourSelves.

What is called "consensus reality" is the male-defined, male-described version of "what is," and we are obliged to live around, under, and sometimes within what men say is "reality," even as we strive to conceive and define a Lesbian "consensus reality." The duality of our position as Lesbians—simultaneously being oppressed by a society in which we are unwanted and marginal, and envisioning for ourselves a culture defined by our values, with Lesbian identity at its core—is, I maintain, a position of strength if we claim it.

First, we must undertake the tedious process of examining and re-examining *every* aspect of how we've been taught to "think," including the process of thinking itself. Every one of us raised in an English-speaking household learned to perceive the world, and ourselves in the world, according to the selective map of the pale male perspective. Any map is always, and only, a *partial* description of the territory it claims to chart. Each map draws attention only to those topographical features that the map creator thinks are "relevant" or "significant"; each map creator perceives only some of the aspects of the territory while other, perhaps equally important, features remain invisible, unperceived. Some things are left out on purpose, others are distorted. Black and dark, for example, are given negative values in the pale male conceptual structure, while white and light are assigned positive values; being able to see is a "good thing"; not being able to see is a "bad thing"; accepting male versions of what is "real" is "rational"; rejecting them is "irrational." These descriptions and the values attached to them are not "the nature of the world," and it's not coincidence. Whatever conceptual changes are eventually condoned by male culture can occur only by enlarging existing category widths, in particular the

referential scope of words like *people* and *gay.* The semantic categories themselves don't change; they aren't allowed to change. They expand and contract, but the essential thought structures remain the same.

One of our difficulties with describing a Lesbian consensus reality is a language problem: we use contradictory labels to name ourselves, terminology that's sometimes useful but often divisive. The way we name ourselves reflects how we understand what we mean in the world. We call ourselves, for example, "people," "human beings," "women," "gays," "Lesbians," "Dykes." Because we're biologically categorized as female, it seems meaningful to say that, by inclusion with heterosexual women, we're oppressed as "women," and our experience of socialization confirms this category overlap. Likewise, because we aren't hetero, we're also oppressed as "homosexuals," so some Lesbians identify with gaymen, in which case they call themselves "gay women," as I did for many years. Our invisibility, even to ourselves, is at least partially due to the fact that our identity is subsumed by two groups: women and gaymen. As a result, Lesbian issues seem to find their way, by neglect or elimination, to the bottom of both liberation agendas. The liberation of Lesbians is supposed to wait for the liberation of all women, or be absorbed and evaporate into the agenda compiled by gaymen. Instead of creating free space for ourselves, we allow men to oppress us invisibly in both categories, as "women" or as "gays," without even the token dignity of being named "Lesbians." How we name ourselves determines how visible we are, even to each other.

If we allow ourselves to imagine ourselves as something other than "woman" or "gay," if we try to conceive of our Selves beyond those labels, what comes into our minds? Is it no-thing, or is it some-thing? Even if it is hazy, vague, without clear definition, isn't it some-thing we know but haven't yet been able to articulate? The issue here is making explicit the basis of our prioritizing, which has been the idea that we are "sub-" somebody else. I think we are much, much more if we choose our Selves. The problem, as I identify it, is calling ourselves *women.* Monique Wittig (1988) and others have argued that the category 'woman' is a manmade category that serves men's purposes. In this case, the label *woman* diffuses Lesbian movement toward ourSelves, diverting our attention from Lesbian issues and Lesbian needs. The label shifts our focus, directing our attention away from Lesbian community. As soon as we name ourselves Lesbians, we step outside of the category 'woman'. What we experience as Lesbians and identify as "women's oppression" is the socialization process that tried to coerce us into 'womanhood'. As a result of this tailoring of our identities, when we change categories from 'woman' to 'Lesbian', we're still oppressed as 'female' and oppressed for daring to be 'not-woman'. While both Lesbians and hetero women experience misogyny as biological females, Lesbians' experience of that oppression is very different.

The L-word continually disappears into the labels *gay* and *woman*, along with our energy, our money, and our hope. So much Lesbian creativity and activity is called "women's this" or "gay that," making Lesbians invisible and giving heterosexual women or gaymen credit for what they can't imagine and haven't accomplished. We need to think *Lesbian*. We need to think *Dyke*. We need to stop being complacent about our erasure.

The male map cannot be trusted because the territory it describes isn't a healthy place for us to live in. Accepting male descriptions of the world endangers Lesbians. We can fight for inclusion within already sanctioned categories, such as 'people', 'human being', or 'woman', thereby forcing other speakers to enlarge them, or we can remain outside of patriarchally given categories and endeavor to construct a different, more accurate map of the Lesbian conceptual territory. We have internalized a description of the world that erodes our self-esteem, damages our self-image, and poisons our capacity for self-love. If the children we were lacked options for the process of self-creation, the Lesbians we've become have the potential, as well as the responsibility, for redefining ourselves, learning to perceive the world in new and different ways from what we were taught, and setting about making maps that accurately describe the territory of our envisioning.

We can choose whether or not we will conform to heterosexual values, and even the degree to which we'll conform to the map men have imposed on reality. How we choose to deal with the defining categories of male culture places us within its boundaries or at its periphery. (See my essay, "Het-

eropatriarchal Semantics and Lesbian Identity: The Ways a Lesbian Can Be" for an analysis of these defining categories.) We are never "outside" the reach of society, because even the negative evaluation of who we are can limit and control our lives. How we describe for ourselves that first wary step into an uncharted world determines how we think of ourselves as Lesbians. The Lesbian situation is essentially *ambiguous,* and that ambiguity provides the foundation of the Lesbian Perspective. We must start from where we are.

TERRA INCOGNITA

Deciding to act on our Lesbian perceptions requires each of us to conceive of ourselves as someone other than who male society has said we are. The Lesbian process of self-definition, however long it takes, begins with the recognition and certainty that our perceptions are fundamentally accurate, regardless of what male societies say. This is a *strong* place in us. In order to trust ourselves, we have to be able to push through the lies and contradictions presented to us as "truths," cast them aside, and stand, for that moment, in our own clarity. Every Lesbian takes that step into *terra incognita*: the undescribed or falsely described, the "unknown," beyond the limits posted by the pale male map of reality. Picture for yourself the map of the "known" world presented to us every moment, every day of our lives. Label that map HETEROPATRIARCHY out to the very neatly trimmed edges. Now read the warning signs along the edge: "Dangerous," "monstrous," "sick," "sinful," "illegal," "unsafe," "Keep Out! Trespassers will be violated!" Remember how long you deliberated with yourself before stepping across that boundary, before you decided you had to ignore the warning signs and take your chances in an ill-defined geography.

It's the clarity of that moment, the confidence of self-creation, that creates the "euphoria" so many Lesbians experience when we first come out. We do not forget that moment of clarity, ever. Lesbians think and behave differently because we've had to fight constantly to establish and maintain our identity in spite of covert and overt attempts, some of them violent, all of them degrading, to coerce us into heterosexuality. The Lesbian Self must stand alone, sometimes for years, against the force of the heterosexual imperative, until she can find other Lesbians who will support and affirm her. The out Lesbian has denied the validity of what men call "reality" in order to be Her Self. We do think differently. We perceive the world as aliens, as outcasts. No matter how hard some Lesbians try to "fit in," pale male societies define us as outside the boundary of the categories that maintain its coherence. We are made outcasts, but we can empower our Selves on that ground.

Although we may look back at times with yearning toward the heterosexual land of make-believe, we know that delusion for what it is: a man-made smog that pollutes and poisons all life. We must choose our own clarity, our willfulness, and reject the orthodoxy, "right-thinking," of men. Being Lesbian *is* nonconforming. The Lesbian Perspective demands heterodoxy, deviant and unpopular thinking, requires us to love ourselves for being outcasts, to create for ourselves the grounds of our being. The Lesbian Perspective isn't something we acquire as soon as we step out of our closets. It's as much a process of unlearning as it is learning. It's something we have to work at, nurture, encourage, and develop. The Lesbian Perspective is furious self-creation.

If we can imagine ourselves into being, if we can refuse to accept the labels and descriptions of men, the "possibilities *are* endless." We *are* outcasts from male society. We have no choice in that. What we can choose is how we define ourselves with respect to our outcast status. The Lesbian Perspective always asks "unpopular" questions. They're not popular because they threaten the interior structure of societies erected by men. What, exactly, does the Lesbian Perspective look like? Because we're already living in a way that men say is impossible, we gradually shed the dichotomies and distinctions we learned as children. The labels, names, and compartmentalizations that accompany them come to have less and less relevance in our thought processes, and we find new ways of interpreting our experience in the world because we perceive it differently. What we once memorized and accepted as "facts" no longer accurately describe our perceptions of reality. We realize that what we were taught to think was "real" or "natural" are only man-made constructs imposed on acts and events, ready-made representations of thoughts and feelings that we can, and must, reject. This is a difficult, gradual, uncertain process only because male societies don't want us to enjoy being outcasts. It's definitely *not* in the interests of men for us to like ourselves. Although it's men who established the boundaries that made us outcasts, what counts is how we organize that information in our minds and act on it in our lives.

The Lesbian Perspective challenges what heterosexuals choose to believe is "fact." As our joy in being outcasts expands, so does our ability to ask dangerous questions and dis-cover magical answers. We have no "givens" beyond that which is "other than": "deviant," "abnormal," "unnatural," "queer," false descriptions we begin with and cannot afford to forget. Indeed, we should wear them proudly. But our major endeavor must be self-definition. We have much to learn yet about ourselves, *our* culture, and we have new maps to draw that show the significant features of our worlds. The Lesbian Perspective makes it possible to challenge the accuracy of male consensus reality, and to create a reality that is Lesbian-defined and Lesbian-sustaining. Once we learn to perceive the world from our own perspective, outside the edges of the pale male map, we'll find it not only recognizable, but familiar.

Bringing Up Baby: Raising a "Third World" Daughter in the "First World"

Shamita Das Dasgupta and Sayantani DasGupta

Daughter Sayantani DasGupta received an MD from Johns Hopkins University. A freelance writer, her work has appeared in such diverse periodicals as Ms., Z Magazine, Contemporary Pediatrics, *and* Journal of the Annals of Behavioral Science in Medical Education, *as well as various anthologies. With her mother, she coauthored* The Demon Slayers and Other Stories: Bengali Folk Tales *(1998).*

Mother Shamita Das Dasgupta teaches psychology at Rutgers and works with battered South Asian women through Manavi, an organization she helped found. In addition to The Demon Slayers, *she edited* A Patchwork Shawl: Chronicles of South Asian Women in America *(1998).*

There are a host of themes explored by this "team" in the following essay: the potentials and treatment of the mother-daughter relationship—in the West and in India; the pleasures of motherhood as well as the uncertainty and strain; the experiences of being an immigrant and a first-generation child in America; heritage viewed from outside the dominant population; White/American feminism and Third World feminism; social consciousness, and several more. Finally, the women give us hope that if we extend our vision and broaden our analyses ever wider to include elements of "race, class, sexuality, and nationality," we can move toward "an intergenerational sisterhood."

SHAMITA

FOR ME, THE MOTHER OF this mother-daughter writing team, attraction to this particular topic mounted

as I watched my U.S.-born daughter grow into a "Third World"[1] activist. As a young and inexperienced Indian mother raising a child in the isolated and somewhat segregated world of a Midwestern town, my task had been complex, even disheartening at times.

As an immigrant to the United States from India in the late 1960s, I did not have the privilege of having my mother or any other female relative close by when my daughter was born. Thus, my early days of childrearing were fraught with self-doubt, advice from Dr. Spock, and a make-up-as-I-go quality. I knew that I wanted a politically aware, activist daughter, but did not have a clue about how to help her get there.

When I joined an undergraduate program in the Midwest as a psychology major, my daughter was three years old. I soon learned from my classes the many ways one can warp a child's mind and development. I became convinced I had already succeeded in doing so. I had surely thwarted my child's individuation by allowing her to sleep in our bed, by instructing her to share with others, by not providing her with a stable, stay-at-home mother. Every time my daughter got into trouble at school or with the neighborhood children, I was sure it was because of some maladjustment process that I had triggered. Later, when I expressed these feelings to my mother in India, she, in her characteristic disregard for psychology, quickly dismissed my fears: "Psychology, shmychology! You can't control everything in life or children. All of you overanalyze and hassle your children about everything. Being a sensible parent is all that one can do. Relax! No parent has ever been perfect up to now." Easier said than done. It took me many more years to realize that in much of Western psychology, the context of an Asian Indian is wholly missing, let alone that of an Asian Indian immigrant.

Shamita Das Dasgupta and Sayantani DasGupta, "Bringing Up Baby: Raising a 'Third World' Daughter in the 'First World,'" in *Dragon Ladies: Asian American Feminists Breathe Fire,* edited by Sonia Shah (Boston: South End Press, 1997) is reprinted with permission of South End Press.

During the early days of my training in feminism, a white American friend in my consciousness-raising group asked me whether, given a choice, I would have opted to have a child. The assumption, of course, was that I had little choice in the matter. Despite women's socialization by patriarchal mores and the presumed absence of free will in the indoctrinated, I could never deny my need to be a mother. For me, the problem was not motherhood, but finding help and advice about how to be a good mother. Feminism and the mainstream women's movement gave me no such direction, but added to my confusion by casting aspersions on my feminist convictions. This need to rear future generations has stayed with me over the years, as I have grown to mentor a new generation of young women, students, and activists.

When I joined the university and began moving in feminist circles, my community predicted dire consequences for my husband and daughter. My friends told me that I was sure to neglect my family's well-being because of my involvements. Nothing good could come out of feminism since it went against family solidarity and attachments. Many of my husband's male acquaintances told him that they pitied him, that they would never allow their wives to be "corrupted" by me. Even my women friends made snide comments about my motives, insinuating that there must be marital discord between my husband and myself. Others told me that my aggressiveness and politics were sure to break my family apart.

Recently, a young activist friend of mine came to me in tears. For some time, she had been trying to move out of her parents' apartment to secure literal and figurative personal space. Even though she had been trying to discuss this move with her parents for a considerable period, they had avoided speaking about it openly. When finally confronted with the inevitable, her parents were horrified and took her move as a rejection of their family. Although her new apartment was close to her parents, her mother swore never to step inside it. To their friends and neighbors, the uncles and aunties of the community, the truth was never revealed. Everyone in her family kept up the pretense that the move had never taken place. It seemed too shameful to admit that a "good" Indian girl could want to live alone.

When five of my friends and I founded Manavi, a battered women's organization for South Asian women, and began addressing the issue of domestic violence, we were quickly dubbed homewreckers and dismissed as fanatic feminists (read: Westernized). Our discussions about incidents of domestic violence within the community usually met with disbelief and skepticism. Even the most sensible members of our community told us that leaving a marriage, regardless of its abusiveness, could never be an option for women from our culture. This attitude of the community is imposed on battered women who end their marital relationships. Most women who decide to leave their abusive husbands anticipate relentless condemnation from the community and terminate their relationship with the latter as well.

Because I and my daughter started writing together on feminist issues, our picture appeared on the cover of the national women's magazine, *Ms.* Although our community friends maintained a stony silence, one of my husband's colleagues sympathetically warned him about the danger of such explicit declarations of our politics. Since no one in our community takes kindly to a nontraditional woman, the colleague explained, my feminist daughter was really hurting her chances of marriage. Besides, who would want to establish a marital alliance with someone whose mother was a feminist?

SAYANTANI

What's the big deal?, I keep asking myself. What's the big deal about my mother and me? I'm not sure I realized exactly how we started getting attention as a "feminist mother/daughter team." For us, we've always been a team. From my days in elementary school, I remember going straight from the school to my mother's college campus. When most kids were playing with other children, I was spending my time playing with my mother's graduate-student colleagues. I was almost constantly with her. On our car rides back and forth from grocery stores, schools, universities, we discussed courses she was taking, books I was reading, our personal thoughts. As I grew older, we started collaborating on writing and other projects. We became collaborators and friends, as well as mother and daughter.

As a medical student, I can't envision spending the same kind of quality time with my future children as my mother did with me. All the way from her bachelor's degree through her Ph.D, and then throughout her career, my mother kept me beside her. We read together, played together . . . she even watched *Sesame Street* with me every single day. I think it was the sheer amount of time we spent together that taught me my politics. I never remember her formally teaching me to be an activist, yet she encouraged me to read and discuss with her everything I could get my hands on. She took me along on the journey of her feminist consciousness. I remember attending progressive rallies and listening in on most of her consciousness-raising meetings; when she formed the South Asian women's group, Manavi,[2] I was right there with her. Yet as I envision the long years of residency and medical practice ahead of me, I don't know how I will teach my children the same lessons my mother taught me. I'm not just scared of raising non-activist children, I'm petrified I will screw mine up! Will my children blame me for not being like their grandmother?

I'm not sure the Great White Foremothers of feminism would call most of the women in my family feminists. Then again, I'm not sure I like the label, either. The narrow definition leaves no room for diversity. But I learned about women's strength from my elderly white-sari-clad grandmothers as well as my activist mother; I had the privilege of meeting their friends, octogenarian grannies who turned out to be nationalist freedom-fighters, double Ph.Ds, or black-belts in judo. A tradition of women's strength leapt out at me from the pages of myth, from stories of the courageous Rani of Jhansi to the tradition of the Durga Puja festival for Bengal's favorite, the warrior goddess.

As a little girl, I remember taking Indian singing and dance classes, attending pujas, and participating in all variety of talent shows, musical dance-dramas, and traditional poetry readings. While I, like most Indian American little girls of my generation, was spending my time swathed in saris and decorated with paper flowers, our Indian American brothers had more freedom in dress, movement, and activity. It was a dual life of being American during the school week and then magically transforming ourselves into perfect little Indian girls during the weekend. I've spent most of my adult life trying to overcome this image of good Indian girlhood.

"You're becoming more and more American every day," my mother would tell me, particularly when she was afraid I was paying too little attention to academics, or too much attention to boys. It was a tricky tension she was referring to, I realize now. While she and I were a constant pair at most mainstream feminist events, we were also Indian women in the U.S. Midwest. My childhood consisted of being ultra-aware of my brownness, my strangeness, my difference. Even at mainstream feminist events, we were two of the few non-white faces. While she had to defend Indian culture to her progressive friends, who were convinced that Indian culture was comprised of nothing but sati, daughter disfavor, and other oppressions, my mother was faced with challenges from within our Indian community about her views. She was balancing my upbringing between two worlds, each with problematic politics.

"It would be much easier if you were a lesbian," friends have joked with me when we have attempted to come up with a list of eligible Indian men for me. The thought being, of course, that there are manifold more interesting South Asian women of my political persuasion than South Asian men. And even though I've used this joking comment frequently in my writing, I know it's not true. As a South Asian woman who dates men, sexuality is a difficult enough arena to negotiate. Yet the uniform silence our community maintains about lesbianism and bisexuality is a veritable minefield. My friend Sarita, 32, who has always been fairly close to her Indian immigrant parents and came out to them a few years ago, still has to field arranged marriage offers from them. "I tell them about my girlfriend," she complains, "and they seem to understand. Then in the next breath, they suggest I meet some nice young man. They seem to think being a lesbian is a phase." This parental reaction is a reflection of larger community attitudes: what doesn't fit their image, they ignore, perhaps thinking that if they ignore it long enough, it will go away.

The Indian American community convinces us that our natal culture consists of nothing but singing, dancing, and happy faces. And yet every time I go to India, I realize how anachronistic the monolithic Indian culture we learn in the United States is. My Indian cousins, who dated and behaved like most U.S. teens, used to appear utterly American, while I, who had been brought up in the Indian American community, fit a more traditional picture of Indianness. There was also more space for me among my Indian relatives than the Indian American community. In fact, while most of the Indian community chided my parents for sending me away from home for college (subtly suggesting that the money would be better spent on my wedding), my grandmother continued to urge me to begin an ambitious career. She seemed to think I had a higher destiny than traditional womanhood, that I could be granted the space of the *virangana* (warrior woman).

Our latest feminist gathering was a mother-daughter event at which we were invited to speak. It had been a long time since either of us attended a primarily mainstream U.S. feminist event, but this one, a speaking engagement for an anthology of feminist mother-daughter oral histories, struck home. But while everyone else was expounding on how moving, revealing, and inspirational it was to be interviewed, neither my mother nor I could figure out what to say. What's the big deal? I kept thinking, we've talked about all of this before. Then someone asked us to relate how the mother-daughter interview process affected our relationship as feminists. We couldn't avoid the question.

"It hasn't," my mother says, smiling at me, "I have been discussing feminism, activism, and politics with my daughter for years. I've been teaching her and learning from her for as long as she's been in my life."

"It's nothing new," I add, "this is what we do together. This is our life!"

MOTHERS–DAUGHTERS, PROFESSIONALLY SPEAKING

In this chapter, we try to articulate our experiences of becoming activist adults in the United States. Being mother and daughter, we are able to view the topic from two differing vantage points: becoming and being brought up as feminist activists. Our own experiences of being a mother and daughter are separated by time and space, as well as circumstances and conditions, since one of us grew up in post-independence India and the other in the post-1970 United States. Our chosen areas of work are also dif-

ferent, with one concentrating on violence against women and the other on healthcare systems. Yet we feel that there are systematic and complementary meanings to be found in our experiences.

How do we, South Asian diasporic mothers, raise activist children, especially daughters, away from our native cultures and our own histories? How do we, as diasporic daughters, accept the teachings of our South Asian mothers, whose lessons often feel culturally inappropriate? Who guides us as we become immigrants and South Asian American activists? Where do we find time-tested templates or our own role models?

Research on relationships between mothers and daughters is scant even in the Western world, let alone in the Third World. In fact, the mother-daughter dyad suffers from deep scholarly neglect, perhaps stemming from the oversight all women have historically experienced in society. When mothers have come into focus, it has been to make them responsible for what has gone wrong with their children. In the recently published anthology of mother-daughter oral histories, *The Conversation Begins*, Barbara Seaman expresses the result of this ubiquitous mother-blame: "For many women—and I am among them—the way you spell mother is G-U-I-L-T. I once began writing a book called 'The American Mother: Whatever You Do, It's Wrong.' I never finished it. I was too 'guilty.'"[3]

FEMINISM DOES MOTHERHOOD

Psychodynamic inquiries have focused on the importance of the mother-daughter dyad in women's emotional well-being.[4] This research suggests that mutuality in mother-daughter relationships is involved in women's social adjustment and the evolution of their self-esteem.[5] Feminists, on the contrary, have examined the same relationship in terms of the development of female autonomy. From the latter explorations two basic arguments have emerged: (a) that mothers stunt their daughter's individuation process; and (b) that being a mother is an obstacle to adult women's independence.

Academic and popular writers advancing the first argument have discussed how mothers have historically instilled guilt in their daughters and consequently have obstructed their metamorphosis into autonomous women.[6] According to these scholars, daughters seem to find their mothers restricting and silencing, rather than empowering compatriots.

Conversely, Western feminists have also openly discussed the constraints of motherhood and its inhibitory influences on women's individual development.[7] Perhaps reacting to the conflation of womanliness with motherhood, these feminists have been most eager to disentangle the two. In favor of encouraging the independent feminine self, at times this effort has led to the denunciation of motherhood itself. Unfortunately, such condemnations have only helped to alienate the majority of women for whom motherhood is still desirable. Even among the praetorian feminists, the issue of motherhood evokes more ambivalence than any other topic. Motherhood, a reality for most of the women on this planet, can hardly be dismissed summarily. Yet the controversy surrounding it is palpable in many feminist analyses.[8] The majority of these investigations have centered on the appropriateness of motherhood in a feminist's life rather than examining the various factors involved in this critical relationship or the vital part it plays in feminist struggles.

After years of neglecting motherhood, we have only recently seen a change of heart among Western feminists. Articles and books about mother/daughter feminist pairs are becoming *de rigeur*.[9] The common perception appears to be that these mothers, products of the 1960s feminist movement, are the first set of women to raise feminist daughters, negotiate relationships with them, and then attempt to "launch" them into the world while retaining strong friendships with them.[10] This perspective may not only be historically egocentric, but culturally narcissistic as well.

Although information about historic mother-daughter relationships in the West is scarce, we manage to catch a glimpse of these through letters and travelogues left behind by some women.[11] No such evidence seems to exist for South Asian women. Yet South Asian women have had a long history not only of activism,[12] but of close-knit female communities. As is wont in segregated societies, South Asian women have depended on each other on a day-to-day basis in the *andar mahal* or *zenana* (women's quarters)[13] and other women's congregations.[14] They have educated, affirmed, and taken care of each other through various *vrata*, or folk rituals.[15] Yet we know little about the relationships women have had with their mothers or daughters. Part of the reason for this silence may be the fact that South Asian women spent very little time in their natal homes due to the traditions of early marriage and patrilocal residency. However, given the numerous high-achieving and activist women in South Asia, such as Pandita Ramabai, Rokeya Sakhawat Hossain, Indira Gandhi, Pritilata Waddedar, Sirimavo Bandaranayake, and Khaleda Zia, it is not easy to understand this total blackout of mother-daughter relationships.

WOMEN, BY MEN

Motherhood, as defined by patriarchy, has historically been problematic for women. In the West, motherhood implies a lack of mobility, an unbreakable chain to home and hearth, and powerless self-sacrifice. In South Asia, motherhood brings with it more complexity. On the one hand, the birth of daughters traditionally brings social shame to women, whereas the birth of sons fortifies their power.[16] This initial reaction at birth translates into widespread daughter disfavor and son privilege in society. On the other hand, motherhood is highly venerated as a powerful role. The association of mortal mothers with the great goddesses in India provides some measure of cultural strength, however hidden or theoretical. It is with this heritage that Asian Indian immigrants arrive at U.S. shores. However, this is not the only factor that influences the relationship between mothers and daughters within our immigrant community in the United States.

Although immigrants from India entered the United States first in the early 1800s, the major influx occurred after the passage of the 1965 Immigration and Naturalization Act. The modified immigration policies that facilitated the passage of Indians to the United States also artificially created an upper-middle-class, Western-educated, technologically oriented homogeneous community within the first decade. That this group would quickly find financial and occupational success in this country is thus of little wonder.[17] In fact, the phenomenal economic achievements of Asian Indian immigrants procured for them the label of "model minority."

The tag was created in the 1970s by the media, which presumed that Asian Indians were free from all social ills such as racism, drug addiction, intergenerational discord, social maladjustment, violence, and unemployment or underemployment. Such assumptions resulted not only in exempting Asian Indians from most governmental assistance, but in creating rifts with other minority groups. In addition, Asian Indian immigrants themselves internalized this myth and became preoccupied with living up to it.

With the acceptance of this immaculate image of themselves, Asian Indians have created a public face that is unblemished by conflicts, dissension, and diversity. This deliberate creation of an uncontentious Indian monolith is typical throughout North America. A speaker at the Federation of Indo-Canadian Associations once said, "The strength of Indians and other South Asians in Canada depends on their ability to project themselves as a united force." He further added, "the whole issue of South Asian unity has to be redefined by South Asian Canadians in the 1990s [to] sell that reality and image to other Canadians."[18] In the process of creating and maintaining this ideal image, Asian Indians have constructed certain icons that are symbolic of the community's cohesion and integrity. Foremost among these is the image of our community's women as loyal, passive, chaste, modest, and obedient. To the immigrant Indian bourgeoisie seeking to establish culturally "familiar essentials" around them, "[T]he woman becomes a metaphor for the purity, the chastity, and the sanctity of the Ancient Spirit that is India."[19] Thus, the validity of our community's image rests on the submissiveness of its women.[20] Lata Mani articulates this issue succinctly: "the burden of negotiating the new world is borne disproportionately by women, whose behavior and desires, real and imagined, become the litmus test for the South Asian community's anxieties or sense of well-being."[21]

In the immigrant community, direct and implicit censure confine both generations of Asian Indian women within boundaries that limit their activities.[22] Mothers are assigned the task of socializing their daughters within prescribed roles, and a daughter is taught to be "a good Indian girl . . . who does not date, is shy and delicate, and marries an Indian man of her parents' choosing."[23] A letter written to the editor of *India Abroad* by a U.S.-raised young woman speaks of this socialization eloquently: "As Indians, we are taught to respect our elders, to remain silent unless spoken to, and especially to be obedient."[24] These strict rules are enforced in the name of preserving the natal culture, the perpetuation of which has become a priority for the community.

The issue of preserving the "Indian culture" has taken on great importance as the children of immigrants have started to come of age in the United States. Asian Indians recognized early on that they are at risk of losing their native culture to ferocious assimilationist pressures in the environment as well as at the hands of their own U.S.-raised children. However well-adapted they may be economically, over the years Asian Indian immigrants have resisted total acculturation and opted to maintain a distinct cultural self. In addition, they believe that the future of their beloved culture depends upon the loyalty of the community's women, especially daughters, who will be socializing agents of the next generation.

Relegating women to the role of keepers of culture, hearth, and home is not a new phenomenon in South Asian traditions. However, to simplify the passage of values, Asian Indian immigrants have fabricated a mythical culture that denies all variability. To be considered an authentic Indian in the Indian community, an individual has to unquestioningly accept an upper-class, heterosexist, Hindu-centric, hierarchical, and sanitized version of "Indian culture." For example, in almost all the regiono-linguistic conferences that take place each year in the United States, such as the Bengali, Tamil, Assam, Havik, Punjabi, and Telegu conferences, activities are limited primarily to Sanskritized versions of visual and performing arts. *India Abroad* described the 1996 Bengali conference as "a strictly cultural event." "Religion and politics were left out of the platform. . . . [W]e waxed philosophical, sang, and made merry," stated one of its organizers.[25] Even when a few seminars are included in these conferences, they are sidelined and stripped of all controversies. Furthermore, in most seminars, issues pertaining to race, class, and sexuality are not discussed, while there is an overall absence of working-class people and their concerns. This reconstructed culture relies heavily on a blatantly androcentric model of gender relationships that is promoted in the community as "true traditions" of India.[26] A letter to the editor of *India Abroad* summarized this communal attitude:

> *I wonder what will make a woman happy in the developed world. In India women are happy just being women. It appears that in the U.S. women don't want to be women, but to be equal to men. But they simply can't be because God never wanted that. It is frightening to visualize the direction toward which the feminist activists are leading unsuspecting women, by destroying the element of love between the sexes.*[27]

To be fair, this reformulated Indian culture is not just for the expediency of the immigrants. It is also a reaction to the dominant U.S. culture that seems to view diversity as deficiency, a view that is paralleled by the recent rise of the highly militant Hindu fundamentalist movement in India. In both the Indian and U.S. forms of this fictional Indian culture, women have been rendered the emblems of purity and authenticity. Consequently, women in general, and the second generation in particular, feel obligated to play the passive, unprotesting, ritual-bound, gender-typed role of a "good Indian woman." Transgressors of these strictures are labeled "Westernized" and are often psychologically, and sometimes literally, banished from the community. "In the U.S., the worst fear of Indian parents by far is their children are becoming 'American.'"[28] Thus, to counteract the host culture's influences and inculcate the children in "authentic" traditions, classes in music, dance, Indian languages, and religion are proliferating all over the United States.[29]

In this mission to sustain the "Indian culture," both young men and women are targeted, but it is second-generation women who bear the brunt.[30] Any questioning of "traditions" are considered cultural betrayals and dealt with harshly. "Many Indian women," writes a reader of an ethnic newspaper, "fully realize the tolls of challenging age-old traditions. They could be ostracized from families."[31] This penalization is not confined to individual levels only, but extends to institutional spheres. A prime example of this was the 1995 India Day parade in New York City, where the organizers, the Federation of Indian Associations in America (FIA), barred groups focusing on battered women, gay

and lesbian rights, communal relations, workers' rights, and anti-racism activities from participating. Each of these groups represents a segment of the population that belies the trouble-free image that the Asian Indian immigrant community has been trying to maintain.

WOMEN ON WOMEN

As women of the community, mothers and daughters play a vital role in the preservation of this re-created Indian culture. Besides being bearers of culture, mothers are positioned as monitors of their daughters' conduct, and their punishment for disregarding the community's dictates is to be identified as "bad mothers." Daughters, on the other hand, are even more restricted within the community's prescriptions, and their transgressions are deemed gross betrayals of the culture. Thus, both generations of women who question "traditions" or express autonomy, diversity, and independence in their behavior are treated as destroyers of the community.

Rejecting the constraints of the Asian Indian immigrant community is not always possible. It is this community that provides us with shelter from mainstream racism and the day-to-day difficulties of negotiating multiple cultural identities. Nonetheless, unquestioning compliance of community rules that strengthen the upper-class patriarchal hierarchy is not possible. As mothers we have to resist the inclination to take the path of least resistance, not only in our own lives, but in the upbringing of our daughters.

Internal cultural critique does not, however, imply cultural betrayal, as the leaders of our immigrant communities would have us believe. Neither feminism nor activism are alien to our culture—they are nested within our heritage.[33] We can draw strength from the tradition of the *virangana*, or "warrior woman," which visualizes women as inherently powerful.[34] In addition, the *virangana* is not marginalized in our natal societies. Rather, she is revered as a savior whom parents urge their daughters to emulate. Claiming this legacy for ourselves and our daughters would only help to empower us. Furthermore, we cannot erase our history of resistance and social change work from the version of "culture" we present to our children. Our "culture" does not only consist of songs and dances, literature and art, but includes activism and the pursuit of social justice.

A MOTHER–DAUGHTER DIALOGUE

Since the Asian Indian immigrant community rejects feminism as a Western phenomenon, many young activists tend to believe that progressive activism and their heritage are incompatible.[35] Thus, young women of Indian descent are often forced to make a choice between their politics and their communities. Those who choose the latter are restricted by the monolithic picture of "good" Indian womanhood that their communities have constructed, their questions silenced by the fear of cultural excommunication. On the other hand, the women who choose the former are not only isolated from their communities, but they often reject their heritage themselves as inherently "backward." By adopting a Western model of feminism, they also run the risk of developing an individualistic feminist politics.

As Third World feminist mothers, we have a responsibility to extend our daughters' social consciousness from the individual to the collective, from the local to the global. In the 1960s, U.S. feminism ran on a platform of "being what you want to be." Despite its superficial inclusion of other agendas, this idea of individual progress has persisted into the feminism of the 1990s. In an interview with *The New York Times,* Katie Roiphe, the author of *The Morning After,* stated, "I thought feminism was a train that you took to end up somewhere better."[36] It is this type of individualistic, looking-out-for-number-one feminism that is particularly dangerous for women from marginalized communities. Indeed, the mainstream feminist movement has a history of exclusion on the bases of class, sexuality, race, and other identities. In the 1990s, U.S. mainstream feminism is trying to overcome this history of oppression by including "other" women—in numbers only. Indeed, it continues to be insensitive to other ideas, agendas, or methodologies.[37] For Third World feminists, our strength arises from our history of collective rather than individualistic action. This does not imply that we should ignore our

new environment. Indeed, in the United States we may learn from other minority groups including African American, Latino/a American, and Native American communities, as well as other Asian communities.

As Third World feminist daughters, it is critical to question from within the community and to root our politics in the rich history of feminist activism in South Asia and the rest of the Third World. A global vision of feminism can only develop if we can extract the empowering parts of our heritage for ourselves and our children. By informing our analyses and work with understandings of race, class, sexuality, and nationality, we broaden our feminist thinking. This process can only take us toward an intergenerational sisterhood, a complex and multidimensional understanding of the forces of oppression at work around us.

Feminist development is a constant process, an interaction rather than merely individual growth. It is dissension, collaboration, and communication with the women around us, our mothers, our sisters, our daughters. It is a pattern of learning where there are no teachers, only participants with different viewpoints. It is a process that grows and continues with the realities of our lives.

Notes

1. We use the term "Third World" in all its subversive power that stems from a history of oppression and resistance. We define the "Third World" activist as a person who recognizes the roles that sexism, classism, racism, imperialism, heterosexism, and nationalism have played in the power differential between the two-thirds and Euro-American worlds and who brings this understanding to his/her social-change agenda.

2. Manavi is the pioneering organization that focuses on violence against South Asian women residing in the United States. It was established in early 1985 in New Jersey.

3. Baker, Christina L., and Christina B. Kline. "Barbara Seaman: A Mother's Story." *The Conversation Begins: Mothers and Daughters Talk About Living Feminism.* New York, NY: Bantam Books, 1996.

4. Chodorow, Nancy. *Feminism and Psychoanalytic Theory.* New Haven, CT: Yale University Press, 1989; and Jordan, June. "The Meaning of Mutuality." *Women's Growth in Connection.* Eds. Jordan, J., A. G. Kaplan, J. B. Miller, I. P. Stiver, and J. L. Surrey. New York: Guilford, 1991. 81–96.

5. Sholomskas, Diane, and Rosalind Axelrod. "The influence of mother-daughter relationships on women's sense of self and current role choices." *Psychology of Women Quarterly* 10 (1986): 171–82; and Goldberg, Joan E. "Mutuality in mother-daughter relationships." *Families in Society* 75 (1994): 236–42.

6. Friday, Nancy. *My Mother, My Self: The Daughters Search for Identity.* New York: Delacorte Press, 1977; Flax, Jane. "The conflict between nurturance and autonomy in mother-daughter relationships and within feminism." *Feminist Studies* 4.2 (1978): 171–189; Rich, Adrienne. *Of Woman Born: Motherhood as Experience and Institution.* New York: Norton, 1976.

7. Rich, op cit., and Firestone, Shulamith. *The Dialectic of Sex: The Case for Feminist Revolution.* New York: William Morrow and Company, Inc., 1970.

8. Hochschild, Arlie R., and Anne Machung. *The Second Shift.* New York: Avon Books, 1990.

9. Webb, Marilyn. "Our Daughters, Our Selves: How Feminists Can Raise Feminists." *Ms.* 3.3 (1992): 30–35; Debold, Elizabeth, Marie Wilson, and Idelisse Malave. *Mother-Daughter Revolution: From Betrayal to Power.* Reading, MA: Addison-Wesley, 1993; Glickman, Rose L. *Daughters of Feminists.* New York, NY: St. Martin's Press, 1993; Rosenzweig, Linda W. *The Anchor of My Life: Middle-Class American Mothers and Daughters, 1880–1920.* New York: New York University Press, 1993; Baker, Christina L., and Christina B. Kline. *The Conversation Begins: Mothers and Daughters Talk About Living Feminism.* New York: Bantam Books, 1996; and "Mothers and Daughters: Honest Talk about Feminism and Real Life. *Ms.* May/June 1996: 45–63.

10. Webb 30–35.

11. Payne, Karen, ed. *Between Ourselves: Letters Between Mothers and Daughters, 1750–1982.* Boston: Houghton Mifflin, 1983.

12. Only 190 years of this history have been recorded, by Kumar, Radha. *The History of Doing: An Illustrated Account of Movements for Women's Rights and Feminism in India, 1800–1990.* New York: Verso, 1993.

13. Chughtai, Ismat. "The Quilt." *The Quilt & Other Stories.* Trans. Tahira Naqvi and Syeda S. Hameed. New Delhi, India: Kali For Women, 1990; and Minault, Gail. "Other Voices, Other Rooms: The View from the Zenana." *Women As Subjects: South Asian Histories.* Ed. Nita Kumar. Calcutta, India: Stree.

14. Oldenburg, Veena T. "Lifestyle as Resistance: The Case of the Courtesans of Lucknow, India." *Feminist Studies* 16.2 (1990): 259–287.

15. Dasgupta, Shamita D. "Nijaswasthan: Bangali nareer brata" (Personal space: Folk rituals of Bengali women).

Sixteenth North American Bengali Conference Magazine. Ed. Chandralekha Sadhu. Houston, TX: Tagore Society of Houston, 1996. 158–160.

16. Cranney, Brenda. "Son Preference in India." *Diva,* 1.2 (October-December 1988): 35–46; Bumiller, Elisabeth. *May You Be the Mother of a Hundred Sons: A Journey Among the Women of India.* New York: Random House, 1990; and Warrier, Sujata. "Patriarchy and Daughter Disfavor in West Bengal." Diss. Syracuse University. Syracuse, NY, 1993.

17. Jensen, Joan M. *Passage from India: Asian Indian Immigrants in North America.* New Haven, CT: Yale University Press, 1988; Helweg, Arthur W., and Uma M. Helweg. *An Immigrant Success Story: East Indians in America.* Philadelphia: University of Pennsylvania Press, 1990; Agarwal, Priya. *Passage from India: Post 1965 Indian Immigrants and Their Children: Conflicts, Concerns, & Solutions.* Palos Verdes, CA: Yuvati Publications, 1991.

18. Jain, Ajit. "Finding a South Asian Identity." *India Abroad* 48 (28 August 1992).

19. Bhattacharjee, Anannya. "The Habit of Ex-Nomination: Nation, Women, and the Indian Immigrant Bourgeoisie." *Public Culture* 5 (1992): 19–44.

20. Dasgupta, Shamita D., and Sayantani DasGupta. "Public Face, Private Space: Asian Indian Women and Sexuality." *"Bad Girls"/"Good Girls": Women, Sex, & Power in the Nineties.* Ed. Nan B. Maglin and Donna Perry. New Brunswick, NJ: Rutgers University Press, 1996. 226–243.

21. Mani, Lata. "Gender, Class, and Cultural Conflict: Indu Krishnans Knowing Her Place." *SAMAR* 1 (Winter 1992): 11–14.

22. Dasgupta, Shamita D. "The Gift of Utter Daring: Cultural Continuity in Asian Indian Communities." *Women in Asian Indian Communities.* Ed. Sucheta Mazumdar and Jyotsna Vaid. Forthcoming.

23. Agarwal, Priya, op. cit.

24. Nigam, Lori. "What Do Women Want to Be? Facing Two Fronts." *India Abroad* 4 (22 January 1993).

25. Easwaran, Ashok. "Bengali Conference: Bengalis Weigh Cultural and Women's Issues." *India Abroad* 42 (19 July 1996).

26. DasGupta, Sayantani, and Shamita Das Dasgupta. "Women in Exile: Gender Relations in the Asian Indian Community in the U.S." *Contours of the Heart: South Asians Map North America.* Ed. Sunaina Maira and Rajini Srikanth. New York: Asian American Writers Workshop, 1996.

27. Nirvitananda, Balaram. "What Do Women Want to Be? Too Much Feminism." *India Abroad* 4 (22 January 1993).

28. Chandran, Jayanti. "Growing up in America." *India Tribune* 20 (May 1995): 23.

29. Anand, Tania. "Instant Initiation." *India Today.* North American special ed. (July 1993): 40e; Tilak, Visi R. "Route to Roots." *India Today.* North American special ed. (31 December 1994): 64c, 64e, 64g; and Jha, Alok K. "Not for God's Sake Alone." *India Today.* North American special ed. (10 April 1995): 64b–64c.

30. Agarwal, Priya, op cit.; and Mani, Lata, op cit.

31. Nigam 4.

32. Names of individuals have been changed to protect their privacy.

33. DasGupta, Sayantani, and Shamita D. Dasgupta. "Journeys: Reclaiming South Asian Feminism." *Our Feet Walk the Sky: Women of South Asian Diaspora.* Ed. Women of South Asian Descent Collective. San Francisco: Aunt Lute Press, 1993; Dasgupta and DasGupta, "Public Face, Private Space" 226–243; and DasGupta and Dasgupta, "Women in Exile."

34. Both Hinduism and Islam believe in active and aggressive feminine forces. In Hinduism, Prakriti and Shakti are representatives of feminine power with the former being the source of all cosmic dynamism and the latter symbolizing autonomous sexuality. For further explanations, see Mernissi, Fatima. *Beyond the Veil: Male-Female Dynamics in Modern Muslim Society.* Cambridge, MA: Schenkman, 1975; Mookerjee, Ajit. *Kali: The Feminine Force.* New York: Destiny Books, 1988; and Wadley, Susan. "Women in Hinduism." *Women in Indian Society: A Reader.* Ed. Rehana Ghadially. Newbury Park, CA: Sage Publications, Inc., 1988.

35. Puar, Jasbir K. "Writing My Way "Home.'" *Socialist Review* 24.4 (1994): 75–108; and Dasgupta and DasGupta, "Public Face, Private Space" 226–243.

36. Noble, Barbara P. "One Daughter's Rebellion or Her Mother's Imprint?" *The New York Times.* Late New York ed. (10 November 1993): C1, C12.

37. Lorde, Audre. "An Open Letter to Mary Daly. *This Bridge Called My Back: Writings by Radical Women of Color.* Ed. Cherrie Moraga and Gloria Anzaldua. New York: Kitchen Table—Women of Color Press, 1981; Davis, Angela Y. *Women, Race & Class.* New York: Vintage Books, 1983; hooks, bell. *Feminist Theory: From Margin to Center.* Boston: South End Press, 1984; and DasGupta, Sayantani. "Reinventing the Feminist Wheel." *Z Magazine* (September 1994): 12–14.

The Black Matriarchy: It Takes a Lioness to Raise Young Lions

Marcia L. McNair

Marcia L. McNair teaches English and journalism at Nassau Community College in New York and is working on her first novel.

The "infamous report" McNair refers to in the following essay was a confidential report made to President Lyndon Johnson by Daniel Patrick Moynihan, who was then assistant secretary of labor (later, senator from New York). Moynihan claimed that "deterioration of the Negro family" was at the heart of deterioration of Black society because a "matriarchal structure" prevailed, and this was out of step with the rest of American society. Surely, any number of assumptions and stereotypes are contained in such a statement. They had great negative impact on many women (and men).

McNair casts off stereotypes when she affirms: "Say it loud, I'm Black, matriarch, and proud." Opposing several pieces of conventional wisdom, she rejects the notions that the "Black matriarchy" is responsible for problems among African-Americans; that African-American women don't make good wives or that there is a shortage of stable African-American men to marry; that children (of any race), especially boys, cannot grow up healthy if they do not have a father living at home; and that a woman needs to apologize if she is a "matriarch," a mother who chooses independence over marriage. McNair remarks, "There's something about stepping across the threshold of my own little house that brings out the lioness in me, and who better than a lioness to raise young lions?"

"BLACK WOMEN DO NOT MAKE good wives," said the well-dressed, articulate black man on *The Ricki Lake Show*. In politically correct disbelief, the audience screamed at his bold remark. Several African-American women rushed to the microphone to challenge his view that they do not possess the requisite qualities of submissiveness and domesticity essential to being a "good wife."

I asked my girlfriends what they thought of the comment. Most found it laughable. But why, underlying their wisecracks ("I don't want to *be* a wife. I *need* a wife," said one upwardly mobile friend), did I sense an uneasiness? As an African American woman, married at the time, the remark reawakened certain latent insecurities in me about desirability and femininity. All African-American women have lived with those insecurities since the 17th century. And as Paula Giddings noted in her landmark historical analysis *When and Where I Enter: The Impact of Black Women on Race and Sex in America*, Victorian ethics dictated that true women did not work outside the home, an unrealistic choice for the majority of black women, past and present, whose men have been denied equal access to employment.

Yet much to my chagrin, even as an African-American woman who had spent a great deal of her life in the study and disputation of stereotypes about us, I found it hard to be angry with the audacious brother because, for the most part, I agreed with him. I, for one, never saw the traditional helpmate as the role I should aspire to in marriage.

My anti-wife conversations were the hint of things to come: A year later, my husband filed for divorce. He seemed to agree with the talk show guest. But after a lifetime of struggling with labels designating who I am, either as a black person or a woman, I am finally able to accept one of the most contentious ones: black matriarch.

I was ten years old in 1967, when Daniel Patrick Moynihan's now infamous report "The Negro Family: The Case for National Action" described the "re-

Marcia L. McNair, "The Black Matriarchy: It Takes a Lioness to Raise Young Lions," *On the Issues* VII, no. 4, pp. 12–13, reprinted with permission of *On the Issues*.

versed role of husband and wife" as the cause of urban social pathologies in nonwhite communities. Every black person of importance, from political activists to sociologists, took up the crusade to discredit the report, mainly by denying the existence of the black matriarchy, and leaving the patriarchal nuclear family unchallenged as the ideal construct. And like so many racially and socially conscious African-American women, my own mother was vociferously opposed to the idea of a black matriarchy, taking little time to consider the fact that she had headed our household alone for nearly six years.

If ever there was a conflicted role model, I'd say my mother was it. She found the idea of a dominant woman contemptible, but she was only able to support our family by being just that. Her journey from welfare mother to director of the local community center embodied the definitive matriarchal qualities of leadership and assertiveness. Yet, despite her professional and personal successes, she always felt herself inadequate when it came to raising my mischievous younger brother. She insisted, in concurrence with society, that his troubles were due to his being a fatherless boy. Like most people, she never focused on the fact that many of the strong black men we knew, or knew of, including the patriarch in our family, were products of the black matriarchy.

My love-hate relationship with the black matriarchy continued through my twenties and into my early thirties, becoming most intense during my first pregnancy. When my son was born, I was happy that he was healthy, but uneasy with the idea that I would be a single mother raising a boy. Though my son, Kahlil, was apparently well-adjusted, everything I had heard and read seemed to predict the contrary. My decisive moment came when, at the age of three, after observing my daily ritual in front of the mirror, Kahlil asked for some lipstick. This was enough to put the fear of God and Revlon into me. I had to find a male role model for my son before he was "emasculated" by me, the "black matriarch." I plunged into the dating scene more to find a father for my son than a mate for myself.

FINDING A SPOUSE WAS EASY

It wasn't difficult to find a husband. Though the image of the single African-American woman as "waiting to exhale" is quite popular, the majority of black single women I know (with and without children) are not unmarried solely because of a lack of marriageable men. There are many black men who are emotionally and financially secure. Yet the notion that there is a shortage of good black men is so prevalent that the Million Man March was needed to disprove it. A little known fact, and I dare say the best-kept secret among African-American women, is that we have plenty of opportunities to get married but often opt not to, for reasons that have little to do with the suitability of black men.

I believe we are simply more comfortable heading our own households, both because most of us grew up in matriarchal households, and because of the strong emphasis black families place on the pursuit of education and employment as the road to racial equality. Race pulls rank on femaleness. A black girl's personal responsibility to elevate the race through academic and professional achievement takes priority over raising children. The familial "when-are-you-going-to-get-married?" is most likely to be asked only after the African-American woman has made it.

My short-lived marriage was a casualty of my independence more than anything else.

Now, several years after my divorce, I've finally come to terms with my matriarchal tendencies. There's something about stepping across the threshold of my own little house that brings out the lioness in me, and who better than a lioness to raise young lions? I teach my boys to imitate my toil, not my toiletry. For the latter, they have plenty of fathers (related and adopted) who are role models for them.

Instead of blaming the black matriarchy for the problems in the African-American community, society needs to attack the real culprits—the oppression of sex, class, and race; for if by some miracle every black household became a two-parent one, the black community would still be disproportionately plagued by high levels of crime, drug abuse, and unemployment as long as these evils exist. Therefore, I am making peace with myself as a black matriarch, ridding myself of the guilt and the shame, reclaiming the label to the point where I often paraphrase James Brown's ode to black power: "Say it loud, I'm black, matriarch, and proud."

Letters to a Young Feminist on Sex and Reproductive Freedom

Phyllis Chesler

Feminist activist and psychologist Phyllis Chesler was one of the founding thinkers of the second wave. Educated at Bard College and the New School for Social Research, she is currently professor of psychology and women's studies at the College of Staten Island, City University of New York. She founded the National Women's Health Network in 1974, was editor-at-large for On the Issues, *a former radical feminist journal, and was recently named the first research scholar to the International Institute for Research on Jewish Women at Brandeis University. Among her works are* Women and Madness *(1972), a groundbreaking work that changed the way psychology thinks about women's emotional lives;* Women, Money and Power *(1976);* About Men *(1978);* With Child: A Diary of Motherhood *(1979);* Mothers on Trial: The Battle for Children and Custody *(1986); and* Patriarchy: Notes of an Expert Witness *(1994).*

In the following selection Professor Chesler addresses issues which, she explains, are both "more complex and simpler" than we have been led to believe: patriarchal attitudes toward sex, women's sexual pleasure, sexual identity, pregnancy, and reproductive choice. She describes her own experiences with abortion, and admonishes us that "rendering abortion illegal is not a feminist option, nor is forcing birth mothers to surrender their infants to adoption."

SEX AND HUMANITY

SEXUAL PLEASURE IS NOT A sin. Nor is it a sacrament. It is your right as a human being to exercise as you

Phyllis Chesler, "Sex and Humanity" and "Not the Church, Not the State, Women Must Decide Their Fate," from *Letters to a Young Feminist* (New York: Four Walls Eight Windows, 1997). Reprinted with the permission of Four Walls Eight Windows. Copyright © 1997 Phyllis Chesler.

see fit. It's amazing that I feel the need to say this, but, given our times, I do.

Feminists are not—and never have been—against sexual pleasure. Patriarchy is—and has always been—against sexual pleasure *for women*. Confusing one's own sexual orgasms with radical actions is silly, pretentious. Feeling good physically is important, but it is not political in the same way as freeing prisoners from concentration camps or feeding the poor. Romanticizing female lust as Goddess-given is as dangerous as romanticizing male war lust as God-given.

If you're a woman, sex is not something you have to submit to (or aspire to) only with a man, or only with your husband, in marriage. Sexual pleasure is not necessarily tied to reproduction. If you're a man, sex is not something you can buy or take by force.

Sex is not something that you can only share with members of the opposite sex. Nor is it something that always results in genital orgasm.

As human beings, we are more than the sum of our sexual parts. However, women are more often reduced to a collection of eroticized body parts: a pretty face, cleavage, breasts, buttocks. Many parts of a woman's body can be eroticized, i.e., can become the focus of orgasm: a foot in a high-heeled shoe, an exposed back, or hip, or thigh, or calf.

In some countries, a woman's exposed (unveiled) face, her eyes, or eyebrows when seen above a half-veil, immediately suggest a forbidden vagina, an orgasm, an orgy, a brothel.

Even in our sex-saturated society, and despite an increase in teenage pregnancies, young girls today, especially of the inner cities, are not having orgasms any more frequently than the young girls of my generation ever did. I didn't believe this either, until I interviewed counselors who are working with precisely this population.

Sex education in the schools and in the media is still being hotly contested and condemned by religious fundamentalists. There is some good information available; it is hard to find. Know that most women cannot have an orgasm without direct clitoral stimulation. Both men and women enjoy oral sex. And, in the era of AIDS and other sexually transmitted diseases, people should not have unprotected sex.

But they do, they do, young people especially.

The solution to unwanted pregnancies, epidemics of sexually transmitted diseases, rape, and incest involves educating the coming generations in radically different ways. Young men must be taught to refrain from using coercion of any sort in matters sexual; young women must be taught how to resist such coercion.

The same experience—having sex—can have different consequences as a function of gender. For example, many young girls still lose their reputations for having sex; boys rarely do. (SOS—Same Old Shit.) Again, contrary to myth, women can and do sexually contract AIDS from men far more often and easily than men do from women, including from prostitutes. Women get pregnant, men don't, and mothers, no matter how young, often bear sole, lifelong responsibility for a child—more so than most fathers ever do. Women also bear the sole, lifelong trauma of having given up a child for adoption.

Sexual desire is fluid, ever-changing, especially if it's more than a masturbation fantasy. Sex may mean one thing when you're eighteen, and an entirely different thing when you're sixty-five. No, all people do not lose their desire for orgasm or affection as they age; some do though, but they're often happy about it. However, health and leisure time free of worry are essential.

You may experience desire one way with one person, another way with another person—or differently over time with the same person.

Some men may experience more sexual desire when they're young, some women when they're older; some men may think the beginnings of sexual relationships are hot, some women that it's hotter when you've come to know and trust your partner.

Trust me, sex is more complex and simpler than you've been led to believe.

Even Dr. Freud said we are all bisexual. This doesn't mean that bisexuals swing from trees, first one way, then another. It means that we all have the potential to love, mate, and experience sexual pleasure with someone of our own sex too. No big deal.

Homophobia is the last acceptable prejudice. I have observed people of all classes, races, and political persuasions bond by mocking homosexuals and lesbians, or by boasting, loudly and non-stop, of their own heterosexuality.

Telling you that I'm either heterosexual or lesbian tells you very little about how often I have genital sex, or how I have orgasms, or what sex or love really means to me. Homosexuals are not what homophobes assume. What being a lesbian means probably has little to do with our culture's general perception of a lesbian.

Both physicists and philosophers tell us that things are not what they seem—sturdy tables, for instance, are no more than molecules in motion—and that all things change, nothing remains the same.

I know women and men who were once heterosexual, parented children together, and who later became homosexuals. They still love their children, they are still good parents. I know closet homosexuals who legally married each other as cover, had children, continue to keep up the heterosexual pretense, but still prefer liaisons with others of their own sex.

Things are not always what they seem. Know that.

"NOT THE CHURCH, NOT THE STATE, WOMEN MUST DECIDE THEIR FATE."

No woman should be forced to have an abortion against her will. No woman should be prevented from having an abortion against her will.

This is what choice is about.

I believe in a woman's absolute right to *choose* whether and when she will have a child. Free choice means that a woman must have access to high-quality, physician-assisted, economically affordable, legal abortion *and* have the option of keeping the child she chooses to bear without having to pay an inhuman price for doing so.

Inhuman prices include: Children having children, having to drop out of school, having a child alone, without family or community, being condemned to poverty because we have no affordable day care, etc. It is also inhuman to have to surrender a child for adoption. This is a trauma from which many birth mothers never recover.

Abortion is not murder. It is the termination of a fetus. This is my view, and the view of the Supreme Court in 1973, in *Roe v. Wade*. However, if women do not have the legal right to decide whether a pregnancy is a future baby or an unacceptable burden, then it is women who are civilly dead.

Anti-abortion crusaders are more concerned with the rights of the unborn than with the rights—including the right to life—of the living. Abortion opponents actually champion the unborn at the expense of the pregnant woman and her other living children. Anti-abortionists do not demand that the state invade a *man's* body against his will for the sake of his living child—who may, for example, die without his father's kidney, lung, or bone marrow.

For at least 10,000 years of recorded history, most women were forced into biological motherhood, and, unlike men, were severely punished and sometimes killed for having sex outside of marriage.

It was therefore obvious to my generation of feminists that women needed to secure the right to safe, legal, and affordable birth control and abortions. Without them, how could a woman pursue life or liberty? She could not—and cannot. I feel as strongly about the importance of birth control and abortion today as I did thirty years ago.

Ideally, a woman's right to choose an abortion should be a civil, not just a privacy right. A woman must have the right to decide if and when to become a mother—not merely the right to choose abortion when her life or health are at stake.

Abortions have always existed. They have not always been illegal, but when they were, wealthy women had them anyway. Poor women either didn't, or risked death at the hands of back-alley practitioners.

In the 1950s, white teenagers who couldn't find or afford an illegal abortion, or who couldn't go through with one, had to endure endless recriminations from their parents; they *had* to drop out of high school or college—no one pregnant was allowed to attend. The "lucky" teenager got to marry someone who didn't really want to marry her and

who wasn't ready to be a husband and father. Or she was forced to surrender her child for adoption.

The teenage father was rarely blamed—only the mother was.

I remember thinking, ah, if you're female, one slip and you're down for the count forever. One night of experimental lovemaking, one brief affair, one tragic episode of rape—and a young woman and her child could be condemned, permanently, to lesser, harsher lives.

In 1959, I traveled alone, between college exams, for an appointment with the famed underground physician Dr. Robert Spencer, of Pennsylvania. (Rumor had it that his daughter had died of a botched, illegal abortion and that this was his way of making sure it didn't happen again to anyone else's daughter.) When I arrived, Dr. Spencer was "out of town." He frequently was. The man lived one step ahead of the law. I remember sitting on a swing in a nearby park, disconsolate, thinking that my life *as I wanted to live it* might be over if I couldn't find another abortionist.

Of course, I went to see Dr. Spencer alone, not with my boyfriend. Back then, men were not supposed to see women in curlers or cold cream, much less in childbirth or having an abortion.

Not all abortionists were trained physicians. They didn't always use anesthesia, and the pain was terrible, but you were more afraid of dying, or of having your parents find out. Some of us also had to contend with the sexual innuendos and gropings of the abortionist. The secrecy and the humiliation were profound.

Over a fourteen-year period, I had other abortions. And yes, I used birth control: first an IUD—until it became embedded in the wall of my uterus, then a diaphragm. Guess what? They failed.

Americans obtained the right to legal abortion in this country not because feminists fought and died for it, but because a sexually positive climate had been created in which both lawyers and physicians emerged who supported a woman's right to choose abortion. They had seen too many women die awful deaths from unsafe, illegal abortions. Perhaps, physicians also viewed abortion as a potentially lucrative practice. Perhaps, both men and women wanted *women* to experience sex without worry, not merely as a way to procreate.

My generation initially focused more on a woman's right to abortion than on her right to motherhood—or on the rights of racially persecuted women to resist sterilization, or the "ideal" of a small family. We were not wrong, nor were we right; no movement can do everything at once. Women were so universally obligated to become mothers, so universally condemned for pursuing independence that our feminist path was clear.

I have never softened about a woman's right to choose: not while I was pregnant, not after I gave birth to my son. I did not think that *my* right to choose to have a baby meant that *all* women had to make this same choice, nor did I think that if they didn't they were, somehow, not respecting my love for my own baby. I experience no contradiction between my *choosing* to have a child and the next woman's *choosing* not to have a child.

Make no mistake, I experienced giving birth as a sacred rite of passage.

In the late 1960s, before abortion was legal, I initiated some meetings to discuss how we could *physically* defend our then-underground clinics and networks. I should have kept notes. But who could have imagined that, only thirty years later, the right to a legal abortion would be under such deadly attack?

Never could I have imagined that, in 1997, abortion clinics and their employees would have to suffer prolonged off-site personal harassment, aggressive anti-abortion demonstrations and endless bomb threats, or that they'd be forced to install metal detectors and help train feminists to escort frightened women into and out of clinics.

Who could have foreseen that so many clinics across the country would be forced to close, would be bombed—not once, but repeatedly—that physicians and clinic workers would be forced to wear bulletproof vests, harassed, even killed so that women could exercise their rights to have a legal abortion. We could never have imagined that physicians and medical students might decide not to perform any abortions, because they seemed too dangerous, too much trouble.

Yes, freedom for women means trouble. But without such freedom, women would be in even more trouble.

Abortion has been under serious siege for more than twenty years, ever since Henry Hyde pushed through his infamous amendment to a federal funding bill that made it much harder for poor women to have federally subsidized abortions.

What can you do? There is more than one feminist thing to do. For example, a feminist might, honorably, do any of the following:

1. vote for pro-choice politicians, write them checks, and actively campaign for them;

2. escort women into and out of abortion clinics;

3. open abortion clinics—currently, at least 84 percent of U.S. counties do not have any abortion providers;

4. educate young men about their responsibilities as fathers; educate young women about their responsibilities, too;

5. pioneer research on more effective, less harmful methods of female birth control;

6. develop and distribute a male birth control pill;

7. lobby your church or religious congregation to change its stance on birth control and abortion;

8. campaign for a guaranteed above-minimum wage for all workers, so the choices are more affordable for everyone;

9. *personally* shelter, or become family to, a particular pregnant woman who wants to keep her baby, but who has no education, no money, and no family support—this option is reserved for saints;

10. become a physician willing to perform abortions; or a lawyer willing to represent physicians who perform abortions, clinic owners, and staff.

The list is endless. However, in my view, there are at least two feminist bottom lines. Rendering abortion illegal is not a feminist option, nor is forcing birth mothers to surrender their infants to adoption. Studies have persuaded me that birth mothers end up surrendering their peace of mind and mental health when they surrender their newborns for adoption. And even loved, well-cared-for adopted children suffer, psychologically, more than other children do.

Do I think the Second Wave of feminism worked as hard on obtaining the right to mother or parent under *feminist* working conditions as they did on keeping abortion legal? No, I don't. But obtaining the right to an abortion is far easier than redefining the family.

As Americans, we shun collective social solutions to what we still view as individual, private matters. We do so at our own peril.

You've inherited the consequence of our failure to redefine the family. The task is yours.

Twenty–Seven Years, But Who's Counting?
Thoughts on Yet Another *Roe v. Wade*

Merle Hoffman

Editor-in-chief of On the Issues *until its closing in 1999, founder of Choices, one of the first women's clinics for reproductive choice in the United States, Merle Hoffman has been an incisive thinker and voice for feminist issues and a courageous activist for women's rights. Her essay recounts some of the history of the struggle to win and maintain women's reproductive autonomy. More importantly, it warns us to be vigilant, to struggle on with passion for this and other rights, because we are under siege and at risk of losing what was won with such effort.*

I USED TO CELEBRATE IT differently—*very* differently.

I remember one January in particular in New York City's Bryant Park. In the midst of the blinding snow and howling winds of what the papers termed "the worst blizzard of the decade," I was part of a band of dedicated pro-choice activists who were passionately celebrating the anniversary of *Roe v. Wade*—and just as passionately attacking those who opposed it. Despite, or perhaps because of, the freezing temperatures, my blood was up. I knew the battle was joined, the troops were marshaled, and I was feeling nothing but transcendent.

Years ago on another anniversary, I debated Nellie Gray, the organizer of the annual anti-abortion march on Washington. She was small, sinewy and angry.

She told me that we were a modern version of the Lincoln-Douglass debates. I smiled in recognition until I realized that she was positioning me as Douglass. "We'll stop our attacks when you put down your knives and stop the killing," she told me. "And your vision of women's roles would be to

butcher them with illegal abortions or turn them into baby-making slaves," I replied.

Past anniversaries were like that—collective, powerful, meaningful, engaged.

Now, as the antis plan their January 22 march, complete with mini-caskets for the "murdered unborn," I receive invitations to pro-choice auctions and black tie gala benefits—cards with hourglasses in the shape of a woman's body reminding me that "the Time is Now"—glittering messages from the glitterati, thousands of miles away from the streets and the battles.

Some say that one only remembers the last memory of a thing—as if the real event becomes transfigured, altered as the present shuts out much of the past. Unlike most anniversaries, which are composites of shared memory and ritual, *Roe* is a Rorschach writ large—a mass of perceptions codified by law that we share with our enemies.

I have grown up with and outgrown "abortion the issue" as it is played every year in stereotype and soundbite. Is it "a woman's right to choose," or is it killing? The arguments change slightly, if at all. The answer to this philosophical challenge is within the realpolitik of each woman's heart.

Was there really a life before abortion and abortion politics, before holding the hands of women in pain and expectation, and why am I still writing about it so many years later?

In the Spring of 1971, when I was 26 years old, abortion had been legal in New York State for almost one year. It would be another two before the Supreme Court would legalize abortion nationally in *Roe v. Wade*.

In the beginning I was not political. I became political when I counseled my first patient. Like so many others, she came from New Jersey because abortion was still illegal in that state. She was 24 years old—white, married, terrified. I don't

"27 Years, But Who's Counting? Thoughts on Yet Another *Roe v. Wade*," *On the Issues*, Vol. VII, no. 8, Winter 1998, pp. 5–7, reprinted with permission of *On the Issues*.

remember her name or a word of what passed between us. It was strangely irrelevant. I do remember that her hand stayed in mine the entire time she was with me, throughout her abortion. Hers was the first of thousands of hands I have held—and her life the first that touched mine in that profound and intimate way.

Simone de Beauvoir has written that the "representation of the world like the world itself is the work of men. They describe it from their own point of view, which they confuse with absolute truth."

When I founded Choices 27 years ago, women's health as a discipline, as a practice and a vision, simply did not exist. Legal abortion brought women's health care out of the closet, radicalized the status of women in society and revolutionized their relationship with the health care establishment.

It was a heady time—a brave new world where one woman's unique yet collective experience of an unplanned and unwanted pregnancy intersected with a new feminist politic of freedom and responsibility. We inhabited a place where we made women's lives matter; a time when feminism resonated with risk and spoke to struggle rather than privilege. There were so many firsts.

For the first time, women were in control of patient referrals and clinics, while physicians were brought down from their godlike pedestals to function as employees of women-owned and feminist-run medical centers. Because the abortion issue was politicized well before legalization (the National Right to Life Committee was founded in 1969), patients often had to run a gauntlet of abuse from demonstrators just as they do now. Counseling sessions were done by young feminist activists trained in women's health; issues of sexuality, religion, love, psychology, and death augmented technical medical explanations of the procedure. As a result, the traditional medical bifurcation of mind/body was imploded by operationally integrating politics, psychology and clinical treatment.

In those early days I treated many women whose unwanted pregnancies stemmed from their victimization by the medical establishment, what I termed "iatrogenic pregnancies" because they were caused by the medical system's ignorance, misinformation or withholding of accurate information. Pregnancies caused by physician arrogance: "I give all my patients the pill"; "I never refit my women's diaphragms"; "My doctor didn't tell me to use anything else for birth control when I went off the pill."

I realized then that women patients constituted an oppressed class in relationship to their physicians. And understanding that power concedes nothing without demand, I developed a philosophy of Patient Power at Choices, which taught that patients had rights that included informed consent to treatment, second opinions, and access to alternative systems. On the other hand, patients were responsible for engaging honestly and directly with providers and educating themselves about their own bodies.

Those nascent feminist ideals have slowly been incorporated and diffused through much of modern medicine—from sensitivity training for doctors in medical schools, to the incorporation of interdisciplinary educational and holistic concepts of healing in general medical practice, to the development of women's health care as a separate medical specialty.

But what's been lost in the years since *Roe*, if it ever really existed, is any authentic link between the providers who, often at the risk of their lives, serve the women who come for abortions, and the activists and theorists who shape national political pro-choice strategy. "Doing" abortions instead of fighting for the right to have them was always considered the dirty end of the business, but now that elitist negativity has spilled over into prejudicial judgments about having them.

For women to be considered "good" abortion patients they have to be hard cases, i.e. victims. They didn't choose sex; it happened to them—abortion only in cases of rape and incest. The current intense debate over so-called partial birth abortions is the epitome of this thinking. President Clinton was quoted in *The New York Times* as saying that while he opposed late-term abortions, he couldn't deny them to that "small group of women in tragic circumstances who need an abortion performed at a late stage of pregnancy to avert death or serious injury." He did at least veto the bill that would have banned them.

This Madonna/whore (hard/soft) labeling of abortion patients has resulted in the continuing disengagement of millions of women from both abortion providers and abortion politics and formed a massive "reluctant constituency." A constituency of 30 million women who have had abortions since legalization but who remain equivocal and removed from the struggle to retain that right for the millions of others who will come after them. Their mantra is the classic "Rape Incest or Me" position.

We are losing the old warhorse abortionists who became committed to the cause when they saw their patients die of botched illegal abortions. No one under forty remembers the days of terror, shame, and extreme personal risk of those desperate pre-*Roe* searches for an abortion you could survive. Instead, we have the negative and ambivalent attitudes of pro-choice "supporters" wanting to be "good girls," who argue that the abortion "issue" has hijacked the women's movement. Why, they ask, must we spend so much time defending a right that was won in 1973? Why must we argue the same old polemics, strategize the same defensive moves? Wouldn't our energies be better spent setting a broader social agenda that addresses issues of economic equity, racism, welfare?

Why? Because we are in a real war with real casualties.

Because doctors and health care workers are shot dead in their clinics.

Because abortion remains unavailable in 86 percent of American counties, and some patients must still risk their lives to have one.

Because *Roe v. Wade,* based on the 14th Amendment's right to privacy has been slowly eviscerated by waiting periods, parental consent, the lack of Medicaid funding for abortion in the majority of states, and the attack on "partial birth" abortion.

Because we are still held hostage to the political agendas that disallow even the smallest move forward (RU-486 is still not produced and distributed in this country).

Because of continuing racial and class divisions that block collective action among women.

Because women who have abortions continue to deny the fact that they did.

Because I recently attended a national meeting of providers who reacted to my description of abortion as a fundamental civil right as "not sellable to the American public"—and because they may be right.

By promulgating a view of abortion as "tragic but necessary," the pro-choice movement has succeeded in remaining in an apologetic and reactive position. Instead of an aggressive visionary strategy we are continually defending things that should require no defense—women's lives and freedom.

We must reclaim and honor our history. We must remember the women who alone and in pain lost their lives for their right to choose.

We must throw off our personal shrouds of shame and tell the stories of our mothers and grandmothers, and ourselves.

We must close the split between the strategists and national leaders of the pro-choice movement and its foot soldiers, the women who have actually had abortions and the providers who make them possible. Together, we must reposition and redefine legal abortion as an integral core of women's health and as the necessary condition for women's freedom. Nothing stops abortion—no law, no government, no religious authority. Making abortion illegal only makes it dangerous and deadly.

The movement must speak with a unified voice that articulates a shared vision. Abortion and reproductive freedom are fundamental human rights, not to be abridged by any entity. We must actively strategize, not only for the next skirmish or the next battle, but for the coming 25 years—to ensure that our daughters and granddaughters do not have to fight the same war.

We must work to regain lost allies (the American Medical Association voted to uphold the ban on "partial birth" abortion). We must move in powerful coalition with other progressive movements—gays and lesbians, civil rights organizations, environmental activists, labor—and demand that the leadership of these movements actively support reproductive freedom.

We must expose the fifth column within our own ranks, feminists who are "pro-choice" but handle their personal discomfort with abortion by naming it a "tragedy" and thus making it more difficult for others to choose freely.

We must expand the definition of pro-choice to include those women living with racism and poverty for whom the right to reproductive freedom means the right to *bear* children with adequate financial and medical support.

We must reach out to the young women who live a feminism of entitlement rather than struggle, and do not understand that freedom requires constant vigilance.

We must be militant when necessary and be ready to sacrifice more then freedom for the cause.

We must creatively develop new legal theories (for one opinion, see "My Body, My Choice, My Consent") that further secure the constitutional basis of reproductive freedom.

Finally, we must be able to speak the truth to ourselves by answering the question, "Is it a woman's right to choose or is it killing?" by saying yes—to both—and taking full responsibility for that profound and powerful truth.

Twenty-seven years and who's counting? I'm counting—counting the days and years and decades until all women will live in a world where reproductive freedom is a fundamental human right and no one will ever again die for her right to choose.

Rape: The Power of Consciousness

Susan Griffin

Susan Griffin has taught women's studies at the University of California at Berkeley and at San Francisco State University. Her play Voices, *produced widely here and in Europe, won an Emmy for a television performance. One of the founders of the Feminist Writer's Guild, she considers her writing a political activity. She is the author of* What Her Body Thought *(1999);* The Eros of Everyday Life: Essays on Ecology, Gender, and Society *(1996);* Chorus of Stones: The Private Life of War *(1992);* Unremembered Country *(1987);* Pornography and Silence: Culture's Revenge Against Nature *(1981); and* Woman and Nature: The Roaring Inside Her *(1978). This essay first appeared in* Ramparts *magazine in 1971. It is a classic in the feminist analysis of violence against women, and one of the classic pieces of writing of the second wave.*

Griffin analyzes the effect of rape not only on the primary victim but on all women: We are all victims of rape, which is a political act of terror against the entire female sex.

PART 1, POLITICS 1971

I

I HAVE NEVER BEEN FREE of the fear of rape. From a very early age I, like most women, have thought of rape as part of my natural environment—something to be feared and prayed against like fire or lightning. I never asked why men raped; I simply thought it one of the many mysteries of human nature.

I was, however, curious enough about the violent side of humanity to read every crime magazine I was able to ferret away from my grandfather. Each issue featured at least one "sex crime," with pictures of a victim, usually in a pearl necklace, and of the ditch or the orchard where her body was found. I was never certain why the victims were always women, nor what the motives of the murderer were, but I did guess that the world was not a safe place for women. I observed that my grandmother was meticulous about locks, and quick to draw the shades before anyone removed so much as a shoe. I sensed that danger lurked outside.

At the age of eight, my suspicions were confirmed. My grandmother took me to the back of the house where the men wouldn't hear, and told me that strange men wanted to do harm to little girls. I learned not to walk on dark streets, not to talk to strangers, or get into strange cars, to lock doors, and to be modest. She never explained why a man would want to harm a little girl, and I never asked.

If I thought for a while that my grandmother's fears were imaginary, the illusion was brief. That year, on the way home from school, a schoolmate a few years older than I tried to rape me. Later, in an obscure aisle of the local library (while I was reading *Freddy the Pig*) I turned to discover a man exposing himself. Then, the friendly man around the corner was arrested for child molesting.

My initiation to sexuality was typical. Every woman has similar stories to tell—the first man who attacked her may have been a neighbor, a family friend, an uncle, her doctor, or perhaps her own father. And women who grow up in New York City always have tales about the subway.

But though rape and the fear of rape are a daily part of every woman's consciousness, the subject is so rarely discussed by that unofficial staff of male intellectuals (who write the books which study seemingly every other form of male activity) that one begins to suspect a conspiracy of silence. And indeed, the obscurity of rape in print exists in marked contrast to the frequency of rape in reality, for *forcible rape is the most frequently committed violent crime in America today*. The Federal Bureau of Investigation classes three crimes as violent: murder, aggravated assault, and forcible rape. In 1968, 31,060 rapes were *reported*. According to the FBI and independent criminologists, however, to approach accuracy this figure must be multiplied by at least a factor of ten to compensate for the fact that most rapes are not reported; when these compensatory mathematics are used, there are more rapes committed than aggravated assaults and homicides.

When I asked Berkeley California's Police Inspector in charge of rape investigation if he knew why men rape women, he replied that he had not spoken with "these people and delved into what really makes them tick, because that really isn't my job. . . ." However, when I asked him how a woman might prevent being raped, he was not so reticent, "I wouldn't advise any female to go walking around alone at night . . . and she should lock her car at all times." The Inspector illustrated his warning with a grisly story about a man who lay in wait for women in the back seats of their cars, while they were shopping in a local supermarket. This man eventually murdered one of his rape victims. "Always lock your car," the Inspector repeated, and then added, without a hint of irony, "Of course, you don't have to be paranoid about this type of thing."

The Inspector wondered why I wanted to write about rape. Like most men he did not understand the urgency of the topic, for, after all, men are not raped. But like most women I had spent considerable time speculating on the true nature of the rapist. When I was very young, my image of the "sexual offender" was a nightmarish amalgamation of the bogey man and Captain Hook: he wore a black cape, and he cackled. As I matured, so did my image of the rapist. Born into the psychoanalytic age, I tried to "understand" the rapist. Rape, I came to believe, was only one of many unfortunate evils produced by sexual repression. Reasoning by tautology, I concluded that any man who would rape a woman must be out of his mind.

Yet, though the theory that rapists are insane is a popular one, this belief has no basis in fact. According to Professor Menachem Amir's study of 646 rape cases in Philadelphia, *Patterns in Forcible Rape*, men who rape are not abnormal. Amir writes, "Studies indicate that sex offenders do not constitute a unique or psychopathological type; nor are

they as a group invariably more disturbed than the control groups to which they are compared." Alan Taylor, a parole officer who has worked with rapists in the prison facilities at San Luis Obispo, California, stated the question in plainer language, "Those men were the most normal men there. They had a lot of hang-ups, but they were the same hang-ups as men walking out on the street."

Another canon in the apologetics of rape is that, if it were not for learned social controls, all men would rape. Rape is held to be natural behavior, and not to rape must be learned. But in truth rape is not universal to the human species. Moreover, studies of rape in our culture reveal that, far from being impulsive behavior, most rape is planned. Professor Amir's study reveals that in cases of group rape—(the "gang-bang" of masculine slang) 90 percent of the rapes were planned; in pair rapes, 83 percent of the rapes were planned; and in single rapes, 58 percent were planned. These figures should significantly discredit the image of the rapist as a man who is suddenly overcome by sexual needs society does not allow him to fulfill.

Far from the social control of rape being learned, comparisons with other cultures lead one to suspect that, in our society, it is rape itself that is learned. (The fact that rape is against the law should not be considered proof that rape is not in fact encouraged as part of our culture.)

This culture's concept of rape as an illegal, but still understandable, form of behavior is not a universal one. In her study *Sex and Temperament*, Margaret Mead describes a society that does not share our views. The Arapesh do not " . . . have any conception of the male nature that might make rape understandable to them." Indeed our interpretation of rape is a product of our conception of the nature of male sexuality. A common retort to the question, why don't women rape men, is the myth that men have greater sexual needs, that their sexuality is more urgent than women's. And it is the nature of human beings to want to live up to what is expected of them.

And this same culture which expects aggression from the male expects passivity from the female. Conveniently, the companion myth about the nature of female sexuality is that all women secretly want to be raped. Lurking beneath her modest female exterior is a subconscious desire to be ravished. The following description of a stag movie, written by Brenda Starr in Los Angeles' underground paper, *Everywoman,* typifies this male fantasy. The movie "showed a woman in her underclothes reading on her bed. She is interrupted by a rapist with a knife. He immediately wins her over with his charm and they get busy sucking and fucking." An advertisement in the *Berkeley Barb* reads, "Now as all women know from their daydreams, rape has a lot of advantages. Best of all it's so simple. No preparation necessary, no planning ahead of time, no wondering if you should or shouldn't; just whang! bang!" Thanks to Masters and Johnson even the scientific canon recognizes that for the female, "whang! bang!" can scarcely be described as pleasurable.

Still, the male psyche persists in believing that, protestations and struggles to the contrary, deep inside her mysterious feminine soul, the female victim has wished for her own fate. A young woman who was raped by the husband of a friend said that days after the incident the man returned to her home, pounded on the door and screamed to her, "Jane, Jane. You loved it. You know you loved it."

The theory that women like being raped extends itself by deduction into the proposition that most or much of rape is provoked by the victim. But this too is only myth. Though provocation, considered a mitigating factor in a court of law, may consist of only "a gesture," according to the Federal Commission on Crimes of Violence, only 4 percent of reported rapes involved any precipitative behavior by the woman.

The notion that rape is enjoyed by the victim is also convenient for the man who, though he would not commit forcible rape, enjoys the idea of its existence, as if rape confirms that enormous sexual potency which he secretly knows to be his own. It is for the pleasure of the armchair rapist that detailed accounts of violent rapes exist in the media. Indeed, many men appear to take sexual pleasure from nearly all forms of violence. Whatever the motivation, male sexuality and violence in our culture seem to be inseparable. James Bond alternately whips out his revolver and his cock, and though there is no known connection between the skills of gunfighting and lovemaking, pacifism seems suspiciously effeminate.

In a recent treatment of the Manson case, Frank Conroy writes of his vicarious titillation when describing the murders to his wife:

"Every single person there was killed." She didn't move.

"It sounds like there was torture," I said. As the words left my mouth I knew there was no need to say them to frighten her into believing that she needed me for protection.

The pleasure he feels as his wife's protector is inextricably mixed with pleasure in the violence itself. Conroy writes, "I was excited by the killings, as one excited by catastrophe on a grand scale, as one is alert to pre-echoes of unknown changes, hints of unrevealed secrets, rumblings of chaos. . . ."

The attraction of the male in our culture to violence and death is a tradition Manson and his admirers are carrying on with tireless avidity (even presuming Manson's innocence, he dreams of the purification of fire and destruction). It was Malraux in his *Anti-Memoirs* who said that, for the male, facing death was the illuminating experience analogous to childbirth for the female. Certainly our culture does glorify war and shroud the agonies of the gunfighter in veils of mystery.

And in the spectrum of male behavior, rape, the perfect combination of sex and violence, is the penultimate act. Erotic pleasure cannot be separated from culture, and in our culture male eroticism is wedded to power. Not only should a man be taller and stronger than a female in the perfect love-match, but he must also demonstrate his superior strength in gestures of dominance which are perceived as amorous. Though the law attempts to make a clear division between rape and sexual intercourse, in fact the courts find it difficult to distinguish between a case where the decision to copulate was mutual and one where a man forced himself upon his partner.

The scenario is even further complicated by the expectation that, not only does a woman mean "yes" when she says "no," but that a really decent woman ought to begin by saying "no," and then be led down the primrose path to acquiescence. Ovid, the author of Western Civilization's most celebrated sex manual, makes this expectation perfectly clear:

. . . and when I beg you to say "yes," say "no."
Then let me lie outside your bolted door. . . . So Love
grows strong. . . .

That the basic elements of rape are involved in all heterosexual relationships may explain why men often identify with the offender in this crime. But to regard the rapist as the victim, a man driven by his inherent sexual needs to take what will not be given him, reveals a basic ignorance of sexual politics. For in our culture heterosexual love finds an erotic expression through male dominance and female submission. A man who derives pleasure from raping a woman clearly must enjoy force and dominance as much or more than the simple pleasures of the flesh. Coitus cannot be experienced in isolation. The weather, the state of the nation, the level of sugar in the blood—all will affect a man's ability to achieve orgasm. If a man can achieve sexual pleasure after terrorizing and humiliating the object of his passion, and in fact while inflicting pain upon her, one must assume he derives pleasure directly from terrorizing, humiliating and harming a woman. According to Amir's study of forcible rape, on a statistical average the man who has been convicted of rape was found to have a normal sexual personality, tending to be different from the normal, well-adjusted male only in having a greater tendency to express violence and rage.

And if the professional rapist is to be separated from the average dominant heterosexual, it may be mainly a quantitative difference. For the existence of rape as an index to masculinity is not entirely metaphorical. Though this measure of masculinity seems to be more publicly exhibited among "bad boys" or aging bikers who practice sexual initiation through group rape, in fact, "good boys" engage in the same rites to prove their manhood. In Stockton, a small town in California which epitomizes silent-majority America, a bachelor party was given last summer for a young man about to be married. A woman was hired to dance "topless" for the amusement of the guests. At the high point of the evening the bridegroom-to-be dragged the woman into a bedroom. No move was made by any of his companions to stop what was clearly going to be an attempted rape. Far from it. As the woman described, "I tried to keep him away—told him of my Herpes Genitalis, et cetera, but he couldn't face the guys if he didn't screw me." After the bridegroom had finished raping the woman and returned with her to the party, far from chastising him, his friends heckled the woman and covered her with wine.

It was fortunate for the dancer that the bridegroom's friends did not follow him into the bedroom for, though one might suppose that in group rape, since the victim is outnumbered, less force would be inflicted on her, in fact, Amir's studies indicate, "the most excessive degrees of violence occurred in group rape." Far from discouraging violence, the presence of other men may in fact encourage sadism, and even cause the behavior. In an unpublished study of group rape by Gilbert Geis and Duncan Chappell, the authors refer to a study by W. H. Blanchard which relates,

> The leader of the male group . . . apparently precipitated and maintained the activity, despite misgivings, because of a need to fulfill the role that the other two men had assigned to him. "I was scared when it began to happen," he says. "I wanted to leave but I didn't want to say it to the other guys—you know—that I was scared."

Thus it becomes clear that not only does our culture teach men the rudiments of rape, but society, or more specifically other men, encourage the practice of it.

II

Every man I meet wants to protect me. Can't figure out what from.
—Mae West

If a male society rewards aggressive, domineering sexual behavior, it contains within itself a sexual schizophrenia. For the masculine man is also expected to prove his mettle as a protector of women. To the naive eye, this dichotomy implies that men fall into one of two categories: those who rape and those who protect. In fact, life does not prove so simple. In a study euphemistically entitled "Sex Aggression by College Men," it was discovered that men who believe in a double standard of morality for men and women, who in fact believe most fervently in the ultimate value of virginity, are more liable to commit "this aggressive variety of sexual exploitation."

(At this point in our narrative it should come as no surprise that Sir Thomas Malory, creator of that classic tale of chivalry, *The Knights of the Round Table,* was himself arrested and found guilty for repeated incidents of rape.)

In the system of chivalry, men protect women against men. This is not unlike the protection relationship which the mafia established with small businesses in the early part of this century. Indeed, chivalry is an age-old protection racket which depends for its existence on rape.

According to the male mythology which defines and perpetuates rape, it is an animal instinct inherent in the male. The story goes that sometime in our pre-historical past, the male, more hirsute and burly than today's counterparts, roamed about an uncivilized landscape until he found a desirable female. (Oddly enough, this female is *not* pictured as more muscular than the modern woman.) Her mate does not bother with courtship. He simply grabs her by the hair and drags her to the closest cave. Presumably, one of the major advantages of modern civilization for the female has been the civilizing of the male. We call it chivalry.

But women do not get chivalry for free. According to the logic of sexual politics, we too have to civilize our behavior. (Enter chastity. Enter virginity. Enter monogamy.) For the female, civilized behavior means chastity before marriage and faithfulness within it. Chivalrous behavior in the male is supposed to protect that chastity from involuntary defilement. The fly in the ointment of this otherwise peaceful system is the fallen woman. She does not behave. And therefore she does not deserve protection. Or, to use another argument, a major tenet of the same value system: what has once been defiled cannot again be violated. One begins to suspect that it is the behavior of the fallen woman, and not that of the male, that civilization aims to control.

The assumption that a woman who does not respect the double standard deserves whatever she gets (or at the very least "asks for it") operates in the courts today. While in some states a man's previous rape convictions are not considered admissible evidence, the sexual reputation of the rape victim is considered a crucial element of the facts upon which the court must decide innocence or guilt.

The court's respect for the double standard manifested itself particularly clearly in the case of the People v. Jerry Plotkin. Mr. Plotkin, a 36-year-old jeweler, was tried for rape last spring in a San Francisco Superior Court. According to the woman who brought the charges, Plotkin, along with three other men, forced her at gunpoint to enter a car one night in October 1970. She was taken to Mr. Plotkin's fashionable apartment where he and the three other men first raped her and then, in the delicate language of the *S. F. Chronicle*, "subjected her to perverted sex acts." She was, she said, set free in the morning with the warning that she would be killed if she spoke to anyone about the event. She did report the incident to the police who then searched Plotkin's apartment and discovered a long list of names of women. Her name was on the list and had been crossed out.

In addition to the woman's account of her abduction and rape, the prosecution submitted four of Plotkin's address books containing the names of hundreds of women. Plotkin claimed he did not know all of the women since some of the names had been given to him by friends and he had not yet called on them. Several women, however, did testify in court that Plotkin had, to cite the *Chronicle*, "lured them up to his apartment under one pretext or another, and forced his sexual attentions on them."

Plotkin's defense rested on two premises. First, through his own testimony Plotkin established a reputation for himself as a sexual libertine who frequently picked up girls in bars and took them to his house where sexual relations often took place. He was the Playboy. He claimed that the accusation of rape, therefore, was false—this incident had simply been one of many casual sexual relationships, the victim one of many playmates. The second premise of the defense was that his accuser was also a sexual libertine. However, the picture created of the young woman (fully 13 years younger than Plotkin) was not akin to the light-hearted, gay-bachelor image projected by the defendant. On the contrary, the day after the defense cross-examined the woman, the *Chronicle* printed a story headlined, "Grueling Day For Rape Case Victim." (A leaflet passed out by women in front of the courtroom was more succinct, "rape was committed by four men in a private apartment in October; on Thursday, it was done by a judge and a lawyer in a public courtroom.")

Through skillful questioning fraught with innuendo, Plotkin's defense attorney James Martin MacInnis portrayed the young woman as a licentious opportunist and unfit mother. MacInnis began by asking the young woman (then employed as a secretary) whether or not it was true that she was "familiar with liquor" and had worked as a "cocktail waitress." The young woman replied (the *Chronicle* wrote "admitted") that she had worked once or twice as a cocktail waitress. The attorney then asked if she had worked as a secretary in the financial district but had "left that employment after it was discovered that you had sexual intercourse on a couch in the office." The woman replied, "That is a lie. I left because I didn't like working in a one-girl office. It was too lonely." Then the defense asked if, while working as an attendant at a health club, "you were accused of having a sexual affair with a man?" Again the woman denied the story, "I was never accused of that."

Plotkin's attorney then sought to establish that his client's accuser was living with a married man. She responded that the man was separated from his wife. Finally he told the court that she had "spent the night" with another man who lived in the same building.

At this point in the testimony the woman asked Plotkin's defense attorney, "Am I on trial? . . . It is embarrassing and personal to admit these things to all these people. . . . I did not commit a crime. I am a human being." The lawyer, true to the chivalry of his class, apologized and immediately resumed questioning her, turning his attention to her children. (She is divorced, and the children at the time of the trial were in a foster home.) "Isn't it true that your two children have a sex game in which one gets on top of another and they—" "That is a lie!" the young woman interrupted him. She ended her testimony by explaining "They are wonderful children. They are not perverted."

The jury, divided in favor of acquittal ten to two, asked the court stenographer to read the woman's testimony back to them. After this reading, the Superior Court acquitted the defendant of both charges of rape and kidnapping.

According to the double standard a woman who has had sexual intercourse out of wedlock cannot be raped. Rape is not only a crime of aggression against the body; it is a transgression against chastity as defined by men. When a woman is forced into a sexual relationship, she has, according to the male ethos, been violated. But she is also defiled if she does not behave according to the double stan-

dard, by maintaining her chastity, or confining her sexual activities to a monogamous relationship.

One should not assume, however, that a woman can avoid the possibility of rape simply by behaving. Though myth would have it that mainly "bad girls" are raped, this theory has no basis in fact. Available statistics would lead one to believe that a safer course is promiscuity. In a study of rape done in the District of Columbia, it was found that 82 percent of the rape victims had a "good reputation." Even the Police Inspector's advice to stay off the streets is rather useless, for almost half of reported rapes occur in the home of the victim and are committed by a man she has never before seen. Like indiscriminate terrorism, rape can happen to any woman, and few women are ever without this knowledge.

But the courts and the police, both dominated by white males, continue to suspect the rape victim, *sui generis,* of provoking or asking for her own assault. According to Amir's study, the police tend to believe that a woman without a good reputation cannot be raped. The rape victim is usually submitted to countless questions about her own sexual mores and behavior by the police. This preoccupation is partially justified by the legal requirements for prosecution in a rape case. The rape victim must have been penetrated, and she must have made it clear to her assailant that she did not want penetration (unless of course she is unconscious). A refusal to accompany a man to some isolated place to allow him to touch her does not in the eyes of the court, constitute rape. She must have said "no" at the crucial genital moment. And the rape victim, to qualify as such, must also have put up a physical struggle—unless she can prove that to do so would have been to endanger her life.

But the zealous interest the police frequently exhibit in the physical details of a rape case is only partially explained by the requirements of the court. A woman who was raped in Berkeley was asked to tell the story of her rape four different times "right out in the street," while her assailant was escaping. She was then required to submit to a pelvic examination to prove that penetration had taken place. Later, she was taken to the police station where she was asked the same questions again: "Were you forced?" "Did he penetrate?" "Are you sure your life was in danger and you had no other choice?" This woman had been pulled off the street by a man who held a 10-inch knife at her throat and forcibly raped her. She was raped at midnight and was not able to return to her home until five in the morning. Police contacted her twice again in the next week, once by telephone at two in the morning and once at four in the morning. In her words, "The rape was probably the least traumatic incident of the whole evening. If I'm ever raped again, . . . I wouldn't report it to the police because of all the degradation. . . ."

If white women are subjected to unnecessary and often hostile questioning after having been raped, third world women are often not believed at all. According to the white male ethos (which is not only sexist but racist), third world women are defined from birth as "impure." Thus the white male is provided with a pool of women who are fair game for sexual imperialism. Third world women frequently do not report rape and for good reason. When blues singer Billie Holliday was 10 years old, she was taken off to a local house by a neighbor and raped. Her mother brought the police to rescue her, and she was taken to the local police station crying and bleeding:

> When we got there, instead of treating me and Mom like somebody who called the cops for help, they treated me like I'd killed somebody. . . . I guess they had me figured for having enticed this old goat into the whorehouse. . . . All I know for sure is they threw me into a cell . . . a fat white matron . . . saw I was still bleeding, she felt sorry for me and gave me a couple glasses of milk. But nobody else did anything for me except give me filthy looks and snicker to themselves.
>
> After a couple of days in a cell they dragged me into a court. Mr. Dick got sentenced to five years. They sentenced me to a Catholic institution.

Clearly the white man's chivalry is aimed only to protect the chastity of "his" women.

As a final irony, that same system of sexual values from which chivalry is derived has also provided womankind with an unwritten code of behavior, called femininity, which makes a feminine woman the perfect victim of sexual aggression. If being chaste does not ward off the possibility of assault, being feminine certainly increases the chances that it will succeed. To be submissive is to defer to masculine strength; is to lack muscular development or

any interest in defending oneself; is to let doors be opened, to have one's arm held when crossing the street. To be feminine is to wear shoes which make it difficult to run; skirts which inhibit one's stride; underclothes which inhibit the circulation. Is it not an intriguing observation that those very clothes which are thought to be flattering to the female and attractive to the male are those which make it impossible for a woman to defend herself against aggression?

Each girl as she grows into womanhood is taught fear. Fear is the form in which the female internalizes both chivalry and the double standard. Since, biologically speaking, women in fact have the same if not greater potential for sexual expression as do men, the woman who is taught that she must behave differently from a man must also learn to distrust her own carnality. She must deny her own feelings and learn not to act from them. She fears herself. This is the essence of passivity and, of course, a woman's passivity is not simply sexual but functions to cripple her from self-expression in every area of her life.

Passivity itself prevents a woman from ever considering her own potential for self-defense and forces her to look to men for protection. The woman is taught fear, but this time fear of the other; and yet her only relief from this fear is to seek out the other. Moreover, the passive woman is taught to regard herself as impotent, unable to act, unable even to perceive, in no way self-sufficient, and finally, as the object and not the subject of human behavior. It is in this sense that a woman is deprived of the status of a human being. She is not free to be.

III

Since Ibsen's Nora slammed the door on her patriarchal husband, woman's attempt to be free has been more or less fashionable. In this nineteenth-century portrait of a woman leaving her marriage, Nora tells her husband, "Our home has been nothing but a playroom. I have been your doll-wife just as at home I was papa's doll-child." And, at least on the stage, "The Doll's House" crumbled, leaving audiences with hope for the fate of the modern woman. And today, as in the past, womankind has not lacked examples of liberated women to emulate:

Emma Goldman, Greta Garbo and Isadora Duncan all denounced marriage and the double standard, and believed their right to freedom included sexual independence; but still their example has not affected the lives of millions of women who continue to marry, divorce and remarry, living out their lives dependent on the status and economic power of men. Patriarchy still holds the average woman prisoner not because she lacks the courage of an Isadora Duncan, but because the material conditions of her life prevent her from being anything but an object.

In the *Elementary Structures of Kinship*, Claude Lévi-Strauss gives to marriage this universal description, "It is always a system of exchange that we find at the origin of the rules of marriage." In this system of exchange, a woman is the "most precious possession." Lévi-Strauss continues that the custom of including women as booty in the marketplace is still so general that "a whole volume would not be sufficient to enumerate instances of it." Lévi-Strauss makes it clear that he does not exclude Western Civilization from his definition of "universal" and cites examples from modern wedding ceremonies. (The marriage ceremony is still one in which the husband and wife become one, and "that one is the husband.")

The legal proscription against rape reflects this possessory view of women. An article in the 1952–53 *Yale Law Journal* describes the legal rationale behind laws against rape:

> *In our society sexual taboos, often enacted into law, buttress a system of monogamy based upon the law of "free bargaining" of the potential spouses. Within this process the woman's power to withhold or grant sexual access is an important bargaining weapon.*

Presumably then, laws against rape are intended to protect the right of a woman, not for physical self-determination, but for physical "bargaining." The article goes on to explain explicitly why the preservation of the bodies of women is important to men:

> *The consent standard in our society does more than protect a significant item of social currency for women; it fosters, and is in turn bolstered by, a masculine pride in the exclusive possession of a sexual object. The consent of a woman to sexual intercourse awards the man a privilege of bodily access, a personal "prize," whose value is enhanced by sole ownership. An additional reason for the man's condemnation of rape may be found in the threat to his status from a decrease in the "value" of his sexual possession which would result from forcible violation.*

The passage concludes by making clear whose interest the law is designed to protect. "The man responds to this undercutting of his status as *possessor* of the girl with hostility toward the rapist; no other restitution device is available. The law of rape provides an orderly outlet for his vengeance." Presumably the female victim in any case will have been sufficiently socialized so as not to consciously feel any strong need for vengeance. If she does feel this need, society does not speak to it.

The laws against rape exist to protect rights of the male as possessor of the female body, and not the right of the female over her own body. Even without this enlightening passage from the *Yale Law Review*, the laws themselves are clear: In no state can a man be accused of raping his wife. How can any man steal what already belongs to him? It is in the sense of rape as theft of another man's property that Kate Millett writes, "Traditionally rape has been viewed as an offense one male commits against another—a matter of abusing his woman." In raping another man's woman, a man may aggrandize his own manhood and concurrently reduce that of another man. Thus a man's honor is not subject directly to rape, but only indirectly, through "his" woman.

If the basic social unit is the family, in which the woman is a possession of her husband, the superstructure of society is a male hierarchy, in which men dominate other men (or patriarchal families dominate other patriarchal families). And it is no small irony that, while the very social fabric of our male-dominated culture denies women equal access to political, economic and legal power, the literature, myth and humor of our culture depict women not only as the power behind the throne, but the real source of the oppression of men. The religious version of this fairy tale blames Eve for both carnality and eating of the tree of knowledge, at the same time making her gullible to the obvious devices of a serpent. Adam, of course, is merely the trusting victim of love. Certainly this is a biased story. But no more biased than the one television audiences receive today from the latest slick comedians. Through a media which is owned by men, censored by a state dominated by men, all the evils of this social system which make a man's life unpleasant are blamed upon "the wife." The theory is: were it not for the female who waits and plots to "trap" the male into marriage, modern man would be able to achieve Olympian freedom. She is made the scapegoat for a system which is in fact run by men.

Nowhere is this more clear than in the white racist use of the concept of white womanhood. The white male's open rape of black women, coupled with his overweening concern for the chastity and protection of his wife and daughters, represents an extreme of sexist and racist hypocrisy. While on the one hand she was held up as the standard for purity and virtue, on the other the Southern white woman was never asked if she wanted to be on a pedestal, and in fact any deviance from the male-defined standards for white womanhood was treated severely. (It is a powerful commentary on American racism that the historical role of Blacks as slaves, and thus possessions without power, has robbed black women of legal and economic protection through marriage. Thus black women in Southern society and in the ghettoes of the North have long been easy game for white rapists.) The fear that black men would rape white women was classic paranoia. Quoting from Ann Breen's unpublished study of racism and sexism in the South, *The New South: White Man's Country,* Frederick Douglass legitimately points out that, had the black man wished to rape white women, he had ample opportunity to do so during the Civil War when white women, the wives, sisters, daughters and mothers of the rebels, were left in the care of Blacks. But yet not a single act of rape was committed during this time. The Ku Klux Klan, who tarred and feathered black men and lynched them in the honor of the purity of white womanhood, also applied tar and feathers to a Southern white woman accused of bigamy, which leads one to suspect that Southern white men were not so much outraged at the violation of the woman as a person, in the few instances where rape was actually committed by black men, but at the violation of his property rights. In the situation where a black man was found to be having sexual relations with a white woman, the white woman could exercise skin-privilege, and claim that she had been raped in which case the black man was lynched. But if she did not claim rape, she herself was subject to lynching.

In constructing the myth of white womanhood so as to justify the lynching and oppression of black men and women, the white male has created a convenient symbol of his own power which has resulted in black hostility toward the white "bitch," accompanied by a fear on the part of many white women of the black rapist. Moreover, it is not surprising that after being told for two centuries that he wants to rape white women, black men have begun to actually commit that act. But it is crucial to note that the frequency of this practice is outrageously exaggerated in the white mythos. Ninety percent of reported rape is intra- not inter-racial.

In *Soul on Ice,* Eldridge Cleaver has described the mixing of a rage against white power with the internalized sexism of a black man raping a white woman.

> Somehow I arrived at the conclusion that, as a matter of principle, it was of paramount importance for me to have an antagonistic, ruthless attitude toward white women. . . . Rape was an insurrectionary act. It delighted me that I was defying and trampling upon the white man's law, upon his system of values and that I was defiling his women—and this point, I believe, was the most satisfying to me because I was very resentful over the historical fact of how the white man has used the black woman.

Thus a black man uses white women to take out his rage against white men. But, in fact, whenever a rape of a white woman by a black man does take place, it is again the white man who benefits. First, the act itself terrorizes the white woman and makes her more dependent on the white male for protection. Then, if the woman prosecutes her attacker, the white man is afforded legal opportunity to exercise overt racism. Of course, the knowledge of the rape helps to perpetuate two myths which are beneficial to white male rule—the bestiality of the black man and the desirability of white women. Finally, the white man surely benefits because he himself is not the object of attack—he has been allowed to stay in power.

Indeed, the existence of rape in any form is beneficial to the ruling class of white males. For rape is a kind of terrorism which severely limits the freedom of women and makes women dependent on men. Moreover, in the act of rape, the rage that one man may harbor toward another higher in the male hierarchy can be deflected toward a female scapegoat. For every man there is always someone lower on the social scale on whom he can take out his aggressions. And that is any woman alive.

This oppressive attitude towards women finds its institutionalization in the traditional family. For it is assumed that a man "wears the pants" in his family—he exercises the option of rule whenever he so chooses. Not that he makes all the decisions—clearly women make most of the important day-to-day decisions in a family. But when a conflict of interest arises, it is the man's interest which will prevail. His word, in itself, is more powerful. He lords it over his wife in the same way his boss lords it over him, so that the very process of exercising his power becomes as important an act as obtaining whatever it is his power can get for him. This notion of power is key to the male ego in this culture, for the two acceptable measures of masculinity are a man's power over women and his power over other men. A man may boast to his friends that "I have 20 men working for me." It is also aggrandizement of his ego if he has the financial power to clothe his wife in furs and jewels. And, if a man lacks the wherewithal to acquire such power, he can always express his rage through equally masculine activities—rape and theft. Since male society defines the female as a possession, it is not surprising that the felony most often committed together with rape is theft. As the following classic tale of rape points out, the elements of theft, violence and forced sexual relations merge into an indistinguishable whole.

The woman who told the following story was acquainted with the man who tried to rape her. When the man learned that she was going to be staying alone for the weekend, he began early in the day a polite campaign to get her to go out with him. When she continued to refuse his request, his chivalrous mask dropped away:

I had locked all the doors because I was afraid, and I don't know how he got in; it was probably through the screen door. When I woke up, he was shaking my leg. His eyes were red, and I knew he had been drinking or smoking. I thought I would try to talk

my way out of it. He started by saying that he wanted to sleep with me, and then he got angrier and angrier, until he started to say, "I want pussy," "I want pussy." Then, I got scared and tried to push him away. That's when he started to force himself on me. It was awful. It was the most humiliating, terrible feeling. He was forcing my legs apart and ripping my clothes off. And it was painful. I did fight him—he was slightly drunk and I was able to keep him away. I had taken judo a few years back, but I was afraid to throw a chop for fear that he'd kill me. I could see he was getting more and more violent. I was thinking wildly of some way to get out of this alive, and then I said to him, "Do you want money? I'll give you money." We had money but I was also thinking that if I got to the back room I could telephone the police—as if the police would have even helped. It was a stupid thing to think of because obviously he would follow me. And he did. When he saw me pick up the phone, he tried to tie the cord around my neck. I screamed at him that I did have the money in another room, that I was going to call the police because I was scared, but that I would never tell anybody what happened. It would be an absolute secret. He said, "okay,' and I went to get the money. But when he got it, all of a sudden he got this crazy look in his eye and he said to me, "Now I'm going to kill you." Then I started saying my prayers. I knew there was nothing I could do. He started to hit me—I still wasn't sure if he wanted to rape me at this point—or just to kill me. He was hurting me, but hadn't yet gotten me into a stranglehold because he was still drunk and off balance. Somehow we pushed into the kitchen where I kept looking at this big knife. But I didn't pick it up. Somehow, no matter how much I hated him at that moment, I still couldn't imagine putting the knife in his flesh, and then I was afraid he would grab it and stick it into me. Then he was hitting me again and somehow we pushed through the back door of the kitchen and onto the porch steps. We fell down the steps and that's when he started to strangle me. He was on top of me. He just went on and on until finally I lost consciousness. I did scream, though my screams sounded like whispers to me. But what happened was that a cab driver happened by and frightened him away. The cab driver revived me—I was out only a minute at the most. And then I ran across the street and I grabbed the woman who was

Yelling, screaming, hitting: they stare at the red blood that trickles through the crying mouth. They cannot believe this pleading, crying woman, this woman who does not fight back, is the same person they know. The person they know is strong, gets things done, is a woman of ways and means, a woman of action. They do not know her still, paralyzed, waiting for the next blow, pleading. They do not know their mama afraid. Even if she does not hit back they want her to run, to run and to not stop running. She wants her to hit him with the table light, the ashtray, the one near her hand. She does not want to see her like this, not fighting back. He notices them, long enough to tell them to get out, go upstairs. She refuses to move. She cannot move. She cannot leave her mama alone. When he says What are you staring at, do you want some, too? she is afraid enough to move. She will not take her orders from him. She asks the woman if it is right to leave her alone. The woman—her mother—nods her head yes. She still stands still. It is his movement in her direction that sends her up the stairs. She cannot believe all her sisters and her brother are not taking a stand, that they go to sleep. She cannot bear their betrayal. When the father is not looking she creeps down the steps. She wants the woman to know that she is not alone. She wants to bear witness.

All that she does not understand about marriage, about men and women, is explained to her one night. In her dark place on the stairs she is seeing over and over again the still body of the woman pleading, crying, the moving body of the man angry, yelling. She sees that the man has a gun. She hears him tell the woman that he will kill her. She sits in her place on the stair and demands to know of herself is she able to come to the rescue, is she willing to fight, is she ready to die. Her body shakes with the answers. She is fighting back the tears. When he leaves the room she comes to ask the woman if she is all right, if there is anything she can do. The woman's voice is full of tenderness and hurt. She is in her role as mother. She tells her daughter to go upstairs and go to sleep, that everything will be all right. The daughter does not believe her. Her eyes are pleading. She does not want to be told to go. She hovers in the shadows. When he returns he tells her that he has told her to get her ass upstairs. She does not look at him. He turns to the woman, tells her to leave, tells her to take the daughter with her.

The woman does not protest. She moves like a robot, hurriedly throwing things into suitcases, boxes. She says nothing to the man. He is still screaming, muttering. When she tries to say to him he is wrong, so wrong, he is more angry, threatening. All the neat drawers are emptied out on the bed, all the precious belongings that can be carried, stuffed, are to be taken. There is sorrow in every gesture, sorrow and pain—like a dust collecting on everything, so thick she can gather it in her hands. She is seeing that the man owns everything, that the woman has only her clothes, her shoes, and other personal belongings. She is seeing that the woman can be told to go, can be sent away in the silent, long hours of the night. She is hearing in her head the man's threats to kill. She can feel the cool metal as if it is resting against her cheek. She can hear the click, the blast. She can see the woman's body falling. No, it is not her body, it is the body of love. She witnesses the death of love. If love were alive she believes it would stop everything. It would steady the man's voice, calm his rage. Love would take the woman's hand, caress her cheek and with a clean handkerchief wipe her eyes. The gun is pointed at love. He lays it on the table. He wants his wife to finish her packing, to go.

She is again in her role as mother. She tells the daughter that she does not have to flee in the middle of the night, that it is not her fight. The daughter is silent, staring into the woman's eyes. She is looking for the bright lights, the care and adoration she has shown the man. The eyes are dark with grief, swollen. She feels that a fire inside the woman is dying out, that she is cold. She is sure the woman will freeze to death if she goes out into the night alone. She takes her hand, ready to go with her. Yet she hopes there will be no going. She hopes when the mother's brother comes he will be strong enough to take love's body and give it, mouth-to-mouth, the life it has lost. She hopes he will talk to the man, guide him. When he finally comes, her mother's favorite brother, she cannot believe the calm way he lifts suitcase, box, sack, carries them to the car without question. She cannot bear his silent agreement that the man is right, that he has done what men are able to do. She cannot take the bits and pieces of her mother's heart and put them together again.

our neighbor and screamed at her, "Am I alive? Am I still alive?"

Rape is an act of aggression in which the victim is denied her self-determination. It is an act of violence which, if not actually followed by beatings or murder, nevertheless always carries with it the threat of death. And finally, rape is a form of mass terrorism, for the victims of rape are chosen indiscriminately, but the propagandists for male supremacy broadcast that it is women who cause rape by being unchaste or in the wrong place at the wrong time—in essence, by behaving as though they were free.

The threat of rape is used to deny women employment. (In California, the Berkeley Public Library, until pushed by the Federal Employment Practices Commission, refused to hire female shelvers because of perverted men in the stacks.) The fear of rape keeps women off the streets at night. Keeps women at home. Keeps women passive and modest for fear that they be thought provocative.

It is part of human dignity to be able to defend oneself, and women are learning. Some women have learned karate; some to shoot guns. And yet we will not be free until the threat of rape and the atmosphere of violence is ended, and to end that the nature of male behavior must change.

But rape is not an isolated act that can be rooted out from patriarchy without ending patriarchy itself. The same men and power structure who victimize women are engaged in the act of raping Vietnam, raping Black people and the very earth we live upon. Rape is a classic act of domination where, in the words of Kate Millett, "the emotions of hatred, contempt, and the desire to break or violate personality," take place. This breaking of the personality characterizes modern life itself. No simple reforms can eliminate rape. As the symbolic expression of the white male hierarchy, rape is the quintessential act of our civilization, one which, Valerie Solanis warns, is in danger of "humping itself to death."

"The Rape" of Mr. Smith

Unknown

This small piece is so clear on the injustices—legal, cultural, and attitudinal—that are visited upon women who are victims of rape that it is used everywhere—in women's studies courses, in rape crisis centers, in training seminars for police and social workers—yet no one seems to know its origin.

It must be remembered that we are all subject to rape: those who have been raped, those who may be raped and therefore have their lives altered, and those who are related to the victims of rape.

THE LAW DISCRIMINATES AGAINST RAPE victims in a manner which would not be tolerated by victims of any other crime. In the following example, a holdup victim is asked questions similar in form to those usually asked a victim of rape.

"Mr. Smith, you were held up at gunpoint on the corner of 16th & Locust?"

"Yes."

"Did you struggle with the robber?"

"No."

"Why not?"

"He was armed."

"Then you made a conscious decision to comply with his demands rather than to resist?"

"Yes."

"Did you scream? Cry out?"

"No. I was afraid."

"I see. Have you ever been held up before?"

"No."

"Have you ever given money away?"

"Yes, of course—"

"And did you do so willingly?"

"What are you getting at?"

"Well, let's put it like this, Mr. Smith. You've given away money in the past—in fact, you have quite a reputation for philanthropy. How can we be sure that you weren't *contriving* to have your money taken from you by force?"

"Listen, if I wanted—"

"Never mind. What time did this holdup take place, Mr. Smith?"

'About 11 p.m."

"You were out on the streets at 11 p.m.? Doing what?"

"Just walking."

"Just walking? You know that it's dangerous being out on the street that late at night. Weren't you aware that you could have been held up?"

"I hadn't thought about it."

"What were you wearing at the time, Mr. Smith?"

"Let's see. A suit. Yes, a suit."

"An *expensive* suit?"

"Well—yes."

"In other words, Mr. Smith, you were walking around the streets late at night in a suit that practically *advertised* the fact that you might be a good target for some easy money, isn't that so? I mean, if we didn't know better, Mr. Smith, we might even think you were *asking* for this to happen, mightn't we?"

"Look, can't we talk about the past history of the guy who *did* this to me?"

"I'm afraid not, Mr. Smith. I don't think you would want to violate his rights, now, would you?"

Naturally, the line of questioning, the innuendo, is ludicrous—as well as inadmissible as any sort of cross-examination—unless we are talking about parallel questions in a rape case. The time of night, the victim's previous history of "giving away" that which was taken by force, the clothing—all of these are held against the victim. Society's posture on rape, and the manifestation of that posture in the courts, help account for the fact that so few rapes are reported.

Witnessing the Death of Love: She Hears Him Tell the Woman That He Will Kill Her . . .

bell hooks

bell hooks, poet, writer, teacher, scholar, born Gloria Jean Watkins in Hopkinsville, Kentucky, in 1952, is one of the most important feminist thinkers in women's studies. Currently, she is professor of English at City College in New York City. An original thinker and prolific writer, she has authored numerous articles and books, beginning with the groundbreaking Black feminist treatise, Ain't I a Woman: Black Women and Feminism *in 1981. Other works include* Feminist Theory: From Margin to Center *(1984);* Talking Back: Thinking Feminist, Thinking Black *(1989);* Yearning: Race, Gender, and Cultural Politics *(1990);* Killing Rage: Ending Racism *(1995);* Reel to Real: Race, Sex & Class at the Movies *(1996); and most recently,* All About Love: New Visions *(2000).*

With infinite tenderness and grief, this narrative, from Bone Black: Memories of Girlhood, *represents the tragedy of male violence against women, of male supremacy, of battering, and the consequences they have not only for the woman who is beaten but for her family, for all women, for society as a whole—a reducing of the person, a loss that brings pain, anger, deceit, and the death of love.*

THEY HAVE NEVER HEARD THEIR mama and daddy fussing or fighting. They have heard him be harsh, complain that the house should be cleaner, that he should not have to come home from work to a house that is not cleaned just right. They know he gets mad. When he gets mad about the house he begins to clean it himself to show that he can do better. Although he never cooks he knows how. He would not be able to judge her cooking if he did not cook himself. They are afraid of him when he is mad. They go upstairs to get out of his way. He does not come upstairs. Taking care of children is not a man's work. It does not concern him. He is not even interested—that is, unless something goes wrong. Then he can show her that she is not very good at parenting. They know they have a good mama, the best. Even though they fear him they are not moved by his opinions. She tries to remember a time when she felt loved by him. She remembers it as being the time when she was a baby girl, a small girl. She remembers him taking her places, taking her to the world inhabited by black men, the barbershop, the pool hall. He took his affections away from her abruptly. She never understood why, only that they went and did not come back. She remembered trying to do whatever she could to bring them back, only they never came. Growing up she stopped trying. He mainly ignored her. She mainly tried to stay out of his way. In her own way she grew to hate wanting his love and not being able to get it. She hated that part of herself that kept wanting his love or even just his approval long after she could see that he was never, never going to give it.

Out of nowhere he comes home from work angry. He reaches the porch yelling and screaming at the woman inside—yelling that she is his wife, he can do with her what he wants. They do not understand what is happening. He is pushing, hitting, telling her to shut up. She is pleading—crying. He does not want to hear, to listen. They catch his angry words in their hands like lightning bugs—store them in a jar to sort them out later. Words about other men, about phone calls, about how he had told her. They do not know what he has told her. They have never heard them talk in an angry way.

She thinks of all the nights she lies awake in her bed hearing the woman's voice, her mother's voice, hearing his voice. She wonders if it is then that he is telling her everything—warning her.

I am always fighting with mama. Everything has come between us. She no longer stands between me and all that would hurt me. She is hurting me. This is my dream of her—that she will stand between me and all that hurts me, that she will protect me at all cost. It is only a dream. In some way I understand that it has to do with marriage, that to be the wife to the husband she must be willing to sacrifice even her daughters for his good. For the mother it is not simple. She is always torn. She works hard to fulfill his needs, our needs. When they are not the same she must maneuver, manipulate, choose. She has chosen. She has decided in his favor. She is a religious woman. She has been told that a man should obey god, that a woman should obey man, that children should obey their fathers and mothers, particularly their mothers. I will not obey.

She says that she punishes me for my own good. I do not know what it is I have done this time. I know that she is ready with her switches, that I am to stand still while she lashes out again and again. In my mind there is the memory of a woman sitting still while she is being hit, punished. In my mind I am remembering how much I want that woman to fight back. Before I can think clearly my hands reach out, grab the switches, are raised as if to hit her back. For a moment she is stunned, unbelieving. She is shocked. She tells me that I must never *ever* as long as I live raise my hand against my mother. I tell her I do not have a mother. She is even more shocked. Enraged, she lashes out again. This time I am still. This time I cry. I see the hurt in her eyes when I say I do not have a mother. I am ready to be punished. My desire was to stop the pain, not to hurt. I am ashamed and torn. I do not want to stand still and be punished but I never want to hurt mama. It is better to hurt than to cause her pain. She warns me that she will tell daddy when he comes home, that I will be punished again. I cannot understand her acts of betrayal. I cannot understand that she must be against me to be for him. He and I are strangers. Deep in the night we parted from one another, knowing that nothing would ever be the same. He did not say good-bye. I did not look him in the face. Now we avoid one another. He speaks to me through her.

Although they act as if everything between them is the same, that life is as it was. It is only a game. They pretend. There is no pain in the pretense. Everything is hidden. Secrets find a way out in sleep. My sisters say to mama She cries in her sleep, calls out. In her sleep is the place of remembering. It is the place where there is no pretense. She is dreaming always the same dream. A movie is showing. It is a tragic story of jealousy and lost love. It is called *Crime of Passion.* In the movie a man has killed his wife and daughter. He has killed his wife because he believes she has lovers. He has killed the daughter because she witnesses the death of the wife. When they go to trial all the remaining family come to speak on behalf of the man. At his job he is calm and quiet, a hardworking man, a family man. Neighbors come to testify that the dead woman was young and restless, that the daughter was wild and rebellious. Everyone sympathizes with the man. His story is so sad that they begin to weep. All their handkerchiefs are clean and white. Like flags waving, they are a signal of peace, of surrender. They are a gesture to the man that he can go on with life.

CHAPTER SEVEN

Discrimination: The Effects
of Sexism on Public Institutions

Sexism affects not only women's personal lives; formalized in both law and custom, it is also reflected in our public institutions—government, education, the health care system, business, the courts and law enforcement, and so on. In the economy, most women are discriminated against, many are poor; in government, and to a large extent in politics, we are nearly powerless; before the law, we are discriminated against and deprived of many rights that aren't even recognized; in health care, we are exploited. In each instance, the discrimination is denied or justified by the same body of myth and mystification that governs women's personal lives. Keep in mind that all social structures are interrelated and reinforcing. An intricate web of rules and practices determines women's circumstance in each arena, and that in turn determines the character of our experiences in our individual lives.

WOMEN IN THE ECONOMY

Much has been written in the last thirty years about the "great strides" women as a group have allegedly made in earning power, professional and social advancement, and opportunity. The truth is that although some women's economic lives have dramatically improved, mainly educated professional women, the great majority of women, in this country and elsewhere, have experienced little or no improvement, and for many women, the situation has grown much worse as the term *feminization of poverty* becomes increasingly descriptive.

The Myth: Lucky Ladies

Every American has heard the tales of pampered wives playing bridge and drinking coffee while their harried husbands labor to win the dollars so carelessly tossed away at the supermarket or dress shop. As the story goes, these wives earn no money of their own, but *because they spend it, they control it;* everyone in America "knows" that. There are tales of "palimony" winners or gay divorcées reveling in windfalls snatched from vanquished ex-husbands, merry widows collecting fat sums from hard-earned insurance policies and Social Security, lazy and comfortable welfare mothers stealing from the state to live on televisions, expensive make-up, and steak. Updated versions of the myth feature high-living married professionals who make a lot of money and secretly invest it in their own mutual funds (for future post-marriage high living) or spend it on endless luxuries, while living well beyond their means on the largesse of their husbands, who will have to pay the piper later. Such types compose a partial list of the privileged, well-off women reputed to represent the majority of the female population in America.

The Reality: Women Are Disadvantaged

In the United States, compared with men, for the most part, women are at a disadvantage. Within and across job classifications, women have lower salaries, generally have less disposable income, are more likely to fall below nationally set poverty standards, and in several ways have far less recourse to remedies.

Facts on Women's Earnings and Income   At present, on the average and across all occupations, year-round, full-time women workers in the United States earn a bit more than three-fourths the salaries of men (in 1998, 76 percent, according to the United States Department of Labor)[1]. In 1998, the median income for women who worked full time was $26,711; for men it was $36,679.[2]

Women are generally employed in the lowest paid occupations and jobs. In 1998, most women worked in technical, sales, and administrative support occupations. Women constituted over 95 percent of workers in child care, household work, and service jobs, and represented only 26.6 percent of physicians, 11.1 percent of engineers, and 28.6 percent of lawyers.[3] Although the number of female lawyers and judges nearly doubled between 1983 and 1998, the income of women lawyers and judges in 1998 was $61,780 compared with men's $114,947. In 1998, women made up 50.3 percent of all salespeople, but they earned a median income of only $23,197 compared with men's $37,248;[4] their much lower income was primarily due to the fact that women constitute only the smallest minority of the

highest paid sales workers (such as auto and boat salespeople) and the majority of the lowest (such as apparel salespeople). Nor is the disparity in sales incomes attributable simply to differences in "product knowledge." As Gloria Steinem pointed out, in department stores, men sell stoves and refrigerators; women sell men's underwear. How shall we account for that? Product knowledge? Even in clerical and administrative support, women's earnings ($23,835) fell seriously behind men's ($31,153).[5] Could we hope that in any occupation, let us say management, women might elude such disparity in earning power? Unfortunately not. Manager/executive median income for women was $34,755 compared with men's $51,351.[6] In fact, women earn less than men in *every* occupation listed by the Bureau of Labor Statistics. In 1998, in the twenty occupations that women are most likely to have, the closest women came to men's earnings was in registered nursing (94.8 percent) and bookkeeping (93.6 percent).[7]

The numbers of single women and single women with children are rising, and they have special economic problems. Contrary to the myth of the gay divorcée, women's economic circumstances after marriage are reduced. Less than 4 percent of divorced women are awarded alimony by the courts. In 1995, only 61 percent of divorced women with children were awarded child support, and fewer than half the fathers ordered to pay that support did so. Of the 10 million women who are eligible for child support, a third live in poverty.[8] The average amount awarded (or paid) for child support is far less than half of what is required for support of a child. We know that within one year after divorce, the standard of living for women and their children drops dramatically, although calculations vary regarding the degree of decline. One very well known study of the late 1980s reported that, after divorce, women's standard of living dropped 73 percent in the first year, while their ex-husbands' standard rose 42 percent.[9] A more recent report placed wives' decline at 33 percent and husbands' increase at 13 percent. Data indicated that the average income of women divorced in their middle years dropped to less than $11,000 one year after divorce.[10]

Because women earn less over a lifetime, their Social Security and retirement benefits are smaller. This situation is worsened because women often retire with benefits at 62 rather than 65, receiving, therefore, even lower rates and having even smaller monthly benefits. If they retire as widows, they receive only their widow's benefits based on their husband's contributions to the Social Security system, not both their widow's pension and their own benefits.

Some Facts About Poverty   By the mid-1980s, the term *feminization of poverty* had become commonplace, because by 1986, women constituted 63 percent of all adults in poverty. Thirty-four percent of all households headed by women were poor (compared with 6 percent of married-couple households), and 54 percent of all children in households headed by women were poor.[11] Half of the Black and Hispanic households headed by women were poor.[12] One-fifth of all women over 60 were poor, and elderly women were twice as likely to be poor as elderly men.[13] By 1990, there had been no improvement; indeed, the situation had actually worsened. Today, more than half of the poor are children and the elderly, and more than half of the homeless are women and their children.

Some Facts About Women's Contribution to the Economy   Women work because we need to. By 1997, more than half of all married-couple families had wives in the paid labor force, and in more than half of those families, the wives earn half or more of their family's income. Married-couple families in which the wife worked had median yearly incomes of $60,669 compared with $36,027 for such families in which the wife did not work for pay.[14] Because incomes in households where wives work are substantially higher than in households where only husbands work, the income of working wives reduces the potential poverty level of families substantially.

Discrimination Everywhere   Women workers are channeled into occupations that are seen as "appropriate" for women. These are continuations of the roles females are expected to fulfill in the wider society: for example, serving and facilitating (secretaries, waitresses, nurses, "gal Fridays"), child care (teachers on the elementary level, pediatricians), sex and decoration (receptionists, flight attendants, entertainers). Occupations historically reserved for women are notoriously underpaid regardless of the

level of expertise needed to perform them, and they are generally controlled by male administrators who make it impossible, one way or the other, for women to set their own market and hence their own demands. Nurses, for example, 92.5 percent of whom are female, are subject to the demands and expectations of the American Medical Association and the American Hospital Association, both of which are controlled by men.

When women try to break out of these occupational ghettos, they face other problems. Various practices, official or otherwise, challenge entry into male-dominated work areas—apprenticeship programs in trade unions, employment traps (for example, odd hours, machines too heavy for females), discriminatory hiring, and so on. (In 1999, for example, only 4 percent of construction workers were women, a tiny gain from the 1 percent of 1979.[15]) Women who do manage entry into nontraditional occupations are generally channeled to the low-earning end of the spectrum. Sales, for example, was shown earlier to favor men financially; high-line items may be reserved for men by seniority rules, for example, which disadvantage women, who more frequently are temporary, part-time, new, or returning workers. Thus, although women's incomes have been rising proportional to men's incomes, due mainly to the efforts of the women's movement, we are still very much involved in a game of catch-up. An additional problem for women, in traditional and nontraditional occupations, is unemployment. Unemployment rates are higher for women than for men, probably even higher than they appear to be, because the number of women who have not yet worked but want to cannot be properly evaluated.

The various welfare programs that are supposed to benefit women and children—and were primary targets of villification during the mid- and late 1990s by those who charged they allowed women to live irresponsibly and handsomely off the state—actually encourage and even ensure female poverty. Welfare benefits in general have never been more than barely sufficient for subsistence and have become even more inadequate since the recent welfare "reforms," which many see as a war on the poor. Often, women are caught between welfare poverty on the one hand and exorbitant costs for child care on the other. The mother with children to care for, no husband, and few skills is in a bind. Very high proportions of unmarried women with children are poor, especially women who were young when they had their first child. (It is also important to note that, according to NOW, more than half the women on welfare have experienced or are fleeing domestic abuse.[16]) Although job "retraining" may be supported, "education" generally is not. Often the kinds of jobs a welfare mother may train for will not yield sufficient income to secure both adequate child care and subsistence living, yet the education that would make work outside the home truly profitable remains generally out of her reach. With aid for abortion and contraception denied her, the mother on welfare has little chance to improve her plight. In the mid-1990s, poor women became the target of racist and sexist politics, and the "reform" of welfare accomplished in 1996 promises to deepen the hardships of thousands of women and their children.

WHY?

What are the ideological factors that underlie the economic position of women? It is not too difficult to guess. Shirley Bernard expresses them in terms of "dominance":

> In a society where money means power, most of the money must come to the dominant group if it is to maintain the status quo. In our society white males are dominant. . . . they earn substantially more than non-whites and females.[17]

The notion of dominance is a shorthand we can decipher to reveal the entire range of beliefs and attitudes inherent in the patriarchal mind-set. Once again, the nature of women's role and the gender ideal are the factors underlying women's disadvantaged position.

The Role: Woman's Work

In earlier chapters, we saw that in patriarchy it is believed that women were created to be helpmeets to men, whereas men are seen as the central actors in society. In addition to performing the functions of procreation and nursing, it is women's central responsibility to serve as under-laborers to men, to manage for them the necessary minutiae that

muddy the waters of real creativity. Women are ideally suited for this function, it is said, being less intelligent and less rational than men—hence, both less capable of true accomplishment and more tolerant of detail and routine.

On the Job

Until very recently—and then only because of advances pressed by the women's movement—the "branch offices" of the public economic sector have been very much a study in patriarchal dominance. In offices, factories, hospitals, schools, and elsewhere, men "did the job," and women "helped." He managed while she answered his phone, sharpened his pencils, typed his letters, and made his coffee. He cured the sick while she followed his orders, applied his prescriptions, and made his coffee. He flew the airplane while she checked the tickets, served the customers, and made his coffee. The rare woman who got to run the show was considered a peculiarity, causing problems for her own self-image as well as for her male colleagues and subordinates.

Salaries reflected these relative positions, for line workers earn more than their assistants. Moreover, women, *by virtue of being women*—regardless of position occupied, regardless of how much education and ability they needed to do their job— earned less, whether in women's occupations or in others. Thus, nurses, schoolteachers, professional secretaries, and others in traditionally female jobs have been notoriously underpaid relative to their education, skill, and experience. But even women in managerial or executive positions could not look forward to the same rank, salary, or privileges of men of the same status. A 1990 survey by *Fortune* magazine exposed a "closely guarded secret":

> The pervasiveness of discrimination against women prevents all but a minuscule number of them from reaching the highest ranks of corporate America.
>
> The magazine examined the 1990 proxy statements of the 799 public companies on its combined list of the 1000 largest U.S. industrial and service companies. It found that of the 4012 people listed as the highest-paid officers and directors, only 19 are women—less than one-half of 1 percent.
>
> Discrimination against women in management also is reflected dramatically in a wide pay gap, according to Labor Department figures. This is shown

in the following data on median weekly wages paid in four categories of managers:

- ★ *Female financial managers, $558; male $837.*
- ★ *Female lawyers and judges, $834; male $1,184.*
- ★ *Female marketing, advertising and public relations managers, $616; male $902.*
- ★ *Female personnel and labor relations managers, $604; male $881.*[18]

By 1998, only two of the Fortune 500 companies had female chief executive officers (CEOs): Mattel Incorporated and Golden West Financial Corporation. Women were 11.2 percent of officers of Fortune 500 companies (up from 10.6 percent in 1997), but men held 94 percent of line positions, the jobs that lead to the most powerful and top-paying positions.[19]

In every category, women are still well behind men in earnings despite the fact that more women are attaining better educations than ever before. More than 53 percent of all students in higher education are female. Increasing numbers of women are earning professional degrees in medicine, law, and engineering, and graduate degrees, including doctorates, in all fields.

It is a current myth that the gender pay gap no longer exists and the task of eliminating discrimination has been completed. Several New Right think tanks have begun to push the notion that because the percentage of women in professional schools has climbed and because there are some women who are earning high salaries, equality has been achieved and affirmative action is no longer necessary. In reality, little has changed. In fact, women have lost ground in some ways. The average salary of full-time women workers relative to men has been slowly increasing and, as we saw earlier, is currently about 76 percent. But considering that the average age of the female labor force is older (35 to 54) than it was even 20 years ago, considering as well the incredible effort women have made to gain parity in opportunity and compensation, even 76 percent is totally unacceptable. Furthermore, while the average salary for women has increased due to the numbers of women entering the professions, the majority of women workers are still confined to the "pink ghetto" (lower-paid jobs, such as clerical and service work, overwhelmingly assigned to women by work segregation) and are

still earning far less than 75 percent of the average male salary.

Even where things seem to have changed, the underlying reality often remains untouched. An executive secretary with ten years' experience may be "promoted" to district sales manager (entry-level position for managerial class) with men several years her junior, but she may be the only one of her group who has reached her ceiling. A female high school teacher may now receive a salary equal to that of her male counterpart for teaching, but if her extra duties at home or her gender preclude her from requesting playground duties or coaching, she may thereby be denied the extra income that raises the job above the average. "Maid" and "janitor" may both be redefined as "maintenance worker–2"and receive equal pay, but if only men make it to "maintenance worker–3" (supervisor), the apparent equal opportunity is only a sham.

It is important to recognize the power of the forces straining to maintain the status quo. The female sex role and gender ideal is a major, if not *the* major, determinant of women's position in the workplace. Michael Korda, a publishing executive in 1972, contended that in the workplace, men perceive women workers, whether colleagues or subordinates, as extensions of their wives or other women in their personal lives. That is, they see women as females first and workers second, and this perception conditions men's attitudes and behavior toward women on the job.[20]

The anthropologist and antifeminist George Gilder offered a further, even more psychologically profound, insight into men's resistance to women's economic equality.[21] In primitive times, Gilder theorized, men proved their masculine identity by facing hardship and death in "the hunt." Today, although industrialization has made the hunt per se unnecessary, men still need to reinforce their sense of masculinity. They have, therefore, substituted their work—whatever it is—making it a kind of symbolic hunt. It is thus crucial for a man to maintain his job's aura of manliness, its rituals and traditions, and most of all its separation from women and all things female. As women encroach upon a field of endeavor, we throw doubt on its manliness, Gilder argues, destroying its ability to function as a symbolic hunt, sending men scurrying to more distant bastions of masculinity. In essence, in Gilder's view, the plain fact of the workplace is that for psychosexual reasons, men simply do not want women there: Other arguments are mere rationales.

Whatever one thinks of the man-the-hunter theory, the truth probably lies somewhere in this deeper region: Men do not want equality with women at work, any more than they want it elsewhere. Gilder concluded that women should stay out, leaving men their bastions and their sources of identity. Feminists, of course, go another way. Martyrdom on the altar of masculinity is a price too high either for women or for all humankind. Women not only *need* to work, but as citizens, women have a right to work, just as men do. Men will have to find other ways to prove their masculinity. Women, however, must change as well.

Gender: Subliminal Effects

It is true that a woman's relationship to a job or career is often different from a man's. Part of that difference comes as a result of external conditions: the double burden of home and child care (sometimes called the "second shift"), barriers to opportunity, as well as misogynist attitudes and behaviors. But added factors in those different relations to work reside within ourselves as women, in our own attitudes and behavior. These are the often hidden or subliminal effects of our gender conditioning.

As detailed earlier, we are raised to see ourselves as being second to men, husbands, and employer-workers; we learn to see our interests as subordinate to their needs and wishes. As wives, our husbands' jobs, desires, and values are to supersede our own. According to traditional rules, we work or fulfill ourselves only after we have accomplished our "primary duties." Even the modern, liberated woman is subject to the tremendous force of that other commitment. Not wanting to choose between work and family—and highly subject to a social structure that decrees her responsible for her home and children—a woman in the workplace is truly doubly burdened. Like it or not, even aware of it or not, and married or not, the weight of that burden is real and does interfere with our work. Even under the best of conditions, no wife clears the bothersome details of living for us, manages child care or housekeeping, or guarantees us unhampered mobility.

Very few of us were intended by popular culture to see ourselves primarily as workers of one kind or another in the public marketplace. Even for women who work full time their entire lives, an inbred image remains of women as temporary or marginal workers, as supplementary rather than central earners. Many of us have often been more apt, then, to accept inadequate incomes, reduced benefits, or poor conditions. To meet home demands, we may settle for part-time shifts (such as "Mommy Tracks"), poor hours, or local jobs, all of which can be terribly exploitative.

The problem goes deeper, though. Added to these reduced expectations of work, until very recently many, if not most, of us were trained to carry reduced expectations of ourselves. There are still many women who, following their mothers' and grandmothers' examples, serving brothers and fathers at home, learned to serve in general. Accustomed to the familiar behavior of subordination, some of us tend not to resist when we experience the same things at work. We may give in to inappropriate use of our energy and time in a way that men would not tolerate. Accustomed to placing our attachments to men above many things, we might be more loyal to an exploitative employer than to a union of female employees.

But even when we learn these things and consciously try to transcend the inherited values of "femininity," we are still subject to the "outposts in our own head." We must not only unlearn the destructive patterns we have been taught, but we must also somehow make up for the experiences many of us did not have, those reserved for males only, experiences such as the competition of team sports or the support system of the male in-group.

WOMEN BEFORE THE LAW: SOME RELEVANT PRINCIPLES

We should keep some essential features of law in mind to help us understand women's relationship to the legal system. Laws are the rules of the game. When we speak of the law in our society, we mean a collection of rules and procedures codified, formalized, made explicit; we mean the conceptual framework within which such "rules" are written, a set of values, attitudes, and general principles toward people, community, and government; we also mean a kind of overriding loyalty to the concept of law as such, to living by the rules we set for ourselves; and finally we mean the whole system of legislation, courts, procedures, and people that is the concrete reflection of the abstract concepts.

Because laws that contradict or clash with social mores are most likely to be disregarded or disobeyed, to carry weight and command obedience in its own right (without undue force) a law must express or coincide with the beliefs and attitudes of a majority of the people governed. Therefore, we can understand law as representing the formal expression of nonformal ideals—norms, mores, values—the unwritten rules of the game for any people.

Laws are written by people who hold power. In our society, law is enacted by legislatures made up of individuals said to represent a majority of voters. It is from this representativeness that legislators in a democracy are supposed to derive their power, and it is from their ability to express the will of the public that they maintain it. To a degree, legislators do express the public will, but to a degree, they do not. What is true, however, is that many of the laws we live by are written and enacted by those people who, one way or the other, maintain their place in the legislatures by being able to satisfy their constituents that they are expressing the common will. That is why laws so clearly reflect the character of current values and specifically the values of those who have and exercise power.

Our legal system relies heavily on precedent, continuity, and conservatism to give it stability and to ensure orderliness, credibility, and respect. Judicial decisions made today are largely based on decisions made earlier and on an interpretation of what is believed to be the original intent of the framers of any law. Change in the body of law is meant to come slowly and cautiously. To a large degree, the past directs the present and the future, and the system strongly tends to maintain the status quo.

Law, Women, and Men

When we relate these principles of law to women's position in society, we can see the source of certain aspects of our situation. The law, in conceptualization, policy, practice, execution, and application, is almost entirely masculine.

In overwhelming proportions, the people in power who have written the laws as well as interpreted, argued, used, and enforced them have been men. Legislators, judges, teachers and philosophers of law, court officials, lawyers, and police have been and still are predominantly male. Women, having been barred one way or another from power and decision making, are represented in absurdly small numbers in every aspect of politics and law. The representation of feminists—that is, women consciously committed to women's rights and needs—is even smaller. Until as recently as 1920, the entire constituency that legislators and public officials had to satisfy was male. Before suffrage in 1920, women had no formal power at all. Today, without unity of common goals, without significant spheres of public influence, women's clout is little better.

It is small wonder, therefore, that the law should reflect a male perspective. Given that the creators of our legal system and the constituency for whom it was created were and to a very large extent still are the sons of patriarchy—and thus conscious and unconscious heirs to all the beliefs, attitudes, and values it entails—our legal system is apt to be highly sexist. It clearly accepts and supports the traditional images of male and female, awards to men privilege and advantage in every sphere of life both public and private, and sanctions the subordination of women to men. Judicial decisions on every level and in every area of concern—domestic relations, civil rights, labor and employment, crime, and others—frequently reflect the common social themes regarding "femininity" and the sexes: that men and women, being "naturally" different in capacities, needs, and function, should occupy different spheres of activity;[22] that because women are weak and dependent, we should be "protected," both from the ugliness of life and the dangers of our own inferiority; that because women are both morally and intellectually less competent than men, less rational and trustworthy, we should be under greater constraint.

What this means to us as women is that the legal system, allegedly designed to protect all citizens, instead often thwarts us. It means that when we go to the courts for redress of crimes or injustice, we go as little girls to a father, as suppliants, and we go to a system that sees us and the world in a way that is very much to our detriment. Although increasing numbers of women are entering the law, becoming lawyers, judges, police officers, and legislators, more frequently male lawyers must argue for us (often missing issues central to our experience), male judges apply masculinist laws to our female circumstances (interpreting them from their privileged male position), and male police must accept the credibility of individuals (women) said to have no credibility. These circumstances make the legal system a very different place for women than for men. The statistics bearing on rape, wife battering, child support, and prison sentences for women —to name just a few conspicuous areas of uneven-handed justice—bear this out. We know, furthermore, that since the law tends to conserve the status quo, we cannot expect change easily or soon, especially without some very powerful catalysts.

Points and Instances: A Short History

Law is based on precedent, and so the past directs the future. Regarding the law, what kind of past do women have?

From earliest times in Western culture, as one might expect in patriarchy, the position of women has been both marginal and shaky. Jo Freeman, like Kate Millett, argues that we can understand our relationship to men in terms of caste.[23] Unlike a class, from which one may emerge, a caste is a rigid category of stratification based on characteristics one has no hand in determining—birth, color, or sex, for example. Women's caste, from which we cannot emerge, entails certain functions and behaviors. It imposes on us a whole separate set of expectations with attendant rewards and punishments. Maintaining this caste (this "place") has been a major occupation of the legal system.

According to Jo Freeman, the current legal status of women in the United States has its roots in the most ancient traditions and prejudices of the Western world. Says Freeman:

The sexual caste system is the longest, most firmly entrenched caste system known to Western civilization. . . . There is a long standing legal tradition reaching back to early Roman law which defines women as perpetual children. This tradition, known as the "Perpetual Tutelage of Women," has not been systematically recognized, but the definition of women as minors who never grow up, who must

always be under the guidance of a male, has been carried down in modified form to the present day.[24]

The early Roman tradition of treating women not as citizens, not even as adults, but rather as "daughters," first of their natural fathers, then of their husbands, found its way into canon law and from there through English common law into our own legal system.

It was Blackstone's *Commentaries on the Laws of England,* written in 1765—a veritable bible on the law in the early United States, according to Freeman—that codified the ancient rules for future generations. Women's status is most clearly reflected in Blackstone's treatment of marriage:

Single women were presumed to have the same rights in private law as single men. But when a woman married, these rights were lost, suspended under the feudal doctrine of "coverture." As Blackstone described: "By marriage, the husband and wife are one person in law; that is, the very being or legal existence of the woman is suspended during the marriage, or at least is incorporated and consolidated into that of the husband, under whose wing, protection, and cover, she performs everything."[25]

Where Do We Go from Here? The ERA?

Historically, ours was a system that, for good or ill, maintained separate justice for women and men. The effect has been a legacy of discrimination and inequality that heavily influences juridical behavior today and supports sexism in the society at large.

Our legal structure will continue to support and command an inferior status for women so long as it permits any differentiation in legal treatment on the basis of sex. This is so for three distinct but related reasons. First, discrimination is a necessary concomitant of any sex-based law because a large number of women do not fit the female stereotype upon which such laws are predicated. Second, all aspects of separate treatment for women are inevitably interrelated; discrimination in one area creates discriminatory patterns in another. Thus a woman who has been denied equal access to education will be disadvantaged in employment even though she received equal treatment there. Third, whatever the motivation for different treatment, the result is to create a dual system of rights and responsibilities in which the rights of each group are governed by a different set of values. History and experience have taught us that in such a dual system one group is always dominant and the other subordinate. As long as woman's place is defined as separate, a male-dominated society will define her place as inferior.[26]

Attempts at change have been spotty and largely ineffectual. The protections of the Fifth and Fourteenth Amendments to the Constitution have not been consistently applied to women's cases; piecemeal legislative changes have been sparse and slow; judicial review has been "casual," peremptory, or sexist itself.[27]

Most feminists and many legislators and judicial experts maintain that what is necessary is a single consistent, coherent principle of equal rights for women and men, a principle of law that would serve as mandate and policy for the public sector and for the courts. The embodiment of that principle is, of course, the Equal Rights Amendment (ERA):

> Section 1: *Equality of rights under the law shall not be denied or abridged by the United States or by any state on account of sex.*
>
> Section 2: *The Congress shall have the power to enforce, by appropriate legislation, the provisions of this article.*
>
> Section 3: *This amendment shall take effect two years after the date of ratification.*

Simply put, the question is whether women are to be counted as full human beings before the law and in society.

Opponents to the amendment argued on grounds both hysterical and spurious: (1) the ERA would legitimate abortion (false), homosexual marriage (false), and extraordinary federal control over personal matters (false); (2) the ERA would deny the sanctity of the family (false), a woman's right not to have outside employment (false), and "privacy" (false); (3) the ERA will require equal numbers of women and men in the army and in combat (false), coed bathrooms (false), women to share barracks with men in the service (false), children to be placed in state-run child-care facilities (false).

Most of these issues were created precisely to frighten both women and men into rejecting the ERA. It was argued, furthermore, that the ERA is

simply not necessary, the Fourteenth Amendment being sufficient to remedy instances of discrimination. Proponents of the ERA pointed out, however, that review under the Fourteenth Amendment has been inconsistent and inefficient, and that the ERA, in making sex an absolutely prohibited classification for law, would go much further toward guaranteeing women equality of economic, educational, and political opportunity.

With all the public controversy, it is sometimes surprising to discover that during the campaign to pass the ERA, the majority of voters favored passage. By 1978, the amendment had been passed by thirty-five states, and even in many states that did not ratify, polls consistently showed a majority of popular approval. The minority opposed to the ERA were apparently entrenched in the power structure, better supported financially, and better organized (as are the minority opposed to women's reproductive freedom). In 1985 the Equal Rights Amendment was reintroduced in both houses of Congress.

The Equal Rights Amendment would be a valuable tool, to be sure, but we must keep in mind that the ERA, like suffrage, cannot guarantee equality. It can function only as a tool, provided it is used properly. To gain equality, women must move to full participation in every sector of American life. Most particularly, women must develop influence in government, for there lies the heart of public power, the formal source of law, policy, and enforcement.

WOMEN, GOVERNMENT, AND POLITICS

To govern is to exercise authority, to wield power, to manage and guide the affairs of state for the citizenry. In this area, people make rules that affect every aspect of our lives, public and private, from how and where we work to whether or not we may terminate a pregnancy. Yet here again—in the creation of law and public policy, in its interpretation, and in its execution—female citizens are absurdly underrepresented.

In 1996, a year that was said to be extraordinary on the federal level in bringing out "the women's vote," the House of Representatives broke a record with 51 women (only about 12 percent of the votes) and the Senate with 9 (out of a possible 100, remember)! No woman has ever been president. Only very recently have women occupied top-level cabinet positions, and proportionally very few American women have had major power in national or international affairs.

So far as formal public power is concerned, at present women have very little. Yet perhaps it would be more accurate to say that we *exercise* very little, for our potential is great. After all, we represent more than half the total population, and we are legally entitled to vote, hold office, and participate in the political process. Until very recently, we have simply not been able to do so to any extent.

A variety of reasons explain women's minimal participation in the political process. Of course, a long history of enforced formal suppression, including disfranchisement and legal discrimination, has left a legacy of prejudicial attitudes and policies. Women do not control large corporations and large sums of money, and we cannot, therefore, control the choices of those people in power who are subject to such pressures. But that, of course, is not the whole story. Informal suppression—the effect of female roles and gender stereotypes—also functions effectively. The negative image of the authoritative woman, the burdens of child rearing and homemaking, and the absence of social support for functioning outside the assigned "place" have all coalesced to keep women from organizing and unifying to challenge discrimination, exploitation, and sexism in the political arena and the wider society.

Most important, women need to identify as a voting bloc in the political process. That is, we need to recognize ourselves as a distinct, meaningful category or class, as a legitimate pressure group formed around and appropriately pressing for our own self-defined needs and goals. We have seen ourselves as Republicans or Democrats, as working class or middle class, as Black or White, as conservative or liberal, and so on—but we have failed to make a most important identification, of ourselves simply as women who, regardless of other loyalties, have common needs and problems and have the right to make civil demands.

The result of reduced participation has been a lack of voice in the decisions that direct our lives. Without proportional representation in government, one is not a free citizen, so one can only endure the whims of those in power; there is no recourse. Such a principle is clearly expressed in the early formulative documents of the American system, and it is obviously reflected in women's position today in society. Men hold power and generally make decisions that they believe to be suitable. Women's perspective can be reflected in law only to the degree that women have public power and a political vote. To achieve this, we must not see ourselves as dependents or supplicants. The United States government is based on the principle that all citizens have a right to make their wishes known and to press for them in orderly fashion so that social balance arises through the interplay of these pressures, and citizens ultimately gain social justice. We as women must affirm ourselves as full citizens, with the full complement of social responsibility and hence the full measure of social rights.

> *We are entering a new phase of feminism—call it Grass Roots Feminism, call it Feminism 2000, call it Global Feminism, call it Life-Preserving Feminism, call it simply New Phase Feminism— whatever it may be, it will make history, as did the first phase of modern feminism. Its horizons are unlimited. Never before have women become possibly the only salvation for the survival of humanity.*
>
> *Not so long ago on a flight from Dallas to Chicago, I sat next to a young woman, not very politically aware, but very appealing, and as so often happens with passing acquaintances, people you never expect to see again, we told each other our life histories. At some point she turned to me and said, "You know, I would like to be an activist; I would like to fight for a cause, but I'm not that type."*
>
> *"What type would you say you are?" I inquired.*
>
> *"A dreamer," was her response.*
>
> *"My dear young friend," I said. "The very first condition for being an activist is that you be a dreamer. Without dreams, without a vision, there can be no hope, and hope is the essence of motivating force in the struggle for social change."*

—Margarita Papandreou[28]
President of the Women's Union of Greece

Notes

1. United States Department of Labor, Bureau of Labor Statistics, *Employment & Earnings*, January 1999.

2. U.S. Census Bureau, Income 1998, Table B: Median Earnings of Full-time, Year-Round Workers by Selected

Characteristics: 1998 (online). Available on http://www.census.gov/hhes/income/income98/in98ern.html.

3. See Elyce Rotella, Table 3, in "Women and the American Economy," among the readings in this chapter.

4. "Median Earnings of Full-time, Year-Round Workers," supra.

5. "Median Earnings of Full-time, Year-Round Workers," supra.

6. "Median Earnings of Full-time, Year-Round Workers," supra.

7. U.S. Department of Labor, Women's Bureau, "20 Leading Occupations of Employed Women, 1998 Annual Averages" (online). Available on http://www.dol.gov/dol/wb/wb_pubs/20lead98.htm.

8. "One in Three Custodial Parents Without Child Support Are Poor, Census Bureau Reports," United States Department of Commerce News, April 23, 1999 (online). Available on http://www.census.gov;80/Press-Release/www/1999/cb99-77.html.

9. Lenore Weitzman, "Women and Children Last: The Social and Economic Consequences of Divorce Law Reforms," in *Feminism, Children, and the New Families,* ed. Sanford M. Dornbusch and Myra H. Strober (New York: Guilford Press, 1988).

10. *The 1995 Information Please Women's Sourcebook,* ed. Lisa DiMona and Constance Herndon (Boston: Houghton Mifflin, 1994), pp. 374, 377.

11. U.S. Department of Labor, Women's Bureau, "20 Facts on Women Workers," 1992.

12. Francine D. Blau and Anna E. Winkler, "Women in the Labor Force: An Overview," in *Women: A Feminist Perspective,* 4th ed., ed. Jo Freeman (Mountain View, CA: Mayfield, 1984). p. 280.

13. Diane Schaffer, "The Feminization of Poverty," in *Women, Power and Policy: Toward the Year 2000,* 2nd ed., ed. Ellen Boneparth and Emily Stoper (New York: Pergamon Press, 1988), p. 224.

14. U.S. Department of Commerce, Bureau of the Census, "Money Income in the United States: 1997."

15. U.S. Department of Labor, Women's Bureau, 1999. "Nontraditional Occupations for Women in 1999" (online). Available on http://www.dol.gov/dol/wb/public/wb_pubs/nontra98.htm.

16. "Pith and Vinegar," *On the Issues* 5, no. 3 (Summer 1996), p. 8.

17. Shirley Bernard, "Women's Economic Status: Some Clichés and Some Facts" in *Women: A Feminist Perspective,* p. 239.

18. Oliver Starr, Jr., "Shatter the Glass Ceiling: Male-Dominated Work Force Erects Barriers to Women's Advancement," *St. Louis Post-Dispatch,* November 5, 1991, p. 3B.

19. *St. Louis Post-Dispatch,* November 10, 1998, p. C6.

20. Michael Korda, *Male Chauvinism! How It Works* (New York: Random House, 1972).

21. George Gilder, *Sexual Suicide* (New York: Quadrangle, 1973).

22. Barbara A. Brown, Thomas I. Emerson, Gail Falk, and Ann E. Freedman, "The Equal Rights Amendment: A Constitutional Basis for Equal Rights for Women," *Yale Law Journal* 80, 1971, p. 876.

23. Jo Freeman, "The Legal Basis of the Sexual Caste System," *Valparaiso University Law Review* 5, no. 2, 1971, p. 203ff.

24. Jo Freeman, "The Legal Basis of the Sexual Caste System," p. 208.

25. Jo Freeman, "The Legal Basis of the Sexual Caste System," p. 210.

26. Brown et al., "The Equal Rights Amendment," pp. 873–874.

27. Brown et al., "The Equal Rights Amendment," p. 876.

28. Margarita Papandreou, "Feminism and Political Power: Some Thoughts on a Strategy for the Future," in *Women, Power, and Policy,* pp. xvii, xix.

The Politics of Women and Medical Care

Hilary Salk, Wendy Sanford, Norma Swenson, and Judith Dickson Luce

With special thanks to David Banta, Gene Bishop, Mary Fillmore, Mary Howell, Judy Norsigian, Sheryl Ruzek, and Karen Wolf.

1992 Update by Amy Alpern, Robin Blatt, David Clarke, Judy Norsigian, Kathy Simmonds, Norma Swenson, and Nancy Worcester.

We usually do not think of the medical care system either as an institution or as an industry, but it is both. It affects the quality of our lives as profoundly as any other, and yet women have little influence over the practice of health care in America—delivery of services, costs, research, laws, or medical training. The argument in this selection is plain: Because women constitute the majority of workers and consumers of the health care industry, we must play a major role in overseeing policy.

THE AMERICAN MEDICAL CARE SYSTEM

I'VE REPEATEDLY DESCRIBED MY SYMPTOMS to physicians—disconcerting symptoms to say the least: sudden menses cessation, elevated temperature, weight loss, anxiety, extreme fatigue, nausea, joint pain, vertigo—but the doctors have made only the catch-all diagnosis of "menopause," unsupported by any testing. They advised me to go into counseling, expecting me to "live with it," despite the fact that I have told them that the symptoms seem extreme, are increasing and have impaired and even curtailed my work, my studies, my personal relationships.

From a letter to the Women's Health Collective in Providence, Rhode Island:

I think you would have been proud of the way I handled the situation with the surgeon. Despite a fair amount of crying on my part (to top it all off, my husband was away when all this happened), I was able to demand a second opinion for my diverticulosis treatment and the most conservative treatment possible. My surgeon was appalled when I balked at surgery Monday without what I felt was adequate time to discuss the situation or get another opinion. By Friday I was able to deal with him, but it took about all I had. I really think that if it wasn't for my experience with the Women's Health Collective and the support of my friends and family, I would have a temporary colostomy right now.

I, extremely well informed, well connected, verbally aggressive, have had to summon all my resources to get what I wanted in my treatment for breast cancer: medical care that was consistent with the findings of the latest literature and that took into account my needs as a woman.

As a young woman interested in one day having a family, I was never told that cimetidine "should not be used in pregnant patients or women of childbearing potential unless, in the judgment of the physician, the anticipated benefits outweigh the potential risks." I should have been informed of this and given the opportunity to make the decision myself in consultation with the doctor. This is one more indication of my rights and indeed my body being violated. My family raised me to trust doctors, but I no longer can do that.

In the words of a visiting nurse:

I learned to listen to patients, to speak their language, to let them set their own priorities for care, to teach them when they were ready. I also learned to evaluate the health care system through their eyes. Each day I confronted an irrelevant, noncaring, inadequate health care system that refused to consider the personal, social, cultural and economic needs of the patient.

It is a sobering time for women using the medical system in this country. Although some women are satisfied with the medical care they get, many are not.* The women quoted above are only a few of the thousands speaking out about the physicians and other medical personnel in medical settings who have:

- Not listened to them or believed what they said.
- Withheld knowledge.
- Lied to them.
- Treated them without their consent.
- Not warned of risks and negative effects of treatments.
- Overcharged them.
- Experimented on them or used them as "teaching material."
- Treated them poorly because of their race, sexual preference, age or disability.
- Offered them tranquilizers or moral advice instead of medical care or useful help from community resources (self-help groups, battered women's services, etc.).
- Administered treatments which were unnecessarily mutilating and too extreme for their problem, or treatments which resulted in permanent disability or even death (*iatrogenesis*).†

- Prescribed drugs which hooked them, sickened them, changed their entire lives.
- Performed operations they later found were unnecessary and removed organs that were in no way diseased.
- Abused them sexually.

WHY FOCUS ON WOMEN AND THE MEDICAL SYSTEM?

Women are part of the medical care system, either for ourselves or our children, spouses or aging parents, more than twice as often as men are. We are 85 percent of all health care workers in hospitals and 75 percent in the system as a whole.* We carry out most doctors' orders—treatment regimens like special diets, medications and bed rest, and so on—either as unpaid workers at home or as paid workers. We teach about health both in the home and in the system—what is good and not good for you. At home we are usually the first to be told when someone doesn't feel well, and we help decide what to do next. Some health care analysts even call us "primary health care workers" or the "layperson on the team." Most "patient" communication for and about family members flows through women: We report signs and changes, symptoms, responses to treatments and medications. The system also depends on women: Our direct reporting forms the basis of much of what medicine calls "scientific results," and our bodies provide the raw material for experimentation and research (e.g., the birth control pill), often without our knowledge and consent.[2]

Yet despite our overwhelming numbers and the tremendous responsibility we carry for people's health, we still have limited power to influence the medical system. Policymakers, usually male, have designed the system primarily for the convenience

---

*We are basing the analysis in this chapter both on thousands of personal accounts and on the work of a wide range of people and groups: feminist writers and other investigative journalists; feminist, radical and progressive physicians; public health researchers; health workers and practitioners of all kinds; medical historians and medical sociologists; public interest groups and government specialists; as well as social and feminist critics of many different persuasions.

†*Iatrogenesis* is the process by which illness, impairment or death results from medical treatment. Some examples are cancers caused by DES, pelvic inflammatory disease (PID) or hysterectomy caused by an IUD, death or disability due to anesthesia accident (particularly when the surgery may not have been necessary), electrocution or burns from hospital equipment, infection from respirators, crippling or fatal strokes due to the birth control pill, addiction to tranquilizers and illness or death resulting from infant formula feeding in hospitals.

---

*While ailing men do report many of the same problems with the medical care system as women, men use the system less. They do not, like women, have to consult physicians for normal events in the reproductive cycle, such as pregnancy. Men tend to come into the system only during crises. Many different studies have shown that medical care providers treat male patients with more respect than women and offer fewer tranquilizers and less moral advice.[1] Also, since only 17 percent of doctors are women, most women see male physicians, a situation which severely exaggerates male-female power imbalances.

and financial gain of physicians, hospitals, administrators and the medical industries. *We believe that women, as the majority of consumers and workers, paid and unpaid, should have the major voice in health and medical care policy-making in this country.*

A previous edition of *Our Bodies, Ourselves* expressed considerable optimism that women would be able to work together to change medical care. In fact, women of all ages have joined together in local communities and nationwide: The resulting women's health movement has significantly changed the way many women look at medical care and is successfully fighting in legislatures, hospital administrations and law courts for improvements. Yet change comes slowly. The medical care system is too often unresponsive to women, deeply entrenched as it is in American economic, political and social structures, and the influence of medicine* in people's lives continues to grow. For example, the insurance and drug industries continue to make unrestrained profits, and physicians are still among the highest paid and among the least accountable of all U.S. professionals.[†] Despite a few governmental programs—Health Systems Agencies (HSAs) and neighborhood health centers—the medical establishment[‡] has the money and status to contain most citizen attempts to achieve community control.

Our critique of medicine has taken on a new dimension. We see basic errors in its fundamental assumptions about health and healing. Although conventional medical care may at times be just what we need, in many situations it may be bad for our health because it emphasizes drugs, surgery, psychotherapy (especially for women) and crisis action rather than prevention.* It is not enough to provide or improve medical care, to have more women physicians, to stop the abuses or to increase access to existing health and medical care for the poor and elderly—even though we support absolutely equal access to care for all classes and groups. We want to reclaim the knowledge and skills that the medical establishment has inappropriately taken over. We also want preventive and nonmedical healing methods to be available to all who need them. We are committed to exposing how the medical establishment works to suppress these alternatives (home birth and nurse-midwifery, for example), contrary to the spirit of the antitrust laws of this country.

Pessimistic as we are about the present system, we believe in the healing powers within all of us— our ability to help one another by listening, talking, caring, touching—and in the power of small groups as sources of information sharing, support and healing. We still believe that we, as women, are the best experts on ourselves. The more we understand how vulnerable we become—both to disease and to dependency on experts—when isolated from one another, the more we see group experience and action as essential resources for health, from small consciousness-raising or self-help groups to large numbers of women organized for political action.

In this chapter we warn you of some of the dangers of this system and offer strategies to make it work for you as well as possible. We hope that you will feel entitled to demand more information about your health and medical needs, more able to distinguish when to turn to professionals, more empowered to take care of yourself and others when that is appropriate and more deeply convinced that good health is a fundamental right worth fighting for.

THE POWER OF MEDICINE IN SOCIETY

Why do most people have an almost religious belief in American medicine? Despite numerous bad or

---

* We use "medicine" to mean both the *tangible* personnel and institutions of the medical system like physicians and hospitals, and the discipline, field or profession of medicine. We also mean the *intangible* institution of beliefs, ideology and assumptions that influence or control our daily habits in ways most of us are not aware of (as do "the family" and "religion").

† Accountability in the case of the medical profession would mean that they be more responsive to our perceived needs and wishes in recognition of the fact that, as taxpayers, we support medical education, research, hospital construction and much of the medical care given in hospitals, nursing homes and clinics.[3]

‡ By *medical establishment* we mean the cluster of organized physician, hospital, drug and insurance groups like the AMA (American Medical Association), the ACOG (American College of Obstetricians and Gynecologists), the AHA (American Hospital Association) and the PMA (Pharmaceutical Manufacturers Association), which pay large sums to influence public opinion, legislation and policy on health and medical matters.

---

* Women consume far more prescription drugs, undergo much more unnecessary surgery and are referred for psychotherapy much more often than men, though crisis care is medicine's model for both sexes. (See relevant chapters for details.)

disappointing experiences, so many women say, "It must be my fault" or "I must just have had the wrong doctor," and fail to see that the system itself has serious faults. The institution and ideology of American medicine has penetrated so totally into the fabric of our lives over the past fifty years that most of us aren't even aware of its influence. Its power rests mainly on several widely held myths, which have in good part been created by an aggressive and highly successful public relations campaign of the wealthy AMA and other such groups.* Brought up as most of us were to "believe" in medicine, it is hard at first to realize how influenced (even at times manipulated) we have been by medical propaganda.

MYTHS AND FACTS

Myth: *American medical care is the best in the world.*

Fact: The United States spends more money on medical care, uses more medical technology per capita than any country on earth and has one of the highest ratios of doctors and hospitals to people. Yet it lags behind other industrialized countries in life expectancy and ranks twenty-fifth in infant mortality rates, two crucial basic indicators of health in the general population.[4] Clearly, we are not getting our money's worth.[†]

Myth: *Medical care has been responsible for the major improvements in world health.*

---

*Misleading tactics have been applied by organized medicine and the drug industry in a variety of situations through their skilled manipulation of the media. Gullible reporters have announced breakthroughs and false reassurances for anything from reselling menopausal estrogens to claiming that the Pill is now totally safe.
†Some physician apologists have claimed that black and minority groups "drag down" our international standing in infant mortality (a clear case of racism and blaming the victim); however, even some of the most racially homogeneous U.S. communities lag considerably below Europe's best.[5] Furthermore, the resources we do spend have not improved certain disparities in health status. For example, in 1990 the National Commission to Prevent Infant Mortality reported that the death rate for black babies in the United States was twice that for white babies (17.9 deaths per 1,000 live births vs. 8.6). Also, from 1980 to 1987 the number of pregnant women not receiving prenatal care increased 50 percent.

Fact: Many dread infectious diseases* were "conquered" in the past century, but this was most likely because of improved nutrition and sanitation, not medical care. *Their incidence rates were already falling* when medical treatments and vaccines were introduced. With the exception of smallpox, vaccines helped speed the decline of these diseases only minimally. *The disappearance of these diseases is the major source of our greater life expectancy in this century, leaving the chronic diseases, for which medicine has provided no cures.* Difficult as it is to believe, mortality from most of the chronic diseases, which are our leading causes of death today, has remained virtually unchanged throughout the century.[6]

Careful studies reveal that medical care has *not* been the most important factor in improving infant mortality rates. Factors such as education, income and race continue to be the most accurate predictors of whether infants live or die. *General improvements, especially in nutrition and fertility control, have contributed most to improvements in neonatal mortality rates.*

Myth: *Medicine is a rigorous science.*

Fact: Medicine has prestige largely because it is associated with science in the public mind and claims objectivity and neutrality. Much of the theory on which modern medical practice is based actually derives from the untested assumptions and prejudices of earlier generations of medical leaders. Even though medical schools vaunt their "scientific method," they never actually teach it.[7] Furthermore, the scientific method is difficult to apply to human beings, since it is rarely possible or ethical to experiment on them as one would on inanimate objects or substances.[†] (However, animal researchers sometimes produce useful results.)

Myth: *Medical treatments in current use have been proven safe and effective.*

---

*The diseases were typhoid, smallpox, scarlet fever, measles, whooping cough, diphtheria, influenza, tuberculosis, pneumonia, diseases of the digestive system and poliomyelitis.
†There are always physicians willing to try if allowed to, which is one reason why ethical review boards have been set up in many institutions to set standards which all investigators must abide by (see Our Rights as Patients, p. 682).

Fact: Most accepted treatments, therapies and medical technologies today have never been *scientifically* evaluated in terms of benefit.* Fetal monitors and radical mastectomies are only two examples of technology coming into widespread use before being fully evaluated. Scientific evaluation (in the form of randomized or controlled clinic trials [RCTs, CCTs])† is difficult, time- and labor-consuming and expensive and gets little funding from public sources. Most doctors have had no training in how to evaluate medical treatments and technology and often base their recommendations simply on what they think may work. As we were told by an assistant professor of medicine at Harvard Medical School:

> *Too frequently practicing physicians indulge in "cookbook medicine": They open the latest medical journal and inflict the latest recipe on patients, assuring their patients that on the one hand they are receiving "the latest thing" and on the other hand that they are "not guinea pigs." . . . In fact, the practicing physician is often extending some scientist's last experiment into the community setting—and without obtaining the patient's informed consent! At the same time, the scientist who performed the original experiment five years ago and who wrote the paper two or three years ago has long abandoned that approach in favor of something with more promise for a real cure.*

Fact: Most nonreproductive medical research has been done only on men and the results have been applied to women. Such a process is also far from scientific. In 1990, the National Institutes of Health (NIH) issued new guidelines to ensure that women would be adequately represented in

all NIH-funded research of potential relevance to women. Thus, this situation should improve.

Myth: *Medical care keeps us healthy.*

Fact: Although deep down many of us believe that medicine has created and sustained our health through the technological advances of the past fifty years, public health* studies show that our health is primarily the result of the food we eat, the water we drink, the air we breathe, the environment we live in, the work we do and the habits we form. These factors in turn result primarily from the education we have, the money we are able to earn and the other resources we are able to command. Still other factors contribute to good health and long life: control over one's personal life, influence over the larger forces that affect all our lives, loving friendships and a supportive community.

Drugs, surgery and medical technology (kidney dialysis machines or blood transfusions, for example) are invaluable tools, and many people would not be alive today without them. While few of us would want to live without these skills and emergency resources available to us and our families, it is fundamentally what *we* do or don't do, not what medicine does, that keeps us healthy.

By focusing on more profitable crisis care after people get sick rather than using its tremendous resources to help us prevent illness before it happens, the medical establishment shows itself unwilling to consider what really can and must be done to keep people healthy. This is a political issue, not simply a medical one, although many medical spokespeople argue that medicine is apolitical, scientific or politically neutral. Because Americans spend increasing health dollars on treating symptoms, we have less to spend on preventing chronic diseases in the first place.† *To consider reallocating the money available would force all of us to confront our economic, political and social system as major contributors to our ill health.*

---

* "No class of [medical] technologies is adequately evaluated for either cost effectiveness or social and ethical implications."[8]
† Although there are other methods of evaluation, RCTs or CCTs are preferable. For these, very large numbers are required. Such trials also require that one group receiving treatment be compared with another (control) group receiving a different treatment or no treatment. This is the most difficult concept for the practicing physician, for whom the withholding of treatment is abhorrent. Without such evaluation, however, there is no way of *proving* that a certain type of medical treatment is effective, even if some people do seem to get better. "Only 10–20 percent of all procedures used in medical practice have been shown by Controlled Clinical Trials to be of benefit."[9]

---

* *Public health,* which is the study of diseases or conditions in groups of people, is to be distinguished from *medicine,* the study and treatment of disease in the individual. *Epidemiology* is the basic science of public health.
† Prevention could reduce our illnesses by about half. (See Derek Bok, *Harvard Magazine,* May–June 1984, p. 430.)

When we go to a physician, clinic or hospital, every one of these myths encourages us to *trust* professionals, to lean on their reassurances and to follow their orders. Especially when we are sick, it is difficult to be anything but trusting and compliant; being sick is frightening and we *need* to feel comforted. Because medical professionals offer false reassurances more often than we'd like to think, we *must* be as critical as we can, get all the information possible and ask friends and family to help us in doing this.

POVERTY, RACISM AND HEALTH

Poverty is the most basic cause of ill health and early death in our society. The poor, who are mostly women and children and disproportionately people of color, have more illnesses and die in greater numbers and earlier than people with more income and education.[10] Many of their health problems are diseases that result from malnutrition, workplace dangers, inadequate housing, environmental pollution or excessive stress.

The medical system blames poor people for suffering the effects of poverty; for instance, accusing poor women of not taking proper care of themselves or their children and seeing alcoholism and depression in working-class families as individual, preventable failures. Medicaid and Medicare programs, which offered the poor and elderly at least minimal access to medical care, have been cut drastically and will take decades to reinstate.* The very programs that reduce people's need for costly medical care—job training, food-assistance programs, health education to the community—have been cut as well. The almost inevitable result will be increasing illness and death among the poor.† The United States and South Africa are the only modern industrialized nations without a universal health service or a national health program. Poor women are increasingly turned away from health facilities.

Racism is a serious threat to health and in some instances creates more barriers to obtaining needed care and to survival than does social class.[11] For example, even allowing for social class, black babies still die at higher rates than white babies living in the same geographic area, due mainly to low birth weight among black babies, which is almost entirely preventable.[12] In many communities, medicine's response to the widening infant death gap between those who are getting adequate nutrition and pre-natal services and those who are not is to propose even more costly neonatal centers.* What's needed is not more expensive machines but a serious attempt to counter the effects of racism or class discrimination on the health of expectant mothers. Leadership for such an effort will not come from the medical establishment, which is heavily invested in technological and pharmacological solutions to problems, not social change.

Although people of color need medical care more often than white people do, they frequently get less. For example, black people are less likely to get the most modern specialty treatment and follow-up care for cancer and do not survive as long after diagnosis. Similarly, even though hypertension is 82 percent higher among women of color, they do not receive any more treatment than white women.[13] Poor women and women of color often receive more abusive and damaging care than other women and are more likely to be used as "teaching material" in hospitals, so that physicians in training can practice the craft they will use later on wealthy private patients.[14] Sterilization abuse is far more frequent. When clients do not speak English fluently, they are often treated as though they are stupid. Stereotypes so govern practitioners' responses that

---

* As it is, Medicaid covers only about 40 percent of the poor. Some states have expanded coverage for pregnant women beyond Medicaid through state-funded programs.

† In Michigan, which has one of the highest unemployment rates in the country, the infant mortality rate in Detroit increased 5.4 percent from 12.8 per 1,000 in 1980 to 19.7 in 1990.

---

*For example, during the economically depressed period of the early 1980s, Rhode Island's Women and Infants Hospital proposed building a $50 million hospital to include a high-technology neonatal intensive care unit to save low-birth-weight infants in distress. Despite massive opposing testimony from citizens who argued that such deaths were preventable through community-based nutrition and midwifery-care programs, the building was approved. Such costly endeavors have become the national trend, displacing funds that could be used not only for nutrition and midwifery programs, but for drug treatment and AIDS prevention efforts as well, which pose increasing threats to women and their children.

a minority or poor patient who has the same symptoms as a white middle-class person will receive a different diagnosis and different treatment. In the words of a woman depicted in the film *Taking Our Bodies Back*:

> It almost doesn't matter what I came in for, the place they send me is the "L" clinic ["L" is a code for sexually transmitted diseases]. They say, "She's black, she's got bladder trouble or a vaginal infection, she must be a prostitute—send her to the 'L' clinic."[15]

When poor women are badly treated, they don't have the money to sue. They may hesitate to complain assertively, fearing that then they will get no care at all, since "free" care may be cut off at any time. Paradoxically, when women decide not to return for care, their absence gives rise to the health administrators' accusation that "they just won't come," although services are available. Again, women are blamed. Poor women also have little access to the more costly nonmedical alternative practices.

Though we are more critical than ever of the present medical system, at the same time we are working for the right of every woman, regardless of race or income, to have access to that system. Above all, we want to promote those social programs that would reduce people's need for expensive medical interventions and work for the deeper societal changes that will help eliminate poverty and racism.

MEDICALIZATION AND SOCIAL CONTROL OF WOMEN'S LIVES

Everywhere you turn, medical professionals are claiming expertise in matters never before considered medical: in criminality, adolescence, overactivity in children, sex, diet, child abuse, exercise and aging. In this takeover, called *medicalization,* medical people become the "experts" on *normal* experiences or social problems.[16] Surely the most striking example of this process is the medicalization of women's lives.

Consider how often we are expected to go to physicians for normal life events. For our early sexual encounters we may expect to go to gynecologists for most birth control devices and perhaps

even for advice about sex.* During pregnancy we are urged to see obstetricians to be sure all is proceeding normally, and few of us have any alternative but the hospital for giving birth. The medicalizing of childbirth has become so complete that it resembles treatment for a severe, life-threatening illness. When birth goes well, we are often grateful to the physician and give her or him the credit for our success; when it goes badly, we are even more grateful for the interventions we believe saved us and our babies. And once the baby is born, we shift our gratitude and dependence to the pediatrician, so that even the first moments of mothering are conducted with an immediate sense of what our pediatrician thinks is right and proper.

When we are depressed or having difficulties in our personal relationships, we are encouraged to seek the advice and help of a psychiatrist instead of talking with friends. Women see psychiatrists in far greater numbers than men.

Medicine has stepped up its treatment of menopause and of aging as diseases. In a sense, the medical world defines women as inherently defective throughout life, in that we "require" a physician's care for all our normal female functions.

Medical "care" offered often extends to value judgments about our behavior, as we hear how a good girl, a good wife, a good mother should behave.

> After advising me on when to put in my diaphragm ("Dinner, dishes, diaphragm," he said), my ob/gyn went on to speak about the fairly serious postpartum depression I was experiencing. "I like to tell my new mothers to get out to the library once in a while to keep their minds alive, but basically to find their happiness in the fact that they are taking care of their husbands and raising a new generation."

> When I told my doctor (foolishly) that I'm a lesbian, the whole visit turned into a moral lecture and he never really paid attention to my problem. I walked out when he recommended a psychiatrist.

---

*Men do not go to urologists for their basic medical care; children are not segregated by sex when visiting pediatricians. Yet for decades many of us are expected to go to an obstetrician-gynecologist to obtain our basic care. We learn to do this without realizing that by doing so we begin to define ourselves and all our bodily needs in terms of our sex organs and reproductive capacities.

These moral judgments carry a weighty power, though they are no more "scientific" than the judgments of a priest or rabbi.[17]

We don't question the role that the physician has taken in our lives because, for one thing, our exposure and acceptance began early. When we were little, our mothers took us regularly to "the doctor," an extremely busy and important person, who may have ignored what our mothers said, and certainly what we said, and had their own answers. It may have seemed that our mothers allowed doctors to do all kinds of embarrassing or uncomfortable things to us and even that they did some of the same things themselves later on on the doctor's orders. Our mothers were very passive and compliant, in part because by the twentieth century male physicians had become the "authorities" on health. They had led a successful campaign during the late nineteenth and early twentieth centuries to eliminate midwives and sharply reduced the number of female physicians. For the first time in the history of the world, women were forbidden by law to be responsible for other women's childbirths and were replaced almost exclusively by male physicians. When this happened, women lost both female role models and caregivers and also the support of a whole system of woman-to-woman guidance.

During the mid-twentieth century, the gradual further moving of childbirth out of the home and into the hospital continued the process of isolating women from one another. Perhaps we have yet to measure how deeply our self-confidence as women may have been damaged by the loss of midwives as role models and respected sources of information and female authority.

All these factors together have brought us into an extreme and enforced dependency on professional experts—usually male physicians or those trained by them.[18]

Through these many medical encounters in the course of our normal life experiences, physicians gradually initiate women into the medical belief system, warning us against listening to other women, belittling the advice of our mothers, aunts, grandmothers and midwives—female lore—by calling it "old wives' tales." In this way, physicians prepare us to be their disciples. As we carry their message into our families and communities, we further contribute to the medicalization of society and a nar-

row, biological/technological perspective on the solution of human problems.*

It is difficult for most of us to recognize how "allopathic" medicine's proponents historically used women and women's central life experiences to initiate our entire society into a belief in and dependency on medicine. Despite much evidence to the contrary, most physicians believe sincerely that modern medicine has always helped women and that it deserves credit for society's overall health improvements since the turn of the century. Thus they tend to feel it is women's moral duty to teach children to place their faith in medicine.

MEDICINE AS AN INSTITUTION OF SOCIAL CONTROL

All societies establish institutions of social control, vested with the authority to define what is right or wrong, good or bad, sick or well. The schools, courts, and churches all play a role in defining our morality, but perhaps none more thoroughly than medicine does today. When we "deviate"—fail to conform to norms of womanhood—we discover how powerful medicine is.† Consider the ugly pronouncements medical authorities have made over the years, in the name of "science," about so-called inferior groups of people like women and blacks, and the way these pseudoscientific statements have been used to deprive these groups of social control and political power. For example, in the nineteenth century physicians claimed that to become a midwife or a doctor would "unsex" a woman: She would see things that would taint her moral character, cause her to "lose her standing as a 'lady' " and, because of the unusual physical and nervous

---

*For a thorough analysis of medicalization and iatrogenesis, see Ivan Illich, *Medical Nemesis: The Expropriation of Health,* New York: Pantheon Books, 1976; Bantam Books, 1977.

†For example, many poor women are sterilized without their knowledge or consent because they are unmarried or a physician thinks they have "too many babies" (see Sterilization, p. 300). Physicians have forced some women to accept cesarean sections, declaring them "unfit mothers" in court when they refuse a recommended section (despite the risk to the mother's own life); some women have had their children taken from them by the courts because a physician judged them "potential child abusers" for refusing medical treatments during pregnancy.[19]

excitement, "would damage her female organs irreparably and prevent her from fulfilling her social role as a wife and mother."[20] About blacks, a nineteenth-century physician wrote:

> The grown-up Negro partakes, as regards his intellectual faculties, of the nature of the child, the female, and the senile White . . .[21]

This misuse of power and these pronouncements continue today: Physicians dismiss females as too much "at the mercy of their hormones" to be trusted with serious responsibility, and cite blacks' "low-degree expectations" as a hurdle to parity in medical schools.*

Partly through the sanctity of the private physician-patient relationship, medicine (primarily obstetrics/gynecology and psychiatry) also achieves social control by encouraging us to see personal problems as individual isolated experiences rather than as problems we have in common with other women.

THE DOCTOR–PATIENT RELATIONSHIP

The relationship between a woman and her doctor is usually one of profound inequality on every level, an exaggeration of the power imbalance inherent in almost all male–female relationships in our society. The scales are even more unbalanced if the doctor is an ob/gyn with special knowledge about and power over our most intimate bodily selves or a psychiatrist with the authority to label us crazy or sane, to decide whether we can keep our children or not. *Doctors also frequently doubt our word simply because we are women.*

As in any relationship in which we are less powerful, we tend to evaluate what happens in a medical encounter in terms of *our* behavior rather than the doctor's. For example, if we don't understand something, we feel inadequate. Often we believe that a doctor's superior education, training, experience, sex and (sometimes) age automatically

produce infallible judgment. "Well, he must know," many women say.

Many of us want to believe that we are in the hands of superior physicians—even though this may well not be true.

> I knew that my doctor had a reputation for being one of the best in the city, and it made me feel good when I said his name and other people would say, "Oh, right, I've heard of him." I expected that he was going to do the best job he could possibly do. When he criticized me, I shrank inside. Sometimes I'd be annoyed that I had to travel so far for him to look at my stomach. But the mysteries still held. He was going to give me the baby. Once he confused me with someone else, and I was very depressed.

There may always be something about the "laying on of hands" that calls up the child in us and makes us feel dependent, especially when pain and fear are present. Many physicians deliberately work to increase this natural phenomenon into a special kind of dependency (psychiatrists call it *transference*) in which the patient turns to the physician for guidance in all kinds of personal problems. Many medical schools and residency training programs teach techniques for eliciting this dependency as a useful way of "managing" patients, using the parent–child relationship as a model.* When a woman raises real, matter-of-fact questions, a doctor is apt to say, "What's the matter, don't you trust me?" For most doctors, the fact that the transference develops is justification for it—that is, a woman becomes overly dependent because she "needs" or wants to be.

> Dr. G. sighed when he saw me. After examining me he sat down and said, "Let me be direct with you, hon." (I flinched at the "hon.") "You have called me or been here no less than four times this fall. You are complaining about a pain that has no apparent organic basis. Quite frankly, my guess is that there are

---

*The kinds of biological (rather than societal) explanations for behavior and social position popular in the nineteenth century are becoming influential once again. Reinforced by such notions as "sociobiology," these myths have dangerous consequences for women, people of color and the poor.[22]

---

*As Diana Scully describes in her 1980 landmark study of obstetrician/gynecologists,[23] the training process prepares the surgeon to gain the patient's trust and confidence primarily for the purpose of controlling or "managing" her and then to *manipulate* her into doing something *the physician wants her to do*—undergoing surgery, for example, or some other procedure. Often, this is done either to gain experience or to generate income and is frequently not in her interests.

areas of your life you are having trouble facing, and the result is a funny pain in your chest and shoulder that flits around and is sometimes here and sometimes there and sometimes not anywhere at all."

"But I can feel exactly where it is," I broke in.

"Why don't you just leave the worrying to me?" he admonished. "I am the doctor. I have everything under control." 24

The work of feminist sociologists such as Sue Fischer and Alexandra Todd shows the importance of changing this imbalance and improving communication. Our stories are crucial for correct diagnoses as well as for control over treatment options.

We can start needed change by pressing for real answers to our questions, using other sources of information besides our doctors (books, magazines, friends, nurses), seeking second opinions (not from a doctor who is our doctor's close colleague, on the same hospital staff or in the same specialty) and by bringing a friend to medical visits. Immersed in the propaganda about women's "need" for dependency, and comfortable with the fatherly, authoritarian role, many physicians react with surprise and even hostility at our "aggressiveness" when we insist on being partners in our health and medical care decisions. We must not let their reactions prevent us from persisting.

Occasionally, over time, you can build a satisfactory relationship with a doctor.

Friends now marvel at my close relationship with my current doctor and my ability to talk back, question and disagree with him and his colleagues. He respects me and trusts me to tell him what is going on, and I in turn trust him to listen, make suggestions and consult with me before any action is taken. When I don't want a procedure done or feel the psychological burden of making yet another trip to the lab or to his office is just too much for me on an occasion, I will tell him and he understands me most of the time. I have finally after many many years found someone willing to take into account my whole medical history and apply it to my current situation.

SEXUAL ABUSE

Not only have women reported increasing numbers of cases of rape by their doctors, but between 5 and 10 percent of doctors have admitted in surveys and interviews to having sexual relations with their patients, sometimes saying that they believed such relations were either harmless or actually beneficial or "therapeutic" to the women involved. Because of the unequal power relationships involved, this sexual abuse may produce severe damage, akin to father–daughter incest. 25 When the woman turns to or is referred to a psychiatrist, she may be blamed for having "caused" the abuse.* Worse still, a few psychiatrists seduce the woman once again. 26

It takes enormous courage for women to come forward and speak out about sexual abuse by doctors. Frequently no one believes them, and in one case, even nurses reporting their eyewitness experiences of patient abuse for three years were ignored by hospital administrators until another physician caught his anesthesiologist colleague in the act. 27

The few cases that do reach state boards of registration in medicine frequently drag on for months and are then resolved with inadequate controls on future abuse. In spite of the fact that the Hippocratic oath and the ethics codes of all medical societies specifically forbid sexual relations with patients, doctors have made no serious effort to discipline those who breach the code. In fact, the medical profession often appears more concerned with covering up for a colleague who commits what are tactfully called "indiscretions." In the words of a woman psychiatrist:

I reported a psychiatrist who had had sex with two of his patients to the medical society. I called back two months later to find out what had been done. They told me the doctor denied everything, and it was his word against the patients'; so they were dropping the matter. When I persisted, the chairman of the ethics committee told me, "You know, my dear, we are not a consumer organization."

Physicians themselves may arrange for a problem physician to go to another community, without telling the unsuspecting new community about his assaultive behavior. In one famous case, medical school faculty members wrote glowing letters of

---

* Another 20 percent believe this. In California alone, one survey reported 36 percent of psychiatrists and 46 percent of psychologists had admitted affairs with clients during therapy.

recommendation for a convicted rapist who had moved to a new community.[28]

It is common for women who are sexually abused by a doctor to be persuaded that he has fallen in love with them. This is not a sign of naiveté or psychopathology on our part. The physicians involved have abused a trust that every woman has learned to place in them.

We want to encourage women to notice any peculiar or irresponsible behavior and discuss these experiences with one another, to feel entitled to take action if necessary, protect ourselves and others and get our genuine needs for trust met appropriately. Keep a record of what happens; call a local women's group or rape crisis center; give serious consideration to mentioning your experience to a reliable lawyer.

THE PROFIT MOTIVE IN MEDICAL CARE

Why doesn't the present U.S. medical system provide affordable services and emphasize prevention and primary care? The profit motive has to be the main reason. From the many individuals who still want to be paid "fee for service" and build up a lucrative practice to the profit-making drug and insurance companies, medical care is now an industry in itself—the second-largest in the country—and a virtual monopoly.

The Medical Monopoly Our present type of medicine created a monopoly at the turn of the century through its control over state licensing laws which defined what the practice of medicine should be and who could be called a doctor. The laws provided state-sanctioned penalties for those who were not "properly" trained and licensed. At the same time the medical profession also gained absolute control over its education process, thus becoming a "legally enforced monopoly of practice."[29] Today medicine continues to set its own priorities and terms, with physicians controlling the majority of the medical decision-making and resource allocation processes. The profession decides what will be taught in medical schools, what medical services will be offered and how and where.* Surgeons gen-

erate most of their own income by self-referral ("I recommend this procedure and I will also perform it"), a practice judged unethical in other countries. Patients or third-party payors pay for services rendered. In many situations there is still no one but another doctor to decide whether or not these services are necessary, and no way of knowing whether or not they are effective. When review of costs occurs (as in the case of insurance), it is often only physicians who undertake that review.

Medicine's monopoly was further consolidated when the government made federal funds available for hospital construction (Hill-Burton law), and the "Blues" (Blue Cross/Blue Shield) were created to reimburse in-hospital care. (Many of the Blue Crosses were created originally by local medical societies and are still physician dominated.) Backed up by the private insurance industry, hospitals became the base of medical care in this country. Substantial federal funding for Medicare, Medicaid and medical research increased the volume of federal money flowing into medicine. At the same time, profit-making hospital and nursing-home chains also began to proliferate. Today, expenditures for medical care grow faster than anything else. The whole system is completely out of control, despite growing cuts. Medicine has been allowed to expand continuously, and virtually without limits or accountability.[†]

In addition, there has been a phenomenal rise in the "corporatization" of medical care; that is,

---

* Because medical care should always involve so much more than the application of technical skills and because it always occurs in a

social context, society should be able to influence both the quality and quantity of medical care available. For example, we have too many specialists crowded into affluent communities and entirely more doctors than we need, although many inner city and rural areas in greater need have severe shortages of physicians. Yet 95 percent of physicians now specialize, despite a continuing shortage of primary-care physicians. Medical schools take no leadership in rectifying the problem, which leaves millions with inadequate access to quality care.

† Because so much of our tax money is involved, we expect public utilities and our public education system, for example, to be somewhat accountable to the users. Through a public process we participate in decisions about cost, services and salaries, and sometimes even the budget itself. Though medical education, research and hospital operations are heavily subsidized by our taxes at all levels, we have virtually no say in how this money is spent. A few federally funded attempts were made in the past to make medicine more accountable, such as the formation of HSAs, but further attempts will now have to depend on local funding and initiative.

In addition, when there are errors or abuses in medical practice, physicians insist on "policing" themselves, leaving our range of options for redress short and unsatisfactory.

profit-making medical care chains that operate laboratories, "emergency rooms," mobile CAT scanners and so on, in addition to hospitals and nursing homes—a proliferation of separate services purely for profit.* Academic centers, medical schools and teaching hospitals have themselves created new and unprecedented arrangements amounting to millions of dollars with profit-making drug firms, all in the name of "scientific research"[30]—the medical-academic-industrial complex.

Those who profit from our illnesses are well organized politically and use their ample resources to keep the medical system free from government intrusion. Although they do not always agree among themselves, an informal coalition—physicians' lobbying groups like the AMA and ACOG, the pharmaceutical industry, hospital associations, the big voluntary "health" associations (Heart Association, Cancer Society, etc.), among others—tend to support the profit motive, the fee-for-service reimbursement system and the present crisis-care medical model.†

Health care has become a commodity or economic good, with profit as a blatant and legitimate goal. However inadequate government involvement in medical care was, it did make it possible for us to partially evaluate the system. It increased access to the system in some regions for a percentage of those who most needed it, and helped us to monitor or check a few of the system's most flagrant abuses. Government agencies were forced to respond *somewhat* to citizen pressure in the name of public interest. But federal regulations have been evaporating, with the result that profit-making enterprises have increased in number and monitoring their practices will be more difficult.

Our best hope is to form groups of workers and friends in the community and to work at the state

---

WHERE DOES THE MONEY GO?

- About 12 percent of the U.S. gross national product, or $666 billion, now goes for health and medical care.

- This 12 percent is at least 25 percent more than Sweden or Canada, two-thirds more than Japan and twice that spent in Great Britain. Yet our infant mortality rate is higher and life expectancy lower than in all these countries.

- Per capita spending on hospital and physician services for the insured are 25 to 50 percent greater than for the uninsured.

- Nursing home costs increase more than 10 percent annually, inching toward $50 billion.

- Unnecessary services, administrative and advertising costs amount to at least $200 billion annually. Administrative costs, due largely to the many health insurers (over 1500), different billing systems and variations in coverage plans, account for more than 20 percent of total health and medical care expenditures—more than in any other nation.

- Physician earnings and hospital costs continue to rise well ahead of inflation; for many, profits are increasing.

- Technological innovations, largely of unproven value, account for 70 percent of health and medical care costs.

- Our tax dollars now support more than half the medical enterprise in all its forms, including medical education.

---

*For example, recent surveys show that half of U.S. physicians are now on salary, many in profit-making corporations that are often physician owned. The fee-for-service system is changing, but not necessarily for the benefit of consumers, because only a few salaried doctors work in nonprofit settings such as health centers.
†The Center for Science in the Public Interest has played an important role in recently challenging how these extremely wealthy national organizations spend the money donated to them and in urging them to play a more effective role in health policy directed toward prevention. We can work locally by getting onto boards of chapters to help influence local projects.

level, making sure that reasonable options for care remain open to as many as possible at reasonable prices.

Insurance   The insurance principle has become increasingly influential in shaping U.S. medical care. All third-party reimbursement systems, whether through private, profit-making insurance systems, non-profit Blue Cross/Blue Shield (the "Blues") or public programs (Medicare, Medicaid), reward doctors and hospitals by reimbursing them for doing the most expensive and complicated procedures on a fee-for-service basis. Yet they pay nothing or even require us to pay out of pocket for basic well-woman or preventive care. The insurance system thus acts as a kind of "blank check": We pay the premiums, directly or through our taxes (both continually rising); the doctors and hospitals bill the third parties (sometimes doctors also bill us for the "difference" between what insurance covers and what their real charges are), and there is no one looking to see if something cheaper or better (or sooner) might have been done. Medical costs skyrocket as a result. The chief beneficiaries of the insurance system are actually the doctors and stockholders, whose incomes and profits are all guaranteed.[31]

The insurance industry discriminates blatantly against women both as health and medical care workers and as consumers. Programs often do not reimburse directly for the services of nonphysician workers like nurse-midwives, nurse-practitioners, physical therapists and nutritionists, the majority of whom are women (this is changing now). Instead they reimburse the physicians, health departments or hospitals who hire or supervise them and indeed profit from their labor.

The Drug Industry   Almost nowhere is the inherent conflict between profit-making and public safety more obvious than with the manufacture and sale of prescription drugs. Yet it is difficult to control the drug industry, which lies at the heart of both the medical system and the capitalist system. According to Dr. James L. Goddard, former commissioner of the Food and Drug Administration (FDA):

> *An American buying prescription drugs buys on faith what his doctor has prescribed. He is like a child who goes to the store with his mother's shopping list, which he cannot even read. He is totally unsophisticated as to the workings of the $5,000,000,000 [1972 figures] industry to which he is contributing and which his tax money is already helping to support. The consumer of drugs pays up and takes his medicine, and the Drug Establishment, about which he knows nothing, scores again.*[32]

Prescription drug sales in 1987 were estimated at about $23 billion, averaging twenty prescriptions per family in the United States. Pharmaceutical companies regularly show a return on investment of over 26 percent, outperforming any other part of the industrial sector. The drug industry is more than three times as price inflationary as all other U.S. industries. Americans have to pay more than twice or three times what Canadians and Europeans spend for drugs.

Although some drugs do save lives and enhance the quality of life for many sick people, research reveals increasing numbers of both new and older drugs to be dangerous or useless.* The GAO (the government's General Accounting Office) reports that Medicare/Medicaid pays $40 million a year for drugs shown to have no effectiveness. Each year, at least 1.5 million people go into the hospital because they have adverse reactions to drugs. Women receive about two-thirds of all prescription drugs, and the most profitable drugs made by the industry are oral contraceptives, injectable contraceptives (like Depo-Provera) and tranquilizers, all risky in some ways and all targeted mainly for women.

The drug industry spends 25 percent of its resources ($10 billion) on marketing—*more than on research*—and most of it for prescription drug promotion targeted to physicians.[34] Despite recent legislative efforts to curb gifts to medical students, the industry continues to woo successfully both practicing physicians, medical residents and medical schools by offering "research" opportunities and luxurious travel symposia, as well as sponsoring educational programs in hospitals and schools. Because medical school training in pharmacology is largely inadequate, doctors become permanently dependent on drug companies for information (or misinformation). As a result, physicians often cannot or do not protect us from ineffective or dangerous drugs. Often they don't know the possibly serious negative effects, or they continue to prescribe

---

*An industry-sponsored study of all drugs approved between 1938 and 1962 showed only 12 percent to be effective for their prescribed use and at least 15 percent to have no effectiveness whatsoever. *Yet most of these drugs are still on the market.*[33]

the drugs anyway,* based on personal observation or the belief that any negative findings (always challenged by the drug companies) have been inaccurate. Doctors also tend to prescribe the advertised brand-name drugs, which are more profitable to the drug companies, rather than using generic drugs, cheaper for the consumer, and often encourage patients' notions that a visit to the doctor is not complete without a prescription to "solve" the problem.

Regulation   The FDA was ostensibly designed to protect the public from the dangers of adulterated food and harmful or useless drugs. (See Chapter 2, "Food," for more on the FDA.) Over many years, the efforts of some conscientious FDA staff, prompted and encouraged by the pressure of consumer groups, activists, investigative reporters and members of Congress, have sometimes led to effective, though limited, protection, as well as increased consumer participation in the regulatory process.

- Barbara Seaman, a founder of the National Women's Health Network and an early researcher on the Pill and menopausal estrogens, helped alert the public to the risk of these drugs in her testimony before Congress.

- Doris Haire, founder of the American Foundation for Maternal and Child Health, has repeatedly challenged the FDA, Congress and physician experts to demonstrate the safety to the infant and mother of drugs administered routinely during pregnancy, labor and delivery.

- Ralph Nader's Health Research Group has publicized the dangers and ineffectiveness of many drugs, successfully pressured the FDA to get them off the market, testified in Congress and worked extensively with the FDA staff on behalf of consumers.

---

*For instance, physicians continued to prescribe progestin for pregnancy tests despite the discovery of a link to birth defects. The FDA warned against the use of the drug in the early stages of pregnancy, yet 75,000 prescriptions for progestin tests were given in 1978, years after the first FDA warning (testimony of Sidney Wolfe before Senator Edward Kennedy's Senate Health subcommittee August 1, 1979).

However, these achievements are being increasingly threatened by the antiregulatory climate of a conservative government and also by the fact that the FDA's small budget has never been able to compete against the huge financial resources the drug industry musters for lobbying, court cases and the production of new products. The FDA is no match for many of the "best" drug companies, which often have substantial criminal records involving bribing of officials in foreign governments, falsifying of test data and failing to comply with FDA requirements to report adverse reactions to drugs.[35] Because drug companies are themselves required to test new drugs for safety and effectiveness, they also hire most of the researchers; if the research lab or doctor can make data look favorable to the company, it is more likely to continue to obtain funding.

At the very least, the drug industry should be required to submit to certain basic reforms, such as the severing of financial connections to those researching the safety and efficacy of the drugs they want to market, and the payment of much more severe penalties for misconduct. Consumer and public-interest groups have to be better watchdogs than ever before and also must serve as pressure groups to establish better regulatory systems at the state and local levels.

MEDICAL EDUCATION AND TRAINING

Physicians have unusually broad powers. They decide which patients will be treated and where, who goes to the hospital, what treatment is given and for how long and which drugs are administered and in what quantities. They also have enormous influence in our most personal decisions. Why do many physicians misuse their power, consciously or unconsciously? Many of the behaviors we complain about in physicians—their authoritarian manner, their insensitivity and condescension—can be traced back to their education and training as doctors.

Who Gets into Medical School?   Traditionally, upper- and upper-middle class white men have been the ones to survive the fierce competition for medical school entrance. In the words of one prestigious medical educator, "The years of premedical education, once considered so rewarding, have become a battleground of ruthless competition."[36] Some students tear out textbook pages so others cannot read them, and distort their fellow-students' experiments. Some also cheat, and it is known that those who do so will continue their deceptive behavior as doctors. Experienced educators have believed for some time that medicine is no longer attracting the best and brightest students, one reason being that they are repelled by the typical pre-med who would become their colleague. Although 1960s and 1970s activism resulted in a surge of women, poor and minority students, this number peaked around 1977 for poor and minority students, in part due to cutbacks in federal funding and in part to the fact that most medical schools were accepting these other candidates only under pressure.* Therefore, most physicians train alongside people more or less exactly like themselves, with teachers formed from the same mold. The result is a kind of cloning: The medical profession reproduces itself.

The Training   Medical schools ask students to absorb an enormous quantity of highly technical information in compressed form, largely through one-way lectures. They place little emphasis on thinking and reasoning and none at all on questioning, criticizing or arguing. Few could learn to think critically in this environment if they did not know how before medical school. Students "are being driven to absorb an enormous amount of science at the sacrifice of just about everything else." Recall is poor after even a short period, however, and many in academic medicine admit that much of this material, irrelevant to competent medical practice, has crowded out crucial skills and subject matter. In the words of a woman physician:

> The training program is disease-oriented, with life-threatening or rare conditions receiving the most attention, and the acquisition of skill in doing procedures (biopsies, punctures) and using diagnostic machines (EKG, X-ray, lab tests) being prized. The day-to-day ills of the public are ignored as "minor

> problems." The promotion of health and the prevention of disease are neglected almost entirely.[37]

The training usually does not challenge students to become more aware of the social and political realities affecting people's health or to work through their own sexism, homophobia, class bias, ageism and racism. A woman doctor who does have a political awareness, wrote:

> When I show a student her own cervix with a mirror, she is fascinated. When she is with me as a student and I offer my white middle-class patient the opportunity, the student thinks it is great. But when I offer a sixty-year-old woman the chance or a twenty-five-year-old working-class black woman, the student is amazed that "that kind" of patient would want to see her cervix. When I say, "This could be done in the clinic and would make women feel more in control," students say to me, "Oh, no, there's no time" (one extra minute?) or, worse, "'Those people' wouldn't be interested."

Glaringly absent from medical training are most of the values, concerns and skills often thought of as "feminine": nurturance, empathy, caring, sensitive listening, encouraging others to take care of themselves, collaboration rather than competition. The medical hierarchy relegates these values and skills to the domain of nurses, other aides and (female) family members of the patients—physicians have "more important" things to attend to. Patients deprived of these elements of caring may not be as quick to recover, may miss absorbing important information about aftercare or preventive care and may end up feeling depressed about their experience because no one has paid attention to the emotional impact of their health problems. Women often complain bitterly of cold, abstract, impersonal or authoritarian doctors. A major study by the Institute of Medicine found that a majority of families were dissatisfied with their doctors and up to half had changed them as a result.[38] These qualities may have less to do with the physician's original personality than with the one-sidedness of her or his training. Similarly vital knowledge needed for optimum patient care—how to evaluate studies and risks accurately, what tests and treatments really cost, how to recognize a patient's rights and identify the

---

*Enrollments for women are still increasing, however.

ethical issues involved in medical decisions, what patients could do for themselves to prevent illness— is either absent altogether or relegated to the status of an elective. Students get the message: This material is not important.[39]

Many medical educators are now alarmed over the erosion of clinical skills caused by the overemphasis on technology in today's training, that is, by the increasing inability of younger physicians to make judgments based on experience, examination and careful listening to the patient rather than on readings from tests and machines.

The focus narrows further at the residency stage, where students aim to specialize because specialization promises more money, prestige and control over one's work.

Specialization and the rapid rate of advancement of knowledge and technology may tend to pre-empt the attention of both teachers and students from the central purpose of medicine, which is to heal the sick and relieve suffering.[40]

Residency programs are grueling, low-paid, often demanding as much as thirty-six hours at a stretch and a hundred hours a week in consistently understaffed conditions, undesirable for both residents and patients alike. Teaching becomes haphazard, and not surprisingly, all types of residents have shown declining scores and performances in recent years, particularly in basic skills.

In short, specialty training is a dehumanizing process. Few working conditions in the industrial age have survived with so little change. Composed of one part sleep deprivation, one part shutting off of all feelings and one part automatic response to orders in what is probably the most militaristic of all civilian disciplines, this training resembles a kind of brainwashing.* The stress contributes to physicians' high rates of mental breakdown, drug addiction, alcoholism, suicide and family disruption.[41] Rates of incompetence among physicians in practice have also grown alarmingly. In addition to

errors, they both perform many useless procedures and fail to perform needed ones.[42]

Studies have shown that while medical students may begin medical training with idealism and a sincere desire to help people, after years of training in the closed worlds of medical school and residency they become almost invariably more cynical, detached and mechanistic than at entry.[43] Their ability to communicate has actually deteriorated during the process.[44] Because of the enormous personal sacrifice medical training requires, and because most of the teachers and the doctors they admire are highly paid specialists, young physicians feel entitled to earn very large sums of money and to command interpersonal authoritarian power once the training is completed. Here is how another distinguished medical educator puts it: "What emerges are physicians without inquiring minds, physicians who bring to the bedside *not* curiosity and a desire to understand but a set of reflexes that allows them to earn a handsome living."[45]

These criticisms are not new; indeed, many were voiced as soon as the medical monopoly was created nearly a century ago. When *Our Bodies, Ourselves* came out in 1973, the then president of the American Association of Medical Colleges said every medical student should read it.

A number of proposals to reform medical training have emphasized the importance of good communication skills and medical care that is culturally, linguistically and racially appropriate. For example, in response to pressure from the women's health movement, which had protested teaching medical students how to do pelvic exams on anesthetized women (often without their consent) and prostitutes, some medical schools now involve specially trained gynecological teaching associates (GTAs) in the teaching of the pelvic exam. These women can offer important, immediate feedback about how well a student is doing an exam, when s/he is doing something that may be hurting and so on.*

Even if educational reforms were to be realized, without substantial input from consumers and their communities, the experience of health and medical

---

*The term *brainwashing* has been used repeatedly by medical educators, students and physicians in conversations with the authors. See also Allan Chamberlain, "Night Life: Sleep Deprivation in Medical Education," *The New Physician* (May 1981), p. 30, for use of this term.

*For more information on GTAs, contact the Program in Introduction to Clinical Medicine, Tulane University Medical Center, 1430 Tulane Avenue, New Orleans, LA 70112.

care will continue to be frustrating for women. Meanwhile, we can look to the many alternative and neighborhood facilities created by women and men over the past twenty years or so for examples of successful efforts to integrate competence, caring and community partnership.

Notes

1. Barbara Bernstein and Robert Kane. "Physicians' Attitudes Toward Female Patients," *Medical Care,* Vol. 19, No. 6 (June 1981), pp. 600–08. See Chapter 3 and Images of Women in Medical Textbooks and Women Physicians, on pp. 666 and 667.

2. Gena Corea. *The Hidden Malpractice: How American Medicine Mistreats Women.* New York: Harper & Row, 1985.

3. Arthur Owens. "Who Says Doctors Make Too Much Money?" *Medical Economics* (March 7, 1983), pp. 66–67. See also Peter Conrad and Rochelle Kern. *The Sociology of Health and Illness: Critical Perspectives,* 3rd ed. New York: St. Martin's Press, 1990. See figures quoted elsewhere in this chapter for taxpayer expenditures for medical care and training.

4. See United Nations Population and Vital Statistics Report in *U.N. Demographic Yearbook 1988.* In 1988 the U.S. infant mortality rate of 10 per 1000 live births was double that of Japan (5 per 1000 live births). The cities of Detroit, Washington and Baltimore all had rates above 19 deaths per 1000 live births. See also U.S. Department of Health and Human Services, *Report of the Secretary's Task Force on Black and Minority Health,* Vol. 6, *Infant Mortality and Low Birth Weight,* January 1986. Low-birth-weight babies are the major cause of high infant mortality rates. In poorer communities, there is what Professor Edward Sparer has called an "infant death gap" between haves and have-nots, which is getting wider.

5. Kathleen Newland. *Infant Mortality and the Health of Societies* (Worldwatch Paper #47). 1981, pp. 6–11. Available from Worldwatch Institute, 1776 Massachusetts Avenue NW, Washington, DC 20036. See also U.S. Department of Health, Education and Welfare, *Factors Associated with Low Birth Weight,* Hyattsville, MD: HEW, April 1980, p. 2.

6. John B. McKinlay and Sonja M. McKinlay. "Medical Measures and the Decline of Mortality," in Peter Conrad and Rochelle Kern, eds., *The Sociology of Health and Illness: Critical Perspectives,* New York: St. Martin's Press, 1981, pp. 12–30. Thomas McKeown. *The Role of Medicine: Dream, Mirage, or Nemesis.* London: Nuffield Provincial Hospitals Trust, 1976. René Dubos, *Mirage of Health: Utopias, Progress, and Biological Change.* New York: Harper Colophon, 1979, p. 23 ff.

7. Lack of teaching of scientific method in medical school is documented in David H. Banta, Clyde J. Behney and Jane Sisk Willems, *Toward Radical Technology in Medicine,* New York: Springer Publishing Co., 1981, p. 30. Additional discussion of the unscientific nature of modern medicine may be found in Rick Carlson, *The End of Medicine,* New York: Wiley-Interscience, 1976. A discussion of how medical decision making might be brought more into line with modern scientific thinking is presented in Harold Bursztajn, Richard I. Feinbloom, Robert M. Hamm and Archie Brodsky, *Medical Choices, Medical Chances,* New York: Routledge, 1990.

8. The Congressional Office of Technology Assessment. "Strategies for Medical Assessment," Publication 052-003-00887-4. Quoted in *The Nation's Health* (November 1982). Available from the U.S. Government Printing Office, Washington, DC 20052.

9. David H. Banta et al. *Toward Rational Technology in Medicine,* p. 122.

10. Leonard S. Syme and Lisa F. Berkman. "Social Class, Susceptibility, and Sickness," in *The Sociology of Health and Illness.*

11. National Academy of Sciences, Institute of Medicine, Division of Health Care Services. "Health Care in a Context of Civil Rights: A Report of a Study," No. 1804. Washington, DC: U.S. Government Printing Office, 1981.

12. Wornie L. Reed. "Racism and Health: The Case of Black Infant Mortality," *The Sociology of Health and Illness,* pp. 34–44.

13. S. Woolhandler et al. "Medical Care and Mortality: Racial Differences in Preventable Deaths," in Phil Brown, ed., *Perspectives in Medical Sociology.* Belmont, CA: Wadsworth, 1989, pp. 71–81.

14. Diana Scully. *Men Who Control Women's Health: The Miseducation of Obstetrician-Gynecologists.* Boston: Houghton-Mifflin, 1980.

15. *Taking Our Bodies Back: The Women's Health Movement,* a 33-minute 1973 color film. Available from Cambridge Documentary Films, Box 385, Cambridge, MA 02139.

16. Irving Zola. "Medicine as an Institution of Social Control," in *Socio-Medical Inquiries—Recollections, Reflections, and Reconsiderations.* Philadelphia: Temple University Press, 1983, p. 262 ff.

17. See Janice Raymond, "Medicine as Patriarchal Religion," *The Journal of Medicine and Philosophy,* Vol. 7 (1982), pp. 197–216.

18. See Barbara Ehrenreich and Deirdre English, *For Her Own Good: 150 Years of the Experts' Advice to Women.* New York: Doubleday/Anchor Books, 1978.

19. George J. Annas. "Forced Cesareans: The Most Un-kindest Cut of All," *The Hastings Center Report* (June 1982), pp. 16–17. Also personal interviews with the authors of *Our Bodies, Ourselves.*

20. Dorothy Wertz and Richard W. Wertz. "The Decline of Midwives and the Rise of Medical Obstetricians," in *The Sociology of Health and Illness,* pp. 173–74.

21. Barbara Ehrenreich and Deirdre English. *For Her Own Good,* p. 117.

22. Estelle P. Ramey. "Men's Cycles (They Have Them Too, You Know)," in A. Kaplan and J. Bean, eds., *Beyond Sex-Role Stereotypes.* Boston: Little, Brown, 1976. See also Ruth Hubbard, Mary Sue Henifin and Barbara Fried, *Biological Woman—The Convenient Myth: A Collection of Feminist Essays and a Comprehensive Bibliography,* Cambridge, MA: Schenkman Publishing Co., 1982 (entire volume).

23. Diana Scully. *Men Who Control Women's Health.* See also Michelle Harrison, *A Woman in Residence.* New York: Random House, 1982.

24. From a woman who was later operated on for a rare form of cancer that had spread to her lungs. Stephani Cook, *Second Life,* New York: Simon & Schuster, 1981.

25. Anita Diamant. "Bedside Manners: Of Doctors, Patient Abuse, and Regulation. Again," *The Boston Phoenix* (November 10, 1981), Section 2, p. 14.

26. Personal communication, women's medical association members investigating physician sexual misconduct. See also "Therapist-Patient Sex Has Negative Effect for Most," *Ob/Gyn News,* Vol. 16, No. 24; D. Sobel, "Sex with Therapist Said to Harm Client"; John Kelly, "Sexually Abusive Doctors"; Ronald Kotulak, "Doctor-Patient Sex."

27. "New Case Alleges Sex Abuse by an M.D. at Rock's Sacramento," *Medical World News* (September 3, 1979), pp. 38–39. See also Anita Diamant. "Bedside Manners," p. 13.

28. "Harvard Medical School Dean's Statement on Letters of Recommendation," *Harvard Medical Area FOCUS* (October 8, 1981), p. 5. See also Fox Butterfield. "Doctors' Praise Assailed for Peer in Rape Case," *The New York Times* (September 24, 1981).

29. E. Freidson, quoted in Peter Conrad and Rochelle Kern, *The Sociology of Health and Illness,* p. 161.

30. Harvard University News Office for the Medical Area. "$6 Million Du Pont Gift for Genetics Research" (September 12, 1981), p. 8; "Johnson & Johnson Gives $500,000 for Basic Research" (September 12, 1981), p. 8; "Gift for Unrestricted Cancer Research from Bristol-Meyers" (April 8, 1982), p. 5. *Harvard Medical Area FOCUS,* 25 Shattuck Street, Boston, MA 02115. See also Barbara J. Culliton, "The Hoechst Department at Mass General (Hospital)" (News and Comment, second in a series on the Academic-Industrial Complex), *Science,* Vol. 216 (June 11, 1982), pp. 1200–03. For a critique, read Arnold S. Relman, "The New Medical-Industrial Complex" (Special Article), *New England Journal of Medicine,* Vol. 303, No. 17 (October 23, 1980), pp. 963–70.

31. William K. Stevens. "High Medical Costs Under Attack as Drain on the Nation's Economy," *The New York Times* (March 28, 1982), pp. 1, 50. Sandra Salmans. "Critics Say Lack of Incentives Hurt Insurers' Efforts to Curb Medical Costs," *The New York Times* (March 31, 1982).

32. *Science for the People,* Science and Society Series, No. 1 (November 1973).

33. Maryann Napoli. *Health Facts,* p. 15. See also "Ineffective Drugs," *The Public Citizen, 1981 Annual Report* (winter 1982), p. 22; Sidney M. Wolfe, Christopher M. Coley and the Health Research Group, *Pills That Don't Work: A Consumer's and Doctor's Guide to Six Hundred Prescription Drugs that Lack Evidence of Effectiveness.* New York: Warner Books, 1982.

34. Staff Report of the Special Select Committee on Aging, U.S. Senate, 102nd Congress, 1st Session, Committee Reprint. Washington, DC: U.S. Government Printing Office, 1991.

35. "Informed Consent," *Health Facts,* Vol. 4, No. 22 (July/August 1980), p. 3. See also Chapter 5, "Bribery and Other Strategies," in Milton Silverman, Philip R. Lee and Mia Lydecker, *Prescription for Death: The Drugging of the Third World,* Berkeley: University of California Press, 1982, pp. 119–30; Barbara Seaman and Gideon Seaman. *Women and the Crisis in Sex Hormones,* New York: Rawson Associates, 1977, pp. 73–74; Mark Dowie et al., "The Illusion of Safety," *Mother Jones* (June 1982), pp. 39, 43, 46–48; Ivan Illich, "The Pharmaceutical Invasion," in *Medical Nemesis,* New York: Pantheon Books, 1976, pp. 63–76; "Eli Lilly is Accused in FDA Documents of Not Reporting Adverse Drug Reactions," *The Wall Street Journal* (August 4, 1982), p. 6.

36. Dr. John Z. Bowers, as quoted in *Medical Area FOCUS* (Harvard Medical School), February 11, 1982.

37. Cynthia Carver. "The Deliverers," in Shelly Romalis, ed., *Childbirth: Alternatives to Medical Control.* Austin: University of Texas Press, 1981, p. 135.

38. Derek Bok, "Needed: A New Way to Train Doctors," president of Harvard University, in his annual report to the Board of Overseers, April 1984, *Harvard Magazine* (May–June 1984), p. 43.

39. Derek Bok, "Needed: A New Way to Train Doctors."

40. "Curriculum Review Panel for Medical School Education Initiated by the Association of American Medical Colleges," *The New York Times* (October 21, 1982).

41. Jack D. McCue. "The Effects of Stress on Physicians and Their Medical Practice," *New England Journal of Medicine*, Vol. 306, No. 8 (February 25, 1982), pp. 458–63.

42. President's Commission for the Study of Ethical Problems in Medicine and Biomedical Research. Washington, DC: U.S. Government Printing Office. *Securing Access to Health Care.* 1983. Also see Marcia Millman, *The Unkindest Cut: Life in the Backrooms of Medicine*, New York: William Morrow, 1977.

43. Howard S. Becker, E.C. Geer, Everett C. Hughes and Anselm L. Straus. *Boys in White*. Chicago: University of Chicago Press, 1961. Though over thirty years old, this classic study appears to apply to most of today's male students as well. No comparable work has yet been done on women. The work of psychiatrist Harold Lief, MD, at the University of Pennsylvania over a twenty-year period has provided similar corroboration, with special reference to sexuality. (The SKAT [Sex Knowledge and Attitude Tests] for physicians was developed by Dr. Lief.) See also Bryce Nelson. "Can Doctors Learn Warmth?" *The New York Times* (September 13, 1983).

44. Derek Bok. *Harvard Magazine*, p. 70.

45. Dr. J. Michael Bishop, in a speech to the American Association of Medical Colleges, November 8, 1983.

The Assault on the Female–Headed Family

Ruth Sidel

A graduate of Wellesley College and the Boston University School of Social Work, Ruth Sidel is professor of sociology at Hunter College in New York City and a frequent speaker on women's issues and social policy. She has studied the role of women, the care of preschool children, and the provision of human services in urban areas in the United States and in several other countries, including the People's Republic of China, Great Britain, Chile, and Sweden. In addition to Keeping Women and Children Last: America's War on the Poor, *from which this selection was taken, her books include* Women and Child Care in China: A Firsthand Report *(1973);* Urban Survival: The World of Working-Class Women *(1978);* Women and Children Last: The Plight of Poor Women in Affluent America *(1986);* On Her Own: Growing Up in the Shadow of the American Dream *(1990); and* Battling Bias: The Struggle for Identity and Community on College Campuses *(1995).*

"While the entire category—single-parent family—is often decried, in reality it is the female-headed family that is under attack," Sidel tells us. Once again, women are being made scapegoats for the ills of society, especially women who don't conform to the regulation patriarchal mold, especially poor women, especially African-American women. The target is the woman who heads a family, the unmarried mother and, in turn, her children. Sidel reveals the sexism and racism buried under the illogical arguments that condemn an entire category of families and make it possible for policy makers to sidestep dealing with real problems.

> *I THINK THIS REASON WHY girls don't do well on multiple choice tests goes all the way back to the Bible, all the way back to Genesis, Adam and Eve. God said, "All right, Eve, multiple choice or mul-*

tiple orgasms, what's it going to be?" We all know what was chosen.[1]

—RUSH LIMBAUGH

The grass-plot before the jail, in Prison Lane, on a certain summer morning, not less than two centuries ago, was occupied by a pretty large number of the inhabitants of Boston; all with their eyes intently fastened on the iron-clamped oaken door. . . . never had Hester Prynne appeared more lady-like, in the antique interpretation of the term, than when she issued from prison. Those who had before known her, and had expected to behold her dimmed and obscured by a disastrous cloud, were astonished, and even startled, to perceive how her beauty shone out, and made a halo of misfortune and ignominy in which she was enveloped. . . . But the point which drew all eyes, and, as it were, transfigured the wearer . . . was that SCARLET LETTER. . . . It had the effect of a spell, taking her out of the ordinary relations with humanity, and inclosing her in a sphere by herself.[2]

Hester Prynne moved from the prison door to the marketplace where, her sentence decreed, she must stand for "a space of three hours"[3] beneath "a sort of scaffold"[4] and "then and thereafter, for the remainder of her natural life, to wear a mask of shame upon her bosom."[5] According to an observer in that Massachusetts marketplace in Nathaniel Hawthorne's novel *The Scarlet Letter*, "thus, she will be a living sermon against sin, until the ignominious letter will be engraved upon her tombstone."[6] Not only must Hester Prynne be punished for violating the customs of her society—for having a child outside of marriage—but her punishment and her shame must serve as a warning to others that behavior outside of the mores of Puritanical New England society would not be tolerated and would be punished by powerful social sanctions.

One hundred and fifty years after the publication of Hawthorne's novel and 350 years after the peak of Puritan power in Massachusetts, an outcry is heard once again against the single-parent family, particularly against families headed by women in which children are born outside of marriage. Once again shame and stigma are being touted as methods of social control.

During the August 1995 debate on overhauling AFDC, Senator John Ashcroft, Republican of Missouri, articulated what has become a virtual litany among elected representatives and those who are featured by the media: "Illegitimacy is a threat to the survival of our nation and our culture."[7] The same day in an Op-Ed piece in *The New York Times*, Lisa Schiffren, a former speechwriter for Dan Quayle, began her article by stating, "America faces no problem more urgent than our skyrocketing illegitimacy rate."[8]

While the entire category—single-parent family—is often decried, in reality it is the female-headed family that is under attack. Of the children in the United States who lived with one parent in 1993, the vast majority, 87 percent, lived with their mother; 13 percent lived with their father.[9] All female-headed families, however, are not perceived as equally reprehensible. Widows are exempt from criticism as they are perceived as victims of tragic circumstances rather than as women who have flouted the conventional moral code of society. Divorced mothers have increasingly come under scrutiny as studies and articles focus on the damage the authors feel divorce has wrought upon the children. But it is the never-married mother and, within that cohort, the poor never-married mother who needs financial assistance from the state, who has been the clearest target of criticism. While some of the discussion of the problems of mother-only families has been scholarly and has attempted to be balanced, much of the recent rhetoric has had a hostile, victim-blaming, hysterical tone reminiscent of other episodes of scapegoating in America's history.

In 1965, a confidential report to President Lyndon Johnson written by a young assistant secretary of labor, Daniel Patrick Moynihan, and entitled *The Negro Family: The Case for National Action*, was leaked to the press and caused a furor. In it, Moynihan, now a Democratic senator from New York, stated:

> At the heart of the deterioration of the fabric of Negro society is the deterioration of the Negro family.

> It is the fundamental source of the weakness of the Negro community. . . . In essence, the Negro community has been forced into a matriarchal structure which, because it is so out of line with the rest of the American society, seriously retards the progress of the group as a whole.[10]

The notion that family structure is at the root of poverty and a wide variety of social ills rather than the social and economic conditions that lead to that structure is the core of the current wave of blaming poor, female-headed families for their own problems and for many of the problems of American society.

The argument that "deviant" values and family structure are primary causes of poverty resurfaced in the mid-1980s with the publication of Charles Murray's *Losing Ground*. Murray labeled out-of-wedlock births "the single most important social problem of our time—more important than crime, drugs, poverty, illiteracy, welfare, or homelessness because it drives everything else." He has also suggested rehabilitating the term "illegitimacy" in order to "make an illegitimate birth the socially horrific act it used to be."[11]

In the summer of 1992, then–Vice President Dan Quayle condemned Murphy Brown, the central character in a popular television program, for having a baby outside of marriage. It is significant that the episode in which Murphy decides to have her baby focuses on her conflict between abortion and bearing the child. Could Quayle have been suggesting that she have an abortion instead of having the baby? Was he suggesting that a single woman in her early forties abstain from sex completely or that she and her partner revert to the shotgun weddings of previous eras despite the fact that the father was not interested in a long-term commitment to Murphy or to the baby? But Dan Quayle's appeal to "family values" went much further than his criticism of a fictional TV character. Quayle also suggested that unmarried women with children were at least partially responsible for the "lawless social anarchy" that erupted in the May 1992 riots in Los Angeles following the acquittal of the four police officers who so brutally beat Rodney King.

Several months after the Quayle speech, an influential and widely read article by Barbara Dafoe Whitehead entitled "Dan Quayle Was Right" was published in *The Atlantic Monthly*. In her article,

Whitehead claims that studies show that children who grow up in single-parent families are at significantly greater risk for a variety of problems than children who are raised in two-parent families. These problems include emotional and behavioral difficulties, dropping out of school, becoming pregnant as teenagers, abusing drugs, getting into trouble with the law, and being victims of physical or sexual abuse. Whitehead stresses, moreover, that children of divorced, separated, or never-married parents are far more likely to live in poverty, commit crimes, fail in school, engage in "aggressive, acting-out behavior," and engage in "assaults on teachers, unprovoked attacks on other children, [and] screaming outbursts in class."[12] The language Whitehead uses clearly indicates her point of view: The terms "stable" marriage and "intact" families are used to describe two-parent families; single-parent families are often referred to as "disrupted" or "broken." The implication of her choice of language is that one-parent families are not "stable" and two-parent families are rarely "disrupted," generalizations that are both simplistic and frequently false.

During the late 1980s, Judith Wallerstein published the results of her study, *Second Chances: Men, Women, and Children a Decade After Divorce.* Wallerstein found that divorce has significant negative implications for many children, leading some to depression, underachievement, or difficulty in forming long-term, intimate relationships of their own. Wallerstein compares children of divorced parents with those of "reasonably happy intact"[13] families, but if we are examining the effects of divorce upon the well-being of children of divorce, does it make sense to compare them to children from "reasonably happy intact" families? If these families were reasonably happy, the parents presumably would not have divorced. Until studies of the impact of divorce on children compare children of divorced parents with children of unhappily married parents—since the parents' conflicts with one another may be at least partially responsible for the problems of the children—we will not be able to disentangle the impact of divorce from the impact of family problems.

David Blankenhorn, founder and president of the Institute for American Values, has broadened the critique of single-parent families by focusing primarily on the impact of fatherlessness. Blankenhorn claims that American society has become a "culture of fatherlessness" and that we are even losing our "idea of fatherhood."[14] Adding to the general tone of panic and imminent disaster embodied in discussions of single parenthood, Blankenhorn's book, *Fatherless America,* is subtitled *Confronting Our Most Urgent Social Problem.* Are mother-only families really our most urgent social problem? More urgent than poverty? Than increasing joblessness and inequality? More urgent than AIDS or massive alienation or violence? Blankenhorn's response is that the critical social problems that plague the United States—"Divorce. Out-of-wedlock childbearing. Children growing up in poverty. Youth violence. Unsafe neighborhoods. Domestic violence. The weakening of parental authority"—are bound together by "the flight of males from their children's lives."[15] While many who bemoan the death of the two-parent family focus primarily on the role of women, Blankenhorn's book is refreshing in that it at least places men in an active role and attempts to hold them somewhat accountable for the increasing number of female-headed homes.

Even thoughtful observers of American society who do not ordinarily look for simplistic answers to complex problems or try to pit one group against another find a way to blame single mothers for some of the most wrenching, deeply rooted, multi-faceted social problems of our time. In May of 1994, Senator Bill Bradley, Democrat from New Jersey, delivered a major speech at the National Press Club on violence in America. Although Bradley decries the social, emotional, and physical cost of violence, and discusses the urgent need for gun control and the glorification of violence by popular culture as well as the issue of domestic violence, and while he does mention urban and rural poverty as well as economic depression as causes of violence, Bradley saves his most vivid rhetoric for single parents and their children. Bradley acknowledges that some single mothers raise law-abiding children but the problems produced by female-headed families—not the profound economic and social inequality that grips this land, or continuing racism or sexism—takes center stage in Senator Bradley's outcry against violence:

> *In Detroit, nearly 80 percent of the kids are born to single parents. In 1991, 30 percent of all children*

born in America were born to a single parent. Among black children, it was two-thirds. Many single mothers do heroic jobs in transmitting values and raising their children well against great odds. Many others are too young, too poor, and too unloved, and their children at birth become 15-year time bombs waiting to explode in adolescence. If you think violence among the young is bad now, wait until this army of neglected, often abused, sometimes abandoned, street-trained, gang-tested, friendless young people reach age 15. Their capacity to have any kind of meaningful attachment will be gone. . . . [16]

Much of Bradley's speech is meant to be a wake-up call that will move people emotionally and stir the press and the citizenry into taking action against the scourge of violence. But the paragraph about single mothers and their children contains some of the most disturbing language of the speech—"this army of neglected, often abused, sometimes abandoned, street-trained, gang-tested, friendless young people"—and of course it was this point that was picked up widely by the press.

Senator Bradley is surely correct when he states that millions of children in the United States are "neglected," "abused," "abandoned," and "friendless," but to suggest that the central cause of their debilitation and despair is that they are the children of single mothers is to isolate one factor in their background and focus on it above all others. Millions of children from single-parent families are, of course, *not* "neglected," "abused," "abandoned," and "friendless."

In a chilling article on the current prevalence of violent crime in the United States and the likelihood of a massive increase in the level of violence in the near future, Adam Walinsky, a lawyer who advocates adding citizen officers to existing police forces, focuses on the violent crimes committed by black youths from single-parent families:

We first notice the children of the ghetto when they grow muscles—at about the age of fifteen. The children born in 1965 reached their fifteenth year in 1980, and 1980 and 1981 set new records for criminal violence in the United States, as teenage and young adult blacks ripped at the fabric of life in the black inner city. Nevertheless, of all the black children who reached physical maturity in those years, three quarters had been born to a married mother

and father. Not until 1991 did we experience the arrival in their mid-teens of the first group of black youths fully half of whom had been born to single mothers—the cohort born in 1976. Criminal violence particularly associated with young men and boys reached new peaks of destruction in black communities in 1990 and 1991. [17]

Walinsky continues by discussing future crime rates based on the number of black males born into mother-only families:

In the year 2000 the black youths born in 1985 will turn fifteen. Three fifths of them were born to single mothers, many of whom were drug-addicted; one in fourteen will have been raised with neither parent at home; unprecedented numbers will have been subjected to beatings and other abuse; and most will have grown up amid the utter chaos pervading black city neighborhoods. [18]

While Walinsky says that "It is supremely necessary to change the conditions that are producing such cohorts," he continues by stating that "no matter what efforts we now undertake, we have already assured the creation of more very violent young men than any reasonable society can tolerate, and their numbers will grow inexorably for every one of the next twenty years."

Has Walinsky truly given up on this generation of disadvantaged young men when he states that "no matter what efforts we undertake" the numbers of "very violent" criminals "will grow inexorably"? Walinsky's solution is to massively increase the police force—by at least a half a million in the next five years and perhaps more after that. He states that this police force is not to imprison citizens but to "liberate" them. But is it really a foregone conclusion that all of these young people will turn to crime? Are there no other ways of intervening in their environment to avert the catastrophe Walinsky describes?

Those who focus on family structure rather than poverty, joblessness, grossly inadequate education, and the lack of community resources—all of which often lead to the despair, rage, and hopelessness that are so often the wellspring of crime—are promoting the view that having a single mother is virtually the only factor of importance shaping the attitudes, behavior, and well-being of young people. What is being neglected in these analyses is that profound changes in family structure do not simply spring up in societies at a certain time but are themselves the result of profound shifts in the broader social structure. The increase in the number of female-headed families is itself caused by social, economic, and political factors that may be key in understanding current social problems.

There is no question that the number of children living with one parent has risen sharply in the United States over the past quarter century. In 1970, 12 percent (11.9) of all children under the age of eighteen lived with one parent; by 1993, nearly 27 percent (26.7) were living with one parent and, as has been mentioned earlier, 87 percent of these young people were living with their mother. If we examine the data more closely we see that, in 1993, 77.2 percent of white children under age eighteen were living with two parents while 20.9 percent were living with one parent. Among children of Hispanic origin, 64.5 percent were living with two parents, 31.8 percent with one parent. The single-parent rate for black children was significantly higher than for either white or Hispanic children. Only 35.6 percent of black children lived with two parents in 1993, a significant decline from 1980 (42.2 percent) and 1970 (58.5 percent), while 57 percent of black children under age eighteen lived with one parent.[19]

But the rise in out-of-wedlock births and single-parent families is not a phenomenon limited to the United States; it is occurring in many parts of the world. The rise in the number of unmarried mothers is most dramatic in Northern and Western Europe as well as in the United States. Divorce rates are also rising rapidly in many other parts of the world. Thus, families in different cultures are changing in similar ways and we must look for structural causes and develop social policy measures that will strengthen all families.

Critics of AFDC and other social welfare programs claim that these very programs and the benefits they provide are the cause of the sharply escalating rate of single parenthood. They claim that the cushion provided by programs for the poor, as meager and tattered as it is, enables women to choose single parenthood and that only when that support is markedly diminished or totally with-

drawn will women choose childbearing within marriage and paid employment. There is, however, no evidence that AFDC payments are a cause of increased childbearing outside of marriage. As mentioned earlier, this issue will be discussed in far greater detail in subsequent chapters, but for now it is important to note that the recent rise in single parenthood has occurred over a period of time during which welfare payments have been sharply curtailed.

Several key demographic factors have contributed to the significant number of young people living with a single parent in the United States and in other countries: the current practice of delaying marriage, the increase in never-married households, and the divorce rate. The estimated median age of marriage has continued to rise over the past quarter century. In the United States in 1970, for example, the median age of marriage for women was 20.8 years and for men, 23.2 years. By 1993, the median age for women was 24.5 and for men, 26.5.[20] Marrying later combined with the earlier onset of menstruation and sexual activity puts unmarried young women at risk of becoming pregnant for several additional years. At the same time, the phenomenon of the never-married parent has been increasing significantly while the divorce rate has been leveling off. Between 1970 and 1981, for example, the percentage of children who lived with a divorced parent rose by 50 percent (from 30.2 to 43.8 percent) while the percentage living with a never-married parent more than doubled (from 6.8 to 15.2 percent). Between 1983 and 1993, the percentage of one-parent children living with a divorced parent declined from 42 to 37.1 percent, while the percentage living with a never-married parent continued to rise from 24 to 35 percent. In other words, a decade ago a child in a single-parent family was almost twice as likely to be living with a divorced parent as with a never-married parent; today a child is slightly more likely to be living with a divorced parent than a never-married parent.[21]

Many factors are responsible for the rise of never-married parents. Some of the key issues include the high divorce rate that peaked in 1981 and has made many young people wary of marriage; the increasing acceptability of having children outside of marriage; women's massive move into the paid labor force and their subsequent increased sense of independence; and the substantial decline in wages of millions of male workers.

While there is no doubt that the number of single-parent families, particularly mother-only families, has risen dramatically in recent years, the central question is what does this trend mean for women, for children, for families, and for American society? *Growing Up With a Single Parent: What Hurts, What Helps* by sociologists Sara McLanahan and Gary Sandefur attempts to explore this issue. The authors begin by stating their position clearly:

> *Children who grow up in a household with only one biological parent are worse off, on average, than children who grow up in a household with both of their biological parents, regardless of the parents' race or educational background, regardless of whether the parents are married when the child is born, and regardless of whether the resident parent remarries.*[22]

McLanahan and Sandefur point out that growing up without a father affects young people in a variety of ways. First, children from single-parent families do less well educationally and are approximately twice as likely to drop out of high school as are young people from two-parent families. Their grades and test scores are lower, their attendance poorer, and their expectations about college lower than that of their peers. Second, young people in one-parent families are less likely to find work in their late adolescent and young adult years. And third, growing up in what these authors term a "disrupted family" significantly increases a female's risk of becoming a teen mother. As the authors state, "Finishing school, finding a job, and starting a family are events that mark the transition from adolescence to adulthood."[23] Young people who have problems in these areas are clearly starting their adult years with a substantial handicap. But, as McLanahan and Sandefur also point out, these issues are often interrelated. Young people who leave school prematurely may well have difficulty finding work and those who have inadequate education and are "idle," to use the authors' term, may well look for gratification and a symbolic transition to adulthood through early childbearing. (Consider once again the use of language to communicate a

point of view. The term "idle" places the onus for lack of work on the individuals—implying they are lolling around the house and perhaps not actively seeking employment; the term "unemployed" or "jobless" implies at least in part a societal contribution to the young person's lack of employment— the recognition that perhaps suitable jobs may be in short supply.) The fact that problems in these three coming-of-age tasks are interconnected may be of greater significance than that each takes place more frequently in single-parent families.

McLanahan and Sandefur themselves stress that many of the disadvantages children of single-parent families experience are directly due to low income or, in the case of divorce, a sudden drop in income. Not only must single-parent families often survive on one salary rather than two but the mother's earning power is likely to be significantly less than the father's. Also, as the authors state, "When a father lives in a separate household, he is usually less committed to his child and less trusting of the child's mother. Hence he is less willing to invest time and money in the child's welfare."[24]

That single-parent families are frequently characterized by poverty, low income, or a sudden drop in income is intimately connected to educational achievement, job prospects, and early childbearing. Children from poor families are likely to attend grossly inadequate schools[25] (as Jonathan Kozol has made abundantly clear in his powerful book *Savage Inequalities: Children in America's Schools*), have few job opportunities, and are at greater risk for early childbearing than more affluent young people. Due to a drop in income, children of divorced parents may well need to move from a more affluent neighborhood, in which they had access to good schools, friends, and familiar faces and surroundings, to a school that is less adequate and a neighborhood that is new and strange. A disruption in the family often sets off a series of other disruptions for all of the family members that are frequently due to abrupt and profound changes in economic status.

Many authors who extol the two-parent family and blame most of the ills of society on the increase in single-parent families compare the problems of 1990s female-headed families with an idealized image of the ways in which families might function. McLanahan and Sandefur state,

When two biological parents share the same household, they can monitor the children and maintain parental control. . . . Having another parent around who cares about the child increases the likelihood that each parent will "do the right thing" even when otherwise inclined. In short, the two-parent family structure creates a system of checks and balances that both promotes parental responsibility and protects the child from parental neglect and, sometimes, abuse.[27]

The parenting McLanahan and Sandefur describe occurs in some families and there is no doubt that having two parents when they are both involved in parenting takes the burden off of each parent and gives the child more than one caregiver and role model. But what about the families in which the father is barely there—because of long hours of work, out-of-town travel, golf, or the notion that domestic affairs are best left to the mother? What about the family in which the father (or the mother) is alcoholic, or emotionally unavailable because of depression or disinterest? What about the family in which the father is frankly abusive—either physically or emotionally—to the mother and/or the children? Why should single-parent families be compared only to ideal two-parent families? McLanahan and Sandefur seem to assume, also, that only fathers can perform certain functions within the family. They state,

Clearly children whose fathers do not reside in the household are at great disadvantage relative to peers with fathers at home when it comes to finding a job, not only because they are less likely to know about job openings but also because they may not know how to apply for a job and how to conduct themselves during interviews.[27] [Emphasis added.]

Can only fathers help young people apply for jobs and tell them how to "conduct themselves during interviews?" This sounds strangely like a 1940s or 1950s image of the American family in which the mother donned an apron, baked pies, did spring cleaning, and was relatively unsophisticated about the world of work. Don't millions of women—particularly single women—have these skills today?

I am not suggesting that being a single parent is easy or, for that matter, that growing up in a single-

parent family doesn't require young people to deal with problems they might not face if they had two parents. What I am suggesting is that comparing the social, emotional, and economic status of single-parent families with idealized versions of two-parent families does not elucidate the issue.

Many of the problems these families, particularly families headed by women, face are due to low economic status, either chronic or sudden. They also suffer from other socially constructed disadvantages such as the gross inequality in the American educational system, a lack of decently paid jobs for those who wish to work, and a profound lack of community-based services that are necessary to families with two working parents and even more essential for single parents and their children. It is the many forms of discrimination based on gender and race, and the stigmatizing of single women and their children, that play a significant role in their economic, social, and psychological disadvantage.

What we are seeing here is strangely circular reasoning: Because women are disadvantaged in the labor force both in the types of jobs they hold and in their wages, because men often feel disconnected from their families and do not pay child support, because post-industrial societies have high rates of divorce that all too often leave mothers and children with insufficient resources, and because the United States has not established the widespread, first-rate services so necessary for families today, women are being blamed for the negative consequences of single parenthood. In other words, because American society has not adjusted to contemporary family patterns, to current economic realities, and to continuing racial, gender, and class inequities, single-parent families are suffering and women are being blamed—for making poor choices, for their children's problems, and indeed for many of the problems of American society. In some sense, women are being blamed because of massive "culture lag"—that is, many elements within American society refusing to adjust to the profound changes that have occurred during the second half of the twentieth century and instead attempting to revert to the norms, values, and patterns of earlier eras.

Many of these problems could have been and could still be addressed by American society, but perhaps one of the central functions of scapegoating individuals and/or groups such as single-parent families is to remove pressure from the society to adapt to present-day reality. In fact, rather than finding ways of helping parents cope with late-twentieth-century life, many leaders are trying to turn the clock back to the 1950s or even some earlier period, to the two-parent patriarchal model as the only legitimate family type.

It is clear that young women who have hopes and dreams and can see the possibility of achieving their goals are far less likely to bear children at an early age. It is clear that young men who have jobs and productive, connected roles in society are far more likely to form long-lasting familial relationships and to take seriously the social role of father. It is clear that if women earned a living wage and were at greater economic parity with male workers, their children—even if they lived in mother-only families—would suffer less economic disadvantage. And it is clear that if fathers were more strongly encouraged to provide child support and to remain a viable presence in their children's lives, the social, economic, and psychological costs of divorce, separation, and never-married parenting would be far less.

Politicians and policy makers need to recognize that the problems of American families are rooted in great part in the socioeconomic conditions of American life and that we as a society can change some of those conditions. If we want to make policy changes that will encourage parents to remain together, we can do so. And when parents choose not to live together, as millions will continue to do for a wide variety of reasons, we can make policy changes that will make life easier for single parents and their children.

Finally, what do those who so strongly deplore single parenthood feel should be done about the increasing number of children in one-parent families? Do they believe couples who have "irreconcilable differences" should remain together "for the sake of the children"? Do they feel women should remain in marriages because their jobs do not pay a living wage? Do they believe women who are battered and abused should remain in abusive relationships because children of single parents seem to do less well in a variety of ways? Or do they believe, as the Puritans of Massachusetts did some 350 years ago, that single mothers and their children should be stigmatized and shunned, thus guaranteeing that they will suffer still further from their single parenthood?

And what of women who have not found an appropriate mate? Must they remain childless? What of women who choose careers with long periods of training and then find that the eligible men are taken? Must they remain childless? What of gay and lesbian adults who want to love and nurture a child? Must they forsake the parenting experience? And what of poor women whose male acquaintances have few job prospects and therefore may make unstable partners? Or black women who have long recognized that far too many black men are chronically unemployed, in jail, or victims of drug and/or alcohol abuse? Must these women take on the responsibility of caring for these men or forsake motherhood? What indeed are the repercussions of establishing the two-parent, heterosexual couple as the only legitimate model of parenthood?

In a recent article, sociologists Christopher Jencks and Kathryn Edin have raised the important question "Do Poor Women Have a Right to Bear Children?" As they point out, in discussing the need to revamp AFDC the Clinton Administration stated that their plan "signals that people should not have children until they are ready to support them." But as Jencks and Edin state, ". . . for many poor women, that time will never come. Sad to say, there are neither enough good jobs nor enough good husbands to provide every American woman with enough money to support a family."[28] In our zeal to discourage single parenting, particularly single parenting among poor women, are we in reality trying to limit the reproduction of low-income women? Is this a legitimate goal of social policy?

Jencks and Edin spell out three commonly heard "fairy tales" about single motherhood and poverty.

> *Fairy Tale #1: "If teen mothers simply held off parenthood until their twenties, they would have enough money to raise a family." Fairy Tale #2: "If single mothers got married they wouldn't need welfare." Fairy Tale #3: "If teen mothers finished high school before having kids, they could get good jobs."* [29]

Jencks and Edin go on to point out the fallacies of each "fairy tale": that delaying childbearing is an extremely complex issue and that teenage pregnancy is driven by many factors, such as poor education and troubled homes, over which young women have no control; that there are not enough men who earn a living wage to go around and that "marrying a man with an unstable work history or low wages is not a good formula for avoiding welfare"; and that finishing high school is no guarantee of a job that will enable a single mother to "make ends meet" and, in fact, "only a minority [of American women] can support children on their earnings alone."[30]

Jencks and Edin correctly point out that many critics of AFDC, including many politicians, would like to "prevent the poor from having children." Andrew Hacker suggests that the campaign to curtail the number of children poor people have is in reality a campaign to curtail black births. Many of those most vociferous about the damaging impact of the poor on their own children and on the wider society think that "most welfare recipients are irresponsible or incompetent parents living in communities that breed lawlessness and promiscuity. Perhaps equally important, they think of welfare recipients as black idlers who live off the labor of industrious whites."[31] Do these policy makers want to prevent the so-called "underclass" from reproducing? But the issue is more complex than those who claim that the poor are the root of all evil would have us believe. Nearly half the children receiving AFDC in any month were born to parents who were married and supporting themselves at the time of the child's birth. Do they want to prevent these couples from bearing children too? And if this is their strategy, how does it jibe with the rhetoric of diminishing the role of government in the lives of the American people?

Notes

1. Rush Limbaugh, T.V., February 23, 1994, quoted in "Big Fat Lies," *Mother Jones*, May/June 1995, 39.

2. Nathaniel Hawthorne, *The Scarlet Letter* (New York: Penguin, 1986), 77, 81.

3. Ibid., 89.

4. Ibid., 82.

5. Ibid., 89.

6. Ibid., 90.

7. Robert Pear, "Dole Courts Conservatives with Changes on Welfare," *New York Times*, August 10, 1995.

8. Lisa Schiffren, "Penalize the Unwed Dad? Fat Chance." *New York Times*, August 10, 1995.

9. Arlene F. Saluter, *Marital Status and Living Arrangements: March 1993*, U.S. Bureau of the Census, Current Population Reports, Series P20–478, U.S. Government Printing Office, Washington, D.C., 1994, XI.

10. Robin L. Jarrett, "Living Poor: Family Life Among Single Parent, African-American Women," *Social Problems*, Vol. 1, No. 1, February 1994: 30–49.

11. Sue Woodman, "How Teen Pregnancy Has Become a Political Football," *Ms.*, January/February 1995, 90–92.

12. Barbara Dafoe Whitehead, "Dan Quayle Was Right," *Atlantic Monthly*, April 1993, 47–84.

13. Ibid.

14. David Blankenhorn, *Fatherless America: Confronting Our Most Urgent Social Problem* (New York: Basic, 1995), 2.

15. Ibid., 2.

16. Senator Bill Bradley, Speech on Violence in America, National Press Club, Washington, D.C., May 11, 1994.

17. Adam Walinsky, "The Crisis of Public Order," *Atlantic Monthly*, July 1995, 39–54.

18. Ibid.

19. Arlene F. Saluter, *Marital Status and Living Arrangements*.

20. Ibid., VII.

21. Ibid., XII.

22. Sara McLanahan and Gary Sandefur, *Growing Up with a Single Parent* (Cambridge, Mass.: Harvard University Press, 1994), 1.

23. Ibid., 39.

24. Ibid., 3.

25. Jonathan Kozol, *Savage Inequalities: Children in America's Schools* (New York: HarperCollins, 1992).

26. McLanahan and Sandefur, *Growing Up with a Single Parent*, 28.

27. Ibid., 35.

28. Christopher Jencks and Kathryn Edin, "Do Poor Women Have a Right to Bear Children?" *The American Prospect*, Winter 1995, 43–52.

29. Ibid.

30. Ibid.

31. Andrew Hacker, "The Crackdown on African-Americans," *The Nation*, July 10, 1995, 45–49.

Women and the American Economy

Elyce J. Rotella

Elyce J. Rotella is Professor of Economics at Indiana University. She was educated at the University of Pittsburgh and the University of Pennsylvania where she received her Ph.D. in economic history. Her research includes work on the growth of women's participation in the U.S. labor force, on clerical workers and school teachers, on the economics of marriage and divorce, on the determinants of urban mortality decline, and on the history of borrowing and saving. Among her published work is the book From Home to Office: U.S. Women at Work, 1870–1930. *She has taught courses that focus on the role of women in the U.S. economy at the University of Pennsylvania, San Diego State University, Tufts University, and Indiana University. In 1998/99, she held the Fulbright Chair in North American Studies at Uppsala University in Sweden.*

In this selection, Rotella explains concepts necessary to analyze women's position in the American economy and details some information on women's present condition and status.

ANY ECONOMY, NO MATTER HOW it is organized, must decide how the resources of the society will be used to produce the goods and services that the members of the society consume. A large portion of the productive resources of any society consists of the labor power of people. Therefore, the amounts and kinds of work that people do is of fundamental interest to anyone trying to understand an economy, and for that reason, economists and other social scientists have long been interested in the ways that tasks are divided among the members of society. There are many reasons for the division of labor among individuals. The most obvious reasons are differences in interest, ability, and acquired skills. If all people were equally able to obtain all kinds of training, we expect that persons would choose tasks

simply according to their interests, abilities, and the remuneration offered. However, we know that in reality, people's choices are limited in a number of ways. For example, some people are expected to follow in their parents' footsteps; some very able people do not go to college or receive other kinds of training because their families are poor; and some people's choices are limited by the expectations society has of the proper roles for them to play.

Both women's and men's choices are limited by sex roles. In all societies, sex is an important determinant of the division of tasks. It is common for people to believe that the sexual division of labor that prevails in their own society is natural and is determined by the biological differences between the sexes. However, there is actually considerable variation among societies in the tasks that are assigned to females and males. For example, farming is thought to be men's work in Western European societies, but in much of Africa, farming was traditionally done by women. One set of tasks that virtually all societies have assigned to women is the care of young children, although there are cultures in which it is customary for men to be quite involved in child rearing.

In this paper, we focus on the economic roles that women play in American society now and in the late twentieth century. Although much of what will be said can also be applied to women in the rest of the world, it should be kept in mind that there are important differences between cultures in the sexual division of labor. In addition, the sexual division of labor has changed considerably over time, so that there are some tasks women frequently perform today that it would have been unthinkable for them to perform in the past.

THE ECONOMIC SYSTEM

Everyone in the economic system plays two basic roles—producer and consumer. People fulfill their

Elyce J. Rotella, "Women and the American Economy" was written expressly for *Issues in Feminism*, 5th edition.

producer role by using the resources they control to make goods and provide services. For most people, their most important productive resource is labor power, and they sell their labor to businesses or agencies that organize the production of goods and services sold in the market. In exchange for their labor, people receive income in the form of wage earnings, which then makes it possible for them to fulfill their other basic economic role, that of consumer. In an advanced market economy, such as the modern U.S. economy, a very large proportion of goods and services produced are sold in markets. This differs from the situation in subsistence economies where most people consume the things they produce themselves and few goods are traded in markets.

Consumers use their earnings to purchase the goods and services they need and want. Clearly, those people who receive the highest earnings in exchange for their labor are able to enjoy the consumption of the largest amounts of goods and services. In addition to spending the earnings that they receive in exchange for their own resources, some people are able to consume more market goods and services because they can use the earned income of others. For example, children are able to consume because of their parents' earnings, and full-time housewives (who work but do not receive a paycheck) consume market goods and services on the basis of their husbands' earnings.

In this paper, we will mostly be examining women's roles as producers in the American economy, but we must keep in mind the close connection that exists among production, earnings, and consumption.

THE CHANGING PARTICIPATION OF WOMEN IN THE U.S. LABOR FORCE

Women may use all of their labor power to work in their homes producing goods and services for themselves and their families. In this case, they do not receive a money wage directly in exchange for their labor. In order to consume market goods and services, they must be able to use the income earned by someone else, usually other family members. Such women are full-time homemakers, and they are fulfilling the economic role that many in our

TABLE 1 Women's Labor Force Participation Rate and Women's Share of the Labor Force

Year	(1) Women's Labor Force Participation Rate[a]	(2) Women's Share of the Labor Force[b]
1900	20.0	18.1
1920	22.7	20.4
1930	23.6	21.9
1940	27.9	25.2
1950	33.9 (men = 86.8)	28.8
1960	37.7	33.4
1970	43.3	38.1
1980	51.5	42.6
1990	57.5	44.9
1995	58.9	46.1
1999	60.0 (men = 74.7)	46.5
2006 (projected)	61.4	47.4

[a] Women's labor force participation rate = $\dfrac{\text{women in the labor force}}{\text{women in the population}}$

[b] Women's share of the labor force = $\dfrac{\text{women in the labor force}}{\text{total labor force}}$

Sources: U.S. Department of Commerce, Bureau of the Census, *Historical Statistics of the United States, Colonial Times to 1970* (1975), pp. 131–132; U.S. Department of Commerce, Bureau of the Census, *Statistical Abstract of the United States, 1999*, p. 411; U.S. Department of Labor, Bureau of Labor Statistics, *Labor Force Statistics from the Current Population Survey*, Series ID: LFU600002, www.dol.gov

culture have considered to be the preferred and "natural" role for married women.

Many other women work for pay, that is, they exchange their labor services for a money wage in the market. Women who work for pay or who are looking for a paying job are said to be members of the labor force. The proportion of all women who are members of the labor force is called the female labor force participation rate.

Column (1) in Table 1 shows how the female labor force participation rate has changed over this century. We can see that in 1900, only 20 percent of all women were at work for pay and that by 1999, 60 percent of all women were in the labor force. This rise in the proportion of all women who work for pay is one of the most dramatic changes that have taken place in the U.S. economy in this century. At the same time, men's labor force participation has been declining largely because of the increased frequency of retirement of older workers. As a result of the rising participation by women and falling participation by men, women are now over 46 percent of the U.S. labor force, and gender differences in labor market experience are smaller than they have ever been.

Although female labor force participation has increased throughout this century, the rate of increase has not been the same in all time periods. The increase was fairly slow until 1940. The period of the Second World War saw a rapid, but temporary, movement of women into the labor force. Right after the war, many women left the labor force. Some left voluntarily, and others were forced out of jobs that were reclaimed by men. By the late 1940s, women's labor force participation was again growing but at a more rapid pace than in the earlier years of the century. Since 1960, the growth of women's labor force participation has been extremely rapid, with the most dramatic increase coming in the 1970s. In the 1990s, we saw a marked slowdown in the rate of increase in women's labor force participation. This slowdown has caused a great deal of comment and debate, with some arguing women's labor force participation rate is nearing its maximum and will grow little in the future. Certainly the rapid increases of the past could not be sustained after we reached a point where the great majority of women were already in the labor force. The U.S. Bureau of Labor Statistics projects that women's labor force participation will continue to grow in the future but at a slower rate than in the past. The projection for 2006 is shown in Table 1.

Column (2) in Table 1 shows how women's share of the total labor force has changed. In 1900, only 18 of every 100 paid workers were women. In 1998, women made up 46.5 percent of the American labor force, and this number is still rising. Clearly then, paid employment is much more important in the lives of American women today than it was in the past, and women are more important in the labor force.

This dramatic increase in women's participation in the labor force has caused economists to investigate the factors that affect women's decisions about how to structure their work lives. Marital status and family responsibilities have been found to have an important effect, but this effect had declined over time. Table 2 shows participation rates by marital status for selected years since 1950; and for married women, it shows the effect of the presence of children in the home. Participation by single (never married) and divorced women is higher than that of married women. Although work force participation by women in all marital status groups has increased, the most notable increases are those of married women (husband present). Since the great majority of American women marry (only 6 percent of women aged 55 to 64 in 1998 had never been married), it is these women whose actions dominate the female work force and who have been responsible for the bulk of the female labor force growth since the Second World War. Some of the increase in participation has also been due to the rise in the proportion of women who are not currently married because of the high divorce rate and because of the recent trend toward later marriage for women. The bottom panel of Table 2 shows the rise in the proportion of divorced and single women and the corresponding decline in the proportion married. So, we can say that the rise in female labor force participation is due both to increased participation by married women and to the fact that fewer women are married.

Since married women are usually expected to bear the primary responsibility for housework and child care, it is not surprising that being married and having children reduces the likelihood that women work for pay. When such women do work in the market, they generally assume the "double burden" of working at a paid job while maintaining nearly complete responsibility for home work. Recent surveys show that husbands' help with housework does not increase substantially when their wives are employed. It is interesting (and perhaps surprising) to see that, even in the face of this "double burden," labor force participation by married women with children is rising very rapidly. Indeed, the greatest increases are occurring among women with young children. In 1960, only 18.6 percent of married women with children under age six were in the labor force; in 1998, this figure was 63.7 percent, an increase of well over threefold. In 1970, 24 percent of all married mothers with children one year old or younger were in the labor force. Just 28

**TABLE 2 Women's Labor Force Participation Rate
by Marital Status and Presence of Children**

Category	1960	1970	1980	1990	1998
Single (never married)	58.6	56.8	64.4	66.9	68.5
Widowed, divorced or separated	41.6	40.3	43.6	47.2	48.8
Divorced	NA	71.5	74.5	NA	NA
Married (husband present)	31.9	40.5	49.9	58.4	61.2
Married (husband present)					
With children 6 to 17 only	39.0	49.2	61.7	73.6	76.8
With children under 6	18.6	30.3	45.1	58.9	63.7
With children under 3	15.3	25.8	41.5	55.5	61.4
With children 1 or under	NA	24.0	39.0	53.9	61.8

Percentage of Women (Age 18 and Over) in Various Marital Status Groups

Category	1960	1970	1980	1990	1998
Single	11.9	13.7	17.1	18.9	20.5
Widowed		13.9	12.8	12.1	10.8
Divorced		3.9	7.1	9.3	10.8
Married		68.5	63.0	59.7	57.9

Sources: U.S. Department of Commerce, Bureau of the Census, *Statistical Abstract of the United States, 1999*, pp. 57, 416–417; *Statistical Abstract of the United States, 1978*, pp. 38, 40. Howard Hayghe, "Rise in Mothers' Labor Force Activity Includes Those with Infants," *Monthly Labor Review* (February 1986), p. 45.

years later, nearly 62 percent of mothers of very young children are labor force participants.

Certainly then, the last half century has seen dramatic changes in the ways that women organize their work lives. We now have a very different pattern of labor force attachment over the life cycle than we had only 30 years ago. Huge changes in labor force participation by age are pictured in Figure 1. A great deal of information is contained in Figure 1, and it deserves careful study. The solid lines show the variation in women's labor force participation by age for various cross sections. A cross section shows behavior by different groups of women at the same date. To see how to understand the graph, let's look at the 1970 cross section, which shows high labor force participation (58 percent) by women in their early 20s, considerably lower participation by women in their mid-20s to mid-30s (45 percent), and then higher participation by older women, with 55 percent of 45- to 49-year-olds in the labor force. Taken together, the solid lines in Figure

1 show enormous changes in labor force behavior by women in all age groups, with the most dramatic increases taking place among women in the ages when household demands are likely to be the greatest. For women ages 25 to 29, labor force participation was 45 percent in 1970 and 77 percent in 1999. In 1999, labor force participation was over 75 percent for all women between the ages of 25 and 49, and the variation by age that we saw in earlier cross sections is nearly gone.

As interesting as is the information presented by the solid lines in Figure 1, we can get more insight into the lives of women by looking at the dashed lines. These lines show the experience of specific groups of women as they age. The dashed lines show the experience of birth cohorts, that is, women who were born at the same time. For example, if we look at the line labeled Cohort III, we see the experience of women born between 1951 and 1955. They were ages 20 to 24 in 1975 and ages 25 to 29 in 1980. These women increased their participation as they

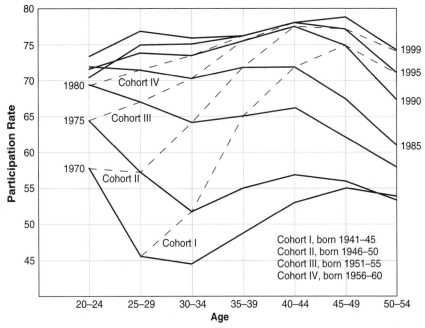

FIGURE 1 Female Labor Force Participation by Age, 1970–1999. **Sources:** U.S. Department of Labor, Bureau of Labor Statistics, *Employment and Earnings,* January 1971, p. 116; January 1976, p. 135; January 1981, p. 165; January 1986, p. 154; January 1991, p. 164; January 1996, p. 106; January 2000, p. 168.

aged (64 percent were in the labor force when they were 20 to 24; 67 percent when they were 25 to 29; 70 percent when they were 30 to 34; 76 percent when they were 35 to 39; 78 percent when they were 40 to 44, and 79 percent when they were 45 to 49).

When we examine cohorts, we get a very different picture of women's behavior than the one we see in the cross sections. Cross sections before 1990 seem to suggest that the typical woman joined the labor force while young, dropped out during the years when she had the heaviest home duties, and then rejoined the labor force when her children were older. Many people, including many employers, still believe that this is the typical pattern of women's labor force behavior. But they are wrong. By looking at the cohorts, we can see that, although some women undoubtedly followed this pattern, it was not the norm and has not been the norm for a long time. The dashed lines rise for every cohort born after the Second World War, showing that more women joined the labor force as they aged.

If we had been around in 1970 and wanted to predict the future participation of women who were ages 25 to 29, we probably would have looked at the current behavior of 30- to 34-year-old women and predicted a slight decline in participation as the 25- to 29-year-old women aged. How wrong we would have been! Look at Cohort I to see that in fact more of these women joined the labor force as they aged; they went from a labor force participation rate of 45 percent at ages 25 to 29 to 52 percent at ages 30 to 34. In fact, we would have been very wrong if we had followed this strategy for almost any age group at any date. To take one other notable example, look at women who were ages 25 to 29 in 1975 (Cohort II, the early baby boom cohort born between 1946 and 1950). These women were ages 30 to 34 in 1980. They had dramatically higher rates of labor force participation when they were 30 to 34 than they had when they were younger. And they continued to increase their participation as they aged to reach a participation rate of 77 percent in 1995 when they were 45 to 49. Suppose that these women had been forming their expectations of their own futures by looking at the lives of their older contemporaries. They would have formed very erroneous expectations.

Look again at Figure 1, this time focusing on the most recent cross sections (1990, 1995, and 1999). We see that labor force participation is high for women in all age groups. Now the differences between cross sections and cohorts is small. To keep the graph from becoming too complicated, the recent cohorts are not drawn in. We have come through the period of revolutionary change in women's behavior and now live in a United States in which the typical pattern is for women to join the labor force while young and maintain continuous attachment throughout their adult lives until retirement. Certainly, some women will still take on the full-time housewife role and live most of their adult lives outside the paid labor force. And some women will withdraw from the labor force for a period when home demands on their time are heaviest. But, the most common pattern for women is continuous labor force attachment. And this pattern is well established so that now most young women expect to spend their entire adult lives in the labor force and therefore make plans to acquire the skills appropriate to a lifetime of market work. These higher levels of education and work experience have resulted in higher wages for women.

THE DIVISION OF WOMEN'S LABOR BETWEEN THE HOME AND THE MARKET: EXPLANATIONS AND IMPLICATIONS

We can gain understanding of the rise in women's labor force participation by focusing on the process through which people make decisions about how to use their time. For everyone, time is a scarce resource, and we must all decide how to allocate our time among the various things that we would like to do. Everyone must spend time every day in sleep and in essential body maintenance functions. Beyond this, we can decide to use our time for work or for leisure. All people (except workaholics) enjoy leisure and hope to have some leisure time each day. The time that we choose to work can be spent either working for pay or working in situations in which

we are not paid for our labor. If we work for pay, we receive earnings that allow us to enjoy consumption of goods and services bought in the market. If we engage in unpaid work, we produce goods and services that we ourselves or someone else consumes. Most unpaid work takes place in the home (dish washing, gardening, child care, and so on), but a substantial amount of unpaid work (for example, volunteer work) is also performed in other settings. Everyone, of course, performs some unpaid work in the home, so everyone must decide how to allocate their work time between paid work and unpaid work. However, since women are expected to be the major producers of goods and services in the home, the decision of dividing time between work at home and work in the market is particularly important for them.

Throughout this century the wages that women can earn in the labor force have increased, and this increase is a major factor that has been shown to be crucial for explaining women's decisions about allocating time to paid work versus unpaid work. When the wage that a woman can earn by being in the labor force increases, the cost to her and her family of having her stay out of the labor force and work at home to produce goods and services for the family to consume will also increase. For example, if a woman could earn $1,000 per week by working as an engineer, she and her family would have to give up $1,000 per week if she stays at home to be a full-time homemaker. And if her potential earnings increase by $100 per week, the cost of staying home rises accordingly. Clearly then, the incentive for a woman to go into the labor force will increase when her market wage increases, and women with high potential wages will be less likely to be full-time homemakers. This is a large part of the reason why women who have high levels of education are much more likely to be in the labor force. Nearly 83 percent of women college graduates are in the labor force compared with 71 percent of high school graduates and 50 percent of those with less than a high school education. Educated women have higher potential earnings, and they can find more pleasant and fulfilling jobs.

As women increase their time in market work and reduce their time in home work, they substitute products they buy in the market for some of the goods and services they might have produced at home. This means that earning women and their families are more likely to eat in restaurants, to send out clothes to laundries, and to use institutional child care and baby-sitters. It is not, however, possible to substitute purchased products for all home production. Therefore, studies have found that women who have the "double burden" of being homemakers and wage earners work more (and sleep fewer) hours per week than any other group in society.

The rise over time in women's wages and in women's labor force participation has a number of implications for the institutions of marriage and the family. In the traditional marriage common in Western cultures, the division of labor has been between the breadwinner husband and the homemaker wife. The husband specialized in paid market work, and the wife specialized in unpaid home work. In this arrangement, the wife was dependent on her husband's earnings to be able to consume market goods and services, and a woman who was concerned with her economic well-being had to be careful to choose a husband with good earning potential. An old joke about searching for a mate says that men seek a "sex object" while women seek a "success object." As more women work in the market and command higher wages, the dependency of wives on their husbands' earnings lessens, with the result that more women choose to marry later, and some may choose not to marry at all. Women with unhappy marriages are more likely to divorce if they can earn their own income.

In the last three decades, we have seen many changes in the marriage behavior of Americans— the kinds of changes that we would expect to result from greater female labor force participation. Overall, women are marrying later; the median age at first marriage for women has risen from 20.3 in 1960 to 25 in 1998. It is quite possible that a substantial number of women may not marry at all; the proportion of women ages 25 to 29 who had never married rose from 10.5 percent in 1970 to 51 percent in 1998. The divorce rate has doubled since 1960. In addition to its implications for the incidence of marriage, we might expect that greater economic independence for women will have implications for courtship and the nature of the marriage relation as well. As they are more able to provide for themselves, women who wish to marry search longer for the ideal mate and are freer to choose husbands on the basis of

affection and attraction rather than on the basis of men's potential as income providers. Perhaps these marriages will be more satisfying to both partners.

The analysis that stresses the increasing value of women's market time (that is, rising wages) also has implications for the decisions that people make about how many children to have. As women's potential market wage rises, the opportunity cost of their time spent in household duties rises. Therefore, the cost to families of having children to care for goes up if the mother is to stay at home to provide child care instead of working for pay. This leads to the incentive to have smaller families and is undoubtedly part of the reason for the low fertility of American women.

The explanation offered above for increased labor force participation by American women emphasizes the central role played by the rising market value of women's time. As women's market wages have risen, women have responded by reallocating time from nonmarket uses to market work. As powerful as this explanation is, we must not lose sight of the fact that women take jobs for the same reasons that men take jobs—they need money to support themselves and their families. Many employed women are married to men who earn low wages, and these women's earnings often make the difference between the family living below or above the poverty level. Earnings of families in which both husband and wife are employed full time are 60 percent higher on average than in families where only the husband is employed. As more and more families choose to send the wife into the labor force in pursuit of this higher income, the "Leave It to Beaver" family with a stay-at-home mother has become increasingly rare. Among all husband-wife families, only 19 percent have the husband as the only earner in the family.

As important as are women's earnings for husband-wife families, they are much more crucial for nonmarried women, especially for the rapidly growing number of nonmarried women who are supporting children. In 1998, nearly 47 percent of all employed women did not have husbands (that is, they were single, widowed, divorced, or married with an absent husband). Most of these women were dependent on themselves alone for financial support. In addition, many of these women were heads of families and used their earnings to support children. In the last 30 years, there has been a dramatic increase in the incidence of divorce in the United States. Although the divorce rate is no longer rising, it remains high so that more than half of all marriages are predicted to end in divorce. The greater prevalence of divorce has led to increased participation by women in the labor force through two avenues. First, divorced women have very high rates of labor force participation. This is because most divorced women bear almost complete responsibility for supporting themselves and their dependent children. Divorce commonly leads to substantially lower economic status for women and their children. In these days of no-fault divorce, alimony is rare—under 4 percent of divorced women are awarded alimony. Child support awards are more common but are far from universal, often hard to collect, and generally cover only a portion of a child's needs. In 1995, 61 percent of women with children of absent fathers had been awarded child support. Of the women who were supposed to receive child support payments in that year, only 40 percent received the full payment, and 30 percent received no child support payments at all. The average child support payment was $3,767 per woman. Clearly divorced women need to be in the labor force to support themselves and their children.

The prevalence of divorce also raises female labor force participation through a second avenue. It gives married women a strong incentive to maintain their attachments to the labor force and therefore their future earning potential. Since so many women will find themselves completely dependent on their own earnings in the future, they find it wise to insure themselves against a low postmarital living standard by remaining in the labor force while married.

In the past, there was a strong inverse relationship between a husband's earnings and a wife's labor force participation. Women with high-earning husbands were much less likely to work for pay than were women who were married to men with lower earnings. Since 1960, this association has been weakening as more highly educated women (who are usually married to high-earning men) enter the labor force. At present, there is no consistent relationship between a husband's earnings and a wife's likelihood of employment. From this we can conclude that married women are more responsive to the positive effects of their own wages, which tend to pull them into the work force, than they are to the negative effects of their husbands' earnings, which in the past tended to keep them at home.

WOMEN'S EARNINGS

We have seen that women's earnings are an important factor affecting the decision of how women allocate their time between work at home and work for pay in the market. Women's earnings have increased over time, which has pulled them into the labor force. In this section, we turn our attention to the determinants of women's earnings and to the gap in earnings between women and men. The earnings of all American workers, males and females, have increased greatly in this century, reflecting the greater productivity of workers. These productivity increases reflect advances in production technology and the higher skill and education levels of workers.

Figure 2 shows what has happened to the gap between women's and men's earnings in the period since 1960. The graph pictures the earnings ratio, which is calculated as the median earnings of year-round, full-time employed women divided by the median earnings of year-round, full-time employed men. We see that from 1960 to 1980, the gap between the earnings of women and men did not change much, remaining around 60 percent. This is followed by the striking rise in the earnings ratio (narrowing in the earnings gap) that took place from 1980 to the mid-1990s. In 1998, women earned on average 74 percent of the earnings of men. Over the entire period since 1960 covered in Figure 2, the earnings of both women and men increased, but the earnings of women increased far faster. Since the 1970s, men's wages have grown very little, while women's wages continue to increase.

Why do women workers earn less than men? And how can we explain changes in the earnings gap over time, both the post-1980 dramatic narrowing and the lack of change that preceded it? Some of the difference between the annual earnings of women and men is due to the fact that more women work part time and part year. In 1998, 71 percent of employed women worked at full-time jobs compared with 87 percent of men. However, since Fig-

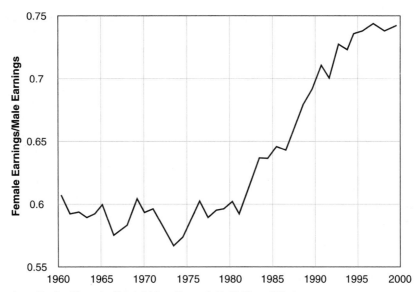

FIGURE 2 Earnings Ratio (Female/Male) Year-Round, Full-Time Workers. **Sources:** U.S. Department of Commerce, Bureau of the Census, "Historical Income Tables—People: Table P-36, Full-Time, Year-Round Workers (All Races) by Median Income and Sex: 1970–1998" (online). Available on www.census.gov

ure 2 compares only the earnings of full-year, full-time workers, we have already controlled for this factor. What we cannot control for is that men who work full time work on average longer hours than do women (44 compared with 41 hours).

In general, economists think that the wages workers receive are related to their productivity. It is not surprising that highly productive workers in skilled jobs receive higher earnings than do less productive workers. We do not usually have accurate direct data on individual worker's productivity, but we have expectations about the qualities that cause workers to be more productive. Education, job training, and experience on the job should lead to higher productivity and therefore to higher earnings. The gap between women's and men's earnings could reflect a gap between women's and men's productivities. The attempt to explain the earnings gap by looking at differences between men and women in education, training, and experience is called the *human capital approach.*

The human capital approach offers some powerful explanations of the pattern of the earnings gap over time. A part of the earnings gap reflects the

fact that some women have lower levels of education and work experience than do men. Until recently, men were more likely to attend college and receive education and training beyond the college level, and there were substantial sex differences in the kinds of postsecondary training received. As important as sex differences in education and training are differences in work experience. Women's lower levels of labor force participation meant that they had lower levels of market experience. Since employers reward education, training, and experience by higher earnings, some of the earnings gap reflects these differences. Although there is more to explaining the earnings gap than just sex differences in education, training, and experience, we can get insight into the changing size of the earnings gap by focusing on these factors. By looking at Figure 2, one can see that during the 1950s, '60s, and '70s, there were periods when the earnings gap widened. This was caused in part by the rapidly increasing participation by women who were new entrants (or reentrants) into the labor force. A large percentage of these women had low levels of prior experience. Many were older women with comparatively low levels of education who were either joining the labor force for the first time or reentering the labor force after a long absence. Such women commonly had low levels of experience and commanded low wages. Since there were so many of them in the labor force, they pulled down women's average earnings.

We can also understand the narrowing of the earnings gap in the 1980s and '90s as being caused partly by the changing human capital characteristics of women workers. Women's educational levels have been rising steadily and more rapidly than men's. Women now earn over 55 percent of bachelor's degrees awarded by American colleges and universities, up from 43 percent in 1971. Beginning in the 1970s, there was considerable change in the kinds of schooling that women got, with many more women educating themselves for employment in nontraditional fields and attending graduate and professional schools. For example, women received 49 percent of the bachelor's degrees in business and management awarded in 1996 compared with under 9 percent in 1970, 16 percent of engineering degrees compared with under 1 percent in 1970, and 41 percent of MD degrees compared with 8 percent in 1970. This rise in women's education has been accompanied by a rise in women's experience levels. As we saw in Figure 1, the period since 1970 has seen rapidly increasing labor force participation by women in their 20s and 30s. What happened was that a growing number of women joined the labor force when young and maintained their attachment while they married and had children. This pattern, common to men, produced a large number of young and middle-aged women with experience levels as high as men of the same age. The rapid rise in women's earnings in the 1980s and '90s reflects this rise in education and experience.

Researchers have tried to calculate how much of the earnings gap can be explained by the human capital approach by comparing the earnings of women and men who have the same education and experience. What they have found is that some of the difference in earnings can be explained by differences in education and experience, but a substantial portion remains unexplained. Even when we compare the earnings of women and men in the same occupational categories, we find that a gap persists.

Most researchers conclude that the part of the earnings gap that cannot be attributed to human capital differences results from discrimination against women in the labor market. Discrimination can take a number of different forms. When women are paid less than equally productive men, they are being discriminated against. When women are excluded from some jobs or training so that they must work in jobs in which their productivity is not as high as it might be, their earnings are lowered due to discrimination. Sometimes employers assume that all women have the same characteristics and make employment decisions about individual women based on the expected average attributes of women as a group. For example, employers may believe that all women will have high labor market turnover because some women drop out of the labor force to fulfill household responsibilities. In such cases, the women who are judged by the expected group characteristics rather than by their own individual characteristics are said to be victims of statistical discrimination.

In most studies, discrimination has been found to be responsible for half or more of the earnings gap. However, the major form that discrimination takes is not "unequal pay for equal work," though there are many cases of women receiving lower pay for doing substantially the same work as men. The biggest cause of the earnings gap and the major form of discrimination against women is that women and men are, by and large, employed in different occupations, and the pay in women's occupations is lower than the pay in men's occupations.

THE SEX DISTRIBUTION OF OCCUPATIONS

In Table 3, we see how women and men workers are distributed among the major occupational categories of the U.S. labor force. Even at the high level of aggregation of these data, there are striking differences in the distributions. Close to 25 percent of all female workers were in administrative support jobs (mostly clerical) compared with 5.6 percent of men. Nearly 19 percent of men, but only 2 percent of women, were precision production, craft, and repair (skilled blue collar) workers. Much higher proportions of women than men were employed as private household workers and as other service

TABLE 3 Occupational Distribution of Females and Males

Occupational group	Percentage of Labor Force in Group, 1998		Percentage of Females	
	Females	Males	1998	1983
Executive, administrative, managerial	15.3	13.7	49.0	40.9
Professional specialty	17.4	13.1	53.3	48.1
Engineers			11.1	5.8
Teachers, college and university			42.3	36.3
Teachers, except college and university			75.3	70.9
Lawyers and judges			28.6	15.8
Dentists			19.8	6.7
Physicians			26.6	15.8
Nurses			92.5	95.8
Pharmacists			44.0	26.7
Technicians and related support	3.7	2.8	53.6	48.2
Sales occupations	13.1	11.1	50.3	47.5
Administrative support, including clerical	23.8	5.6	78.6	79.9
Secretaries, stenographers and typists			97.6	98.2
Private household workers	1.3	0.1	94.6	96.1
Child care workers			96.5	96.9
Protective service workers	0.7	2.8	17.8	12.8
Other service workers	15.5	7.3	64.4	64.0
Precision production, craft, repair	2.0	18.7	8.3	8.1
Construction trades			2.0	1.8
Machine operators, assemblers, inspectors	4.8	6.9	37.3	42.1
Transportation and material moving	0.9	6.8	10.2	7.8
Truck drivers			5.3	3.1
Handlers, equipment cleaners, helpers, laborers	1.7	5.6	20.3	16.8
Farming and forestry	1.1	3.9	19.1	16.2
TOTAL	100.0	100.0	46.2	47.3

Source: U.S. Department of Commerce. Bureau of the Census, *Statistical Abstract of the United States, 1999*, pp. 424–426.

workers. In the professional and technical fields, where the figures for females and males are more similar, the degree of aggregation in the data hides the substantial differences that actually exist because a large proportion of female professionals are teachers, nurses, librarians, and social workers, whereas male professionals are in a much broader mix of fields.

When we look at occupational breakdowns of the U.S. labor force that are more detailed than the breakdown in Table 3, we see even greater disparity between women's and men's jobs. Women's employment is concentrated in a much smaller number of occupations than is men's employment. Not only are women workers concentrated in a fairly small number of jobs, but many of the jobs that women hold are held almost exclusively by women. That is, the occupational structure is highly segregated by sex, with many women being employed in jobs in which the overwhelming majority of workers are women. We can get some sense of this by looking at the few detailed occupations listed in Table 3 and by concentrating on the last two columns, which show the percentage of all workers in the occupation who were female in 1998 and 1983. For example, we see that in 1998, women were 97.6 percent of secretaries, stenographers, and typists but only 2 percent of construction workers. They were 75.3 percent of grade school and high school teachers but only 11.1 percent of engineers.

Despite the continuing high degree of concentration and sex segregation that persists in the U.S. occupational structure, there have been notable changes in the last two decades as women have made substantial inroads into some professional and managerial fields. A few of these changes (as well as some examples of lack of change) can be seen by comparing the last two columns of Table 3. For example, we see that 28.6 percent of all lawyers and judges were women in 1998 compared to 15.8 percent in 1983. Women's employment has also grown rapidly among physicians, dentists, veterinarians, pharmacists, accountants, and business executives. These occupational changes are taking place mainly among highly educated young women. The higher earnings of these women are responsible for much of the narrowing of the earnings gap since 1980. For less educated women, there has been little change in occupational or earnings prospects. Few women are employed in the skilled blue-collar trades that provide the best earnings prospects for workers with less than college educations. The employment of women without higher education is still concentrated in clerical jobs, in a few traditionally female factory occupations, and in the service jobs of the "pink collar ghetto."

The concentration and segregation we observe in the occupational structure has implications for women's earnings and for the male-female earnings gap. If women's ability to enter occupations is circumscribed so that they are able to take fewer kinds of jobs than men, then women's wages will be lowered because so many women are available to work in a limited set of occupations. If more women enter the labor force and most of them seek jobs in traditional women's occupations, then there will be extreme competition for these jobs and therefore downward pressure on women's wages. If discrimination limits women's access to some occupations, it increases competition for "women's jobs" and reduces competition for "men's jobs." The result is that

women's wages are artificially low and men's wages are artificially high. Economists call this mechanism *occupational crowding*. The existence of occupational crowding implies that the gap between women's and men's earnings will persist until the sex stereotyping of occupations lessens substantially.

THE FEMINIZATION OF POVERTY

Over the same period that many American women have been improving their economic position, other women have suffered severe economic hardship. Women now make up a larger share of the population living in poverty—a phenomenon that has come to be called the feminization of poverty. The most notable economic advances have taken place among young, well-educated women who succeeded in entering nontraditional jobs, solidified their attachment to the labor force, and experienced above-average increases in earnings. For women at the other end of the economic scale, the picture is bleak. Seventy percent of persons with incomes under $5,000 are women. Women's greater likelihood of living in poverty is due in large part to women's lower earnings; a great many women who work full time, year round do not earn enough to support a family above the poverty line. The effect of low earnings combines with the fact that a large and growing number of families are maintained by women (that is, families in which no adult male is present) to produce very high poverty rates for women and the children who are dependent on them.

Table 4 presents figures on poverty among American families. We can see that families maintained by women are much more likely to be poor than are husband-wife families. Nearly 39 percent of families with children maintained by women are poor compared with 7% of those living in husband-wife families with children. The increase in the share of the poverty population represented by families maintained by women is due to the marked rise in the prevalence of these families. (See the top half of Table 4.) Whereas in 1970, 10.7 percent of all American families were maintained by women, by 1998, this number had grown to 17.9 percent (24 percent of families with children under 18).

The growth in the number of families maintained by women and the attendant feminization of

TABLE 4 Proportion of U.S. Families Maintained by Women (No Husband Present)

Year	Total	White	Black	Hispanic
1970	10.7	8.9	28.0	15.3
1980	14.6	11.6	40.3	20.1
1990	17.0	13.2	45.9	23.8
1998	17.9	14.2	45.1	23.8

Proportion of U.S. Families with Children Under 18 Maintained by Mothers (No Husband Present)

Year	Total	White	Black	Hispanic
1970	11.5	8.9	33.0	NA
1980	19.4	15.1	48.7	24.0
1990	22.4	16.4	53.2	26.3
1998	24.0	19.0	53.5	26.7

Proportion of Families Living Below the Poverty Line, 1998

	Families Maintained by Women	Husband-Wife Families
Total	29.9	5.3
White	24.9	5.0
Black	40.9	7.3
Hispanic	43.8	15.7

Proportion of Families with Children Under 18 Living Below the Poverty Line, 1994

	Families Maintained by Women	Husband-Wife Families
Total	38.7	6.9
White	33.9	6.6
Black	47.5	8.6
Hispanic	52.2	19.3

Sources: U.S. Department of Commerce, Bureau of the Census, Current Population Reports, Series P-60, No. 207, *Poverty in the United States, 1998;* and U.S. Census Bureau, "Historical Poverty Tables–Families" (online). Available on www.census.gov

poverty is related to the increased incidence of divorce, the rise in the age at marriage, the apparent higher proportion of women not marrying at all, and the increase in childbearing by single women. As a result, in 1998, only 57.9 percent of women age 18 and over were married and living with a spouse—a smaller proportion than at any other time in U.S. history. This means that a large and growing proportion of women and their children are dependent on women's earnings, and we have already seen that women's earnings are much lower than men's.

Looking at Table 4, we see striking differences among Black, White, and Hispanic women. Since the 1950s, racial and ethnic differences in women's labor force participation, average earnings, and occupational distribution have declined substantially. The same cannot be said of racial/ethnic differences in poverty. Over 40 percent of families maintained by Black and Hispanic women are poor compared with 25 percent of persons in families maintained by White women. The figures are considerably higher for families with children under age 18. The top of Table 4 shows that there are also substantial differences among the three groups in the proportion of families maintained by women. Black families are particularly likely to be economically dependent on women, with 45.1 percent of all Black families and 53.5 percent of all Black families with children being maintained by women. These figures reflect the recent rapid decline in the proportion of Black women who are married. In 1998, only 39 percent of Black women were married and living with a spouse, and over 69 percent of Black babies were born to nonmarried women. These women and their children are very likely to live in poverty. Although the feminization of poverty is a phenomenon that cuts across racial and ethnic lines, the striking differences we see in proportions of families maintained by women has led to widening differences in incidence of poverty among the races.

SUMMARY

The twentieth century witnessed very dramatic increases in participation by women in the American labor force. The bulk of this increase has taken place since the Second World War and has been largely due to increased participation by married women. Since 1970, the greatest changes have come from mothers of young children. Now the most common pattern of labor force behavior for women is one of continuous attachment throughout adulthood.

Studies of women's labor force participation have found that increases in women's wages are very important for explaining the greater propensity of women to work for pay. As women's education and experience levels have risen, thereby raising their potential market wage, the implied price of home-produced goods and services has also risen, thus increasing the incentive to work for pay instead of working full-time in the home.

After many years during which the gap between women's and men's average earnings changed little, the gap has narrowed substantially since 1980. This narrowing is related closely to the growth in experience levels of women who have maintained continuous attachment to the labor force and to changes in the amounts and kinds of education that women receive. Well-educated young women have had notable successes in gaining access to professional and managerial jobs that have not until recently been held by women.

Although the earnings gap has narrowed, very large differences remain between the earnings of men and women. Studies have found that individual differences between women and men in education, training, and job experience can account for only a part of the earnings gap. The remainder reflects discrimination, particularly the kinds of discrimination that lead to widely differing occupational distributions of women and men workers. Despite notable increases in women's employment in some jobs that were previously reserved for men, much of women's work is still concentrated in a relatively small number of low-paid jobs. Since the growth in women's labor force participation has not been accompanied by integration of the occupational structure, most new women workers have sought jobs in traditional women's fields. This development has increased competition for those jobs and exerted downward pressure on women's earnings. Further substantial decrease in the size of the female-male earnings gap will require reduced sex segregation in the occupational structure.

Despite economic gains by well-educated women workers, the picture for women who are close to the bottom of the economic ladder is disturbing. The number of families maintained by women is increasing as the incidence of marriage falls and the divorce and nonmarital birth rates remain high. Such families have a very high chance of falling into poverty.

It is difficult to predict how women's economic roles will change in the future. We are seeing improvements for some women but difficulties for others. Most employed women bear the "double burden" of working in the labor force while they maintain primary responsibility for work in the home. Perhaps equality in the labor market will only come about when women achieve equality in other areas of life.

Suggestions for Further Reading

Francine D. Blau, Marianne A. Ferber, and Anne E. Winkler, *The Economics of Women and Work,* 3rd ed. (New York: Prentice-Hall, 1998).

Claudia Goldin, *Understanding the Gender Gap: An Economic History of American Women* (New York: Oxford University Press, 1989).

Nancy Folbre, *Who Pays for the Kids? Gender and the Structures of Constraint* (New York: Routledge, 1994).

Barbara Reskin, *The Realities of Affirmative Action in Employment* (Washington, DC: American Sociological Association, 1998).

Affirmative Action:
Building a National Community That Works

National Council for Research on Women

Antiwoman and racist forces would have Americans believe that affirmative action should be eradicated, either because it does not work, or because it is unfair to men, or because it is unnecessary—having already accomplished its goal. The truth is that it has worked, it is very fair—in that it is creating some level of equality in work opportunity—and its task is far from complete.

ABOVE ALL THE POLITICAL AND legal wrangling over affirmative action, an important set of national principles and commitments holds steady. The Constitution provides "equal protection under the law" to *all* US citizens, while history defines the nation as the "land of opportunity" and a place where hard work pays off. Affirmative-action programs and policies turn these and other laws and ideals into real-life practices in the nation's classrooms, workrooms, and executive offices.

So why has affirmative action come under fire in recent months? Why are some calling for its demise, claiming it encourages—even legislates—reverse discrimination, while others, including President Clinton, want to amend it, not end it?

"It is one thing to believe in a meritocracy, and it is another to believe it is here right now," says Reginald Wilson, senior scholar at the American Council on Education and author of "Affirmative Action: Yesterday, Today, and Beyond."[1] "Educating and presenting the facts about affirmative action to the American public is only part of the job ahead. Making sure people realize that many of the things we aspire toward are just that, aspirations, is the other side of the battle," adds Wilson.

Numerous studies support this conclusion: affirmative action is not a done deal. Just as the issue

began to heat up in the media, inside the Beltway, and on the Supreme Court, the Federal Glass Ceiling Commission released its fact-finding report, *Good for Business: Making full use of the nation's human capital: The environmental scan.*[2] Based on a series of public hearings, commissioned research reports, surveys with chief executive officers, discussions with focus groups, and analyses of US Bureau of the Census data and other materials, the report demonstrates that there are glass ceilings all over corporate America.

Good for Business presents staggering figures:

97 percent of the senior managers of Fortune 1000 industrial and Fortune 500 service companies are white; 95 to 97 percent are male.

In Fortune 2000 industrial and service companies, only 5 percent of senior managers are women—and of that 5 percent, virtually all are white.

In 1994, only two women were CEOs of Fortune 1000 companies. In 1990, a woman with an MBA from one of the top 20 business schools earned an average of 12 percent less in her first year of work than her male classmates.

African American men with professional degrees earn only 79 percent and African American women with professional degrees earn only 60 percent of what white men in similar positions earn.[3]

How people are perceived affects how far they advance up the corporate ladder, concludes *Good for Business.* In many instances, stereotypes about women and different ethnic and racial groups still determine who gets hired and who gets promoted. As one corporate executive told Glass Ceiling Commission researchers, "What's important is comfort, chemistry, relationships, and collaborations. That's what makes a shop work. When we find minorities and women who think like we do, we snatch them up."[4] From a business perspective this approach makes sense; from an affirmative-action point of view—one committed to opening up rather than limiting opportunity—it doesn't.

"Thinking like we do" implies that people have the same educational opportunities and that they come to the personnel office with a similar set of values and professional and personal needs. According to the Hudson Institute's landmark report, *Workforce 2000,* between 1987 and the year 2000, "non-whites, women, and immigrants will make up more than five-sixths of the net additions to the workforce," with black women constituting the majority of non-whites.[5] Heeding these projections, many businesses have hired "diversity management" consultants to make cultural differences work for rather than against the bottom line.[6] "The issue of diversity is critical to American businesses," says Michelle Carpenter, director of Work/Family Strategies at Aetna. "We have a competitive advantage over the rest of the world because we have a diverse workforce.... We can't afford infighting and segregation," cautions Carpenter.

MISPERCEPTIONS DO NOT A DIALOGUE MAKE

Unfortunately, in the midst of the current acrimony, infighting and segregation prevail because the public does not fully comprehend the legal parameters of affirmative action. When Governor of California Pete Wilson issued an executive order on July 1, 1995 to "End Preferential Treatment and Promote Individual Opportunity Based on Merit," he stirred up the already turbulent public discussion on affirmative action by adding misperceptions on top of layers of misunderstandings.

Put simply: affirmative action is not about quotas or hiring, promoting, or admitting unqualified employees or students. It is about actively ensuring that everyone has equal access to quality schools and viable employment and business opportunities and about taking reasonable measures to redress enduring histories of discrimination. Concretely, affirmative action is a set of public policies, laws, and executive orders, as well as voluntary and court-ordered practices designed to promote fairness and diversity.

For the most part, they have. According to the Equal Employment Opportunity Commission—the federal body charged with enforcing civil-rights acts as they pertain to employment—of the more than 10,000 reverse-discrimination cases filed between 1987 and 1994; only 10 percent had merit.[7] Likewise, while affirmative-action policies have opened some doors, at least partially, they do not guarantee future access. When Catalyst, a New York City-based research and advocacy group for business and professional women, tracked the presence of women on corporate boards, they found a mixed bag. The good news: in 1995, 81 percent of Fortune 500 companies had at least one female director, compared with 69 percent in 1993. The bad news: women currently hold only 600 of the 6274 Fortune 500 board seats available.[8] The world has changed, but not enough to warrant a laissez faire attitude toward making American ideals everyday realities.

Historically, the courts and federal government have only cautiously expanded affirmative-action policies and often sought to keep them in check. Women were not included in President Nixon's 1969 executive order imposing hiring "goals and timetables" on federal building contractors until 1971. In the Bakke decision of 1978, the Supreme Court established that colleges and universities could consider race when admitting students, but they could not use racial quotas. And the Supreme Court's *Adarand Construction v. Pena* ruling on June 12, 1995 did not so much strike down as clarify the limits of affirmative action. The 5–4 vote held that any race-based affirmative-action programs are "constitutional only if they are narrowly tailored measures that further compelling governmental interests."[9] Helen Norton, director of the Equal Opportunity Program at the Women's Legal Defense Fund in Washington, DC, explains: "Adarand was a setback but not a disaster. The Court made it harder for the federal government to set up affirmative-action programs, but they also made it clear that affirmative action is legal." The spate of headlines and articles pronouncing the end of affirmative action that followed this decision further polarized the mounting public discord.

Hyperbole does not lead to workable solutions. A recent survey sponsored by the Feminist Majority Foundation demonstrates that when people understand that affirmative-action programs seek to level the educational and economic playing fields for women and minorities without resorting to numerical quotas, they overwhelmingly register their support.[10] "People know that discrimination is alive and well," says Fran Buchanan, deputy executive director at Equal Rights Advocates, a group that recently conducted focus groups on affirmative action in California. "When we asked, 'Have you seen discrimination?' people were real clear that they had." As a result, Buchanan advocates making sure the public knows that affirmative action benefits everyone. "It brings hiring practices under scrutiny. . . . *Qualified* used to mean knowing somebody; [under affirmative action] everybody has to have the opportunity to apply, even white men," stresses Buchanan.

BEYOND THE RHETORIC AND TOWARD COMMITMENTS

Affirmative action is a tool not a goal. As with any tool, it can be misused, it needs periodic sharpening, and it doesn't work on its own. Rather than perceiving current anti-affirmative-action efforts as tolling the death of a 30-year civil-rights era, we need to attend to what can be done to turn the principles of affirmative action into policy and common practice. Helen Neuborne, program officer at the Ford Foundation, cautions: "The level playing field language is used without understanding what it is and how it happens. The approach to affirmative action needs to be broad." In other words, equal access is a deceptively simple concept. Though affirmative-action laws have been limited to race and gender, antidiscrimination measures have cast wider nets, protecting people on the basis of race, religion, sex, national origin, age, and disability. Opening doors means transforming the nation's institutions to account for people's many differences.

THE PRIMACY OF EDUCATION

The debate over who gets admitted to state universities and colleges largely focuses on the symptom rather than the problem. Given that currently African Americans and Hispanics constitute 37 percent of California's high-school graduates, the fact that the University of California, Berkeley counts only 5.5 percent or 1127 African Americans and 13.8 percent or 2800 Hispanics among its more than 21,000 undergraduates raises questions about who gets admitted and why.[11] Do California high schools prepare all their students equally? Furthermore, what happens to these students once they matriculate? How many stay in school? How many find mentors to help them navigate the university and reach their full potential as students and citizens? Recent figures show that six-year graduation rates at Berkeley vary from 59 percent for African Americans, 64 percent for Hispanics, 84 percent for whites, and 88 percent for Asians.[12] To what extent do institutional conditions explain these numbers?

Admissions, retention, and graduation problems are not California's alone. Nationally, 70 percent of African American college students drop out of school, as compared with 40 percent of their classmates from other racial and ethnic backgrounds. Similarly, African Americans rarely exceed 7 percent of the undergraduate student populations at elite universities across the country.[13] Reassessments of public education occasioned by the 40th anniversary of the Supreme Court's landmark desegregation case, *Brown v. Board of Education*, found that nationwide nearly 70 percent of all black students attend elementary and secondary schools with mostly black and Hispanic enrollments.[14] Adding these facts together suggests that separate is not equal and not every kid gets a running start.

Despite existing desegregation programs and attempts by some states to distribute state-educational dollars evenly across districts, not all public primary and secondary schools are created equal. More needs to be done to ensure that kids of *all* backgrounds—from suburban, rural, and urban school districts alike—acquire comparable academic skills and develop the capacity to do college-level work so that they can imagine and pursue productive and challenging futures for themselves. Only then will we begin to experience the social and economic benefits of a level playing field.

BELOW EVERY GLASS CEILING LIES A STICKY FLOOR

When matters turn to work, dismantling the glass ceiling addresses only half the problem. The "sticky floor" of low-paying, low-mobility jobs curtails the advancement of many more white women and women and men of color than does the CEO old-boys network.[15] According to Karen Nussbaum, director of the Women's Bureau, US Department of Labor, "You still find a very large group of women in clerical and low-wage service work, and 75 percent of working women still earn less than $25,000" a year.[16] Of these working women, two-thirds are the principal breadwinners in their families. One-third of the female-headed households lives in poverty.[17] And women make up 60 percent of the country's minimum-wage workers. At $4.25 an hour, this wage puts less on the dinner table today than it did 40 years ago.[18] In light of these figures, increasing the minimum wage, making health care and other benefits affordable and accessible, and expanding job-training programs for women and girls of all backgrounds will go a long way toward broadening the reach and effectiveness of affirmative-action and equal-opportunity policies. A tool is only as good as the people who use it. If white women and women of color are not given the skills and resources they need to take advantage of opening doors, equal access is a hollow concept.

MISSING NUMBERS AND DOUBLE EXCLUSIONS

What remains largely unsaid in the haggling over affirmative action is the tenacity with which US institutions discriminate on the basis of race and gender. To a great extent, Congress, the courts, the media, and researchers have placed women of color outside the frame of this critical national discussion. Most talk about "women" and "minorities" without specifying where women of color fall in these breakdowns. If they are counted among "minorities," such numbers only tell half their story. "You're either a woman or a person of color; women of color fall in some nether world, making it difficult to discern if discrimination has happened on the basis of race or gender [or both]. If an employer doesn't need to consider race or gender, women of color experience a double exclusion," notes Fran Buchanan of Equal Rights Advocates.

Existing numbers do tell us that women of color generally fare less well than either white women or

men of color. For example, in 1994, for every dollar earned by white men, African American men earned 75 cents, white women earned 72 cents, Hispanic men earned 64 cents, African American women earned 63 cents, and Hispanic women earned only 56 cents.[19] Given this playing field, if the states, federal government, and the Supreme Court hamstring or abolish affirmative-action initiatives, women of color have the most to lose.

THE WORK–FAMILY CONNECTION

In reassessing affirmative action, the country is indirectly looking at who it is and who it wants to be. If women of color are not an integral part of this analysis, policies will fall short of meeting the demands of the nation's schools, workplaces, *and* families. One study, *Defining Work and Family Issues: Listening to the Voices of Women of Color,* by Jennifer Tucker and Leslie R. Wolfe of the Center for Women Policy Studies in Washington, DC, finds that women of color identify racism and sexism in the workplace as "work and family conflicts."[20] Tucker explains, "Women of color experience work and family and workplace diversity issues as intrinsically linked." While many large companies make work-family consulting services available to their employees, most of these programs attend to the ways family life can interfere with workplace productivity. *Defining Work and Family Issues* shows that when women face sexual harassment and racial discrimination on the job their home lives suffer and in the end so do their employers. Productivity and attendance drops. Women become distracted, angry, unmotivated, and eventually leave their jobs. Tucker recommends that companies encourage collaboration between their work-family and workplace-diversity programs.

Elizabeth Kuhn, regional director at Work/Family Directions, a Boston-based company providing work-family services to hundreds of thousands of employees throughout the country, sees her work as affirmative action. In the early 1980s, Work/Family Directions helped employers meet the childcare needs of their workers. Today they offer advice, training, and resource referrals on topics ranging from caring for elderly parents to parenting adolescents to adopting young children. Through an

800 number, Work/Family Directions responds to about 300,000 calls a year. Kuhn reports that women make 90 percent of the calls pertaining to childcare, 75 percent of those asking about elder care, and 50 percent of those requesting information about college planning. "The primary care for family matters rests with women. There are many reasons that women have not cracked the glass ceiling. A complex strategy is needed to help women advance," observes Kuhn.

REACHING FOR A DIVERSE AND EQUAL FUTURE

Part of that strategy entails blocking attempts to annul affirmative-action policies on the federal and state levels. The situation calls for "defensive lobbying," asserts the Women's Legal Defense Fund's (WLDF) Helen Norton. In the past year, WLDF and several other groups have been actively educating members of Congress so that they understand the impact affirmative action has had on educating and employing the nation's women. According to Norton, affirmative action is a "smoke screen," a "diversionary tactic. . . . White men, white women, people of all colors are not doing as well as their parents and they're worried about their kids. [WLDF is] trying to make it clear that this fight shouldn't be about affirmative action but about economic security for everybody. It is much easier to oppose affirmative action than it is to address economic issues," concludes Norton.

By working in coalitions that bridge the women's and civil-rights communities, as well as legal, educational, business, and labor constituencies, women's and civil-rights organizations across the country are attempting to reshape the affirmative-action debate so that the discussion broadens and the solutions multiply.

Affirmative action is about race, gender, and class in America. As such it is everyone's issue and in everyone's best interest. In its first 30 years, it has laid the groundwork for changing the way America does business and educates its population. Using the current public discussion to rearticulate our commitment to affirmative action is the first step toward ensuring that the next 30 years will witness the elimination of the glass ceiling and the sticky

floor and the institution of a more equitable public-education system and more effective work-family policies in the public and private sectors. Such changes will make the principles behind affirmative action more than a set of ideals to which we aspire; they will become part of the fabric of everyday life, making discrimination part of our history, not an impediment to our future.

EYE OPENERS: THE EVIDENCE IS IN: THE CASE FOR AFFIRMATIVE ACTION

1. Women currently make up nearly half of the nation's workforce.[1]

   99 percent of women in the US will work for pay sometime during their lives.[2]

   In 1968, on average, women left work for 10 years after their children were born; in 1987, they left for six months.[3]

2. Between 1980 and 1990, the proportion of all managers who are white women grew by about one-third, from 27 to 35 percent, while the proportion of all managers who are women of color more than doubled, increasing from 3 to 7 percent.

   In 1990, among full-time salaried managers, only 6.3 percent of white women and 3.6 percent of women of color earned incomes in the top 20 percent.[4]

   In 1992, when 42 percent of all managers were women, only 13 percent of the business experts named in the *New York Times, Wall Street Journal, Fortune,* and *Business Week* were women.[5]

3. A 1995 study by Catalyst found that 68 percent of the CEOs at America's leading corporations consider recruiting female directors a top priority, and 86 percent consider increasing the number of women on their boards "important."[6]

4. As of March 31, 1995, women or people of color owned a total of 110 banks, or about 1 percent of all commercial banks. Women alone owned only .05 percent of the total.[7]

   Even under affirmative action, businesses owned by people of color or women get fewer than 6 percent of all federal contracts.[8]

In 1980, women-owned firms received 0.8 percent of federal-contract awards over $25,000 and 0.9 percent in 1991. In 1993, 1.8 percent of all federal-procurement awards and 1.2 percent of prime contracts went to women-owned businesses.[9]

In 1994, the National Foundation for Women Business Owners found that the 7.7 million women-owned businesses in the US employed 15.5 million people—white people and people of color, including white men—35 percent more than all Fortune 500 companies combined.[10]

5. Between 1987 and 1994, 10,501 race-based reverse-discrimination charges were filed by white men and resolved by the Equal Employment Opportunity Commission (EEOC). Of these cases, the EEOC found that only 1072, approximately 10 percent, had merit. In 1994 alone, this number fell to a mere 0.2 percent.

   In reverse-discrimination cases filed by either women or men in 1994, the EEOC found in favor of the complainants in 13.2 percent of race-based, 12.7 percent of national origin-based, and 16.6 percent of gender-based cases.[11]

6. In 1966, two and one-half million women attended college. In 1975, three years after President Nixon signed into law Title IX of the Education Amendments Act, the number of women in college doubled to over five million. In 1979, women college students outnumbered men for the first time in US history. Currently, over eight million women attend college, composing 55.1 percent of the total enrollment.[12]

   According to the EEOC, college-educated women earn 29 percent less than college-educated men and make only $1950 more per year than high-school-educated white men.[13]

7. The US Department of Education estimates that only 40 cents of every $1000 of federal-educational assistance funds minority-targeted scholarships.[14]

8. When Richmond, VA suspended its affirmative-action programs in 1987, city contracts to minorities dropped from 41.6 percent to 2.2 percent.[15]

In Los Angeles, where nonwhites make up two-thirds of the population, only 5 percent of every public-works dollar goes to minority-owned contractors.[16]

9. In the mid 1990s, white men make up 33 percent of the population. They are: 85 percent of tenured professors; 85 percent of partners in law firms; 80 percent of the US House of Representatives; 90 percent of the US Senate; 95 percent of Fortune 500 CEOs; 97 percent of school superintendents; 99.9 percent of athletic team owners; and 100 percent of all US presidents.[17]

Notes

1. Reginald Wilson, "Affirmative Action: Yesterday, Today, and Beyond" (Washington, DC: American Council on Education, May 1995). Photocopy.

2. Federal Glass Ceiling Commission, *Good for Business: Making full use of the nation's human capital: The environmental scan* (Washington, DC: US Department of Labor, 1995). President Bush appointed the Federal Glass Ceiling Commission, a 21-member bipartisan group, under the Civil Rights Act (CRA) of 1991 after Senator Robert Dole introduced the Glass Ceiling Act, which became Title II of the CRA. The commission also plans to publish *A Strategic Plan*, which will recommend ways to dismantle artificial barriers to advancement for white women and men and women of color.

3. Federal Glass Ceiling Commission, iii–iv, 12, 13, 9.

4. Ibid., 28.

5. William B. Johnston and Arnold H. Packer, *Workforce 2000: Work and Workers for the 21st Century* (Indianapolis, IN: Hudson Institute, 1987), xx, 89.

6. A February 1994 article in *Entrepreneur* reported that diversity training workshops typically last from half a day to three days and cost companies from $500 to $5000. Jane Easter Bahls, "Culture Shock," *Entrepreneur* (February 1994): n.p. For a critique of "diversity management," see Avery Gordon, "The Work of Corporate Culture: Diversity Management," *Social Text* 44 vol. 13, no. 3 (Fall/Winter 1995): 3–30.

7. Equal Employment Opportunity Commission, "EEOC Charge Resolution Statistics Reflecting Type of Reverse Discrimination." Photocopy.

8. "Catalyst Fact Sheet: National Business Women's Week, October 16–20, 1995." Photocopy.

9. "Excerpts from the Decision on Justifying Affirmative Action Programs," *New York Times* (June 13, 1995): D24.

10. Louis Harris, *Women's Equality Poll,* 1995 (Arlington, VA: Feminist Majority Foundation, 1995): Photocopy.

11. Peter Applebome, "The Debate on Diversity in California Shifts," *New York Times* (June 4, 1995): 22.

12. Ibid.

13. Claude M. Steele, "Black Students Live Down to Expectations," *New York Times* (August 31, 1995): A25.

14. William Cellis, "40 Years After Brown, Segregation Persists," *New York Times* (May 18, 1994): A1. And Steven A. Holmes, "Look Who's Saying Separate is Equal," *New York Times* (October 1, 1995): Sec. 4, p. 5.

15. For a report that links the glass ceiling and the sticky floor, see Sharon L. Harlan and Catherine White Berheide, *Barriers to Workplace Advancement Experienced by Women in Low-Paying Occupations* (Albany, NY: Center for Women in Government, 1994).

16. Sam Roberts, "Women's Work: What's New, What Isn't," *New York Times* (April 27, 1995): B6.

17. Coalition of Labor Union Women, "What Is Affirmative Action?" Photocopy.

18. Orna Feldman, "Secretary of Labor Robert Reich: Public Policies Must Address Investment in Human Capital," *Radcliffe News* (September 1995): 2. And *1993 Handbook on Women Workers: Trends & Issues* (Washington, DC: US Department of Labor, Women's Bureau, 1994), 201.

19. US Bureau of the Census, reported by the Institute for Women's Policy Research, Washington, DC.

20. Jennifer Tucker and Leslie R. Wolfe, *Defining Work and Family Issues: Listening to the Voices of Women of Color* (Washington, DC: Center for Women Policy Studies, 1994).

EYE OPENERS

1. Women's Bureau, US Department of Labor, *Working Women Count! A Report to the Nation* (Washington, DC: US Department of Labor, 1994), 4.

2. Ibid.

3. Jeffrey Rosen, "Affirmative Action: A Solution," *New Republic* vol. 4, no. 190 (May 8, 1995): 20.

4. Jill Braunstein, Heidi I. Hartmann, and Lois Shaw, "Restructuring Work: How Have Women and Minority Managers Fared?" (Washington, DC: Institute for Women's Policy Research, 1995). Pamphlet.

5. Carol Wheeler, "How Much Ink Do Women Get?" *Executive Female* (September / October 1994): 51.

6. Catalyst, "CEOs Seek More Female Directors," *Perspectives* II (Spring 1995).

7. Board of Governors of the Federal Reserve System, conversation with NCRW.

8. Tamar Lewin, "Reactions: 5–4 Decision Buoys Some; For Others It's a Setback," *New York Times* (June 13, 1995): D25.

9. Women's Transportation Seminar, "Fact Sheet on Women-Owned Businesses." Photocopy.

10. Catalyst, "Catalyst Fact Sheet: National Business Women's Week, October 16–20, 1995." Photocopy.

11. Equal Employment Opportunity Commission, "EEOC Charge Resolution Statistics Reflecting Type of Reverse Discrimination." Photocopy.

12. American Civil Liberties Union, memo (March 6, 1965). Photocopy, 3. And "The Nation," *Chronicle of Higher Education Almanac* vol. XLII, no. 1 (September 1, 1995): 5.

13. Equal Employment Opportunity Commission, "Wage Gap." Photocopy, 1.

14. *Affirmative Action Review: Report to the President* (Washington, DC: The White House, 1995), 87.

15. Californians for Equal Opportunity (June 14, 1995). Email.

16. American Civil Liberties Union of Southern California, "Why We Still Need Affirmative Action—A Few Statistics." Photocopy.

17. Ibid.

Sexual Harassment: The Nature of the Beast

Anita F. Hill

Anita F. Hill is professor of law at the University of Oklahoma College of Law. In 1991, her allegations of sexual harassment against Clarence Thomas at his confirmation hearings for appointment to the Supreme Court touched off a furor that pitted gender against race but placed the issue of sexual harassment before the public as never before. It is interesting to note that although Hill was demonized on television by Thomas's supporters, and she was disbelieved and vilified by many at the time of the hearings, one year later polls showed that the public had reversed its opinions.

Sexual harassment is no joke, although it is frequently treated as trivial or funny. It affects not only our ability to support ourselves and our families, but also our health and well-being. Furthermore, it is illegal discrimination under the provisions of Title VII of the Civil Rights Act. According to the guidelines of the federal Equal Employment Opportunity Commission (EEOC), sexual harassment is defined as "unwelcome sexual advances, requests for sexual favors, and other verbal or physical conduct of a sexual nature" when (1) submission to such conduct is made either explicitly or implicitly a term or condition of employment or learning; (2) submission to or rejection of such conduct is used as the basis for employment or course decisions; or (3) such conduct has the purpose or effect of interfering with the individual's work or educational performance or has the effect of creating an intimidating, hostile, or offensive working or learning environment.

THE RESPONSE TO MY SENATE Judiciary Committee testimony has been at once heartwarming and heartwrenching. In learning that I am not alone in experiencing harassment, I am also learning that there are far too many women who have experienced a

range of inexcusable and illegal activities—from sexist jokes to sexual assault—on the job.

My reaction has been to try to learn more. As an educator, I always begin to study an issue by examining the scientific data—the articles, the books, the studies. Perhaps the most compelling lesson is in the stories told by the women who have written to me. I have learned much; I am continuing to learn; I have yet ten times as much to explore. I want to share some of this with you.

"The Nature of the Beast" describes the existence of sexual harassment, which is alive and well. A harmful, dangerous thing that can confront a woman at any time.

What we know about harassment, sizing up the beast:

Sexual harassment is pervasive . . .

1. It occurs today at an alarming rate. Statistics show that anywhere from 42 to 90 percent of women will experience some form of harassment during their employed lives. At least one percent experience sexual assault. But the statistics do not fully tell the story of the anguish of women who have been told in various ways on the first day of a job that sexual favors are expected. Or the story of women who were sexually assaulted by men with whom they continued to work.

2. It has been occurring for years. In letters to me, women tell of incidents that occurred 50 years ago when they were first entering the workplace, incidents they have been unable to speak of for that entire period.

3. Harassment crosses lines of race and class. In some ways, it is a creature that practices "equal opportunity" where women are concerned. In other ways it exhibits predictable prejudices and reflects stereotypical myths held by our society.

Hill, *Sexual Harassment: The Nature of the Beast*, 65 S. Cal. L. Rev. 1445-1449, reprinted with the permission of the *Southern California Law Review.*

We know that harassment all too often goes unreported for a variety of reasons . . .

1. Unwillingness (for good reason) to deal with the expected consequences;

2. Self-blame;

3. Threats or blackmail by coworkers or employers;

4. What it boils down to in many cases is a sense of powerlessness that we experience in the workplace, and our acceptance of a certain level of inability to control our careers and professional destinies. This sense of powerlessness is particularly troubling when one observes the research that says individuals with graduate education experience more harassment than do persons with less than a high school diploma. The message: when you try to obtain power through education, the beast harassment responds by striking more often and more vehemently.

That harassment is treated like a woman's "dirty secret" is well known. We also know what happens when we "tell." We know that when harassment is reported the common reaction is disbelief or worse . . .

1. Women who "tell" lose their jobs. A typical response told of in the letters to me was: I not only lost my job for reporting harassment, but I was accused of stealing and charges were brought against me.

2. Women who "tell" become emotionally wasted. One writer noted that "it was fully eight months after the suit was conducted that I began to see myself as alive again."

3. Women who "tell" are not always supported by other women. Perhaps the most disheartening stories I have received are of mothers not believing daughters. In my kindest moments I believe that this reaction only represents attempts to distance ourselves from the pain of the harassment experience. The internal response is: "It didn't happen to me. This couldn't happen to me. In order to believe that I am protected, I must believe that it didn't happen to her." The external response is: "What did you do to provoke that kind of behavior?" Yet at the same time that

I have been advised of hurtful and unproductive reactions, I have also heard stories of mothers and daughters sharing their experiences. In some cases the sharing allows for a closer bonding. In others a slight but cognizable mending of a previously damaged relationship occurs.

What we are learning about harassment requires recognizing this beast when we encounter it, and more. It requires looking the beast in the eye.

We are learning painfully that simply having laws against harassment on the books is not enough. The law, as it was conceived, was to provide a shield of protection for us. Yet that shield is failing us: many fear reporting, others feel it would do no good. The result is that less than 5 percent of women victims file claims of harassment. Moreover, the law focuses on quid pro quo, but a recent New York *Times* article quoting psychologist Dr. Louise Fitzgerald says that this makes up considerably less than 5 percent of the cases. The law needs to be more responsive to the reality of our experiences.

As we are learning, enforcing the law alone won't terminate the problem. What we are seeking is equality of treatment in the workplace. Equality requires an expansion of our attitudes toward workers. Sexual harassment denies our treatment as equals and replaces it with treatment of women as objects of ego or power gratification. Dr. John Gottman, a psychologist at the University of Washington, notes that sexual harassment is more about fear than about sex.

Yet research suggests two troublesome responses exhibited by workers and by courts. Both respond by . . .

1. Downplaying the seriousness of the behavior (seeing it as normal sexual attraction between people) or commenting on the sensitivity of the victim.

2. Exaggerating the ease with which victims are expected to handle the behavior. But my letters tell me that unwanted advances do not cease—and that the message was power, not genuine interest.

We are learning that many women are angry. The reasons for the anger are various and perhaps all too obvious . . .

1. We are angry because this awful thing called harassment exists in terribly harsh, ugly, demeaning, and even debilitating ways. Many believe it is criminal and should be punished as such. It is a form of violence against women as well as a form of economic coercion, and our experiences suggest that it won't just go away.

2. We are angry because for a brief moment we believed that if the law allowed for women to be hired in the workplace, and if we worked hard for our educations and on the job, equality would be achieved. We believed we would be respected as equals. Now we are realizing this is not true. We have been betrayed. The reality is that this powerful beast is used to perpetuate a sense of inequality, to keep women in their place notwithstanding our increasing presence in the workplace.

What we have yet to explore about harassment is vast. It is what will enable us to slay the beast.

Research is helpful, appreciated, and I hope will be required reading for all legislators. Yet research has what I see as one shortcoming: it focuses on our reaction to harassment, not on the harasser. How we enlighten men who are currently in the workplace about behavior that is beneath our (and their) dignity is the challenge of the future. Research shows that men tend to have a narrower definition of what constitutes harassment than do women. How do we expand their body of knowledge? How do we raise a generation of men who won't need to be reeducated as adults? We must explore these issues, and research efforts can assist us.

What are the broader effects of harassment on women and the world? Has sexual harassment left us unempowered? Has our potential in the workplace been greatly damaged by this beast? Has this form of economic coercion worked? If so, how do we begin to reverse its effects? We must begin to use what we know to move to the next step: what we will do about it.

How do we capture our rage and turn it into positive energy? Through the power of women working together, whether it be in the political arena, or in the context of a lawsuit, or in community service. This issue goes well beyond partisan politics. Making the workplace a safer, more productive place for ourselves and our daughters should be on the agenda for each of us. It is something we can do for ourselves. It is a tribute, as well, to our mothers—and indeed a contribution we can make to the entire population.

I wish that I could take each of you on the journey that I've been on during all these weeks since the hearing. I wish that every one of you could experience the heartache and the triumphs of each of those who have shared with me their experiences. I leave you with but a brief glimpse of what I've seen. I hope it is enough to encourage you to begin—or continue and persist with—your own exploration. And thank you.

This article is based on remarks delivered by Anita Hill (professor of law, University of Oklahoma) as part of a panel on sexual harassment and policymaking at the National Forum for Women State Legislators convened by the Center for the American Woman and Politics (CAWP) late last year. Other panel members were Deborah L. Rhode, professor of law at Stanford; Susan Deller Ross, professor of law and director of the Sex Discrimination Clinic at Georgetown University Law School; and Kimberle Williams Crenshaw, professor of law at UCLA. A transcript of the entire proceedings (the largest meeting of elected women ever held) is available from CAWP, Eagleton Institute of Politics, Rutgers University, New Brunswick, New Jersey 08901.

Law and Equality: The Continuing Struggle for Women's Rights

Susan Gluck Mezey

Susan Gluck Mezey is a professor of political science at Loyola University, Chicago. She received her MA and PhD from Syracuse University and her JD from De-Paul University in Chicago. She has published articles on women's issues in political science journals and law reviews. She is the author of four books: No Longer Disabled: The Federal Courts and the Politics of Social Security Disability *(Greenwood Press, 1988);* In Pursuit of Equality: Women, Public Policy, and the Federal Courts *(St. Martin's Press, 1992);* Children in Court: Public Policymaking and the Federal Courts *(State University of New York Press, 1996); and* Pitiful Plaintiffs: Child Welfare Litigation and the Federal Courts *(University of Pittsburgh Press, 2000).*

Here Professor Mezey outlines the current major legal issues for women and explains the relevant concepts and terms. She recounts the history of women's struggle for equality before the law in the nineteenth century and its continuation to the present. Regarding the future, she reminds us that "the law is a powerful weapon in the struggle for social, political and economic equality between women and men." Over the years the feminist movement has made a great deal of progress, but "there is more work ahead in the struggle to produce a society where sex is no longer a barrier to equality."

INTRODUCTION

IN A LETTER TO HER husband, future president John Adams, Abigail Adams urged that he "remember the ladies and . . . not put such unlimited power into the hands of the husbands." The letter reached John Adams at the constitutional convention in Philadelphia where he was engaged in drafting a constitution to govern the newly created United States. When the Constitution was finished, however, it showed that the founders of the new nation had paid little attention to Abigail's concerns. Throughout much of the nineteenth century, in most states, women remained subordinate to men in public and private life—unable to vote, unable to own or sell property if they were married, unable to serve on juries or in public office, and restricted from entering many professions.

The first formal gathering of women's rights activists was in 1848 at the Women's Rights Convention, held in Seneca Falls, New York. Borrowing from the nation's Declaration of Independence, the delegates issued this Declaration of Sentiments:

> *We hold these truths to be self evident, that all men and women are created equal, that they are endowed by their Creator with certain inalienable rights, that among these are life, liberty, and the pursuit of happiness.*

After the Civil War, spurred by their role in the abolition and temperance struggles, women turned their energy to winning the vote. Although women were allowed to vote in some states, a constitutional amendment was necessary to allow women to vote in all states. The battle for national enfranchisement was won when the Nineteenth Amendment, stating "the right of the citizens of the United States to vote will not be denied or abridged by the United States or by any State on account of sex," was ratified in 1920.[1]

By the 1960s, it was clear to many women that, although their victory in 1920 had been an important one, they needed to mount a new campaign for equal rights. Arising, in part, out of their involvement in the civil rights and antiwar movements of the 1960s, the second women's movement was born.[2] Spearheaded by feminists, this women's movement had an extensive agenda aimed at creating equality between the sexes—in public and private life.[3] Al-

Susan Gluck Mezey, "Law and Equality: The Continuing Struggle for Women's Rights" was written expressly for *Issues in Feminism,* 5th edition.

though feminists do not always agree on the best way to close the political, economic, and social gaps between women and men, most recognize the importance of legal equality in reaching their goals.[4]

CONSTITUTIONAL REVIEW

The equal protection clause of the Fourteenth Amendment of the U.S. Constitution prohibits a state from "deny[ing] to any person within its jurisdiction equal protection of the laws." This clause puts states on notice that differential treatment is permissible only when it is based on *relevant* distinctions among individuals, that is, it requires "similarly situated" persons to be treated alike.

The U.S. Supreme Court is an important voice in determining women's legal status. Its decisions, however, are often influenced by prevailing beliefs about the role of women in society; until 1971, the Court raised no objection to laws that deprived women of equal rights. The modern phase of legal equality for women was, in part, prompted by Congress's enactment of federal sex discrimination legislation and its approval of the Equal Rights Amendment.[5] The courts were also encouraged to adopt a new approach to women's rights as a result of the arguments made in litigation brought on behalf of women.[6]

The Supreme Court struck its first sex-based law in 1971. In 1976, it applied a new, more rigorous level of analysis to sex-based laws by insisting that they be "substantially related" to the achievement of "important" governmental interests.[7] In a 1982 opinion, Justice Sandra Day O'Connor added that states must provide an "exceedingly persuasive justification" for laws that distinguish between the sexes. And in announcing the majority opinion for the Court in *United States v. Virginia,* Justice Ruth Bader Ginsburg reiterated that this strict standard of proof must apply in gender discrimination cases.

Overall, the Supreme Court has invalidated laws based on "archaic or overbroad generalizations" about men and women by striking an Idaho probate statute preferring males to females, a military regulation requiring women officers to prove their husband's dependency to receive benefits, a social security regulation limiting survivors' benefits to widows, an Alabama law allowing alimony payments to women only, and a Mississippi law denying men admission to a state nursing college.

Despite its commitment to legal equality between men and women, the Supreme Court has upheld sex-based laws that seem designed to compensate women for past discrimination; it let stand two Social Security regulations allowing women a more favorable method of computing benefits, a Navy rule permitting women more time in rank than men, and a Florida law granting a property tax exemption to widows only.

Aside from these compensatory laws, the Supreme Court has also sustained laws related to physical differences between the sexes—on the grounds that men and women are not "similarly situated." Thus, it upheld a congressional statute limiting military registration to men only, a California law punishing men only for the crime of statutory rape, and several laws distinguishing between unwed mothers and fathers.

Women on the U.S. Supreme Court

Sworn in on September 25, 1981, by President Ronald Reagan, Sandra Day O'Connor became the first woman to sit among the brethren on the high court. Feminists, who thought her presence on the Supreme Court would elevate women's rights, lobbied the Senate in support of her confirmation. However, for a number of reasons, primarily because of her position in abortion cases, Justice O'Connor's performance on the high court has often been disappointing to feminists.[8]

Ruth Bader Ginsburg, the second woman justice in U.S. history, was appointed to the Supreme Court by President Bill Clinton in 1993. Unlike Justice O'Connor, Justice Ginsburg proclaimed herself solidly in favor of abortion rights during her confirmation hearings. Moreover, before becoming a judge, she advocated many women's rights issues, urging the Supreme Court to rule against most sex-based classifications.[9]

EQUAL EMPLOYMENT OPPORTUNITY

Equal Pay Act

In the 1960s and '70s, Congress enacted legislation prohibiting pay disparity between men and women and barring sex discrimination in employment, credit, housing, and education. Women increasingly turned to the courts to seek judicial enforcement of these rights.

The 1963 Equal Pay Act (EPA), passed during President John Kennedy's administration, commanded employers to provide "equal pay for equal work"; early federal court cases interpreting the EPA ruled that the jobs need not be "identical" but only "substantially equal."

Early EPA challenges frequently succeeded in court because many employers were paying women less than men for performing "substantially" the same work. However, despite these victories, the Equal Pay Act has not eliminated the earnings gap between men and women in the United States (with women who work full time earning about seventy cents for every dollar men earn). Because the EPA has been unable to overcome the problem of occupational sex segregation—that is, women working in jobs predominantly held by women and commanding lower wages than jobs primarily held by men—feminists formulated the theory of comparable worth, or pay equity.[10] Arguing that jobs of "similar skill, effort, responsibility, and working conditions" should receive comparable pay, comparable worth advocates sought to reduce sex-based pay differentials.

Unlike EPA cases, however, the comparable worth cases, filed under Title VII (of the 1964 Civil Rights Act) as wage discrimination suits, frequently lost. In such cases, when courts were asked to decide whether nursing was comparable to truck driving and should command comparable pay, they ruled that market conditions, such as the supply of available workers, the wages that workers can command from other employers, and the rate of unionization, constituted sufficient nondiscriminatory reasons for pay disparity between male truck drivers and female nurses. Although some states and municipalities have attempted to remedy pay inequities through legislation, occupational segregation still persists and, consequently, so does pay inequity.

Title VII

The biggest step toward equal employment opportunity for women was the passage of Title VII of the 1964 Civil Rights Act, making it unlawful for em-

ployers, labor unions, and employment agencies "to discriminate against any individual with respect to his [or her] compensation, terms, conditions or privileges of employment, because of such individual's race, color, religion, sex, or national origin."[11] In 1972, Title VII was expanded to cover private employers or unions with 15 or more employees, as well as employees of federal, state, and local governments, and educational institutions. Then in 1991, Congress broadened the protections of Title VII, making it easier for victims to prove discrimination, allowing workers to collect money damages in cases of intentional discrimination, and permitting jury trials.

Although, as originally proposed, Title VII was not intended to reach discrimination based on sex, in the final vote on the floor of the House of Representatives, Congresswoman Martha Griffiths proposed an amendment to include a ban on sex discrimination. Accepted in part by opponents who hoped to defeat the entire bill, the prohibition on sex discrimination was included in the final version of the law.

Title VII does not ban all sex-based employment. It allows employers to hire on the basis of sex where it is a "bona fide occupational qualification" (BFOQ) for the job, that is, when the nature of the business requires workers of only one sex. The courts soon narrowed the exception in a 1971 case involving an airline that refused to hire a man seeking a job as a flight attendant on the grounds that customers preferred women flight attendants. In *Diaz v. Pan American,* the circuit court ruled that customer preferences do not constitute a BFOQ.

The most recent situation involving the BFOQ defense occurred in the 1991 case of *United Automobile Workers v. Johnson Controls.* The Supreme Court held that an employer's fetal protection policy violated Title VII; the employer required women seeking jobs in which they were exposed to potentially harmful chemicals to be sterilized or prove their infertility.[12] Sex was not a "bona fide occupational qualification," said the Court, because the employer was unable to prove that pregnancy (or fertility) actually interfered with a woman's ability to perform the job. The Court noted that by passing Title VII (as amended by the Pregnancy Discrimination Act of 1978), Congress intended to allow women to decide for themselves whether (and where) to work while pregnant.

Pregnancy in the Workplace

One of the most important debates about women and employment concerns the treatment of pregnant women. Some feminists argue that pregnancy should be treated like any other disability or condition that affects the ability to work, because making exceptions for pregnant women denies equality between the sexes. Other feminists believe employers must treat women differently from men and that failing to acknowledge the constraints that pregnancy imposes on working women minimizes the physical and financial burdens of childbearing.

In a much criticized 1974 decision, *Geduldig v. Aiello*, the Supreme Court upheld a California law denying working women pregnancy disability benefits on the grounds that differentiating on the basis of pregnancy was *not* an impermissible sex classification; in a now-infamous footnote the Court explained that "the [California] program divides potential recipients into two groups—pregnant women and nonpregnant persons. While the first group is exclusively female, the second includes members of both sexes."

A few years later in *General Electric Company v. Gilbert*, a 1976 case, the Supreme Court held that the company could deny disability benefits to pregnant women while extending coverage to men for a variety of disabilities without violating Title VII. On October 31, 1978, Congress enacted the Pregnancy Discrimination Act (PDA), clarifying that discrimination on the basis of pregnancy constituted illegal sex discrimination under Title VII. The heart of the PDA stated that: "women affected by pregnancy . . . shall be treated the same for all employment-related purposes . . . as other persons not so affected but similar in their ability or inability to work. . . ." In enacting the PDA, Congress reversed *Gilbert* and placed pregnancy on a par with other disabilities. However, it only required employers to cover pregnancy-related disabilities if they offered disability benefits to all workers.

Passage of the PDA raised questions about whether pregnant women workers should be treated differently from men. During the 1970s, some states enacted laws granting pregnant workers reasonable periods of leave time, reinstatement, and protection of fringe benefits.[13] Shortly before the PDA was passed, the California legislature approved a law guaranteeing female employees covered by Title VII up to four months of unpaid pregnancy disability leave and reinstatement in their jobs. In *California Federal Savings and Loan Association v. Guerra*, decided in 1987, the U.S. Supreme Court held that California's law was consistent with the PDA's principle of nondiscrimination because although the PDA did not "require" preferential treatment, neither did it "prohibit" it.

Another law aimed at assisting women in the workplace, the Family and Medical Leave Act (FMLA), was enacted on February 5, 1993. In signing the bill, President Clinton said: "now millions of our people will no longer have to choose between their jobs and their families." The FMLA provided that workers in companies with fifty or more employees were entitled to take up to twelve weeks of unpaid leave for their serious illness, or for the birth or adoption of a child, or to care for a sick family member.

Although it furthers the nondiscrimination principle of the PDA, because it only provides for unpaid leaves of absence, the FMLA does not ease the financial burden of pregnancy on working women and falls short of achieving Title VII's goal of equal opportunity for women in the workplace. Recognizing the limited effects of the FMLA for workers unable to take time from work without pay, near the end of his administration, President Clinton suggested a new approach to state unemployment compensation programs that would allow states to provide paid leave for new parents. The Clinton proposal, leaving implementation to the states on a voluntary basis, would give states the authority to provide funds for a parent to have a paid leave of absence of twelve weeks during the baby's first year (or the first year after a child is adopted).

SEXUAL HARASSMENT IN EMPLOYMENT

The issue of sexual harassment was brought to the nation's attention when, in October 1990, Professor Anita Hill of the University of Oklahoma Law

School testified before the Senate Judiciary Committee on national television that she had been sexually harassed by Supreme Court nominee Clarence Thomas when she worked for him at the Equal Employment Opportunity Commission. Although Thomas was narrowly confirmed by the Senate and took his seat on the high court, the controversy created a greater awareness of the problems of harassment that many women face on their jobs.

Sexual harassment reflects an imbalance of power in the workplace and sends a message that workers may be viewed as objects of sexual gratification. Feminist legal scholar Catharine MacKinnon has identified two types of sexual harassment in employment. The first, called *quid pro quo,* exists when women are forced to exchange sexual favors for employment benefits. The second, called workplace (or environmental) harassment, occurs when the atmosphere in which women work is permeated with unwelcome sexuality, but no explicit demands are made on them as a condition of their employment.[14]

In the 1970s, when women began to bring claims of sexual harassment as violations of Title VII, the courts largely dismissed their complaints. After a number of cases, however, the courts agreed that sexual harassment could constitute the type of sex discrimination in employment that was forbidden by Title VII. Judges generally proved more willing to believe *quid pro quo* harassment claims because the victim was able to point to an adverse employment decision resulting from her refusal to comply with her employer's demands.

The courts eventually also accepted the legitimacy of workplace harassment claims. In the 1981 case of *Bundy v. Jackson,* the federal court ruled in favor of Sandra Bundy, agreeing that she was in a hostile work environment because her boss said to her, among other things, "any man in his right mind would want to rape you." The court also noted that employers could be held responsible for hostile environments created by their employees.

In a unanimous opinion in the 1986 case of *Meritor Savings Bank v. Vinson,* the Supreme Court agreed with the lower courts that a hostile work environment created by sexual harassment, that is, "unwelcome" sexual advances, violates Title VII when it is sufficiently "severe and pervasive." The high court did not settle the question of the extent of the company's liability for sexual harassment, rul-

ing, however, that the employer cannot simply escape liability by claiming ignorance of the harassment nor by pointing to a company policy against it.

In 1991, in *Robinson v. Jacksonville Shipyards,* a Florida federal court judge ruled that pornographic pictures of women in various stages of undress as well as suggestive and lewd remarks by male employees created a hostile work environment for women shipyard workers. And following the example set by the Ninth Circuit in *Ellison v. Brady,* another 1991 decision, many federal courts also began to view the harassing behavior from the perspective of the "reasonable woman."[15] The Ninth Circuit defended this approach by pointing out that conduct that might appear normal to a man could reasonably be seen by a woman as offensive, abusive, or "hostile."

In 1993, victims of sexual harassment won another victory in the Supreme Court in *Harris v. Forklift.* In this unanimous opinion, the Court held that women were not required to demonstrate that the sexual harassment they complained of was so severe that they suffered psychological injury, but only that it was abusive and affected the employee's job performance.

In a 1998 decision, *Oncale v. Sundowner Offshore Services,* the Supreme Court held that Title VII also applies to sexual harassment between people of the same sex. The case involved the claim of Joseph Oncale, who quit his job on a Louisiana oil rig because of abuse by male coworkers who molested him, insulted him, and threatened to rape him. Despite his complaints to the company, nothing was done.

The lower federal court dismissed his case, ruling that Title VII does not apply to a man claiming he was victimized by other men. In a unanimous opinion, the Supreme Court made it clear that neither the harasser nor the victim's sex or sexual orientation was relevant in determining whether the law was being broken; what mattered was the conduct and whether it was "severely hostile or abusive." The Supreme Court returned the case to the lower court to allow Oncale to prove that he was discriminated against on the basis of sex, as the law requires.

Some months later, in June 1999, the Supreme Court handed down two 7 to 2 sexual harassment decisions in which it held that, under most circumstances, employers could be responsible for the harassing acts of their employees, depending in part on whether they had a policy against sexual harassment and whether they had made it known to their employees.

In its rulings, the Court reviewed three sets of circumstances involving sexual harassment of employees. First, there were the *quid pro quo* cases that occur when a supervisor retaliates against an employee who does not accede to demands for sexual favors. In these situations, said the Court, the employer is automatically liable whether it knew of the harassment or not and whether it had an antiharassment policy or not. Second, the Court stated, were the hostile work environment cases where there is a severe and pervasive sexually charged atmosphere. And last, maintained the Court, is the case where a supervisor threatens an adverse job action but does not carry out the threat. In the latter two situations, the Court ruled, an employer would be liable unless it could show it "exercised reasonable care to prevent and correct promptly any sexually harassing behavior." Employers could avoid liability, added the Court, by proving that the employee "unreasonably failed to take advantage of any preventive or corrective opportunities provided by the employer."

In one of the cases, *Burlington Industries v. Ellerth*, Kimberly Ellerth worked as a salesperson in one of Burlington's divisions in Chicago. She charged that a supervisor, the vice-president of the company, threatened her with adverse job consequences if she did not respond more positively to his lewd remarks and sexual overtures. He said he could make her life "very hard or very easy," depending on her reaction to him. Although his threats were never carried out, she eventually quit her job but waited three weeks before attributing her resignation to his behavior. She never informed anyone in authority about his conduct, despite her knowledge that the company had a sexual harassment policy.

Adapting principles of employer liability used in *quid pro quo* cases, the high court held that employers are liable for the supervisor's harassment in cases such as Ellerth's because they put the supervisor in a position of power over employees. The company can escape liability, however, said the Court, if it can show that it tried to prevent the harassment and that the employee failed to take advantage of the opportunity to avoid the harm. Such

a defense, reiterated the Court, is not available in cases where a threatened job action is carried out by the supervisor.

In the other case, *Faragher v. City of Boca Raton*, Beth Faragher had worked as a lifeguard for the city of Boca Raton, Florida, from 1985 to 1990 to pay her college expenses. In 1992, while attending law school, she sued the city and her two male supervisors, claiming they created a hostile work environment by repeatedly touching her and making lewd comments to her. Faragher collected $10,000 in damages from the supervisors but did not recover fees from the city because, as the lower court held, city officials were unaware of the harassment.

On appeal, the Supreme Court held that although the city had a formal sexual harassment policy, it was liable for the acts of the supervisory employees because it had not done enough to make the policy known among its employees, nor had it attempted to keep track of the conduct of its supervisors. The problem was, in part, that the city's sexual harassment policy specified that complaints must be reported to the employee's supervisors, and the city had neglected to convey to employees that they might bypass their supervisors when necessary. Thus, the Court concluded that, as a matter of law, the city had not exercised reasonable care in preventing the supervisors' harassing conduct.

Both employers and women's rights advocates applauded the Supreme Court's decisions, saying that the Court had gone a long way toward clarifying a confusing area of law and underscoring the fact that employers could not easily escape responsibility when their supervisory employees engage in sexual harassment.

EQUAL EDUCATIONAL OPPORTUNITY

Separate but Equal

In 1954 in *Brown v. Board of Education*, the Supreme Court announced that "separate but equal" has no place in public education and that schools segregated on the basis of race are unconstitutional. Refusing to apply the principle to sex-segregated education, the Court has never held that "separate but equal" on the basis of sex is inherently unconstitutional.

The Supreme Court's first ruling on sex-segregated education was the 1982 case of *Mississippi*

University for Women v. Hogan in which nurse Joe Hogan sued for admission to the all-women nursing program at Mississippi University for Women (MUW). Mississippi argued that its policy was intended to compensate women for past discrimination. Speaking for a 5–4 majority, Justice O'Connor rejected MUW's argument because there was no evidence that the school had ever discriminated against women. Actually, she noted, rather than compensating women, the policy had the opposite effect of maintaining the stereotypical image of nursing as a female occupation. However, while the Court held that MUW's nursing program must open its doors to men, it stopped short of declaring that "separate but equal" on the basis of sex was unconstitutional.

Military School Education

More recently, the debate over "separate but equal" centered on the admission of women to state-funded military schools, specifically, Virginia Military Institute (VMI) and South Carolina's Citadel.[16] These two institutions, the last two male-only military colleges in the nation, had refused to admit women on an equal basis with men, claiming that the presence of women would undermine the institutional mission of training men for the military.

The six-year battle to win admission for women to VMI and the Citadel began when the U.S. Department of Justice filed suit against VMI in 1990. VMI argued that it would lose its distinctiveness and destroy its educational mission if forced to admit women.

Following a trial, in June 1991, Federal Court Judge Jackson L. Kiser ruled for the state, holding that to allow women into VMI would significantly impair the educational environment. Concluding his opinion in *United States v. Virginia*, the judge stated that "VMI truly marches to the beat of a different drummer, and I will permit it to continue to do so."

On appeal, the Fourth Circuit Court of Appeals ruled that VMI had justified its single-gender policy on the basis of its institutional mission but had failed to answer "the larger question of whether the unique benefit offered by VMI's type of education can be denied to women." In the case that would be known as *VMI I*, the appellate court declined to order VMI to admit women. Instead, the court gave the school three options; the court said VMI could stop accepting state funds (it was receiving more than a third of its funding from the state), offer a parallel program at another institution, or admit women. The case was sent back to Judge Kiser to allow him to determine whether the state's response was constitutionally acceptable.

Meanwhile, the state began to formulate a plan to establish a military-style training program for women at neighboring Mary Baldwin College, a private school thirty miles away. Called "Virginia Women's Institute for Leadership" (VWIL), this "separate but equal" program allowed women to attend VMI for reserve officer training, while taking leadership and liberal arts courses at Mary Baldwin. In May 1994, Judge Kiser ruled that VMI could keep its doors open without admitting women because the alternative program at Mary Baldwin College satisfied equal protection requirements. Kiser wrote: "if VMI marches to the beat of a drum, then Mary Baldwin marches to the melody of a fife, and when the march is over, both will have arrived at the same destination."

In *VMI II*, the appellate court agreed that VWIL provided an adequate remedy for the constitutional violation, holding that the Constitution merely required that men and women receive "substantively comparable benefits" from the state. VWIL's doors opened in August 1995 with forty-two women enrolled.

The Supreme Court announced its 7–1 opinion (Justice Thomas recused himself because his son attended VMI) in *United States v. Virginia* in the last week of June 1996. Speaking for the Court, Justice Ginsburg reiterated that states must offer an "exceedingly persuasive justification" for sex-based classifications. "The burden of justification," she declared, "is demanding, and it rests entirely on the State."

The state had argued that "single-sex education provides important educational benefits" that contribute to "diversity in educational approaches"; it contended that admitting women to VMI would require the school to modify its approach and thus lose its unique "adversative" character. The Court, however, found "no persuasive evidence" in the record that VMI's single-sex admission policy was intended to further educational diversity throughout the state. Moreover, said the Court, the state's assumption that women would fail in VMI's method of education was inappropriately based on "fixed notions concerning the roles and abilities of males and females." Refusing to place sex in the same proscribed category as race or national origin, the Court nevertheless ruled that Virginia had not shown a sufficient justification for excluding all women from VMI. Turning to the VWIL program, Ginsburg characterized it as "separate" and "unequal" and not a remedy for VMI's constitutional violation.

The Citadel case began in 1993 when Shannon Faulkner sued the university for rejecting her application for admission, charging that the Citadel's all-male cadet corps was unconstitutional. In August, a federal judge ruled in favor of her admission but barred her from participating in the corps of cadets. Following numerous legal delays, she was finally permitted to enroll in January 1994—the first woman ever to sit in regular day classes at the Citadel. After a trial, in July 1994, the same federal judge ordered Faulkner into the corps of cadets, but because of appeals and other legal challenges, during which time the state made a half-hearted attempt at creating an alternative program such as VWIL, Faulkner did not become a member of the corps until August 1995.

About a week after she became the first woman cadet at the Citadel, Faulkner unexpectedly resigned—with about thirty other new cadets. Citing ill health and emotional stress, she explained that the lengthy battle with its 2½ years of stress had "all crashed in" on her during the last week.[17] Another plaintiff was substituted in the suit against the Citadel, but the suit was placed on hold while the VMI case was on appeal before the high court.

On the day that the Supreme Court announced that VMI would have to admit women or forfeit state funding, the Citadel declared it would immediately begin to accept women; four were admitted into the Citadel's entering class. In contrast, VMI alumni began to explore the possibility of buying the college from the state and maintaining it as a private institution. Three months after the Court's ruling, in a 9 to 8 vote, the Governing Board of VMI finally ended its attempt to keep women out of VMI and announced that henceforth VMI would be coeducational.

Women now attend both institutions, studying and living alongside the men cadets.

Title IX

In 1972, Congress enacted Title IX of the Educational Amendments, a law providing that "no person in the United States shall, on the basis of sex, be excluded from participation in, be denied the benefits of, or be subjected to discrimination under any education program or activity receiving Federal financial assistance." Title IX bans discrimination in vocational, professional, and graduate schools; it encompasses physical education classes, extracurricular activities, scholarships, and counseling. Although by its terms, Title IX only authorizes the federal government to terminate federal funds to schools that violate the act, in 1979, in *Cannon v. University of Chicago*, the Supreme Court held that individuals who have been discriminated against on the basis of sex have the right to sue educational institutions to enforce the protections of Title IX.

Although Title IX represented an important step toward equality in education, it allowed exceptions to sex equality in two major areas: admissions and athletics. The law exempted single-sex admissions in most elementary and secondary schools, private undergraduate schools, and traditionally single-sex public undergraduate institutions, as well as military and religious schools.

The Supreme Court's initial approach to Title IX was an expansive one, allowing the individual discrimination suits and including employees as well as students within the ban on sex discrimination.[18] Then, in 1984, in *Grove City College v. Bell*, the Court narrowed the statutory definition of "program or activity."

Grove City College argued that it was exempt from Title IX regulations because it received no direct federal aid. If the law did apply to it, the college insisted, it was restricted to the program receiving aid—in this case, the financial aid office. Ruling that educational institutions receiving indirect aid through student grants and loans were subject to Title IX, the Supreme Court nevertheless agreed with Grove City College that Title IX only applied to the specific program receiving the federal aid; other units within the college were not within the reach of Title IX.

In 1988, over President Reagan's veto, Congress enacted the Civil Rights Restoration Act (CRRA) to reverse part of the *Grove City* decision. The CRRA defined "program or activity" to include the entire institution if any part of it received federal funds. Although there continues to be resistance to the principle of sex equality in athletic programs, Title IX, strengthened by passage of the CRRA, is credited with producing greater equity in college and high school sports programs. The influence of Title IX in the lives of younger women can be seen in the performance of the U.S. women athletes in the 1996 Olympics as well as the victory of the U.S. women's soccer team in the 1999 World Cup.

In addition to its role in equality in athletics, Title IX has also been used to protect women and girls from sexual harassment in educational settings. In *Alexander v. Yale University,* a federal court ruled that Title IX forbids sexual harassment of students.[19] Since then, the Supreme Court has decided three cases involving Title IX and sexual harassment in schools, in each case deciding the circumstances under which a school may be held liable for harassment to students under Title IX.

In *Franklin v. Gwinnett County Public Schools,* decided in 1992, the Supreme Court extended the principle of "workplace" harassment, announced in *Meritor Savings Bank v. Vinson,* to the public school setting. The suit was brought by a high school student who claimed that a teacher had repeatedly sexually abused her and that school officials knew about it and did nothing to stop it. They even, she alleged, tried to prevent her from filing charges. The Supreme Court reversed the lower court action dismissing her suit, ruling that money damages were available in cases involving sexual harassment of students by teachers. The high court did not, however, specify under what circumstances a school would be held liable for a teacher's sexual harassment of a student.

The next case, *Gebser v. Lago Vista Independent School District,* provided the Court with an opportunity to address the issue of school liability in a case in which school officials were unaware of the teacher's misconduct. The case involved a sexual harassment suit brought by a high school student who had a sexual relationship with her teacher during her first year of high school. She had not reported the relationship to school authorities, and

they had not known about it. When it was discovered and the teacher was fired, the student sued the school for damages under Title IX. The lower federal courts dismissed the case, ruling that the school was not responsible because it had no actual knowledge of the relationship between the teacher and the student. In a 1998 decision, the Supreme Court affirmed the lower court rulings. The high court held that the school would only be held liable if a district official who had the authority to take corrective measures on behalf of the school knew of the teacher's misconduct and was "deliberately indifferent" to it. Any other policy, the Court held, was unfair to the school and would go beyond what Congress intended in Title IX.

One of the disputed areas remaining in the law following *Franklin* and *Gebser* was whether the school could be held liable for the sexual harassment of one student by another.[20]

A year after *Gebser* was decided, the Supreme Court addressed the question of the limits of the school's responsibility under Title IX for harassing behavior by classmates in *Davis v. Monroe County Board of Education.* LaShonda Davis was a fifth grader in a Monroe County, Georgia, public school who was physically and verbally abused for months by the boy who sat next to her in class. His behavior included grabbing her breasts, rubbing against her, and making lewd comments to her. Despite LaShonda and her mother's repeated complaints to her teacher and the school principal, nothing was done to stop her classmate's harassing behavior, including ignoring LaShonda's pleas to change his seat. Her grades began to suffer and she threatened suicide. Eventually, the Davis family filed criminal charges against the boy and he pleaded guilty to sexual battery in juvenile court. On behalf of her daughter, LaShonda's mother sued the school district under Title IX.

The issue for the Supreme Court was the extent of the school's responsibility for harassing behavior by students. The appellate court, holding that Title IX only protected students from harassment by school employees, not other students, dismissed the case. School officials argued that applying Title IX to student-on-student harassment would open schools up to an "avalanche" of litigation against them for situations involving children teasing and calling each other names. Announcing the opinion for a 5–4 majority, Justice O'Connor restated the *Gebser* position and held that a school may be held liable in cases involving sexual harassment of students by students when it knows of the harassment and is deliberately indifferent to it. Schools that decide "to remain idle in the face of known student-on-student harassment in its schools," said O'Connor, are responsible in damages when the behavior is "so severe, pervasive, and objectively offensive that it denies its victims the equal access to education" guaranteed under Title IX.

Although the standards set by the Supreme Court set the bar of the school's liability quite high, it conveyed to schools that if they choose to ignore the legitimate complaints of their students about other students' harassing behavior, they will have to pay for their neglect.

REPRODUCTIVE RIGHTS

In 1973, the Supreme Court issued a ruling in *Roe v. Wade* that would have an enormous impact on a woman's reproductive decision making, that is, whether a women had the right to control her pregnancy. The case involved a constitutional challenge to a Texas law that allowed legal abortions only in cases where the woman's life was endangered by the pregnancy.[21]

In a 7 to 2 vote, the Supreme Court proclaimed that the constitutional right to privacy was "broad enough to encompass a woman's decision whether or not to terminate her pregnancy." But, said Justice Harry Blackmun, the right was not "unqualified." Although the state could not ban abortions during the first three months (first trimester) of pregnancy, during the next three months (second trimester), it could make rules and regulations that reasonably relate to maternal health. In the last three months of pregnancy (third trimester), because the fetus may be able to survive outside the womb, the state could prohibit abortions entirely unless the woman's life or health was at risk.

Despite the sweeping principles of *Roe*, the Supreme Court refused to require states to provide public funds for poor women seeking abortions. In three 1977 cases, the Court held that although women had a right to terminate their pregnancies, the government was not obligated to fund the exer-

cise of that right. And, according to the Supreme Court, because the government's decision placed no obstacle "in the pregnant woman's path," her right of privacy was not diminished. Thus, although *Roe* established a woman's "right to choose," over time it became apparent that the right was largely limited to women with sufficient financial resources.[22]

Following *Roe,* states passed laws limiting young women's access to abortion. In a number of decisions beginning in 1976, the Supreme Court upheld laws requiring minors seeking abortions to obtain parental consent, or at least notify them, before the abortion could be performed. The Court has not permitted parents to exercise full veto power over their daughter's decision to have an abortion though; state laws requiring parental involvement must contain judicial bypass provisions allowing the minor to petition a court for approval instead.

Reproductive Rights Diminished

In two cases decided in 1983 and 1986, the Supreme Court struck regulations requiring second-trimester abortions to be performed in hospitals, specifying that physicians must provide pregnant women with information regarding fetal development and the risks of the abortion, establishing waiting periods, and requiring the presence of a second physician at abortions performed late in the pregnancy.

In 1989, the antiabortion forces won a victory when the Supreme Court upheld a Missouri law imposing significant restrictions on women's reproductive choices. Although the Supreme Court did not take the ultimate step of overturning *Roe*, the 5 to 4 decision in *Webster v. Reproductive Health Services* marked a setback for abortion rights advocates.

Webster revolved around a 1986 Missouri abortion law that included a preamble declaring life begins at conception, a provision requiring a test to determine fetal viability, a ban on using public funds to encourage or counsel women to have abortions not necessary to save their lives, and a prohibition on using public facilities for abortions—even for women willing and able to pay.

Speaking for a plurality of the Supreme Court, Chief Justice William Rehnquist held that the Court need not decide on the constitutionality of the preamble because it simply reflected the state's view on the onset of life. Justice Rehnquist also found no constitutional problem in prohibiting the use of public funds and public facilities for abortion or the fetal testing provision even though the latter clashed with *Roe* by allowing viability tests during the second trimester.

Justice Blackmun, author of *Roe*, defended the opinion he announced almost twenty years ago, arguing that *Roe* still represented the best way of balancing the state's interest in regulating abortion with the woman's interest in privacy. He concluded his dissent by warning of dire consequences for the future: "for today, at least . . . the women of this Nation still retain the liberty to control their destinies. But the signs are evident and very ominous, and a chill wind blows."

The "chill wind" Blackmun feared arose within months after *Webster* as a number of state legislatures enacted laws restricting abortion, often including provisions previously declared unconstitutional by the Supreme Court. The Pennsylvania Abortion Control Act of 1989, among other provisions, required married women to notify their husbands of a planned abortion, imposed a 24-hour waiting period, and ordered the doctor to warn women of the dangers of abortion.

With two strongly prochoice justices, Thurgood Marshall and William Brennan, retired from the bench, there was a realistic possibility that the Supreme Court would abolish the reproductive guarantees established in *Roe*.

In a sharply divided ruling in *Planned Parenthood of Southeastern Pennsylvania v. Casey,* in 1992, the Supreme Court "reaffirmed the essential holding" of *Roe* that women have a constitutional right to terminate a pregnancy. The Court abolished *Roe*'s trimester framework, however, essentially dividing the pregnancy into two stages based on the viability of the fetus. As in *Roe*, the state's interest in the viable fetus justifies regulations or even bans on abortion except when necessary to preserve the life or health of the mother. Departing from *Roe*, the high court held that states could enact abortion regulations during the previability stage as long as the regulations did not impose an "undue burden" on the woman seeking an abortion. Indicating the extent to which the Court had shifted in its support for abortion rights since *Roe*, the only regulation found "unduly burdensome" was the mandate that

women notify their husbands of their intention to have an abortion.

The Debate Continues

The most recent controversy over abortion rights revolves around a procedure known as "dilation and extraction," almost always performed in the last months of pregnancy when women's lives are endangered or when their fetuses have severe abnormalities.[23] In 1995, Congress approved a bill to criminalize the procedure unless a doctor could show it was necessary to save the woman's life and no other procedure would be effective. The bill aimed at deterring the doctor from performing the abortion; it exempted the woman from criminal penalties and allowed her parents or husband to sue the physician. President Clinton vetoed the bill, saying it provided no exemption for situations where a woman's health was at risk. His veto message accused Congress of "fashion[ing] a bill that is consistent neither with the Constitution nor with sound public policy."[24]

More than half the states also attempted to ban the procedure, with the majority of courts holding these laws unconstitutional. In September 1999, a federal court ruled in *Carhart v. Stenberg* that a Nebraska law was written so broadly that it also barred doctors from performing abortions on nonviable fetuses by the most common second-trimester method ("dilation and evacuation"). Thus, ruled the court, the Nebraska law imposed an undue burden on a woman's right to choose to have an abortion and was unconstitutional.

The U.S. Supreme Court accepted the case for review and will likely decide it at the end of the 1999–2000 term.

Abortion Protests

Largely prompted by the militant tactics of antiabortion groups, abortion clinics began to seek the protection of federal marshals when local law enforcement officials were incapable of curbing violence against clinics. In *Bray v. Alexandria Women's Health Clinic,* decided in January 1993, the Supreme Court barred federal court judges from invoking the Ku Klux Klan Act, a Reconstruction-era civil rights law, to block protest activity that interfered with the work of the clinics. The Court held that women seeking abortions were not within the class of people intended to be protected by the federal law.

Reacting in part to the *Bray* decision, and to the often violent tactics of the antiabortion protestors, Congress passed a law called the Freedom of Access to Clinic Entrances Act (FACE), signed into law by President Clinton on May 26, 1994. FACE makes it a federal crime to use force, the threat of force, or physical obstruction, such as sit-ins, to interfere with, injure, or intimidate clinic workers or women seeking abortions or other reproductive health services. Violators are subject to imprisonment, fines, and civil suit. It was passed in reaction to the increasing number of blockades of abortion clinics by antiabortion groups, such as Operation Rescue, and the inability or unwillingness of local law enforcement officials to remove them from the scene. Shortly before the law was passed; two doctors were shot, one fatally, by antiabortion activists near the entrances to their clinics.[25]

In two 1994 decisions, the Supreme Court held that the First Amendment did not entitle protestors to engage in unrestricted protest activity. In *National Organization for Women v. Scheidler,* the Court unanimously held that the Racketeer Influenced and Corrupt Organizations (RICO) Act could be applied to conspiracies that sought to close the doors of abortion clinics nationwide. RICO is a powerful weapon, enabling the government to file criminal charges as well as allowing private plaintiffs to collect triple damages if successful. The effect of the Supreme Court's decision was to allow clinics to present evidence to a judge that the defendants committed serious felonies, like bombings or murder, to further the conspiracy.

The second case that year, *Madsen v. Women's Health Center,* involved a legal confrontation between a Melbourne, Florida, abortion clinic and Operation Rescue. In a partial victory for the clinic, the Supreme Court upheld a lower court order establishing a 36-foot buffer zone around clinic entrances and driveways as well as a ban on excessive noise (singing, chanting, whistling, shouting, yelling, and the use of bullhorns and car horns) during the hours of morning surgery. Citing the First Amendment, the high court refused to allow a buffer zone at the back and sides of the clinic, the restriction on picket signs, and a 300-foot buffer at the homes of clinic

staff, and a ban on unsolicited approaches to clinic patients.

A number of state laws also aimed at protecting persons at clinic entrances from verbal or physical harassment from protestors. A Colorado law, enacted in 1993 before FACE, attempted to protect women seeking abortions by establishing a 100-foot zone around health care facilities and barred persons inside this zone from moving closer than eight feet to pass out literature or counsel or protest abortion activity without the listener's consent. In *Hill v. Colorado,* decided in February 1999, the Colorado Supreme Court held that the law did not violate the protestors' First Amendment right to free speech. In January 2000, the U.S. Supreme Court agreed to review the case.

Violence Against Women

After extensive hearings lasting four years, during which it determined the severity of violence against women and the lack of adequate response by state law enforcement authorities, Congress enacted the Violence Against Women Act (VAWA) as part of the Violent Crime Control and Law Enforcement Act of 1994. VAWA had been introduced by Senator Joseph Biden (Democrat from Delaware) in 1990. Data from the Department of Justice introduced during consideration of the bill showed that most of the violence against women, including rapes and sexual assaults, was committed by someone known to them, and in a third of those cases, the perpetrator was a husband, ex-husband, boyfriend, or ex-boyfriend; moreover, women were six times more likely than men to experience violence committed by an intimate.[26] VAWA made it a federal crime to cross state lines with the intent to injure a partner or spouse or violate an order of protection. In an attempt to focus the efforts of state law enforcement agencies on gender-motivated violence, Congress authorized $1.6 billion for six years to a program called S.T.O.P. (Services*Training*Officers*Prosecutors) in which states receive funding to improve strategies among police, prosecutors, and prevention services to deal with crimes of sexual violence or domestic abuse. The law also established a Violence Against Women Office in the Department of Justice and created a national 800 hotline number.

In May 1995, a West Virginia man, who severely beat his wife, locked her in the trunk of their car, and then drove through West Virginia and Kentucky, was the first person convicted under VAWA. He was sentenced to life in prison for the kidnaping and abuse that resulted in her suffering irreversible brain damage. The second conviction followed shortly thereafter against a man who beat his domestic partner in Oregon and forced her to drive with him to California. He was convicted in a California federal court and sentenced to 87 months in prison and ordered to pay her restitution.

Perhaps the most controversial section of VAWA, known as the "civil rights provision," declared that "all persons within the United States shall have the right to be free from crimes of violence motivated by gender." Intended to complement existing federal civil rights laws, this provision granted victims of gender-motivated violence, such as rape or domestic violence, the right to sue their attackers for damages, including punitive damages.[27]

In 1994, first-year student Christy Brzonkala claimed she was sexually assaulted by two football players in her dormitory room at Virginia Polytechnic Institute and State University (VPI). Several months later, when she learned the identity of her attackers, she reported them to the university under VPI's Sexual Assault Policy. The university's judicial committee found one of the players guilty of sexual assault and suspended him; no action was taken against the other man. After a number of appeals, the university set aside the offender's suspension and allowed him to return to school and continue to play football.[28] Fearful for her safety, Brzonkala left school and sued the university and her two attackers under the civil rights provision of VAWA, providing the first opportunity for the federal courts to rule on its constitutionality. The defendants argued that the "civil rights" section of VAWA was unconstitutional because Congress lacked the constitutional authority to grant victims of gender-motivated violence the right to sue their attackers for damages and that laws regarding sexual assault were exclusively within the purview of state criminal justice systems.

Judge Jackson Kiser, the judge who had ruled in VMI's favor, agreed with the defendants that the statute was unconstitutional and dismissed the case. After lauding the purpose of the statute, the appel-late court upheld his ruling. In doing so, the appeals court relied on a case decided in 1995 in which the U.S. Supreme Court held that the Gun-Free School Zones Act, which made it a crime to possess a gun within 1,000 feet of a school, was insufficiently linked to interstate commerce and therefore Congress lacked the authority to pass it. The *Brzonkala* court rejected the argument that violence affected interstate commerce by limiting women's opportunity to participate in the labor force.

On May 15, 2000, the Supreme Court upheld the appellate court, striking the civil rights provision of the act. The high court ruled that despite congressional findings that gender-motivated violence has a serious impact on the economy, there is an insufficient link between interstate commerce and the criminal behavior to permit Congress to establish a federal right to sue the perpetrators of such violence.[29]

CONCLUSION

This chapter has demonstrated that the law is a powerful weapon in the struggle for social, political, and economic equality between women and men. In the last thirty to forty years, building on the efforts of the first women's movement, the feminist movement has advocated increased equality in employment opportunity and pay equity, ending sexual harassment at work and in school, eliminating violence against women, and expanding reproductive rights. Although their efforts have helped lessen inequality between the sexes, there is more work ahead in the struggle to produce a society where sex is no longer a barrier to equality.

References

Baron, Ava. "Feminist Legal Strategies: The Powers of Difference." In *Analyzing Gender,* ed. Beth Hess and Myra Marx Ferree, pp. 474–503. Beverly Hills: Sage, 1987.

Cahn, Naomi R. "The Looseness of Legal Language: The Reasonable Woman Standard in Theory and Practice." *Cornell Law Review* 77 (1992), pp. 1398–1446.

Collins, Kathy Lee. "Student-to-Student Sexual Harassment under Title IX: The Legal and Practical Issues." *Drake Law Review* 46 (1998), pp. 789–834.

Cowan, Ruth. "Women's Rights Through Litigation: An Examination of the American Civil Liberties Union

Women's Rights Project, 1971–1976." *Columbia Human Rights Law Review 8* (Spring–Summer 1976), pp. 373–412.

Craig, Barbara Hinkson, and O'Brien, David M. *Abortion and American Politics.* Chatham, NJ: Chatham House, 1993.

Dziech, Billie Wright, and Weiner, Linda. *The Lecherous Professor: Sexual Harassment on Campus.* Boston: Beacon Press, 1984.

Evans, Sara. *Personal Politics.* New York: Vintage Books, 1980.

Faux, Marian. *Roe v. Wade.* New York: Macmillan, 1988.

Freeman, Jo. *The Politics of Women's Liberation.* New York: David McKay, 1975.

Gelb, Joyce, and Palley, Marian Lief. *Women and Public Policies.* Princeton: Princeton University Press, 1987.

Ginsburg, Ruth Bader. "The Burger Court's Grapplings with Sex Discrimination." In *The Burger Court,* ed. Vincent Blasi, pp. 132–156. New Haven: Yale University Press, 1983.

Hembacher, Brian. "Fetal Protection Policies: Reasonable Protection or Unreasonable Limitation on Female Employees." *Industrial Relations Law Journal 11* (1989), pp. 32–44.

Houck, Danielle M. "VAWA After *Lopez:* Reconsidering Congressional Power Under the Fourteenth Amendment in Light of *Brzonkala v. Virginia Polytechnic and State University,*" *U.C. Davis Law Review 31* (1998), pp. 625–653.

Kraditor, Aileen. *The Ideas of the Woman Suffrage Movement 1890–1920.* New York: Anchor Books, 1971.

McCann, Michael. *Rights At Work: Pay Equity Reform and the Politics of Legal Mobilization.* Chicago: University of Chicago Press, 1994.

MacKinnon, Catharine. *Sexual Harassment of Working Women.* New Haven: Yale University Press, 1979.

Mezey, Susan Gluck. "The Persistence of Sex Segregated Education in the South." *Southeastern Political Review 22* (June 1994), pp. 371–395.

———. *In Pursuit of Equality: Women, Public Policy and the Federal Courts.* New York: St. Martin's Press, 1992.

Miller, Margaret. "Justice Sandra Day O'Connor: Token or Triumph From a Feminist Perspective." *Golden Gate Law Review 15* (1985), pp. 493–525.

Note. "Rethinking (M)otherhood: Feminist Theory and State Regulation of Pregnancy." *Harvard Law Review 103* (1990), pp. 1325–1343.

O'Brien, Christine Neylon, and Madek, Gerald A. "Pregnancy Discrimination and Maternity Leave Laws." *Dickinson Law Review 93* (1989), pp. 311–337.

O'Connor, Karen. *Women's Organizations' Use of the Courts.* Lexington: Lexington Books, 1980.

Salomone, Rosemary. *Equal Education Under Law.* New York: St. Martin's Press, 1986.

Samuels, Suzanne Uttaro. *Fetal Rights, Women's Rights: Gender Equality in the Workplace.* Madison: University of Wisconsin Press, 1995.

Smith, Christopher E., Baugh, Joyce Ann, Hensley, Thomas R., and Johnson, Scott Patrick. "The First-Term Performance of Justice Ruth Bader Ginsburg." *Judicature 78* (1994), pp. 74–80.

Smith, Sheila. "Justice Ruth Bader Ginsburg and Sexual Harassment Law: Will the Second Female Supreme Court Justice Become the Court's Women's Rights Champion?" *University of Cincinnati Law Review 63* (1995), pp. 1893–1945.

Sullivan, Patricia A., and Goldzwig, Steven R. "Abortion and Undue Burdens: Justice Sandra Day O'Connor and Judicial Decision-Making." *Women and Politics 16* (1996), pp. 27–53;

Taub, Nadine, and Schneider, Elizabeth. "Perspectives on Women's Subordination and the Role of Law." In *The Politics of Law,* ed. David Kairys, pp. 117–139. New York: Pantheon Books, 1982.

Tong, Rosemarie. *Feminist Thought: A Comprehensive Analysis.* Boulder: Westview Press, 1989.

Tribe, Laurence H. *Abortion: The Clash of Absolutes.* New York: Norton, 1992.

United States Department of Justice, *The Violence Against Women Act: Breaking the Cycle of Violence* (online). Available on http://www.ojp.usdoj.gov/vawo/laws/cycle.htm

Whalen, Charles, and Whalen, Barbara. *The Longest Debate.* New York: New American Library, 1985.

Williams, Wendy. "Equality's Riddle: Pregnancy and the Equal Treatment/Special Treatment Debate." *New York University Review of Law and Social Change 13* (1984–85), pp. 325–380.

———. "Firing the Woman to Protect the Fetus: The Reconciliation of Fetal Protection with Employment Opportunity under Title VII." *Georgetown Law Journal 69* (1981), pp. 641–704.

Notes

1. Tennessee, the last state needed, ratified the Nineteenth Amendment on August 26, 1920. Aileen Kraditor, *The Ideas*

of the Woman Suffrage Movement 1890–1920 (New York: Anchor Books, 1971).

2. Sara Evans, *Personal Politics* (New York: Vintage Books, 1980).

3. There are different types of feminists, for example, radical feminists, Marxist feminists, and liberal feminists; they urge different approaches to achieve equality. Rosemarie Tong, *Feminist Thought: A Comprehensive Analysis* (Boulder: Westview Press, 1989).

4. Ava Baron, "Feminist Legal Strategies: The Powers of Difference," in *Analyzing Gender,* ed. Beth Hess and Myra Marx Ferree (Beverly Hills: Sage, 1987), pp. 474–503; Nadine Taub and Elizabeth Schneider, "Perspectives On Women's Subordination and the Role of Law," in *The Politics of Law,* ed. David Kairys (New York: Pantheon Books, 1982), pp. 117–139.

5. Ruth Bader Ginsburg, "The Burger Court's Grapplings with Sex Discrimination," in *The Burger Court,* ed. Vincent Blasi (New Haven: Yale University Press, 1983), pp. 132–156.

6. Karen O'Connor *Women's Organizations' Use of the Courts* (Lexington: Lexington Books, 1980); Ruth Cowan, "Women's Rights Through Litigation: An Examination of the American Civil Liberties Union Women's Rights Project, 1971–1976," *Columbia Human Rights Law Review 8* (Spring–Summer 1976), pp. 373–412; Jo Freeman, *The Politics of Women's Liberation* (New York: David McKay, 1975).

7. With this formulation, the Supreme Court created an intermediate level of scrutiny for sex-based classifications. Susan Gluck Mezey, *In Pursuit of Equality: Women, Public Policy and the Federal Courts* (New York: St. Martin's Press, 1992).

8. Patricia A. Sullivan and Steven R. Goldzwig, "Abortion and Undue Burdens: Justice Sandra Day O'Connor and Judicial Decision-Making," *Women and Politics 16* (1996), pp. 27–53; Margaret Miller, "Justice Sandra Day O'Connor: Token or Triumph from a Feminist Perspective," *Golden Gate Law Review 15* (1985) pp. 493–525.

9. Christopher E. Smith, Joyce Ann Baugh, Thomas R. Hensley, and Scott Patrick Johnson, "The First-Term Performance of Justice Ruth Bader Ginsburg," *Judicature 78* (1994), pp. 74–80; Sheila Smith, "Justice Ruth Bader Ginsburg and Sexual Harassment Law: Will the Second Female Supreme Court Justice Become the Court's Women's Rights Champion?" *University of Cincinnati Law Review 63,* (1995), 1893–1945.

10. Michael McCann, *Rights At Work: Pay Equity Reform and the Politics of Legal Mobilization* (Chicago: University of Chicago Press, 1994).

11. Charles Whalen and Barbara Whalen, *The Longest Debate* (New York: New American Library, 1985).

12. Suzanne Uttaro Samuels, *Fetal Rights, Women's Rights: Gender Equality in the Workplace* (Madison: University of Wisconsin Press, 1995); Brian Hembacher, "Fetal Protection Policies: Reasonable Protection or Unreasonable Limitation on Female Employees," *Industrial Relations Law Journal 11* (1989), pp. 32–44; Note, "Rethinking (M)otherhood: Feminist Theory and State Regulation of Pregnancy," *Harvard Law Review 103* (1990), pp. 1325–1343; Wendy Williams, "Firing the Woman to Protect the Fetus: The Reconciliation of Fetal Protection with Employment Opportunity under Title VII," *Georgetown Law Journal 69* (1981), pp. 641–704.

13. Christine Neylon O'Brien and Gerald A. Madek, "Pregnancy Discrimination and Maternity Leave Laws," *Dickinson Law Review 93* (1989), pp. 311–337; Wendy Williams, "Equality's Riddle: Pregnancy and the Equal Treatment/Special Treatment Debate," *New York University Review of Law and Social Change 13* (1984–85), pp. 325–380.

14. Catharine MacKinnon, *Sexual Harassment of Working Women* (New Haven: Yale University Press, 1979).

15. Naomi R. Cahn, "The Looseness of Legal Language: The Reasonable Woman Standard in Theory and Practice," *Cornell Law Review 77* (1992), pp. 1398–1446.

16. Susan Gluck Mezey, "The Persistence of Sex Segregated Education in the South," *Southeastern Political Review 22* (June 1994), pp. 371–395.

17. Newspaper accounts revealed the abuse Faulkner had taken from the public, including death threats, for her attempt to become a member of the corps. After she announced her departure, the Citadel's students displayed an unseemly glee, yelling, chanting, and running around cheering in the rain. *Houston Chronicle,* August 19, 1995.

18. Joyce Gelb and Marian Lief Palley, *Women and Public Policies* (Princeton: Princeton University Press, 1987); Rosemary Salomone, *Equal Education Under Law* (New York: St. Martin's Press, 1986).

19. Billie Wright Dziech and Linda Weiner, *The Lecherous Professor: Sexual Harassment on Campus* (Boston: Beacon Press, 1984).

20. Kathy Lee Collins, "Student-to-Student Sexual Harassment under Title IX: The Legal and Practical Issues," *Drake Law Review 46* (1998), pp. 789–834.

21. Marian Faux, *Roe v. Wade* (New York: Macmillan, 1988).

22. Barbara Hinkson Craig and David M. O'Brien, *Abortion and American Politics* (Chatham, NJ: Chatham House,

1993); Laurence H. Tribe, *Abortion: The Clash of Absolutes* (New York: Norton, 1992).

23. This method is known by abortion rights supporters as "late-term" abortion and by opponents of abortion rights as "partial birth" abortion.

24. *Congressional Quarterly Weekly,* April 13, 1996.

25. From 1977 to 1994, there were more than 1,000 violent incidents at abortion clinics, including at least 36 bombings, 81 cases of arson, 131 death threats, 84 assaults, 2 kidnappings, and the shooting of 2 doctors. *The New York Times,* May 27, 1994.

26. United States Department of Justice, *The Violence Against Women Act: Breaking the Cycle of Violence* (online). Available on http://www.ojp.usdoj.gov/vawo/laws/cycle.htm

27. Danielle M. Houck, "VAWA After *Lopez:* Reconsidering Congressional Power Under the Fourteenth Amendment in Light of *Brzonkala v. Virginia Polytechnic and State University,*" *U.C. Davis Law Review 31* (Winter 1998), pp. 625–653.

28. Because she did not identify her assailants for several months and no physical evidence of the attack was preserved, criminal charges could not be filed against the two men.

29. The high court decision was not surprising given the Court's recent approach to cases involving Congress's authority to enact laws in areas traditionally considered within the power of the states. The Court expressed concern that if this provision of VAWA were allowed to stand, Congress would have virtually free rein to regulate all manner of criminal conduct that was within the purview of state criminal justice systems. The Court also found that Congress exceeded its authority to act under the Fourteenth Amendment because the Constitution only applies to actions by states, not private citizens.

The Equal Rights Amendment: What Is It, Why Do We Need It, and Why Don't We Have It Yet?

Riane Eisler and Allie C. Hixson

Riane Eisler was born in Vienna and studied anthropology, sociology, and law at the University of California at Los Angeles, where she also taught. She is the author of numerous articles and books, among them The E.R.A. Handbook *(1978);* The Chalice and the Blade: Our History, Our Future *(1987);* The Partnership Way: New Tools for Living and Learning, *coauthored with David Loye (1990),* Sacred Pleasure *(1996); and* Tomorrow's Children: A Blueprint for Partnership Education in the 21st Century *(2000). She is also an international activist for women, peace, and human rights issues. She is cofounder of the Center for Partnership Studies in Pacific Grove, California.*

Dr. Allie Corbin Hixson holds a master's degree in humanities and was the recipient of an American Association of University Women College Faculty Program Award leading to her doctorate in English from the University of Louisville (1969). She is the author of A Critical Study of Edwin Muir, Orcadian Poet. *After a fifteen-year teaching career, Hixson retired from academia to become a full-time volunteer activist for women's rights. She led the Kentucky International Women's Year (IWY) delegation to the 1977 First National Women's Conference in Houston, served as one of the vice chairs for that conference, and is past cochair of the IWY continuing committee, the National Women's Conference Committee.*

The Equal Rights Amendment was first introduced in Congress in 1923 under the leadership of Alice Paul, not three full years after the passage of the Nineteenth Amendment, which guaranteed women the right to vote. After a well-organized and well-financed campaign by conservative and radical right forces such as the John Birch Society, the Eagle Forum, and fundamentalist religious groups, the ERA was defeated in 1982.

Down but not out, the ERA was reintroduced in Congress on January 3, 1985. It is currently out of the news but not off the feminist agenda. It is astonishing and frightening how many young women are unfamiliar with the ERA. Where do you stand on the issue?

THE EQUAL RIGHTS AMENDMENT

Section 1. Equality of rights under the law shall not be denied or abridged by the United States or by any State on account of sex.

Section 2. The Congress shall have the power to enforce, by appropriate legislation, the provisions of this Article.

Section 3. This Amendment shall take effect two years after the date of ratification.

THE STATUE OF LIBERTY IS the symbol of American opportunity, of the promise of equality and justice for all. For American women, in this year of 1986 when we celebrate her hundredth anniversary, our Statue of Liberty has a very special meaning. As she too is female, she has always stood for compassion, caring, and other qualities associated with women's great contribution to our nation, with our love for our country and our service to it. But at this time, when the promise of constitutional protection for the half of our nation born female has not yet been fulfilled—when the United States is the only major industrialized nation other than South Africa that does not yet have a constitutional clause guaranteeing women equal rights with men—she is also our inspiration: the emblem of our *inalienable* rights.

Throughout the world, the Statue of Liberty is the symbol of democracy. In our nation, the modern cradle of democracy, this noble female figure is also a reminder to all American women and men of good will that we cannot countenance any failure of the democratic process: that in a nation where poll after poll shows that the majority of the people favor the proposed Equal Rights Amendment to our Constitution, it is our responsibility as American citizens to see that the people's will is done.

THE MORAL IMPERATIVE: JUSTICE AND EQUALITY FOR ALL CITIZENS

We hold this truth to be self evident: that all Americans are entitled to the equal protection of our laws. This is the American creed, the best and finest of the American spirit, the promise of the American dream. For over half a century, this promise has been expressed in twenty-four simple words: "Equality of rights under the law shall not be denied or abridged by the United States or by any state on account of sex."

That is the text of the proposed Equal Rights Amendment to the U.S. Constitution. When Americans are asked whether they approve or disapprove of these words, in poll after poll over 60% express approval. Until 1980, both the Democratic and the Republican Party platforms endorsed the ERA. Every major American women's organization from the National Organization for Women to the YWCA, the American Association of University Women, the National Federation of Business and Professional Women's Clubs, the National Council of Negro Women, the League of Women Voters, the National Women's Political Caucus, Federally Employed Women, the Older Women's League, the National Woman's Party and hundreds more support the ERA. So do the American Bar Association, the United Auto Workers, the AFL-CIO, the National Council of Churches, the National Assembly of Women Religious, the National Association of Social Workers, the American Federation of Governmental Employees, the American Jewish Congress, the National Council of Senior Citizens, and most other mainstream American organizations. Four American first ladies—Lady Bird Johnson, Patricia Nixon, Betty Ford, and Rosalyn Carter—backed the ERA. Why? Because, as Lady Bird Johnson said, "everyone in our democracy deserves to be treated with fairness and justice, and to have that right assured in our Constitution."

How, then, is it that we do not yet have an Equal Rights Amendment? As Betty Ford put it in 1981, when the ERA was only three states short of the thirty-eight states needed for ratification, "as a woman and as a Republican, I do not understand how we, as a people, can continue to hold our heads high and be proud of what this nation stands for if we have not guaranteed the rights of half our nation." When, as Ford summed it up, "all we are asking is that our rights be protected under the law," how could a handful of men in a handful of states deprive all American women of the constitutional protection that is our rightful due?

The answer is that these men voted their prejudices, aided and abetted by a well-financed campaign of slanderous lies against women and the ERA.

. . .

PUBLIC INFORMATION

Facts, Strategies, and Tactics

Proponents of the ERA sometimes have difficulty getting across the fact that women are legally "second class" citizens, particularly when those who feel threatened by the ERA are declaring vociferously that they do not "feel" second-class! A major reason is that until very recently there has been a dearth of FACTS about women, with most of what is taught us presenting primarily data about men.

Until the advent of "Women's Studies" departments on college campuses in the 1970s, the writing of history has been, by and large, the work of men. For nearly two centuries, female school children have suffered the drawing of a veil over their mind's eye as they have been fed a carefully controlled diet of the exploits of "great men" of history, interspersed only briefly with an anecdote about Betsy Ross sewing the flag or Molly Pitcher carrying water to the battlefield.

Not a word was there ever to enlighten a young girl when she was taught to recite the Declaration of Independence that the glowing words of "all men are created equal" did not include her. Nor did she hear about the long and bitter struggle of our foremothers to gain their property rights and the right to vote.

Too many of these young girls have first had to grow up from being "cheerleaders" to "displaced homemakers" before the veil of illusion was pierced and they understood all too painfully the real status of females in the United States.

It is a sad fact that still today too many females, of all ages, cannot name the year or the number of the amendment to the Constitution that won for women the vote. Nor do they know about the long struggle women had even to obtain this most elementary of all political rights.

In June 1982, during the close contest over the ERA in the Illinois Legislature, the campaign for ratification was brought to a point of intensity with the arrival of the little band of "hunger fasters." Under the leadership of Sonia Johnson, the excommunicated Mormon who wrote the story of her life and battle with the Mormon hierarchy in the book *From Housewife to Heretic* (Doubleday, 1981), these women gained attention for ERA by announcing they would fast until the critical vote. But, as she recounts in the film documentary about the Illinois campaign (*Fighting for the Obvious*), former Illinois Representative Susan Catania had to explain to her "shocked" colleagues in the Illinois Assembly— both pro-ERA women and men—that these tactics were hardly new. Quite the contrary, the "fast" and the incident of women chaining themselves to the chamber galleries were strictly in the tradition of the tactics used by the suffragists who had gone to jail, had fasted and were force-fed, beaten, with at least one woman dying in a dungeon for the right of women to go to the polls. Still, not one of these Illinois legislators was familiar with this story of the bitter struggles of the suffragists.

The general ignorance about our real history was undoubtedly a major factor behind the failure of the proposed twenty-seventh amendment to the Constitution. The next campaign in Illinois and elsewhere will be successful only if the American public has the indisputable historical facts about the necessity for the Equal Rights Amendment to perfect a flawed democratic blueprint. More women and men will be spokespersons for the Equal Rights Amendment when they have it clear in their own minds how women got into the current dilemma. And when this information is more widely spread, ERA opponents will no longer be able to delude our countrywomen and men with the myth that American women are—and have traditionally been— truly honored both in law and life.

. . .

SHORT HISTORY OF THE EQUAL RIGHTS AMENDMENT

1848. First Women's Rights Convention in Seneca Falls, New York, marks official birth of movement for equal rights in the United States. Elizabeth Cady Stanton proclaims all men *and women* are created equal.

1868. Fourteenth Amendment, including clause guaranteeing all persons equal protection under the law, becomes part of U.S. Constitution. Clause 2 provides for lowered representation for states that restrict right to vote of any qualified *male* citizen.

1870. Fifteenth Amendment guaranteeing black males right to vote becomes part of U.S. Constitution. Despite efforts by feminists, provision guaranteeing white and black women right to vote is not included.

1920. After more than three quarters of a century of struggle, Nineteenth Amendment guaranteeing women right to vote becomes part of U.S. Constitution.

1923. Because U.S. courts consistently fail to include women under the definition of persons protected under Equal Protection clause of the Fourteenth Amendment, under leadership of Alice Paul, Equal Rights Amendment is first introduced in U.S. Congress. Called the "Lucretia Mott Amendment," original version authored by Alice Paul reads: "Men and women shall have equal rights throughout the United States and in every place subject to its jurisdiction."

1943. Convinced that amendment would not pass with original wording, Alice Paul consents to rewording: "Equality of rights under the law shall not be denied or abridged by the United States or any state on account of sex."

1972. After introduction in Congress for forty-nine years, with numerous Congressional hearings, ERA is passed by U.S. Congress.

1973. ERA has been ratified by thirty-one states; only seven more states are needed.

1974. Two more states ratify ERA. The total is now thirty-three, so that only five more states are needed. But a well-financed, slanderous anti-ERA campaign is launched. John Birch Society, Phyllis Schlafly, and Christian Anti-Communist Crusade call ERA a subversive communist plot—even though Communist Party USA went on record in 1970 opposing ERA!

1975. North Dakota ratifies the ERA. Four more states are needed.

1977. January 18—Indiana becomes 35th state to ratify ERA. November 18–21—First National Women's Conference held in Houston, Texas, attended by 20,000 women, including Rosalyn Carter, Betty Ford, and Lady Bird Johnson. Conference is part of formal U.S. participation in First United Nations Decade for Women. It adopts a National Plan of Action which has passage of ERA as its first priority. National Women's Conference Committee is charged with implementation of National Plan of Action.

1978. Anti-ERA campaign has successfully blocked further state ratifications. As March 22, 1979, deadline approaches, ERA is still three states short of ratification. ERA Extension March for Equality of 100,000 in Washington, D.C. is spearheaded by NOW. U.S. Congress approves bill introduced by Representative Elizabeth Holtzman (D.N.Y.) extending ratification deadline to June 30, 1982.

1979. ERA opponents file suit in Federal Court challenging the constitutionality of the ERA deadline extension. Case is assigned to Judge Marion Callister, a high official in the Mormon Church, which that same year excommunicates Sonia Johnson for her activities in support of ERA.

1980. Republican Party platform and presidential candidate Ronald Reagan reverse Republican Party's traditional pro-ERA position.

Democratic National Convention reaffirms support for ERA and adds Platform pledge to withhold campaign funds and assistance from candidates who do not support ERA.

1981. Judge Callister rules ERA extension void, but Supreme Court stays ruling pending ERA ratification.

1982. Despite close votes in Florida, Illinois, and North Carolina, no more states ratify and ratification deadline expires.

Although ERA has been ratified by states representing the numerical majority of American population and polls show majority of Americans favor proposed amendment, it fails to be ratified by three additional states needed for it to become part of the United States Constitution. July 14, ERA is reintroduced in Ninety-seventh Congress.

1983. Equal Rights Amendment is again reintroduced in Congress (Ninety-eighth) on January 3rd with 230 co-sponsors in the House, but passage falls six votes short in November 1983 House vote.

1984. First woman in American history to be nominated for vice president, Geraldine Ferraro, runs on Democratic ticket, strongly endorsing ERA.

1985. Equal Rights Amendment is reintroduced in both houses of Ninety-ninth Congress on January 3, first day of new legislative session.

Women and Environmental Activism

Marta Benavides

Marta Benavides is from El Salvador, where she works with the Women's Environment and Development Program. In Nellie Stromquist's Women in the Third World, *from which this essay is taken, she is described as a biologist, theologian, and educator, committed to social justice, who has worked in rural development and on soil and water recovery.*

"Death of humans and death of nature result from the same causes: abuse, disrespect, lack of recognition of the natural laws, and a persistent determination to continue to exploit human beings and the environment for economic profit," explains Benavides. She describes some of the history that has led to a global environmental crisis and to disastrous conditions for people of the "South" or what is frequently termed the "Third World."*

In many ways, women have been most disadvantaged by the consequences of colonialization and by the biological and economic exploitation of the planet. Perhaps in part this is why women have been in the forefront of ecological/environmental movements. Here Benavides describes what women are doing all over the world to save the environment.

INTRODUCTION

THIS ESSAY EXAMINES THE ACTIONS of women, particularly women of the nonindustrialized Third World

---

*Stromquist tells us that there is considerable controversy regarding the term *Third World* and others that would take its place, such as *developing countries, less developed countries,* and *The South.* Third World is a concept that originated during the 1950s, when the First World designated capitalist countries with developed economies, such as the United States, the Second World referred to socialist countries with planned economies, like the U.S.S.R, and the Third World referred to nonaligned countries, or, essentially, what was left.

Marta Benavides, "Women and Environmental Activism," from *Women in the Third World: An Encyclopedia of Contemporary Issues,* edited by Nelly P. Stromquist (New York: Garland Publishing, Inc., 1998). Copyright © 1998 Nellie P. Stromquist. Published by permission of Garland Publishing Company and the editor.

nations, to live healthily and in a healthy environment. It reflects on the meaning of such concepts as environment, development, progress, and consumer and looks at conditions in the late twentieth century and how we arrived at them. In the process, it presents examples of effective work to achieve a healthy environment at local, national, regional, and global levels.

We live in the 1990s in the knowledge that we face an environmental crisis of such dimensions that we can predict the destruction of the human race and life as we know it on the planet. Across the world, soil is constantly eroding, the result in some countries of centuries of monoculture and export economies; in others, of agribusiness, cash crops, and the ever-increasing use of chemical fertilizers, pesticides, and herbicides; in others, of strip mining, the clearing of thousands of acres, the felling of trees for export purposes, and war. Water supplies are also drying, a usual consequence of erosion of the land. Potable water was a promise that did not materialize for the majority of peoples of nonindustrialized nations, and more of their water sources have not only dried but become polluted, a result of the dumping of toxic wastes into lakes and rivers, oceans, and the countryside. This is a reality that an increasing number of communities of color, impoverished communities in the industrialized nations, face as a daily fact of life.

Thousands of children and adults die of hunger every day in the nonindustrialized world, while in industrialized nations the number of elderly and of infants younger than one year of age dying as a result of malnutrition and lack of medicine has reached alarming levels. The air is polluted, the result of untreated toxic emissions from industries and cars. We talk of the impending warming of the Earth and its potential destructiveness, while U.N. studies affirm that the process has started, and the United Nations demands rigorous, urgent, and enforced controls of the causes behind this situation.

Death of humans and death of nature result from the same causes: abuse, disrespect, lack of recognition of the natural laws, and a persistent determination to continue to exploit human beings and the environment for economic profit. Profit and suffering are not equally distributed. Very few people profit; most suffer. How did it come to be this way? What we see today is the result of the process of globalization for profit that started more than 500 years ago. At that time, various processes of regionalization, present in varying degrees in the continents of the world, reached an economic level in Europe that demanded expansion. This expansion was for new trade, for economic gains that would enable the countries involved to become powers, to develop an effective military force that would enable them to move and gain control of raw materials and peoples necessary to consolidate their industrial development.

At the time, women and children were not considered fully human and thus did not have rights to property or decisions. Those with power mounted an aggressive witch hunt to do away with those who had special knowledge, such as medicine in its various forms, or who knew too much—those who knew how to think creatively and critically, that is, people with wisdom. Most of those hunted were women. In this way, the pursuers effectively destroyed leaders, knowledge, and wisdom, rendering those people remaining subservient to their ways of thought. They also pursued ethnic cleansing, as is evident in the history of the persecution and killing of the Moors and the Jews. In Christian Europe, the Roman Catholic Church supported and justified these actions and even contributed by way of the Crusades. The Church also purged those who thought and believed differently, as happened with Galileo, who stated that the Earth turned around the sun, yet, it blessed the adventures of Columbus in search of new routes for silk and spice.

It is this kind of understanding that became globalized by force and gunboat diplomacy. If these people could think that women and children were not fully human, if they could destroy thinkers and wise persons under the guise of paganism (and in defense of the one true God), if they could persecute those different among them (to keep their businesses and gold), if they could militarily invade strategically located nations to gain control as they strove to Christianize, what wouldn't they do to exploit the people and control the natural resources of other continents? Imagine the fate of many cultures, the fate of spirituality and religion, the fate of women and men, the fate of Mother Earth. England needed timber for its navy to have the best battle and trade ships. Besides various raw materials, it specialized in trading the most important natural resource—that is, in the kidnaping, transportation, and sale of people as slaves.

The people and "discovered" continents became the raw materials for the industrialization of the European nations, and that is when the former's "development" began. This power, or "development," has always been dependent on assured "free" or cheap raw materials. It is this logic that has evolved into today's globalized condition of ecological, social, economic, and moral deterioration. It is these needs and priorities that have determined what profit is (and for what and for whom), influenced the domestic policies of industrialized nations, and decided the imposition of laws and military, even dictatorial, powers on the nonindustrialized nations. This is the reason we should hesitate to call ourselves "Third World." We are not underdeveloped, or developing nations—we are the direct result of the creation of the "First World."

In the last decades, the globalized situation of the world resulted in the "development" of high interest rates that brought most countries with dependent economies to bankruptcy through foreign or external debt. As a result of this and technological advances, as well as market competition, a new globalization has occurred. The new forms of internal and external relations have been regulated with the advent of the GATT (General Agreement for Tariffs and Trade) regulations, the WTO (World Trade Organization), and the three new economic world blocs that have replaced the "Big Seven" industrialized nations: NAFTA (North American Free Trade Agreement), the European Economic Community, and the Pacific Rim. At this point, the struggle is for control of food and for biodiversity, which includes the patenting of all forms of life, to be exploited when and how it is deemed necessary by those corporations holding the patents. Already some indigenous peoples are fighting the patenting of their genes.

Today it is understood that a better terminology for the two sides of this division of the world's nations is the "North" for those that are industrialized and have a relatively high standard—though not necessarily quality—of life, and the "South" for those nonindustrialized nations that generally have been formally or informally a colony of one or various nations of the North. We have been forced to live at the periphery, while the North has been the center. The people and the natural materials of the South have been seen as resources, and we have been used as such, so there is depletion as a result of abuse and careless use (Luxemburg, 1951). A few years before the fall of the Berlin Wall in 1989, it became rather clear that a new world order had evolved. The industrialized nations of the North and the impoverished nations of the South are economic and sociological concepts that deal with the quality of social conditions in the countries of the world. We recognize that, due to economic readjustments, there is an increasing South in the North and a small North in the South. We have to be mindful of the real meaning of development. There are destruction and war, inequality and injustice where there must be peace; there are disintegration and erosion where there should be health and wholeness; there are oppression, repression, violation of the right to be human where there should be freedom. This is, then, the background needed to understand the disabling and eroding environment we face today and to understand the unhappy fate of women and of the Earth (Boserup, 1970).

Development, defined as the making of a more advanced or effective state, and progress, defined as advancement in general, cannot be fostered if they depend on the exploitation of half of the human race—women—or on the destruction of that which sustains life itself. In this context, those people who live in affirmation of all and cooperate with nature should be the ones considered developed and progressive. As we reflect on the way women work, we are able to see that, over the course of thousands of years, they have learned from nature the ways of sustenance and have worked with nature to maintain health and to heal, knowing that the best medicine was food and a balanced life. They have developed a practice of wholeness, which is a more integral expression of permaculture, for the maintenance of their homesteads.

"Environment" is not only about natural surroundings, but about all that constitutes our life, and, for that matter, the mind-set, logic, or understanding of the world that guides our thinking, analysis, and actions. "Environment" is not only about ecology, but about our ways of being, about what is important in life, and the nature and meaning of healthy relations within ourselves and with others, starting with those closest and with that which provides our sustenance. It is about awareness of the partnership in which we live with each other and with nature, and the respect and humbleness in which we carry ourselves while we are on Earth. Would we live in a way that would enable us to leave a legacy of wisdom, of understanding, of affirmation and respect for diversity, of cooperation and collaboration among peoples, nations, and nature to guarantee quality of life for the seventh generation? Or will we be the mindless or mere consumer? The word "consumer" comes from the word "consume"—to destroy or expend by use, use up, spend wastefully. These words tell us the reality of what is going on; they give the definition of how we are. The way in which we exist in the world determines that, for us to have a full, secure, and meaningful life, we can and must do it only in partnership with others and with nature. The planet was not created for consumption, regardless of the fact that there are theoreticians, scientists, and theories that support such conduct (Singh, 1987). We must develop the appropriate language and understandings to describe the world we want. We have the power to name, thus to create.

WOMEN OF THE SOUTH SHAPING THEIR ENVIRONMENT

The Women of Color of North America at the First World Women's Congress for a Healthy Planet (Miami, 1991) made a statement to define a more integral concept of environment when they said that they believe that a women's environmental agenda will be nothing without an embodiment of economic justice, political democracy, and a respect for the contributions of all civilizations and cultures. They believe that we must be guided by principles of equity in the quality of life for all (WEDO, 1991). This position resonates with the concerns and aspirations of women and peoples from all over the world, as is evident by their efforts to achieve a plenitude of life. Many women do the work of healing the environment as they create new understandings and appropriate practices. We are naming ourselves, our ways, and our relations. Women are partners, facilitators, coordinators, and creators. It is not at all, as some people of the North believe, that women are just not interested in the environment and, thus, do nothing about it and continue to degrade it.

The work of women around the world reflects their efforts for the well-being of their families, their homes, and their communities, and their consistent efforts to shape their immediate environments in ways that affirm the best possible quality of life. All we must do is be mindful of all that women do, and it will be evident. For what else is it to keep a home, and keep everyone fed, clean, healthy, and growing, even while one has to suffer a double journey, unvalued work, or the stigma of racism or classism, not to mention sexism? What else is it to be a *comadre*, the godmother committed to take care of the neighbors' children; the *curandera*, who keeps and shares the knowledge of the medicinal plants to heal or nourish whoever needs it; or the *partera*, the midwife who cares for women as they bring a new baby to life? What else is it to carry the water in a clay basin on one's head or the firewood on one's back, or wash the clothes in the river, or carry the baby in one's womb, or give birth and raise the future farmers, scientists, factory and construction workers, and the young women who will give birth to future ones?

The women in the "Third World"—a high percentage of whom have lived for centuries in impoverishment generally due to colonialism—are the miracle makers, the ones who multiply the bread and the fish, the ones who heal by touching. These are the women who are now facing, because of the globalized economy, a new world order of economic and ecological crisis and devastation. They are working and searching to find partners among their community peers, and cooperating with other women nationally, or across borders, using their experience to develop recommendations and actions for a healthy planet, as the bases for their own fulfillment and health.

Women of all countries and from various backgrounds—small farms, indigenous communities and networks, grass-roots groups, consumer organizations, neighborhood leagues, and flower and horticul-ture clubs, as well as governments and universities, and women who are social and physical scientists, technicians, doctors, geographers, parliamentarians, lawyers, church members, bureaucrats, and bankers—have joined at local, national, regional, and international levels to work with determination to improve the quality of life for themselves and their families, for their community, for their country, and for the world. This can be seen concretely in the local, national, and regional participation of women's nongovernmental organizations (NGOs), and the movements culminating in the U.N.-sponsored Earth Summit (Rio de Janeiro, 1992), the Second World Conference on Human Rights (Vienna, 1993), the International Conference on Population and Development (Cairo, 1994), and the World Summit on Social Development (Copenhagen, 1995). Through these, women have created an environment of participatory governance for quality of life for themselves and for the healing of their societies and the planet. These women, often joined by men, want healthy environmental standards to be upheld in their factories in the provision of water, light, and ventilation, and similar standards to be applied to sewage and recycled waters. They are pressuring to prevent regular and toxic waste from being dumped in their communities or rivers; to stop desertification, the sale of public lands, and legislation that permits the sale or "urbanization" of wetlands; and to pass legislature that guarantees the right to clean water and air and asbestos-free schools. They are also applying pressure to legalize their right to health, to control their reproduction, and to have their rights and those of the girl child be recognized as human rights.

Women are uniting in efforts around the world to transform the conditions of the home, the community, and the workplace; to acquire access to water; to develop appropriate and compatible technologies; and to manage and recycle waste to create jobs, energy, and fuel production. They are also carrying out research that will impact biodiversity and bioengineering work and they are working to enact laws to bring the international financial systems under the control of people-centered systems and to value unpaid work.

Indigenous and peasant women are working to preserve medicinal plants and indigenous knowledge, as is occurring in communities aiming toward sustainability in El Salvador. In an effort to stop desertification, women university students are studying and documenting the increasing number of animal and plant species at the verge of extinction (Benavides, 1991, p. 95).

Winona LaDuke, an indigenous woman whom the Spirits call Thunderbird Woman and who lives on the White Earth Reservation in North America, is a good example of this coming of age. She tells us:

> I am coming home. Coming home. That is, I believe the challenge we all face is making a home, restoring, building, investing in, and reclaiming a community, a destiny, a way of life. . . . That is the essence of becoming part of the Land. There are no more frontiers, and no greener pastures. This is what we are fortunate enough to have. . . . From here I try to look back, and look forward. I am looking at the community 20 years from now, and trying to do my part to make it what I dream it will be. In the future I plan to hear in my community primarily Ojibwa/Anishinabeg. . . . I plan to see a recovered traditional economy—from wild rice to buffalo, deer, maple sugar, and the ecosystem that supports them. . . . I see the restoration of our traditional religious institutions, and I see non-Indians, as well as Anishinabeg on this reservation, sharing common land, values, and language. . . . In short, I wrestle personally, politically, intellectually with how to restore my home, and how to come home (Utne Reader, 1995, p. 80).

In Bhopal, India (where a toxic gas leak caused hundreds of deaths in 1984), women continue to protest Union Carbide operations, educate nationally and internationally on the dangers they present, go to court about various related issues, and look for programs to heal those affected by the emissions. In Ecuador, women have organized to stop local factories' chemical emissions; indigenous women participate with their husbands, friends, and brothers to defend their rights to land, territoriality, and all resources within. In Puerto Rico, a free associated state of the United States, women and men, in coordination with churches and universities, have organized industrial-mission campaigns to press factories to respect U.S. environmental protection regulations because the factory emissions are causing skin, breathing, and hormonal diseases

and disorders in women, men, and children. They also have sought to stop the construction of port facilities that were to bring the largest oil tankers to the island, which would continue to pollute and destroy the already deteriorated environment.

Thousands of women work to have a nuclear free South Pacific. They denounce the destructions of their islands and the pollution of the seas, and, with each new nuclear test, they know that more babies will be born without spinal columns. The nuclear-bomb tests in the area by foreign powers continue in violation of human rights and the international principles for the rights of nations. The coalition working in educational and political campaigns to have a nuclear-free region and future spans oceans and involves people of the South and the North.

In the United States, women and men of the United Farmworkers of America (UFW) have led successful strikes against grape and lettuce growers, who contaminate their crops with pesticides that poison the milk of breast-feeding women, causing sickness, deformation, and death among babies. They defend their economic and health rights, demand environmental regulations, and campaign for the protection of consumers and their rights. Leaders of the UFW have crossed the border to inform people, trade unions, and the government to promote Mexico's support of environmental laws and the defense of the rights of Mexican men and women who work in the United States, especially as they relate to environmental hazards.

In India, the first major contemporary environmental movement was Chipco, which means "to embrace":

> Though this resistance movement had predecessors in the 1800s, now in the late 60s women created the movement to resist logging in the Himalayan region. For over a decade, villages and communities protected a particular patch of land from being logged. The people brought food, and kept the children of those "embracing" the trees, until equipment and contractors had moved from the area, and the patch removed from the list to be logged. The people were conscious that forests on mountain tops are the source of one's water, that water is the source of life, and that it must be protected. This is a good

example of protracted nonviolent action. (Indigenous Women, *n.d., pp. 18–19.*)

The Alternative Nobel Prize (Right Livelihood Award) was granted to this movement in 1987.

ENVIRONMENTAL MOVEMENTS AND PROCESSES FACILITATED BY WOMEN

All of the activities presented so far as examples of women's actions for a healthy and better environment have resulted in movements and processes that have protected the quality of life of women in general. There is no way that the status and condition of women would be considered important if it were not for the work that women have been carrying out at various levels.

The 80,000 members of Kenya's Green Belt Movement (GBM), started in 1977, have planted more than seven million trees to prevent desertification and have set up more than 600 income-producing nurseries, in spite of the Kenyan government's direct interference. GBM has also documented and campaigned actively against official corruption, misuse of funds, and structural-adjustment programs and policies (SAPs), which leave the people without social safety nets.

Crucial actions have been initiated by individual women. Chee Yoke Ling of Friends of the Earth led effective mass protests in Malaysia against the use of poisonous pesticides and the dumping of radioactive waste. Laila Kamel of Egypt worked with a Cairo garbage-collector community in the Mokattam hills recycling garbage and generating jobs and educational opportunities for the people of this community. Tuenjai Deetes cofounded the Hill Area Development Foundation to increase the self-sufficiency of marginal communities, which, having fled ethnic wars and hardships in Burma and Laos, settled in the mountainous area of northern Thailand. The foundation promotes self-sufficiency for the marginal communities while protecting the natural resources against deforestation and soil erosion and respecting tribal culture.

Ester Yazzie is an indigenous Navajo woman who lives in the state of Arizona and uses her law-enforcement training to sustain traditional values. After uranium was discovered in their land, hundreds of Navajos worked in the open-pit and deep mines without being told about the dangers of radiation, and now they die of radiation-related diseases. They leave their widows and children with no support. Most homes are also contaminated since Navajos use the earth to build the traditional hogans (Navajo dwellings built of earth walls supported by timbers). Yazzie works with her people to get the uranium-mining industry to stop the exploitation of lands and peoples for nuclear-power generation, nuclear testing, and radioactive-waste dumping; to clean and restore all homelands; to end the secrecy about the nuclear industry and its dangers; and to provide full and fair compensation for damage to peoples, families, and communities. Her people share a vision for the future: Given the unity of humanity and the world, they appeal on behalf of future generations to those in the present to use sustainable, renewable, and life-enhancing energy alternatives. The need to live in harmony and respect for life, as a means of peace, leads people to discuss the concept of Gaia, the planet as a living thing (*Indigenous Women*, n.d).

Leonor Briones, professor at the University of the Philippines, president of the Freedom from Debt Coalition, declared:

In 1988, the Philippines paid $2 billion a year interest on its [foreign] debt to the wealthy nations of the North—and received a pitiful $236 million in return. It's foreign aid in reverse . . . and we are only one of 50 countries that annually pay the North $50 billion more than we get . . . Many of our people live in absolute, grinding, unimaginable poverty. . . . We are paying $350,000 interest a day on a corrupt nuclear plant that is now mothballed because it was defective from the start. The leaders knew that the project was riddled with bribery; the whole world knew. Yet they gave the money. And now they insist that to pay back such fraudulent loans, our government must cut subsidies on food, education, health, and social services. . . . Our women hold four and five jobs at once, struggling to pay for medicines for their babies, begging the schools to let their children write exams. Our country is hemorrhaging its people, its financial and natural resources. . . . To get the foreign currency we need to pay our debt, we are pushed to encroach on the environment. Only *one-fifth of our beautiful coral reefs are healthy. Fish stocks have plummeted by 50 per cent . . . (WEDO, 1991).*

Moema Viezzer of Sao Paulo, Brazil, directs Women in Citizenship Action. This group struggles against hunger and poverty and in defense of life. It educates women and their impoverished communities about nutrition, food security, and how to create urban community orchards. It also studies the national and international policies that bring the women and their country to these conditions.

Marta Benavides of El Salvador carries out an initiative, the Women's Environment and Development Program, for people's land and human rights, environmental education, and ecological action for sustainability. In this process, each community participates in the creation of a healthy and natural environment. Sustainability is about how we treat ourselves, each other, and our environment, and about how we live, using and affirming our strengths and differences, sharing common goals and resources.

In all of these cases, we can see the need for dialogue and analysis, and the importance of committed, collaborative, and consistent action, which comes from the grass roots to impact on their communities and groups and on social institutions and governments agencies as well as on other NGOs.

Let us review the example of a multinational project that has a direct impact on future programs and commitments of women, churches, ecumenical groups, and NGOs. At the Mexican–U.S. border, 50 women of all races, representing impoverished communities, Protestant and Catholic churches, and women's groups in the United States and Canada and from Mexico, Guatemala, and El Salvador, gathered to learn about each other's situations and about the impacts of the *maquiladora* industry—factories of free-trade zones—on the quality of life of women, children, families, communities, nations, and the environment. The meeting was called and sponsored by Agricultural Missions of the Commission of Women in Development. The representatives learned that NAFTA recently signed by the United States, Mexico, and Canada, had already had resulted in severe detrimental consequences for some working people in the United States, as it depended primarily on Mexican "cheap" (low-

wage) labor, especially that of young women. They learned about increased family violence, disruption of homes, impoverished communities, pollution of the environment, babies born without spines or eyes or with other deformations, and chronic illnesses of women—on both sides of the border. They learned that these are the result of a way of doing business that is a common practice across the United States, Mexico, Central America, and the Caribbean. Having visited, studied, and reflected on these conditions, the representatives at the meeting recommended that the churches study and monitor NAFTA for the purpose of taking effective action on behalf of both male and female workers and the environment. The representatives further recommended that actions in this regard be included in the work of churches in Canada and that the women's division of each denomination be educated about it, in the context and spirit of the Program of Justice, Peace, and the Integrity of Creation sponsored by the World Council of Churches. They challenged the churches to continue this type of work, to maintain close ties with one another, and to keep a spiritual dimension in the work on the environment. They also recommended that this challenge be shared with all of the partner communities and programs supported by sponsors in the NAFTA nations and in the rest of the world (National Council of Churches-USA, 1993).

GLOBAL CONNECTIONS AND THEIR IMPACT

The work and the impact of women in environmental processes and efforts show that they must become full partners in local, national, and global environmental plans and strategies for the new paradigm of sustainable social and human development to be a success. In this context, DAWN (Development Alternatives with Women for a New Era), a women's NGO from the South led by Barbadian Peggy Antrobus, states:

Women must be seen neither as victims nor saviours but as people whose interlocking roles in reproduction and production in the household and in the economy offer them a special vantage point for addressing the issue of the current debates in development theory, policy and practice—the debates revolving around the role of States vs. Markets, as well as those revolving around issues of Population, Environment and Development (quoted in DAWN Informs, 1994).

DAWN works also with other women's networks of the South, and actively coordinates with women's networks from the North, which share these perspectives.

Gus Speth, United Nations Development Program (UNDP) administrator, shares his views on the relationship among women, development, and the environment:

> *Sustainable human development is . . . people-centered . . . , participatory . . . , pro-poor and pro-nature. It gives highest priority to poverty alleviation, to environmental regeneration, and to job-led growth. And it recognizes that none of this is possible unless the status of women is elevated. Sustainable human development is an essential precondition to bringing human numbers into balance with the carrying capacities of nature and the coping capacities of societies* (UN-NGLS Go-Between, 1993).

Women's lives and roles profoundly shape and affect every aspect of the environment. Women total more than half the population of the world. People are the most valuable natural resource of a nation; women can say that they are the planet's most valuable resource. Yet, women are overexploited and neglected; it is they who face higher illiteracy rates and who live in poverty in the highest numbers. The United Nations, in its Women, Environment, and Development Program, implemented with the support of its United Nations Development Fund for Women (UNIFEM), states:

> *Although women grow, process, and market between 50 and 80 per cent of the food consumed in developing countries, governments rarely record these inputs or support them with financial credit, technologies, education or training—inputs which could raise productivity while safeguarding the environment and reducing the physical burdens involved. Overlooking the central role which women play in the economic and social life of their countries constrains national development and jeopardizes the natural resource base on which growth is founded. For millions of women in the developing world, the struggle for survival and environmental protection are inseparable. Women are among the first to suffer*

> *when land is degraded, when trees disappear, and when water supplies are polluted. As the main providers of food, fuel and water for their families, women are acutely aware of the need to protect their surroundings and to manage natural resources. In rural areas, where they spend many hours of every day fetching and carrying fuelwood and water, they know from harsh experience that the depletion of woodlands or watersources will eventually force them to walk farther afield in search of new supplies. Experience has taught them that soil erosion, caused by intense agriculture on fragile soils, will ultimately reduce the amount of food they can put on the table. . . . They do whatever is necessary to survive from day to day. Poverty and environmental degradation embrace in a daily downward spiral. . . . In the poorest communities of Africa, Asia and the Pacific, Latin America and the Caribbean, an often destructive quest for survival is fueled by high rates of population growth and the failure of policymakers to recognize obvious truth: That as long as women remain poor, fragile eco-systems will remain at risk* (UNIFEM, n.d.).

It is clear that the U.N. findings and documents of the conferences and summits of the 1990s contradict the blessings heralded in the new world order of peace, prosperity, and progress for all peoples and nations following the fall of the Berlin Wall and of the socialist and communist camps. All of them—the Children's Summit (New York, 1990); the Earth Summit (Rio, 1992), where the intimate relation of poverty, development, environment, and women was clearly presented; the Second World Conference on Human Rights (Vienna, 1993), where women pressed for women's and children's rights to be accepted and affirmed as human rights; the International Conference on Population and Development (Cairo, 1994); and the World Summit on Social Development (Copenhagen, 1995), at which delegates worked on poverty alleviation and eradication, productive-quality employment, and social integration—have shown that the existing model of development has resulted in serious illness for humans and the planet.

The United Nations has begun to use Human Development Indexes: Each country must show its development as measured not only by the gross national product or per-capita income, but also by the literacy rate, housing, employment, education, health, transportation services, and environmental protection available to its citizens and by the possibilities for improved quality of life being created for future generations. This is a process to assure sustainable human and social development, which is an important way to follow up on, and interconnect, all of the international U.N. conferences, especially the Earth Summit. The United Nations produced the Women's Human Development Index in August 1995, in time for the Fourth World Conference on Women in Beijing.

The U.N. conferences and summits provide an excellent example of the partnership and collaboration among women of the South and the North, women and men in general, young and old people, peasants and city dwellers, officials of civil society and of government, and the importance and relevance of this work. Each of the U.N. meetings is preceded by preparatory commissions, and on these occasions 200–300 women and men representing organizations from 50–70 countries from all over the world come together daily to inform one another, develop analysis and strategy, and monitor and lobby the texts being worked line by line by government representatives. This process enables participants in the Women's Caucus at each U.N. conference to learn of the processes, plans, actions, and interest of governments and the United Nations. It also enables them to have an impact not only on global governance but also on the forging of a new society.

Bella Abzug, the cochair of WEDO (Women's Environment and Development Organization, a highly active NGO) speaking for the international women's caucus and addressing the official U.N. delegates at a preparatory commission of the 1995 Social Development Summit, summarized the way women are working in this process and the effect they are achieving:

As women who seek an equal voice for women in international and national decision-making and democratic and human rights for all people, we have a simple test for evaluating progress. We ask, what is happening to women around the world? Women have been the shock absorbers for the dramatic changes the world has witnessed in the last five years and for the so-called structural adjustments

that put corporate profiteering ahead of human needs. . . . In some parts of the world, women are losing whatever rights and benefits they had, and those who never had either are bearing the burdens of unpaid labor in factories owned by absentee, faceless owners. For many women and girls the alternative is exploitation and prostitution in the international sex market. We propose a major capitalization strategy for a people-centered economy. This would redirect World Bank and other financial institutions' resources into small-scale credit without collateral for self-employment. We propose to work for an international agreement on corporate responsibility that assures factory and field workers in the South, many of them women, of their right to decent wages, social benefits, health and child care facilities, and working conditions free of industrial pollutants and other environmental hazards. We urge education and awareness strategies that teach the poor, both children and adults; that make technology an ally, not a job-destroying, health-destroying foe; that penalize male violence against women; that recast gender stereotypes which subordinate women and deny them an equal share in fate-of-the-earth decisions (Statement presented at PrepCom I, World Social Development Summit, 1995).

The Asia-Pacific Women Action Network, in the context of the Social Summit, submitted a formal declaration to be placed in the docket of documents. The way these women carried out their process of self-awareness and education, and lifted it to the international arena both for NGOs as well as officially, shows how helpful this process can be for the region, and participants, and for all the other areas of the world. It states, among other positions, that:

The realities of women's lives are shaped by contextual and perceptual paradigms. A combination of market-driven, profit-oriented development and patriarchal values have placed the vast majority of our women in extremely marginalized and vulnerable positions. Women become the object of development, first as impoverished citizens of Asia-Pacific, and second by facing specific gender discrimination and violence. . . . Sustainable development, poverty alleviation, and social integration cannot be attained without the full participation and co-leadership of women at all levels of society and decision making. A gender perspective is one of the most forward looking and socially just approaches for social development. The different and irreversible impacts that structural adjustment policies, trade liberalization, and the trickle-down programs have on women have not been responsibly dealt with by our nations. . . . Women have always been and still are in Asia-Pacific primary food producers. Therefore, agricultural sustainability cannot be achieved without women's active participation in setting and implementing policy. Food security is a basic right, inextricably tied to sustainable agriculture. Food security is the access by all peoples at all times to food needed for a healthy life. It is in this context that food for domestic consumption must override agriculture products for trade. Food security can only be a reality when women's rights to land and resources are protected. . . . Women, in their role as primary food producers, have necessarily been custodians of biodiversity in all forms. They have maintained a relationship with nature without ownership and degradation. Modern agricultural biotechnologies have begun to displace women from their central role as food producers and gatherers of medicinal plants. . . . The corruption of traditional lifestyles, the deprivation of productive land, lack of income opportunities and increasing violence have resulted in large-scale migration of women to already overcrowded urban centers where they live in abject poverty . . . (Asian-Pacific NGOs, 1994, pp. 68–69).

Vandana Shiva of India, a physicist, philosopher, feminist, ecologist, and director of the Research Foundation for Science, Technology, and Natural Resource Policy in Dehradun, India, has made a great contribution to the establishment of the connections between the personal and the global and to the recognition of the importance of local, national, and international work. She details in her writings the link among women, ecology, development, health, and the agricultural conditions of the "Third World" (Shiva, 1989, 1991a, 1991b, 1991c, 1993). Shiva is concerned with the protection of cultural and biological diversity. She argues that, unless we can put limits and boundaries on commercial activity and on new technologies, the violence against nature and against people will become uncontrollable. "The question I constantly ask myself is, "What are the creative catalytic linkages that strengthen community and enable communities of people to exer-

cise social and ecological control on economic and technological processes?'" (*Utne Reader,* 1995, p. 81).

Women met at the regional level to work on the development of the *Platform for Action* decided during the Fourth World Conference on Women (Beijing, 1995) and at similar meetings for the other U.N. conferences and summits. Women are learning from each experience to establish, lobby, and defend their positions and to work cooperatively with other women in their community, nation, region, and the world. During these meetings, women have analyzed and affirmed past agreements. They have developed quality benchmarks, bottom-line goals, commitments, and deadlines; they have also produced an economic analysis and demands for democratization, transparency, and accountability for U.N. programs and the Bretton Woods institutions: the International Monetary Fund (IMF) and the World Bank. They have disseminated the information and have been negotiating with their governments and other delegates. They are using the experience gained for local and national quests and legislation, and they are firmly defending what has been achieved.

It is important to see that the work that we, as women, are carrying out in favor of the environment is much more than mere activism. We are consciously and tenaciously bringing about a new world order of equality, equity, peace, justice, and people-centered development. What we are doing is not just saving the Earth but also working to establish an enabling environment in which we can reach our whole potential as human beings and live in harmony with a healthy natural environment: This is the exercise of our power. Women are doing this at national, regional, and international levels, attempting then to bring about the era of being in fullness, creating from all of these interrelations and work platforms an impact on national and international laws, agreements, accords, and practices.

We are intent not simply to live, but to achieve quality of life, and a life lived simply. Our task is to think and understand globally and work effectively locally so that we may have an impact both locally and globally. To be effective, we understand that we must learn self-knowledge and the universal principles of life. We recognize the need to work and participate cooperatively for human and social fulfillment on a healthy planet. We know that, in the interrelatedness of life, to be working for a healthy environment does not necessarily mean that we must work only on those issues directly linked to the health of nature and the planet; rather, we acknowledge that all of those people who, conscientiously and with love, work for lasting peace, for quality of life, for equity and equality, for justice, for the elimination of all forms of discrimination and exploitation, and for understanding among peoples are making a contribution to these ends. Together we are creating an environment and a climate that allow humans and the planet to live in harmony and be healthy. This, then, would be the enabling and healthier environment—and practices—that can result in an enriched and meaningful life for us, our societies, future generations, and our planet.

References

Asian-Pacific NGOs. *Breaking a Common Ground in the Pursuit of Alternatives.* Declarations of the Asian Pacific NGOs in the Preparatory Activities to the World Summit on Social Development, Manila: Asian-Pacific NGOs, June-October 1994.

Benavides, Marta. *La Mujer y Medio Ambiente en América Latina: El Papel de la Mujer.* Quito: CEPLAES, 1991.

Boserup, Ester, *Woman's Role in Economic Development.* New York: St. Martin's, 1970.

DAWN Informs. (St. Michael, Barbados). February 1994.

Indigenous Women, vol. 2, no. 1, n.d.

Luxemburg, Rosa. *The Accumulation of Capital.* London: Routledge and Kegan Paul, 1951.

National Council of Churches-USA. *Women Crossing Boundaries: Fighting Back.* New York: Agricultural Missions, National Council of Churches-USA, 1993.

Shiva, Vandana. *Staying Alive: Women, Ecology, and Development.* London: Zed, 1989.

———— (ed.). *Biodiversity: Social and Ecological Perspectives.* London: Zed, 1991a.

————. *Ecology and the Politics of Survival.* Tokyo: United Nations University Press, 1991b.

————. *The Violence of the Green Revolution: Third World Agriculture.* London: Zed, 1991c.

————. *Monocultures of the Mind.* London: Zed, 1993. Singh, Narendra. "Robert Solow's Growth Hickonomics," *Economic and Political Weekly,* vol. 23, no. 45, 1987.

UN-NGLS Go-Between, no. 42, November 1993.

United Nations Development Fund for Women (UNIFEM). *Women, Environment, Development.* Educational pamphlet. New York: UNIFEM, n.d.

Utne Reader, no. 67, January/February 1995.

Women's Environment and Development Organization (WEDO). *Findings of the Tribunal: World Women's Congress for a Healthy Planet.* New York: WEDO, 1991.

The Global Women's Human Rights Movement

Human Rights Watch

Human Rights Watch, founded in 1978, is a nongovernment organization that monitors and investigates human rights abuses in over seventy countries around the world. It documents practices from denial of due process to murder, torture, exile, and so on.

This report tells us that "few movements have made so large an impact in so short a time as the women's human rights movement." It describes widespread abuses of women, whether they are institutional and perpetrated by governments or they are habits of culture to which governments turn a blind eye. Although the international community now at last speaks of women's human rights, it points out, there is still a vast gap between "rhetoric and reality," and there is very much to be done.

INTRODUCTION

FEW MOVEMENTS HAVE MADE SO large an impact in so short a time as the women's human rights movement. Working across national, cultural, religious and class lines, advocates promoting the human rights of women have waged a campaign to ensure respect for women's rights as fundamental human rights. The movement's emergence and growth over the past decade have, to a large extent, also transformed the way human rights issues are understood and investigated, both by intergovernmental bodies and by nongovernmental human rights organizations. The result has been to turn the spotlight on—and to place at the center of the social and political debates at the United Nations and between governments—the role that human rights violations play in maintaining the subordinate status of the world's women. Their impact was

Excerpted from "Introduction," *The Human Rights Watch Global Report on Women's Human Rights: Human Rights Watch Women's Rights Project*, published by Human Rights Watch, 350 Fifth Avenue, New York, NY 10118. Copyright © 1995 by Human Rights Watch.

powerfully apparent at the World Conference on Human Rights in Vienna in 1993, when governments recognized women's rights as "an inalienable, integral and indivisible part of universal human rights."

Clearly the international women's human rights movement has raised the visibility of abuses against women, and the international community has made welcome statements supporting women's human rights. But the gap between government rhetoric and reality is vast. The challenge now is to ensure that governments that should be combatting violations of women's rights do not get credit for deploring abuse when they do nothing to stop it.

The Range and Severity of Abuse

In 1990 Human Rights Watch began working with colleagues in the human rights and women's movements around the world to apply the fact-finding and advocacy tools of the international human rights movement to documenting violations of women's human rights and seeking remedies for such abuse. We have exposed state-directed and state-approved violence against women; violence against women by private actors that is legally endorsed; violence against women by private actors that is illegal but is tolerated by the state through discriminatory enforcement of the law; and discriminatory laws and practices. We have explored abuses that are gender-specific either in their form—such as forced pregnancy and forced virginity exams—or in that they target primarily women—such as rape and the forced trafficking of women for purposes of sexual servitude.

Rampant abuses against women have traditionally been excused or ignored. Rape in situations of conflict by combatants is prohibited under international humanitarian law but until recently was dismissed as part of the inevitable "spoils of war." Domestic violence was regarded as a "private" matter only, not as a crime that the state must prosecute and punish. To the extent that control of women's sexuality and physical integrity is regarded as a matter of family or community honor rather than personal autonomy and individual rights, women in much of the world still face enormous obstacles in their search for redress when they have suffered abuse committed in the name of custom or tradition. Throughout the world, women are still relegated to second-class status that makes them more vulnerable to abuse and less able to protect themselves from discrimination.

As the country studies in this report show, governments often are directly implicated in abuses of women's human rights. Prison guards in many countries—studies in this report include the United States, Pakistan and Egypt—sexually assault women prisoners and detainees. Rape of women by combatants is frequently tolerated by commanding officers in the course of armed conflict and by abusive security officials in the context of political repression, as the examples of Kashmir, Bosnia-Hercegovina, Peru, Somalia, and Haiti illustrate. And, as our investigations of the trafficking of women and girls into forced prostitution have demonstrated, this ostensibly private commercial trade in human beings would be impossible without the active involvement of government officials, such as corrupt border guards and police who alternate between raiding brothels and profiting from them. Refugee and displaced women, in zones where U.N. or governmental protection is inadequate, are robbed and raped by security forces and camp officials, as described in the case study on Burmese women in this report.

Governments also have imposed, or refused to amend, laws that discriminate against women. In Pakistan, discriminatory evidentiary standards not only deny rape survivors access to justice, but also result in their arbitrary detention and thus expose them to further sexual violence by their jailers. As mothers or potential mothers, women face *de jure* discrimination in many countries. For example, Botswana men who marry foreigners have the right to pass Botswana citizenship on to their children; Botswana women do not.[1] In Russia, women are routinely turned away from public sector jobs because they are considered less productive workers on account of their maternal responsibilities.

In other situations, governments apply gender-neutral laws in discriminatory ways or fail to enforce constitutional and other guarantees of non-discrimination. In Thailand, laws that penalize both prostitution and procurement are applied in a discriminatory manner resulting in the arrest of female prostitutes but impunity for their predominately male agents, pimps, brothel owners, and clients. The Brazilian constitution, in another example, guarantees women equality before the law yet courts in Brazil have exonerated men who kill their allegedly adulterous wives in order to protect their honor.

The women's human rights movement has prompted investigation into another important area of human rights abuse: violence against women carried out by private actors that is tolerated or ignored by the state. As intractable as state-perpetrated violence against women is, women's health and lives are equally endangered by abuse at the hands of husbands, employers, parents, or brothel owners. Domestic violence, for example, is a leading cause of female injury in almost every country in the world and is typically ignored by the state or only erratically punished, as the studies of Brazil, Russia, and South Africa in this report reveal. In Kuwait, employers assault Asian women domestic workers, driving hundreds of women to flee to their embassies each year. Yet only a handful of abusive employers are investigated or prosecuted. To fulfill their international obligations, states are required not only to ensure that women, as victims of private violence, obtain equal protection of the law, but also that the conditions that render women easy targets for attack—including sex discrimination in law and practice—are removed.

Women's lack of social and economic security has compounded their vulnerability to violence and sex discrimination. We have found, for example, that numerous Burmese, Nepali, and Bangladeshi women and girls, seeking to escape poverty at home, accept fraudulent job or marriage offers that result in their being trafficked into forced prostitution. In South Africa, women's lack of access to alternative housing is one reason why some of them hesitate to report domestic violence. At the same time, the lack of access to political power and to equal justice—through the right to organize, to express opinions freely, to participate in the political process, and to obtain redress for abuse—is a central obstacle to women seeking to improve their social and economic status within their societies. At the International Conference on Population and Development in Cairo in 1994, governments recognized that "advancing gender equality and equity and the empowerment of women, and the elimination of all kinds of violence against women, and ensuring women's ability to control their own fertility, are cornerstones of population and development-related programs." Similarly, the stated goals of the Fourth World Conference on Women in Beijing—peace, equality and development—suggest that protection of women's human rights is inextricably connected to the improvement of women's status more generally.

Silence and Impunity

Silence about abuses against women hides the problems that destroy, and sometimes end, women's lives. Governments excuse and fail to take action against soldiers and prison guards who rape, police officers who forcibly traffick women, immigration officials who assault, judges who exonerate wife-murderers, and husbands who batter. They accept and defend domestic laws that discriminate on their face or in practice. Until recently, local and international human rights organizations, the United Nations and regional human rights bodies have approached human rights advocacy by focusing on a narrow interpretation of politically motivated abuse, while often failing to respond to the repression of women even when they challenge existing legal, political or social systems. Also neglected by governments and international organizations have been the range of abuses that women suffer because many of these violations did not conform to standard ideas of what constitutes human rights abuse. Thus, "Nada," a Saudi woman who sought political asylum in Canada in 1992, initially was denied refuge because persecution for her feminist views on the status of women in her country and her activities flowing from those beliefs—attempting to study in the field of her choice, to refuse to wear the veil, and to travel alone—was not deemed political. Similarly, in a notorious case in 1988, a U.S. immigration judge denied political asylum to Catalina Mejia, a Salvadoran woman who was raped by soldiers. In the judge's opinion, Mejia's rape by a

Salvadoran soldier, who accused her of being a guerrilla, was not an act of persecution but rather the excess of a soldier acting "only in his own self-interest."[2]

The lack of documentation of violations of women's rights reinforces governments' silence; without concrete data, governments have been able to deny the fact of and their responsibility for gender-based abuse. Where human rights violations against women remain undocumented and unverified, governments pay no political or economic price for refusing to acknowledge the problem and their obligation to prevent and remedy abuse. One of the first challenges faced by the women's human rights movement has been to transform women's experiences of violence and discrimination into fact-based proof of the scale and nature of such abuse and governments' role in its perpetuation.

Just as human rights groups historically have been the primary force in ensuring accountability for politically motivated human rights abuse, women's rights advocates are the vanguard in the fight for justice for gender-based violations. Thus, for example, they have won recognition that traditional notions of the political actor must be modified to acknowledge the political nature of women's efforts to challenge their subordinate status and the violence and discrimination that reinforce it. Women's rights advocacy has rejected the argument that governments bear no responsibility for the wide range of abuses perpetrated by private actors and argued to the contrary that governments must remedy and prevent such acts.

By building regional and international linkages that extend across cultural religious, ethnic, political, class, and geographic divides, women have developed effective political and legal strategies that strengthen their work domestically. Women's ability to secure their rights domestically is always subject to their countries' laws and willingness to enforce those laws. By calling upon the protections of the international human rights system, women are claiming rights that are not only morally desirable but also legally enforceable. Thus, for example, women's rights groups combating rape in custody in Pakistan cast the abuse not only as a criminal act under domestic law, but also as torture, a gross violation of international human rights norms. This strategy helped them to secure legal reform in Pakistan and to influence the approach of the international human rights community to the problem of custodial rape in their country.

In the past, absent support from their domestic legal systems, human rights organizations, and intergovernmental agencies, women often chose not to seek redress rather than risk reprisal and social ostracism in cultures that often blame the victim. As the international human rights system becomes more responsive to gender-based human rights violations, women who have previously been silent about their experiences of abuse are speaking up. Their testimonies add to the evidence of the scale and prevalence of abuses against women that the international community simply cannot afford to ignore.

The Challenge Ahead

The global women's human rights movement has won important battles in the international arena as well as on the home front. In March 1993 the U.N. Commission on Human Rights adopted for the first time a resolution calling for the integration of the rights of women into the human rights mechanisms of the United Nations. Later that year, governments participating in the World Conference on Human Rights declared:

> *the human rights of women and of the girl-child are an inalienable, integral and indivisible part of universal human rights. The full and equal participation of women in political, civil, economic, social and cultural life, at the national, regional and international levels, and the eradication of all forms of discrimination on grounds of sex are priority objectives of the international community.*
>
> *Gender-based violence and all forms of sexual harassment and exploitation, including those resulting from cultural prejudice and international trafficking, are incompatible with the dignity and worth of the human person, and must be eliminated.[3]*

This declaration was a milestone for the women's human rights movement because governments around the world had for a long time refused to acknowledge that women, too, are entitled to enjoy their fundamental human rights. In December 1993 the General Assembly took another key step

toward integrating women into the U.N.'s human rights work by adopting the Declaration on Violence Against Women. With this declaration, the U.N. member states recognized explicitly that states are obliged to fight specific forms of violence against women and called on governments to exercise due diligence to prevent, investigate, and punish acts of violence against women.

With the appointment in 1994 of a Special Rapporteur on Violence against Women, its Causes and Consequences, the U.N. recognized the need to address the gender-specific aspects of violence against women.[4] The special rapporteur was given the authority to investigate violence against women, to recommend measures to eliminate this violence, and to work closely with other special rapporteurs, special representatives, working groups, and independent experts of the Commission on Human Rights and the Sub-Commission on Prevention of Discrimination and Protection of Minorities and treaty bodies to combat violence against women.

Despite such indicators of progress in promoting women's rights, the dismal record on preventing abuse persists. Even those governments that profess a strong commitment to promoting human rights in general have balked at fulfilling their obligation to protect women's rights. On the international level, the Special Rapporteur on Violence against Women lacks sufficient technical and financial support from the U.N. to carry out her work. Similarly, despite the strengths of the Committee on the Elimination of Discrimination Against Women, its effectiveness in promoting women's rights remains severely compromised by inadequate technical and financial resources and its inability to consider individuals' complaints against states. Moreover, the U.N. has failed to integrate women's human rights into its treaty-based and non-treaty-based bodies' system-wide work on human rights. International financial institutions are also in a position to influence the governmental response to abuses against women, yet they generally have refused to address the discriminatory barriers to women's participation in development, or gross violations of women's human rights.

In far too many cases—many of them documented in this report—overwhelming evidence of human rights violations goes unheeded by repressive governments with the tacit acceptance of other governments and international institutions. In very few instances has the international community denounced abuses against women and pressured abusive governments to prevent and remedy them. Thus, in Peru, President Alberto Fujimori has not prosecuted one soldier accused of rape in the context of the counterinsurgency offensive; instead he declared an amnesty for all security forces that makes it legally impossible to investigate the many egregious abuses, including rape by soldiers and police, committed over the past fifteen years. In the United States, the federal government has failed to use its authority to stop torture and other cruel and inhuman treatment of women prisoners in state prisons. In Turkey, the government has yet to investigate police and state doctors for forcing women and girls to undergo virginity exams; indeed the government tried recently to adopt regulations specifically endorsing such exams. And, in the former Yugoslavia, Serbian forces reportedly have renewed their campaign of massive human rights abuse, including rape, to drive non-Serbs out of so-called safe areas. . . .

RECOMMENDATIONS

In each of the thematic chapters that follow, we present a series of recommendations for responsible governments and the wider international community—including donor countries, the United Nations and other intergovernmental bodies—to end impunity and to prevent future abuse. More generally, the challenge to the women's rights and human rights movements, and to governments that support the goal of gender equality, is to insist that women's human rights be continually integrated into all official programs, legislation, and discourse related to human rights.

Governments should review national legislation and practices in order to eliminate discrimination on the basis of sex and adopt necessary legislation for promoting and protecting women's right to be free from sex discrimination in all spheres. This requires governments to amend criminal, civil, family, and labor laws that discriminate on the basis of sex, including pregnancy and maternity. Governments further should eliminate gender bias in the administration of justice and particularly discriminatory

laws and practices that contribute to the wrongful incarceration of women. All victims of discrimination on the basis of sex should be afforded an appropriate forum to challenge the practice and obtain an effective remedy.

As a matter of urgency, governments should protect women's human rights and fundamental freedoms regardless of whether such abuses are attributed to tradition or custom. In countries where customary and/or religious law co-exist with statutory law, governments should ensure that each legal regime is in full compliance with international human rights norms, with particular attention to matters of family and personal status law.

Governments should also implement existing laws and policies that protect women from and guarantee them remedies for gender-based violence. States must guarantee women equal protection of the law through rigorous enforcement of criminal laws prohibiting violence against women, and reform legislation and practices that mischaracterize domestic violence, marital rape and wife-murder as private matters or crimes of honor, and thus allow perpetrators to receive lenient treatment or to go unpunished altogether. Governments should exercise their obligations to investigate and prosecute alleged instances of torture or other forms of cruel, inhuman and degrading treatment, including rape, that occur within their territories and to exercise jurisdiction over torturers who enter their territories.

Governments should promote the universal ratification of the International Covenant on Civil and Political Rights, the International Covenant on Economic, Social and Cultural Rights, the Convention against Torture and Other Cruel, Inhuman or Degrading Treatment or Punishment, and the Convention on the Elimination of All Forms of Discrimination Against Women (CEDAW). Governments should further withdraw all reservations to these treaties that undermine their object and purpose.

Finally, governments should integrate considerations of women's human rights into bilateral and multilateral foreign policy. To this end, governments should systematically use all available leverage to combat violations of women's rights, including bilateral, diplomatic, trade, and military relations; their voice and vote at international and regional financial institutions; and the stigma of public condemnation of abusive governments.

The international community should also do more to promote and protect women's human rights. Member states of the U.N. should adopt and ratify a protocol to CEDAW that would allow women whose domestic legal systems have failed them to submit complaints directly to the Committee on the Elimination of Discrimination Against Women. The committee's current inability to consider individual communications or complaints against states severely limits its effectiveness in promoting the rights embodied in CEDAW. Further, countries that are parties to CEDAW should include information in their periodic reports on efforts to combat all forms of abuse identified in this report.

The international community further should integrate women's human rights into the system-wide activities of the United Nations' treaty-based and non-treaty-based bodies on human rights. Member states should seek to ensure that existing thematic and country-specific special rapporteurs, working groups, and special representatives consistently address violations of women's human rights that fall within their mandates. In this regard, the international community should ensure adequate support for the work of the Special Rapporteur on Violence against Women and renew her mandate beyond the first term of three years.

United Nations agencies, particularly the U.N. Development Program and the U.N. Population Fund, donor governments, and regional and multilateral development banks should seek to ensure that population programs and policies that they support include safeguards for the protection of basic civil and political rights. International financial institutions, such as the World Bank, as well as donor governments should extend the concept of "good governance" to include a firm commitment to the protection of human rights.

Notes

1. Human Rights Watch/Africa and Women's Rights Project, "Botswana: Second Class Citizens: Discrimination Against Women Under Botswana's Citizenship Act," *A Human Rights Watch Short Report*, vol. 6, no. 7 (September 1994).

2. Susan Forbes Martin, *Refugee Women* (London: Zed Books, Ltd., 1991), p. 24.

3. "The Vienna Declaration and Program of Action," adopted by the World Conference on Human Rights, June 25, 1993, pp. 33–34.

4. U.N. Commission on Human Rights, Fiftieth Session, Resolution 1994/45, March 4, 1994. Endorsed by Economic and Social Council, decision of 1994/254, July 22, 1994.

CHAPTER EIGHT

How Sexist Ideology Affects Our Understanding of the World– and How Feminists Respond

"MIND CONTROL" AS AN INSTRUMENT OF PATRIARCHY

Despite the incredible injustices done to women everywhere in the world, too few people of either sex have taken the matter seriously enough. Today, even after the dramatic social changes initiated in the West by the women's movement (or because of it), there are many who consider feminism to be deluded, if not meaningless. They argue either that the women's movement should just quietly go away because women's liberation (once termed "emancipation") from patriarchy/discrimination has now been accomplished, and women never had it so good; or they argue that women do not need liberating, have never needed it (or need only small adjustments in the status quo, especially in the West), and that the women's movement is upsetting the balance of nature and, if continued (and, heaven help us, proves successful), can end only in catastrophe.

Such people contend that not only men but women, perhaps the majority of women, are in the nonfeminist or antifeminist camp: Are there not thousands of women who would never accept the label "feminist"? Are there not women who make fun of feminists? Are there not women from all walks of life—single women, wives, mothers, working women, old women, young women—who decry the very changes feminists are proud of? Are there not even increasing numbers of accomplished, professional women who oppose so-called women's rights legislation, even academic women who used to teach women's studies? And, besides that, they argue, don't many women say that even if some of the nonsense feminists harp about has something to it, the things they fret about are mostly frivolous compared to the wonderful privilege and comfort women already enjoy, especially in the United States? Women who look to change the balance of gender relationships are their own worst enemies, now, aren't they? Was that not Phyllis Schlafly's thesis in her battle against the Equal Rights Amendment?

It is true that there have been women who have acted side by side with men in the control of women by patriarchy. And it is true that women as well as men participate in passing patriarchal culture from one generation to the next. If one thinks for

445

a minute of what a tremendous feat it is for one-half of the world's population to have been subjugated by the other half, one sees that it has to be so. More than half the human population comprises women, and had that numerical superiority ever been tapped, it could have given women great power. Women can be creative, resourceful, and courageous, and we could have stood on our own behalf. Yet for centuries, women have very often supported the patriarchal status quo, have "backed their men," and have demanded that our daughters and granddaughters do so as well, binding their feet and their minds and instructing them in the duties of being "good girls" and women. How are we to account for that? Is there something to the charge that we women are our own worst enemies or that there is simply nothing to bother about? Or does the answer lie elsewhere?

People who study history and government often talk of the impossibility of a monolithic power dominating the entire world because of the enormity of the task. It would be unlikely, they argue, that any power could maintain a policing network so encompassing or an executive agency so vast that it could preserve worldwide control. And yet, although patriarchal societies are not themselves monolithic, patriarchy *per se* is, and for centuries it has maintained control over women and over the institutions that guide the political, economic, and cultural arrangements governing our lives. How does it do this?

It is neither a new nor a surprising idea that the most potent form of control is one that reigns not over the body but over the mind. Science fiction and Cold War drama are full of stories about brainwashing and mind control. To place into the belief system of an individual the idea that the restraints governing her or him are inevitable, right, proper, and desirable is to place a perpetual sentry at the door to a free existence. Given this, there is no need for external guards. So long as the belief remains, the job is done and the control is intact.

Some time ago, at a conference of the Society for Women in Philosophy, as the members were discussing the nature of domination and control, one woman suggested that the most stable and effective form of slavery was one in which members of the oppressed group were socialized to love their slav-ery. A second woman countered that an even more perfect form of slavery was one in which the slaves were *unaware* of their condition, unaware that they were controlled, believing instead that they had freely chosen their life and situation. The control of women by patriarchy is effected just this way, by mastering our beliefs and attitudes through the management of all the agencies that influence our understanding.

For the most part, without ideas that challenge the patriarchal system, most women (and men) are unaware that their actions and life possibilities are controlled by the gender system and that women do not freely come to choose male-defined "femininity" and its trappings.

Women and men see the world and ourselves differently because patriarchy has arranged for women and men to have two different conceptual universes for women and men to live in and to learn what we think. In a sexist world, education, religion, media, art, science, philosophy, and other agencies of enculturation foster two separate realities for people to absorb; not only are women and men trained to see the world differently, but we also come to have divergent postures to life and to ourselves. We come to answer differently the questions, Who am I? What am I? What shall I be? Nor are these mechanisms specific to our society alone. All cultures are transmitted from one generation to the next through processes like these. Although the degree of difference and subordination varies from one society to the next, all societies effect the compliance of women with patriarchy in this fashion.

If patriarchy is to prevail, it must instill its consciousness into the minds of its subjects, particularly women, because the rebellion of women would mean its demise. We must sharpen our comprehension of the many ways that patriarchal society exerts control over our understanding. Let us look at some of the more powerful agencies of idea formation, how they work and what they produce.

EDUCATION

In the United States, as elsewhere, one learns patriarchal consciousness in many ways, from formal teaching to informal or subliminal messages.

Schools, from the primary grades through college, teach not only the three Rs and the officially recognized "knowledge" we find in books and curricula. Self-consciously or not, they also foster values, attitudes, expectations, and worldviews. In functioning both as a trainer for participation in the wider society and as a reflection of that society, the schools generally transmit the traditional views on sexual identity, and very early they convey and reinforce in girls and boys the segregated conceptual systems of the sexes.

The Environment

Consider the hierarchy of the typical American primary school and high school. Parallel to the arrangement of women and men in most institutions (male doctor to female assistants, male manager to female clerks or secretaries, male pilot to female flight attendants—male always in charge), the school presents to the students the traditional picture of masculine power. On the front lines, in the classrooms and in the outer offices behind typewriters or computer screens, one finds women—accessible, concrete, "live" personnel. In the inner office, apart from the common folk, distant and powerful, resides the principal, who, in the great majority of cases, is a male. Further removed and even more powerful are the school boards and the superintendents, of whom, again, a majority are male.

Female teachers often function in relation to the principal in the same way that female parents often function in relation to male parents. The former maintain policy set by the latter (authority figure), but when children are very difficult, they are sent to that ultimate power for more "meaningful" discipline. When, on occasion, the principal visits the classroom, students can feel that something special is happening. The effect on both female and male children is powerful and enduring. The arrangement says something very different to boys and girls about what they may become, what they can expect of people in life, and what they can do and accomplish. Given such environmental cues, the consciousness of the two sexes forms rather differently.

The cues gain credence and deepen in meaning as they are played out in the same environment among the children themselves. Children are separated and reminded that they are different: *Boys on this side of the room, girls over there.* Their sense of competition is deepened: *Let's have a contest, the boys against the girls.* Their place on the power-strength continuum is fixed: *I want three boys to carry the projector for me.* Little girls are taught to "behave like ladies": *Keep your legs down. Don't be rowdy.* Boys are told to be nice young *men* or to help little Debbie climb down from the seesaw. In my daughter's kindergarten room, toys were arranged against two walls: dolls, cradle, ironing board, brooms, and cupboards on one side; trucks, blocks, and a horse on the other. Circumstances do not change in high school. Boys gravitate to science and technology, girls to literature. Boys begin to excel and girls to channel their interest away from study and toward pleasing the boys. In my high school, girls were required to take shop, but we spent that semester making jewelry while the boys made wooden cabinets. It was "natural," after all; we were encouraged to do what interested us.

Physical education—with its different expectations for girls and boys—trains differently not only the body but the mind. Team sports—competitive, aggressive, and demanding—teach teamwork, the value of practice and readiness, the effectiveness of perseverance and determination, the willingness to face risk for gain. Girls interested in team sports are usually poorly supported, financially or emotionally. The most popular women in high school sports lead cheers. They are more apt to win their kudos standing on the sideline in tiny little outfits, tossing their hair and their bodies and shouting, "Come on, boys! Let's go."

Consider for a moment the effects of those two different vantage points and the lessons gleaned from them. Think about those two very different sets of perceptions—*I, player* and *I, cheerleader; I, center* and *I, periphery*—and the consequences they may have twenty years later.

The Curriculum

The school system, through its administrative structures and its curriculum, says different things to female and male students because it evolves out of a sexist society. So do the people within the system. Teachers, principals, authors, and scientists who learn and work in a sexist environment quite predictably incline toward sexist beliefs and perspectives. What they say and teach is therefore also sexist. Books, films, magazines, pamphlets, and papers are usually sexist; they are used by teachers who often do not notice or question that perspective, and so they are presented as truth. Primers that picture Dad in his easy chair and Mother in her apron, history books that discuss the lives of farmers and their wives, anthropology texts entitled *Man in All His Aspects,* and many other such instances converge to paint a clear picture of the different status of women and men. Sexist theories presented as truth in books have the weight of all history behind them. Even more than propositions about women and men that are pointedly spoken, the unspoken or subliminal statement has power because it is not even available for critique.

From nursery school through college, then, the learning experience—both formal and informal—is different for females and males. Different images of what women and men are and should be are communicated by the people in institutions and validated by the history of "truth" as maintained in the books.

One of the earliest targets of the women's movement in the United States was the school system, particularly textbooks. The feminists' goal was to revise textbooks to present people realistically, rather than showing all children (White) living in perfectly manicured middle-class suburban neighborhoods, all Moms washing dishes with happy smiles on their faces, and all Dads cheerfully mowing grass. Feminists meant to create positive models that both girls and boys could aspire to, models that would lead them to stretch their minds and reach for full participation in society. Antifeminists responded vehemently, marshalling legal, political, and economic strength against the textbook initiatives. The battle is still going on.

In schools, females are presented with the same vision of themselves that we meet in the culture at large. From books, teachers, counselors, extracurricular activities, and aptitude tests, we learn that we are expected to be passive, quiet, nurturing, surreptitiously bossy, incompetent ladies, wives, and mothers, and all the rest of the baggage that makes up the content of sexism. Given the power of the school experience—and given its early, continuous,

and pervasive entry into our lives—it is hardly surprising that we should absorb its formulations, believe them, and, finally, internalize them.

Education is, therefore, one of the major contributors to building a patriarchal ideology, a social belief system that affirms a sexist stance to life. Without feminist intervention, education helps lead to the fixing of a "feminine" (that is, masculinist) consciousness in women, the consciousness that allows patriarchy to prevail in our own private worlds because it appears "right." If the schools, the teachers, and the textbooks say this picture is right, who, then, are we to say it is wrong?

Change

Since the impetus of the women's movement and Title IX, sensitivity to sexual asymmetry is increasing at the college level, in high schools, and even in parent-teachers associations and school boards. For teachers now in training, courses on sexism in education are frequently available. Book publishers, sensitized to the issue by groups such as the National Organization for Women (NOW) and the Women's Equity Action League (WEAL), are setting new, nonsexist guidelines. Schools are integrating physical education classes and even sports teams. Universities and professional schools are under pressure to add women to their faculty and staff not only for their own benefit but also as role models for the next generation of contributors. Antifeminists, of course, are equally active in resisting such change.

In any society, the educational process, both formal or otherwise, is a primary effector of enculturation and a major arm of social control. We must, on the one hand, expect it to reflect the beliefs of the wider society and thus to be basically conservative. On the other hand, education is supposed to be a purveyor of knowledge and truth, a foil to hardening of the intellectual arteries, a proponent of personal and social growth. That is an impressive image, believed by many, that carries with it an impressive responsibility: the duty to ensure that, however difficult the task, new understanding will be absorbed and integrated into the existing body of knowledge and passed on to the next generation. In that duty lies the hopeful optimism of women's studies and contemporary feminists. It is the reason that both feminists and our opponents treat the educational system as a primary target for vigilance and activity.

THE MEDIA

A *medium,* in the sense referred to here, is a mode or agency for communicating ideas. In our society, the important media include newspapers, radio and television, magazines, art, advertising, books, and films. They are the primary means of carrying ideas among the various segments of the population. Media not only carry information, they are also very powerful in framing attitudes and forming opinions. In a word, media teach, and they teach not only with what they say but also with how they say it.

Television, Magazines, News Reporting

One of the most powerful media in our lives is television. More than any other modern invention, it has affected our thinking because, beginning early in life for most of us, it so thoroughly pervades our waking time—for some people as much as six hours a day or more. During those hours, we see programs and advertising replete with the traditional stereotypes, the age-old misogynistic and racist attitudes. On the sitcoms and weekly dramas are the long-suffering wives, the manipulative young beauties, the wronged lovers, the half-naked seductresses, the mindless child-women pursuing husbands, lovers, or other fantasies, and most of these characters are White. Or we may be treated to street prostitutes, broken druggies, poor and hapless single mothers, or, for the really hip television show, escapees into the professions that are mostly women of color. In the westerns, women are dance-hall queens (prostitutes) with hearts of gold, "fiery" Mexican girls, or damsels in distress; sometimes they are gun-totin' toughies who, after a bath and the right guy to tame them, turn out to be damsels in distress. In the crime dramas, women are mostly the victims of bizarre crimes or the neglected wives and girlfriends of policemen; sometimes they are gun-totin' cops, and often, under the right circumstances, they too turn out to be damsels in distress, suffering role reversal inner torment. Often when women manage to get into nontraditional jobs, they can usually be counted on to mess things up or become victimized in some way and to require saving

by the male heroes of the program. Exceptions now exist, thanks to the women's movement, but they are rare. The occasional single women, even the self-sufficient ones, tend to appear in light comedy. Seen in drama only since the women's movement fought for it, but still fairly uncommon, are realistic and positive representations of staunch women, older women, ordinary working women, non-White, non-Christian, not nondescript, realistically presented, wrestling with the simple and not-so-simple human problems that we are all heir to.

Advertising, more insidious even than programming because it communicates beliefs more covertly, offers even more destructive fare. Here we see women, almost always White, still groaning over which laundry soap will work best on their teenager's dirt, twittering to one another over the advantages of some toilet paper, and "doctoring" their husbands with cough syrup or laxatives. We see younger women smiling seductively, undulating to some jingle, willing to sell themselves to sell a product. Now and again we are presented with a professional woman, but she is generally a wife or mother juggling her time with the aid of product X so as not to neglect her family. We also see the straight sexual ads: This perfume, hair color, soap, or toothpaste will give you the sex appeal you now lack; if you buy it, you will finally capture your elusive prince. Of course, more numerous now than any are ads for "fitness": half-naked youngsters with bulging muscles and breasts that could not possibly have affixed to those skinny bodies naturally, touting this or that diet or machine to reorganize one's flesh according to the latest body image. Worse yet are ads that use female bodies as a shill to the male buyer: sexpots smiling seductively, draped across speedboats or cooing over shaving cream.

Where are the real women, the millions of struggling working women, the divorced and widowed women, the professional women, the intelligent, competent women? Where are the women of color in roles that are not either comical or supportive of White stereotypes, roles that actually portray life in African-American or Mexican-American communities? Where are the ideas truly important to us, truly meaningful: dramas about women trying to break into decent jobs and decent salaries; working to stay emotionally intact; struggling to hold down jobs, care for children, and maintain peace of mind all at the same time? Where are the products truly useful to us, those that really might save work rather than create it?

Magazines and newspapers are no better. Women's magazines typically are owned and published by men, supported by patriarchal agencies through advertising money. It is they who select the articles and the ads. It is they who decide *and tell us* what women want to see or think about. Women's magazines are most commonly found at the checkout counter of supermarkets and discount stores. They are easily identifiable. On their covers generally are pictures of food, artistically presented, side by side with the scoop on the latest quick weight loss diet, or pictures of movie and television stars. Inside, one finds details on how to prepare wonderful recipes that make the family sit up and take notice (finally); details on how to follow that diet, lose pounds and inches, look young again, and make one's husband sit up and take notice (finally); and, failing that, details on how to lose oneself in the lives of those who *were* able to get people to sit up and take notice.

The problem of what is "real" and what is not is rather complex in terms of social presentation. The media not only reflect cultural images but also create, teach, and reify them. Girls and young women, constantly bombarded with certain images of beauty, are being taught that those images *are* beauty, are required, that they should and must have it. It does not matter if the images do not fit. For young or old, big or small, abled or differently abled, rich or poor, healthy or sick, African-American, Asian-American, Jewish-American or other: one size fits all. Women who see themselves portrayed only as willing subordinates (happy or otherwise), nasty-natured villains, or sexy bombshells are being taught that this is the way women are and that we are anomalous in any other guise. Watching these portrayals, the woman who does not fit into one or the other required category rarely says to herself, "Those images aren't real." Because she comes to those images with the unconscious working assumption that the media offer true representations of reality, she believes the images. For her, the images are real; thus, it is she who is not real. She must either accept herself as the anomaly (with all the personal conflict that goes with it) or change to conform. Until alternative visions are given realistic treatment by the

mass media, until they are given social approval by that treatment, they will remain subversive, alien, or abnormal. Media treatment of alternative visions, however, has been sparse at best and generally well within the bounds of traditionally acceptable images. Most often, they are sexist and racist. Women work, but they are models, highly paid executives in three-piece suits, waitresses, or gorgeous, chic detectives. Unskinny women do occasionally show up, but with very few exceptions, they are the clowns, not the lovers.

Language, of course, is central. The repeated use of certain language, particularly words in juxtaposition, can either hide the real meaning of a concept or distort it radically. Consider the term *beauty pageant.* The name alone proclaims that the contestants are beautiful, that they represent beauty *per se.* But standards of beauty are not absolute. In 1956, for example, when I was 16 years old, my nineteenth-century European grandmother worried about me endlessly, concerned that my size 9 frame was far too skinny ever to lure a husband. Would she find the undernourished contestants of today's pageants beautiful? And I wonder if, after coming to terms with the artifice of contemporary feminine makeup and mannerisms, after spending time with and learning to admire very different kinds of women, most women would indeed find the pageant contestants beautiful. I find them silly and plastic. Can the term itself be wrong? The power of language is such that it can distort reality to its own image. That is why the language and images the media employ have been such a focal point of the movement.

Art and Films

In a university where I taught, a young art instructor was forced to remove his painting from a student-faculty art exhibit because his subject was a nude male with full portrayal of genitals. Several nudes (female nudes are always referred to simply as "nudes") remained on display without comment, their breasts and pubes in plain view.

An avant-garde festival of "erotic" films at another university was advertised by a poster picturing the face of the devil superimposed on the nude lower torso of a woman. Complaints to the administration by female faculty and students did not, however, bring it down.

Pop music, rock particularly, has become intensely misogynistic and savagely aggressive. Many all-male rock groups wear their sexuality as costume and chant diatribes against "silicone sisters" and "delectable poison," even depicting how they would kill, rape, and cut them up. Album covers have appeared depicting chained women, naked or half naked, their chests to the floor, their heads beneath the shoe of some arrogant male, the leader of the group. The girls in the audience, "liberated" and "modern," scream for more, pay for the concerts, and buy the albums. The number of female rock groups or females in the groups is proportionately minuscule.

The sexism of current rock music is particularly destructive. Modern technology, with its plug-yourself-in, take-anywhere radios and its high-gloss videos, has made popular music culture an even more prominent and more attitude-forming phenomenon than it was in generations past. It is ever present, totally penetrating, and inside the head. Thus, its images come to pervade our awareness.

A popular video of the late 1980s, for example, "Addicted to Love," presented a conservatively suited, well-dressed young man surrounded by several women, all identical. The women—each alike in costume, size, and thin, angular shape— were bizarrely made up so that only their lips, darkened eyes, and hairlines were prominent. Undulating in unison to the rhythm of the music, like mechanized dolls, they were completely without expression or any sign of emotion. They were "sexy." The effect, in its way mesmerizing, was to depict the women not as persons but as caricatures, as clone-like robots, without individuality, identity, thought, or will. They had no humanity. They were props—interesting, decorative, seductive, but not fully alive. What lesson does such an image teach men about women? What lesson does it teach women about ourselves? What behaviors does it justify or create?

The point of looking at these representative instances is that in each of the cases, the perspective was male/masculinist. Paintings of nude women are considered respectable because men find them "beautiful," men like to look at them, and feel justified in keeping pictures of nude women. Paintings of nude males are not socially respectable because they are not favored by heterosexual/martial males.

They do not want women to fancy them (which would suggest that women were in charge of their own sexuality), nor do they countenance the interests of gay males, since homosexuality is particularly threatening to the martial self-image. Further, the blatant presentation of the unadorned male body tends to remove their aura of godliness, distance, and power, and reduces them to the common, as women have been reduced. It is fashionable today for women to dress so as to reveal their bodies, and modern chic decrees that those who object are just not "with it." Women who deplore videos, places (Hooters, for example), or fashions because of their contemptuous treatment of women are simply dismissed as prudes and poor sports.

The male hegemony sets the rules and standards. This is art; this is not. This is presentable; this is not. The depiction of naked women, invitingly arranged, is presentable art; the same depiction of men is irresponsible (and probably perceived as antimale). Literature portraying war, the conflicts of manhood, or cataclysm is grand art; that involving childbirth, families, or women's experiences is petty craft of marginal interest.

The same is true of the movies, that great shaper of American attitudes. In her study of the treatment of women in film, Molly Haskell explained that as the film industry has grown more and more to resemble an "art," with production of a film in the hands of one great "artist" (such as Bergman or Antonioni), the films increasingly reflect that (male) artist's point of view, and women's images have plunged.[1] Increasing *the camera's eye* (the point of view of a film, which is conveyed by the stance of the director and his positioning of the camera and the action) is male; the film presents a man's view of reality. Most often, however, both men and women fail to realize that the film reflects a masculine consciousness because, as Beauvoir pointed out, in patriarchy maleness is taken as universality. What effect does this have on society? What is the effect on men and women, respectively?

SOCIAL SCIENCE

Scientific theory is extremely important in the lives of twentieth-century people. Side by side with its data, procedures, and theories stands the scientific worldview, an entire way of looking at reality and of relating to life. Some social analysts have suggested that in contemporary times science functions much as a god or as a substitute for God, providing a basis for truth and knowledge, an agent to be trusted and depended on for salvation, even a ground of value.

Placing very high trust in the judgments of science and scientists is part of Western cultural ethos. A large segment of the public maintains the belief that "Science *is* Truth," the only dependable, sane truth for up-to-date, rational, right-minded people. The corollary to the "Science is Truth" theme is the notion that we should all live our lives in accordance with the truths of Science. Although the idea is rarely articulated in quite this way, a close appraisal of the new intellectual scene reveals the "modern" dictum: Live your life in such a way that Science would be proud of you. As medievals yearned to please God and achieve a state of grace, moderns yearn for a state of "health."

Because people today want so badly to be judged "healthy," social science—that part of science that focuses specifically on human behavior—has become very much like a faith. On at least two levels, as a technical-academic enterprise and as a "philosophy" of life for popular culture, social science, especially psychology, serves as a kind of religion. It posits eternal verities about human nature and goals, decrees standards of perfection (health) toward which one is advised to strive, separates the "good" people (healthy, normal) from the bad (unhealthy, abnormal), determines social priorities both for individuals and for the state, and carries sufficient esteem in the community to socialize the population according to a certain vision of behavior.

Current attitudes toward child rearing and parental responsibility provide an example of how "scientific" theory and masculinist interests can interlock to support one another, creating accepted beliefs or values that operate to preserve patriarchy. In this case, the sciences are sociology and child psychology; the goal for patriarchy is to dislodge women from our newly won independence and place us back under the control of the domestic sphere.

When my parents were young children (in the early 1920s), they often told me, they were encouraged to be self-reliant, independent, and responsible.

They were expected to contribute to family interests at a very early age; in addition to school work they had "chores," which included caring for younger children, cleaning or cooking, driving a tractor, and so on. By the time they were in their very early teens, both were working part time and turning over their salaries to their households. Their managing independently when left alone at home, to work, do their homework, or even to play by themselves, was taken as a point of pride both by themselves and their parents. Today, they would be considered "neglected." Yesterday's "mature, responsible children" would be today's "latchkey kids," and their parents would be rebuked (or prosecuted!) for leaving their youngsters unsupervised or treating them so badly.

Today's conventional beliefs regarding children and families tell us (1) that nothing is more important or valuable than a child; that nothing is or should be more important or meaningful than having them, caring for them, or meeting their needs; and, covertly, that children's interests supersede those of the adults in their families; (2) that for mental health, children in the early years of their life require the presence and attention of their mothers almost all the time; (3) that for their safety and happiness, children should never be by themselves, but instead their whereabouts and activities should be carefully monitored and organized as much as possible; (4) that both for its own proper social adjustment and for the good of society, every child requires two parents, female and male, to be present in their lives, preferably in their homes; and (5) that mothers who do not adhere to these principles and do everything they can to satisfy them are unnatural and neglectful.

The hypotheses of this model of child rearing are essentially speculation, certainly they could not even remotely be deemed verified, yet they are promulgated with passion by many in the social sciences and repeated with equal passion by various other institutions of society, including health care, education, and the popular media. It is a construction rarely questioned.

How children should best be raised or best be cared for by their mothers is, of course, a large issue. There are real and serious questions to be asked and answered here. Additionally, however, when considering these questions, we need to keep in mind that the terms *child, mother, parent,* and so on are social terms, constructions, as well as material entities. What is a child, for example? Do we mean someone under the age of 21, under 13, or under 7? (These are ages that various societies during different periods of history identified as the age of transition into adulthood.)

The subject here is not child rearing or motherhood *per se,* but "motherhood," "childhood," or models of child rearing as social constructions. Because social science has so great a potential as an enforcer of the status quo, it is reasonable, probably crucial, for feminists to ask what may have prompted social scientists at this time in history to adopt a particular philosophy of children and parenting, what sociologist Sharon Hays refers to as an *ideology of intensive mothering.*

> *It is my argument that the contemporary cultural model of socially appropriate mothering takes the form of an ideology of* intensive mothering. *The ideology of intensive mothering is a gendered model that advises mothers to expend a tremendous amount of time, energy, and money in raising their children. In a society where over half of all mothers with young children are now working outside of the home, one might well wonder why our culture pressures women to dedicate so much of themselves to child rearing. And in a society where the logic of self-interested gain seems to guide behavior in so many spheres of life, one might further wonder why a logic of unselfish nurturing guides the behavior of mothers. These two puzzling phenomena make up what I call the cultural contradictions of contemporary motherhood.[2]*

We might well wonder, remarks Hays. Indeed, we might. It is not unreasonable for feminists to speculate whether there might be connections among women's increased freedom and opportunity, a nearly obsessive societal fixation on "kids" and their needs, and the sexist determination to get women back in the home and out of the workplace. Is it scandalous today to wonder who benefits from the unverified hypothesis that children fare better when their activities are always "managed" and that they should never be left alone or left to their own devices? It certainly does not benefit mothers, and there is very good reason to question whether it benefits children. Dare we ask who benefits from

the proposition that there "needs" to be a dad in every household, that male children must be emotionally disfigured without one?

Clearly, the impact that theories of social science have on the conduct of our lives is tremendous. For women, that can spell disaster, because both the technical enterprise of social science and the contemporary ethic that has evolved from it are still rabidly sexist.

The Formal Enterprise

For a variety of reasons—the newness of the study, the complexity of its subject matter, and the absence of clearly articulated concepts and procedures—social science, at least for now and possibly far into the future, requires a far greater degree of interpretive latitude than its natural science counterpart. That is a polite way of saying that social science is still quite subjective and thus resistant to the traditional forms of verification. Because of this, theories of the social sciences generally bear the mark of the people who develop them, and they tend to be "culture bound," reflective of both their time and place.

The majority of the people doing social science, even before it became "science," has always been male. For the most part, it was men who developed the methods of research and the procedures for verification; they also originated the earliest ideas from which current developments have evolved; and they ultimately fixed the application of those ideas, carrying theory out of the laboratory into the streets. With few exceptions, until fairly recently, most of the women who gained some recognition for their work were adherents and popularizers of the existent male-identified systems rather than creators of their own models. In fact, their female support lent those antifemale systems greater weight not only in academia but also in the minds of the people who received them. Theories from the pens of men immersed in the Victorian worldview brought all the familiar misogynistic stereotypes into greater respectability and enshrined them as science, or truth. At last it was not only taught by experience but also explained by science that women are petty, self-centered, and unprincipled. Sigmund Freud, for example, showed how such traits were caused by penis envy, masculine protest, and the castration complex.

Although some of the most blatant expressions of misogyny have changed (the expression, not the beliefs), the situation is little better today. Sexism in the social sciences is absolutely crucial in the formation of women's consciousness in contemporary society. The precepts of science and social science have become the theoretical underpinnings of education, social service, psychology, medicine, even law, and through them, misogynistic doctrines masquerading as scientific truth are being formally infused into our entire conceptual environment. Every teacher, social worker, nurse, and doctor has received the rudiments of elementary psychology and has been properly oriented to the importance of social "adjustment," strong male models, and clear sexual identity distinction. It is a rare child who escapes Erikson or Piaget, a rare ob-gyn patient who eludes Freud. Women are getting extra doses of distortion, officially sanctioned and therefore extremely powerful and convincing.

The other branch of the formal enterprise, the so-called helping professions, is similarly suffused with sexist ideology and perspective. As Phyllis Chesler pointed out, especially in *Women and Madness*,[3] the helping professions may turn out to be more hindrance than help for the woman staggering under the collective weight of patriarchy's consciousness shapers.

In the nineteenth century, science taught women that "self-abuse" (masturbation) was so damaging that it warranted removal of the clitoris if no other way could be found to stop the sinner-victim from practicing this "foul habit." It taught that "ladies" (if not women) never had orgasms and would not want to. Using the label "ladies nostrums," it dosed women up with morphine and barbiturates so that they would not mind their boredom or their overwork or their frustration or their resentment at being controlled. For those few who would not be so easily cured and who could afford it, science recommended lobotomies or incarceration in "rest homes" or mental asylums! It is hard for us today to imagine, but it is quite true.

The twentieth century brought us Freud, Spock, and others who held us responsible for our family's mental health—as if responsibility for their physical health was not enough! Any slip in toilet training, any lack of vigilance in answering questions immediately as they arise, and *wham!*, mother makes a crazy child. During the 1950s, a period of conservative retrenchment much like today, scientific and pop literature was full of warnings about the hazards for children whose mothers worked outside the home. "Latchkey kids" were likely to be maladjusted at best, prone to crime and drugs at worst, nearly certain to become "juvenile delinquents," a term rarely used anymore. Today, as the economy *requires* mothers and wives to work, and as more women enter the fields of sociology and psychology, studies are emerging that document the unreliability of earlier "evidence" that children reared in homes where mothers work are at all different from children of the "Leave it to Beaver" model home. In fact, evidence shows a slightly higher inclination to autonomy and adaptability in children whose moms work, not bad traits altogether. But how much guilt have women suffered and are still suffering because "science" scared them to death? Now, once again, as social conservatism reemerges, so does the principle of total mothering.

Today science tells us that juvenile violence is caused by single mothers (not poverty, media, or a generally violent culture), that comparable worth programs are unfeasible, that fetuses are babies, that healthy people are heterosexual (and preferably married), and that physical fitness requires us to be skinny. All of us must turn a critical eye to anything we are taught—and certainly to received opinion. That is the heart of learning and wisdom. But women must be especially wary because so often we are barred from participating in the creation of "received opinion," and so often the opinion that becomes accepted is simply an amalgam of flimsy data and a political agenda created by those who benefit from it.

RELIGION

Religion, as it is practiced through the social institutions of a people, is as much a reflection of that culture's ideals, attitudes, and needs as it is their creator. The Judeo-Christian tradition of the West, for the most part, is no exception. As Western culture is patriarchal, so typically is its religion, and most often so is its god.

Although most major religions contend that God is without sex, neither female nor male, that contention is contradicted by a host of beliefs and language indicating the maleness of their anthropomorphic gods. Currently, some fathers of the various Christian churches have opposed the ordination of women on the grounds that it would be sacrilegious because the maleness of Christ proves that only men were meant for the priestly office. In medieval times, the Church explained that women rather than men were likely to be witches because, among other things, men had been saved from that most awful danger by the fact that Christ was male. Today the use of feminine pronouns, *she* or *her,* to refer to the deity brings a very hostile response. Certainly, the Catholic imagery of the Church standing analogously to Christ as a wife stands to a husband once more supports the identification of the deity as male. Whatever the argument to the contrary, *He,* God the *Father,* most definitely is presented as male.

So in our culture, we traditionally conceive of god as male. What can we make of that? A great deal. The relationships among the concrete, material conditions of a culture, including its social organization and its myths, mores, and ideals, are intricate and close. The maleness of the Western god, his character and behavior, is as much a source of the content of our culture's masculinist perspectives as it is an indicator. If men are to be gods, their god must be male. Likewise, if God in His heaven is male, then on earth men can be the only true gods. The entire conceptual system of Martial thought is elevated and deified by its incarnation in the person of the "One True God," ultimate male, just as the sociopolitical structures of patriarchy are reinforced by their justification through theology. The relationship between masculinist theology and patriarchal society is the reason it is both possible and necessary to insist on the masculinity of the priesthood or the authority of the hierarchy. It is the source of the masculine tone in biblical imagery and of male privilege in church doctrine.

Consider the Genesis story of Adam and Eve, a story whose theme appears in numerous mythologies in other cultures. Through feminist analysis we can see how the story serves both as a resolution for a thorny male psychological conflict as well as a justification of male domination of women. Early in the creation, Adam appears, formed *in the likeness and image of God* (a concept, though unclear, frequently employed to support the ascendancy of

maleness). Pure and happy, Adam spends his hours exercising his divinely given dominion over the earth until God decides that he needs a helpmeet. As Adam sleeps, Eve is taken by God from Adam's rib, from his body, formed into a "woman" (so called because she was "taken out of man"), and presented to him. Shortly thereafter, Eve is beguiled into disobedience by a serpent, and taking Adam along with her into disfavor with God, she causes their expulsion from the Garden of Eden, the downfall of all humankind, and the specter of certain death for all of us. The serpent is henceforth sentenced to the dust, Eve to her husband's yoke, and Adam, because he "hearkened to the voice of [his] wife," condemned to labor, sweat, and sorrow.

People have pulled many meanings from this story. Freud made much of the phallic symbolism of the serpent, building around the tale a sexual interpretation. Others have focused on the matter of human growth through separation from parental protection and subsequent trial by life. As feminists, however, we can see another, more pragmatic application.

We can see the masculinist myth of Adam, the man, created "in the image of God" (in appearance? in power?), the first progenitor, the first earthly parent. So what if women and not men are able to conceive and bear young? Man did it *first* and produced woman, who produces young only secondarily. And man did it best—cleanly and neatly while he slept, without the fuss and mess of human conception, labor, and childbirth. We can see Eve, the woman—second in creation, an afterthought, a helpmeet—the first to be approached by the snake, easily seduced, equally seducing, placed for sinfulness and stupidity under the authority of her husband, condemned to painful childbirth and suffering. In a single stroke, the awesome female power of procreation is discounted (as punishment for sin); supreme parenting is comfortably settled upon the male (God and Adam, a theme reiterated and developed in the doctrine of the Virgin Birth); the man is firmly fixed in a position of dominance over women (his wife and, one assumes, other females); and the exploitation and subjection of woman is justified: She sinned, she was stupid and evil and led humanity into disgrace and misery, she was condemned to the yoke by God. Men must work, and women must bring forth children. Men rule and leave off hearkening to their wives, whereas woman's desire is to her husband. All is conveniently explained, justified, and resolved.

As one might expect, the impact of the masculinist character of theology and religion is vast, not only on women's lives and perspectives but on the entire culture as well.

Patriarchal Religion and Women

If the religion into which we are given and by which we are expected to live is masculinist and misogynist, what does it mean to be a "religious" woman in that context? Although we may rarely focus on them, we are all aware of certain realities of Western religious tradition.

- The god of this tradition (Judaism, Christianity, and Islam) generally is referred to as *he* (almost never *she,* and rarely *it*). God is male. So are his priests, potentates, hierarchies, and power centers; so are his philosophers, apologists, and policymakers; so are his favorite sons. Encyclicals of the pope to this day are addressed: "Honored Brothers and Dear Sons. . . ."

- The savior and messiah of the Christian tradition, Jesus, was himself male; so were the apostles and disciples. Never did the question arise of his faithful female followers becoming disciples; it was outside the realm of consideration, a fact often pointed out today by religious conservatives.

- In the tradition, women are conspicuously absent from power, from participation in theory or policy, from full human status. (Aquinas, remember, said that women's souls were not fully developed, and a Jewish male begins his morning prayers with thanksgiving for not having been born a woman.)

- In Judaism, Christianity, and Islam, the ideal woman is a fecund animal who tends to her young, to her husband's home and service, and who "humbly" accepts the dominion of her husband and the male hegemony. Docile, quiet, passive, obedient, and meek, she neither questions nor challenges.

- The Christian ideal, Mary, perfect in submission ("Thy will be done") and sexual "pu-

rity," took no active part in the drama of Christ. Receptacle only of God's seed, she nurtured her young male god; she herself neither directed nor taught nor hazarded an intrusion into the march of events. She is the female model.

- According to the tradition, woman's progenitor was Eve, mother of evil, precipitator of the Fall. She resides in each of us.

- According to the early fathers of Christianity, women's bodies are evil, seductive, damning, dirty. Women are carnal; men are spiritual. Women are body; men are mind. Women dare sex, and sex is evil. Women are pleasure and passion, and that, too, is condemned.

Consider the impact on your self-image of being "in the likeness of God," like Jesus, the pope, and the "Brothers of the Church," and contrast it with never finding yourself reflected in the sacred pronoun. Utter: "God, He . . ." or "God, Him. . . ." Now say: "God, She. . . ." Imagine the experience of seeing oneself reflected in the sacred images of power: Christ walking on clouds, God forming Adam with His powerful arm. Imagine, instead, modeling after the suffering Mary or shamefully hiding one's inner Eve, one's sexuality. Think of looking high into the pulpit, seeing the Man proclaiming the Word of Him, knowing that this is ever out of the grasp of oneself or any of one's kind because of one's lesser excellence and status. Ask again: If one's religion is sexist, masculinist, and misogynist, what does it mean to be a religious woman?

No wonder victimization is a sacred principle of womanhood, sacrifice a magic contribution, self-effacement a high.

Patriarchal religion adds to the problem by intensifying the process through which women internalize the consciousness of the oppressor. The males' judgment having been metamorphosed into God's judgment, it becomes the religious duty of women to accept the burden of guilt, seeing the self with male chauvinist eyes. What is more, the process does not stop with religion's demanding that women internalize such images. It happens that those conditioned to see themselves as "bad" or "sick" in a real sense become such. Women who are conditioned to live out the abject role assigned to the female sex actually appear to "deserve" the contempt heaped upon "the second sex."

—MARY DALY, *Beyond God the Father*[4]

God, Mars, and Culture

Consider the impact that the deification of maleness has on society. Remember that in any society the forms of religious worship are a reflection of cultural ideals, expressed in a different language. What makes the religious expression of those ideals so powerful is its claim to absolute validity and its subsequent persuasive force over people who believe it.

What we find when we analyze the patriarchal Western tradition is precisely what we would expect to find: a martial god, an authoritarian ethic, and a warrior consciousness. The worship of Mars, the religion of masculinism, means for society an obeisance to all the warrior values.

In patriarchy, with few exceptions, god is a ruler, a king. Superior to all, he commands. He does not tolerate disobedience, rewards and punishes according to how well one meets his expectations, and trains his followers through a series of trials and challenges.

The masculinity of god is underscored smartly by comparison with Mary as the image of mercy and kindness. The Queen of Heaven, to whom most of the finest churches in the West are dedicated, is the Mother, free from the angry, frightening qualities of Mars/God: forgiving where he is stern, understanding where he is legalistic, accessible where he is distant.

God is good, we are told, although there are no standards outside of his own will against which we may judge him. He is good (right) because he is God, that is, King, the top of the hierarchy. Everybody else is expected to be good, too; that is, obedient to the will of the King. If one is not good (obedient), then God punishes. If one suffers sufficiently, one might be redeemed (forgiven), but that, too, is solely up to God. The pattern of the god-person relationship is clearly disciplinarian and authoritarian.

Other relationships in which god resides are equally authoritarian although in a different context. The relationships are generally expressed as dualistic oppositions in which god has ascendancy: God against nature, spirit against body, life against death, god vis-à-vis humanity. The relations are ones of strain and conflict.

The tone is certainly not humanistic: You are bad, it tells us. Your body is bad; sex is bad; pleasure is bad. You may be saved from yourself, but only if you deny your earthly self.

And, of course, the ethos of strain and contention permeates the lives of the people who are both its subject and its instigators. One strives constantly to "be good," to conform, to measure up to an image that is not in harmony with what it is to be human because, among other things, it is derived from only one aspect of humanity: maleness.

The character of this Mars-Father-God permeates our culture conceptually and spiritually. It is difficult to be self-affirming, constructively self-confident, healthily self-loving in the face of an image of humanity that is subordinated and debased.

Feminist Alternatives

There are other ways to treat religion than as the submission of one's will and understanding to the prescriptions of a powerful, antagonistic authority. There are those who view worship as a total experience of life's elements, so beautiful, meaningful, and profound that they transcend temporary matters and deserve our most concentrated attention and respect. Perhaps such an experience may be possible through a very sensitive portrayal of the father-god tradition, but certainly not through the secularized, garden variety, patriarchal projections to which we are accustomed.

Many feminists question whether a reformed, nonsexist portrayal of such religions is possible, whether the historical identification of God as male can be reversed, whether its hierarchical, authoritarian character can be purged without obliterating its nature altogether.[5] Feminists ask whether women can or should participate in a religion that worships male gods and ideals in male language, demeans women's full humanity, and prohibits the full exercise of women's potential. Can or should we participate in religious institutions that have historically been misogynistic and that even now form policy for our lives while blocking our power to contribute to those formulations? Is reform possible or even worthwhile?

Feminists both within and outside of the traditional religious institutions raise some rather intriguing questions about "God-talk"[6] and by doing so perhaps point the way to a revitalization of religious experience. We might wonder whether a feminist theology would be less authoritarian, less demanding and constraining than the ones we know? In such a perspective, would the deity Herself, free of masculinist ideals, have been visualized as a more tolerant, accepting being, and would such a religion have been more affirming? Is there need for a deity at all, or could we, as Mary Daly proposes, think of God not as a person at all, not as a noun, but rather as a verb, the Holy Verb *to be*? Thus, life itself and each moment in it are both deity and divine.

Some feminists reject entirely any forms of worship, arguing that religion channels one's energy in the wrong directions, that women's situation requires strong political action, not "wasteful dreaming." One can certainly sympathize with such a view, given the history of religion for women. On the other hand, there are those who perceive feminism to be at base a spiritual movement. Feminists seek increased opportunity for participation and gain not as ends in themselves, not simply for the power they entail, but rather for the growth in the quality of life they represent, and that is a spiritual matter. In such a context, "religion," worship, or reverence may prove fruitful, and it should not be dismissed without careful scrutiny simply because of its past association and its usurpation by patriarchy.[7]

CONCLUSION

As we examine the agencies that form beliefs in our culture, we see a network of interlocking institutions and ideas that direct the consciousness of society.

Ideas that appear repeatedly in varying forms throughout the network become highly powerful forces of indoctrination because they are continually reinforced by their constant repetition in many contexts. Their repetitiveness alone gives them a cumulative effect that renders them nearly unquestionable. We have seen, in case after case, that our society's institutions promote the traditional misogynistic themes of women's inferiority. The wonder is not that women absorb them, that many of us participate in our own oppression, but that any of us at all ever break through to a new vision!

And yet we do break through, we do come to recognize the falsehoods and the injustices, and we do strive to live by a more constructive point of view. That, in a nutshell, is what feminism is. However heterogeneous some of the theories, methods, or goals, feminism is constant in recognizing the falseness and perversity of masculinist images of womanhood; it is constant in its affirmation of the worth of women.

Notes

1. Molly Haskell, *From Reverence to Rape: The Treatment of Women in the Movies* (New York: Holt, Rinehart & Winston, 1973).

2. Sharon Hays, *The Cultural Contradictions of Motherhood* (New Haven, CT: Yale University Press, 1996), p. *x.*

3. Phyllis Chesler, *Women and Madness* (New York: Doubleday, 1972). Reissued with a new introduction by Harcourt Brace Jovanovich, 1989.

4. Mary Daly, *Beyond God the Father* (Boston: Beacon Press, 1973), p. 49.

5. See particularly the works of Mary Daly: *Beyond God the Father* (1973) and *Gyn/Ecology* (1978).

6. See the works of Rosemary Radford Ruether, Carol Christ, Starhawk, Merlin Stone, Margot Adler, Anne Kent Rush, Charlene Spretnak, Naomi Goldenberg, Judith Plaskow, Penelope Washbourn, Nelle Morton, Barbara G. Walker, Carol Ochs, Elaine Pagels, Elisabeth Fiorenza, and many other women now participating in the feminist "Womanspirit" movement.

7. For further discussion of feminist spirituality, see Sheila Ruth, *Take Back the Light: A Feminist Reclamation of Spirituality and Religion* (Lanham, MD: Rowman & Littlefield, 1994).

Consciousness Raising

Catharine A. MacKinnon

Catharine A. MacKinnon is professor of law at the University of Michigan Law School. She pioneered the legal claim for sexual harassment and has been active against pornography and for sex equality in the United States and around the world. Her publications include Sexual Harassment of Working Women: A Case of Sex Discrimination *(1987);* Feminism Unmodified: Discourses on Life and Law *(1987);* Toward a Feminist Theory of the State *(1989);* Only Words *(1996); and* In Harm's Way: The Pornography Civil Rights Hearings, *co-edited with Andrea Dworkin (1998).*

Here, MacKinnon describes the process of developing a feminist consciousness, of beginning to "see" previously invisible realities of gender and of women's lives. "The key to feminist theory consists in its way *of knowing," she says. This aspect of feminism is crucial and explains in part the contribution of feminist politics, activism, and pedagogy.*

CONSCIOUSNESS RAISING IS THE PROCESS through which the contemporary radical feminist analysis of the situation of women has been shaped and shared. As feminist method and practice, consciousness raising is not confined to groups explicitly organized or named for that purpose. In fact, consciousness raising as discussed here was often not practiced in consciousness-raising groups. Such groups were, however, one medium and forum central to its development as a method of analysis, mode of organizing, form of practice, and technique of political intervention. The characteristic structure, ethic, process, and approach to social change which mark such groups as a development in political theory and practice are integral to many of the substantive

contributions of feminist theory. The key to feminist theory consists in its *way* of knowing. Consciousness raising is that way. "[An] oppressed group must at once shatter the self-reflecting world which encircles it and, at the same time, project its own image onto history. In order to discover its own identity as distinct from that of the oppressor, it has to become visible to itself. All revolutionary movements create their own way of seeing."[1] One way to analyze feminism as a theory is to describe the process of consciousness raising as it occurred in consciousness-raising groups.

As constituted in the 1960s and 1970s, consciousness-raising groups were many women's first explicit contact with acknowledged feminism. Springing up spontaneously in the context of friendship networks, colleges and universities, women's centers, neighborhoods, churches, and shared work or workplaces, they were truly grassroots. Many aimed for diversity in age, marital status, occupation, education, physical ability, sexuality, race and ethnicity, class, or political views. Others chose uniformity on the same bases. Some groups proceeded biographically, each woman presenting her life as she wished to tell it. Some moved topically, using subject focuses such as virginity crises, relations among women, mothers, body image, and early sexual experiences to orient discussion. Some read books and shared literature. Some addressed current urgencies as they arose, supporting women through difficult passages or encouraging them to confront situations they had avoided. Many developed a flexible combination of formats. Few could or wanted to stick to a topic if a member was falling apart, yet crises were seldom so clarifying or continuous as entirely to obviate the need for other focus.

Participants typically agreed on an ethic of openness, honesty, and self-awareness. If a member felt she could not discuss an intimate problem or felt coerced to do so, this was typically taken as a group failure. Other usual norms included a commitment to attend meetings and to keep information confidential. Although leadership patterns often emerged, and verbal and emotional skills recognizably varied, equality within the group was a goal that reflected a value of nonhierarchical organization and a commitment to confronting sources of inequality on the basis of which members felt subordinated or excluded.

What brought women to these groups is difficult to distinguish from what happened once they were there. As with any complex social interaction, from laboratory experiment to revolution, it is often difficult to separate the assumptions from the discoveries, the ripeness of conditions from the precipitating spark. Where does consciousness come from? The effectiveness of consciousness raising is difficult to apportion between the process itself and the women who choose to engage in it. The initial recruiting impulse seems to be a response to an unspecific, often unattached, but just barely submerged discontent that in some inchoate way women relate to being female. It has not escaped most women's attention that their femaleness defines much of who they can be. Restrictions, conflicting demands, intolerable but necessarily tolerated work, the accumulation of constant small irritations and indignities of everyday existence have often been justified on the basis of sex. Consciousness raising coheres and claims these impressions.

Feminists tend to believe that most if not all women resent women's status on some level of their being; even women's defense of their status can be a response to that status. Why some women take the step of identifying their situation with their status as women, transforming their discontents into grievances, is a crucial unanswered question of feminism (or, for that matter, of marxism). What brings people to be conscious of their oppression as common rather than remaining on the level of bad feelings, to see their group identity as a systematic necessity that benefits another group, is the first question of organizing. The fact that consciousness-raising groups were there presupposes the discovery that they were there to make. But what may have begun as a working assumption becomes a working discovery: women are a group, in the sense that a shared reality of treatment exists sufficient to provide a basis for identification—at least enough to be-

gin talking about it in a group of women. This often pre-articulate consensus shapes a procedure, the purpose of which becomes to unpack the concrete moment-to-moment meaning of being a woman in a society that men dominate, by looking at how women see their everyday experience in it. Women's lives are discussed in all their momentous triviality, that is, as they are lived through. The technique explores the social world each woman inhabits through her speaking of it, through comparison with other women's experiences, and through women's experiences of each other in the group itself. Metaphors of hearing and speaking commonly evoke the transformation women experience from silence to voice. As Toni McNaron put it, "within every story I have ever heard from a woman, I have found some voice of me. The details are of course unique to the speaker—they are our differences. But the meaning which they make is common to us all. I will not understand what is common without hearing the details which reveal it to me."[2] The particularities become facets of the collective understanding within which differences constitute rather than undermine collectivity.

The fact that men were not physically present was usually considered necessary to the process. Although the ways of seeing that women have learned in relation to men were very much present or there would be little to discuss, men's temporary concrete absence helped women feel more free of the immediate imperative to compete for male attention and approval, to be passive or get intimidated, or to support men's version of reality. It made speech possible. With these constraints at some remove, women often found that the group confirmed awarenesses they had hidden, including from themselves. Subjects like sexuality, family, body, money, and power could be discussed more openly. The pain of women's roles and women's stake in them could be confronted critically, without the need every minute to reassure men that these changes were not threatening to them or to defend women's breaking of roles as desirable. The all-woman context valued women to each other as sources of insight, advice, information, stimulation, and problems. By providing room for women to be close, these groups demonstrated how far women were separated and how that separation deprived women of access to the way their treatment is systematized. "People who are without names, who do not know themselves, who have no culture, experience a kind of paralysis of consciousness. The first step is to connect and learn to trust one another."[3] This context for serious confrontation also revealed how women had been trivialized to each other. Pamela Allen called these groups "free space."[4] She meant a respectful context for interchange within which women could articulate the inarticulate, admit the inadmissible. The point of the process was not so much that hitherto-undisclosed facts were unearthed or that denied perceptions were corroborated or even that reality was tested, although all these happened. It was not only that silence was broken and that speech occurred. The point was, and is, that this process moved the reference point for truth and thereby the definition of reality as such. Consciousness raising alters the terms of validation by creating community through a process that redefines what counts as verification. This process gives both content and form to women's point of view.[5]

Concretely, consciousness-raising groups often focused on specific incidents and internal dialogue: what happened today, how did it make you feel, why did you feel that way, how do you feel now? Extensive attention was paid to small situations and denigrated pursuits that made up the common life of women in terms of energy, time, intensity, and definition—prominently, housework and sexuality. Women said things like this:

> I am nothing when I am by myself. In myself, I am nothing. I only know I exist because I am needed by someone who is real, my husband, and by my children. My husband goes out into the real world. Other people recognize him as real, and take him into account. He affects other people and events. He does things and changes things and they are different afterward. I stay in my imaginary world in this house, doing jobs that I largely invent, and that no-one cares about but myself. I do not change things. The work I do changes nothing; what I cook disappears, what I clean one day must be cleaned again the next. I seem to be involved in some sort of mysterious process.[6]

Intercourse was interrogated: how and by whom it is initiated, its timing, woman's feelings during and after, its place in relationships, its meaning, its place in being a woman.[7] Other subjects included interactions in routine situations like walking down the street, talking with bus drivers, interacting with cocktail waitresses. Women's stories—work and how they came to do it; children; sexual history, including history of sexual abuse—were explored. Adrienne Rich reflects the process many women experienced and the conclusion to which many women came:

> I was looking desperately for clues, because if there were no clues then I thought I might be insane. I wrote in a notebook about this time: "Paralyzed by the sense that there exists a mesh of relationships— e.g., between my anger at the children, my sensual life, pacifism, sex (I mean sex in its broadest significance, not merely sexual desire)—an interconnectedness which, if I could see it, make it valid, would give me back myself, make it possible to function lucidly and passionately. Yet I grope in and out among these dark webs." I think I began at this point to feel that politics was not something "out there" but something "in here" and of the essence of my condition.[8]

Woman's self-concept emerged: who she thinks she is, how she was treated in her family, who they told her she was (the pretty one, the smart one), how she resisted, how that was responded to, her feelings now about her life and herself, her account of how she came to feel that way, whether other group members experience her the way she experiences herself, how she carries her body and delivers her mannerisms, the way she presents herself and interacts in the group. Contradictions between messages tacitly conveyed and messages explicitly expressed inspired insightful and shattering criticism, as with women who behave seductively while complaining that men accost them. Complicity in oppression acquires concrete meaning as women emerge as shapers of reality as well as shaped by it. A carefully detailed and critically reconstructed composite image is built of women's experienced meaning of "being a woman." From women's collective perspective, a woman embodies and expresses a moment-to-moment concept of herself in the way she walks down the street, structures a household, pursues her work and friendships, shares her sexuality—a certain concept of how she has survived and who she survives as. A minute-by-minute moving picture is created of women becoming, refusing, sustaining their condition.

Interactions usually overlooked as insignificant if vaguely upsetting proved good subjects for detailed scrutiny. A woman mentions the way a man on the subway looked at her. How did this make her feel? Why does she feel so degraded? so depressed? Why can the man make her hate her body? How much of this feeling comes from her learned distrust of how men use her sexually? Does this show up in other areas of her life? Do other women feel this way? What form of power does this give the man? Do all men have, or exercise, such power? Could she have done anything at the time? Can the group do anything now? Women learn that the entire structure of sexual domination, the tacit relations of deference and command, can be present in a passing glance.

Realities hidden under layers of valued myth were unmasked simply by talking about what happens every day, such as the hard physical labor performed by the average wife and mother, the few women who feel strictly vaginal orgasms and the many who pretend they do. Women confronted collectively the range of overt violence represented in the life experience of their group of women, women who might previously have appeared "protected." They found fathers who raped them; boyfriends who shot at them; doctors who aborted them when they weren't pregnant or sterilized them "accidentally"; psychoanalysts who so-called seduced them, committing them to mental hospitals when they exposed them; mothers who committed suicide or lived to loathe themselves more when they failed; employers who fired them for withholding sexual favors or unemployment offices that refused benefits when they quit, finding their reasons personal and uncompelling. Women learned that men see and treat women from their angle of vision, and they learned the content of that vision.

These details together revealed and documented the kind of world women inhabit socially and some of what it feels like for them to inhabit it, how women are systematically deprived of a self and how that process of deprivation constitutes socialization to femininity. In consciousness raising, women become aware of this reality as at once very specific—a woman's social condition and self-concept as it is lived through by her—and as a social reality in which all women more or less participate, however diversely, and in which all women can be identi-fied. Put another way, although a woman's specific race or class or physiology may define her among women, simply being a woman has a meaning that decisively defines all women socially, from their most intimate moments to their most anonymous relations. This social meaning, which is unattached to any actual anatomical differences between the sexes, or to any realities of women's response to it, pervades everyday routine to the point that it becomes a reflex, a habit. Sexism is seen to be all of a piece and so much a part of the omnipresent background of life that a massive effort of collective concentration is required even to discern that it has edges. Consciousness raising is such an effort. Taken in this way, consciousness means a good deal more than a set of ideas. It constitutes a lived knowing of the social reality of being female.

What women become conscious of—the substance of radical feminist analysis—is integral to this process. Perhaps most obviously, it becomes difficult to take seriously accounts of women's roles or personal qualities based on nature or biology, except as authoritative appeals that have shaped women according to them. Combing through women's lives event by event, detail by detail, it is no mystery that women are who they are, given the way they have been treated. Patterns of treatment that would create feelings of incapacity in anybody are seen to connect seamlessly with acts of overt discrimination to deprive women of tools and skills, creating by force the status they are supposed to be destined for by anatomy. Heterosexuality, supposed natural, is found to be forced on women moment to moment. Qualities pointed to as naturally and eternally feminine—nurturance, intuition, frailty, quickness with their fingers, orientation to children—or characteristics of a particular subgroup of women—such as married women's supposed talent for exacting, repetitive, simple tasks, or Black women's supposed interest in sex—look simply like descriptions of the desired and required characteristics of particular occupants of women's roles. Meredith Tax summarized this insight: "We didn't get this way by heredity or by accident. We have been molded into these deformed postures, pushed into these service jobs, made to apologize for existing, taught to be unable to do anything requiring any strength at all, like opening doors or bottles. We have been told to be stupid, to be silly."[9]

If such qualities are biological imperatives, women conform to them remarkably imperfectly. When one gets to know women close up and without men present, it is remarkable the extent to which their so-called biology, not to mention their socialization, has failed. The discovery that these apparently unchangeable dictates of the natural order are powerful social conventions often makes women feel unburdened, since individual failures no longer appear so individualized. Women become angry as they see women's lives as one avenue after another foreclosed by gender.

More than their content, it is the relation to lived experience which is new about these insights. It is one thing to read a nineteenth-century tract describing a common problem of women. It is quite another for women to hear women speak the pain they feel, wonder what they have to fall back on, know they need a response, recognize the dilemmas, struggle with the same denial that the pain is pain, that it is also one's own, that women are real. Susan Griffin expressed it: "We do not rush to speech. We allow ourselves to be moved. We do not attempt objectivity. . . . We said we had experienced this ourselves. I felt so much for her then, she said, with her head cradled in my lap, she said, I knew what to do. We said we were moved to see her go through what we had gone through. We said this gave us some knowledge."[10]

It was common for women in consciousness-raising groups to share radical changes in members' lives, relationships, work, life goals, and sexuality. This process created bonds and a different kind of knowledge, collective knowledge built on moving and being moved, on changing and being changed. As an experience, it went beyond empirical information that women are victims of social inequality. It built an experienced sense of how it came to be this way and that it can be changed. Women experienced the walls that have contained them as walls—and sometimes walked through them. For instance, when they first seriously considered never marrying or getting a divorce, women often discovered their economic dependency, having been taught to do little they can sell or having been paid less than men who sell comparable work. Why? To understand the precise causation would be to identify the supportive dynamics of male supremacy and capitalism. But an equivalency, at least, was clear:

women's work is defined as inferior work, and inferior work is defined as work for women. Inferior work is often considered appropriate for women by the same standards that define it as inferior, and by the same standards that define "women's work" as inferior work—its pay, status, interest or complexity, contacts with people, its relation to cleanliness or care of bodily needs. Inextricably, women may find themselves inwardly dependent as well: conditioned not to think for themselves, to think that without a man they are nothing, or to think that they are less "woman" when without one. The point is not how well women conform to this standard but that there is such a standard and women do not create it. The power dynamic behind these facts is brought into the open when women break out, from the panic they feel at the thought and from the barriers they encounter when they try. It becomes clear, from one horror story after another, that men's position of power over women is a major part of what defines men as men to themselves, and women as women to themselves. Challenge to that power is taken as a threat to male identity and self-definition. Men's reaction of threat is also a challenge to women's self-definition, which has included supporting men, making men feel masculine, and episodically being treated better as a reward. Men's response to women's redefinition as in control is often to show women just how little control they have by threatening women's material or physical survival or their physical or sexual or emotional integrity. Women learn they have learned to "act independently in a dependent fashion."[11] And sometimes they find ways to resist all of this.

This place of consciousness in social construction is often most forcefully illustrated in the least materially deprived women, because the contrast between their economic conditions and their feminist consciousness can be so vivid:

> As suburban women, we recognize that many of us live in more economic and material comfort than our urban sisters, but we have come to realize through the women's movement, feminist ideas and consciousness raising, that this comfort only hides our essential powerlessness and oppression. We live in comfort only to the extent that our homes, clothing, and the services we receive feed and prop the status and egos of the men who support us. Like

dogs on a leash, our own status and power will reach as far as our husbands and their income and prestige will allow. As human beings, as individuals, we in fact own very little and should our husbands leave us or us them, we will find ourselves with the care and responsibility of children without money, jobs, credit or power. For this questionable condition, we have paid the price of isolation and exploitation by the institutions of marriage, motherhood, psychiatry and consumerism. Although our life styles may appear materially better, we are, as all women, dominated by men at home, in bed, and on the job, emotionally, sexually, domestically and financially.[12]

Women found they face these conditions sharply through nonmarriage or divorce or on becoming openly lesbian. Women who do not need men for sexual fulfillment can suddenly be found "incompetent" on their jobs when their bosses learn of their sexual preference. Similarly, when a women's health clinic is opened, and women handle their own bodies, male-controlled hospitals often deny admitting privileges, threatening every woman who attends the clinic. These conditions arise when women suggest that if housework is so fulfilling men should have the chance to do it themselves: it is everybody's job, women just blame themselves or do it when it is not done or done well. Always in the background, often not very far, is the sanction of physical intimidation, not because men are stronger but because they are willing and able to use their strength with relative social impunity; or not because they use it, but because they do not have to. In addition, identity invalidation is a form of power a man has for the price of invoking it: you are an evil woman, you are a whore (you have sex on demand), you are a failure as a woman (you do not have sex on demand). Women learn they have to become people who respond to these appeals on some level because they are backed up by material indulgences and deprivations. The understanding that a social group that is accorded, possesses, and uses such tools over others to its own advantage is powerful and that it exercises a form of social control or authority becomes not a presupposition or rhetorical hyperbole but a substantiated conclusion.

Perhaps the most pervasive realization of consciousness raising was that men as a group benefit from these same arrangements by which women are deprived. Women see that men derive many advantages from women's roles, including being served and kept in mind, supported and sustained, having their children cared for and their sexual needs catered to, and being kept from the necessity of doing jobs so menial they consider them beneath them unless there is no other job (or a woman) around. But the major advantage men derive, dubious though it may seem to some, is the process, the value, the mechanism by which their interest itself is enforced and perpetuated and sustained: power. Power in its socially male form. It is not only that men treat women badly, although often they do, but that it is their choice whether or not to do so. This understanding of power is one of the key comprehensions of feminism. The reality it points to, because it is everywhere and relatively invariant, appears to be nowhere separable from the whole, from the totality it defines.

Women, it is said, possess corresponding power. Through consciousness raising, women found that women's so-called power was the other side of female powerlessness. A woman's supposed power to deny sex is the underside of her actual lack of power to stop it. Women's supposed power to get men to do things for them by nagging or manipulating is the other side of the power they lack to have their every need anticipated, to carry out the task themselves, to be able to deliver upon sharing the responsibility equally, or to invoke physical fear to gain compliance with their desires without even having to mention it. Once the veil is lifted, once relations between the sexes are seen as power relations, it becomes impossible to see as simply unintended, well-intentioned, or innocent the actions through which women are told every day what is expected and when they have crossed some line. From the male point of view, no injury may be meant. But women develop an incisive eye for routines, strategems, denials, and traps that operate to keep women in place and to obscure the recognition that it is a place at all. Although these actions may in some real way be unintentional, they are taken, in some other real way, as meant.[13]

These discussions explored the functioning of sex roles in even one's closest "personal" relations, where it was thought women were most "ourselves," hence most free. Indeed, the reverse often seemed to be the case. The measure of closeness often seemed to be the measure of the oppression. When shared with other women, one's most private events often came to look the most stereotypical, the most for the public. Each woman, in her own particular, even chosen, way reproduces in her most private relations a structure of dominance and submission which characterizes the entire public order. The impact of this insight can be accounted for in part by the fact that it is practiced on the level of group process, so that what could be a sociopsychological or theoretical insight becomes a lived experience. That is, through making public, through discussing in the group, what had been private, for example sexual relations, it was found that the split between public and private, at least in the context of relations between the sexes, made very little sense, except as it functioned ideologically to keep each woman feeling alone, particularly in her experiences of sexual violation.

> *After sharing, we* know *that women suffer at the hands of a male supremacist society and that this male supremacy intrudes into every sphere of our existence, controlling the ways in which we are allowed to make our living and the ways in which we find fulfillment in personal relationships. We know that our most secret, our most private problems are grounded in the way that women are treated, in the way women are allowed to live.*[14]

The analysis that the personal is the political came out of consciousness raising. It has four interconnected facets. First, women as a group are dominated by men as a group, and therefore as individuals. Second, women are subordinated in society, not by personal nature or by biology. Third, the gender division, which includes the sex division of labor which keeps women in high-heeled low-status jobs, pervades and determines even women's personal feelings in relationships. Fourth, since a woman's problems are not hers individually but those of women as a whole, they cannot be addressed except as a whole. In this analysis of gender as a nonnatural characteristic of a division of power in society, the personal becomes the political.

. . . Consciousness raising is a face-to-face social experience that strikes at the fabric of meaning of social relations between and among women and men by calling their givenness into question and reconstituting their meaning in a transformed and critical way. The most apparent quality of this method is its aim of grasping women's situation as it is lived through. . . .

. . .

Consciousness raising has revealed that male power is real. It is just not the only reality, as it claims to be. Male power is a myth that makes itself true. To raise consciousness is to confront male power in its duality: as at once total on one side and a delusion on the other. In consciousness raising, women learn they have learned that men are everything, women their negation, but the sexes are equal. The content of the message is revealed as true and false at the same time; in fact, each part reflects the other transvalued. If "Men are all, women their negation" is taken as social criticism rather than as simple description, it becomes clear for the first time that women are men's equals, everywhere in chains. The chains become visible, the civil inferiority—the inequality—the product of subjection and a mode of its enforcement. Reciprocally, the moment it is seen that this life as we know it is not equality, that the sexes are not socially equal, womanhood can no longer be defined in terms of lack of maleness, as negativity. For the first time, the question of what a woman is seeks its ground in and of a world understood as neither of its making nor in its own image, and finds, within a critical embrace of woman's fractured and alien image, the shadow world women have made and a vision of the possibility of equality. As critique, women's communality describes a fact of male supremacy, a fact of sex "in itself": no woman escapes the meaning of being a woman within a gendered social system, and sex inequality is not only pervasive but may be universal (in the sense of never having not been in some form), though "intelligible only in . . . locally specific forms."[24] For women to become a sex "for itself"[25] is to move community to the level of vision.

Notes

1. Sheila Rowbotham, *Woman's Consciousness, Man's World* (Harmondsworth: Penguin, 1973), p. 27.

2. Toni McNaron, *The Power of Person: Women Coming into Their Own* (Minneapolis: Women's Caucus of the National Association of Social Workers, 1982).

3. Rowbotham, *Woman's Consciousness*, p. 27.

4. Pamela Allen, *Free Space: A Perspective on the Small Group in Women's Liberation* (New York: Times Change Press, 1970).

5. In addition to the citations in Chapter 1, note 4, see Jo Freeman, *The Politics of Women's Liberation: A Case Study of an Emerging Social Movement and Its Relation to the Policy Process* (New York: David McKay, 1975), chap. 4; Carol Hanisch, *Notes from the Second Year* (New York: Radical Feminism, 1970), pp. 76–77. For possible parallels in Chinese "speak bitterness" sessions, see Richard H. Solomon, *Mao's Revolution and the Chinese Political Culture* (Berkeley: University of California Press, 1971), pp. 195–197, 209, 439, 441, 514, 523, 571.

6. Meredith Tax, "Woman and Her Mind: The Story of Everyday Life," in *Radical Feminism,* ed. Ann Koedt, Ellen Levine, and Anita Rapone (New York: Quadrangle Books, 1973), pp. 26–27.

7. An excellent example in writing, of which there are few, is Ingrid Bengis, *Combat in the Erogenous Zone: Writings on Love, Hate, and Sex* (New York: Alfred A. Knopf, 1973). See also Kate Millett, *Flying* (New York: Ballantine Books, 1974).

8. Adrienne Rich, "When We Dead Awaken: Writing as Re-Vision," in *On Lies, Secrets, and Silence: Selected Prose, 1966–1978* (New York: Norton, 1979), p. 44.

9. Tax, "Woman and Her Mind," pp. 26–27.

10. Susan Griffin, *Woman and Nature: The Roaring Inside Her* (New York: Harper & Row, 1978), p. 197.

11. This is Steven Hymer's description of the results of Robinson Crusoe's socialization of Friday. Steven Hymer, "Robinson Crusoe and the Secret of Primitive Accumulation," *Monthly Review* 23 (September 1971): 16.

12. Westchester Radical Feminists, "Statement of Purpose, May, 1972," in Koedt, Levine, and Rapone, *Radical Feminism,* pp. 385–386.

13. Pat Mainardi, "The Politics of Housework," in *Sisterhood Is Powerful: An Anthology of Writings from the Women's Liberation Movement,* ed. Robin Morgan (New York: Random House, 1970), pp. 447–454, written in 1965, is an early and brilliant example of this perception.

14. Allen, *Free Space,* p. 27. See also Irene Peslikis, "Resistances to Consciousness," in Morgan, *Sisterhood Is Powerful,* pp. 337–339.

15. Michelle Z. Rosaldo, "The Use and Abuse of Anthropology: Reflections on Feminism and Cross-Cultural Understanding," *Signs: Journal of Women in Culture and Society* 5 (Spring 1980): 417.

16. Marx discusses the in itself/for itself distinction in *Poverty of Philosophy,* p. 195 and in *The Eighteenth Brumaire of Louis Bonaparte,* in *Selected Works.* See L. Kolakowski, *Main Currents of Marxism,* trans. P. S. Falla, vol. 1 (Oxford: Clarendon Press, 1978), 356.

Disappearing Tricks

Dale Spender

Dale Spender is a researcher, writer, editor, broadcaster, and teacher. She is a member of the Queensland Women's Consultative Council and the Australian Society of Authors. She is a consultant in the areas of information technology and management, in education and the construction of knowledge, as well as an international expert in the fields of language, communication, writing, editing, publishing, and equity. She has taught in universities in many countries, has given more than 300 keynote addresses, has appeared regularly on radio and television in Australia and overseas, and has written for many popular publications and newspapers. She contributes a regular column, "Data Crit," to the Australian Author. *Her more than 30 books include* Nattering on the Net: Women, Power and Cyberspace *(1996);* Life Lines: Australian Women's Letters and Diaries 1788 to 1840, *with Patricia Clarke (1992);* The Knowledge Explosion: Generations of Feminist Scholarship, *with Cheris Kramarae (1992);* The Writing or the Sex?: Or Why You Don't Have to Read Women's Writing to Know It's No Good *(1989);* Women of Ideas (and What Men Have Done to Them): From Aphra Behn to Adrienne Rich *(1988);* Reflecting Men at Twice Their Natural Size *(1987);* For the Record: The Making and Meaning of Feminist Knowledge *(1985);* Man Made Language *(1985);* There's Always Been a Women's Movement This Century *(1983);* Feminist Theorists: Three Centuries of Key Women Thinkers *(1983); and* Men's Studies Modified: The Impact of Feminism on the Academic Disciplines *(1981). Her newest work, co-edited with Cheris Kramarae, is the* Routledge International Encyclopedia of Women's Studies, *due to be published sometime in 2000.*

Spender shows us how sexism inserts itself into our thinking process—in this case, through language.

MAN: 'Human being, especially *an adult male human being*'

—Webster's Collegiate Dictionary

Words are symbols. They stand for, or represent, an object. In the last decade there has been a debate about the symbol *man* (and its pronoun, *he*) for there is ambiguity about what these symbols represent. On the one hand, the prescriptive grammarians of the past not only ruled that *man* and *he* represented the male of the species; they also ruled that *man* and *he* represented the species as well, and therefore included women. Many people have taken the prescriptive grammarians at their word and accepted their ruling without always being familiar with their reasons. There are, however, individuals, many of them feminists, who have declared that this was a rather ridiculous rule partly because it has led to ambiguity and confusion, and partly because the reasons for the rule were blatantly sexist. While some may still be content to accept that the use of *man* and *he* which we have been taught is legitimate and inoffensive, and that its sexist overtones of rendering women invisible are nothing but a mere linguistic *accident*, there are others of us who regard this rule as most unacceptable and who wish to change it. There was nothing accidental about the way in which the rule was introduced and there is nothing accidental about the consequences which ensue. Because it was a rule which was intended to promote the primacy of *man* at the expense of *woman*, we are committed to its elimination and to the introduction of more equitable linguistic forms which favour neither sex.

The rationalisation that *man embraces woman* is a relatively recent one in the history of our language.

Using *man* and *he* to encompass *woman* is a practice that was unknown in the fifteenth century. In 1553 we have the record of a certain Mr Wilson who argued that it was more 'natural' to place the man before the woman (as, for example, in male and female, husband and wife, brother and sister) and as he was writing for an almost exclusively male population of educated people who were interested in the art of rhetoric, there were few women in a position to protest against the so-called 'natural order'. By 1646, however, the argument had taken a different turn. Not only was it by then considered natural that the male should take precedence, it was also, according to one Mr Poole, that the male gender was the *worthier* gender and therefore deserved priority. Claims for the superiority of man over woman increased and were strengthened when, in 1746, Mr Kirkby invented his *Eighty-Eight Grammatical Rules*; Rule Twenty-One stated that the male gender was more *comprehensive* than the female. This marks an interesting shift in the argument. The Oxford English Dictionary defines *comprehensive* as *including much,* so Mr Kirkby was claiming that the male gender included much more than the female. This is of course a personal opinion which Mr Kirkby and his colleagues were entitled to hold, but it is not a linguistic opinion and these are not grounds for making linguistic judgements and for formulating rules to be imposed on all users of the language. Again, however, it seems that there were few protests about Rule Twenty-One; certainly Mr Kirkby had no women colleagues who could have objected to the rule and pointed to the flaws in his reasoning. And so the grammatical rule that *man embraces woman,* because *man* is more important, came into being and has been imposed upon the speakers of the language.

Mr Kirkby's rule however, was not always taken up with enthusiasm. Many people were unaware of it (and could therefore be labelled as ignorant) and some ignored it. People persisted in using *man* to mean male and *woman* to mean female, and *they* to refer to a person whose sex was unknown (as for example in 'Anyone can say what *they* like' or 'Everyone has *their* rights'). But the male grammarians were upset by this flagrant disregard of their rules and began to insist on *correctness*—meaning conformity to their rules—as a necessary characteristic of 'an educated man'. Their efforts were successful; being correct became important and so that there could be no doubt about what was correct or incorrect in the case of *man* and *he,* an Act of Parliament was passed in 1850 in which *man* was legally made to stand for *woman* (Bodine, 1975). There were of course no women members of parliament who could have cast opposing votes.

There can be no mistake about the reasons for the introduction of this rule and the consequent Act of Parliament. They were to give prominence and primacy to the male sex, and to give linguistic substance to the sexist bias of influential men. There is little likelihood that this usage would have evolved of its own accord; it required considerable intervention on the part of grammarians to introduce it and to insist on its use.

The current moves, then, by feminists to take out what the male grammarians put in, cannot be referred to as 'tampering' with the language. We are not trying to change something which is pure and unadulterated. On the contrary, we are trying to remove an artificial linguistic rule which should never have been given credence and which has never been justified on linguistic grounds. However, although the efforts of the male grammarians were not justified, they were, nonetheless, successful. We have in the past accepted their rule but if we continue to operate it we will help to support a practice of making man visible at the expense of woman. We will also be influenced by this practice for it has been found that one of the results of using the term *man* has been that the image of the male sex becomes foremost in our thoughts; while *man* is the favoured linguistic term, it is the male sex which is the favoured image in our consciousness.

There is evidence that people think of the male when they use the term *man.* Alleen Pace Nilsen (1973) found that young children thought that *man* meant male in sentences such as 'man needs food'; Linda Harrison (1975) found that science students thought of male people when talking of the evolution of *man*; J. Schneider and Sally Hacker (1972) found that college students thought of males when confronted with titles such as *Political Man* and *Urban Man.* And both Linda Harrison and Wendy Martyna (1978) found that men used the term *man* much more frequently than women. When Wendy

Martyna asked the people in her sample what they thought of when they used the word *man,* the men said they thought of themselves. Women, however, said that they used the term *man* because they had been taught that it was grammatically correct. In Martyna's sample, at least, the women, who ranged from kindergarten to college students, recognised that they were not encompassed in the term *man;* they could not think of themselves when they used the word. If *man* was truly an encompassing word, a generic term, then women, as well as men, should be able to see their own image within it. That men think of themselves and not of women when they use the term *man* is an hypothesis which can readily be put to the test. Muriel Schulz (1978) examined the writings of many leading sociologists (past and present) and found that although they may have used terms like 'men of ideas' and 'the nature of man', supposedly to include *all* members of the species, they in fact meant only males. Alma Graham also found that many men revealed that although they may claim vehemently that man *includes* woman, their usage indicates otherwise:

> *In practice, the sexist assumption that man is a species of male becomes the fact. Erich Fromm certainly seemed to think so when he wrote that man's 'vital interests' were 'life, food, access to females etc.'. Loren Eisley implied it when he wrote of man that 'his back aches, he ruptures easily, his women have difficulties in childbirth. . .' . If these writers had been using* man *in the sense of the human species rather than male, they would have written that man's vital interests are life, food, and access to the opposite sex, and that man suffers backaches, ruptures easily, and has difficulties in giving birth (Graham, 1975; 62).*

With examples like this it is difficult to maintain the argument that *man* includes *woman* as the grammarians of old absurdly (but conveniently) claimed. For these are not just examples of occasional slips, they are the logical outcome of the grammarians' law that the world is to be considered male unless proven otherwise. There are yet more illustrations of the way in which the word *man* is used by us to mean just *men.* We can say that *man makes wars,* that *man plays football,* and that *he is an aggressive animal* without suggesting that we are mistaken or that we are being funny, even though we realise that these statements apply to only half the population. When women are left out of the activities that are being described, it seems that there is something wrong. But what happens when men are left out? The human species does a great deal more than make wars and play football but there is a problem when we use the word *man* to refer to other, equally human, but not necessarily male activities. Can we say *man devotes about forty hours a week to housework* without sounding as though we have made a mistake? Can we say *man lives an isolated life when engaged in child-rearing,* or that *man is usually hospitalised for birth in our society* without saying something that sounds absurd? *Are menopause and menstruation significant events in the life of man?* When we think about it, it becomes increasingly clear that in our language, *man* means male. It is an example of the way in which the world is male unless proved otherwise; and housework, childcare and menstruation and menopause are otherwise. They are not classified with men and we therefore cannot use *man,* which means men, to refer to them!

> *One may be saddened but not surprised at the statement 'man is the only primate that commits rape'. Although, as commonly understood, it can apply to only half the human population, it is nevertheless semantically acceptable. But 'man, being a mammal breastfeeds his young' is taken as a joke (Miller and Swift, 1976; 25–6).*

If we could say *man has been engaged in a constant search for the means to control his fertility,* we would have very different meanings embedded in our language; we would have a very different consciousness. We would be starting to make women with their problems and their pleasures visible and real.

While *woman* has been forced out of the language in many contexts, and the invisibility of women has been reinforced, our present society, which is predicated on the principle of male supremacy (and the accompanying male visibility) has not seen fit to protest because the issue has not been regarded as a problem. Women are socially devalued so it is not inconsistent to devalue them linguistically. Mainly as a response to feminist efforts, however, this issue is beginning to be seen as a problem and already there are changes underway. Many government agencies in America have tried to dismantle the mechanisms which maintain asymmetry between the sexes. When the evidence that *man* made *woman* invisible was put to certain government agencies, many were persuaded of its validity. The argument was enough to convince the United States Department of Labour to issue a revision of occupational titles in order to provide more equal employment opportunities. The old job titles were considered to be discriminatory towards women because they excluded women and suggested that their entry into such jobs was inappropriate.

Three thousand five hundred job titles were revised to eliminate reference to age and sex so that *policeman* became *police officer,* for example, and *salesman* became *sales agent.* Of course, the Manpower Administration had to begin with itself, changing its own title to that of The Employment and Training Administration and renaming its publication *Worklife,* recognising that the old name, *Manpower,* excluded the sizeable workforce of women:

> *Since children learn about society from language it is an easy lesson for girls to learn that many situations described by male identified words do not include them. Implicit in the omission is the understanding that a large part of the world is inappropriate to them (Berger & Kachuk, 1977; 3).*

Of course, boys may learn the same things from language, but the words which exclude males are much less frequent, and of much lower status. Boys might not feel so offended by exclusion. Being left out of housework (*housewife*), or out of child care (*governess, au pair girl*), may not be as hard to take as being left out of politics (*congressman, chairman*), religion (*clergyman, priest*), work (*businessman, foreman, craftsman* and, of course, the verb *to man*) or society (*gentleman*).

The use of *man* to include *woman,* however, reveals not only sexist prejudice but also linguistic ignorance. It contradicts another grammatical rule, which is that English has *natural* gender. When a language has natural gender objects are supposed to be labelled on the basis of sex so that the world is divided into masculine, feminine and neuter according to its sexual attributes (or lack of them). English is *supposed* to have natural gender and this is *supposed* to make it superior to languages which

have grammatical gender, such as French and German for example. Grammatical gender is not based on sex, but on arbitrary decisions (which are considered to be confusing) so that in German, for example, a tree is masculine, a tomcat is feminine and a wife neuter. English did once have grammatical gender (Anglo-Saxon was similar to modern German in this respect) and it is often claimed that the move to natural gender was a big improvement. The reason given for this is that natural gender is so much less confusing; people are classified according to their sex. In English, sex and gender are supposed to correspond and are therefore called *natural.*

But in describing the language in this way, one significant factor has been overlooked. English is only natural and unproblematic *if one is male.* There is nothing natural about women being referred to as *man* and *he;* they are not being classified on the basis of sex, and they do constitute half the population. The claim for natural gender in English is a claim based purely on the male experience of language and while *they* may not feel that there is any confusion, women may not share their assessment. It is confusing for women; it can be even more confusing than is the case with languages that have grammatical gender. At least if one is learning French or German one does not expect a correlation between sex and gender and one can become accustomed to being a woman and referred to as male or neutral. But in English we are specifically taught that sex and gender do correspond linguistically, and that it is wrong to refer to a tomcat as she, a tree as he, or a wife as it. But it is all right to refer to women as *men* or *he.*

So, there is inconsistency in the claims of the grammarians. If English does have natural gender then it is wrong to refer to women as *he/man.* And if *man* does include *woman* then it is wrong to claim that English has natural gender. One could ask why the male grammarians have not noticed this inconsistency?

In my work with secondary school students in a London mixed comprehensive I decided to investigate whether they felt excluded when they were excluded from the language. I wanted to find out how they felt about the use of *man* and *he* to encompass *woman,* so I tried to overcome any difficulties by presenting the concepts in a simple and concrete way. I began with a discussion of magic and that favourite conjuring trick of making things disappear. We talked about whether or not it was possible to make people invisible and I held out the carefully baited hook that it probably was possible and that, in fact, it wasn't even unusual as we were all magicians, making people invisible every day. The bait was taken and I began to focus upon language. I had some pictures of men and women which had captions using the so-called generic *he* and *man*. Illustrations of males and females reading were subtitled with 'Each student needs individual attention if *he* is to master reading'. Pictures of the Football Association Cup Final were accompanied with statements such as 'Everyone wants to grow up to be a football hero'. Newspaper photographs which prominently displayed Ms Thatcher in her proverbial hat were followed by 'Politicians remove their hats in the presence of the Queen'. I do not think it would be biased on my part to state that the girls caught on to the idea more quickly than the boys. They took no more than three to four minutes to formulate the rule and the following is an extract from some of the comments made by one of the young women:

> *Can't you see you just pretend. . . . You pretend you're talking about everybody, but you don't, you're not. It's only men. . . . Look at this, no, look D, Come one. He says 'Everybody', but he doesn't mean that, you don't think he means me do you? That I want to be a football hero? He doesn't, course not!* Men's *everybody . . . and that's the trick.*

At this stage their involvement was in the 'game' and although they were able to use the rule (adequately summed up by this student as 'Men's everybody') there was no comment about the injustice of the rule in that it made only women disappear. The boys were very eager to play, we made a lot of magic and many women disappeared:

> *Australians are beer-drinking surfies.*
> *All Americans play baseball.*
> *Teenagers have to become members of gangs if they want to be accepted.*

These were some of the 'tricks' which were performed, but after having spent about twenty minutes making women disappear, I changed the focus. I reminded the students that only half the magic

trick had been performed by making people invisible. There wouldn't be many magicians making a living if they could not complete the magic and bring people back again. I did not know what the students would do with this information. I envisaged that they would put women back into the picture in some way, but I neither predicted nor determined what that way should be. There was some discussion about bringing people back again and then C. began to alter some of the captions. She did so by simply applying the principle of reversal. Among some of her 'magic' was the following:

> *Adolescents think only of marriage and make-up.*
> *Australians look good in bikinis.*

She certainly made the female 'visible' by this process and was both pleased and amused by her efforts. Although I tried to indicate that she had made females visible at the expense of males, her only comment was 'About time' and with the other girls in the group she proceeded to give new captions to many of the pictures and to provide captions for those pictures which were without them and which included women and men.

It would be an understatement to say that the girls were thoroughly enjoying themselves. The boys, however, did not share their enthusiasm and passed from discomfort to hostility. They declared the whole thing 'stupid' and one of them withdrew from the group. I could only surmise that the feeling of exclusion which they experienced made them feel extremely uncomfortable and caused them to protest. Perhaps not being accustomed to 'not counting' and being made invisible, made it more difficult for them. My assumption about the reason for their behaviour was reinforced by an event described by Casey Miller and Kate Swift in which a group of males, who were being 'left out', also protested. Although the boys in my group had less sophisticated rationales for their behaviour, I suspect that their reaction might well have been the same.

> *Men who work in fields where women have traditionally predominated—as nurses, secretaries and primary school teachers for example—know exactly how . . . (the) . . . proposed generic pronoun . . . (she) . . . would affect them; they've tried it and they don't like it. Until a few years ago most publications,*

writers and speakers on the subject of primary and secondary education used she in referring to teachers. As the proportion of men in the profession increased, so did their annoyance with the generic use of feminine pronouns. By the mid 1960's, according to the journal of the National Education Association, some of the angry young men in teaching were complaining that references to the teacher as 'she' were responsible in part for their poor image and consequently, in part, for their low salaries. One man, speaking on the floor of the National Education Association Representative Assembly, said 'The incorrect and improper use of the English language is a vestige of the nineteenth-century image of the teacher and conflicts sharply with the vital image we attempt to set forth today. The interests of neither the women nor of the men in our profession are served by grammatical usage which conjures up an anachronistic image of the nineteenth-century school marm.'

Here is the male as norm argument in a nutshell. Although the custom of referring to elementary and secondary school teachers as 'she' arose because most of them were women, it becomes grammatically 'incorrect and improper' as soon as men enter the field in more than token numbers. . . . Women teachers are still in the majority but the speaker feels that it is neither incorrect not improper to exclude them linguistically (Miller and Swift, 1976; 33–4).

References

Berger, G. and Kachuk, B. 1977. *Sexism, Language and Social Change*, US Dept. of Health, Education and Welfare, National Institute of Education

Bodine, A. 1975. 'Androcentrism in Prescriptive Grammar: Singular "they", Sex Indefinite "he" and "he" and "she" ', *Language in Society*, Vol. 4, no. 2

Graham, A. 1975. 'The Making of a Nonsexist Dictionary', in Thorne, B. and Henley, N. (eds), *Language and Sex: Difference and Dominance*, Newbury House, Rowley, Mass.

Harrison, L. 1975. 'Cro-Magnon Woman–in Eclipse', *The Science Teacher*, April

Miller, C. and Swift, K. 1976. *Words and Women: New Language in New Times*, Penguin

Nilsen, A. P. 1973. 'Grammatical Gender and Its Relationship to the Equal Treatment of Males and Females in Children's Books', unpublished Ph.D thesis, University of Iowa

Schneider, J. and Hacker, S. 1972. 'Sex Role Imagery and the Use of the Generic "man" in Introductory Texts: A Case in the Sociology of Sociology', paper presented at Sociology of Sex Roles, American Sociological Association, New Orleans, August

Schulz, M. 1978. 'Man (Embracing Woman): The Generic in Sociological Writing', paper presented at Sociolinguistics: Language and Sex, Ninth World Congress on Sociology, Uppsala, 14–20 August

The Egg and the Sperm: How Science Has Constructed a Romance Based on Stereotypical Male–Female Roles

Emily Martin

Anthropologist Emily Martin reveals how the largely unconscious sexism of scientific researchers embeds itself in science itself, in its language, its perspectives, and its explanations. If not properly aware of their own sexist bias and stereotypical thinking, scientists may "project cultural imagery onto what they study." She points out that the models scientists use to explain or describe their findings "can have important social effects." Indeed, they may support or even magnify sexist institutions and social structures.

The theory of the human body is always a part of a world-picture. . . . The theory of the human body is always a part of a fantasy.

—JAMES HILLMAN, *The Myth of Analysis*[1]

AS AN ANTHROPOLOGIST, I AM intrigued by the possibility that culture shapes how biological scientists describe what they discover about the natural world. If this were so, we would be learning about more than the natural world in high school biology class; we would be learning about cultural beliefs and practices as if they were part of nature. In the course of my research I realized that the picture of egg and sperm drawn in popular as well as scientific accounts of reproductive biology relies on stereotypes central to our cultural definitions of male and female. The stereotypes imply not only that female biological processes are less worthy than their male counterparts but also that women are less worthy than men. Part of my goal in writing this article is to shine a bright light on the gender stereotypes hidden within the scientific language of biology. Exposed in such a light, I hope they will lose much of their power to harm us.

Reprinted from *Signs*, Vol. 16, No. 3, 1991, pp. 485–501, by permission of The University of Chicago Press.

EGG AND SPERM: A SCIENTIFIC FAIRY TALE

At a fundamental level, all major scientific textbooks depict male and female reproductive organs as systems for the production of valuable substances, such as eggs and sperm.[2] In the case of women, the monthly cycle is described as being designed to produce eggs and prepare a suitable place for them to be fertilized and grown—all to the end of making babies. But the enthusiasm ends there. By extolling the female cycle as a productive enterprise, menstruation must necessarily be viewed as a failure. Medical texts describe menstruation as the "debris" of the uterine lining, the result of necrosis, or death of tissue. The descriptions imply that a system has gone awry, making products of no use, not to specification, unsalable, wasted, scrap. An illustration in a widely used medical text shows menstruation as a chaotic disintegration of form, complementing the many texts that describe it as "ceasing," "dying," "losing," "denuding," "expelling."[3]

Male reproductive physiology is evaluated quite differently. One of the texts that sees menstruation as failed production employs a sort of breathless prose when it describes the maturation of sperm: "The mechanisms which guide the remarkable cellular transformation from spermatid to mature sperm remain uncertain. . . . Perhaps the most amazing characteristic of spermatogenesis is its sheer magnitude: the normal human male may manufacture several hundred million sperm per day."[4] In the classic text *Medical Physiology*, edited by Vernon Mountcastle, the male/female, productive/destructive comparison is more explicit: "Whereas the female *sheds* only a single gamete each month, the seminiferous tubules *produce* hundreds of millions of sperm each day" (emphasis mine).[5] The female author of another text marvels at the length of the microscopic seminiferous tubules, which, if uncoiled and placed end to end, "would span almost one-third of a mile!" She writes, "In an adult male these structures produce millions of sperm cells each day." Later she asks, "How is this feat accomplished?"[6] None of these texts expresses such intense enthusiasm for any female processes. It is surely no accident that the "remarkable" process of making sperm involves precisely what, in the medical view, menstruation does not: production of something deemed valuable.[7]

One could argue that menstruation and spermatogenesis are not analogous processes and, therefore, should not be expected to elicit the same kind of response. The proper female analogy to spermatogenesis, biologically, is ovulation. Yet ovulation does not merit enthusiasm in these texts either. Textbook descriptions stress that all of the ovarian follicles containing ova are already present at birth. Far from being *produced,* as sperm are, they merely sit on the shelf, slowly degenerating and aging like overstocked inventory: "At birth, normal human ovaries contain an estimated one million follicles [each], and no new ones appear after birth. Thus, in marked contrast to the male, the newborn female already has all the germ cells she will ever have. Only a few, perhaps 400, are destined to reach full maturity during her active productive life. All the others degenerate at some point in their development so that few, if any, remain by the time she reaches menopause at approximately 50 years of age."[8] Note the "marked contrast" that this description sets up between male and female: the male, who continuously produces fresh germ cells, and the female, who has stockpiled germ cells by birth and is faced with their degeneration.

Nor are the female organs spared such vivid descriptions. One scientist writes in a newspaper article that a woman's ovaries become old and worn out from ripening eggs every month, even though the woman herself is still relatively young: "When you look through a laparoscope . . . at an ovary that has been through hundreds of cycles, even in a superbly healthy American female, you see a scarred, battered organ."[9]

To avoid the negative connotations that some people associate with the female reproductive system, scientists could begin to describe male and female processes as homologous. They might credit females with "producing" mature ova one at a time, as they're needed each month, and describe males

as having to face problems of degenerating germ cells. This degeneration would occur throughout life among spermatogonia, the undifferentiated germ cells in the testes that are the long-lived, dormant precursors of sperm.

But the texts have an almost dogged insistence on casting female processes in a negative light. The texts celebrate sperm production because it is continuous from puberty to senescence, while they portray egg production as inferior because it is finished at birth. This makes the female seem unproductive, but some texts will also insist that it is she who is wasteful.[10] In a section heading for *Molecular Biology of the Cell,* a best-selling text, we are told that "Oogenesis is wasteful." The text goes on to emphasize that of the seven million oogonia, or egg germ cells, in the female embryo, most degenerate in the ovary. Of those that do go on to become oocytes, or eggs, many also degenerate, so that at birth only two million eggs remain in the ovaries. Degeneration continues throughout a woman's life: by puberty 300,000 eggs remain, and only a few are present by menopause. "During the 40 or so years of a woman's reproductive life, only 400 to 500 eggs will have been released," the authors write. "All the rest will have degenerated. It is still a mystery why so many eggs are formed only to die in the ovaries."[11]

The real mystery is why the male's vast production of sperm is not seen as wasteful.[12] Assuming that a man "produces" 100 million (10^8) sperm per day (a conservative estimate) during an average reproductive life of sixty years, he would produce well over two trillion sperm in his lifetime. Assuming that a woman "ripens" one egg per lunar month, or thirteen per year, over the course of her forty-year reproductive life, she would total five hundred eggs in her lifetime. But the word "waste" implies an excess, too much produced. Assuming two or three offspring, for every baby a woman produces, she wastes only around two hundred eggs. For every baby a man produces, he wastes more than one trillion (10^{12}) sperm.

How is it that positive images are denied to the bodies of women? A look at language—in this case, scientific language—provides the first clue. Take the egg and the sperm.[13] It is remarkable how "femininely" the egg behaves and how "masculinely" the sperm.[14] The egg is seen as large and passive.[15] It does not *move* or *journey,* but passively "is transported," "is swept,"[16] or even "drifts"[17] along the fallopian tube. In utter contrast, sperm are small, "streamlined,"[18] and invariably active. They "deliver" their genes to the egg, "activate the developmental program of the egg,"[19] and have a "velocity" that is often remarked upon.[20] Their tails are "strong" and efficiently powered.[21] Together with the forces of ejaculation, they can "propel the semen into the deepest recesses of the vagina."[22] For this they need "energy," "fuel,"[23] so that with a "whiplashlike motion and strong lurches"[24] they can "burrow through the egg coat"[25] and "penetrate" it.[26]

At its extreme, the age-old relationship of the egg and the sperm takes on a royal or religious patina. The egg coat, its protective barrier, is sometimes called its "vestments," a term usually reserved for sacred, religious dress. The egg is said to have a "corona,"[27] a crown, and to be accompanied by "attendant cells."[28] It is holy, set apart and above, the queen to the sperm's king. The egg is also passive, which means it must depend on sperm for rescue. Gerald Schatten and Helen Schatten liken the egg's role to that of Sleeping Beauty: "a dormant bride awaiting her mate's magic kiss, which instills the spirit that brings her to life."[29] Sperm, by contrast, have a "mission,"[30] which is to "move through the female genital tract in quest of the ovum."[31] One popular account has it that the sperm carry out a "perilous journey" into the "warm darkness," where some fall away "exhausted." "Survivors" "assault" the egg, the successful candidates "surrounding the prize."[32] Part of the urgency of this journey, in more scientific terms, is that "once released from the supportive environment of the ovary, an egg will die within hours unless rescued by a sperm."[33] The wording stresses the fragility and dependency of the egg, even though the same text acknowledges elsewhere that sperm also live for only a few hours.[34]

In 1948, in a book remarkable for its early insights into these matters, Ruth Herschberger argued that female reproductive organs are seen as biologically interdependent, while male organs are viewed as autonomous, operating independently and in isolation:

> At present the functional is stressed only in connection with women: it is in them that ovaries, tubes, uterus, and vagina have endless interdependence. In the male, reproduction would seem to involve "organs" only.
>
> Yet the sperm, just as much as the egg, is dependent on a great many related processes. There are secretions which mitigate the urine in the urethra before ejaculation, to protect the sperm. There is the reflex shutting off of the bladder connection, the provision of prostatic secretions, and various types of muscular propulsion. The sperm is no more independent of its milieu than the egg, and yet from a wish that it were, biologists have lent their support to the notion that the human female, beginning with the egg, is congenitally more dependent than the male.[35]

Bringing out another aspect of the sperm's autonomy, an article in the journal *Cell* has the sperm making an "existential decision" to penetrate the egg: "Sperm are cells with a limited behavioral repertoire, one that is directed toward fertilizing eggs. To execute the decision to abandon the haploid state, sperm swim to an egg and there acquire the ability to effect membrane fusion."[36] Is this a corporate manager's version of the sperm's activities—"executing decisions" while fraught with dismay over difficult options that bring with them very high risk?

There is another way that sperm, despite their small size, can be made to loom in importance over the egg. In a collection of scientific papers, an electron micrograph of an enormous egg and tiny sperm is titled "A Portrait of the Sperm."[37] This is a little like showing a photo of a dog and calling it a picture of the fleas. Granted, microscopic sperm are harder to photograph than eggs, which are just large enough to see with the naked eye. But surely the use of the term "portrait," a word associated with the powerful and wealthy, is significant. Eggs have only micrographs or pictures, not portraits.

One depiction of sperm as weak and timid, instead of strong and powerful—the only such representation in western civilization, so far as I know—occurs in Woody Allen's movie *Everything You Always Wanted to Know About Sex* *But Were Afraid to Ask*. Allen, playing the part of an apprehensive sperm inside a man's testicles, is scared of the man's approaching orgasm. He is reluctant to launch himself into the darkness, afraid of contraceptive devices, afraid of winding up on the ceiling if the man masturbates.

The more common picture—egg as damsel in distress, shielded only by her sacred garments; sperm as heroic warrior to the rescue—cannot be proved to be dictated by the biology of these events. While the "facts" of biology may not *always* be constructed in cultural terms, I would argue that in this case they are. The degree of metaphorical content in these descriptions, the extent to which differences between egg and sperm are emphasized, and the parallels between cultural stereotypes of male and female behavior and the character of egg and sperm all point to this conclusion.

NEW RESEARCH, OLD IMAGERY

As new understandings of egg and sperm emerge, textbook gender imagery is being revised. But the new research, far from escaping the stereotypical representations of egg and sperm, simply replicates elements of textbook gender imagery in a different form. The persistence of this imagery calls to mind what Ludwik Fleck termed "the self-contained" nature of scientific thought. As he described it, "the interaction between what is already known, what remains to be learned, and those who are to apprehend it, go to ensure harmony within the system. But at the same time they also preserve the harmony of illusions, which is quite secure within the confines of a given thought style."[38] We need to understand the way in which the cultural content in scientific descriptions changes as biological discoveries unfold, and whether that cultural content is solidly entrenched or easily changed.

In all of the texts quoted above, sperm are described as penetrating the egg, and specific substances on a sperm's head are described as binding to the egg. Recently, this description of events was rewritten in a biophysics lab at Johns Hopkins University—transforming the egg from the passive to the active party.[39]

Prior to this research, it was thought that the zona, the inner vestments of the egg, formed an impenetrable barrier. Sperm overcame the barrier by mechanically burrowing through, thrashing their tails and slowly working their way along. Later research showed that the sperm released digestive enzymes that chemically broke down the zona; thus, scientists presumed that the sperm used mechanical *and* chemical means to get through to the egg.

In this recent investigation, the researchers began to ask questions about the mechanical force of the sperm's tail. (The lab's goal was to develop a contraceptive that worked topically on sperm.) They discovered, to their great surprise, that the forward thrust of sperm is extremely weak, which contradicts the assumption that sperm are forceful penetrators.[40] Rather than thrusting forward, the sperm's head was now seen to move mostly back and forth. The sideways motion of the sperm's tail makes the head move sideways with a force that is ten times stronger than its forward movement. So even if the overall force of the sperm were strong enough to mechanically break the zona, most of its force would be directed sideways rather than forward. In fact, its strongest tendency, by tenfold, is to escape by attempting to pry itself off the egg. Sperm, then, must be exceptionally efficient at *escaping* from any cell surface they contact. And the surface of the egg must be designed to trap the sperm and prevent their escape. Otherwise, few if any sperm would reach the egg.

The researchers at Johns Hopkins concluded that the sperm and egg stick together because of adhesive molecules on the surfaces of each. The egg traps the sperm and adheres to it so tightly that the sperm's head is forced to lie flat against the surface of the zona, a little bit, they told me, "like Br'er Rabbit getting more and more stuck to tar baby the more he wriggles." The trapped sperm continues to wiggle ineffectually side to side. The mechanical force of its tail is so weak that a sperm cannot break even one chemical bond. This is where the digestive enzymes released by the sperm come in. If they start to soften the zona just at the tip of the sperm and the sides remain stuck, then the weak, flailing sperm can get oriented in the right direction and make it through the zona—provided that its bonds to the zona dissolve as it moves in.

Although this new version of the saga of the egg and the sperm broke through cultural expectations, the researchers who made the discovery continued to write papers and abstracts as if the sperm were the active party who attacks, binds, penetrates, and enters the egg. The only difference was that sperm were now seen as performing these actions weakly.[41] Not until August 1987, more than three years after the findings described above, did these researchers reconceptualize the process to give the egg a more active role. They began to describe the zona as an aggressive sperm catcher, covered with adhesive molecules that can capture a sperm with a single bond and clasp it to the zona's surface.[42] In the words of their published account: "The innermost vestment, the *zona pellucida*, is a glycoprotein shell, which captures and tethers the sperm before they penetrate it. . . . The sperm is captured at the initial contact between the sperm tip and the *zona*. . . . Since the thrust [of the sperm] is much smaller than the force needed to break a single affinity bond, the first bond made upon the tip-first meeting of the sperm and *zona* can result in the capture of the sperm."[43]

Experiments in another lab reveal similar patterns of data interpretation. Gerald Schatten and Helen Schatten set out to show that, contrary to conventional wisdom, the "egg is not merely a large, yolk-filled sphere into which the sperm burrows to endow new life. Rather, recent research suggests the almost heretical view that sperm and egg are mutually active partners."[44] This sounds like a departure from the stereotypical textbook view, but further reading reveals Schatten and Schatten's conformity to the aggressive-sperm metaphor. They describe how "the sperm and egg first touch when, from the tip of the sperm's triangular head, a long, thin filament shoots out and harpoons the egg." Then we learn that "remarkably, the harpoon is not so much fired as assembled at great speed, molecule by molecule, from a pool of protein stored in a specialized region called the acrosome. The filament may grow as much as twenty times longer than the sperm head itself before its tip reaches the egg and sticks."[45] Why not call this "making a bridge" or "throwing out a line" rather than firing a harpoon? Harpoons pierce prey and injure or kill them, while this filament only sticks. And why not focus, as the Hopkins lab did, on the stickiness of the egg, rather than the stickiness of the sperm?[46] Later in the article, the Schattens replicate the common view of the sperm's perilous journey into the warm darkness of the vagina, this time for the purpose of explaining its journey into the egg itself: "[The sperm] still has an arduous journey ahead. It must penetrate farther into the egg's huge sphere of cytoplasm and somehow locate the nucleus, so that the two cells' chromosomes can fuse. The sperm dives down into the cytoplasm, its tail beating. But it is soon interrupted

by the sudden and swift migration of the egg nucleus, which rushes toward the sperm with a velocity triple that of the movement of chromosomes during cell division, crossing the entire egg in about a minute."[47]

Like Schatten and Schatten and the biophysicists at Johns Hopkins, another researcher has recently made discoveries that seem to point to a more interactive view of the relationship of egg and sperm. This work, which Paul Wassarman conducted on the sperm and eggs of mice, focuses on identifying the specific molecules in the egg coat (the zona pellucida) that are involved in egg-sperm interaction. At first glance, his descriptions seem to fit the model of an egalitarian relationship. Male and female gametes "recognize one another," and "interactions . . . take place between sperm and egg."[48] But the article in *Scientific American* in which those descriptions appear begins with a vignette that presages the dominant motif of their presentation: "It has been more than a century since Hermann Fol, a Swiss zoologist, peered into his microscope and became the first person to see a sperm penetrate an egg, fertilize it and form the first cell of a new embryo."[49] This portrayal of the sperm as the active party—the one that *penetrates* and *fertilizes* the egg and *produces* the embryo—is not cited as an example of an earlier, now outmoded view. In fact, the author reiterates the point later in the article: "Many sperm can bind to and penetrate the zona pellucida, or outer coat, of an unfertilized mouse egg, but only one sperm will eventually fuse with the thin plasma membrane surrounding the egg proper (*inner sphere*), fertilizing the egg and giving rise to a new embryo."[50]

The imagery of sperm as aggressor is particularly startling in this case: the main discovery being reported is isolation of a particular molecule *on the egg coat* that plays an important role in fertilization. Wassarman's choice of language sustains the picture. He calls the molecule that has been isolated, ZP3, a "sperm receptor." By allocating the passive, waiting role to the egg, Wassarman can continue to describe the sperm as the actor, the one that makes it all happen: "The basic process begins when many sperm first attach loosely and then bind tenaciously to receptors on the surface of the egg's thick outer coat, the zona pellucida. Each sperm, which has a large number of egg-binding proteins on its surface, binds to many sperm receptors on the egg. More specifically, a site on each of the egg-binding proteins fits a complementary site on a sperm receptor, much as a key fits a lock."[51] With the sperm designated as the "key" and the egg the "lock," it is obvious which one acts and which one is acted upon. Could this imagery not be reversed, letting the sperm (the lock) wait until the egg produces the key? Or could we speak of two halves of a locket matching, and regard the matching itself as the action that initiates the fertilization?

It is as if Wassarman were determined to make the egg the receiving partner. Usually in biological research, the *protein* member of the pair of binding molecules is called the receptor, and physically it has a pocket in it rather like a lock. As the diagrams that illustrate Wassarman's article show, the molecules on the sperm are proteins and have "pockets." The small, mobile molecules that fit into these pockets are called ligands. As shown in the diagrams, ZP3 on the egg is a polymer of "keys"; many small knobs stick out. Typically, molecules on the sperm would be called receptors and molecules on the egg would be called ligands. But Wassarman chose to name ZP3 on the egg the receptor and to create a new term, "the egg-binding protein," for the molecule on the sperm that otherwise would have been called the receptor.[52]

Wassarman does credit the egg coat with having more functions than those of a sperm receptor. While he notes that "the zona pellucida has at times been viewed by investigators as a nuisance, a barrier to sperm and hence an impediment to fertilization," his new research reveals that the egg coat "serves as a sophisticated biological security system that screens incoming sperm, selects only those compatible with fertilization and development, prepares sperm for fusion with the egg and later protects the resulting embryo from polyspermy [a lethal condition caused by fusion of more than one sperm with a single egg]."[53] Although this description gives the egg an active role, that role is drawn in stereotypically feminine terms. The egg *selects* an appropriate mate, *prepares* him for fusion, and then *protects* the resulting offspring from harm. This is courtship and mating behavior as seen through the eyes of a sociobiologist: woman as the hard-to-get prize, who, following union with the chosen one, becomes woman as servant and mother.

And Wassarman does not quit there. In a review article for *Science,* he outlines the "chronology of fertilization."[54] Near the end of the article are two subject headings. One is "Sperm Penetration," in which Wassarman describes how the chemical dissolving of the zona pellucida combines with the "substantial propulsive force generated by sperm." The next heading is "Sperm-Egg Fusion." This section details what happens inside the zona after a sperm "penetrates" it. Sperm "can make contact with, adhere to, and fuse with (that is, fertilize) an egg."[55] Wassarman's word choice, again, is astonishingly skewed in favor of the sperm's activity, for in the next breath he says that sperm *lose* all motility upon fusion with the egg's surface. In mouse and sea urchin eggs, the sperm enters at the *egg's* volition, according to Wassarman's description: "Once fused with egg plasma membrane [the surface of the egg], how does a sperm enter the egg? The surface of both mouse and sea urchin eggs is covered with thousands of plasma membrane-bound projections, called microvilli [tiny "hairs"]. Evidence in sea urchins suggests that, after membrane fusion, a group of elongated microvilli cluster tightly around and interdigitate over the sperm head. As these microvilli are resorbed, the sperm is drawn into the egg. Therefore, sperm motility, which ceases at the time of fusion in both sea urchins and mice, is not required for sperm entry."[56] The section called "Sperm Penetration" more logically would be followed by a section called "The Egg Envelops," rather than "Sperm-Egg Fusion." This would give a parallel—and more accurate—sense that both the egg and the sperm initiate action.

Another way that Wassarman makes less of the egg's activity is by describing components of the egg but referring to the sperm as a whole entity. Deborah Gordon has described such an approach as "atomism" ("the part is independent of and primordial to the whole") and identified it as one of the "tenacious assumptions" of Western science and medicine.[57] Wassarman employs atomism to his advantage. When he refers to processes going on within sperm, he consistently returns to descriptions that remind us from whence these activities came: they are part of sperm that penetrate an egg or generate propulsive force. When he refers to processes going on within eggs, he stops there. As a result, any active role he grants them appears to be assigned to the parts of the egg, and not to the egg itself. In the quote above, it is the microvilli that actively cluster around the sperm. In another example, "the driving force for engulfment of a fused sperm comes from a region of cytoplasm just beneath an egg's plasma membrane."[58]

SOCIAL IMPLICATIONS: THINKING BEYOND

All three of these revisionist accounts of egg and sperm cannot seem to escape the hierarchical imagery of older accounts. Even though each new account gives the egg a larger and more active role, taken together they bring into play another cultural stereotype: woman as a dangerous and aggressive threat. In the Johns Hopkins lab's revised model, the egg ends up as the female aggressor who "captures and tethers" the sperm with her sticky zona, rather like a spider lying in wait in her web.[59] The Schatten lab has the egg's nucleus "interrupt" the sperm's dive with a "sudden and swift" rush by which she "clasps the sperm and guides its nucleus to the center."[60] Wassarman's description of the surface of the egg "covered with thousands of plasma membrane-bound projections, called microvilli" that reach out and clasp the sperm adds to the spiderlike imagery.[61]

These images grant the egg an active role but at the cost of appearing disturbingly aggressive. Images of woman as dangerous and aggressive, the femme fatale who victimizes men, are widespread in Western literature and culture.[62] More specific is the connection of spider imagery with the idea of an engulfing, devouring mother.[63] New data did not lead scientists to eliminate gender stereotypes in their descriptions of egg and sperm. Instead, scientists simply began to describe egg and sperm in different, but no less damaging, terms.

Can we envision a less stereotypical view? Biology itself provides another model that could be applied to the egg and the sperm. The cybernetic model—with its feedback loops, flexible adaptation to change, coordination of the parts within a whole, evolution over time, and changing response to the environment—is common in genetics, endocrinology, and ecology and has a growing influence in medicine in general.[64] This model has the potential to shift our imagery from the negative, in which the female reproductive system is castigated both for

not producing eggs after birth and for producing (and thus wasting) too many eggs overall, to something more positive. The female reproductive system could be seen as responding to the environment (pregnancy or menopause), adjusting to monthly changes (menstruation), and flexibly changing from reproductivity after puberty to nonreproductivity later in life. The sperm and egg's interaction could also be described in cybernetic terms. J. F. Hartman's research in reproductive biology demonstrated fifteen years ago that if an egg is killed by being pricked with a needle, live sperm cannot get through the zona.[65] Clearly, this evidence shows that the egg and sperm *do* interact on more mutual terms, making biology's refusal to portray them that way all the more disturbing.

We would do well to be aware, however, that cybernetic imagery is hardly neutral. In the past, cybernetic models have played an important part in the imposition of social control. These models inherently provide a way of thinking about a "field" of interacting components. Once the field can be seen, it can become the object of new forms of knowledge, which in turn can allow new forms of social control to be exerted over the components of the field. During the 1950s, for example, medicine began to recognize the psychosocial *environment* of the patient: the patient's family and its psychodynamics. Professions such as social work began to focus on this new environment, and the resulting knowledge became one way to further control the patient. Patients began to be seen not as isolated, individual bodies, but as psychosocial entities located in an "ecological" system: management of "the patient's psychology was a new entrée to patient control."[66]

The models that biologists use to describe their data can have important social effects. During the nineteenth century, the social and natural sciences strongly influenced each other: the social ideas of Malthus about how to avoid the natural increase of the poor inspired Darwin's *Origin of Species*.[67] Once the *Origin* stood as a description of the natural world, complete with competition and market struggles, it could be reimported into social science as social Darwinism, in order to justify the social order of the time. What we are seeing now is similar: the importation of cultural ideas about passive females and heroic males into the "personalities" of gametes.

This amounts to the "implanting of social imagery on representations of nature so as to lay a firm basis for reimporting exactly that same imagery as natural explanations of social phenomena."[68]

Further research would show us exactly what social effects are being wrought from the biological imagery of egg and sperm. At the very least, the imagery keeps alive some of the hoariest old stereotypes about weak damsels in distress and their strong male rescuers. That these stereotypes are now being written in at the level of the *cell* constitutes a powerful move to make them seem so natural as to be beyond alteration.

The stereotypical imagery might also encourage people to imagine that what results from the interaction of egg and sperm—a fertilized egg—is the result of deliberate "human" action at the cellular level. Whatever the intentions of the human couple, in this microscopic "culture" a cellular "bride" (or femme fatale) and a cellular "groom" (her victim) make a cellular baby. Rosalind Petchesky points out that through visual representations such as sonograms, we are given "*images* of younger and younger, and tinier and tinier, fetuses being "saved.'" This leads to "the point of visibility being "pushed back' *indefinitely.*"[69] Endowing egg and sperm with intentional action, a key aspect of personhood in our culture, lays the foundation for the point of viability being pushed back to the moment of fertilization. This will likely lead to greater acceptance of technological developments and new forms of scrutiny and manipulation, for the benefit of these inner "persons": court-ordered restrictions on a pregnant woman's activities in order to protect her fetus, fetal surgery, amniocentesis, and rescinding of abortion rights, to name but a few examples.[70]

Even if we succeed in substituting more egalitarian, interactive metaphors to describe the activities of egg and sperm, and manage to avoid the pitfalls of cybernetic models, we would still be guilty of endowing cellular entities with personhood. More crucial, then, than what *kinds* of personalities we bestow on cells is the very fact that we are doing it at all. This process could ultimately have the most disturbing social consequences.

One clear feminist challenge is to wake up sleeping metaphors in science, particularly those involved in descriptions of the egg and the sperm. Although the literary convention is to call such metaphors "dead," they are not so much dead as sleeping, hidden within the scientific content of texts—and all the more powerful for it.[71] Waking up such metaphors, by becoming aware of when we are projecting cultural imagery onto what we study, will improve our ability to investigate and understand nature. Waking up such metaphors, by becoming aware of their implications, will rob them of their power to naturalize our social conventions about gender.

Notes

Portions of this article were presented as the 1987 Becker Lecture, Cornell University. I am grateful for the many suggestions and ideas I received on this occasion. For especially pertinent help with my arguments and data I thank Richard Cone, Kevin Whaley, Sharon Stephens, Barbara Duden, Susanne Kuechler, Lorna Rhodes, and Scott Gilbert. The article was strengthened and clarified by the comments of the anonymous *Signs* reviewers as well as the superb editorial skills of Amy Gage.

1. James Hillman, *The Myth of Analysis* (Evanston, Ill.: Northwestern University Press, 1972), 220.

2. The textbooks I consulted are the main ones used in classes for undergraduate premedical students or medical students (or those held on reserve in the library for these classes) during the past few years at Johns Hopkins University. These texts are widely used at other universities in the country as well.

3. Arthur C. Guyton, *Physiology of the Human Body*, 6th ed. (Philadelphia: Saunders College Publishing, 1984), 624.

4. Arthur J. Vander, James H. Sherman, and Dorothy S. Luciano, *Human Physiology: The Mechanisms of Body Function*, 3d ed. (New York: McGraw Hill, 1980), 483–84.

5. Vernon B. Mountcastle, *Medical Physiology*, 14th ed. (London: Mosby, 1980), 2:1624.

6. Eldra Pearl Solomon, *Human Anatomy and Physiology* (New York: CBS College Publishing, 1983), 678.

7. For elaboration, see Emily Martin, *The Woman in the Body: A Cultural Analysis of Reproduction* (Boston: Beacon, 1987), 27–53.

8. Vander, Sherman, and Luciano, 568.

9. Melvin Konner, "Childbearing and Age," *New York Times Magazine* (December 27, 1987), 22–23, esp. 22.

10. I have found but one exception to the opinion that the female is wasteful: "Smallpox being the nasty disease it is, one might expect nature to have designed antibody molecules with combining sites that specifically recognize the

epitopes on smallpox virus. Nature differs from technology, however: it thinks nothing of wastefulness. (For example, rather than improving the chance that a spermatozoon will meet an egg cell, nature finds it easier to produce millions of spermatozoa.)" (Niels Kaj Jerne, "The Immune System," *Scientific American* 229, no. 1 [July 1973]: 53). Thanks to a *Signs* reviewer for bringing this reference to my attention.

11. Bruce Alberts et al., *Molecular Biology of the Cell* (New York: Garland, 1983), 795.

12. In her essay "Have Only Men Evolved?" (in *Discovering Reality: Feminist Perspectives on Epistemology, Metaphysics, Methodology, and Philosophy of Science,* ed. Sandra Harding and Merrill B. Hintikka [Dordrecht: Reidel, 1983], 45–69, esp. 60–61), Ruth Hubbard points out that sociobiologists have said the female invests more energy than the male in the production of her large gametes, claiming that this explains why the female provides parental care. Hubbard questions whether it "really takes more 'energy' to generate the one or relatively few eggs than the large excess of sperms required to achieve fertilization." For further critique of how the greater size of eggs is interpreted in sociobiology, see Donna Haraway, "Investment Strategies for the Evolving Portfolio of Primate Females," in *Body/Politics,* ed. Mary Jacobus, Evelyn Fox Keller, and Sally Shuttleworth (New York: Routledge, 1990), 155–56.

13. The sources I used for this article provide compelling information on interactions among sperm. Lack of space prevents me from taking up this theme here, but the elements include competition, hierarchy, and sacrifice. For a newspaper report, see Malcolm W. Browne, "Some Thoughts on Self Sacrifice," *New York Times* (July 5, 1988), C6. For a literary rendition, see John Barth, "Night-Sea Journey," in his *Lost in the Funhouse* (Garden City, N.Y.: Doubleday, 1968), 3–13.

14. See Carol Delaney, "The Meaning of Paternity and the Virgin Birth Debate," *Man* 21, no. 3 (September 1986): 494–513. She discusses the difference between this scientific view that women contribute genetic material to the fetus and the claim of long-standing Western folk theories that the origin and identity of the fetus comes from the male, as in the metaphor of planting a seed in soil.

15. For a suggested direct link between human behavior and purportedly passive eggs and active sperm, see Erik H. Erikson, "Inner and Outer Space: Reflections on Womanhood," *Daedalus* 93, no. 2 (Spring 1964): 582–606, esp. 591.

16. Guyton (n. 3 above), 619; and Mountcastle (n. 5 above), 1609.

17. Jonathan Miller and David Pelham, *The Facts of Life* (New York: Viking Penguin, 1984), 5.

18. Alberts et al., 796.

19. Ibid., 796.

20. See, e.g., William F. Ganong, *Review of Medical Physiology,* 7th ed. (Los Altos, Calif.: Lange Medical Publications, 1975), 322.

21. Alberts et al. (n. 11 above), 796.

22. Guyton, 615.

23. Solomon (n. 6 above), 683.

24. Vander, Sherman, and Luciano (n. 4 above), 4th ed. (1985), 580.

25. Alberts et al., 796.

26. All biology texts quoted above use the word "penetrate."

27. Solomon, 700.

28. A. Beldecos et al., "The Importance of Feminist Critique for Contemporary Cell Biology," *Hypatia* 3, no. 1 (Spring 1988): 61–76.

29. Gerald Schatten and Helen Schatten, "The Energetic Egg," *Medical World News* 23 (January 23, 1984): 51–53, esp. 51.

30. Alberts et al., 796.

31. Guyton (n. 3 above), 613.

32. Miller and Pelham (n. 17 above), 7.

33. Alberts et al. (n. 11 above), 804.

34. Ibid., 801.

35. Ruth Herschberger, *Adam's Rib* (New York: Pelligrini & Cudaby, 1948), esp. 84. I am indebted to Ruth Hubbard for telling me about Herschberger's work, although at a point when this paper was already in draft form.

36. Bennett M. Shapiro, "The Existential Decision of a Sperm," *Cell* 49, no. 3 (May 1987): 293–94, esp. 293.

37. Lennart Nilsson, "A Portrait of the Sperm," in *The Functional Anatomy of the Spermatozoan,* ed. Bjorn A. Afzelius (New York: Pergamon, 1975), 79–82.

38. Ludwik Fleck, *Genesis and Development of a Scientific Fact,* ed. Thaddeus J. Trenn and Robert K. Merton (Chicago: University of Chicago Press, 1979), 38.

39. Jay M. Baltz carried out the research I describe when he was a graduate student in the Thomas C. Jenkins Department of Biophysics at Johns Hopkins University.

40. Far less is known about the physiology of sperm than comparable female substances, which some feminists claim is no accident. Greater scientific scrutiny of female reproduction has long enabled the burden of birth control to be placed on women. In this case, the researchers' discovery did not depend on development of any new technology.

The experiments made use of glass pipettes, a manometer, and a simple microscope, all of which have been available for more than one hundred years.

41. Jay Baltz and Richard A. Cone, "What Force Is Needed to Tether a Sperm?" (abstract for Society for the Study of Reproduction, 1985), and "Flagellar Torque on the Head Determines the Force Needed to Tether a Sperm" (abstract for Biophysical Society, 1986).

42. Jay M. Baltz, David F. Katz, and Richard A. Cone, "The Mechanics of the Sperm-Egg Interaction at the Zona Pellucida," *Biophysical Journal* 54, no. 4 (October 1988): 643–54. Lab members were somewhat familiar with work on metaphors in the biology of female reproduction. Richard Cone, who runs the lab, is my husband, and he talked with them about my earlier research on the subject from time to time. Even though my current research focuses on biological imagery and I heard about the lab's work from my husband every day, I myself did not recognize the role of imagery in the sperm research until many weeks after the period of research and writing I describe. Therefore, I assume that any awareness the lab members may have had about how underlying metaphor might be guiding this particular research was fairly inchoate.

43. Ibid., 643, 650.

44. Schatten and Schatten (n. 29 above), 51.

45. Ibid., 52.

46. Surprisingly, in an article intended for a general audience, the authors do not point out that these are sea urchin sperm and note that human sperm do not shoot out filaments at all.

47. Schatten and Schatten, 53.

48. Paul M. Wassarman, "Fertilization in Mammals," *Scientific American* 259, no. 6 (December 1988): 78–84, esp. 78, 84.

49. Ibid., 78.

50. Ibid., 79.

51. Ibid., 78.

52. Since receptor molecules are relatively *immotile* and the ligands that bind to them relatively *motile*, one might imagine the egg being called the receptor and the sperm the ligand. But the molecules in question on egg and sperm are immotile molecules. It is the sperm as a *cell* that has motility, and the egg as a cell that has relative immotility.

53. Wassarman, 78–79.

54. Paul M. Wassarman, "The Biology and Chemistry of Fertilization," *Science* 235, no. 4788 (January 30, 1987): 553–60, esp. 554.

55. Ibid., 557.

56. Ibid., 557–58. This finding throws into question Schatten and Schatten's description (n. 29 above) of the sperm, its tail beating, diving down into the egg.

57. Deborah R. Gordon, "Tenacious Assumptions in Western Medicine," in *Biomedicine Examined*, ed. Margaret Lock and Deborah Gordon (Dordrecht: Kluwer, 1988), 19–56, esp. 26.

58. Wassarman, "The Biology and Chemistry of Fertilization," 558.

59. Baltz, Katz, and Cone (n. 42 above), 643, 650.

60. Schatten and Schatten, 53.

61. Wassarman, "The Biology and Chemistry of Fertilization," 557.

62. Mary Ellman, *Thinking about Women* (New York: Harcourt Brace Jovanovich, 1968), 140; Nina Auerbach, *Woman and the Demon* (Cambridge, Mass.: Harvard University Press, 1982), esp. 186.

63. Kenneth Alan Adams, "Arachnophobia: Love American Style," *Journal of Psychoanalytic Anthropology* 4, no. 2 (1981): 157–97.

64. William Ray Arney and Bernard Bergen, *Medicine and the Management of Living* (Chicago: University of Chicago Press, 1984).

65. J. F. Hartman, R. B. Gwatkin, and C. F. Hutchison, "Early Contact Interactions between Mammalian Gametes In Vitro," *Proceedings of the National Academy of Sciences (U.S.)* 69, no. 10 (1972): 2767–69.

66. Arney and Bergen, 68.

67. Ruth Hubbard, "Have Only Men Evolved?" (n. 12 above), 51–52.

68. David Harvey, personal communication, November 1989.

69. Rosalind Petchesky, "Fetal Images: The Power of Visual Culture in the Politics of Reproduction," *Feminist Studies* 13, no. 2 (Summer 1987): 263–92, esp. 272.

70. Rita Arditti, Renate Klein, and Shelley Minden, *Test-Tube Women* (London: Pandora, 1984); Ellen Goodman, "Whose Right to Life?" *Baltimore Sun* (November 17, 1987); Tamar Lewin, "Courts Acting to Force Care of the Unborn," *New York Times* (November 23, 1987), A1 and B10; Susan Irwin and Brigitte Jordan, "Knowledge, Practice, and Power: Court Ordered Cesarean Sections," *Medical Anthropology Quarterly* 1, no. 3 (September 1987): 319–34.

71. Thanks to Elizabeth Fee and David Spain, who in February 1989 and April 1989, respectively, made points related to this.

Teaching Resistance: The Racial Politics of Mass Media

bell hooks

Previously (in Chapter 6 of this text), we read bell hooks's memoir in which she described her childhood experience of observing the abuse of her mother and the consequences it had for her and her family. Here hooks takes a more didactic tack. She describes not only the racist content of television and film depictions of African-Americans but also the insidious way the constant bombardment of messages from the media gets inside our heads and distorts our perception of reality. Television, says hooks, damages African-Americans' ability to maintain "oppositional worldviews," reducing resistance to racist ideology and encouraging compliance with White supremacy. It has the same effect on women's ability to detect and resist sexist ideology.

Consider the meaning of the term oppositional worldview, *a concept important in multicultural feminism. Evaluate its place in a "raised consciousness," and then determine what the best response should be to the problem hooks describes.*

WHEN I BEGAN THE PROCESS of education for critical consciousness to radicalize my thinking and action, I relied on the writings and life practices of Malcolm X, Paulo Freire, Albert Memmi, Frantz Fanon, Amical Cabral, Walter Rodney, and a host of other thinkers. The work of these teachers and political mentors led me to think about the absence of a discourse on colonialism in the United States. When thinking about the kind of language commonly evoked to talk about black experience in white supremacist capitalist patriarchal North America, I was often struck by the pervasive use of euphemisms, words like "Jim Crow," "Uncle Tom," "Miss Ann," etc. These colorful terms obscured the underlying structures of domination that kept white supremacy in place. By socializing white and black citizens in the

From bell hooks, *Killing Rage: Ending Racism* (New York: Henry Holt and Company, 1995). Copyright © 1995 by Gloria Watkins. Reprinted by permission of Henry Holt and Company, LLC.

United States to think of racism in personal terms, individuals could think of it as having more to do with inherent prejudicial feelings than with a consciously mapped-out strategy of domination that was systematically maintained. Even though African Americans in the United States had no country, whites took over and colonized; as a structure of domination that is defined as the conquest and ownership of a people by another, colonialism aptly describes the process by which blacks were and continue to be subordinated by white supremacy.

In the beginning black folks were most effectively colonized via a structure of ownership. Once slavery ended, white supremacy could be effectively maintained by the institutionalization of social apartheid and by creating a philosophy of racial inferiority that would be taught to everyone. This strategy of colonialism needed no country, for the space it sought to own and conquer was the minds of whites and blacks. As long as a harsh brutal system of racial apartheid was in place, separating blacks from whites by laws, coercive structures of punishment, and economic disenfranchisement, many black people seemed to intuitively understand that our ability to resist racist domination was nurtured by a refusal of the colonizing mindset. Segregation enabled black folks to maintain oppositional worldviews and standpoints to counter the effects of racism and to nurture resistance. The effectiveness of those survival strategies was made evident by both civil rights movements and the militant resistance that followed in their wake. This resistance to colonialism was so fierce, a new strategy was required to maintain and perpetuate white supremacy. Racial integration was that strategy. It was the setting for the emergence of neo-colonial white supremacy.

Placed in positions of authority in educational structures and on the job, white people could oversee and eradicate organized resistance. The new neo-colonial environment gave white folks even greater access and control over the African-American mind.

Integrated educational structures were the locations where whites could best colonize the minds and imaginations of black folks. Television and mass media were the other great neo-colonial weapons. Contemporary African Americans often ponder how it is possible for the spirit of resistance to be so diminished today even though the structures of our lives continue to be shaped and informed by the dictates of white supremacy. The spirit of resistance that remained strong from slavery to the militant sixties was displaced when whites made it seem as though they were truly ready to grant black folks social equality, that there were indeed enough resources to go around, that the imperialist wealth of this country could be equitably shared. These assumptions were easy to believe given the success of sixties black militant struggle. By the time the bubble burst, collectively black folks had let our guard down and a more insidious colonization of our minds began to take place. While the Eurocentric biases taught to blacks in the educational system were meant to socialize us to believe in our inherent inferiority, it was ultimately the longing to have access to material rewards granted whites (the luxury and comfort represented in advertising and television) that was the greatest seduction. Aping whites, assimilating their values (i.e., white supremacist attitudes and assumptions) was clearly the way to achieve material success. And white supremacist values were projected into our living rooms, into the most intimate spaces of our lives by mass media. Gone was any separate space apart from whites where organized militant resistance could emerge. Even though most black communities were and remain segregated, mass media bring white supremacy into our lives, constantly reminding us of our marginalized status.

With the television on, whites were and are always with us, their voices, values, and beliefs echoing in our brains. It is this constant presence of the colonizing mindset passively consumed that undermines our capacity to resist white supremacy by cultivating oppositional worldviews. Even though most African Americans do not identify with the experiences of whites in real life or have intimate relationships with them, these boundaries are crossed when we sit facing the television. When television was first invented and many black folks could not afford TVs or did not have the luxury of time to consume representations of whiteness all day long, a barrier still existed between the value system of the dominant white culture and the values of most black folks. That barrier was torn down when televisions entered every living room. Movies function in a similar way. Not surprising, when black Americans were denied easy access to white movies, black cinema thrived. Once the images of whiteness were available to everyone there was no black movie-going audience starving for black images. The hunger to see black folks on the screen had been replaced by the desire to be close to the Hollywood image, to whiteness. No studies have been done that I know of which look at the role mass media have played since 1960 in perpetuating and maintaining the values of white supremacy. Constantly and passively consuming white supremacist values both in educational systems and via prolonged engagement with mass media, contemporary black folks, and everyone else in this society, are vulnerable to a process of overt colonization that goes easily undetected. Acts of blatant racism are rarely represented in mass-media images. Most television shows suggest via the liberal dialogues that occur between white characters, or racially integrated casts, that racism no longer serves as a barrier. Even though there are very few black judges in the United States, television courtroom dramas cast black characters in these roles in ways so disproportionate to the reality that it is almost ludicrous. Yet the message sent to the American public and folks all over the world watching American TV is that our legal system has triumphed over racial discrimination, that not only is there social equality but that black folks are often the ones in power. I know of no studies that have examined the role television has played in teaching white viewers that racism no longer exists. Many white folks who never have intimate contact with black folks now feel that they know what we are like because television has brought us into their homes. Whites may well believe that our presence on the screen and in their intimate living spaces means that the racial apartheid that keeps neighborhoods and schools segregated is the false reflection and that what we see on television represents the real.

Currently black folks are often depicted on television in situations where they charge racist victimization and then the viewer is bombarded with evidence that shows this to be a trumped-up charge, that whites are indeed far more caring and able to be social equals than "misguided" blacks realize. The message that television sends then is that the problem of racism lies with black people—that it exists in our minds and imaginations. On a recent episode of *Law and Order* a white lawyer directs anger at a black woman and tells her, "If you want to see the cause of racism, look in the mirror." Television does not hold white people responsible for white supremacy; it socializes them to believe that subjugation and subordination of black people by any means necessary is essential for the maintenance of law and order. Such thinking informed the vision of white folks who looked at the tape showing the brutal beating of Rodney King by a group of white men and saw a scenario where he was threatening white lives and they were merely keeping the peace.

Movies also offer us the vision of a world where white folks are liberal, eager to be social equals with blacks. The message of films like *Grand Canyon, Lethal Weapon, The Bodyguard,* and a host of other Hollywood films is that whites and blacks live together in harmony. Contemporary Hollywood films that show strife between races situate the tension around criminal behavior where black characters may exist as good or bad guys in the traditional racist cowboy scenario but where most whites, particularly heroic ones, are presented as capable of transcending the limitations of race.

For the most part television and movies depict a world where blacks and whites coexist in harmony although the subtext is clear; this harmony is maintained because no one really moves from the location white supremacy allocates to them on the race-sex hierarchy. Denzel Washington and Julia Roberts may play opposite one another in *The Pelican Brief* but there will not be a romance. True love in television and movies is almost always an occurrence between those who share the same race. When love happens across boundaries as in *The Bodyguard, Zebrahead,* or *A Bronx Tale,* it is doomed for no apparent reason and/or has tragic consequences. White and black people learning lessons from mass media about racial bonding are taught that curiosity about those who are racially different can be expressed as long as boundaries are not actually crossed and no genuine intimacy emerges.

Many television viewers of all races and ethnicities were enchanted by a series called *I'll Fly Away* which highlighted a liberal white family's struggle in the South and the perspective of the black woman who works as a servant in their home. Even though the series is often centered on the maid, her status is never changed or challenged. Indeed she is one of the "stars" of the show. It does not disturb most viewers that at this moment in history black women continue to be represented in movies and on television as the servants of whites. The fact that a black woman can be cast in a dramatically compelling leading role as a servant does not intervene on racist/sexist stereotypes, it reinscribes them. Hollywood awarded its first Oscar to a black person in 1939 when Hattie McDaniel won as Best Supporting Actress in *Gone With the Wind.* She played the maid. Contemporary films like *Fried Green Tomatoes* and *Passion Fish,* which offer viewers progressive visions of white females, still image black women in the same way—as servants. Even though the black female "servant" in *Passion Fish* comes from a middle-class background, drug addiction has led to her drop in status. And the film suggests that working secluded as the caretaker of a sick white woman redeems the black woman. It was twenty-four years after McDaniel won her Oscar that the only black man to ever receive this award won Best Actor. Sidney Poitier won for his role in the 1960s film *Lilies of the Field.* In this film he is also symbolically a "mammy" figure, playing an itinerant worker who caretakes a group of white nuns. Mass media consistently depict black folks either as servants or in subordinate roles, a placement which still suggests that we exist to bolster and caretake the needs of whites. Two examples that come to mind are the role of the black female FBI agent in *The Silence of the Lambs,* whose sole purpose is to bolster the ego of the white female lead played by Jodie Foster. And certainly in all the *Lethal Weapon* movies Danny Glover's character is there to be the buddy who because he is black and therefore subordinate can never eclipse the white male star. Black folks confront media that include us and subordinate our representation to that of whites, thereby reinscribing white supremacy.

While superficially appearing to present a portrait of racial social equality, mass media actually work to reinforce assumptions that black folks should always be cast in supporting roles in relation to white characters. That subordination is made to appear "natural" because most black characters are consistently portrayed as always a little less ethical and moral than whites, not given to rational reasonable action. It is not surprising that it is those black characters represented as didactic figures upholding the status quo who are portrayed as possessing positive characteristics. They are rational, ethical, moral peacemakers who help maintain law and order.

Significantly, the neo-colonial messages about the nature of race that are brought to us by mass media do not just shape whites' minds and imaginations. They socialize black and other non-white minds as well. Understanding the power of representations, black people have in both the past and present challenged how we are presented in mass media, especially if the images are perceived to be "negative," but we have not sufficiently challenged representations of blackness that are not obviously negative even though they act to reinforce white supremacy. Concurrently, we do not challenge the representations of whites. We were not outside movie theaters protesting when the white male lead character in *Paris Trout* brutally slaughters a little black girl (even though I can think of no other image of a child being brutally slaughtered in a mainstream film) or when the lead character in *A Perfect World* played by Kevin Costner terrorizes a black family who gives him shelter. Even though he is a murderer and an escaped convict, his character is portrayed sympathetically whereas the black male father is brutally tortured presumably because he is an unloving, abusive parent. In *A Perfect World* both the adult white male lead and the little white boy who stops him from killing the black man are shown to be ethically and morally superior to black people.

Films that present cinematic narratives that seek to intervene in and challenge white supremacist assumption, whether they are made by black or white folks, tend to receive negative attention or none at all. John Sayles's film *The Brother from Another Planet* successfully presented a black male character in a lead role whose representation was oppositional. Rather than portraying a black male as a sidekick of a more powerful white male, or as a brute and sex fiend, he offered us the image of a gentle, healing, angelic black male spirit. John Waters's film *Hair-*

spray was able to reach a larger audience. In this movie, white people choose to be antiracist, to critique white privilege. Jim Jarmusch's film *Mystery Train* is incredibly deconstructive of racist assumptions. When the movie begins we witness a young Japanese couple arriving at the bus station in Memphis who begin to speak Japanese with a black man who superficially appears to be indigent. Racist stereotypes and class assumptions are challenged at this moment and throughout the film. White privilege and lack of understanding of the politics of racial difference are exposed. Yet most viewers did not like this film and it did not receive much attention. Julie Dash's film *Daughters of the Dust* portrayed black folks in ways that were radically different from Hollywood conventions. Many white viewers and even some black viewers had difficulty relating to these images. Radical representations of race in television and movies demand that we be resisting viewers and break our attachment to conventional representations. These films, and others like them, demonstrate that film and mass media in general can challenge neo-colonial representations that reinscribe racist stereotypes and perpetuate white supremacy. If more attention were given these films, it would show that aware viewers long for mass media that act to challenge and change racist domination and white supremacy.

Until all Americans demand that mass media no longer serve as the biggest propaganda machine for white supremacy, the socialization of everyone to subliminally absorb white supremacist attitudes and values will continue. Even though many white Americans do not overtly express racist thinking, it does not mean that their underlying belief structures have not been saturated with an ideology of difference that says white is always, in every way, superior to that which is black. Yet so far no complex public discourse exists that explains the difference between that racism which led whites to enjoy lynching and murdering black people and that wherein a white person may have a black friend or lover yet still believe black folks are intellectually and morally inferior to whites.

Mainstream media's endorsement of *The Bell Curve* by Richard J. Herrnstein and Charles Murray reflects the American public's willingness to support racist doctrine that represents black people as genetically inferior. Anti-racist white male thinker and activist Edward Herman reminds us of the danger of such acceptance in his essay "The New Racist Onslaught":

> *Built on black slavery, with segregation and poverty helping reinforce stereotypes after 1865, racism has deep and persistent roots in this country. Today, racist Bob Grant has a radio audience of 680,000 in New York City, and racist Rush Limbaugh has a supportive audience of millions (extending to Supreme Court Justice Clarence Thomas). Reagan with his repeated imagery of black welfare mothers exploiting the taxpayer, Bush with Willie Horton and the menace of "quotas," and a slew of code words bandied about by politicians, show that polarizing racist language and political strategies are acceptable and even integral parts of mainstream culture today.*

When black psyches are daily bombarded by mass media representations that encourage us to see white people as more caring, intelligent, liberal, etc., it makes sense that many of us begin to internalize racist thinking.

Without an organized resistance movement that focuses on the role of mass media in the perpetuation and maintenance of white supremacy, nothing will change. Boycotts remain one of the most effective ways to call attention to this issue. Picketing outside theaters, turning off the television set, writing letters of protest are all low-risk small acts that can become major interventions. Mass media are neither neutral nor innocent when it comes to spreading the message of white supremacy. It is not far-fetched for us to assume that many more white Americans would be anti-racist if they were not socialized daily to embrace racist assumptions. Challenging mass media to divest of white supremacy should be the starting point of a renewed movement for racial justice.

Women's Spirit and Men's Religion

Sheila Ruth

The violence done to women in the name of religion has often been devastating. Among the injuries are the blemishing or eradication of many of our uniquely female experiences and the denial of our right to construct our own spiritual expression.

MY MOTHER HAD DIED. ON her seventieth birthday, three years into her widowhood, missing her husband and tired of being tired, she had finally let go. I sat alone, uncomfortable, on a rickety wooden folding chair in a small, seedy funeral home in the Bronx. "Guests" sat silently, half listening to a rabbi—part pompous, part well-meaning—as he chanted and intoned in a language neither my mother nor I had learned to understand. (Only the men in our transplanted European neighborhood had been taught to read and pray in Hebrew. The women had been taught how to keep kosher and "make a Jewish home.")

My mother had been JEWISH, like so many working-class women of her generation in New York City in the 1940s and 1950s. It was not so much a theological matter, nor even a religious one, in the strictest sense. It had to do with her sense of herself, with her belonging in the Jewish community, with her wholehearted embrace of "yiddishness." In her apartment, beside the photographs of long-forgotten European relatives, artifacts from Israel, plaques of the Ten Commandments and various holy ornaments had festooned the walls and tabletops of each room. She had always worn a Star of David around her neck, and *Fiddler on the Roof* was the only Broadway play she had ever made an effort to see. Never having been educated, she had known very little about the Books, the Talmud and the Torah, except

that they were sacred. She could not chant prayers or perform any rituals except for the lighting of sabbath candles, a task specifically assigned to the "woman of the house." In earlier years she had carried out the laws she knew to the letter, keeping kosher, minding the sabbath, going to mikvah, although she had not known why except that God had ordered it so, and that had been good enough for her. Later, after the death of her parents, the strictness of her observances had diminished, but never her commitment to Jewish identity or her absolute belief in God.

Following my father's death, the prescribed rituals had been carried out precisely and without question: immediate burial, closed casket, the requisite number of men to join my brother in a minyan, chanting the Kaddish, the prayer for the dead. Stark as they were, these rigors were comforting to my mother. To die and be buried as a Jew was to take the worst sting out of death, she had once said. On this my parents had agreed: one of the primary reasons for having children (sons, actually) was to leave behind someone who would see to a proper passing and who would say the Kaddish when it was time.

I remembered these things as I sat in the late afternoon sunlight, musing upon the woman who was my mother, missing her (hard as she had often been to take), experiencing a mix of intricate emotions. I fingered a giant bag of m&m's I was carrying in my purse. I had bought them for her some days before, planning to mail them in time for her birthday, as I did each year. Half guiltily indulging our taste for these candies and giving them to each other for special occasions was a private ritual we had shared; touching them now evoked poignant memories and sharpened my sense of separation.

I needed comfort. I didn't like having to sit so long in that half-lit, dusty little room, staring at the box that housed my mother's body. There were no small amenities, no flowers nor music to soften the bleak setting of the scene; this being an orthodox ceremony, such things were forbidden. I sought some small solace in the familiarity of the satin cloth draped across the coffin, dark purple with a golden star, but I felt none. The "eulogy," some *good words* spoken in English about the dead woman by the rabbi-who-did-not-know-her added nothing for me but a further note of irony and alienation. It seemed rotten to me that after seventy years of being and doing, the end of one's time should be marked by such barren contrivance.

After a time, we left the funeral home and reassembled at a Jewish cemetery in New Jersey, an equally stark, relentlessly depressing place, marked only by plain marble headstones—some slightly askew—by uneven tufts of scrub grass and a scattering of untrimmed bushes. There were few people at the grave site (most of her close friends and relatives having died or moved away from the city): a handful of old women who had recently been her neighbors, her sister, two younger brothers and their wives, my brother and I, and the rabbi. I stood beside a mound of sandy earth, looking down at her coffin, resting now in a giant pit. I had not realized that six feet would be so deep, could look so far. The ceremony began, the rabbi chanted a few lines in Hebrew. Switching to English, he looked around at the party and explained in his everyday voice (which seemed almost a conspiratorial whisper), "Here we would say Kaddish, but we don't have a minyan, so we'll finish." Intoning again, he said, "Let us not tarry among the dead, but make our way back to the living."

Not realizing that the ceremony had concluded and that I was supposed to file through the small row of people and return to the car, I stood there, vacantly, and waited. My brother tapped my arm. "Come on. We're supposed to go."

"Already? What about Kaddish?" I asked under my breath. "No Kaddish," my brother said, taking my arm, "we don't have a minyan."

No minyan. We needed ten men, any ten, to say the prayers, and there weren't enough.

Like the Hindu woman facing suttee, my mother too had committed the unpardonable *faux pas* of outliving her relevant males. I thought to myself, now isn't that a hell of a note! A Jew had died and could not have her Kaddish because she had failed to die soon enough or to produce enough sons. Worse, it seemed to me, a woman had died and could not have her prayers because the number present, being women, did not count for sufficient company to call upon their God.

For a moment I considered rebellion, a scene, perhaps, although I knew it wouldn't change a thing. I was not even to be permitted to stay awhile to say my own goodbyes and make my own unauthorized bidding of the gods. It would be forbidden, of course. In my head I heard my mother's piercing Bronx voice, "Sheila, don't start. Do what you're told!" They had me. Again.

There would be one small act of resistance, though, before I left. For myself, if not for my mother, I would have a "Kaddish" of my own. I reached into my purse and drew out the package I still carried there. Deliberately, tearing open the bag with a flourish, I scattered the little colored candies up and down the giant pit. They clattered noisily, almost happily, along the wooden cover of the box below, and I thought with some satisfaction that they lent a bit of sweetness and color to the place—and to the connection I forged once again with the spirit of my mother.

RE-LIGO: THE LINK

The story of my mother's funeral is paradigmatic. What happened there and what failed to happen tells us much about religion: what it can accomplish, and should accomplish, when it is functioning well, and what damage it does when it goes awry.

The term *religion* is derived from the Latin *re-ligo, to bind back, to rebind,* which reveals its meaning. In one sense, we may understand binding to suggest a shackling, the kind of bullying by rules and rulers so vividly apparent at my mother's funeral service. Because it exercises illegitimate power over the most profound experiences of life, such binding results in an alienation of spirit and a lost opportunity to confront and make sense of existence. It creates an estrangement among people who are not joined together by their common, intimate sharing of one another's experience, but who instead, being separated from their authentic selves, must remain apart from one another.

At its best, however, religion represents a binding of a very different kind.

> *Latin religio meant re-linking or reunion, a restoration of the umbilical bond between nature and man, or between the Mother Goddess and her son—consort, typified by human sexual union. The Sanskrit equivalent was* yoga, *which also meant linking or joining, root of the English "yoke."*
>
> —BARBARA G. WALKER[1]

So the operative questions for religion are: How am I linked to the rest of life, to the source of life? What is the significance of that link? How do I make use of it, how shall it, should it, make use of me, and what is my duty to that process? How may I take the best out of my bond with life; how can that enhance and beautify my existence, perhaps all existence? How do I and should I understand and direct all the events of my life from the perspective of my profound attachment to the whole of being? What are the ways that I can protect, strengthen, and enjoy the bond?

The function of religion is to continuously cement a conscious re-linking of the individual with the infinite universe. It is to help us acknowledge and make use of the tie that holds us to the Source. The infant takes nourishment from the mother, sustaining its life through their interaction by way of the umbilicus. We as individuals take our spiritual nourishment and survive as selves through interaction with our "Mother," the universe that gave us being. . . .

The death of someone significant to us is an extraordinary event in our lives and potentially disintegrative. To meet death in a way that affirms life is a complex task for mind and emotion. Not only must we deal with the raw sense of loss, we must also integrate a whole array of everyday changes the death will have upon our lives.

On a deeper level, because we are faced with death in such an immediate way, we also must come to terms with our own death and other coming losses, with death in general, and with the fragility and impermanence of life. We must consider once again "the meaning of life." One more time, we must reassess our orientation to being, of which death is a part.

To manage such a powerful event well, we require strategies to pull things back together for us, within ourselves, between ourselves and meaning, and between us and our community; we must resociate. Part of the work is rational, cognitive. But the most powerful portion of the experience centers in the emotions and in the spirit, and there the healing must take place, in the deepest, central core of our beings. Fragmented by an event that tears apart all our carefully soldered relationships and psychic structures, we need to reestablish or remodel our connectedness, our "friendship" with life. Providing us the materials to achieve that is a major function of religion and their rituals.

To accomplish the purpose of integration and healing, rituals must speak to our felt condition and in our own tongue. My mother's burial was barren to me not for want of enough men (or even people) to carry on the prescribed observances. Rather, the ceremony failed to pull together for me the disparate elements of the event—my absent mother, the dead woman, the people present and not present, the place, my feelings, my thoughts, the fact of death, the fact of life, the cosmos—and present them to me in some sensible bundle. It failed absolutely to touch the woman who had died (more accurately, to touch the woman who had lived); it failed to speak of her and for her to those connected with her. The surroundings were sterile, not because they were poor or ugly, but because they were alien to her and to those present. What had that stark little storefront room to do with the life (not just the death) of this person? Had she ever been to that room or to one like it? Did it hold anything of her or hers? Was it a place she might love, like, or relate to in any way? In fact, given choice, she would never have entered there voluntarily. The incantations were meaningless, not simply because they were in a foreign language, but because they had little to do with the life the woman had led, her days, her dreams. Indeed, because they had never really been connected to the lives any of us had led, they could not evoke even the sense of the extraordinary that they were meant to. By defining the situation in terms of the missing males, the ceremony had discounted the women present; it therefore had negated us, all of us, including the one being buried, separating us from the proceedings, the deity, and the wider community. In so doing, it severed the bonds that should have been cemented. For those who came seeking meaning and solace, there could be only fragmentation.

In the end, at the burial of my mother, in a space that was totally alien and therefore alienating, the only voice of Spirit left to me was the symbolic sharing that had bonded us so many times before. In words that were my own, the candies we both savored, I spoke to my mother, to the gathering, and to myself as well.

Scattering the candies was an act of religion. It is this kind of speaking, and everything that surrounds it, this kind of connecting and everything that surrounds it, this kind of marking of a life-changing event, and everything that surrounds it, that forms the core of religion, done well.

Death, of course, is not the only "moment" in life that is critical to the spirit. Various rites of passage are very familiar: vital biological events, such as birth or death, or those more obviously socially constructed, such as reaching the age of majority, retiring from work, or completing periods of training. Every society recognizes its own collection of milestones, and they are assigned meaning and value through particular activities and symbols. A person is raised to a new level of authority, for example. There is a ceremony. Now one may wear special clothes—a certain cap, a feather, a color. A title may change—chief, Madame, professor.

When an event or experience is given special recognition, when it is set apart by reverence or celebration, when members of the community are asked to bear witness, in these and in other ways, the event is *marked*. It is designated as an important occurrence to the individual and to the community. The raw event is given meaning, even granted "reality" by the symbols attached to it. Because it is focused upon, formally "spoken," the awareness of the event is sharpened in the consciousness, brought into the foreground of thought, so that it can be dealt with in the particular way determined by the society.

Just how much marking contributes to the meaning or reality of an event may be seen more readily when compared with events or moments for which marking is denied. Just as events may be brought into existence by marking, it is equally possible to

drop them from existence or distort their meaning either by not marking them at all or by giving them a false marking. . . .

All markings have force, but those markings which are said to connect with the Ultimate are particularly powerful. To make a promise before a judge of the land, surrounded by leather-bound volumes housed in mahogany, in the old marble courthouse in the county seat is impressive. The judge, to be sure, represents not only the people of the state, but the force of law and tradition and the granting of social approbation. Yet how much greater is the force of validation when it represents not only society, but God! To make a promise *in the temple* signifies that the promise has particular meanings because it places itself in relation to the Infinite. The vow is made not only to oneself and to the community, but to the eternal, to deity, which represents society's most fundamental mores and its hopes and expectations for the future. What is more, it is expected that the deity will respond with like for like—promises kept for promises kept. The whole fabric of the event is altered: There are additional responsibilities, expectations and prohibitions; attitudes and emotions are invested here that do not exist in other contexts; and this promise is perceived differently even by those outside the culture, even by those who are not believers, because they comprehend the implications of the religious element.

Of course, things other than life events may be marked. Designating a day to honor Martin Luther King Jr. not only honors the man, but what he stood for. Having such a celebration says as much about American culture, history, racism, and law as it did about Dr. King. That is why it meant so much to those who pressed for it, and why it was so equally resisted by its opponents. Obviously, markings are as meaningful and as consequential in their absence as in their presence, for if the presence of the mark denotes acknowledgment, response, and importance, consider what the withholding of a mark signifies.

For women, the violence done to us by absent or false marking is commonplace and crucial. How many of our most profound life experiences are lost in silence—menarche and menopause (both of them a coming-of-age), rape, the moving on and moving out of our children, taking to ourselves a close friend? How many others are distorted or perverted, turned upside down by no marking or the wrong marking, no words or the wrong words? A purification ceremony at the close of each menstruation, assuring that the woman will return to her men "cleansed" and harmless, common in patriarchy, is the wrong marking. Rather there should be affirmations of femaleness, celebrations for the bringers of life. After rape, secrecy and shame are the wrong "words"; what is required is some dramatically transforming reassertion of absolute, *inviolate* dignity and power, a communal "naming" of the vileness of the wrong, a ceremony of outrage, retribution, and compensation. In a reality constructed by men for men, no words, no ceremonies, no constructive markings have ever been permitted to evolve for women's life-altering moments.

A gathering assembles itself around a dinner table dressed for a feast, covered with flowers, wonderful foods, sweet-smelling herbs, and incense. The girl who has just had her first menstruation is seated at the head of the table, dressed in what she loves best, adorned with ribbons and flowers, surrounded by the women close and dear to her. There is laughter, play. From each one present she receives women's gifts. Finally it is her mother's turn. The woman gives her daughter a jewel with red beads or stones, marking the blood, celebrating the sign of femaleness, welcoming her into the family of women. The daughter returns a gift, honoring the birth, honoring the line. They are very proud.

In a darkened classroom the only light comes from a scented candle placed on a desk in the center of the room. A group of students are constructing a woman's ceremony by giving their teacher a "croning," a ritual to celebrate her becoming a "crone," a woman of maturity, wisdom, and consequence. The teacher is given a white robe to wear, signifying youth, beginningness, purity of intention. To symbolize her gifts to them, a sweet drink is poured into a silver cup, and she is asked to bring the cup to each woman, standing in a circle, and offer her a sip. Then she is blindfolded and led gently around the circle of students, as each one in turn takes her hands, rubs perfumed lotion into them, and thanks her for something she has given them—new insight, compassion, humor, permission to be powerful, and so on. When the circle is completed, a tinkling bell is sounded, the blindfold is removed, the white robe is replaced by a black one, signifying maturity, fullness, power. They all share some

cookies and drink and laugh together. There is affection among them, acceptance, validation, but even more. There is a collective granting of respect to certain abstractions, learning, the sharing of knowledge, caring, maturity, aging.

In women, aging is rarely venerated. Quite the contrary. The gifts we may receive with age, uncelebrated may become invisible; maligned, they may be denied, lost. In honoring those gifts in their teacher, the students are making an equally strong statement about their own futures, their expectations for themselves and for other women.

What happens to powerful experiences that go unmarked or unremarked by the communities where we make our psychic homes? In our deepest selves and in our awareness, what is their status, and what is the consequence of their going unnoticed or of their being inverted? Are they erased? Are they distorted? Do they toxify?

That women's uniquely female "moments" go unmarked or falsely marked is no accident, but one more reflection of the fact that the "world's great religions" and the patriarchies that created them are not of us nor for us.

How are we to respond to patriarchal religion's contempt for our lives? Do we simply reject the religious altogether and opt for purely social, secular markings? Does that meet our needs? Isn't there an insufficiency in stipulating or recognizing meanings that do not go beyond the social order? The relativity of social norms always leaves the force of their conviction incomplete. We must make some attempt to reach a truth that lies beneath the social form and lends it veracity. Anything less will leave us feeling incomplete.

Let us take for example an adoption. If no religious ceremony exists to mark an extraordinary new relationship with a child, a parent may go to court, swear an oath, rename the child (a powerfully symbolic act). A party may be arranged or a special dinner. These are social rituals, and clearly understood they may be significant. But is this sufficient? Are these acts truly equal in power to religious ceremony? Without some processing at a very deep level of what the adoption is—what it involves in the very widest sense, not only for the child, but for the community, the family, the parent, *for parenting itself, for one's whole reading of the nature of things*—is everything said that needs to be said, is everything marked clearly enough, deeply enough?

If we are spiritually strong, each of us may find our meanings by ourselves, make our own peace with life-events, and create our own markings; sometimes we do that very well. Of course, at some level we must do this for ourselves even when positive sacred ceremonies exist. But how much more powerful can it be to join with others in our affirmations and join all together with some symbolic connector to ultimate being. . . .

WOMEN'S SPIRIT AND MEN'S RELIGION

Sunday morning. I had slept in. Relishing a day with few obligations, I let myself wake slowly, opening one eye, then the other, measuring the amount of light that was seeping into my room from behind the window shade, trying to judge how pretty a day was waiting for me and how quickly I should rise to meet it. Deciding to poke, I lay a few moments longer, then turned drowsily toward the table near my bed to check the clock. As I moved, I became aware of a warm wetness between my legs and beneath me. Like a properly housebroken puppy, I reacted at once: Oh, no! My period. I wasn't due yet. What a mess! Oh, damn!

I whined and crabbed and clucked as I had seen my mother do a hundred times before, years ago when I had lived in her house. Always, when she had "the curse," she would sit in the big kitchen chair beside the stove and, rocking back and forth, she would hold her stomach and groan. When I "came around," I had not felt as much pain as she had, but, like a dutiful daughter, I did what was expected: I grunted and grimaced and complained, displayed the proper disgust for all the necessary apparatus—belts, pads, pins, and such—and maintained a level of secrecy that would have impressed the CIA.

At 15, when I had my first period, I was pleased, proud to be a woman at last, an adult, one of the girls. I could telephone Jeanie and Marian and whisper that I had "gotten a letter from a girl friend," just as they did. (In the 1950s, young women didn't even utter the words among themselves, among close friends.) I could refuse to take a shower after gym class (in 1955 everyone knew it was dangerous

to get your hair wet when you were . . .), and I could (blush) find excuses not to go swimming with the rest of the gang.

My mother too had been pleased. After all, I had been "late," older than usual, and she had worried that "oh-my-god-what-if-Sheila-couldn't-have-children?" Still living out of her roots in the small Austrian village where she was born, she had called every aunt, cousin, and woman friend she knew to spread (very decorously, of course) the good news.

To mark the event, my mother delivered the requisite lecture: "Now, Sheila, this means you're a big girl, and you have to . . . uh . . . be careful. Not that I mean you aren't good . . . I know you're a good girl. But, you know, this means, uh. . . ." A new tack: "We keep the napkins here, on the top of the closet in the back, behind the toilet paper" (where the men of the family never ventured). "This is the belt that holds it on. It goes here like this, around here, under there, pinned to this, and when you change, you wrap the old pad in toilet paper, like this, then in newspaper; fold it several times so it stays closed. Don't leave it in the bathroom waste basket because it will *smell*." (Worse than . . . ?) "Take it to the big garbage pail outside behind the garage and close the lid tight." (So it can't get away?) ". . . and don't let your father or brother see. If you need to buy a new box of pads, go to the store when Mrs. R. is there, not Mr. R., and ask her for Modess when she's alone." Mrs. R. had indeed been discrete, giving and getting in hushed tones, wrapping the box in a paper bag and placing that one in a larger one, disguising as best she could that so distinctive package. Her efforts rarely succeeded, and I was always left to hide it as best I could beneath my coat, lurking along in the shadows as I hurried home and into the house (by the back door, closest to the bathroom). It was a far less funny drama then than it is now in memory.

Soon after leaving my mother's house, I had relinquished most of the charade, the ceremony of hiding, the outward groaning and apologies—at least in my head. Yet more than twenty years later, in my own home, quite alone, here I was, daughter of Miriam, the daughter of Esther, a daughter of patriarchy, responding to stimulus as prescribed, following the proper cues: "Ugh, what a mess! Oh, the sheets are ruined (?). I've got to get to the bathroom. Omigod, what if I get blood on the rug? It'll never come up. Ugh. Ick. Damn."

Cupping one hand between my legs, I hobbled to the bathroom and the safety of the tile floor. It was a gusher. Dumping my nightgown in the tub, I went to the business of cleaning up. What first? The potty or the sink? The sink. Clean your . . . ugh . . . hands. They're full of . . . I reached for the faucet with my "cleaner" hand, watching the other (for signs of decay?), making sure not to touch anything. I looked down. My hand was covered with red. I stopped. I just stopped. I looked. Standing there, naked, blood trickling down my thighs, not staring or inspecting or analyzing or anything complex, I just looked.

Time shifted, and I was in another bathroom in another day, during my married-to-L time, flushing the red down the toilet. I was pained, grieving and disappointed because the red told me that I wasn't pregnant, again, and I wanted so much to be. Every red said no.

Red and pregnancy. Red and babies. They meant each other. They mean each other.

Flash. Lightening bolt. Back to Sunday morning, to red in my hand. Red and pregnancy. Red and babies. Red and Life! Blood and Life. They mean each other. I looked again. I looked anew. This time I did inspect. Blood. Darker, thicker, slightly viscous, but blood. I smeared it between my fingers, raised it to my nose to smell. No "stink." Nothing that needed to be "deodorized." Just blood. The same stuff that spills from the rest of me when my skin is opened. If I cut my hand, would I squeal and grimace and guard the floor from pollution? From the stuff of Life? I am disgusted with the flow of Life, because it comes from between my legs, from my own vagina?!

A parade of obscenities marched through my head: the pads in the top of the closet, in the back, behind . . . the drugstore embarrassments, the synagogue humiliations, my mother sharing her secrecy, my father who (very decently) never spoke of it, my "orthodox" uncle, refusing my handshake in the synagogue, pulling back his hand from my contamination—taboo, taboo. The blood of Life, reviled, ridiculed.

I started to cry, almost to wail, almost to howl. Some measure of feminist consciousness had been part of me even in my childhood, to be crystallized years later as a politic, but this, this level of experiential recognition was different—deeper, wrenching, powerful in the extreme.

I cried, first pain, then relief, then rage, fury. "You bastards," I hurled, "you fuckers, you sneer and growl and make your damn rules. How dare you?"

How dare they malign FEMALE, how dare they malign the symbol of Life, the source, the center, the beginning? How dare they try to separate me from me, from a portion of myself that is uniquely female, that marks me as woman? To hate this is to hate me, to hate the womanness of me, to hate women, to hate what we are, let alone what we can do. We, women, collectively, make life. We are Life. And they revile it? For what? For themselves, for their hatred of us, their fear of us, for their inability to match this capacity, for their need to control and direct it . . . us, for their own self-glorification, for power for themselves and the power of their gods, for God . . . the Father . . .

Thunderbolt again. God the Father? Fathers don't have periods, they don't make blood, and they don't make babies. They partly make pregnant, but they don't make babies. Not never. Not no time. Not no species. Women make babies. We make Life. Earth makes Life. Universe makes Life. Life makes life. God, if you are to have one, would not be a father; it would be a MOTHER! *God is a woman,* damn it, like me. She's a sister, my sister. We're alike in this. We make living things. If you want a deity, try this one on for size: God the Mother–Sister. That had a ring to it. It certainly rang my bell!

I started to laugh (to hell with crying). I laughed and laughed and laughed some more and never gave a damn that I was bleeding all over the floor.

Not their words. Mine. Not their experience, Mine. Not their consciousness, Mine. Not their awareness, Ours. Not their (S)pirit, Ours. Not their signs, Ours!

Where in all their books could we find signs for this? Not possible. You had to be there.

RELIGION: WHY SPEAK THE WORD?

For many feminists, memories of religion are memories of alienation and servitude. For those of us who fled, religion had functioned as the worst kind of binding, as an unfriendly master we had been expected to serve and revere. Our religions and the people who administered them told us how to behave and what to think, how to make judgments, what to choose, and when to defer. The authority of religion over our conceptual lives and our behavior was final and absolute. In its rigid exclusivity, its nice demarcations of social groups, it proposed to determine who was friend and who was enemy, whom we might seek out and who must be shunned. (These are good people, those are bad; these are right, those are wrong; these are "ours," those are not.) As source of all Truth, religion was primary arbiter in matters of conscience and morality. (Thou shalt not disobey thy parents—even if every fiber of life and thought judge them wrong; thou shalt not enjoy thy body—regardless of how sane it seems to do so; thou shalt not doubt God or priests or book—for this you will suffer death or hell or both or worse.)

Even more than "God," religion ruled; ours was to serve and thus to garner our due measure of approval, respectability, security (such as it was), and self-esteem. Not to conform ourselves to religious expectation was to invite rejection, slurs on our "reputation," and not a little physical risk.

A bumper sticker on the rear of a pick-up truck parked outside a tavern in southern Missouri proclaimed in bold letters:

> *God said it.*
> *I believe it.*
> *And that's the end of it.*

I felt cold when I saw it, because it undoubtedly implied something to the effect of, "and I and we believe better than you, and if you don't think so, keep your mouth shut, because if we catch you alone, we're gonna beat your ass!" What is more, in my memory such violent insistence on conformity applied even more to women than to men, and the punishment for deviation was far more severe.

It has been suggested, even by those who are very positively oriented toward spirituality, that it would be more judicious for a project like this book to avoid the term *religion* altogether and opt for some more neutral term that would be less offensive. They argue that the hostility many people, especially feminists and other activists, feel for religion

would contaminate both the ideas I wish to preserve and the chances those ideas might have for a fair hearing.

In fact, it is a strong argument. Many activists often have a negative knee-jerk reaction to the very idea of religion. Although this is an inappropriate response, it is understandable and hard to counter; and it makes the task of encouraging a reconsideration of religion extraordinarily difficult.

Yet there is an equal risk in abandoning the language of religion precisely because of the history and the associations it has developed. Could it not be argued that religion *as religion* must not be relinquished just because it carries such authority, just because of the respect it engenders, because of the magnitude of its themes? For centuries unknown, the most crucial elements of human existence have fallen under the purview of religion—the setting of values and ideals, the design of primal metaphors, the arbitration of morality, the call to the deep mind, the dispensing of sacred rites. For most of the population these things are still centered in religion and will never be seen anywhere else. Are not these aspects of life far too significant to ignore or to leave in the hands of the twisted, the ignorant, and the power-hungry? Not to "take over" religion in mean spiritedness so the thugs will not have it, but with all authenticity, we must face these matters and cleanse, clarify, and refine these ideas, because they reflect a rich and vital portion of human experience that does persist, will persist, and should persist.

Because what properly belongs to religion profoundly and pervasively affects our lives, and because it holds positive possibilities for society, the power that religion as religion carries must be tapped and turned to human good. If the term religion evokes associations of awe, reverence, and respect, then that is the very best reason to use it in the service of Life.

I am reminded of an incident that took place several years ago at a conference on feminist scholarship. A professor of literature, also a Roman Catholic nun and a director of a women's studies program, had delivered a paper on sexism in literary criticism. The piece was insightful and was very well received by the audience. During the discussion period that followed, the professor revealed a more radically feminist orientation than she had in her paper. Perplexed by the combination of a strong feminist consciousness and an equally committed Catholicism, the students abandoned the subject of literary criticism to question the woman, to challenge her about her religious identification. She stoutly defended that identification, arguing that for her the sacraments were ultimately important, more so than the matter of who administered them. Dismayed and not a little frustrated, one young woman asked, "How can you tolerate remaining in a church so populated by sexist oppressors?" "It's *my* church," the nun answered. "Let them leave. Why should I?"

The incident raises a vital feminist issue, that of the "proprietorship" of ideas, or knowledge. Who, if anyone, *owns* ideas? Are squatters' rights to be granted to those who get there first and lay claim to them by usage? If religion and many of its terms and concepts—*sacred, holy, sacrament, deity, worship, grace*—have been kidnapped and pressed into service by the ultimate pirates, must they languish forever in captivity? It is said that possession is nine-tenths of the law. Surely that principle does not apply to ideas!

The feminist nun was defending her right to the use and interpretation of certain concepts that were meaningful to her, the idea of the holy, the sanctity of sacrament, the relevance to her life of Jesus, in fact of Christianity, particularly Roman Catholicism. Regardless of whether we experience the sacred as she did, the force and the reasonableness of her presupposition are clear: the religion, if not the power structure, is no less hers because it has been (illegitimately) appropriated by others.

We may make the same analysis of all religion. It does not belong to the patriarchs, no matter how strong their claims to the contrary. Why should it be surrendered to them? Why should we freely grant them this one more larceny without resistance?

Just because we are appalled by the errors of the "world's great religions," we must not commit an equally egregious error. We must not allow the assumption that patriarchy's treatment of religion is the only possible treatment. To do so would be to commit the androcentric fallacy: the error of treating masculinist perspectives as universals.

Rather than quit religion, we need to recover it and to create for it a different and better treatment than it has been given—one in which life and humanity are served by its content and not the other way around. We need to construct a sense of religion that serves people, and not one in which people are the servants of priests and books. Service to people's living needs is the proper and probably original intention for religion. Patriarchy's religions become catastrophic when the adherents commit terrible sins: they steal people's spiritual birthright; they gain power over people by lying, they appropriate their energy and their goods; they manipulate human affairs in order to gain the vilest political ends; they abuse trust and exploit the weakness of those who come seeking help.

It is not the exercise of power over individuals that is the province of religion, but the empowerment of individuals to define and gain their own liberation.

Canto, Locura y Poesia

Olivia G. Castellano

Born in 1944 in Del Rio, Texas, Olivia Castellano is currently professor of English at California State University at Sacramento. She has had wide experience in teaching, having taught English literature, composition, women's studies, and the social sciences on the college level, and English, French, and Spanish on the high school level. She has published several poems and three books of poetry, Blue Mandolin: Yellow Field *(1980),* Blue Horse of Madness *(1983), and* Spaces that Time Missed *(1986). Her articles on pedagogy and the Chicana experience have appeared in various journals and anthologies.*

Professor Castellano describes her childhood as the daughter of a farmworker. She portrays a youth in which books and education were her passion, her friends, and also her path to spiritual growth and freedom. She wanted to be a "warrior," to "sabotage society" with its racism and sexism. Today that is exactly what she is and does—through her writing and her teaching. As Castellano demonstrates, education has revolutionary potential; and words and ideas are revolutionary tools, for societies and for individuals. Through them we can not only detect ideological distortion but demolish it.

I AM A WALKING CONTRADICTION. I have no Ph.D. yet I'm a full professor of English at a state university. By all definitions and designs I should not even have made it to college. I am the second of five children of a Southern Pacific Railroad worker with a fifth-grade education and a woman who dropped out of the second grade to help raise ten siblings—while her mother worked ten hours a day cleaning houses and doing laundry for rich Texan ranchers.

In Comstock, the Tex-Mex border town about fifteen miles from the Rio Grande where I spent the first twelve years of my life, I saw the despair that poverty and hopelessness had etched in the faces of young Chicano men who, like my father, walked back and forth on the dusty path between Comstock and the Southern Pacific Railroad station. They would set out every day on rail carts to repair the railroad. The women of Comstock fared no better. Most married early. I had seen them in their kitchens toiling at a stove, with one baby propped on one hip and two toddlers tugging at their skirts. Or they followed their working mothers' route, cleaning houses and doing laundry for rich Texan ranchers who paid them a pittance. I decided very early that this was not the future I wanted.

In 1958 my father, tired of seeing his days fade into each other without promise, moved us to California where we became farmworkers in the San Jose area (then a major agricultural center). I saw the same futile look in the faces of young Chicanos and Chicanas working beside my family. Those faces already lined so young with sadness made me deadly serious about my books and my education.

At a young age—between eleven and fourteen—I began my intellectual and spiritual rebellion against my parents and society. I fell in love with books and created space of my own where I could dare to dream. Yet in school I remained shy and introverted, terrified of my white, male professors. In my adolescence I rebelled against my mother's insistence that Mexican girls should marry young, as she did at eighteen. I told her that I didn't care if my cousins Alicia and Anita were getting married and having babies early. "I was put on this earth to make books, not babies!" I announced and ran into my room.

Books were my obsession. I wanted to read everything that I was not supposed to. By fourteen I was already getting to know the Marquis de Sade, Rimbaud, Lautréamont, Whitman, Dostoyevsky, Marx. I came by these writers serendipitously. To get from home to Sacramento High School I had to walk through one of the toughest neighborhoods in

Olivia G. Castellano, "Canto, Locura y Poesia," *The Women's Review of Books* 7, no. 5, February, 1990, pp. 18–20. Reprinted by permission of the author.

the city, Oak Park. There were men hanging out with liquor in brown paper bags, playing dice, shooting craps and calling from cars: "Hey, baby, get in here with me!" I'd run into a little library called Oak Park Library, which turned out to have a little bit of everything. I would walk around and stare at the shelves, killing time till the shifty-eyed men would go away.

The librarians knew and tolerated me with skepticism: "Are you sure you're going to read the Marquis de Sade? Do your parents know you're checking out this material? What are you doing with the *Communist Manifesto?*" One librarian even forbade me to check the books out, so I'd sit reading in the library for hours on end. Later, at sixteen or seventeen, I was allowed to check anything and everything out.

So it was that I came to grapple with tough language and ideas. These books were hot! Yet I also was obsessed with wanting to be pretty, mysterious, silent and sexy. I wanted to have long curly hair, red lips and long red nails; to wear black tight dresses and high heels. I wanted desperately to look like the sensuous femmes fatales of the Mexican cinema— María Féliz, one of the most beautiful and famous of Mexico's screen goddesses, and Libertad Lamarque, the smoky-voiced, green-eyed Argentinian singer. These were the women I admired when my mother and I went to the movies together. So these were my "outward" models. My "inward" models, the voices of the intellect that spoke to me when I shut the door to my room, were, as you have gathered, a writer of erotica, two mad surrealists, a crazy Romantic, an epileptic literary genius and a radical socialist.

I needed to sabotage society in a major, intellectually radical way. I needed to be a warrior who would catch everyone off guard. But to be a warrior, you must never let your opponent figure you out. When the bullets of racism and sexism are flying at you, you must be very clever in deciding how you want to live. I knew that everything around me— school, teachers, television, friends, men, even my own parents, who in their internalized racism and self-hatred didn't really believe I'd amount to much though they hoped like hell that life would prove them wrong—everything was against me, and I understood this fully.

To protect myself I fell in love with language— all of it, poems, stories, novels, plays, songs, biog-

raphies, "cuentos" or little vignettes, movies—all manifestations of spoken and written language. I fell in love with ideas, with essays by writers like Bacon or Montaigne. I began my serious reading crusade around age eleven, when I was already convinced that books were central to my life. Only through them and through songs, I felt, would I be free to structure some kind of future for myself.

I wanted to prove to anyone who cared to ask (though by now I was convinced no one gave a damn) that I, the daughter of a laborer-farmworker, could dare to be somebody. Try to imagine what it is like to be always full of rage—rage at everything: at white teachers who could never even pronounce my name (I was often called anything from "Odilia" to "Otilia" to "Estela"); rage at those teachers who asked me point-blank, "But how did you get to be so smart? You are Mexican, aren't you?"; rage at my eleventh-grade English teacher who said to me in front of the class, "You stick to essay writing; never try to write a poem again because a poet you are not!" (This, after I had worked for two diligent weeks on an imitation of "La Belle Dame Sans Merci"! Now I can laugh. Then it was pitiful.)

From age thirteen I was also angry at boys who hounded me for dates. When I'd reject them they'd yell, "So what do you plan to do for the rest of your life, fuck a book?" I was angry at my Chicana classmates in high school who, perhaps jealous of my high grades, would say, "What are you trying to do, be like the whites?" I regret to say that I was also angry at my parents, exasperated by their docility, their limited expectations of me. Oh, I knew they were proud; but sometimes, in their own misdirected rage (maybe afraid of my little successes), they would make painful comments. "Te vas a volver loca con esos jodidos libros" ("You'll go nuts with those fucking books") was my mother's frequent statement. Or the even more sickening, "Esta nunca se va a casar." ("Give up on this one; she'll never get married.") This was the tenor of my adolescent years. When nothing on either side of the two cultures, Mexican or Anglo-American, affirms your existence, that is how rage is shaped.

While I managed to escape at least from the obvious entrapments—a teen pregnancy, a destructive early marriage—I did not escape years of being told I wasn't quite right, that because of my ethnicity and gender I was somehow defective, incomplete. Those years left wounds on my self-esteem, wounds so deep that even armed with my books and stolen knowledge I could not entirely escape deep feelings of unworthiness.

By the time I graduated from high school and managed to get a little scholarship to California State University in Sacramento, where I now teach (in 1962 it was called Sacramento State College), I had become very unassertive, immensely shy. I was afraid to look unfeminine if I raised my hand in class, afraid to seem ridiculous if I asked a "bad" question and all eyes turned on me. A deeper part of me was afraid that my rage might rear its ugly head and I would be considered "an angry Mexican accusing everybody of racism." I was painfully concerned with my physical appearance: wasn't I supposed to look beautiful like Féliz and Lamarque? Yet while I wanted to look pretty for the boys, the thought of having sex terrified me. What if I got pregnant, had to quit college and couldn't read my books any more? The more I feared boys, the more I made myself attractive for them and the more they would make advances, the more I rejected them.

The constant tension sapped my energy and distracted me from my creative journeys into language. Oh, I would write little things (poems, sketches for stories, journal entries), but I was afraid to show them to anyone. Besides, no one knew I was writing them. I was so frightened by my white, male professors, especially in the English department—they looked so arrogant and were so ungiving of their knowledge—that I didn't have the nerve to major in English, though it was the major I really wanted.

Instead, I chose to major in French. The "Parisiens" and "Québecois" in the French department faculty admired my French accent: "Mademoiselle, êtes-vous certaine que vous n'êtes pas parisienne?" they would ask. In short, they cared. They engaged me in dialogue, asked why I preferred to study French instead of Spanish. ("I already know Spanish," I'd say.) French became my adopted language. I could play with it, sing songs in it and sound exotic. It complemented my Spanish; besides, I didn't have to worry about speaking English with my heavy Spanish accent and risk being ridiculed. At one point, my spoken French was better than my oral Spanish; my written French has remained better than my written Spanish.

At 23, armed with a secondary school teaching credential and B.A. in French with an English minor, I became a high school teacher of French and English. Soon after that I began to work for a school district where the majority of the students were Chicanos and Blacks from families on welfare and/or from households run by women.

After two years of high school teaching, I returned to Cal State at Sacramento for the Master's degree. Professionally and artistically, it was the best decision I have ever made. The Master's program to which I applied was a pilot program in its second year at CSUS. Called the Mexican American Experienced Teachers' Fellowship, it was run by a team of anthropology professors, central among whom was Professor Steven Arvizu. The program was designed to turn us into "agents of cultural change." It was 1969 and the program was one of the first federally funded (Title V) ones to address Mexican American students' needs by re-educating their teachers.

My interests were literary, but all twenty of us "fellows" had to get an M.A. in social anthropology, since this experiment took the "anthropologizing education" approach. We studied social dynamics, psycholinguistics, history of Mexico, history of the American Southwest, community activism and confrontational strategies and the nature of the Chicano movement. The courses were eye-openers. I had never heard the terms Chicano, biculturalism, marginality, assimilation, Chicanismo, protest art. I had never heard of Cesar Chavez and the farmworkers nor of Luis Valdez and the Teatro Campesino. I had never studied the nature of racism and identity. The theme of the program was that culture is a powerful tool for learning, self-expression, solidarity and positive change. Exploring it can help Chicano students understand their bicultural circumstances.

The program brought me face to face with nineteen other Chicano men and women, all experienced public school teachers like myself, with backgrounds like mine. The program challenged every aspect of my life. Through group counseling, group encounter, classroom interaction, course content and community involvement I was allowed to express my rage and to examine it in the company of peers who had a similar anger. Most of our instructors, moreover, were Chicano or white professors sensitive to Chicanos. For the first time, at 25, I had found my role models. I vowed to do for other students what these people had done for me.

Eighteen years of teaching primarily white women students, Chicanos and Blacks at California State University, Sacramento, have led me to see myself less as a teacher and more as a cultural worker, struggling against society to undo the damage of years of abuse. I continue to see myself as a warrior empowered by my rage. Racism and sexism leave two clear-cut scars on my students; internalized self-hatred and fear of their own creative passion, in my view the two most serious obstacles in the classroom. Confronting this two-headed monster has made me razor-sharp. Given their tragic personal stories, the hope in my students' eyes reconfirms daily the incredible beauty, the tenacity of the human spirit.

Teaching white women students (ages 30–45) is no different from working with Chicano and Black students (both men and women): you have to bring about changes in the way they view themselves, their abilities, their right to get educated and their relation to a world that has systematically oppressed them simply for being who they are. You have to help them channel and understand the seething rage they carry deep inside, a rage which, left unexpressed, can make them turn against each other and, more sadly, against themselves.

I teach four courses per semester: English 109G, Writing for Proficiency for Bilingual/Bidialectal Students (a course taken mainly by Chicano and Black students, ages 19–24); English 115A, Pedagogy/Language Arts for Prospective Elementary School Teachers (a course taken mainly by women aged 25–45, 50 percent white, 50 percent Chicano); English 180G, Chicano Literature, an advanced studies General Education course for non-English majors (taken by excellent students, aged 24–45, about 40 percent white, 40 percent Chicano, 20 percent Black/Vietnamese/Filipino/South American). The fourth course is English 1, Basic Language Skills, a prefreshman composition course taken primarily by Black and Chicano freshmen, male and female, aged 18–22, who score too low on the English Placement Test to be placed in "regular" Freshman Composition.

Mine is a teaching load that, in my younger days at CSUS, used to drive me close to insanity from physical, mental and spiritual exhaustion—

spiritual from having internalized my students' pain. Perhaps not fully empowered myself, not fully emplumed in the feathers of my own creativity (to borrow the wonderful "emplumada" metaphor coined by Lorna Dee Cervantes, the brilliant Chicana poet), I allowed their rage to become part of mine. This kind of rage can kill you. And so through years of working with these kinds of students I have learned to make my spirit strong with "canto, locura y poesia" (song, madness, and poetry). Judging from my students' progress, the songs have worked.

Truly, it takes a conjurer, a magus with all her teaching cards up her sleeve, to deal with the fragmented souls that show up in my classes. Among the Chicanos and Blacks I get ex-offenders (mostly men but occasionally a woman who has done time), orphans, single women heads of household, high school dropouts who took years to complete their Graduation Equivalency Diploma.

I get women who have been raped and/or who have been sexually abused either by a father figure or by male relatives—Sylvia Tracey, for example, a 30-year-old Chicana feminist, mother of two, whose parents pressured her to marry her (white) rapist and who is going through divorce after ten years of marriage. I get women who have been battered. And, of course, I get the young Chicano and Black little yuppies who don't believe the world existed before 1970, who know nothing about the sixties' history of struggle and student protest, who—in the case of the Chicanos—feel ashamed that their parents speak English with an accent or were once farmworkers. I get Chicanos, Blacks and white women, especially, who are ashamed of their writing skills, who have never once been told that they could succeed in school.

Annetta Jones is typical. A 45-year-old Black woman, who single-handedly raised three children, all college-educated and successful, she is still married to a man who served ten years in prison for being a "hit man." She visited him faithfully in prison and underwent all kinds of humiliation at the hands of correctional officers—even granting them sexual favors just to be allowed to have conjugal visits. When her husband completed his time he fell in love with a young woman from Chicago, where he now lives.

Among my white women students (ranging in age from 25 to 40, though occasionally I get a 45-

year-old woman who wants to be an elementary or high school teacher and "help out young kids so they won't have to go through what I went through"—their exact words) I get women who are either divorced or divorcing; rarely do I get a "happily" married woman. This is especially true of the white women who take my Chicano literature and my credential-pedagogy classes. Take Lynne Trebeck, for instance, a white woman about 40 years old who runs a farm. When she entered the university her husband objected, so she divorced him! They continue to live in the same house (he refused to leave), "but now he has no control over me," she told me triumphantly midway through the semester. She has two sons, fifteen and eighteen years old; as a young woman she did jail time as the accomplice of a convicted drug dealer.

Every semester I get two or three white lesbian feminists. This semester there was Vivianne Rose, about 40, in my Chicano literature class. Apparently sensing too much conservatism in the students, and knowing that she wanted to be an elementary school teacher, she chose to conceal her sexual orientation. On the first day of class she wore Levi pants, a baggy sweat shirt, white tennis shoes and a beige baseball cap. By the end of the first week she had switched to ultrafeminine dresses and skirts, brightly colored blouses, nylons and medium-heeled black shoes, not to mention lipstick and eye makeup. When she spoke in class she occasionally made references to "my husband who is Native American." She and Sylvia Tracey became very close friends. Halfway through the course they informed me that "Shit, it's about time we tell her." (This, from Sylvia.) "Oh hell, why not," Vivianne said; "my 'husband' is a woman." The woman *is* Native American; Vivianne Rose lived on a reservation for years and taught young Native American children to read and write. She speaks "Res" talk (reservation speech) and has adopted her "husband's" last name.

Among my white women students there are also divorced women who are raising two to four children, usually between the ages of eight and seventeen. Sometimes I get older widowed white women who are taking classes for their own enjoyment, not for a degree. These women also tell stories of torment: rapes, beatings, verbal and emotional harassment from their men. On occasion I get women who have done jail time, usually for taking the rap

for drug-connected boyfriends. I rarely get a married woman, but when I do there is pain: "My husband doesn't really want me in school." "My husband doesn't really care what I do in college as long as I take care of his needs and the kids' needs." "My husband doesn't really know what I'm studying—he has never asked and I've never told him."

Most of the white women as well as the minority students come to the university under special programs. There is the "Educational Opportunity Program" for students who do not meet all university entrance requirements or whose grade point average is simply too low for regular admission. There is the "Student Affirmative Action Program" for students who need special counseling and tutoring to bring their academic skills up to par or deal with emotional trauma. There is the "College Assistance Migrant Program" for students whose parents are migrant farmworkers in the agricultural areas surrounding Sacramento. There is a wonderful program called PASAR for older women students entering the university for the first time or returning after a multiple-year absence. The Women's Resource Center also provides small grants and scholarships for re-entry women. A large number of my students (both white and minority women) come severely handicapped in their basic language, math and science skills; many have never used a computer. It is not uncommon (especially among Chicanos and Blacks) to get an incoming student who scores at the fifth- and sixth-grade reading levels.

The task is herculean, the rewards spiritually fulfilling. I would not have it any other way. Every day is a lesson in humility and audacity. That my students have endured nothing but obstacles and putdowns, yet still have the courage and strength to seek a college education, humbles me. They are, like me, walking paradoxes. They have won against all the odds (their very presence on campus attests to that). Yet really they haven't won: they carry a deeply ingrained sense of inferiority, a firm conviction that they are not worthy of success.

This is my challenge: I embrace it wholeheartedly. There is no place I'd rather be, no profession more noble. Sure, I sometimes have doubts: every day something new, sad, even tragic comes up. Just as I was typing this article, for instance, Vicky, one of the white students in my Chicano literature class, called in tears, barely able to talk. "Professor, I can't possibly turn in my paper to your mailbox by four o'clock," she cried. "Everything in my house is falling apart! My husband just fought with my oldest daughter [from a previous marriage], has thrown her out of the house. He's running up and down the street, yelling and threatening to leave us. And I'm sitting here trying to write your paper! I'm going crazy. I feel like walking away from it all!" I took an hour from writing this article to help her contain herself. By the end of our conversation, I had her laughing. I also put her in touch with a counselor friend of mine and gave her a two-day extension for her final paper. And naturally I was one more hour late with my own writing!

I teach in a totally non-traditional way. I use every trick in the book: lots of positive reinforcement, both oral and written; lots of one-on-one conferences. I network women with each other, refer them to professor friends who can help them; connect them to graduate students and/or former students who are already pursuing careers. In the classroom I force my students to come up in front of their classmates, explain concepts or read their essays aloud. I create panels representing opposing viewpoints and hold debates—lots of oral participation, role-playing, reading their own texts. Their own writing and opinions become part of the course. On exams I ask them questions about their classmates' presentations. I meet with individual students in local coffeehouses or taverns: it's much easier to talk about personal pain over coffee or a beer or a glass of wine than in my office. My students, for the most part, do not have a network of support away from the university. There are no supportive husbands, lovers (except on rare occasions, as with my lesbian students), no relatives saying, "Yes, you can do it."

Is it any wonder that when these students come to me they have a deep sense of personal shame about everything—poor skills, being older students? They are also very angry, not only at themselves but at the schools for having victimized them; at poor, uninspired teaching; at their parents for not having had high enough expectations of them or (in the case of the women) for having allowed them to marry so young. Sylvia, my Chicana feminist student, put it best when I was pointing out incomplete sentences in her essay: "Where the hell was I when all this was being taught in high school? And why didn't anybody give a damn that I wasn't learning it?"

I never teach content for the first two weeks of any of my courses. I talk about anger, sexism, racism and the sixties—a time when people believed in something larger than themselves. We dialogue—about prisons and why so many Chicano and Black young men are behind bars in California; why people fear differences; why they are so homophobic. I give my students a chance to talk about their anger ("coraje" in Spanish). I often read them the poem by my friend and colleague Jose Montoya, called "Eslipping and Esliding," where he talks about "locura" (craziness) and says that with a little locura, a little eslipping and esliding, we can survive the madness that surrounds us. We laugh at ourselves, sharing our tragic, tattered pasts; we undo everything and let the anger out. "I know why so many of you are afraid of doing well," I say. "You've been told you can't do it, and you're so pissed off about it, you can't concentrate." Courage takes pure concentration. By the end of these initial two or three weeks we have become friends and defined our mutual respect. Only then do we enter the course content.

I am not good at endings; I prefer to celebrate beginnings. The struggle continues and the success stories abound. Students come back, year after year, to say "Thank you." Usually I pull these visitors into the classroom: "Tell my class that they can do it. Tell them how you did it!" They start talking and can't stop. "Look, Olivia, when I first came into your class," said Sylvia, "I couldn't even put a fucking sentence together. And now look at me, three years later I'm even writing poetry!"

PART III

WOMEN ON THE MOVE

"So—against odds, the women inch forward."

—ELEANOR ROOSEVELT, 1946

AS WE LOOK NOW AT some of women's past thoughts and activities on behalf of women, it is worthwhile to consider afresh a point made earlier—that the "history of history" has been almost entirely male. Given the masculinist emphasis on political power and its contempt for things female, it is clear why women's history is, by and large, omitted from the books and why the few appearances women do make are trivialized or distorted. If, as in this final chapter, we conceive of the women's movement as a centuries-old process of women coming to awareness of their condition *as women*, then we can see that it is not enough simply to have passively absorbed what little history has to tell us about women's drive for freedom and authority. To know and to understand the women's movement requires of us all that we search for the totality of women's experience throughout history, seek out previously hidden facts, look at old information in new ways, keep our minds open to reinterpretations of traditional recountings, and be ready for surprises from the lost past of women on the move.

CHAPTER NINE

Our Feminist Foremothers:
Events and Arguments

WHEN DID THE WOMEN'S MOVEMENT BEGIN?

It is often asked: When did the women's movement begin? Some *her*storians attempt to fix the origins of feminist ideas in relatively recent times, specifically, in the Enlightenment and the French Revolution, in the drive for the abolition of slavery, or in the American civil rights and war resistance movements. These attempts have a certain logic, because those events did give birth to some of the ideas and values that have become fundamental to feminism, but they can be misleading. First, they isolate Western or American women's activism from that in other parts of the world, and second, they tend to focus attention not on one long progression of activity but on many discrete, though related periods of activism: on eighteenth-, nineteenth-, or twentieth-century movements, each with a discernible starting point, each built around distinct goals, and each with separate and characteristic political attitudes, personalities, and strategies. A traditional reading in this vein might be summed up as follows:

> *The first stirrings of the women's movement were felt with the publication of Mary Wollstonecraft's* A Vindication of the Rights of Woman *in 1792. The Women's Rights Movement in the United States was born during the drive for abolition of slavery during the nineteenth century. It culminated in the winning of the vote in 1920; and then, because women had exhausted themselves in the fight for suffrage, it died, until Betty Friedan's* The Feminine Mystique *brought it back to life in 1963.*

It is probably more accurate to think of the women's movement as a march of events and an evolution of thought and action that has, over the centuries, and in many different locations, moved women toward greater strength and freedom both in our awareness of ourselves as women and in our position in various societies. This has been happening for a very long time, often for individuals, sometimes collectively. It has progressed, and it has receded; it has sometimes been subterranean, and sometimes it crests into waves of activism. It has expressed itself in many ways: in political action, in the writing of novels, treatises, biographies, and poetry, in marches on courthouses and town squares, in participation in revolutions, or in the quiet but sturdy resistance of women in their households. It has been expressed in various contexts—political, economic, psychological, or even physical—and it is not easily confined to one model. From this perspective, no discernible "beginning" to the women's movement exists. We need not exclude the Roman women demonstrating in the forum in 195 B.C.E. for repeal of the antifemale Oppian laws or the poems of Sappho or the struggles for survival of a thirteenth-century group of women called the Beguines (who chose to abjure marriage, live and work together, help the poor in the name of Christianity, but maintain independence from the control of the male church). We can include among the ideas of the women's movement the themes of female worth from medieval mystic Hildegard of Bingen; the egalitarian ideals of the British Quakers; the arguments of American colonial agitator Anne Hutchinson or of "Constantia," the twentieth-century resistance of Chinese women workers to foot binding; or Rosa Park's courageous decision to take an empty seat in the front of the bus.

Such an approach has manifold value. First, it reveals the universality of women's concerns. It reveals the startling continuity over time of feminist issues, values, goals, and challenges and, in so doing, allows us to see that each wave of activism is not separate and anomalous, destined for an end or for limited achievement at best but rather is an integral part of a progressive development. Finally, this approach affords us a context for evaluating challenges not only to feminist goals but also to the very legitimacy of feminism as a world movement.

KEY THEMES OF WOMEN'S MOVEMENT

For centuries, in groups and as individuals, women have spoken out consistently on certain key issues. Although they may reflect the character of the times and the issues prominent in their age, the goals of feminist women's efforts have been remarkably consistent: They have to do with the *quality* of life for women and for the entire human community.

It is also interesting to note that opponents' reactions have been consistent as well. Adversaries generally attack feminists' "femininity" (we aren't real women), good sense, and morality, and they charge activism on women's behalf with triviality

or destructiveness or both (however inconsistent that may seem).

MAJOR ISSUES FOR WOMEN

It is a revelation to read "The time has come to take this world muddle that men have created and strive to turn it into an ordered, peaceful, happy abiding place for humanity"[1] and discover that those words, which sound so contemporary, were spoken by Alva Belmont in 1922. Mary Wollstonecraft chides the affectations and destructive results of traditional "femininity," and were it not for the habits of language current in her time, she would sound quite like modern activists.

Again and again in poetry, political treatises, personal letters, speeches, and social analyses, we see these themes reiterated: the folly of grossly distorting women's physical, emotional, and intellectual development; the injustice of denying to half the world's population their rights, opportunities, and contributions; the great need for humanitarian treatment of the young, the sick, and the powerless in the face of the insensitive and selfish values of traditional masculinist institutions; the unlikeliness of peace and harmony in a world permeated with the aggressiveness and arrogance of martial power values.

The consistency of the themes in our history underscores the continuity of the movement, the character of feminist concerns, and, it would appear, the legitimacy of our claims. Feminist analysis is not transitory but rather is part of the mainstream of ongoing political thought, although it has not been perceived or treated that way.

CHARGES AND COUNTERCHARGES

Feminist women all say to the masculinists: You make little effort to truly understand us, you misrepresent and malign us; you thwart us; you deny to the world our abilities and contributions; you distort the quality of life; you cause war and unhappiness; you are arrogant and mean-spirited. They answer: You, feminists, are misled and confused; your goals are contrary to reason, nature, God, and order; your behavior is immoral, unnatural, and unseemly; you are either ill (unfeminine) or evil; your actions will cause your own downfall and that of your family, *the* family, the nation, and the world; you are unable to see this, or you don't care.

It crystallizes one's own sense of place and helps to resolve certain personal conflicts to realize that activist women in any age have met the same misogynist accusations. Cato exclaimed of the Roman women: "It is complete liberty, or rather complete license they desire. If they win in this, what will they not attempt? The moment they begin to be your equals, they will be your superiors."[2] Doesn't that sound like: Give them an inch and they'll take a mile; they want to dominate men? Mary Wollstonecraft commented in 1792: "From every quarter have I heard exclamations against masculine women."[3] The same charge of "masculinity" was made against nineteenth-century activists, and what contemporary feminist has not been called masculine or "unwomanly"? Lucy Stone reported in 1855: "The last speaker [at the National Convention, Cincinnati] alluded to this movement as being that of a few disappointed women."[4] How modern! Feminists today are called "disappointed" (that is, frigid, jilted, or crabby) and are always taken to be "in the minority," not in the mainstream of female life.

JUST A DISAPPOINTED FEW

The contention that feminists are not of the majority of women or are not like "normal" women bears looking at, first, because it is an attack so often made, and second, because it raises the question of how accurately feminists may claim to represent women's concerns. The argument is phrased in various ways: "Feminists are just a bunch of losers who couldn't make it in the man-woman world." "Feminism is just a White middle-class movement." "Feminists are just a bunch of bored, selfish middle-class women trying to get more for themselves when there is *real* oppression in the world that affects millions of people." Let us consider those charges one by one.

A Bunch of Losers

To the charge that her movement was composed of a few disappointed women, Lucy Stone answered, "In education, in marriage, in religion, in everything, disappointment is the lot of woman! It shall be the business of my life to deepen this disappointment in every woman's heart until she bows down to it no longer."[5] That, of course, is the proper answer. Women *are* losers in a patriarchal society, not losers in ourselves, as the epithet implies, not losers because of some personal inadequacy, but losers in a game where the rules and the rewards are so heavily stacked against us. It is the business of the movement to clarify to all women what we are losing and to help us understand that we are the victims and not the perpetrators of loss.

A White Middle-Class Movement

To a movement that proposes to speak to all women, a movement in which the term *sisterhood* has been of first priority, the charge that we are composed of and concerned with only a small part of the female community, and that part the more privileged segment, is a serious matter.

For a period in feminism in the early twentieth century, in seeking the vote, activist groups put aside their original convictions and exploited themes of ethnic, racial, and class bigotry. It was a period in feminist history that bears scrutiny for the lessons it reveals, yet it does not represent the greatest part of feminist history and thought, but rather the smallest. Eighteenth-century analysis, growing as it did out of the Enlightenment, was strongly egalitarian. The next wave of activism, in the nineteenth century, developed out of abolition, out of the theory of human rights, and out of an absolute conviction in the worth and equality of all people. The first feminists of the second wave came out of the civil rights and antiwar movements of the 1950s and 1960s. Their work, *in its intention,* is both internationalistic and egalitarian in its treatment of class, sex, and race. What is now being called the third wave, the developing consciousness and activism of the newest, youngest feminists, is even more internationalistic, more multicultural than previously.

Certainly, a great deal of writing and activism originated with middle-class women (some from working-class backgrounds). An examination of history reveals, however, that almost all movements for liberation and change have originated among those people who appear privileged beyond the means of those most sorely oppressed. It was they who had the education and training to see beyond their condition to reasons and alternatives, they who could articulate issues and instigate strategies for change, and it was they who had the time and the wherewithal to act. The themes *liberte, egalite* and *fraternite* of the French Revolution originated among the well-educated, well-placed philosophers of the Enlightenment, not among the wretched poor who suffered most and most needed change, and to whom help eventually flowed. Marx and Lenin were intellectuals, and although they hoped for a rising of the masses, Lenin ultimately came to believe in the necessity of an educated vanguard of leadership.

Although the movement may appear to have been instigated by the White middle class (and even this appearance is misleading), it was not meant to be a movement *of* the White middle class. That is, it was not about only the White middle class, nor is it today. Obviously, ending violence against women is the concern of every woman on the globe. The drive for jobs and occupational equity certainly concerns working-class and poor women as much as it does middle-class women. Opening skilled and semi-skilled unions to women, reforming clerical and secretarial occupations, and expanding women's place in government-funded poverty relief projects are all goals of the feminist movement. Securing the right of women to control our own bodies affects poor women even more than it does the affluent. Welfare reform *in favor of women and their children* has long been a feminist goal. The extinction of racism, homophobia, and other forms of bigotry is a major feminist target.

Where the women's movement originally erred was not in its intentions but in individuals' failure to see; this was a result of lack of development, lack of sufficient perceptiveness. Like much of the society around us, feminists need greater sensitivity to *difference* and to the difference in our lives that difference makes. This has led many of us to lump all women into one category—woman—and to assume that female experience is always the same. Hester Eisenstein described the error as

a false universalism that generalized about the experience of women, ignoring the specificities of race, class, and culture. A feminist perspective assumed that all women in the world, whatever their race, religion, class, or sexual preference, had something

fundamentally in common. Some versions of feminism took this assumption a step further: they insisted that what women had in common, by virtue of their membership in the group of women, outweighed all of their other differences, or (to put this another way) that the similarity of their situation as female was more fundamental than their economic and cultural differences. The second step in this argument is what I term "false" universalism. To some extent, this habit of thought grew inevitably from the need to establish gender as a legitimate intellectual category. But too often it gave rise to analysis that, in spite of its narrow base of white, middle-class experience, purported to speak about and on behalf of all women, black or white, poor or rich.[6]

Feminists, like the wider society, have suffered from ethnocentrism, or heterosexism, or classism, or ageism, and so on, and it has had the same effect as this always does: It is destructive.

Notable, however, is the seriousness of purpose with which the movement has responded to the problem. All of us have made efforts to increase our sensitivity, to talk and *listen* to one another, to refrain from speaking for others, to make it possible for each to speak and act for herself, and for all to act for each other.

To the question, What are the central challenges for feminist scholars in the future? Catharine Stimpson replied:

To end stupid oversimplifications about "all women" and to speak of the differences among women created by race, class, religion, sexuality, nationality, region and age. I believe that the study of differences among women, which I have named "heterogeneity," is a laboratory in which we can learn how to think about and live with "human differences" themselves.[7]

Tension arises over strategies and issues and between Black and White, Anglo and Latina, gay and straight, moderate and radical feminists, and so on—but diversity and interchange are creative. The ultimate values have stood.

A Diversion from "Real" Oppression

Feminists have been told that the movement, being about "peripheral" and "trivial" matters, dangerously diverts resources away from "real" problems that are far more serious than that of women. That charge is neither new nor unique to our times, as you will see in the selections ahead. When Abigail Adams—a young, intelligent, spunky woman of the emerging republic—wrote to her husband to "remember the ladies," she met with little success. Husband John, at that time a young firebrand in the cause of liberty, eventually the second president of the United States, cautioned her to be patient, for *more important matters* were at stake. In a letter to his compatriot James Sullivan, Adams revealed that although good reasons existed to consider the rights of "the ladies," it was consciously decided *not* to ensure the rights of women citizens in the new society because it would be impractical and raise too many problems.[8] The egalitarian founders of the new republic were too busy, it seems, to open such a messy can of worms as rights of women.

After the Civil War, when Congress forged the new constitutional amendments for human rights, feminists who had worked tirelessly for abolition asked that women be included among the newly protected persons. They were denied their request, told that it was the Negro's day. Paradoxically, only black men, not black women, were guaranteed their rights. You will see in the debate over the Equal Rights Amendment that the omission of women from those civil rights amendments (the Thirteenth through the Fifteenth) continues to haunt us into the present.

During the early 1920s, the new government of the USSR revoked gains made by women in the 1918 revolution on the grounds that the country was under siege and other needs must take priority over women's rights. Last, women have always come last.

In the 1970s, feminists were chided for "muscling in" on affirmative action, federal programs, and educational opportunities; female activists in political parties are even now ridiculed for harping on "trivia" (women's issues) while men worry about "important" things like troop reductions and state-of-the-art bombers.

Today there are those who would go cheerfully to prison for the protection of fetuses, but they would just as happily sacrifice the liberty, autonomy, and quality of life of the women who bear them. The right of a fetus to develop is important.

The right of children, once born, to health and opportunity is not even a consideration. The right of a woman to live well as she sees fit is trivial.

The charge of triviality is a constant in women's history and should not surprise us. Reducing women's suffering to trivia is not only an enduring masculinist perspective but a misogynist strategy as well. To the sane and right-minded, it is self-evident that denial of autonomy and freedom, denial of political, economic, and educational equity, and daily exploitation and violence are as destructive in women's lives as they would be in men's. A revolution that advanced only the position of men could not justly be called a revolution for human rights. Similarly, "affirmative action" that guarantees jobs for men but not for women cannot claim to be a program for "equal" human rights. When political activists demand parity for the poor, the colonized, and the oppressed, they must remember that more than half of those poor, colonized, and oppressed are female and that women are doubly tyrannized in being exploited even within their own subgroups, *as women,* by men. History shows that, when all is said and done, women's movement has been a drive to free all women from the tyranny of misogyny and all humanity from the tyrannies of masculinism—hardly trivial.

EARLIER SISTERS, ONGOING THEMES

To begin to get a clear picture of women's movement through the centuries, we need the widest treatment of history and anthropology. There are paintings on the walls of caves in France that are believed to have been put there by women who were recording their social organization; there are poems by ancient Sumerian and African mothers, letters written by a Renaissance woman to her daughter entering marriage, speeches attributed to condemned "witches," psychological tracts and social treatises—and all carry powerful political messages and implications. By rights, a student of women's experience should see them all. Space, however, precludes so wide a sample. What this chapter presents is just a small segment of women's material, limited for the most part to the United States and to the last two centuries, selected primarily for its representativeness, in period or attitude, and for its fame.

As you sample the writings of foremothers at the end of this chapter, notice how the analyses and arguments of each woman reflect the currents and ideas of her time yet maintain the continuity of the concerns just discussed. Many of the arguments remain powerful and timely today. Consider, too, how drives for progress in women's affairs have often come out of human liberation movements and how necessary it has been for women in every age to remind (male) society that its altruism must be extended to include women in its definition of "humanity."

ENLIGHTENMENT THEMES

The eighteenth century was a period of tremendous upheaval and change both in its social organization and in the philosophical themes that developed out of it. The major issues focused on what rights people should have in society and in government. Certain ideals, although hotly debated and often maintained more in principle than in fact, came to occupy a central position in political philosophy. New importance was given to the ancient idea of *natural human worth*—that is, the value of the individual, which was held to be cosmic in its source (Nature or God) and prior to any privilege or status that could be bestowed by "civilized" society. Men were said to be equal in that value, brothers to one another, rational, and essentially good. Education for all, freedom of opportunity, and the exercise of reason were seen as supplying the major ingredients of progress and harmonious community. Privilege, hereditary wealth and power, and unearned status were represented as villainous. Authority unchecked and exercised without consent was tyranny. Human excellence was composed of rationality, responsibility, emotional and physical health, independence, and tolerance. These were the major ideals of the political thought that we later called the Enlightenment. Although there was often great controversy over how these ideals might be instituted, the values themselves were taken as fundamental by a very large portion of the intelligentsia.

Note that *men* were said to be equal in worth. "All *men* are created equal"—not women. It was left to thinkers like Mary Wollstonecraft to remind the great liberal egalitarians that all they had said re-

garding worth, rights, opportunity, and freedom, as well as the condition and potential of the poor and oppressed and uneducated, could and should be applied to women also. Although Abigail Adams's letter to her husband may have been, in her husband's own words, "saucy," it revealed an important truth. The framers of the great experiment in political rights were themselves guilty of the same tyranny against which they had just rebelled in righteous indignation.

HUMAN RIGHTS AND ABOLITION

Among radical activists of the 1960s, it was a common belief that the best way to attract people to reform movements was not to preach at them, but rather to let them just once confront the establishment, and its barbarity would radicalize them. That, indeed, in large measure was what happened to women activists in the nineteenth century. Incensed by the injustice of slavery, they moved to correct that social sin; then, finding themselves equally sinned against, they became radicalized on their own behalf.

The women learned much from their work in the abolition movement. It was a combination of the Quaker conviction in the equality of people and the Enlightenment commitment to human liberty that they brought against slavery, and it was not a far distance from the rights of slaves to the rights of women. Many women learned for the first time about the effectiveness of political organization, and they experienced the potential and the joy of female unity and assertiveness. They learned to say openly, "Me too. I count also." As women came to see clearly the hypocrisy and cruelty of oppression against Blacks, they gained the insight to recognize it in the lives of all women, and the strength to reject the absurdity and meanness of masculinist values, behavior, and rules.

Presenting so well the analogy between the oppression and liberation of Blacks and that of women is the speech of Sojourner Truth at a rights convention in Ohio in 1851. An ex-slave who had become a lecturer and a preacher, Truth was described by the convention's president, Frances Gage, as an "almost Amazon form, which stood nearly six feet high, head erect, and eyes piercing the upper air like one in a dream." Truth's "Ain't I a Woman?" speech is a most powerful and stirring statement of masculinist injustice and irrationality.

THEMES OF THE FIRST HALF
OF THE TWENTIETH CENTURY

The first half of the twentieth century saw the people of the world drawing closer together, albeit painfully. The rise of industrialism, the need for increased trade, the Great War, the rise of Marxism, and other factors all brought internationalistic questions to the foreground and forced reexamination of many issues. People in the United States had to place themselves in a wider context and reconsider the limits of authority; the sources of government; the uses of knowledge; the concepts of community, social responsibility, and freedom; and even the nature of happiness. During this period the social sciences—sociology, psychology, and anthropology—were evolving, and they, too, were raising new questions: What have we learned about what is desirable and undesirable in our own society, and how should we change it for the better? What does the new study of human behavior tell us about possibilities for the future of life and society? What are the proper limits of science in changing our lives? That is, what should we not or could we not tamper with? What part of us comes from nature (and is therefore unchangeable), and what part originates somewhere else?

The debate over women's issues was affected by the emerging intellectual models. A belief, prevalent among some feminists and nonfeminists alike, is that the women's movement simply died in 1920 with the passage of the Nineteenth Amendment and the winning of suffrage. It is claimed that because the movement narrowed in the latter part of the nineteenth century from very wide-ranging concerns to a total involvement in suffrage, and because the winning of that goal required a Herculean effort, when it was won, activists simply folded in exhaustion. This argument has some basis. Certainly, political activity on a scale of the preceding seven decades did diminish. One could look for reasons in the Depression of the 1930s, in the political turmoil of the entire world during that same decade, and in the vast output of human energy in World War II during the 1940s. Such monumental

events, coupled with the belief that suffrage created the opportunity to cure all women's ills, might indeed have led to a decrease in organized activism.

Yet we can bring the idea that the movement died (or even went to sleep) into different focus by placing it in the context of events from the wider intellectual scene. As general political activism in the 1930s centered mainly in socialism and Marxism, so did feminism. Many of the questions raised by the original American feminists in the nineteenth century were debated by female socialists of this time—the isolation of housework, the opportunity for salaried work, the right to an independent identity, the oppressive elements of marriage and romance. (In fact, feminist groups of all kinds during these years and later were accused of Bolshevist sympathies.)

During this time, just as the impetus for social change often came out of the newly developing social sciences, so, too, did speculation about new possibilities for women's personal lives. In the 1920s, Freud's theories of female sexuality (among others, that females *had* sexuality) touched off a whole set of issues that were carried into the 1930s and '40s by psychologists like Karen Horney and her contemporaries. Reinforced by the research of various feministically inclined anthropologists, like Margaret Mead and Ruth Benedict, more positive attitudes toward women's sexuality occasioned lively activism on behalf of biological freedom. The birth control and planned parenthood movement was born and flourished between the 1920s and the 1950s; birth control became "legalized" in the mid-1930s, and the birth control pill and other advances in contraception were made available during the 1960s.

In the 1920s, the suffragist Alice Paul and her coworkers of the radical Congressional Union introduced the Equal Rights Amendment and lobbied for its passage. The National Council of Women, the Women's International League for Peace and Freedom, the League of Women Voters, and other organizations like these, each with its own political agenda, came into existence during this period. Many still function today.

In the first half of the twentieth century, America's economic system underwent tremendous changes, as did women's participation in it. After World War I, women moved into the public workplace in growing numbers on every level. Frequently, as they grew in numbers, they organized. Women were particularly active in the trade union movement. In the professions, organizations such as Business and Professional Women (BPW) not only supported women in gaining better educational and business opportunities but also lobbied—and still do—for other women's goals in the legislatures and with presidential commissions.

Given all this activity, it is clearly not the case that exhausted women let their movement die. It is more accurate to say that many suffrage activists moved into different areas of activity and that new feminist women expressed their values through these different models. The movement—less centralized, less political, less visible in some ways, even less populous— was nonetheless alive.

THE SECOND HALF AND
THE SECOND WAVE

Although women's issues as a major focus of public discussion receded in importance during the 1940s, conditions that would change this continued to ferment. The Depression had had a negative effect on women's position in the economy. What jobs existed had gone to men, and women lost ground in education, professional status, work rights, and salary. During World War II, however, conditions changed. Positions left empty by men gone to war and jobs in the burgeoning industrial sector had to be filled by women. Laboring in factories and offices, managing small businesses, running farms, teaching college, and building tanks, women did very well. Jobs that, until then, had been deemed "for men only" were effectively accommodated by women, and they learned an unforgettable lesson: There is no masculine or feminine occupation.

From 1945 on, even immediately after the war, when many women lost their jobs to returning veterans, the number and percentage of working women of all kinds—married and unmarried, young and mature, parent and nonparent—increased dramatically, and the realities of women's lives changed. But what changed very little, and what eventually was to cause much of the conflict that crystallized in the 1950s and exploded in the 1960s, was the cultural mythology, the projected ideals of feminin-

ity and the "place" of women. Except for the brief wartime appearance of the patriotic Rosie the Riveter, America's dream-girl image never adjusted to women's new realities and changing needs. In fact, the gap between myth and reality widened. In the late 1940s and the 1950s, popular culture stressed the vision of the virginal, naive girl-next-door and the softly pliant housewife in cotton dress and three-inch spike heels tending single-mindedly to family and home. On the surface, at least, it was a time of traditional values and "togetherness."

Betty Friedan, in *The Feminine Mystique,* credits the wars, especially the Korean War, for this period of retrenchment. Disillusioned and emotionally exhausted, people (particularly men) craved the security and nurturance of a stable family and home, and they retreated to the familiar comforting arrangement of marriage, or at least the image of it, and to the concept of the nurturing, tender wife-mother. This is at least partly true.

Again, however, one must be careful not to oversimplify, and one must seek explanations for women's situation with an eye to events in the wider culture. A period of apparent quiescence in the 1950s harbored within it the seeds of turmoil. Although the decade was known for a kind of apathy toward political and national events, underneath it broiled with dissention; it saw the Cold War, the second "red scare," Joseph McCarthy's cynicism and hate, and McCarthyism. "The corporation man" and the man in gray flannel flourished, but so did Jack Kerouac and anticonformist "beatniks." In 1954, the landmark case *Brown vs. the Board of Education,* judged educational segregation unconstitutional, and it was a day in 1955 when Rosa Parks' refusal to stand in the back of the bus touched off the civil rights marches and boycotts. These and other events were as much a part of the personal history of the new feminist women of the 1960s as were the television images of superwife.

Somewhere between the opposing realities, between prom gowns and Rosa Parks, between affluence and Vietnam, between maternal admonitions of sexual purity and the realities of displaced homemakers, the feminists of the second wave emerged alive and kicking.

Early in the 1950s, Simone de Beauvoir's book *The Second Sex* had appeared in English in the

United States, offering a profound philosophical analysis not only of certain aspects of injustice toward women, such as economic and political discrimination, but of the whole distorted conceptualization of femaleness in a patriarchal world. In 1963, Betty Friedan published *The Feminine Mystique,* treating the hidden disappointment and unhappiness of many American women in male-female relationships, in the structures of marriage and motherhood, in their lives, and exploding the cultural myth of the happy homemaker. These and other writings in novels, newspapers, and magazines were part of a widening examination of women's lives, not only among academics but among a growing number of ordinary women.

In the mid-to-late 1960s, civil rights activism and opposition to the Vietnam War generated scores of activist groups and organizations on college campuses all over the United States. Women's participation in these activities and groups had a variety of consequences. Just as their ill treatment by many men in the abolitionist movement made nineteenth-century women reflect on their own circumstances, discrimination and misogyny in twentieth-century activism had the same effect—young women began to question society and politics not only from a class or racial perspective but from a *female* perspective, a gender perspective. Furthermore, they found that concepts and strategies learned in a drive for international or racial justice could be employed in a drive for *women's* justice, and increasingly they were. Finally, as many women activists were students, they carried the perspectives, terminology, ideas, values, attitudes, and expectations they had developed in social activism into their studies and their writing. What emerged was the feminist analysis of the "women's liberation movement," as it was called in the early years of the second wave.

One of the most influential works of that time—both among feminists and in the public eye—was the book *Sexual Politics* by Kate Millett, a Columbia University graduate student finishing a doctorate in English. In some ways, Millett was typical of early second-wave activists: She had served in CORE (Congress of Racial Equality) in the 1950s, supported student strikes while teaching at Barnard College in New York City, and served in NOW when it was formed. When *Sexual Politics* was pub-

lished in 1970, it not only received wide press attention, bringing the women's liberation movement into public awareness, but also contributed to the developing women's movement both a powerful theoretical base and a terminology that is today still a vibrant part of feminist analysis. "Can the relationship between the sexes be viewed in a political light at all?" she asked. Well, that would depend on how "politics" was defined, wouldn't it? Millett proceeded to offer a new, thoroughly modern definition of politics and applied it to the relationship of women and men in society:

> *The term "politics" shall refer to power-structured relationships, arrangement whereby one group of persons is controlled by another. . . . [S]ex is a status category with political implications. . . .*
>
> *In America, recent events have forced us to acknowledge at last that the relationship between the races is indeed a political one which involves the general control of one collectivity, defined by birth, over another collectivity, also defined by birth. Groups who rule by birthright are fast disappearing, yet there remains one ancient and universal scheme for the domination of one birth group by another— the scheme that prevails in the area of sex. . . .*
> *. . . a disinterested examination of our system of sexual relationship must point out that the situation between the sexes now, and throughout history, is a case of . . . a relationship of dominance and subordinance. What goes largely unexamined, often even unacknowledged (yet is institutionalized nonetheless) in our social order, is the birthright priority whereby males rule females. Through this system a most ingenious form of "interior colonization" has been achieved. It is one which tends moreover to be sturdier than any form of segregation, and more rigorous than class stratification, more uniform, certainly more enduring. However muted its present appearance may be, sexual domination obtains nevertheless as perhaps the most pervasive ideology of our culture and provides its most fundamental concept of power.*
> *This is so because our society, like all other historical civilizations, is a patriarchy.*[9]

And there it is, the kernel of an idea that was to be enlarged, developed, spun out for decades. It is hard to realize today, after nearly thirty years of theorizing, how radical, how pivotal this insight was in 1970.

INTO THE FUTURE: THE NEXT WAVE

Feminists must decide many issues for the future. We are feeling the full brunt of an antifeminist, anti-woman backlash, not only in the United States but all over the world. A strong reactionary wave of political and economic "conservatism" has reversed many of women's hard-won victories of the past. In many countries, women are being pushed out of education, employment, and public affairs and back into economic dependency, if not outright physical seclusion. In the United States, affirmative action, comparable worth, and many upward mobility programs lie almost in tatters. Religious fundamentalism in many parts of the globe has vowed absolute enmity to women's reproductive liberty, and they are making progress. Everywhere increasing numbers of women and their children are poor, homeless, and hungry. The earth we have vowed to protect is being devoured for its resources. All over the world, war, famine, and political repression hit women worst.

Fewer young women today are actively involved in politics or social activism. Indeed, they seem less aware, less concerned, than they were thirty years ago. Yet some observers of society see the possibilities of the tide turning. Precisely because of the intensity of the horrors women are suffering—the wholesale rape and murder of female populations in ethnic wars, the expansion worldwide of the purchase and abuse of women and girls, increasing degrees of oppression for women under theocratic regimes, starvation and illiteracy, and so much more—it is possible to see seeds of the rebirth of activism in the present that will flourish in the coming century just as the worst repressions of the 1950s gave birth to the energy of the 1960s. This is already visible. Women around the globe are coming together, working at building a worldwide women's movement; they are agitating within their own countries for the recognition of women's rights at home and elsewhere. In the United States the "women's vote" was considered a major factor in the last presidential election, as were the issues of reproductive and sexual freedom. Women's groups here are joining with international environmentalist groups and organizations working for peace and hunger relief.

We are the ones who can decide how the energy of the new millennium will be employed. What shall we do? Where shall we put our greatest efforts? What should be our priorities? How can we revitalize the energy, optimism, and power of women's movement, and where shall we take it?

These questions are put to all of us. For serious feminists, these tough questions should be asked and kept ever in mind as we go about our business. As we grow in sophistication and influence, we need greater unity, a better sense of our ultimate direction, ever more effective strategies. We need ideas more carefully defined and strongly supported to communicate with one another, to persuade the outsider, and to counter our challengers.

In 1977, Barbara Jordan, legislator and political leader, gave the keynote speech at the First National Women's Conference in Houston. She said:

> *If Americans were asked to differentiate or distinguish between what characterized other countries and what characterizes us, we would say our high regard for the individual. That's the thing which makes us different.*
>
> *We endorse personal and political freedom as a national right of human pride. Human rights are more than abstractions, particularly when they are limited or non-existent. . . .*
>
> *Women are human. We know our rights are limited. We know our rights are violated. We need a domestic human rights program. . . .*
>
> *At a time when this country is drifting, if it is not shifting to the right, civil rights and affirmative action efforts are lagging.*
>
> *Not making a difference is a cost we cannot afford. . . .*
>
> *The cause of equal and human rights will reap what is sown November 18th through November 21st, 1977.*
>
> *What will you reap?*
> *What will you sow?*[10]

More than twenty years have passed since Jordan's words were spoken, and, extraordinarily, the country is *still* drifting, if not shifting to the right; civil and human rights are still lagging; and not making a difference is still a cost we cannot afford.

Indeed, the only thing that we must change about Jordan's comments is this: The cause of equality will reap what is sown *today* and tomorrow and thereafter—by all of us and each of us.

What will *you* sow?

Notes

1. *Ladies' Home Journal,* September 1922, p. 7; quoted in Judith Papachristou, ed., *Women Together* (New York: Knopf, 1976), p. 203.

2. Quoted in Vern L. and Bonnie Bullough, *The Subordinate Sex* (Baltimore: Penguin Books, 1974), p. 88.

3. Author's Introduction to Mary Wollstonecraft, *A Vindication of the Rights of Woman* (New York: Dutton, Everyman Library, 1929), p. 3.

4. Quoted in Papachristou, *Women Together,* p. 32.

5. Papachristou, *Women Together,* p. 32.

6. Hester Eisenstein, *Contemporary Feminist Thought* (Boston: G. K. Hall, 1983), p. 132.

7. Catharine R. Stimpson, "Setting Agendas, Defining Challenges," *The Women's Review of Books* 6, no. 5 (February 1989), p. 14.

8. See the Adams letters in this chapter.

9. Kate Millett, *Sexual Politics* (New York: Doubleday, 1970), pp. 23–25, passim.

10. Keynote speech, First Plenary Session, the First National Women's Conference, November 19, 1977. Reported in Helene Mandelbaum, ed., *The Spirit of Houston* (Washington, DC: National Commission on the Observance of International Women's Year, 1978), p. 223.

Rediscovering American Women—A Chronology Highlighting Women's History in the United States . . .

National Commission on the Observance of International Women's Year

The first part of this chronology was included in The Spirit of Houston, *the report to President Carter following the conference in Texas of the National Commission on the Observance of International Women's Year, the First National Women's Conference in 1977. No doubt it was meant to remind us that women* have *been a force in American history, sometimes against all odds.*

The update following the Houston Chronology was compiled by Kim Blankenship, a young feminist activist, leader, and attorney in St. Louis; Anne Bezdek, a doctoral candidate in philosophy and women's studies; and Sheila Ruth, author of this volume. We must remind ourselves and the world that a chronology of women's history should require constant updating. Time and events do not stand still, and neither must women's activism.

THE REFORMATION WHICH WE PROPOSE, in its utmost scope, is radical and universal. It is not the mere perfecting of a progress already in motion, a detail of some established plan, but it is an epochal movement—the emancipation of a class, the redemption of half the world, and a reorganization of all social, political, and industrial interests and institutions.

—PAULINA WRIGHT DAVIS
Woman's Rights Convention
Worcester, Massachusetts, 1850

"Rediscovering American Women" was reprinted from *The Spirit of Houston,* the First National Women's Conference, an Official Report to the President, the Congress and the People of the United States, March 1978. Washington, DC: National Commission on the Observance of International Women's Year, U.S. Department of State, 1978.

NATIONAL COMMISSION ON THE OBSERVANCE OF INTERNATIONAL WOMEN'S YEAR

1587
Virginia Dare, a girl, was the first baby born to English colonists in the New World. The daughter of Elenor White Dare and Ananias Dare, she was born on August 18 in Roanoke Island, Virginia.

circa 1600
The Constitution of the Iroquois Confederation of Nations guaranteed women the sole right and power to regulate war and peace. The women also selected tribal leaders.

1607
Princess Pocahontas saved the life of Captain John Smith, one of the founders of the Jamestown Colony, by interceding with her father, king of the Powhatan Confederacy.

1620
The Mayflower Compact was signed aboard ship by 39 men and male servants among the 102 passengers aboard the Pilgrim vessel. Women, who were not considered free agents, were not asked to sign. Only five of the 18 wives who arrived in Plymouth on the *Mayflower* survived the first harsh winter in the new land.

1638
Anne Hutchinson was excommunicated by the Puritan church in Boston for challenging its religious doctrines. One of her followers, Mary Dyer, later became a Quaker and was hanged in 1660 in Boston for refusing to accept a sentence of banishment. An-

other woman who fought for freedom of conscience was Lady Deborah Moody, who moved from Massachusetts to Gravesend, Long Island where she and her companions established a community based on religious tolerance and self-government.

1648

The first attempt by a white woman to obtain political power in America originated with Margaret Brent. In a petition to the Colony of Maryland House of Delegates she requested two votes in votes in the Assembly. She believed she merited one vote as a landowner, a vote a man would have obtained without question, and one vote as the executrix for the deceased brother of Lord Baltimore. Her request was denied.

1652

Elizabeth Poole formed a joint stock company in Taunton, Massachusetts to manufacture iron bars. This was one of the first successful iron production plants in the colonies.

1717

Twenty young women sent by King Louis XIV aboard a "brides' ship" to Louisiana to marry French settlers there refused to do so when they arrived in the primitive colony. Their revolt became known as the "petticoat rebellion."

1735

During the eight months that printer Peter Zenger was in jail in New York awaiting trial on charges of printing seditious materials, his wife, Catherine, kept his printshop running. She set type, read proof, wrote, and continued publication of his *New York Weekly Journal*. After her husband's death in 1746, Catherine Zenger continued to publish the newspaper.

The first woman publisher in the Colonies was believed to be Elizabeth Timothy, who took over her late husband's paper, the weekly *South Carolina Gazette*, in Charleston, South Carolina. An estimated 30 women were newspaper publishers in the 18th century Colonies.

1761

The first black poet whose work was to be preserved arrived in Boston harbor on a slave ship

from western Africa. Then seven years old, Phyllis Wheatley was taught to read and write English and Latin, and her poetry became a focus for antislavery forces.

American Revolution

Women's groups, such as the Daughters of Liberty, organized to boycott tea and later to provide clothing and supplies for the Army. Deborah Sampson served as a soldier, for which she received a military pension, and Molly Pitcher assisted in the battlefield.

Groups of New Jersey women took vigorous action against husbands who abused their wives. Entering the home of a known wife-beater in the evening, they stripped the man and spanked him with sticks, shouting, "Woe to the men that beat their wives."

1777

Abigail Adams wrote to her husband, John Adams, and suggested, ". . . in the code of laws . . . I desire you to remember the ladies and be more generous and favorable to them than your ancestors. Do not put such unlimited power into the hands of the husbands. Remember all men would be tyrants if they could. If particular care and attention is not paid to the ladies, we are determined to foment a rebellion and will not hold ourselves bound by any laws in which we have no voice or representation." The future President replied: "Depend upon it, we know better than to repeal our Masculine systems."

In the years immediately following the American Revolution, women had the right to vote in some parts of Virginia and New Jersey. Later, the adoption of State constitutions limited the franchise to white males and excluded women.

1788

Mercy Otis Warren, the first American woman historian, a political satirist and playwright, wrote her *Observations on the New Constitution* in which she deplored the absence of a Bill of Rights. The first 10 Amendments (the Bill of Rights) were added to the Constitution in 1791.

1800–1820

Deborah Skinner operated the first power loom. In the first two decades of the 19th century, factories were established employing large numbers of women and children, particularly in the New England textile industry.

1804

Sacajawea, a young Indian woman, accompanied the Lewis and Clark expedition to the West. Her skill and courage were credited with helping to make the exploration a success.

1805

Mercy Otis Warren published a three-volume history of the American Revolution which is still used by historians.

1810

Mother Elizabeth Bayley Seton founded and became head of the first sisterhood in America, the Sisters of Charity of St. Joseph's. She was canonized as the Catholic Church's first U.S.-born Saint by Pope Paul VI in 1975.

1821

Emma Willard founded a female seminary at Troy, N.Y., the first effort to provide secondary education for women. In 1837 Mary Lyon founded Mt. Holyoke Seminary (later College), which provided education similar to that offered to men at the better men's colleges.

1828

The first known strike of women workers over wages took place in Dover, N.H. Similar strikes were waged in Lowell, Mass., in 1834 and 1836 by women textile workers protesting reduced real wages.

1833

Prudence Crandall opened a school for black girls in her Connecticut home. She was arrested, persecuted, and forced to give up the school to protect her pupils from violence.

1837

First national Anti-Slavery Convention of American Women met in New York City. This was the first national gathering of women organized for action without the assistance or supervision of men.

1839

After this time, most states began to recognize through legislation the right of married women to hold property. In New York State, Ernestine Rose and Susan B. Anthony led a petition campaign for women's rights. Mrs. Rose, Polish-born daughter of a rabbi, addressed the New York state legislature on at least five occasions until the body enacted a married women's property law in 1848.

1841

The first woman graduated from Oberlin College, having completed an easier "literary" course. At Oberlin, female students were required to wash male students' clothing, clean their rooms, serve them at meals, and were not permitted to recite in public or work in the fields with male students.

1845

Woman in the Nineteenth Century, written by Margaret Fuller, was an early and influential publication urging women's rights. Fuller wrote: "We would have every path laid open to Woman as freely as to Man."

1847

Trained by her father as an astronomer, Maria Mitchell at age 29 discovered a comet while standing on a rooftop scanning the sky with a telescope. In 1848 she became the first woman elected to the American Academy of Arts and Sciences in Boston.

1848

The first Women's Rights Convention was held in Seneca Falls, N.Y., led by Lucretia Mott and Elizabeth Cady Stanton. Its Declaration of Sentiments, paraphrased from the Declaration of Independence, stated that "all men and women are created equal." Eleven resolutions were approved, including equality in education, employment, and the law. A resolution advocating the right to suffrage passed by a narrow margin, with some delegates feeling that it was too daring a proposal.

The first issue of *The Lily,* a temperance paper, appeared with an editorial by Amelia Bloomer, later known for her experiment in clothing reform.

1849

Elizabeth Blackwell received her medical degree at Geneva, N.Y., becoming the first woman doctor in the United States.

1851

Sojourner Truth, ex-slave, electrified an audience in Akron, Ohio by drawing a parallel between the struggle for women's rights and the struggle to abolish slavery. In answer to arguments that women were delicate creatures who necessarily led sheltered lives, she described the hard physical labor she had done as a black woman slave and demanded, "And ain't I a Woman?"

1854

The first American day nursery opened in New York City for children of poor working mothers. In later years, licensing standards were established, but only minimal Federal funding was provided, except during the Depression and World War II.

1860

Elizabeth Peabody, a teacher, writer, and associate of the Transcendentalists, organized in Boston the first formal kindergarten in the United States. It was modeled on the Froebel kindergarten system in Germany.

Civil War

Women were responsible for the establishment of the U.S. Sanitary Commission. Dorothea Dix, Clara Barton, and Mother Bickerdyke served as nurses and trained others. Dr. Mary Walker was one of several women who served as doctors and surgeons at the front.

Susan B. Anthony organized the National Women's Loyal League to collect signatures for passage of the 13th amendment abolishing slavery. Women's rights leaders were prominent in the struggle to end slavery.

Women entered government offices to replace clerks who went to war. This established women not only in Government service but in clerical work. After the invention of the typewriter in 1867, women flocked to white collar office work, which began to be considered a women's specialty.

1864

Working Women's Protective Union was founded in New York to ensure fair treatment for women wage earners. Thousands of women were working in factories.

1865

Vassar College opened, offering the first college-level curriculum for women. Five years later, Wellesley and Smith Colleges were founded. Although women were admitted to some coeducational institutions, their opportunities to study with men were limited until the University of Michigan admitted women in 1870 and Cornell University became coeducational in 1872.

1866

Elizabeth Cady Stanton became the first woman candidate for Congress, although women could not vote. She received 24 votes.

1868

The first women's suffrage amendment to the Constitution was introduced by Senator S. C. Pomeroy of Kansas. In 1878 another proposal for woman suffrage, which came to be known as the Anthony Amendment, was introduced.

1869

After passage of the 14th and 15th amendments granting suffrage to all males, both black and white, leaders of the women's movement determined to press their own claims more vigorously. Because of differences over strategy, two organizations were formed. The National Woman Suffrage Association was led by Elizabeth Cady Stanton and Susan B. Anthony while the more conservative American Women Suffrage Association was directed by Lucy Stone and Julia Ward Howe. Unification of these two groups was not achieved until 1890.

1870

Women gained the right to vote and to serve on juries in the Territory of Wyoming.

1872

Susan B. Anthony attempted to vote in Rochester, N.Y. She was tried and convicted of voting illegally but refused to pay the $100 fine.

1873

Belva Lockwood was admitted to the bar of the District of Columbia and in 1879 won passage of a law granting women lawyers the right to practice law before the U.S. Supreme Court. She ran for President in 1884 as candidate of the National Equal Rights Party and got 4,149 votes.

1874

Under the leadership of Frances Willard, the Women's Christian Temperance Union became the largest women's organization in the Nation. During this same period, the Young Women's Christian Association evolved to meet the needs of working women away from home. Other women organized for cultural purposes and by 1890 the General Federation of Women's Clubs was formed. The Association of Collegiate Alumnae, organized in 1882 to investigate the health of college women, eventually became the American Association of University Women.

1878

The Knights of Labor advocated equal pay for equal work, the abolition of child labor under age 14, and in 1881 opened their membership to working women. By 1886, 50,000 women were members.

1880s

Lucy Gonzalez Parson, a labor organizer, traveled in 16 states to raise funds to help organize women garment workers and others. She founded *The Alarm* newspaper and edited *The Liberator*.

1890

Elizabeth Cady Stanton was elected first president of the unified suffrage organization, the National American Woman Suffrage Association. She also studied organized religion as a major source of women's inferior status and in 1895 published *The Woman's Bible*.

1893

Rebelling against an invitation to organize a Jewish women's committee to serve at receptions during Chicago's big Columbian Exposition, Hannah Greenbaum Solomon invited Jewish women from all over the country to attend a conference at the same time as the Exposition. The result was formation of the National Council of Jewish Women, dedicated to education, social reform, and issues of concern to women.

1896

The National Association for Colored Women, the first national organization of black women, was established, and Mary Church Terrell served as first president.

1898

Charlotte Perkins Gilman published *Women and Economics,* in which she decried the wasted efforts and the low economic status of the housewife. Gilman advocated the industrialization of housework and the socialization of child care.

1899

Florence Kelley became general secretary of the National Consumers League and worked for legislation in behalf of working women and children.

1900

The first decade of the 20th century showed the greatest increase in the female labor force of any period prior to 1940. New groups were formed to protect women and children from exploitation by industry. Several unions were organized at this time composed largely of women in the garment trades. Mother Jones, a labor organizer, led a march of children who worked in the Pennsylvania textile mills to the home of President Roosevelt in Oyster Bay, Long Island to call public attention to their plight.

1902

Carrie Chapman Catt organized the International Suffrage Alliance to help establish effective women's groups in other countries.

1904

Mary McLeod Bethune founded Bethune-Cookman College in Daytona Beach, Florida.

1907

The landmark case, *Muller* v. *Oregon,* established sex as a valid classification for protective legislation. The sociological type of evidence assembled by Florence Kelley and Josephine Goldmark to convince the court that overlong hours were harmful to the future of the race provided a model brief for later laws. While labor laws applying only to women were on the whole beneficial to women in the early part of the century, when jobs were largely sex segregated, the laws did result in loss of job opportunities for those seeking "male" jobs.

1908

A poem, "The New Colossus," written by Emma Lazarus, a poet who had died in 1887, was inscribed on a tablet in the pedestal of the Statue of Liberty in New York harbor. Its most famous lines: "Give me your tired, your poor, Your huddled masses yearning to be free . . ."

1909

The first significant strike of working women, "The Uprising of the 20,000," was conducted by shirt-waist makers in New York to protest low wages and long working hours. The National Women's Trade Union League (founded in 1903) mobilized public opinion and financial support for the strikers.

1911

The Triangle fire on March 25, in which 146 women shirtwaist operators were killed, dramatized the poor working conditions of immigrant women. A report of the Senate Investigation of the Condition of Women and Child Wage Earners led to establishment of the Children's Bureau (1912) and later the Women's Bureau of the Department of Labor (1920).

Liga Feminil Mexicanista was founded in Laredo, Texas to insure that the Mexican American culture and heritage would be preserved and transmitted.

1913

Harriet Tubman, ex-slave and most famous "conductor" on the Underground Railroad, died in poverty. Before the Civil War, she made 19 rescue trips to save hundreds of slaves. During the war, she served as a nurse, spy, and scout and led daring raids into the South.

1914

The Alaska Native Sisterhood was formed as an auxiliary of the Alaska Native Brotherhood, the most powerful union of native peoples in Alaska.

1915

Jane Addams, "the angel of Hull House," Carrie Chapman Catt and other women leaders held a meeting of 3,000 women in Washington, D.C. on January 10 which organized the Women's Peace Party. They called for the abolition of war.

Margaret Sanger, having studied birth control clinics abroad, returned home to campaign against the legal barriers to the dissemination of contraceptive information. She and other women, including Emma Goldman, were jailed for their efforts.

1916

Impatient with the slow pace of the woman suffrage campaign, Alice Paul organized the National Woman's Party to conduct a more militant strategy. Its followers organized suffrage parades, picketed the White House, and chained themselves to its fence. Repeatedly arrested and imprisoned, the women protested their illegal and harsh confinement by going on hunger strikes. They were force-fed by prison authorities. Their suffering aroused widespread public outrage and was credited with hastening ratification of the suffrage amendment.

1917

Jeannette Rankin, a Republican from Montana, was the first woman elected to serve in Congress. The first vote she cast opposed American entry into World War I. She was the only woman to serve in Congress before adoption of the Federal suffrage amendment.

1919

An outgrowth of women suffrage organizations, the League of Women Voters was set up to educate women for their new political and social responsibilities. The National Federation of Business and Professional Women's Clubs was also organized.

1919

Jane Addams led a delegation of American women to a Women's Conference in Zurich, which paralleled the official peace conference in Paris. They formed the Women's International League for Peace and Freedom, with Jane Addams as president and Emily Green Balch as secretary-treasurer.

1920

On August 26, the 19th amendment was ratified and 26 million women of voting age finally gained the right to vote.

1923

The Equal Rights Amendment, advocated by Alice Paul and the National Woman's Party, was introduced in Congress for the first time. Most women did not support this effort because they feared it would threaten protective legislation for women workers who labored in sweatshop conditions.

In the following years, the momentum of women's campaigns for access to equal education, employment, and professional achievement waned. Discrimination against women intensified. From 1925 to 1945 medical schools placed a quota of five percent on female admissions. Columbia and Harvard law schools refused to consider women applicants.

1928

Doris Stevens became the first president of the Inter-American Commission of Women, the Organization of American States.

1930

The Depression encouraged reaction against any change in women's traditional domestic role. Legislation restricted the employment of married women, and there was strong public disapproval of women working when men were unable to find employment. Nevertheless, many women performed low-paid labor to support their families. Opportunities for women to obtain college educations and graduate training were limited by lack of financial support.

1931

Suma Sugi, the first Nisei lobbyist (American born of Japanese ancestry), succeeded in amending the Cable Act of 1922 to permit American-born Asian women to regain their American citizenship upon termination of their marriage to an alien.

1933

Frances Perkins, the first woman to hold a Cabinet post, was appointed to head the Department of Labor by President Roosevelt and served in his cabinet for 12 years.

Eleanor Roosevelt turned her 12 years in the White House into a model of activism and humanitarian concern for future First Ladies.

1935

The National Council of Negro Women was founded in New York, with Mary McLeod Bethune as its first president.

1940

The percentage of working women was almost the same as it had been in 1900, when one of every five women worked for wages. After the U.S. entered World War II, wartime needs required the employment of large numbers of women. "Rosie the Riveter" became a national symbol. After the war, many women remained in the labor force, although many were displaced by returning veterans. Between 1940–60, the number of working women and the proportion of working wives doubled. More women over 35 were employed in rapidly expanding business and industry. Inequities in pay and advancement opportunities became more obvious limitations affecting large numbers of women. Economic conditions produced a favorable environment for the increasing demands for equity voiced by the women of the 1960's.

1950

A repressive decade for Chicana activists. Several were deported for their attempts to organize communities. Also deported was film actress Rosaura Revueltas, featured in the film, "Salt of the Earth," about striking miners in the Southwest.

1952

The Constitution of the Commonwealth of Puerto Rico was enacted, embodying the Equal Rights Amendment.

1953

Simone de Beauvoir's *The Second Sex*, a scholarly and historical analysis of the inferior status of women, was published in the United States.

1956

Rosa Parks, a black seamstress, refused to give up her bus seat to a white man and was arrested, touching off the Montgomery, Alabama, bus boycott.*

1957

Daisy Bates, coeditor with her husband of a black newspaper and president of the Arkansas National Association for the Advancement of Colored People, acted as spokesperson and counselor for the nine black youths who desegrated Little Rock Central High School.

1960

Women Strike for Peace was formed as an outgrowth of protests against resumption of nuclear testing by the Soviet Union and United States.

---

*Rosa Parks' action took place in December of 1955, setting off the boycott, which came to fruition in 1956.

1961

The President's Commission on the Status of Women, chaired by Eleanor Roosevelt, was established by Executive Order 10980, with a charge to study seven areas: education, private and Federal employment, social insurance and tax laws, protective labor laws, civil and political rights and family law, and home and community. Esther Peterson, Director of the Women's Bureau, was the moving force in its establishment, with the assistance of then Vice President Lyndon Johnson.

1962

In Michigan, the Governor's Commission on the Status of Women became the first State commission. Union women Mildred Jeffrey and Myra Wolfgang were the leaders in obtaining its establishment.

1962

Acting on a recommendation of his Commission on the Status of Women, President Kennedy issued an order requiring Federal employees to be hired and promoted without regard to sex. Prior to this order, Federal managers could restrict consideration to men or women.

1963

The National Federation of Business and Professional Women's Clubs adopted as its top priority the nationwide establishment of State commissions on the status of women. By June 1964 when the first national conference was held, there were 24 commissions, and by the end of the year there were 33.

The Equal Pay Act was passed in June, effective June 1964, after formation of a coalition of women's organizations and unions to support it in Congress.

The Feminine Mystique by Betty Friedan was published. Describing social pressures that sought to limit women to roles as wives and mothers, it became a national and influential best seller.

The Interdepartmental Committee on the Status of Women and Citizens Advisory Council on the Status of Women were established by Executive Order 11126, with Margaret Hickey as its first chairperson. The Committee and Council sponsored national meetings of the State commissions, issued annual reports on issues affecting women, and made legislative and administrative recommendations. Subsequent chairpersons were Maurine

Neuberger and Jacqueline Gutwillig. (The Council was terminated on August 22, 1977 by Executive Order 12007.)

1964

The Spring issue of *Daedalus,* Journal of the American Academy of Arts and Sciences, devoted an entire issue to "The Woman in America," enhancing the academic respectability of the subject. Alice Rossi's "Equality Between the Sexes: An Immodest Proposal," probably the most widely reproduced article in the women's movement, first appeared here.

Title 7 of the Civil Rights Act, enacted in 1964, prohibited discrimination in employment because of sex, race, color, religion, and national origin.

The first meeting of the First National Institute on Girls' Sports was held "to increase the depth of experience and expand opportunities for women."

1965

The U.S. Supreme Court found that a Connecticut law banning contraceptives was unconstitutional because it violated the right to privacy. *Griswold* v. *State of Connecticut,* 381 U.S.C. 479.

1966

A Federal court declared that an Alabama law excluding women from State juries was in violation of the equal protection clause of the 14th amendment, the first time in modern times a Federal court had found a law making sex distinctions unconstitutional. *White* v. *Crook,* 251 F. Supp. 401.

The National Organization for Women (NOW) was organized at the Third National Conference of Governors' Commissions on the Status of Women as a culmination of dissatisfaction with the failure to enforce Title 7 of the Civil Rights Act. Among the 28 women who founded NOW were: Betty Friedan, Aileen Hernandez, Dr. Kathryn Clarenbach, Dr. Pauli Murray, Marguerite Rawalt, Catherine Conroy, Dorothy Haener, and Dr. Nancy Knaak.

1967

The first "women's liberation" group was formed in Chicago, partially in rebellion against the low status of young women in civil rights and "new left" campus movements. Similar groups were independently organized in New York, Toronto, Detroit, Seattle, San Francisco, and other cities. Initially concerned with analyzing the origins, nature, and extent of women's subservient status in society, some groups used the technique of "consciousness-raising" sessions to help women liberate themselves from restricting inferior roles. Most of the groups were small, egalitarian and opposed to elitism. They called for far-reaching and radical change in almost all aspects of American society.

Executive Order 11246, prohibiting discrimination by Federal contractors, was amended to include sex discrimination, with an effective date of October 1968.

A law repealing arbitrary restrictions on military rank held by women was signed by the President.

1968

The Church and the Second Sex by Dr. Mary Daly, a scholarly critique of Catholic Church doctrine, influenced Protestant as well as Catholic women. The first stirrings of Catholic feminist dissent occurred at the Second Vatican Council. The American branch of St. Joan's Alliance, an international Catholic feminist organization, had been formed in 1965 by Frances McGillicuddy.

Beginning in 1968, a number of distinguished Native American women, including Lucy Covington (Colville), Ramona Bennett (Puyallup), Joy Sundberg (Yurok), and Ada Deer (Menominee), were elected as tribal chairs.

Federally Employed Women was organized in September to press for equality in Federal employment, with Allie Weedon, a black attorney, as first president.

The Women's Equity Action League was organized in December by Dr. Elizabeth Boyer and other members of the National Organization for Women and concentrated on attacking sexism in higher education.

Women liberationists picketed the Miss America beauty pageant in Atlantic City. Contrary to myth, they did not burn bras. They carried signs that said: Women Are People, Not Livestock.

1969

Shirley Chisholm, Democrat of New York City, was the first black woman elected to Congress.

Weeks v. *Southern Bell Telephone Co.*, 408 F. 2d 228, was the first appeals court decision interpreting sex provisions of Title 7 of the Civil Rights Act of 1964. The lawsuit was brought by a blue collar union woman protesting discriminatory effects of State labor laws applying only to women. Marguerite Rawalt, NOW legal counsel, located a Louisiana lawyer, Sylvia Roberts, to represent Mrs. Weeks, and NOW paid court costs. The excellent decision, the great courage of the plaintiff, and the important victory of a volunteer woman lawyer and a women's organization over highly paid corporation lawyers were a great boost to the women's movement.

An equally important Title 7 case was decided by the Seventh Circuit Court of Appeals, *Bowe* v. *Colgate Palmolive*, 416 F. 2d 711. Union women and volunteer women attorneys were the pattern in this case, too. These and later Title 7 cases illustrated the real effects of State labor laws applying only to women and led to their early demise and broadened support for the Equal Rights Amendment.

The first Commission on the Status of Women appointed by a professional association began to function inside the Modern Language Association. In its early years, that Commission assumed responsibility for collecting and disseminating data on women's studies courses and programs. In December 1970 the Commission published a list of 110 women's studies courses taught at 47 colleges and universities. There were by then two Women's Studies Programs at Cornell University and San Diego State University.

In Fall 1972, the *Women's Studies Newsletter*, edited by Florence Howe, began to appear quarterly on the SUNY College at Old Westbury campus, published by The Feminist Press. *Annually,* the newsletter lists Women's Studies Programs; in 1977, there were 276. There are also groups of women's studies courses on more than 1,000 other campuses. The total number of courses now offered exceeds 15,000.

A women's caucus was organized at the Chicano Liberation Conference held in Denver.

The Boston Women's Health Collective was organized, one of a number of women's self-help groups that emerged in various parts of the country. The group researched and wrote *Our Bodies, Ourselves,* which later became a worldwide bestseller.

The four Republican Congresswomen—Florence Dwyer, Margaret Heckler, Catherine May, and Charlotte Reid—asked for an unprecedented audience with President Nixon to discuss women's issues. They presented a letter which outlined a proposed administration program and provided data on discrimination. Their program became the agenda of the President's Task Force on Women's Rights and Responsibilities, which the President later established with Virginia Allan as chair.

Women in the American Sociological Association formed the first caucus within a professional association, after presentation of a survey by Dr. Alice Rossi on the status of women in graduate departments of sociology. By the end of 1971 every professional association had an activist women's caucus or official commission to study the status of women.

1970
Women's Equity Action League officer, Dr. Bernice Sandler, filed the first formal charges of sex discrimination under Executive Order No. 11246 against the University of Maryland. The charges were well documented. By the end of 1971 women professors had filed formal charges of sex discrimination against more than 300 colleges, largely through the efforts of Dr. Sandler and WEAL.

The first statewide meeting of AFL-CIO women was held in Wisconsin in March. The women endorsed the ERA, opposing AFL-CIO national policy. The next month the United Auto Workers became the first major national union to endorse ERA. Later the AFL-CIO executive council changed its position and announced its support for the ERA.

The Subcommittee on Constitutional Amendments of the Senate Judiciary Committee, chaired by Senator Birch Bayh, held three days of hearings on the ERA in May. Leaders of women's organizations and unions, women lawyers, and Members of Congress testified.

The NAACP adopted a women's rights platform at its annual national convention in June.

The first national commercial newsletters to serve the women's movement—*Women Today*, published in Washington by Myra and Lester Barrer, and *Spokeswoman*, published in Chicago by Susan Davis—were issued.

The Interstate Association of Commissions on the Status of Women were organized to provide a national voice and greater autonomy for the State commissions. Elizabeth Duncan Koontz, newly appointed Director of the Women's Bureau, arranged

the organized meetings, and Dr. Kathryn Clarenbach was elected first president.

The Women's Bureau held its 50th anniversary conference, attended by more than 1,000 women. The Conference endorsed the ERA and other recommendations of the President's Task Force on Women's Rights and Responsibilities.

On the first day of the Women's Bureau Conference, Congresswoman Martha Griffiths filed a petition to discharge the ERA from the House Judiciary Committee, where it had rested without hearings since 1948. The petition was successful, and the ERA was debated in the House on August 10, passing overwhelmingly. It was then defeated in the Senate by the addition of unacceptable amendments.

Hearings on discrimination in education were held in June and July by Congresswoman Edith Green, chairing a special House Subcommittee on Education. The two-volume report is a classic in documenting discrimination against women in education.

The Women's Affairs Division of the League of United Latin American Citizens was organized at the convention in Beaumont, Texas, with Julia Zozoya and Ada Pena in the forefront.

The National Conference of Commissioners on Uniform State Laws published the Uniform Marriage and Divorce Act, based on the assumption that marriage is an economic partnership and recognizing homemakers' contributions as having economic value.

A nationwide celebration of the 50th anniversary of the suffrage amendment, including a mammoth parade in New York City, was held in all major cities on August 26 by a wide spectrum of organizations and individual women. The parade became an annual event.

Sixty-three Native American women from 43 tribes and 23 States met at Colorado State University to discuss their common concerns. They organized the North American Indian Women's Association.

Patsy Mink, Democrat of Hawaii, was the first and only Asian woman elected to Congress. In New York City, Democrat Bella Abzug was the first woman elected to Congress on a women's rights platform. They were among only 11 women in the 435-member House of Representatives.

The Women's Action Organization of State, AID and ICA, the first women's caucus in the federal government, was formed to eliminate discrimination and promote equality of opportunity for women in the foreign affairs agencies.

1971

The National Women's Political Caucus was organized at a meeting in Washington in July, with Congresswoman Bella Abzug, Gloria Steinem, Aileen Hernandez, Fannie Lou Hamer, Edith Van Horn, Liz Carpenter, Koryne Horbal, Congresswoman Shirley Chisholm, Brownie Ledbetter, Betty Friedan, Bobby Kilberg, Jo Ann Gardner, LaDonna Harris, and Virginia Allan among the early leaders.

The U.S. Supreme Court held in *Reed* v. *Reed* that an Idaho law giving preference to males as executors of estates was invalid under the 14th amendment, the first in a series of Supreme Court cases expanding the application of the 5th and 14th amendments to sex discrimination, 404 U.S. 71, 1971.

A preview issue of *Ms.* magazine was published in December with Gloria Steinem as editor. Established to give voice to the ideas of the women's movement, it was an immediate success.

The Women's National Abortion Coalition was organized to work for repeal of anti-abortion laws.

1972

The Equal Rights Amendment was overwhelmingly approved by the Congress and submitted to the States for ratification. Hawaii was the first State to ratify.

The Equal Employment Opportunity Act of 1972, extending coverage and giving the EEOC enforcement authority, passed. The EEOC issued greatly improved sex discrimination guidelines.

Title 9 of the Education Amendments of 1972 was passed, prohibiting discrimination on account of sex in most Federally assisted educational programs. The Equal Pay Act was extended to cover administrative, professional, and executive employees, and the Civil Rights Commission was given jurisdiction over sex discrimination.

The Democratic and Republican Party platforms endorsed the ERA and vigorous enforcement of anti-discrimination laws. As a result of campaigns by the National Women's Political Caucus, the participation of women as convention delegates was higher than in previous conventions. At the Democratic convention, women were 40 percent

of the delegates; at the Republican convention, 30 percent.

The National Conference of Puerto Rican Women was organized in Washington, with Carmen Maymi and Paquito Viva in leading roles.

The November elections brought more women into elective office. The number of women elected to State legislatures was 28.2 percent higher than those serving in the preceding year. In the House of Representatives, the number of Congresswomen increased to 16, but with the retirement of Margaret Chase Smith, the U.S. Senate once again became all-male.

Members of the National Council of Jewish Women conducted a study of day-care facilities in 176 areas. The NCJW report, written by Mary Keyserling, concluded that while the need for day-care centers was enormous, facilities were nonexistent in most places or were of poor quality, underfunded, and understaffed.

1973

AT&T signed an agreement with the EEOC and the Labor Department providing goals and timetables for increasing utilization of women and minorities. About $15 million in back pay was paid to some 15,000 employees.

In a historic decision on January 22, the U.S. Supreme Court held that during the first trimester of pregnancy, the decision to have an abortion must be left solely to a woman and her physician. The only restriction a State may impose is the requirement that the abortion be performed by a physician licensed by the State. In the second and third trimesters, the Court held, the States may impose increasingly stringent requirements. Lawyers for the plaintiffs were Sarah Weddington and Marjorie Hames. *Doe* v. *Bolton* and *Roe* v. *Wade*, 93 S. Ct. 739 and 755.

The National Black Feminists Organization was formed. Eleanor Holmes Norton, leading attorney and head of the New York City Human Rights Commission, was one of the leaders.

The Foreign Assistance Act (Public Law 93-189, 87 Stat. 714) included the Percy Amendment providing that in administering financial aid, particular attention be given to "programs, projects, and activities which tend to integrate women into the national status and assisting the total development effort." Dr. Irene Tinker and the Federation of Organizations for Professional Women were leading proponents.

Billie Jean King beat Bobby Riggs in straight sets in their "Battle of the Sexes" tennis match.

1974

The Coalition of Labor Union Women was organized in Chicago with over 3,000 women in attendance. Olga Madar, former UAW vice president, was elected president.

More than 1.5 million domestic service workers were brought under the coverage of the Fair Labor Standards Act by Public Law 93-259, approved April 8. A rate of $1.90 per hour was effective May 1, 1974, with increases slated for later periods.

The Wisconsin Commission on the Status of Women, chaired by Dr. Kathryn Clarenbach, inaugurated a series of six regional conferences to examine the status of the homemaker.

A national newsletter, *Marriage, Divorce and the Family,* edited by Betty Blaisdell Berry, began publication.

The Mexican American Women's Association (MAWA) was founded.

A study by Dr. Constance Uri, a Cherokee/Choctaw physician, revealed the widespread use and abuse of sterilization of Native American women in Indian health care facilities. The exposé led to the investigation of excessive sterilization of poor and minority women and to the 1977 revision of the Department of Health, Education, and Welfare's guidelines on sterilization.

Congresswoman Bella Abzug's bill to designate August 26 "Women's Equality Day" in honor of the adoption of the Suffrage Amendment became Public Law 93-392.

The Housing and Community Development Act of 1974, Public Law 93-383, prohibited sex discrimination in carrying out community development programs and in making federally related mortgage loans. The Civil Rights Act of 1968 was also amended to prohibit sex discrimination in financing, sale or rental of housing, or the provision of brokerage services.

The Equal Credit Opportunity Act became Public Law 93-495 after Congresswomen Bella Abzug, Margaret Heckler, and Leonor Sullivan led the fight for it in the House. It prohibited discrimination in credit on the basis of sex or marital status. Later, Congresswoman Abzug led a delegation of women members of Congress to meet with Chairman Arthur Burns of the Federal Reserve Board to protest unsatisfactory regulations designed to implement the new law. The regulations were revised.

The Screen Actors Guild reported a nationwide survey of 10,000 viewers on their opinions of women in the media. The majority wanted a more positive image of women, wanted to see women appearing on TV in positions of authority and in leading roles, and felt the media did not encourage young girls to aspire to a useful and meaningful role in society.

Following a "Win With Women" campaign by the National Women's Political Caucus, 18 women were elected to the 94th Congress. A 19th member was elected in a special election in early 1975. In the State legislatures there was a 29.5 percent increase in the numbers of women (465 to 604). The first woman governor to be elected in her own right, Ella Grasso, was elected Governor of Connecticut. Mary Anne Krupsak was elected Lieutenant Governor of New York, and many more women were elected to statewide offices.

1975

The U.S. Supreme Court held in *Wiesenfeld* v. *Wineberger* that a widower with minor children whose deceased wife was covered by social security is entitled to a social security benefit under the same circumstances as a widow would be. The Court held unanimously that the fifth amendment prohibited the present difference in treatment. 43 USLW 4393.

The Supreme Court also held that, in the context of child support, a Utah statute providing that the period of minority extending for males to age 21 and for females to age 18 denies equal protection of the laws guaranteed by the 14th amendment. *Stanton* v. *Stanton,* 43 USLW 4167.

Ms. magazine published a petition for sexual freedom signed by 100 prominent women. They pledged to work for repeal of all laws and regulations that discriminate against homosexuals and lesbians.

The National Commission on the Observance of International Women's Year, 1975, was appointed by President Ford with Jill Ruckelshaus as presiding officer. Elizabeth Athanasakos became presiding officer in 1976. Members of the Commission represented the United States at the United Nations International Women's Year Conference in Mexico City in June.

The First American Indian Women's Leadership Conference met in New York City, sponsored by the International Treaty Council in conjunction with IWY.

A bill introduced by Congresswoman Bella Abzug directed the National Commission to organize and convene a National Women's Conference, preceded by State meetings. The bill was passed by both Houses, was signed by President Ford and became Public Law 94-167.

1976

The number of women delegates to the political party conventions rose to 31.4 percent at the Republican convention and declined to 34 percent at the Democratic convention. A large and effective women's caucus at the Democratic convention in New York met with Presidential nominee Jimmy Carter and obtained pledges from him to appoint significant numbers of women to his administration, to take other steps to improve the position of women, and to campaign for ratification of the ERA.

The major parties nominated 52 women for the House of Representatives, eight more than in 1974, but 31 ran against incumbents. Eighteen were elected, one less than in the previous Congress. Although women won seats in Maryland and Ohio and all incumbents won reelection, Congresswomen Bella Abzug and Patsy Mink gave up their seats to make unsuccessful campaigns for the Senate, and Congresswoman Leonor Sullivan retired. The number of women in State legislatures increased to 685, representing nine percent of legislative seats.

1977

President Carter named a new National Commission on the Observance of IWY and appointed Bella Abzug presiding officer. He named two women, Patricia Harris and Juanita Kreps, to his Cabinet and made other major appointments of women. An analysis of the Presidential personnel plum file appointments list in October, however, showed that of 526 top positions in the Carter administration, only 60 (11 percent) were held by women.

The drive for final ratification of ERA was stalled at 35 States, with three more States needed to meet the 1979 deadline for ratification.

The National Women's Conference met in Houston, Texas, November 18–21, attracted almost 20,000 people, including 2,005 delegates, adopted a National Plan of Action, and was acclaimed a success.

Editor's Note: In highlighting some of the notable women and events affecting women in American history, this chronology makes no pretense to being complete or even comprehensive. It is intended rather to remind readers that the role of women in America has too often been overlooked and that the struggle for equality for women is as old as our Nation.

Special thanks to Catherine East for compiling the original chronology on which this is based, which appeared as an IWY publication in 1975.

UPDATE: THE PROCESS CONTINUES

Kim Blankenship, Anne Bezdek,
and Sheila Ruth

1978

President Carter nominated Col. Margaret A. Brewer, forty-seven, as the first female general of the Marine Corps. She became the Director of Information.

Sea duty was opened to Navy women after a court battle. A U.S. district judge in Washington ruled a federal law unconstitutional which prohibited women from serving on anything other than transport and hospital ships. A few months later, in November, 8 women reported to serve on Navy ships. They were the first of 5,130 the Navy planned to assign over the following five years.

1979

The Jaycees ousted a chapter which retained women as members. Their national executive board revoked the charters of six units, five of which were in Alaska, for noncompliance with the bylaws that restricted the membership to men.

The first woman rabbi headed a congregation. Rabbi Linda Joy Holtzman became a recognized spiritual leader of Conservative Beth Israel Congregation in Coatesville, Pennsylvania. Rabbi Holtzman was a graduate of Reconstructionist Rabbinical College in Philadelphia.

Diana Nyad swam from the Bahamas to Florida. Nyad, a New Yorker, reached Juno Beach after a 60-mile swim in 27 hours and 38 minutes from North Bimini Island off the Bahamas. The thirty-year-old woman fought currents, sharks, and jellyfish.

1980
Firefighter Linda Eaton quit her job in Iowa City, alleging harassment after she had won a 16-month legal battle for the right to breastfeed her baby at the firehouse. The Iowa Civil Rights Commission found her the victim of sex discrimination. Eaton was the fire department's only female firefighter. Eaton received from the case back pay of $145, $2,000 in damages, and $26,000 in legal fees.

The first women graduated from service academies in May. The Coast Guard commissioned 14 women and 142 men at the New London academy's ninety-eighth graduation ceremony.

The U.S. Military Academy graduated 61 women in a class of 809.

At the Naval Academy, 55 women were a part of the graduating class of 938 midshipmen.

The Air Force Academy graduated 97 women and 970 men.

Women were placed on the AFL-CIO Executive Board for the first time. Joyce Miller, the president of the Coalition of Labor Union Women, was the first female to serve on the council since the federation's formation twenty-five years ago.

1981
The first woman Supreme Court justice was seated. On September 21 the Senate, with a 99–0 vote, confirmed Sandra Day O'Connor as a Supreme Court justice. O'Connor, a judge from Arizona, was the 102nd justice to sit on the Supreme Court. She was confirmed on September 25.

The first test-tube baby was born in a U.S. hospital. Elizabeth Jordan Carr—5 pounds, 12 ounces, and healthy—was delivered at Norfolk General Hospital in Virginia. She was conceived in a laboratory dish. She was the fifteenth child born in this manner; the others were born in Britain and Australia.

1982
The new editor of the *Roget's Thesaurus* eliminated sexism from its publication. This edition of the 130-year-old book of synonyms and antonyms barred categories that the woman editor said were biased. "Mankind" became "humankind," and "countryman" was referred to as a "country dweller." The category heads were edited to be as neutral as possible.

The Equal Rights Amendment was defeated. It was three states short of the thirty-eight needed to ratify it as the twenty-seventh amendment to the Constitution. The supporters vowed to fight on.

1983
The first U.S. woman traveled in space. Sally Ride became the first U.S. woman to travel in space in June when the space shuttle *Challenger* was launched from Cape Canaveral, Florida. The *Challenger*, on its second flight, also carried four men in its crew. Ride, a physicist, held the position of mission specialist. The crew members deployed a Canadian communications satellite to hover over the Pacific Ocean at an altitude of 22,000 miles, and a similar satellite was deployed for Southeast Asian nations.

The House of Representatives defeated a plan to revive the proposed Equal Rights Amendment by only six votes short of the two-thirds majority needed.

Alice Walker became the first African American woman to win the Pulitzer Prize for ficiton for her novel *The Color Purple*.

1984
The thirty-ninth Democratic National Convention nominated former Vice President Walter F. Mondale of Minnesota as candidate for president. He then chose Rep. Geraldine A. Ferraro of Queens, N.Y., by acclamation for vice-president. She was the first woman to be named for the office on a major party ticket.

The Jaycees finally admitted women members. The all-male civic organization bowed to the Supreme Court decision which opened up male-only organizations to female membership.

Marital rape was outlawed in New York. The State Court of Appeals, the highest tribunal, ruled that married men could be prosecuted for raping their wives.

1985
The Equal Rights Amendment was introduced in both houses of the Ninety-Ninth Congress in January.

The first woman conservative rabbi was ordained. Amy Eilberg entered the clergy with a ceremony in New York.

1987

A surrogate mother contract was tested in court for the first time in 1987, and the custody decision handed down favored the biological father and his wife over the surrogate. The case, known as the "Baby M" case, held that the contract was "constitutionally protected" and that the father was better able to care for the child than the biological mother.

In October, lesbian and gay rights supporters marched on Washington. Over 500,000 people attended the march, but major news sources opted not to report the event.

1988

The New Jersey Supreme Court overturned a lower court ruling on the "Baby M" case. The court in its ruling prohibited a natural parent from being deprived of parental rights absent any proof that the parent had neglected or abandoned the child. The court also ruled that surrogacy contracts were legal if there was no fee, and they had no binding agreement forcing the natural mother to give up the child.

1989

Rev. Barbara Harris was consecrated as the first female bishop in the Angelican Church.

In April a march on Washington supported a pro-choice stand on reproductive freedom. One of the largest such marches in U.S. history, it brought over 500,000 people to the Capitol steps.

The Bush administration attorneys requested the Supreme Court to overturn *Roe* v. *Wade.*

In *Webster* v. *Reproductive Health Services,* the Supreme Court upheld states' rights to regulate abortion, gutting much of *Roe* v. *Wade* and leaving abortion rights at risk. Feminists vowed never to give up the right to reproductive freedom.

A pro-choice "March for Women's Lives" sponsored by the National Organization for Women drew between 300,000 and 500,000 marchers to the Capitol.

1990

President George Bush vetoed the Civil Rights Act of 1990 on the grounds that it supported quotas in the workplace. He had also vetoed the family-leave bill that gave workers the right to take unpaid leave to care for sick family members or newborn or newly adopted babies.

Cardinal John J. O'Connor, Catholic archbishop of New York City, threatened politicians who supported abortion rights with excommunication.

Antonia C. Novello was appointed the first woman Surgeon General of the United States Public Health Service. She was sworn in by the first female Supreme Court Justice, Sandra Day O'Connor.

1991

Judge Clarence Thomas was confirmed as justice of the Supreme Court after being accused of sexual harassment by Anita Hill, a law professor and Thomas's former aide. The televised hearings brought the issue of sexual harassment before the public as never before, and Professor Hill's ill treatment and the sexism expressed by members of the Senate Judiciary Committee so angered American women that they emerged in the 1992 election as a formidable voting bloc.

After a 1990 veto by President George Bush, Congress enacted the Civil Rights Act of 1991, reversing several rulings by the Supreme Court that made it easier for employers to prevail in discrimination suits.

The Supreme Court upheld the federal "gag rule" barring counselors at federally funded family planning clinics from informing patients of the option of abortion.

Nadine Strossen, graduate of Harvard University Law School, was named the first woman president of the American Civil Liberties Union.

Ileana Ros-Lehtinen (R-FL) became the first Hispanic woman elected to the U.S. House of Representatives.

Feminist author and activist Audre Lorde became the first African American woman to be named Poet Laureate of New York State.

1992

The "Year of the Woman" saw a record number of women run for public office, with record numbers in the House and Senate. Carol Moseley-Braun (D-IL) became the first African American woman elected to the U.S. Senate. She defeated Senator Alan Dixon, long-time incumbent, who had supported Clarence Thomas's nomination to the Supreme Court after Anita Hill's accusation of sexual harassment. Nydia Velazquez (D-NY) became the first Puerto Rican congresswoman.

The governing body of the Church of England narrowly voted to allow women to become priests. The action was described as one of the most important since the church broke with the Roman Catholic Church in 1534.

Colonel Margarethe Cammermeyer, a decorated Vietnam veteran, was discharged from the Washington State Army National Guard because she was an acknowledged lesbian. The Colonel, who had served in the military for 26 years, had been the chief nurse of the State National Guard. Her firing furthered public discussion of the civil rights of gays.

Televangelist Pat Robertson, a leader of the Christian Right and a powerful force in Republican Party politics, was reported by the Associated Press to have written in a fund-raising letter that a proposed amendment to the Iowa constitution guaranteeing equality for women would advance "a feminist agenda . . . that encourages women to leave their husbands, kill their children, practice witchcraft, destroy capitalism and become lesbians."

Vice President Dan Quayle created a public furor when (in a speech before the Commonwealth Club of California) he criticized a television character, Murphy Brown, for bearing a child out of wedlock. Diane English, executive producer of the show, answered, "If the vice president thinks it's disgraceful for an unmarried woman to bear a child, and if he believes that a woman cannot raise a child without a father, then he'd better make sure abortion remains safe and legal."

1993

Maya Angelou read her original poem, "On the Pulse of Morning," at President Bill Clinton's inauguration.

Lucille Roybal-Allard became the first Mexican American congresswoman.

President Clinton issued executive orders overturning several restrictions on abortion, including the infamous "gag rule."

Opponents to reproductive rights became more violent. Two physicians known to perform abortions were shot, one of them fatally.

Ruth Bader Ginsburg, an advocate for women's rights and avowedly pro-choice, was appointed the second female justice of the U.S. Supreme Court.

Rita Dove, winner of the Pulitzer Prize for Poetry, was named Poet Laureate of the United States, the first African American and the youngest person ever to be so honored.

Toni Morrison became the first African American to win the Pulitzer Prize for Literature.

Faye Wattleton, President of Planned Parenthood Federation of America, 1978–1992, was inducted into the National Women's Hall of Fame.

Janet Reno was the first woman to be appointed Attorney General of the United States.

1994

Shannon Faulkner became the first woman admitted to classes at The Citadel, South Carolina's military school, after a discrimination suit begun in 1993. She won her battle to become a member of the Corps of Cadets in 1995, but resigned shortly thereafter, saying that she was exhausted and ill. Another woman was substituted in the suit against The Citadel (which was dropped in 1996 after the school abandoned its male-only policy).

Joycelyn Elders became the first woman to be appointed U.S. Surgeon General. She resigned her office after controversy caused by her outspoken views on sex education, the prevention of AIDS, and U.S. policy on illegal drugs.

1995

Nancy Kassebaum (R-KS) became the first woman to chair a major Senate committee.

Pope John Paul II issued the encyclical, *In Evangelium Vitae*, reiterating the church's opposition to abortion, birth control, and in vitro fertilization.

The United Nation's Fourth World Congress on Women met in Beijing, China, with over 180 nations represented and 30,000 women attending. The congress forged a "Platform for Action" to address injustice and inequality of women worldwide.

1996

The Supreme Court ruled that the male-only policy of the Virginia Military Institute (VMI) was discriminatory and that the school would have to open its doors to women. One day after the Court announced its decision, The Citadel declared that it too would begin to accept women.

Rosa Parks, the woman who touched off the antisegregation civil rights movement in 1955 by refusing to move to the back of the bus as required of blacks, was awarded the Presidential Medal of Freedom.

President Bill Clinton vetoed a congressional bill banning late-term abortions (referred to medically as "intact dilation and evacuation"), used in situations necessary to save the life of the mother or in cases of severe, life-threatening malformation of the fetus. The House, but not the Senate, overrode the veto.

President Clinton signed into law the Defense of Marriage Act, which denies federal marriage benefits to same-sex couples and allows states to deny recognition of same-sex marriages performed in other states. Opponents to the law maintained that it was unconstitutional based on the "full faith and credit" clause of the U.S. Constitution.

The U.S. Food and Drug Administration found the drug RU-486 (mifepristone) to be a safe and effective alternative to surgical abortion. Its sponsor, the Population Council, a family planning organization, said that they hoped to make the drug available to American women by the following year. Because it could be used in the privacy of a doctor's office, it was hoped that RU-486 would end most of the violence and abuses of antichoice activists. (By 2000, the drug was still not available in the United States.)

1997

Madeleine Albright, a naturalized citizen born in Czechoslovakia in 1937, formerly U.S. Ambassador to the United Nations, became the first woman to be nominated (and then to serve) as U.S. secretary of state.

The Women in Military Service for America Memorial, honoring the nearly two million women who served in the military over the past two centuries, was dedicated at Arlington National Cemetery in Virginia.

Debby Krenek was appointed editor in chief of the New York *Daily News*, the first woman to hold that position in the 77-year history of the newspaper.

The Justice Department released its first annual "survey of stalking" report as part of its report on violence against women, mandated under the 1994 Violence Against Women Act. It reported that one million women are stalked every year in the United States.

1998

January 22 marked the twenty-fifth anniversary of *Roe v. Wade,* the Supreme Court case that legalized abortion.

Rita R. Colwell was named director of the National Science Foundation, the first woman ever to be appointed to that post.

Bella Abzug, author, activist, politician, and tireless worker for women's rights, died on March 31. She served as U.S. Representative from New York from 1970 to 1976, was cofounder and first chair of the National Women's Political Caucus, first chair of the National Commission on the Observance of International Women's Year in 1976, and organizer of the National Women's Conference in Houston in 1977.

Julie Taymor (for the *Lion King*) and Garry Hynes (for *The Beauty Queen of Leenane*) became the first women ever to win Tony awards for best director.

Mary Calderone, advocate for contraception during the 1960s and later for sex education in public schools and high schools, died at the age of 94.

Winter Olympics XVIII, held in Nagano, Japan, included women's hockey for the first time. The United States won over Canada, 3–1.

Dr. Barnett Slepian, an obstetrician who, as part of his practice, performed abortions at a clinic in Buffalo, was shot and killed in his home. He was the third doctor, the seventh person, killed by antiabortionists since 1993.

Virginia Military Institute enrolled its first female cadets after a protracted struggle to bar them.

Delegates to the annual convention of Southern Baptists, the largest Protestant denomination in the United States, overwhelmingly ratified a statement directing that wives should submit graciously to their husbands, reflecting the decided turn to the right of that body.

1999

Nancy Mace became the first woman to graduate from The Citadel in Charleston.

Radcliffe College in Cambridge, Massachusetts, founded in 1879 for the education of women (not admitted to all-male Harvard), merged with Harvard

University. Radcliffe College became Radcliffe Institute for Advanced Study, specializing in women's issues.

Texaco, Inc. agreed to pay $3.1 million to 186 female managers and support personnel because they had been paid less than male peers 1993–1996. It was the largest settlement ever granted under the federal affirmative action compliance program.

Carleton Fiorina became the first woman to run one of the United States' twenty largest publicly held companies when she was named CEO of Hewlett-Packard Company, the world's second largest computer maker.

Col. Eileen Collins became the first woman to command a shuttle mission when she commanded the Columbia to deploy the Chandra X-Ray Observatory, an orbiting x-ray telescope.

Karen Jurgensen was named editor of *USA Today,* becoming the first woman in the United States to head a large national newspaper.

Among the books which the editors found particularly useful in compiling [the first part of the] chronology were:

Chafe, William. The American Woman: Her Changing Social, Economic and Political Roles, 1920–1970. *Oxford University Press.*

DePauw, Linda Grant. Fortunes of War, New Jersey Women and the American Revolution. *New Jersey Historical Commission.*

Flexner, Eleanor. Century of Struggle. *Atheneum.*

Freeman, Jo. Women: A Feminist Perspective. *Mayfield.*

Hole, Judith, and Ellen Levine. Rebirth of Feminism. *Quadrangle.*

Lerner, Gerda. "The Lady and the Mill Girl: Changes in the Status of Women in the Age of Jackson." Ameri-can Studies Journal, *Spring 1969.*

Lerner, Gerda. Black Women in White America. *Vintage.*

O'Neill, William. Everyone Was Brave. *Quadrangle.*

Papachristou, Judith. Women Together, A History in Documents of the Women's Movement in the United States. *A Ms. Book.*

Wertheimer, Barbara. We Were There: The Story of Working Women in America. *Pantheon.*

Sources used in compiling the Update include:

Dimona, Lisa, and Constance Herndon, eds. The 1995 Information Please Women's Sourcebook. *Boston: Houghton Mifflin, 1995.*

Facts on File, *World News Digest, 1990–1999.*

Potter, Joan, and Constance Claytor. African-American Firsts. *Elizabethtown, NY: Pinto Press, 1994.*

Read, Phyllis J., and Bernard L. Witlieb. The Book of Women's Firsts. *New York: Random House, 1992.*

Tobias, Sheila. "Chronology," Faces of Feminism: An Activist's Reflection on the Women's Movement. *Boulder, CO: Westview Press, 1997.*

"Twenty Years of the U.S. Women's Movement," Ms. 3, no. 1 (July/August 1992).

The World Almanac and Book of Facts, 1991–1996.

A Vindication of the Rights of Woman

Mary Wollstonecraft

It is not uncommon to begin the history of the nineteenth-century wave of feminism and women's rights movements with the work of the eighteenth-century British writer and radical thinker Mary Wollstonecraft. After all, her work had great influence in Europe and the United States, and The Rights of Woman *was read as inspiration by the founders of the Seneca Falls Convention—Lucretia Mott, Elizabeth Cady Stanton, and others.*

Born in Spitalfields, a poor district near London, in 1759, Wollstonecraft was destined to live a hard and extraordinary life for women of her time and to learn from experience both the value and the elusiveness of strength and independence in the lives of women. Her father became a drunkard after financial failure and periodically beat his wife and family and trifled away their remaining money. To escape conditions at home, her sister Eliza had married badly while still in her teens, and Wollstonecraft believed she had to spirit Eliza away to safety. On their own, the two sisters found it very hard to earn a living. All but two or three occupations were closed to them as women, and Eliza was not well. With a friend, Fanny Blood, they opened a school for girls; but, ill prepared and untrained, they failed financially, and the school closed.

Having educated herself, Wollstonecraft moved to London and began earning a living at writing—at first books about educating girls and stories for children. But through her publisher she began to move in intellectual and radical circles and to grow in insight and awareness. In 1792 she published the Vindication of the Rights of Woman, *which was well read and earned her some fame. Later in that year, she moved to Paris to observe firsthand the revolution in France. There she began a history of the French Revolution, later published, and met the American Gilbert Imlay, with whom she lived and had a daughter, Fanny. After Imlay left her in 1795, she returned to London, depressed and heartbroken, to rebuild her life and move once again with the friends she had known. Soon she met the radical philosopher William Godwin, whom she agreed to marry when she became pregnant. In 1797, shortly after the birth of her daughter Mary, she died at the age of 38.*

The following excerpts from The Rights of Woman *are from the introduction and the dedication, in which Wollstonecraft sets forth her main principles: Women are turned into weak, petty creatures—mere "alluring objects" (sex objects?)—by neglected education, by manners and morals (what we today would probably call sex-role socialization), and by flattery and dependence. She chides M. Talleyrand-Périgord, and with him the nation of men, for not applying to women the same concern and commitment for "human" rights and freedom that they hold for men.*

AUTHOR'S INTRODUCTION

AFTER CONSIDERING THE HISTORIC PAGE, and viewing the living world with anxious solicitude, the most melancholy emotions of sorrowful indignation have depressed my spirits, and I have sighed when obliged to confess that either Nature has made a great difference between man and man, or that the civilisation which has hitherto taken place in the world has been very partial. I have turned over various books written on the subject of education, and patiently observed the conduct of parents and the management of schools; but what has been the result?—a profound conviction that the neglected education of my fellow-creatures is the grand source of the misery I deplore, and that women, in particular, are rendered weak and wretched by a variety of concurring causes, originating from one hasty conclusion. The conduct and manners of women, in fact, evidently prove that their minds are not in a healthy state; for, like the flowers which are planted

From *The Rights of Woman* by Mary Wollstonecraft. Everyman's Library Edition.

in too rich a soil, strength and usefulness are sacrificed to beauty; and the flaunting leaves, after having pleased a fastidious eye, fade, disregarded on the stalk, long before the season when they ought to have arrived at maturity. One cause of this barren blooming I attribute to a false system of education, gathered from the books written on this subject by men who, considering females rather as women than human creatures, have been more anxious to make them alluring mistresses than affectionate wives and rational mothers; and the understanding of the sex has been so bubbled by this specious homage, that the civilised women of the present century, with a few exceptions, are only anxious to inspire love, when they ought to cherish a nobler ambition, and by their abilities and virtues exact respect.

In a treatise, therefore, on female rights and manners, the works which have been particularly written for their improvement must not be overlooked, especially when it is asserted, in direct terms, that the minds of women are enfeebled by false refinement; that the books of instruction, written by men of genius, have had the same tendency as more frivolous productions; and that, in the true style of Mahometanism, they are treated as a kind of subordinate beings, and not as a part of the human species, when improvable reason is allowed to be the dignified distinction which raises men above the brute creation, and puts a natural sceptre in a feeble hand.

Yet, because I am a woman, I would not lead my readers to suppose that I mean violently to agitate the contested question respecting the quality or inferiority of the sex; but as the subject lies in my way, and I cannot pass it over without subjecting the main tendency of my reasoning to misconstruction, I shall stop a moment to deliver, in a few words, my opinion. In the government of the physical world it is observable that the female in point of strength is, in general, inferior to the male. This is the law of Nature; and it does not appear to be suspended or abrogated in favour of woman. A degree of physical superiority cannot, therefore, be denied, and it is a noble prerogative! But not content with this natural preeminence, men endeavour to sink us still lower, merely to render us alluring objects for a moment; and women, intoxicated by the adoration which men, under the influence of their senses, pay them, do not seek to obtain a durable interest in their hearts, or to become the friends of the fellow-creatures who find amusement in their society.

I am aware of an obvious inference. From every quarter have I heard exclamations against masculine women, but where are they to be found? If by this appellation men mean to inveigh against their ardour in hunting, shooting, and gaming, I shall most cordially join in the cry; but if it be against the imitation of manly virtues, or, more properly speaking, the attainment of those talents and virtues, the exercise of which ennobles the human character, and which raises females in the scale of animal being, when they are comprehensively termed mankind, all those who view them with a philosophic eye must, I should think, wish with me, that they may every day grow more and more masculine.

This discussion naturally divides the subject. I shall first consider women in the grand light of human creatures, who, in common with men, are placed on this earth to unfold their faculties; and afterwards I shall more particularly point out their peculiar designation.

I wish also to steer clear of an error which many respectable writers have fallen into; for the instruction which has hitherto been addressed to women, has rather been applicable to *ladies*, if the little indirect advice that is scattered through "Sandford and Merton" be excepted; but, addressing my sex in a firmer tone, I pay particular attention to those in the middle class, because they appear to be in the most natural state. Perhaps the seeds of false refinement, immorality, and vanity, have ever been shed by the great. Weak, artificial beings, raised above the common wants and affections of their race, in a premature unnatural manner, undermine the very foundation of virtue, and spread corruption through the whole mass of society! As a class of mankind they have the strongest claim to pity; the education of the rich tends to render them vain and helpless, and the unfolding mind is not strengthened by the practice of those duties which dignify the human character. They only live to amuse themselves, and by the same law which in Nature invariably produces certain effects, they soon only afford barren amusement.

But as I purpose taking a separate view of the different ranks of society, and of the moral character of women in each, this hint is for the present sufficient; and I have only alluded to the subject because it appears to me to be the very essence of an introduction to give a cursory account of the contents of the work it introduces.

My own sex, I hope, will excuse me, if I treat them like rational creatures, instead of flattering their *fascinating* graces, and viewing them as if they were in a state of perpetual childhood, unable to stand alone. I earnestly wish to point out in what true dignity and human happiness consists. I wish to persuade women to endeavor to acquire strength, both of mind and body, and to convince them that the soft phrases, susceptibility of heart, delicacy of sentiment, and refinement of taste, are almost synonymous with epithets of weakness, and that those beings who are only the objects of pity, and that kind of love which has been termed its sister, will soon become objects of contempt.

Dismissing, then, those pretty feminine phrases, which the men condescendingly use to soften our slavish dependence, and despising that weak elegancy of mind, exquisite sensibility, and sweet docility of manners, supposed to be the sexual characteristics of the weaker vessel, I wish to show that elegance is inferior to virtue, that the first object of laudable ambition is to obtain a character as a human being, regardless of the distinction of sex, and that secondary views should be brought to this simple touchstone.

This is a rough sketch of my plan; and should I express my conviction with the energetic emotions that I feel whenever I think of the subject, the dictates of experience and reflection will be felt by some of my readers. Animated by this important object, I shall disdain to cull my phrases or polish my style. I aim at being useful, and sincerity will render me unaffected; for, wishing rather to persuade by the force of my arguments than dazzle by the elegance of my language, I shall not waste my time in rounding periods, or in fabricating the turgid bombast of artificial feelings, which, coming from the head, never reach the heart. I shall be employed about things, not words! and, anxious to render my sex more respectable members of society, I shall try to avoid that flowery diction which has slided from essays into novels, and from novels into familiar letters and conversation.

These pretty superlatives, dropping glibly from the tongue, vitiate the taste, and create a kind of sickly delicacy that turns away from simple unadorned truth; and a deluge of false sentiments and overstretched feelings, stifling the natural emotions of the heart, render the domestic pleasures insipid, that ought to sweeten the exercise of those severe duties, which educate a rational and immortal being for a nobler field of action.

The education of women has of late been more attended to than formerly; yet they are still reckoned a frivolous sex, and ridiculed or pitied by the writers who endeavour by satire or instruction to improve them. It is acknowledged that they spend many of the first years of their lives in acquiring a smattering of accomplishments; meanwhile strength of body and mind are sacrificed to libertine notions of beauty, to the desire of establishing themselves—the only way women can rise in the world—by marriage. And this desire making mere animals of them, when they marry they act as such children may be expected to act—they dress, they paint, and nickname God's creatures. Surely these weak beings are only fit for a seraglio! Can they be expected to govern a family with judgment, or take care of the poor babes whom they bring into the world?

If, then, it can be fairly deduced from the present conduct of the sex, from the prevalent fondness for pleasure which takes place of ambition and those nobler passions that open and enlarge the soul, that the instruction which women have hitherto received has only tended, with the constitution of civil society, to render them insignificant objects of desire—mere propagators of fools!—if it can be proved that in aiming to accomplish them, without cultivating their understandings, they are taken out of their sphere of duties, and made ridiculous and useless when the short-lived bloom of beauty is over,[1] I presume that *rational* men will excuse me for endeavouring to persuade them to become more masculine and respectable.

Indeed the word masculine is only a bugbear; there is little reason to fear that women will acquire too much courage or fortitude, for their apparent inferiority with respect to bodily strength must render them in some degree dependent on men in the various relations of life; but why should it be increased by prejudices that give a sex to virtue, and confound simple truths with sensual reveries?

Women are, in fact, so much degraded by mistaken notions of female excellence, that I do not mean to add a paradox when I assert that this artificial weakness produces a propensity to tyrannise, and gives birth to cunning, the natural opponent of strength, which leads them to play off those contemptible infantine airs that undermine esteem even whilst they excite desire. Let men become more chaste and modest, and if women do not grow wiser in the same ratio, it will be clear that they have weaker understandings. It seems scarcely necessary to say that I now speak of the sex in general. Many individuals have more sense than their male relatives; and, as nothing preponderates where there is a constant struggle for an equilibrium without it has naturally more gravity, some women govern their husbands without degrading themselves, because intellect will always govern.

TO M. TALLEYRAND-PÉRIGORD
LATE BISHOP OF AUTUN

Sir, ... Contending for the rights of woman, my main argument is built on this simple principle, that if she be not prepared by education to become the companion of man, she will stop the progress of knowledge and virtue; for truth must be common to all, or it will be inefficacious with respect to its influence on general practice. And how can woman be expected to cooperate unless she knows why she ought to be virtuous? unless freedom strengthens her reason till she comprehends her duty, and see in what manner it is connected with her real good. If children are to be educated to understand the true principle of patriotism, their mother must be a patriot; and the love of mankind, from which an orderly train of virtues spring, can only be produced by considering the moral and civil interest of mankind; but the education and situation of woman at present shuts her out from such investigations.

In this work I have produced many arguments, which to me were conclusive, to prove that the prevailing notion respecting a sexual character was subversive of morality, and I have contended, that to render the human body and mind more perfect,

chastity must more universally prevail, and that chastity will never be respected in the male world till the person of a woman is not, as it were, idolised, when little virtue or sense embellish it with the grand traces of mental beauty, or the interesting simplicity of affection.

Consider, sir, dispassionately these observations, for a glimpse of this truth seemed to open before you when you observed, "that to see one-half of the human race excluded by the other from all participation of government was a political phenomenon that, according to abstract principles, it was impossible to explain." If so, on what does your constitution rest? If the abstract rights of man will bear discussion and explanation, those of woman, by a parity of reasoning, will not shrink from the same test; though a different opinion prevails in this country, built on the very arguments which you use to justify the oppression of woman—prescription.

Consider—I address you as a legislator—whether, when men contend for their freedom, and to be allowed to judge for themselves respecting their own happiness, it be not inconsistent and unjust to subjugate women, even though you firmly believe that you are acting in the manner best calculated to promote their happiness? Who made man the exclusive judge, if woman partake with him of the gift of reason?

In this style argue tyrants of every denomination, from the weak king to the weak father of a family; they are all eager to crush reason, yet always assert that they usurp its throne only to be useful. Do you not act a similar part when you *force* all women, by denying them civil and political rights, to remain immured in their families groping in the dark? for surely, sir, you will not assert that a duty can be binding which is not founded on reason? If, indeed, this be their destination, arguments may be drawn from reason; and thus augustly supported, the more understanding women acquire, the more they will be attached to their duty—comprehending it—for unless they comprehend it, unless their morals be fixed on the same immutable principle as those of man, no authority can make them discharge it in a virtuous manner. They may be convenient slaves, but slavery will have its constant effect, degrading the master and the abject dependent.

But if women are to be excluded, without having a voice, from a participation of the natural rights of mankind, prove first, to ward off the charge of injustice and inconsistency, that they want reason, else this flaw in your NEW CONSTITUTION will ever show that man must, in some shape, act like a tyrant, and tyranny, in whatever part of society it rears its brazen front, will ever undermine morality.

I have repeatedly asserted, and produced what appeared to me irrefragable arguments drawn from matters of fact to prove my assertion, that women cannot by force be confined to domestic concerns; for they will, however ignorant, intermeddle with more weighty affairs, neglecting private duties only to disturb, by cunning tricks, the orderly plans of reason which rise above their comprehension.

Besides, whilst they are only made to acquire personal accomplishments, men will seek for pleasure in variety, and faithless husbands will make faithless wives; such ignorant beings, indeed, will be very excusable when, not taught to respect public good, nor allowed any civil rights, they attempt to do themselves justice by retaliation.

The box of mischief thus opened in society, what is to preserve private virtue, the only security of public freedom and universal happiness?

Let there be then no coercion *established* in society, and the common law of gravity prevailing, the sexes will fall into their proper places. And now that more equitable laws are forming your citizens, marriage may become more sacred; your young men may choose wives from motives of affection, and your maidens allow love to root out vanity.

The father of a family will not then weaken his constitution and debase his sentiments by visiting the harlot, nor forget, in obeying the call of appetite, the purpose for which it was implanted. And the mother will not neglect her children to practise the arts of coquetry, when sense and modesty secure her the friendship of her husband.

But, till men become attentive to the duty of a father, it is vain to expect women to spend that time in their nursery which they, "wise in their generation," choose to spend at their glass; for this exertion of cunning is only an instinct of nature to enable them to obtain indirectly a little of that power of which they are unjustly denied a share; for, if women are not permitted to enjoy legitimate rights, they will render both men and themselves vicious to obtain illicit privileges.

I wish, sir, to set some investigations of this kind afloat in France; and should they lead to a confirmation of my principles when your constitution is revised, the Rights of Woman may be respected, if it be fully proved that reason calls for this respect, and loudly demands JUSTICE for one-half of the human race.

I am, Sir,
Yours respectfully,
M. W.

Notes

1. A lively writer (I cannot recollect his name) asks what business women turned of forty have to do in the world?

The Adams Letters

Abigail and John Adams

Abigail Adams (1744–1818) was born in Massachusetts the daughter of an upper-middle-class woman and her husband, who was a minister. Typical of her day, she received no formal education. Her husband, John, of course, fared differently. The son of a respected farmer, he graduated from Harvard in 1755, taught school for a while, studied law, and was admitted to the bar in 1758. Finally, he carried on an active political life culminating in his becoming the second president of the United States in 1796.

How different, how predictably different, their lives were; how much opportunity to express his intelligence and energy John had and how little Abigail had. No wonder she had to request of him in 1776 that he "remember the ladies" as John Adams, together with Jefferson and Franklin, was composing the Declaration of Independence. No wonder he quite purposely (as his letter to Sullivan shows) turned her down, calling her a "saucy" girl.

It would be nearly three-quarters of a century later before another such declaration could be written—in Seneca Falls.

FROM ABIGAIL TO JOHN

Braintree
March 31, 1776

—I LONG TO HEAR THAT you have declared an independancy—and by the way in the new Code of Laws which I suppose it will be necessary for you to make I desire you would Remember the Ladies, and be more generous and favourable to them than your ancestors. Do not put such unlimited power

---

The first two letters reprinted by permission of the publishers from *Adams Family Correspondence, Volume I, December 1761 to May 1776,* ed. L. H. Butterfield, Cambridge, Mass.: The Belknap Press of Harvard University Press, Copyright © 1963 by the Massachusetts Historical Society. The third letter (to Sullivan) is from Charles Francis Adams, ed., *Works of John Adams,* Vol. ix. Boston: Little, Brown, 1854, p. 375.

into the hands of the Husbands. Remember all Men would be tyrants if they could. If perticuliar care and attention is not paid to the Laidies we are determined to foment a Rebelion, and will not hold ourselves bound by any Laws in which we have no voice, or Representation.

That your Sex are Naturally Tyrannical is a Truth so thoroughly established as to admit of no dispute, but such of you as wish to be happy willingly give up the harsh title of Master for the more tender and endearing one of Friend. Why then, not put it out of the power of the vicious and the Lawless to use us with cruelty and indignity with impunity. Men of Sense in all Ages abhor those customs which treat us only as the vassals of your Sex. Regard us then as Beings placed by providence under your protection and in immitation of the Supreem Being make use of that power only for our happiness.

FROM JOHN TO ABIGAIL

April 14, 1776

As to your extraordinary Code of Laws, I cannot but laugh. We have been told that our Struggle has loosened the bands of Government every where. That Children and Apprentices were disobedient—that schools and Colledges were grown turbulent—that Indians slighted their Guardians and Negroes grew insolent to their Masters. But your Letter was the first Intimation that another Tribe more numerous and powerfull than all the rest were grown discontented.—This is rather too coarse a Compliment but you are so saucy, I wont blot it out.

Depend upon it, We know better than to repeal our Masculine systems. Altho they are in full Force, you know they are little more than Theory. We dare not exert our Power in its full Latitude. We are obliged to go fair, and softly, and in Practice you know We are the subjects. We have only the Name of Masters, and rather than give up this, which would compleatly subject us to the Despotism of the Peticoat, I hope General Washington, and all our brave Heroes would fight.

FROM JOHN ADAMS
TO JAMES SULLIVAN

Philadelphia, 26 May, 1776

. . . It is certain, in theory, that the only moral foundation of government is, the consent of the people. But to what an extent shall we carry this principle? Shall we say that every individual of the community, old and young, male and female, as well as rich and poor, must consent, expressly, to every act of legislation? No, you will say, this is impossible. How, then does the right arise in the majority to govern the minority, against their will? Whence arises the right of the men to govern the women, without their consent? Whence the right of the old to bind the young, without theirs?

But let us first suppose that the whole community, of every age, rank, sex, and condition, has a right to vote. This community is assembled. A motion is made, and carried by a majority of one voice. The minority will not agree to this. Whence arises the right of the majority to govern, and the obligation of the minority to obey?

From necessity, you will say, because there can be no other rule.

But why exclude women?

You will say, because their delicacy renders them unfit for practice and experience in the great businesses of life, and the hardy enterprises of war, as well as the arduous cares of state. Besides, their attention is so much engaged with the necessary nurture of their children, that nature has made them fittest for domestic cares. And children have not judgment or will of their own. True. But will not these reasons apply to others? Is it not equally true, that men in general, in every society, who are wholly destitute of property, are also too little acquainted with public affairs to form a right judg-

ment, and too dependent upon other men to have a will of their own? If this is a fact, if you give to every man who has no property, a vote, will you not make a fine encouraging provision for corruption, by your fundamental law? Such is the frailty of the human heart, that very few men who have no property, have any judgment of their own. They talk and vote as they are directed by some man of property, who has attached their minds to his interest. . . .

Your idea that those laws which affect the lives and personal liberty of all, or which inflict corporal punishment, affect those who are not qualified to vote, as well as those who are, is just. But so they do women, as well as men; children, as well as adults. What reason should there be for excluding a man of twenty years eleven months and twenty-seven days old, from a vote, when you admit one who is twenty-one? The reason is, you must fix upon some period in life, when the understanding and will of men in general, is fit to be trusted by the public. Will not the same reason justify the state in fixing upon some certain quantity of property, as a qualification?

The same reasoning which will induce you to admit all men who have no property, to vote, with those who have, for those laws which affect the person, will prove that you ought to admit women and children; for, generally speaking, women and children have as good judgments, and as independent minds, as those men who are wholly destitute of property; these last being to all intents and purposes as much dependent upon others, who will please to feed, clothe, and employ them, as women are upon their husbands, or children on their parents. . . .

Depend upon it, Sir, it is dangerous to open so fruitful a source of controversy and altercation as would be opened by attempting to alter the qualifications of voters; there will be no end of it. New claims will arise; women will demand a vote; lads from twelve to twenty-one will think their rights not enough attended to; and every man who has not a farthing, will demand an equal voice with any other, in all acts of state. It tends to confound and destroy all distinctions, and prostrate all ranks to one common level.

Declaration of Sentiments and Resolutions

Seneca Falls Convention of 1848

The "woman question" had been bubbling heatedly among the intelligentsia and great reformers of the times and in the press at least since women had begun to emerge as strong and active movers in the antislavery societies. A major precipitating factor of early feminist activism occurred in 1840 in London at the World Anti-Slavery Convention attended by many Americans, among them Lucretia Mott, a strong, intelligent Quaker minister and delegate of the American Anti-Slavery Society, and Elizabeth Cady Stanton, then the bride of Henry Stanton, delegate of the American and Foreign Anti-Slavery Society. Although debate over the issue of women's participation in the abolition movement had been sharp in the United States, women had gained some degree of tolerance, if not wholehearted acceptance. Furthermore, the women involved here were educated, spirited women, accustomed to speaking out. They were not prepared for their reception in London: After a full day of debate on the question, on the grounds of morality and propriety (not to mention incompetence), women were finally allowed only to attend, not to participate actively in the discussion. Barred from the central gathering, they were required to sit in a separate curtained gallery, hidden from view, forbidden to speak. Humiliated and furious at the hypocrisy of liberals who could see one brand of oppression but not another, the American women determined to call their own convention on their own issue upon their return home.

Although diverted for nearly eight years, they made good their plan on July 19, 1848, at Seneca Falls, New York. The convention brought forth the following document, written primarily by Stanton and ultimately adopted by the gathering. The decision to use the language of the Declaration of Independence was done pointedly to remind all that women had been omitted from the concerns and safeguards of the original U.S. Constitution. The arguments are clearly in the tradition of eighteenth-century Enlightenment liberalism and nineteenth-century reformism. Notice the breadth of concerns voiced here, suffrage being only a part (and not a well-supported one!) of the commitment. Notice, too,

the parallels between these ideas and those of today's women's movement.

WHEN, IN THE COURSE OF human events, it becomes necessary for one portion of the family of man to assume among the people of the earth a position different from that which they have hitherto occupied, but one to which the laws of nature and of nature's God entitle them, a decent respect to the opinions of mankind requires that they should declare the causes that impel them to such a course.

We hold these truths to be self-evident: that all men and women are created equal; that they are endowed by their Creator with certain inalienable rights; that among these are life, liberty, and the pursuit of happiness; that to secure these rights governments are instituted, deriving their just powers from the consent of the governed. Whenever any form of government becomes destructive of these ends, it is the right of those who suffer from it to refuse allegiance to it, and to insist upon the institution of a new government, laying its foundation on such principles, and organizing its powers in such form, as to them shall seem most likely to effect their safety and happiness. Prudence, indeed, will dictate that governments long established should not be changed for light and transient causes; and accordingly all experience hath shown that mankind are more disposed to suffer, while evils are sufferable, than to right themselves by abolishing the forms to which they were accustomed. But when a long train of abuses and usurpations, pursuing invariably the same object evinces a design to reduce them under absolute despotism, it is their duty to throw off such government, and to provide new guards for their future security. Such has been

Elizabeth Cady Stanton, Susan B. Anthony, and Matilda Joslyn Gage, eds. *History of Woman Suffrage,* 2d ed., Vol. 1. Rochester, NY: Charles Mann, 1889.

the patient sufferance of the women under this government, and such is now the necessity which constrains them to demand the equal station to which they are entitled.

The history of mankind is a history of repeated injuries and usurpations on the part of man toward woman, having in direct object the establishment of an absolute tyranny over her. To prove this, let facts be submitted to a candid world.

He has never permitted her to exercise her inalienable right to the elective franchise.

He has compelled her to submit to laws, in the formation of which she had no voice.

He has withheld from her rights which are given to the most ignorant and degraded men—both natives and foreigners.

Having deprived her of this first right of a citizen, the elective franchise, thereby leaving her without representation in the halls of legislation, he has oppressed her on all sides.

He has made her, if married, in the eye of the law, civilly dead.

He has taken from her all right in property, even to the wages she earns.

He has made her, morally, an irresponsible being, as she can commit many crimes with impunity, provided they be done in the presence of her husband. In the covenant of marriage, she is compelled to promise obedience to her husband, he becoming, to all intents and purposes, her master—the law giving him power to deprive her of her liberty, and to administer chastisement.

He has so framed the laws of divorce, as to what shall be the proper causes, and in case of separation, to whom the guardianship of the children shall be given, as to be wholly regardless of the happiness of women—the law, in all cases, going upon a false supposition of the supremacy of man, and giving all power into his hands.

After depriving her of all rights as a married woman, if single, and the owner of property, he has taxed her to support a government which recognizes her only when her property can be made profitable to it.

He has monopolized nearly all the profitable employments, and from those she is permitted to follow, she receives but a scanty remuneration. He closes against her all the avenues to wealth and distinction which he considers most honorable to himself. As a teacher of theology, medicine, or law, she is not known.

He has denied her the facilities for obtaining a thorough education, all colleges being closed against her.

He allows her in Church, as well as State, but a subordinate position, claiming Apostolic authority for her exclusion from the ministry, and, with some exceptions, from any public participation in the affairs of the Church.

He has created a false public sentiment by giving to the world a different code of morals for men and women, by which moral delinquencies which exclude women from society, are not only tolerated, but deemed of little account in man.

He has usurped the prerogative of Jehovah himself, claiming it as his right to assign for her a sphere of action, when that belongs to her conscience and to her God.

He has endeavored, in every way that he could, to destroy her confidence in her own powers, to lessen her self-respect, and to make her willing to lead a dependent and abject life.

Now, in view of this entire disfranchisement of one-half the people of this country, their social and religious degradation—in view of the unjust laws above mentioned, and because women do feel themselves aggrieved, oppressed, and fraudulently deprived of their most sacred rights, we insist that they have immediate admission to all the rights and privileges which belong to them as citizens of the United States.

In entering upon the great work before us, we anticipate no small amount of misconception, misrepresentation, and ridicule; but we shall use every instrumentality within our power to effect our object. We shall employ agents, circulate tracts, petition the State and National legislatures, and endeavor to enlist the pulpit and the press in our behalf. We hope this Convention will be followed by a series of Conventions embracing every part of the country.

WHEREAS, The great precept of nature is conceded to be, that "man shall pursue his own true and substantial happiness." Blackstone in his Commentaries remarks, that this law of Nature being coeval with mankind, and dictated by God himself, is of course superior in obligation to any other. It is binding over all the globe, in all countries and at all times; no human laws are of any validity if contrary to this, and such of them as are valid, derive all their force, and all their validity, and all their authority, mediately and immediately, from this original; therefore,

Resolved, That such laws as conflict, in any way, with the true and substantial happiness of woman, are contrary to the great precept of nature and of no validity, for this is "superior in obligation to any other."

Resolved, That all laws which prevent woman from occupying such a station in society as her conscience shall dictate, or which place her in a position inferior to that of man, are contrary to the great precept of nature, and therefore of no force or authority.

Resolved, That woman is man's equal—was intended to be so by the Creator, and the highest good of the race demands that she should be recognized as such.

Resolved, That the women of this country ought to be enlightened in regard to the laws under which they live, that they may no longer publish their degradation by declaring themselves satisfied with their present position, nor their ignorance, by asserting that they have all the rights they want.

Resolved, That inasmuch as man, while claiming for himself intellectual superiority, does accord to woman moral superiority, it is pre-eminently his duty to encourage her to speak and teach, as she has an opportunity, in all religious assemblies.

Resolved, That the same amount of virtue, delicacy, and refinement of behavior that is required of woman in the social state, should also be required of man, and the same transgressions should be visited with equal severity on both man and woman.

Resolved, That the objection of indelicacy and impropriety, which is so often brought against woman when she addresses a public audience, comes with a very ill-grace from those who encourage, by their attendance, her appearance on the stage, in the concert, or in feats of the circus.

Resolved, That woman has too long rested satisfied in the circumscribed limits which corrupt customs and a perverted application of the Scriptures have marked out for her, and that it is time she should move in the enlarged sphere which her great Creator has assigned her.

Resolved, That it is the duty of the women of this country to secure to themselves their sacred right to the elective franchise.

Resolved, That the equality of human rights results necessarily from the fact of the identity of the race in capabilities and responsibilities.

Resolved, therefore, That, being invested by the Creator with the same capabilities, and the same consciousness of responsibility for their exercise, it is demonstrably the right and duty of woman, equally with man, to promote every righteous cause by every righteous means; and especially in regard to the great subjects of morals and religion, it is self-evidently her right to participate with her brother in teaching them, both in private and in public, by writing and by speaking, by any instrumentalities proper to be used, and in any assemblies proper to be held; and this being a self-evident truth growing out of the divinely implanted principles of human nature, any custom or authority adverse to it, whether modern or wearing the hoary sanction of antiquity, is to be regarded as a self-evident falsehood, and at war with mankind.

Resolved, That the speedy success of our cause depends upon the zealous and untiring efforts of both men and women, for the overthrow of the monopoly of the pulpit, and for the securing to woman an equal participation with men in the various trades, professions, and commerce.

Ain't I a Woman?

Sojourner Truth

Sojourner Truth (1795–1883)—born Isabella, a slave, in New York State—became a well-known antislavery speaker some time after gaining her freedom in 1827. This speech, given extemporaneously at a woman's rights convention in Akron, Ohio, in 1851, was recorded by Frances Gage, feminist activist and one of the authors of the huge compendium of materials of the first wave, **The History of Woman Suffrage.** *Gage, who was presiding at the meeting, describes the event:*

> *The leaders of the movement trembled on seeing a tall, gaunt black woman in a gray dress and white turban, surmounted with an uncouth sunbonnet, march deliberately into the church, walk with the air of a queen up the aisle, and take her seat upon the pulpit steps. A buzz of disapprobation was heard all over the house, and there fell on the listening ear, "An abolition affair!" "Woman's rights and niggers!" "I told you so!" "Go it, darkey!" . . . Again and again, timorous and trembling ones came to me and said, with earnestness, "Don't let her speak, Mrs. Gage, it will ruin us. Every newspaper in the land will have our cause mixed up with abolition and niggers, and we shall be utterly denounced." My only answer was, "We shall see when the time comes."*

> *The second day the work waxed warm. Methodist, Baptist, Episcopal, Presbyterian, and Universalist ministers came in to hear and discuss the resolutions presented. One claimed superior rights and privileges for man, on the ground of "superior intellect"; another, because of the "manhood of Christ; if God had desired the equality of woman, He would have given some token of His will through the birth, life, and death of the Saviour." Another gave us a theological view of the "sin of our first mother."*

> *There were very few women in those days who dared to "speak in meeting"; and the august teachers of the people were seemingly getting the better of us, while the boys in the galleries, and the sneerers among the pews, were hugely enjoying the discomfiture as they supposed, of the "strong-minded." Some of the tender-skinned friends were on the point of losing dignity, and the atmosphere betokened a storm. When, slowly from her seat in the corner rose Sojourner Truth, who, till now, had scarcely lifted her head. "Don't let her speak!" gasped half a dozen in my ear. She moved slowly and solemnly to the front, laid her old bonnet at her feet, and turned her great speaking eyes to me. There was a hissing sound of disapprobation above and below. I rose and announced, "Sojourner Truth," and begged the audience to keep silence for a few moments.*

> *The tummult subsided at once, and every eye was fixed on this almost Amazon form, which stood nearly six feet high, head erect, and eyes piercing the upper air like one in a dream. At her first word there was a profound hush. She spoke in deep tones, which, though not loud, reached every ear in the house, and away through the throng at the doors and windows.*

One cannot miss that there were those who were staunch for women's rights but yet were racist. It was not until later, much later, that there was much sophisticated analysis linking sexism, racism, and expressions of other kinds.

Truth's speech is reproduced here exactly as Gage recorded it in History of Woman Suffrage.

"WALL, CHILERN, WHAR DAR IS so much racket dar must be somethin' out o' kilter. I tink dat 'twixt de niggers of de Souf and de womin at de Norf, all talkin' 'bout rights, de white men will be in a fix pretty soon. But what's all dis here talkin' 'bout?

"Dat man ober dar say dat womin needs to be helped into carriages, and lifted ober ditches, and to hab de best place everywhar. Nobody eber helps me into carriages, or ober mud-puddles, or gibs me any

---

Elizabeth Cady Stanton, Susan B. Anthony, and Matilda Joslyn Gage, eds., *History of Woman Suffrage,* 2d ed., Vol. 1. Rochester, NY: Charles Mann, 1889.

best place!" And raising herself to her full height, and her voice to a pitch like rolling thunder, she asked. "And a'n't I a woman? Look at me! Look at my arm! (and she bared her right arm to the shoulder, showing her tremendous muscular power). I have ploughed, and planted, and gathered into barns, and no man could head me! And a'n't I a woman? I could work as much and eat as much as a man—when I could get it—and bear de lash as well! And a'n't I a woman? I have borne thirteen chilern, and seen 'em mos' all sold off to slavery, and when I cried out with my mother's grief, none but Jesus heard me! And a'n't I a woman?

"Den dey talks 'bout dis ting in de head; what dis dey call it?" ("Intellect," whispered some one near.) "Dat's it, honey. What's dat got to do wid womin's rights or nigger's rights? If my cup won't hold but a pint, and yourn holds a quart, wouldn't ye be mean not to let me have my little half-measure full?" And she pointed her significant finger, and sent a keen glance at the minister who had made the argument. The cheering was long and loud.

"Den dat little man in black dar, he say women can't have as much rights as men, 'cause Christ wan't a woman! Whar did your Christ come from?" Rolling thunder couldn't have stilled that crowd, as did those deep, wonderful tones, as she stood there with outstretched arms and eyes of fire. Raising her voice still louder, she repeated, "Whar did your

Christ come from? From God and a woman! Man had nothin' to do wid Him." Oh, what a rebuke that was to that little man.

Turning again to another objector, she took up the defense of Mother Eve. I can not follow her through it all. It was pointed, and witty, and solemn; eliciting at almost every sentence deafening applause; and she ended by asserting: "If de fust woman God ever made was strong enough to turn de world upside down all alone, dese women togedder (and she glanced her eye over the platform) ought to be able to turn it back, and get it right side up again! And now dey is asking to do it, de men better let 'em." Long-continued cheering greeted this. "'Bleeged to ye for hearin' on me, and now ole Sojourner han't got nothin' more to say."

Amid roars of applause, she returned to her corner, leaving more than one of us with streaming eyes, and hearts beating with gratitude. She had taken us up in her strong arms and carried us safely over the slough of difficulty turning the whole tide in our favor. I have never in my life seen anything like the magical influence that subdued the mobbish spirit of the day, and turned the sneers and jeers of an excited crowd into notes of respect and admiration. Hundreds rushed up to shake hands with her, and congratulate the glorious old mother, and bid her God-speed on her mission of "testifyin' agin concerning the wickedness of this 'ere people."

Speech Before the Legislature, 1860

Elizabeth Cady Stanton

Elizabeth Cady was born in Johnstown, New York, in 1815. As the daughter of a judge of comfortable means, she encountered people and situations that afforded her more than the usual opportunities for education allowed girls of her time. Having displayed an earnest zest and ability for learning, she was granted special permission to attend the Boys Academy in Johnstown. Prevented by her sex from attending college, she was graduated from the rather conservative Emma Willard Seminary in Troy, New York. Afterward she studied law with her father but, again because of her sex, was prevented from gaining admission to the bar. She had learned, however, precisely how the law burdened women and wives.

Elizabeth's family and friends included many of the brightest thinkers of the Northeast, all of whom taught and influenced her. Her marriage to the activist Henry Stanton in 1840, their trip to the World Anti-Slavery Convention in London, and their move in 1842 to Boston further developed her social sensitivities, knowledge, and thirst for intellectual stimulation. After the family returned from Boston in 1846 to settle in Seneca Falls, New York, Elizabeth became isolated from friends and society. She became immersed in the duties and experiences of a housewife and mother of seven. It suffocated her. Only her visits to her friend Lucretia Mott in Waterloo, New York, revived her. There, with Lucretia and her sister Martha Wright, with Jane Hunt and Mary Ann McClintock, in what could only be called consciousness-raising sessions, seated around a table for tea, the women talked, vented their frustration, and finally planned the convention at Seneca Falls.

After that time, Elizabeth Cady Stanton worked determinedly for the whole range of women's freedoms—from discrimination in marriage and divorce, to freedom from the misogyny of traditional religion (she published the Woman's Bible *in 1895), to suffrage, and more. In 1851 she met Susan B. Anthony, with whom she worked until the end. They founded a radical magazine,* The Revolution, *in 1868, and in 1869 Stanton was elected president of the National Woman's Suffrage Association, an organization she served for over 20 years. Stan-*

ton was always brave and outspoken, often ahead of her time, and sometimes considered too radical even for many of the feminists. She died still at work in New York City in 1902.

Early in 1860, Stanton was invited to address the New York legislature on a pending bill (subsequently passed) for an enlargement of women's property rights. Her speech, presented here, expressed the themes of natural human rights, the necessary limits of authority, and the parallels between blacks and females. Here she introduced, furthermore, another extremely important concept, one that should be carried into the present, that of woman as citizen. We are, after all, citizens of the United States, and our inalienable right is full participation in all the opportunities of this country.

GENTLEMEN OF THE JUDICIARY:—THERE are certain natural rights as inalienable to civilization as are the rights of air and motion to the savage in the wilderness. The natural rights of the civilized man and woman are government, property, the harmonious development of all their powers, and the gratification of their desires. There are a few people we now and then meet who, like Jeremy Bentham, scout the idea of natural rights in civilization, and pronounce them mere metaphors, declaring that there are no rights aside from those the law confers. If the law made man too, that might do, for then he could be made to order to fit the particular niche he was designed to fill. But inasmuch as God made man in His own image, with capacities and powers as boundless as the universe, whose exigencies no mere human law can meet, it is evident that the man must ever stand first; the law but the creature of his wants; the law-giver but the mouthpiece of human-

Elizabeth Cady Stanton, Susan B. Anthony, and Matilda Joslyn Gage, eds., *History of Woman Suffrage*, 2d ed., Vol. 1. Rochester, NY: Charles Mann, 1889. Currently available from Ayer Company Publishers, POB 958, Salem, NH 03079.

ity. If, then, the nature of a being decides its rights, every individual comes into this world with rights that are not transferable. He does not bring them like a pack on his back, that may be stolen from him, but they are a component part of himself, the laws which insure his growth and development. The individual may be put in the stocks, body and soul, he may be dwarfed, crippled, killed, but his rights no man can get; they live and die with him.

Though the atmosphere is forty miles deep all round the globe, no man can do more than fill his own lungs. No man can see, hear, or smell but just so far; and though hundreds are deprived of these senses, his are not the more acute. Though rights have been abundantly supplied by the good Father, no man can appropriate to himself those that belong to another. A citizen can have but one vote, fill but one office, though thousands are not permitted to do either. These axioms prove that woman's poverty does not add to man's wealth, and if, in the plenitude of his power, he should secure to her the exercise of all her God-given rights, her wealth could not bring poverty to him. There is a kind of nervous unrest always manifested by those in power, whenever new claims are started by those out of their own immediate class. The philosophy of this is very plain. They imagine that if the rights of this new class be granted, they must, of necessity, sacrifice something of what they already possess. They can not divest themselves of the idea that rights are very much like lands, stocks, bonds, and mortgages, and that if every new claimant be satisfied, the supply of human rights must in time run low. You might as well carp at the birth of every child, lest there should not be enough air left to inflate your lungs; at the success of every scholar, for fear that your draughts at the fountain of knowledge could not be so long and deep; at the glory of every hero, lest there be no glory left for you. . . .

If the object of government is to protect the weak against the strong, how unwise to place the power wholly in the hands of the strong. Yet that is the history of all governments, even the model republic of these United States. You who have read the history of nations, from Moses down to our last election, where have you ever seen one class looking after the interests of another? Any of you can readily see the defects in other governments, and pronounce sentence against those who have sacri-

ficed the masses to themselves; but when we come to our own case, we are blinded by custom and self-interest. Some of you who have no capital can see the injustice which the laborer suffers; some of you who have no slaves, can see the cruelty of his oppression; but who of you appreciate the galling humiliation, the refinements of degradation, to which women (the mothers, wives, sisters, and daughters of freemen) are subject, in this the last half of the nineteenth century? How many of you have ever read even the laws concerning them that now disgrace your statute-books? In cruelty and tyranny, they are not surpassed by any slaveholding code in the Southern States; in fact they are worse, by just so far as woman, from her social position, refinement, and education, is on a more equal ground with the oppressor.

Allow me just here to call the attention of that party now so much interested in the slave of the Carolinas, to the similarity in his condition and that of the mothers, wives, and daughters of the Empire State. The negro has no name. He is Cuffy Douglas or Cuffy Brooks, just whose Cuffy he may chance to be. The woman has no name. She is Mrs. Richard Roe or Mrs. John Doe, just whose Mrs. she may chance to be. Cuffy has no right to his earnings; he can not buy or sell, or lay up anything that he can call his own. Mrs. Roe has no right to her earnings; she can neither buy nor sell, make contracts, nor lay up anything that she can call her own. Cuffy has no right to his children; they can be sold from him at any time. Mrs. Roe has no right to her children; they may be bound out to cancel a father's debts of honor. The unborn child, even by the last will of the father, may be placed under the guardianship of a stranger and a foreigner. Cuffy has no legal existence; he is subject to restraint and moderate chastisement. Mrs. Roe has no legal existence; she has not the best right to her own person. The husband has the power to restrain, and administer moderate chastisement.

Blackstone declares that the husband and wife are one, and learned commentators have decided that that one is the husband. In all civil codes, you will find them classified as one. Certain rights and immunities, such and such privileges are to be secured to white male citizens. What have women and negroes to do with rights? What know they of government, war, or glory?

The prejudice against color, of which we hear so much, is no stronger than that against sex. It is produced by the same cause, and manifested very much in the same way. The negro's skin and the woman's sex are both *prima facie* evidence that they were intended to be in subjection to the white Saxon man. The few social privileges which the man gives the woman, he makes up to the negro in civil rights. The woman may sit at the same table and eat with the white man; the free negro may hold property and vote. The woman may sit in the same pew with the white man in church; the free negro may enter the pulpit and preach. Now, with the black man's right to suffrage, the right unquestioned, even by Paul, to minister at the altar, it is evident that the prejudice against sex is more deeply rooted and more unreasonably maintained than that against color. As citizens of a republic, which should we most highly prize, social privileges or civil rights? The latter, most certainly.

To those who do not feel the injustice and degradation of the condition, there is something inexpressibly comical in man's "citizen woman." It reminds me of those monsters I used to see in the old world, head and shoulders woman, and the rest of the body sometimes fish and sometimes beast. I used to think, What a strange conceit! but now I see how perfectly it represents man's idea! Look over all his laws concerning us, and you will see just enough of woman to tell of her existence; all the rest is submerged, or made to crawl upon the earth. Just imagine an inhabitant of another planet entertaining himself some pleasant evening in searching over our great national compact, our Declaration of Independence, our Constitutions, or some of our statute-books; what would he think of those "women and negroes" that must be so fenced in, so guarded against? Why, he would certainly suppose we were monsters, like those fabulous giants or Brobdignagians of olden times, so dangerous to civilized man, from our size, ferocity, and power. Then let him take up our poets, from Pope down to Dana; let him listen to our Fourth of July toasts, and some of the sentimental adulations of social life, and no logic could convince him that this creature of the law, and this angel of the family altar, could be one and the same being. Man is in such a labyrinth of contradictions with his marital and property rights; he is so befogged on the whole question of maidens, wives,

and mothers, that from pure benevolence we should relieve him from this troublesome branch of legislation. We should vote, and make laws for ourselves. Do not be alarmed, dear ladies! You need spend no time reading Grotius, Coke, Puffendorf, Blackstone, Bentham, Kent, and Story to find out what you need. We may safely trust the shrewd selfishness of the white man, and consent to live under the same broad code where he has so comfortably ensconced himself. Any legislation that will do for man, we may abide by most cheerfully. . . .

But, say you, we would not have woman exposed to the grossness and vulgarity of public life, or encounter what she must at the polls. When you talk, gentlemen, of sheltering woman from the rough winds and revolting scenes of real life, you must be either talking for effect, or wholly ignorant of what the facts of life are. The man, whatever he is, is known to the woman. She is the companion, not only of the accomplished statesman, the orator, and the scholar; but the vile, vulgar, brutal man has his mother, his wife, his sister, his daughter. Yes, delicate, refined, educated women are in daily life with the drunkard, the gambler, the licentious man, the rogue, and the villain; and if man shows out what he is anywhere, it is at his own hearthstone. There are over forty thousand drunkards in this State. All these are bound by the ties of family to some woman. Allow but a mother and a wife to each, and you have over eighty thousand women. All these have seen their fathers, brothers, husbands, sons, in the lowest and most debased stages of obscenity and degradation. In your own circle of friends, do you not know refined women, whose whole lives are darkened and saddened by gross and brutal associations? Now, gentlemen, do you talk to woman of a rude jest or jostle at the polls, where noble, virtuous men stand ready to protect her person and her rights, when, alone in the darkness and solitude and gloom of night, she has trembled on her own threshold awaiting the return of a husband from his midnight revels?—when, stepping from her chamber, she has beheld her royal monarch, her lord and master—her legal representative—the protector of her property, her home, her children, and her person, down on his hands and knees slowly crawling up the stairs? Behold him in her chamber—in her bed! The fairy tale of "Beauty and the Beast" is far too often realized in life. Gentlemen, such scenes as woman has witnessed at her own fireside, where no eye save Omnipotence could pity, no strong arm could help, can never be realized at the polls, never equaled elsewhere, this side the bottomless pit. No, woman has not hitherto lived in the clouds, surrounded by an atmosphere of purity and peace—but she has been the companion of man in health, in sickness, and in death, in his highest and in his lowest moments. She has worshiped him as a saint and an orator, and pitied him as madman or a fool. In Paradise, man and woman were placed together, and so they must ever be. They must sink or rise together. If man is low and wretched and vile, woman can not escape the contagion, and any atmosphere that is unfit for woman to breathe is not fit for man. Verily, the sins of the fathers shall be visited upon the children to the third and fourth generation. You, by your unwise legislation, have crippled and dwarfed womanhood, by closing to her all honorable and lucrative means of employment, have driven her into the garrets and dens of our cities, where she now revenges herself on your innocent sons, sapping the very foundations of national virtue and strength. Alas! for the young men just coming on the stage of action, who soon shall fill your vacant places—our future Senators, our Presidents, the expounders of our constitutional law! Terrible are the penalties we are now suffering for the ages of injustice done to woman.

Again, it is said that the majority of women do not ask for any change in the laws; that it is time enough to give them the elective franchise when they, as a class, demand it.

Wise statesmen legislate for the best interests of the nation; the State, for the highest good of its citizens; the Christian, for the conversion of the world. Where would have been our railroads, our telegraphs, our ocean steamers, our canals and harbors, our arts and sciences, if government had withheld the means from the far-seeing minority? This State established our present system of common schools, fully believing that educated men and women would make better citizens than ignorant ones. In making this provision for the education of its children, had they waited for a majority of the urchins of this State to petition for schools, how many, think you, would have asked to be transplanted from the street to the school-house? Does the State wait for the criminal to ask for his prison-house? the insane, the idiot, the

deaf and dumb for his asylum? Does the Christian, in his love to all mankind, wait for the majority of the benighted heathen to ask him for the gospel? No; unasked and unwelcomed, he crosses the trackless ocean, rolls off the mountain of superstition that oppresses the human mind, proclaims the immortality of the soul, the dignity of manhood, the right of all to be free and happy.

No, gentlemen, if there is but one woman in this State who feels the injustice of her position, she should not be denied her inalienable rights, because the common household drudge and the silly butterfly of fashion are ignorant of all laws, both human and Divine. Because they know nothing of governments, or rights, and therefore ask nothing, shall my petitions be unheard? I stand before you the rightful representative of woman, claiming a share in the halo of glory that has gathered round her in the ages, and by the wisdom of her past words and works, her peerless heroism and self-sacrifice, I challenge your admiration; and, moreover, claiming, as I do, a share in all her outrages and sufferings, in the cruel injustice, contempt, and ridicule now heaped upon her, in her deep degradation, hopeless wretchedness, by all that is helpless in her present condition, that is false in law and public sentiment, I urge your generous consideration; for as my heart swells with pride to behold woman in the highest walks of literature and art, it grows big enough to take in those who are bleeding in the dust.

Now do not think, gentlemen, we wish you to do a great many troublesome things for us. We do not ask our legislators to spend a whole session fixing up a code of laws to satisfy a class of most unreasonable women. We ask no more than the poor devils in the Scripture asked, "Let us alone." In mercy, let us take care of ourselves, our property, our children, and our homes. True, we are not so strong, so wise, so crafty as you are, but if any kind friend leaves us a little money, or we can by great industry earn fifty cents a day, we would rather buy bread and clothes for our children than cigars and champagne for our legal protectors. There has been a great deal written and said about protection. We, as a class, are tired of one kind of protection, that which leaves us everything to do, to dare, and to suffer, and strips us of all means for its accomplishment. We would not tax man to take care of us. No, the Great Father has endowed all his creatures with the necessary powers for self-support, self-defense, and protection. We do not ask man to represent us; it is hard enough in times like these for man to carry backbone enough to represent himself. So long as the mass of men spend most of their time on the fence, not knowing which way to jump, they are surely in no condition to tell us where we had better stand. In pity for man, we would no longer hang like a millstone round his neck. Undo what man did for us in the dark ages, and strike out all special legislation for us; strike the words "white male" from all your constitutions, and then, with fair sailing, let us sink or swim, live or die, survive or perish together.

At Athens, an ancient apologue tells us, on the completion of the temple of Minerva, a statue of the goddess was wanted to occupy the crowning point of the edifice. Two of the greatest artists produced what each deemed his masterpiece. One of these figures was the size of life, admirably designed, exquisitely finished, softly rounded, and beautifully refined. The other was of Amazonian stature, and so boldly chiselled that it looked more like masonry than sculpture. The eyes of all were attracted by the first, and turned away in contempt from the second. That, therefore, was adopted, and the other rejected, almost with resentment, as though an insult had been offered to a discerning public. The favored statue was accordingly borne in triumph to the place for which it was designed, in the presence of applauding thousands, but as it receded from their upturned eyes, all, all at once agaze upon it, the thunders of applause unaccountably died away—a general misgiving ran through every bosom—the mob themselves stood like statues, as silent and as petrified, for as it slowly went up, and up the soft expression of those chiselled features, the delicate curves and outlines of the limbs and figure, became gradually fainter and fainter, and when at last it reached the place for which it was intended, it was a shapeless ball, enveloped in mist. Of course, the idol of the hour was now clamored down as rationally as it had been cried up, and its dishonored rival, with no good will and no good looks on the part of the chagrined populace, was reared in its stead. As it ascended, the sharp angles faded away, the rough points became smooth, the features full of expression, the whole figure radiant with majesty and beauty. The rude hewn mass, that before had

scarcely appeared to bear even the human form, assumed at once the divinity which it represented, being so perfectly proportioned to the dimensions of the building, and to the elevation on which it stood, that it seemed as though Pallas herself had alighted upon the pinnacle of the temple in person, to receive the homage of her worshippers.

The woman of the nineteenth century is the shapeless ball in the lofty position which she was designed fully and nobly to fill. The place is not too high, too large, too sacred for woman, but the type that you have chosen is far too small for it. The woman we declare unto you is the rude, misshapen, unpolished object of the successful artist. From your stand-point, you are absorbed with the defects alone. The true artist sees the harmony between the object and its destination. Man, the sculptor, has carved out his ideal, and applauding thousands welcome his success. He has made a woman that from his low stand-point looks fair and beautiful, a being without rights, or hopes, or fears but in him—neither noble, virtuous, nor independent. Where do we see, in Church or State, in school-house or at the fireside, the much talked-of moral power of woman? Like those Athenians, we have bowed down and worshiped in woman, beauty, grace, the exquisite proportions, the soft and beautifully rounded outline, her delicacy, refinement, and silent helplessness— all well when she is viewed simply as an object of sight, never to rise one foot above the dust from which she sprung. But if she is to be raised up to adorn a temple, or represent a divinity—if she is to fill the niche of wife and counsellor to true and noble men, if she is to be the mother, the educator of a race of heroes or martyrs, of a Napoleon, or a Jesus— then must the type of womanhood be on a larger scale than that yet carved by man.

In vain would the rejected artist have reasoned with the Athenians as to the superiority of his production; nothing short of the experiment they made could have satisfied them. And what of your experiment, what of your wives, your homes? Alas! for the folly and vacancy that meet you there! But for your club-houses and newspapers, what would social life be to you? Where are your beautiful women? your frail ones, taught to lean lovingly and confidingly on man? Where are the crowds of educated dependents—where the long line of pensioners on man's bounty? Where all the young girls, taught to believe that marriage is the only legitimate object of a woman's pursuit—they who stand listlessly on life's shores, waiting, year after year, like the sick man at the pool of Bethesda, for some one to come and put them in? These are they who by their ignorance and folly curse almost every fireside with some human specimen of deformity or imbecility. These are they who fill the gloomy abodes of poverty and vice in our vast metropolis. These are they who patrol the streets of our cities, to give our sons their first lessons in infamy. These are they who fill our asylums, and make night hideous with their cries and groans.

The women who are called masculine, who are brave, courageous, self-reliant and independent, are they who in the face of adverse winds have kept one steady course upward and onward in the paths of virtue and peace—they who have taken their gauge of womanhood from their own native strength and dignity—they who have learned for themselves the will of God concerning them. This is our type of womanhood. Will you help us raise it up, that you too may see its beautiful proportions—that you may behold the outline of the goddess who is yet to adorn your temple of Freedom? We are building a model republic; our edifice will one day need a crowning glory. Let the artists be wisely chosen. Let them begin their work. Here is a temple to Liberty, to human rights, on whose portals behold the glorious declaration, "All men are created equal." The sun has never yet shone upon any of man's creations that can compare with this. The artist who can mold a statue worthy to crown magnificence like this, must be godlike in his conceptions, grand in his comprehensions, sublimely beautiful in his power of execution. The woman—the crowning glory of the model republic among the nations of the earth—what must she not be?

Constitutional Argument

Susan B. Anthony

Susan B. Anthony was born in Adams, Massachusetts, in 1820. Her father, a Quaker steeped in that religion's historical principle of sexual equality, held Susan in high regard. He educated her as he would a son, taught her responsibility and self-reliance, entrusted her with the management of his farm, and introduced her to the people and ideas of the liberal reform movements current in Rochester, New York, where they had come to live in about 1839. In her teens, Susan taught at the Canajoharie Institute, but teaching was not a sufficient challenge for her. Later, having returned to Rochester, she became active in a reform movement to which several of her friends belonged—temperance. It was through the Rochester Daughters of Temperance that she met Amelia Bloomer of Seneca Falls, who, in 1851, introduced her to Elizabeth Cady Stanton.

The women quickly became friends. Anthony was soon invited to Stanton's home to discuss ideas, and Anthony's views developed rapidly to coalesce with Stanton's. The two lectured, worked together, and founded The Revolution, *a radical magazine. In 1872, to bring to the test of the Supreme Court her conviction that as a citizen she was guaranteed by the Fourteenth Amendment the right to vote, Anthony "knowingly, wrongfully, and unlawfully" cast a vote in the election in Rochester. Arrested, convicted, and fined, she refused to pay, hoping for an appeal path, but the fine was not pursued. Nonetheless, she brought her principle into view and gained considerable sympathy. Later she was to lecture on coeducation (deemed radical at the time) and on all the various women's issues and to serve in the National American Woman's Suffrage Association and on the International Council of Women. In 1902, shortly after her retirement, she died.*

Like Stanton, Anthony was one of the strongest models in feminist history. The following selection is from a speech delivered during a tour of New York State prior to her trial in 1873. In it Anthony argued her thesis that both the original conception and the current law
of the U.S. Constitution guaranteed her a citizen's right to vote.

DELIVERED IN TWENTY-NINE OF THE post-office districts of Monroe, and twenty-one of Ontario, in Miss Anthony's canvass of those counties prior to her trial in June, 1873.

Friends and Fellow-Citizens:—I stand before you under indictment for the alleged crime of having voted at the last presidential election, without having a lawful right to vote. It shall be my work this evening to prove to you that in thus doing, I not only committed no crime, but instead simply exercised my citizen's right, guaranteed to me and all United States citizens by the National Constitution beyond the power of any State to deny.

Our democratic-republican government is based on the idea of the natural right of every individual member thereof to a voice and a vote in making and executing the laws. We assert the province of government to be to secure the people in the enjoyment of their inalienable rights. We throw to the winds the old dogma that government can give rights. No one denies that before governments were organized each individual possessed the right to protect his own life, liberty and property. When 100 or 1,000,000 people enter into a free government, they do not barter away their natural rights; they simply pledge themselves to protect each other in the enjoyment of them through prescribed judicial and legislative tribunals. They agree to abandon the methods of brute force in the adjustment of their differences and adopt those of civilization. Nor can you find a word in any of the grand documents left

From Ida H. Harper, *Life and Work of Susan B. Anthony,* Vol. II. Indianapolis, IN: Bowen-Merrill, 1898.

us by the fathers which assumes for government the power to create or to confer rights. The Declaration of Independence, the United States Constitution, the constitutions of the several States and the organic laws of the Territories, all alike propose to *protect* the people in the exercise of their God-given rights. Not one of them pretends to bestow rights.

All men are created equal, and endowed by their Creator with certain inalienable rights. Among these are life, liberty and the pursuit of happiness. To secure these, governments are instituted among men, deriving their just powers from the consent of the governed.

Here is no shadow of government authority over rights, or exclusion of any class from their full and equal enjoyment. Here is pronounced the right of all men, and "consequently," as the Quaker preacher said, "of all women," to a voice in the government. And here, in this first paragraph of the Declaration, is the assertion of the natural right of all to the ballot; for how can "the consent of the governed" be given, if the right to vote be denied? Again:

Whenever any form of government becomes destructive of these ends, it is the right of the people to alter or abolish it, and to institute a new government, laying its foundations on such principles, and organizing its powers in such form, as to them shall seem most likely to effect their safety and happiness.

Surely the right of the whole people to vote is here clearly implied; for however destructive to their happiness this government might become, a disfranchised class could neither alter nor abolish it, nor institute a new one, except by the old brute force method of insurrection and rebellion. One-half of the people of this nation today are utterly powerless to blot from the statute books an unjust law, or to write there a new and a just one. The women, dissatisfied as they are with this form of government, that enforces taxation without representation—that compels them to obey laws to which they never have given their consent—that imprisons and hangs them without a trial by a jury of their peers—that robs them, in marriage, of the custody of their own persons, wages and children—are this half of the people who are left wholly at the mercy of the other half, in direct violation of the spirit and letter of the declarations of the framers of this government, every one of which was based on the immutable principle of equal rights to all. By these declarations, kings, popes, priests, aristocrats, all were alike dethroned and placed on a common level, politically, with the lowliest born subject or serf. By them, too, men, as such, were deprived of their divine right to rule and placed on a political level with women. By the practice of these declarations all class and caste distinctions would be abolished, and slave, serf, plebeian, wife, woman, all alike rise from their subject position to the broader platform of equality.

The preamble of the Federal Constitution says:

We, the people of the United States, in order to form a more perfect union, establish justice, insure domestic tranquillity, provide for the common defence, promote the general welfare and secure the blessings of liberty to ourselves and our posterity, do ordain and establish this Constitution for the United States of America.

It was we, the people, not we, the white male citizens, nor we, the male citizens; but we, the whole people, who formed this Union. We formed it not to give the blessings of liberty but to secure them; not to the half of ourselves and the half of our posterity, but to the whole people—women as well as men. It is downright mockery to talk to women of their enjoyment of the blessings of liberty while they are denied the only means of securing them provided by this democratic-republican government—the ballot. . . .

But I submit that in view of the explicit assertions of the equal right of the whole people, both in the preamble and previous article of the constitution, this omission of the adjective "female" should not be construed into a denial; but instead should be considered as of no effect. Mark the direct prohibition, "No member of this State shall be disfranchised, unless by the law of the land, or the judgment of his peers." "The law of the land" is the United States Constitution; and there is no provision in that document which can be fairly construed into a permission to the States to deprive any class of citizens of their right to vote. Hence New York can get no power from that source to disfranchise one entire half of her members. Nor has "the judgment of their peers" been pronounced against women exercising their right to vote; no disfranchised person is allowed to be judge or juror—and none but disfranchised persons can be women's peers. Nor has the legislature passed laws excluding women as a class on account of idiocy or lunacy; nor have the courts convicted them of bribery, larceny or any infamous crime. Clearly, then, there is no constitutional ground for the exclusion of women from the ballot-box in the State of New York. No barriers whatever stand today between women and the exercise of their right to vote save those of precedent and prejudice, which refuse to expunge the word "male" from the constitution. . . .

For any State to make sex a qualification, which must ever result in the disfranchisement of one entire half of the people, is to pass a bill of attainder, an ex post facto law, and is therefore a violation of the supreme law of the land. By it the blessings of liberty are forever withheld from women and their female posterity. For them, this government has no just powers derived from the consent of the governed. For them this government is not a democracy; it is not a republic. It is the most odious aristocracy ever established on the face of the globe. An oligarchy of wealth, where the rich govern the poor; an oligarchy of learning, where the educated govern the ignorant; or even an oligarchy of race, where the Saxon rules the African, might be endured; but this oligarchy of sex which makes father, brothers, husband, sons, the oligarchs over the mother and sisters, the wife and daughters of every household; which ordains all men sovereigns, all women subjects— carries discord and rebellion into every home of the nation. This most odious aristocracy exists, too, in the face of Section 4, Article IV, which says: "The United States shall guarantee to every State in the Union a republican form of government."

What, I ask you, is the distinctive difference between the inhabitants of a monarchical and those of a republican form of government, save that in the monarchical the people are subjects, helpless, powerless, bound to obey laws made by political superiors; while in the republican the people are citizens, individual sovereigns, all clothed with equal power to make and unmake both their laws and lawmakers? The moment you deprive a person of his right to a voice in the government, you degrade him from the status of a citizen of the republic to that of a

subject. It matters very little to him whether his monarch be an individual tyrant, as is the Czar of Russia, or a 15,000,000 headed monster, as here in the United States; he is a powerless subject, serf or slave; not in any sense a free and independent citizen.

It is urged that the use of the masculine pronouns *he*, *his* and *him* in all the constitutions and laws, is proof that only men were meant to be included in their provisions. If you insist on this version of the letter of the law, we shall insist that you be consistent and accept the other horn of the dilemma, which would compel you to exempt women from taxation for the support of the government and from penalties for the violation of laws. There is no *she* or *her* or *hers* in the tax laws, and this is equally true of all the criminal laws.

Take for example the civil rights law which I am charged with having violated; not only are all the pronouns in it masculine, but everybody knows that it was intended expressly to hinder the rebel men from voting. It reads, "If any person shall knowingly vote without *his* having a lawful right." It was precisely so with all the papers served on me—the United States marshal's warrant, the bail-bond, the petition for habeas corpus, the bill of indictment—not one of them had a feminine pronoun; but to make them applicable to me, the clerk of the court prefixed an "s" to the "he" and made "her" out of "his" and "him"; and I insist if government officials may thus manipulate the pronouns to tax, fine, imprison and hang women, it is their duty to thus change them in order to protect us in our right to vote.

So long as any classes of men were denied this right, the government made a show of consistency by exempting them from taxation. When a property qualification of $250 was required of black men in New York, they were not compelled to pay taxes so long as they were content to report themselves worth less than that sum; but the moment the black man died and his property fell to his widow or daughter, the black woman's name was put on the assessor's list and she was compelled to pay taxes on this same property. This also is true of ministers in New York. So long as the minister lives, he is exempted from taxation on $1,500 of property, but the moment the breath leaves his body, his widow's name goes on the assessor's list and she has to pay taxes on the $1,500. So much for special legislation in favor of women! . . .

The only question left to be settled now is: Are women persons? I scarcely believe any of our opponents will have the hardihood to say they are not. Being persons, then, women are citizens, and no State has a right to make any new law, or to enforce any old law, which shall abridge their privileges or immunities. Hence, every discrimination against women in the constitutions and laws of the several States is today null and void, precisely as is every one against negroes. . . .

If once we establish the false principle that United States citizenship does not carry with it the right to vote in every State in this Union, there is no end to the petty tricks and cunning devices which will be attempted to exclude one and another class of citizens from the right of suffrage. It will not always be the men combining to disfranchise all women; native born men combining to abridge the rights of all naturalized citizens, as in Rhode Island. It will not always be the rich and educated who may combine to cut off the poor and ignorant; but we may live to see the hard-working, uncultivated day laborers, foreign and native born, learning the power of the ballot and their vast majority of numbers, combine and amend State constitutions so as to disfranchise the Vanderbilts, the Stewarts, the Conklings and the Fentons. It is a poor rule that won't work more ways than one. Establish this precedent, admit the State's right to deny suffrage, and there is no limit to the confusion, discord and disruption that may await us. There is and can be but one safe principle of government—equal rights to all. Discrimination against any class on account of color, race, nativity, sex, property, culture, can but embitter and disaffect that class, and thereby endanger the safety of the whole people. Clearly, then, the national government not only must define the rights of citizens, but must stretch out its powerful hand and protect them in every State in this Union.

If, however, you will insist that the Fifteenth Amendment's emphatic interdiction against robbing United States citizens of their suffrage "on account of race, color or previous condition of servitude," is a recognition of the right of either the United States or any State to deprive them of the

ballot for any or all other reasons, I will prove to you that the class of citizens for whom I now plead are, by all the principles of our government and many of the laws of the States, included under the term "previous condition of servitude."

Consider first married women and their legal status. What is servitude? "The condition of a slave." What is a slave? "A person who is robbed of the proceeds of his labor; a person who is subject to the will of another." By the laws of Georgia, South Carolina and all the States of the South, the negro had no right to the custody and control of his person. He belonged to his master. If he were disobedient, the master had the right to use correction. If the negro did not like the correction and ran away, the master had the right to use coercion to bring him back. By the laws of almost every State in this Union today, North as well as South, the married woman has no right to the custody and control of her person. The wife belongs to the husband; and if she refuse obedience he may use moderate correction, and if she do not like his moderate correction and leave his "bed and board," the husband may use moderate coercion to bring her back. The little word "moderate," you see, is the saving clause for the wife, and would doubtless be overstepped should her offended husband administer his correction with the "cat-o'-nine-tails," or accomplish his coercion with blood-hounds.

Again the slave had no right to the earnings of his hands, they belonged to his master; no right to the custody of his children, they belonged to his master; no right to sue or be sued, or to testify in the courts. If he committed a crime, it was the master who must sue or be sued. In many of the States there has been special legislation, giving married women the right to property inherited or received by bequest, or earned by the pursuit of any avocation outside the home; also giving them the right to sue and be sued in matters pertaining to such separate property; but not a single State of this Union has ever secured the wife in the enjoyment of her right to equal ownership of the joint earnings of the marriage copartnership. And since, in the nature of things, the vast majority of married women never earn a dollar by work outside their families, or inherit a dollar from their fathers, it follows that from the day of their marriage to the day of the death of their husbands not one of them ever has a dollar, except it shall please her husband to let her have it.

In some of the States, also, laws have been passed giving to the mother a joint right with the father in the guardianship of the children. Twenty-five years ago, when our woman's rights movement commenced, by the laws of all the States the father had the sole custody and control of the children. No matter if he were a brutal, drunken libertine, he had the legal right, without the mother's consent, to apprentice her sons to rumsellers or her daughters to brothel-keepers. He even could will away an un-born child from the mother. In most of the States this law still prevails, and the mothers are utterly powerless.

I doubt if there is, today, a State in this Union where a married woman can sue or be sued for slan-der of character, and until recently there was not one where she could sue or be sued for injury of person. However damaging to the wife's reputation any slander may be, she is wholly powerless to in-stitute legal proceedings against her accuser unless her husband shall join with her; and how often have we heard of the husband conspiring with some out-side barbarian to blast the good name of his wife? A married woman can not testify in courts in cases of joint interest with her husband. . . .

I submit the question, if the deprivation by law of the ownership of one's own person, wages, prop-erty, children, the denial of the right as an individ-ual to sue and be sued and testify in the courts, is not a condition of servitude most bitter and abso-lute, even though under the sacred name of mar-riage? Does any lawyer doubt my statement of the legal status of married women? I will remind him of the fact that the common law of England prevails in every State but two in this Union, except where the legislature has enacted special laws annulling it. I am ashamed that not one of the States yet has blot-ted from its statute books the old law of marriage, which, summed up in the fewest words possible, is in effect "husband and wife are one, and that one the husband."

Thus may all married women and widows, by the laws of the several States, be technically in-cluded in the Fifteenth Amendment's specification of "condition of servitude," present or previous. The facts also prove that, by all the great fundamen-tal principles of our free government, not only married women but the entire womanhood of the nation are in a "condition of servitude" as surely as were our Revolutionary fathers when they rebelled against King George. Women are taxed without rep-resentation, governed without their consent, tried, convicted and punished without a jury of their peers. Is all this tyranny any less humiliating and degrad-ing to women under our democratic-republican government today than it was to men under their aristocratic, monarchial government one hundred years ago? . . .

Is anything further needed to prove woman's condition of servitude sufficient to entitle her to the guarantees of the Fifteenth Amendment? Is there a man who will not agree with me that to talk of free-dom without the ballot is mockery to the women of this republic, precisely as New England's orator, Wendell Phillips, at the close of the late war de-clared it to be to the newly emancipated black man? I admit that, prior to the rebellion, by common con-sent, the right to enslave, as well as to disfranchise both native and foreign born persons, was conceded to the States. But the one grand principle settled by the war and the reconstruction legislation, is the su-premacy of the national government to protect the citizens of the United States in their right to freedom and the elective franchise, against any and every interference on the part of the several States; and again and again have the American people asserted the triumph of this principle by their overwhelming majorities for Lincoln and Grant. . . .

It is upon this just interpretation of the United States Constitution that our National Woman Suf-frage Association, which celebrates the twenty-fifth anniversary of the woman's rights movement next May in New York City, has based all its arguments and action since the passage of these amendments. We no longer petition legislature or Congress to give us the right to vote, but appeal to women everywhere to exercise their too long neglected "cit-izen's right."

Woman and the New Race

Margaret Sanger

Nothing has contributed so much to women's growing liberation as the increasing control women can exercise over their reproductive capacities. Although some forms of birth control had been practiced in antiquity, it did not become a major force in the lives of ordinary women, especially poor women, until the twentieth century. In this country, into the 1930s, the so-called Comstock Laws of 1873 forbade the distribution of birth control information through the mails, and many states had laws prohibiting the use and sale of contraceptives. The efforts of the Birth Control League and, particularly, Margaret Sanger eventually resulted in the social acceptance of "planned parenthood."

Sanger was born in Corning, New York, in 1883. She studied nursing in White Plains and New York City. Early in her first marriage, she worked as an obstetrical nurse on New York's impoverished Lower East Side, where she saw the destructive burdens unchecked reproduction imposed on the poor and underprivileged. After studying contraception in Europe in 1913, she returned to New York, where she founded the magazine Woman Rebel *and, in 1916, opened her first clinic with her sister, Ethel Byrne, and a friend, Fania Mindell. All were arrested, and Byrne was subsequently jailed and mistreated. The episode brought this until-then rarely discussed issue into public view, and 1917 saw the founding of the National Birth Control League, with a growing membership.*

Although the birth control campaign did not have the support of many of the established women's rights organizations, who feared the controversy, various reform groups (including some trade unions) and women activists, many from the suffrage movement, pressed vehemently for birth control. Circumstances were in many ways analogous to today's abortion debate. Then, as now, opposition was highly charged and well organized in both religious and political circles; the poor were in even greater need of the reform than were the more affluent; and issues centered on matters of morality and "nature." Sanger ultimately won her fight. By 1952 in Bombay, she was well respected and was named first

president of the International Planned Parenthood Federation. She died in Arizona in 1966. She had founded various journals and leagues and had written six books, including Woman and the New Race *(1920). In the section reprinted here, Sanger argues the claims of women's right to personal freedom and autonomy in procreative decisions, points out the implications for the world community of unchecked reproduction, and focuses on the centrality of women alone in carrying the burdens and responsibilities of having and rearing children. These remain contemporary themes.*

WOMAN'S ERROR AND HER DEBT

THE MOST FAR-REACHING SOCIAL DEVELOPMENT of modern times is the revolt of woman against sex servitude. The most important force in the remaking of the world is a free motherhood. Beside this force, the elaborate international programmes of modern statesmen are weak and superficial. Diplomats may formulate leagues of nations and nations may pledge their utmost strength to maintain them, statesmen may dream of reconstructing the world out of alliances, hegemonies and spheres of influence, but woman, continuing to produce explosive populations, will convert these pledges into the proverbial scraps of paper; or she may, by controlling birth, lift motherhood to the plane of a voluntary, intelligent function, and remake the world. When the world is thus remade, it will exceed the dream of statesman, reformer and revolutionist.

Only in recent years has woman's position as the gentler and weaker half of the human family been emphatically and generally questioned. Men assumed that this was woman's place; woman herself accepted it. It seldom occurred to anyone to ask whether she would go on occupying it forever.

From Margaret Sanger, *Woman and the New Race*. New York: Brentano's Publishers, 1920.

Upon the mere surface of woman's organized protests there were no indications that she was desirous of achieving a fundamental change in her position. She claimed the right of suffrage and legislative regulation of her working hours, and asked that her property rights be equal to those of the man. None of these demands, however, affected directly the most vital factors of her existence. Whether she won her point or failed to win it, she remained a dominated weakling in a society controlled by men.

Woman's acceptance of her inferior status was the more real because it was unconscious. She had chained herself to her place in society and the family through the maternal functions of her nature, and only chains thus strong could have bound her to her lot as a brood animal for the masculine civilizations of the world. In accepting her rôle as the "weaker and gentler half," she accepted that function. In turn, the acceptance of that function fixed the more firmly her rank as an inferior.

Caught in this "vicious circle," woman has, through her reproductive ability, founded and perpetuated the tyrannies of the Earth. Whether it was the tyranny of a monarchy, an oligarchy or a republic, the one indispensable factor of its existence was, as it is now, hordes of human beings—human beings so plentiful as to be cheap, and so cheap that ignorance was their natural lot. Upon the rock of an unenlightened, submissive maternity have these been founded; upon the product of such a maternity have they flourished.

No despot ever flung forth his legions to die in foreign conquest, no privilege-ruled nation ever erupted across its borders, to lock in death embrace with another, but behind them loomed the driving power of a population too large for its boundaries and its natural resources.

No period of low wages or of idleness with their want among the workers, no peonage or sweatshop, no child-labor factory, ever came into being, save from the same source. Nor have famine and plague been as much "acts of God" as acts of too prolific mothers. They, also, as all students know, have their basic causes in over-population.

The creators of over-population are the women, who, while wringing their hands over each fresh horror, submit anew to their task of producing the multitudes who will bring about the *next* tragedy of civilization.

While unknowingly laying the foundations of tyrannies and providing the human tinder for racial conflagrations, woman was also unknowingly creating slums, filling asylums with insane, and institutions with other defectives. She was replenishing the ranks of the prostitutes, furnishing grist for the criminal courts and inmates for prisons. Had she planned deliberately to achieve this tragic total of human waste and misery, she could hardly have done it more effectively.

Woman's passivity under the burden of her disastrous task was almost altogether that of ignorant resignation. She knew virtually nothing about her reproductive nature and less about the consequences of her excessive childbearing. It is true that, obeying the inner urge of their natures, *some* women revolted. They went even to the extreme of infanticide and abortion. Usually their revolts were not general enough. They fought as individuals, not as a mass. In the mass they sank back into blind and hopeless subjection. They went on breeding with staggering rapidity those numberless, undesired children who become the clogs and the destroyers of civilizations.

To-day, however, woman is rising in fundamental revolt. Even her efforts at mere reform are, as we shall see later, steps in that direction. Underneath each of them is the feminine urge to complete freedom. Millions of women are asserting their right to voluntary motherhood. They are determined to decide for themselves whether they shall become mothers, under what conditions and when. This is the fundamental revolt referred to. It is for woman the key to the temple of liberty.

Even as birth control is the means by which woman attains basic freedom, so it is the means by which she must and will uproot the evil she has wrought through her submission. As she has unconsciously and ignorantly brought about social disaster, so must and will she consciously and intelligently *undo* that disaster and create a new and a better order.

The task is hers. It cannot be avoided by excuses, nor can it be delegated. It is not enough for woman to point to the self-evident domination of man. Nor does it avail to plead the guilt of rulers and the exploiters of labor. It makes no difference that she does not formulate industrial systems nor that she is an instinctive believer in social justice. In her submission lies her error and her guilt. By her failure to withhold the multitudes of children who have made inevitable the most flagrant of our social evils, she incurred a debt to society. Regardless of her own wrongs, regardless of her lack of opportunity and regardless of all other considerations, *she* must pay that debt.

She must not think to pay this debt in any superficial way. She cannot pay it with palliatives—with child-labor laws, prohibition, regulation of prostitution and agitation against war. Political nostrums and social panaceas are but incidentally and superficially useful. They do not touch the source of the social disease.

War, famine, poverty and oppression of the workers will continue while woman makes life cheap. They will cease only when she limits her reproductivity and human life is no longer a thing to be wasted.

Two chief obstacles hinder the discharge of this tremendous obligation. The first and the lesser is the legal barrier. Dark-Age laws would still deny to her the knowledge of her reproductive nature. Such knowledge is indispensable to intelligent motherhood and she must achieve it, despite absurd statutes and equally absurd moral canons.

The second and more serious barrier is her own ignorance of the extent and effect of her submission. Until she knows the evil her subjection has wrought to herself, to her progeny and to the world at large, she cannot wipe out that evil.

To get rid of these obstacles is to invite attack from the forces of reaction which are so strongly entrenched in our present-day society. It means warfare in every phase of her life. Nevertheless, at whatever cost, she must emerge from her ignorance and assume her responsibility.

She can do this only when she has awakened to a knowledge of herself and of the consequences of her ignorance. The first step is birth control. Through birth control she will attain to voluntary motherhood. Having attained this, the basic freedom of her sex, she will cease to enslave herself and the mass of humanity. Then, through the understanding of the intuitive forward urge within her, she will not stop at patching up the world; she will remake it.

BIRTH CONTROL—A PARENTS' PROBLEM OR WOMAN'S?

The problem of birth control has arisen directly from the effort of the feminine spirit to free itself from bondage. Woman herself has wrought that bondage through her reproductive powers and while enslaving herself has enslaved the world. The physical suffering to be relieved is chiefly woman's. Hers, too, is the love life that dies first under the blight of too prolific breeding. Within her is wrapped up the future of the race—it is hers to make or mar. All of these considerations point unmistakably to one fact—it is woman's duty as well as her privilege to lay hold of the means of freedom. Whatever men may do, she cannot escape the responsibility. For ages she has been deprived of the opportunity to meet this obligation. She is now emerging from her helplessness. Even as no one can share the suffering of the overburdened mother, so no one can do this work for her. Others may help, but she and she alone can free herself.

The basic freedom of the world is woman's freedom. A free race cannot be born of slave mothers. A woman enchained cannot choose but give a measure of that bondage to her sons and daughters. No woman can call herself free who does not own and control her body. No woman can call herself free until she can choose consciously whether she will or will not be a mother.

It does not greatly alter the case that some women call themselves free because they earn their own livings, while others profess freedom because they defy the conventions of sex relationship. She who earns her own living gains a sort of freedom that is not to be undervalued, but in quality and in quantity it is of little account beside the untrammeled choice of mating or not mating, of being a mother or not being a mother. She gains food and clothing and shelter, at least, without submitting to the charity of her companion, but the earning of her own living does not give her the development of her inner sex urge, far deeper and more powerful in its outworkings than any of these externals. In order to have that development, she must still meet and solve the problem of motherhood.

With the so-called "free" woman, who chooses a mate in defiance of convention, freedom is largely a question of character and audacity. If she does attain to an unrestricted choice of a mate, she is still in a position to be enslaved through her reproductive powers. Indeed, the pressure of law and custom upon the woman not legally married is likely to make her more of a slave than the woman fortunate enough to marry the man of her choice.

Look at it from any standpoint you will, suggest any solution you will, conventional or unconventional, sanctioned by law or in defiance of law, woman is in the same position, fundamentally, until she is able to determine for herself whether she will be a mother and to fix the number of her offspring. This unavoidable situation is alone enough to make birth control, first of all, a woman's problem. On the very face of the matter, voluntary motherhood is chiefly the concern of the woman.

It is persistently urged, however, that since sex expression is the act of two, the responsibility of controlling the results should not be placed upon woman alone. Is it fair, it is asked, to give her, instead of the man, the task of protecting herself when she is, perhaps, less rugged in physique than her mate, and has, at all events, the normal, periodic inconveniences of her sex?

We must examine this phase of her problem in two lights—that of the ideal, and of the conditions working toward the ideal. In an ideal society, no doubt, birth control would become the concern of the man as well as the woman. The hard, inescapable fact which we encounter to-day is that man has not only refused any such responsibility, but has individually and collectively sought to prevent woman from obtaining knowledge by which she could assume this responsibility for herself. She is still in the position of a dependent to-day because her mate has refused to consider her as an individual apart from his needs. She is still bound because she has in the past left the solution of the problem to him. Having left it to him, she finds that instead of rights, she has only such privileges as she has gained by petitioning, coaxing and cozening. Having left it to him, she is exploited, driven and enslaved to his desires.

While it is true that he suffers many evils as the consequence of this situation, she suffers vastly more. While it is true that he should be awakened to the cause of these evils, we know that they come home to her with crushing force every day. It is she who has the long burden of carrying, bearing and rearing the unwanted children. It is she who must watch beside the beds of pain where lie the babies who suffer because they have come into overcrowded homes. It is her heart that the sight of the deformed, the subnormal, the undernourished, the overworked child smites first and oftenest and hardest. It is *her* love life that dies first in the fear of undesired pregnancy. It is her opportunity for self expression that perishes first and most hopelessly because of it.

Conditions, rather than theories, facts, rather than dreams, govern the problem. They place it squarely upon the shoulders of woman. She has learned that whatever the moral responsibility of the man in this direction may be, he does not discharge it. She has learned that, lovable and considerate as the individual husband may be, she has nothing to expect from men in the mass, when they make laws and decree customs. She knows that regardless of what ought to be, the brutal unavoidable fact is that she will never receive her freedom until she takes it for herself.

Having learned this much, she has yet something more to learn. Women are too much inclined to follow in the footsteps of men, to try to think as men think, to try to solve the general problems of life as men solve them. If after attaining their freedom, women accept conditions in the spheres of government, industry, art, morals and religion as they find them, they will be but taking a leaf out of man's book. The woman is not needed to do man's work. She is not needed to think man's thoughts. She need not fear that the masculine mind, almost universally dominant, will fail to take care of its own. Her mission is not to enhance the masculine spirit, but to express the feminine; hers is not to preserve a man-made world, but to create a human world by the infusion of the feminine element into all of its activities.

Woman must not accept; she must challenge. She must not be awed by that which has been built up around her; she must reverence that within her which struggles for expression. Her eyes must be less upon what is and more clearly upon what should be. She must listen only with a frankly questioning attitude to the dogmatized opinions of man-made society. When she chooses her new, free course of action, it must be in the light of her own opinion—of her own intuition. Only so can she give play to the feminine spirit. Only thus can she free her mate from the bondage which he wrought for himself when he wrought hers. Only thus can she restore to him that of which he robbed himself in restricting her. Only thus can she remake the world.

The world is, indeed, hers to remake, it is hers to build and to recreate. Even as she has permitted the suppression of her own feminine element and the consequent impoverishment of industry, art, letters, science, morals, religions and social intercourse, so it is hers to enrich all these.

Woman must have her freedom—the fundamental freedom of choosing whether or not she shall be a mother and how many children she will have. Regardless of what man's attitude may be, that problem is hers—and before it can be his, it is hers alone.

She goes through the vale of death alone, each time a babe is born. As it is the right neither of man nor the state to coerce her into this ordeal, so it is her right to decide whether she will endure it. That right to decide imposes upon her the duty of clearing the way to knowledge by which she may make and carry out the decision.

Birth control is woman's problem. The quicker she accepts it as hers and hers alone, the quicker will society respect motherhood. The quicker, too, will the world be made a fit place for her children to live.

Woman as "Other"

Simone de Beauvoir

French existentialist Simone de Beauvoir (1908–1986) is one of the most important figures of the women's movement in the twentieth century. The Second Sex was one of the earliest inquiries into the social construction of "femininity" and sparked a great deal of debate. Beauvoir was a political activist all her life and participated in the women's movement in France during the second wave.

Le Deuxième Sexe (The Second Sex) was published in France in 1949 and in the United States in 1953, a time and climate hospitable neither to feminist scholarship nor to activism. Coming at a time of transition for the women's movement, between the social-psychological debates of the twenties and thirties and the liberation movement of the sixties, the book was a work of great creativity and courage. Broad in range and at times complex in argument, it covers issues in philosophy, biology, psychology, sociology, anthropology, education, politics, history, and more. The unifying theme is summarized by H. M. Parshley in the translator's preface:

> *Since patriarchal times women have in general been forced to occupy a secondary place in the world in relation to men, a position comparable in many respects with that of racial minorities in spite of the fact that women constitute numerically at least half of the human race, and further that this secondary standing is not imposed of necessity by natural "feminine" characteristics but rather by strong environmental forces of educational and social tradition under the purposeful control of men. This, the author maintains, has resulted in the general failure of women to take a place of human dignity as free and independent existents, associated with men on the plane of intellectual and professional equality, a*

condition that not only has limited their achievement in many fields but also has given rise to pervasive social evils and has had a particularly vitiating effect on the sexual relations between men and women.

Beauvoir's thesis is not new and was not new in 1949, but it had been ignored, and her treatment of it was unique. Today, she has been faulted for being nonpolitical in her orientation, not sufficiently concerned with remedy, and at times even sexist in her perspective. Although that may be true of the work in its present context, it was a criticism far less applicable in its day, and the book was widely read.

As a philosophy, existentialism emphasizes direct experience, feeling, awareness, choice, commitment, and honestly. It strives for living "authentically," being true to one's own values and insights, living fully and freely, taking responsibility for one's actions, sharpening one's understanding, and ultimately moving beyond the confines of the brute here and now as determined by the concrete social environment. In this, one is said to strive for transcendence. *A major theme of* The Second Sex *is that women's peripheral existence denies them the chance for transcendence.*

In the following selection, Beauvoir analyzes the female condition of otherness *or* alterity. *It is natural, she argues, for people—either individually or collectively—to understand their existence in terms of a fundamental duality: I (Self) and things not myself (Other). The mature adult juxtaposes her or his own needs and perceptions against those of others, understanding at the same time that the other person is doing so as well. To me, I am Self, you are Other; but to you, you are Self, I am Other. I realize and accept this as so. Beauvoir terms the equality of claims to Self and Otherness from different perspectives* reciprocity. *She points out, however, that the typical reciprocity of claims to Selfness does not obtain between women and men. Men perceive themselves as Self and women as Other. That is as it should be. The problem Beauvoir emphasizes is that women too perceive men as Self (as subject) and them-*

selves as Other. Commonly, neither men nor women recognize the reciprocity of Selfness for women.

A MAN WOULD NEVER GET the notion of writing a book on the peculiar situation of the human male.[1] But if I wish to define myself, I must first of all say: "I am a woman"; on this truth must be based all further discussion. A man never begins by presenting himself as an individual of a certain sex; it goes without saying that he is a man. The terms *masculine* and *feminine* are used symmetrically only as a matter of form, as on legal papers. In actuality the relation of the two sexes is not quite like that of two electrical poles, for man represents both the positive and the neutral, as is indicated by the common use of *man* to designate human beings in general; whereas woman represents only the negative, defined by limiting criteria, without reciprocity. In the midst of an abstract discussion it is vexing to hear a man say: "You think thus and so because you are a woman"; but I know that my only defense is to reply: "I think thus and so because it is true," thereby removing my subjective self from the argument. It would be out of the question to reply: "And you think the contrary because you are a man," for it is understood that the fact of being a man is no peculiarity. A man is in the right in being a man; it is the woman who is in the wrong. It amounts to this: just as for the ancients there was an absolute vertical with reference to which the oblique was defined, so there is an absolute human type, the masculine. Woman has ovaries, a uterus; these peculiarities imprison her in her subjectivity, circumscribe her within the limits of her own nature. It is often said that she thinks with her glands. Man superbly ignores the fact that his anatomy also includes glands, such as the testicles, and that they secrete hormones. He thinks of his body as a direct and normal connection with the world, which he believes he apprehends objectively, whereas he regards the body of woman as a hindrance, a prison, weighed down by everything peculiar to it. "The female is a female by virtue of a certain *lack* of qualities," said Aristotle; "we should regard the female nature as afflicted with a natural defectiveness." And St. Thomas for his part pronounced woman to be an "imperfect man," an "incidental" being. This is symbolized in Genesis where Eve is depicted as made from what Bossuet called "a supernumerary bone" of Adam.

Thus humanity is male and man defines woman not in herself but as relative to him; she is not regarded as an autonomous being. Michelet writes: "Woman, the relative being. . . ." And Benda is most positive in his *Rapport d' Uriel*: "The body of man makes sense in itself quite apart from that of woman, whereas the latter seems wanting in significance by itself. . . . Man can think of himself without woman. She cannot think of herself without man." And she is simply what man decrees; thus she is called "the sex," by which is meant that she appears essentially to the male as a sexual being. For him she is sex—absolute sex, no less. She is defined and differentiated with reference to man and not he with reference to her; she is the incidental, the inessential as opposed to the essential. He is the Subject, he is the Absolute—she is the Other.[2]

The category of the *Other* is as primordial as consciousness itself. In the most primitive societies, in the most ancient mythologies, one finds the expression of a duality—that of the Self and the Other. This duality was not originally attached to the division of the sexes; it was not dependent upon any empirical facts. It is revealed in such works as that of Granet on Chinese thought and those of Dumézil on the East Indies and Rome. The feminine element was at first no more involved in such pairs as Varuna-Mitra, Uranus-Zeus, Sun-Moon, and Day-Night than it was in the contrasts between Good and Evil, lucky and unlucky auspices, right and left, God and Lucifer. Otherness is a fundamental category of human thought.

Thus it is that no group ever sets itself up as the One without at once setting up the Other over against itself. If three travelers chance to occupy the same compartment, that is enough to make vaguely hostile "others" out of all the rest of the passengers on the train. In small-town eyes all persons not belonging to the village are "strangers" and suspect; to the native of a country all who inhabit other countries are "foreigners"; Jews are "different" for the anti-Semite, Negroes are "inferior" for American racists, aborigines are "natives" for colonists, proletarians are the "lower class" for the privileged.

Lévi-Strauss, at the end of a profound work on the various forms of primitive societies, reaches the following conclusion: "Passage from the state of Nature to the state of Culture is marked by man's ability to view biological relations as a series of contrasts; duality, alternation, opposition, and symmetry, whether under definite or vague forms, constitute not so much phenomena to be explained as fundamental and immediately given data of social reality."[3] These phenomena would be incomprehensible if in fact human society were simply a *Mitsein* or fellowship based on solidarity and friendliness. Things become clear, on the contrary, if, following Hegel, we find in consciousness itself a fundamental hostility toward every other consciousness; the subject can be posed only in being opposed—he sets himself up as the essential, as opposed to the other, the inessential, the object.

But the other consciousness, the other ego, sets up a reciprocal claim. The native traveling abroad is shocked to find himself in turn regarded as a "stranger" by the natives of neighboring countries. As a matter of fact, wars, festivals, trading, treaties, and contests among tribes, nations, and classes tend to deprive the concept *Other* of its absolute sense and to make manifest its relativity; willy-nilly, individuals and groups are forced to realize the reciprocity of their relations. How is it, then, that this reciprocity has not been recognized between the sexes, that one of the contrasting terms is set up as the sole essential, denying any relativity in regard to its correlative and defining the latter as pure otherness? Why is it that women do not dispute male sovereignty? No subject will readily volunteer to become the object, the inessential; it is not the Other who, in defining himself as the Other, establishes the One. The Other is posed as such by the One in defining himself as the One. But if the Other is not to regain the status of being the One, he must be submissive enough to accept this alien point of view. Whence comes this submission in the case of woman?

There are, to be sure, other cases in which a certain category has been able to dominate another completely for a time. Very often this privilege depends upon inequality of numbers—the majority imposes its rule upon the minority or persecutes it. But women are not a minority, like the American Negroes or the Jews; there are as many women as men on earth. Again, the two groups concerned have often been originally independent; they may have been formerly unaware of each other's existence, or perhaps they recognized each other's au-

tonomy. But a historical event has resulted in the subjugation of the weaker by the stronger. The scattering of the Jews, the introduction of slavery into America, the conquests of imperialism are examples in point. In these cases the oppressed retained at least the memory of former days; they possessed in common a past, a tradition, sometimes a religion or a culture.

The parallel drawn by Bebel between women and the proletariat is valid in that neither ever formed a minority or a separate collective unit of mankind. And instead of a single historical event it is in both cases a historical development that explains their status as a class and accounts for the membership of *particular individuals* in that class. But proletarians have not always existed, whereas there have always been women. They are women in virtue of their anatomy and physiology. Throughout history they have always been subordinated to men,[4] and hence their dependency is not the result of a historical event or a social change—it was not something that *occurred.* The reason why otherness in this case seems to be an absolute is in part that it lacks the contingent or incidental nature of historical facts. A condition brought about at a certain time can be abolished at some other time, as the Negroes of Haiti and others have proved; but it might seem that a natural condition is beyond the possibility of change. In truth, however, the nature of things is no more immutably given, once for all, than is historical reality. If woman seems to be the inessential which never becomes the essential, it is because she herself fails to bring about this change. Proletarians say "We"; Negroes also. Regarding themselves as subjects, they transform the bourgeois, the whites, into "others." But women do not say "We," except at some congress of feminists or similar formal demonstration; men say "women," and women use the same word in referring to themselves. They do not authentically assume a subjective attitude. The proletarians have accomplished the revolution in Russia, the Negroes in Haiti, the Indo-Chinese are battling for it in Indo-China; but the women's effort has never been anything more than a symbolic agitation. They have gained only what men have been willing to grant; they have taken nothing, they have only received.[5]

The reason for this is that women lack concrete means for organizing themselves into a unit which can stand face to face with the correlative unit. They have no past, no history, no religion of their own; and they have no such solidarity of work and interest as that of the proletariat. They are not even promiscuously herded together in the way that creates community feeling among the American Negroes, the ghetto Jews, the workers of Saint-Denis, or the factory hands of Renault. They live dispersed among the males, attached through residence, housework, economic condition, and social standing to certain men—fathers or husbands—more firmly than they are to other women. If they belong to the bourgeoisie, they feel solidarity with men of that class, not with proletarian women; if they are white, their allegiance is to white men, not to Negro women. The proletariat can propose to massacre the ruling class, and a sufficiently fanatical Jew or Negro might dream of getting sole possession of the atomic bomb and making humanity wholly Jewish or black; but woman cannot even dream of exterminating the males. The bond that unites her to her oppressors is not comparable to any other. The division of the sexes is a biological fact, not an event in human history. Male and female stand opposed within a primordial *Mitsein,* and woman has not broken it. The couple is a fundamental unity with its two halves riveted together, and the cleavage of society along the line of sex is impossible. Here is to be found the basic trait of woman: she is the Other in a totality of which the two components are necessary to one another.

One could suppose that this reciprocity might have facilitated the liberation of woman. When Hercules sat at the feet of Omphale and helped with her spinning, his desire for her held him captive; but why did she fail to gain a lasting power? To revenge herself on Jason, Medea killed their children; and this grim legend would seem to suggest that she might have obtained a formidable influence over him through his love for his offspring. In *Lysistrata* Aristophanes gaily depicts a band of women who joined forces to gain social ends through the sexual needs of their men; but this is only a play. In the legend of the Sabine women, the latter soon abandoned their plan of remaining sterile to punish their ravishers. In truth woman has not been socially emancipated through man's need—sexual desire and the desire for offspring—which makes the male dependent for satisfaction upon the female.

Master and slave, also, are united by a reciprocal need, in this case economic, which does not liberate the slave. In the relation of master to slave the master does not make a point of the need that he has for the other; he has in his grasp the power of satisfying this need through his own action; whereas the slave, in his dependent condition, his hope and fear, is quite conscious of the need he has for his master. Even if the need is at bottom equally urgent for both, it always works in favor of the oppressor and against the oppressed. That is why the liberation of the working class, for example, has been slow.

Now, woman has always been man's dependent, if not his slave; the two sexes have never shared the world in equality. And even today woman is heavily handicapped, though her situation is beginning to change. Almost nowhere is her legal status the same as man's,[6] and frequently it is much to her disadvantage. Even when her rights are legally recognized in the abstract, long-standing custom prevents their full expression in the mores. In the economic sphere men and women can almost be said to make up two castes; other things being equal, the former hold the better jobs, get higher wages, and have more opportunity for success than their new competitors. In industry and politics men have a great many more positions and they monopolize the most important posts. In addition to all this, they enjoy a traditional prestige that the education of children tends in every way to support, for the present enshrines the past—and in the past all history has been made by men. At the present time, when women are beginning to take part in the affairs of the world, it is still a world that belongs to men—they have no doubt of it at all and women have scarcely any. To decline to be the Other, to refuse to be a party to the deal—this would be for women to renounce all the advantages conferred upon them by their alliance with the superior caste. Man-the-sovereign will provide women-the-liege with material protection and will undertake the moral justification of her existence; thus she can evade at once both economic risk and the metaphysical risk of a liberty in which ends and aims must be contrived without assistance. Indeed, along with the ethical urge of each individual to affirm his subjective existence, there is also the temptation to forgo liberty and become a thing. This is an inauspicious road, for he who takes it—passive, lost, ruined—becomes henceforth the creature of another's will, frustrated in his transcendence and deprived of every value. But it is an easy road; on it one avoids the strain involved in undertaking an authentic existence. When man makes of woman the *Other,* he may, then, expect her to manifest deep-seated tendencies toward complicity. Thus, woman may fail to lay claim to the status of subject because she lacks definite resources, because she feels the necessary bond that ties her to man regardless of reciprocity, and because she is often very well pleased with her role as the *Other.*

But it will be asked at once: how did all this begin? It is easy to see that the duality of the sexes, like any duality, gives rise to conflict. And doubtless the winner will assume the status of absolute. But why should man have won from the start? It seems possible that women could have won the victory; or that the outcome of the conflict might never have been decided. How is it that this world has always belonged to the men and that things have begun to change only recently? Is this change a good thing? Will it bring about an equal sharing of the world between men and women?

These questions are not new, and they have often been answered. But the very fact that woman *is the Other* tends to cast suspicion upon all the justifications that men have ever been able to provide for it. These have all too evidently been dictated by men's interest. A little-known feminist of the seventeenth century, Poulain de la Barre, put it this way: "All that has been written about women by men should be suspect, for the men are at once judge and party to the lawsuit." Everywhere, at all times, the males have displayed their satisfaction in feeling that they are the lords of creation. "Blessed be God . . . that He did not make me a woman," say the Jews in their morning prayers, while their wives pray on a note of resignation: "Blessed be the Lord, who created me according to His will." The first among the blessings for which Plato thanked the gods was that he had been created free, not enslaved; the second, a man, not a woman. But the males could not enjoy this privilege fully unless they believed it to be founded on the absolute and the eternal; they sought to make the fact of their supremacy into a right. "Being men, those who have made and compiled the laws have favored their own sex, and jurists have elevated these laws into principles," to quote Poulain de la Barre once more.

Legislators, priests, philosophers, writers, and scientists have striven to show that the subordinate position of woman is willed in heaven and advantageous on earth. The religions invented by men reflect this wish for domination. In the legends of Eve and Pandora men have taken up arms against women. They have made use of philosophy and theology, as the quotations from Aristotle and St. Thomas have shown. Since ancient times satirists and moralists have delighted in showing up the weaknesses of women. We are familiar with the savage indictments hurled against women throughout French literature. Montherlant, for example, follows the tradition of Jean de Meung, though with less gusto. This hostility may at times be well founded, often it is gratuitous; but in truth it more or less successfully conceals a desire for self-justification. As Montaigne says, "It is easier to accuse one sex than to excuse the other." Sometimes what is going on is clear enough. For instance, the Roman law limiting the rights of woman cited "the imbecility, the instability of the sex" just when the weakening of family ties seemed to threaten the interests of male heirs. And in the effort to keep the married woman under guardianship, appeal was made in the sixteenth century to the authority of St. Augustine, who declared that "woman is a creature neither decisive nor constant," at a time when the single woman was thought capable of managing her property. Montaigne understood clearly how arbitrary and unjust was woman's appointed lot: "Women are not in the wrong when they decline to accept the rules laid down for them, since the men make these rules without consulting them. No wonder intrigue and strife abound." But he did not go so far as to champion their cause.

It was only later, in the eighteenth century, that genuinely democratic men began to view the matter objectively. Diderot, among others, strove to show that woman is, like man, a human being. Later John Stuart Mill came fervently to her defense. But these philosophers displayed unusual impartiality. In the nineteenth century the feminist quarrel became again a quarrel of partisans. One of the consequences of the industrial revolution was the entrance of women into productive labor, and it was just here that the claims of the feminists emerged from the realm of theory and acquired an economic basis, while their opponents became the more aggressive. Although landed property lost power to some extent, the bourgeoisie clung to the old morality that found the guarantee of private property in the solidity of the family. Woman was ordered back into the home the more harshly as her emancipation became a real menace. Even within the working class the men endeavored to restrain women's liberation, because they began to see the women as dangerous competitors—the more so because they were accustomed to work for lower wages.[7]

In proving women's inferiority, the antifeminists then began to draw not only upon religion, philosophy, and theology, as before, but also upon science—biology, experimental psychology, etc. At most they were willing to grant "equality in difference" to the *other* sex. That profitable formula is most significant; it is precisely like the "equal but separate" formula of the Jim Crow laws aimed at the North American Negroes. As is well known, this so-called equalitarian segregation has resulted only in the most extreme discrimination. The similarity just noted is in no way due to chance, for whether it is a race, a caste, a class, or a sex that is reduced to a position of inferiority, the methods of justification are the same. "The eternal feminine" corresponds to "the black soul" and to "the Jewish character." True, the Jewish problem is on the whole very different from the other two—to the anti-Semite the Jew is not so much an inferior as he is an enemy for whom there is to be granted no place on earth, for whom annihilation is the fate desired. But there are deep similarities between the situation of woman and that of the Negro. Both are being emancipated today from a like paternalism, and the former master class wishes to "keep them in their place"—that is, the place chosen for them. In both cases the former masters lavish more or less sincere eulogies, either on the virtues of "the good Negro" with his dormant, childish, merry soul—the submissive Negro—or on the merits of the woman who is "truly feminine"—that is, frivolous, infantile, irresponsible—the submissive woman. In both cases the dominant class bases its argument on a state of affairs that it has itself created. As George Bernard Shaw puts it, in substance, "The American white relegates the black to the rank of shoeshine boy; and he concludes from this that the black is good for nothing but shining shoes." This vicious circle is met with in all analogous circumstances; when an individual (or a group of individuals) is kept in a situation of inferiority, the fact is that he *is* inferior. But the significance of the verb *to be* must be rightly understood here; it is in bad faith to give it a static value when it really has the dynamic Hegelian sense of "to have become." Yes, women on the whole *are* today inferior to men; that is, their situation affords them fewer possibilities. The question is: should that state of affairs continue?

Many men hope that it will continue; not all have given up the battle. The conservative bourgeoisie still see in the emancipation of women a menace to their morality and their interests. Some men dread feminine competition. Recently a male student wrote in the *Hebdo-Latin:* "Every woman student who goes into medicine or law robs us of a job." He never questioned his rights in this world. And economic interests are not the only ones concerned. One of the benefits that oppression confers upon the oppressors is that the most humble among them is made to *feel* superior; thus, a "poor white" in the South can console himself with the thought that he is not a "dirty nigger"—and the more prosperous whites cleverly exploit this pride.

Similarly, the most mediocre of males feels himself a demigod as compared with women. It was much easier for M. de Montherlant to think himself a hero when he faced women (and women chosen for his purpose) than when he was obliged to act the man among men—something many women have done better than he, for that matter. And in September 1948, in one of his articles in the *Figaro littéraire,* Claude Mauriac—whose great originality is admired by all—could[8] write regarding woman: "*We* listen on a tone [*sic!*] of polite indifference . . . to the most brilliant among them, well knowing that her wit reflects more or less luminously ideas that come from *us.*" Evidently the speaker referred to is not reflecting the ideas of Mauriac himself, for no one knows of his having any. It may be that she reflects ideas originating with men, but then, even among men there are those who have been known to appropriate ideas not their own; and one can well ask whether Claude Mauriac might not find more interesting a conversation reflecting Descartes, Marx, or Gide rather than himself. What is really remarkable is that by using the questionable *we* he identifies himself with St. Paul, Hegel, Lenin, and Nietzsche, and from the lofty eminence of their grandeur looks down disdainfully upon the bevy of women who make bold to converse with him on a footing of equality. In truth, I know of more than one woman who would refuse to suffer with patience Mauriac's "tone of polite indifference."

I have lingered on this example because the masculine attitude is here displayed with disarming ingenuousness. But men profit in many more subtle ways from the otherness, the alterity of woman. Here is miraculous balm for those afflicted with an inferiority complex, and indeed no one is more arrogant toward women, more aggressive or scornful, than the man who is anxious about his virility. Those who are not fear-ridden in the presence of their fellow men are much more disposed to recognize a fellow creature in woman; but even to these the myth of woman, the Other, is precious for many reasons.[9] They cannot be blamed for not cheerfully relinquishing all the benefits they derive from the myth, for they realize what they would lose in relinquishing woman as they fancy her to be, while they fail to realize what they have to gain from the woman of tomorrow. Refusal to pose oneself as the Subject, unique and absolute, requires great self-denial. Furthermore, the vast majority of men make no such claim explicitly. They do not *postulate* woman as inferior, for today they are too thoroughly imbued with the ideal of democracy not to recognize all human beings as equals.

In the bosom of the family, woman seems in the eyes of childhood and youth to be clothed in the same social dignity as the adult males. Later on, the young man, desiring and loving, experiences the resistance, the independence of the woman desired and loved; in marriage, he respects woman as wife and mother, and in the concrete events of conjugal life she stands there before him as a free being. He can therefore feel that social subordination as between the sexes no longer exists and that on the whole, in spite of differences, woman is an equal. As, however, he observes some point of inferiority—the most important being unfitness for the professions—he attributes these to natural causes. When he is in a co-operative and benevolent relation with woman,

his theme is the principle of abstract equality, and he does not base his attitude upon such inequality as may exist. But when he is in conflict with her, the situation is reversed: his theme will be the existing inequality, and he will even take it as justification for denying abstract equality.[10]

So it is that many men will affirm as if in good faith that women *are* the equals of man and that they have nothing to clamor for, while *at the same time* they will say that women can never be the equals of man and that their demands are in vain. It is, in point of fact, a difficult matter for man to realize the extreme importance of social discriminations which seem outwardly insignificant but which produce in woman moral and intellectual effects so profound that they appear to spring from her original nature.[11] The most sympathetic of men never fully comprehend woman's concrete situation. And there is no reason to put much trust in the men when they rush to the defense of privileges whose full extent they can hardly measure. We shall not, then, permit ourselves to be intimidated by the number and violence of the attacks launched against women, nor to be entrapped by the self-seeking eulogies bestowed on the "true woman," nor to profit by the enthusiasm for woman's destiny manifested by men who would not for the world have any part of it.

We should consider the arguments of the feminists with no less suspicion, however, for very often their controversial aim deprives them of all real value. If the "woman question" seems trivial, it is because masculine arrogance has made of it a "quarrel"; and when quarreling, one no longer reasons well. People have tirelessly sought to prove that woman is superior, inferior, or equal to man. Some say that, having been created after Adam, she is evidently a secondary being; others say on the contrary that Adam was only a rough draft and that God succeeded in producing the human being in perfection when He created Eve. Woman's brain is smaller; yes, but it is relatively larger. Christ was made a man; yes, but perhaps for his greater humility. Each argument at once suggests its opposite, and both are often fallacious. If we are to gain understanding, we must get out of these ruts; we must discard the vague notions of superiority, inferiority, equality which have hitherto corrupted every discussion of the subject and start afresh.

Notes

1. The Kinsey Report [Alfred C. Kinsey and others: *Sexual Behavior in the Human Male* (W. B. Saunders Co., 1948)] is no exception, for it is limited to describing the sexual characteristics of American men, which is quite a different matter.

2. E. Lévinas expresses this idea most explicitly in his essay *Temps et l'Autre.* "Is there not a case in which otherness, alterity [*altérité*], unquestionably marks the nature of a being, as its essence, an instance of otherness not consisting purely and simply in the opposition of two species of the same genus? I think that the feminine represents the contrary in its absolute sense, this contrariness being in no wise affected by any relation between it and its correlative and thus remaining absolutely other. Sex is not a certain specific difference . . . no more is the sexual difference a mere contradiction. . . . Nor does this difference lie in the duality of two complementary terms, for two complementary terms imply a pre-existing whole. . . . Otherness reaches its full flowering in the feminine, a term of the same rank as consciousness but of opposite meaning."

I suppose that Lévinas does not forget that woman, too, is aware of her own consciousness, or ego. But it is striking that he deliberately takes a man's point of view, disregarding the reciprocity of subject and object. When he writes that woman is mystery, he implies that she is mystery for man. Thus his description, which is intended to be objective, is in fact an assertion of masculine privilege.

3. See C. Lévi-Strauss: *Les Structures élementaires de la parenté.* My thanks are due to C. Lévi-Strauss for his kindness in furnishing me with the proofs of his work, which, among others, I have used liberally in Part II.

4. With rare exceptions, perhaps, like certain matriarchal rulers, queens, and the like—TR.

5. See Part II, ch. viii.

6. At the moment an "equal rights" amendment to the Constitution of the United States is before Congress.—TR. [*Note:* Today, nearly fifty years after the writing of *Second Sex,* that amendment is still before Congress—still not yet law.—S. Ruth]

7. See Part II.

8. Or at least he thought he could.

9. A significant article on this theme by Michel Carrouges appeared in No. 292 of the *Cahiers du Sud.* He writes indignantly: "Would that there were no woman-myth at all but only a cohort of cooks, matrons, prostitutes, and bluestockings serving functions of pleasure or usefulness!" That is to say, in his view woman has no existence in and for herself; he thinks only of her *function* in the male world. Her reason for existence lies in man. But then, in fact, her poetic "function" as a myth might be more valued than any other. The real problem is precisely to find out why woman should be defined with relation to man.

10. For example, a man will say that he considers his wife in no wise degraded because she has no gainful occupation. The profession of housewife is just as lofty, and so on. But when the first quarrel comes he will exclaim: "Why, you couldn't make your living without me!"

11. The specific purpose of Book II of this study is to describe this process.

The Problem That Has No Name

Betty Friedan

Betty Friedan, born in Peoria, Illinois, in 1921 and edu-cated at Smith College and the University of California at Berkeley, has been active in the Second Wave from its beginning. She had been a housewife, journalist, and freelance writer before publishing her landmark work, The Feminine Mystique, *in 1963. Some have credited the book with generating the popular dialogue on women's issue during the 1960s, thereby having a major role in precipitating the modern women's movement. Later, Friedan took part in founding the National Orga-nization for Women in 1966, in organizing the Women's Strike for Equality in 1970, and in convening the Na-tional Women's Political Caucus in 1971. Her other books include* It Changed My Life *(1976),* The Sec-ond Stage *(1981),* The Fountaion of Age *(1993), and* Life So Far *(2000).*

In this excerpt from the first chapter of The Femi-nine Mystique, *Friedan describes the inchoate sense of something not quite right that was lodged in the minds and feelings of countless middle-class American house-wives of the 1950s, newly returned to their traditional roles and "domestic bliss" after the social chaos of World War II and the Korean War. Friedan's work, though lim-ited mainly to middle-class, White, married women of a particular time and place, is important, not only because it so accurately delineated the nature of the "mystique" and the feelings of those women who experienced it, but because it so clearly captures the flaws in the traditional ideal, the fall from grace of happily-ever-after land, and the dangers that land holds for those who believe in or seek it.*

THE PROBLEM LAY BURIED, UNSPOKEN, for many years in the minds of American women. It was a strange stirring, a sense of dissatisfaction, a yearning that women suffered in the middle of the twentieth cen-tury in the United States. Each suburban wife strug-gled with it alone. As she made the beds, shopped for groceries, matched slipcover material, ate pea-nut butter sandwiches with her children, chauf-feured Cub Scouts and Brownies, lay beside her husband at night—she was afraid to ask even of herself the silent question—"Is this all?"

For over fifteen years there was no word of this yearning in the millions of words written about women, for women, in all the columns, books and articles by experts telling women their role was to seek fulfillment as wives and mothers. Over and over women heard in voices of tradition and of Freudian sophistication that they could desire no greater destiny than to glory in their own feminin-ity. Experts told them how to catch a man and keep him, how to breastfeed children and handle their toilet training, how to cope with sibling rivalry and adolescent rebellion; how to buy a dishwasher, bake bread, cook gourmet snails, and build a swimming pool with their own hands; how to dress, look, and act more feminine and make marriage more excit-ing; how to keep their husbands from dying young and their sons from growing into delinquents. They were taught to pity the neurotic, unfeminine, un-happy women who wanted to be poets or physicists or presidents. They learned that truly feminine women do not want careers, higher education, po-litical rights—the independence and the opportu-nities that the old-fashioned feminists fought for. Some women, in their forties and fifties, still re-membered painfully giving up those dreams, but most of the younger women no longer even thought about them. A thousand expert voices applauded their femininity, their adjustment, their new matu-rity. All they had to do was devote their lives from earliest girlhood to finding a husband and bearing children. . . .

The suburban housewife—she was the dream image of the young American woman and the envy, it was said, of women all over the world. The American housewife—freed by science and labor-saving appliances from the drudgery, the dangers of child-birth and the illnesses of her grandmother. She was healthy, beautiful, educated, concerned only about her husband, her children, her home. She had found true feminine fulfillment. As a housewife and mother, she was respected as a full and equal part-ner to man in his world. She was free to choose automobiles, clothes, appliances, supermarkets; she had everything that women ever dreamed of.

In the fifteen years after World War II, this mys-tique of feminine fulfillment became the cherished and self-perpetuating core of contemporary Ameri-can culture. Millions of women lived their lives in the image of those pretty pictures of the American suburban housewife, kissing their husbands good-bye in front of the picture window, depositing their station-wagonsful of children at school, and smiling as they ran the new electric waxer over the spotless kitchen floor. They baked their own bread, sewed their own and their children's clothes, kept their new washing machines and dryers running all day. They changed the sheets on the beds twice a week instead of once, took the rug-hooking class in adult education, and pitied their poor frustrated mothers, who had dreamed of having a career. Their only dream was to be perfect wives and mothers; their highest ambition to have five chil-dren and a beautiful house, their only fight to get and keep their husbands. They had no thought for the unfeminine problems of the world outside the home; they wanted the men to make the major decisions. They gloried in their role as women, and wrote proudly on the census blank: "Occupa-tion: housewife." . . .

If a woman had a problem in the 1950's and 1960's, she knew that something must be wrong with her marriage, or with herself. Other women were satisfied with their lives, she thought. What kind of a woman was she if she did not feel this mysterious fulfillment waxing the kitchen floor? She was so ashamed to admit her dissatisfaction that she never knew how many other women shared it. If she tried to tell her husband, he didn't understand what she was talking about. She did not really un-derstand it herself. For over fifteen years women in America found it harder to talk about this problem than about sex. Even the psychoanalysts had no name for it. When a woman went to a psychiatrist

for help, as many women did, she would say, "I'm so ashamed," or "I must be hopelessly neurotic." "I don't know what's wrong with women today," a suburban psychiatrist said uneasily. "I only know something is wrong because most of my patients happen to be women. And their problem isn't sex-ual." Most women with this problem did not go to see a psychoanalyst, however. "There's nothing wrong really," they kept telling themselves. "There isn't any problem."

But on an April morning in 1959, I heard a mother of four, having coffee with four other moth-ers in a suburban development fifteen miles from New York, say in a tone of quiet desperation, "the problem." And the others knew, without words, that she was not talking about a problem with her husband, or her children, or her home. Suddenly they realized they all shared the same problem, the problem that has no name. They began, hesitantly, to talk about it. Later, after they had picked up their children at nursery school and taken them home to nap, two of the women cried, in sheer relief, just to know they were not alone.

Gradually I came to realize that the problem that has no name was shared by countless women in America. As a magazine writer I often inter-viewed women about problems with their children, or their marriages, or their houses, or their commu-nities. But after a while I began to recognize the telltale signs of this other problem. I saw the same signs in suburban ranch houses and split-levels on Long Island and in New Jersey and Westchester County; in colonial houses in a small Massachusetts town; on patios in Memphis; in suburban and city apartments; in living rooms in the Midwest. Some-times I sensed the problem, not as a reporter, but as a suburban housewife, for during this time I was also bringing up my own three children in Rockland County, New York. I heard echoes of the problem in college dormitories and semi-private maternity wards, at PTA meetings and luncheons of the League of Women Voters, at suburban cocktail parties, in station wagons waiting for trains, and in snatches of conversation overheard at Schrafft's. The groping words I heard from other women, on quiet afternoons when children were at school or on quiet evenings when husbands worked late, I think I understood first as a woman long before

I understood their larger social and psychological implications.

Just what was this problem that has no name? What were the words women used when they tried to express it? Sometimes a woman would say "I feel empty somehow . . . incomplete." Or she would say, "I feel as if I don't exist." Sometimes she blotted out the feeling with a tranquilizer. Sometimes she thought the problem was with her husband, or her children, or that what she really needed was to re-decorate her house, or move to a better neighbor-hood, or have an affair, or another baby. Sometimes, she went to a doctor with symptoms she could hardly describe: "A tired feeling . . . I get so angry with the children it scares me . . . I feel like crying without any reason." (A Cleveland doctor called it "the housewife's syndrome.") A number of women told me about great bleeding blisters that break out on their hands and arms. "I call it the housewife's blight," said a family doctor in Pennsylvania. "I see it so often lately in these young women with four, five and six children who bury themselves in their dishpans. But it isn't caused by detergent and it isn't cured by cortisone." . . .

In 1960, the problem that has no name burst like a boil through the image of the happy American housewife. In the television commercials the pretty housewives still beamed over their foaming dish-pans and *Time*'s cover story on "The Suburban Wife, an American Phenomenon" protested: "Having too good a time . . . to believe that they should be un-happy." But the actual unhappiness of the American housewife was suddenly being reported—from the *New York Times* and *Newsweek* to *Good Housekeeping* and CBS Television ("The Trapped Housewife"), al-though almost everybody who talked about it found some superficial reason to dismiss it. It was attrib-uted to incompetent appliance repairmen (*New York Times*), or the distances children must be chauf-feured in the suburbs (*Time*), or too much PTA (*Red-book*). Some said it was the old problem—education: more and more women had education, which na-turally made them unhappy in their role as house-wives. "The road from Freud to Frigidaire, from Sophocles to Spock, has turned out to be a bumpy one," reported the *New York Times* (June 28, 1960). "Many young women—certainly not all—whose education plunged them into a world of ideas feel stifled in their homes. They find their routine lives out of joint with their training. Like shut-ins, they feel left out. In the last year, the problem of the edu-cated housewife has provided the meat of dozens of speeches made by troubled presidents of women's colleges who maintain, in the face of complaints, that sixteen years of academic training is realistic preparation for wifehood and motherhood."

There was much sympathy for the educated housewife. ("Like a two-headed schizophrenic . . . once she wrote a paper on the Graveyard poets; now she writes notes to the milkman. Once she de-termined the boiling point of sulphuric acid; now she determines her boiling point with the overdue repairman. . . . The housewife often is reduced to screams and tears. . . . No one, it seems, is apprecia-tive, least of all herself, of the kind of person she becomes in the process of turning from poetess into shrew.")

Home economists suggested more realistic preparation for housewives, such as high-school workshops in home appliances. College educators suggested more discussion groups on home man-agement and the family, to prepare women for the adjustment to domestic life. A spate of articles ap-peared in the mass magazines offering "Fifty-eight Ways to Make Your Marriage More Exciting." No month went by without a new book by a psychia-trist or sexologist offering technical advice on find-ing greater fulfillment through sex.

A male humorist joked in *Harper's Bazaar* (July, 1960) that the problem could be solved by taking away women's right to vote. ("In the pre-19th Amendment era, the American woman was placid, sheltered and sure of her role in American society. She left all the political decisions to her husband and he, in turn, left all the family decisions to her. Today a woman has to make both the family *and* the political decisions, and it's too much for her.")

A number of educators suggested seriously that women no longer be admitted to the four-year col-leges and universities: in the growing college crisis, the education which girls could not use as house-wives was more urgently needed than ever by boys to do the work of the atomic age.

The problem was also dismissed with drastic solutions no one could take seriously. (A woman writer proposed in *Harper's* that women be drafted for compulsory service as nurses' aides and baby-sitters.) And it was smoothed over with the age-old panaceas: "love is their answer," "the only answer is inner help," "the secret of completeness—children," "a private means of intellectual fulfillment," "to cure this toothache of the spirit—the simple formula of handing one's self and one's will over to God."[1]

The problem was dismissed by telling the housewife she doesn't realize how lucky she is—her own boss, no time clock, no junior executive gunning for her job. What if she isn't happy—does she think men are happy in this world? Does she really, secretly, still want to be a man? Doesn't she know yet how lucky she is to be a woman? . . .

Even so, most men, and some women, still did not know that this problem was real. But those who had faced it honestly knew that all the superficial remedies, the sympathetic advice, the scolding words and the cheering words were somehow drowning the problem in unreality. A bitter laugh was beginning to be heard from American women. They were admired, envied, pitied, theorized over until they were sick of it, offered drastic solutions or silly choices that no one could take seriously. They got all kinds of advice from the growing armies of marriage and child-guidance counselors, psychotherapists, and armchair psychologists, on how to adjust to their role as housewives. No other road to fulfillment was offered to American women in the middle of the twentieth century. Most adjusted to their role and suffered or ignored the problem that has no name. It can be less painful for a woman, not to hear the strange, dissatisfied voice stirring within her.

It is no longer possible to ignore that voice, to dismiss the desperation of so many American women. This is not what being a woman means, no matter what the experts say. For human suffering there is a reason; perhaps the reason has not been found because the right questions have not been asked, or pressed far enough. I do not accept the answer that there is no problem because American women have luxuries that women in other times and lands never dreamed of; part of the strange newness of the problem is that it cannot be understood in terms of the age-old material problems of man: poverty, sickness, hunger, cold. The women who suffer this problem have a hunger that food cannot fill. . . .

Can the problem that has no name be somehow related to the domestic routine of the housewife? When a woman tries to put the problem into words, she often merely describes the daily life she leads. What is there in this recital of comfortable domestic detail that could possibly cause such a feeling of desperation? Is she trapped simply by the enormous demands of her role as modern housewife: wife, mistress, mother, nurse, consumer, cook, chauffeur; expert on interior decoration, child care, appliance repair, furniture refinishing, nutrition, and education? Her day is fragmented as she rushes from dishwasher to washing machine to telephone to dryer to station wagon to supermarket, and delivers Johnny to the Little League field, takes Janey to dancing class, gets the lawnmower fixed and meets the 6:45. She can never spend more than 15 minutes on any one thing; she has no time to read books, only magazines; even if she had time, she has lost the power to concentrate. At the end of the day, she is so terribly tired that sometimes her husband has to take over and put the children to bed.

Thus terrible tiredness took so many women to doctors in the 1950's that one decided to investigate it. He found, surprisingly, that his patients suffering from "housewife's fatigue" slept more than an adult needed to sleep—as much as ten hours a day—and that the actual energy they expended on housework did not tax their capacity. The real problem must be something else, he decided—perhaps boredom. Some doctors told their women patients they must get out of the house for a day, treat themselves to a movie in town. Others prescribed tranquilizers. Many suburban housewives were taking tranquilizers like cough drops. "You wake up in the morning, and you feel as if there's no point in going on another day like this. So you take a tranquilizer because it makes you not care so much that it's pointless."

It is easy to see the concrete details that trap the suburban housewife, the continual demands on her time. But the chains that bind her in her trap are chains in her own mind and spirit. They are chains made up of mistaken ideas and misinterpreted facts, of incomplete truths and unreal choices. They are not easily seen and not easily shaken off.

How can any woman see the whole truth within the bounds of her own life? How can she believe that voice inside herself, when it denies the conventional, accepted truths by which she has been living? And yet the women I have talked to, who are finally listening to that inner voice, seem in some incredible way to be groping through to a truth that has defied the experts.

Note

1. See the Seventy-fifth Anniversary Issue of *Good Housekeeping*, May, 1960, "The Gift of Self," a symposium by Margaret Mead, Jessamyn West, *et al.*

NOW Bill of Rights

National Organization for Women

The National Organization for Women (NOW) was formed in 1966 by a group of feminist legislators, authors, professionals, labor workers, and academics. Set off by a series of events—the publication of Betty Friedan's Feminine Mystique, *the addition of "sex" to the Civil Rights Act of 1964, the decade's climate of social criticism and change—the formation of the organization was one of the major events responsible for increasing feminist activism of the second wave. Notice that among its goals were passage of the ERA and access to day care and to legal abortion, issues that at the time were controversial and yet galvanizing to many women, even those who might not have formerly been politically active.*

N.O.W.
BILL OF RIGHTS

I   Equal Rights Constitutional Amendment

II   Enforce Law Banning Sex Discrimination in Employment

III   Maternity Leave Rights in Employment and in Social Security Benefits

IV   Tax Deduction for Home and Child Care Expenses for Working Parents

V   Child Care Centers

VI   Elimination of Discrimination in Education

VII   Anti-Poverty Measures Which Protect Human Dignity

VIII   The Right of Women to Control Their Reproductive Lives

IX   Equal Access to Public Accommodations and Housing

X   Partnership Marriages of Equalized Rights and Shared Responsibilities

WE DEMAND:

I That the Equal Rights Amendment to the Constitution, passed by the Congress be immediately ratified by the several states to provide that "Equality of rights under the law shall not be denied or abridged by the United States or by any State on account of sex."

II That equal employment opportunity be guaranteed to all women, as well as men, by insisting that the Equal Employment Opportunity Commission enforces the prohibitions against sex discrimination in employment under Title VII of the Civil Rights Act of 1964 with the same vigor as it enforces the prohibitions against racial discrimination.

III That women be protected by law to ensure their rights to return to their jobs within a reasonable time after childbirth without loss of seniority or other accrued benefits, and be paid maternity leave as a form of social security and/or employee benefit.

IV Immediate revision of tax laws to permit the deduction of home and child care expenses for working parents.

V That child care facilities be established by law on the same basis as parks, libraries, and public schools, adequate to the needs of children from the pre-school years through adolescence, as a community resource to be used by all citizens from all income levels.

VI That the right of women to be educated to their full potential equally with men be secured by Federal and State legislation, eliminating all discrimination and segregation by sex, written and unwritten, at all levels of education, including colleges, graduate and professional schools, loans and fellowships, and Federal and State training programs such as the Job Corps.

VII The right of women in poverty to secure job training, housing, and family allowances on equal terms with men, but without prejudice to a parent's right to remain at home to care for his or her children; revision of welfare legislation and poverty programs which deny women dignity, privacy and self-respect.

VIII   The right of women to control their own reproductive lives by removing from penal codes laws limiting access to contraceptive information and devices and laws governing abortion.

IX   Amendment of Title II of the Civil Rights Act and state laws to include prohibition of sex discrimination in places of public accommodation, housing.

X   Revision of marriage, divorce and family laws to equalize the rights of men and women to own property, establish domicile, maintain individual identity and economic independence, etc., and promote marriage as an equal partnership of shared responsibility in all its aspects.

Theory of Sexual Politics

Kate Millett

Kate Millett, feminist, author, and sculptor, was born in 1934 in St. Paul, Minnesota. She studied English at the University of Minnesota and at Oxford University and finished a doctorate at Columbia University with a dissertation that became the book Sexual Politics. *Millett has taught English and women's studies, worked as a sculptor, and codirected a film,* Three Lives. *An activist early in her career, she served in CORE (Congress of Racial Equality) in the 1950s, supported student strikes while teaching at Barnard, and served in NOW as chair of the Education Committee. During the early days of the Iranian revolution, she traveled to Iran to study the effects of the revolution on women there and to talk to feminist leaders. In addition to* Sexual Politics, *her works include* The Prostitution Papers *(1973),* Flying *(1974),* Sita *(1976),* Going to Iran *(1982),* The Loony-Bin Trip *(1990), and* The Politics of Cruelty: An Essay on the Literature of Political Imprisonment *(1995).*

The publication of Sexual Politics *in 1970 was an important development in the current movement. It received wide press attention, focused public attention on women's liberation, and was one of the first books to articulate a broad theoretical base for the ideas of the growing movement. Millett widens the term* politics *(which traditionally means simply "that which pertains to the* polis, *or city") to refer to "power-structured relationships . . . whereby one group of persons is controlled by another" then shows how this concept captures the essence of male-female arrangements. Using literary and historical models to support her thesis, she argues that social and sexual relations between women and men are not-so-nice power arrangements, grounded in misogyny, expressing themselves as a life view (patriarchy), and resulting in the worldwide oppression of women on both an institutional and a personal level.*

. . . IN INTRODUCING THE TERM "SEXUAL politics," one must first answer the inevitable question "Can the relationship between the sexes be viewed in a political light at all?" The answer depends on how one defines politics.[1] This essay does not define the political as that relatively narrow and exclusive world of meetings, chairmen, and parties. The term "politics" shall refer to power-structured relationships, arrangements whereby one group of persons is controlled by another. By way of parenthesis one might add that although an ideal politics might simply be conceived of as the arrangement of human life on agreeable and rational principles from whence the entire notion of power *over* others should be banished, one must confess that this is not what constitutes the political as we know it, and it is to this that we must address ourselves.

The following sketch, which might be described as "notes toward a theory of patriarchy," will attempt to prove that sex is a status category with political implications. Something of a pioneering effort, it must perforce be both tentative and imperfect. Because the intention is to provide an overall description, statements must be generalized, exceptions neglected, and subheadings overlapping and, to some degree, arbitrary as well.

The word "politics" is enlisted here when speaking of the sexes primarily because such a word is eminently useful in outlining the real nature of their relative status, historically and at the present. It is opportune, perhaps today even mandatory, that we develop a more relevant psychology and philosophy of power relationships beyond the simple conceptual framework provided by our traditional formal politics. Indeed, it may be imperative that we give some attention to defining a theory of politics which treats of power relationships on grounds less conventional than those to which we are accustomed.[2] I have therefore found it pertinent to define them on grounds of personal contact and interaction between members of well-defined and coherent groups: races, castes, classes, and sexes. For it is precisely because certain groups have no representation in a number of recognized political structures that their position tends to be so stable, their oppression so continuous.

In America, recent events have forced us to acknowledge at last that the relationship between the races is indeed a political one which involves the general control of one collectivity, defined by birth, over another collectivity, also defined by birth. Groups who rule by birthright are fast disappearing, yet there remains one ancient and universal scheme for the domination of one birth group by another—the scheme that prevails in the area of sex. The study of racism has convinced us that a truly political state of affairs operates between the races to perpetuate a series of oppressive circumstances. The subordinated group has inadequate redress through existing political institutions, and is deterred thereby from organizing into conventional political struggle and opposition.

Quite in the same manner, a disinterested examination of our system of sexual relationship must point out that the situation between the sexes now, and throughout history, is a case of that phenomenon Max Weber defined as *herrschaft*, a relationship of dominance and subordinance.[3] What goes largely unexamined, often even unacknowledged (yet is institutionalized nonetheless) in our social order, is the birthright priority whereby males rule females. Through this system a most ingenious form of "interior colonization" has been achieved. It is one which tends moreover to be sturdier than any form of segregation, and more rigorous than class stratification, more uniform, certainly more enduring. However muted its present appearance may be, sexual dominion obtains nevertheless as perhaps the most pervasive ideology of our culture and provides its most fundamental concept of power.

This is so because our society, like all other historical civilizations, is a patriarchy.[4] The fact is evident at once if one recalls that the military, industry, technology, universities, science, political office, and finance—in short, every avenue of power within the society, including the coercive force of the police, is entirely in male hands. As the essence of politics is power, such realization cannot fail to carry impact. What lingers of supernatural authority, the Deity, "His" ministry, together with the ethics and values, the philosophy and art of our culture—its

very civilization—as T. S. Eliot once observed, is of male manufacture.

If one takes patriarchal government to be the institution whereby that half of the populace which is female is controlled by that half which is male, the principles of patriarchy appear to be two fold: male shall dominate female, elder male shall dominate younger. However, just as with any human institution, there is frequently a distance between the real and the ideal; contradictions and exceptions do exist within the system. While patriarchy as an institution is a social constant so deeply entrenched as to run through all other political, social, or economic forms, whether of caste or class, feudality or bureaucracy, just as it pervades all major religions, it also exhibits great variety in history and locale. In democracies,[5] for example, females have often held no office or do so (as now) in such miniscule numbers as to be below even token representation. Aristocracy, on the other hand, with its emphasis upon the magic and dynastic properties of blood, may at times permit women to hold power. The principle of rule by elder males is violated even more frequently. Bearing in mind the variation and degree in patriarchy—as say between Saudi Arabia and Sweden, Indonesia and Red China—we also recognize our own form in the U.S. and Europe to be much altered and attenuated by the reforms described in the next chapter.

I IDEOLOGICAL

Hannah Arendt[6] has observed that government is upheld by power supported either through consent or imposed through violence. Conditioning to an ideology amounts to the former. Sexual politics obtains consent through the "socialization" of both sexes to basic patriarchal polities with regard to temperament, role, and status. As to status, a pervasive assent to the prejudice of male superiority guarantees superior status in the male, inferior in the female. The first item, temperament, involves the formation of human personality along stereotyped lines of sex category ("masculine" and "feminine"), based on the needs and values of the dominant group and dictated by what its members cherish in themselves and find convenient in subordinates: aggression, intelligence, force, and efficacy in the male; passivity, ignorance, docility, "virtue," and ineffectuality in the female. This is complemented by a second factor, sex role, which decrees a consonant and highly elaborate code of conduct, gesture and attitude for each sex. In terms of activity, sex role assigns domestic service and attendance upon infants to the female, the rest of human achievement, interest, and ambition to the male. The limited role allotted the female tends to arrest her at the level of biological experience. Therefore, nearly all that can be described as distinctly human rather than animal activity (in their own way animals also give birth and care for their young) is largely reserved for the male. Of course, status again follows from such an assignment. Were one to analyze the three categories one might designate status as the political component, role as the sociological, and temperament as the psychological— yet their interdependence is unquestionable and they form a chain. Those awarded higher status tend to adopt roles of mastery, largely because they are first encouraged to develop temperaments of dominance. That this is true of caste and class as well is self-evident.

IV CLASS

It is in the area of class that the castelike status of the female within patriarchy is most liable to confusion, for sexual status often operates in a superficially confusing way within the variable of class. In a society where status is dependent upon the economic, social, and educational circumstances of class, it is possible for certain females to appear to stand higher than some males. Yet not when one looks more closely at the subject. This is perhaps easier to see by means of analogy: a black doctor or lawyer has higher social status than a poor white sharecropper. But race, itself a caste system which subsumes class, persuades the latter citizen that he belongs to a higher order of life, just as it oppresses the black professional in spirit, whatever his material success may be. In much the same manner, a truck driver or butcher has always his "manhood" to fall back upon. Should this final vanity be offended, he may contemplate more violent methods. The literature of the past thirty years provides a staggering number of incidents in which the caste

of virility triumphs over the social status of wealthy or even educated women. In literary contexts one has to deal here with wish-fulfillment. Incidents from life (bullying, obscene, or hostile remarks) are probably another sort of psychological gesture of ascendancy. Both convey more hope than reality, for class divisions are generally quite impervious to the hostility of individuals. And yet while the existence of class division is not seriously threatened by such expressions of enmity, the existence of sexual hierarchy has been re-affirmed and mobilized to "punish" the female quite effectively.

The function of class or ethnic mores in patriarchy is largely a matter of how overtly displayed or how loudly enunciated the general ethic of masculine supremacy allows itself to become. Here one is confronted by what appears to be a paradox: while in the lower social strata, the male is more likely to claim authority on the strength of his sex rank alone, he is actually obliged more often to share power with the women of his class who are economically productive; whereas in the middle and upper classes, there is less tendency to assert a blunt patriarchal dominance, as men who enjoy such status have more power in any case.[7] . . .

One of the chief effects of class within patriarchy is to set one woman against another, in the past creating a lively antagonism between whore and matron, and in the present between career woman and housewife. One envies the other her "security" and prestige, while the envied yearns beyond the confines of respectability for what she takes to be the other's freedom, adventure, and contact with the great world. Through the multiple advantages of the double standard, the male participates in both worlds, empowered by his superior social and economic resources to play the estranged women against each other as rivals. One might also recognize subsidiary status categories among women: not only is virtue class, but beauty and age as well.

Perhaps, in the final analysis, it is possible to argue that women tend to transcend the usual class stratifications in patriarchy, for whatever the class of her birth and education, the female has fewer permanent class associations than does the male. Economic dependency renders her affiliations with any class a tangential, vicarious, and temporary matter. Aristotle observed that the only slave to whom a commoner might lay claim was his woman, and the service of an unpaid domestic still provides working-class males with a "cushion" against the buffets of the class system which incidentally provides them with some of the psychic luxuries of the leisure class. Thrown upon their own resources, few women rise above working class in personal prestige and economic power, and women as a group do not enjoy many of the interests and benefits any class may offer its male members. Women have therefore less of an investment in the class system. But it is important to understand that as with any group whose existence is parasitic to its rulers, women are a dependency class who live on surplus. And their marginal life frequently renders them conservative, for like all persons in their situation (slaves are a classic example here) they identify their own survival with the prosperity of those who feed them. The hope of seeking liberating radical solutions of their own seems too remote for the majority to dare contemplate and remains so until consciousness on the subject is raised.

As race is emerging as one of the final variables in sexual politics, it is pertinent, especially in a discussion of modern literature, to devote a few words to it as well. Traditionally, the white male has been accustomed to concede the female of his own race, in her capacity as "his woman" a higher status than that ascribed to the black male.[8] Yet as white racist ideology is exposed and begins to erode, racism's older protective attitudes toward (white) women also begin to give way. And the priorities of maintaining male supremacy might outweigh even those of white supremacy; sexism may be more endemic in our own society than racism. For example, one notes in authors whom we would now term overtly racist, such as D. H. Lawrence—whose contempt for what he so often designates as inferior breeds is unabashed—instances where the lower-caste male is brought on to master or humiliate the white man's own insubordinate mate. Needless to say, the female of the non-white races does not figure in such tales save as an exemplum of "true" womanhood's servility, worthy of imitation by other less carefully instructed females. Contemporary white sociology often operates under a similar patriarchal bias when its rhetoric inclines toward the assertion that the "matriarchal" (e.g. matrifocal) aspect of black society and the "castration" of the black male are the most deplorable symptoms of black oppression in white racist society, with the implication that racial inequity is capable of solution by a restoration of masculine authority. Whatever the facts of the matter may be, it can also be suggested that analysis of this kind presupposes patriarchal values without questioning them, and tends to obscure both the true character of and the responsibility for racist injustice toward black humanity of both sexes. . . .

VI FORCE

We are not accustomed to associate patriarchy with force. So perfect is its system of socialization, so complete the general assent to its values, so long and so universally has it prevailed in human society, that it scarcely seems to require violent implementation. Customarily, we view its brutalities in the past as exotic or "primitive" custom. Those of the present are regarded as the product of individual deviance, confined to pathological or exceptional behavior, and without general import. And yet, just as under other total ideologies (racism and colonialism are somewhat analogous in this respect) control in patriarchal society would be imperfect, even inoperable, unless it had the rule of force to rely upon, both in emergencies and as an ever-present instrument of intimidation.

Historically, most patriarchies have institutionalized force through their legal systems. For example, strict patriarchies such as that of Islam, have implemented the prohibition against illegitimacy or sexual autonomy with a death sentence. In Afghanistan and Saudi Arabia the adulteress is still stoned to death with a mullah presiding at the execution. Execution by stoning was once common practice through the Near East. It is still condoned in Sicily. Needless to say there was and is no penalty imposed upon the male corespondent. Save in recent times or exceptional cases, adultery was not generally recognized in males except as an offense one male might commit against another's property interest. In Tokugawa Japan, for example, an elaborate set of legal distinctions were made according to class. A samurai was entitled, and in the face of public knowledge, even obliged, to execute an adulterous wife, whereas a chonin (common citizen) or peasant might respond as he pleased. In cases of cross-class adultery, the lower-class male convicted of sexual intimacy with his employer's wife would, because he had violated taboos of class and property, be beheaded together with her. Upper-strata males had, of course, the same license to seduce lower-class women as we are familiar with in Western societies.

Indirectly, one form of "death penalty" still obtains even in America today. Patriarchal legal systems in depriving women of control over their own bodies drive them to illegal abortions; it is estimated that between two and five thousand women die each year from this cause.[9]

Excepting a social license to physical abuse among certain class and ethnic groups, force is diffuse and generalized in most contemporary patriarchies. Significantly, force itself is restricted to the male who alone is psychologically and technically equipped to perpetrate physical violence.[10] Where differences in physical strength have become immaterial through the use of arms, the female is rendered innocuous by her socialization. Before assault she is almost universally defenseless both by her physical and emotional training. Needless to say, this has the most far-reaching effects on the social and psychological behavior of both sexes.

Patriarchal force also relies on a form of violence particularly sexual in character and realized most completely in the act of rape. The figures of rapes reported represent only a fraction of those which occur,[11] as the "shame" of the event is sufficient to deter women from the notion of civil prosecution under the public circumstances of a trial. Traditionally rape has been viewed as an offense one male commits upon another—a matter of abusing "his woman." Vendetta, such as occurs in the American South, is carried out for masculine satisfaction, the exhilarations of race hatred, and the interests of property and vanity (honor). In rape, the emotions of aggression, hatred, contempt, and the desire to break or violate personality, take a form consummately appropriate to sexual politics. In the passages analyzed at the outset of this study, such emotions were present at a barely sublimated level and were a key factor in explaining the attitude behind the author's use of language and tone.[12]

Patriarchal societies typically link feelings of cruelty with sexuality, the latter often equated both with evil and with power. This is apparent both in the sexual fantasy reported by psychoanalysis and that reported by pornography. The rule here associates sadism with the male ("the masculine role") and victimization with the female ("the feminine role").[13] Emotional response to violence against women in patriarchy is often curiously ambivalent; references to wife-beating, for example, invariably produce laughter and some embarrassment. Exemplary atrocity, such as the mass murders committed by Richard Speck, greeted at one level with a certain scandalized, possibly hypocritical indignation, is capable of eliciting a mass response of titillation at another level. At such times one even hears from men occasional expressions of envy or amusement. In view of the sadistic character of such public fantasy as caters to male audiences in pornography or semi-pornographic media, one might expect that a certain element of identification is by no means absent from the general response. Probably a similar collective *frisson* sweeps through racist society when its more "logical" members have perpetrated a lynching. Unconsciously, both crimes may serve the larger group as a ritual act, cathartic in effect.

Hostility is expressed in a number of ways. One is laughter. Misogynist literature, the primary vehicle of masculine hostility, is both an hortatory and comic genre. Of all artistic forms in patriarchy it is the most frankly propagandistic. Its aim is to reinforce both sexual factions in their status. Ancient, Medieval, and Renaissance literature in the West has each had a large element of misogyny.[14] Nor is the East without a strong tradition here, notably in the Confucian strain which held sway in Japan as well as China. The Western tradition was indeed moderated somewhat by the introduction of courtly love. But the old diatribes and attacks were coterminous with the new idealization of woman. In the case of Petrarch, Boccaccio, and some others, one can find both attitudes fully expressed, presumably as evidence of different moods, a courtly pose adopted for the ephemeral needs of the vernacular, a grave animosity for sober and eternal Latin.[15] As courtly love was transformed to romantic love, literary misogyny grew somewhat out of fashion. In some places in the eighteenth century it declined into ridicule and exhortative satire. In the nineteenth century its more acrimonious forms almost disappeared in English. Its resurrection in twentieth-century attitudes and literature is the result of a resentment over patriarchal reform, aided by the growing permissiveness in expression which has taken place at an increasing rate in the last fifty years.

Since the abatement of censorship, masculine hostility (psychological or physical) in specifically *sexual* contexts has become far more apparent. Yet as masculine hostility has been fairly continuous, one deals here probably less with a matter of increase than with a new frankness in expressing hostility in specifically sexual contexts. It is a matter of release and freedom to express what was once forbidden expression outside of pornography or other "underground" productions, such as those of De Sade. As one recalls both the euphemism and the idealism of descriptions of coitus in the Romantic poets (Keats's *Eve of St. Agnes*), or the Victorian novelists (Hardy, for example) and contrasts it with Miller or William Burroughs, one has an idea of how contemporary literature has absorbed not only the truthful explicitness of pornography, but its anti-social character as well. Since this tendency to hurt or insult has been given free expression, it has become far easier to assess sexual antagonism in the male.

The history of patriarchy presents a variety of cruelties and barbarities: the suttee execution in India, the crippling deformity of footbinding in China, the lifelong ignominy of the veil in Islam, or the widespread persecution of sequestration, the gynacium, and purdah. Phenomena such as clitoroidectomy, clitoral incision, the sale and enslavement of women under one guise or another, involuntary and child marriages, concubinage and prostitution, still take place—the first in Africa, the latter in the Near and Far East, the last generally. The rationale which accompanies that imposition of male authority euphemistically referred to as "the battle of the sexes" bears a certain resemblance to the formulas of nations at war, where any heinousness is justified on the grounds that the enemy is either an inferior species or really not human at all. The patriarchal mentality has concocted a whole series of rationales about women which accomplish this purpose tolerably well. And these traditional beliefs still invade our consciousness and affect our thinking to an extent few of us would be willing to admit.

Notes

1. The American Heritage Dictionary's fourth definition is fairly approximate: "methods or tactics involved in managing a state or government." *American Heritage Dictionary*

(New York: American Heritage and Houghton Mifflin, 1969). One might expand this to a set of strategems designed to maintain a system. If one understands patriarchy to be an institution perpetuated by such techniques of control, one has a working definition of how politics is conceived in this essay.

2. I am indebted here to Ronald V. Samson's *The Psychology of Power* (New York: Random House, 1968) for his intelligent investigation of the connection between formal power structures and the family and for his analysis of how power corrupts basic human relationships.

3. "Domination in the quite general sense of power, i.e. the possibility of imposing one's will upon the behavior of other persons, can emerge in the most diverse forms." In this central passage of *Wirtschaft und Gesellschaft* Weber is particularly interested in two such forms: control through social authority ("patriarchal, magisterial, or princely") and control through economic force. In patriarchy as in other forms of domination "that control over economic goods, i.e. economic power, is a frequent, often purposively willed, consequence of domination as well as one of its most important instruments." Quoted from Max Rheinstein's and Edward Shil's translation of portions of *Wirtschaft und Gesellschaft* entitled *Max Weber on Law in Economy and Society* (New York: Simon and Schuster, 1967), pp. 323–24.

4. No matriarchal societies are known to exist at present. Matrilineality, which may be, as some anthropologists have held, a residue or a transitional stage of matriarchy, does not constitute an exception to patriarchal rule, it simply channels the power held by males through female descent—, e.g. the Avunculate.

5. Radical democracy would, of course, preclude patriarchy. One might find evidence of a general satisfaction with a less than perfect democracy in the fact that women have so rarely held power within modern "democracies."

6. Hannah Arendt, "Speculations on Violence," *The New York Review of Books*, Vol. XII No. 4, February 27, 1969, p. 24.

7. Goode, *op. cit.,* p. 74.

8. It would appear that the "pure flower of white womanhood" has at least at times been something of a disappointment to her lord as a fellow-racist. The historic connection of the Abolitionist and the Woman's Movement is some evidence of this, as well as the incident of white female and black male marriages as compared with those of white male and black female. Figures on miscegenation are very difficult to obtain: Goode (*op. cit.,* p. 37) estimates the proportion of white women marrying black men to be between 3 to 10 times the proportion of white men marrying black women. Robert K. Merton "Intermarriage and the Social Structure" *Psychiatry,* Vol. 4, August

1941, p. 374, states that "most intercaste sex relations—not marriages—are between white men and Negro women." It is hardly necessary to emphasize that the more extensive sexual contacts between white males and black females have not only been extramarital, but (on the part of the white male) crassly exploitative. Under slavery it was simply a case of rape.

9. Since abortion is extralegal, figures are difficult to obtain. This figure is based on the estimates of abortionists and referral services. Suicides in pregnancy are not officially reported either.

10. Vivid exceptions come to mind in the wars of liberation conducted by Vietnam, China, etc. But through most of history, women have been unarmed and forbidden to exhibit any defense of their own.

11. They are still high. The number of rapes reported in the city of New York in 1967 was 2432. Figure supplied by Police Department.

12. It is interesting that male victims of rape at the hands of other males often feel twice imposed upon, as they have not only been subjected to forcible and painful intercourse, but further abused in being reduced to the status of a female. Much of this is evident in Genet and in the contempt homosexual society reserves for its "passive" or "female" partners.

13. Masculine masochism is regarded as exceptional and often explained as latently homosexual, or a matter of the subject playing "the female role"—e.g., victim.

14. The literature of misogyny is so vast that no summary of sensible proportions could do it justice. The best reference on the subject is Katherine M. Rogers, *The Troublesome Helpmate, A History of Misogyny in Literature* (Seattle, University of Washington Press, 1966).

15. As well as the exquisite sonnets of love, Petrarch composed satires on women as the "De Remediis utriusque Fortunae" and *Epistolae Seniles*. Boccaccio too could balance the chivalry of romances (Filostrato, Ameto, and Fiammetta) with the vituperance of Corbaccio, a splenetic attack on women more than medieval in violence.

The Beijing Declaration

The United Nations Fourth World Conference on Women was held in Beijing, China, September 4–15, 1995, with over 30,000 women attending.* This document was adopted by the 181 governments represented, which committed themselves to implementing the Platform for Action formulated there. In the context of an organization (the UN) that professes commitment to human rights, it is only proper that they did so. However, we must keep in mind the words of Boutros Boutros-Ghali, then secretary-general of the UN: "Despite the progress made since the First World Conference on Women, twenty years ago, women and men still live in an unequal world." He calls upon all governments that have not yet done so to "ratify UN human rights instruments and labour conventions," among them CEDAW, the Convention on the Elimination of Discrimination Against Women, which was drafted in Mexico City during the First World Conference, adopted by the UN General Assembly in 1979, and ratified by the membership in 1981. We must note that the United States is one of those governments that has never ratified it. It was signed by President Carter in 1980 and submitted to the Senate, where no action was taken. In 1995 it was placed before the Senate Foreign Relations Committee, but again no action was taken.[†] This could not simply be an oversight.

INTRODUCTION

Translating the Momentum of Beijing into Action[‡]

By Boutros Boutros-Ghali
United Nations Secretary-General

ALL OF US OWE A debt of gratitude to the People's Republic of China, which has hosted one of the largest global conferences ever held, with some 17,000 participants, including 6,000 delegates from 189 countries, over 4,000 representatives of accredited non-governmental organizations, a host of international civil servants and about 4,000 media representatives. More than 30,000 people also participated in the NGO* Forum.

My special thanks also go to the President of the Conference, Madame Chen Muhua, and to the Secretary-General of the Fourth World Conference on Women, Mrs. Gertrude Mongella.

Now the momentum of Beijing must be translated into concrete action. We must all ensure that the decisions reached in Beijing will change the world.

The commitments made in Beijing are not only the result of diplomatic negotiation. Behind them lies the strong and organized power of the women's movement. The entire continuum of global conferences and summits has been shaped by the growing influence, passion and intellectual conviction of the women's movement.

At Rio, Vienna, Cairo and Copenhagen the importance of issues related to the improvement of the status of women was stressed. From each of these global conferences emerged a more powerful recognition of the crucial role of women in sustainable development and protecting the environment; of the human rights of women as an inalienable, integral and indivisible part of universal human rights; of violence against women as an intolerable violation of these rights; of health, maternal care and family planning facilities, and of access to education and information, as essential to the exercise by women of their fundamental rights.

In the United Nations, the women's movement has a staunch ally. Starting from the assertion in the Charter, calling for full equality of men and women,

---

Published by the Department of Public Information, United Nations, New York, 1996.

*The first was held in Mexico City in 1975, the second in Copenhagen in 1980, and the third in Nairobi in 1985.

[†] "The UN Fourth World Conference on Women," by Beatrice W. Dierks, *NWSA Journal*, vol. 8, no. 2 (Summer 1996), provides an excellent history and description of the Beijing conference. Many of the facts reported in this note are found in that article.

[‡] From the statement of the secretary-general read on the concluding day of the Fourth World Conference on Women, Beijing, 15 September 1995.

---

* NGO—nongovernmental organization [editor's note]

the United Nations has worked with the women's movement to realize this goal of our founders. The Commission on the Status of Women was one of the first bodies established by the United Nations after its foundation. Over the past 20 years, World Conferences on Women, held in Mexico City, Copenhagen and Nairobi, have contributed to the progressive strengthening of the legal, economic, social and political dimensions of the role of women. In 1979, the General Assembly adopted the landmark Convention for the Elimination of all Forms of Discrimination against Women.

The movement for gender equality the world over has been one of the defining developments of our time. I am proud and honoured that the United Nations has been part of this movement.

Despite the progress made, much, much more remains to be done. While women have made significant advances in many societies, women's concerns are still given second priority almost everywhere. Women face discrimination and marginalization in subtle as well as in flagrant ways. Women do not share equally in the fruits of production. Women constitute 70 per cent of the world's poor.

The sign at the entrance to the NGO Forum at Huairou calls on us to "Look at the world through women's eyes." For the past two weeks, the world has done just that. We have seen that, despite the progress made since the First World Conference on Women, 20 years ago, women and men still live in an unequal world. Gender disparities and unacceptable inequalities persist in all countries. In 1995 there is no country in the world where men and women enjoy complete equality.

The message of this Conference is that women's issues are global and universal. Deeply entrenched attitudes and practices perpetuate inequality and discrimination against women, in public and private life, on a daily basis, in all parts of the world. At the same time, there has emerged a consensus that equality of opportunity for all people is essential to the construction of just and democratic societies for the twenty-first century. The fundamental linkages between the three objectives of the Conference—equality, development and peace—are now recognized by all.

The Platform for Action has emerged from a preparatory process more participatory and inclusive than any in history. Never before have so many women, representing both Governments and non-governmental organizations, gathered to share experiences and chart the way ahead. The United Nations has provided the venue and the framework to move issues of gender equality to the top of the global agenda. The women of the world have been the driving force to shape this agenda and move it forward.

The Platform for Action is a powerful agenda for the empowerment of women. It calls for the integration of gender perspectives in all policies and programmes. It focuses on concrete measures to address the critical areas of concern worldwide. The Platform for Action must be our guide and constant point of reference. I ask that it receive wide dissemination globally, regionally and locally. The implementation of its goals, objectives and measures must be actively monitored. And it must be further strengthened, as needed, to take account of new developments as they emerge.

As we set out on the road from Beijing, the Platform is a call for concrete action to make a difference:

- Action to protect and promote the human rights of women and the girl child as an integral part of universal human rights;
- Action to eradicate the persistent and increasing burden of poverty on women;
- Action to remove the obstacles to women's full participation in public life and decision-making, at all levels—including the family;
- Action to eliminate all forms of violence against women;
- Action to ensure equal access for girl children and women to education and health services;
- Action to promote economic autonomy for women, and ensure their access to productive resources; and
- Action to encourage an equitable sharing of family responsibilities.

The Platform for Action places heavy responsibilities on the United Nations system. It calls upon United Nations organizations to play a key role in follow-up, implementation and monitoring. It poses a challenge to the capacity and commitment of the United Nations. As Secretary-General, I accept that challenge. I will ensure that the recommendations addressed to me are implemented swiftly and effectively. I am committed to placing the gender perspective into the mainstream of all aspects of the work of the Organization. I will work with my colleagues, the Executive Heads of the United Nations specialized agencies and the United Nations Programmes and Funds, to ensure a coordinated system-wide response, integrating the follow-up of this Conference with that of other global conferences. And I will keep Member States regularly informed of the progress that is made.

Executive Heads of the organizations of the United Nations system have expressed their commitment to the advancement of women in the secretariats of the system as a policy priority. They have all committed themselves to developing specific policies and monitoring mechanisms to improve the status of women and, in particular, to increase the number of women in senior and policy-making positions.

The United Nations system is already active on a number of fronts which will prove critical to the implementation of the Platform. Reversing the trend towards the feminization of poverty. Raising the educational levels and health standards of women and girls. Expanding legal protection for women in the home. Establishing stronger protection for women in times of war. All these must be given priority.

I call on all Governments that have not yet done so to accede to and ratify United Nations human rights instruments and labour conventions—in particular the Convention on the Elimination of Discrimination Against Women and the Convention on the Rights of the Child.

In conclusion, let me emphasize the institutions of civil society which have played such an important role in preparing for this Conference. Since I assumed the office of Secretary-General, I have spoken often of the evolution of civil society and its importance for economic, cultural and democratic advancement. More effective mechanisms to ensure partnership between Governments and civil society will contribute significantly to the implementation of the policies and measures that are called for in the Platform. The United Nations will intensify the close ties and working relationships that already exist with the NGO community at the global and na-

tional levels. The United Nations will be prepared to support Governments in their endeavours to foster and strengthen the institutions of civil society.

In a few weeks, the leaders of the world will meet at United Nations Headquarters in a Summit of Heads of State and Government. There they will mark the fiftieth anniversary of the founding of the United Nations.

As the world celebrates this anniversary, let us work together to ensure that the equal rights of men and women, enshrined in the Charter, become a reality.

Let us work together to implement the Platform for Action adopted here at Beijing. Let us tell the world—and let us tell it with pride: the empowerment of women is the empowerment of all humanity!

BEIJING DECLARATION

1. We, the Governments participating in the Fourth World Conference on Women,

2. Gathered here in Beijing in September 1995, the year of the fiftieth anniversary of the founding of the United Nations,

3. Determined to advance the goals of equality, development and peace for all women everywhere in the interest of all humanity,

4. Acknowledging the voices of all women everywhere and taking note of the diversity of women and their roles and circumstances, honouring the women who paved the way and inspired by the hope present in the world's youth,

5. Recognize that the status of women has advanced in some important respects in the past decade but that progress has been uneven, inequalities between women and men have persisted and major obstacles remain, with serious consequences for the well-being of all people,

6. Also recognize that this situation is exacerbated by the increasing poverty that is affecting the lives of the majority of the world's people, in particular women and children, with origins in both the national and international domains,

7. Dedicate ourselves unreservedly to addressing these constraints and obstacles and thus enhancing further the advancement and empowerment of women all over the world, and agree

that this requires urgent action in the spirit of determination, hope, cooperation and solidarity, now and to carry us forward into the next century.

We reaffirm our commitment to:

8. The equal rights and inherent human dignity of women and men and other purposes and principles enshrined in the Charter of the United Nations, to the Universal Declaration of Human Rights and other international human rights instruments, in particular the Convention on the Elimination of All Forms of Discrimination against Women and the Convention on the Rights of the Child, as well as the Declaration on the Elimination of Violence against Women and the Declaration on the Right to Development;

9. Ensure the full implementation of the human rights of women and of the girl child as an inalienable, integral and indivisible part of all human rights and fundamental freedoms;

10. Build on consensus and progress made at previous United Nations conferences and summits— on women in Nairobi in 1985, on children in New York in 1990, on environment and development in Rio de Janeiro in 1992, on human rights in Vienna in 1993, on population and development in Cairo in 1994 and on social development in Copenhagen in 1995 with the objective of achieving equality, development and peace;

11. Achieve the full and effective implementation of the Nairobi Forward-looking Strategies for the Advancement of Women;

12. The empowerment and advancement of women, including the right to freedom of thought, conscience, religion and belief, thus contributing to the moral, ethical, spiritual and intellectual needs of women and men, individually or in community with others and thereby guaranteeing them the possibility of realizing their full potential in society and shaping their lives in accordance with their own aspirations.

We are convinced that:

13. Women's empowerment and their full participation on the basis of equality in all spheres of society, including participation in the decision-making process and access to power, are fundamental for the achievement of equality, development and peace;

14. Women's rights are human rights;

15. Equal rights, opportunities and access to resources, equal sharing of responsibilities for the family by men and women, and a harmonious partnership between them are critical to their well-being and that of their families as well as to the consolidation of democracy;

16. Eradication of poverty based on sustained economic growth, social development, environmental protection and social justice requires the involvement of women in economic and social development, equal opportunities and the full and equal participation of women and men as agents and beneficiaries of people-centred sustainable development;

17. The explicit recognition and reaffirmation of the right of all women to control all aspects of their health, in particular their own fertility, is basic to their empowerment;

18. Local, national, regional and global peace is attainable and is inextricably linked with the advancement of women, who are a fundamental force for leadership, conflict resolution and the promotion of lasting peace at all levels;

19. It is essential to design, implement and monitor, with the full participation of women, effective, efficient and mutually reinforcing gender-sensitive policies and programmes, including development policies and programmes, at all levels that will foster the empowerment and advancement of women;

20. The participation and contribution of all actors of civil society, particularly women's groups and networks and other non-governmental organizations and community-based organizations, with full respect for their autonomy, in cooperation with Governments, are important to the effective implementation and follow-up of the Platform for Action;

21. The implementation of the Platform for Action requires commitment from Governments and the international community. By making national and international commitments for action,

including those made at the Conference, Governments and the international community recognize the need to take priority action for the empowerment and advancement of women.

We are determined to:

22. Intensify efforts and actions to achieve the goals of the Nairobi Forward-looking Strategies for the Advancement of Women by the end of this century;

23. Ensure the full enjoyment by women and the girl child of all human rights and fundamental freedoms and take effective action against violations of these rights and freedoms;

24. Take all necessary measures to eliminate all forms of discrimination against women and the girl child and remove all obstacles to gender equality and the advancement and empowerment of women;

25. Encourage men to participate fully in all actions towards equality;

26. Promote women's economic independence, including employment, and eradicate the persistent and increasing burden of poverty on women by addressing the structural causes of poverty through changes in economic structures, ensuring equal access for all women, including those in rural areas, as vital development agents, to productive resources, opportunities and public services;

27. Promote people-centred sustainable development, including sustained economic growth, through the provision of basic education, lifelong education, literacy and training, and primary health care for girls and women;

28. Take positive steps to ensure peace for the advancement of women and, recognizing the leading role that women have played in the peace movement, work actively towards general and complete disarmament under strict and effective international control, and support negotiations on the conclusion, without delay, of a universal and multilaterally and effectively verifiable comprehensive nuclear-test-ban treaty which contributes to nuclear disarmament and the prevention of the proliferation of nuclear weapons in all its aspects;

29. Prevent and eliminate all forms of violence against women and girls;

30. Ensure equal access to and equal treatment of women and men in education and health care and enhance women's sexual and reproductive health as well as education;

31. Promote and protect all human rights of women and girls;

32. Intensify efforts to ensure equal enjoyment of all human rights and fundamental freedoms for all women and girls who face multiple barriers to their empowerment and advancement because of such factors as their race, age, language, ethnicity, culture, religion, or disability, or because they are indigenous people;

33. Ensure respect for international law, including humanitarian law, in order to protect women and girls in particular;

34. Develop the fullest potential of girls and women of all ages, ensure their full and equal participation in building a better world for all and enhance their role in the development process.

We are determined to:

35. Ensure women's equal access to economic resources, including land, credit, science and technology, vocational training, information, communication and markets, as a means to further the advancement and empowerment of women and girls, including through the enhancement of their capacities to enjoy the benefits of equal access to these resources, *inter alia*, by means of international cooperation;

36. Ensure the success of the Platform for Action, which will require a strong commitment on the part of Governments, international organizations and institutions at all levels. We are deeply convinced that economic development, social development and environmental protection are interdependent and mutually reinforcing components of sustainable development, which is the framework for our efforts to achieve a higher quality of life for all people. Equitable social development that recognizes empowering the poor, particularly women living in poverty, to utilize environmental resources sustainably is

a necessary foundation for sustainable development. We also recognize that broad-based and sustained economic growth in the context of sustainable development is necessary to sustain social development and social justice. The success of the Platform for Action will also require adequate mobilization of resources at the national and international levels as well as new and additional resources to the developing countries from all available funding mechanisms, including multilateral, bilateral and private sources for the advancement of women; financial resources to strengthen the capacity of national, subregional, regional and international institutions; a commitment to equal rights, equal responsibilities and equal opportunities and to the equal participation of women and men in all national, regional and international bodies and policy-making processes; and the establishment or strengthening of mechanisms at all levels for accountability to the world's women;

37. Ensure also the success of the Platform for Action in countries with economies in transition, which will require continued international cooperation and assistance;

38. We hereby adopt and commit ourselves as Governments to implement the following Platform for Action, ensuring that a gender perspective is reflected in all our policies and programmes. We urge the United Nations system, regional and international financial institutions, other relevant regional and international institutions and all women and men, as well as non-governmental organizations, with full respect for their autonomy, and all sectors of civil society, in cooperation with Governments, to fully commit themselves and contribute to the implementation of this Platform for Action.

Bibliography and Further Readings

Abbott, Deborah, and Ellen Farmer. 1995. *From Wedded Wife to Lesbian Life: Stories of Transformation.* Freedom, CA: Crossing Press.

Abramovitz, Mimi. 1996. *Regulating the Lives of Women* (Rev. ed.). Boston: South End Press.

———. 1996. *Under Attack, Fighting Back: Women and Welfare in the United States.* New York: Monthly Review Press.

Afkhami, Mahnaz. 1995. *Faith and Freedom: Women's Human Rights in the Middle East.* Syracuse, NY: Syracuse University Press.

Afkhami, Mahnaz, and Erika Friedl, eds. 1994. *In the Eye of the Storm: Women in Post-Revolutionary Iran.* Syracuse, NY: Syracuse University Press.

Afshar, Haleh, ed. 1993. *Women in the Middle East: Perceptions, Realities and Struggles for Liberation.* New York: St. Martin's Press.

Agosín, Marjorie, ed. 1999. *A Map of Hope: Women's Writing on Human Rights—An International Literary Anthology.* Piscataway, NJ: Rutgers University Press.

———. 1999. *Uncertain Travelers: Conversations with Jewish Women Immigrants to America.* Hanover, NH: University Press of New England.

Albelda, Randy, and Chris Tilly. 1997. *Glass Ceilings and Bottomless Pits: Women's Work, Women's Poverty.* Boston: South End Press.

Allen, Jeffner. 1990. *Lesbian Philosophies and Cultures.* New York: State University of New York Press.

———. 1986. *Lesbian Philosophy: Explorations.* Palo Alto, CA: Institute of Lesbian Studies.

———. 1996. *Sinuosities: Lesbian Poetic Politics.* Bloomington, IN: Indiana University Press.

Allen, Paula Gunn. 1992. *Grandmothers of the Light: A Medicine Woman's Sourcebook.* Boston: Beacon Press.

———. 1996. *Life Is a Fatal Disease: Selected Poems 1964–1994.* Albuquerque, NM: West End Press.

———. 1998. *Off The Reservation: Reflections on Boundary-Busting, Border-Crossing Loose Canons.* Boston: Beacon Press.

———. 1986. *The Sacred Hoop: Recovering the Feminine in American Indian Traditions.* Boston: Beacon Press.

Altink, Sietske. 1996. *Stolen Lives: Trading Women into Sex and Slavery.* Binghamton, NY: Haworth.

Amott, Teresa L., and Julie A. Matthaei. 1996. *Race, Gender, and Work: A Multicultural Economic History of Women in the United States* (Rev. ed.). Boston: South End Press.

Andersen, Margaret L., and Patricia Hill Collins, eds. 1992. *Race, Class, and Gender: An Anthology.* Belmont, CA: Wadsworth Publishing.

Anderson, Sherry Ruth, and Patricia Hopkins. 1991. *The Feminine Face of God: The Unfolding of the Sacred in Women.* New York: Bantam.

Angelou, Maya. 1991. *All God's Children Need Traveling Shoes.* New York: Random House.

———. 1995. *Brave and Startling Truth.* New York: Random House.

———. 1981. *The Heart of a Woman.* New York: Random House.

———. 1999. *I Dream a World: Portraits of Black Women Who Changed America.* New York: Stewart Tabori & Chang.

———. 1969. *I Know Why the Caged Bird Sings.* New York: Random House.

———. 1991. *I Shall Not Be Moved.* New York: Bantam.

Angelou, Maya, et al. 1993. *Double Stitch: Black Women Write About Mothers and Daughters.* New York: Harper & Row.

Angier, Natalie. 1999. *Woman: An Intimate Geography.* New York: Anchor Books.

Anzaldúa, Gloria, ed. 1987. *Borderlands/La Frontera: The New Mestiza.* San Francisco: Spinsters/Aunt Lute.

———. 1990. *Making Face, Making Soul/Haciendo Caras: Creative and Critical Perspectives by Women of Color.* San Francisco: Aunt Lute Foundation Books.

Ardrey, Robert. 1966. *The Territorial Imperative.* New York: Atheneum.

Arendell, Terry. 1995. *Fathers & Divorce.* Thousand Oaks, CA: Sage Publications.

Ashley, Jo Ann. 1976. *Hospitals, Paternalism, and the Role of the Nurse* (Athene Series). New York: Teachers College Press.

Asian Women United of California, eds. 1989. *Making Waves: An Anthology of Writings By and About Asian American Women.* Boston: Beacon Press.

Aswad, Barbara C., and Barbara Bilge, eds. 1996. *Family and Gender Among American Muslims: Issues Facing*

Middle Eastern Immigrants and Their Descendants. Philadelphia, PA: Temple University Press.

Babcox, Deborah, and Madeline Belkin, comps. 1971. *Liberation Now!* New York: Dell.

Bacon, Margaret Hope. 1986. *Mothers of Feminism: The Story of Quaker Women in America.* San Francisco: Harper & Row.

Baehr, Helen, and Ann Gray, eds. 1996. *Turning It On: A Reader in Women and Media.* London, UK: Arnold.

Baker, Christina Looper, and Christina Baker Kline. 1996. *The Conversation Begins: Mothers and Daughters Talk About Living Feminism.* New York: Bantam.

Bambara, Toni Cade. 1996. *Deep Sightings and Rescue Missions: Fiction, Essays, and Conversations.* New York: Pantheon.

Bancroft, Anne. 1996. *Women in Search of the Sacred.* New York: Penguin.

Banner, Lois W. 1983. *American Beauty.* New York: Alfred A. Knopf.

———. 1980. *Elizabeth Cady Stanton: A Radical for Women's Rights.* Boston: Little, Brown.

———. 1993. *In Full Flower: Aging Women, Power, and Sexuality.* New York: Random House.

Bardwick, Judith. 1981. *Feminine Personality and Conflict.* Westport, CT: Greenwood Press. (Originally published by Brooks/Cole, 1970.)

Barker-Benfield, G. J. 1999. *The Horrors of the Half-Known Life: Male Attitudes Toward Women and Sexuality in 19th Century America.* New York: Routledge. (Originally published by Harper Colophon, 1976.)

Barnett, Ola W., and Alyce D. LaViolette. 1993. *It Could Happen To Anyone: Why Battered Women Stay.* Thousand Oaks, CA: Sage Publications.

Barrington, Judith, ed. 1991. *An Intimate Wilderness: Lesbian Writers on Sexuality.* Portland, OR: Eighth Mountain Press.

Barry, Kathleen. 1984. *Female Sexual Slavery.* New York: New York University Press.

———. 1995. *The Prostitution of Sexuality.* New York: New York University Press.

———. 1988. *Susan B. Anthony: A Biography of a Singular Feminist.* New York: New York University Press.

Bart, Pauline B., and Eileen Geil Moran. 1993. *Violence Against Women: The Bloody Footprints.* Thousand Oaks, CA: Sage Publications.

Bean, Constance A. 1993. *Women Murdered by the Men They Loved.* New York: Haworth Press.

Beauvoir, Simone de. 1953. *The Second Sex.* Trans. and ed. H. M. Parshley. New York: Alfred A. Knopf.

Belenky, Mary Field, Blythe McVicker Clinchy, Nancy Rule Goldberger, and Jill Mattuck Tarule. 1996. *Women's Ways of Knowing: The Development of Self, Voice, and Mind* (10th ann. ed.). New York: Basic Books.

Bell, Diane, and Renate Klein, eds. 1996. *Radically Speaking: Feminism Reclaimed.* Australia: Spinifex Press.

Bell, Linda A., and David Blumenfeld, eds. 1995. *Overcoming Racism and Sexism.* Lanham, MD: Rowman & Littlefield.

Bell-Scott, Patricia, Beverly Guy-Sheftall, Jacqueline Jones Royster, Janet Sims-Wood, Miriam DeCosta-Willis, and Lucie Fultz, eds. 1993. *Double Stitch: Black Women Write About Mothers and Daughters.* New York: HarperPerennial.

Bem, Sandra Lipsit. 1993. *The Lenses of Gender: Transforming the Debate on Sexual Inequality.* New Haven, CT: Yale University Press.

Bergen, Raquel Kennedy. 1996. *Wife Rape: Understanding the Response of Survivors and Service Providers* (Sage Series on Violence Against Women, Vol. 2). Thousand Oaks, CA: Sage Publications.

Bernard, Jessie. 1973. *American Family Behavior.* New York: Russell & Russell.

———. 1981. *The Female World.* New York: Free Press.

———. 1987. *The Female World from a Global Perspective.* Bloomington: Indiana University Press.

———. 1973. *The Future of Marriage.* New York: Bantam.

———. 1974. *The Future of Motherhood.* New York: Dell.

———. 1971. *Remarriage.* New York: Russell & Russell.

———. 1972. *The Sex Game.* New York: Atheneum.

———. 1971. *Women and the Public Interest.* Chicago: Aldine.

———. 1975. *Women, Wives, Mothers: Values and Options.* Chicago: Aldine.

Berry, Mary Frances. 1986. *Why ERA Failed: Politics, Women's Rights and the Amending Process of the Constitution.* Bloomington: Indiana University Press.

Bielecki, Tessa. 1996. *Teresa of Avila: Ecstasy and Common Sense.* Boston: Shambhala Publications.

Bird, Caroline. 1995. *Lives of Our Own: Secrets of Salty Old Women.* Boston: Houghton Mifflin.

Black, Allida. 1996. *Casting Her Own Shadow: Eleanor Roosevelt and the Shaping of Postwar Liberalism.* New York: Columbia University Press.

Blanchard, Dallas A., and Terry J. Prewitt. 1993. *Religious Violence and Abortion: The Gideon Project.* Gainesville: University Press of Florida.

Blau, Francine D., and Ronald Ehrenberg, eds. 1997. *Gender and Family Issues in the Workplace.* New York: Russell Sage Foundation.

Blea, Irene I. 1991. *La Chicana and the Intersection of Race, Class, and Gender.* New York: Praeger.

Bleier, Ruth H., ed. 1986. *Feminist Approaches to Science.* New York: Pergamon.

———. 1984. *Science and Gender: A Critique of Biology and Its Theories on Women.* New York: Pergamon.

Bly, Robert. 1990. *Iron John: A Book About Men.* Reading, MA: Addison-Wesley.

Bordo, Susan. 1997. *Twilight Zones: The Hidden Life of Cultural Images from Plato to O. J.* Berkeley, CA: University of California Press.

———. 1993. *Unbearable Weight: Feminism, Western Culture, and the Body.* Berkeley, CA: University of California Press.

The Boston Women's Health Book Collective. 1996. *The New Our Bodies, Ourselves: A Book By and For Women* (25th ann. ed.) New York: Simon & Schuster.

Boulding, Elise. 1992. *The Underside of History: A View of Women Through Time* (Rev. ed., Vols. 1 & 2). Thousand Oaks, CA: Sage Publications.

Boumil, Marcia Mobilia, and Joel Friedman. 1996. *Deadbeat Dads: A National Child Support Scandal.* Westport, CT: Praeger Publishers.

Boxer, Marilyn Jacoby. 1998. *When Women Ask the Questions: Creating Women's Studies in America.* Baltimore, MD: The Johns Hopkins University Press.

Brod, Harry. 1987. *The Making of Masculinities: The New Men's Studies.* Boston: Allen and Unwin.

———. 1988. *A Mensch Among Men: Explorations in Jewish Masculinity.* Freedom, CA: Crossing Press.

Brod, Harry, and Michael Kaufman, eds. 1994. *Theorizing Masculinities* (Research on Men and Masculinities Series, Vol. 5). Thousand Oaks, CA: Sage Publications.

Brooks, Geraldine. 1995. *Nine Parts of Desire: The Hidden World of Islamic Women.* New York: Anchor Books.

Brown, Lyn M. and Carol Gilligan. 1992. *Meeting at the Crossroads: Women's Psychology and Girls' Development.* Cambridge, MA: Harvard University Press.

Brown, Rita Mae. 1988. *Bingo.* New York: Bantam.

———. 1988. *In Her Day.* New York: Bantam.

———. 1987. *The Poems of Rita Mae Brown.* Freedom, CA: Crossing Press.

———. 1979. *Rubyfruit Jungle.* New York: Bantam.

———. 1988. *Starting From Scratch: A Different Kind of Writer's Manual.* New York: Bantam.

———. 1983. *Sudden Death.* New York: Bantam Books.

———. 1993. *Venus Envy.* New York: Bantam Books.

Brownmiller, Susan. 1975. *Against Our Will: Men, Women, and Rape.* New York: Simon & Schuster.

———. 1984. *Femininity.* New York: Simon & Schuster

———. 1999. *In Our Time: Memoir of a Revolution.* New York: Dial Press.

———. 1989. *Waverly Place.* New York: Grove Press.

Budapest, Zsuzsanna E. 1989. *The Grandmother of Time: A Woman's Book of Celebrations, Spells, and Sacred Objects for Every Month of the Year.* San Francisco: HarperSanFrancisco.

———. 1989. *The Holy Book of Women's Mysteries.* Oakland, CA: Wingbow.

Bullough, Vern L. and Bonnie Bullough. 1995. *Sexual Attitudes: Myths and Realities.* Amherst, NY: Prometheus Books.

Bullough, Vern L., Brenda Shelton, and Sarah Slavin. 1988. *The Subordinated Sex.* Athens: University of Georgia Press.

Bunch, Charlotte. 1987. *Passionate Politics: Feminist Theory in Action.* New York: St. Martin's Press.

Bunch, Charlotte, and Nancy Myron, eds. 1974. *Class and Feminism: A Collection of Essays from the Furies.* Baltimore: Diana Press.

———. 1975. *Lesbianism and the Women's Movement.* Baltimore: Diana Press.

Bunch, Charlotte, and Sandra Pollack, eds. 1983. *Learning Our Way: Essays in Feminist Education.* Trumansburg, NY: Crossing Press.

Bushnell, Dana E., ed. 1995. *"Nagging" Questions: Feminist Ethics in Everyday Life.* Lanham, MD: Rowman and Littlefield.

Butler, Judith. 1999. *Gender Trouble* (10th ann. ed.). New York: Routledge.

Buzawa, Eves S., and Carl G. Buzawa. 1996. *Domestic Violence: The Criminal Justice Response,* 2d ed. Thousand Oaks, CA: Sage Publications.

Cade, Toni, ed. 1970. *The Black Woman: An Anthology.* New York: Signet.

Cahill, Lisa Sowle. 1996. *Sex, Gender, and Christian Ethics.* New York: Cambridge University Press.

Cahill, Susan, ed. 1996. *Wise Women: Over 2000 Years of Spiritual Writing by Women.* New York: W. W. Norton.

Caine, Lynn. 1974. *Widow.* New York: Morrow.

Caldicott, Helen. 1996. *A Desperate Passion: An Autobiography.* New York: W. W. Norton.

Camp, Helen. 1995. *Iron in Her Soul: Elizabeth Gurley Flynn and the American Left.* Pullman, WA: Washington State University Press.

Cannon, Katie G. 1988. *Black Womanist Ethics.* Atlanta: Scholars Press of Georgia.

———. 1995. *Katie's Canon: Womanism and the Soul of the Black Community.* New York: The Continuum Publishing Group.

Caraway, Nancie. 1991. *Segregated Sisterhood: Racism and the Politics of American Feminism.* Knoxville: University of Tennessee Press.

Case, Sue-Ellen. 1988. *Feminism and Theatre.* New York: Methuen.

Chafetz, Janet Saltzman. 1986. *Female Revolt: Women's Movements in World and Historical Perspective.* Totowa, NJ: Rowman and Allenheld.

———. 1978. *Masculine/Feminine or Human?: An Overview of the Sociology of Gender Roles.* Itasca, IL: Peacock.

Chang, Jung. 1992. *Wild Swans: Three Daughters of China.* New York: Anchor Doubleday.

Chang, Pang-Mei Natasha. 1996. *Bound Feet & Western Dress: A Memoir.* New York: Doubleday.

Chernin, Kim. 1987. *The Flame Bearers.* New York: Perennial Library, Harper & Row.

———. 1985. *The Hungry Self: Women, Eating, and Identity.* New York: Perennial Library, Harper & Row.

———. 1996. *In My Father's Garden: A Daughter's Search for a Spiritual Life.* Chapel Hill, NC: Algonquin Books.

———. 1983. *In My Mother's House.* New Haven, CT: Ticknor & Fields.

———. 1982. *The Obsession: Reflections on the Tyranny of Slenderness.* New York: Harper & Row.

———. 1987. *Reinventing Eve: Modern Woman in Search of Herself.* New York: Harper & Row.

———. 1989. *Sex and Other Sacred Games: Love, Desire, Power, and Possession.* New York: Times Books.

Chesler, Ellen. 1992. *Woman of Valor: Margaret Sanger and the Birth Control Movement in America.* New York: Simon & Schuster.

Chesler, Phyllis. 1978. *About Men.* New York: Simon & Schuster. Reissued by Harcourt Brace Jovanovich, 1989.

———. 1999. *Letters to a Young Feminist.* New York: Four Walls Eight Windows.

———. 1986. *Mothers on Trial: The Battle for Children and Custody.* New York: McGraw-Hill. Reprinted by Harcourt Brace Jovanovich, 1991.

———. 1994. *Patriarchy: Notes of an Expert Witness.* Munroe, ME: Common Courage Press.

———. 1989. *Sacred Bond: The Legacy of Baby M.* New York: Times Books.

———. 1979. *With Child: A Diary of Motherhood.* New York: Crowell.

———. 1972. *Women and Madness.* New York: Doubleday. Reissued with a new introduction by Harcourt Brace Jovanovich, 1989.

Chesler, Phyllis, et al., eds. 1995. *Feminist Foremothers in Women's Studies, Psychology, and Mental Health.* Binghamton, NY: Haworth Press.

Chicago, Judy. 1996. *Beyond the Flower: The Autobiography of a Feminist Artist.* New York: Viking.

Chisholm, Shirley. 1971. *Unbought and Unbossed.* New York: Avon.

Chodorow, Nancy J. 1989. *Feminism and Psychoanalytic Theory.* New Haven, CT: Yale University Press.

———. 1978. *The Reproduction of Mothering: Psychoanalysis and the Sociology of Gender.* Berkeley, CA: University of California Press.

Chopin, Kate. 1972. *The Awakening,* New York: Avon. (Originally published in 1899.)

Chow, Esther Ngan-Ling, Doris Wilkinson, and Maxine Baca Zinn, eds. 1996. *Race, Class & Gender: Common Bonds, Different Voices.* Thousand Oaks, CA: Sage Publications.

Christ, Carol P. 1995. *Diving Deep and Surfacing: Women Writers on Spiritual Quest,* 3d ed. Boston: Beacon Press.

———. 1987. *Laughter of Aphrodite: Reflections on a Journey to the Goddess.* San Francisco: Harper & Row.

———. 1997. *Rebirth of the Goddess: Finding Meaning in Feminist Spirituality.* Reading, MA: Addison-Wesley.

———. 1989. *Weaving the Visions: New Patterns in Feminist Spirituality.* San Francisco: Harper & Row.

Christ, Carol P., and Judith Plaskow, eds. 1992. *Womanspirit Rising: A Feminist Reader in Religion,* 2d ed. San Francisco: Harper & Row.

Clack, Beverley, ed. 1999. *Mysogyny in the Western Philosophical Tradition: A Reader.* New York: Routledge.

Clark, Marcia, with Teresa Carpenter. 1997. *Without a Doubt.* New York: Viking.

Clatterbaugh, Kenneth. 1996. *Contemporary Perspectives on Masculinity: Men, Women and Politics in Modern Society,* 2d ed. Boulder, CO: Westview Press.

Clausen, Jan. 1997. *Beyond Gay or Straight: Understanding Sexual Orientation.* Philadelphia: Chelsea House Publishers.

Clement, Grace. 1996. *Care, Autonomy, and Justice: Feminism and the Ethic of Care.* Boulder, CO: Westview Press.

Clements, Marcelle. 1998. *The Improvised Woman: Single Women Reinventing Single Life.* New York: W.W. Norton.

Cline, Sally. 1990. *Just Desserts: Women and Food.* London: Andre Deutsch.

Cline, Sally, and Dale Spender. 1987. *Reflecting Men at Twice Their Natural Size.* New York: Seaver Books / Henry Holt.

Clover, Carol J. 1993. *Men, Women, and Chain Saws: Gender in the Modern Horror Film.* Princeton, NJ: Princeton University Press.

Collard, Andree, and Joyce Contrucci. 1989. *Rape of the Wild: Man's Violence Against Animals and the Earth.* Bloomington: Indiana University Press.

Collins, Patricia Hill. 2000. *Black Feminist Thought: Knowledge, Consciousness, and the Politics of Empowerment* (10th ann. ed). New York: Routledge. (Originally published by Unwin Hyman, 1990.)

———. 1998. *Fighting Words: Black Women and the Search for Justice.* Minnesota: University of Minnesota Press.

Conover, Pamela Johnston, and Virginia Gray. 1983. *Feminism and the New Right: Conflict over the American Family.* Westport, CT: Praeger.

Cook, Blanche Wiesen. 1992. *Eleanor Roosevelt: 1884–1933,* Vol. 1. New York: Viking.

———. 1999. *Eleanor Roosevelt: 1933–1938,* Vol. 2. New York: Viking.

Cook, Sandy, and Susanne Davies, eds. 1999. *Harsh Punishment: International Experiences of Women's Imprisonment.* Boston: Northeastern University Press.

Coole, Diana H. 1993. *Women in Political Theory: From Ancient Misogyny to Contemporary Feminism,* 2d ed. Boulder, CO: Lynne Rienner Publishers.

Coontz, Stephanie. 1997. *The Way We Really Are: Coming to Terms with America's Changing Families.* New York: Basic Books.

Corea, Gena. 1985. *The Hidden Malpractice: How American Medicine Mistreats Women.* New York: Harper & Row.

———. 1992. *Invisible Epidemic: The Story of Women and AIDS.* New York: HarperCollins.

———. 1985. *The Mother Machine.* New York: Harper & Row.

Corea, Gena et al. 1987. *Man-Made Women: How New Reproductive Technologies Affect Women.* Bloomington: Indiana University Press.

Cotera, Martha P. 1976. *The Chicana Feminist.* Austin, TX: Information Systems Development.

———. 1976. *Diosa y Hembra: The History and Heritage of Chicanas in the United States.* Austin, TX: Information Systems Development.

Cott, Nancy F. 1987. *The Grounding of Modern Feminism.* New Haven, CT: Yale University Press.

Cott, Nancy F., et al., eds. 1996. *Root of Bitterness: Documents of the Social History of American Women,* 2d ed. Boston: Northeastern University Press.

Craig, Steve, ed. 1992. *Men, Masculinity, and the Media* (Research on Men and Masculinity Series, ed. Michael Kimmel, Vol. 1). Thousand Oaks, CA: Sage Publications.

Crawford, Mary. 1995. *Talking Difference: On Gender and Language.* Thousand Oaks, CA: Sage Publications.

Cuklanz, Lisa M. 2000. *Rape on Prime Time: Television, Masculinity, and Sexual Violence.* Philadelphia: University of Pennsylvania Press.

———. 1996. *Rape on Trial: How the Mass Media Construct Legal Reform and Social Change.* Philadelphia: University of Pennsylvania Press.

Culliver, Concetta C., ed. 1992. *Female Criminality: The State of the Art.* New York: Garland.

Daly, Mary. 1973. *Beyond God the Father.* Boston: Beacon Press.

———. 1975. *The Church and the Second Sex.* New York: Harper Colophon.

———. 1978. *Gyn/Ecology: The Metaethics of Radical Feminism.* Boston: Beacon Press.

———. 1992. *Outercourse: The Be-Dazzling Voyage. Containing Recollections from My* Logbook of a Radical Feminist Philosopher *(Being an Account of My Time/Space Travels and Ideas—Then, Again, Now, and How).* San Francisco: HarperSanFrancisco.

———. 1984. *Pure Lust.* Boston: Beacon Press.

———. 1998. *Quintessence . . . Realizing the Archaic Future: A Radical Elemental Feminist Manifesto.* Boston: Beacon Press.

Daly, Mary, in cahoots with Jane Caputi. 1987. *Webster's First New Intergalactic Wickedary of the English Language.* Boston: Beacon Press.

Davis, Angela. 1974. *Angela Davis: An Autobiography.* New York: Random House.

———. 1971. *If They Come in the Morning: Voices of Resistance.* New Rochelle, NY: Okapaku Communications Corporation.

———. 1971. "Reflections on the Black Woman's Role in the Community of Slaves." *The Black Scholar* 3, No. 4 (December): 2–16.

———. 1989. *Women, Culture, and Politics.* New York: Random House.

———. 1981. *Women, Race, and Class.* New York: Random House.

Davis, Elizabeth Gould. 1971. *The First Sex.* New York: Putnam.

Davis, Flora. 1991. *Moving the Mountain: The Women's Movement in America Since 1960.* New York: Simon & Schuster.

DeCrow, Karen. 1975. *Sexist Justice.* New York: Vintage.

Decter, Midge. 1972. *The New Chastity and Other Arguments Against Women's Liberation.* New York: Coward, McCann & Geoghegan.

DeLamotte, Eugenia C., Natania Meeker, and Jean F. O'Barr, eds. 1997. *Women Imagine Change: A Global Anthology of Women's Resistance from 600 BCE to Present.* New York: Routledge.

Delaney, Janice, Mary Jane Lupton, and Emily Toth. 1988. *The Curse: A Cultural History of Menstruation* (Rev. ed.). Champaign: University of Illinois Press.

Diamond, Irene, and Gloria F. Orenstein, eds. 1990. *Reweaving the World: The Emergence of Ecofeminism.* San Francisco: Sierra Club Books.

Digby, Tom, ed. 1997. *Men Do Feminism.* New York: Routledge.

Dines, Gail, and Jean M. Humez, eds. 1995. *Gender, Race, and Class in Media: A Critical Text-Reader.* Thousand Oaks, CA: Sage Publications.

Diquinzio, Patrice. 1999. *The Impossibility of Motherhood: Feminism, Individualism and the Problem of Mothering.* New York: Routledge.

Donovan, Josephine, and Carol J. Adams, eds. 1996. *Beyond Animal Rights: A Feminist Caring Ethic for the Treatment of Animals.* New York: Continuum.

Doress, Paula Brown, Diana Laskin Siegal, and the Midlife and Older Women Book Project. 1987. *Ourselves Growing Older: Women Aging With Knowledge and Power.* New York: Simon & Schuster.

Dow, Bonnie J. 1996. *Prime-Time Feminism: Television, Media Culture, and the Women's Movement Since 1970.* Philadelphia, PA: University of Pennsylvania Press.

Dowling, Colette. 1996. *Red Hot Mamas: Coming Into Our Own at Fifty.* New York: Bantam.

Dubeck, Paula J., and Kathryn Borman, eds. 1996. *Women and Work: A Handbook.* Hamden, CT: Garland.

Dubois, Ellen Carol, and Vicki Ruiz, eds. 2000. *Unequal Sisters: A Multicultural Reader in U.S. Women's History.* New York: Routledge.

DuCille, Ann. 1996. *Skin Trade.* Cambridge, MA: Harvard University Press.

Due, Linnea. 1995. *Joining the Tribe: Growing Up Gay and Lesbian in the '90s.* New York: Anchor Doubleday.

Dujon, Diane, and Ann Withorn, eds. 1996. *For Crying Out Loud: Women's Poverty in the United States.* Boston: South End Press.

DuPlessis, Rachel Blau, and Ann Snitow, eds. 1998. *The Feminist Memoir Project: Voices From Women's Liberation.* New York: Three Rivers Press.

Dusky, Lorraine. 1996. *Still Unequal: The Shameful Truth About Women and Justice in America.* New York: Crown.

Dworkin, Andrea. 1987. *Ice and Fire: A Novel.* New York: Weldenfeld & Nicolson.

———. 1987. *Intercourse.* New York: Free Press.

———. 1997. *Life and Death: Unapologetic Writings on the Continuing War Against Women.* New York: Free Press.

———. 1991. *Mercy.* New York: Four Walls Eight Windows.

———. 1976. *Our Blood: Prophecies and Discourses on Sexual Politics.* New York: Harper & Row.

———. 1987. *Pornography: Men Possessing Women.* New York: Free Press.

———. 1983. *Right-Wing Women.* New York: Putnam.

———. 1974. *Woman-Hating.* New York: E. P. Dutton.

Dynes, Wayne R., ed. 1990. *Encyclopedia of Homosexuality.* New York: Garland.

Easlea, Brian. 1983. *Fathering the Unthinkable: Masculinity, Scientists and the Nuclear Arms Race.* London: Pluto Press.

Edin, Kathryn, and Laura Lein. 1997. *Making Ends Meet: How Single Mothers Survive Welfare and Low-Wage Work.* New York: Russell Sage.

Edut, Ophira. 1998. *Adiós, Barbie: Young Women Write About Body Image and Identity.* Seattle: Seal Press.

Ehrenreich, Barbara, Elizabeth Hess, and Gloria Jacobs. 1987. *Re-Making Love: The Feminization of Sex.* New York: Anchor.

Eisenstein, Hester. 1983. *Contemporary Feminist Thought.* Boston: G. K. Hall.

————. 1991. *Gender Shock: Practicing Feminism on Two Continents.* Boston: Beacon Press.

Eisler, Riane. 1987. *The Chalice and the Blade.* New York: Harper & Row.

————. 1996. *Sacred Pleasure: Sex, Myth, and the Politics of the Body.* San Francisco: HarperSanFrancisco.

————. 2000. *Tomorrow's Children: A Blueprint for Partnership Education in the 21st Century.* Boulder, CO: Westview Press.

Eisler, Riane, and David Loye. 1990. *The Partnership Way: New Tools for Living and Learning, Healing Our Families, Our Communities, and Our World.* San Francisco: HarperSanFrancisco.

Eller, Cynthia. 1993. *Living in the Lap of the Goddess: The Feminist Spirituality Movement in America.* New York: Crossroad.

Ellman, Mary. 1968. *Thinking About Women.* New York: Harcourt Brace Jovanovich.

Elshtain, Jean Bethke. 1992. *Meditations on Modern Political Thought: Masculine/Feminine Themes from Luther to Arendt.* University Park, PA: Penn State Press.

————. 1993. *Public Man, Private Woman: Women in Social and Political Thought,* 2d ed. Princeton, NJ: Princeton University Press.

Elshtain, Jean Bethke, and Sheila Tobias, eds. 1989. *Women, Militarism, and War: Essays in History, Politics, and Social Theory.* Lanham, MD: Rowman & Littlefield.

English, Jane, ed. 1977. *Sex Equality.* Englewood Cliffs, NJ: Prentice-Hall.

Epstein, Cynthia Fuchs. 1988. *Deceptive Distinctions: Sex, Gender, and the Social Order.* New Haven, CT: Yale University Press.

————. 1970. *Woman's Place.* Berkeley: University of California Press.

Erikson, Erik H. 1964. "Inner and Outer Space: Reflexions on Womanhood." *Daedalus* 93:582–606.

Esfandiari, Haley. 1997. *Reconstructed Lives: Women and Iran's Islamic Revolution.* Baltimore, MD: Johns Hopkins University Press.

Espin, Oliva M., and Ellen Cole. 1993. *Refugee Women and Their Mental Health.* New York: Haworth Press.

Espiritu, Yen Le. 1996. *Asian American Women and Men: Labor, Laws, and Love.* Thousand Oaks, CA: Sage Publications.

Estrich, Susan. 1987. *Real Rape: How the Legal System Victimizes Women Who Say No.* Cambridge, MA: Harvard University Press.

Evans, Judith. 1986. *Feminism and Political Theory.* Thousand Oaks, CA: Sage Publications.

————. 1995. *Feminist Theory Today: An Introduction to the Political Theories of Second Wave Feminism.* Thousand Oaks, CA: Sage Publications.

Evans, Mary. 1996. *Simone de Beauvoir.* Thousand Oaks, CA: Sage Publications.

Evans, Sara. 1990. *Born for Liberty: A History of Women in America.* New York: Free Press.

————. 1978. *Personal Politics: The Roots of Women's Liberation in the Civil Rights Movement and the New Left.* New York: Alfred A. Knopf.

Faludi, Susan. 1991. *Backlash: The Undeclared War Against American Women.* New York: Crown.

————. 1999. *Stiffed: The Betrayal of the American Man.* New York: William Morrow.

Farganis, Sondra. 1996. *The Social Reconstruction of the Feminine Character,* 2d ed. Lanham, MD: Rowman & Littlefield.

Fasteau, Marc Feigen. 1974. *The Male Machine.* New York: McGraw-Hill.

Felder, Raoul, and Barbara Victor. 1996. *Getting Away with Murder: Weapons for the War Against Domestic Violence.* New York: Simon & Schuster.

Ferrato, Donna. 1991. *Living With the Enemy* (Introduction by Ann Jones). New York: Aperture.

Festle, Mary Jo. 1996. *Playing Nice: Politics and Apologies in Women's Sports.* New York: Columbia University Press.

Fiorenza, Elisabeth Schussler, and M. Shawn Copeland, eds. 1996. *Feminist Theology in Different Contexts.* Maryknoll, NY: Orbis Books.

————. 1994. *Violence Against Women.* Maryknoll, NY: Orbis Books.

Figert, Anne E. 1996. *Women and the Ownership of PMS: The Structuring of a Psychiatric Disorder.* Hawthorne, NY: Aldine de Gruyter.

Figes, Eva. 1971. *Patriarchal Attitudes.* Greenwich, CT: Fawcett.

Firestone, Shulamith. 1971. *The Dialectic of Sex.* New York: Bantam.

Flexner, Eleanor and Ellen Fitzpatrick. 1996. *A Century of Struggle: The Woman's Rights Movement in the United States* (Enlarged ed.). Cambridge, MA: Harvard University Press.

Forbes, Geraldine. 1996. *The New Cambridge History of India: Women in Modern India.* Cambridge, UK: Cambridge University Press.

Forster, Margaret. 1986. *Significant Sisters: The Grassroots of Active Feminism, 1839–1939.* New York: Oxford University Press.

Francis, Leslie, ed. 1996. *Date Rape: Feminism, Philosophy, and the Law.* University Park, PA: Penn State Press.

Francis, Leslie Pickering. 1997. *Sexual Harassment In Academe: The Ethical Issues.* Lanham, MD: Rowman & Littlefield.

Franck, Irene M., and David M. Brownstone. 1995. *Women's World: A Timeline of Women in History.* New York: HarperCollins.

Frankfort, Ellen. 1972. *Vaginal Politics.* New York: Quadrangle.

Frazer, Elizabeth, Jennifer Hornsby, and Sabina Lovibond, eds. 1992. *Ethics: A Feminist Reader.* Cambridge, MA: Blackwell.

French, Marilyn. 1986. *Beyond Power: On Women, Men, and Morals.* New York: Ballantine.

———. 1985. *Bleeding Heart.* New York: Ballantine.

———. 1988. *Her Mother's Daughter.* New York: Ballantine.

———. 1996. *My Summer With George.* New York: Alfred A. Knopf.

———. 1992. *The War Against Women.* New York: Ballantine.

———. 1977. *The Women's Room.* New York: Jove Publications.

Freyd, Jennifer J. 1996. *Betrayal Trauma: The Logic of Forgetting Childhood Abuse.* Cambridge, MA: Harvard University Press.

Friday, Nancy. 1996. *The Power of Beauty.* New York: HarperCollins.

Fried, Heidi. 1996. *The Road to Auschwitz: Fragments of a Life.* Lincoln: University of Nebraska Press.

Fried, Marlene Gerber, ed. 1990. *From Abortion to Reproductive Freedom: Transforming a Movement.* Boston: South End Press.

Friedan, Betty. 1963. *The Feminine Mystique.* New York: Dell. (20th ann. ed. published by W. W. Norton, 1983.)

———. 1993. *The Fountain of Age.* New York: Simon & Schuster.

———. 1976. *It Changed My Life: Writings on the Women's Movement.* New York: Random House.

———. 1986. *The Second Stage* (Rev. ed.). New York: Summit.

Friedman, Sara Ann. 1996. *Work Matters: Women Talk About Their Jobs and Their Lives.* New York: Viking.

Frye, Marilyn. 1983. *The Politics of Reality: Essays in Feminist Theory.* Freedom, CA: Crossing Press.

———. 1992. *Willful Virgin: Essays in Feminism.* Freedom, CA: Crossing Press.

Fujimura-Fanselow, and Atsuko Kameda, eds. 1995. *Japanese Women: New Feminist Perspectives on the Past, Present, and Future.* New York: The Feminist Press at the City University of New York.

Garcia, Alma M., ed. 1997. *Chicana Feminist Thought: The Basic Historical Writings.* New York: Routledge.

Gates, Henry Louis, ed. 1990. *Reading Black, Reading Feminist: A Critical Anthology.* New York: Meridian/Penguin Books.

Gamble, Sarah. 2000. *Routledge Critical Dictionary of Feminism and Postfeminism.* New York: Routledge.

Gerami, Shahin. 1996. *Women and Fundamentalism: Islam and Christianity.* New York: Garland.

Gifford, Carolyn De Swarte, and Donald Dayton, eds. 1988. *The American Ideal of the "True Woman" as Reflected in Advice Books to Young Women.* New York: Garland.

Gilligan, Carol. 1982. *In a Different Voice.* Cambridge, MA: Harvard University Press.

———. 1988. *Mapping the Moral Domain: A Contribution of Women's Thinking to Psychological Theory and Education.* Cambridge, MA: Harvard University Press.

Gilman, Charlotte Perkins. 1973. *The Yellow Wallpaper.* Old Westbury, NY: Feminist Press. (Originally published in 1892.)

———. 1979. *Herland: A Lost Feminist Utopian Novel.* New York: Random House.

Goldberg, Herb. 1976. *The Hazards of Being Male.* New York: Penguin.

Goldberg, Steven. 1974. *The Inevitability of Patriarchy.* New York: Morrow.

Goldenberg, Naomi. 1979. *Changing of the Gods: Feminism and the End of Traditional Religions.* Boston: Beacon Press.

———. 1990. *Returning Words to Flesh: Feminism, Psychoanalysis, and the Resurrection of the Body.* Boston: Beacon Press.

Goldin, Claudia. 1990. *Understanding the Gender Gap: An Economic History of American Women.* New York: Oxford University Press.

Gordon, Linda. 1992. *Good Boys and Dead Girls (and Other Essays).* New York: Penguin.

———. 1988. *Heroes of Their Own Lives: The Politics and History of Family Violence.* New York: Viking.

———. 1976. *Woman's Body, Woman's Right: A Social History of Birth Control.* New York: Viking.

Gordon, Linda, ed. 1991. *Women, the State, and Welfare.* Madison: University of Wisconsin Press.

Gorna, Robin. 1996. *Vamps, Virgins and Victims: How Can Women Fight AIDS?* New York: Cassell.

Gottlieb, Lynn. 1995. *She Who Dwells Within: A Feminist Vision of a Renewed Judaism.* San Francisco: HarperSanFrancisco.

Grauerholz, Elizabeth, and Mary Koralweski, eds. 1991. *Sexual Coercion: A Sourcebook on Its Nature, Causes, and Prevention.* New York: Lexington Books.

Greer, Germaine. 1992. *The Change: Women, Aging, and Menopause.* New York: Alfred A. Knopf.

———. 1990. *Daddy We Hardly Knew You.* New York: Alfred A. Knopf.

———. 1971. *The Female Eunuch.* New York: McGraw-Hill.

———. 1986. *The Madwoman's Underclothes: Essays and Occasional Writings.* New York: Atlantic Monthly Press.

———. 1979. *The Obstacle Race: The Fortunes of Women Painters and Their Work.* New York: Farrar, Straus & Giroux.

———. 1984. *Sex and Destiny: The Politics of Human Fertility.* New York: Harper & Row.

Griffin, Susan. 1992. *A Chorus of Stones: The Private Life of War.* New York: Doubleday.

———. 1996. *The Eros of Everyday Life.* New York: Anchor Doubleday.

———. 1981. *Pornography and Silence: Culture's Revenge Against Nature.* New York: Harper & Row.

———. 1979. *Rape: The Power of Consciousness.* San Francisco: Harper & Row.

———. 1987. *Unremembered Country.* Port Townsend, WA: Copper Canyon.

———. 1999. *What Her Body Thought: A Journey Into the Shadows.* San Francisco: HarperSanFrancisco.

———. 1978. *Woman and Nature: The Roaring Inside Her.* New York: Harper & Row.

Grimké, Sarah. 1988. *Letters on the Equality of the Sexes and Other Essays.* Ed. Elizabeth Ann Bartlett. New Haven, CT: Yale University Press.

Gross, Rita M. 1996. *Feminism and Religion: An Introduction.* Boston: Beacon Press.

Gubar, Susan, and Joan Hoff, eds. 1989. *For Adult Users Only: The Dilemma of Violent Pornography.* Bloomington: Indiana University Press.

Guinier, Lani. 1995. *The Tyranny of the Majority: Fundamental Fairness in Representative Democracy.* New York: The Free Press.

Guinier, Lani, Michelle Fine, and Jane Balin, eds. 1997. *Becoming Gentlemen: Women, Law School, and Institutional Change.* Boston: Beacon Press.

Gurko, Miriam. 1976. *The Ladies of Seneca Falls: The Birth of the Women's Movement.* New York: Schocken.

Guy-Sheftall, Beverly. 1995. *Words of Fire: An Anthology of African-American Feminist Thought.* New York: The New Press.

Hackstaff, Karla B. 2000. *Marriage in a Culture of Divorce.* Philadelphia, PA: Temple University Press.

Haddad, Tony, ed. 1993. *Men and Masculinities: A Critical Anthology.* Toronto: Canadian Scholars' Press.

Hadley, Janet. 1996. *Abortion: Between Freedom and Necessity.* Philadelphia, PA: Temple University Press.

Hagan, Kay Leigh, ed. 1992. *Women Respond to the Men's Movement.* San Francisco: HarperSanFrancisco.

Harding, Sandra. 1991. *Whose Science? Whose Knowledge?: Thinking from Women's Lives.* Ithaca, NY: Cornell University Press.

Harjo, Joy, and Gloria Bird, eds. 1997. *Reinventing the Enemy's Language: Contemporary Native Women's Writings of North America.* New York: W. W. Norton.

Harris, Sharon M., ed. 1996. *American Women Writers to 1800.* New York: Oxford University Press.

Hartsock, Nancy C. M. 1997. *The Feminist Standpoint Revisited and Other Essays.* Boulder, CO: Westview Press.

Haskell, Molly. 1997. *Holding My Own in No Man's Land: Women and Men and Film and Feminism.* New York: Oxford University Press.

Hays, H. R. 1964. *The Dangerous Sex.* New York: Putnam.

Hays, Sharon. 1996. *The Cultural Contradictions of Motherhood.* New Haven, CT: Yale University Press.

Hearn, Jeff, ed. 1991. *Critical Studies on Men.* London: Routledge.

Heilbrun, Carolyn G. 1995. *The Education of a Woman: The Life of Gloria Steinem.* New York: The Dial Press.

———. 1997. *The Last Gift of Time: Life Beyond Sixty.* New York: The Dial Press.

Held, Virginia, ed. 1995. *Justice and Care: Essential Readings in Feminist Ethics.* New York: Westview Press.

Hemmons, Willa Mae. 1996. *Black Women in the New World Order: Social Justice and the African American Female.* Westport, CT: Praeger Publishers.

The Hen Co-op. 1993. *Growing Old Disgracefully: New Ideas for Getting the Most Out of Life.* Freedom, CA: Crossing Press.

Henley, Nancy, Mykol Hamilton, and Barrie Thorne. 1984. *Womanspeak and Manspeak: Sex Differences and Sexism in Communication, Verbal and Nonverbal.* St. Paul, MN: West.

Hennessy, Rosemary, and Chrys Ingraham, eds. 1997. *Materialist Feminism: A Reader in Class, Difference, and Women's Lives.* New York: Routledge.

Herdt, Gilbert, ed. 1993. *Gay Culture in America: Essays from the Field.* Boston: Beacon Press.

Hesse-Biber, Sharlene. 1996. *Am I Thin Enough Yet? The Cult of Thinness and the Commercialization of Identity.* New York: Oxford University Press.

Heyzer, Noeleen, and Vivienne Wee. 1996. *Gender, Poverty, and Sustainable Development: Towards a Holistic Framework.* New York: Weatherhill.

Heyn, Dalma. 1997. *Marriage Shock: The Transformation of Women into Wives.* New York: Villard Books.

Hill, Anita Faye, and Emma Coleman Jordan, eds. 1995. *Race, Gender, and Power in America: The Legacy of the Hill-Thomas Hearings.* New York: Oxford University Press.

Hill, George H., Lorraine Raglin, and Chas Floyd Johnson. 1990. *Black Women in Television: An Illustrated History and Bibliography.* New York: Garland.

Hirsch, Marianne, and Evelyn Fox Keller, eds. 1990. *Conflicts in Feminism.* New York: Routledge.

Hirshfield, Jane, ed. 1995. *Women in Praise of the Sacred: 43 Centuries of Spiritual Poetry by Women.* New York: HarperPerennial.

Hirschmann, Nancy J., and Christine Di Stenano, eds. 1996. *Revisioning the Political: Feminist Reconstructions of Traditional Concepts in Western Political Theory.* Boulder, CO: Westview Press.

Hite, Shere. 1987. *The Hite Report: A Study of Male Sexuality.* New York: Ballantine.

———. 1994. *The Hite Report on the Family: Growing Up Under Patriarchy.* New York: Grove Press.

———. 1974. *Sexual Honesty: By Women for Women.* New York: Warner.

———. 1987. *Women and Love: A Cultural Revolution in Progress.* New York: Alfred A. Knopf.

Hoagland, Sarah Lucia. 1988. *Lesbian Ethics: Toward New Values.* Palo Alto, CA: Institute of Lesbian Studies.

Hochschild, Arlie. 1989. *The Second Shift.* New York: Viking.

Hoff, Joan. 1991. *Law, Gender, and Injustice: A Legal History of U.S. Women.* New York: New York University Press.

Hole, Judith and Ellen Levine. 1971. *Rebirth of Feminism.* New York: Quadrangle.

Hood, Jane, ed. 1993. *Men, Work, and Family* (Research on Men and Masculinities Series, Vol. 4). Thousand Oaks, CA: Sage Publications.

hooks, bell. 1981. *Ain't I a Woman: Black Women and Feminism.* Boston: South End Press.

———. 1995. *Art on My Mind: Visual Politics.* New York: New Press.

———. 1992. *Black Looks: Race and Representation.* Boston: South End Press.

———. 1996. *Bone Black: Memories of Girlhood.* New York: Henry Holt & Company.

———. 1992. *Breaking Bread: Insurgent Black Intellectual Life.* Boston: South End Press.

———. 1984. *Feminist Theory: From Margin to Center.* Boston: South End Press.

———. 1995. *Killing Rage: Ending Racism.* New York: Henry Holt & Company.

———. 1996. *Reel to Real: Race, Sex & Class at the Movies.* New York: Routledge.

———. 1993. *Sisters of the Yam: Black Women and Self Recovery.* Boston: South End Press.

———. 1989. *Talking Back: Thinking Feminist, Thinking Black.* Boston: South End Press.

———. 1994. *Teaching to Transgress: Education as the Practice of Freedom.* New York: Routledge.

———. 1992. *A Woman's Mourning Song.* New York: Writers and Readers.

———. 1990. *Yearning: Race, Gender, and Cultural Politics.* Boston: South End Press.

Horner, Matina. 1969. "A Bright Young Woman Is Caught in a Double Bind," *Psychology Today* 3, No. 6 (November).

Hoshiko, Sumi. 1993. *Our Choices: Women's Personal Decisions about Abortion.* Binghamton, NY: Harrington Park Press.

Howe, Florence, and Marsha Saxton. 1987. *With Wings: An Anthology of Literature By and About Women with Disabilities.* New York: Feminist Press at City University of New York.

Hoy, Suellen. 1995. *Chasing Dirt: The American Pursuit of Cleanliness.* New York: Oxford University Press.

Hubbard, Ruth. 1990. *The Politics of Women's Biology.* New Brunswick, NJ: Rutgers University Press.

Hubbard, Ruth, and Mary S. Henefin, eds. 1979. *Women Look at Biology Looking at Women: A Collection of Feminist Critiques.* Boston: G.K. Hall.

Hubbard, Ruth, and Brenda Miller Power, eds. 1991. *Literacy in Process.* Portsmouth, NH: Heinemann.

Hubbard, Ruth, et al. 1982. *Biological Woman: The Convenient Myth.* Cambridge, MA: Schenkman.

Hughes, Jean O., and Bernice R. Sandler. 1987. *"Friends" Raping Friends: It Could Happen to You.* Washington, DC: Association of American Colleges, Project on the Status and Education of Women.

Hughes, Sarah Shaver, and Brady Hughes. 1995. *Women in World History.* Vol. 1: *Readings from Prehistory to 1500.* Vol. 2: *1500 to the Present* (1996). Armonk, NY: M.E. Sharpe.

Hull, Gloria T., et al. 1982. *All the Women Are White, All the Blacks Are Men, But Some of Us Are Brave: Black Women's Studies.* Old Westbury, NY: Feminist Press.

Human Rights Watch. 1995. *The Human Rights Watch Global Report on Women's Human Rights.* New York: Human Rights Watch.

Humm, Maggie. 1995. *The Dictionary of Feminist Theory*, 2d ed. Columbus: Ohio State University Press.

Humm, Maggie, ed. 1992. *Modern Feminisms: Political, Literary, Cultural.* New York: Columbia University Press.

Hunter College Women's Studies Collective. 1995. *Women's Realities, Women's Choices: An Introduction to Women's Studies*, 2d ed. New York: Oxford University Press.

Hurston, Zora Neale. 1991. *Dust Tracks on the Road: An Autobiography.* New York: HarperCollins.

———. 1986. *The Gilded Six-Bits.* Minneapolis, MN: Redpath Press.

———. 1979. *I Love Myself When I Am Laughing . . . and Again When I Am Looking Mean and Impressive: A Zora Neale Hurston Reader.* Ed. Alice Walker. Old Westbury, NY: Feminist Press.

———. 1985. *Spunk: The Selected Stories of Zora Neale Hurston.* San Francisco: Turtle Island Foundation.

———. 1978. *Their Eyes Were Watching God.* Champaign: University of Illinois Press.

Ireland, Patricia. 1996. *What Women Want.* New York: Dutton.

Ishtar, Zohl de. 1995. *Daughters of the Pacific.* Australia: Spinifex.

Jack, Dana Crowley. 1993. *Silencing the Self: Depression and Women.* New York: HarperPerennial.

Jackson, Stevi, and Sue Scott, eds. 1996. *Feminism and Sexuality: A Reader.* New York: Columbia University Press.

Jacobus, Mary, Evelyn Fox Keller, and Sally Shuttleworth, eds. 1990. *Body/Politics: Women and the Discourses of Science.* New York: Routledge.

Jaggar, Alison M. 1983. *Feminist Politics and Human Nature.* Lanham, MD: Rowman & Littlefield.

———. 1989. *Gender/Body/Knowledge: Feminist Reconstructions of Being and Knowing.* New Brunswick, NJ: Rutgers University Press.

Jaggar, Alison M., ed. 1994. *Living With Contradictions: Controversies in Feminist Social Ethics.* New York: Westview Press.

Jaggar, Alison M., and Paula S. Rothenberg, eds. 1993. *Feminist Frameworks: Alternative Theoretical Accounts of the Relations Between Women and Men*, 3d ed. New York: McGraw-Hill.

———. 1983. *Feminist Politics and Human Nature.* Lanham, MD: Rowman & Littlefield.

Jahan, Rounaq. 1995. *The Elusive Agenda: Mainstreaming Women in Development.* United Kingdom: Zed Books. (Distributed by Humanities International Press, Atlantic Highlands, NJ.)

Janeway, Elizabeth. 1982. *Cross Sections from a Decade of Change.* New York: Morrow.

———. 1987. *Improper Behavior.* New York: Morrow.

———. 1971. *Man's World, Woman's Place: A Study in Social Mythology.* New York: Delta Books.

———. 1980. *Powers of the Weak.* New York: Alfred A. Knopf.

Jaquith, Cindy. 1988. *Surrogate Motherhood, Women's Rights and the Working Class.* New York: Pathfinder Press.

Jardine, Alice, and Paul Smith, eds. 1987. *Men in Feminism.* New York: Methuen.

Jayawardena, Kumari. 1986. *Feminism and Nationalism in the Third World.* New Delhi: Kali for Women. Distributed by Biblio Distribution Center, Totowa, NJ.

Jesser, Clinton J. 1996. *Fierce and Tender Men: Sociological Aspects of the Men's Movement.* Westport, CT: Praeger Publishers.

Joffe, Carole. 1995. *Doctors of Conscience: The Struggle to Provide Abortion Before and After* Roe v. Wade. Boston: Beacon Press.

Johnson, Allan G. 1997. *The Gender Knot: Unraveling Our Patriarchal Legacy.* Philadelphia, PA: Temple University Press.

Johnson, Sonia. 1989. *From Housewife to Heretic*. Albuquerque, NM: Wildfire Books.

———. 1987. *Going Out of Our Minds: The Metaphysics of Liberation*. Freedom, CA: Crossing Press.

———. 1991. *The Ship That Sailed into the Livingroom: Sex and Intimacy Reconsidered*. Albuquerque, NM: Wildfire Books.

Johnston, Jill. 1973. *Lesbian Nation*. New York: Simon & Schuster.

Jonas, Susan, and Marilyn Nissenson. 1997. *Friends for Life: Enriching the Bond Between Mothers and Their Adult Daughters*. New York: William Morrow.

Jones, Ann. 1994. *Next Time She'll Be Dead: Battering and How to Stop It*. Boston: Beacon Press.

———. 1996. *Women Who Kill: With Previously Unpublished Material About the "Battered Women's Syndrome."* Boston: Beacon Press..

Jong, Erica. 1989. *Any Woman's Blues*. New York: Harper & Row.

———. 1979. *At the Edge of the Body*. New York: Holt, Rinehart and Winston.

———. 1992. *Becoming Light: Poems New and Selected*. New York: HarperCollins.

———. 1980. *Fanny: Being the True History of the Adventures of Fanny Hackabout-Jones*. New York: New American Library.

———. 1994. *Fear of Fifty: A Midlife Memoir*. New York: HarperCollins.

———. 1973. *Fear of Flying*. New York: Holt, Rinehart and Winston.

———. 1977. *How to Save Your Own Life*. New York: Holt, Rinehart and Winston.

———. 1976. *Loveroot*. New York: Holt, Rinehart and Winston.

———. 1983. *Ordinary Miracles: New Poems*. New York: New American Library.

———. 1984. *Parachutes and Kisses*. New York: New American Library.

———. 1987. *Serenissima: A Novel of Venice*. Boston: Houghton Mifflin.

———. 1981. *Witches*. New York: H. A. Abrams.

Jordan, June. 1998. *Affirmative Acts: Political Essays*. New York: Anchor Books.

Kahn, Karen, ed. 1995. *Front Line Feminism, 1975–1995: Essays from* Sojourner's *First 20 Years*. San Francisco: Aunt Lute Books.

Kaminer, Wendy. 1990. *A Fearful Freedom: Women's Flight from Equality*. New York: Addison-Wesley.

———. 1996. *True Love Waits: Essays and Criticism*. Reading, MA: Addison-Wesley.

Kandall, Stephen R. 1996. *Substance and Shadow: Women and Addiction in the United States*. Cambridge, MA: Harvard University Press.

Kaplan, Laura. 1995. *The Story of Jane: The Legendary Underground Feminist Abortion Service*. New York: Pantheon.

Kass-Simon, G., and Patricia Farnes, eds. 1990. *Women of Science: Righting the Record*. Bloomington: Indiana University Press.

Kaufman, Michael. 1993. *Cracking the Armour: Power, Pain and the Lives of Men*. Toronto: Penguin.

Kaufman, Michael, ed. 1987. *Beyond Patriarchy*. Toronto: Oxford University Press.

Kawar, Amal. 1996. *Leading Women of the Palestinian National Movement*. Albany, NY: State University of New York Press.

Keen, Sam. 1991. *Fire in the Belly*. New York: Bantam.

Keith, Lois, ed. 1996. *"What Happened to You?" Writing by Disabled Women*. New York: The New Press.

Keller, Evelyn Fox, and Helen E. Longino, eds. 1996. *Feminism and Science* (Oxford Readings in Feminism). New York: Oxford University Press.

Kerber, Linda K., and Jane Sherron De Hart, eds. 1995. *Women's America: Refocusing the Past*. New York: Oxford University Press.

Kessler-Harris, Alice. 1982. *Out to Work: A History of Wage-Earning Women in the United States*. New York: Oxford University Press.

———. 1990. *A Woman's Wage: Historical Meanings and Social Consequences*. Lexington: University Press of Kentucky.

Kim, Elaine H., and Lilia V. Villanueva, eds. 1997. *Making More Waves: New Writing by Asian-American Women*. Boston: Beacon Press.

Kimmel, Michael. 1995. *Manhood in America: A Cultural History*. New York: Free Press.

Kimmel, Michael S., ed. 1987. *Changing Men: New Directions in Research on Men and Masculinity* (Sage Focus Editions, Vol. 88). Thousand Oaks, CA: Sage Publications.

———. 1991. *Men Confront Pornography*. New York: New American Library.

———. 1995. *The Politics of Manhood: Profeminist Men Respond to the Mythopoetic Men's Movement (and the*

Mythopoetic Leaders Answer). Philadelphia, PA: Temple University Press.

Kimmel, Michael S., and Michael Messner, eds. 1992. *Men's Lives*, 2d ed. New York: Macmillan.

Kimmel, Michael S., and Thomas E. Mosmiller. 1993. *Against the Tide: Pro-Feminist Men in the United States 1776–1990.* Boston: Beacon Press.

Kingfisher, Catherine Pelissier. 1996. *Women in the American Welfare Trap.* Philadelphia: University of Pennsylvania Press.

Kirkham, Pat, and Janet Thumim, eds. 1995. *Me Jane: Masculinity, Movies and Women.* New York: St. Martin's Press.

———. 1993. *You Tarzan: Masculinity, Movies and Men.* New York: St. Martin's Press.

Klein, Renate D., and Deborah Lynn Steinberg, eds. 1989. *Radical Voices: A Decade of Feminist Resistance from Women's International Forum.* New York: Pergamon.

Knapp, Bettina L. 1998. *Women, Myth and the Feminine Principle.* Albany, NY: State University of New York Press.

Koedt, Anne, Ellen Levine, and Anita Rapone. 1973. *Radical Feminism.* New York: Quadrangle.

Kolbenschlag, Madonna. 1996. *Eastward Toward Eve: A Geography of the Soul.* New York: Crossroad.

Korda, Michael. 1972. *Male Chauvinism! How It Works.* New York: Random House.

Kozol, Jonathan. 1988. *Rachel and Her Children: Homeless Families in America.* New York: Fawcett Columbine.

Kraditor, Aileen S. 1965. *The Ideas of the Woman Suffrage Movement, 1890–1920.* New York: Columbia University Press.

Kraditor, Aileen S., ed. 1968. *Up From the Pedestal.* Chicago: Quadrangle.

Kramarae, Cheris. 1984. *Language and Power.* Thousand Oaks, CA: Sage Publications.

———. 1983. *Language, Gender, and Society.* Rowley, MA: Newbury House.

Kramarae, Cheris, ed. 1988. *Technology and Women's Voices.* New York: Routledge & Kegan Paul.

Kramarae, Cheris, and Dale Spender, eds. 1992. *The Knowledge Explosion: Generations of Feminist Scholarship* (Athene Series). New York: Teachers College Press.

Kramarae, Cheris, and Paula Treichler, eds. 1985. *A Feminist Dictionary.* Boston: Pandora Press.

Kuhn, Annette. 1988. *Cinema, Censorship and Sexuality, 1909–1925.* New York: Routledge, Chapman and Hall.

Kurz, Demie. 1995. *For Richer, For Poorer: Mothers Confront Divorce.* New York: Routledge.

Kushner, Eve. 1997. *Experience Abortion: A Weaving of Women's Words.* New York: Harrington Park Press.

Langer, Cassandra L. 1996. *A Feminist Critique: How Feminism Has Changed American Society, Culture, and How We Live from the 1940s to the Present.* New York: HarperCollins.

Larson, Rebecca. 1999. *Daughters of Light: Quaker Women Preaching and Prophesying in the Colonies and Abroad, 1700–1775.* New York: Alfred A. Knopf.

Lawless, Elaine J. 1988. *Handmaidens of the Lord: Pentecostal Women Preachers and Traditional Religion.* Philadelphia: University of Pennsylvania Press.

Lederer, Wolfgang. 1968. *The Fear of Women.* New York: Grune & Stratton.

Lelwica, Michelle Mary. 1999. *Starving for Salvation: The Spiritual Dimensions of Eating Problems Among American Girls and Women.* New York: Oxford University Press.

LeMoncheck, Linda, and Mane Hajdin. 1997. *Sexual Harassment: A Debate.* Lanham, MD: Rowman & Littlefield.

Lerner, Gerda. 1993. *The Creation of Feminist Consciousness: From the Middle Ages to Eighteen-Seventy (Women and History*, Vol. 2). New York: Oxford University Press.

———. 1986. *The Creation of Patriarchy. (Women and History*, Vol. 1.) New York: Oxford University Press.

———. 1992. *The Female Experience: An American Documentary* (Updated ed. with new preface). New York: Oxford University Press. (Original Bobbs, Merrill edition, 1977).

———. 1998. *The Feminist Thought of Sarah Grimké.* New York: Oxford University Press.

———. 1998. *The Grimké Sisters From South Carolina: Pioneers for Women's Rights and Abolition.* New York: Oxford University Press.

———. 1979. *The Majority Finds Its Past: Placing Women in History.* New York: Oxford University Press.

———. 1997. *Why History Matters.* New York: Oxford University Press.

Lerner, Gerda, ed. 1973. *Black Women in White America: A Documentary History.* New York: Vintage.

Lessing, Doris. 1976. *The Golden Notebook.* New York: Simon & Schuster.

LeVay, Simon. 1996. *Queer Science: The Use and Abuse of Research into Homosexuality.* Cambridge, MA: MIT Press.

Lopata, Helena Znaniecka. 1995. *Current Widowhood: Myths & Realities.* Thousand Oaks, CA: Sage Publications.

Lorber, Judith. 1994. *Paradoxes of Gender.* New Haven, CT: Yale University Press.

Lowe, Marian, and Ruth Hubbard, eds. 1983. *Woman's Nature: Rationalizations of Inequality.* New York: Pergamon.

Ludtke, Melissa. 1997. *On Our Own: Unmarried Motherhood in America.* Berkeley, CA: University of California Press.

Luebke, Barbara F., and Mary Ellen Reilly. 1995. *Women's Studies Graduates: The First Generation.* New York: Teachers College Press, Athene Series.

Luker, Kristin. 1996. *Dubious Conceptions: The Politics of Teenage Pregnancy.* Cambridge, MA: Harvard University Press.

Lunneborg, Patricia. 1992. *Abortion: A Positive Decision.* Westport, CT: Greenwood.

Maccoby, Eleanor E., ed. 1966. *The Development of Sex Differences.* Stanford, CA: Stanford University Press.

Maccoby, Eleanor E., and C. N. Jacklin. 1974. *The Psychology of Sex Differences.* Stanford, CA: Stanford University Press.

Maccoby, Eleanor E., and Robert H. Mnookin. 1992. *Dividing the Child: Social and Legal Dilemmas of Custody.* Cambridge, MA: Harvard University Press.

Macdonald, Myra. 1995. *Representing Women: Myths of Femininity in the Popular Media.* New York: St. Martin's Press.

MacKinnon, Catharine A. 1987. *Feminism Unmodified: Discourses on Life and Law.* Cambridge, MA: Harvard University Press.

———. 1993. *Only Words.* Cambridge, MA: Harvard University Press.

———. 1987. *Sexual Harassment of Working Women: A Case of Sexual Discrimination.* New Haven, CT: Yale University Press.

———. 1989. *Toward a Feminist Theory of the State.* Cambridge, MA: Harvard University Press.

Maggio, Rosalie. 1996. *The New Beacon Book of Quotations by Women.* Boston: Beacon Press.

Mairs, Nancy. 1996. *Waist-High in the World: A Life Among the Nondisabled.* Boston: Beacon Press.

Mak, Grace C. L., ed. 1996. *Women, Education, and Development in Asia: Cross-national Perspectives.* Hamden, CT: Garland.

Manning, Beverly. 1988. *We Shall Be Heard: An Index to Speeches by American Women, 1978–1985.* Metuchen, NJ: Scarecrow Press.

Martin, Jane Roland. 2000. *Coming of Age in Academe: Rekindling Women's Hopes and Reforming the Academy.* New York: Routledge.

Marshall, Paule. 1981. *Brown Girl, Brownstones.* New York: Feminist Press. (First published in 1959.)

———. 1969. *The Chosen Place, The Timeless People.* New York: Harcourt, Brace and World.

———. 1991. *Daughters.* New York: Atheneum.

———. 1983. *Praisesong for the Widow.* New York: Putnam.

———. 1984. *Reena & Other Stories.* New York: Feminist Press.

Martin, Wendy. 1972. *The American Sisterhood.* New York: Harper & Row.

Martin, Wendy, ed. 1996. *The Beacon Book of Essays by Contemporary American Women.* Boston: Beacon Press.

Mathews, Donald G., and Jane Sherron De Hart. 1990. *Sex, Gender, and the Politics of ERA: A State and the Nation.* New York: Oxford University Press.

Matthews, Glenna. 1987. *"Just a Housewife": The Rise and Fall of Domesticity in America.* New York: Oxford University Press.

Matthews, Jean V. 1997. *Women's Struggle for Equality: The First Phase, 1828–1876.* Chicago: Ivan R. Dee, Inc.

May, Larry, and Robert A. Strikwerda, eds. 1996. *Rethinking Masculinity: Philosophical Explorations in Light of Feminism,* 2d ed. Lanham, MD: Rowman & Littlefield.

Mayerson, Connie. 1996. *Goin' to the Chapel: Dreams of Love, Realities of Marriage.* New York: HarperCollins.

Mazel, Ella, ed. 1996. *Ahead of Her Time: A Sampler of the Life and Thought of Mary Wollstonecraft.* New York: Brunner/Mazel.

McAlister, Linda Lopez, ed. 1996. *Hypatia's Daughters: 1500 Years of Women Philosophers.* Bloomington: Indiana University Press.

McLennan, Karen Jacobsen, ed. 1996. *Nature's Ban: Women's Incest Literature.* Boston: Northeastern University Press.

Mead, Margaret. 1928. *Coming of Age in Samoa.* New York: Morrow.

———. 1949. *Male and Female.* New York: Dell.

———. 1935. *Sex and Temperament in Three Primitive Societies.* New York: Morrow.

Medea, Andrea, and Kathleen Thompson. 1974. *Against Rape: A Survival Manual for Women.* New York: Farrar, Straus, and Giroux.

Melich, Tanya. 1996. *The Republican War Against Women.* New York: Bantam.

Mernissi, Fatima. 1975. *Beyond the Veil: Male-Female Dynamics in Modern Muslim Society.* Bloomington: Indiana University Press.

———. 1995. *Dreams of Trespass: Tales of a Harem Girlhood.* Reading, MA: Addison-Wesley.

———. 1991. *The Veil and the Male Elite: A Feminist Interpretation of Women's Rights in Islam.* Trans. Mary Jo Lakeland. Reading, MA: Addison-Wesley.

Messer, Ellen, and Kathryn E. May. 1988. *Back Rooms: Voices from the Illegal Abortion Era.* New York: St. Martin's Press.

Meyer, Leisa D. 1996. *Creating GI Jane: Sexuality and Power in the Women's Army Corps During World War II.* New York: Columbia University Press.

Mezey, Susan Gluck. 1996. *Children in Court: Public Policymaking and the Federal Courts.* New York: State University of New York Press.

———. 1992. *In Pursuit of Equality: Women, Public Policy, and the Federal Courts.* New York: St. Martin's Press.

———. 1988. *No Longer Disabled: The Federal Courts and the Politics of Social Security Disability.* Westport, CT: Greenwood Press.

———. 2000. *Pitiful Plaintiffs: Child Welfare Litigation and the Federal Courts.* Pittsburgh, PA: University of Pittsburgh Press.

Miller, Patricia G. 1993. *The Worst of Times: Illegal Abortions— Survivors, Practitioners, Coroners, Cops, and Children of the Women Who Died Talk About Its Horrors.* New York: HarperCollins.

Millett, Kate. 1979. *The Basement: Meditations on a Human Sacrifice.* New York: Simon & Schuster.

———. 1990. *Flying.* New York: Simon & Schuster Trade.

———. 1990. *The Loony Bin Trip.* New York: Simon & Schuster Trade.

———. 1995. *The Politics of Cruelty: An Essay on the Literature of Political Imprisonment.* New York: W.W. Norton.

———. 1970. *Sexual Politics.* New York: Doubleday.

———. 1992. *Sita.* New York: Simon & Schuster Trade.

Minh-ha, Trinh T. 1989. *Woman, Native, Other: Writing Postcoloniality and Feminism.* Bloomington: Indiana University Press.

Mink, Gwendolyn, ed. 1999. *Whose Welfare?* New York: Cornell University Press.

Minnich, Elizabeth Kamarck. 1990. *Transforming Knowledge.* Philadelphia, PA: Temple University Press.

Mitchell, Juliet. 1975. *Psychoanalysis and Feminism.* New York: Vintage.

———. 1973. *Woman's Estate.* New York: Vintage.

———. 1984. *Women: The Longest Revolution.* New York: Pantheon Books.

Mitchell, Juliet, and Ann Oakley, eds. 1986. *What Is Feminism?* New York: Pantheon Books.

Mitter, Sara S. 1991. *Dharma's Daughters: Contemporary Indian Women and Hindu Culture.* New Brunswick, NJ: Rutgers University Press.

Modleski, Tania. 1991. *Feminism Without Women: Culture and Criticism in a "Postfeminist" Age.* New York: Routledge.

Moghadam, Valentine M. 1993. *Modernizing Women: Gender and Social Change in the Middle East.* Boulder, CO: Lynne Rienner Publishers.

Mohanty, Chandra Talpade, Ann Russo, and Lourdes Torres, eds. 1991. *Third World Women and the Politics of Feminism.* Bloomington: Indiana University Press.

Moi, Toril. 1990. *Feminist Theory and Simone de Beauvoir.* Cambridge, MA: Basil Blackwell.

Mondimore, M. D., and Francis Mark. 1996. *A Natural History of Homosexuality.* Baltimore, MD: Johns Hopkins University Press.

Money, J., and A. A. Ehrhardt. 1972. *Man and Woman, Boy and Girl.* Baltimore, MD: Johns Hopkins University Press.

Montague, Ashley. 1974. *The Natural Superiority of Women.* New York: Collier Books.

Moore, Brenda L. 1996. *To Serve My Country, To Serve My Race: The Story of the Only African American WACs Stationed Overseas During World War II.* New York: New York University Press.

Moore, Robert, and Douglas Gillette. 1990. *King, Warrior, Magician, Lover: Rediscovering the Archetypes of the Mature Masculine.* New York: HarperCollins.

Moraga, Cherríe. 1986. *Giving up the Ghost: Teatro in Two Acts.* Los Angeles: West End Press.

———. 1993. *The Last Generation.* Boston: South End Press.

———. 1983. *Loving in the War Years: Lo Que Nunca Paso Por Sus Labios.* Boston: South End Press.

———. 1997. *Waiting in the Wings: Portrait of a Queer Motherhood.* Ithaca, NY: Firebrand Books.

Moraga, Cherríe, and Gloria Anzaldúa, eds. 1983. *This Bridge Called My Back: Writings by Radical Women of Color.* 2d ed. New York: Kitchen Table: Women of Color Press.

Morales, Aurora Levins, and Rosario Morales. 1986. *Getting Home Alive.* Ithaca, NY: Firebrand Books.

Morbeck, Mary Ellen, Alison Galloway, and Adrienne L. Zihlman, eds. 1997. *The Evolving Female: A Life-History Perspective.* Princeton, NJ: Princeton University Press.

More, Ellen S. 1999. *Restoring the Balance: Women Physicians and the Profession of Medicine, 1850–1995.* Cambridge, MA: Harvard University Press.

Morgan, Elaine. 1972. *The Descent of Woman.* New York: Stein & Day.

Morgan, Robin. 1994. *The Anatomy of Freedom: Feminism in Four Dimensions.* New York: W. W. Norton.

———. 1990. *The Demon Lover: On the Sexuality of Terrorism.* New York: W.W. Norton.

———. 1978. *Going Too Far: The Personal Chronicle of a Feminist.* New York: Vintage Books.

———. 1992. *The Word of a Woman: Feminist Dispatches, 1968–1992.* New York: W.W. Norton.

Morgan, Robin, ed. 1997. *Sisterhood Is Global: The International Women's Movement Anthology.* New York: The Feminist Press at The City University of New York. (Revision of the 1984 anthology.)

———. 1970. *Sisterhood Is Powerful: An Anthology of Writings from the Women's Movement.* New York: Vintage.

Morris, Desmond. 1968. *The Naked Ape.* New York: McGraw-Hill.

Morrison, Toni. 1987. *Beloved.* New York: Alfred A. Knopf.

———. 1972. *The Bluest Eye.* New York: Washington Square Press.

———. 1992. *Jazz.* New York: McKay.

———. 1993. *Playing in the Dark: Whiteness and the Literary Imagination.* New York: Random House.

———. 1978. *Song of Solomon.* New York: New American Library.

———. 1973. *Sula.* New York: Alfred A. Knopf.

———. 1981. *The Tar Baby.* New York: Alfred A. Knopf.

Morrison, Toni, ed. 1992. *Race-ing Justice, En-gendering Power: Essays on Anita Hill, Clarence Thomas, and the Construction of Social Reality.* New York: Pantheon Books.

Moynihan, Daniel Patrick. 1965. *The Negro Family: The Case for National Action.* Washington, DC: U.S. Department of Labor.

Mulhern, Chieko Irie, ed. 1991. *Heroic with Grace: Legendary Women of Japan.* Armonk, NY: M.E. Sharpe.

Murphy-Milano, Susan. 1996. *Defending Our Lives: Getting Away from Domestic Violence and Staying Safe.* New York: Anchor Books.

Murray, Pauli. 1989. *Pauli Murray: The Autobiography of a Black Activist, Feminist, Lawyer, Priest, and Poet.* Knoxville: University of Tennessee Press.

National Commission of the Observance of International Women's Year. 1976. "To Form a More Perfect Union . . .": *Justice for American Women.* Washington, DC: U.S. Department of State.

———. 1978. *The Spirit of Houston: The First National Women's Conference.* Washington, DC: U.S. Department of State.

Nicholson, Linda, ed. 1990. *Feminism/Postmodernism.* New York: Routledge.

———. 1997. *The Second Wave: A Reader in Feminist Theory.* New York: Routledge.

Norris, Pippa, ed. 1997. *Women Media and Politics.* New York: Oxford University Press.

Nussbaum, Martha, ed. 1996. *Women, Culture, and Development: A Study of Human Capabilities.* New York: Oxford University Press.

Oakley, Ann. 1974. *The Sociology of Housework.* New York: Pantheon.

———. 1976. *Woman's Work: The Housewife Past and Present.* New York: Vintage.

Ochs, Carol. 1989. *An Ascent to Joy: Transforming Deadness of Spirit.* New York: Meyer Stone Books.

———. 1977. *Behind the Sex of God: Toward A New Consciousness Transcending Matriarchy and Patriarchy.* Boston: Beacon Press.

———. 1992. *When I'm Alone.* Minneapolis, MN: Carolrhoda Books.

———. 1996. *Women and Spirituality,* 2d ed. Lanham, MD: Rowman & Littlefield.

Osborn, Torie. 1996. *Coming Home to America: A Roadmap to Gay and Lesbian Empowerment.* New York: St. Martin's Press.

Painter, Nell Irvin. 1996. *Sojourner Truth: A Life, a Symbol.* New York: W. W. Norton & Company.

Paludi, Michele A., ed. 1996. *Sexual Harassment on College Campuses: Abusing the Ivory Power* (Revised and updated edition of *Ivory Power: Sexual Harassment on Campus*). Albany, NY: State University of New York Press.

Papachristou, Judith, ed. 1976. *Women Together: A History in Documents of the Women's Movement in the United States.* New York: Alfred A. Knopf.

Parrish, Jenni, ed. 1995. *Abortion Law in the United States* (Three vols.). Hamden, CT: Garland.

Passaro, Joanne. 1996. *The Unequal Homeless: Men on the Streets, Women in Their Place.* New York: Routledge.

Patai, Daphne, and Noretta Koertge. 1994. *Professing Feminism: Cautionary Tales from the Strange World of Women's Studies.* New York: Basic Books.

Pearsall, Marilyn, ed. 1997. *The Other Within Us: Feminist Perspectives on Women and Aging.* Boulder, CO: Westview Press.

Penelope, Julia. 1992. *Call Me Lesbian: Lesbian Lives, Lesbian Theory* (Introduction by Sarah Hoagland.) Freedom, CA: Crossing Press.

Penelope, Julia, ed. 1994. *Out of the Class Closet: Lesbians Speak.* Freedom, CA: Crossing Press.

Penelope, Julia, and Susan J. Wolfe, eds. 1994. *Lesbian Culture: An Anthology.* Freedom, CA: Crossing Press.

Penley, Constance, ed. 1988. *Feminism and Film Theory.* New York: Routledge, Chapman and Hall.

Peters, Margot. 1997. *May Sarton: A Biography.* New York: Alfred A. Knopf.

Peterson, V. Spike, ed. 1992. *Gendered States: Feminist (Re)Visions of International Relations Theory.* Boulder, CO: Lynne Rienner Publishers.

Pérez, Emma. 1999. *The Decolonial Imaginary: Writing Chicanas into History.* Bloomington: Indiana University Press.

Pharr, Suzanne. 1988. *Homophobia: A Weapon of Sexism.* Little Rock, AR: Chardon Press.

———. 1996. *In the Time of the Right: Reflections on Liberation.* Inverness, CA: Chardon Press.

Pipher, Mary. 1994. *Reviving Ophelia: Saving the Selves of Adolescent Girls.* New York: Ballantine.

Plath, Sylvia. 1971. *The Bell Jar.* New York: Harper & Row.

Pogrebin, Letty Cottin. 1991. *Deborah, Golda, and Me: Being Female and Jewish in America.* New York: Crown Publishing Group.

Poppema, Suzanne T., M.D. 1996. *Why I Am an Abortion Doctor.* Amherst, NY: Prometheus Books.

President's Task Force on Women's Rights and Responsibilities. 1970. *A Matter of Simple Justice.* Washington, DC: Government Printing Office.

Purdy, Laura M. 1996. *Reproducing Persons: Issues in Feminist Bioethics.* Ithaca, NY: Cornell University Press.

Rabuzzi, Kathryn Allen. 1988. *Motherself: A Mythic Analysis of Motherhood.* Bloomington: Indiana University Press.

Radford, Jill, and Diana E. H. Russell, eds. 1992. *Femicide: The Politics of Woman Killing.* New York: Twayne.

Rakow, Lana, and Cheris Kramarae, eds. 1990. *The Revolution in Words: Righting Women, 1868–1871.* New York: Routledge.

Ralston, Meredith L. 1996. *"Nobody Wants to Hear Our Truth": Homeless Women and Theories of the Welfare State.* Westport, CT: Greenwood Press.

Randall, Margaret. 1987. *This Is About Incest.* Ithaca, NY: Firebrand Books.

Ranke-Heinemann, Uta. 1991. *Eunuchs for the Kingdom of Heaven: Women, Sexuality and the Catholic Church.* New York: Penguin.

Rapp, Sandy. 1991. *God's Country: A Case Against Theocracy.* New York: Haworth Press.

Rapping, Elayne. 1996. *The Culture of Recovery: Making Sense of the Self-Help Movement in Women's Lives.* Boston: Beacon Press.

———. 1994. *Media-tions: Forays Into the Culture and Gender Wars.* Boston: South End Press.

Ratner, Rochelle, ed. 2000. *Bearing Life: Women's Writing on Childlessness.* New York: The Feminist Press.

Raymond, Janice. 1986. *A Passion for Friends: Toward a Philosophy of Female Affection.* Boston: Beacon Press.

Raymond, Janice, et al. 1991. *RU–486: Myths, Misconceptions, and Morals.* North Amherst, MA: Institute on Women and Technology.

Réage, Pauline. 1965. *The Story of O.* Trans. Sabine d'Estrée. New York: Grove Press.

Redfern, Bernice J. 1989. *Women of Color in the United States: A Guide to the Literature.* New York: Garland.

Reed, Evelyn. 1971. *Problems of Women's Liberation.* New York: Pathfinder Press.

———. 1970. *Woman's Evolution.* New York: Pathfinder Press.

Reilly, Lee. 1996. *Women Living Single: Thirty Women Share Their Stories of Navigating Through a Married World.* Boston: Faber & Faber.

Rich, Adrienne. 1975. *Adrienne Rich's Poetry.* New York: Norton.

———. 1991. *An Atlas of the Difficult World: Poems, 1988–1991.* New York: Norton.

———. 1986. *Blood, Bread, and Poetry: Selected Prose, 1979–1985.* New York: Norton.

———. 1995. *Dark Fields of the Republic, Poems 1991–1995.* New York: Norton.

———. 1978. *The Dream of a Common Language: Poems, 1974–1977.* New York: Norton.

———. 1986. *Of Woman Born: Motherhood as Experience and Institution.* New York: Norton.

———. 1979. *On Lies, Secrets, and Silence: Selected Prose, 1966–1978.* New York: Norton.

———. 1983. *Sources.* Woodside, CA: Heyeck Press.

———. 1990. *Women and Honor: Some Notes on Lying.* Pittsburgh, PA: Cleis Press.

———. 1986. *Your Native Land, Your Life: Poems.* New York: Norton.

Richards, Dell. 1990. *Lesbian Lists: A Look at Lesbian Culture, History, and Personalities.* Boston: Alyson Publications.

Rierden, Andi. 1997. *The Farm Life: Inside a Women's Prison.* Amherst, MA: University of Massachusetts Press.

Rimmerman, Craig, ed. 1996. *Gay Rights, Military Wrongs: Political Perspectives on Lesbians and Gays in the Military.* Hamden, CT: Garland.

Rogers, Mary Beth. 2000. *Barbara Jordan: American Hero.* New York: Bantam.

Rollins, Judith. 1995. *All Is Never Said: The Narrative of Odette Harper Hines.* Philadelphia, PA: Temple University Press.

Roman, Leslie, Linda K. Christian-Smith, and Elizabeth Ellsworth, eds. 1988. *Becoming Feminine: The Politics of Popular Culture.* New York: Falmer.

Rosen, Ruth. 2000. *The World Split Open: How the Modern Women's Movement Changed America.* New York: Penguin Putnam.

Ross, John Munder. 1994. *What Men Want: Mothers, Fathers, and Manhood.* Cambridge, MA: Harvard University Press.

Rosser, Sue V. 1992. *Biology and Feminism: A Dynamic Interaction.* New York: Twayne.

———. 1990. *Female-Friendly Science: Applying Women's Studies Methods and Theories to Attract Students to Science.* New York: Pergamon.

———. 1989. *Feminism and Science: In Memory of Ruth Bleier.* New York: Pergamon.

———. 1988. *Feminism Within the Science and Health Care Professions: Overcoming Resistance.* New York: Pergamon.

———. 1986. *Teaching Science and Health from a Feminist Perspective: A Practical Guide.* New York: Pergamon.

———. 1994. *Women's Health—Missing From U.S. Medicine.* Bloomington: Indiana University Press.

Rosser, Sue V., ed. 1995. *Teaching the Majority: Breaking the Gender Barrier in Science, Mathematics, and Engineering.* Williston, VT: Teachers College Press.

Roses, Lorraine Elena, and Ruth Elizabeth Randolph, eds. 1996. *Harlem's Glory: Black Women Writing, 1900–1950.* Cambridge, MA: Harvard University Press.

Rossi, Alice S., ed. 1988. *The Feminist Papers: From Adams to de Beauvoir.* Boston: Northeastern University Press.

Rossiter, Amy. 1988. *From Private to Public: A Feminist Exploration of Early Mothering.* Toronto: Women's Press.

Rothenberg, Paula S. 1992. *Race, Class, and Gender in the United States: An Integrated Study.* New York: St. Martin's Press.

Rothman, Barbara Katz. 1989. *Recreating Motherhood: Ideology and Technology in a Patriarchal Society.* New York: W.W. Norton.

Rotundo, E. Anthony. 1994. *American Manhood: Transformations in Masculinity from the Revolution to the Modern Era.* New York: HarperCollins.

Rountree, Cathleen. 1991. *Coming into Our Fullness: On Women Turning Forty.* Freedom, CA: Crossing Press.

Rowbotham, Sheila. 1976. *Hidden from History.* New York: Vintage.

———. 1991. *The Past Is Before Us: Feminism in Action Since the 1960s.* Boston: Beacon Press.

———. 1973. *Woman's Consciousness, Man's World.* Baltimore, MD: Penguin.

———. 1992. *Women in Movement: Feminism and Social Action.* New York: Routledge.

———. 1974. *Women, Resistance and Revolution.* New York: Vintage.

Rubin, Lillian B. 1994. *Families on the Fault Line: America's Working Class Speaks About the Family, the Economy, Race, and Ethnicity.* New York: HarperCollins.

Ruether, Rosemary Radford. 1992. *Gaia & God: An Ecofeminist Theology of Earth Healing.* San Francisco: Harper SanFrancisco.

———. 1974. *Religion and Sexism.* New York: Simon & Schuster.

———. 1983. *Sexism and God-Talk: Toward a Feminist Theology.* Boston: Beacon Press.

———. 1996. *Womanguides: Readings Towards a Feminist Theology.* Boston: Beacon Press. (With a new preface. Originally published in 1985.)

Ruether, Rosemary Radford, and Rosemary Skinner Keller, eds. 1995. *In Our Own Voices: Four Centuries of American Women's Religious Writing.* San Francisco: HarperCollins.

———. 1986. *Women and Religion in America.* San Francisco: Harper & Row.

Ruether, Rosemary, and Eleanor McLaughlin, eds. 1979. *Women of Spirit: Female Leadership in the Jewish and Christian Traditions.* New York: Simon & Schuster.

Ruiz, Vicki L. 1998. *From Out of the Shadows: Mexican Women in Twentieth-Century America.* New York: Routledge.

Rupp, Leila. 1999. *A Desired Past: A Short History of Same-Sex Love in America.* Chicago: The University of Chicago Press.

Russell, Diana E. H. 1994. *Against Pornography: The Evidence of Harm.* Phoenix, AZ: Russell Publications.

Russell, Diana E. H., ed. 1993. *Making Violence Sexy: Feminist Views of Pornography* (Athene Series). New York: Teachers College Press.

Ruth, Sheila. 1994. *Take Back the Light: A Feminist Reclamation of Spirituality and Religion.* Lanham, MD: Rowman & Littlefield.

Salem, Dorothy. 1990. *To Better Our World: Black Women in Organized Reform, 1890–1920.* Brooklyn, NY: Carlson.

Sanday, Peggy Reeves. 1996. *A Woman Scorned: Acquaintance Rape on Trial.* New York: Doubleday.

Sapiro, Virginia. 1984. *The Political Integration of Women: Roles, Socialization, and Politics.* Champaign: University of Illinois Press.

———. 1992. *A Vindication of Political Virtue: The Political Theory of Mary Wollstonecraft.* Chicago: University of Chicago Press.

———. 1986. *Women in American Society.* Palo Alto, CA: Mayfield.

———. 1988. *Women, Political Action, and Political Participation.* Women and Politics Series. Washington, DC: American Political Science Association.

Sarton, May. 1995. *At Eighty-two: A Journal.* New York: W. W. Norton.

———. 1993. *Collected Poems: 1930–1993.* New York: W.W. Norton.

———. 1973. *Journal of a Solitude.* New York: W.W. Norton.

———. 1983. *Plant Dreaming Deep* (illustrated). New York: W.W. Norton.

Sayers, Janet. 1991. *Mothers of Psychoanalysis: Helen Deutsch, Karen Horney, Anna Freud, Melanie Klein.* New York: W.W. Norton.

Scarf, Mimi. 1988. *Battered Jewish Wives: Case Studies in the Response to Rage.* Lewiston, NY: E. Mellen Press.

Scharf, Lois, and Joan M. Jensen. 1983. *Decades of Discontent: The Women's Movement, 1920–1940.* Westport, CT: Greenwood Press.

Schmidt, Alvin John. 1989. *Veiled and Silenced: How Culture Shaped Sexist Theology.* Macon, GA: Mercer University Press.

Schein, Virginia E. 1995. *Working from the Margins: Voices of Mothers in Poverty.* New York: ILR Press.

Schneir, Miriam, ed. 1994. *Feminism in Our Time: The Essential Writings, World War II to the Present.* New York: Vintage.

———. 1971. *Feminism: The Essential Historical Writings.* New York: Random House.

Schwalbe, Michael. 1996. *Unlocking the Iron Cage: The Men's Movement, Gender Politics, and American Culture.* New York: Oxford University Press.

Schwartz, Lewis M. 1993. *Arguing About Abortion.* Belmont, CA: Wadsworth Publishing.

Scott, Hilda. 1985. *Working Your Way to the Bottom: The Feminization of Poverty.* Boston: Pandora.

Scott, Joan Wallach, ed. 1996. *Feminism and History* (Oxford Readings in Feminism). New York: Oxford University Press.

Seidler, Victor. 1991. *Recreating Sexual Politics: Men, Feminism and Politics.* New York: Routledge, Chapman & Hall.

Sered, Susan Starr. 1996. *Priestess, Mother, Sacred Sister: Religions Dominated by Women.* New York: Oxford University Press.

Shah, Sonia, ed. 1997. *Dragon Ladies: Asian American Feminists Breathe Fire.* Boston: South End Press.

Shapiro, Patricia Gottlieb. 1996. *My Turn: Women's Search for Self After the Children Leave.* Princeton, NJ: Peterson's.

Sharma, Arvind, ed. 1987. *Women in World Religions.* New York: State University of New York Press.

Shehadeh, Lamia Rustum, ed. 1999. *Women and War in Lebanon.* Gainesville, FL: University Press of Florida.

Shulman, Alix Kates. 1972. *Memoirs of an Ex-Prom Queen.* New York: Alfred A. Knopf.

Sidel, Ruth. 1996. *Keeping Women and Children Last: America's War on the Poor.* New York: Penguin.

———. 1990. *On Her Own: Growing Up in the Shadow of the American Dream.* New York: Viking Penguin.

———. 1995. *Urban Survival: The World of Working Class Women.* Lincoln: University of Nebraska Press.

———. 1986. *Women and Children Last: The Plight of Poor Women in Affluent America.* New York: Penguin. (Rev. ed. 1992.)

Simon, Barbara Levy. 1987. *Never Married Women.* Philadelphia, PA: Temple University Press.

Simon, Rita J., and Jean Landis. 1991. *The Crimes Women Commit, The Punishments They Receive.* New York: Lexington.

Simonds, Wendy. 1996. *Abortion at Work: Ideology and Practice in a Feminist Clinic.* New Brunswick, NJ: Rutgers University Press.

Sinclair, Marianne. 1988. *Hollywood Lolitas: The Nymphet Syndrome in the Movies.* New York: Henry Holt.

Sipe, Beth, and Evelyn J. Hall. 1996. *I Am Not Your Victim: Anatomy of Domestic Violence* (Sage Series on Violence Against Women, Vol. 1). Thousand Oaks, CA: Sage Publications.

Sjöö, Monica. 1999. *Return of the Dark/Light Mother or New Age Armageddon? Towards a Feminist Vision of the Future.* Austin, TX: Plain View Press.

Skeggs, Beverly, ed. 1996. *Feminist Cultural Theory: Process and Production.* New York: St. Martin's Press.

Smith, Barbara, ed. 1983. *Home Girls: A Black Feminist Anthology.* New York: Kitchen Table/Women of Color Press.

Smith, Patricia. 1993. *Feminist Jurisprudence.* New York: Oxford University Press.

Soble, Alan, ed. 1997. *The Philosophy of Sex: Contemporary Readings,* 3d ed. Lanham, MD: Rowman & Littlefield.

Sochen, June. 1987. *Enduring Values: Women in Popular Culture.* Westport, CT: Greenwood Press.

———. 1974. *Movers and Shakers: American Women Thinkers and Activists, 1900–1970.* New York: Quadrangle.

———. 1991. *Women's Comic Visions.* Detroit, MI: Wayne State University Press.

Spallone, Patricia. 1989. *Beyond Conception: The New Politics of Reproduction.* Granby, MA: Bergin & Garvey.

Spallone, Patricia, and Deborah Lynn Steinberg, eds. 1987. *Made to Order: The Myth of Reproductive and Genetic Progress* (Athene Series). New York: Pergamon.

Spelman, Elizabeth V. 1988. *Inessential Woman: Problems of Exclusion in Feminist Thought.* Boston: Beacon Press.

Spender, Dale. 1987. *The Education Papers: Women's Quest for Equality in Britain.* Boston: Routledge.

———. 1983. *Feminist Theorists: Three Centuries of Key Women Thinkers.* New York: Pantheon.

———. 1985. *For the Record: The Making and Meaning of Feminist Knowledge.* London: Women's Press.

———. 1985. *Man Made Language,* 2d ed. Boston: Routledge, Chapman & Hall.

———. 1981. *Men's Studies Modified: The Impact of Feminism on the Academic Disciplines.* New York: Pergamon Press.

———. 1986. *Mothers of the Novel: 100 Good Women Writers Before Jane Austen.* London: Pandora Press.

———. 1995. *Nattering on the Net: Women, Power & Cyberspace.* Staten Island, NY: Spinifex Press.

———. 1983. *There's Always Been a Women's Movement This Century.* Boston: Pandora.

———. 1984. *Time and Tide Wait for No Man.* London: Pandora Press.

———. 1988. *Women of Ideas (and What Men Have Done to Them): From Aphra Behn to Adrienne Rich.* Boston: Pandora Press.

———. 1988. *Writing a New World.* London: Pandora.

———. 1989. *The Writing or the Sex?: Or Why You Don't Have to Read Women's Writing to Know It's No Good.* New York: Pergamon.

Spender, Dale, and Elizabeth Sarah. 1988. *Learning to Lose: Sexism and Education.* London: Women's Press.

Spender, Dale, and L. Spender, eds. 1984. *Gatekeeping: The Denial, Dismissal, and Distortion of Women.* Tarrytown, NY: Pergamon.

Spiegel, Marcia Cohn, and Deborah Lipton Kremsdorf, eds. 1987. *Women Speak to God: The Prayers and Poems of Jewish Women.* San Diego, CA: Women's Institute for Continuing Jewish Education.

Stabile, Carol A. 1994. *Feminism and the Technological Fix.* New York: St. Martin's Press.

Stacey, Judith, Susan Bereaud, and Joan Daniels, eds. 1974. *And Jill Came Tumbling After: Sexism in American Education.* New York: Dell.

Stan, Adele M., ed. 1995. *Debating Sexual Correctness: Pornography, Sexual Harassment, Date Rape, and the Politics of Sexual Equality.* New York: Delta.

Stanton, Elizabeth Cady. 1972. *The Woman's Bible.* New York: Arno Press.

Stanton, Elizabeth Cady, Susan B. Anthony, and Matilda Joslyn Gage, eds. 1881–1886. *History of Woman Suffrage.* Vols. 1–3. New York: Fowler and Wells. (1886–1904, Vols. 4-6, ed. Ida Husted Harper, National Woman Suffrage Association.)

Starhawk. 1989. *Dreaming the Dark: Magic, Sex, and Politics.* Boston: Beacon Press.

———. 1994. *Fifth Sacred Thing.* New York: Bantam.

———. 1979. *The Spiral Dance: A Rebirth of the Ancient Religion of the Great Goddess.* San Francisco: Harper & Row.

———. 1989. *Truth or Dare.* San Francisco: HarperSanFrancisco.

———. 1997. *Walking to Mercury.* New York: Bantam.

Stark, Evan, and Anne Flitcraft, M.D. 1996. *Women at Risk: Domestic Violence and Women's Health.* Thousand Oaks, CA: Sage Publications.

Starr, Tama. 1991. *The "Natural Inferiority" of Women: Outrageous Pronouncements by Misguided Males.* New York: Poseidon.

Steinem, Gloria. 1994. *Moving Beyond Words.* Los Angeles, CA: S & S Enterprises.

———. 1983. *Outrageous Acts and Everyday Rebellions.* New York: Holt, Rinehart and Winston.

———. 1992. *Revolution from Within: A Book of Self-Esteem.* Boston: Little, Brown.

Stephenson, June. 1991. *Men Are Not Cost-Effective.* Napa, CA: Smith Publishing.

———. 1991. *The Two-Parent Family Is Not the Best.* Napa, CA: Smith Publishing.

Stockdale, Margaret S., ed. 1996. *Sexual Harassment in the Workplace: Perspectives, Frontiers, and Response Strategies.* Thousand Oaks, CA: Sage Publications.

Stoltenberg, John. 1993. *The End of Manhood: A Book For Men of Conscience.* New York: Dutton.

———. 1989. *Refusing to Be a Man: Essays on Sex and Justice.* New York: Penguin.

Stone, Merlin. 1979. *Ancient Mirrors of Womanhood: Our Goddess and Heroine Heritage.* Vols. 1 & 2. New York: New Sibylline Books.

———. 1978. *When God Was a Woman.* New York: Harcourt Brace Jovanovich.

Stoner, K. Lynn, ed. 1989. *Latinas of the Americas: A Source Book.* New York: Garland.

Stromquist, Nelly P., ed. 1998. *Women in the Third World: An Encyclopedia of Contemporary Issues.* New York: Garland Publishing, Inc.

Sumrall, Amber Coverdale. 1984. *Bless Me Father: Stories of a Catholic Childhood.* New York: New American Library.

Sumrall, Amber Coverdale, and Patrice Vecchione. 1992. *Catholic Girls.* New York: New American Library.

Swirski, Barbara, and Marilyn P. Safir. 1991. *Calling the Equality Bluff: Women in Israel* (Athene Series). New York: Pergamon Press.

Szekely, Eva. 1988. *Never Too Thin.* Toronto: Women's Press.

Tanner, Leslie B., ed. 1970. *Voices from Women's Liberation.* New York: Signet.

Taylor, Dena. 1988. *Red Flower: Rethinking Menstruation.* Freedom, CA: Crossing Press.

Taylor, Jill McLean, Carol Gilligan, and Amy M. Sullivan. 1995. *Between Voice and Silence: Women and Girls, Race and Relationship.* Cambridge, MA: Harvard University Press.

Terborg-Penn, Rosalyn, Sharon Harley, and Andrea Benton Rushing, eds. 1988. *Women in Africa and the African Diaspora.* Washington, DC: Howard University Press.

Thesander, Marianne. 1997. *The Feminine Ideal.* London: Reaktion Books.

Thiam, Awa. 1986. *Black Sisters, Speak Out.* Trans. Dorothy Blair. London: Pluto Press.

Thompson, Mary Lou, ed. 1970. *Voices of the New Feminism.* Boston: Beacon Press.

Thorne, Barrie. 1993. *Gender Play: Girls and Boys in School.* Newark, NJ: Rutgers University Press.

———. 1992. *Rethinking the Family: Some Feminist Questions* (Rev. ed.). Boston: Northeastern University Press.

Thornham, Sue. 1997. *Passionate Detachments: An Introduction to Feminist Film Theory.* New York: St. Martin's Press.

Thornhill, Randy, and Craig T. Palmer. 2000. *A Natural History of Rape: Biological Bases of Sexual Coercion.* Cambridge, MA: The MIT Press.

Tiger, Lionel. 1969. *Men in Groups.* New York: Random House.

Tiger, Lionel, and Robin Fox. 1971. *The Imperial Animal.* New York: Holt, Rinehart and Winston.

Tigert, Leanne McCall. 1999. *Coming Out Through Fire: Surviving the Trauma of Homophobia.* Cleveland OH: United Church Press.

Tinker, Irene. 1990. *Persistent Inequalities: Women and World Development.* New York: Oxford University Press.

Thomas, Sue. 1994. *How Women Legislate.* New York: Oxford University Press.

Tobias, Sheila. 1997. *Faces of Feminism: An Activist's Reflections on the Women's Movement.* Boulder, CO: Westview Press.

Tong, Rosemarie. 1993. *Feminine and Feminist Ethics.* Belmont, CA: Wadsworth Publishing.

———. 1996. *Feminist Approaches to Bioethics: Theoretical Reflection and Practical Applications.* Boulder, CO: Westview Press.

———. 1989. *Feminist Thought: A Comprehensive Introduction.* Boulder, CO: Westview Press.

———. 1984. *Women, Sex and the Law.* New Feminist Perspective Series. Lanham, MD: Rowman & Littlefield.

Trebilcot, Joyce, ed. 1984. *Mothering: Essays in Feminist Theory.* Lanham, MD: Rowman & Littlefield.

Tsomo, Karma Lekshe. 1996. *Sisters in Solitude: Two Traditions of Buddhist Monastic Ethics for Women.* Albany, NY: State University of New York Press.

Tucker, Susan. 1988. *Telling Memories Among Southern Women: Domestic Workers and Their Employees in the Segregated South.* Baton Rouge: Louisiana State University Press.

Umansky, Lauri. 1996. *Motherhood Reconceived: Feminism and the Legacies of the Sixties.* New York: New York University Press.

Valdivia, Angharad L., ed. 1995. *Feminism, Multiculturalism, and the Media: Global Diversities.* Thousand Oaks, CA: Sage Publications.

Vaz, Kim Marie, ed. 1995. *Black Women in America.* Thousand Oaks, CA: Sage Publications.

Verschuur-Basse, Denyse. 1996. *Chinese Women Speak.* Westport, CT: Praeger Publishers.

Villani, Sue Lanci, with Jane E. Ryan. 1997. *Motherhood at the Crossroads: Meeting the Challenge of a Changing Role.* New York: Insight Books of Plenum Press.

Wade-Gayles, Gloria, ed. 1995. *My Soul Is a Witness: African-American Spirituality.* Boston: Beacon Press.

Wagner-Martin, Linda, and Cathy N. Davidson, eds. 1995. *The Oxford Book of Women's Writing in the United States* and *The Oxford Companion to Women's Writing in the United States.* New York: Oxford University Press.

Walker, Alice. 1997. *Anything We Love Can Be Saved: A Writer's Activism.* New York: Random House.

———. 1982. *The Color Purple.* New York: Harcourt Brace Jovanovich.

———. 1991. *Her Blue Body Everything We Know: Earthling Poems 1965–1990 Complete.* New York: Harcourt Brace Jovanovich.

———. 1973. *In Love and Trouble: Stories of Black Women.* New York: Harcourt Brace Jovanovich.

———. 1983. *In Search of Our Mother's Gardens: Womanist Prose.* San Diego, CA: Harcourt Brace Jovanovich.

———. 1992. *Possessing the Secret of Joy.* New York: Harcourt Brace Jovanovich.

———. 1989. *The Temple of My Familiar.* New York: Harcourt Brace Jovanovich.

———. 1981. *You Can't Keep a Good Woman Down: Stories.* New York: Harcourt Brace Jovanovich.

Walker, Barbara G. 1992. *Amazon: A Novel.* San Francisco: HarperSanFrancisco.

———. 1985. *The Crone: Woman of Age, Wisdom, and Power.* San Francisco: Harper & Row.

———. 1986. *The I Ching of the Goddess.* San Francisco: Harper & Row.

———. 1987. *The Skeptical Feminist: Discovering the Virgin, Mother, and Crone.* San Francisco: Harper & Row.

———. 1988. *The Woman's Dictionary of Symbols and Sacred Objects.* San Francisco: Harper & Row.

———. 1983. *The Woman's Encyclopedia of Myths and Secrets.* San Francisco: Harper & Row.

———. 1990. *Women's Rituals: A Sourcebook.* San Francisco: Harper & Row.

Walker, Robbie Jean. 1992. *The Rhetoric of Struggle: Public Address of African-American Women.* New York: Garland.

Warren, Karen J. 2000. *Ecofeminism: A Western Philosophical Perspective on What It Is and Why It Matters.* Lanham, MD: Rowman & Littlefield.

Warren, Karen J., ed. 1996. *Ecological Feminist Philosophies.* Bloomington: Indiana University Press.

Weisser, Susan, and Jennifer Fleischner, eds. 1994. *Feminist Nightmares: Women at Odds: Feminism and the Problem of Sisterhood.* New York: New York University Press.

Weitzman, Lenore. 1987. *The Divorce Revolution: The Unexpected Social and Economic Consequences for Women and Children in America.* New York: Free Press.

Welter, Barbara. 1966. "The Cult of True Womanhood: 1820–1860." *American Quarterly* 18, No. 2, Pt. 1: 151–174.

Wendell, Susan. 1996. *The Rejected Body: Feminist Philosophical Reflections on Disability.* New York: Routledge.

Whelehan, Imelda. 1995. *Modern Feminist Thought: From the Second Wave to "Post Feminism."* New York: New York University Press.

Wiehe, Vernon R., and Ann L. Richards. 1995. *Intimate Betrayal: Understanding and Responding to the Trauma of Acquaintance Rape.* Thousand Oaks, CA: Sage Publications.

Wiley, Catherine, and Fiona Barnes, eds. 1996. *Homemaking: Women Writers and Politics and Poetics of Home.* Hamden, CT: Garland.

White, Evelyn C., ed. 1990. *The Black Women's Health Book: Speaking for Ourselves.* Seattle, WA: Seal Press.

Wilkinson, Sue, and Celia Kitzinger, eds. 1993. *Heterosexuality: A Feminism and Psychology Reader*. Thousand Oaks, CA: Sage Publications.

Williams, Joan. 1999. *Unbending Gender: Why Family and Work Conflict and What To Do About It*. New York: Oxford University Press.

Williams, Patricia J. 1991. *The Alchemy of Race and Rights: Diary of a Law Professor*. Cambridge, MA: Harvard University Press.

———. 1995. *The Rooster's Egg: On the Persistence of Prejudice*. Cambridge, MA: Harvard University Press.

Wilson, Edward O. 1975. *Sociobiology: The New Synthesis*. Cambridge, MA: Harvard University Press.

Winner, Karen. 1996. *Divorced From Justice: The Abuse of Women by Divorce Lawyers and Judges*. New York: HarperCollins.

Wittig, Monique. 1973. *Les Guérillères*. Trans. David Le Vay. New York: Avon.

———. 1992. *The Straight Mind and Other Essays*. Boston: Beacon Press.

Wolf, Naomi. 1994. *Fire With Fire: The New Female Power and How to Use It*. New York: Fawcett.

———. 1991. *The Beauty Myth*. New York: William Morrow.

Yayori, Matsui. 1989. *Women's Asia*. Trans. Mizuko Matsuda. London: Zed Books.

Young, Elise G. 1991. *Keepers of the History: Women of the Israeli-Palestinian Conflict* (Athene Series). New York: Pergamon Press.

Young-Bruehl, Elisabeth. 1996. *The Anatomy of Prejudices*. Cambridge, MA: Harvard University Press.

Yu-ning, Li, ed. 1992. *Chinese Women Through Chinese Eyes*. Armonk, NY: M.E. Sharpe.

Yung, Judy. 1995. *Unbound Feet: A Social History of Chinese Women in San Francisco*. Berkeley: University of California Press.

———. 1999. *Unbound Voices: A Documentary History of Chinese Women in San Francisco*. Berkeley: University of California Press.

Zahava, Irene, ed. 1996. *Feminism3: The Third Generation in Fiction*. Boulder, CO: Westview Press.

Zakaria, Rafiq. 1990. *Women & Politics in Islam: The Trial of Benazir Bhutto*. New York: New Horizons Press.

Zaman, Habiba. 1996. *Women and Work in a Bangladesh Village*. Dhaka, Bangladesh: Narigrantha Prabartana.

Zappone, Katherine. 1991. *The Hope for Wholeness: A Spirituality for Feminists*. Mystic, CT: Twenty-Third Publications.

Index